John William McCo

John William McCormack

A Political Biography

Garrison Nelson

Bloomsbury Academic
An imprint of Bloomsbury Publishing Inc

B L O O M S B U R Y

NEW YORK · LONDON · OXFORD · NEW DELHI · SYDNEY

Bloomsbury Academic
An imprint of Bloomsbury Publishing Inc

1385 Broadway	50 Bedford Square
New York	London
NY 10018	WC1B 3DP
USA	UK

www.bloomsbury.com

BLOOMSBURY and the Diana logo are trademarks of Bloomsbury Publishing Plc

First published 2017

Library of Congress Cataloging-in-Publication Data
A catalog record for this book is available from the Library of Congress.

ISBN: HB: 978-1-6289-2516-6
ePDF: 978-1-6289-2517-3
ePub: 978-1-6289-2518-0

Cover design: David A Gee
Cover image © Boston University's Howard Gotlieb Archival Research Center Archive

Typeset by Deanta Global Publishing Services, Chennai, India
Printed and bound in the United States of America

Contents

List of Photographs

Acknowledgments

In 1968, I left graduate school at the University of Iowa and was hired by the University of Vermont (UVM) shortly after the birth of my daughter, Shyla. UVM has been my academic home for close to five decades. In September that year, I attended my first national meeting of the American Political Science Association in Washington, DC. On Friday of the Labor Day weekend, I went to the U.S. Capitol in hopes of arranging meetings with congressional leaders who were the subjects of my doctoral dissertation. In a surprisingly fortuitous circumstance, Speaker of the U.S. House John W. McCormack was not only in his office but I was granted an hour-long meeting with him. As we sat in his office, I rattled off the names of prominent members with whom he served—Cactus Jack Garner, Will Bankhead, Sam Rayburn, and Billy Connery from my hometown of Lynn, Massachusetts, who had been McCormack's closest friend in the state delegation. He was delighted to be asked about these people and as he reminisced, he offered me a cigar. It was a wonderful hour for this 26-year-old new college instructor to enjoy a good smoke with the 76-year-old House Speaker in the U.S. Capitol. This remarkable experience was the inspiration for this particular book as well as for most of my published research on the U.S. Congress.

This book is the first ever full-length biography of John W. McCormack, 1891–1980, who at the time of his death weeks from his 89th birthday was then the second longest-lived Speaker of the U.S. House of Representatives. McCormack was one of the very few political leaders who openly resisted a biography written about him even going so far as to repeatedly warn his office staff about preparing a manuscript of their service with him. As Dr. Martin Sweig, his longtime assistant once contended to me, "John McCormack was the most secretive man I ever met." Consequently, the search for sources documenting his life and political career had to go well beyond his apparently sanitized congressional papers located at Boston University's Howard Gotlieb Archival Research Center. Also presenting a problem was trying to interview McCormack's key constituents, the South Boston Irish, who honored the code most succinctly stated by Martin Lomasney, the political boss of Boston's polyglot West End: "Never write what you can speak; never speak what you can nod." During the many months that I lived in South Boston and on my frequent trips to that unique peninsula as well as the Prince Edward Island birthplace of John's Canadian Scottish father, I learned many McCormack family stories whose sources refused to let me name them in print. Most of the stories were benign but they were too good to leave out of the book and so they are included in spite of many not being fully fact-checked. Without sounding too ominous, there is no one more wholly disdained among the Irish than the informer.

The two people who most encouraged my work on John McCormack were Edward J. "Eddie" McCormack, Jr., the Speaker's nephew and onetime attorney general of

Massachusetts, and Dr. Howard Gotlieb, the founder-director of Boston University's renowned Gotlieb Archival Research Center, where John McCormack's Papers were stored. Howard was a friend of my father's and was delighted that I had chosen to write about McCormack. Howard's staff associates Charles Niles, Vita Paladino, and Sean Noel were unstintingly supportive of my efforts to wade through the thousands of McCormack documents in their collection. Also, Eddie McCormack gave me six boxes of material—family photographs, personal letters, news clippings, and gavels—that were not included in the BU files. It was there I found documents and letters that unlocked John McCormack's hidden past. It was the successful reinvention of his family history that made it possible for John to escape the twin cruelties of abject childhood poverty and deadly disease that shortened the lives of five siblings and his beloved mother enabling him to ascend politically to the Speakership of the U.S. House just one heartbeat away from the presidency between November 1963 and January 1965.

Two other researchers whose prior work has been invaluable were Dr. Lester Gordon, whose BU dissertation *John McCormack and the Roosevelt Era* was distilled from hours of taped interviews with McCormack, and Mr. Paul Wright of the University of Massachusetts-Boston, whose copious notes and interviews with McCormack relatives and South Boston associates provided much context for this narrative. Close McCormack friends Mr. Bill McSweeny and his wife Dorothy also interviewed John and their tapes are at the Gotlieb Center. Eileen Hanerfeld Crosby ably prepared the transcripts from the Lester Gordon and McSweeny tapes. John was both very voluble and concealing in his interviews. He could talk at length about a topic yet reveal very little about it. Noticing this tendency was none other than his favorite protégé Thomas P. "Tip" O'Neill, Jr. who described John as "a windbag" after their initial meeting. John mentored Tip's career and was pleased when Tip joined the House leadership in 1971 upon John's retirement and eventually became House Majority Leader, 1973–77, and Speaker, 1977–87. John McCormack's unique self-effacing personality allowed him to hide "in plain sight," avoiding public scrutiny as he attended to the nation's business.

In the course of researching the book, I was aided by the highly competent staffs of four Presidential Libraries and Museums: the Franklin D. Roosevelt Library in Hyde Park, NY; the Harry S. Truman Library in Independence, Missouri; the John F. Kennedy Library in Dorchester, Massachusetts; and the Lyndon B. Johnson Library in Austin, Texas. Congressional libraries that were especially valuable were the Carl Albert Congressional Research Center at the University of Oklahoma in Norman, Oklahoma, and the Richard W. Bolling Papers at the University of Missouri-Kansas City. I also visited the Joseph W. Martin Papers at Stonehill College in Easton, Massachusetts, and Tip O'Neill's Papers at Boston College. Knowledgeable archivists are the salvation of a biographer without whose assistance any researcher would drown in the enormity of the papers contained in these collections. Three in particular deserve special mention, Bob Clark at the Roosevelt Library, Steven Plotkin at the Kennedy Library, and Carolyn G. Hanneman at the Albert Center. The able staffs of the U.S. Senate Historical Office, the U.S. House Historical Office, as well as longtime friends at the Congressional Research Service of the Library of Congress helped fill in missing details about a man whose congressional career spanned 42 years. Special mention should be made of

Mr. Waldron Leard of Joe McCormack's hometown of Souris, PEI, whose encyclopedic knowledge of Canada's smallest province was invaluable to my understanding of the unique relationship between the Canadian Maritimes and New England.

I learned of the importance of mentorship as an undergraduate at Boston University where I was mentored by Professor Murray B. Levin and in graduate school at the University of Iowa by Professors Sam Patterson and John C. Wahlke. It is a central tenet of a successful life as well as an academic career. My research was facilitated by an extraordinary cadre of UVM undergraduate mentees. Among them, I would list Alana Chain, Brad Carlson, and Heather Purdie, who provided assistance at critical points in the research. Seven students in particular stand out: Maggie Taylor Steakley, who mined the Kennedy Library for thousands of pages of oral history documents; Alexandra Gero, who photocopied thousands of pages of the *Congressional Record* in search of relevant John McCormack remarks; Jade Harberg, whose careful reading of documents could find the most illuminating quotes; Lindsey Nelson, who created the photo record of McCormack's life and career that has been invaluable in public presentations of this research; Liz Kane, whose organizational skills produced order from the disorder of multiple hundreds of file folders of 20-plus years of research; and Katie Alexander, who read through thousands of pages of newspaper accounts to provide the contemporaneous scaffolding for the book's narrative. This past year, the book was completed thanks to the determination of Sophie Scharlin-Pettee, who oversaw the book's final rewrite with clarity and insight, and Brenna Marie Rosen, who helped tighten the final editing and prepared the book's mammoth bibliography. The wonderful intelligence and good humor of Sophie and Brenna were essential to the completion of the manuscript as I tried to juggle my multiple responsibilities of classroom instruction and political commentary.

While I funded most of the book personally, I was aided by timely grants from the Earhart Foundation in Michigan, the Carl Albert Center at the University of Oklahoma, and the John F. Kennedy Library and Museum. The most recent source of funding came this past year from the generous endowment of UVM alumnus Elliott A. Brown, whose memories of the wonderful mentoring that he received from many of the UVM colleagues with whom I taught in my early years on campus enabled us to establish an intergenerational bridge of mentoring that I have been able to extend into this present generation of UVM students.

Any research project that extends beyond 20 years could not be completed had it not been for the information and sage counsel of multiple individuals. Listed here are many of the individuals with whom I spoke during the two decades that I worked irregularly on this book regarding John McCormack's life and political career as well as those who provided information and advice on how best to present the relevant materials. Undoubtedly, there are many others who provided valuable insights for the book but whose names have been lost to memory. A number of the interviews were formal, but most of the others, especially those at professional meetings or in telephone calls and e-mails, were more conversational. Among those with whom I spoke were: Tyler Abell, Professor Scott Adler, Jack Anderson, Professor Samuel Beer, Dr. Richard Baker, Professor Edmund Beard, Hon. Francis X. Bellotti, Richard Ben-Veniste, Professor

Steven D. Berkowitz, Gerald A. Berlin, Hon. Richard W. Bolling, Professor David W. Brady, Dr. W. Ross Brewer, Professor Frank Bryan, Gerry Burke, Hon. William M. Bulger, Professor James McGregor Burns, Canadian Consulate—Boston, Cecelia Cancellaro, Robert A. Caro, Professor Anthony Champagne, Christine Chinlund, Robert (Bob) Clark, Adam Clymer, Ellen Coffey, Hon. Tom Costin, Professor R. Bruce Craig, Professor William Crotty, Maryann McLeod Crush, Professor Maurice Cunningham, Professor Robert Dallek, Professor Roger Davidson, Terry Dean, Professor Bruce J. Dierenfield, Hon. Gerard F. Doherty, Hon. Michael S. Dukakis, Professor Susan Dunn, Hon. Thomas H. Eliot, Michael Esslinger, Professor Richard Fenno, Finn Galloway-Kane, Professor Gregory Gause, Hon. Newton L. Gingrich, Dr. Howard Gotlieb, Professor Matthew Green, Hon. Harry F. Greene, Professor Samuel B. Hand, D. B. Hardeman, Professor Douglas B. Harris, Robert (Bob) Healy, Professor Raul Hilberg, Professor Richard Hogarty, Gary Hymel, Ira Jackson, Ambrose Joyce, Professor Morton Keller, Professor David King, Dr. Betty Koed, Hon. Thomas Kuchel, Albert LaFarge, John C. Lally, Waldron Leard, Hon. Patrick J. Leahy, Scott Lehigh, Professor Burdett Loomis, Scot MacKay, Ralph G. Martin, Harvey Matusow, Professor David Mayhew, Hon. Edward J. McCormack Jr., Edward J. McCormack III, Hon. John W. McCormack, Sean McCormack, Marlaine McLean, William (Bill) McSweeny, Bruce Meredith, Metropolitan Opera Company in New York City, Mary Ellen McWalters Melder, Hon. Wilbur D. Mills, John Monahan, Ken Moody, Anna Murphy, Charles Niles, Sean Noel, Professor Thomas H. O'Connor, Padraig O'Malley, Hon. Thomas P. O'Neill, III, Dr. Norman Ornstein, Rev. Art O'Shea, Vita Paladino, Professor Samuel C. Patterson, Professor Robert L. Peabody, Professor Ronald M. Peters, Jr., Andrew Pierce, Professor Nelson Polsby, Professor James Riddlesperger, Jr., Clay Risen, Dr. Donald Ritchie, W. R. Rohrbaugh, Paul Rundquist, Professor Larry Sabato, Dr. David B. Sacher, Professor Howard Sacher, Hon. Thomas P. Salmon, John Sears, Professor Charles Stewart III, Professor Mark Stoler, James Sundquist, Dr. Martin Sweig, Dr. Raymond Smock, Professor Benn Steil, Carol Tank-Day, Sharon Tomasello, Celeste Walsh, Professor Thomas Whalen, Dr. George Abbott White, Professor Robert C. Wood, Dr. Robert Woodbury, Hon. Jim Wright, Paul Wright, and Professor Julian Zelizer.

Special thanks are extended to Matthew Kopel who signed my prior book, *Pathways to the U.S. Supreme Court: From the Arena to the Monastery* (Palgrave Macmillan, 2013) and as an acquisitions editor for Bloomsbury obtained a contract for this manuscript. He never lost faith in the book even when I felt overwhelmed by its enormity and wished to walk from it.

To my longtime partner and extraordinary companion Rosemary Malone, my beloved children, Shyla and Ethan, and my adored grandchildren Emily, Sophia, Addie, and Chase, I offer this book in heartfelt thanks for your loving support.

November 27, 1963: The Troubling Public Introduction

Three dates are embedded deep in the memory of Americans. Two led to the enormous loss of American lives: December 7, 1941, "the day of infamy," when Japanese warplanes attacked the U.S. Navy base at Pearl Harbor, Hawaii, ending the lives of 2,400 Americans and wounding another 1,100; and September 11, 2001, when nineteen Islamic terrorists hijacked four commercial airliners and flew three of them into the World Trade Center Towers in New York City and the Pentagon in Arlington, Virginia, with a total death toll of 3,000. The Pearl Harbor attack led to World War II. The 9/11 attack prompted the international "war on terrorism."

The third date, November 22, 1963, did not claim thousands of lives, nor did it lead to armed conflict. It did, however, have an equally devastating impact. On that date in Dallas, Texas, 46-year-old President John Fitzgerald Kennedy, the nation's youngest elected president, became the fourth American president to be murdered in less than a century. Fifty years after his death, conspiracy theories abound as many Americans continue to be confounded as to how this young, vibrant leader of the world's most powerful nation could have been felled by a single misfit loner with a mail-order rifle.

Much American innocence was lost as a result of the Kennedy assassination; the emotional damage to the nation remains incalculable. But the nation would go on. The Founding Fathers had prepared for these circumstances with the vice presidency. And for the eighth time in American history, a vice president assumed the presidential mantle following the death of a predecessor. President Kennedy's successor, Lyndon B. Johnson, with 27 combined years as a U.S. Representative, a U.S. Senator, and Vice President, was the most politically experienced of the successor presidents. The nation was only thirteen months away from the October 1962 Cuban Missile Crisis that placed millions of Americans at risk of nuclear annihilation. The hope was that President Johnson would assuage those fears and bring a calming presence to the anxious American people.

When President Johnson addressed Congress on November 27, five days after the murder and a day after the burial, a disquieting picture emerged. Seated behind Johnson were two very old white men. To the President's left was seated the 86-year-old U.S. Senator Carl Hayden (Dem-Ariz.), the President pro tempore of the Senate and second in line to President Johnson. To his right was U.S. Representative John W. McCormack (Dem-Mass.), the Speaker of the U.S. House and next in line to President Johnson with

Figure 1.1 President Lyndon Johnson's first address to Congress on November 27, 1963, with U.S. House Speaker John McCormack (Dem-Mass.) on the president's right and Senate President pro tem Carl Hayden (Dem-Ariz.) on his left (U.S. House Historian's Office).

only two weeks to his 72nd birthday (Figure 1.1). Their places in the line of succession had been established in the Presidential Succession Act of 1947,[1] a measure for which both had voted 16 years earlier, but neither hoped would ever be used.

Senator Hayden entered the Congress during the Taft Administration as Arizona's first elected U.S. Representative in 1912, the year it joined the Union. Hayden left the House for the Senate in 1927 and served in that chamber until 1969, when he retired at the age of 91. Speaker McCormack was first elected to the House in 1928 during the closing days of the Coolidge Administration and served until 1971 when he retired at the midpoint of President Richard Nixon's first term at the age of 79.

Standing before them was Lyndon Johnson, who had served with both men in their respective chambers—12 years for each. Although only 55, President Johnson suffered from a well-known heart condition which had kept him out of the 1956 presidential nominating contest. It was a condition that would end his life in 1973 at 64. The widely circulated photograph of Speaker McCormack and Senator Hayden seemed to represent the ghosts of "Congress Past." But they were now the ghosts of Congress Present and, most likely, Congress Yet-to-Come. In an effort to diminish the likelihood of either of these two gaining the presidency through the legislated line of succession, a constitutional amendment was proposed by Senator Birch Bayh (Dem-Ind.), entitled the "Presidential Succession and Disability Amendment." This amendment would allow the Congress to fill the vice presidency if it became vacant and to limit the operation of the 1947 Presidential Succession Act which placed the Speaker and the Senate's President pro tempore right behind the Vice President. To hammer home his point about the necessity of the amendment, the fateful 1963 photograph graced the cover of Senator Bayh's book *One Heartbeat Away*.[2]

Senator Bayh's proposal was successful and the 25th Amendment was ratified on February 23, 1967, one year and ten months after Congress had approved it and sent it to the states for ratification. The time it took to move through the state legislatures was close to the median of other constitutional amendments. The photograph had alerted the nation, but it had not panicked it.

With the solution approved, Senator Hayden was spared further speculation about his fitness for the presidency; however, Speaker McCormack was not so fortunate. Questions about his fitness continued to dog his speakership and he had to defend himself for much of his time in the chair as efforts to oust him surfaced during his years as Speaker.[3]

A private man in public life

From 1962 through 1970, Boston's John W. McCormack served as the 44th Speaker of the U.S. House of Representatives. He was a major legislative architect of both the New Deal and the Great Society. Forty-six years have passed since he left the House in 1971 and more than 30 years since his death in 1980. If he remains relatively unknown, that was his plan.

John McCormack was a very private man in a public office. In the words of his longtime Administrative Assistant Dr. Martin Sweig, "John McCormack was the most secretive man I have ever met."[4] Why?

The Austin-Boston Speakers: From 1940 through 1989, the U.S. House of Representatives had only six Speakers—Sam Rayburn, Joe Martin, John McCormack, Carl Albert, Thomas P. "Tip" O'Neill, Jr., and Jim Wright. Five were Democrats; only Joe Martin was a Republican. Three came from Massachusetts, two from Texas, and Carl Albert came from an Oklahoma district just across the Red River from Rayburn's.[5] During this same half-century, there were ten presidents and six Chief Justices of the Supreme Court. The presidents were born in eight different states and elected from nine of them. The Chief Justices were born in six different ones and chosen from five. The Speakers were born in four states and elected from only three. That an elected political institution with the shortest fixed term of any national legislature would have so few presiding officers is not the least of the House leadership's many ironies. That a national political institution with a constitutionally mandated requirement that its membership reflect population shifts in that nation should have been presided over by members from only three of the nation's fifty states enriches the irony. And that the one Speaker, John W. McCormack of Massachusetts, whose leadership in that body spanned over 30 years during that half-century remains unknown to the American public turns irony to mystery.

In the years between 1940, when John McCormack was first elected House Majority Leader, and 2016, twelve different individuals have held the office of Speaker of the U.S. House of Representatives. As the first public officer listed in the Constitution, the Speaker matters. Thus, it is not surprising that multiple books have been written about the occupants of the Speaker's chair. Eleven of the last twelve Speakers from Democrat

Sam Rayburn of Texas to Republican Paul Ryan of Wisconsin have been the subjects of biographies and autobiographies. Twenty-four biographies and autobiographies alone cover the lives and public careers of five Austin-Boston Speakers with nine on Sam Rayburn,[6] seven on Jim Wright,[7] five on Tip O'Neill,[8] two on Joe Martin,[9] and one on Carl Albert.[10] But there are none on John McCormack.

The forgotten speakership

John McCormack, who held the speakership for nine years, is the lone exception. Is it because he was unimportant and irrelevant to the politics of his time? No. It is because he chose not to share the full dimensions of his life that we know so little. Four reasons would seem to account for his lack of public attention.

1. *He did not want to be Speaker*: In an April 1977 interview, McCormack told me that he preferred being Majority Leader working the floor and assembling voting coalitions than presiding at a distance from the Speaker's chair.[11] In a postscript to a letter to H. G. Dulaney, Sam Rayburn's former secretary, McCormack wrote in 1967, six years after Sam's death, "I miss very much our late friend, Speaker Sam Rayburn. I wish he was here—he as Speaker and I as Majority Leader."[12]

2. *He was too deferential to the presidency*: McCormack's relationship to the presidency was reactive, not proactive. He saw his speakership as providing support for presidential initiatives. Presidential support scores on House floor votes during the nine years of John's speakership are the highest among the eleven Speakers who have served in the 60-plus years since 1953 when *Congressional Quarterly* began calculating that factor. The House's average presidential support score during John's nine years as Speaker was 84.2%–84.0% for his two years with Kennedy (1962–63); 86.5% for his five years with Johnson (1964–68); and 78.4% for his two years with Republican Nixon (1969–70).[13] Johnson's success rate in the House was so high that conservative columnist Robert Novak contended that Speaker McCormack was virtually on Johnson's staff.[14]

   Washington State's Tom Foley, who served as Majority Whip, 1981–87, and became the first post–Austin-Boston Speaker in 1989, recalled that "Speaker John McCormack made only marginally more use of the Whip [than Rayburn] and the White House congressional liaison staff performed most of the vote-counting function during the Kennedy and Johnson Administrations."[15]

   That may account for the high regard that John received from Democratic Presidents Franklin D. Roosevelt, Harry Truman, and Lyndon Johnson. However, it placed the House in a subordinate role and not the coequal one envisioned by the framers of the Constitution, who gave the all-important taxing power to the House.

3. *He was overshadowed in Boston*: John McCormack's career was intertwined for years with fellow Boston Irish-descended political leaders, all of whom were far more colorful than he, most notably his semi-mentor, Boston Mayor James Michael

Curley, his protégé Thomas P. "Tip" O'Neill, Jr., and the powerful and glamorous Fitzgerald-Kennedy clan of Mayor John F. "Honey Fitz" Fitzgerald, Ambassador Joseph P. Kennedy, President John F. Kennedy, and U.S. Senator Edward M. Kennedy. All cast huge shadows over both the Boston and national landscapes. The most succinct depiction of the relationship appeared as an aside in Rose Kennedy's memoirs, "The Fitzgeralds, Kennedys, and McCormacks had had many encounters in Massachusetts' political life: usually as friends, sometimes as foes, sometimes friendly enemies."[16]

Jack Kennedy's assassination created a martyrdom that has elevated his presidential reputation high in the estimation of both historians and the general public. In Boston, he was a secular saint. Consequently, any criticism of Jack Kennedy, no matter how mild or innocuous, was seen as dishonoring the memory of this beloved president and would lead to vehement denunciations from the Boston Irish, the very people who John McCormack had been elected to represent.

McCormack was very reluctant to discuss the complex relationship he had with John Kennedy. Two instances stand out. In Herbert S. Parmet's second biographical volume about Kennedy, *JFK: The Presidency of John F. Kennedy*, he quotes an unnamed historian as a "confidential source" who recounted[17]:

> One historian who interviewed McCormack shortly before his death in 1981 [*sic*] came away from that meeting and immediately recorded his observation that "when I turned to his relationship with John Kennedy . . . the change in atmosphere was quite dramatic. The speaker stiffened in his chair, his voice changed, and he became quite formal and quite strained. I knew at once that it would not be possible to probe realistically into the Kennedy-McCormack relationship. The speaker refused to discuss or even admit that any differences existed and repeatedly insisted that his ties to Kennedy were very positive. . . . It is my considered view as an historian that Speaker McCormack's response demonstrated that his relationship with John Kennedy was charged with tension, which, for personal and other reasons, the speaker does not intend to discuss or document."

Similarly, Lester Gordon, a Boston University graduate student hired by the university in 1972 to conduct a series of hour-long oral history interviews with McCormack, had the following exchange on his Tape 15. After John had provided an extensive and detailed answer describing the role of the relatively unimportant General Services Administration, Gordon prefaced his next question with, "The next time we meet in a couple of weeks, we'll talk about Kennedy's administration."[18]

McCormack responded, "Who?"

The interview ended and there was never another one.

4. *He did not want a biography*: John McCormack limited the number of his papers donated to the Gotlieb Archival Research Center at Boston University. Only the post-1950 papers have any completeness about them. The inference is that John's nephew and former Massachusetts Attorney General Eddie McCormack, an alumnus of BU

Law, and Dr. Martin Sweig, his chief of staff who spent time in prison for perjury, "sanitized" the files. The remaining papers are well catalogued but bereft of the extensive and candid correspondence found in the papers of other congressional luminaries with whom he served, like his allies Sam Rayburn (at the Rayburn Library in Bonham, Texas) and Carl Albert (at the University of Oklahoma), and his longtime liberal adversary Richard W. Bolling (at the University of Missouri-Kansas City). Furthermore, John's oral histories tend to be overlong and dissembling. He preferred to talk around questions rather than address them directly.

It was during the early 1970s while BU was completing John's documentary record that his beloved South Boston erupted in nationally publicized white opposition to the racial integration of its public schools. Leaders of the vocal opposition were two of South Boston's most powerful politicians: Boston School Committee member Louise Day Hicks, who would succeed John as the U.S. Representative of the 9th Massachusetts District, and State Senator William M. "Billy" Bulger, a protégé of John's brother Edward, best known as "Knocko" McCormack. South Boston, then the city's least diverse and most defensive of its ethnic enclaves, wanted no further scrutiny.

Lastly, John McCormack, who had successfully reinvented himself as the oldest son of a poor, widowed Irish mother, knew that his backstory might be revealed so he chose to hide in plain sight, with a conscious effort to be the least interesting major political figure of his time. There were serious personal reasons why he chose to operate in this self-effacing manner and these will be explored in this book, but his life and career are far too important to remain in the shadows of history.

John McCormack "in the room"

For almost 40 years, McCormack was near the epicenter of political power in the nation. The most fascinating aspect of his life is not his oft-told "rags-to-riches," Horatio Alger–like rise from the South Boston Irish tenements to the Speaker's chair on Capitol Hill,[19] but the fact that he was "in the room" for so many major political events which altered the course of American life.

—1928: McCormack was elected to the House to fill the unexpired term of the late Representative James A. Gallivan (Dem-Mass.) and to the subsequent term. He would win 22 consecutive elections to Congress.

—1931: With the support of newly installed Speaker John Nance "Cactus Jack" Garner of Texas, McCormack was elected to the Ways and Means Committee. At this time, the Democratic members of Ways and Means served as "the committee on committees" for other Democrats. McCormack finished second among the members elected to the new vacancies, ahead of Fred Vinson (Dem-Ky.), who would later become Secretary of the Treasury and Chief Justice of the United States. Fred Vinson was a "poker pal" of McCormack.[20]

—1933: FDR's New Deal measures moved quickly through the tax-writing House Ways and Means Committee on which McCormack was a member. These were the legendary "100 days."

—1934: The House named its first Special Committee on Un-American Activities to investigate fascist and communist movements. McCormack was chosen as chair with Sam Dickstein (Dem-NY) as vice chair.[21] Not known at the time was that Dickstein was on the payroll of the Soviet Embassy where he was referred to as "crook."[22] It was this committee that exposed the so-called businessmen's plot to overthrow FDR.

—1937: Commerce Committee Chair Sam Rayburn (Dem-Texas), a New Deal supporter, was elected House Majority Floor Leader over Rules Committee Chair John J. O'Connor (Dem-NY), a New Deal opponent, with the help of northern urban Catholic votes provided by McCormack.[23]

—1940: Working closely with conservative Virginia Representative Howard W. Smith, McCormack helped write the controversial Alien Registration Act, known as the "Smith Act." This act required all foreigners to register and be fingerprinted. It also made it unlawful to be a member of any organization that advocated the overthrow of the government by force or violence, or to advocate or conspire to advocate such overthrow.[24]

—1940: Sam Rayburn succeeded the deceased Will Bankhead (Dem-Ala.) as Speaker and McCormack succeeded Rayburn as House Majority Floor Leader. McCormack defeated Clifton Woodrum (Dem-Va.) in the Democratic Caucus with the help of FDR Cabinet Secretaries Harry Hopkins and Harold Ickes and led by Eugene "Goober" Cox (Dem-Ga.), an avowed segregationist.[25] Cox was another "poker pal" of McCormack. Once elected, Rayburn and McCormack served as the House's top two Democrats for 21 years and never had a vote recorded against them.

—1941: Newly elected Majority Leader McCormack was assigned by President Roosevelt to be the House Floor Manager for the $7 billion dollar Lend-Lease bill that was intended to rescue Britain from the Axis powers. Fearful of anti-British sentiments among American Irish urban Democrats, McCormack's role is seen as pivotal in managing this bill through the House.[26]

—1941: Following the bombing of Pearl Harbor, Majority Floor Leader McCormack introduced the resolutions of war against Japan and the other Axis powers, Germany and Italy.[27]

—1944: Meeting in the office of Speaker Sam Rayburn with Minority Leader Joe Martin (Rep-Mass.), Majority Leader McCormack first learned of the Manhattan Project. Army Chief of Staff George Marshall, Secretary of War Henry Stimson, and

Director of Scientific Research Vannevar Bush briefed the House leaders and urged them to appropriate money for the atomic bomb project without public knowledge or congressional scrutiny.[28]

—1944: The Democratic National Convention renominated President Franklin Roosevelt but replaced Vice President Henry A. Wallace with U.S. Senator Harry S. Truman (Dem-Mo.). Senator Truman played poker with McCormack, who chaired the 1944 Resolutions Committee.[29]

—1945: President Franklin Roosevelt died. Vice President Harry Truman received a call from the White House while seated with Speaker Rayburn in "the Board of Education," the Speaker's Capitol Hill hideaway.[30] Truman, who enjoyed poker and bourbon, would drink with Rayburn, who didn't play cards, and play poker with McCormack, who didn't drink. While they waited for McCormack, Harry Truman was summoned to the White House to learn of FDR's fate. Later that evening McCormack and other key officials attended President Truman's swearing-in by Chief Justice Harlan Fiske Stone.

—1947: With the Democratic loss in 1946, McCormack was now minority whip. In this new role, he circulated a petition among House members to urge President Harry Truman to pardon ex-Representative and newly elected Boston Mayor James Michael Curley for mail fraud and enable him to leave prison to serve as mayor for the fourth time. Over eighty House members signed the petition. Only one Massachusetts Democratic member refused, and that was John F. Kennedy, who succeeded Curley in the seat.[31]

—1949: Majority Leader McCormack made possible the return of segregationist William Colmer (Dem-Miss.) to the Rules Committee in 1949 over the opposition of Speaker Rayburn. But at the same time, McCormack, whose committee service was optional, remained seated on the Expenditures Committee when it installed William Dawson of Chicago as the first ever black chair of a congressional committee. John declared that his continuance was "to show what a great pleasure it is for me to serve under him as chairman."[32] This averted a southern walkout.

—1952: U.S. Representative John F. Kennedy challenged the reelection of Republican U.S. Senator Henry Cabot Lodge, Jr. of Massachusetts, who released documents indicating that John Kennedy's father, former Ambassador Joseph P. Kennedy, was a "defeatist" and accepting of a Nazi victory in Europe. McCormack, a longtime favorite of Jewish voters, was known as "Rabbi John."[33] He campaigned vigorously for Kennedy in the Jewish wards of Boston and helped him gain a 70,000 Democratic vote plurality over Lodge in spite of General Eisenhower's 209,000 Republican vote plurality over Illinois Governor Adlai E. Stevenson.[34]

—1956: After McCormack easily won the state's presidential preference primary over Kennedy-backed Adlai Stevenson,[35] Kennedy operatives took control of the state party away from McCormack loyalists to give Kennedy the delegation chairmanship. But it was McCormack's efforts at the Democratic National Convention that apparently undermined Kennedy's bid for the vice presidency.[36]

—1957: In October, the Soviets launched Sputnik, an earth-orbiting satellite. When a panicked American nation turned to the Congress for help, the House of Representatives created the Special Committee on Astronautics and Space Exploration and named 67-year-old John McCormack as chair.[37] At the time, McCormack had yet to fly on an airplane. Senate Majority Leader Lyndon B. Johnson (Dem-Texas) headed the Senate's panel.

—1960: In a surprising move, McCormack was selected by Senator John F. Kennedy to manage his nomination on the convention floor. A friend to both Sam Rayburn and Lyndon Johnson, McCormack helped put together the Kennedy-Johnson ticket which won the closest election in the twentieth century and installed the nation's first Roman Catholic president. Bobby Kennedy and Sam Rayburn opposed the ticket for different reasons. Ambassador Joseph Kennedy wanted Johnson and McCormack helped deliver him to the ticket.[38]

—1961: With the final illness and eventual death of Speaker Rayburn, McCormack assumed the chair in an acting capacity. During this year Ambassador Kennedy approached John McCormack with an offer intended to gain the Senate nomination for his youngest son Teddy and a gubernatorial nomination for the Speaker's nephew Eddie.[39] The ambassador's stroke in December voided the deal.

—1962: McCormack was elected as the first Roman Catholic Speaker of the U.S. House of Representatives.

—1962: Ted Kennedy and Eddie McCormack engaged in the fratricidal "Teddy-Eddie" contest for the Senate nomination. A bruising debate at South Boston High School led to a denunciation of Ted Kennedy by Ed McCormack. The attack backfired and Ted Kennedy gained the nomination with a two-to-one margin[40] and would serve in the U.S. Senate for 48 years.

—1963: John F. Kennedy's assassination placed 71-year-old Speaker McCormack next in line to President Lyndon Johnson for fourteen months. The prospect discomforted many Americans and the 25th Amendment, allowing the vice presidency to be filled by presidential appointment with confirmation by the Congress, was ratified quickly.

—1964: Speaker McCormack presided over the Democratic National Convention that nominated President Lyndon Johnson and U.S. Senator Hubert Humphrey (DFL-Minn.) as their ticket. Johnson and Humphrey captured 44 states and the District of Columbia with over 61% of the vote, the Democrats' highest percentage in the two-party era.[41]

—1965: Speaker McCormack presided over the House when the 1st Session of the 89th Congress gave LBJ a then record-setting 93% success rate for his Great Society legislative measures, including Medicare and Medicaid. This session rivaled 1933's "100 days" for legislative accomplishment, a time when McCormack also served.[42]

—1967: Ousted African-American U.S. Representative Adam Clayton Powell (Dem-NY) sued Speaker McCormack after being denied his seat and the chairmanship of the House Education and Labor Committee. The U.S. Supreme Court granted Powell his seat, but the House refused to let him resume his chairmanship.[43]

—1969: U.S. Representative Morris Udall (Dem-Ariz.) challenged Speaker McCormack within the Democratic Caucus. It was the first challenge to a sitting Speaker since 1923. McCormack handily won renomination in the Caucus by a vote of 178 to 62.[44]

—1970: Speaker John McCormack completed nine consecutive years as Speaker. It was the longest consecutive speakership on record until 1986 when his protégé Speaker Thomas P. "Tip" O'Neill Jr. (Dem-Mass.) completed his tenth consecutive year.

The political dimension: Preserving the New Deal and containing race politics

The realization that the Supreme Court's opposition was undermining the New Deal led FDR to unveil his Court expansion plan early in 1937. With huge majorities in both the House and the Senate, FDR assumed that it would sail through the Congress. But Sam Rayburn and John McCormack were well aware that House Judiciary Chair Hatton Sumners, a longtime Texas ally, was opposed to the plan and suggested that the bill first be introduced in the Senate.[45] It was in the Senate that the bill was stymied. In December 1937, North Carolina Senator Josiah Bailey issued the "Conservative Manifesto," and with southern Senators joined by a handful of Republicans they created what would become popularly known as the Conservative Coalition.[46] Before the 75th Congress ended, an informal alliance between them was formed in both houses and the coalition brought a virtual stop to the legislative expansion of the New Deal. With economic uncertainty returning in the 1937 recession and the impending loss of dozens of House seats in the 1938 midterm election, FDR loyalists were fearful that the New Deal would crash in Congress. To protect the New Deal's gains, FDR had intervened in the 1937 Senate majority leadership contest tilting toward moderate Alben Barkley of Kentucky over conservative Pat Harrison of Mississippi.[47]

The House was another story. Anticipated losses would be heaviest in those regions of the country recently voting for Democrats in the West and the agricultural Midwest. Only the South and the big-city Democrats would likely survive the anti–New Deal backlash. Texan Sam Rayburn, the newly elected House Majority Leader, and Bostonian John McCormack, the soon-to-be chair of the Democratic Caucus, held safe seats and were Roosevelt loyalists. They were well known to FDR's most politically savvy Cabinet members—Interior Secretary Harold Ickes, Commerce Secretary Harry Hopkins, and David K. Niles, Hopkins's assistant and longtime McCormack ally from Boston who handled political matters for the Works Progress Administration. Whether this was the original intent of the alliance can be argued, but it did prevent the Conservative Coalition from rolling back much of the New Deal's most significant gains, notably Social Security and the pro-labor Wagner-Connery National Labor Relations Act. The Rayburn-McCormack team led a "blocking" coalition that preserved the New Deal.

The Connection's later and more important impact was to help facilitate the transition of the Democratic Party from its 130-year dependence on its electoral base of white rural southern native-born voters into a more national party open to urban ethnic, religious, and racial minorities.

On the political level, the longtime Austin-Boston linkage between McCormack's Massachusetts and Rayburn's Texas was no surprise. Texas is the largest southern state with the smallest black population and Boston is the largest northern city with the smallest black population. Southerners with few blacks in their districts did not have to engage in racist posturing. This made it possible for them to have friends who were Catholic, Jewish, liberal, northern, and even black. They could deal with the disparate elements of the Democratic coalition without an electoral backlash in their districts.[48]

Boston is the northern urban analogue of this phenomenon. The decade-ending censuses of the 1950s and 1960s revealed that Boston ranked 12th in the 1960 Census and 11th in the 1970 Census regarding the proportion of blacks in the Standard Metropolitan Statistical Areas' (SMSA) "core city" of the twelve largest SMSAs in the country.[49] These were the decades of McCormack's power. Without a sizable number of blacks in their districts, Boston-area Representatives were not obliged to become advocates for civil rights issues. As Martin Sweig recalled, "John McCormack never made a civil rights speech, but he always voted for civil rights bills."[50] Voting for civil rights bills would not have antagonized the South, but speaking for civil rights would have.

Boston-area members were able to accommodate some of the more vocal and vehement racists that have sat in the House. John McCormack's best friend in the House was Eugene "Goober" Cox of Georgia, a leading segregationist. "We never agreed on anything," McCormack recounted, "but he was a damn good pal."[51]

In the 1948 Democratic National Convention and the general election, the Democratic Party confronted the political ramifications of the race crisis head on. Following the passage of a pro–civil rights plank to the Democratic platform, dozens of angry white southern Democrats left the convention to nominate Governor J. Strom Thurmond of South Carolina as the presidential nominee of the States Rights Party, best known as the "Dixiecrats." With Thurmond's hard-core segregationists out of the Democratic Party, liberals and urban blacks renewed their commitment to the party and President Harry Truman was elected in his own right.

This made continuing the balancing act between the white South and urban blacks even more imperative. It was John McCormack who adjusted the balance by making possible the return of segregationist William Colmer of Mississippi to the Rules

Committee in 1949 over the opposition of Speaker Sam Rayburn.[52] But it was also John McCormack, as majority leader that same year, whose decision to remain seated on the Expenditures Committee headed off a southern walkout when William Dawson of Chicago was installed as the first ever black chair of a congressional committee. The message was simple: If the majority leader had no problem with a black chairing his committee, why should anyone else have a problem with it?

McCormack was able to manage this balancing act because he was in a position to negotiate with southern hard-liners without fear of electoral retribution back home. It was the ability to finesse the race issue that made the original "Austin-Boston connection" of Rayburn and McCormack so powerful. This was because it was (and is) the race issue, more than any other, that has disrupted the Democratic Party.

Presidential politics within the Democratic Party have been plagued by race issues as well.[53] It was race that forced Democratic nominating conventions to adopt the "two-thirds rule" for selecting their presidential candidates. This rule gave the South a century-long veto over presidential nominees from 1831 to 1932. It was race that led to two separate Democratic nominating conventions in 1860 and it was race that resulted in 103 ballots at the 1924 convention.

In the postwar years, it was the racial divide which led not only to many southern delegates storming out of the 1948 Democratic Convention to create the Dixiecrat presidential candidacy of Governor Thurmond, but also the "loyalty oath" battle at the 1952 convention; the "independent elector" movement in the 1960 election for Virginia Senator Harry Flood Byrd; and the presidential candidacies of Alabama Governor George Wallace in 1964, 1968, and 1972. The "Willie Horton" campaign against Massachusetts Governor Michael Dukakis in the 1988 election was a dramatic example of how race politics play havoc with Democratic presidential fortunes.

But the House remained relatively unaffected and the Democrats were able to hold the House for 60 out of 64 years between 1931 and 1994. Democratic leaders in the House sought to finesse, control, and contain racial politics, the most vehement and volatile of the issues with which the party has had to contend in its lengthy existence. The most effective way to do this was to bring into the leadership members who could accommodate this divisiveness. These members had districts that permitted them flexibility to have friends on both sides of the issue. Members from Texas and Massachusetts—Austin and Boston—met the requirement. These leaders could direct the U.S. House of Representatives to contain the race question but not necessarily to address it.

The personal dimension: Poverty and probity

On a personal level, John McCormack was a mainstay "in the room" because he was reliable. A lifelong teetotaler, he always had his wits about him; he remembered everything. A Boston Irishman, McCormack could keep secrets, knowing full well that the most disdained person among the Irish was an informant. A devout Roman Catholic, he valued loyalty above all other virtues. He needed no press attention to feel good about himself. His solid marriage of 51 years provided him with all of the emotional sustenance that he needed. His background of poverty led him to value minor financial comforts and the steadiness of a job that lasted 42 years. His modesty, frugality, and integrity made McCormack the "moral compass" of the House of Representatives.

Furthermore, John McCormack was "a poor boy who had made good." The "poor boy" motif is played out again and again among the Austin-Boston Speakers. It was true of Sam Rayburn, whose farmer father uprooted the family from the dwindling fields of Roane County in the mountains of east Tennessee to the more productive ones of northeast Texas; of Joe Martin, whose blacksmith father made too little money to educate his oldest son; of Carl Albert, whose coal miner father had located in a community only large enough to support a one-room schoolhouse; of Tip O'Neill, who grew up the motherless son of a Boston Irish bricklayer; and of Jim Wright, whose itinerant father roamed through the Southwest as a traveling salesman. The shared hardships of their early lives united these men and sensitized them to the deprivations that continued in America and the role that the federal government could play in alleviating them.

But McCormack's life history was different. His early hardships were genuine, but the story of his life was altered to fit the realities of gaining public office in Boston, a city hopelessly fractured by ethnic and religious conflicts. McCormack had often told people of his early life, of a poor Irish-born immigrant father who died young, leaving 13-year-old John, the oldest son, to care for his Irish-born mother and two younger siblings.[54]

It was a powerful story and had been recounted often. The greatest of the early-twentieth-century Boston Irish politicians—James Michael Curley, the presumed hero of the classic novel *The Last Hurrah*, and both of President John F. Kennedy's grandfathers, John F. "Honey Fitz" Fitzgerald and Patrick "P.J." Kennedy—had stories identical to this. The power of this tale of Irish fathers, widowed mothers, and younger siblings had elevated them to positions of high station within Irish Boston. Once John McCormack had convinced the gatekeepers that he was "one of them," he ascended quickly through the ranks of the Boston Irish, and once elevated to the U.S. House of Representatives he was able to play a large and lasting role in American political life.

An Early Alliance: While it was Sam Rayburn of Texas and John McCormack of Boston who were the original "Austin-Boston Connection," both men were linked by their respective mentors. Rayburn's was Speaker John Nance "Cactus Jack" Garner of Uvalde, Texas, while McCormack's was James Michael Curley, Boston's four-time mayor. Garner and Rayburn had both been mentored by fellow Texan Joe Bailey, one-time House Minority Leader. Jack Garner and Jim Curley got to know one another when they served together on the House Foreign Affairs Committee, 1911–13. Twenty years later, in July 1932, pro-FDR Bostonians Jim Curley and Joe Kennedy lobbied William Randolph Hearst to shift California's delegates to FDR with Cactus Jack named as vice president. Curley delivered a resounding seconding speech for Garner. Just months before, in December 1931, John McCormack in only his third year was elected to the House Ways and Means Committee with support from Speaker Garner and all of the Texans. "It was a record," recounted McCormack as he remembered his early ascension to this most formidable seat of power.[55] The first step had been taken.

In 1940 Sam Rayburn would be elected as Speaker and John McCormack would be elected as Majority Leader. They would take the reins of the House Democrats and never face a challenging vote in the 21 years that they served together as the party's top two leaders. And their respective protégés—Rayburn's Carl Albert of Oklahoma and Jim Wright of Texas along with McCormack's protégé Thomas P. "Tip" O'Neill, Jr.— would extend the reach of the "Austin-Boston Connection" into June 1989 and Speaker Jim Wright's resignation from the House.

The Austin-Boston Speakers kept the Democratic majority in the House together for a half-century. They did this by defining race politics in a way that limited the divisiveness of the issue as long as possible through containment and deflection.

Regional divisions could be handled through taxation and appropriations policies that would redistribute the substantial post–New Deal federal tax revenues from the wealthy industrial states of the Northeast and Midwest to the relatively benighted ones of the South and Southwest. Defense expenditures were the best vehicle for this interregional transfer of funds because national security was the one issue that enjoyed a wide consensus of popular support. The members of the tax-writing Ways and Means Committee, the spending Appropriations Committee, and the Armed Services Committee all knew their respective roles in the reallocation of these revenues to those places most in need of financial uplift. The South had benefited most from the World War II build-up and its military bases were the major beneficiaries of defense appropriations. Keeping Democrats in power protected the seniority of the southern Representatives and the committee chairmanships they held.

In the northern urban areas, the House redistributed federal revenues to alleviate the economic hardships of families. The key to the success of these programs was to make them income-targeted and not race-targeted. The fact that minority families were disproportionately poor made them disproportionately the beneficiaries of federal welfare policy. Many of these families endured financial hardships similar to those of the "poor boy" Austin-Boston Speakers, who used their legislative powers to insure that future generations would not have to undergo the financial deprivations that they had overcome.

Religious divisions, which disrupted national presidential politics in the Al Smith candidacy of 1928, were handled within the House. No religious tests were imposed upon those Democrats who would gain power within the chamber, either at the elected level of floor leadership as in the case of Roman Catholics like Boston's McCormack and Tip O'Neill and New Orleans's Hale Boggs or in the elevation of committee chairs with Jewish Representatives like New York City's Sol Bloom of the Foreign Affairs Committee and Emanuel Celler of the Judiciary Committee, and Chicago's Adolph Sabath on the Rules Committee. By protecting the seniority system, the House Democratic leadership was able to reward those members whose ethnically homogeneous enclaves had made them immune enough to defeat to accumulate the seniority needed for a committee chairmanship.

For these House leaders, their ascents through the social structure were vivid affirmations of the "American Dream." The posts they held were hard-won, and they had come much too far to risk these posts for abstract principles. They contained disruptive issues. Containing issues may not have always been good social policy or ideologically consistent, but it guaranteed institutional survival in the House. A major architect of this strategy was John McCormack.

After McCormack left the House in 1971, the Austin-Boston speakership continued for another 18 years with his friends and protégés Carl Albert, Tip O'Neill, and Jim Wright following him to the Speaker's chair. The forced departure of Fort Worth's Jim Wright in 1989 due to the ethics onslaught of Georgia Republican Newt Gingrich ended the Austin-Boston speakership.[56]

The vacuum left by its collapse was filled by the most agenda-driven of the House's various legislative groupings—the Congressional Black Caucus. Following Wright's departure, it was they who got Philadelphia's William Gray elected as majority whip, the first black in the top ranks of House leadership. It was the Congressional Black Caucus that also pushed President George H. W. Bush's Justice Department to create "majority-minority" districts that would more than double minority representation in the 1992 House elections but would "bleach" adjacent congressional districts.[57]

The racial "bleaching" of these districts placed the white southern Democratic moderates representing them at risk. Two years later, in 1994, more than twenty southern Democrats fell before the young white conservative zealots recruited by Newt Gingrich, the man who had ended the career of Jim Wright. It was the defeats of the southern Democratic moderates that gave Newt Gingrich the seats he needed to install himself as Speaker of the House.[58] Perhaps it was fitting that the man who would end the Austin-Boston speakership would be the beneficiary of its demise.

The end of the Austin-Boston speakership unleashed racial forces which led to the loss of Democratic control of the House. This would have dismayed John McCormack but would not have surprised him. The public speakership, fashioned in large part by his protégé Tip O'Neill, would have also dismayed him.[59] Endless rounds of press conferences, C-SPAN coverage, Sunday morning talk show interviews, and all the other aspects of the "public speakership" would have sent him scurrying from office. McCormack's public life was a very private one. It was not the only irony of his 42-year congressional career, but the most obvious one.

No one in national public life disliked the limelight more than John McCormack. No political figure of his era was more resistant than he about a biography. But times have changed. Today's speakership of the House is on daily public display, with six years of a Republican House of Representatives committed to dismantling much of the economic legislation passed to lighten the burdens of America's underprivileged citizens. The time has arrived for an assessment of John McCormack, one of the congressional architects of both the New Deal and the Great Society, and the last private Speaker of the House. In the process we will learn more about how the U.S. House of Representatives operated and how a small group of long-serving congressional leaders managed the nation's business while containing the divisive politics of race, region, and religion.

Notes

1   Presidential Succession Act of 1947, approved July 18, 1947 (Public law 80-199; 61 Statutes 380-381). Public Law (P.L.) refers to the numeric order of legislation passed within a Congress.

2   Birch Bayh, *One Heartbeat Away: Presidential Disability and Succession* (Indianapolis: Bobbs-Merrill, 1968).

3   The most critical accounts of the McCormack speakership are contained in two books by U.S. Representative Richard Bolling (Dem-Mo.): *House Out of Order* (New York: E.P. Dutton, 1965); and *Power in the House: A History of the Leadership of the House of Representatives* (New York: E.P. Dutton, 1968), pp. 230–38. Bolling was a protégé of Sam Rayburn, who anticipated that he would follow Rayburn as Speaker. Bolling contended that McCormack as Speaker had surrendered power to the conservative committee chairs.

4   Author's telephonic interview with Dr. Martin Sweig, Winthrop, MA, June 1998.

5   The only work to deal with the five Democratic Austin-Boston Speakers is Anthony Champagne, Douglas B. Harris, James W. Riddlesperger, Jr., and Garrison Nelson, *The Austin-Boston Connection: Five Decades of House Democratic Leadership* (College Station: Texas A+M University Press, 2009). While Joe Martin, the lone Republican Speaker, is excluded, two Texas Democratic mentors are included: House Minority Leader Joseph W. Bailey and Speaker John Nance Garner.

6   The best biographies and memoirs on Sam Rayburn include C. Dwight Dorough, *Mr. Sam* (New York: Random House, 1962); Booth Mooney, *Roosevelt and Rayburn: A Political Partnership* (Philadelphia: J.B. Lippincott, 1971); Alfred Steinberg, *Sam Rayburn: A Biography* (New York: Hawthorn Books, 1975); two books by Anthony Champagne, *Congressman Sam Rayburn* (New Brunswick, NJ: Rutgers University Press, 1984) and *Sam Rayburn: A Bio-bibliography* (New York: Greenwood Press, 1988); H. G. Dulaney and Edward H. Phillips, eds., *"Speak, Mister Speaker"* (Bonham, TX: Sam Rayburn Foundation, 1978); and D. B. Hardeman and Donald C. Bacon, *Rayburn: A Biography* (Austin, TX: Texas Monthly Press, 1987).

7   Books and memoirs on Jim Wright include John Barry, *The Ambition and the Power: The Fall of Jim Wright* (New York: Viking, 1989); Wright's memoirs, *Worth It All: My War for Peace* (New York: Brasseys, 1993) and *Balance of Power: Presidents and Congress from the Era of McCarthy to the Age of Gingrich* (Atlanta: Turner Publishing, 1996); and collections of his writings, *Reflections of a Public Man* (Fort Worth, TX: Allied, 1984); as well as the compilation by James W. Riddlesperger, Jr., Anthony Champagne, and Dan Williams, eds., *The Wright Stuff: Reflections on People and Politics* (Fort Worth, TX: Texas Christian University Press, 2013).

8   Books and memoirs on Thomas P. "Tip" O'Neill, Jr. include Paul Clancy and Shirley Elder, *Tip: A Biography of Thomas P. O'Neill, Speaker of the House* (New York: Macmillan, 1980); his best-selling memoir with William Novak, *Man of the House: The Life and Political Memoirs of Speaker Tip O'Neill* (New York: Random House, 1987). The best account is John Aloysius Farrell, *Tip O'Neill and the Democratic Century* (Boston: Little, Brown, 2001). Chris Matthews, who served on O'Neill's staff, has just published a wonderful joint biography of President Reagan and Speaker O'Neill entitled, *Tip and the Gipper: When Politics Worked* (New York: Simon & Schuster, 2013).

9   On Joe Martin, see his autobiography as told to Robert J. Donovan, *My First Fifty Years in Politics* (New York: McGraw-Hill, 1960); and the James J. Kennealy's biography,

A Compassionate Conservative: A Political Biography of Joseph W. Martin, Jr., Member of the U.S. House of Representatives (Lanham, MD: Lexington Books, 2003).

10 Carl Albert's autobiography with Danney Goble, *Little Giant: The Life and Times of Speaker Carl Albert* (Norman: University of Oklahoma Press, 1990).

11 Author's telephonic interview with the Hon. John W. McCormack, April 1977.

12 Letter from John W. McCormack to H. G. Dulaney, quoted in Champagne et al., *The Austin-Boston Connection*, p. 130.

13 "Presidential Victories on Votes in Congress, 1953–2007," in Norman J. Ornstein, Thomas E. Mann, and Michael J. Malbin, eds., *Vital Statistics on Congress, 2008* (Washington, DC: The Brookings Institution, CQ Press, 2008), pp. 144–45, and updated with *Congressional Quarterly Almanacs*.

14 Robert D. Novak, *The Prince of Darkness: 50 Years of Reporting in Washington* (New York: Crown Forum, 2007), p. 301.

15 Jeffrey R. Biggs and Thomas S. Foley, *Honor in the House: Speaker Tom Foley* (Pullman: Washington State University, 1999), pp. 69–70.

16 Rose Fitzgerald Kennedy, *Times to Remember* (Garden City, NY: Doubleday & Company, 1974), p. 428.

17 Herbert S. Parmet, *JFK: The Presidency of John F. Kennedy* (New York: The Dial Press, 1983), p. 205. Parmet lists the interview with the unnamed historian as "Confidential source" (p. 378, n. 14).

18 Lester Gordon, oral history interviews for Boston University with John McCormack, "Eisenhower Years, 1952–1960," Tape 15, June 1, 1973.

19 A typical article about John McCormack in the Horatio Alger genre is Richard W. O'Connor, "From Andrew Square to the Speaker's Chair," *Yankee*, XL (April 1976), pp. 90–95 and 132–34. McCormack loved the Horatio Alger stories and his onetime residence at 470 Dorchester Street met Alger Street at the curb, which was named for Boston's own Horatio Alger. John's nickname in South Boston was "Little Dick" because of his affinity for the Burt L. Standish dime novels about Frank and Dick Merriwell, the star baseball-playing brothers at Yale.

20 Author's interview with U.S. House Speaker John W. McCormack, Washington, DC, September 1968.

21 Among the relevant accounts are Sander Diamond, *The Nazi Movement in the United States, 1924–1941* (Ithaca, NY: Cornell University Press, 1974); Walter Goodman, *The Committee: The Extraordinary Career of the House Committee on Un-American Activities* (New York: Farrar, Straus and Giroux, 1968); and Earl Latham, *The Communist Conspiracy in Washington from the New Deal to McCarthy* (Cambridge, MA: Harvard University Press, 1966).

22 See "'Crook': A Soviet Agent in Congress," in Allen Weinstein and Alexander Vassiliev, eds., *The Haunted Wood: Soviet Espionage in America—The Stalin Era* (New York: Random House, 1999), chapter 7.

23 Hardeman and Bacon, *Rayburn: A Biography*, p. 212.

24 The Alien Registration Act (Smith Act) was approved on June 28, 1940 (Public Law 76-670; 54 Statutes 670-76). McCormack's role was described in the author's interview with Dr. Martin Sweig, May 1997.

25 Author's telephonic interview with the Hon. John W. McCormack, Boston, MA, April 1977.

26 McCormack's role in deflecting Irish-American opposition to legislation aiding Britain may be found in T. Ryle Dwyer, *Irish Neutrality and the USA: 1939–1947* (Dublin: Gill

and Macmillan, 1977), p. 39. See also Edward R. Stettinius, Jr., later to become secretary of state, who describes McCormack's role in his account, *Lend-Lease: Weapon for Victory* (New York: Macmillan, 1944), on pp. 68 and 70. McCormack's Irish-American connection is made in Leon Martel, *Lend-Lease, Loans, and the Coming of the Cold War: A Study of the Implementation of Foreign Policy* (Boulder, CO: Westview, 1979), pp. 216–17.

27   McCormack resolutions: Declaration of a State of War with Japan was approved December 8, 1941 (Public Law 77-328; 55 *Statutes* 795). Roll call vote 130, *Congressional Record*, 77th Congress, 1st Session, pp. 9536–37. Declaration of a State of War with Germany was approved December 11, 1941 (Public Law 77-331; 55 *Statutes* 796); and Declaration of a State of War with Italy was approved December 11, 1941 (Public Law 77-332; 55 *Statutes* 797). Roll call votes 131 and 132, *Congressional Record*, 77th Congress, 1st Session, pp. 9665–67.

28   See Joe Martin's book, *My First Fifty Years in Politics*, pp. 100–101; and Henry L. Stimson and McGeorge Bundy, *On Active Service in Peace and War* (New York: Harper & Bros., 1947), p. 614.

29   Robert H. Ferrell, *Choosing Truman: The Democratic Convention of 1944* (Columbia: University of Missouri Press, 1994). McCormack is not mentioned in Ferrell's book, even though he chaired the Resolutions Committee that wrote the platform. See "McCormack Asks Collaboration," *NYT* (July 10, 1944), p. 16; James A. Hagerty, "Wallace Backers in Chicago Gloomy . . . Brief Platform Sought—McCormack and Mrs. Norton Put It at 500 to 1,000 Words—Foreign Policy Stressed," *NYT* (July 15, 1944), p. 26; and "Foreign-Policy Day Set by Democrats—McCormack Says the Platform Makers Will Devote All of Wednesday to This Issue," *NYT* (July 17, 1944), p. 8.

30   Robert Donovan's version of that fateful afternoon has only Lewis Deschler, the House parliamentarian, and James M. Barnes, a former Illinois congressman and White House legislative liaison, in the room with Truman and Rayburn. Others were expected at the close of House business. See Robert J. Donovan, *Conflict and Crisis: The Presidency of Harry S. Truman, 1945–1948* (New York: W. W. Norton, 1977), pp. 3–5. See also President Truman's own recollection in Volume I of his memoirs, *Year of Decisions* (Garden City, NY: Doubleday, 1955), p. 4; and David M. McCullough, *Truman* (New York: Simon & Schuster, 1995), p. 4 and 7 for the swearing-in.

31   James Michael Curley noted John Kennedy as "the glaring exception," in his autobiography, *I'd Do It Again: A Record of All My Uproarious Years* (Englewood Cliffs, NJ: Prentice-Hall, 1957), pp. 333–34. Jack Beatty contends that the decision not to sign the petition was JFK's own and it countered his father's wishes. JFK wished to avenge Curley's attacks on his namesake and his mother's father, John F. "Honey Fitz" Fitzgerald, *The Rascal King: The Life and Times of James Michael Curley, 1884–1958* (Reading, MA: Addison-Wesley, 1992), p. 480. President Truman gave John McCormack the credit for the Curley pardon. "I did it for you, John," was the president's statement (p. 481).

32   The episode is recounted in Christopher Manning's valuable biography, *William L. Dawson and the Limits of Black Electoral Leadership* (Dekalb: Northern Illinois Press, 2009), p. 128. Associated Press, "McCormack Aids Dawson: Steps Aside to Open Committee Chairmanship to Negro," *NYT* (January 1, 1949), p. 24.

33   On John McCormack's electoral appeal to the voters of heavily Jewish Ward 14 (Mattapan), see Lawrence H. Fuchs, *The Political Behavior of American Jews* (Glencoe, IL: The Free Press, 1956), p. 138n.

34 Joe Kennedy's anti-Semitism was long suspected. See "The Jewish Question," in Ronald Kessler's *The Sins of the Father: Joseph p. Kennedy and the Dynasty He Founded* (New York: Warner Books, 1996), pp. 161–76. It is also noted in the highly critical book by Nigel Hamilton, *JFK: Reckless Youth* (New York: Random House, 1992), pp. 108, 247, 512, and 669. John McCormack's assistance to John Kennedy with Jewish voters is recounted in his interview with T. Harrison Baker of the University of Texas Oral History Project, Lyndon Baines Johnson Library, September 23, 1968, pp. 21–22.

35 "1956 Primaries," in *Congressional Quarterly, Presidential Elections, 1789–1992* (Washington, DC: Congressional Quarterly, 1995), p. 172. Only write-ins were recorded in the April 24, 1956, Massachusetts primary. McCormack captured 26,128 votes (47.9%) to Adlai Stevenson's 19,024 (34.9%). John Kennedy finished in fifth place with 949 votes behind McCormack, Stevenson, Tennessee Senator Estes Kefauver (4,547 votes), and Republican President Dwight D. Eisenhower (1,859 votes).

36 On McCormack's presumed anti-Kennedy efforts at the 1956 Democratic Convention, see "National Affairs: The Wide Open Winner," *TIME* (August 27, 1956).

37 The House Select Committee on Astronautics and Space Exploration was created on March 5, 1958, by H.Res. 496 of the 85th Congress. The committee was created that day with House Majority Leader John W. McCormack named as chair.

38 Given the fact that this selection led to two important presidencies, this decision has been analyzed countless times. The narrow success of the Kennedy-Johnson ticket has led many to take credit for putting it together. Even though John McCormack was named by John Kennedy to be his convention floor manager, he is most often left out of accounts that focus on decision-making within the Kennedy camp. See Arthur M. Schlesinger, Jr., *A Thousand Days: John F. Kennedy in the White House* (Boston, MA: Houghton, Mifflin, 1965), pp. 50–57; Jules Witcover, *Crapshoot: Rolling the Dice on the Vice Presidency* (New York: Crown, 1992), pp. 140–63; and Jeff Shesol, "The Affront," in *Mutual Contempt: Lyndon Johnson, Robert Kennedy, and the Feud That Defined a Decade* (New York: W. W. Norton, 1997), pp. 41–60. John McCormack's role, if acknowledged, was presumably to convince his good friend Sam Rayburn, Johnson's floor manager, that John Kennedy was offering the vice presidency to Lyndon Johnson in good faith and not as an empty gesture with the assumption that the offer would be rejected. See John McCormack's interview with T. Harrison Baker of the University of Texas Oral History Project, Lyndon Baines Johnson Library, September 23, 1968, pp. 13–17. See also Robert Dallek, *Lone Star Rising; Lyndon Johnson and His Times* (New York: Oxford University Press, 1991), pp. 574–82.

39 See John McCormack's interview with T. Harrison Baker of the University of Texas Oral History Project, Lyndon Baines Johnson Library, September 23, 1968, pp. 24–25.

40 The fullest account of this conflict appears in Murray B. Levin, *Kennedy Campaigning: The System and the Style as Practiced by Senator Edward Kennedy* (Boston: Beacon Press, 1966). The Teddy-Eddie debates and their aftermath are covered in chapter 4, pp. 181–232.

41 Theodore H. White's *The Making of the President, 1964* (New York: Atheneum, 1965) covered the convention in chapter 9, "Lyndon Johnson's Convention," pp. 243–93.

42 See *Congressional Quarterly*, "Congress, 1965—the Year in Review: Johnson Leadership, Large Majorities Win Legislative Grand Slam for Democrats," *Congressional Quarterly Almanac, 1964*, XXI (Washington, DC, 1965), pp. 65–79. And in "Congress Backs Johnson on 93% of Roll Call Votes," pp. 1099–1110. The success rate for Johnson in the House itself was 94% (105 successes on 112 votes).

43   A day-by-day recounting of the Powell case may be found in U.S. Representative Andy
     Jacobs Jr.'s (Dem-Ind.) book *The Powell Affair: Freedom Minus One* (Indianapolis:
     Bobbs-Merrill, 1973). Secondary accounts of this event may be found in p. Allan
     Dionisopoulos, *Rebellion, Racism and Representation* (DeKalb: Northern Illinois
     University Press, 1970), pp. 1–18; and Charles V. Hamilton, *Adam Clayton Powell,
     Jr.: The Political Biography of an American Dilemma* (New York: Atheneum, 1991),
     pp. 445–78.

44   *Congressional Quarterly Almanac, 1969*, XXV (Washington, DC: Congressional
     Quarterly, 1970), p. 25.

45   Sumners's opposition may be found in the daily recounting of the battle in Joseph
     Alsop and Turner Catledge's *The 168 Days* (Garden City, NY: Doubleday, Doran, 1938),
     p. 67. See also the analysis of Sumners's crucial role in Anthony Champagne, "Hatton
     Sumners and the 1937 Court-Packing Plan," *East Texas Historical Journal*, 26 (Spring
     1988), pp. 46–49.

46   James T. Patterson, *Congressional Conservatism and the New Deal: The Growth of the
     Conservative Coalition in Congress, 1933–1939* (Lexington: University of Kentucky
     Press, 1967).

47   Polly Davis, "Court Reform and Alben W. Barkley's Election as Majority Leader,"
     Southern Quarterly, XV (1976), pp. 15–31.

48   This argument gets a fuller treatment in Garrison Nelson, "Congressional Race
     Politics and the End of the Austin-Boston Connection," a paper presented at the
     Annual Meeting of the New England Political Science Association in Portland, Maine,
     April 1990.

49   Of the 12 largest Standard Metropolitan Statistical Areas (SMSAs) in the country,
     Boston ranked 12th in the 1960 Census and 11th in the 1970 Census with regard to
     the proportion of blacks in the SMSA's "core city." In 1960, Boston's 9.1% proportion
     of blacks fell 15.5 points below the 24.6 median for these 12 urban places. In 1970,
     Boston's 16.3 was 16.9 points below that year's median for black populations in the
     core cities of the 12 largest SMSAs. Figures are recomputed from data presented in the
     1977 edition of the Statistical Abstract of the U.S. (Washington, DC: U.S. Department
     of Commerce, Bureau of the Census, 1977), pp. 22–24.

50   Author's telephonic interview with Dr. Martin Sweig, Winchester, MA, May 1997.

51   Author's telephonic interview with the Hon. John W. McCormack, Boston, April 1977.

52   Rayburn's opposition to Colmer is stated in a letter to Jere Cooper (Dem-Tenn.), the
     second-ranking Democrat on the House Ways and Means Committee, November 22,
     1948, in the Rayburn Papers, Rayburn Library, 1948 files, Miscellaneous A-2, July–
     December, as cited in James A. Robinson, *The House Rules Committee* (Indianapolis:
     Bobbs-Merrill Co., 1963), pp. 104–105.

53   A well-written reminder of the Democratic Party's unfortunate racist legacy is
     recounted in Bruce Bartlett's *Wrong on Race: The Democratic Party's Buried Past*
     (New York: Palgrave Macmillan, 2008). A solid overview of the role played by race
     politics in presidential decision-making over the course of American history may
     be found in Kenneth O'Reilly, *Nixon's Piano: Presidents and Racial Politics from
     Washington to Clinton* (New York: The Free Press, 1995). See also Thomas Byrne
     Edsall with Mary D. Edsall, *Chain Reaction: The Impact of Race, Rights, and Taxes on
     American Politics* (New York: W. W. Norton & Co., 1991).

54 The biographical accounts of John McCormack's early life all contain this version. See: Donald R. Kennon, ed., "John William McCormack," in *The Speakers of the U.S. House of Representatives: A Bibliography, 1789–1984* (Baltimore: The Johns Hopkins University Press, 1986), p. 266; Charles Moritz, ed., "John W. McCormack," in *Current Biography, 1962* (New York: H.W. Wilson, 1963), pp. 275–77; Richard H. Gentile, "John William McCormack," in Kenneth T. Jackson, ed., *DAB, Supplement Ten, 1975–1980* (New York: Charles Scribner's Sons, 1995), pp. 483–87. *Mea culpa.* I accepted the story in my profile of John McCormack in Donald C. Bacon, Roger H. Davidson, and Morton H. Keller, eds., *The Encyclopedia of the United States Congress*, III (New York; Simon & Schuster, 1995), pp. 1328–30.

55 Author's interview with the Hon. John W. McCormack in the Speaker's Office, Washington, DC, September 1968.

56 Needless to say the Wright and Gingrich accounts of this event differ. For Wright's version, see his *Balance of Power*, pp. 474 and 484–85. For Gingrich's version of the removal of Wright, see Newt Gingrich, *Lessons Learned the Hard Way: A Personal Report* (New York: HarperCollins, 1998), pp. 88 and 92–94.

57 Only a few contemporaneous accounts described the racial "bleaching" in southern congressional districts for the 1994 victory. See Richard E. Cohen, "Campaigning for Congress: The Echo of 1994," in Larry Sabato, ed., *Towards the Millennium: The Elections of 1996* (Boston: Allyn and Bacon, 1997), pp. 174–77. One early account anticipated the potential problem for the Democrats; see the Occasional Paper prepared for the McCormack Institute of Public Affairs by Maurice T. Cunningham and Edmund Beard, *The Re-segregation of America: The Racial Politics of Legislative Redistricting* (Boston: University of Massachusetts-Boston, 1993). The unintended consequences are described in David Canon's prize-winning *Race, Redistricting, and Representation: The Unintended Consequences of Black Majority Districts* (Chicago: University of Chicago Press, 1999) and that it may have been intended by the G.H.W. Bush Justice Department in Maurice T. Cunningham's *Maximization, Whatever the Cost: Race, Redistricting and the Department of Justice* (Westport, CT: Praeger, 2001).

58 Accounts of the 1994 congressional election include James A. Finefrock, "The Republican Tsunami," *San Francisco Examiner* (December 9, 1994), p. A-11. Among the more evocative descriptions were "Stampede!," the cover story for *TIME*, CXLIV (November 21, 1994), pp. 46–49ff; J. Weisberg's "After the Deluge," *New York*, XXVII (November 14, 1994), pp. 28ff.; Meg Greenfield's "After the Big One," *Newsweek*, CXXIV (November 21, 1994), p. 108; and R. Lacayo's "After the Revolution," *TIME*, CLXIV (November 28, 1994), pp. 28–33.

59 Douglas B. Harris, "The Rise of the Public Speakership," *Political Science Quarterly*, CXIII (Summer 1998), pp. 193–212.

2

Irish Emigration and the Cauldron
of Yankee Boston

Seldom does the misery of others provide as much joy as did the plight of the Irish for the British. As the Great Famine of the 1840s ravaged the Irish countryside and depopulated Ireland of its citizenry through death, disease, and departure, the *London Times* gleefully announced[1]:

> They are going! They are going! The Irish are going with a vengeance. Soon a Celt . . . will be as rare in Ireland as a Red Indian on the shore of Manhattan. Law has ridden through Ireland; it has been taught with bayonets, and interpreted with ruin. Townships leveled with the ground, straggling columns of exiles, workhouses multiplied, and still crowded, express the determination of the legislature to rescue Ireland from its slovenly old barbarism, and to plant there the institutions of this more civilised land.

The goal of British policy was to rid the Irish countryside of its impoverished small farmers with their large families—the "cotters"—and to claim their lands for more lucrative agricultural pursuits.

No one of Irish descent in Boston has been able to escape the oft-told tale of how the sad and destitute immigrants left their once beloved Ireland in the 1840s to escape its squalor, poverty, and misery, seeking refuge in North America, three thousand miles across the frigid Atlantic. A nation of eight million was almost halved by the potato blight that led to the deaths of more than 1 million Irishmen and the diaspora of well more than 1 million others who fled the island during that horrendous half-decade from 1845 to 1850. No country has ever been as depopulated by out-migration as Ireland. Only the German immigrants outnumbered the Irish and there were far more Germans remaining in Europe than arriving in America.

Often weakened and enfeebled by disease, most notably cholera, many others died shipboard as they contracted "boat fever"—or typhus—and were tossed overboard to awaiting sharks or sent back on ships after American and Canadian immigration officials deemed them unworthy of landing safely in North America. That the worst of these boats, where as many as 30% of the immigrants would not survive, came to be known as "coffin ships" is no surprise.[2] The death rate among Irish immigrants to North America was lower among immigrants to the United States because the

American immigration officials turned back ships filled with sickly Irishmen. Many of these ships would sail north to Canada rather than return across the Atlantic with passengers who had already paid their transit fees. The Irish émigrés to Canada were worse off because they were poorer. Twenty percent of them died either en route or shortly after landing.

In the United States, the East Coast ports of New York, Philadelphia, Baltimore, and Boston all became destinations for the Irish and receptions differed. New York City with its preexisting multiple ethnic and religious communities had little problem accepting the Irish. There was no dominant ethnic group to displace with Englishmen, Scots, Walloons, Danes, Norwegians, and Germans all finding homes in the Dutch-founded province of New Netherland, its major encampment in the city then known as New Amsterdam.[3] As early as 1644, 20 years before it was named New York, it was contended that 18 different languages were represented in the population of Manhattan and its environs. The Irish were not among the city's early settlers, but that would change two centuries later as the Great Famine ravaged the Irish countryside. Journalist Edward E. Hale reported that "the total arrivals in New York from all countries, are generally about three fourths of the arrivals in our ports," and it is estimated that between 1847 and 1860, more than one million Irishmen entered the United States through the Port of New York.

Philadelphia's mantra as "the city of brotherly love" and Pennsylvania's state motto of "Virtue, Liberty, and Independence" produced a culture of tolerance that made these states hospitable for the newer immigrants.[4] Philadelphia's political and economic elite was predominantly Quaker, and having faced discrimination of their own from the Puritans to the north and the Anglicans to the south of them, they were more accepting of the later Irish Catholic newcomers.

Most of the early pre-Famine Irish immigrants to Philadelphia were Scots-Irish Protestants, largely Presbyterians, from the Ulster Plantation in the north of Ireland. Many had come from Scottish families that had been previously relocated to Ireland's northeastern province as a consequence of the euphemistically labeled "Highland Clearances."[5] Other Scottish immigrants to North America had already been settled in the fertile lands of the Canadian Maritimes, most notably Nova Scotia or "New Scotland," displacing the French Acadians who had settled in those places earlier.

Scots-Irish who came to the American colonies moved through Pennsylvania westward into the Alleghenies and down the spine of the Appalachian chain.[6] They settled in the mountains of the western Carolinas, creating enclaves in what would become the states of Kentucky and Tennessee after the Revolution. It was the congressional descendants of these settlers with whom John McCormack would find his closest friends and most like-minded allies.

Baltimore, which had been founded by the English Catholic Calvert family, was the initial seat of Roman Catholicism in the United States; so Irish Catholics arriving in their port was not disquieting.[7] It was not a major destination of the Famine Irish, with Hale reporting that only 6,772 émigrés landed in Baltimore of the 270,570 recorded as having arrived in American ports in 1850.[8]

Boston transformed

Boston was different. It was to be the chosen destination of the righteous that would reform and purify the Church of England that had been corrupted by the Stuarts.[9] They were "Puritans." Boston was not their initial landing place but other locations were less appealing—Salem with its rocky harbor, Marblehead with its narrow one, and Lynn with its deep tides and long landfall. And the hill upon which their settlement would beam righteousness across the Atlantic to the benighted souls of Europe would be known as Beacon Hill—to transmit rectitude and godliness in this New England, this better England, this uncorrupted England.[10]

It was an immodest goal, but these were an immodest people. The Puritans were far wealthier, better educated, and much more politically powerful than the impoverished and bedraggled settlers who arrived in Plymouth a decade earlier. Led by Governor John Winthrop, the Puritans of Boston had begun their "errand into the wilderness" to accomplish great things.[11] Boston was to be a "City upon a Hill" that the Gospel of Matthew contends is one that "cannot be hid," while the eyes of the world would watch this city and learn from it.

Although Boston was the largest English settlement for most of the seventeenth century, it was bypassed by Philadelphia and New York in the eighteenth century—cities with better climates and more rivers for commerce. Most importantly, New York and Philadelphia were far more welcoming of the newer immigrants.[12] With the Massachusetts state motto, "By the Sword She Seeks Peace Under Liberty," they were forewarned. This was the place of the Boston Massacre, the Boston Tea Party, the battles of Lexington, Concord where the "shot heard around the world" was fired, and Bunker Hill. It was the colonial capital that most violently resisted English authority.

Consequently, Boston did not have to confront other European immigrants who might have challenged their white English Congregationalist hegemony. Certainly not the Scots-Irish whose Presbyterianism made them unwelcome in Massachusetts Bay, nor did the Bostonians have to deal with the German and Scandinavian Lutherans who wanted land and moved west to the wide fertile fields of Michigan, Wisconsin, and Illinois. Unlike the Germans and Scandinavians, the agricultural skills of the Irish were not well regarded. The regular potato harvest cycle of good years and bad years had finally taken their toll as an unbroken succession of bad years in the 1840s and a quasi-permanent potato blight led many of them to lose confidence in the agricultural way of life. When they came to North America, most chose urban life.

Because the Irish were predominantly English speakers, they were able to intermingle with the predominantly English-speaking citizens of the United States. Their brogues and accents may have set them apart as did the illiteracy imposed upon them by the English landholders back in Ireland. But it was the deep-seated commitment of the immigrant Irish to Roman Catholicism with its conservative Jansenist orientation which made them appear most mysterious and threatening to Protestant America.

In many ways, Boston was the least diverse of the large American cities on the eve of the Irish immigration.[13] It was an English-speaking Protestant city and its

Protestants were primarily Congregationalist or Unitarians, that unique Boston quasi-heresy. Other denominations including the Episcopalians and Methodists existed in the city, but Boston of the 1840s was remarkably racially, religiously, and linguistically homogenous.

The pre–Civil War years of Yankee Boston were remarkable. Its industry and commerce flourished and the city's literary output staggered belief. Its authors and poets, including Nathaniel Hawthorne, Ralph Waldo Emerson, Henry Wadsworth Longfellow, John Greenleaf Whittier, Henry David Thoreau, and the senior Oliver Wendell Holmes, had achieved widespread fame and approbation throughout the English-speaking world.[14] Boston, the "City on a Hill," had become "the Athens of America" and was worth its attention.[15] These Protestant Yankees were clearly superior beings.

The Resistant Mindset: But who were these Irish people? Was this Puritan city now under Catholic siege? Why had these people come to this center of enlightenment? To many Bostonians, Irish barbarians had arrived at the docks and with them came destitution and disease. Newly elected Harvard-educated Mayor John Prescott Bigelow faced a major outbreak of cholera in the city. In 1849, over 5,000 people died out of a population of 130,000, approximately 4% of the city's citizens. In his 1850 inaugural address, Bigelow blamed the deaths on "palpable indiscretions in diet, or intemperance" as the wave of Irish immigrants and "its throng of disabled mariners, destitute strangers, and reckless and dissolute persons from every clime. [as] Foreign paupers are rapidly accumulating on our hands. . . . Numbers of helpless beings, including imbeciles in both body and mind—the aged, the blind, the paralytic, and the lunatic have been landed from immigrant vessels to become instantly, and permanently a charge upon our public charities."[16]

Even that most cherished of the Yankee intellectuals, Henry David Thoreau, who empathized with all of God's creatures, displayed remarkable callousness and condescension to his Irish neighbors on Walden Pond, the Fields. The disdain felt by Thoreau, who had often come to the spot in the woods where the Fields settled long before "the ship was built that floated this family to America," was palpable[17]: "An honest, hard-working, but shiftless man plainly was John Field and his wife . . . with round greasy face and bare breast, still thinking to improve her condition one day; with the never absent mop in one hand, and yet no effects of it visible any where." The insensitive Thoreau described the infant child of the Fields as a "poor starveling brat" and felt that any serious discussion with one of John Field's ancestry was doomed. "But alas! The culture of an Irishman is an enterprise to be undertaken with a moral bog hoe."[18]

Apart from their growing numbers, the most troubling aspect of the Irish emigrants to Boston's Brahmins, the self-designated elite of well-educated Puritan descendants, was their devotion to the Roman Catholic Church and the slavery-supporting Democratic Party. In 1864, Thoreau's neighbor and landlord, the estimable Ralph Waldo Emerson, wrote to his friend the British essayist Thomas Carlyle concerning the Democratic Party, "Take from it the wild Irish element imported in the last 25 years into this country, and led by Romish Priests, who sympathize, of course, with despotism, and you would bereave it of all its numerical strength."[19]

In spite of the seemingly insuperable odds against them, immigrants still came to Boston and its environs. This was where New England's jobs were. Both the immigrant Irish from across the ocean and the poor mountain Yankees and French Canadians from northern New England, who filled the mills and the factories, made possible the prosperity of New England that enabled the literary and well-educated Brahmins to sit comfortably in their book-lined studies and write their elegiac poems and prose for appreciative national audiences.[20]

Nineteenth-century industrialization in Boston did not grow as rapidly or penetrate the city's social and economic structure as it did elsewhere.[21] The lack of private sector employment placed greater demands upon public sector employers—the police force, the fire department, the public schools and libraries, and the sanitation and sewer systems. These were the jobs that could be filled by political intervention providing the currency of electoral campaigns. Consequently, the arrival of waves of Irish immigrants in Boston was greeted with a great deal of local apprehension. The leaders of the city saw little to be gained by this massive influx of cheap labor whose bumptious ways and relative illiteracy would disrupt Boston's self-styled role as "the Athens of America."[22]

Furthermore, the city and its neighboring environs already had a pool of skilled and semiskilled artisans for its private workforce and a number of marginally skilled souls for its public workforce—the "swamp Yankees." The designation derived from their settlements along the marshy regions north and south of the city. Nothing of agricultural value could be grown on them and using their water-soaked straw and peat to heat one's home required more energy than it was worth. Primarily small artisans and early factory workers, the swamp Yankees added troops to the Brahmin aristocracy and its resistance to the Irish Catholic immigrant invasion. The swamp Yankees were both tough and threatened. Violence often broke out between them and the newly arrived Irish who sought the same jobs near the bottom of the economic ladder.

Race Politics: Of all the nation's major cities, Boston had the fewest blacks and the most active antislavery societies. These antislavery societies were led by the city's array of intellectuals, Protestant clerics, and the Brahmin aristocracy.[23] With prominent abolitionist activists like William Lloyd Garrison, editor of *The Liberator*; Theodore Parker, the city's leading Unitarian minister; and the powerful orator Wendell Phillips, Boston led the antislavery movement in the North. It was in Boston that the escaped slave Frederick Douglass would first make his mark with the publication in 1845 of his stirring autobiography, *Narrative of the Life of Frederick Douglass, An American Slave Written by Himself.*[24]

Seven years later in 1852, American presidential politics took a dramatic turn as the Whig Party of Henry Clay and Daniel Webster, who would both die that year, nominated its last presidential candidate General Winfield Scott, who lost badly to Democratic ex-Senator Franklin Pierce of New Hampshire. Pierce was one of the proslavery northerners labeled as "doughfaces" by the abolitionist press. Pierce's classmates at Maine's Bowdoin College included Nathaniel Hawthorne, who wrote his campaign biography, and Henry Wadsworth Longfellow. Pierce married Jane Means Appleton, the daughter of Bowdoin's president. But it was another Bowdoin personage who truly altered the national landscape: Harriet Beecher Stowe, the wife of a Bowdoin professor, whose novel, entitled simply *Uncle Tom's Cabin or Life among the Lowly*, was published by Boston publisher John P. Jewett & Co. It became the best-selling American novel of the nineteenth century. While President Abraham Lincoln's supposed greeting to Mrs. Stowe, "So this is the little lady who started this great war," is generally regarded as apocryphal, the quotation's continued existence is proof of the book's powerful impact in mobilizing the Northern public toward the antislavery cause.[25]

New England's antislavery crusade in Congress was led by former President John Quincy Adams (Whig-Mass.). During his time in the U.S. House, Adams battled against the proslavery "gag rule" that prevented abolitionist petitions from reaching the House floor. For ten of his seventeen illustrious years in the U.S. House, Adams's 12th Massachusetts District (1833–43) contained the town of Dorchester that would be the heart of John McCormack's 12th Massachusetts District 90 years later.[26] And in 1856, U.S. Senator Charles Sumner (Rep-Mass.) was almost fatally caned on the Senate floor by U.S. Representative Preston Brooks (Dem-SC) for his antislavery speeches,[27] further signaling to the nation the powerful antipathy of Boston's leading citizens toward that "peculiar institution" of slavery. The abolitionist descendants of Pilgrims and Puritans were also very well aware that in the rival southern colony of Virginia, African slaves were imported to the English settlements in 1619, a year before the *Mayflower* landed in Plymouth.[28] Chained slaves in Virginia predated religious liberty in Massachusetts.

However, many of the Bostonians who led the antislavery societies were among those who most resisted the growing Irish presence. The irony is that two of the five lives lost in the nation-defining Boston Massacre of 1770 were those of the African-American Crispus Attucks and the young Irish immigrant Patrick Carr. That irony was ignored in their assessment of the Irish Catholic threat to the city.[29] There was no community of compassion here. For the upscale antislavery leaders, ridding the nation of its "original sin" of slavery was a daunting enough task. To them, the prospect of feeding, housing, employing, and policing the Irish victims of Europe's last Great Famine seemed an unwanted and unnecessary burden.[30]

It is important to remember that the Irish were the only one of the nation's newer ethnic groups whose majority came to North America when slavery was "the law of the land" in the United States. As a result, Irish Catholics were socialized into a legal system that considered blacks to be subhuman and not entitled to any of the privileges of citizenship.[31] It was Supreme Court Chief Justice Roger Brooke Taney, a Maryland-born Catholic, who wrote in the infamous 1857 case of *Dred Scott v. Sandford* that slaves were property and as such had no standing to sue in the nation's federal courts. It was patriotic of the Irish to defend proslavery legislation emanating from the U.S. Congress. At last, the Irish had arrived in a place where someone other than them was at the bottom of the economic and social heap. How comforting this fact may have been to these bedraggled immigrants is debatable, but it was certainly well known.

When the Boston Irish gazed upon the stern and righteous faces of the Boston abolitionists with their long noses and doleful countenances, it was not New England Congregationalists and Unitarians that they saw. No, it was the harsh Anglican and Methodist faces of the British landowners and magistrates that came most readily to memory. Protestant denominationalism and its subtle nuances were a mystery not worth exploring to most of America's Catholics. The adverse consequences for the Irish Catholics were real and common enough to transcend the denominational identity of their Protestant oppressors.

For Boston's Irish immigrants, the willingness of Boston's Brahmins and Yankees to risk arrest and imprisonment for these black fugitive slaves was a fearful portent of their own potential displacement in the economic and social hierarchy. The abolition of slavery carried with it fears of what the Irish had escaped thousands of miles away: a return to the bottom of the social ladder.

Many Irishmen cheered on the federal marshals who came to Boston to arrest the slaves and those who had harbored them.[32] Tensions deepened and resentment grew. Compassion on either side had few takers and toughness became a virtue. The resentment and resistance of Yankee Boston contributed to the defiant and confrontational attitudes of the Boston Irish that made them the toughest and most politically successful of the nation's urban ethnic "tribes."

The Dimension of Class: This was the Boston that the Famine Irish would encounter and transform. While Boston ranked 5th among the nation's cities in 1840, it returned to 3rd place in the 1850 Census, as its population grew during the decade from 93,383 to 136,881—an increase of 46.6%.[33] The population explosion caused by the arrival of thousands of Irishmen in the small and land-poor city of Boston led to ghettoized crowding of the Irish and dilapidated housing stock abandoned by Yankees who had moved into better quarters. In these and the temporary and jerry-built houses could be found the poorest immigrants, those whose diseases had escaped detection by immigration officials, or whose lack of education or knowledge only of Gaelic limited their employability. "Sean ti" is Gaelic for "old house" and their homes were "shanties" and their occupants were the disdained "shanty Irish."

The "lace curtain Irish" were those who aspired to a better life. They had lace curtains on their windows, lace doilies on their furniture, and fruit in their homes when no one was ill. While the shanty Irish saw America as a place to survive, the lace curtain Irish saw America as a place to thrive.

The political history of the Irish Catholic-Yankee Protestant competition too often takes on an ethno-religious dimension by focusing on the wealthy Boston Brahmin and impoverished Irish Catholic conflict.[34] This was the approach favored by Mayor James Michael Curley and William Henry Cardinal O'Connell, two sworn enemies: it tends to fuse social class origins with religion and ethnic origin downplaying the intra-class tensions that existed within each group. Not only does it understate the intra-Irish social class clash between the "shanty Irish" and the "lace curtain Irish," it also overlooks the fact that the vast majority of Boston's Protestants were poor and many lived on the city's outlying tidal marshes where little could be grown—"swamp Yankees."[35] It was the inhospitality of their land that led the swamp Yankees to become workers in the grim factory towns that surrounded the city, including Lynn, Brockton, Lawrence, and Lowell. Boston's urbane, well-educated, and wealthy Brahmins were almost as disdainful of the poorer Protestants as they were of the Irish Catholic immigrants.

Defining Boston's Brahmins: Few of the Boston Brahmins were as unsparing as Harvard's Dr. Oliver Wendell Holmes, the physician and essayist father of U.S. Supreme Court Justice Oliver Wendell Holmes, Jr. The elder Holmes is credited with popularizing the term "Brahmin" for Boston's upper-crust WASPs (White Anglo-Saxon Protestants). He airily dismissed lesser status Protestants in his 1860 essay in the *Atlantic Monthly*: "The (non-Brahmin) youth is the common country boy, whose race has been bred to bodily labor. . . . You must not expect too much of any such." To Holmes and his fellow Brahmins, social class linked to educational attainment triumphed over religion and ethnicity.

The Harvard Political Factor: No discussion of Boston's Brahmins can leave out the extraordinary role of Harvard College and its impact upon the Brahmin mindset and the politics of both the state and the nation that began more than two centuries ago and continues to the present day.[36] Founded in 1636 as the nation's first college, its early preeminence in training the nation's leaders was not surprising with the eighteenth century ending with Harvard graduate John Adams as the nation's first vice president and its second president. In the 58 presidential elections that have been held since 1789, Harvard alumni have received 36 presidential and vice presidential nominations.[37] With 25 of those nominations, only its arch rival and fellow Congregationalist-founded Yale University comes close. All twelve presidential elections between 1972 and 2016 have had at least one Harvard or Yale alumnus as a major party presidential or vice presidential nominee.

No private university has dominated the public offices of any state more than Harvard has dominated Massachusetts. It is unmatched anywhere else in the United States. Of the fifty-two U.S. Senators who represented Massachusetts from 1789 to the present day, twenty-seven are alumni of Harvard College and its law school.[38] Moreover, of the nation's 114 Congresses, 97 (85.1%) have convened with at least one Harvard alumnus occupying one of Massachusetts's two Senate seats; Twenty-five Congresses have had both Massachusetts seats occupied by Harvard men. Harvard's dominance also appears in the governorship of Massachusetts where 32 of the state's 71 (45.7%) elected and acting governors from John Hancock in 1780 to its latest occupant Charles Baker have been Harvard alumni including its first five and last three.[39]

The link between Ivy League education and the State House also extended to the presiding offices of the Massachusetts Great and General Court. The years between the Civil War and World War II were clearly dominated by Ivy Leaguers: of the 22 Republican Speakers of the Massachusetts House in this era, twelve were Harvard alumni and three graduated from Dartmouth.[40] Of the 32 Senate Presidents, fifteen were Harvard alumni and Dartmouth once again provided three. Old school ties eliminated the need for organizational loyalty among the state's Republicans. Who needed a political party organization to recruit and vet candidates when you already had the Harvard Alumni Association? Shared memories of youthful life in Harvard Yard were clear indicators of the existence of social and economic safety nets in the lives of these young Ivied Yankees. They did not enter political life to ensure their economic security nor would the loss of public office cast them into personal financial deprivation. Unlike their immigrant rivals educated at other universities and colleges, they had large and deep safety nets.

The Slow Takeover: Although its population grew in "Irishness," political power would be slow in coming because Boston had powerful, entrenched, and homogeneous elites in place that would not acquiesce in their own displacement. This made Boston unlike polyglot New York and Philadelphia and the newer cities of Chicago, St. Louis, and Cincinnati where the Irish arrived at the start of settlement.[41] Furthermore, Boston was not only the Commonwealth's largest city, it was also the seat of its government for the state's legislature; the Great and General Court regularly convened in the glorious Charles Bulfinch–designed State House atop Beacon Hill. Those who controlled Massachusetts also controlled Boston, because the Great and General Court could and would amend the city's charter as circumstances arose.

In the 1860 Census, it was reported that 26% of Boston's residents were born in Ireland—the highest of any American city.[42] It would remain in first position for the remainder of the century with 13% Irish-born in the 1900 Census. In terms of size, Boston had settled into fifth place among the nation's fourteen largest cities, but Irish political power was slow to appear. Only one Irish mayor had been elected by the turn of the twentieth century: Hugh O'Brien, who won four one-year terms from 1884 to 1887. O'Brien's dubious reward for his electoral success was to have the Great and General Court remove his power to appoint the city's chief of police and lodge it in a governor-appointed three-member Police Commission.[43]

Boston was not the first of the nation's major cities to elect an Irish mayor or a Catholic mayor. It was the 10th of the 14 largest cities to elect a Catholic mayor and the 12th to elect an Irish Catholic one, but they clearly made up for it in a hurry.[44]

U.S. Representative Patrick Collins, a native of Fermoy in County Cork and educated at Harvard Law, was Boston's second Irish-born mayor.[45] His death in 1905 led to the short term of Daniel Whelton of the West End as the city's first native-born Irish-descended mayor. But it was John Francis "Honey Fitz" Fitzgerald who would signal the arrival of Irish political hegemony. Although Fitzgerald would lose his reelection bid in 1907, it was his second victory in 1910 that marked a major sea change in Boston politics and the close of the competitive Yankee-Irish political conflict.

Over the next century, only two Protestants would capture Boston's City Hall—Brahmin Democrat Andrew J. Peters in 1917 and Yankee Republican Malcolm Nichols in 1925. In 1929, Fitzgerald's hated rival, James Michael Curley, won his third contest for mayor against Nichols and no Protestant or Republican has come close since—a span exceeding 80 years.

As twenty-first-century ethnic and racial diversity increases, Boston may no longer be the Irish Mecca that it once was, but influence in this largest of the original Puritan settlements remains far more politically powerful for those of Irish descent than for their long-displaced Brahmin adversaries. Perhaps there was more than a kernel of truth in Archbishop William Henry O'Connell's haughty observation at the 1908 centennial of the Boston diocese at Boston's magnificent Cathedral of the Holy Cross that "the Puritan has passed; the Catholic remains."[46]

Archbishop O'Connell's 1908 pronouncement may have been premature for that year, as George Hibbard, a Yankee Republican, was Boston's mayor, but within two years it would be prophetic, as John Fitzgerald returned in triumph to City Hall. As Fitzgerald resumed the mayoralty, John McCormack, an 18-year-old law clerk, had learned his most important lesson: if he was to escape poverty and obscurity, public office was the route to take. And to succeed politically in Boston, one had to be of undeniable Irish descent.

John McCormack knew that he needed the votes from his Irish-descended fellow citizens of South Boston if he was to hold public office. But he also knew that he could not claim undeniable Irish ancestry until he underwent a major reconstruction of his life and background. This would be "the greening" of John McCormack, and it would allow him to hold public office in Irish Boston for more than half a century.

The Political Gatekeepers of Irish Boston: Young John McCormack learned quickly that the only way to a successful political career in the highly fragmented and ethnically divided city of Boston was to maneuver your way through the baronial structure of the city's politics. The city had no single political machine. It had multiple power centers and local factions dominated both before and after the European War.[47] Commanding and competing personalities set the tone for Irish Boston's political life. The best known of these included Mayors John F. "Honey Fitz" Fitzgerald and James Michael Curley, and the ward bosses of the West End and East Boston, Martin Lomasney and Patrick Joseph "P.J." Kennedy respectively (Figure 2.1). These were the barons of Irish Boston's politics, and they were a tough and skeptical lot with similar life histories.

Martin Lomasney (1859–1933) from the West End was born to Mary Murray from Lismore, County Waterford. His father Maurice Lomasney was born in Fermoy, County Cork. They married when she was 30 and he 34; they had four sons, only two survived—Martin and Joseph. His father died when Martin was eleven, followed shortly by his mother. Martin and Joseph lived with their aunt and maternal grandmother who spoke only Gaelic. He left school in the 6th grade to work at a railway station selling newspapers.[48]

John F. Fitzgerald (1863–1950) from the North End had a more complicated background. Most sources agree that Fitzgerald's father, Tom Fitzgerald, was from County Wexford, but there is much confusion about his mother's real name and her Irish background. A number of biographies state that her name was Rosanna Cox,[49] while others contend that it was Rose Mary Murray.[50] The last word on the subject should belong to Rose Kennedy herself who stated in her autobiography, "My paternal grandparents Thomas Fitzgerald and Rose Mary Murray, made that grim voyage in the 1840s."[51]

All are agreed that Rose Fitzgerald Kennedy was named for her grandmother and the biographies all locate her Irish location as Wexford. According to Jack Kennedy, it was for political advantage that his grandfather John Fitzgerald chose to move his great-grandmother's birthplace from county to county—Limerick and Tipperary in the southernmost kingdom of Munster, Wexford in the eastern kingdom of Leinster, and Cavan in the northern kingdom of Ulster.[52]

a. Martin Lomasney   b. Patrick J. Kennedy

c. John F. Fitzgerald   d. James Michael Curley

Figure 2.1a–d The gatekeepers of Irish Boston: Martin Lomasney, Patrick J. Kennedy, John F. Fitzgerald, and James Michael Curley (Wikipedia.com portraits).

There is also agreement that both emigrated in the 1840s at the height of the Famine. Tom Fitzgerald started as a farmer in South Acton and later moved to Boston's North End becoming a grocer and liquor storeowner. He died when John was eighteen, three years after his mother's death. John Fitzgerald was the third of seven boys, two of whom died at an early age. He graduated from Boston Latin; and attended Boston College, but had to drop out of Harvard Medical School to support the younger boys. His first job was as a clerk at the Custom House.[53]

Patrick J. Kennedy (1858–1929) from East Boston was the son of Bridget Murphy and Patrick Kennedy, who were both born in County Wexford. They married in the United States and had four children, three daughters and a son. Patrick Sr. was dead at 35, shortly after the birth of his only son. Never finishing grade school, P.J. began work in his teens as a stevedore and longshoreman who eventually took over a bar in Haymarket Square and moved into the retail liquor business.[54]

James Michael Curley (1874–1958) of Roxbury was born to Sarah Clancy and Michael Curley both from the County Galway in the western kingdom of Connacht. They immigrated to the United States as teenagers and married when he was 21 and she 19. She had three babies, but only James Michael and his brother John survived. Curley's father was a hod carrier who died in 1884 at the age of 34, when James Michael, was only 10.[55]

The four gatekeepers were not born in Ireland, but their parents were and tales of Ireland's tragic history were carried by their parents and regularly refreshed by their recently arrived neighbors. Death was omnipresent and each of them had family members who had died young. If they seemed to be young men in a hurry to scamper up the political ladder in search of power and security, one should not be surprised.

Jim Curley was the youngest of the four and just 18 years older than John McCormack. He was the Irish gatekeeper with whom John would have the deepest relationship. While the fiefdoms of the other three were closer to downtown Boston and Beacon Hill, Curley's Roxbury base extended into South Boston and Dorchester where housing was cheap and jobs were scarce. The residents of these neighborhoods are the people who would have benefited most from Curley's four terms in City Hall. Jim Curley's family came from the western Irish county of Galway as did the family of McCormack's wife M. Harriet Joyce. Another connection between the two men was that both had been tutored for the law by the corruptible Republican Judge Charles Innes with McCormack qualifying for the bar while Curley dropped the course and never took the exam.

While McCormack knew the other gatekeepers, it was Joseph P. Kennedy, P. J. Kennedy's lone surviving son and Honey Fitz's son-in-law, with whom his dealings were the most problematic. As Jim Curley and Joe Kennedy made their respective moves in Boston, there was a key difference. Joe Kennedy's father, the East Boston barkeep and liquor dealer, provided much of the capital that Joe was able to parlay into the presidency of the Columbia Trust Company at the age of 25, Jim Curley's father was destitute and left ten-year-old Jim nothing when he died. Curley was sensitive about being a fatherless boy and it defined much of his response to life. According to Boston historian Charles Trout, "throughout Curley's career, he reserved a special place for prominent men who had lost their fathers at an early age, or for men whose fathers had been so greatly reduced in circumstances that they could not protect their sons."[56]

When it came to their children, both men would provide paternal protection in the form of quality education; especially their sons. Joe Kennedy and Jim Curley each fathered nine children. Joe had five daughters and four sons, all of whom would reach adulthood and five would survive him: Rosemary, Eunice, Patricia, Jean, and Teddy. All four of his boys went to quality prep schools and Harvard and he guaranteed each one million dollars. While Joe Kennedy's nine children would provide him with almost thirty grandchildren, Jim Curley's nine children provided him with none.

Jim Curley's children had mixed educational experiences and unfortunate histories.[57] Curley had two daughters and seven sons, two of whom, twin sons John and Joseph, died in infancy.[58] Dorothea, his second daughter, would die at the age of fourteen of pneumonia. Only six of the Curleys survived to adulthood. Mary, the oldest girl, took courses at Harvard Extension, and it was she who would replace her mother Mary (Mae) Herlihy at Jim's side after her death left him a widower in 1930. Jack Beatty contends that she was the family liberal,[59] but her divorce from the abusive advertising executive Edward Donnelly would have closed the door to a political career in Irish Catholic Boston. Mary and Leo, the fifth child, would die on subsequent days in 1950 of reported cerebral hemorrhages. Leo's visible despondency at his sister's death led to rumors of suicide while other old-timers suspected that Mary and Leo had shared a deadly drug concoction at Mary's apartment.[60] Sadly, their fatal vice was alcoholism.

The two Curley sons best suited for successful lives were Francis, the youngest, who obtained two advanced degrees from the nearby Shadowbrook Seminary, then went into the Jesuit priesthood and served at Weston College; and James Jr., the eldest, who went to Boston Latin, Boston College, and Harvard Law. But James Jr., the Curley family's prince, was dead at 24 of a stomach embolism. He had been successful at Harvard Law and had caught the favorable attention of Professor Felix Frankfurter who found similar qualities in Joseph P. Kennedy, Jr.[61] Jim apparently chose not to invest himself as deeply in the other boys although he was able to provide quality educations for each of them: Paul went to Boston Latin, Boston College, and Georgetown and was dead at 32 of alcoholism; Leo left Harvard Law after a professor criticized his father and transferred to Boston University Law to get his degree; and George went to New Prep, Andover, and Holy Cross. Curley's anger with Harvard at this time was such that when George received an acceptance letter from Harvard, Curley confessed in his autobiography that he had "torn up the letter informing him that his application had been acted upon favorably."[62] Survived by only two sons—Francis, the priest, and George, who was gay—Jim Curley was unable to pass down his political legacy. This was a harsh fate that Joe Kennedy clearly escaped.

Jim Curley had to ascend the political ladder on his own without a mentor.[63] As a result, Curley became a quintessential "loner" and never developed the sense of political interdependence that other politicians, including John McCormack, used to create successful coalitions.

Jim Curley and John McCormack: An Irish Poor Boy Alliance: Knowing Curley's temper and his great power to ridicule opponents, McCormack was always careful around him. In his dealings with Curley, McCormack had two advantages that many of the other would-be Curley acolytes did not—a credible tale of a fatherless boyhood and a younger brother, Edward J. "Knocko," who would provide Curley with the South Boston "muscle" so necessary in the rough and tumble ward politics of the early-twentieth-century Boston Irish. Curley regularly included Knocko in his mayoral campaigns and named him assistant superintendent of markets, a job that gave Knocko the opportunity to inspect the meat lockers of the city's better restaurants and make off with sides of beef for his own restaurant in South Boston.

Boston's ambitious, poor Irish boys were linked by their ethnic origins and the Roman Catholic religion, but they had no common socializing experience in the region's prep schools and private colleges to reinforce those links. Unlike their Yankee rivals, they had no social and economic safety nets to break their falls from grace. Risks were real and the loss of public office could and did cast them into personal deprivation. With adverse consequences omnipresent in their lives, the young Irish Democratic politicians had to choose their factional loyalties carefully. Given that most factional loyalties were fluid and that many of the ward bosses' had mercurial tempers, their careers could end before they had begun if they made an unwise decision. Maintaining and furthering their career trajectories while they danced between the city's factions was a clear test of their political skills. Silence was a virtue. Today's ally could become tomorrow's enemy. John McCormack understood these risks.

Risky Business: Young John McCormack had to impress the gatekeepers if he was to become a player in Boston politics. It was these tough and cynical men to whom John McCormack would present himself and his altered ancestry.

John McCormack's hardships were real and similar to those that had been overcome by Curley, Fitzgerald, Kennedy, and Lomasney, giving him a leg up over the hordes of other young Boston Irish aspirants. His hardships had made him "one of them," and he could be trusted. Had they known of his true ancestral background, he would not have been as well regarded. He might have been forgiven for altering the circumstances of his father's disappearance from his life and recasting his place among his surviving brothers. These were minor details. Undoubtedly, each of these men had relatives whom they disdained and had banished from their consciousness, but who continued to occupy earthly places. Their common Irishness provided a link between them that defined them against the Protestant political hierarchy whose power they coveted.

However, John McCormack was far less Irish than they. Only his maternal grandparents had come from Ireland. John knew that his Irishness was stretched, even if the gatekeepers did not. His ambivalence about his ancestry was so pronounced that it even appeared in the 1920 U.S. Census. John McCormack is reported to be a 28-year-old lawyer lodging at 29 Mt. Vernon Street in Dorchester, with a father born in Scotland and a mother born in Massachusetts.[64] For the third census in succession, the birthplace of John's father had been changed. In the 1900 Census, John's father Joseph McCormack reported his own birthplace as Canada. In 1910, his abandoned wife Mary Ellen made him a native of Ireland, and in 1920, John, his oldest surviving son, chose to make him a Scot. For John McCormack, who was then an elected member of the Massachusetts House of Representatives, this was a risky decision. Fortunately for McCormack, at the time no Freedom of Information forms were available to catch the shifting birthplaces of his father.

Most troubling to his advancement was his paternal link to Scottish Canada. Joe McCormack's Canadian Scottish heritage was one that had to be well concealed if young John was to have any chance of success in Irish Boston. A Canadian heritage was a potentially career-ending problem. But to the powerful players in Boston's Irish political drama, John McCormack's tales of family poverty were verifiably authentic. They all knew the hardships of life along Dorchester Avenue and the numbered and lettered streets of South Boston. McCormack's aspirations to escape the circumstances of his upbringing were as real as their own. They had no need to examine it closely. Most important to them was that John McCormack himself was born in Southie and none of them had to travel to Andrew Square to establish the difficulties of his life. McCormack understood as clearly as did they how politics could be used to advance oneself and to alleviate the economic hardship of their Irish-descended constituents.

Notes

1   The delight of the British press at the departure of the Irish is captured in this editorial from the *London Times*, as quoted in Seamus MacManus, *The Story of the Irish Race*, 4th rev. ed. (New York: Devin-Adair, 1945), p. 610n.

2   A first-person account of one such vessel is given by Robert Whyte, listed as "A Cabin Passenger," in *The Ocean Plague: Or a Voyage to Quebec in an Irish Emigrant Vessel* (Boston: Coolidge and Willey, 1848). Books commemorating the Famine's sesquicentennial include Edward Laxton, *The Famine Ships: The Irish Exodus to America, 1846–51* (London: Bloomsbury, 1996); and Jim Rees, *A Farewell to Famine* (Arklow, Ireland: Dee-Jay Publications, 1995). MacManus lists a number of ships where more than half of the passengers died in the Atlantic crossing to Canada (*The Story of the Irish Race*, pp. 609–10.

3   New York City's settlements are recounted in Charles H. Andres, *Our Earliest Colonial Settlements: Their Diversities of Origin and Later Characteristics* (New York: New York University Press, 1933); and Edward R. Ellis, *The Epic of New York City* (New York: Coward-McCann, 1966).

4   On Philadelphia's early settlements, see David Hackett Fischer's section, "North Midlands to the Delaware: The Friends Migration, 1675–1725," in his magisterial *Albion's Seed: Four British Folkways in America* (New York: Oxford University Press, 1989), pp. 419–609; and the early three-volume compilation of John F. Watson, *Annals of Philadelphia and Pennsylvania in the Olden Time*, revised by Willis P. Hazard (Philadelphia: E.S. Stuart, 1905).

5   A brief account of the "Highland Clearances" and their impact upon Canadian settlement may be found in J. D. Mackie, *A History of Scotland*, 2nd rev. ed. by Bruce Lenman and Geoffrey Parker (London: Penguin Books, 1978), pp. 320–24. The original version appeared in 1964. See also John Prebble, *The Highland Clearances* (London: Penguin Books, 1963).

6   Books recounting the influence of the Scots-Irish in America include Ronald Chepesiuk, *The Scotch-Irish: From the North of Ireland to the Making of America* (Jefferson, NC: McFarland, 2000); Barry Vann, *In Search of Ulster-Scots Land: The Birth and Geotheological Imagings of a Transatlantic People, 1603–1703* (Columbia: University of South Carolina Press, 2008). The most colorful of these books was written by U.S. Senator James Webb (Dem-Va.), *Born Fighting: How the Scots-Irish Shaped America* (New York: Broadway Books, 2004).

7   George Calvert, Lord Baltimore, intended that the settling of Maryland and Newfoundland would be religious sanctuaries for English Catholics; see T. K. Rabb, *Enterprise and Empire: Merchant and Gentry Investment in the Expansion of England* (Cambridge, MA: Harvard University Press, 1967), p. 89. A fuller account of the family and its colony may be found in Clayton C. Hall, *The Lords Baltimore and the Maryland Palatinate: Six Lectures on Maryland's Colonial History* (Baltimore: Johns Hopkins University Press, 1902).

8   Edward Everett Hale, Letter I; "Preparations for Passage," dated December 3, 1851 in *Letters on Irish Emigration First Published in the Boston Daily Advertiser* (Boston: Phillips, Samson & Co., 1852), p. 7.

9   Useful books documenting the faith brought to North America by the Puritans are Selma R. Williams, *Kings, Commoners, and Colonists: Puritan Politics in Old and New England, 1603–1660* (New York: Atheneum, 1974); Edmund S. Morgan, *The Puritan Family: Religion and Domestic Relationships in 17th Century New England* (New York: Harper & Row, 1944); and Perry Miller, *Errand into the Wilderness* (Cambridge, MA: Belknap Press of Harvard University Press, 1956).

10 A book on early New England settlements from an English perspective provocatively contends that there were more economic refugees than religious ones; see David Cressy, *Coming Over: Migration and Communication between England and New England* (Cambridge, England: Cambridge University Press, 1980). More recent scholarship includes Virginia DeJohn Anderson, *New England's Generation: The Great Migration and the Formation of Society and Culture in the Seventeenth Century* (Cambridge, GB: Cambridge University Press, 1991); and Alison Games, *Migration and the Origins of the English Atlantic World* (Cambridge, MA: Harvard University Press, 1999).

11 The original quotation is "Consider that wee shall be as a Citty upon a Hill, the eies of all people are uppon us; soe that if wee shall deale falsely with our god in this worke wee have undertaken and soe cause him to withdrawe his present help from us, wee shall be made a story and a byword through the world." John Winthrop, "A Model of Christian Charity," a sermon delivered aboard the *Arbella* (1630). A clearer rendition may be found in Emily Morison Beck, ed., *Bartlett's Familiar Quotations*, 15th ed. (Boston: Little, Brown, 1980), p. 264.

12 As contended by Oscar Handlin in *Boston's Immigrants: A Study in Acculturation, 1790–1880*, new and revised edition (New York: Atheneum, 1969), p. 25. The contrast between Boston and Philadelphia is wonderfully recounted in E. Digby Balzell's *Puritan Boston and Quaker Philadelphia* (New York: The Free Press, 1979).

13 See Handlin, *Boston's Immigrants*; and Thomas H. O'Connor's indispensable *The Boston Irish: A Political History* (Boston: Northeastern University Press, 1995).

14 The enduring treatments of this era are Van Wyck Brooks's Pulitzer Prize–winning *The Flowering of New England* (New York: E.P. Dutton, 1936); and F. O. Matthiesen's *American Renaissance: Art and Expression in the Era of Emerson and Whitman* (London and New York: Oxford University Press, 1941).

15 The most evocative depiction of Boston's social and cultural life in the two decades before the arrival of the Famine Irish may be found in Thomas H. O'Connor's fascinating *The Athens of America: Boston, 1825–1845* (Amherst: University of Massachusetts Press, 2006).

16 Quoted in Alan Lupo, *Liberty's Chosen Home: The Politics of Violence in Boston*, rev. ed. (Boston: Beacon Press, 1988), p. 22.

17 Henry David Thoreau, *The Variorum Walden*, annotated by Walter Harding (New York: Twayne, 1962), p. 173. My thanks are given to Mr. Andrew McLean for bringing this quotation to my attention.

18 Ibid., p. 174. The "brat" quotation appears on p. 173. A later effort to explain Thoreau's anti-Irish prejudice was undertaken in Frank Buckley, "Thoreau and the Irish," *New England Quarterly*, XIII (1940), pp. 389–400.

19 Letter of Ralph Waldo Emerson to Thomas Carlyle, September 26, 1864, *The Correspondence of Thomas Carlyle and Ralph Waldo Emerson, 1834–1872*, Vol. 2 (Boston: Ticknor, 1886), p. 322.

20 Peter Temin, "The Industrialization of New England, 1830–1880," in Peter Temin, ed., *Engines of Enterprise: An Economic History of New England* (Cambridge, MA: Harvard University Press, 2000), pp. 109–52. See also Thomas H. O'Connor's *Lords of the Loom, the Cotton Whigs and the Coming of the Civil War* (New York: Scribner's, 1968). This point is made in Robert Dalzell's *Enterprising Elite: The Boston Associates and the World They Made* (Cambridge, MA: Harvard University Press, 1987), chapter 5, "Philanthropy and the Uses of Wealth," pp. 113–63.

21 Books describing Boston's nineteenth-century growth include Lawrence W. Kennedy, *Planning the City upon a Hill: Boston since 1630* (Amherst: University of Massachusetts Press, 1992); Sam Bass Warner, *Streetcar Suburbs: The Process of Growth in Boston (1870–1900)* (Cambridge, MA: Harvard University Press, 1978); and Walter Muir Whitehill's classic, *Boston: A Topographical History*, 2nd ed. (Cambridge, MA: Harvard University Press, 1978).

22 Yankee Boston's resistance to the Irish has been told often; see O'Connor's *The Boston Irish*, chapters 2 and 3; and Oscar Handlin's *Boston's Immigrants, 1790–1880: A Study in Acculturation* (Cambridge, MA: Belknap Press, 1979).

23 Yankee Boston's antislavery societies and their activities are recounted in Lawrence Lader, *The Bold Brahmins: New England's War against Slavery* (New York: E. P. Dutton, 1961). There was also substantial statistical evidence of working-class resistance to slavery as well in New England; see Edward Magdol's *The Antislavery Rank and File: A Social History of the Abolitionist's Constituency* (Westport, CT: Greenwood Press, 1986).

24 Frederick Douglass, *Narrative of the Life of Frederick Douglass, An American Slave Written by Himself* (Boston: Published at the Anti-Slavery Office, 1845).

25 The Lincoln-Stowe account appears in Charles Edward Stowe, *Harriet Beecher Stowe: The Story of Her Life* (1911), p. 203, and is refuted in Daniel R. Vollaro, "Lincoln, Stowe, and the 'Little Woman/Great War' Story: The Making, and Breaking of a Great American Anecdote," *Journal of the Abraham Lincoln Association*, XXX (Winter 2009), pp. 1ff.

26 Kenneth Martis (ed.) with Ruthe Anderson Rowles (cartographer), *The Historical Atlas of United States Congressional Districts, 1789–1983* (New York: Free Press; London: Collier Macmillan, 1982), pp. 236 for Adams and 238 for McCormack.

27 See the Pulitzer Prize–winning biography, David H. Donald, *Charles Sumner and the Coming of the Civil War* (New York: Alfred A. Knopf, 1960).

28 Lerone Bennett, Jr., *Before the Mayflower: A History of Black America* (New York: Penguin Books, 1984).

29 The fullest treatment of the event remains Hiller B. Zobel's *The Boston Massacre* (New York: W. W. Norton, 1970).

30 See Frederick Cople Jaher, "The Politics of the Boston Brahmins, 1800–1860," in Ronald P. Formisano and Constance K. Burns, eds., *Boston 1700–1980: The Evolution of Urban Politics* (Westport, CT: Greenwood Press, 1984), pp. 59–86. This appeared initially in Jaher's book, *The Urban Establishment: Upper Strata in Boston, New York Charleston, Chicago, and Los Angeles* (Urbana: University of Illinois Press, 1982).

31 American Catholic anxieties about the antislavery conflict's impact upon the church's emerging place in America are recounted in Madeleine H. Rice, *American Catholic Opinion in the Slavery Controversy* (New York: Columbia University Press, 1944). A harsh characterization of antebellum Irish antipathy toward American blacks may be found in Noel Ignatiev's *How the Irish Became White* (New York: Routledge, 1995).

32 O'Connor, *The Boston Irish*, pp. 83–85.

33 The sixth census of 1840 listed Boston in fifth place with 93,383 residents, and the seventh census of 1850 listed it in third place with 136,881 residents.

34 Both James Michael Curley and his longtime adversary William Henry O'Connell were past masters of fomenting this particular ethno-class conflict interpretation.

35 The academic definition of "swamp Yankee" may be found in Ruth Schell's 1963 article "Swamp Yankee" in *American Speech*. She contends that it is a colloquialism for rural southern rural New England Yankee Protestants who lived in Rhode Island, Connecticut, and southeastern Massachusetts. See Ruth Schell, "Swamp Yankee," *American Speech*, XXXVIII (1963), pp. 121–23.

36 See Ronald Story, *The Forging of an Aristocracy: Harvard and the Boston Upper Class, 1800–1870* (Middletown, CT: Wesleyan University Press, 1980).

37 Garrison Nelson, "Running from New England: Will It Ever Lead the Nation Again?" for the online *New England Journal of Political Science*, III (Fall 2009), pp. 112–65; and "New England and the Presidency: Voting Bloc Shrinks as Educational Role Grows," *Boston Sunday Globe, Ideas* (December 28, 2003), p. D12.

38 The major source for the U.S. Senators is the *Biographical Directory of the United States Congress: Bicentennial Edition, 1774–1989* (Washington, DC: U.S. Government Printing Office, 1989) with online updates. Hereinafter referred to as *BDUSC* (1989 ed.).

39 The major source for governors is Robert Sobel and John Raimo (eds.), *Biographical Directory of the Governors of the United States, 1789–1978* (Westport, CT; Meckler Books, 1978), 4 vols. with online updates.

40 "The Presiding Officers, 1780–1980," in Cornelius Dalton, John Wirkkala, and Anne Thomas, eds., *Leading the Way: A History of the Massachusetts General Court, 1629–1980* (Boston: Office of the Secretary of State, 1984), pp. 373–427.

41 William V. Shannon, *The American Irish* (New York: Macmillan, 1966), p. 153.

42 U.S. Census Office, *Population of the United States in 1860* from the 8th Census (Washington, DC: 1864), pp. 31–32. A valuable summary of these data may be found in Stephan Thernstrom (ed.), *Harvard Encyclopedia of American Ethnic Groups, 1972–1980* (Cambridge: Belknap Press of Harvard University Press, 1980), p. 531.

43 Cornelius Dalton, John Wirkkala, and Anne Thomas, *Leading the Way: A History of the Massachusetts General Court, 1629–1980* (Boston: Office of the Secretary of State, 1984), p. 201.

44   Ethnic and religious data of the mayors may be found in Melvin G. Holli and Peter d'A. Jones (eds.), *Biographical Dictionary of American Mayors, 1820–1980: Big City Mayors, Baltimore, Boston, Buffalo, Chicago, Cincinnati, Cleveland, Detroit, Los Angeles, Milwaukee, New Orleans, New York, Philadelphia, Pittsburgh, San Francisco, St. Louis* (Westport, CT: Greenwood Press, 1981).

45   *BDUSC* (1989 ed.), pp. 810–11. See O'Connor, *The Boston Irish*, pp. 160–65; and Michael P. Curran, *Life of Patrick A. Collins* (Norwood, MA: Norwood Press), 1906.

46   O'Connell's remarks were delivered on October 28, 1908, as quoted in James M. O'Toole's *Militant and Triumphant: William Henry O'Connell and the Catholic Church in Boston, 1859–1944* (Notre Dame, IN: University of Notre Dame Press, 1992), p. 121. Earlier that year on January 29, 1908, at the same church, O'Connell had been installed as Boston's Archbishop; Dorothy G. Wayman, *Cardinal O'Connell of Boston: A Biography* (New York: Farrar, Strauss and Young, 1955), p. 139.

47   In addition to Thomas H. O'Connor's *The Boston Irish: A Political History*, a much more recent and livelier account is Gerard O'Neill's enjoyable *Rogues and Redeemers: When Politics Was King in Irish Boston* (New York: Crown, 2012).

48   Books on Martin Lomasney include Leslie G. Ainley's biography, *Boston Mahatma* (Boston: Brice Humphries, 1949), and a fictionalized account in Joseph Dinneen's 1938 novel, *Ward Eight* (New York: reprinted by Arno Press, 1976).

49   Rosanna Cox is named as John Fitzgerald's mother in Doris Kearns Goodwin, *The Kennedys and the Fitzgeralds: An American Saga* (New York: Simon & Schuster, 1987), p. 13; Cindy Adams and Susan Crump, *Iron Rose: The Story of Rose Fitzgerald Kennedy and Her Dynasty* (Dove, 1995), p. 27; and in Gerard O'Neill, *Rogues and Redeemers: When Politics Was King in Irish Boston* (New York: Crown, 2012), p. 12. *Wikipedia* places Tom Fitzgerald's birthplace in Limerick and Rosanna Cox's in Cavan.

50   She is also identified as Rose Mary Murray in John Henry Cutler, *"Honey Fitz": Three Steps to the White House* (Indianapolis: Bobbs-Merrill, 1962), pp. 37–38; Thomas Maier, *The Kennedys: America's Emerald Kings* (New York: Basic Books, 2003), p. 52; Michael O'Brien, *John F. Kennedy: A Biography* (New York: Thomas Dunne Books/ St. Martin's Press, 2005); Barbara A. Perry, *Rose Kennedy: The Life and Times of a Political Matriarch* (New York: W. W. Norton, 2013), p. 10.

51   Rose Fitzgerald Kennedy, *Times to Remember* (Garden City, NY: Doubleday, 1974), p. 5.

52   Robert Dallek, *An Unfinished Life: John F. Kennedy, 1917–1963* (Boston: Little, Brown, 2003), p. 1.

53   Books on John F. "Honey Fitz" Fitzgerald include Cutler, *"Honey Fitz": Three Steps to the White House*; and Goodwin, *The Kennedys and the Fitzgeralds: An American Saga*.

54   Goodwin, *The Kennedys and the Fitzgeralds*, pp. 264–68. The County Wexford location of Bridget Murphy Kennedy's birthplace came from the author's telephonic interview with Mr. Andrew Pierce of the Boston Genealogical Research Associates, July 1999.

55   Books on Curley include Jack Beatty, *The Rascal King: The Life and Times of James Michael Curley (1874–1958)* (Reading, MA: Addison-Wesley, 1992); Joseph Dinneen, *The Purple Shamrock: The Hon. James M. Curley of Boston* (New York: W.W. Norton, 1949); and Curley's autobiography, *"I'd Do It Again": A Record of All My Uproarious Years* (Englewood Cliffs, NJ: Prentice-Hall, 1956); and most recently, Curley's best-known appearance is as the model for Mayor Frank Skeffington in the best-selling novel by Edwin O'Connor, *The Last Hurrah* (Boston: Little, Brown & Co., 1956).

56 Charles H. Trout, "Curley of Boston: The Search for Irish Legitimacy," in Formisano and Burns, *Boston, 1789–1980*, pp. 165–95; the quotation is on p. 191.

57 This section is derived from the two biographies, Dinneen's *The Purple Shamrock* and Beatty's *The Rascal King*, and Curley's autobiography, *"I'd Do It Again,"* ghostwritten by John Henry Cutler.

58 Curley's autobiography reported their deaths in 1921, *"I'd Do It Again,"* pp. 79 and 363, while Beatty reported it as 1922, *The Rascal King*, p. 236.

59 Beatty, *The Rascal King*, p. 15.

60 Old-time Boston reporters were always careful never to let harsh tales of powerful families enter their columns, but they were reporters after all and had a felt need to share those tales with others on an unattributed basis. It was from them that I heard this tale.

61 Frankfurter on James M. Curley Jr., "Since last we met, one of our number has gone forever. It is always terrible when death strikes youth and most terrible when there as the promise of a good life for himself and his community, as was true of young Curley." Quoted in Beatty, *The Rascal King*, p. 288.

62 Curley, *"I'd Do It Again,"* p. 79.

63 Dinneen, *The Purple Shamrock*, pp. 21–22.

64 Fourteenth Census return for 1920:

State: Massachusetts; County: Suffolk; Township: Boston; Ward: 11 Enumeration District No. 303 indicates that John W. McCormack, was then lodging at 29 Mt. Vernon Street in Dorchester.

Race/				Place of Birth		
Name	Relationship	Sex	Age	Person	Father	Mother
McCormack, John W.	Lodger	WM	28 s	Mass.	Scotland	Mass.

The Reinvention of John McCormack

Tombstones tell tales. Not only do they indicate the final whereabouts of those lying beneath them, they also reveal the character and history of the survivors who pay to have the stones erected and inscribed.

Boston's most prestigious graveyards are downtown, two blocks from the crest of Beacon Hill where the majestic Bulfinch-designed State House looks down upon the hustling metropolis the city has become. Boston never became the "Hub of the Universe" which it hoped for in the nineteenth century, but today its citizens are sufficiently diverse to give the city an international flavor. The city's other title, "the Athens of America," has come closer to the mark. With more than a quarter of a million college students attending almost one hundred institutions of higher learning in the city and its neighboring suburbs, Boston can qualify as the nation's and perhaps the world's biggest college town.

Part of Boston's allure and much of its curse can be found in the graveyards of King's Chapel and the Old Granary wherein lie the city's Puritan aristocracy, who brought equal helpings of enlightenment and prejudice to this unique place. The Massachusetts Bay Puritans intended for Boston to radiate its goodness throughout the New World and reflect back to the Old World that a band of educated and devout worshippers could make an "errand into the wilderness" and create a Christian community to serve as a model of renewal and salvation for the benighted and decadent civilizations of Europe.

But the tombstones that have relevance for the life of U.S. Representative John W. McCormack lie in the further reaches of the city.[1]

The first tombstone, Sandbanks in Watertown

The first tombstone is located in Sandbanks, a small cemetery occupying a corner of Watertown. Across the town line in Cambridge, the adjacent Mount Auburn Cemetery dwarfs Sandbanks. Mount Auburn is where the luminaries of Massachusetts's intellectual life have been laid to rest. Situated only a few blocks from Harvard, Mount Auburn Cemetery has buried within it many of the school's most illustrious scholars. Among them are four Supreme Court Justices Joseph Story, Benjamin Curtis, Horace Gray, and Felix Frankfurter; the essayist Oliver Wendell Holmes, Sr.; U.S. Senators Edward Everett and Charles Sumner; and the poets James Russell Lowell and John

Ciardi. Others buried there include Henry Wadsworth Longfellow and Julia Ward Howe, who wrote the Union anthem, "The Battle Hymn of the Republic."

The Mount Auburn Cemetery has been wonderfully landscaped with gardens and small ponds and flowered walkways leading one to the mausoleums and graves of its occupants. Part of the landscaping was a large 10-foot wall erected on the Cambridge-Watertown line separating the "garden cemetery" of Mount Auburn from Sandbanks. The wall is thickly made and was erected in 1920 to provide a clear boundary between the growing burial needs of Mount Auburn and the diminishing ones of Sandbanks. The wall was built shortly after the city's bitter and ethnically divisive Boston Police Strike of 1919.

The 1906 death certificate of James J. McCormack, the first of John McCormack's adolescent siblings to die, indicates that James was buried in "Mt. Auburn Cemetery (Watertown)."[2] A call to Mount Auburn in search of James's gravesite elicited a response which was hard to mistake. After being told that James J. McCormack was not located in the cemetery's registry, I was asked, "Was he a Catholic?" I said, "Yes" and was told that his gravesite was likely in the adjacent cemetery of Sandbanks and that I should call another cemetery in nearby Waltham where information about the occupants of Sandbanks could be found.

In Waltham at the Diocesan office of New Calvary Cemetery, I was presented with a small well-worn notebook with loose pages and a map of the Sandbanks graveyard. A search of the old record book indicated that 16-year-old James Joseph McCormack would be found in grave C of the 5th row in the East Range.

Finding Sandbanks was not easy. No street sign or guidepost led one to it and no sign on the dilapidated gates indicated its unique past. It had been years since anyone had been buried in Sandbanks, and maintenance had slipped. Many of the stones were askew and a number were broken. A longtime native Irish maintenance man who cared for three cemeteries contended that one can sometimes "feel a chill" from Sandbanks that is absent elsewhere. It was he who alerted me to the presence of the concrete fortress wall separating the two cemeteries. "The Protestants built that wall to keep us from them," he declaimed in a tone softened by an Irish brogue but hardened by the realization that the two defining cultures of this "City on a Hill" had to remain separated even in death.

Once arriving there, the next step of locating James's gravesite was less difficult. The cemetery map had accurately captured the unique land configuration of Sandbanks and the wall separating it from Mount Auburn Cemetery. No tombstone identified James's final location, but a small oblong one near grave C indicated that a Julia O'Brien had erected a tombstone with two of its sides inscribed.

On the side facing the graveyard, it read:	On the left side of the stone facing the entrance, it read:
Erected by Julia O'Brien in memory of her son Patrick J. O'Brien b. Boston May 18, 1853 d. Rochester, N.Y. October 17, 1882	Michael J. O'Brien b. Boston June 5, 1819 d. Boston October 13, 1881

Julia O'Brien had purchased this gravesite for her husband Michael, herself and her two children, Patrick and Mary Ellen. Julia and Michael O'Brien were the parents of Mary Ellen O'Brien McCormack and the maternal grandparents of James J. McCormack, who would always remain sixteen. But the tombstone contained an inaccuracy, for Michael J. O'Brien was not born in Boston. According to his naturalization papers, Michael O'Brien was born in County Cork, the most populous of the counties along Ireland's southern coast in the kingdom of Meinster. Those who arrived in Boston from Ireland in the years before the Civil War had to confront the Yankee ascendancy in its fullest glory.

There was no welcome in Yankee Boston for the immigrant Irish, so concealing an Irish birthplace was essential for economic survival, and both Michael and Julia O'Brien knew this well. This was the time of the "NINA" employment signs—"No Irish Need Apply."[3] In a jaunty doggerel rejoinder to these signs, it was often intoned, "Whoe'er writ it, writ it well, the same is writ on the gates of Hell, 'No Irish Need Apply.'"

On a cold February morning in 1906, 14-year-old John McCormack with his brothers Patrick, Edward, and Donald and his sister Catherine stood over this open grave. Mary Ellen bid farewell to James, the first of her three grown children to predecease her. No tombstone for James was placed there as he was laid in the plot reserved for Mary Ellen. It was in the gravesite of her parents and her brother Patrick for whom her oldest son was named. It may have been her only consolation that day. James's own father, Joseph H. McCormack, did not accompany his wife and the five remaining children to this gravesite. He had left the family apartment sometime the previous year and his whereabouts were unknown. Now they were six.

Some thought that Joe McCormack had returned to his native Prince Edward Island (PEI), the smallest of the Canadian Maritimes. Others believed that he was in an alcoholic haze between Boston and PEI. Perhaps he was dead. Where he went or why he left did not matter to the hardy band of Boston Irishmen he left behind. Joe McCormack was dead to them.

Fourteen-year-old John learned a number of important lessons that day. One was that Yankee Boston needed to separate itself even from dead Irishmen. Another was that altering a family history to escape poverty and gain employment was no sin, for there on the 1883 gravestone of his grandfather was the inscribed birthplace of Boston, but as John may well have known, Michael J. O'Brien was born in Ireland. Grandma Julia who paid to have the tombstone erected and inscribed knew this. If altering ancestry was the way to survival, so be it. It was good enough for Grandma Julia and it would be good enough for John when he too would be faced with providing his family history.

The Greening of Joe McCormack: Who was Joe McCormack? He was the absent father of a clan that would produce a son who was a heartbeat away from the presidency of the United States for fourteen months from November 22, 1963, to January 20, 1965. Joseph was born in Grant's Crossing, a small village located near Souris, a coastal town on the rough northeastern edge of PEI. He was raised by natives of the island whose ancestry could be traced back to the 1700s in Scotland. The names on Joe McCormack's baptismal document are those of Donald McCormack and Mary McPhee, both Roman Catholic natives of Souris. As recounted in the *Memorial Volume, The Scottish Catholics of Prince Edward Island, 1772–1922*[4]: "A settlement was formed at Launching Place in Kings County about the year 1796, composed of MacDonalds, MacPhees, MacCormacks and Walkers, all of whom had come from Scotland with Father MacEachern, and had spent the intervening years at Scotchfort."

In *Ten Farms Become a Town: A History of Souris, Prince Edward Island, 1700–1920*, local historian George Leard lists the names of both Scottish and Irish settlers arriving in Souris in the late eighteenth century. Special note is made of Scottish settlers in 1772, "That year five families who came out on the *Alexander*: John McCormack, Donald McCormack, Roderick McDonald, Roderick McIntosh, and Angus McIntyre settled in Lot 43."[5] The McPhees arrived six years later in 1778. The baptismal records of Joe McCormack and his siblings remain today in the parish hall of the first large Roman Catholic Church, St. Margaret of Scotland, established in that corner of the island. There were six children in the household of Donald McCormack and Mary McPhee[6]:

Catherine, born in 1839
Sarah, born in 1840
John, born in 1843
Raphael, born in 1845
P. Edward, born in 1854
Joseph, born in 1857

It was Mrs. Viva E. Noyes, Joe McCormack's landlady, who filled out Joe's 1929 death certificate in Maine. Joe's father's name is listed as "unknown," but he is listed as having been a farmer born in Scotland. His mother's maiden name is listed as "Annie McCormick," and her place of birth is also listed as Scotland.[7] Yet, how much anyone shares with a landlady is debatable. In a place as tight as PEI, where only one divorce was recorded over a four-hundred-year period,[8] illegitimate children were acknowledged but relocated quickly among the God-fearing intact families of the community. Had the child been the offspring of an illicit interreligious Catholic-Protestant coupling, illegitimacy was declared and efforts would be made to place the child in a religiously appropriate home that would welcome yet another mouth to feed. Tensions between Catholics and Protestants on the island were genuine. Sometimes, but not always, the children of these misalliances might be fully integrated within the new families. Other times they may have shared the dinner table and the household chores, but not the inheritances. Those would only go to the acknowledged family members. And so it was with Joseph McCormack. When Donald McCormack died in 1891, none of his estate went to Joseph. All of it went to P. Edward McCormack, the one boy in the family who chose to remain on the farm.[9]

The site of Joe's crossing into the United States was Lewiston, Maine, during October 1877. Joseph H. McCormack of PEI had come to begin his new life. It was probably not his first trip to the States, but this time he had a purpose and that was to become an American citizen. On the official U.S. document recording his arrival, Joe McCormack contended that he was born on October 29, 1860, making him 17 years of age and "being then a minor under the age of 18 years."[10] On the baptismal document back in PEI, Joseph McCormack was listed as being born in November 1857. This would have made him nineteen when he crossed into the United States. Joe McCormack's birth year as reported to the census takers in the 1900 U.S. Census Bureau was 1862. So from the very beginning of his arrival in the United States, Joe McCormack's American life history underwent occasional alteration.

Lying about his age at the outset would make no sense if one did not understand the suspicious mindset of immigrants who resented the paperwork demands of the American federal bureaucracy and gave them any answer which suited their personal purpose that day. For Joe McCormack on that October day, the toll exacted from minors was undoubtedly less than that exacted from adults. So why pay the full amount if you could escape it? Joe was now over the first hurdle.

Truth and fiction often intermingled in Joe McCormack's life.

Joe never concealed his PEI heritage. It is recorded as his birthplace in the immigration document that he filled out in 1877 in Lewiston, Maine, and in his 1885 marriage license. It is also recorded on all six of the Boston birth notices of his census-enumerated children, on the three death certificates of his deceased adult children, on the 1900 Census in Massachusetts, the 1920 Census in Maine, and in his 1929 obituary.

When his name first appeared in the July 1881 *Boston City Directory*, Joseph McCormack was listed as a "laborer."[11] Four months later and after he and many of South Boston's laborers promoted themselves to "engineer," Joe married Miss Margaret Degnan of Newton, Massachusetts.[12] She was of Irish ancestry and Joe was married as a Catholic. By altering his job description, he undoubtedly placated her parents and hopefully impressed the neighbors.

Margaret Degnan McCormack died of typhoid fever in 1883 at the age of 26.[13] Little is known of her, but the perils of childbirth and the travails of tenement life shortened the existence of many young Irishwomen. Margaret gave birth to a son, Henry, but shortly after his birth, Margaret took ill and died. Joe McCormack, the young widower, sent his infant son north to PEI to be raised by his eldest sister Catherine (Kate) McCormack Haley. Kate McCormack had married Thomas Haley. According to family legend, the Haleys had a "wonderful farm" and Henry would be raised away from the suffocating slums of South Boston. It was the first time that Joe McCormack had shifted his parental responsibilities to others. It would not be the last.

Henry McCormack would be eighteen when he died from tuberculosis in 1902, the same disease that would take the lives of Joe McCormack's three grown children from his second marriage.

The Resilient Mother: Margaret's death and Henry's departure for Canada forced a new beginning for Joe McCormack, and on April 7, 1885, the young widower married Miss Mary Ellen O'Brien of Boston, Massachusetts.[14] However, Margaret's death haunted young Joe and he began to fall heavily under the influence of alcohol. Mary Ellen was born in Boston and raised in nearby Medford. It was her first and only marriage. Joe's sister Sarah McCormack Keller, who lived in nearby Field's Corner Dorchester, tried to warn young Mary Ellen not to marry Joe due to his alcohol problem, among other things, but Mary Ellen persisted. Charlotte Walsh Hannaway, the granddaughter of Sarah McCormack Keller, recalled that Mary Ellen fell victim to that great triumph of hope over experience with the declaration that "I love him and I will change him."[15] Charlotte Hannaway also recalled that "it was a tragedy" that drinking had ruined Joe McCormack.

Mary Ellen's father, Michael O'Brien, was born in County Cork, Ireland, and it is believed that her mother Julia Devereux was born in County Kerry. Michael and Julia would be John McCormack's most direct links to Ireland.

In Boston's *Registry of Marriages*, Joe McCormack is listed once again as an "engineer," and it was in Medford, a small city in Middlesex County outside of Cambridge, that the first child of Joe and Mary Ellen McCormack, Patrick Daniel, was born on January 17, 1886.[16] The priest officiating at the baptism at St. Joseph's on January 25, 1886, was Father William Henry O'Connell, who later became cardinal archbishop of Boston and the legendary nemesis of Boston's Mayor James Michael Curley.

The children came quickly for young Mary Ellen. By the time of the next birth, Joe and Mary Ellen had returned to South Boston. Catherine Amelia (Emily) was born on August 7, 1887, at 213 East Eighth Street and[17] barely a year passed when in August 1888, Robert was born. Robert only lived for ten months, and upon his death, he was buried in a corner of the Sandbanks cemetery where Mary Ellen's father and brother lay.[18] James Joseph was born on May 23, 1889, down the block at 432 East Eighth Street.

John William was born on December 21, 1891, three doors away at 426 East Eighth Street. Another baby, this time a girl, Mary, named for her mother, arrived on August 7, 1893, and would be baptized ten days later, but little can be found of her death and burial.[19] She did not live long enough to be recorded by the census. From her first pregnancy in 1885 to her 1902 miscarriage, Mary Ellen carried twelve babies in 17 years. Eight were born but only six lived long enough to be enumerated in the Federal Census. Sadness may have been her one constant companion.

To feed his growing family, Joe worked as a stonemason. But like many of his neighbors, he had an uneven occupational and residential history. As the family's financial prospects increased, larger and more expensive places were sought for housing. Joe once even owned a building, but apparently lost it during the Panic of 1893, one of America's market-based economic collapses.[20] The money to pay for the home would have come from the estate of Julia O'Brien, Mary Ellen's mother who died of "senile dementia" in 1892.[21]

In 1894 and 1895, the *City Directory* recorded Joseph McCormack living in two places—Joseph McCormack, the mason, living at 261 East Eighth Street; and Joseph

McCormack, the clerk, living at 33 Seneca Street in the city's South End. It appears as if Joe was then living apart from the family. It was his first separation from Mary Ellen, but not his last.

Only one Joseph McCormack appeared in the 1896 *Directory*, and he is listed at 1 Ellery Terrace in South Boston. The births resumed. Edward was born on New Year's Day in January 1896.[22] And the moves continued. In 1897, the family moved a few blocks down from Andrew Square to 788 Dorchester Avenue, and in 1898 and 1899, they are listed at 2 Woodward Place. The last child to survive infancy was born in April 1899 and named Daniel. Often listed as Donald, he was the youngest and smallest boy. Part of the confusion lay in the fact that in Gaelic, the name is "Donal" and it is the root of both names. But within the family, Donald's nickname was "Buttons." His birth certificate lists the family home at 470 Dorchester Avenue, a South Boston residence smaller in size and value than most of their neighbors.[23] This was where both the 1900 *Directory* and Census found the McCormack clan.

In periods of financial decline the family was obliged to move to more modest and inexpensive housing. This surely weighed on their sense of well-being and security. This was the context for John McCormack's childhood. By the time of his ninth birthday, John had moved six times. More would follow.

By the time John McCormack was 17, the family had moved at least fourteen times according to the annual *City Directory*. Each of these moves was within a six-block radius in Boston's Andrew Square, a rough-edged crossroads linking South Boston to Dorchester. Most of the residences were small two-bedroom apartments that were far too small for a family of eight. How many other places the McCormack family occupied between their recorded addresses in the *City Directories* is unknown, but there is little doubt these moves were often made quickly and without notice.

It was not unusual for poor families to ricochet around the neighborhood to beat the rent. As John's brother Edward "Knocko" McCormack recalled, "You never had no regular address. You just stayed in one place as long as the landlord let you and then you moved on."[24] According to historian Lester Gordon, based on interviews with John, rent was about $1.50 a week for a three-room tenement and some weeks that was too much to pay.[25] Food, most often dried fish and potatoes, came from the local welfare office. Driftwood for the family's stove was provided by the boys' scavenger hunts along the mud flats of Carson Beach, while trips to the railroad yards would yield stray lumps of coal for heat to counter the harsh chill winds that blew off the bay.

The weekly rentals had become increasingly difficult for Joe McCormack. Every move meant a new configuration of beds. Adjustments in sleeping arrangements accompanied the birth of each new child. Essential furniture such as beds and dressers became increasingly dilapidated with each successive move. Mary Ellen's kitchen pots and pans as well as her dishes and cutlery were also damaged in the frequent moves. The children's few possessions—toys, dolls, and books—were always moved and they were likely the only constants in their young lives. Their school clothes shifted from older child to younger child and the McCormack children surely stood out as they sat among their slightly more affluent classmates. Their poverty accompanied them everywhere.

Construction in Boston was not booming as it was elsewhere in urban America. Boston had lost ground to the newer metropolises of the Midwest. In the 1850 Census—the first following the arrival of the Famine Irish—Boston ranked third among the nation's cities trailing only New York City and Baltimore. By the 1870 Census, the city had slipped to seventh place. This meant that there were fewer construction jobs and the competition for them was heated. The hiring agents who placed men for these jobs were immensely aware of their power, and they made sure that "their own kind" were first in line to receive them. For Irish hiring agents, the initial determinant was an Irish birthplace and if scarcity was even more severe, the counties of origin within Ireland would determine the assignment of jobs. "Kerries" and "Corkies" often battled it out at the hiring halls.

By this time Joe McCormack had become a day laborer. His Maritime ancestry limited his employment opportunities. While he was a big man and well suited for construction work, his Canadian accent and the Scottish cast of his countenance placed him near the end of the line at the hiring halls. These jobs were fundamentally unstable. They paid well when you worked, but work was not always available. Often Boston's rainy weather and harsh winters would shut down job sites. Over that you had no control. Other times you weren't paid when intemperance gained the upper hand in your personal life and you didn't show up for work.

Most of Joe's daily wages were left at the tavern long before he arrived home, if he arrived home at all. Joe was a hard drinker. He was not the first man to find solace in a bottle, nor the last. All of the wonderful tales of drinking bonhomie among the Irish, be they native or Bostonian, reverberate in the cultural ethos. A man with little self-control like the Canadian Scotsman Joe McCormack, Irish Boston's drinking ethos quickly engulfed him.

"Were it not for whiskey, the Irish would rule the world" is a phrase trotted out to explain why the wonderful affability, charm, and eloquence so often attributed to the Irish did not result in their attainment of great material possessions or places of earthly prominence. But those who utter this phrase most often are Irishmen themselves who seem to gain wry enjoyment from this acknowledgment of their inability to match their promise with their performance.[26]

The family shrinks

The family snapshot as recorded in the 1900 Census has Joseph H. McCormack, age 38, a stonemason living at 470 Dorchester Avenue.[27] His wife Mary E. is listed at age 36. The McCormack household as recorded in the Twelfth Census return for 1900:

State: Massachusetts; County: Suffolk; Township: Boston; Ward: 15 Enumeration District No. 1370

Name	Relationship	Race/ Sex	Birthdate	Age	Place of Birth Person	Father	Mother.
Joseph H.	Head	WM	Apr 1862	38 M	Canada Eng.	same	same
Mary E.	Wife	WF	Oct 1863	36 M	Mass.	Ireland	Ireland
Patrick D.	Son	WM	Jan 1886	14 s	Mass.	Canada Eng.	Mass.
Catherine E.	Daughter	WF	Aug 1887	12 s	Mass.	Canada Eng.	Mass.
James J.	Son	WM	May 1889	11 s	Mass.	Canada Eng.	Mass.
John W.	Son	WM	Dec 1891	8 s	Mass.	Canada Eng.	Mass.
Edward	Son	WM	Jan 1896	4 s	Mass.	Canada Eng.	Mass.
Daniel	Son	WM	Apr 1899	1 s	Mass.	Canada Eng.	Mass.

And the whereabouts of the household's six children:

Patrick D. McCormack, Son, 14.

Catherine E. McCormack, Daughter, 12, at school.

James J. McCormack, Son, 11, at school.

John W. McCormack, Son, 8, at school.

Edward McCormack, Son, 4.

Daniel McCormack, Son, 1.

In the 1900 U.S. Census, Joe reported three months of unemployment in the previous year. But it was his commitment to his wife and children that was even shakier. A year later, the family left 470 Dorchester Avenue to return to 1 Ellery Terrace. Joe's irregular work history was familiar to his Canadian neighbors. Those who had known Joe McCormack back on PEI regarded him as a drunk, a rake, a small-time swindler, and an abusive husband.[28] Those behaviors continued in Boston, leading to further tension within the family.

Flight to Canada: Sometime in 1901, a pregnant Mary Ellen McCormack gathered up her six children—Patrick, Catherine, James, John, Edward, and Donald—and fled from Boston to escape Joe's alcoholic rages. She fled to the farm of Thomas and Kate McCormack Haley near Souris on PEI. Kate Haley was the oldest daughter of Donald McCormack and Mary McPhee McCormack, the farm family that raised Joe. The town of Souris, a small community of farmers and fishermen, is on the east coast of PEI in Kings County. Poor soil in Souris led farm families to export their children as well as their produce. The farms are small, mostly between fifty and one hundred acres. The Haley farm, the "wonderful farm" of family legend, was one of the smaller ones—a fifty-acre hillside farm with a one-a-half story farmhouse. It was barely large enough for Kate and Tom Haley, their daughter Mary Ellen, the young farmhand, Archie Howlett, and the sickly Harry McCormack, the only child of Joe McCormack's first marriage and half-brother to John McCormack.

The dwelling was much too small for Mary Ellen's brood. Three adults and nine children in one small house stretched the meager resources of the Haleys and Mary Ellen's presence was not wholly welcomed. A further tragedy befell Mary Ellen when the child she was carrying died.

News of the death of her infant son reached Father Ronald Bernard McDonald, the parish priest of St. Mary's in Souris, but he refused to bury the baby in consecrated ground because Mary Ellen had "abandoned the family home" in Boston.[29] So shortly afterward, Mary Ellen, her six children, and the Haleys buried the baby's body in the field behind St. Mary's Cemetery. Harry McCormack, the baby's 18-year-old half-brother, soon followed in February 1902. Unlike the baby, Harry got a tombstone and consecrated ground.

Word of Joe McCormack's impending arrival on the Island led to another flight. Mary Ellen gathered up the remaining six children and returned to Boston. Neither she nor John ever returned to PEI. To an intelligent and impressionable ten-year-old such as John McCormack, the inhospitality of the Canadian townsmen toward his mother and his siblings may have contributed to his desire to conceal his Canadian heritage. Forgiveness is in short supply when family extinction is at hand.

Another story about Joe McCormack that residents of Souris retell is how he came back from Boston and agreed to paint the house of a family in town, whose prominence in Catholic circles was established by having a bishop among their forebears. Joe painted the house with inferior paint that washed away during the first serious rainstorm. He then elicited more money from the family for better paint but disappeared with the money, leaving this prominent family with an unpainted house and some serious chagrin. This was the last that Souris would see of Joe McCormack. When he later abandoned the family household, he went to Maine to avoid his former neighbors in PEI.

Back in Boston, Joe resumed his paternal role in the McCormack household. It was 1902. Mary Ellen's pregnancies ceased and the coldness of the dinner table can only be imagined. The household continued to move as Joe's economic deficiencies continued. The *Directory* located the family at 499 Southampton Street in 1903 and then up to the Dorchester line at 15 Boston Street in 1904 and next door to 17 Boston Street in 1905. Family legend contends that Joseph H. McCormack died that year.

Whatever demons that beset Joe, they won. By 1905, failing fortunes and an ailing family had taken their toll. Married to a practicing Catholic, divorce was not possible, so Joe opted for desertion—the "poor man's divorce"—abandoning his family to the hardships of urban life in America. This was how one ended marriages in Joe's native PEI; so one afternoon he hopped the Boston & Maine Railroad and headed north, deserting his family to gain employment as a stonecutter along the Atlantic's edge, which served as the major corridor between PEI and the city of Boston.

The fatherless family

Again the diminished family moved. This time to 93 Mercer Street, back to the edge of East Eighth Street where the early births had occurred. It is here that the family would suffer its greatest losses. From the summer of 1905 through the autumn of 1906, the McCormack family agonized through the illness and loss of two of its grown children, James and Catherine.

The first piece of tragic news arrived in August 1905, when James Joseph McCormack was diagnosed with "phthisis." James Joseph was the second surviving son, the one who bore his father's name, and he was to be the family standard-bearer. James Joseph was closest in age to John who turned fourteen in December 1905. However, "phthisis" is a Latin euphemism, for what truly ailed James Joseph was active tuberculosis and its diagnosis would have terrible ramifications for the McCormack family. James Joseph lingered for six months until he died on February 15, 1906, at the age of sixteen. Now they were six. With the departure of Joe McCormack from the household and James Joseph taking ill, sleeping arrangements would have been adjusted once again. Sister Catherine would have moved into her mother's bed. Her bed would have been given over to James. The three younger boys—John, Edward, and Daniel—would have slept together.

The family rallied around James Joseph, but their resources were dwindling. Mary Ellen's health had suffered greatly from her twelve pregnancies and she had developed "chronic nephritis" a lingering back pain that sapped her extraordinary strength and robbed her of her once-proud erect bearing. Her decreased mobility and the lack of proper nutrition led her to gain far more weight than her frame could bear making it physically difficult for her to move her dying 16-year-old son James Joseph from his sickbed to the toilet.

In other cultures and societies, Catherine, Mary Ellen's 18-year-old daughter, would have handled this difficult chore, but among the Catholic Irish, be they native or Bostonian, any intimacy among young adults was prohibited. Brothers and sisters were not exempt from this proscription.[30] Worse however was that the family's unawareness of James Joseph's ailment led them to believe that he did not have the dreaded and highly contagious TB bacillus.

Mary Ellen's nephritis was exacerbated by tuberculosis, but because she did not have the coughing and wheezing symptoms most common to the disease known as "consumption," it was not known that she had become a carrier. By having Catherine sleep beside her, Mary Ellen carried the disease from her son James to her daughter Catherine, regularly exposing her to the TB bacillus. Three months after James Joseph died, Catherine was diagnosed with tuberculosis.

John's eighth grade graduation from the John Andrew Grammar School that June may have been the family's only triumph that year, for it meant that he was now employable. It was John's long hours in school and delivering newspapers that may have saved his life by keeping him away from the disease-ridden apartment. His immediate post-school employment by the Western Union Telegraph Company and later by the Boston Curb Exchange kept him even further away. John did suffer a partially collapsed lung as a result of being grazed by tuberculosis, but it never took full hold.

Throughout the horrible summer of 1906, the slender, blond, and pretty Catherine Amelia, known as "Kitty" to her younger Walsh cousins, struggled to breathe through the narrowing passages of her TB-infested lungs. Four months after she had come under a doctor's care, on October 2, 1906, John McCormack's only surviving sister, who had just turned nineteen, succumbed to acute tuberculosis. Celeste Walsh, granddaughter of Sarah McCormack Keller, vividly remembered the McCormack family's recounting of this death and the reaction of her cousin John. "Jack was so young when she died. There was nothing he could do."[31]

The family was more prepared for this death than they were for that of James. With the meager earnings of her brothers Patrick and John, a cemetery plot was purchased for Catherine in Mt. Benedict Cemetery in West Roxbury. This cemetery was in a rural part of the city, but it was Catholic, new, and clearly a cut above Sandbanks. Twice within the year of Joe McCormack's disappearance and John McCormack's last full year of formal education, death had come to the McCormacks. Now they were five.

Good Irish Catholic families annually honored the memories of those babies who had died before their births and those who died before their baptisms and whose souls resided in the "limbo of the infants." In the McCormack household where death already reigned, its return to their home and its claim on two more children—two beloved teenagers—further scarred the family's survivors.

It is doubtful if John realized that his first major outlay as a full-time worker was to pay for a cemetery plot for his teenage sister. Sometimes there are no choices. On that October morning, the four remaining siblings—Patrick, John, Edward, and Donald—gathered at their sister's grave. Once again, Mary Ellen stood alone over her daughter's grave with no comfort from her husband, Catherine's father.

From 1905 to 1910, Mary Ellen tried to keep up appearances and continued to list Joe with the *City Directory* as living in the family apartment in their next three moves to 3 Vinton Place, 49 Vinton Street, and to 47 Vinton Street. By the 1910 U.S. Census, Joe was no longer listed among the inhabitants of 47 Vinton Street in South Boston. Five years after his "death," the illusion of Joe's return to the apartment was finally put to rest. The census takers arrived once again and it was considered unwise to lie to them. Unlike the *City Directory* which only required the completion of a simple form, the census takers came into the home and counted heads. Joe's departure would not be concealed any longer.

The 1910 family snapshot was a diminished one.

Thirteenth Census return for 1910:

State: Massachusetts; County: Suffolk; Township: Boston; Ward: 16 Enumeration District No. 1492

Mary E. McCormack of 47 Vinton Street.

Name	Relationship	Race/Sex	Age	Place of Birth Person	Father	Mother
Mary E.	Head	WF	50 M1	Mass.	Ire-English	Ire-English
Patrick D.	Son	WM	24 s	Mass.	Ire-English	Mass.
John W.	Son	WM	18 s	Mass.	Ire-English	Mass.
Edward	Son	WM	14 s	Mass.	Ire-English	Mass.
Daniel	Son	WM	11 s	Mass.	Ire-English	Mass.

Under occupation,

> Mary E. McCormack, is listed as "none";
> Patrick D. McCormack, "Hostler, Stable'"
> John W. McCormack, "Clerk lawyer's Office";
> Edward, "Messenger boy, Telegraph"; and
> Donald [*sic*] "none."

Although Mary Ellen's occupation was listed as "none," John remembered vividly how hard his mother worked to provide aid and comfort to her neighbors. "My dear mother wielded a tremendous influence upon me. I had an intense love for her. She was a good neighbor to the other families that lived in the community; whenever they had any troubles, they'd come to her and she was sort of the counselor and the advisor."[32]

But Mary Ellen harbored anger about Joe's departure and disappointment with her Canadian in-laws. It led her to provide the 1910 census taker with an altered history for the father of her four remaining sons. Rather than have her boys listed as having a Canadian father, the boys were given a paternal ancestry matching her own. The country from whence the father of the boys came was now listed was "Ire. English." Joe McCormack had been reinvented as an English-speaking Irishman. Canada was disappearing from the family history.

Gone are the names of Catherine and James, the siblings closest to John and the ones whose deaths may have pained him the most. The loss of her daughter was undoubtedly the deepest hurt of all for Mary Ellen McCormack. It was family tradition to say that Joe McCormack had died, but Boston newspaper records, coroner accounts, and archdiocesan reports indicate no formal notice of Joseph's death.

The post-Census changes

As recorded in the 1910 Census, John was now employed as a "Clerk lawyer's Office." It was a step up from his initial full-time job as a messenger boy, the job that enabled him to be discovered by William Way of Plymouth who had a Boston office. Way's initial offer was a raise of fifty cents a week to work for him. It was a half dollar that would change young John's life forever.[33] Now elevated to a clerk in Way's office, John was eagerly devouring the law books on Way's shelves. But death struck once again. This time it was 24-year-old Patrick, John's oldest brother whose 1911 death certificate is the last Massachusetts document to identify Joe McCormack as a Canadian and Mary Ellen as a Bostonian. Now they were four.

Once again, the diminished family gathered at Mt. Benedict in West Roxbury and Patrick was buried beside his sister Catherine. For Mary Ellen McCormack, this was the third of her grown children to depart this life. Two others, Robert and Mary, had died in infancy and four miscarried. Death had been a constant companion in these harsh years of her life and her motherhood. Twenty-seven years of carrying her children from one cramped and dreary apartment to another had dramatically shortened her life and filled it with unspeakable hardships. Two years later in 1913, she would join her daughter and sons in death, a victim of myocardial disease, exacerbated by chronic nephritis and abetted by tuberculosis—a disease that, in retrospect, she may well have unknowingly spread among her children. She was only 52. Now they were three.

It was at this time that 21-year-old John McCormack, ready to pass the bar examination, began the reinvention of his life. It was a successful reinvention, carrying him far from Andrew Square to the Speaker's chair in the nation's Capitol, third in line to the presidency. But on this day, filling out his mother's death certificate, his only concern was with the family remnants of himself and his two young brothers.

The first step

Mary Ellen's 1858 birth certificate, 1885 marriage license, and church records listed her parents as Michael and Julia O'Brien. But her 1913 death certificate listed her parents as Patrick O'Brien and Bridget Daley, both of Ireland. As the oldest living son, it was almost certainly John who would have given this information to the funeral home.

There are many possible explanations for the discrepancy, some more generous than others. Perhaps John did not know the names of his maternal grandparents. Michael O'Brien died before John was born and Grandmother Julia died when he was less than a year old. A second possibility may have been that Patrick and Bridget O'Brien were indeed his grandparents, but they had died early. Perhaps Mary Ellen had been raised by godparents whose names were, as noted on marriage and church records, Michael and Julia Devereux O'Brien.

However, John was 14 when James was buried in Sandbanks and he stood beside the tombstone of Michael and Patrick O'Brien, erected by his grandmother Julia. He was aware of how his grandmother had reinvented his grandfather as a Bostonian. John also knew that this inscription was literally chiseled in stone so when John filled out his own mother's death certificate seven years later, he chose not to identify Michael and Julia as his mother's parents, but instead took the names of two others and placed them on his mother's death certificate. Patrick and Bridget were the names of the patron saints of Ireland, so these names were common throughout Irish Boston. Patrick O'Brien was the name of his mother's deceased brother. Bridget Daley was the maiden name of a woman whose son, Bernard Twitchell, was born eight days after James and was baptized on the same day and at the same church, South Boston's Gate of Heaven.[34] She and her husband Paul lived on Dorchester Street near where it joined East Eighth Street. Who knows how many times Mary Ellen and Bridget may have walked together carrying their baby boys?

It was a dangerous move to place Bridget Daley's name on the certificate, but John and his two young brothers, Edward and Donald, no longer had a generational barrier between them and their own mortality. The document was partially true; Mary Ellen's parents had been born in Ireland. It was her parents' names on the certificate that were false. Grandma Julia understood that to be Irish in nineteenth-century Boston jeopardized the welfare of a family. John understood that to be Irish in twentieth-century Boston was essential for family success so there should be no surprise that the death certificates of both Edward McCormack in 1963 and John in 1980 list Ireland as the birthplaces of each of their parents. Apart from John's father listed as a native of Scotland in the 1920 Census, the surviving McCormacks were now officially Irish.

As John McCormack and his two brothers buried their mother in Mt. Benedict in 1913, alongside her oldest son and her last daughter, Joe McCormack once again made no appearance. On her death certificate, Mary Ellen McCormack's marital status is listed as "M" for "Married," not "W" for "Widowed." Joe had been gone for eight years but John knew that his father was still alive. After all, Joe's sister Sarah McCormack Keller, the younger of the two McCormack girls whose parents had raised Joe McCormack in PEI, lived in Dorchester's Fields Corner less than three miles away from South Boston's Andrew Square.

In the condolence letter that Sarah's granddaughter Charlotte Walsh Hannaway sent to her second cousin Eddie McCormack after John's death in 1980, she wrote that John visited Aunt Sarah frequently and that John once told her[35]:

> Do you think I ever forget the past. How good Aunt Sarah was to my dear Mother—Then he told me a story which took place before I was born. As he said I used to go to see Aunt Sarah often and I would walk from South Boston to Fields Corner. I would hurry for I knew when I reached the house she would open the door and with her arms out wide draw me in to her and I was cold and it was good. Then she would take me in to the kitchen where there was always a fire which Uncle Dan kept going from the day he started until the day he put it out. She would feed me and have me lay down on the couch. She was a bright spot in my early life and she had so little for herself. This day she took off my shoes and the hole was the first thing she saw. She called Uncle Dan and showed it to him—saying look in the shop and see if you have a pair to fit Jack, if not fix these shoes for him. My grandfather in years back had a shoe store even in those days there were thefts and after a number of them he gave up the store but saved the merchandise. Jack went on to say that on his way back to S.B. it took him twice as long to get there as he stopped every so often to admire his new shoes.

John knew as did Sarah, her daughter Amy Keller Walsh and Amy's husband Chauncey Walsh that Joe McCormack was still alive somewhere, but he was dead to the boys if not yet to God.

John was 21, Edward was 18, and Daniel was just 14. They were three young fatherless boys who had just buried their mother. Living in a city with little compassion for its ethnic poor, despair might have been the expected response. But John McCormack would not be denied. He was on the verge of becoming a lawyer and he would have a professional credential to make his way in Boston. But which Boston: Yankee Boston or Irish Boston?

Knocko and Buttons, the surviving brothers

In the 1910 Census, the four McCormack boys—Patrick, John, Edward, and Daniel—were listed as living at home with their mother. This would be the last census to record

Mary Ellen and Patrick McCormack. By decade's end, Mary Ellen and Patrick would both be dead and the surviving members of the McCormack family would materialize elsewhere. Patrick, then 24 years old, was working in a stable; 14-year-old Edward was out of school and working as a messenger boy for the Telegraph Company; and eleven-year-old Daniel was out of school with no occupation. That an eleven-year-old boy should be unemployed would not be surprising in present times, but Daniel was apparently old enough to work in the eyes of the census takers. John and the younger boys supplemented the family income with a large paper route, but only John had a regular income and had become the family's breadwinner before he left his teens.

The two younger boys, Edward and Daniel, stayed at home for a while. Edward remained in Boston and became a highly visible and colorful part of Irish Boston's political pageant. Within the family, Daniel's nickname was "Buttons." Following the death of his mother, Donald McCormack was considered an orphan and he left South Boston to escape the clutches of the good sisters at the Catholic orphanage known then as the Catholic Home for Destitute Children, but later euphemistically renamed the Home for Little Wanderers. Family legend had Buttons disappearing into the Southwest where he was employed selling paraphernalia to traveling carnival shows. He was not a "carnie," but he spent most of his time in their company.

Buttons was built tall and lean like John McCormack, much in the family mold of their father but thinner than John. He never married and spent most of his adult life in Texas.[36] His most promising business venture according to his cousins, the Walsh sisters, was to engage in Texas land speculation, but those endeavors failed. He was once employed as an elevator operator at the U.S. Capitol Building. Clearly, this was a favor from his older brother as a way of qualifying him for a federal government pension.

At one time, Daniel returned home to Boston, ill with cancer and lived for a short time with Charlotte Walsh Hannaway, the eldest daughter of his cousin Amy Keller Walsh. But the cold dampness of Boston and the warm dampness of Washington held no long-term appeal for Buttons, so he returned to Texas to die. Buttons lived in Aransas Pass, a small town on Texas's Gulf Coast, and died in Temple, Texas, at the Veterans Hospital in 1966.[37] Then Speaker John McCormack had the remains of his last brother flown home to Boston and buried in the Mt. Benedict Cemetery with his mother Mary Ellen, his sister Catherine, and his oldest brother, Patrick. It had been 60 years since all four of these McCormacks had been together on earth.

Knocko McCormack: A local icon

It was John McCormack's brother Edward J. McCormack, Sr. who was perceived to be the real deal in Irish South Boston.[38] Edward's loud, boisterous, and raucous ways were the stuff of local legend. To John McCormack who disdained nicknames, his brother was always Edward, but to South Boston, Edward was always known as "Knocko," an echo of his early career as a prizefighter. John's tall and lean physique was a sharp contrast to the burly one of Knocko who stood a little less than six feet, but weighed close to three hundred pounds.

Initially, Edward followed in John's path and worked as a messenger boy for the Telegraph Company. Like John, Edward dropped out of school to help the family's finances. But unlike John, Edward's beefy build suited him for rough and tumble work and he gravitated toward more physical labor as a stevedore on the docks of South Boston. These jobs paid more than delivering messages, but they did not hold the same promise of discovery and protégéship.

Edward grew strong and tough. He became an accomplished street fighter and a semiprofessional boxer who was accorded the nickname "Knocko" for obvious reasons. He was a human locomotive whose quick temper and powerful fists earned him local repute.

Knocko was a finalist at the 1918 New England Amateur Boxing matches in the 158-pound class, but lost when eventual champion "Billy Rush found Ed McCormack an easy proposition in the final bout. McCormack covered up from the start of the bout, preferring to take a licking than boxing."[39] Knocko's domain then became the taverns and bars of South Boston and Dorchester. He worked as a bouncer, barkeep, and a bookmaker. Knocko's was a life that placed him outside of respectable Boston and on the edges of its underworld.

He was a bootlegger during Prohibition and a tavern keeper after it. For many years, Knocko McCormack was the Grand Marshal of the annual St. Patrick's Day Parade in South Boston. This is akin to being declared emperor in Southie. Every year, there would be a photograph of Knocko, wearing a tam-o-shanter and dressed in full military regalia from the highly decorated Yankee Division, riding astride his poor horse Jerry, leading the St. Patrick's Day Parade down Broadway. To the old-timers of South Boston, Knocko was a quintessential "Irish boyo" and in the words of former Massachusetts Senate President William M. Bulger, "while brother John was soft-spoken and courteous, brother Knocko was as self-effacing as a bass drum."[40]

One of Knocko's official roles was as assistant commissioner of markets for the city. Appointed most often during Jim Curley's administrations, Knocko would cruise through the city and drop in on its finest restaurants, Durgin Park and Lock-Obers among them, and decree that particular cuts of meat that hung in their refrigerated lockers had become spoiled. Not eager to offend the assistant commissioner of markets, the restaurant owners would surrender the "spoiled" meat to the commissioner without compensation. And the meat would make a miraculous recovery en route to South Boston where the regulars at his restaurant, the Wave Cottage, would be treated to a fine meaty sandwich for the simple price of a nickel. Knocko knew how to keep his friends and patrons well fed and well entertained.[41] And as reported in *Blood and Power*, "Knocko's Wave Cottage restaurant boasted a gambling den on the second floor."[42]

Knocko generally referred to his brother as "the Congy." To those who knew them both, such as Bill Bulger and U.S. House Speaker Tip O'Neill, John was "his complete opposite." But Knocko provided John with the Irish ethnic cover that he needed to maintain the support of his South Boston and Dorchester constituents. Knocko McCormack was a clear embodiment of Carl Wittke's stereotypical characterization of the Irish as a "warm-blooded and warm-hearted people . . . convivial and generous, sometimes to a fault, frequently improvident, and do not often come in conflict with the law except for intemperance, minor offenses, and occasional difficulties arising from the political graft of some of our larger cities."[43]

This characterization does not fit John McCormack. John was better described by Wittke's depiction of the Scotch-Irish, "The Scotch-Irishman's tenacity, firmness, and determination, his courage and his self-reliance, have helped him to make a notable record in political leadership."[44] Wit, humor, and charm seem to be absent here. Of John McCormack, his protégé Tip O'Neill contended "that John McCormack was so conservative that he didn't burn the candle at one end."[45]

Knocko endeared himself to many of Southie's less fortunate souls. As described by Bill Bulger, "He had a special relationship with the Public Works Department and would pass out what he called 'snow buttons' entitling each recipient to a stint shoveling for the city in the winter."[46] With winter storms roaring off the ocean to regularly pelt the South Boston peninsula, these buttons were to be treasured during those harsh winters when heat and employment were scarce.

Knocko was an enforcer for the faction of Mayor James Michael Curley, It was a time when bare-knuckled brawls often defined the respective turf occupied by the various barons of the city. Having Knocko and his gang gave Curley an intimidating phalanx that could guarantee highly visible places for Curley placards and campaign leaflets. Tracking down rumors of illegal payoffs or illicit love affairs were also part of the trade practiced by the Knocko McCormacks of Boston. "Getting the goods" on someone was essential in the highly personalized campaign realm of Boston city politics. Sometimes, it wasn't really necessary to get the "goods," just let loose a few rumors that you had the "goods" in some of the city's major gathering posts and the city's hyperactive rumor mill would run amuck. It did not take much to kick that rumor mill in gear and a positive reputation that had taken years to build would evaporate overnight.

Jack Beatty's excellent biography of Jim Curley, *The Rascal King*, contended that Knocko McCormack was a man whose feelings Curley did not want to hurt.[47] The fact that Knocko had done many a "dirty deed" for James Michael and knew where many of the mayor's "bones were buried" gave Knocko a prominent place at Curley's table. Contributing to Knocko's uniqueness was the fact that his older brother John, "the Congy," held a post of great power within the U.S. House of Representatives. Should Knocko ever need federal immunity protections as encouragement to provide state's evidence against James Michael, John "the Congy" could arrange it. This would make it possible for Knocko to elude imprisonment, a fate which had befallen Jim Curley twice before. Fortunately, Knocko would be John McCormack's protection from the mercurial and grandiose ambitions of Jim Curley. It was more than Knocko's "feelings" which worried Jim Curley.

Knocko's family

In 1919, young Edward married Mary T. Coffey, a 19-year-old stenographer from Cambridge across the Charles River. She was a tall, slender brunette with a sharp wit and an ability to stay out of the way of Knocko's quick temper. There were three children born to them: Mary E. (known as Mae), John W. II, and Edward J. Jr. Knowing that Harriet, John's wife, had shared with Mary, her sister-in-law, that "women's problems" had prevented her from conceiving a child, Knocko chose to name his oldest son John W. McCormack II. It was a way to honor his older brother who had kept the diminished family together.

Mae was tall and brunette like her mother and was a family favorite. On November 28, 1942, a horrendous fire broke out in Boston's Cocoanut Grove nightclub[48] and the life of Mae McCormack was lost along with hundreds of other revelers all unaware of how little care had been given by the nightclub's owners to the safety of its patrons. Rumors of payoffs by the nightclub's owner to corrupt city building inspectors were common throughout the stricken city.

Boston legend contends that Mayor Maurice Tobin, a Jim Curley rival, appeared at the wake of Mae McCormack to express his condolences to the McCormacks. Believing as did many in the city that corrupt city officials had winked at the Grove's multiple fire code violations, a disconsolate Knocko brushed aside the mayor's extended hand and sent a sledgehammer fist into his face.[49] The powerful punch did double duty for Mae's memory and for Tobin's disloyalty to Jim Curley in the previous two mayoral contests.

The Walsh cousins remembered that Mary T. was slow to recover from the death of her only daughter. It haunted her for the remaining half-century of her own life. Mary T. McCormack died early in 1997, outliving Knocko by more than 33 years and two of her three children, and she came within months of outliving her last child Edward Jr. who died shortly after her in the spring of the same year.

Knocko's two sons, John II and Edward Jr., were as dissimilar as he and his brother John. Although named John W. McCormack II to honor Knocko's brother, he soon acquired his father's talent for clocking various citizens of South Boston. Within the family, he was known as "Jacko" by his mother and brother.[50] But outside the family he was best known as "Jocko" McCormack.[51] Edward, the younger brother, was nicknamed "Bubba," and remembered his brother as "the best street fighter in South Boston."[52] It was a memory that Edward held with great pride. The boys had contrasting styles. Longtime residents of Southie have very fond memories of Jocko. "He was a lovable rogue," Anna Murphy of the Cork and Bull restaurant and bar recalled one afternoon, "he didn't give a shit for nothing."[53] As for Eddie, she opined, "He didn't do shit for South Boston." Not all of Southie's citizens appreciated Eddie's efforts to help implement the court-ordered desegregation school busing plan.

Jocko and Bubba played on Knocko's baseball and softball teams. From his command post at the Wave Cottage on P Street, Knocko made sure that his players performed competently on the field. For the player who struck out at the wrong time or whose error cost Knocko's team a victory, banishment from the bar was the usual punishment.[54] After a while, Knocko would forgive the misplay and the critical strike out and the teammate would be returned to the bar at the Wave Cottage. How often some teammates may have been through this cycle of banishment and forgiveness is hard to say, but this too was all part of the legend of Knocko McCormack.

Jocko McCormack was tall and good-looking, but he was similar to his father in his street-savvy and his hard edge. He too made it into the pantheon of Southie legends. One of the most endearing portraits of Jocko is contained in a column written by widely syndicated political columnist and author Jim Bishop, who got to know Jocko in the U.S. Navy during World War II and came to appreciate the fullness of his unique personality.[55] Jocko enlisted five days after the attack on Pearl Harbor and served on a few naval vessels that were hit and sunk by Japanese warships. He became known as "Cruiser-a-day McCormack." After the war, he went into private business eventually working for the Canteen Corporation servicing food and vending machines.

Jocko had a raconteur's gift for spinning colorful South Boston yarns, many featuring his father's exploits. Bill Bulger, who knew the McCormack boys well, observed that "unlike his brother, Jocko, who was a pie in the face of society, Eddie was smart and debonair, a study in silk; very smooth, very smooth."[56] Eddie was far more studious and conscientious. Respectability was his goal. A hockey player at South Boston High School, Edward had his share of local brawls, but it was the family's hope that he would develop more along the lines of Uncle John McCormack. So Edward was pointed on a course of academic achievement and legal training. He began his collegiate career at Colby College in Maine but transferred to the U.S. Naval Academy at Annapolis. Eddie shared that his big sister Mae had suggested that if he had to choose between West Point or Annapolis after transferring from Colby College that he go to the Naval Academy because the "honor code" at West Point would oblige him to "rat out" his classmates.[57] These were behaviors held in little regard by the very wary longtime residents of Irish South Boston.

The transfer was expedited by his uncle's position in the U.S. House, and it had the benefit of keeping Edward out of combat in World War II. This was a controversial decision. Knocko had fought in World War I with Massachusetts's highly decorated Yankee Division and sending his sons off to war was something his patriotism demanded, but his paternalism resisted. So Jocko went off to war and joined the navy while Edward remained at Annapolis. The fragility of the McCormack family, so vividly revealed again with the Cocoanut Grove fire, had to be protected. Uncle John had served in the army without facing combat in the Great War and had not been adversely affected politically by this occurrence, so why should the Annapolis stint hurt Eddie? Edward received his commission from the Naval Academy and met his noncombat postwar service requirements. Following his discharge from the navy, Edward enrolled at Boston University Law School. As the top student at the Law School, he served as editor of the *BU Law Review* in his senior year. But politics was still the family trade and Eddie began to position himself for advancement within the increasingly powerful Democratic Party of Massachusetts.

John McCormack's brothers and nephews gave him as much family as he was to have. Jocko married Lorna Izzo and had one son, Sean. Eddie married Emily Ruplis, who came from a family in South Boston's small but active Lithuanian community. She and Eddie had two boys, Edward J. III "Skip" and John W., named for Eddie's father and uncle. John McCormack was closer to Eddie's family than to Jocko's and after the death of his wife Harriet in 1971, John and Emily would go to the movies together in Boston. As Eddie's cousin Charlotte Walsh Hannaway recalled in her condolence letter to Eddie and Emily[58]:

> So Emily as Jack grew older and was alone he needed someone and you filled that spot for him dear. I was always so happy and a lump would come in my throat when I would see you and Jack together especially at Uphams Corner at the Movies. Not that I liked a rememberance [sp] of a McCormack in that area but the two of you together father and daughter. Thank you dear for your sweetness to him.

Emily was as close to John as he was to having a daughter.

The Canadian shadow

John McCormack's family alterations, making his mother Irish-born, might have been forgiven. Her parents were Irish-born after all, but his father's Scottish Canadian ancestry would have been far more difficult to overcome. Young John's prospects for political advancement would have been seriously derailed had it been fully known. It was better glossed over than acknowledged. Forgiveness for this part of the reinvention would have been very slow in coming, if it came at all.

Canadian ancestry was not esteemed within the Boston Irish community. In the years following the Civil War, a number of Canadian-born Protestants arrived in Boston. Calling themselves "British-Americans," these Canadians had left behind a newly confederated Canada and a disdain for its mandated tolerance of French-speaking Roman Catholics in Quebec. These Maritime Protestants chose Boston over Toronto as the nearest metropolis within which to seek economic advancement. Boston was just a few hundred miles away by boat. Toronto seemed almost a continent away and it had to be traversed on land for hundreds of miles through hostile French-speaking Catholic villages and towns.

It was the Maritime Anglo-Scot Protestants, the self-identified British Americans, stout defenders of the Empire and Queen Victoria, who were seen as largely responsible for an outbreak of anti-Catholicism during the 1880s—the Gilded Age.[59] Boston's Brahmins seem to have avoided the more virulent of the anti-Catholic groups.[60] Succinctly stated by James J. Connolly[61]:

> While Boston's tradition of Catholic-Protestant tensions stretched back to the Pope's Day rioting of the colonial era, its late nineteenth-century manifestation had more immediate sources. The arrival of British Americans from Canada in the 1870s and 1880s on the heels of the great prewar Irish migration sparked conflict between the two groups as they wrestled for social, political, and economic advantage in Boston. It was these Canadian immigrants, rather than Boston's Yankee elite, who spearheaded the attack on Boston's Irish-Catholic community.

The anti-Irish violence was real. Future Roosevelt Administration U.S. Secretary of Labor Frances Perkins, a Congregationalist native of Worcester, Massachusetts, remembered how horrified she was by the hooliganism of the anti-Irish gangs in Boston when she visited the city as a young girl.[62]

To the future gatekeepers of Irish Boston—Patrick Kennedy (b. 1858), John Fitzgerald (b. 1863), Martin Lomasney (b. 1859), and Jim Curley (b. 1874)—whose youth was spent dodging anti-Irish Catholic prejudice, whether the Protestant hands hurling the stones at them were native-born or Canadian imports were distinctions without differences. The insults and indignities all seemed to have Protestant origins.

Needless to say, Canada and its relocated citizenry—the "Noveys"—held no vaunted location in the Boston Irish view of the world. To Boston's Irish, the term "Novey" meant anyone who had come from the Canadian Maritimes. Like most derisive appellations, it was applied with little distinction and it covered all of the Maritimers: the Nova Scotians, the New Brunswickers, Islanders from PEI, and the "Newfies" of Newfoundland and Labrador.

It was in the Maritimes in 1755 that the English undertook a major rehearsal of the forcible relocation of Catholics from a homeland. Aided with an expeditionary force of New Englanders, the English moved the French Catholics from Acadia to locations along the Eastern Seaboard in colonies such as Virginia and the Carolinas, as far from Acadia as possible.[63] By burning their villages and trampling their lands, it was hoped by the English that the defeated and dispirited Acadians would not return. Many Acadians returned to France, but for most of those families for whom North America had been home for more than a century, they chose to remain on the continent, hoping for the day when Acadia would once again be theirs. The best known of their relocations was down the Atlantic Coast and along the Gulf of Mexico, where thousands were brought to New Orleans in the French colony of Louisiana. From these refugees comes that wonderful tradition that defines much of that most unique of American cities—the "Cajun."[64] Replacing the Catholic Acadians on the fertile lands of the Maritimes were Highland Scots who had also been moved from their homelands as part of the euphemistically labeled "Highland Clearances."[65] These new settlements would be collectively known as "Nova Scotia" or "New Scotland."

Maine-born and Bowdoin-educated Henry Wadsworth Longfellow in his extraordinarily popular poem "'Evangeline: A Maid of Acadia,'" the first epic poem of American literature, chronicled the tragic tale of the 1755 French Catholic diaspora from the land that they called Acadia and their beloved community of Grand Pre. "Evangeline" taught the children of the nineteenth century (and much of the twentieth century) that it was the noble and devout Catholic French who were the true white settlers of the Maritimes and that it was the English who were bullying interlopers and the disrupters of a peaceful idyllic community.[66] In his telling of the tale, Longfellow, a descendant of Yankees from Massachusetts and Maine, was careful to leave the unfortunately eager involvement of his New England Yankee forebears in this event from his rendering of the destruction of Grand Pre. However, citizens of Grand Pre remember to this day that it was not the British, but rather New England soldiers from Massachusetts, Rhode Island, and New Hampshire who disrupted its peaceable community.[67]

The anti-Catholic eruptions that accompanied the arrival of these Canadian descendants of Catholic displacers appeared as if they had similar designs on the Irish of Boston. To a people once displaced, such fears are not trivial. To be a "Novey," real or suspected, was a designation to be avoided in Irish Boston. And a Catholic "Novey" was no exception.

Easily the most conflicted of the Boston Irish gatekeepers on this issue was Boss Martin Lomasney, "the Mahatma" of the ethnically diverse Ward Eight in the city's West End. Lomasney was so sensitive about challenges to his Irish heritage that he was the only member of the 300-plus members of the Massachusetts Constitutional Convention in 1917 to declare that he was the issue of "Irish parents."[68] Lomasney's father had once spent time in Nova Scotia and his rivals suggested that Lomasney was a "Novey." Lomasney's parents were both gone in 1871, by the time that he was eleven, but he was so sensitive to these accusations that he carried his parent's marriage license and his own birth certificate in his waistcoat for the next 50 years. Lomasney's personal possession of these official documents created difficulty for those individuals who sought independent verification of his ancestry.[69]

Carrying the marriage license of one's deceased parents in the inner pocket of your waistcoat or in the top drawer of your desk indicates the defensiveness of these Irish-descended politicians to any hint that their Irish ancestry was tainted. These were documents that John McCormack did not possess and thankfully did not have to produce. There might have been no tale to tell here had they been requested.

John McCormack completes the reinvention

Armed with his bar examination credential, 21-year-old John McCormack planned his ascent into a successful career. Would it be Yankee Boston or Irish Boston that would be the path to success? John was well aware that success in Yankee Boston required a Pilgrim or a Puritan ancestor and a Harvard degree, and that the New England Historic Genealogical Society and the Harvard Alumni Association held the names of those on their lists close to their breasts. His name was not on either list, so he would have to launch his career in Irish Boston.

Irish Boston had its own requirements but they were less strict than those of Yankee Boston. Documentation was not necessary, but it helped. Being Catholic was essential but also expected. The successful combination of life experiences for advancement within Irish Boston was to be the son of an Irish immigrant and a widowed mother with younger siblings to support. These were the family histories of the political gatekeepers of the Boston Irish. It was they who controlled access to the lower rungs of the political ladder. Martin Lomasney of the West End on the backside of Beacon Hill, John F. "Honey Fitz" Fitzgerald of the North End, Patrick J. "P.J." Kennedy of East Boston, and James Michael Curley of Roxbury were the four most powerful of the Irish gatekeepers.

In a May 18, 1971, interview shortly after leaving the House, John McCormack recounted his early life and it made him one of them[70]:

> Well, at the time of the death of my father I was a young man, a boy—thirteen years old. He was a stonemason. The family was left in very bad financial circumstances. I had graduated from the grammar school and I had to leave the grammar school to go to work in order to try to keep the family together. Our family consisted of my mother and two younger brothers.

Whatever he may have told the city, the reality was that John McCormack did not have "the right stuff" for these people. His father Joe McCormack was not born in Ireland but instead was a Canadian from the Maritimes. To South Boston, this made Joe McCormack a "two-boater" or "herring choker." As recounted to me by Boston College Professor of History Thomas O'Connor, a South Boston native and author of *The Boston Irish*, "two-boaters" were unwelcome.[71] "Rory, get the dory. There's a herrin' in the bay" was the anti-Maritimer refrain heard around Southie. The implication of this remark is that Maritimers would hop into their small boats and chase herring around the bays and inlets and once found, they would pull the fish out of the water with their bare hands and choke them.[72]

Furthermore, Joe McCormack was not only a "two-boater," but he may have even been a Scot. Heaven forbid. John's mother, Mary Ellen McCormack, was born in Boston. Her father and mother were born in Ireland, but she was not. And John was not the family's oldest sibling; Patrick, Catherine, and James were all older than John and past adolescence and into adulthood at the time of Joe McCormack's departure from the household. Desperation and ambition can work wonders, and John McCormack set about to recast himself in the prevailing model of Irish Boston's successful politicians.

This was a lesson he had learned from his grandfather's tombstone in Sandbanks. Family histories could be altered if survival was at stake. So John McCormack altered his history. Joe McCormack, born the son of a Scotswoman in PEI, was trouble. He may have been emotionally dead to his surviving sons, but there was no certainty that he was truly dead and gone. While the McCormack boys may not have known where Joe was living or working, one person who did know if Joe still lived was Sarah McCormack Keller. But Sarah was embarrassed by her brother's behavior and may not have known that John McCormack recast his father as a native Irishman who had died in 1905.

Mary Ellen O'Brien McCormack, who was born in Boston of Irish parents, would also be recast as a native of Ireland. It is doubtful if Mary Ellen would have appreciated this posthumous relocation of her birthplace, but she would have understood why it was necessary. The three older siblings—Patrick, Catherine, and James—would be recast as having died in infancy. That Patrick was 25, Catherine 19, and James 16 at the time of their deaths would have to be finessed. The three surviving McCormack brothers and their cousins may have remembered their departed siblings, but to the world their identities were lost to history. It is perhaps no coincidence that the Murphy gravesite with its Celtic cross at Mt. Benedict, a short 18 feet away from the final resting place of Mary Ellen, Patrick, and Catherine, bore the names of three deaths on the tombstone. The three names of the Murphy dead were eerily identical to those of his own dead siblings—Patrick, James, and Catherine. Two of the Murphys had died in infancy. And so it would be. To those who would ask the Speaker, he would say that he, Edward, and Donald survived while the other McCormacks died in infancy and childhood.

The second tombstone, Mount Benedict, West Roxbury

In 1966, Donald died in Temple, Texas, leaving John as the family's last surviving son.[73] Brother Knocko had predeceased them both in 1963 and so it was left up to John to deal with Donald's remains. John was now Speaker of the House, and he had the remains of Donald, his youngest brother, flown to Boston and driven to Mt. Benedict Cemetery. John had the tombstone inscribed:

> In Memory of My Mother
> Mary
> 1861–1913
> Donald
> 1901–1966
> McCORMACK

Mary Ellen and Donald were memorialized on that tombstone but two other children—Patrick, the oldest son, and Catherine, the oldest daughter—who lay beside them were not memorialized. John knew that they were there. He had stood over both of their graves while his mother wept. But he could not acknowledge their presence. Acknowledging their presence in his mother's gravesite would have unraveled part of the life history that he had used to ascend the heights of Irish Boston. How could John McCormack have grown siblings when he had told people throughout his district and in Washington that his siblings had died in infancy? How indeed? The Boston Catholic Cemetery Association knew that there were four McCormacks, not just two, buried in Mt. Benedict Cemetery as indicated in their letter.[74]

Leaving their names off his mother's tombstone may have been the most difficult decision of his life at this time, the moment of his greatest success. During the previous twelve months of 1965, John McCormack had triumphantly presided over the U.S. House of Representatives during the 1st Session of the 89th Congress. This was "the Great Society Congress" and its legislative achievements came close to President Lyndon Johnson's goal of "out-Rooseveling Roosevelt." Even at the height of his political power and influence, John McCormack's altered life history had to remain in place.

If it was discovered that he had lied about the ages of his deceased siblings, then it was possible that there were other lies. Was his mother really born in Ireland as stated on Edward's death certificate[75] and on John's?[76] Or was she born in Boston as it says on her own death certificate and those of James, Catherine, and Patrick and on the census returns of 1900 and 1910 and on all six of the birth notices of her enumerated children? What of Joe McCormack? Had he died in 1905 as contended in the family history? If so, why was there no Massachusetts death certificate or Boston obituary, funeral mass, or cemetery plot to mark his passing? John McCormack was obliged to reinvent his family history in order to account for these anomalies.

James in Watertown and Catherine and Patrick in West Roxbury are buried in unmarked graves. These three siblings had shared most of John McCormack's conscious childhood memories. Leaving them out of the family history must have been horribly painful. Failing to memorialize his brother and sister on the tombstone that they shared with his mother was not a grievous sin but it was a sin nevertheless. He had knowingly and deliberately dealt improperly with his family's dead.

Did he confess these sins to a Catholic priest? Most likely, it would have been to his dear South Boston pal Richard Cardinal Cushing. John was an active churchgoer and a man of extraordinary rectitude. The guilt and remorse of these events would have burdened him greatly. Did he live an exemplary life? Yes, he did. No more devoted husband has ever sat in the House of Representatives. John McCormack's devotion to Harriet, his wife of 51 years, was not only legendary but true.

To a man with John McCormack's integrity, these tales in the reconstruction of his life were undoubtedly troubling. This may explain his lifelong resistance to prying reporters and biographers. The third oldest son of a Canadian immigrant father and an abandoned mother is not as dramatic a life story as that of the oldest son of an Irish immigrant father and a widowed mother. Nor did it have the same resonance among those tough Boston Irish politicians whose help he would need to climb the political ladder.

John McCormack never talked of his father Joe, leading others to believe that he had died when John was young. John McCormack also never spoke of that horrible year which robbed him of both his brother James and his sister Catherine. No one knew of these losses. Some pains must remain private forever. But he talked often and lovingly of his mother. When the City of Boston renamed the Old Harbor Housing Project in South Boston the "Mary Ellen McCormack Development," it was Speaker of the U.S. House of Representatives John W. McCormack who was invited to give the main address at its rededication. It was a speech about his mother that the Speaker could not complete. More than 50 years had passed since her death, but her memory moved him still.

Complementary identities

To his South Boston and Dorchester constituents, John McCormack was Irish. However, he was not as Irish as many might have liked. To South Boston natives such as historian Thomas O'Connor, John McCormack "looked like a herrin" or "herring choker"—a Maritimer.[77] He was tall and gaunt and dressed like an undertaker with his dark suits and white shirts. Never during his speakership and not even during his retirement did John McCormack relinquish that formality.

The *Irish Echo's* anniversary article on John McCormack's death contrasted him with some other giants of the Boston Irish.[78] "John McCormack isn't as colorful a celt as was Richard Cardinal Cushing. Nor does he have the shamrock style of the legendary James Michael Curley or the celtic charisma of our much loved and missed President John Fitzgerald Kennedy."

Given the Scottishness of his roots, John McCormack would have been hard-pressed to generate a "shamrock style," never mind colorfulness and charisma. Such traits are seldom associated with the Scots. However, John McCormack was a quick study. In his years at the Constitutional Convention in Boston and at the Massachusetts State House, John McCormack gravitated toward those who had power. In his early years in Boston, it was the Yankee Protestants. In the U.S. House of Representatives, he gravitated toward the southerners. John McCormack learned early that in the House, "It was the southerners who had the power and you had to be friendly with the southerners if you wanted to succeed."[79] But among the southerners, there was an important regional element in his choice of best friends and political allies. The southerners he was closest to were from eastern Tennessee and eastern Kentucky, western North Carolina, north Georgia, and north Alabama. These locales were situated in the southern end of the Appalachian Mountains—the regional heart of the Scotch-Irish. These curious hyphenated souls were the descendants of predominantly Presbyterian Scottish Lowlanders who first relocated to the Ulster Plantation in Northern Ireland and then moved westward across the Atlantic Ocean through Pennsylvania, the most religiously tolerant of the colonies, to the Alleghenies and down the Appalachian chain. They preceded by a century the arrival of the Catholic Irish on this continent.[80]

The southern Appalachian congressmen, both those born in and those representing that part of the nation, included a number of John McCormack's closest friends—Fred Vinson of Kentucky, Jere Cooper of Tennessee, Gene Cox of Georgia, Will Bankhead of north Alabama, and Alfred Bulwinkle of western North Carolina. Speaker Sam Rayburn of Texas was John McCormack's greatest partner in shaping the legislative destiny of the House. Unbeknownst to Rayburn, John McCormack shared his ethnic origins. Rayburn's ancestors had originally come to Pennsylvania from the Ulster Plantation in Northern Ireland during the 1700s migration of the Scotch-Irish to America.[81] Moving first to the Shenandoah Valley of Virginia, the Rayburn family continued westward into east Tennessee. It was there in Roane County, a stronghold of the American Scotch-Irish in the southern Appalachian chain, that Sam Rayburn was born in 1882.

There was something about John McCormack that Rayburn and his fellow Scotch-Irishmen liked. Perhaps it was his Scotch-Irish "tenacity, firmness and determination." But John McCormack could not tell them what it was they liked, for if it had become known in South Boston that John McCormack was more Scotch-Irish and Canadian than immigrant Irish, his career in the House would have come to an abrupt and painful end.

So John McCormack concealed his true ethnic identity. His reinvented Irish identity helped him hold his South Boston seat, and his genuine Scotch-Irish behavioral style gained him friends and legislative allies in a chamber dominated by these men of the mountains of the Southeast. In the end, both of his identities paid political dividends.

John McCormack learned his lesson well. As a young man, he had been careful not to play the Irish ethnic card, because he knew that his ancestry was tainted and those for whom Irishness was a defining feature of their candidacies would have called him on it. But because he didn't play that card, he was able to gain the support of non-Irishmen like his early Boston Yankee mentors William Way and Charles Innes, and the redoubtable Boston Brahmins Augustus Peabody Loring and Henry Lee Shattuck. In this way, he was able to bridge the rival tribes of Boston.

This lesson came in handy for the U.S. House of Representatives as well. John did not play the northern Catholic card with his southern Baptist and Presbyterian mentors in the House. He learned earlier than most that identity politics limit the height of one's reach and that those trusted by both sides in a conflict can ascend the quickest.

Before John McCormack could play his unique role in the U.S. House of Representatives in Washington, DC, he first had to navigate the troublesome and often treacherous shoals of Boston politics and the more subtle political dangers lurking within the Massachusetts State House. Designed by legendary architect Charles Bulfinch, the State House stood atop Beacon Hill. This was the place from which Boston was intended to send its message of godliness and righteousness to the world. It would not be an easy journey for John McCormack to make, but nothing in his life would be any harder than getting beyond the tragedy and poverty of his youth in Andrew Square. These circumstances may have left private scars but they toughened him for the public struggles that lay ahead.

Notes

1 Earlier versions of this research may be found in Garrison Nelson, "In the Shadows of John McCormack's Past Lie New Truths about His Life," *Boston Globe* (July 25, 1999), pp. E1–E3; "Irish Identity Politics: The Reinvention of Speaker John W. McCormack," *New England Journal of Public Policy*, XV (Fall/Winter 1999/2000), pp. 7–34; and "Unraveling the Reinvention of Speaker John W. McCormack," in Burdett A. Loomis, ed., *Extension of Remarks* of the Legislative Studies Section of the American Political Science Association (January 2000), pp. 2–7.

2 Death certificate of James J. McCormick [*sic*] at the Massachusetts Registry of Vital Records and Statistics filed February 19, 1906:

> Name of Father: Joseph H McCormick [*sic*]
> Birthplace of Father: Sawyer [*sic*], PEI
> Name of Mother: Mary E O'Brien
> Birthplace of Mother: Boston

3 In a fascinating article by historian Richard Jensen, he contends that the NINA signs were less prevalent than assumed and that Irish hardships were less than generally described in his article "'No Irish Need Apply': A Myth of Victimization," *Journal of Social History*, XXXVI (Winter 2002), pp. 405–29.

4 From the "The Arrival of the First Scottish Emigrants in Prince Edward Island and After," *Memorial Volume, The Scottish Catholics of Prince Edward Island, 1772–1922*, Chapter XIII (Summerside, P.E.I.: Journal Publishing Co., 1922), p. 50. A fascinating history of the MacCormack family that traces its origins from Scotland through Ireland to the Canadian Maritimes is John R. MacCormack, *Highland Heritage & Freedom's Quest: Three Centuries of MacCormacks in Ireland, Scotland, Prince Edward Island and West Lake Ainslie, Nova Scotia* (Halifax, Nova Scotia, Canada: Kinloch Books, 1998).

5 Adele Townshend compiled from the Leard Papers, *Ten Farms Become a Town: A History of Souris, Prince Edward Island, 1700–1920* (Town of Souris, 1986; reprinted 1997), p. 13. George Leard's nephew Waldron Leard was the source of much of my information about the McCormack family in Souris.

6 The baptismal records were originally located in the now-closed St. Columba's Church and were moved to the larger St. Margaret of Scotland Church. The only addition that I believe need adding is the Charlottetown location of the PEI Provincial Archives.

7 Scotland is listed on both the death certificate of Joseph McCormick [*sic*] in the Maine Office of Vital Records State Archives dated February 7, 1929, and the 1929 burial certificate of Joseph McCormick [*sic*] in the Town of Waldoboro, Maine.

8 This unique datum may be found in William S. Dutton, "Prince Edward—The Island Where There Is No Divorce and No Crime," *The American Magazine* (December 1929), pp. 48 ff.

9 This is the assertion contained in Michael T. Meggison's "Feature Article" in the *P.E.I. Genealogical Society's Records*, entitled, "The P.E.I. Scottish and Irish Ancestry of John William McCormack, Speaker of the U.S. House of Representatives" (2000), p. 2.

10 U.S. naturalization papers on file at the Federal Records Center in Waltham, MA, indicate that Joseph McCormack of Prince Edward Island who entered the United States in 1877 at Lewiston, Maine, completed the naturalization process in Boston, MA, on October 20, 1884.

11 *Boston City Directory*, July 1881.

12 Marriages registered in the City of Newton, 1882, p. 203. On November 9, 1882, Joseph McCormick [*sic*] of Boston, 23, an engineer, born in Prince Edward Island, son of Daniel and Mary, was married for the first time to Margaret Degnan of Newton, 24, born in Ireland, daughter of John and Anna E., also married for the first time by the Reverend Dolan in Newton, Mass.

13 Death notice of Margaret Degnal [*sic*] McCormick [*sic*], 26, at 65 Baxter Street on December 29, 1883. She is listed as having died of typhoid fever. The notice lists her birthplace and that of her parents, John and Margaret, as Ireland, *Record of Deaths in Massachusetts, 1883*.

14 *Marriages Registered in the City of Boston, for 1885*. On April 7, 1885, Joseph McCormick [*sic*] of Boston, 25, an engineer, born in Prince Edward Island, son of Daniel and Mary, married for the second time to Mary O'Brien of Boston, 25, born in Boston, daughter of Michael and Julia, for the first time. The church records of St. James the Greater in Boston for that date are in Latin and indicate that "*Josephus McCormick [sic], ex loco Boston, Filium [of] Danielis et Mariam*" was married to "*Mariam O'Brien, ex loco eodum, Filiam [of] Michaelis et Julia*," were presented by "*D. J. McLane et Barbara Foley*" and were married by "*Giacobus J. O'Brien*," p. 54.

15 The quotation comes from a condolence letter of Mrs. Charlotte Walsh Hannaway to
    the Hon. Edward J. McCormack, Jr., 1982, McCormack Family Papers. The letter was
    postmarked February 23, 1982. Mrs. Hannaway was the eldest daughter of Amy Keller
    Walsh whose mother Sarah McCormack Keller was the second daughter of Donald
    McCormack and Mary McPhee of Prince Edward Island. In her letter, she states that
    she is "nearing the age of seventy-five" which would establish her year of birth as 1907.
    She was born two years after the disappearance of Joe McCormack from the family
    household.

16 Baptismal record indicates that Patrick Daniel McCormick [*sic*] born on January 17,
    1886, was baptized on January 25, 1886. He was born to Joseph McCormick [*sic*] of
    Prince Edward Island and Mary O'Brien of Boston. The godparents were David
    McClean and Barbara Foley, who had been the witnesses at the wedding of Joe and Mary
    Ellen the previous year. The Reverend W. H. O'Connell presided, *Baptismal Register of
    St. Joseph's,* Vol. I, p. 34. Father O'Connell later became the first cardinal archbishop
    of Boston; see the excellent biography, James M. O'Toole, *Militant and Triumphant:
    William Henry O'Connell and the Catholic Church in Boston, 1859–1944* (Notre Dame,
    IN: University of Notre Dame Press, 1992), pp. 18–19, on his years in Medford.

17 Birth notice of Catherine Amelia McCormick [*sic*], born on August 7, 1887, at 213 East
    Eighth Street, South Boston to Joseph H., a mason, born in Prince Edward Island, and
    Mary E., born in Boston. *Index to Births in Massachusetts, 1886–1890*, 378: 156. On
    the baptism she is listed as Catherine E. McCormack in *St. Augustine's Register*, Vol. 2,
    p. 260.

18 Robert's burial is reported in *Registry of Deaths, Sandbanks, Watertown, Mass.*, June
    1889, p. 68. I could not locate a birth notice or a baptismal record for him.

19 Birth notice of Mary McCormick [*sic*], born on August 17, 1893 at 426 East Eighth
    Street, South Boston to Joseph H., a stonemason, born in Prince Edward Island and
    Mary E., born in Boston. *Index to Births in Massachusetts, 1891–1895*, 432: 173. The
    baptism is recorded at Gate of Heaven Church in South Boston, on August 27, 1893,
    p. 174.

20 This item appears in Ellen Coffey's 1994 Senior Honors Thesis at Stanford University,
    The Impact of the New Deal on Boston Politics: The Early Career of John W. McCormack,
    pp. 1–3. Ms. Coffey is the grandniece of Mary Coffey McCormack, the wife of Edward
    "Knocko" McCormack and John's sister-in-law. Ms. Coffey's well-written thesis depicts
    the house as "a wooden A-frame three stories high, perched on a hill overlooking the
    Boston Harbor," and "spacious, and light-filled" is more romantic than accurate. It is a
    tenement house slammed together with similar others on the densely populated East
    Eighth Street.

21 Death notice of Julia O'Brien on September 25, 1892, widow of Michael (maiden name
    Deady [*sic*]), at age 71 of "senile insanity" in Boston. She was living at 103 Mercer Street
    prior to her hospitalization. Her place of birth was listed as Ireland and her parents
    were listed as Michael and Margaret Boyle, both born in Ireland. *Deaths Registered in
    Boston, 1892*, p. 366.

22 Birth notice of Edward McCormack, born on January 1, 1896, at I Ellery Terrace,
    South Boston to Joseph H., a stonemason, born in Prince Edward Island and Mary E.,
    born in Boston. *Index to Births in Massachusetts, 1896–1900*, 459: 355. The baptism
    on January 11, 1896, is recorded at St. Augustine's Church in South Boston, *Baptismal
    Register, 1894–1899*, Vol. III, p. 189.

23   Birth notice of Daniel McCormick [*sic*], born on April 14, 1899, at 470 Dorchester Avenue, South Boston to Joseph H., a stonemason, born in Prince Edward Island and Mary O'Brien, born in Boston. *Index to Births in Massachusetts, 1896–1900*, 487: 85. The baptism of Daniel McCormack on April 23, 1899, is recorded at St. Augustine's Church in South Boston, *Baptismal Register, 1894–1899*, Vol. III, p. 543.

24   Edward J. McCormack, Sr. as quoted in "Mr. Speaker," *TIME*, January 19, 1962, p. 17.

25   Lester Ira Gordon, *John McCormack and the Roosevelt Era*, PhD dissertation, Boston University, 1976, p. 15.

26   See J. R. Barrett, "Why Paddy Drank: The Social Importance of Whiskey in Pre-Famine Ireland," *Journal of Popular Culture*, XI (1977), pp. 155–66; and Edward Wakin, *Enter the Irish-American* (New York: Crowell, 1976), pp. 59–60; and O'Connor, *The Boston Irish*, pp. 64–66 and 156–57.

27   Twelfth Census return for 1900: State: Massachusetts; County: Suffolk; Township: Boston; Ward: 15 Enumeration District No. 1370 indicates that Joseph H. McCormack of 470 Dorchester Street was born in "Canada Eng [lish]" and his wife Mary E. was born in Massachusetts.

28   These accounts were derived from a two-week research sojourn in 1997 where a number of Prince Edward Islanders spoke to me without attribution and sent me anonymous letters detailing events recounted to them by their parents and grandparents.

29   Correspondence with a person in Prince Edward Island familiar with the McCormack family history in Canada, May 28, 1998. A century later, this is still a sore point in Souris.

30   This insight was provided in an interview with Ms. Mary Ellen McWalters Melder of Rochester, NY, a U.S.-born descendant of Irish-born parents, July 1997.

31   Author's telephonic interview with John McCormack's cousin Miss Celeste Walsh, April 1997. Celeste Walsh was the granddaughter of Joe McCormack's sister Sarah McCormack Keller and the younger sister of Charlotte Walsh Hannaway.

32   John on Mary Ellen helping neighbors, Lester Gordon interviews, Tape 1, p. 5.

33   James Colbert, "50 Cent Raise in Pay Started McCormack on Political Career," *Boston Post*, April 10; 1956, p. 1.

34   Baptismal records of Gate of Heaven Church, South Boston, Mass. and kept on file at the Archdiocese of Boston Archives in Brighton, Mass. Bridget Daley was married to James Twitchell. Bernard Twitchell was born on May 31, 1889, and baptized on June 2, 1889, at Gate of Heaven. The names of James McCormack and Bernard Twitchell are only three lines apart on pages 83–84.

35   Condolence letter from Charlotte Walsh Hannaway to Eddie McCormack, in the McCormack Family Papers.

36   Most of my information about "Buttons" McCormack came from my telephonic interviews with John's cousin, Miss Celeste Walsh, April and May 1998.

37   Death certificate of Donald J. McCormack, died January 6, 1966, of "carcinoma of the breast," Texas Department of Health, February 14, 1966. "McCormack Rites Thronged in Dorchester," *Boston Globe*, January 12, 1966, p. 29.

38   Edward "Knocko" McCormack appears in the autobiography of William M. Bulger, *While the Music Lasts: My Life in Politics* (Winchester, MA: Faber and Faber, 1997), pp. 14–16. William Bulger is a longtime South Boston politician who served as president of the Massachusetts State Senate and as president of the University of Massachusetts.

39 "Boston Boxers Take Five of the New England Titles," *Boston Daily Globe*, March 19, 1918, p. 4.

40 Bulger, *While the Music Lasts*, pp. 14–16. The quotation appears on p. 14. See also Tip O'Neill's depiction of Knocko in *Man of the House*, pp. 121–22.

41 This account comes from Knocko's South Boston pals, eager to talk about him but reluctant to be identified.

42 Stephen Fox, *Blood and Power: Organized Crime in Twentieth Century America* (New York: William Morrow, 1989), p. 264.

43 Carl Wittke, *We Who Built America: The Saga of the Immigrant* (Cleveland: Case Western Reserve University, 1967), p. 178. The book was originally published in 1939.

44 Ibid., p. 63.

45 O'Neill with Novak, *Man of the House*, p. 121.

46 Bulger, *While the Music Lasts*, p. 16.

47 Jack Beatty, *The Rascal King: The Life and Times of James Michael Curley (1874–1958)* (Reading, MA: Addison-Wesley, 1992), p. 492.

48 The fire has been recounted in three books: Paul Benzaquin, *Holocaust! Fire in Boston's Cocoanut Grove* (Boston: Braden Press, 1967) originally published by Henry Holt & Co. in New York in 1959; and Edward Keyes, *Cocoanut Grove* (New York: Atheneum, 1984). Benzaquin's book contends that 490 died. The Benzaquin and the Keyes books make no mention of Mae McCormack among the victims. The one book that does is the most recent one by John C. Esposito, *Fire in the Grove: The Cocoanut Grove Tragedy and Its Aftermath* (Cambridge, MA: Da Capo Press, 2005).

49 This account comes from Esposito, *Fire in the Grove*, p. 211.

50 E-mails from Knocko McCormack's grandsons, Sean and Edward III, to the author, July 31, 2015.

51 See his newspaper obituary, "John W. (Jocko) McCormack, 62, vending machine representative," *Boston Globe*, September 28, 1982, p. 21.

52 Author's interview with the Hon. Edward J. McCormack Jr., Boston, May 1995.

53 Author's interview with Ms. Anna Murphy, South Boston, March 1997.

54 Multiple South Boston informants told me this including Boston's former mayor, the Hon. Raymond Flynn, November 1999.

55 Jim Bishop, "Hail and Farewell [to Jocko McCormack]," King Features, *Reading (Pa.) Eagle*, October 20, 1982, p. 7. When Jocko died, the *Back of the Yards Journal*, a local Chicago paper on the city's Southwest side, republished the *Boston Globe*'s obituary and an even longer one of their own reminiscences of Jocko's visits, "Back of the Yards mourns loss, a patriot and father eulogized by friend," October 6, 1982, pp. 1 and 15.

56 Bulger, *While the Music Lasts*, p. 91.

57 Author's interview with the Hon. Edward J. McCormack, Boston, July 1995.

58 The quotation comes from a February 23, 1982, condolence letter of Mrs. Charlotte Walsh Hannaway to the Hon. Edward J. McCormack, Jr., 1982, McCormack Family Papers.

59 See Arthur Mann's valuable *Yankee Reformers in the Urban Age: Social Reform in Boston, 1880–1900* (New York: Harper Torchbooks edition, 1966), pp. 42–43, for instances of British-American anti-Catholic prejudice in the Gilded Age of Boston.

60 This is the contention of Barbara Miller Solomon, in her "Brahmins and Irishmen in the 1880's," in her *Ancestors and Immigrants: A Changing New England Tradition* (New York: John Wiley & Sons, 1965), p. 49.

61 James J. Connolly, *The Triumph of Ethnic Progressivism: Urban Political Culture in Boston, 1900–1925* (Cambridge, MA: Harvard University Press, 1998), p. 18.

62 Matthew and Hannah Josephson, *Al Smith: Hero of the Cities A Political Portrait Drawing on the Papers of Frances Perkins* (Boston: Houghton Mifflin Co., 1969), p. 105.

63 The most recent account of Acadia and its troubles may be found in Charles D. Mahaffie, Jr., *A Land of Discord Always: Acadia from the Beginning to the Expulsion of Its People, 1604-1755* (Camden, ME: Down East Books, 1995).

64 William Faulkner Rushton, *The Cajuns: From Acadia to Louisiana* (New York: Farrar Straus Giroux, 1979).

65 A brief account of the "Highland Clearances" and their impact upon Canadian settlement may be found in J. D. Mackie, *A History of Scotland*, 2nd rev. ed. by Bruce Lenman and Geoffrey Parker (London: Penguin Books, 1978), pp. 320–24. The original version appeared in 1964.

66 Evangeline was translated throughout the world and was the inspiration for a number of operas and one movie. A nineteenth-century account of the poem's early popularity may be found in Noah Porter, *Evangeline: The Place, the Story, and the Poem* (New York: Cassell, Petter, Galpin, 1892).

67 The long-standing involvement of New Englanders in the region is presented in John Bartlet Brebner, *New England's Outpost: Acadia before the Conquest of Canada* (New York: B. Franklin, 1927) reprinted by Archon Books of Hampden, CT, in 1965.

68 Lomasney's entry reads: "5th Suffolk, Boston, born there of Irish parents, Dec. 3, 1859." *A Souvenir of the Massachusetts Constitutional Convention; Boston, 1917-18-19* (Stoughton, MA: A.M. Bridgman, 1919), p. 78. At the convention, Lomasney served on the Committee on the Bill of Rights while 26-year-old John McCormack served on the Committee on Form and Phraseology, p. 81.

69 In his chapter on "'Czar' Martin Lomasney," Tulane University political scientist Harold Zink states that "Mr. Lomasney claims Boston as native city in spite of persistent rumors to the effect that Nova Scotia deserves that honor. The doubt as to his birthplace arises from the absence of record in parish or public archives of Boston. However, Mr. Lomasney has never taken out naturalization papers, has repeatedly insisted that he was born in Boston down on South Margin Street, and states that he has a birth certificate and a baptismal record bearing out his claim." See his book, *City Bosses in the United States: A Study of Twenty Municipal Bosses* (Durham, NC: Duke University Press, 1930), p. 69.

70 Transcribed interview with John W. McCormack conducted by Mr. Edward Kraft, May 18, 1971. The family history quotation appears on pp. 2–3. These papers, hereinafter referred to as McCormack Family Papers, were provided to me by the Speaker's late nephew, the Hon. Edward J. McCormack, Jr. in March 1997. A more public recounting of the tale appears in a reminiscing article by McCormack in "I Remember When I Was Thirteen," in Leo P. Danwer, ed., *I Remember Southie* (Boston: Christopher Publishing House, 1976), pp. 119–21. Thanks are extended to Mr. Paul Wright of the University of Massachusetts-Boston for locating this short article.

71 Author's telephonic interview with Professor Thomas H. O'Connor of Boston College, June 1997.

72 Author's interviews with three Maritime-descended Bostonians including a staff member of the Canadian Consulate in Boston confirmed this interpretation, August 1999.

73 Death certificate of Donald J. McCormack, filed at the Texas Department of Health, Bureau of Vital Statistics, on January 11, 1966, indicates that Donald J. McCormack, a painter, died at the Veterans Administration Center in Temple, Texas, on January

7, 1966, of carcinoma of the breast exacerbated by chronic bronchitis and his parents are listed as Joseph McCormack and Mary O'Brien. His birthplace is listed as Massachusetts and his birth date as "4-14-1900" which varies from that on the birth notice, the baptismal record, and the census returns.

74   A letter to the author from Mr. John Kelley, the Business Agent of the Boston Catholic Cemetery Association, dated April 7, 1997, contains a list of the McCormack's buried in grave 1915—section 2 of Mt. Benedict Cemetery in West Roxbury, Massachusetts contains the names of:

> Catherine A. McCormick Age 19 Date 10/3/1906
> 93 Mercer St., So. Boston
>
> Patrick H. McCormick Age 24 Date 3/30/1911
> 47 Vinton St., So. Boston
>
> Mary McCormick Age 52 Date 5/12/1913
> 47 Vinton St., So. Boston
>
> Donald J. McCormack Age 65 Date 1/10/1966
> Temple, Texas

However, the records are slightly askew. Patrick was 25 (January 17, 1886 to April 4, 1911) when he died and Donald or Daniel was 66 (April 14, 1899 to January 7, 1966). Also, the records have Patrick buried five days before he died. Apparently, there was some confusion at the funeral home.

75   Death certificate of Edward J. McCormack in the Massachusetts Registry of Vital Records and Statistics filed on November 20, 1963:

> line 17: Name of Father: Joseph H. McCormack
> line 18: Birthplace of Father (City) (State or country) Ireland
> line 19: Maiden Name of Mother: Mary E. O'Brien
> line 20: Birthplace of Mother (City) (State or country) Ireland

76   Death certificate of John William McCormack in the Massachusetts Registry of Vital Records and Statistics filed on November 24, 1980:

> line 15a: Father-Full Name: Joseph McCormack
> line 15b: State of Birth (if not in U.S.A., name country) Ireland
> line 16a: Mother-Name (Given) (Maiden): Mary O'Brien line
> 16b: State of Birth (if not in U.S.A., name country) Ireland

77   Author's telephonic interview with Professor Thomas H. O'Connor, Boston College, July 1998.

78   Maureen Connell, "Remembrances of Those Who Died on November 22 . . . especially John W. McCormack," *Boston Irish Echo* (November 21, 1981), p. 10.

79   Author's telephonic interview with the Hon. John W. McCormack, Boston, April 1977. William V. Shannon makes just this point about McCormack's House career, in *The American Irish* (New York: Macmillan, 1963), pp. 341–42. Shannon also indicated that McCormack seldom returned to Boston and spent most of his weekends in Washington.

80   Books on the Scotch-Irish in America, *infra.* Chapter 2, note 17.

81   Hardeman and Bacon, *Rayburn: A Biography*, p. 12. A wonderful account of the Scotch-Irish migration and its impact upon America may be found in "Borderlands to the Backcountry: The Flight from North Britain, 1717–1775," in David Hackett Fischer's *Albion's Seed*, pp. 605–782.

4

The Ascent: Yankee Mentors, Irish Gatekeepers, and Harriet

From Messenger Boy to Attorney-at-Law: A True Horatio Alger Tale: Happy childhoods were rare among the poorer South Boston Irish. Tenement apartments were small, cramped, and poorly ventilated. They were breeding grounds for disease. Consequently, one had to go outside for fresh air and any semblance of social life. For the Boston Irish, social life revolved around the neighborhood squares. John McCormack's adolescence was filled with activities in and around Andrew Square and Everett Square named for two of Boston's notable statesmen, the Civil War Governor John Andrew and the redoubtable U.S. Senator Edward Everett.

Other places that provided a haven from the harshness of tenement life for John McCormack were the Catholic Church which gave comfort and the John A. Andrew School that instilled a love of learning and inspiration for a better life.

Young John was a great reader who devoured the "rags-to-riches" tales of Boston-born Horatio Alger Jr. The side street defining the South Boston block where 470 Dorchester Avenue met the curb was named for Horatio Alger. Alger's books were among the most widely read in the years of John McCormack's youth for they held out the glorious possibility of social mobility in this land of opportunity. By the time of World War I, it is estimated that sales of his books totaled over sixteen million.[1]

Social analysts have often challenged the "rags-to-riches" theme and have marshaled impressive evidence to suggest that it is more myth than reality.[2] In political life, it is usually called the "log cabin myth," which states that every young person, regardless of social origins, can rise to the top of the political ladder by dint of hard work, native intelligence, and unassailable integrity. The urban equivalent of the "log cabin" would be the "three-decker" and the "tenement apartment."

While President Abraham Lincoln is the best-known example of this myth, it has been regularly refueled. Three examples suffice: President Bill Clinton, the son of a widowed nurse from Hope, Arkansas; Governor Michael Dukakis, the Massachusetts-born son of struggling Greek immigrants; and President Barack Obama, the Hawaiian-born mixed-race son of a Kansas-born mother and a Kenya-born father.

John McCormack enjoyed the Alger stories and urged Americans to continue reading them. As he recalled in a 1973 interview, "I was an intense reader of Horatio Alger and also of Dick and Frank Merriwells in the dime novels because they'd always overcome great difficulties."[3] John's nephew Edward J. McCormack, Jr., the onetime attorney general of Massachusetts, related that John was called "little Dick" because of his affinity for the Burt L. Standish dime novels about Frank and Dick Merriwell, the star baseball-playing brothers at Yale.[4] John was a good athlete and at six-foot-two and rangy, he often played first base on the neighborhood baseball teams in Andrew Square, the rough-edged intersection that joined South Boston and Dorchester.

Tailoring his life to fit the Alger-like models would not be difficult. John had all of the raw materials. Long hours of work supporting one's widowed mother and younger siblings defined the Alger hero. However, the truly successful Alger hero did not toil obscurely in the coalmines and sweatshops, but visibly on street corners and at newsstands. This enabled their discovered by a prominent older man who would sponsor them after witnessing some heroic deed.

John McCormack's jobs gave him the necessary visibility. He took his first job in 1906 at the age of 14 with the Western Union Telegraph Company at $3.00 per week. He took this job shortly after his graduation from the John Andrew Grammar School in South Boston. This was the horrible year marked painfully by the deaths of his 16-year-old brother James and his 19-year-old sister Catherine. Ironically, it was John's time in school and at work that kept him far from the tenement apartment where the tuberculosis bacillus raged and laid waste to his vulnerable siblings.

Later that year, he changed employers and joined the Boston Curb Exchange as a messenger boy for a brokerage firm at $3.50 per week. This multiplied his trips into the city's financial districts where he could be more visible and more likely to be discovered. Sure enough, it happened.

William Way and Charles Innes: Two Yankee Protestant mentors

In 1907, John McCormack's life would change forever. While on his errands for the Boston Curb Exchange, he was discovered by the most important person of his early career—Mr. William T. Way, Esq. Way was a lawyer born in Boston's Roxbury section, back when it was a Yankee enclave, and not the Irish one of Jim Curley. Way was impressed enough with young John to hire him as a messenger boy for his Summer Street law firm at $4.00 per week.[5] With $4.00 a week in his pocket, John McCormack could cover the $2.00 per week rent for the family apartment. The sadly diminished McCormack family could remain together in one place for a little while longer. Mary Ellen McCormack's good boy would provide.

William Way was an old Yankee. His mother came from a long-established Roxbury family and his father was born in Rochester, Vermont. Like the oldest of the Yankees, William Way was a descendant of a Revolutionary War veteran, Nathaniel Maynard, his grandfather. Way himself was born in 1864, the last full year of the Civil War. He was a public school graduate who had trained for the law in his father's office and admitted to the Massachusetts Bar in 1890.[6]

In 1907 when he discovered 15-year-old John McCormack, Way was 43 years old and in his seventh year as a Master in Chancery. Way married late in life and had no children so in the classic mold of Horatio Alger benefactors, he was amenable to discovering and promoting protégés. In William Way, John McCormack had found his first great mentor and an Alger-like route out of poverty and obscurity.

> He looked upon me as sort of a son and encouraged me to study law. Then there was some of his clients would take an interest in me and encourage me to study law in the office. Mr. Way played a very, very important part—William T. Way—in my whole life, particularly those years in his office.

John McCormack placed himself wholly in the care of Attorney Way. In the 1910 Census, 18-year-old John McCormack still lived at home at 47 Vinton Street in South Boston, but his employment was listed as "clerk, lawyer's office." With the encouragement of William Way; John McCormack had begun the formal study of the law in 1909 at the age of 17.[7] It was Way who raised young McCormack from messenger boy to office clerk and the white-collar world that had eluded his father. It was Way who would also provide for his legal training and a bar examination tutelage which would elevate him further from the streets of Andrew Square.

A native of Jim Curley's Roxbury, William Way had moved to Plymouth but kept a Boston office. During the seven years of John McCormack's apprenticeship, Way sought a legislative seat in the House of Representatives of the Massachusetts Great and General Court. He ran unsuccessfully four times in five years. He ran in his Plymouth district three times for the Massachusetts House in 1910, 1913, and 1914.[8] In 1912, he sought a Plymouth County Senate seat hoping that the civil war within the Republican Party between the Taft regulars and Teddy Roosevelt Progressives would open a place for him. However, he lost all four contests. He came close twice, but by 1914, his vote total fell to 30% and it was clear to him that the electoral route would remain forever closed.

William Way was a political anomaly. He ran from Republican-dominated Plymouth County as a Democrat. That provided little electoral help. He was also a practicing Unitarian, the Boston-based Protestant faith which many Christians felt bordered on heresy. Known as "the Boston religion," Unitarianism's major belief was that Jesus Christ was not the Son of God, but simply His greatest prophet. As for the Holy Ghost, no such entity existed. By eliminating the Trinity and believing in the Unity of God alone, the Unitarians were at great variance from all Roman Catholics and most fellow Protestants. As some wry observers contended, Unitarianism was based on three beliefs, "The fatherhood of God, the brotherhood of Man, and the neighborhood of Boston." Way's Unitarianism was his political liability to the Irish Catholic voters in Plymouth County and his Democratic Party affiliation made him unpalatable to fellow Protestants who voted Republican in Yankee Plymouth. Put simply, William Way did not have "the right stuff" for political advancement. John McCormack learned a major lesson and his reinvented life story contained all the "right stuff"—an Irish father, a widowed mother, and younger siblings.

Way's legal practice in Boston and his political aspirations brought him into the orbit of the city's Democratic politicians. It was his hobnobbing with Jim Curley and the others that would reap benefits for young John McCormack. It was William Way who likely first introduced John to Curley. Long after Way's political ambitions had evaporated and his memory lost to history, the political careers of these two contrasting Boston Irishmen, the grandiose and self-dramatizing James Michael Curley and the proper and circumspect John McCormack, would intersect frequently for the better part of 40 years.

Another important connection Way established for John McCormack was with Judge Charles H. Innes, the city's formidable Republican boss. Although Way had been taught in his father's law office and knew how to prepare someone for a career in the law, he was less certain of his ability to prepare someone for the bar examination so Way arranged for John to receive legal instruction from Judge Innes.[9]

Charles Innes, the Great Poobah

Charles Hiller Innes was from Boston's elite Ward 4, the Back Bay. He was a graduate of Boston English High School and Boston University Law, both cuts below the Brahmin touchstones of Boston Latin and Harvard Law. He had served on the Boston City Council, in both the Massachusetts State House and Senate, and as a delegate to four Republican National Conventions.[10] He was close to fellow non-Brahmin Yankee Protestants including Vermont-born Massachusetts Governor Calvin Coolidge, who would become vice president in 1921 and president in 1923; New Hampshire–born Channing Cox who succeeded Coolidge in 1921 and defeated John Fitzgerald in 1922, and Maine-born Malcolm Nichols, the last Protestant mayor of Boston who held the post from 1925 to 1929 between Jim Curley's second and third terms as mayor. With powerful allies in the White House, the State House, and City Hall, there is little wonder that Innes was known as "the Great Poobah." He represented large firms and lobbied for them on Beacon Hill.

Innes's most unique enterprise was to provide legal training to students at his suite of offices at 53 State Street. For 26 years, from 1892 until 1918, Innes prepared about 900 young men and women for legal careers.[11] This enabled Innes to create a large network of contacts throughout the city and state. For many years, there were annual dinners sponsored by the Charles H. Innes Law Association honoring Innes and frequently presided over by his Republican beneficiaries Governor Cox and Mayor Nichols with many of Innes's grateful graduates invited to rub shoulders with the power brokers of the city and state.[12] The Hon. John McCormack was listed as a member of 1930s official dinner committee. Innes himself was invited by another of his beneficiaries, President Coolidge, to attend the 1927 Gridiron Dinner in Washington with its smattering of Cabinet members, U.S. Senators, and Representatives.

James Michael Curley and John McCormack were two of the many future Democratic leaders benefitting from the tutelage of Judge Innes.[13] As Joseph Dinneen, a Curley biographer, described it: "Jim Curley had only a grammar school education, but in his thirties he spent two evenings a week in the home of another political tutor, Charles H. Innes. Here he read books and reported on them like a schoolboy." He also studied "law" under Innes, who, Dinneen said, controlled the "royal purple vote," as well as the "vote of the red light district of the South End."[14] Despite Innes's guidance, Jim Curley dropped out of the program even though the probabilities of bar passage were always high for Innes-trained candidates. John Henry Cutler, Honey Fitz's biographer and Jim Curley's ghostwriter, said, "Innes was part of Boston's invisible government with a knack for anticipating bar examination questions."[15] Judge Innes's "knack" may be surmised: he bought questions and sold answers. Whether they were sold for money or for political favors does not really matter.

Many of his "law" students became jurists and politicians whom he controlled. As late as 1931, the *Boston Post*'s political writer said: "I doubt if there is any single Republican in the state who has so much power today." He had lieutenants planted everywhere in the city who "could deliver the goods," and was once characterized as the leader of the "crooks who run City Hall." And when Republicans controlled Boston City Hall, it was said that the elected officials were the "day mayors" of the city while Charles Innes remained the city's "night mayor." The pun was intended.

Judge Innes was able to keep the Boston Republican Party afloat in a city that was becoming more Democratic. If that meant playing the various Irish factions against one another that is what had to be done. Judge Innes was surprisingly successful. In the words of the *Boston Post*'s John Bantry (the pen name of Clifton B. Carberry, the paper's managing editor), "As compared with Charles H. Innes as a politician, the Democratic leaders, Mayor Curley, John F. Fitzgerald, and even Martin Lomasney, are mere children in the game."[16] Thanks to his influence and a Republican-dominated state legislature, one of Boston's three seats in the U.S. House retained a Republican congressman from the 1930s to 1962. This was in a city that regularly returned huge Democratic majorities for president and governor.

With Way's sponsorship and Innes's tutelage, John McCormack passed the Massachusetts Bar at the age of twenty-one with no law school, no college, and no high school training. All John McCormack had was an eighth grade diploma from the John Andrew Grammar School and the benign intervention of two Boston Yankees, the Democrat William Way who loaned him law books and the Republican Judge Charles Innes whose unique "knack for anticipating bar examination questions" got him into the legal profession. John learned an important lesson from these two: not all of Boston's Yankees stood in the way of Irish advancement. Unlike Jim Curley, John McCormack would not have to play the ethnic Irish card to insure his success. As a young man, he had been careful not to play this card because he knew that his ancestry was tainted, and those for whom Irishness was a defining feature of their candidacies would have called him on it. But because he didn't play it, he was able to gain the support of non-Irishmen like his two early Boston Yankee mentors. John McCormack was able to bridge the rival tribes of Boston.

Passing the Bar: John McCormack's triumph was dimmed by the loss of his 52-year-old mother. She died in May, the month before he would pass the bar. With the death of his mother and his admittance to the Massachusetts Bar shortly afterward,

John McCormack would put his reinvented life history to the ultimate test. It was a bittersweet memory for John McCormack as he recounted in a 1973 interview, "So, shortly prior to my passing the bar, my dear mother died as if the good lord left her on earth long enough to see the foundation for my future was laid."[17] Mary Ellen McCormack came close, but she never lived to see John attain the credential that would move him far beyond the narrow world of Andrew Square and ultimately to a virtual heartbeat from the presidency of the United States.

John would now begin the practice of law in Boston, one of the most contentious and legally competitive cities in America. The city was rife with attorneys. The best known had trained at Harvard's Law School then close to its second century of existence. Seated on the U.S. Supreme Court bench was its most distinguished alumnus, Justice Oliver Wendell Holmes, Jr., who would be joined in a few years by another of its prestigious graduates, Louis D. Brandeis. Other attorneys graduated from Boston University's law school, then in its 41st year of existence; who would be joined by the graduates of Suffolk Law School that had been created just seven years earlier. Their numbers were dwarfed by the hundreds of lawyers in the city that had read for the bar in lawyer's offices and had passed the bar examination with no formal education beyond grade school. John McCormack was one of these.

The proliferation of lawyers in the city had become troublesome to many of the profession's guardians and legislation was passed in the Great and General Court of Massachusetts requiring at least attendance in high school, if not necessarily a high school diploma, to go before the Board of Bar Examiners. The West End's Representative Martin Lomasney objected vociferously. He had already become legendary for his succinct advice to fellow politicians, "Never write if you can speak; never speak if you can nod; never nod if you can wink." Lomasney, who left school in the eighth grade, contended that the law discriminated against the poor boys of the city, but it passed the lawyer-filled legislature fearful of increased competition. John McCormack got in just under the wire.

John's Legal Practice: After leaving William Way's office, John McCormack hung out his own shingle in 1913 and began his law practice in his old Andrew Square neighborhood. He moved from the family apartment and boarded in the Dorchester section of the city. But the young lawyer was well aware of the deep ambivalence that the Catholic Irish had toward the law and its practitioners.

Irish Catholic sensibilities about the law were generally hostile. The English of William III's occupying army had used the law to subjugate the Irish, no more so than in the infamous Penal Codes of 1691 which mandated the following[18]:

> The Irish were forbidden to: receive education; exercise his religion; enter a profession; hold public office; engage in trade or commerce; live in a corporate town or within five miles thereof; own a horse of greater value than 5 pounds; purchase land; lease land; accept a mortgage on land in security for a loan; vote; keep any arms for his protection; hold a life annuity; buy land from a Protestant; receive a gift of land from a Protestant; rent any land worth more than thirty shillings a year; reap from his land; be a guardian to a child; leave his infant child under Catholic guardianship when dying; attend Catholic worship; and compelled

by law to attend Protestant worship. The priest was banned and hunted with bloodhounds. The schoolmaster was banned and hunted with bloodhounds. There sprang up in those days the infamous trade of priest-hunting, "five pounds" being equally the government price for the head of a priest or the head of a wolf.

For Yankee Boston, the law had almost a religious quality and its practitioners formed a secular priesthood. Its presumed neutrality and even handedness were values to be cherished. But for those steeped in Irish history, the English cousins of New England's Yankees had distorted the legal process. Not only had the English passed punitive legislation to drive the Irish from their lands and make them more amenable to relocation, their enforcement of these laws by judicial officials lacked even a semblance of even handedness or neutrality. As George Dangerfield pointed out in *The Damnable Question*[19]: "Years of oppression had taught the Catholic Irish that they could not look to the law for protection; that every one of its representatives, from judge to juror, was an enemy; that to reveal what was really in their minds would be dangerous; that the truth, while great and prevailing, commonly prevailed against them."

The Holy Roman and Apostolic Church was different. It was unchanging. Its values were immutable and transcended time and place. That which was "illegal" could be defined into legality; but that which was "immoral" was forever inscribed upon one's immortal soul. As a Catholic and as a lawyer, John McCormack understood the difference. When any conflict would ensue, it was his Catholicism that took precedence. It may have not always been the most pragmatic course, but it was one which guided him through troubled times. Armed with his reconstituted life and anchored in his fundamental values, John McCormack was now ready to test the political waters.

As a barely credentialed lawyer in a city filled with them, John would be competing with hundreds of others for the bottom-end clients. It was the better-trained and better-credentialed lawyers who would negotiate complex high-end contracts and multimillion dollar wills, and provide the legal foundations of the city's growing number of family trusts. These are the cases that would not be brought to John McCormack. John's caseload generally consisted of personal injury lawsuits and minor (and not so minor) criminal matters such as public drunkenness, assaults, robberies, and burglaries. As a good Catholic, divorces were unlikely to be brought to him. John's clientele was primarily impoverished Irishmen and other ethnics from Southie. Like most struggling ethnic lawyers for whom admittance to the larger Boston law firms was denied, politics provided an avenue of opportunity. But to succeed in that realm he had to pass through the gatekeepers of the Boston Irish.

A Perilous Journey through the Boston Irish Gates: John McCormack was born seven years after Irish-born Hugh O'Brien was elected as Boston's 31st mayor and its first Irish Catholic mayor. After four one-year terms in office, O'Brien lost to Thomas N. Hart in 1889, a Yankee Republican. Hart's first term as mayor was short-lived and it was Democrat Nathan Matthews Jr. who was the city's mayor at the time of John McCormack's birth.

Boston's second Irish mayor was Patrick A. Collins, a native of Fermoy in County Cork. Collins was a three-term congressman, 1883–89, who was named American

Consul General to Great Britain by President Grover Cleveland, 1893–97. He served as mayor from 1902 to 1905. Upon his death, Chairman of the Board of Aldermen Daniel Whelton, a Lomasney ally from the West End, became the city's first native-born mayor of Irish descent as well as its first native-born Catholic mayor.

The Boston of John McCormack had long since survived the Civil War and the ending of slavery. Blacks did not leapfrog the Irish at the bottom of the ladder. The later immigrant groups, particularly those that were Catholic, such as the Italians, the French Canadians, and the East Europeans generally, but not always, deferred to the Irish, their English-speaking coreligionists. After all, the Irish had gained control of the key socializing institutions for the new immigrants—the Catholic churches and the parochial schools. The non–Irish Catholics gave the elected Irish hierarchy political troops of their own to outvote the Yankees and to place Irishmen in the posts of power and privilege previously owned by the Boston Brahmins. However, before they could gain power from one another, they first had to gain power over the city, and for Boston's Irish Democrats, this was an arduous and bitter struggle to displace a longtime ruling Yankee Republican elite. This fact alone dramatically differentiated Boston's Irish Democratic politics from those of New York City and Chicago.

The Irish Democrats in New York City and Chicago differed from Boston's in their dealings with the Republican-controlled state legislatures. Both the New York City and Chicago machines operated more than a hundred miles distant from their state capitals of Albany and Springfield respectively. But Boston is the state capital and the Irish Democrats–controlled City Hall was only three blocks from the Yankee Republican–dominated Massachusetts State House. Boston's Democratic politicians knew they were far less autonomous than their brethren in Chicago and New York City. There would be little tolerance of the strong-arm tactics used elsewhere to build citywide machines. So the State House Republicans were not displeased that Democratic politics in the city took on the character of medieval fiefdoms with many of the wards controlled by rival barons. A divided enemy was easier to control.

The decentralization of political power within the city and the ongoing struggles between City Hall and the State House made political life especially challenging for the young and ambitious politicians of Boston, be they Yankee or Irish. Apart from the obvious similarity of ethnicity and religion, the young Yankee Republican politicians had educational and social bonds that reinforced their political ties. The vast majority of the prominent ones had graduated from New England's prestigious universities with those linked to Harvard and Dartmouth College moving most rapidly up the ladder. Those who did not have these degrees had to serve in subsidiary roles. The years between the Civil War and World War II were clearly dominated by Ivy Leaguers.

Young Boston Irish Democratic politicians like John McCormack had a more difficult time. Their ethnic origins and religion may have linked them together but they had no common socializing experience in the region's colleges to reinforce those links. They did not have the social and economic safety nets to break their falls from grace. The Irish gatekeepers had survived the economic hurdles of deprivation and the political ones set by their rivals. It was they who would emphasize these facts to the newer men who wished to hold public office.

Past the Gatekeepers: Two Irish gatekeepers, Martin Lomasney of the West End and P. J. Kennedy of East Boston, were content to control their respective fiefdoms and hold state legislative offices in the Great and General Court. Lomasney never married and had no children. His life was totally consumed by his management of the political hangout he called the Hendricks Club (named in honor of Thomas Hendricks, Grover Cleveland's first vice president) and his fourteen-hour days dispensing patronage and cutting deals in the ethnic hodgepodge of the West End. The Irish, black, Jewish, Italian, and Chinese citizens of Ward Eight would come to Lomasney for help. Martin Lomasney preferred to manipulate the process and to enrich himself. He chose a less visible role but appreciated others' awareness of his political dexterity. Of all the many nicknames that he collected over the years, the one he appreciated most was "the Mahatma."[20]

Like Lomasney, P. J. Kennedy limited his own reach to the Massachusetts Senate, but his son Joseph Patrick became one of the richest men in America and Ambassador to Great Britain and three of his grandsons sat in the U.S. Senate, one of whom became President of the United States.[21] P. J. Kennedy married and had four children: two boys—Joseph Patrick (1888–1969) and Francis (1891–92), and two girls—Loretta (1892–1972) and Margaret (1898–1974). Young Francis died as an infant in 1892. Like his own father before him, P.J. had only one surviving son. But what a son! The grade-school educated P.J. was a tavern keeper who later entered the wholesale liquor business. But P.J.'s surviving son went to Boston Latin and Harvard College and according to legend, by the time he was 25, Joe Kennedy had been chosen president of a bank.[22] Joe Kennedy's financial exploits were legendary. Irish Boston had insufficient capital for Joe Kennedy's dreams while Yankee Boston had no inclination to share its capital for the financial grandiosity of the son of an East Boston saloon keeper. Each of P.J.'s three Kennedy grandsons—John F., Robert F., and Edward M.—would be elected to the U.S. Senate and seek the presidency. But P.J. had no such ambitions. He enjoyed his prosperous liquor business and watched bemusedly as two of the other Irish gatekeepers—John Francis Fitzgerald of the North End, the father of Rose Fitzgerald, his son's new wife and James Michael Curley of Roxbury—wrestled each other for political prominence.

Fitzgerald and Curley both had grand public office ambitions. Both sought and achieved the mayoralty of the city and election to the U.S. House of Representatives. Both sought seats in the U.S. Senate, Fitzgerald in 1916 (and in 1942) and Curley in 1936, but neither succeeded. Fitzgerald lost to Henry Cabot Lodge and Curley lost to Lodge's grandson, Henry Cabot Lodge, Jr.

Prior to his election as mayor, Fitzgerald was first elected to the U.S. House in the Democrats' 1894 catastrophic defeat. In both 1894 and 1896, only John Fitzgerald had been able to win a seat for the Democrats of New England. Not many of Fitzgerald's fellow Democrats served in those hopelessly depleted Congresses that closed out the nineteenth century. However, two of them would leave their imprint upon the life and career of John McCormack. One was the low-key Henry Naphen, first elected in 1898 from the Boston district adjacent to Fitzgerald's. Naphen's daughter Mary was the best friend and maid of honor for Miss M. Harriet Joyce when she wed the young Boston lawyer John W. McCormack in 1920. The other was the brilliant but erratic House

Minority Floor Leader Joseph Weldon Bailey of Texas. Bailey's sponsorship of the House candidacies of his Texas protégés, John Nance "Cactus Jack" Garner and Sam Rayburn, would have a lasting impact upon the congressional life of John McCormack and the political life of the nation.[23] But those days were yet to come.

To the Democrats of Boston, Fitzgerald's three House victories were relatively unimpressive: 53.3% in 1894, 54.7% in 1896, and 48.7% in 1898.[24] In both 1896 and 1898, fellow Democrats had run against him in the general election, including the ambitious 30-year-old James A. Gallivan who would later help Fitzgerald derail Jim Curley's 1917 reelection for mayor. Hanging on to a marginal seat and serving in a hopeless minority diminished the allure of U.S. House politics for Fitzgerald. Fitz might have run for a seat in the U.S. Senate but the U.S. Constitution's original design limited access to the Senate through the state legislatures. The Great and General Court had controlled admittance to the U.S. Senate sufficiently so that none of the state's Irish Catholics had yet broken through that barrier. After his last reelection in 1898, Fitzgerald redirected his energies toward Boston.

Returning to a Boston-centered career, Fitzgerald was nominated by the Democrats to succeed the late Mayor Patrick A. Collins, who died in 1905. Pat Collins was the city's second Irish-born mayor and his unexpected death left the Democratic kingmakers in a bind. Fitzgerald was a proven vote-getter and the various barons of Irish Boston sponsored him. With an 8,100-vote plurality election over Brahmin Republican Louis Frothingham, John F. Fitzgerald became the city's first elected Boston-born Irish-descended Catholic mayor. Always eager to please his sizable cadre of relatives and friends, Fitzgerald let them feast heartily on Boston's municipal wealth. Public sector employment was to be protected by the city's Finance Commission staffed primarily by "Goo-Goos"—members of the Good Government Association. Fitz and his henchmen found their way around Civil Service requirements by concocting jobs that were not on the approved list, including city dermatologist and tea warmer.[25] Scandal after scandal ensued and Fitzgerald was voted out of office two years later.[26] In 1907, the Yankees reclaimed the office with city Postmaster George Hibbard defeating Fitzgerald by 2,177 votes after Martin Lomasney and the other anti-Fitzgerald barons sponsored a third candidate, State Representative John A. Coulthurst, to split the Irish vote.

Two years later in 1909, John Fitzgerald sought electoral redemption. The Boston City Charter was amended in 1909 to remove party designations from the ballot. This was yet another sign of "goo-gooism's" anti-political stance. One needed only 3,000 signatures on petitions to obtain a place on the ballot. With no party designations to deal with, public prominence would suffice for the politically ambitious, and Fitzgerald's public prominence was great indeed. Fitzgerald's slogan "Manhood Over Money" and his posters depicting Brahmin financier James J. Storrow as "$torrow" worked and he returned to hold the office's first four-year term in a close contest: 47,177 votes for Fitzgerald and 45,775 for Storrow.[27] Martin Lomasney returned to Fitzgerald's camp for this battle. However, Fitzgerald's success was made possible by the presence of incumbent swamp Yankee Mayor George Hibbard, whose 1,614 votes enabled him to avenge the Republicans' denial of his renomination in favor of the Brahmin Storrow. The city's Protestants also knew how to "get even" with one another.

Although Honey Fitz was only 46 at the time and would live for another 41 years, this would be his last successful election.

A year later in 1910, wheels spun again. This time the key factor in the political calculus was to rid the city, if only temporarily, of the young and ambitious James Michael Curley of Roxbury and the South End. One account suggests that it was William S. McNary, a former Democratic congressman, who enticed Curley into the race in order to avenge his 1906 defeat by the incumbent Joe O'Connell, the father of twelve and a graduate of both Boston College and Harvard Law.[28] Once Curley entered the race, McNary hoped that Curley would siphon enough votes from O'Connell to permit McNary's return to Washington. But Curley won the Democratic nomination and triumphed by 4,562 votes over Republican J. Mitchell Galvin who had come within 16 votes of O'Connell two years earlier. Another version is that Lomasney and Fitzgerald encouraged the 35-year-old Curley to take the congressional seat and await a later opportunity to run for City Hall.[29] Much later, they hoped. Perhaps Curley might be lured by the Capitol's revenue-enhancing opportunities and never return.

Curley arrived in the House of Representatives following the "revolt" against Republican Speaker Joseph G. Cannon of Illinois in 1909–10. Succeeding Cannon in 1911 was the new Democratic Speaker James Beauchamp "Champ" Clark of Missouri. While in Washington, Curley made an effort to ingratiate himself with Clark by adopting Clark's style of wearing white vests at public meetings. In his autobiography, Curley contended that he served Clark as the Democratic whip, the member whose responsibility is to round up the votes.[30] However, published accounts of House leadership indicate that Champ Clark ran the House Democrats without a floor whip during most of the ten years of his leadership both on the floor and as Speaker.[31]

Clark enjoyed the support of the Massachusetts Democratic delegation for most of the ballots in his 1912 bid for that year's presidential nomination, but he looked upon the vainglorious claims of Bostonians with a wary eye. As the Missourian wrote in his autobiography[32]:

> To merely walk the streets of Boston and read the inscriptions on her monuments, her statues, and her buildings is a liberal education in patriotism. Should an inhabitant of another planet, versed in both Latin and English, descend upon that city, without any prior knowledge of our history, he would naturally conclude that Massachusetts, single-handed and alone, originated and achieved the Revolution, created the Republic, and has sustained and governed it from the first. If he should read Massachusetts books, a great multitude which no man can number, he would be confirmed in this erroneous impression.

Jim Curley's embellishments would not have surprised Champ Clark. Jim Curley's grandiosity was part of his style as was discussing himself in the third person. During his four years in the U.S. House, Curley got better committee assignments than did Fitzgerald. He began his congressional career in the 62nd Congress (1911–13), assigned to the eighth slot on the important Foreign Affairs Committee and to the seventh one on the lesser Immigration and Naturalization Committee.[33] Curley's interests in the well-being of his immigrant constituents were well suited for these assignments. During his first term on Foreign Affairs, he served with John Nance Garner of Texas, who occupied the third majority slot. By 1913, Garner had moved on to the all-powerful Ways and Means Committee, but their shared service on Foreign Affairs in 1911–13 bonded them and it would help Jack Garner gain the vice presidency 20 years later and pave the way for Curley's protégé, John McCormack, to gain a seat on Ways and Means in 1931.

For Fitzgerald and Lomasney, the hopes that Washington might entice Jim Curley for more than a few years were dashed. He much preferred to be at his comfortable home in the Jamaica Plain section of Boston, with his family that eventually grew to nine children, while he planned his campaign for City Hall. Jim Curley was now ready to make the first of his ten runs for City Hall. Observing the mayoral shenanigans was 21-year-old John W. McCormack, now a young lawyer in the city, and his name would be linked to Curley's for most of the next four decades.

The Fitzgerald-Curley feud and its lingering impact

It was 1913 when young John McCormack first hung out his shingle as Boston's voters returned to the polls to elect a mayor. Party labels had been done away with and so two Irish-descended Democrats would face off against one another: the incumbent John F. Fitzgerald, a "lace curtain Irishman" originally of the North End who had attended Harvard Medical School; and U.S. Representative James Michael Curley, a "shanty Irishman" from Roxbury who had no education beyond grammar school but had extended his influence into Dorchester and South Boston, the largest wards within his congressional district.

Fitzgerald was well aware of the power of Boston's moralizing Watch and Ward Society that was founded originally as the New England Society for the Suppression of Vice in 1878. The Society gave the phrase "Banned in Boston" its unique cachet.[34] Eager to stamp out vice, the Society monitored books and plays to prevent "objectionable" material such as sex scenes and swearing from reaching the eyes and ears of Boston's citizenry. Eager to place himself on the side of his righteous citizens, Mayor Fitzgerald banned the foxtrot contending that the bodies of men and women came dangerously close to one another.

Mayor Fitzgerald's anticipated reelection campaign in 1913 would be his fourth successive contest for City Hall. Fitzgerald was confident that he would easily be reelected, and as a November 8, 1913, *Boston Post* cartoon indicates, he intended to keep dancing with Dame Boston for years to come. Having decreed that the foxtrot and the tango were too immoral for the sensibilities of good old Boston, Fitzgerald's dancing with Dame Boston is of a very chaste nature. Standing in the background of the cartoon were the younger ambitious Boston politicians who waited for the moment when Fitzgerald's hubris would sink him. This would also be the first time that Fitzgerald would deal directly with the man who would become his greatest nemesis, Jim Curley, who stood at the far left in the cartoon. There would be no contest.

"Toodles" Ryan: The day before the dancing cartoon appeared, a small item appeared in the *Boston Globe* that would alter Fitzgerald's life and political career forever. Tucked away in the clipping was a four-paragraph statement[35]:

Mansfield denies he promised

Henry K. Mansfield of Middleton, proprietor of Ferncroft Inn, in an answer filed in Superior Court yesterday in the suit of Elizabeth M. Ryan of New Haven against him, denied he promised to marry her in July 1908, or that he ever reaffirmed the alleged promise or that he ever said he did or did not intend to marry her.

If the plaintiff should offer evidence that he did promise to marry her then he says he was justified in refusing to keep such promises.

He denies he owes her $50,000 on account of any agreement to marry her.

He inquires when, where and before whom the alleged promise to marry her was made. He asks her if the mutual promise was expressed or implied or if in writing; how many times, when, where and in whose presence, if any one's, the promise was reaffirmed, and the time and place and in whose presence he ever declared he no longer intended to marry her.

In his trips from Washington back to Boston, Curley had learned of Mayor Fitzgerald's reputed dalliance with Elizabeth Ryan, better known as "Toodles." Fitzgerald had a flirtatious nature and was considered to be the best dancer among the city's politicians, but this was another matter. Toodles was an ample-breasted 23-year-old blond cigarette girl, who was quite skilled at taking men's minds off their gambling debts at the Ferncroft Inn, many miles north of the city. She was the mistress of Henry K. Mansfield, the owner of the Ferncroft Inn who was not above loaning her out to powerful men. Curley had heard the story from Dan Coakley, a disreputable and later disbarred Boston attorney, who had turned sexual blackmail into a profitable and powerful business.[36]

Dan Coakley had once been appointed superintendent of parks by John Fitzgerald and had a deep antipathy toward Honey Fitz stemming from the mayor's requesting the resignation of Coakley's scandal-plagued client Michael Mitchell from the post of superintendent of Boston's supplies. Mitchell's onetime closeness to the Fitzgerald family and Fitz's later damaging grand jury testimony about Mitchell made a lifetime enemy of the dangerous and vengeful Coakley. But how could one expect loyalty from a man such as Fitzgerald who would cheat on his long-suffering wife? Coakley would later go on to concoct "badger game" schemes of sexual entrapment of wealthy ultra-Yankees with his ally Joseph Pelletier, the district attorney of Suffolk County.[37] Eventually, the unraveling of these tales would lead to Dan Coakley's disbarment and to Joe Pelletier's suicide. But at this time in his career, Coakley's criminal instincts had not yet seized total control of his being, and he had some credibility and a ready listener in Jim Curley.

A black-bordered letter signifying death was sent to Fitzgerald's home. It was sent by Congressman Jim Curley to Josie Hannon Fitzgerald. Mrs. Fitzgerald summoned

Rose, the oldest of her three daughters to the house. Rose Kennedy, recently married to Joseph P. Kennedy, the surviving son of Fitz's ally, East Boston's boss P. J. Kennedy, came home to confront her beloved father as he danced across the family doorstep.[38] (It may have been Rose Fitzgerald Kennedy's first encounter with infidelity of the men in her family, but it would be far from her last.) Chagrined and mortified, Fitz "took ill" and withdrew from the race. This would happen every time that he would deign to challenge Curley directly as Curley would call the newspapers to announce his upcoming series of public lectures entitled "Graft in Ancient Times and Modern," "Great Lovers from Cleopatra to Toodles," and "Libertines: From Henry VIII to the Present Day."[39] Only one was delivered, but the threat did its job as Honey Fitz was "Toodled" out of the 1913 race.

The Toodles case generated front-page attention. She had left Massachusetts to become an actress in New Haven but returned for the trial. Every day she would appear in court with a new flamboyant outfit and a dramatic hat. She had become the talk of Boston and on January 19, 1915, what had been a salacious rumor became news fodder as her attorney, the corruptible Dan Coakley, elicited testimony from 71-year-old retired wine merchant James F. Mullen stating that he saw four men kiss Miss Ryan.[40]

"Now I want those names!" turning to the witness.

Mullen answered: "Frank Hall of the Adams House, John F. Fitzgerald, Gus Seeley, and myself."

"Is the John F. Fitzgerald you mention the ex-Mayor of Boston?"

"Yes sir."

Blaring from the front page, the Fitzgerald-Toodles episode was now a matter of official court record and seared into the consciousness of Boston's voters. It was the beginning of the end of the public career of John F. Fitzgerald.

Many feared Curley and rightly so. In an effort to emulate New York's machine, Curley dubbed his organization the Tammany Club of Boston. But unlike New York's Tammany Hall, Curley's Tammany Club was a personal fiefdom, dedicated almost solely to keeping the self-aggrandizing Jim Curley and no one else in public office.

Having removed Fitzgerald from the mayoralty contest of 1913, Jim Curley defeated fellow Irish-descended Democrat Tom Kenny. It was the first time since the city's founding in 1630 that the two leading contenders for mayor were both Irish Democrats. But this election was a portent of things to come as Irish Democrats went on to win 20 of the 22 mayoralty contests between 1910 and 1991, and were the runners-up in 19 of the 22 contests between 1914 and 1993. Most of Boston's twentieth-century politics had become the domain of Irish Democrats.

Young John McCormack watched closely and learned that even as distinguished a public career as that of John Fitzgerald could be quickly overtaken by a foolish scandal. John McCormack learned of the power of rumor to alter and even to end the careers of public men and of the one rumor most to be feared in Irish Boston—marital infidelity. After all, Boston was a city founded by Puritans. Most importantly, he learned that Jim Curley played hardball with his opponents and must be watched carefully.

Protestant politicians could and did cheat on their wives but theirs were marriages unsanctified by the true Holy Roman and Apostolic Church. To some of the more devout Irish Catholics, Protestant marriages hardly counted. Could a religion that accepted divorces ever sanctify marriage? It appeared to many of the Irish that the widely reported marriages among Boston's most prominent ultra-Yankees were more like commercial mergers than romantic couplings. Extensive lists of the corporate board memberships of the brides, and grooms, their fathers, and grandfathers accompanied engagement notices often overwhelming the amount of space allotted to naming all of the proper schools which had prepared them for these particular alliances.

On the other hand, marital infidelity was the "third rail" for political careers within the Boston Irish enclaves. Public drunkenness could be forgiven and often was. Larceny from the public treasury and nepotism on the public payroll could be rationalized, as helping one's family and thereby forgivable. Confession of these sins was sometimes not even necessary. But adultery was a mortal sin and no amount of "Hail Marys" and "Our Fathers" could ever expunge this sin from your immortal soul. It was this fact of Catholic existence that guided John McCormack throughout his public career and private life.

The Lodge-Fitzgerald Senate contest, 1916

Fitz later sought redemption in the 1916 U.S. Senate contest as he would run against Senator Henry Cabot Lodge of Nahant, a town along Boston's North Shore. Now serving in his fourth term, Lodge was the quintessential Brahmin. His great-grandfather George Cabot had served in the U.S. Senate from 1791 to 1796, during the presidency of George Washington. Lodge himself had earned the first PhD degree in political science ever granted by Harvard University. But his formidable intellect and arrogant bearing had repelled voters almost as often as it had attracted them.[41] Twice, in 1882 and 1884, Lodge had failed to be elected as a Republican to the U.S. House. But in 1886, he was elected to the 50th Congress. After three terms in the U.S. House, Lodge moved on to the Senate with the support of the Yankee-dominated legislature and served from 1893 until his death in 1924.[42] At the time of the 1916 election, Lodge was the Republican floor leader of the Senate. If the Yankee Brahmins of Massachusetts had tolerated a king, it would have been Henry Cabot Lodge.

The upcoming 1916 contest would be Senator Lodge's first public election since 1890 and his first for the Senate since the passage of the 17th Amendment obliged U.S. Senators to be elected by the citizens and not the state legislatures. It was Honey Fitz's hope that the condescending patrician Lodge would turn off voters and that he would become the state's first Irish Catholic U.S. Senator. By leaving the mayoralty to Jim Curley, he could also avoid the time-consuming distractions of city hall politics as he learned of voters' needs in the outer reaches of Massachusetts, west of Dedham, north of Everett, and south of Quincy. Boston may have been the state's largest political venue, but not its only one.

The race was surprisingly close. Lodge defeated Fitzgerald with a plurality of 32,939 votes of 517,000 total and a percentage breakout of 51.7% to 45.3%. Lodge had run slightly ahead of the presidential margin racked up by New York's Charles Evans

Hughes, a fellow three-named Ivy Leaguer, who thwarted President Wilson's reelection bid in Massachusetts. Despite losing Massachusetts, President Wilson returned to the White House but he was soon to learn that his life might have been lengthened and his presidency enhanced had he found more ways to help Honey Fitz unseat his personal nemesis Henry Cabot Lodge in this campaign.

Honey Fitz failed in that quest for the U.S. Senate. His three Kennedy grandsons—John Fitzgerald, Robert Francis, and Edward Moore—would win election to the U.S. Senate eleven times between them. Honey Fitz saw young Jack elected to the U.S. House in 1946 and 1948 but never lived to see his grandsons extract revenge from the Lodge clan. His death in 1950 robbed him of the delight he would have taken from Jack's defeat of incumbent U.S. Senator Henry Cabot Lodge, Jr., the grandson of his protagonist, in 1952 and Teddy's defeat of Cabot's son George Lodge in 1962. The family revenge on the Lodges took two generations. "Getting even" with Jim Curley would take less time.

The Irish card

Boston's first two Irish mayors, Hugh O'Brien (1885–89) and Patrick Collins (1903–1905) of County Fermoy, were reluctant to play the "Irish card." Both were born in Ireland and believed that the best way to insure Irish advancement was through an acceptance of Yankee dominance of the city, and they encouraged their supporters to adopt many of the nobler behaviors of the native New Englanders, such as temperance, frugality, and hard work.[43]

John Fitzgerald and Jim Curley were less convinced of this strategy, and both played ethnic politics with great eagerness. They used the "us-them" strategy to mobilize their fellow Irish-descended voters to move the Yankees out of City Hall for most of the twentieth century.[44] While John Fitzgerald craved approbation and affection from Boston's citizens, Jim Curley polarized the city along ethno-class lines to gain office and to enrich himself. Jim Curley's long-lasting impact upon the city's finances and its demography led two Harvard economists, Edward L. Glaeser and Andrei Shleifer, in a 2005 article for the *Journal of Law, Economics, and Organization* to label this phenomenon as "the Curley effect."[45]

Stated succinctly, "James Michael Curley, a four-time mayor of Boston, used wasteful redistribution [of city resources] to his poor Irish constituents and incendiary rhetoric to encourage richer citizens to emigrate from Boston, thereby shaping the electorate in his favor. As a consequence, Boston stagnated, but Curley kept winning elections."

This was the tenor of the city in which John McCormack, son of a Canadian Scotsman from Prince Edward Island, sought to make his way. By making Irishness a defining feature of a successful political career, John Fitzgerald and Jim Curley contributed to ethnic polarization. For those ambitious up-and-comers like John McCormack, who's Irishness was debatable, concealing the non-Irish aspects of one's ancestry was essential for political survival.

John McCormack studied both men closely and learned from each. Both Jim Curley and John Fitzgerald were masterful orators. Organizational matters were left to others. Curley and Fitzgerald did not confront one another directly; it was through their intermediaries that they most often battled. Curley's wit was a biting one and a style with far more acidity than that of the "hail fellow" bonhomie style of Fitzgerald. Curley took special delight in tweaking Fitzgerald. Jim Curley's major offense to the Fitzgerald wing was to threaten regularly the grandfather of the future president with widening the Boston public's awareness of Honey Fitz's dalliance with Toodles Ryan. Although the Toodles episode was well known among the city's political class, the ambitious Fitzgerald and Kennedy clans had nothing to gain by having this tale wend its way through the Irish Catholic parishes of the city.

After taking the mayor's office in 1914, Curley "cleaned up" City Hall, most notably by firing Honey Fitz's retainers and replacing them with his own. So there was ample motivation for revenge among the Fitzgerald wing as Curley prepared for reelection in 1917. Burying Curley would best serve their purpose—the quicker and more completely the better. Honey Fitz's 1916 loss to Senator Lodge had been expected but he hoped to come back in the 1917 mayoralty contest.

Stopping Curley

Fearing Fitzgerald's return in 1917, Curley again rattled off to city reporters his set of public lectures to be delivered at various Boston venues, the most incendiary of which was "Great Lovers of All Time: From Cleopatra to Toodles." Each was intended to sink Fitzgerald's candidacy. The first speech, "Graft in Ancient Times and Modern," was given in Dorchester, but before the Toodles speech could be delivered, Fitz withdrew.[46] Fitz, more convinced than ever that it was Curley who had sent the black-bordered letter to his home, began working with Martin Lomasney, an occasional ally, to finish Curley.

Fitzgerald and Lomasney each sponsored Democratic candidates with Irish ancestries to split the Irish vote and cost Curley his reelection. Fitzgerald induced into the race U.S. Representative James A. "Big Jim" Gallivan of the 12th District. This district encompassed the southern sections of the city—South Boston, Dorchester, and Roxbury. Lomasney brought U.S. Representative Peter Tague of the 10th District that encompassed the northern sections of the city—the North End, Charlestown, and East Boston—into the contest. The solidly Republican bastions of Back Bay and Beacon Hill were left out of the fray.

Almost 90,000 votes were cast in that mayoral election. Turnout was high as it always was when Curley was on the ballot. Pro-Curley and anti-Curley sentiments were on display and mobilization on both sides was easy to generate. Also, there were some obvious urban politics reasons for the heightened turnout. Not all of those who appeared at the polling booths to cast their votes on Election Day were the bearers of the names on the voter checklist and occasionally someone who had died over the weekend was resurrected to cast a vote. And there were always the "mattress voters" who resided elsewhere in the Commonwealth yet chose to vote in Boston on Election Day.

Gallivan's presence had the intended effect as he took third place with almost 20,000 votes.[47] Martin Lomasney's candidate Congressman Peter Tague, who would later thwart Honey Fitz's congressional comeback in 1918, took less than 2,000 votes from the city's smaller Irish wards in Charlestown and East Boston. The deed had been done. Mayor James Michael Curley had been voted out of City Hall for the first time.

The beneficiary of the three-way split among the city's Irish voters was former Congressman Andrew James Peters, a Yankee Democrat who had been named as assistant secretary of the treasury by President Woodrow Wilson. Peters had served under Secretary of the Treasury William Gibbs McAdoo, and President Wilson's onetime son-in-law. Mayor Peters had also served in the subcabinet with Assistant Secretary of the Navy Franklin D. Roosevelt of New York. Franklin D. Roosevelt's career is another one that would touch the lives of Boston's Irish barons and that of John McCormack.

Fitzgerald and Lomasney had united successfully against Curley. The Mahatma wanted to help Fitz's comeback by giving him Congressman Peter Tague's seat in the U.S. House in the 1918 election. Tague's contribution to Curley's defeat had been minuscule. Lomasney was unimpressed by Tague's efforts and may have suspected that Tague's dispirited campaign for mayor was intended to limit the lingering antagonism of Curley supporters from costing him future elections to the U.S. House. Tague also understood the game and chose not to accommodate Fitzgerald and Lomasney.

The "mattress voters" of Martin Lomasney arrived to do their duty—sleep over in Ward 8, vote the following day, and then disappear. Lomasney's support in the House primary led to Fitz being named on more ballots than Tague who then brought an official challenge to Fitzgerald's election. The challenge was an especially bitter one and it was not wholly resolved until 1919. Lomasney came to Washington to testify on Fitzgerald's behalf. The challenge eventually went to the floor of the U.S. House of Representatives to be settled.[48] Even though Fitzgerald had been assigned to the Public Buildings and Grounds Committee, he was asked to give up the House seat. Tague, the incumbent, returned to his seat and held it for two more terms in spite of Lomasney's efforts to topple him. Tague's victory was the usual outcome of intra-party contests that arrived on the House floor. Incumbents generally won.

Albeit brief, it was Fitz's last service in a major elective post. In 1922, Honey Fitz lost his only general election contest for Governor of Massachusetts. And he never got out of the 1930 gubernatorial primary or the 1942 senatorial one. The tale of Honey Fitz and "Toodles" had ended Fitzgerald's once-illustrious electoral career.

For the last 30 years of Fitzgerald's life, 1920–50, it would be Jim Curley, the publicly corrupt but privately moral man, who would continue to win elections—three more for Mayor of Boston, one for Governor of Massachusetts, and two more for the U.S. House. Jim Curley won fewer victories than he hoped for, but Curley's uncorrupted private life extended his elective career for eighteen of 30 years beyond that of Fitzgerald's.[49] It would be a lesson learned by young John McCormack.

John's testing begins: The Constitutional Convention

Massachusetts, the second oldest colony and the sixth state to ratify the U.S. Constitution, labored for years with a hopelessly outdated state constitution. The Industrial Revolution of the 1800s had impacted Massachusetts greatly. The limited availability of fertile farmland had made the economy much more dependent on manufacturing and commerce than on farming and agriculture. Far more than the other states of New England and certainly more than those in the fast-developing Midwest, Massachusetts was becoming an industry-dependent state. Boston, its capital, was a major commercial and financial city and the neighboring industrial cities of Lawrence, Lynn, Lowell, and Brockton produced goods which could be marketed throughout the United States and exported to the world.

Developments in commerce and industry seriously outpaced those in government and the state's constitution had no sense of what these changes entailed for Massachusetts and its residents. What should be done about the growing immigration and requirements for citizenship of the European newcomers who were put to work in the factories and mills of the Bay State? Should there be policies to deal with the frequent labor disturbances such as strikes that presumably impeded industrial progress? Should statutory regulations exist to limit the growth of the more successful of the economic entrepreneurs to protect competition within the markets? Should regulations exist to guarantee safe working conditions for these employees of the factories and mills, so that the labor disturbances would cease and the preconditions for industrial unionism could be avoided?

The governorship was then a greatly weakened institution. Colonial feuds between the legislative assemblies and the royal governors had permeated constitutional discourse, and the governors of Massachusetts were locked into one-year terms and had to contend with a Governor's Council that could and did limit the power of executive appointment. It was a gubernatorial structure far weaker than those of the other large industrial states within the Northeast. It also had the political consequence of placing Massachusetts's governors at a relative disadvantage in their occasional quests for national political office. But this would soon change.

The lieutenant governor who opened the Constitutional Convention in 1917 was Calvin Coolidge of Northampton. Coolidge was from small town Plymouth Notch, Vermont, and a graduate of the prestigious Amherst College. He found himself vaulting from that office through the first two-year governorship in 1919 and into the vice presidential nomination a year later. In 1923, upon the death of President Warren G. Harding, Calvin Coolidge would become the only Massachusetts Governor installed in the White House as President of the United States.

John McCormack, a junior member of the 1917–18 Massachusetts Constitutional Convention, would also reap benefits from the convention but his wait would be longer. McCormack ran for and was elected to one of the two seats from the 11th Suffolk District. He was only 25.

It was at the Constitutional Convention that John McCormack learned of his affinity for legislating. As a young member of the body, he was not assigned to any

COMMITTEE FORM AND PHRASEOLOGY.
Paul R. Blackmur (R.M.). A. P. LORING (Ch.). Horace I. Bartlett.
Theodore W. Ellis.* John W. McCormack, C. W. Hobbs, Jr.†

COMMITTEE ON CONTINGENT EXPENSES AND PAY ROLL.
C. W. Wonson (Cl.), ARTHUR B. CURTIS (Ch.), John C. Twomey (R.M.).
Patrick F. Nestor, Charles S. Bird, Jr.
* Resigned Aug. 22, 1917. † Appointed Sept. 20, 1917.

Figure 4.1 John W. McCormack: A Delegate to the 1917–19 Constitutional Convention. (Gerry Burke Family Photographs)

of the major committees, but it was working the floor that appealed to him most. He also developed a knack for sensing where power was located and who had it. At the convention, McCormack was assigned to the five-member Committee on Form and Phraseology chaired by the estimable Brahmin Augustus Peabody Loring, a state senator from Beverly on the North Shore (Figure 4.1). It was Loring who prepared *A Trustee's Handbook* for the Overseers of his alma mater, Harvard College. John McCormack was the committee's lone Democrat and its youngest member. Its other committeemen were college graduates and Republicans: Paul R. Blackmur, a BU law graduate from Quincy; Amherst alumnus Horace I. Bartlett from Newburyport; and

Theodore W. Ellis of Springfield who had graduated from Harvard College and its law school. State Senator Clarence W. Hobbs, Jr., a Republican from Worcester with two degrees from Harvard, replaced Ellis in 1917. This was heady company for young John McCormack, the 1906 graduate of the John A. Andrew Grammar School in South Boston. McCormack was now in regular contact with the members of the state's power elite. Here was an opportunity to learn the ways of the Republican Yankees under the extraordinary tutelage of Augustus Peabody Loring, a Brahmin of the old school. John later recalled, "It was a place where I made important friends and gained political experience."[50]

Democrats were in attendance throughout the convention but they only chaired three of the twenty-four committees and the only Irish Democratic chair was ex-Governor David I. Walsh on the Committee on State Administration. Of the Boston Irish gatekeepers, only Martin Lomasney representing the 5th Suffolk District was officially at the Constitutional Convention but he was everywhere. The Index of the Convention's *Proceedings* contains a column and one-half listing of Lomasney's various utterances to the convention.[51]

Among the others at the convention whose lives would intersect with John McCormack was U.S. Representative James A. Gallivan, whose seat McCormack would eventually occupy. Big Jim Gallivan spoke before the delegates and delivered an address on a memorial to nuns. Gallivan's speech may not have sat well with the predominantly Protestant male audience of the convention but the news accounts of it would have positive resonance back home in Catholic South Boston and Dorchester. During the convention, Jim Curley attempted to avenge his mayoral defeat by challenging Gallivan in the 1918 congressional primary, but Gallivan easily won reelection. After his 1917 foray into mayoral politics, Jim Gallivan limited his ambitions to holding on to his U.S. House seat. All he needed to do for that was to please the Irish Catholic portion of the city.

Sergeant John McCormack

On April 16, 1917, the U.S. Congress voted to enter the Great War against the Imperial Government of Germany. It was not universally supported. Fifty members of the U.S. House voted against the declaration, including House Majority Leader Claude Kitchin of North Carolina.[52] It was never a stance that John McCormack would take. With the Great War expanded to the United States, John McCormack left the Constitutional Convention to serve in the U.S. Army. Shortly before basic training, 26-year-old McCormack was asked to preside over the Constitutional Convention on July 24, 1918.[53] It was a modest start but it clearly foreshadowed the life he wished to lead.

After basic training at Camp Devens in Ayer, Massachusetts, McCormack returned to Boston, and had dinner with one of the convention's more active members, Mr. Joseph J. Leonard. Leonard was a 41-year-old Boston-born Democrat from the 22nd Suffolk District.[54] He was a lawyer and a former state legislator who had served in the House in 1904–05 and been assigned to the House committees on Harbors and Lands and Ways and Means. Leonard was chosen president of the United Improvement Association of Boston in 1912–13, a reform organization. At the convention, Leonard was assigned to the State Finance Committee with the estimable Republican Brahmin Henry Parkman serving as chair. In a debate over granting Civil Service "preference to honorably discharged soldiers and sailors from the army and navy of the United States," Leonard addressed the convention and described his dinner with McCormack[55]:

> I had the privilege last week of dining with one of our fellow-members, Mr. McCormack of Boston, a young man who had established himself in his chosen profession, and when I say that members of this Convention know what it is to be a young lawyer, to feel that one has made good in his practice. He told me of his experience in Camp Devens,—he is now, I believe, a sergeant, drawing his $36 or so a month,—he would not change conditions with me, or any other man in civil life for any consideration, and I know he meant it and was not merely saying it as a matter of effective talk.

McCormack was transferred to Fort Lee in Virginia where he readied himself for officer training and overseas combat, but he was not sent overseas nor saw any formal combat. On November 23, 1918, the armed forces were demobilized and McCormack left the service honorably discharged with the rank of sergeant. It would be his brother Knocko who would see combat in France with the Yankee Division.

John McCormack entered the crowded field for one of the two seats from the 11th Suffolk District. He was one of six candidates in the September 1919 primary. These were seats that the Republicans did not challenge so it was in the primary that the winners would be selected. The young veteran John McCormack campaigned vigorously and finished second behind incumbent James B. Troy.[56] Democrats Troy and McCormack won the general election unopposed with McCormack slightly outpolling Troy: 2,925 to 2,849. It was the last one-year session of the General Court. The Constitutional Convention upon which he had served lengthened the term of office to two years. In the following year, Representatives Troy and McCormack were easily reelected to the General Court's first two-year legislative terms

A city in peril: The Boston Police Strike

It was during John McCormack's first campaign for a seat in the General Court that the city experienced its most violent eruption of civil disorder since the Boston Massacre of 1770 claimed five lives. Not even the 1863 Boston draft riots with its six fatalities[57] compared with the Boston Police Strike of September 1919.[58] The predominantly Yankee Police Commission had frozen wages for the predominantly Irish Boston police force at prewar levels. Since 1885 and the first election of Hugh O'Brien, an Irish-born mayor, the Boston Police Commission had been appointed by the state legislature.[59] Compounding their financial woes, the Boston policemen had to purchase their own uniforms and encountered horrendous working conditions in overcrowded and rat-infested station houses. The policemen asked for and received a charter from the American Federation of Labor to organize their own union. This set the stage for the confrontation. Despite a series of meetings between the nascent police union and the ineffectual Yankee Democratic Mayor Andrew James Peters, the Police Commission, led by former Republican Yankee Mayor Edwin U. Curtis, would not budge. There would be no raises and any policemen who chose to strike would be fired on the spot.

This was a time when labor issues were especially troubling to American conservatives. They were still recoiling from Lenin's Bolshevik takeover of Imperial Russia and its replacement by what the Communists would call a "dictatorship of the proletariat." Their anxieties were further fueled in this country by the government raids on foreign-born workingmen led by President Wilson's ambitious Attorney General, A. Mitchell Palmer.[60]

The hope of the Yankees was that if they stood firm the Irish policemen and their supporters would retreat into the sullen silence that had characterized the Boston Irish response on so many of their previous encounters. But this did not happen. The inevitable consequence of the stalemate was a strike by 1,100 of the 1,500-plus members of the police force and a city left imperiled by their absence. Riots, looting, robberies, and rapes erupted throughout the city and when it was finally over, eight people had been killed, twenty-one wounded, at least fifty injured and an estimated third of a million dollars had been lost.[61]

The riots were the worst in South Boston. Here lived many families of the policemen whose secure city jobs were lost forever. And lurking in Southie, there was an organized opposition to police authority, the infamous Gustin Gang led by the Wallace brothers. As recounted by Boston historian Francis Russell[62]: "Here was located the Gustin Gang—its name abbreviated from St. Augustine's, the towering brick Gothic-revival Church on Dorchester Street—the most feared gang in all Boston. Here was the spawning ground of politicians and prize-fighters, policemen and plug-uglies."

St. Augustine's Church was located on Dorchester Street where John McCormack's fiancée Harriet and her mother lived, and it was at St. Augustine's Church where John and Harriet would be wed a short nine months later.

But on these September nights in 1919, Dorchester Street was rife with violence, and the people most involved in it were the people from whom John McCormack would seek votes two months later. It was near St. Augustine's that one of the street gangs stoned policemen while chanting, "Kill them! Kill the dirty sons of bitches." Andrew Square, where much of John's formative years had been spent, was filled with looters who stripped the premises of the small retailers who had dared to venture into this harsh crossroads of the divided city.

Ethnic and class polarization were everywhere. One of the temporary solutions was to recruit burly Harvard students and graduates to provide a police force for the city. Included among them would be future governor and U.S. Senator Leverett Saltonstall.[63] This was yet another reminder to the Irish that the Yankees would not surrender their "City on a Hill" without a fight. With Irish Boston and Yankee Boston at each other's throats, neutrality was impossible. Perhaps this is why John chose to identify his father's birthplace as "Scotland" in the 1920 Census. John was not displeased that the legislature had adjourned in July and was not obliged to address this divisive issue as were the city and state's executive officers, eager as they were to position themselves as champions of law and order. The enemies John McCormack would have made among his future constituents would have been fatal. The memories of South Boston's Irish linger for years.

The once glorious reputations of civic officials charged with the responsibility of maintaining order were eviscerated, particularly those of Mayor Peters and Police Commissioner Curtis who shifted blame back and forth. There was one notable exception. Governor Calvin Coolidge mobilized the newly formed militia, the Massachusetts State Guard, and it was they who brought order to the city and a national reputation for the governor.

Samuel Gompers, the head of the American Federation of Labor, was deeply fearful of the adverse public reaction to municipal unions and he pleaded with Governor Coolidge to remove Curtis as the police commissioner to bring about an "opportunity for cool deliberate consideration when the passions aroused shall have subsided."[64] But it was Governor Coolidge who made the best use of this opportunity. Contained in the middle of his telegrammed reply to Gompers was the deathless phrase, "There is no right to strike against the public safety by anybody, anywhere, any time." Coolidge's simple sentence was picked up by the newspapers and repeated throughout the nation transforming him into a folk hero. The strike had ended, but the city remained divided. Young John McCormack had to tread lightly.

Mayor Andrew James Peters, a man Curley described as having the "names of three Apostles," was an indifferent mayor at best and while knowledge of his own personal scandals involving his teenaged ward Starr Faithfull awaited future disclosure,[65] his hands-off management of the city led to wide-ranging accusations of corruption. Mayor Peters had behaved so ineptly during the Boston Police Strike that few tears were shed at his departure from City Hall. So once again, the citizens of Boston returned Jim Curley to City Hall in 1921. During Curley's absence the Great and General Court, fearful of Curley's entrenchment in office, passed a special act on March 25, 1918, decreeing that no mayor of Boston could succeed himself in office.[66]

Curley returns to City Hall

During his second stint in City Hall, other troubles beset the city. But politics continued unabated and one can only imagine the delight he took from serving as mayor while his deadly rival John Fitzgerald lost his comeback contest for governor in 1922 to the incumbent Republican Channing H. Cox, a New Hampshire native who won 52.2%. Cox was one of three Northern New England Republicans who played key roles in Massachusetts politics in the post–World War I era. Cox along with Vermont-born Governor Calvin Coolidge and Maine native, Boston Mayor Malcolm Nichols were

Protestants but not Brahmins.[67] Each of these mountain Yankees had been tutored in Bay State politics by Charles H. Innes, Boston's most powerful "swamp Yankee."

Ineligible to run for reelection in 1925, Mayor Jim Curley made his initial statewide bid in 1924 running for governor. However, with former Governor Coolidge now serving as President of the United States and topping the national ticket, Curley was swamped by Republican auto dealer Alvan T. Fuller—56.0% for Fuller to 42.2% for Curley. Curley had fared worse than Fitzgerald's failed run two years earlier. Running in place of Curley was his ally, Democratic Irishman Teddy Glynn who lost to Republican Malcolm Nichols, the last Yankee Republican mayor of Boston. Although he graduated from Harvard College, Nichols was a native of Maine and not a Brahmin. Political "Brahminism" was on the wane and Charley Innes seized the opening.

Following Curley's first major defeat as the incumbent Mayor of Boston in 1917, he was down but not out. Curley demonstrated levels of resilience and vengeance that were legendary. The phrase, most often associated with Fitz's son-in-law, Joseph P. Kennedy, "Don't get mad, get even," epitomized the Curley style. Curley's electoral resilience would lead him back to City Hall and scores would be settled. Memories are long among the Boston Irish and congressional terms are short. He had finished off John Fitzgerald. Martin Lomasney could control his ward and the congressional district that surrounded it but the city would never completely be his. Big Jim Gallivan had stuck his nose into a contest where it didn't belong and his time would come too. Young John McCormack would be there.

It was at the start of his state legislative career that John met and married the single-most important person of his life, M. Harriet Joyce, who would be his lifelong companion for the next half century.

M. Harriet Joyce

Marrying late for men was a feature of life back in Ireland. It was not as common to marry late in America, but John McCormack was eager to establish himself in his legal career before he would choose a bride. Marriages in the United States were seldom arranged and social class differences, while often discussed, rarely impeded a couple truly in love. For the upwardly striving politician, "marrying up" was a way of solidifying one's newly attained social position and providing something of a safety net so that one need not fall too far down should success be more elusive than anticipated.

John McCormack's marriage confirmed his new standing in the middle class but it did far more. It was the most defining alliance of his life. John McCormack's devotion to his wife took on legendary proportions. For the entire 51 years of his marriage, they never dined apart.

Born in the city's suburban Jamaica Plain district in 1883, Miss M. (for Marguerite) Harriet Joyce and her family moved to one of the better sections of South Boston. While Southie's Irish Catholics were ethnically homogeneous, this unique peninsula displayed a wide range of housing choices and economic circumstances. Contained within it were large pockets of tightly packed tenement poverty in the Bayview section where John McCormack's mother and her expanding family were housed and smaller pockets of upper-middle-class comfort in South Boston's City Point section. Harriet's family lived on Dorchester Avenue, comfortably if not opulently.

Harriet's parents, Garrett G. and Margaret Joyce, were both born in County Galway on the western shore of Ireland, within that part of the island known as Connaught in ancient times and which contended less with the British and most with the fierce and stormy winters of the icy Atlantic. The Galway Joyces were known as the "merchant princes," and they shared power over the region in ancient times with the O'Flahertys.[68] County Galway was also the ancestral location of both of James Michael Curley's parents and may have endeared Miss Joyce to the redoubtable mayor. This was another fortuitous Irish coincidence for John McCormack and even further confirmation of the centrality of Harriet's role in John's political ascendance.

Harriet was a small woman with dark eyes and long flowing brown hair. She was attractive but not a beauty in the conventional sense. Her most distinctive feature was her rich contralto voice that brought her a great deal of local prominence.[69] She was a classical singer with a repertoire of operatic arias sung in French, Italian, and German. But she was a contralto. Contraltos have the lowest range among female voices reaching approximately two octaves upward from E or F below middle C. They do not get the leads in opera. Those belong to the prima donna sopranos and the mezzos. The roles contraltos usually get are secondary characters.

Even the greatest contraltos, such as Italy's Marietta Alboni (1823–94), and Americans Sophie Braslau of New York (1892–1935) and the indomitable Marian Anderson of Philadelphia (1902–93), were hard-pressed to find sufficient operatic employment and found more opportunity in giving recitals than in singing grand opera. Anderson, the first African-American woman to sing at the Metropolitan Opera, played a major political role in the efforts of President Roosevelt's wife, Eleanor, to desegregate American society when she sang at a 1940 concert at the Lincoln Memorial for 70,000 people after being denied permission to sing at Constitution Hall, a venue owned by the Daughters of the American Revolution.[70]

So it was with Boston's M. Harriet Joyce. Recitals and music lessons would be her major sources of income during her singing career. Harriet's first major appearance in the Boston newspapers came in 1910 when she was invited to sing for the annual dinner of the Ladies Catholic Club at the Hotel Vendome. In attendance that evening would be the formidable Archbishop of the Boston Diocese, the Reverend William Henry O'Connell, a well-known music lover.[71] On the day of her performance before his Grace, Harriet Joyce was pictured in the *Boston Herald* with her long brown hair mounted upon her head in the style of a Gibson girl. The reviews the following day were enthusiastic and Archbishop O'Connell decreed her to be "the little girl with the large voice." This quote from so distinguished a source would appear repeatedly in the pre-performance announcements of Miss Joyce's various singing engagements throughout the city of Boston and New England.

Harriet was a woman of some sophistication. Her activities were widely reported and in one news account of her single life she was described as operating her motorcar "with great skill." She was a great contrast to John's mother, the unfortunate Mary Ellen. In an occasional account of Miss Joyce's performances, it was contended that she studied abroad but the evidence remains unclear. What is clear is that she was a celebrity in Boston's music circles, and her many performances had made Harriet well known to the city's most prominent citizens and powerful politicians long before John McCormack was known to them.

At her professional debut in the city's Steinert Hall she sang with an octet from the Boston Symphony.[72] It was a snowy day at the end of April in 1912, but the hall was packed and in attendance were most of the event's patronesses, most notably the wife of the governor, Mrs. Eugene Noble Foss, and the wife of the mayor, Mrs. John Francis Fitzgerald. Once again, Miss Joyce dazzled her audience. As recounted in the *Boston Globe's* opening paragraph[73]:

> The sweet notes of the contralto rendering Gounod's "Recitative a cantilena" (Cinq Mars) died away and the vast audience in Steinert Hall, overawed, sat quietly for a moment as though spell-bound, and then as one, the many hundreds burst forth into one round of applause. Miss M. Harriet Joyce had made her debut and it was a magnificent success.

She sang at the Lynn Women's Club on the North Shore to an audience which included a patroness, Mrs. William P. Connery, whose husband would enter the U.S. House in 1923 preceding John McCormack's arrival by five years. Connery became a close ally and served with John for nine years. Harriet sang throughout Massachusetts and Rhode Island and performed as far north as Orono, Maine, and as far south as Little Rock and Pine Bluff, Arkansas.

One of her more memorable performances was delivered at the Boston Press Club on the occasion of the departure of Florencio Constantino, the Spanish tenor, described in one account as "the world's famous opera singer." Constantino sang his favorite aria as Verdi's Duke of Mantua, "Le donna e mobile." Although Constantino was the featured performer that evening, Harriet's reviews were just as glowing as his. And one amusing clipping recounts that the great tenor was so taken by her performance that he presented her with a wonderful gift—a photograph of himself. And the clipping goes on to state that the Spanish tenor made Miss Joyce "a fine offer to sing in his opera house down in South America."[74] Accompanied as she always was with her best friend, Mary T. Naphen, and her widowed mother, Miss Joyce passed on the offer and forsook South America for South Boston.

Not the least of the ironies of Harriet's singing career was the fact that at the time of her 1912 debut, the Boston Opera Company's principal tenor was the Irishman John F. McCormack (1884–1945).[75] Considered by many to be a serious rival to the legendary Enrico Caruso, McCormack made his American debut in New York in 1909 and then moved on to the Boston Opera for two years. In 1912, while the renowned 28-year-old singer John F. McCormack of Athlone on Ireland's River Shannon was leaving Boston for the Philadelphia Opera, the obscure 20-year-old law clerk John W. McCormack of South Boston was attempting to escape Andrew Square for a law firm downtown.

Who knows how many of Harriet's close friends were delighted to hear of her intentions to marry John McCormack, only to be disappointed when they learned it was not the man whose recordings so thrilled them, but a young gangly lawyer from East Eighth Street in South Boston. Harriet's friends were too well-mannered to make the comparison public, but to the sensitive John W. McCormack, there would always be the sense that he had married well above his station. And what later prominence he was to attain came through the sophisticating ministrations of Harriet.

Harriet's constant companion during her travels and performances was Mary T. Naphen. She was the daughter of the late Congressman Henry F. Naphen (Dem-Mass.), who served in the House for four years from 1899 to 1903 and whose 10th Congressional District abutted Honey Fitz's 9th District.[76] It was Mary who shared her father's comfortable living quarters in Washington's Shoreham Hotel northwest of the Capitol. She was familiar with the social responsibilities of the congressional hostesses whose entertaining skills were deemed essential to the advancement of their husband's or father's House careers. But illness led Henry Naphen to depart the swamp-like atmosphere of the Capitol and return to Boston where he would die in 1905 at the relatively young age of 52. Henry Naphen's district would later provide the bulk of the Massachusetts 12th Congressional District that John McCormack would represent for 42 years. And it is well within the realm of possibility that it was Mary Naphen who convinced her best friend Harriet that the young gawky lawyer from the Bayview neighborhood had enough potential to be remolded as a congressman.

When John McCormack first saw Harriet is not really clear, but she was one of the featured performers at the 1914 Evacuation Day Commemoration in South Boston. Evacuation Day is one of those peculiarly Boston holidays which celebrates the evacuation of British troops from the City of Boston during the American Revolution. It falls on March 17, St. Patrick's Day, and it is a day when the Governor of Massachusetts comes to South Boston and presumably allows both the city's Yankees and its Irishmen to put aside their antagonisms and jointly celebrate the day's festivities. Fondly recalled by Brahmin Governor Leverett Saltonstall, "the fusion of the two anniversaries generates an emotional and spirited warmth in the historic part of Boston."[77]

On Evacuation Day, 1914, at the South Boston Municipal Building, both the state's first native-born Irish Catholic Governor David I. Walsh of Fitchburg and the city's second native-born Irish-descended Mayor James Michael Curley were the featured speakers.[78] Harriet sang her two favorite arias, "Arioso" from Bemberg's *The Death of Joan d'Arc* and "Le Parlate d'Amor" from Gounod's *Faust*. Then 31 years old, Miss Harriet Joyce was a rising star in their midst and the 22-year-old aspiring lawyer John McCormack knew it. All of the state's prominent Irish-descended politicians— Archbishop O'Connell, Governor Walsh, Congressman Connery, and Mayors Fitzgerald and Curley—knew who she was and had heard her perform. For John it would be a feat of some significance if he were able to marry her.

They first met in 1917 before John joined the army. He and two of his friends met Miss Joyce and her mother while they vacationed at Nantasket Beach, a favorite South Shore resort, which was readily accessible to Boston. McCormack's friends had rented rooms in a home owned by family friends of Miss Joyce. It was on a visit to the home that John had an opportunity to meet Harriet and her mother. His gallant behavior in putting up the canvas top of her convertible during a rainstorm and driving Harriet and her mother back home to South Boston was much appreciated, and they entered into a year-long courtship.[79]

She was closely tied to her mother and brothers and agreed to marry John McCormack at the age of 35, late even for American Irish women. She gave up her successful local singing career to marry John. Her presumed sacrifice was later embellished to include giving up an opportunity to sing with the Metropolitan Opera Company in New York City. It adds more drama to her decision but apparently the choice was less difficult. There appears to be no formal record at the Metropolitan Opera of their interest in her.[80]

An unmarried Irishwoman in her mid-thirties, even one as talented as Harriet, whose father had died was faced with diminishing prospects. A young Irish Catholic lawyer with ambition, albeit from the wrong side of the tracks, became more attractive with each passing month. John's election to the State House that fall made it clear that he had genuine goals.

How far John intended to rise is not known. But with Harriet at his side, his horizons would be greatly broadened. She was able to introduce John to those influential men who controlled access to the positions of power in Irish Boston. She knew them before they knew John. It is doubtful if John McCormack would have risen as high or as quickly without her. She took John McCormack far beyond the narrow world of Andrew Square.

At John and Harriet McCormack's wedding on June 9, 1920, a large number of local notables were in attendance (Figure 4.2). The various news accounts described "a distinguished gathering" with "persons prominent in all walks of life" who were attending "the scene of a brilliant wedding" and which was decreed to be "one of the most elaborate weddings of the season."[81]

This was clearly a gathering of Boston's "lace curtain Irish." Priests, professors, and various officeholders including Suffolk County Sheriff John A. Kelliher and Acting Mayor James T. Moriarty gathered at South Boston's venerable St. Augustine's Church for the wedding. Leading the small delegation of fellow State Representatives was the Hon. Henry L. Shattuck, a Brahmin Republican and chair of the powerful Ways and Means Committee.

The maid of honor was Miss Mary T. Naphen and the best man was fellow attorney and Army Captain John P. Buckley of Charlestown. Harriet's older brother, J. Harry Joyce, gave her away. There were six ushers including the bride's younger brother, Daniel F. Joyce, but no brothers of John accompanied him on this important day. Knocko and Buttons McCormack were missing from the wedding party. Whether they were even in attendance is not known, or if they were too plebeian to be mentioned in the news accounts is unclear. Painful memories of John's early tenement life were now being buried.

Harriet was 36 when they married, eight years older than John. But he, ever the nobleman, added ten years to his age making him two years older than her on their marriage license.[82] It was a simple deception, one that did little harm and spared his

John W. McCormack and Harriet (Joyce) McCormack, wedding day (1920)

Figure 4.2 The wedding of John W. McCormack and M. Harriet Joyce, 1920 (Edward J. McCormack, Jr. Family Papers).

bride some unnecessary embarrassment. John McCormack did not abandon the women of his life. He was not his father's son.

Joe McCormack made no appearance at John's wedding. However, during the same month as John's wedding, the elusive Joe McCormack was recorded in the 1920 Census. He had escaped the 1910 Census takers, but in 1920 he was reported as living in Waldoboro, Maine, and working in the woods.[83] Joe's disappearance from the previous census was likely due to the fact that the two youngest boys, Edward and Donald, were still young enough to require support. By 1920, even Donald, his youngest son, had reached the age of maturity and Joe need not fear efforts to wring support money out of him.

John and Harriet honeymooned in Quebec and in Atlantic City. Harriet's fluency in French was invaluable as they motored deep into the French Canadian countryside. Whether Harriet learned of her new husband's Scottish Canadian ancestry while visiting there is unknown. It would have been the appropriate time to let her in on the truth. This was a honeymoon after all and it was spent in the faded grandeur and religious mysticism of French Canada. It was a vivid contrast from the tiny Maritime farmhouse of Grants Crossing four hundred miles to the east in Prince Edward Island where John and his family spent a harsh and painful few months two decades earlier.

During the entirety of his congressional career, Harriet and John lived in the Hotel Washington and dined on room service. It is likely that as a "lace curtain Irishwoman" she never learned to cook. Maids and cooks were readily available in the years before the end of World War I and the high level of aspiration which she carried from her family most likely spared her training in such mundane skills.

Harriet's role as John's dinner mate for 50-plus years is part of both the reality and the legend.[84] John McCormack was one of very few politicians who had a lifetime loving partner. Unlike his fellow House politicians and good friends, he did not suffer from the emotional angst which bedeviled Sam Rayburn, whose marriage lasted less than three months, or that of Joe Martin, who never married and lived with his mother until his seventies.

There were no children from the marriage. Harriet confided to her sister-in-law Mary T. McCormack, Knocko's wife, that it was "women's problems" which prevented her from conceiving.[85] We can never know if John was disappointed. This most private of public officials would never share the most private of his feelings. To him, parenthood may have been a mixed blessing. After all, John McCormack had seen how his beloved mother's twelve pregnancies had shortened her stay on earth. Perhaps, the pride of fatherhood gave way to protectiveness toward Harriet's health. For John McCormack, the risk of losing his wonderful Harriet was not one that he wished to take. It was well known that both President Theodore Roosevelt, whose daughter Alice was married to Nick Longworth, John's first Speaker, and Speaker Will Bankhead with whom John served had lost their young wives in childbirth.

John rewarded Harriet with devotion unmatched among major twentieth-century American politicians. And her devotion to him gave him an emotional solidity that he cherished. Having lost both his only sister and his mother too early in his life, John McCormack appreciated the validation of his existence by this, the most important woman of his life.

Harriet stayed in the hotel room for most of every day. She occasionally shopped and went for walks, but most of her day was spent in anticipation of John's return from Capitol Hill. Harriet Joyce McCormack may have been reclusive but she was astute and she knew enough of the world and how people behaved to give John advice on whom to promote and whom to avoid. She was his most sagacious counsel.

John would regularly leave evening meetings to meet Harriet for dinner, either at the Hotel Washington, in the Capitol dining rooms, or even at local diners. It kept him away from much of the alcohol served at those late evening meetings, whose consumption by others often undermined their powers of argumentation and concentration. It was also further reassurance to his Irish Boston constituents that he would not succumb to the temptations of the flesh which had ruined the political careers of the beloved nationalist leader Charles Parnell back in Ireland and their own John Fitzgerald in Boston.

In June 1968, in the 48th year of their marriage, John wrote a simple note on the Speaker's office stationary to his 84-year-old Harriet then in failing health.[86]

Darling Harriet:

> My love for you is deep and intense. With your love, God has blessed me during our married life. I again repeat my unlimited love for you.
>
> Your Sweetheart,
> John

With no children at home, John McCormack was freed from serious family responsibilities but his familial needs made him attentive to promising House newcomers as a mentor. Unlike parenting, mentoring had limits. You could pick and choose your protégées. In an institution as complex as the House of Representatives, finding a way to bring young men into the fold who would maintain its values and serve the nation would be John McCormack's lifelong task.

John would return to their corner suite on the eighth floor of the Hotel Washington that very night to dine with Harriet as he had every night of their years together. On his last day as Speaker, observers noted the House galleries were filled not with the usual faces of congressional staffers and Capitol Hill reporters, but with the wives of the members themselves who were there to honor arguably the House's greatest husband.[87]

Notes

1   The estimate is based on Frank Luther Mott, *Golden Multitudes: The Story of Best Sellers in the United States* (New York: Macmillan, 1947), p. 158. Among the assessments of Alger's influence on American life, both positive and negative, are Richard Wohl, "The 'Rags to Riches' Story: An Episode of Secular Idealism," in Reinhard Bendix and Seymour Martin Lipset, eds., *Class, Status, and Power* (Glencoe, IL: The Free Press, 1953), pp. 388–93; and "Horatio Alger, Jr. and the Gilded Age," in Richard Weiss, ed., *The American Myth of Success: From Horatio Alger to Norman Vincent Peale* (New York: Basic Books, 1969), pp. 48–64.

2   A typical debunking of the myth may be found in Richard B. Morris, "Where Success Begins: Rags to Riches—Myth and Reality," *The Saturday Review*, XXXVI (November 21, 1953), pp. 15–16 and 65–71. For a political science audience, see Kenneth W. Prewitt, "Social Bias in Leadership Selection, Political Recruitment and Electoral Context," *Journal of Politics*, XXXIII (May 1971), pp. 293–315.

3   Lester Gordon interview with the Hon. John W. McCormack, Tape 1, 1973.

4   Author's interview with the Hon. Edward J. McCormack, Jr., October 1996. Burt L. Standish was one of the many pen names of Maine-born author Gilbert Patten (1866–1945) who accounted for more than 200 book titles. See Stewart Holbrook, "Frank Merriwell at Yale Again and Again and Again," *American Heritage*, XII (June 1961), pp. 24–27.

5   James Colbert, "50 Cent Raise in Pay Started McCormack on Political Career," *Boston Post*, April 10, 1956, p. 1.

6   "Way, William T.," *Who's Who in New England*, Vol. 2 (Chicago: A.N. Marquis, 1916), p. 1122.

7   On John's June 18, 1913, application for admission to the bar, Way lists "on or about the first of February 1909" as the date that John "actually pursued the study of law." Paul Wright files.

8   William Way's election returns, Massachusetts State Archives, 1910–14.

9   "Innes, Charles H," *Who's Who in New England*, Vol. 3 (Chicago: A.N. Marquis, 1938), p. 686.

10 The best account of Innes's career and teaching activities appears in John T. Galvin, "One Man Pulls the Strings in Wild 1925 Mayor's Race," *Boston Globe*, August 21, 1983.

11 "Charley Innes Prouder of Teaching Law Than of Being a 'Political Boss,'" *Boston Sunday Advertise*, April 9, 1933.

12 The Boston Public Library has a valuable Charles H. Innes file with useful clippings as well as programs and menus from the many annual dinners honoring Innes.

13 Letter from Charles H. Innes regarding McCormack's two years of instruction to the Board of Bar Examiners, dated June 24, 1913. Paul Wright Papers, University of Massachusetts-Boston Archives. See also Joseph F. Dinneen, *The Purple Shamrock: The Hon. James Michael Curley of Boston* (New York: W. W. Norton, 1949), pp. 50–51, for Innes's tutelage of Curley.

14 Cutler, *"Honey Fitz": Three Steps to the White House*, p. 184.

15 Cutler, ibid. Cutler also quotes a *Boston Post* political writer who in describing Innes in 1931 contended, "I doubt if there is any single Republican in the state who has so much power today."

16 John T. Galvin, "1925 Campaign for Mayor Was a Four-Ring Circus," *Boston Globe*, August 21, 1983, p. A23.

17 Lester Gordon interview with the Hon. John McCormack, January 11, 1973.

18 Alexander M. Sullivan, *New Ireland* (London: S. Low, Marston, Searle, and Rivington, 1878), p. 79, as quoted in Edward M. Levine, *The Irish and Irish Politicians: A Study of Cultural and Social Alienation* (Notre Dame, IN: University of Notre Dame Press, 1966), p. 16.

19 George Dangerfield, *The Damnable Question: A Study in Anglo-Irish Relations* (Boston: Little, Brown, 1976), p. 9.

20 See Leslie G. Ainley's biography of Lomasney, *Boston Mahatma* (Boston: Brice Humphries, 1949).

21 Apart from John Quincy Adams and George W. Bush, whose fathers were also President of the United States, only President John F. Kennedy's father has been the topic of several books. Among them are Richard J. Whalen, *The Founding Father: The Story of Joseph P. Kennedy* (New York: New American Library, 1964); Ronald Kessler, *The Sins of the Father: Joseph P. Kennedy and the Dynasty He Founded* (New York: Warner Books, 1996); and the best by David Nasaw, *The Patriarch: The Remarkable Life and Turbulent Times of Joseph P. Kennedy* (New York: Penguin Books, 2012).

22 The bank president claim is disputed in a short biography, "Joseph P. Kennedy Sr. (1888–1969)," in Jeff C. Young, ed., *Fathers of American Presidents: From Augustine Washington to William Blythe and Roger Clinton* (Jefferson, NC: McFarland & Co., 1997), pp. 180–89, esp. p. 182.

23 See "Joe Bailey," in Champagne et al., *The Austin-Boston Connection*, pp. 16–46.

24 *Congressional Quarterly, Guide to U.S. Elections* (Washington, DC: Congressional Quarterly, 1975), pp. 673, 678, and 683 respectively.

25 See "John the Bold: Boston's John F. 'Honey Fitz' Fitzgerald," in Francis Russell's, ed., *The Knave of Boston and Other Ambiguous Massachusetts Characters* (Boston: Quinlan Press, 1987), pp. 20–45.

26 Vote counts in the 1907 mayoralty reported in Peter d'A. Jones, "John Francis Fitzgerald," in Melvin Holli and Peter d'A. Jones, eds., *Big City Mayors* (Westport, CT: Greenwood Press, 1981), pp. 116–17.

27 *Boston's 45 Mayors from John Phillips to Kevin H. White* (Boston: City Record, 1975).

28 This account appears in Alfred Steinberg's chapter, "James Michael Curley: The Joyous Scourge of Boston," in his *The Bosses* (New York: Macmillan, 1972), pp. 144–46.

29 Russell, *The Knave of Boston*, p. 36. Steinberg contends that Fitzgerald covertly tried to help O'Connell defeat Curley but backed down after having Jim Curley's fist shaken in his face (Steinberg, *The Bosses*, p. 146).

30 Curley, *I'd Do It Again*, pp. 99 and 104.

31 On Clark's nonuse of named Whips, see Randall B. Ripley, "Party Whip Organizations in the United States House of Representatives," *APSR*, LVIII (September 1964), pp. 561–76; and *Party Leaders of the House of Representatives* (Washington, DC: Brookings Institution, 1967), p. 37n.

32 Champ Clark, *My Quarter Century of American Politics* (New York: Harper & Bros., 1920), p. 120.

33 Source for Curley's House committee assignments is David T. Canon, Garrison Nelson, and Charles Stewart III, *Committees in the U.S. Congress, 1789–1946: Members* (Washington, DC: Congressional Quarterly, 2002), 3:256.

34 See Neil Miller, *Banned in Boston: The Watch and Ward Society's Crusade against Books, Burlesque, and the Social Evil* (Boston: Beacon Press, 2010).

35 "Award of $1300 in Promise Suit—Jury Acts on Default of Defendant—Miss Palatnick says Goldfarb Refused to Marry Her—Mansfield Denies Promise to Elizabeth Ryan," *Boston Globe*, November 7, 1913.

36 A vivid portrait of Dan Coakley and his activities may be found in Russell's "The Knave of Boston," in his collection of essays, *The Knave of Boston and Other Ambiguous Massachusetts Characters*, pp. 1–19; and "The Art of the Double Deal: 'Dapper Dan' Coakley and the 'Toodles Ryan' Case," in Peter F. Stevens delightful collection of short essays in *Hidden History of the Boston Irish: Little-known Stories from Ireland's "Next Parish Over"* (Charleston, SC: The History Press, 2008), pp. 51–54.

37 The Coakley-Pelletier blackmail scheme is vividly recounted in "The Badger Game," in Gerard O'Neill's lively *Rogues and Reformers: When Politics Was King in Irish Boston* (New York: Crown, 2012), pp. 101–13.

38 Doris Kearns Goodwin's account of the rumored affair is balanced; see *The Fitzgeralds and the Kennedys: An American Saga*, pp. 287–91, esp. 290. John Henry Cutler's *"Honey Fitz": Three Steps to the White House* makes no mention of the episode.

39 While Cutler leaves out the Toodles allegations, he lists these as the titles of Curley's speeches in *"Honey Fitz,"* pp. 215–16.

40 "Says He Saw 4 Kiss Miss Ryan: Mullen Accused of Lying—Ex-Mayor Fitzgerald Brands Ferncroft Episode Silly and False," *Boston Post*, January 20, 1915, p. 1.

41 A solid general overview of Lodge's life is John A. Garraty, *Henry Cabot Lodge: A Biography* (New York: Knopf, 1953).

42 "Henry Cabot Lodge," *BDUSC* (1989 ed.), p. 1384.

43 O'Connor, *The Boston Irish*, pp. 118–33. O'Connor refers to a contrast made by John William Ward between the "rational politics" practiced by the Yankees and the "ethnic politics" of the immigrants based on Ward's lecture at the John F. Kennedy Library, "The Common Weal and the Public Trust," 350 *Forum* (October 21, 1980).

44 The almost total Irish-descended domination of the mayoralty of Boston is documented in Peter K. Eisenger's *The Politics of Displacement: Racial and Ethnic Transition in Three American Cities* (New York: Academic Press, 1980), pp. 29–54; and "Ethnic Political Transition in Boston, 1884–1933: Some Lessons for Contemporary Cities," *Political Science Quarterly*, XCIII (1978), pp. 217–39.

45 Edward L. Glaeser and Andrei Shleifer, "The Curley Effect: The Economics of Shaping the Electorate," *Journal of Law, Economics and Organization*, XXI (April 2005), pp. 1–19. See also Reinhard H. Luthin, "James M. Curley: The Boston Brahmin-Baiter," in his *American Demagogues: Twentieth Century* (Boston: The Beacon Press. 1954), p. 71.

46 Francis Russell, "John the Bold: Boston's John F. 'Honey Fitz' Fitzgerald," in *The Knave of Boston*, p. 39.

47 Vote totals: Peters, 37,900 (43.6%); Curley, 28,000 (32.3%); Gallivan, 19,400 (22.3%); and Tague, 1,700 (2.0%). The numbers have been rounded and may be found in Dinneen, *The Purple Shamrock*, p. 122.

48 The case *Tague v. Fitzgerald* is described in Zink, *City Bosses in the United States*, pp. 82–83.

49 The monogamist character of Jim Curley is recounted in both Dinneen's *The Purple Shamrock*, pp. 142–49; and in Beatty's depiction of his family life in *The Rascal King*, pp. 232–37.

50 Lester Gordon interview with the Hon. John W. McCormack, February 7, 1973, in the PhD dissertation, *John McCormack and the Roosevelt Era* (Boston: Boston University, 1976).

51 *Debates in the Massachusetts Constitutional Convention 1917–1918*, Vol. IV, pp. 500–501.

52 Alex M. Arnett, *Claude Kitchin and the Wilson War Policies* (Boston: Little, Brown, 1937), pp. 224–40.

53 *Journal of the Constitutional Convention of the Commonwealth of Massachusetts, 1917* (Boston: Wright & Potter, 1917), p. 730. The printing date is 1917 but the cover of the journal indicated 1917–19.

54 A short biography of Joseph Leonard appears in *A Souvenir of the Massachusetts Constitutional Convention, Boston 1917-18-19* (Stoughton, MA: A.M. Bridgman, 1919), p. 78.

55 *Debates in the Massachusetts Constitutional Convention 1917–1918*, Vol. IV, pp. 201–02.

56 Secretary of the Commonwealth, *Number of Assessed Polls, Registered Voters and Persons Who Voted in Each Voting Precinct at the State, City and Town Elections*, 1919, Pub. Doc. 43 (Boston, 1920), p. 174, for the September Democratic Primary, and p. 299 for the General Election. The tally for the primary was James B. Troy of Boston, 1,179 votes; John W. McCormack of Boston, 949 votes; Patrick M. Costello of Boston, 724 votes; Michael J. Reidy of Boston, 482 votes; Owen Gallagher of Boston, 476 votes; and Michael A. O'Brien, Jr. of Boston, 111 votes.

57 O'Connor, *The Boston Irish*, p. 90. O'Connor contends that unlike the infamous New York City riots, the Boston riot "involved no looting of shops, no destruction of property, and no attacks on the city's black population." A fuller treatment appears

in William F. Hanna, "The Boston Draft Riot," *Civil War History*, XXXVI (September 1990), pp. 262–73.

58   The most compelling account of this episode remains Francis Russell, *A City in Terror: 1919 The Boston Police Strike* (New York: Viking Press, 1975). Reissued as *A City in Terror: Calvin Coolidge and the Boston Police Strike* (Boston: Beacon Press, 2005). A shorter version written by Russell, "The Strike That Made a President," *American Heritage*, October 1963, pp. 44–47 and 90–94.

59   *Boston City Charter, Acts 1878*, Chapter 244, Section 1: "The mayor of the city of Boston may appoint, subject to the approval of the city council, three able and discreet persons to constitute a board of police commissioners in said city" (p. 229). The revision was in the *Acts, 1885*, Chapter 323, Section 1. "The governor of the Commonwealth with the advice and consent of the council shall appoint from the two principal political parties three citizens of Boston who shall have been residents therein two years immediately preceding the date of their appointment, who shall constitute a board of police for said city, and who shall be sworn before entering upon the duties of their office" (p. 261).

60   See Robert K. Murray's valuable *Red Scare: A Study in National Hysteria* (Minneapolis: University of Minnesota Press, 1955). The Boston Police Strike is covered in pp. 122–34.

61   Russell, *A City in Terror*, p. 170.

62   Ibid., p. 124.

63   Ibid., pp. 142–43. See the memoir of Harvard-educated U.S. Senator Leverett Saltonstall's service as a temporary policeman during the strike in Leverett Saltonstall as told to Edward Weeks, *Salty: Recollections of a Yankee in Politics* (Boston: Boston Globe, 1976), pp. 19–20.

64   Russell, *A City in Terror*, p. 191.

65   Francis Russell, "The Mayor and the Nymphet," in *The Knave of Boston*, pp. 69–85; and Morris Markey, "The Mysterious Death of Starr Faithfull," in Isabel Leighton, ed., *The Aspirin Age, 1919–1941* (New York, 1949), pp. 258–74.

66   The statute limiting mayoral succession is in the *Boston City Charter*, Special Acts, 1918—Chapter 94: An Act Relative to the Term of the Mayor of the City of Boston, *Section 45*, "The mayor of the city of Boston shall be elected at large to hold office for the term of four years from the first Monday in February following his election and until his successor is chosen and qualified and *shall not be eligible for election to the following term*" (p. 825; emphasis added).

67   Kerry W. Buckley's assessment of Calvin Coolidge as "a swamp Yankee" was due to his being "a scion of an old family that was no longer elite or monied," in the essay, "A President for the Great Silent Majority: Bruce Barton's Construction of Calvin Coolidge," *New England Quarterly*, LXXVI (December 2003), pp. 593–628.

68   Author's interview with Mr. Ambrose Joyce of the Connemara Marble Works, Connemara, County Galway, Ireland, May 2000.

69   Harriet's singing dates were regularly reported in the Boston press. Many clippings of her performances may be found in Folder 46, Box 2, of the files assembled by Paul Wright which are housed in the archives at the University of Massachusetts-Boston.

70   The fullest account of Marian Anderson's Lincoln Memorial concert is Raymond Arsenault, *The Sound of Freedom: Marian Anderson, the Lincoln Memorial, and the Concert That Awakened America* (New York: Bloomsbury Press, 2009).

71   "South Boston Girl Will Sing Before Archbishop," *Boston Herald* (June 21, 1910). She is reported to possess "an unusual contralto voice." The clipping goes on to say that "the archbishop had heard about the voice of the South Boston girl and a short time ago he

expressed a desire to hear it." On Cardinal O'Connell's music interests, see Dorothy G. Wayman's laudatory biography, *Cardinal O'Connell of Boston: A Biography of William Henry O'Connell, 1895–1944* (New York: Farrar, Straus and Young, 1955), pp. 16–17. He was named Cardinal in 1911.

72   "Young Singer to Make Debut," *Boston Sunday Herald*, April 28, 1912.

73   "Miss Joyce Makes Debut, Society Braved Storm Monday Night to Hear Sweet Singer," *Boston Globe*, April 30, 1912.

74   Paul Wright files, University of Massachusetts-Boston, Box 2, File 46.

75   The operatic John McCormack enjoyed his time in Boston and recounted, "My reception by Bostonians has always been cordial and most enthusiastic. I regard them as discriminating judges of music and musicians, and quick to show how they feel. If I have a favorite audience in America it is in Boston" (John Scarry, *John McCormack: His Own Life Story* [New York: Vienna House, 1973; originally published by Small, Maynard & Co. in 1918], p. 291).

76   Naphen was born in Ireland in 1852, emigrated to Lowell with his parents and graduated from Harvard College and the Boston University Law School. A biographical sketch of Henry Naphen may be found in James Bernard Cullen, ed., *The Story of the Irish in Boston* (Boston: James. B. Cullen, Co., 1889), pp. 296–97. His congressional career is recounted in the *BDUSC* (1989, ed.), p. 1557. He was elected to the School Committee, 1882–85; and the State Senate, 1885–86. In the U.S. House, he served on the Accounts (1899–1901) and Foreign Affairs (1901–1903). On the Foreign Affairs Committee, he served with two future Speakers, Champ Clark (Dem-Mo.) and Frederick Gillett (Rep-Mass.), and with Albert Burleson (Dem-Tex.) who served as President Wilson's Postmaster General.

77   Saltonstall, as told to Edward Weeks, *Salty: Recollections of a Yankee in Politics*, pp. 70–71.

78   South Boston Citizens' Association, *Official Programme, Evacuation Day*, March 17, 1914. Paul Wright files.

79   This account is from the tapes of the Hon. John W. McCormack in the Special Collections of Boston University and is retold in the doctoral dissertation of Lester I. Gordon, *John McCormack and the Roosevelt Era*, Department of History, Boston University, 1976, p. 46.

80   Author's telephonic interviews with the Metropolitan Opera Company in New York City, June 1997 and December 2007.

81   Typical of the wedding accounts was "Prominent Couple United," *Boston Globe*, June 10, 1920, and "Wedded in St. Augustine's Church: John W. McCormack and Miss M. Harriet Joyce," *Boston Herald*, June 10, 1920. The wedding accounts were part of the Boston University Special Collection and may also be found in the Paul Wright files at the University of Massachusetts-Boston.

82   See the June 9, 1920, Boston marriage listing of John William McCormack and Marguerite H. Joyce on file at the Massachusetts Registry of Vital Records and Statistics.

83   Fourteenth Census return of 1920 from Waldoboro, Maine indicates that Joseph McCormick [*sic*], a 58-year-old white male, born in Prince Edward Island is a "Laborer" living "in Woods." Joe's previous census listing in 1900, twenty years earlier in Boston, gave his age at 38.

84   Lester Gordon interview with the Hon. John W. McCormack, February 7, 1973, Gordon, *John McCormack and the Roosevelt Era*, p. 47.

85   Paul Wright taped interview with Mary T. Coffey McCormack, Paul Wright files, UMass-Boston Archives.

86 Letter from Speaker John W. McCormack to Harriet McCormack, June 1968, in the McCormack Family Papers.

87 This account came from a telephonic interview with William McSweeny, Washington, DC, October 1996. Bill McSweeny and his wife, Dorothy, were regular dinner guests of the Speaker and Mrs. McCormack in the 1960s. McSweeny was from Haverhill, Mass., and served as an executive at Occidental Petroleum under its legendary leader Armand Hammer. Bill McSweeny worked with the Speaker in 1970, his last full year in office after the departure of his scandal-plagued associates, Dr. Martin Sweig and Nathan Voloshen. Dorothy McSweeny worked on the oral histories with the Speaker.

5

From Beacon Hill to Capitol Hill

International reshuffling and domestic discord

The end of the Great War in 1918 led to a massive reconfiguration of Europe. The Austro-Hungarian Empire was dissolved with Austria and Hungary becoming separate and smaller entities, while two nations were formed from its remains: Czechoslovakia and Yugoslavia. Imperial Russia, which lost its czar to an overthrow in 1917 and had been taken over by the Bolsheviks led by V. I. Lenin, would be renamed the Russian Socialist Federative Soviet Republic. It lost much of its western frontier as Poland, Finland, Estonia, Latvia, and Lithuania gained national independence, albeit short-lived.

The new nationalism of postwar Europe would also impact the victors, as Great Britain encountered emboldened Irish Republicans who hoped that Britain's preoccupation with the war effort would let them escape the grasp of what most of them considered a brutal Anglican occupation of their land. The Easter Rising of April 1916 in Dublin was a foreshadowing of what eventually would lead to most of Ireland's independence from Great Britain. The Rising was quickly crushed and fourteen of its leaders were executed by British firing squads. One of its captured leaders escaped execution—Éamon de Valera, commandant of the 3rd Battalion, who did so partly due to his American birth.[1] But the movement for Irish independence would continue until the creation of the Irish Free State in 1922. De Valera had been named President of the Irish Republic in 1919, and because of his New York City birth, he was the logical choice to travel the United States to raise money. He came to Boston in June 1919, often described as Ireland's "next parish over" and was greeted as a conquering hero by more than 50,000 of mostly Irish-descended Bostonians who filled Fenway Park.[2] Among the dignitaries welcoming de Valera were U.S. Senator David I. Walsh and Boston Mayor Andrew James Peters, but the initial greeting to de Valera was made by Daniel H. Coakley, the man whose discovery of the "Toodles" Ryan episode had brought an end to the electoral success of John Fitzgerald.

June 30, 1919, was also the date that the Wartime Prohibition Act took effect. Ostensibly this act was to conserve grain for the war effort, but it was one part of the crusade by the Anti-Saloon League to outlaw the distribution and sale of alcohol by Americans. These two presumably dissimilar events would be joined during the

"Roaring Twenties," and the ambitious young lawyer John McCormack would find his political and legal careers caught in this conjoining.

Prohibition: The triumph of rural Protestant America

With the nation fully engaged in the war effort in 1917, the mostly Methodist leaders of the Prohibition movement—the Anti-Saloon League and the Women's Christian Temperance Union—pushed for the adoption of the 18th Amendment to outlaw the sale and distribution of alcoholic beverages.[3] While both chambers gave the measure the two-thirds vote necessary for adoption, it was not a party vote in either chamber. Senate Democrats supported the amendment 36 to 12 and Senate Republicans followed suit 29 to 8. The House vote was similar: Democrats split 140–64, Republicans 138–62, and third-party members 4–2. But it was a regional vote with most of its support from the rural southern and Midwestern states, hotbeds of American Protestantism. Massachusetts was the eleventh and first New England state to ratify the amendment—the only one of the three heavily Catholic states of southern New England to do so. The amendment was only defeated in Connecticut and Rhode Island.

Since Prohibition was considered to be a measure that "bettered" Americans, it is often listed as one of the four Progressive Era amendments along with the 16th Amendment that created the federal income tax, the 17th Amendment that obliged U.S. Senate candidates to be elected by popular vote and removed the state legislatures from their selection, and the 19th Amendment granting voting suffrage to women.

Congressionally mandated Prohibition was one item of a multipronged agenda by white native rural Protestants to wrest control of American politics from the perceived pernicious influence of urban immigrants. After all, they believed it was those foreign city-dwelling heavy drinkers who had intentionally involved the United States in that European War, presumably to settle scores with the nations that had treated them poorly on the other side of the Atlantic.

Other legislative attacks were directed at urban America including restrictions on immigration. The arrival in the United States of more than one million people per year in the years before the World War was no longer desirable. Since most new immigrants chose to settle in cities, the 1920 Census documented that urban residents outnumbered rural ones for the first time in American history. In both 1921 and 1924, Congress passed immigration quota acts to control the foreign influx and to limit immigration to those whose countrymen were already situated in the United States. The First Immigration Quota Act, passed in 1921, established a policy whereby the number of aliens of any nationality to be admitted under immigration laws should be limited to 3% of the number of persons of that nationality listed in the 1910 Census, providing that not more than 20% of any nationality admissible during any one year should be admitted during any single month, and set a total limit of 357,803 immigrants per year.[4]

Not content with this limitation, Congress returned to the issue in 1924 with the passage of the Second Immigration Quota/National Origins Act.[5] The 1924 Act pushed the effective date back to the 1890 Census—clearly intending to stem the tide of Italian and Polish Catholics and Russian Jews who had entered the United States in the closing decade of the nineteenth century. This act lowered the annual immigration quota of each nationality to 2% and completely excluded Japanese immigration. It also provided that only 150,000 immigrants should be admitted in any one year. The million-fold annual immigration waves of immigrants ended. The hope of the rural congressmen was that the cities would be limited in their growth and the composition of these newer immigrants would look very much like those whose ancestors had already settled here. The demographic transformation of America would be slowed, and the inevitability of urban America's conquest of the nation would be postponed for at least another generation.

In 1926, during his fourth year in the State Senate, John McCormack was able to secure the passage of a challenge to that act, albeit initially limited to those of Irish descent.[6]

> *Ordered,* That the Massachusetts Senate view with favor the adoption of an amendment to the Federal Immigration Law which will operate as a basis for the computation of the proposed quota for immigrants which will not be discriminatory nor inequitable in its proportions to American citizenship and particularly to those of Irish blood; be it further
>
> *Ordered*, That the Massachusetts Senate is opposed to the adoption or retention of any provision which will tend to promote national or racial prejudice, or which suggests the inferiority of any element of our citizenship . . .

John McCormack's "maiden speech" in the U.S. House on February 14, 1929,[7] was a challenge to the National Origins Act, but the act remained in place for another 36 years until the passage of the Immigration and Nationality Act of 1965 finally abolished it.[8] It was a very delighted U.S. House Speaker John McCormack presiding on October 3, 1965, when that anti-immigrant statute was tossed into history's dustbin.

Congress's most direct rebuff to urban America was the decision in the 67th Congress not to reapportion the U.S. House of Representatives in the wake of the 1920 Census.[9] Here was a nation that had reapportioned its congressional districts every census year since 1790, including one during the Civil War when the nation was coming apart. By not passing enabling legislation to permit the House to be reapportioned, Congress would not let urban America gain House seats in this census year of its first-ever statistical majority.

Even with all of these legislative triumphs over urban Catholics and Jews, it was not enough. For the first time since Reconstruction, the militant and violent arm of rural Protestant America returned to terrorize the nation's citizens. The Ku Klux Klan was back. It was a 1915 movie by acclaimed pioneering director D. W. Griffith entitled *Birth of a Nation* that glorified the Reconstruction Era Klan that led to its revival. Fueled by a combustible mixture of prohibitionism, anti-unionism, and anti-immigrant prejudice, the Klan's hate-filled agenda was newly broadened to include Catholics and Jews along with their original target of blacks.[10] As a consequence, it spread well beyond the South and had an insidious and disastrous impact upon the Democratic Party of the 1920s.

Boston: An epicenter of panic

Boston was the site of two events that riled the consciousness of white native rural Protestants and provided the link between immigration and urban crime that justified their efforts to put these newcomers back in their place. The first was the Boston Police Strike of September 1919 led by mostly Irish-descended patrolmen, whose unionizing efforts with the American Federation of Labor presumably placed the city in jeopardy. The outrage went national with Democratic President Woodrow Wilson calling the strike "a crime against civilization" that left the city "at the mercy of an army of thugs"[11] and the state's senior Republican U.S. Senate Majority Leader Henry Cabot Lodge contending that "if the American Federation of Labor succeeds in getting hold of the police in Boston it will go all over the country, and we shall be in measurable distance of Soviet government by labor unions."[12]

The second troubling event was the April 1920 armed robbery of a shoe factory and the murders of its paymaster and his guard in nearby Braintree, Massachusetts. Accused of the robbery and the murders were two Italian-born anarchists, Nicola Sacco and Bartolomeo Vanzetti. The Sacco-Vanzetti case with its heavy ethnic and political overtones stirred international attention and outrage.[13] A novel by Upton Sinclair entitled *Boston*; a play by Maxwell Anderson titled *God of the Lightning*; and sonnets by Edna St. Vincent Millay were part of the literary protest against their trial and 1927 executions. Harvard Law Professor and future Supreme Court Justice Felix Frankfurter also weighed in.[14] Their executions were loudly condemned throughout much of the nation and the world. Most of the criticism was directed at the Dartmouth-educated Yankee Judge Webster Thayer, who presided over the trial and denied multiple defense motions and requests for a new trial. Not all of Boston's Brahmins rallied behind Thayer, but even those who supported the case's outcome had their own rectitude seriously dented by evidence of Judge Thayer's anti-immigrant prejudice.[15]

Boston's Ford Hall Forum became the center of the protests. It was in this capacity that the Forum's young manager David K. Niles made the acquaintance of prominent liberal activists that would eventually launch him into the White House as assistant director of the Works Progress Administration, undersecretary to Harry Hopkins at the Department of Commerce, and one of FDR's original six special assistants.[16] David Niles would also become John McCormack's closest link to the White House.

These were the troubled times that John McCormack would encounter as he began his service in the Massachusetts House of Representatives in 1919. John had to be discreet and move carefully in these tumultuous times, and his reinvented Irishness may have become less of a virtue. This may have accounted for his decision to relocate the birthplace of his father from Canada to Scotland in the 1920 Census.[17]

Crime and corruption, the ethnics' revenge

Fewer unintended consequences were greater than the eruption of crime and corruption unleashed by Prohibition. As liquor disappeared from store shelves and reputable restaurants, it flourished in the urban "speakeasy" hideaways where bootlegger-provided illegal liquor flowed freely. Prohibition launched a generation of "scofflaws" with disdain for the government efforts to enforce the 18th Amendment. Ironically, the major beneficiaries of this ill-guided effort to reform America were the very ethnics—the Irish, Italians, and Jews—that the righteous Protestant backers of Prohibition sought to tame. Crime syndicates emerged in every major city with each of the dominant ethnic groups gaining hegemonic control of the liquor traffic and its attendant vices of gambling and prostitution.

With the sale and transportation of intoxicating beverages criminalized, Boston's underworld saw an opportunity for profit. The rugged coast of Massachusetts filled with jagged inlets and open bays, allowed the bootleggers to launch an increasingly large flotilla of small boats known as "rum runners" to bring contraband alcohol from Canada to the thirsty patrons of Boston's innumerable speakeasies.[18]

South Boston's Gustin Gang

Blue-stocking Boston was not immune from these criminal enterprises and the conflict between the Irish gangs of South Boston and Dorchester and the Italian gangs of the North End and East Boston for control of the city's underworld turf often erupted into gunfire. A key set of criminal constituents in the South Boston portion of John's legislative district were a group of disreputable souls known as the "Gustin Gang." Frankie Wallace and his three brothers—Stevie, Billy, and Jimmy—were bootleggers who were headquartered on Gustin Street, a tiny backstreet scarcely more than a wide alleyway, in South Boston.[19] They gave themselves the surname of "Gustin" to the police and to reporters. In an effort to consolidate control of the docks, Frankie Wallace and two associates—Barney "Dodo" Walsh and Timothy Coffey—went to 317 Hanover Street in the North End in 1931 to settle matters with Joe Lombardo, a leader of the Italian bootleggers. It was a fatal mistake. Waiting in ambush were Lombardo and his associates. Both Frankie Wallace and Barney Walsh were killed and Tim Coffey barely escaped with his life. Never again would the Gustins venture far from Southie.

On occasion, John McCormack defended the Gustins in court as he would in 1927 when he was able to get "Stephen Wallace, alias Steve Gustin, of South Boston" freed on a charge of robbing Frank A. Brown of Hyde Park at a filling station. Although Stevie fit the description of "short and stocky, with flaming red hair and a freckled face," Mr. Brown, undoubtedly aware of the Gustins' reputation for reprisal, thought better of the accusation and as the *Boston Globe* reported,[20] "Cross-examined by Senator John W. McCormack, counsel for Wallace, Brown said positively that

Wallace was not the man who held him up and taken $50 from the till in the garage." John's willingness to defend a Gustin in open court would pay dividends when Congressman Jim Gallivan's death five months later opened a U.S. House seat in the 12th Congressional District.

The General Court

In his first run for the General Court in 1919, John finished behind incumbent James B. Troy and both were unopposed for the two seats in the general election.[21] The Yankee-dominated General Court treated Boston and its Irish-American citizens like unruly children, much in need of parental guidance. This patronizing and condescending attitude irritated many of the Irish Catholic members. Representative John McCormack was not one of them. He had come too far to let resentment and minor slights interfere with his legislative agenda that called for financial relief for parochial schools and help for veterans. Yankee Republican lawmakers were resistant. And they had the votes.

During John McCormack's first term in 1920, Democrats were badly outnumbered 64 to 176 in the Massachusetts House of Representatives.[22] Minority members, particularly new ones, had to accept lesser roles with equanimity. Twenty-eight-year-old McCormack was placed on the three-member House Standing Committee on Bills in the Third Reading and on the eleven-member Joint Standing Committee on Labor. Being a Democratic labor supporter on a Labor Committee in a Republican-dominated legislature was a thankless task and dealing with bills in the "third reading" would appear to border on irrelevance. Despite its name, the Committee on Bills in the Third Reading was the last committee that dealt with bills before they reached the floor for debate and a vote. It operated in a fashion similar to that of the Rules Committee in the U.S. House of Representatives in that it arranged the conditions of the debate and the vote. The committee often dropped clauses from bills that it felt might hinder their passage and renumbered them in their revised versions. John McCormack was the only Democrat on the committee and his fellow committee members included the formidable Republican Henry Lee Shattuck, a leading Boston Brahmin.

A year later, newly married John McCormack stood for reelection, the first one with a two-year term, and with his seatmate, James Troy, he was able to withstand a massive landslide for the Republican ticket of U.S. Senator Warren G. Harding of Ohio and Massachusetts's own Governor Calvin Coolidge.[23] The Harding-Coolidge ticket carried 68.6% of the Massachusetts vote, capturing the City of Boston by more than 30,000 votes. The Democratic ticket of Ohio Governor James M. Cox and Assistant Navy Secretary Franklin D. Roosevelt was buried in the onslaught. Republicans won all of the statewide executive posts and reduced the four Democratic seats among the sixteen-member U.S. House delegation to two—Peter Tague of the 10th District and Jim Gallivan of the 12th District. These two survivors were the two House members who had undermined Jim Curley's mayoral reelection bid in 1917. Their numbers had yet to be called.

The entwining of John's political and legal careers

During the 1920s, John McCormack was everywhere in Boston as he readied himself for a move up the political ladder. He spoke at multiple ethnic dinners and to local schools, churches, women's groups, and veterans' organizations. He seldom missed a birthday celebration or a funeral.[24] John regularly introduced bills to the General Court, well aware that as a member of a small political minority few would get out of committee, but he persevered and steadily raised his public profile.

John became known as one of the more successful defense attorneys in the city representing the entire range of the city's criminals, including alleged murderers. In a 1980 letter from Paul T. Smith, John's personal lawyer, to Mr. Henry J. Nicholson, Smith recounted that[25]

> prior to [John's] election, he had 21 criminal cases pending in the Suffolk Superior Court. He tried all of these cases and obtained verdicts of not guilty in 20 of the 21. Of the 21st case, which was tried before Judge Fosdick, there was a finding of guilty. Just before John McCormack was to leave to go to Washington, Judge Fosdick called him into his chambers and asked John to make a motion for a new trial. Which John did, and the Judge found his client not guilty as that John had a 100% record of the cases that were pending at the time of his election to Congress.

Family members ran afoul of the law during these years. The most serious crime involved Dr. Thomas H. Walsh, the brother of Chauncey Walsh, whose wife Amy Keller Walsh was John's first cousin. Dr. Walsh was known locally as "the Irish abortionist" and it was a failed abortion that led to the death of Miss Edith Greene, a state ward and the pregnant girlfriend of James V. Ford, a local boxer. In an effort to conceal the death, Miss Greene was dismembered and two lowlifes were hired to bury her remains in an open gravesite. They were arrested and implicated Dr. Walsh, who was convicted and sentenced to seven years in prison.[26]

The other crime involved John's incorrigible younger brother Knocko, who was arrested as an accessory before and after the May 27, 1924, holdup and armed robbery of Herbert Hume, a messenger for the Guaranty Trust Company of Cambridge who was carrying the substantial sum of $15,500. As described in the *Globe*, "The men are Edward J. McCormack, alias 'Knocker' McCormack, aged 28 of 78 Middle Street of South Boston, and Thomas E. Davies, aged 22, of 14 Magnolia av., Cambridge."[27] When the case came to trial, John had assembled a list of witnesses, including his onetime law partner J. Arnold Farrar. They provided Knocko with a suitable alibi and he was cleared.[28]

John's ability to deal successfully with hard-core South Boston criminals some days of the week and with well-mannered, well-educated Republican Protestants in the General Court on other days involved a level of compartmentalization that would serve him well when he moved from the State House on Beacon Hill to the U.S. House on Capitol Hill. No greater evidence of this appears than in his dealings with Boston Brahmin legislators, most notably Henry Lee Shattuck.

Henry Lee Shattuck, a new Brahmin mentor

Henry Lee Shattuck came from one of the city's most distinguished medical aristocracies. Many of the Shattucks, including Henry's father and brothers, had been trained at Harvard and its Medical School.[29] Fortunately for John McCormack, Henry Shattuck was not one of the Irish-disdaining Yankees. According to former U.S. Senator Leverett Saltonstall, who served with Shattuck in 1923 after John McCormack had left the House for the State Senate, Shattuck was known to be partial to the young Irishmen who sought social advancement. In his memoirs, Saltonstall recalled that "[Shattuck] loved the Irish and had a romantic feeling for Ireland, which he was fond of visiting. On Sundays he would entertain groups of boys from South Boston at his private club in Dover, and no one will ever know how many students he helped through college."[30]

Serving closely on the three-member House Standing Committee on Bills in the Third Reading committee with Henry Shattuck early in his legislative career gave John McCormack another opportunity to learn the ways of the Yankees. He learned from his initial mentor, William Way, that not all of the Massachusetts Yankees were hostile to the Catholic Irish. They had ruled the Commonwealth for three centuries and had much to teach. The better Yankees knew that their days of total control were over and many were eager to socialize the more receptive of the immigrant children into the ways of sound and responsible governance. By not playing the Irish ethnic card, McCormack was able to avoid the defensiveness of many of the South Boston Irish that had deafened them to the sage counsel of the thoughtful Yankees.

John's relationship with Henry Shattuck developed along lines similar to those he had with Augustus Peabody Loring at the Massachusetts Constitutional Convention. Loring chaired the Committee on Form and Phraseology that John served on at the Constitutional Convention, and Henry Lee Shattuck chaired the investigating committee that McCormack served on in the State House. The committee was tasked to investigate rampant corruption in the building of Boston's Elevated Railway. Well aware that a number of fellow legislators had been paid off to support the 1918 passage of the Elevated Public Control Act that provided state money for "the El," most of the chamber's legislators quickly disappeared from view when the investigating committee was formed. John McCormack was not one of them and his willingness to serve as the lone Democrat on the panel impressed Shattuck, who was quoted stating that McCormack "promptly accepted the appointment as a duty no legislator could shirk."[31] While John was not happy with the committee's final report, his commitment to serve on it greatly impressed Henry Shattuck and his fellow Brahmins in the State House.[32]

Loring and Shattuck were "ultra Brahmins" both having served as Overseers of Harvard. When McCormack left the House to move to the State Senate, Shattuck's next protégé would be a younger Brahmin, Leverett Saltonstall, a future governor and U.S. Senator.[33] Shattuck's nephew Elliott Lee Richardson would be elected Massachusetts attorney general, but his greatest distinction was to be appointed to four Cabinet posts by Republican Presidents Richard Nixon and Gerald Ford.

Much of John McCormack's appeal to these Boston Brahmins was that he did not fit the stereotype of the Irish politician—a hard-drinking, loud-mouthed, glad-handing politician. Alcoholism in the family line had led to Joe McCormack's desertion and the shortened life of John's oldest brother Patrick. The teetotaling John McCormack was almost as Protestant as they, and his obvious devotion to his wife Harriet elevated him in their estimation. But then again, John was not as Irish as those others who claimed links to Erin.

The second House term appeared to be more promising. John sat on both the Rules and Judiciary Committees, but his party was so minuscule—52 seats out of 240—he could do little but watch. The emptiness of the term gave way to a new ambition—a run for the State Senate. It was a much smaller body and although McCormack would be badly outnumbered by Republicans, there would be a greater opportunity to speak and debate.

When the incumbent State Senator Bill McDonald announced that he would not run for reelection, McCormack offered his name. His opponent in the primary was Robert E. Bigney, who had lost to McDonald two years earlier and who would not enjoy the support of McDonald's voters. McCormack watched as Bigney struggled to extricate himself from the enemies he had made in his earlier run. It was a lesson about how to challenge an incumbent positively that he would apply four years later. The victory was solid, but no landslide.[34] The general election was no contest as John McCormack won unopposed. Republicans already held 33 of the 40 State Senate seats and conceded this particular seat to the Democrats.

John McCormack was now a Massachusetts State Senator. His reputation grew and his name was often featured in news accounts of the General Court's activities that reached beyond Boston and into the other New England states. That publicity had an unanticipated cost as a shadow appeared on the near horizon, a shadow that could have easily ended John McCormack's ascent in public life. Joe McCormack, John's errant father, who John declared to have died in 1905, had returned to Boston.

The return of a dead man

When Joe McCormack arrived on the Dorchester doorstep of Amy Keller Walsh and her husband Chauncey Walsh is unclear. Joe's reappearance was recalled by one of the surviving Walsh cousins in a 1982 letter from Charlotte Walsh Hannaway to her second cousin Edward McCormack, Jr. Charlotte was the oldest daughter of Joe's favorite niece Amy and the granddaughter of Sarah McCormack, the younger of the two McCormack sisters who had raised Joe in Souris, Prince Edward Island. In her letter, she recounted[35]:

> Years ago your Grandfather came to Fields Corner and stayed with us saying he was going to see Jack in the morning to see if he could put him someplace. He had come from Maine where he had stayed for years. What a tragedy it was. What a handsome Man he was I couldn't take my eyes from him. So my Dad said "Joe, you can't go in to see Jack looking like that. Wear my suit" and so he did and the next morning he left in pa's suit. When he didn't come home or rather back to the house

Ma called Jack and Jack said he had given him five dollars and he left. Jack said he
would think of something for his Father but Joe went back to Maine . . .

The fact that Joe McCormack went to his niece's home and not to that of either of his
sons indicates he knew he would be unwelcome. Joe had abandoned their mother and
left her alone to fend off the twin terrors of poverty and disease. He had also avoided
her funeral and those of his own three grown children. John would have received his
father with a distant coldness. Knocko might have beaten him senseless.

This ghost from the past could have been troublesome for John McCormack who
had told people that his father was dead. The least that Joe owed John was to disappear
forever and never again return to Boston. The five dollars placed in Joe McCormack's
hands by his oldest surviving son was about the limit of John McCormack's compassion
for his father.

Later that day, probably wearing Chauncey Walsh's unreturned suit, Joe McCormack
returned to Waldoboro in Lincoln County, Maine. Located along the old Boston &
Maine Railroad line—$2.50 away from Boston—Waldoboro is a small mining town
arching along high-pitched hills with a few narrow streets. It is a worker's town and a
Protestant town. Occasional efforts to organize a parish among the town's few Catholics
had failed and priests from the nearby towns were called in to officiate at religious
functions. But it was home to Joe McCormack. Waldoboro was close to the city of
Rockland and its surrounding environs included the limestone quarries in Thomaston.
Stoneworkers assembled in these towns along the Lincoln and Knox County borders;
many were Canadian Scotsmen and Irishmen from Prince Edward Island.

Joe worked in the quarries along Route 1 and boarded with George and Viva
Noyes.[36] It was Viva Noyes who would drive Joe the fifteen miles to Rockland's Knox
County Hospital on February 5, 1929, for treatment for his worsening bronchitis. Joe
was gone the following day, dead of bronchial pneumonia exacerbated by influenza.[37]
Work cracking rocks filled the stonecutters' lungs with dust. Ironically, it was an
industrial equivalent of the dreaded tuberculosis that had shortened the lives of his
children years before.

A fellow worker of Joe's came down from Waldoboro and informed Buster Hartrey,
John's longtime Boston secretary, of Joe's passing. John was now seated in the U.S.
House of Representatives and was on the floor that week in February when Hartrey
relayed the news. For John McCormack, the prospect of returning to New England to
bury a man he despised was an unpleasant one that he chose to avoid.

It was Harold W. Flanders, Waldoboro's busiest undertaker, who removed Joe
McCormack's body from the Knox County Hospital and it was the Reverend Henry
O. Megert, pastor of the Methodist Church, who officiated at the service.[38] Flanders
received John McCormack's instructions and his personal check. What John told
Flanders to do is not known but can easily be imagined. What is known was reported
in the *Lincoln County News:* Joseph McCormack; late of Waldoboro, Maine these past
25 years—a native of Prince Edward Island, Canada, born in 1862, and a stone cutter—
was laid to rest in the unmarked town portion of the Waldoboro Rural Cemetery.

It was a pauper's grave and paid for by the town. That Harold Flanders might have taken John McCormack's money to bury his father "decently" and money from the town to bury Joe McCormack as a pauper was not surprising to longtime residents of Waldoboro.

Expectations of a mass, a wake, and consecrated ground—the marks of a "decent burial" to Roman Catholics—appear to have been unfulfilled. None of the three Roman Catholic parishes in the area—St. Bernard's in Rockland, St. Denis's in North Whitfield, or the venerable St. Patrick's in Newcastle—provided a priest for the burial of Joe McCormack, the family deserter. So it was a Methodist minister who oversaw the burial of Joe McCormack from the Flanders Funeral Home.

John McCormack did not attend his father's burial. Ostensibly, it was congressional business that kept him away that day. He also never intended to visit the gravesite. Flanders, a non-Catholic, knew that and acted accordingly. Nor was Joe McCormack a person whose remains would ever be sited in Boston's Mt. Benedict Cemetery, close to those of John's beloved mother Mary Ellen and his siblings. One can only imagine the deep and abiding shame of his father's abandonment and the hatred that young John McCormack felt for him.

So John McCormack reinvented a family history. The reconstruction of John's life treated his father's disappearance as a death and his own place within the family as the oldest surviving brother of three boys. This version left Patrick, the eldest out of the surviving family. Patrick was laid to rest in 1911 in the Mt. Benedict gravesite originally purchased with John's earnings by Mary Ellen to bury her only daughter. In 1913, it was Mary Ellen's turn and she was buried in the same gravesite with 24-year-old Patrick and 19-year-old Catherine whose names were not inscribed on the tombstone. With the death of Joe McCormack in Maine, the reinvention would remain secure but the guilt remained.

State Senator McCormack

Forty State Senators assembled in the General Court for his first term in 1923. Of these, seven were Democrats and 33 were Republicans. But there would be two hundred fewer members clamoring for the floor. John could play a larger role here than in the chamber on the other side of the State House. McCormack's personal recollection in 1970 made the party ratio even more daunting[39]: "When I was elected to the Massachusetts Senate we were five Democrats out of forty members. We could hold our party caucus in a phone booth."

John's initial committee assignments included the Senate Standing Committee on Rules and the Joint Committees on Cities and Election Laws.[40] Social issues predominated in this session as the Senate debated the Chamberlain bill. Named for state Senator George Chamberlain, a Republican from Springfield, the bill was intended to increase the State Department of Education's control over parochial and private schools by authorizing the board to enforce laws regarding the compulsory classroom use of English. The targets of this legislation were the increasing number of Italians and French Canadians who had joined the Irish to enhance Catholic political power.

Catholic leaders vehemently opposed the bill. Parochial schools were a key bulwark in the socialization of young Catholics and in the preservation of the faith in Protestant America. Catholic leaders lobbied against the bill and with the support of Irish Catholic lawmakers and hesitant non-Catholics, it was defeated.[41]

The other key social issue was Prohibition. For many Roman Catholics, Prohibition was seen as yet another effort of America's secular Protestants to impose their religious values upon the ever-growing Roman Catholic population. By criminalizing behavior that the fundamentalist Protestants associated with immigrant ethnics, you could criminalize an entire substratum of society. The whiskey-drinking Irish immigrants, the beer-drinking German immigrants, and the wine-drinking Italian and Jewish immigrants could be behaviorally marginalized in one simple step.

Although a lifelong teetotaler, John was a stalwart opponent of the Anti-Saloon League's efforts to broaden police power to crack down on alcohol consumption. In his 1928 list of legislative achievements, he stated[42]:

> I have always vigorously opposed PROHIBITION LEGISLATION. The resolve memorializing Congress in favor of light wines and beer was filed by me and adopted under my leadership. I opposed the so-called Padlock Bill, and the measure providing for the confiscation of private automobiles which might be carrying a small amount of stimulants for medicinal purposes. These bills, sponsored by the Anti-Saloon League, were defeated as of the fight led by me. Since my retirement, both bills have become law.

This was also a time when the once-dormant Ku Klux Klan was riding high. To Catholics, any nativist legislation that placed immigrant behavior beyond the law was seen as anti-Catholic and anti-immigrant. The national Democratic Party was bitterly divided over the Klan and Prohibition. Social issues polarize and have far greater political resonance than economic ones.

At the 1924 national convention in New York City, Democratic delegates were so immobilized by these issues that they refused to condemn the Klan and a bitter floor battle over the party's presidential nomination forced the convention to hold 103 ballots before it was able to come up with its national ticket.[43] The Democratic Party's "first team" of potential presidential nominees—Senate Minority Leader Oscar W. Underwood of Alabama, New York's Roman Catholic Governor Alfred E. Smith, and Woodrow Wilson's Secretary of the Treasury, William Gibbs McAdoo of California—was decimated by the protracted multi-ballot nominating conflict. This led to the nomination of a weak slate with John W. Davis of West Virginia as its presidential nominee and Nebraska Governor Charles W. Bryan as vice president. Davis had been Woodrow Wilson's solicitor general and later ambassador to the United Kingdom. Governor Bryan's older brother William Jennings Bryan had led Democrats to three presidential defeats in 1896, 1900, and 1908. This was not a formidable team, and it would carry only twelve states, the Confederacy and Oklahoma.

McCormack stood for reelection in 1924, vanquishing the hapless Mr. Bigney in the Democratic primary once again.[44] Republican opposition in this heavily Democratic district was almost nonexistent and Senator McCormack won 15,833 votes of 18,525 easily defeating Republican Henry J. Kogel.

Democratic strength in the State Senate was still minuscule and the election had decreased the number of State Senators to six. Given the fact that former Massachusetts Governor Calvin Coolidge was now president and had topped the Republican ticket as the party's incumbent nominee, the Democrats were left only with a few seats in their urban enclaves. This hearty band of half-dozen Democrats in the State Senate elected John McCormack as their floor leader in 1925.[45] It may have been a dubious honor, but it was real enough to validate a career. It was as floor leader that McCormack found his lifelong calling. This was what he enjoyed doing: assembling voting coalitions and debating the opposition on the floor. He much preferred the visible rough and tumble of floor work to laborious closed-door committee service and to the tedious business of presiding over the chamber. Working the floor was John's favorite role as may be seen in the frequency of his name cited in the *Senate Journals* of those four years. In the 1923 *Senate Journal*, John appeared on 133 of its first 804 pages (17.3%); in the 1924 *Journal*, 244 of 933 pages (26.0%); in the 1925 *Journal*, 139 of 711 pages (19.5%); and in the 1926 *Journal*, 134 of 725 pages (18.5%).[46] He would repeat this floor debate omnipresence in the U.S. House.

As minority leader, John was able to move between committees serving on Standing Rules in both sessions but moving from the Joint Committees on Constitutional Law and Taxation in 1925 to the Joint Committees on Legal Affairs and Public Safety in 1926.[47] Legislatively, his successes were few. On March 25, 1926, in a motion that would foreshadow John's deep commitment to President Franklin Roosevelt's New Deal agenda and Social Security, John submitted an amendment to the State Senate that was a "Bill to provide for a system of old age pensions, with an old age pension fund to protect citizens from want in old age."[48] The bill was voted down twenty Nays to eight Yeas.[49] John's most notable success and one that would foreshadow his 1965 efforts for Medicare and Medicaid was his effort to retrofit the Pondville Hospital originally built for alcoholics and requisitioned by the army in World War One into the first state-supported public cancer hospital in the United States. Senator McCormack successfully managed the floor vote for its $100,000 appropriation. John considered it his "greatest legislative accomplishment."[50] But for the most part, the session was spent in a defensive mode fending off challenges to undermine labor legislation and social gains made in previous terms. John McCormack preferred to create rather than to defend. After four years in the State Senate and two as its Minority Floor Leader, John McCormack felt he was now ready to move up the ladder yet again. This time, it would be for the U.S. House of Representatives.

McCormack passed on a reelection bid in 1926 to challenge six-term incumbent Representative James A. Gallivan, the inheritor of the House seat once held by James Michael Curley. Had Jim Gallivan's number been called at last?

The quest for the 12th: Waiting for Jim Gallivan

Boston's James "Big Jim" Gallivan first gained the Massachusetts 12th Congressional District seat in a special election in 1914 when James Michael Curley chose to leave the relative obscurity of 435 House members to gain center stage as mayor of the nation's fifth largest city. Jim Curley's departure from the House was also related to his national ambitions. In the two previous Congresses, Curley had allied himself with the Democratic floor leader, James Beauchamp "Champ" Clark of Missouri, and told people in Boston that he served as Clark's whip or deputy leader, but no such formal record of this service exists.

Champ Clark had been the Democratic architect of the "revolt" against four-term Speaker of the U.S. House Joseph G. Cannon of Illinois. Working with "insurgent" Republicans, who had been victimized by Cannon's prejudicial committee assignments, Clark had participated in the political emasculation of that office.[51] Clark used his prominence to seek the Democratic nomination for president in 1912 against New Jersey Governor Woodrow Wilson. Massachusetts Democrats stuck with Clark through the first twenty-plus ballots until they shifted their commitment to their favorite son, Governor Eugene Noble Foss.[52] On the 46th and final ballot, Massachusetts joined the two-thirds delegate vote total for New Jersey Governor Wilson that was needed for the nomination. Champ Clark returned to the speakership, now an office with little power. So it was back to Boston for Jim Curley.

Jim Gallivan and Jim Curley were occasional allies but not friends, and as such, running against one another was never out of the question. This became apparent in 1917 when Gallivan, then in his third House term, entered the lists of mayoral candidates at the apparent behest of former Mayor John F. "Honey Fitz" Fitzgerald. With Gallivan on the ballot, Irish voters in South Boston and Dorchester had an alternative to Jim Curley and out of City Hall went James Michael for the first time.

For Jim Gallivan who had inherited Curley's 12th Congressional District in a 1914 special election, this would be a demonstration of independence from Curley. Longtime *Boston Globe* politics editor Michael E. Hennessy contended that "as a campaigner [Gallivan] had few equals."[53] Furthermore, Gallivan's electoral percentages were more than a dozen points greater than Curley's in the district, and so he had already demonstrated to himself and the city that he had more vote-getting ability than James Michael.[54] And he had nothing to lose. No law prevented Gallivan from running for Mayor of Boston, a local office, while he served in the U.S. House, a federal one. Curley had done the same just four years earlier. So Big Jim Gallivan accepted Honey Fitz's offer to run against Curley in the 1917 mayoral race. Curley knew exactly why Gallivan was in the race and denounced Big Jim as a "desperado" and lumped Tague and Gallivan together as "the two Congressional Hessians in charge of [the] mud batteries."[55]

Always the greatest peril confronting Curley's foes was the mayor's well-known penchant for sharing his knowledge of one's human frailties, real or alleged, as frequently as he could and to as wide an audience as he could find. Of Jim Gallivan, Curley intoned to the city[56]:

> Congressman Gallivan has two degrees. One from Harvard and the other from the Washingtonian Institution for Dipsomaniacs. As you know, the hotel rooms in which Congressmen live in Washington have bells that summon members of the House to a roll-call vote. Unfortunately, the pubs and taverns in Baltimore frequented by my opponent are not equipped with bells, which accounts for Gallivan's impressive absentee record.

Having helped to oust Jim Curley from City Hall, Jim Gallivan continued to serve in the House and never again renewed his active involvement in city politics. Big Jim knew that the former and future mayor's more devout supporters wanted his scalp. Washington was a safer venue. From 1914 on, the 12th District became more Democratic and Jim Gallivan attained victory totals regularly in the 60-plus percent range and had extended his control to corners of the district that were beyond the reach of Jim Curley.

In the House, Gallivan began his service filling Curley's vacancy on the Foreign Affairs Committee, but in 1915, he was named to the Appropriations Committee. As a "Harvard man" and one of the few Ivy League–educated Democrats in the House, the House Democratic hierarchy undoubtedly considered Gallivan a comer. Also, his state delegation had been one of the most steadfast in its support of Speaker Clark's presidential bid.

Created during the Civil War, the Appropriations Committee was intended to take pressure off the beleaguered Ways and Means Committee that was responsible for both the revenue and spending policies of the nation at that time.[57] When Jim Gallivan joined the Appropriations Committee in 1915 as the 13th and last majority member, it included a collection of formidable legislative talent. In the sixth minority slot was former Speaker of the House, the irrepressible Joseph G. "Uncle Joe" Cannon (Rep-Ill.). Even though Cannon had once been the committee's chair and had served on it in twelve previous Congresses, his 1912 election defeat during the Will Taft-Teddy Roosevelt civil war had voided his prior seniority and he had to work his way up the ladder once again. Ironically, the rigidity of the House seniority system was one of the by-products of Uncle Joe's regime as Speaker.[58]

Also on the Appropriations Committee were two future Speakers, Frederick H. Gillett, the unassuming Republican Ranking Minority Member from Springfield in Western Massachusetts and Tennessee Democrat Joseph Wellington Byrns; and one future Majority Floor Leader, Frank W. Mondell (Rep-Wyoming). During his seven terms of service on Appropriations, Gallivan would serve in the majority for only four years (1915–19) but in the minority for nine years.

Republicans used the Appropriations Committee as a launching pad for their leadership talent much as the Democrats used the Ways and Means Committee. The major difference between these two powerful money committees was that prominent members of Ways and Means often got national recognition and external power because so many of the tariff bills were named after their authors on the committee.[59] Appropriations Committee members had a lower external profile, but they held internal power. By controlling congressional spending legislation, Appropriations Committee members adopted a collective cost-containment commitment that obliged other members of the House to come to them with their spending requests.[60] Many members needed these appropriations for their districts as proof of their effectiveness to constituents back home. Friends could be made on the Hill by acceding to these appropriations requests and careers could be ended if the committee failed to deliver funds for a member's constituency. The members of the Appropriations Committee may have escaped national attention, but they were well known within the chamber and their internal power was formidable.

Jim Gallivan moved steadily up the committee's seniority ladder as his safe district in South Boston and Dorchester enabled him to survive while other Democrats faced electoral disaster throughout the 1920s. He had moved into the third minority slot on Appropriations by 1925 and held that rank at the time of his 1926 challenge by young John McCormack.

Back in Boston, Republicans despaired of capturing Gallivan's seat. His most serious challenge had come in the 1918 Democratic primary when he handily beat back a challenge from the seat's previous occupant James Michael Curley.[61] The former mayor was still seething over Gallivan's role in knocking him out of City Hall, but Gallivan's command of the district and his placement on a prominent House committee denied Jim Curley revenge at this time. But Jim Curley never took Gallivan out of his sight.

The coattails of the 1920 Republican presidential team of Ohio Senator Warren G. Harding and Massachusetts Governor Calvin Coolidge enabled one Republican challenger of Gallivan's to keep him under 60%, but that was the closest any Republican ever got to "Big Jim." By 1926, Republican futility had reached such a point that they chose not to run anyone against Gallivan. His election challenge would come from within the Democratic Party in the candidacy of State Senator John W. McCormack.

Big Jim had no trouble with his electoral foes. It was his other demons that would fell him. He had ruined his once robust health with too much alcohol. The alcoholic bonding with his fellow Boston Irishmen had led to far too many rounds of drinks in the taverns and pubs of Southie and Dorchester. American women had yet to be enfranchised by the 19th Amendment, so the only votes that counted for most of Jim Gallivan's career belonged to men. And these men wanted to know if you thought they were good enough to drink with.

Jim Gallivan's problems were exacerbated by Prohibition. Like many Prohibition-era urban Democrats, the legislated hypocrisy of alcoholic temperance in the 18th Amendment irritated him. He and many others saw Prohibition as yet another rural Protestant tyranny to alter and punish the behaviors of their Catholic immigrant rivals for power. Jim Gallivan had the talent and the position to assist his fellow urban Catholics in thwarting these negative thrusts but time was no longer on his side. His lifetime of intemperance had cost him the full flush of color that had once filled his face. His complexion was now pale and sallow. To Southie's old-timers who witnessed and often partook of Jim Gallivan's bonding binges, he had been renamed as "Chalkface" or "Chalkie." They knew that the change in Gallivan's facial coloring meant that the days left in Big Jim's dance on earth were numbered.

The young challenger

John McCormack also knew. He had witnessed Jim Gallivan passed out on the floor of a men's room at the Boston Athletic Club.[62] When John and his closest friend, contractor James Fitzgerald, reached for Gallivan's pulse, they had difficulty finding it. It was at this point that McCormack surmised that Gallivan's seat would soon be open. As Fitzgerald reportedly said to John, "You better run against him. The fellow isn't going to live long. He's going to drop dead."

The story of McCormack's discovery of the condition in which he found Jim Gallivan is part of Boston political lore. John McCormack was always hesitant to be critical of fellow politicians, particularly those who were Irish Catholic. As a devout believer in the afterlife, the prospect of spending eternity with those whom he had maligned on earth was more than he could have handled.

In late July, John declared his candidacy for election to the 70th Congress with words that would presage his later efforts on behalf of Social Security and Medicare. John declared, "I shall continue to fight for legislation to protect and to better the lot of women and children in industry: low-salaried public employees, all who labor, the sick and afflicted, and to defend family life against invasion."[63]

The 12th District seat could be McCormack's if he campaigned as a successor to Gallivan and not as a rival. Jim Gallivan correctly suspected what John's motivation for this contest was and in their first debate on August 28, the *Globe* reported that[64]

> Gallivan charged that McCormack was not a serious candidate for the office and said that a conversation had been reported to him that McCormack had said that McCormack did not expect to beat Gallivan.
>
> "But he thinks I am going to die," said the Congressman, "and McCormack wants to be runner-up."

Someone had apparently shared Jim Fitzgerald's ghoulish observation.

McCormack's campaign focused on two basic themes. The first was that Gallivan had been insufficiently supportive of Governor David I. Walsh's candidacy for reelection to a third one-year term in 1915 and had not been wholly supportive of Walsh's 1924 Senate reelection bid. With popular incumbent President Calvin Coolidge, the state's former governor topping the Republican ticket maintaining some distance from fellow Democrats made sense especially when the Democratic candidate for governor that year was Gallivan's bitter enemy Jim Curley. McCormack further contended that Gallivan was not supporting Walsh's 1926 comeback in the special election to fill the vacant seat of the deceased U.S. Senator Henry Cabot Lodge.[65] McCormack's linking himself with the popular Irish Catholic Walsh who sought a return to the U.S. Senate was a reminder to the thousands of supporters of James Michael Curley that Gallivan had undermined their man's reelection bid for mayor in 1917. Gallivan did not support "his own."

The second issue was to challenge Representative Gallivan's claim that he had voted against the passage of the Volstead Act that had enacted the 18th Amendment implementing prohibition. This involved researching the *Congressional Record* and determining that Gallivan had not voted on any of the roll calls concerning the Volstead Act. It was a vote seven years earlier and one with some resonance for the district's voters, but its major impact was to unsettle Gallivan and goad him into a debate. Popular incumbents like Jim Gallivan had no need to share a stage and equal billing with challengers.

McCormack's tactic worked. After stalling for months, Jim Gallivan accepted the challenge to debate John McCormack. Two debates were scheduled. The first on August 28 at South Boston's old Municipal Building was especially contentious with the *Globe*'s headline declaring that "Gallivan and Rival Cheered and Hissed."[66] The second debate took place on September 11. John McCormack had prepared for that debate by carefully researching Gallivan's voting record. He contended that Gallivan had missed 1,214 roll calls out of 2,170 cast in Big Jim's 12-year congressional career.[67] It was a serious charge indicating that Gallivan had become clearly indifferent to his congressional responsibilities. Gallivan was especially angered by John's accusations of his not voting against the Volstead Act.[68]

While Gallivan blithely contended that the missed votes were quorum calls and procedural ones lacking in legislative substance, the damage had been done and John McCormack scored serious points. Gallivan was now obliged to campaign much more energetically than in the past. This was a serious challenge and Gallivan fired back in a speech at Dorchester's Municipal Hall contending that John had missed more votes than he had.[69]

> Although I have attempted to deal with him with kindness, McCormack has become too ridiculous to argue with and too stupid to attempt to convince by his repeated assertions that I was absent when the Volstead act was passed in the House. Not only was I present during every minute that this wicked piece of legislation was under discussion but I had charge of the opposition on the floor of the House.

While John McCormack was ready on the attendance facts, it was clear that Big Jim still had some cards to play. In a story recounted by a South Boston old-timer, Gallivan lured John into a public trap.[70] "Stand up, young man," Jim Gallivan requested from the podium at the debate, and John McCormack stood up. "Sit down, young man," and a chagrined John McCormack sat down. A triumphant Jim Gallivan turned to the South Boston audience and asked, "Ladies and gentlemen, do you want a puppet like this to be your Congressman? Or do you want a real leader to represent you?"

It was a successful gambit and it won much of the crowd to Gallivan's side. Years of Boston Irish battles had provided Gallivan with debating tactics useful in scoring points with an audience. But he had been in the arena long enough to know that he was in trouble. There was one possible savior for his diminished prospects: former Mayor James Michael Curley.

Shortly before the primary, an anxious Jim Gallivan had to make a call to Jim Curley. And Curley, whose first term in City Hall had ended in 1917 with Gallivan dividing the Irish vote, was called upon to rescue Big Jim. As John McCormack recalled[71]:

> I picked up the *[Boston] Post* about 10 days or two weeks before the primary and I saw a big picture on the front page of Jim Curley and Jim Gallivan meeting each other [on] Court Street and the photographer from the *Post* being there at the time and both of them shaking hands with one another. . . . I evaluated that Curley and him shaking hands would be very helpful from the Curley angle because everybody knew they had an intense dislike for each other for years prior to that. "When I saw that I said 'Goodby John.'"[72]

The ex-mayor's rescuing endorsement did not come immediately. Making a desperate Jim Gallivan squirm must have given great joy to Curley, but the endorsement finally arrived. Curley did not fall over himself in lugubrious praise of Gallivan, but it was enough. John realized that Big Jim's begrudging endorsement from Curley could move thousands of voters that James Michael could command on his side and Jim Gallivan's prospects of returning once again to the House had vastly improved.

What reasons impelled Curley to support Gallivan can be speculated. There is little doubt that Curley enjoyed his old rival's discomfort and his need to be rescued by the man whose career he had derailed earlier. In later years, John McCormack speculated that Curley had supported Gallivan in order to prevent McCormack from challenging Curley for mayor after upsetting the popular Gallivan. This was a semi-grandiose recollection 40 years after the contest. But there was a kernel of truth in it. At one point in 1937, John McCormack's old Republican State House Mentor Henry L. Shattuck approached McCormack about returning home to run for mayor.[73] But John McCormack seldom demonstrated any discernible interest in executive office or Boston city politics, nor had he built the network of citywide connections that would be necessary to overcome the well-funded and well-organized Curley machine. John McCormack was moving rapidly up the ladder of U.S. House leadership and any detour would have ended that ascent. Jim Gallivan had also brought the shadow of Canada into the race and it was alleged that John McCormack was a "two-boater" whose Boston Irish ancestry was tainted.[74]

When the dust had cleared, the *Boston Globe* reported that Big Jim Gallivan "beat McCormack to the tune of two to one and swept the district's five wards, scoring 20,443 votes to McCormack's 10,838."[75] For a defeat, it was a successful first run. John McCormack had placed himself in the big leagues. Jim Gallivan was impressed. In a post-election letter to McCormack, Gallivan wrote: "Let me congratulate you on the splendid and clean manner in which you conducted your campaign. It was a source of sincere regret that I had to have you as my opponent."[76]

Even more important for a young politician, the Boston press was pleased with his performance. In the words of the Democratic-leaning *Boston Post*,

> The Democrats of Boston will do well to keep an eye on Senator John McCormack. This young man, though decisively defeated by Congressman Gallivan, showed himself to be a sportsman and a gentleman, as well as a resolute determined fighter. Senator McCormack accepted his defeat so gracefully and his whole bearing in the campaign was so thoroughly manly and likable that he looms now as perhaps the most promising young political figure in the Democratic party. It is upon the shoulders of such men as Senator McCormack that the future of the party in the city rests.[77]

John McCormack had assured himself of the inside position when intemperance would take its final toll on Big Jim.

From South Station to Union Station: John McCormack, the member from Massachusetts

Following his loss to Gallivan, John McCormack returned to the private practice of law. His newfound fame had benefited his legal practice and he was reportedly grossing over $30,000 a year. Like most of the smaller firms, Hardy, McCormack and Farrar handled both criminal and civil cases with John McCormack, its ablest courtroom advocate, specializing in the criminal cases, including a few accused of murder. Most of his clients were acquitted and none was executed.

But the lure of politics remained, and Jim Gallivan's fate had shifted. On April 3, 1928, Congressman James Gallivan died, little more than a year after he had begun his service as a member of the 70th Congress and only four months into the 1st Session of that Congress.[78]

Nine Democratic candidates were announced for the seat. Only three were viable: State Senator William Hennessey, School Committeeman Edward Sullivan, and John McCormack. McCormack presented himself as "the logical Democratic candidate for Congress" (Figure 5.1). The issues he chose to emphasize were consistent with Democratic candidacies of the time: repeal of the National Origins Act that restricted immigration, collective bargaining in labor disputes, and an enhanced defense. McCormack committed himself to modifying the Volstead Act that had implemented Prohibition and granted states greater control over alcohol consumption within their borders.

The Democratic Party's presidential nomination of New York Governor Alfred E. Smith raised Catholic political consciousness to new heights in Boston. John eagerly pledged his commitment to the presidential ticket calling for a "determined effort to be made to increase the number of voters in the district by 10,000 to assure the carting of Massachusetts for Alfred E. Smith."[79] John benefited as well from his earlier championing in 1926 of the comeback candidacy of popular U.S. Senator David I. Walsh, the state's first Irish Catholic governor and U.S. Senator who easily defeated Republican B. Loring Young for the full Senate term in 1928.[80]

The Life and Public Record of

Hon. JOHN W. McCORMACK

The Logical
Democratic Candidate
For CONGRESS
And the Issues of the Campaign

Primaries: Tuesday, Sept. 18, 1928   Polls Open 6.00 A.M. to 4.00 P.M.

Page one of a 1928 brochure for John W. McCormack's first successful campaign for Congress

Figure 5.1 The Hon. John W. McCormack: The Logical Democratic Candidate for Congress, 1928. (Gotlieb Archival Research Center, Boston University)

The Gustin Gang also weighed in. This was a time when their influence over South Boston was at its peak and before they made their foolhardy and fatal visit to the North End in the 1931 ambush by Joe Lombardo. Big Jim Gallivan had helped them prosper and remain out of jail during his tenure in office, and with his death the gang went looking for a favorable deal with his successor.

John McCormack was a good choice because he had defended the gang in court. He had few illusions about the ways in which they made their money and was sufficiently well acquainted with the folkways of South Boston to understand the perceived benefits of their product. He was especially impressed with their distributive skills. A key to their support would be a place for Eugene T. Kinnaly, Jim Gallivan's secretary. Whoever promised to retain Kinnaly would be the beneficiary of the gang's electoral clout. John understood this simple fact of South Boston politics and declared in his campaign brochure that he would have Kinnaly as his secretary should he win.[81]

John appointed Kinnaly to serve as his campaign manager throughout the election.[82] Following the election, McCormack promised Kinnaly the same administrative assistant role he had held under Gallivan. Keeping Kinnaly was a brilliant but necessary move made possible by his careful campaign in the 1926 primary when he dealt with Gallivan as Big Jim's successor and not as his rival. By guaranteeing Kinnaly's continuity, the McCormack candidacy would seem more of an extension of the Gallivan presence than a change from it.

The primary was held on September 18, 1928, to fill the vacancy remaining on Gallivan's term in the 70th Congress and to nominate a Democratic candidate for the 71st Congress. John McCormack won the special election to fill the vacancy and the Democratic nomination for the subsequent full term. In both cases Edward Sullivan and William Hennessey came in second and third respectively.[83] The Gustin Gang had delivered for McCormack and Kinnaly. With Buster Hartrey in John's Boston office and Gene Kinnaly in the Washington office, he was well staffed for the next three decades.

The women of South Boston and Dorchester were now able to vote. A teetotaler and devoted husband such as McCormack would get their votes. And for those old-time Boston Irish pub-dwellers who needed to bond alcoholically with the candidate, John McCormack had a ready and willing surrogate: his irrepressible brother Knocko.

John McCormack later attributed his success in that contest to his decision to challenge Jim Gallivan in 1926.[84]

> If I hadn't run in 1926, I would probably never have won in 1928 because two candidates in the other end of the district where the big vote was, were both outstanding men. . . . It was because when I ran two years before, so many hundreds of persons wanted to vote for me but couldn't, saying though, that if they had another opportunity they would do so, that I was elected.

Although he risked Gallivan's ire by doing so, McCormack was able to meet thousands of voters who had expressed satisfaction with the way he campaigned and to lock up the inside track in the district at a time when he knew that Big Jim Gallivan's days in the House were numbered.

The general election in the district was no contest. Martin Lomasney and James Michael Curley added their names to the list of McCormack's endorsers. Governor Al Smith led a triumphant Democratic ticket in Massachusetts and McCormack dispatched his Republican opponent, Herbert W. Burr, with 62,435 votes to Burr's 19,164 for the remainder of the term in the 70th Congress and 64,351 votes to Burr's

19,937 for election to the 71st Congress.[85] He was in Boston's big leagues now and on his way to Washington.

To the nation's Capitol

The trip to Washington was not difficult for Representative-elect John W. McCormack and his wife, Harriet. Train travel was comfortable and Boston's South Station was less than a day's trip to Union Station at the base of Capitol Hill. John McCormack had learned to live with being in the Democratic minority of the State House but it would not be the same in Washington. John knew that but he was unsure of what to expect.

The 1928 presidential election had been especially painful for America's Catholics. The bitter anti-Catholic campaign toward Al Smith's candidacy had made them aware of how deep religious prejudice had been ingrained in American politics. Five southern states—Virginia, North Carolina, Texas, Tennessee, and Florida—had all abandoned Smith for the Republican nominee Herbert Hoover.[86] Especially bitter was the widespread assertion that Roman Catholics, by definition, were beholden to a foreign power and that as long as they maintained their faith, they could never be fully considered as American. The "ultra-American" zealotry in some Catholic circles during the post–World War II anti-Communist years was undoubtedly linked to this perceived need for proving one's loyalty to the nation.

The American electorate had not wholly repudiated Al Smith. Two northern states, the Catholic bastions of Massachusetts and Rhode Island, had joined the six Deep South states of Alabama, Arkansas, Mississippi, Georgia, Louisiana, and South Carolina in providing Smith with his only electoral votes. Numerically, Smith's electoral vote count of 82 was the lowest for a Democratic nominee since the election of 1868 when the Civil War hero General Ulysses S. Grant had swamped New York Governor Horatio Seymour.

Below the electoral votes, a major change was in process. The turnout of voters in American cities had increased dramatically. This was true among the ethnic Catholic populations of Chicago's Polish and New York City's Italians.[87] The rise among Irish voters was not surprising. Had the Republicans campaigned as anti-Irish instead of anti-Catholic, it is likely that they might have split the ethnic Catholic community but they did not. The unity of America's ethnic Catholics that had frayed badly during the aftermath of World War I was now fully restored. Much of that unity was a by-product of legislature passed by Republican-dominated Congresses, most notably, the 1919 Volstead Act that implemented the 18th Amendment that decreed Prohibition, the two anti-immigration Acts of 1921 and 1924, and the resistance of the House to reapportion itself following the 1920 Census.

The 1928 presidential election provided the quintessential urban-rural contest as it pitted the champion of urban America, the Irish-German Catholic New York City-born Al Smith, against the Iowa-born Quaker Herbert Hoover of California. Al Smith's defeat amidt the backdrop of anti-Catholicism and anti-urbanism cut the nation's urban Catholics deeply. In spite of the defeat, the choice represented an historic effort on the part of the Democrats to reach into non-Protestant and nonrural America for a candidate well beyond their southern base. Five southern states—Virginia, Texas, Florida, Tennessee, and North Carolina—voted for Herbert Hoover indicating the risks for Democratic presidential kingmakers who wished to broaden the base of the party.

By the 1930 Census, urban America's growth could no longer be denied and the nation's largest cities demanded and received more political representation in the U.S. House. Their collective electoral impact upon the nation's politics was finally being felt. Finding Democratic presidential and vice presidential candidates who could successfully link the disparate wings of the South and the cities would be the challenge of those who managed the presidential party at its nominating conventions. A similar challenge confronted those who controlled the fortunes of the Democratic congressional parties in the House and Senate caucuses.

If the Democratic Party was ever to replace the Republican Party as the nation's dominant political affiliation, it would require that the Democrats create an alliance between the South and the cities. The multireligious and multiethnic heavily immigrant urban voters had the numbers to provide enough electoral votes to deliver presidential victories to Democratic candidates but to gain Democratic legislative success in Congress required that the agenda requests of the white native-born Protestants of the South had to be addressed as well. It was a tough balancing act, and it was one that Boston's John McCormack understood and helped to achieve.

Notes

1   S. J. Connolly, ed., *Oxford Companion to Irish History* (New York: Oxford University Press, 2004), p. 607.

2   A. J. Philpott, "Eamon De Valera pleads Irish cause at Fenway Park," *Boston Globe*, June 30, 1919.

3   The most extensive rendering of the political success of the Prohibition movement may be found in Daniel Okrent's superb *Last Call: The Rise and Fall of Prohibition* (New York: Scribner, 2010). Its anti-immigration stance may be found in ibid., on pp. 85–87 and 235–39.

4   First Immigration Quota Act (The Emergency Quota Act) was approved May 19, 1921 (42 Stat. 5–7) in Stephen J. Stathis, *Landmark Legislation, 1774–2002: Major U.S. Acts and Treaties* (Washington, DC: CQ Press, 2003), p. 183.

5   Second Immigration Quota Act (National Origins Act) was approved May 26, 1924. (Public Law 68-139; 43 Stat. 153-169) in Stathis, *Landmark Legislation*, p. 186. A thoughtful critique of the legislation may be found in John Higham, *Strangers in the Land: Patterns of American Nativism, 1860–1925* (New Brunswick, NJ: Rutgers University Press, 1955).

6   "Orders of the Day," *Journal of the [Massachusetts] State Senate, 1926*, May 27, 1926, p. 711.

7   *Congressional Record*, 70th Congress, Second Session, February 14, 1929, pp. 3472–77.

8   Immigration and Nationality Act of 1965 was approved October 3, 1965 (Public Law 89-236; 79 Stat. 911-922), in Stathis, *Landmark Legislation*, p. 267.

9   The official congressional explanation for the non-reapportionment of the House following the 1920 Census is listed on the website of the History, Art, and Archives: U.S. House of Representatives, "The Permanent Apportionment Act of 1929, June 11, 1929," as "Gradually, however, the method for calculating apportionment caused smaller rural states to lose representation to larger urbanized states. A battle erupted between rural and urban factions, causing the House (for the only time in its history) to fail to reapportion itself following the 1920 Census. Signed into law on June 18, 1929, the Permanent Apportionment Act capped House Membership at the level established after the 1910 Census [435] and created a procedure for automatically reapportioning House seats after every decennial census."

10 The Klan's resurfacing in the 1920s and its spread beyond the South are depicted in Kenneth T. Jackson, *The Ku Klux Klan in the City 1915–1930* (New York: Oxford University Press, 1967); Thomas R. Pegram, *One Hundred Percent American: The Rebirth and Decline of the Ku Klux Klan in the 1920s* (Chicago: Ivan R. Dee, 2011); and Kelly J. Baker, *Gospel According to the Klan: The KKK's Appeal to Protestant America, 1915–1930* (Lawrence: University Press of Kansas, 2011).

11 David Pietrusza, *1920: The Year of the Six Presidents* (New York: Carroll and Graf, 2007), p. 99; "Wilson Denounces Police Strike That Left Boston a Prey to Thugs," *NYT*, September 12, 1919. Two Boston-area writers who addressed the strike's causes and consequence are Francis Russell in *A City in Terror: 1919 The Boston Police Strike* (New York: Viking Press, 1975) and a distinctly South Boston perspective in Thomas H. O'Connor's *South Boston, My Home Town: The History of an Ethnic Neighborhood*, 2nd ed. (Boston: Northeastern University Press, 1994), pp. 165–72.

12 Philip S. Foner, *History of the Labor Movement in the United States*, Vol. 8, *Postwar Struggles, 1918–1920* (New York: International Publishers, 1947), p. 97.

13 The Sacco-Vanzetti trial and execution became an international event. See Francis Russell's *Tragedy in Dedham: The Story of the Sacco-Vanzetti Case* (New York: McGraw-Hill, 1962).

14 Felix Frankfurter, *The Case of Sacco and Vanzetti: A Critical Analysis for Lawyers and Laymen* (Boston: Little, Brown, 1927). Frankfurter's wife Marion Denman Frankfurter and Gardner Jackson, eds., *The Letters of Sacco and Vanzetti* (New York: Vanguard Press, 1930).

15 The outpouring of books on the case continues to the present day. The most widely read author on the case is Francis Russell, who followed up *Tragedy in Dedham* with *Sacco and Vanzetti: The Case Resolved* (New York: Harper & Row, 1986), in which he contended that Vanzetti was innocent but Sacco was guilty. Other books captivated by the case include Herbert B. Ehrmann, *The Case That Will Not Die: Commonwealth vs. Sacco and Vanzetti* (Boston: Little, Brown, 1969); William Young and David E. Kaiser, *Postmortem: New Evidence in the Case of Sacco and Vanzetti* (Amherst: University of Massachusetts Press, 1985); and Susan Tejada, *In Search of Sacco and Vanzetti: Double Lives, Troubled Times, and the Massachusetts Murder Case that Shook the World* (Boston: Northeastern University Press, 2011).

16 Garrison Nelson, "'A Mania for Anonymity': The Mysterious Presidential Aide, David K. Niles of Boston," a paper for the April 2012 Meeting of the New England Political Science Association in Portsmouth, NH, pp. 3–7.

17 Fourteenth Census return for 1920:

State: Massachusetts; County: Suffolk; Township: Boston;

Ward: 11 Enumeration District No. 303 indicates that John W. McCormack, was then lodging at

29 Mt. Vernon Street in Dorchester.

Name Relationship	Race/	Sex	Age	Place of Birth		
				Person	Father	Mother
McCormack, John W. Lodger	WM	28 s		Mass.	Scotland	Mass.

18 David J. Hanson, "National Prohibition and Repeal in Massachusetts," an entry on the Alcohol Problems and Solutions website, accessed October 1, 2014.

19 The Gustin Gang's shoot-out with Italian bootleggers in the North End is recounted in Gerard O'Neill and Dick Lehr, *The Underboss: The Rise and Fall of a Mafia Family* (New York: St. Martin's Press, 1989), pp. 15–20. See also Stephen Fox, *Blood and Power: Organized Crime in Twentieth Century America* (New York: William Morrow, 1989), pp. 73–74. Thomas H. O'Connor's otherwise estimable memoir misnames Stevie Wallace as "Stevie" Gustin which was the surname by which they identified themselves to the authorities (*South Boston, My Home Town*, p. 166).

20 "Asserts Wallace Not Hold-up Man: Filling Station Attendant Describes Robbery, Dentist on Stand as Alibi Witness for Defendant," *Boston Globe*, November 4, 1927, p. 17.

21 Secretary of the Commonwealth, Public Document No. 43: *Number of Assessed Polls, Registered Voters in Each Voting Precinct, 1919* (Boston: Wright & Potter, 1920), p. 175, for the primary and p. 299 for the election.

22 See Dalton, Wirkkala, and Thomas, *Leading the Way: A History of the Massachusetts General Court, 1629–1980*, p. 442. Accounts of Massachusetts history in that era include J. Joseph Huthmacher, *Massachusetts People and Politics: 1919–1933* (New York: Atheneum, 1969); and Michael E. Hennessy, *Four Decades of Massachusetts Politics, 1890–1935* (Norwood, MA: The Norwood Press, 1935).

23 Secretary of the Commonwealth, Public Document No. 43: *Number of Assessed Polls, Registered Voters in Each Voting Precinct, 1920* (Boston: Wright & Potter, 1921), p. 255 for the primary and p. 519 for the election.

24 The *Boston Globe* lists 60 of John's appearances throughout the city from 1920 to 1927.

25 Letter from Attorney Paul T. Smith to Henry J. Nicholson, dated December 29, 1980, and included in the McCormack Family Papers.

26 The Edith Greene case is first described in the *Boston Daily Globe* on July 18, 1926, "Hunt for Hanson, Walsh Is Bailed, Former Gland Doctor Accused as Accessory in Disposing of Edith Greene's Body, Five Relatives Provide Bonds for Roxbury Physician After His day in Cell," p. B1. The fullest depiction is in Curt Norris, "New England Mysteries: Shady Doctor Leaves Trail of Horror," the *Quincy (Mass.) Patriot Ledger*, October 27 (1984), p. 13. I was told of this case by Celeste Walsh, Dr. Walsh's niece and daughter of Amy Keller Walsh, John's first cousin. Mr. Norris supplied the clipping.

27 "Two Arrests in Cambridge Holdup, Messenger of Bank Robbed, South Boston and Cambridge Men Arraigned," *Boston Globe*, May 29, 1924, p. 1A.

28 "Was in Boston, Witnesses Say, Testify for McCormack in Cambridge Robbery Case," *Boston Globe*, November 21, 1924, p. 1A.

29   On the Shattuck medical dynasty, see E. Digby Baltzell, *Puritan Boston and Quaker Philadelphia*, rev. ed. (New Brunswick, NJ: Transaction Publishers, 1996), pp. 353–56 and 496. The Shattucks and the Warrens were the only Boston first families to produce four physicians.

30   Leverett Saltonstall as told to Edward Weeks, *Salty: Recollections of a Yankee in Politics* (Boston: Boston Globe, 1976), p. 30.

31   John T. Galvin, *The Gentleman Mr. Shattuck: A Biography of Henry Lee Shattuck, 1879–1971* (Boston: Tontine Press, 1996), p. 175. The quotation appeared in the *Boston Herald*, April 1, 1921.

32   Michael Hennessy contended that "John W. McCormack of Boston, secretary of the committee, dissented from some of the findings of his associates. In his opinion, members of the [original] committee had used their inside official knowledge for personal profit. The committee's report was regarded as a whitewash." In Michael E. Hennessy's reminiscences, *Four Decades of Massachusetts Politics, 1890–1933* (Norwood, MA: The Norwood Press, 1935), pp. 310–13, quoted p. 313.

33   Saltonstall as told to Edward Weeks, *Salty: Recollections of a Yankee in Politics*, p. 30.

34   Secretary of the Commonwealth, *Number of Assessed Polls, Registered Voters and Persons Who Voted in Each Voting Precinct at the State, City and Town Elections*, 1922, Pub. Doc. 43 (Boston, 1923). McCormack's victory over Bigney in the September 1922 Democratic Primary is reported on p. 196 and his unopposed November election is reported on p. 334.

35   Letter from Mrs. Charlotte Walsh Hannaway to the Hon. Edward J. McCormack, Jr., postmarked February 23, 1982, in the McCormack Family Papers.

36   Excerpted from an earlier article, Garrison Nelson, "Irish Identity Politics: The Reinvention of Speaker John W. McCormack of Boston," New England Journal of Public Policy, XV (Fall/Winter 1999–2000), pp. 7–34.

37   Death certificate of Joseph McCormick [*sic*], filed February 7, 1929, in State of Maine Archives. Also burial records at the Rural Cemetery, Town of Waldoboro, Maine, February 1929.

38   *Lincoln County News* accounts: "Joseph McCormack was taken to Knox hospital for treatment Tuesday," February 7, 1929; and on February 14, 1929, "Joseph E. McCormack passed away, Wednesday, Feb. 6 at Knox hospital, Rockland, of pneumonia. He was born at Prince Edward Island 66 years ago. He was a paving cutter by trade and came to this place at the beginning of the stone-cutting industry 25 years ago, making his home with Mr. and Mrs. George W. Noyes. He is survived by one brother. Funeral services were held from Flanders' funeral parlor Saturday afternoon with the Rev. H.O. Megert, pastor of the Methodist Church officiating. Burial was in rural cemetery" (p. 7). I thank Ms. Libby Lorusso for locating this information.

39   Ellen Beswick's interview with the Hon. John McCormack in "My Fifty Years in Government," *Boston Herald Traveler*, December 13, 1970, p. 16.

40   *Journal of the [Massachusetts] Senate, 1923*, January 3, 1923, pp. 11–13.

41   Gordon, *John McCormack and the Roosevelt Era*, pp. 56–57; and J. Joseph Huthmacher, *Massachusetts People and Politics, 1919–1933* (Cambridge, MA: Belknap Press of Harvard University Press, 1959), pp. 68–69. For Cardinal William Henry O'Connell's involvement in state legislation, see James O'Toole's *Militant and Triumphant: William Henry O'Connell and the Catholic Church in Boston, 1859–1944* (Notre Dame, IN: University of Notre Dame Press, 1992), pp. 129–36.

42   The 1928 campaign brochure entitled, *The Life and Public Record of Hon. John W. McCormack, The Logical Candidate for Congress and the Issues of the Campaign.*

43   The best account of the 1924 Democratic National Convention may be found in Robert K. Murray, *The 103rd Ballot: Democrats and the Disaster in Madison Square Garden* (New York: Harper & Row, 1976).

44   Secretary of the Commonwealth, *Number of Assessed Polls, Registered Voters and Persons Who Voted in Each Voting Precinct at the State, City and Town Elections, 1924,* Pub. Doc. 43 (Boston, 1925). In the September 1924 Democratic Primary for the 3rd Suffolk District, John W. McCormack of Boston defeated Robert E. Bigney of Boston: 7136 (56.2%) to 5551 (43.8%), p. 160. In the November 1924 General Election, McCormack defeated Republican Henry J. Kogel of Boston: 15,833 (85.5%) to 2,692 (14.5%), p. 341.

45   Gordon, *John McCormack and the Roosevelt Era*, p. 58.

46   Counts based on pages in the *Journals of the [Massachusetts] Senate*, Massachusetts Great and General Court, 1923–26.

47   *Journal of the Massachusetts Senate, 1925*, January 7, 1925, pp. 11–15.

48   *Journal of the Massachusetts Senate, 1926*, January 6, 1926, pp. 6–9.

49   Ibid., pp. 446–47. There were six pairs and four absent or non-votes. McCormack who was present paired "Yea" with Republican Senator Eben S. Draper of Worcester.

50   The 1928 campaign brochure entitled, *The Life and Public Record of Hon. John W. McCormack, The Logical Candidate for Congress and the Issues of the Campaign.*

51   An account that focuses on Clark's role is Geoffrey F. Morrison, "Champ Clark and the Rules Revolution of 1910," *Capitol Studies*, II (Winter 1974), pp. 43–56.

52   Bain and Parris, "Appendix C: The Voting Records," p. 350ff.

53   An essay extolling Gallivan may be found in "Passing of Frothingham and Gallivan," in Michael E. Hennessy's reminiscences, *Four Decades of Massachusetts Politics, 1890–1933* (Norwood, MA: The Norwood Press, 1935), pp. 398–400. The quote is on p. 399.

54   *Congressional Quarterly, Guide to U.S. Elections* (Washington, DC: Congressional Quarterly, 1976), pp. 726 and 731 respectively.

55   James Michael Curley, *I'd Do It Again: A Record of All My Uproarious Years* (Englewood Cliffs, NJ: Prentice-Hall, 1957), p. 141.

56   Ibid., pp. 144–45.

57   The history of the House Appropriations Committee was first documented in Edward T. Taylor, *History of the Committee on Appropriations* (Washington, DC: U.S. Government Printing Office, 1941).

58   On the reform of the seniority system's imposition in the House to remove the Speaker's authority over committee assignments, see Nelson W. Polsby, Miriam Gallaher, and Barry S. Rundquist, "Growth of the Seniority System in the U.S. House of Representatives," *APSR*, LXIII (September 1969), pp. 787–807.

59   Tariffs authored by Ways and Means Committee notables included the McKinley Tariff of 1890, the Wilson-Gorman Tariff of 1894, the Dingley Tariff of 1897, the Payne-Aldrich Tariff of 1909, and the Hawley-Smoot Tariff of 1930.

60   The best-ever assessment of the unique role of the House Appropriations Committee remains, Richard F. Fenno, *The Power of the Purse: Appropriations Politics in Congress* (Boston: Little, Brown, 1973); and "The House Appropriations Committee as a Political System: The Problem of Integration," *APSR*, LVI (June 1962), pp. 310–24.

61 Secretary of the Commonwealth, *Number of Assessed Polls, Registered Voters and Persons Who Voted in Each Voting Precinct at the State, City and Town Elections*, 1918, Pub. Doc. 43 (Boston, 1919), p. 157.

62 The story of McCormack's discovery of Jim Gallivan passed out at the Boston Athletic Club surfaced in the national news in *TIME Magazine* in "The Congress: Mr. Speaker" (January 19, 1962), p. 18. It had long been part of the local folklore.

63 "Asks Congressional Nomination as Wet; State Senator McCormack Candidate in 12th; Favors Light Wines and Beers, Also Stimulants as Medicine," *Boston Globe*, July 19, 1926, p. 9.

64 "Gallivan and Rival Cheered and Hissed; Debate in South Boston Is Enlivened by Crowd; McCormack Loses Rebuttal Chance as Congressman Presides," *Boston Globe*, August 29, 1926, p. B10.

65 *Boston Globe*, September 13, 1926, quoted in Gordon, *John McCormack and the New Deal*, p. 62.

66 "Gallivan and Rival Cheered and Hissed," *Boston Globe*, August 29, 1926, p. B1.

67 "McCormack Again Attacks Gallivan Failure to Vote," *Boston Daily Globe*, September 5, 1926, p. B8. A recent online source govtrack.us.com reported: "From Feb 1914 to Mar 1928, Gallivan missed 625 of 1,484 roll call votes, which is 42.1%. This is worse than the median of 14.1% among the lifetime records of representatives serving in Mar 1928." Retrieved March 4, 2013.

68 "Gallivan Reviews Work against Volstead's Bill," *Boston Globe*, September 12, 1926, p. B22. None of Gallivan's purported anti-Volstead activities appear in the close to forty pages of Daniel Okrent's exhaustive review of the congressional battle over Prohibition in *Last Call: The Rise and Fall of Prohibition*. It was a mixed record. Gallivan was one of 100 to vote against the bill when it passed the House 287–100, on July 22, 1919, (*Congressional Record*, 66th Congress, 1st Session, p. 3005) but was a nonvoter on October 10, 1919, when the conference report passed the House 230–69 (*Congressional Record*, 66th Congress, 1st Session, p. 6698). Gallivan got into an exchange with House Judiciary Chair Andrew Volstead (Rep-Minn.) over the likely cost of enforcement when Volstead contended that the cost would be a relatively modest $7,100,000, but Gallivan who knew better contended, "Why not $100,000,000?" *Congressional Record*, 66th Congress, 3rd Session, January 21, 1921, p. 1329.

69 "Gallivan Turns Fire on Rival's Absence; Asserts McCormack Missed More Roll Call Than He," *Boston Globe*, September 5, 1926, p. B8.

70 A story recounted to the author in 1995 from a South Boston eyewitness to the event at the Municipal Building.

71 Lester Gordon interview with John McCormack, February 7, 1973.

72 Gordon, *John McCormack and the Roosevelt Era*, p. 66.

73 See Alan Lupo's *Liberty's Chosen Home: The Politics of Violence in Boston* (Boston: Beacon Press, 1977), p. 81.

74 John P. Roche's syndicated column following Speaker McCormack's death, "John McCormack, One of a Kind," *Columbus (Ind.) Republic*, December 1, 1980.

75 Vote totals from *Boston Globe*, September 15, 1926, pp. 1ff.

76 "The Congress: Mr. Speaker," *TIME* (January 19, 1962), p. 18.

77 *Boston Post*, September 15, 1926.

78 "A FEW OF THOUSANDS OF MOURNERS UNABLE TO GAIN ADMITTANCE TO CHURCH AT FUNERAL OF CONGRESSMAN JAMES A. GALLIVAN: SILENT

CROWDS PAY TRIBUTE TO GALLIVAN. Thousands Turned Away at Church at Funeral of Congressman Nation, State, City and 'Jimmy's' Friends Mourn His Death—Streets Thronged," *Boston Globe*, April 6, 1928, p. 1.

79 McCormack's taped interview with Lester Gordon, February 7, 1973.

80 *CQ Guide to U.S. Elections* (1975 ed.), p. 494.

81 The 1928 campaign brochure, *The Life and Public Record of Hon. John W. McCormack, The Logical Candidate for Congress and the Issues of the Campaign.*

82 "McCormack Seeks Seat in Congress; Opposed Gallivan for Nomination Last Term; Kinnaly to Be Secretary if Nomination Is Won," *Boston Globe*, June 12, 1928.

83 McCormack won the 1928 Democratic primary victory with 14,196 votes; Edward M. Sullivan of Boston, 10,152 votes; William I. Hennessey of Boston, 9,289 votes; John H. Dunn of Boston, 3,119 votes; Daniel M. Lyons of Boston, 2,812 votes; William A. Fish of Boston, 385 votes; Thomas F. Curley of Boston, 369 votes; Frederick F. Carroll of Boston, 257 votes; and Thomas J. Collins of Boston, 224 votes in Secretary of the Commonwealth, *Primaries and Elections, 1928* (Boston, 1929).

84 Gordon, *John McCormack and the Roosevelt Era*, pp. 67, 71–72.

85 Secretary of the Commonwealth, *Primaries and Elections, 1928* (Boston, 1929), p. 450 for the 70th Congress vacancy and p. 380 for the election to the 71st Congress.

86 Differing interpretations of the 1928 election have led some authors to contend that Prohibition had a more important impact than Al Smith's Catholicism. On the Prohibition side, see Ruth B. Silva, *Rum, Romanism and Votes: 1928 Reexamined* (College Park: Pennsylvania State University Press, 1962). Greater negative weight to Smith's religion is presented in Alan J. Lichtman, *Prejudice and the Old Politics: The Presidential Election of 1928* (Chapel Hill: University of North Carolina Press, 1979).

87 David Burner, *The Politics of Provincialism: The Democratic Party in Transition, 1918–1932* (New York: Knopf, 1968). The 1928 election receives special consideration in V. O. Key. Jr.'s seminal "A Theory of Critical Elections," *Journal of Politics*, XVII (February 1955), pp. 3–18.

6

The 1928–33 Game Change

The Education of a Freshman Member: One of the remnants of the original Constitution was the curious timing of elections and swearing-in dates. Elections would occur in Novembers of even numbered years, and the new Congress would convene on March 4th. However, the normal start date for Congresses would be in early December. Consequently, there would be thirteen months between the election and the effective start date of the new Congress. During that interval, the old Congress would meet between early January and the 4th of March. Many members of the old Congress would not be members of the new Congress due to retirements or electoral defeats. These were "lame duck" sessions.

John McCormack entered the House for the balance of the 70th Congress at the opening of the 2nd Session on December 3, 1928. He was also simultaneously elected to the 71st Congress. Democrats had done poorly in the election with a net loss of 28 House seats and seven Senate seats. McCormack sat among a number of members whose careers had been terminated in the Hoover landslide.[1] The uniqueness of the double election gave John McCormack a three-month head start over the other freshmen elected that year, enabling him to gain seniority and begin his socialization into congressional mores early.

The 1928 Election: It was the greatest Electoral College triumph in the history of the Republican Party. Led by Secretary of Commerce Herbert Hoover with Senate Majority Leader Charles Curtis of Kansas as his running mate, Republicans captured 444 electoral votes. Among Hoover's high of forty states were five from the Old Confederacy—Florida, North Carolina, Tennessee, Texas, and Virginia. Four of those five had not always voted Democratic. Texas was the surprise. Apart from the 1864 and 1868 elections impacted by the Civil War and Reconstruction, Texas had voted Democratic in every election in which its votes were counted since its admission to the Union in 1848. To Republicans, this was the culmination of their strategy to break off the outer southern states and diminish the Democrats' hold over the Solid South.

To Texas Democrats, this was not a presidential candidacy they ever wished to see again. One Texan, five-term Representative John C. Box of Jacksonville, was especially dismayed. Box had become acting minority whip upon the November 19th death of William A. Oldfield of Arkansas. Oldfield's death and the defeat of Minority Leader Finis Garrett in the Tennessee Senate primary opened the door for John Nance Garner as Minority Leader. Box was the second-ranking Democrat on the House Immigration and Naturalization Committee sandwiched between two Jewish immigrants—Adolph

Sabath of Chicago, its ranking Democrat; and Sam Dickstein of New York City, its third-ranking member. As the son of a Confederate veteran and a lay Methodist minister, Box was clearly bothered by the demographic changes wrought within the Democratic Party.

In a letter to newly elected New York Governor Franklin D. Roosevelt, Box emphatically declared that "the future success of the Democratic party depends on ridding the organization of those forces which nominated Governor Al Smith and controlled his campaign." Clearly, the intended target was Tammany Hall and, by implication, Tammany's Irish Catholic hierarchy and its ethnic immigrant allies.

John McCormack was infuriated by Box's letter. John's easy general election victory in 1928 over Republican Herbert W. Burr[2] gave him a level of confidence that might have been close to hubris. With less than three months in the House and shortly after the election, the newly elected John McCormack sent an incensed public letter to Box through the *New York Times* declaring,[3]

> As the Representative of one of the strongest Democratic Congressional districts in the entire country, and as one who has always had the interests of the party constantly in mind, I cannot permit your sectional, emotional, and to my mind unnecessary reference to Governor Smith to go unchallenged.

It may not have been John's intent but an open letter in the *New York Times* would surely get him noticed by the House's Democratic power brokers, not the least of whom was Box's fellow Texan John Nance Garner who had become the new Democratic floor leader.

Nick Longworth: John's First Speaker: Presiding over John McCormack's first House session was one of its most colorful figures and contradictory characters, Speaker Nicholas Longworth, the elegant Republican from Cincinnati. The aristocratic Nick Longworth was an unlikely Speaker of the House. After all, the House was America's cauldron of democracy—the "people's house" in the words of Alexander Hamilton. The House that had been the scene of shouting matches, fistfights, and spittoon tosses seemed an inappropriate place for the likes of Nick Longworth, a Harvard-educated dandy who wore spats.

Longworth was well known in Washington during his early years as a congressman and as a wealthy and sophisticated but confirmed bachelor.[4] He became truly famous in the capital's social circles when the 36-year-old Longworth married 22-year-old Alice Lee Roosevelt, the beautiful and tempestuous daughter of President Theodore Roosevelt in the White House.[5] It was a politically powerful coupling but not a particularly happy one. During the frequent poker-playing and whiskey-drinking meetings of what he called the "Bureau of Education"—the Speaker's hideaway in the Capitol—Longworth would excuse himself from his colleagues for romantic dalliances with women far more likely to be impressed than the daughter of a president with the attentions of a Speaker of the House. According to William "Fishbait" Miller, the longtime Doorkeeper of the House, Longworth was "one of the greatest womanizers in history on Capitol Hill."[6]

Alice was Teddy Roosevelt's daughter from his first marriage to Boston Brahmin belle Alice Hathaway Lee of Chestnut Hill. Alice Lee Roosevelt would die at the age of

22 following the birth of her only child and was followed in death by her mother-in-law Martha Bulloch Roosevelt later that same day in the same house. A despondent Teddy left New York shortly afterward to console himself in the wilds of the Dakotas, leaving Alice in the care of his sister Anna, "Auntie Bye." Alice's abandonment by her father left psychic scars that manifested themselves in brutal verbal sarcasm and romantic infidelities. Nick Longworth's infidelities matched Alice's own, but hers resulted in a child, Paulina Longworth, who was actually the daughter of U.S. Senator William P. Borah, the "Idaho Stallion."[7]

However, Alice's greatest victory over Nick was by outliving him by almost fifty years and becoming such an extraordinarily amusing and acerbic wit that she almost totally eclipsed Nick Longworth's fame within Washington.

Nick was first elected to the House in 1902 along with Cactus Jack Garner with whom he would share center stage in the late 1920s. Longworth's political career was entwined with that of fellow Cincinnati Republican William Howard Taft. Longworth remained loyal to Taft and lost his House seat by a scant 101 votes when the fratricidal battle between his father-in-law and his longtime family friend spilled over into his congressional district.[8] He was defeated by what he would call the "Bullmeese." Two years later, in 1915, he returned to the House and quickly became a major figure in that chamber. He was elected Majority Leader in 1923 and two years later succeeded Frederick Gillett of Massachusetts as Speaker of the House. Nick was a very successful leader of the House.[9] Although Longworth was a defender of Republican orthodoxy, his personal style was dissimilar from other orthodox Republicans, and in the words of one observer, Nick Longworth "ruled as a crony rather than a czar."[10]

The Hotel Washington, Suite 820: Newly elected U.S. Representative John McCormack had more mundane business to transact upon his arrival at the Capitol. He had moved to Washington shortly after the November 1928 election and was able to secure lodgings for himself and Harriet in the Hotel Washington. It was a fortuitous choice. They enjoyed the hotel so much that they resided there when in Washington for the next 42-plus years. John McCormack was a man of simple tastes and regular habits. The Hotel Washington was located across the street from the Department of the Treasury and a block away from the White House, and it was readily accessible to downtown Washington and Capitol Hill.

The McCormack's settled easily into Suite 820, a corner suite with not much of a view. Why did the McCormack's choose a hotel suite over an apartment? The answer is surprisingly simple: room service. As a well-brought-up "lace curtain Irish lady," Harriet Joyce McCormack never had to learn to cook or clean. Her father's upper-middle-class lifestyle had enabled her to escape the mundane responsibilities of other less well-connected Irish-American women.

Every morning at eight, a waiter would arrive at the door with eggs, bacon, and orange juice.[11] John McCormack would take the table and roll it into the room. He was always careful to place the table on a white tablecloth on the floor covering an oriental rug that he and Harriet had purchased in Boston. Harriet would not come to the door. That was John's responsibility.

In the evening, John and Harriet would take their dinners in their room or upstairs in the hotel's dining room. As in the morning, John McCormack asked the hotel to provide only one waiter for their evening meal. When they dined upstairs, they sat at the same table every evening. They would have sirloin steak chopped into hamburger and mixed with onions. On the side was a bowl of mashed potatoes garnished slightly au gratin. The couple's meals were as unaltered as were their schedules.

The suite was modestly furnished with tables, desks, and rugs that they brought from Boston. The Hotel Washington was opened in 1918 and when John and Harriet moved into the room, it had not been remodeled for a decade. No remodeling of the room occurred until 1972, a year and a half after John McCormack's retirement.[12] Even the toilet fixtures of Suite 820, the bathtub and sink, remained the same for 54 years. To say that John McCormack was a man of regular habits is a vast understatement.

John's First White House Visit: Seated in the White House with less than three months left in his term was President Calvin Coolidge. Already a "lame duck," Coolidge had become disinclined to carry out the duties of his office. It has been contended that the death of his young son Calvin, Jr. due to blood poisoning following an accident at the White House contributed to a state of presidential depression.[13] Coolidge's long daily naps and his extended sleeps left him with only twelve hours a day for governmental business. But then to Coolidge, "the business of government is business."

President Calvin Coolidge was no stranger to Representative John McCormack. It was Massachusetts Governor Calvin Coolidge who broke the Boston Police Strike with the rallying cry, "There is no right to strike against the public safety by anybody, anywhere, anytime." It was this event that launched Coolidge into the national arena and his nomination as Warren Harding's vice presidential running mate in 1920. In 1919, John spent his first years in the State House during Coolidge's last years as governor, and he knew all too well that it was Coolidge's breaking of the bitterly divisive strike that helped propel Cal into the White House. John saw the strike differently than did Coolidge. He had constituents both among the Boston Police strikers who were Irish and among many of the South Boston looters. He took no clear public stands nor did he demonize Governor Coolidge; so his bridges remained intact. Other Democrats would be less cautious.

Shortly after arriving in Washington, McCormack was invited to the White House to be presented to President Coolidge. The two men were aware of one another but had not formally met. President Coolidge called for a servant to bring him a cigar. The servant promptly arrived with a humidor filled with high quality cigars. Coolidge selected one, cut off its tip, and began to smoke it, relatively unmindful of U.S. Representative McCormack's willingness to enjoy the experience.

Coolidge finally noted McCormack's eagerness to share this moment with him, and as recounted by McCormack to John P. Roche, Coolidge said[14]:

"Oh," Congressman Mc . . . Mc . . .
"Cormack,"
". . .would you like a cigar?"
He rang the bell again and said, "Give the congressman a cigar."
The servant returned with a White Owl on a silver server.

John knew very well that White Owls were then modestly priced at two for five cents. The status differential was a lesson John McCormack already knew. Being reminded of it even in the White House brought back the unfortunate echoes of Boston's ethnic unpleasantness.

John's First Committees and the North Texans: With barely three months left in the 70th Congress and as a freshman member of the House minority, John was aware that only minor committees would be available. The Democratic minority had been shrunken further by the 1928 election and it was in no position to lobby effectively for its freshmen. Having been an elected floor leader in the Massachusetts Senate, John could have lobbied the leadership for more powerful committee slots. But he remembered his own experience in that capacity when he found freshmen so full of hubris that they would take nothing less than prestigious assignments, and the resentments caused by their demands lingered long afterward.[15] He would take what was assigned and make the best of it. John McCormack had come from too great a distance to feel deprived with lesser committee assignments. He was now a member of the U.S. House of Representatives. It would be his political home for half of his life and getting comfortable was how he wanted to start.

Representative McCormack was assigned to the Committees on Territories and Elections No. 3.[16] He filled two of the vacancies of Arkansas's Heartsill Ragon, who had just moved onto the powerful Ways and Means Committee. On both of these committees he would sit on the minority side with Texas Representative Guinn Williams, who was then in his fourth term.[17] Williams would provide McCormack with access to the Texas delegation, then as now, the largest southern Democratic delegation in the House. Williams was elected from the 13th Congressional District along the Red River separating north Texas from Oklahoma. Williams's district was bordered by the 18th District on the west represented by Amarillo's Marvin Jones of the Texas Panhandle and directly to the east was the 4th Congressional District represented by Bonham's Sam Rayburn.[18] For a short time in 1927, Sam Rayburn and Marvin Jones would be brothers-in-law. However, Sam's marriage to Marvin's young sister Metze scarcely survived three months.[19] The southeastern corner of Guinn Williams's district also linked him to that of the Texas 5th represented by Sam Rayburn's oldest friend in the House, Hatton W. Sumners of Dallas.

Joining this clique upon his entrance to the House in March 1929, just months after Boston's John McCormack was sworn in, would be the irrepressible J. W. Wright Patman who would hold onto the 1st District in the northeastern corner of Texas for 47 years.[20] It was among the men of north Texas that John McCormack of Boston would find his earliest and most valued House colleagues. His life and House career were shaped by their influence.

One fortuitous occurrence for John took place when John Box, the one Texan who could have scuttled John's embrace by his fellow Texans, failed to gain renomination in 1930 and was defeated by Martin Dies, Jr. Dies would be a major headache to John later in the decade, but for now, he was just a 30-year-old freshman.

It would be Guinn Williams, the least well known of these Texans, who would be their initial link to John McCormack. The Territories Committee was relatively active compared to Elections No. 3. When asked what the Committee on Elections No. 3 did, McCormack answered, "I don't know. They never met."[21] When pressed further as to what he did when he was not in committee, McCormack added, "I watched the floor debates."

McCormack's minor committee assignments gave him time to prowl the floor and learn the tricks of the parliamentary trade by watching the Democrats' newly elected Minority Floor Leader Cactus Jack Garner. Although Garner represented a south Texas district, it was his origins in north Texas that gave his career its boost. Garner was a protégé of the highly talented but ethically challenged U.S. Representative Joseph Weldon Bailey, who served as Minority Leader for one Congress from 1897 until 1899 and left his House post to protest congressional commissions to serve in the Spanish-American War.[22] With Garner organizing the Texas Legislature on his behalf, Bailey would move on to the Senate in 1903 and would later recruit then Texas House Speaker Sam Rayburn to lead his legislative faction after Garner had been elected to the U.S. House.[23]

Cactus Jack Garner: John McCormack's First Floor Leader: Cactus Jack Garner, Joe Bailey's senior protégé, was on the Ways and Means Committee when Rayburn's initial request for committee assignments was presented in 1913. The Ways and Means Democrats had just obtained the power to assign their fellow Democrats to committees, and thanks to Garner the newly elected Sam Rayburn was able to escape assignment to the dead-end committees generally reserved for incoming freshmen. On June 3, 1913, Rayburn was assigned to the 12th majority slot on Interstate and Foreign Commerce Committee,[24] just behind another freshman, Alben W. Barkley of Kentucky. Barkley would later serve as Senate Majority Leader (1937–49) and as Vice President (1949–53). Barkley and Rayburn worked together as members of the congressional "Big Four" during the Roosevelt and Truman administrations. Young Sam Rayburn knew that this was a good assignment and that Garner had delivered for him. He remained on the Commerce Committee until his election as House Majority Leader in 1937. It was his only House committee assignment.

Garner's major argument on Rayburn's behalf rested on the fact that Rayburn had been elected to the speakership of the Texas House. Rayburn had received yet another benefit from Joe Bailey, his boyhood idol. Unlike Joe Bailey, these two Texans, Garner and Rayburn, took well to House life. Jack Garner became Democratic floor leader in 1929 and Speaker two years later. It was from this post that Garner was nominated and elected to be vice president in 1932. Sam Rayburn became House Majority Leader in 1937 and Speaker for the first time in 1940. It was a post that he held for seventeen years—the longest occupancy of the speakership in American history. Throughout the entirety of the Rayburn speakership, only one man served as majority leader: John W. McCormack of Boston.

The relationship between Garner and Rayburn was not always a smooth one. In 1923, following the death of Minority Leader Claude Kitchin of North Carolina, Garner sought the Democratic leadership position. Rayburn was then chairman of the Democratic Caucus that was to make the selection. Garner had hoped that Rayburn would help him gain the leadership post, but Rayburn supported the candidacy of Finis Garrett of Tennessee.[25] So close was Garrett's friendship that Rayburn began the Washington portion of his short-lived marriage to Metze Jones in Garrett's Washington apartment.[26]

Cactus Jack Garner was not always an easy man to like. His cigar-chomping, hot-tempered style cost him House allies and Sam Rayburn, a man more comfortable away from the spotlight, did not always appreciate Garner's self-promoting tendencies. After Rayburn told Garner, "You can't win, John," Garner withdrew his challenge to Garrett.[27] Garner sulked but made no effort to displace William Oldfield of Arkansas as the party's whip, the second-in-command. Sam Rayburn was loyal to his region if not always to his adopted state. The crushing Senate primary defeat of Garrett in 1928 opened up the floor leadership again. Cactus Jack entered the lists once more, and this time he was successful.

Garner greatly enjoyed his new responsibilities and the power and public prominence that went with them. Across the Capitol, the Senate Democrats were led by Arkansas's Joseph T. Robinson, who had suffered political embarrassment as the vice presidential candidate on Al Smith's losing presidential ticket. Robinson's Arkansas had held firm for the Democrats, but five of the remaining ten states of the Confederacy had voted for Republican Herbert Hoover. So Senator Robinson lowered his profile while Garner was raising his. Cactus Jack had waited a long time to occupy the top leadership post among the Democrats, and he quickly asserted himself.

Cactus Jack was like a bantam rooster, bouncing around the floor with a cigar in hand during debate.[28] He'd raise his bushy eyebrows and squint at those members who disagreed with him, and would gesticulate furiously at those who failed to appreciate the wisdom of his utterances. He had a quick temper and a ferocious wit. His prickliness was well known. "Cactus Jack" is not a nickname for those guided by empathy and compassion.

Cactus Jack first entered the House in 1903 and was eager to attain the trappings of congressional power. But this was the time of Republican Speaker Joe Cannon, and minority members were not treated well. In his first ten years, Garner served on four lesser committees, the best known of which was Foreign Affairs where he served for six years. While serving on Foreign Affairs in 1911, Garner first encountered the most colorful and disreputable of the Boston Irishmen—James Michael Curley. But it was not until 1913 that Garner, then in his eleventh year in the House, was named to his seventh committee—Ways and Means. By this time in the life of the House, the Ways and Means Democrats not only had control over the initiation of revenue legislation, they also held the significant power to appoint all other Democratic members to the remaining standing committees.

Many House leaders eschewed floor debate. They believed the successful passage of desired legislation required behind-the-scenes coalition building. Public displays of oratorical brilliance might gain you the notice of the press gallery, but it was unlikely to gain you the votes of your colleagues. Furthermore, debating on the House floor was not an activity for the faint of heart. Members frequently interrupted one another and often took verbal potshots that would be followed shortly by grandiose but unconvincing apologies. The insults were remembered; the apologies seldom were. Cactus Jack enjoyed debate and was very good at it.

McCormack appreciated Garner's combativeness. It was on his side that Garner was doing battle. John McCormack also learned that enemies could be made in the process of legislating who would never appreciate what you stood for, no matter how well-argued or how important it may have been for the nation. Garner was also watching John McCormack as he did so many of the new Democrats. "From 1926 on," according to Bascom Timmons, Garner's biographer, "Mr. Garner's interest in the new men was heightened." Timmons reported of Garner[29]: "He kept his eye on the new men in the back rows. . . . He thought a good line could be got on them in their second term."

Cactus Jack was an alumnus of the Ways and Means Committee which had become the Democratic "committee on committees" where taking the measure of the new men was a requirement, and John McCormack was about to be discovered.

The Hoover Presidency Begins: On March 4, 1929, the cerebral and chilly Herbert Hoover was inaugurated as president. Earlier that morning, the 71st Congress had been sworn in, quite unaware of the legislative burdens which would befall them before the year would end and the economic catastrophe which would engulf the nation for a decade to come.

The immediate economic crisis facing the nation was an agricultural one. The "Roaring Twenties" had led to a major out-migration from the nation's rural areas to its urban ones, where industrial expansion offered higher-paid employment than could be found on the farms. As the orphaned son of eastern Iowa farmers, President Hoover moved quickly on a campaign promise to find relief for the nation's farmers who had been locked in a decade-long price depression. He called a special session of Congress to provide relief for American farmers through the passage of the Agricultural Marketing Act of 1929.[30] This act created the Federal Farm Board with eight members and the secretary of agriculture to promote the marketing of farm commodities through agricultural cooperatives and price stabilization corporations. It also authorized a revolving fund of $500 million for low-interest loans to such agencies in the interest of the orderly purchasing, handling, and selling of surplus commodities. It became law in June 1929 and the Congress adjourned, eager as ever to escape the suffocating heat of a capital city built on a swamp. The Agricultural Marketing Act contained tariff protection for agricultural commodities, but conservative Republicans Senate Finance Chair Reed Smoot of Utah and House Ways and Means Chair Willis C. Hawley sought even higher tariff protections for industrial goods.

After a nine-year bull market run fueled by rampant speculation, the stock market began to experience double-digit losses in October 1929[31]—dropping 10% on October 24, 13% on October 28, and 12% on October 29. Panicky investors began a major sell-off while Congress continued its debate on the Smoot-Hawley Tariff. The Crash had begun.

Only seven months after President Herbert Hoover's triumphant inaugural, the stock market's Crash revealed that President Hoover had few answers for the nation's economic woes. In spite of his own serious misgivings, Hoover signed Smoot-Hawley into law, and the resulting tariff war with our trading partners expanded the Crash worldwide, leading to the Great Depression of the 1930s.

The First session of the 71st Congress ended on November 22, 1929, and the members left town not fully aware of how their constituents back home had been devastated.

Like most of his colleagues, Representative John McCormack was one of those stunned by the economic collapse. In his last year in the House, McCormack discussed his first year on Capitol Hill[32]:

> When I came here in December, 1928 as a young Congressman, filling out an unexpired term, there were no serious problems to speak of. The stock market was floating along nicely and Americans by and large were enjoying life. Some of us worried about an over-extension in construction, but nobody believed that we were heading into a business recession that would develop into a deep depression.

Congress reconvened just ten days later on December 2, 1929, after witnessing the early devastation of the Crash. The Second Session of the 71st Congress would be a less civil place than the first. To the Republican lawmakers who ran the Congress, the Crash was "the normal business cycle" at work and Americans would recover from this disruption as they had from so many others. Urgency was in the air, but not enough to undertake extraordinary measures. Listening with partially closed ears, the House's conservative Republicans did what they almost always did in times of fiscal travail. They raised tariff rates in the Smoot-Hawley bill to their highest levels ever and contributed substantially to the exporting of the Depression to Europe. It was not a sensible solution, but it was a familiar one for the congressional Republicans. With a 267–167 seat-edge in the House and a 56–39 seat-edge in the Senate, Republicans had more than enough votes as the Smoot-Hawley Tariff passed easily.[33]

The Smoot-Hawley Tariff of 1930 raised import duties on imported agricultural products from 38% to 45%, their highest levels in almost a century, and most economists feared that these usurious tariffs would trigger tariff wars with America's major trade partners.[34] The bill gave some special protection to southern agricultural commodities such as sugar, textile, citrus fruit, and cotton, but it removed many other items from the free list. Having carried five southern states in the 1928 election, Hoover's Republicans wanted to use the agricultural protection portion of the bill to break the Democratic unity of the "Solid South."

Hoover was reportedly displeased with Smoot-Hawley and was urged by many individuals including a group of 1,028 economists who signed a petition to veto it.[35] In June 1930, the president acquiesced to the congressional Republicans and rationalized his signing of the bill by contending that the legislation's revitalized tariff provision would resolve all the objections to its higher rates by instituting a process for their systematic reduction.

John McCormack did not believe Hoover's argument and like most of his fellow Democrats, John voted against it twice—the original House bill and its even more onerous conference report—the version that President Hoover would sign in spite of his own publicly expressed misgivings. With the tariff issue settled, John hoped that this session of Congress would address the social issues dearest to his constituents such as the repeal of Prohibition and the liberalization of the immigration laws.

It is not known when John McCormack first caught Jack Garner's eye, but John made his maiden speech to the House on February 14, 1929, in the closing days of the 70th Congress. On this day, McCormack challenged the "National Origins" clause of the 1924 Immigration Control Act. He was especially displeased that it seemed to discriminate against Irish and Italians, the nation's two largest Catholic immigrant groups. "We want Americans," he declaimed. "We want the immigrants who come over here to be filled with a love of our institutions."[36]

With his move into the top minority slot, Jack Garner's talent searches took on a new urgency. Now was the time for Garner to build a team of his own and to promote junior members whose loyalty could be established. John McCormack was about to be discovered.

The one positive step taken in the months leading up to the 1930 election was for Congress to create the Veterans Administration, consolidating all of the federal servicemen's programs,[37] but no further legislative action was taken to alleviate the Depression's economic agonies. President Coolidge had been publicly hostile to the monetary claims of World War veterans, and President Hoover wished to stave off an unpleasant protest. Hoover like Coolidge in 1924 vetoed the "Bonus Bill" formally known as the "Emergency Adjusted Compensation Bill," and like Coolidge, Hoover's veto was overridden with the session drawing to a close.[38] This time ex-Sergeant McCormack could honor his comrades and cast his first ever successful veto override vote.

The Partial Victory of 1930: The initial results of the 1930 midterm election were mixed. Democrats made a net gain of eight seats in the Senate and had reduced the Republican majority to one seat (48-47-1). In the House, the Republicans slim margin would shift to a Democratic one of three seats (217–214) by the December 1931 convening of the 72nd Congress. With so much uncertainty about the upcoming Congress, meaningful legislation ceased and one of the few items Congressmen could agree on in the closing days of the lame duck 3rd Session of 71st Congress was the adoption of "The Star-Spangled Banner" as the national anthem.[39] On the final day of the session, its longest lasting legislative legacy was signed into law—the Davis-Bacon Act of 1931 (P.L. 71-793, 46 Stat. 1494). Coauthored by Republicans U.S. Senator James J. Davis of Pennsylvania and U.S. Representative Robert L. Bacon of New York, the law requires that local prevailing wages are to be paid to workers on federal public works projects.[40]

A number of key Republicans had narrowly escaped defeat in 1930, including Speaker Nicholas Longworth. A crueler fate awaited Longworth and the House Republicans as death would rob the Republicans of their House majority when a number of elderly House incumbents died.[41] Included among them was 61-year-old Speaker Nicholas Longworth.

The loss of Nick Longworth was especially troubling because he was the glue that kept the Republican majority together. Even the cynical inside reporters Drew Pearson and Robert S. Allen contended that Longworth was "unfailingly good-natured and courteous, and even when he was bludgeoning the House, he was never disagreeable about it."[42] His dapper appearance and gracious manner made him an unlikely but very successful leader of the House. His less able allies, Majority Leader John Q. Tilson of Connecticut and Rules Committee Chair Bertrand H. Snell of upstate New York, bickered with one another over the succession and Tilson, the presumed heir-apparent, was bested by Snell on the eighth ballot in the Republican Conference.[43]

The Failed Good Intentions of Republican Recovery Plans: President's Hoover's most ambitious effort was his sponsorship of the Reconstruction Finance Corporation Act that became law in January 1932.[44] This act created the RFC as a lending agency with the authority to issue tax-exempt bonds and with wide powers to extend credit. The RFC began with $500 million in capital and was authorized to borrow an additional $1.5 billion by issuing tax-exempt bonds. It was intended to provide emergency financing for banking institutions, life insurance companies, farm mortgage associations, building and loan corporations, railroads, and other businesses. But the RFC was a program focused on institutions and not individuals, and its fundamental "top-down" focus was unlikely to reach the growing millions of unemployed citizens who drifted onto bread lines and would eventually throw Herbert Hoover out of office, keeping his fellow Republicans from controlling Congress for fourteen years.

On February 27, 1932, the first Glass-Steagall Act was passed.[45] Coauthored by two southern Democratic conservatives, U.S. Senator Carter Glass (Dem-Va.) and U.S. Representative Henry B. Steagall (Dem-Ala.), it was designed to counteract the contraction of credit due to foreign withdrawals and the domestic hoarding of gold and currency by authorizing the sale of $750 million worth of the government's gold supply for industrial and business needs. It also liberalized the Federal Reserve System's power to discount commercial paper.

The inability of the market-based economy to guarantee jobs and security to the nation's citizenry was no surprise to John McCormack. It was a confirmation of his painful childhood experiences during the financial collapse of the 1890s, but now he could do something about it. What he could do and what he would do awaited the next Congress.

Boston and the Depression: Because Boston itself was not a manufacturing city, the impact of the Depression was less direct, but it had a devastating effect upon all of the neighboring factory towns. The Boston Stock Exchange (BSE) suffered as greatly as Wall Street, as capital investment evaporated and jobs disappeared. The once booming textile cities of Lowell, Lawrence, and Maynard, like most of the mill towns in the Blackstone Valley, as well as the shoe cities of Lynn, Brockton, Stoneham, Haverhill, and Newburyport faced massive layoffs. The negative effects of these plant closings rippled throughout Massachusetts until 25% unemployment was reached in 1934.[46]

As had happened in previous economic crises, the opportunity for political gain presented itself to the minority. The November election would be a telling one. Republicans fearfully went to the nation while Democrats hoped that economic disaster would lead to a revival of their political fortunes. The tides of political fortune in American politics had often shifted following economic catastrophe.

Unexpected Help from Jim Curley: With the House out of session for much of the year, John and Harriet would return to Boston, and it was during this time that John would reconnect with Mayor James Michael Curley who had been elected to his third nonconsecutive term as mayor in 1929, defeating the Good Government's Irish Catholic candidate Frederick Mansfield. A photo captured second-term U.S Representative McCormack and Mayor Curley together as Curley readied himself for an appearance at the 1930 Democratic State Convention. It is one of the very few photographs of the two men together as John McCormack was careful to keep a respectful distance from Curley.[47]

It was also during this period that John would make the acquaintance of the very mysterious David K. Niles, the Russian-born Jew who ran the city's major and internationally known arena for public debate, the Ford Hall Forum. The Forum had been relocated to the New England Conservatory of Music on Huntington Avenue and every Sunday night its seats would fill with Bostonians eager to engage in debates over national and international issues. The Forum had been the locus for much of the opposition to the 1921 trial and 1927 electric chair executions of the two Italian anarchists, Nicola Sacco and Bartolomeo Vanzetti. Leading the intellectual challenge to that trial was the brilliant Austrian-born Harvard Law Professor Felix Frankfurter, whose path would frequently cross that of David K. Niles, just as Niles's path would frequently cross that of John McCormack.[48] Niles became a member of Mayor Jim Curley's third term "brain trust" and is listed in Curley's autobiography along with members of the MIT, Tufts, and Suffolk faculties.[49] However, Harvard, the Brahmin bastion and Curley's favorite academic target, was not included.

John McCormack's Boston victory in the 1930 contest was a convincing one. He finished with 50,894 votes (76.7%) to Republican Samuel Abrams's 15,422 votes (23.3%).[50] Abrams hoped to upset McCormack by mobilizing Jewish voters in the city's 14th Ward—the Mattapan section of the district—but John McCormack had already learned how to reach beyond the South Boston and Dorchester Irish to build a broad-based electoral coalition. McCormack's predecessor Jim Gallivan chose not to appeal to the district's large Jewish population, content to let Southie and Irish Dorchester send him back to Washington.

The First House Majority and Speaker Cactus Jack Garner

The new 72nd Congress was sworn in under the original constitutional mandate of March 4. It would be during the subsequent 73rd Congress that the 20th Amendment, the "lame duck" amendment would move the opening day of Congress to January 3 of odd-numbered years.

John McCormack's reelection permitted him to join a legislative majority for the first time in his political career. The House Democrats were poised to enjoy majority status for the first time since 1918 and to elect their first new Speaker since Champ Clark. Ready to assume control of the House upon its convening in December 1931 was John Nance Garner of Texas.[51] He would be the first southern Democratic Speaker elected since 1857, when South Carolina's James L. Orr presided over the House just before the Civil War, and the first Texan ever. Garner's victory was easy.[52] The real battle in the leadership was over Majority Floor Leader.

A number of House Democrats were mentioned for the leadership post—Joseph W. Byrns of Tennessee, Charles R. Crisp of Georgia, the son of a former Speaker, John E. Rankin of Mississippi, and John J. O'Connor of New York. It was anticipated that the contest would narrow to Garner's choice John McDuffie of Alabama, the Democratic whip, and Henry T. Rainey of Illinois. Rainey was first elected to the House in 1903 and had been a loyal Champ Clark lieutenant and like Garner, he served on the Ways and Means Committee. Rainey was then 71 years old and heavily supported by House old-timers.[53]

Now 39 years old, John McCormack supported the two southerners, Jack Garner and John McDuffie.[54] It is doubtful if John knew how this support of southern congressmen would change his congressional life, but it did. And the change came quickly and decisively. John McDuffie understood that John McCormack was the only New Englander supporting his candidacy, and he gained a great fondness for McCormack that placed him high in the estimation of the House's southerners. Like so many of the southerners who regarded John McCormack fondly, John McDuffie was Scottish-descended.[55]

Most important to McCormack was his knowledge that John O'Connor was living openly with his mistress.[56] O'Connor, like other New York Irish Catholic politicians Representative Bourke Cockran and New York City Mayor Jimmy Walker, may have played fast and loose with women other than their wives, but the Boston Irishmen did not. After all, Boston had been founded by Puritans; New York had not. The multiple electoral defeats that befell Honey Fitz after the Toodles Ryan disclosure were proof of that fact. John's obvious fidelity to Harriet was undoubtedly appreciated by Jack Garner whose relationship with his wife who served as his secretary was "one of the most remarkable partnerships political Washington has known."[57]

In the name of party harmony, John McDuffie stepped aside and Rainey went on to defeat O'Connor, whose difficulties were attributed to his being a Tammany wet.[58] Rainey's election was a sign to Jack Garner that he did not hold full rein over the House Democrats in his upcoming term as Speaker. But Garner held enough power to appoint the party's whip and he renewed John McDuffie's hold on that post.[59]

The Ways and Means Committee: Now the House's majority party, the returning Democrats, arrived in Washington eager to upgrade their committee assignments and take advantage of the newly opened majority slots on the committees. It was their first majority opportunity since the reelection of Woodrow Wilson in 1916, and they were ready to move up the committee hierarchy.

John McCormack had patiently bided his time with another two years on Territories and Elections No. 3.[60] He was added to the Civil Service Committee in 1929, but this committee too held little promise of advancement within the House. Joining McCormack on the Civil Service Committee that year was Robert Ramspeck (Dem-Georgia), whom Rayburn and McCormack would name as Democratic whip in 1945.[61] McCormack was ready to move up and hoped to land a slot on the House Judiciary Committee. After all, he had served on the Judiciary Committee back in the Massachusetts General Court and had paid his dues by dutifully accepting lesser committee assignments. It was not a sense of entitlement that he brought to the Speaker's office that day, but one of hopeful expectation.

In December 1931, John went to meet new Speaker John Nance Garner. He was not ready for what he would hear. According to McCormack, Garner greeted him with a gruff but friendly outburst: "John, where the hell have you been?" asked Garner. McCormack was stunned to learn that Speaker Garner knew his name, never mind that he had been looking for him. "We wanted you for chairman of the caucus. Bill Arnold [of Illinois] came in and I gave it to him but I wanted you."[62]

Bill Arnold, an Appropriations Committee member from Illinois, then in his ninth year in the House, was a logical selection. McCormack was only in his third year. "I didn't even know that Garner knew that I was a member," McCormack recounted. Clearly, the House Democratic leadership had big plans for the tall young member from Boston.

"We want you for Ways and Means," Garner continued, "But you have to be elected to it." McCormack was dumbfounded. Once the Democratic Caucus selected the party's leaders, it would then elect new members of the House Ways and Means Committee. There were seven vacancies. Five seats were awarded for the incoming majority while the additional two openings were created when Cactus Jack was elected Speaker and Cordell Hull of Tennessee was elected to the U.S. Senate.

Young John McCormack listened for further advice from Cactus Jack. Garner's recommendation was simple: "Just have Billy Connery blow his nose at you and we will get you elected to it." Billy Connery came from the north shore industrial city of Lynn and was the senior Democrat from Massachusetts.[63] Connery had entered the House in 1923 and was only three years older than John McCormack, but at the relatively young age of 42, he had become the Democratic "dean" of the Massachusetts congressional delegation. As the state's senior Democrat, his recommendations carried great weight. Connery wrote a letter of endorsement and the race was on. Backed by the unanimous support of the New England and Texas Democratic delegations, information that had been relayed to him by Garner ally Sam Rayburn,[64] McCormack finished first among the twelve contenders for the open slots on Ways and Means with 164 votes from the 218-member Democratic Caucus, 24 votes more than the second-place finisher, Edward Eslick of Tennessee.[65] But Eslick had more seniority than John and was chosen for the eleventh slot just ahead of John.[66] Fittingly enough, making the phone call to inform John that the Texans had voted unanimously for his election to Ways and Means was Sam Rayburn.

John McCormack was the youngest and the most junior of the members elected to the committee.[67] Finishing behind McCormack and assigned to the last slot was fourth-term Representative Fred M. Vinson of Kentucky,[68] whose friendship with John would continue for the next 22 years during which Vinson would be named as a Federal Judge and Director of War Mobilization by President Roosevelt, and Secretary of the Treasury and Chief Justice of the U.S. Supreme Court by President Harry Truman. Later in the 72nd Congress, Eslick would die and be replaced by Jere Cooper of Tennessee who would play an important role in the postwar Congresses. Surrounded by the powerhouses of Washington, John McCormack knew that he had arrived. "It was a record," recounted McCormack, as he remembered his early ascension to this most formidable seat of power within the U.S. House.[69]

Of the more than fifty standing committees then functioning in the U.S. House of Representatives, none was more important to Democrats than the Ways and Means Committee. The U.S. Constitution mandates in Article I, Section 7, that "all Bills for raising Revenue shall originate in the House of Representatives." The House lodged that authority in the Committee on Ways and Means early in the nation's first decade.[70] Its primary institutional responsibility was in writing tariff and taxation legislation—the primary mission of the House itself. Given its link to the House's historic mission, it was not surprising that the chairs of the Ways and Means Committee in the nineteenth century had served as the de facto floor leaders of the House's majority party, ranking behind only the elected Speakers of the House. Ways and Means was ranked the most eminent committee in a statistical assessment prepared by Professor John C. Eberhart of Northwestern University for the Library of Congress, covering 4,841 standing committee assignments between 1914 and 1941. To Professor Eberhart, "The [committee] hierarchy is a pyramid with the Ways and Means Committee at its peak, and a layer of very unimportant minor committees at the bottom."[71]

Statistics aside, the easiest way to describe the importance of the House Ways and Means Committee is to list the names of its illustrious members throughout its two centuries. Thirteen of its members were elected either president—James Madison, Andrew Jackson, James K. Polk, James A. Garfield, William McKinley, and George H. W. Bush; or vice president—Elbridge Gerry, John Tyler, Richard M. Johnson, Millard Fillmore, John C. Breckinridge, Charles Curtis, and John Nance Garner. Presidents Polk, Fillmore, and McKinley all chaired the Ways and Means Committee. Four Justices of the Supreme Court, including John McCormack's fellow committeeman Chief Justice Fred M. Vinson, were Ways and Means alumni as were 34 presidential Cabinet appointees. Most importantly, 22 future Speakers used the committee as springboards to the chair including Wisconsin's Paul D. Ryan chosen in 2015.[72] In 1931, Garner moved from Ways and Means to the speakership and seated on the committee during McCormack's first term on the committee was Henry T. Rainey (Dem-Ill.), who would follow Garner to the Speaker's chair after Garner's inauguration as vice president in 1933.

The Ways and Means Committee served as the committee on committees for the House Democrats for more than 60 years. This was a practice instituted after the House overthrew its dictatorial Speaker Joseph G. Cannon (Rep-Ill.) in 1909–10 and removed his power to name all the members of each of the House's standing committees.[73] To become a Democratic member of Ways and Means, one had to be elected to it by the full membership of the Democratic Caucus. Once there, the assignment-making power could make you many friends.

Jack Garner liked John McCormack for a number of reasons, not the least of which was McCormack's enjoyment of poker. He and McCormack lived in the same hotel in Washington, but contrary to popular legend, John told me that he was not a poker-playing pal of Garner. Jack Garner and John McCormack were both from humble origins and strangers to formal higher education, but it was not just McCormack's similarity that motivated Garner's interest in him.

As the Democratic Speaker of the House in a Republican administration, Garner was the highest ranking member of his party in the federal government and as a Texan,

Garner could expect the full backing of the South should he contend for the 1932 presidential nomination.[74] John McCormack was from Massachusetts, the only major industrial state to cast its eighteen electoral votes for Al Smith in the 1928 election. Coming from South Boston, John was considered by most to be a Jim Curley protégé, and it would appear that Garner's sponsorship of McCormack's membership on Ways and Means was a signal to Mayor Curley that Garner was open to a nomination alliance. After all, Garner and Curley knew each other from their time together on the House Foreign Affairs Committee during the early years of the Wilson Administration.[75]

It is doubtful if John McCormack had any idea that Jack Garner's sponsorship of his membership on Ways and Means was related to Garner's nascent presidential aspirations, but John might very well have been an essential ingredient in Garner's plan to achieve the presidency. However, it was at the point of John McCormack's joining the Ways and Means Committee that the "Austin-Boston connection" had begun. This link between the north Texans and their associates from the South with urban Catholics from the Boston area created the single-most important congressional alliance in House history. For many people, this would have been the time to forget the hardships of Andrew Square and to enrich oneself with the emoluments of office. This was not the case for John McCormack. This was the time to address the hardships of all the Andrew Squares throughout the nation. With the 1932 Democratic National Convention scheduled to meet in late June, just seven short months away, a new president might accomplish that task. But first, the dispirited Republicans would gather in Chicago.

Hoover's political collapse

More layoffs, more bankruptcies, and more foreclosures brought more difficulty to the Hoover Administration. Politically, the president's own party began to abandon him. Opposition to Hoover's 1932 renomination grew to such a degree that a relatively obscure former U.S. Senator Joseph France from Maryland openly challenged Hoover's renomination in the presidential preference primaries. France finished ahead of Hoover in Nebraska, Pennsylvania, Ohio, West Virginia, New Jersey, and Oregon and tallied 1,137,948 total votes (48.5%) to Hoover's 781,165 (33.3%).[76] In spite of France's showing in the primaries, the glum Republicans met in Chicago in mid-June and chose to renominate Hoover with 1,126.5 of the 1,154 delegate votes (97.6%). Their anxiety played out on the vice presidential ballot, where Vice President Charles Curtis received only 634.25 votes (55.0%).[77] Like President William Howard Taft before him in 1912, the Republican primary voters rejected President Hoover's bid for an uncontested renomination. And Joe France was no Teddy Roosevelt.

The president's faction was in such total control of the nomination that Joe France was escorted from the convention hall before he was allowed to address the assemblage and received only 4 delegate votes of the 1,154 cast (0.3%).[78] The heavy-handedness of the Hoover organization was clearly in evidence. A minor eruption concerning the renomination of Vice President Charles Curtis was not enough to slow the Hoover operatives. Curtis barely regained renomination as the angry delegates chose to take out their frustrations on his candidacy rather than Hoover's. Although the renomination of the Hoover-Curtis ticket may have been secured, many Republicans left the hall in despair over the party's November prospects while still others left the hall in anger sufficient to vote against Hoover a few months hence. Despite the size of Hoover's renomination vote, November's general election prospects for the G.O.P. were now as grim as the economy.

President Hoover's popularity continued to sink and the arrival in Washington of thousands of "Bonus Marchers" reinforced his negative image. Photographs of impoverished World War veterans, storming the Capitol in hopes that Congress would expedite the payment of the postwar bonuses that they had been promised, were widely published.[79] Hoover called out the army to disperse the veterans and with young General Douglas MacArthur, aided by Colonel Dwight D. Eisenhower, the Bonus Marchers were driven off the Capitol grounds. Republicans became even more dispirited and the Democrats, who also gathered in Chicago eleven days later, became more hopeful.

The 1932 Democratic Convention

Democratic optimism was high in anticipation of the 1932 presidential nominating convention. Gaining control of the House in the off-year congressional elections was often a harbinger of gaining control of the presidency in the subsequent election. As 1932 opened, three major candidates emerged among the eager Democrats—former New York Governor Al Smith, present New York Governor Franklin D. Roosevelt, and newly installed Speaker of the House John Nance Garner of Texas. Roosevelt and Smith locked horns in the northern primaries while Garner was able to defeat both in the California primary with the support of the powerful conservative Democratic newspaper publisher William Randolph Hearst.

Both Smith and Roosevelt had failed in their previous national bids—Smith for president in 1928 and Roosevelt for vice president in 1920. Neither New Yorker had dazzled the nation in their earlier runs but with its 47 electoral votes, New York was the nation's largest state and the most necessary building block for victory in the Electoral College. The media reach of New York City was unrivaled in the nation, and virtually every presidential election season would begin with the governor of New York near the top of the list of prospective candidates, regardless of party. Governors had generally fared better than congressional leaders in gaining nomination and election. Both Presidents James K. Polk (Dem-Tenn.), a former Speaker of the House; and William McKinley (Rep-Ohio), a former Ways and Means chair, discovered in the previous century that their presidential prospects were enhanced after leaving the House and serving as governor of their states.[80]

Jack Garner was not one who paid much attention to history, and he had some genuine resources. As the Speaker of the House, Garner was the most nationally situated of the Democratic candidates. He had positioned himself to thwart President Hoover's business-based solutions to the deepening economic crisis, but the media reach of Washington was then very limited and so he was little known in the further precincts of American politics. Garner came to the convention with two key allies, both of whom would play a role in the future leadership career of John McCormack. Garner's fellow Texan Sam Rayburn served as the Speaker's floor manager and Alabama's John McDuffie, the House Democratic whip, would place Garner's name into nomination. Despite the obvious ability of these two House members, Garner's presidential candidacy appeared to be a regional one concentrated in the South and in California. Any Protestant Democrat should be able to hold the South. After all, even Al Smith the Catholic had won six states of the Confederacy.

Massachusetts had bucked the national Republican trend in 1928 and cast its eighteen electoral votes for New York Governor Al Smith. It was the largest state to cast electoral votes for Smith and the only major northern industrial state in his column. It now stood out in dramatic relief creating an opportunity for Boston's Irish-linked Catholic Democrats John McCormack, Jim Curley, and Joseph P. Kennedy to engage in national politics.

Not all of the Bay State's prominent Democrats were eager to see a rematch between President Hoover and Al Smith, most notably Jim Curley and Joe Kennedy.[81] For these two men, Governor Roosevelt was the preferred choice for the Democratic nomination. FDR was seen as electable; Smith was not. Joe Kennedy had already relocated his family to New York so his commitment made more sense than did Curley's decision. But Curley's commitment to FDR was enmeshed in his ongoing rivalry with Governor Joseph Ely, a Yankee Democrat, who later would be asked by Al Smith to present his name to the convention.

The state's leading politicians took sides. John McCormack joined Williams College and Harvard Law graduate Governor Joseph B. Ely, a Protestant from Westfield, and Senator David I. Walsh, who had been both the state's first Catholic governor and U.S. Senator, in backing Al Smith in the Massachusetts primary. Boston Mayor Jim Curley convinced FDR's key tactician, the gnome-like Louis McHenry Howe, whose wife was from Fall River, to get FDR on the primary ballot. It was a disaster and Smith buried FDR 73.1% to 26.9% thus committing the delegation to Smith.[82] John McCormack was named to the pro-Smith convention delegation, but Jim Curley was not. Howe became convinced that Curley was more concerned with unsettling Governor Ely than he was in helping FDR. Louis Howe and FDR were displeased by these results. Their previous faith in Jim Curley's political acumen diminished greatly.[83]

Most states did not hold primaries at this time, and for many of the states that did hold them, they were merely advisory. But in the absence of national public opinion polls, the primaries were a rough guide to the relative strength of the contenders. Governor Roosevelt had his name entered in most of the presidential preference primaries and came away with victories in nine states with 44.5% of the total primary vote cast. Only three states were recorded for Roosevelt's principal rivals. In Massachusetts and New Jersey, Roosevelt finished behind Al Smith, and in California, he finished behind Jack Garner.[84]

Curley knew Cactus Jack during his first two terms in the U.S. House (1911–14). Although he was now Boston's mayor for the third time, Curley suffered for his support of the Roosevelt candidacy. The Smith loyalists among the Massachusetts delegates were so committed to renominating "the happy warrior" that Curley was excluded from the delegation. In the words of the *Cleveland Plain Dealer*, "James Michael Curley is the most battered political casualty of the Massachusetts primary. He is still Mayor, but his political prestige is ground into dust and blowing all over the Common."[85]

It was anticipated that New York City's Tammany Hall with its heavily Catholic machine would be committed to Al Smith and not to the state's current governor, Franklin Roosevelt, the Dutch Reformed aristocrat from Dutchess County. Massachusetts could be an effective Catholic counterweight if it produced a united delegation for FDR headed by Jim Curley. It was not to be. Curley's failed efforts for FDR kept him off the pro-Smith delegation. It would be headed by Governor Ely who was joined by both of the state's two Democratic U.S. Senators from Fitchburg, David I. Walsh and Marcus A. Coolidge, and all four of the state's Democratic U.S. Representatives, William P. Connery of Lynn, William J. Granfield of Longmeadow, and Boston's John J. Douglass and John W. McCormack.

Excluded from the state delegation, Jim Curley had to think fast and move quickly if he was to resume his ambitious political trajectory. First, he had to get to the Chicago convention. Ever the opportunist, he had no intention of missing this nominating convention, awash in so much enthusiasm and positive anticipation. Through some typical machinations and the apparent "illness" of the chair of the Puerto Rican delegation, the chair stepped aside and Jim Curley became "Don Jaime Miguel Curleo," a voting delegate from Puerto Rico.[86] He was seated close to the Massachusetts delegates who thought they had left him on the railroad platform at South Station. Their delight at freezing Curley out had been premature.

Governor Ely, a Protestant and sworn enemy of Jim Curley, was called upon to make the nominating speech for Al Smith. Smith's Tammany Hall loyalists had stacked the New York delegation sufficiently to thwart FDR. Of New York's 94 delegates, Smith outpolled FDR 65 ½ to 28 ½ on the first ballot and Smith maintained his edge in New York throughout the balloting.[87] Allied with New York in the Smith column were the delegations from Massachusetts, New Jersey, and Connecticut. These four states provided virtually all of Smith's support and the delegate count among them was sufficiently large to keep FDR from the nomination.

Nominating conventions differed from preference primaries and Democratic conventions differed from Republican ones. Because the Democratic Party had been traditionally anchored in the South, Democrats from that region who wished to protect slavery prior to the Civil War insisted upon a two-thirds requirement in each of their conventions from 1831 on for the nominations of president and vice president. This gave the South a veto over any candidate who would interfere with their "peculiar institution" of chattel slavery. Even after the war ended, southern Democrats held fast to the two-thirds rule to preserve their post-Reconstruction Jim Crow racial segregation laws. While the rule may have guaranteed Democratic victories in the South, it had been fatal to Democratic presidential prospects and contributed to Democratic defeats in fourteen of the eighteen presidential contests from 1860 to 1928. The rule led to three previous Democratic conventions with front-running candidates losing the nomination because of the two-thirds vote requirement—Champ Clark in 1912 and William Gibbs McAdoo in 1920 and 1924.[88] Franklin Roosevelt, the 1932 front-runner, needed to overcome that rule if he was to be nominated.

William Randolph Hearst was adamantly opposed to American involvement in the League of Nations and had rallied his newspapers behind the candidacy of California U.S. Senator and former Treasury Secretary William Gibbs McAdoo, a onetime Woodrow Wilson son-in-law. But McAdoo had run afoul of the two-thirds rule twice, and Hearst needed another horse to ride to carry on his anti-League crusade. Jack Garner was Hearst's choice, and if Garner could hold enough southern delegates, the Democratic two-thirds requirement would deadlock the convention once again and prevent any internationalist, like former Secretary of War Newton D. Baker, from being nominated.[89]

A serious problem had developed on the convention floor as FDR's nomination bid fell short. His first ballot tally of 666.25 had only grown to 682.79 by the third ballot—still 87 votes short of the 769.33 votes needed for the required two-thirds of the 1,154 delegates. The key to the nomination was to dislodge the 101.25 votes held by Garner—90 of which were in the California (44) and Texas delegations (46). Both Jim Curley and Joe Kennedy knew that convincing William Randolph Hearst, Garner's major backer, to release the California and Texas delegations would break the deadlock and give FDR the nomination. Both men went to Jim Farley's hotel suite and each called Hearst's home at San Simeon, but Hearst refused to take Curley's calls.

Although Curley's old foe John F. Fitzgerald was a delegate, it was Fitzgerald's son-in-law Joseph P. Kennedy, a native of East Boston, with whom Curley had to deal at this convention. Joe Kennedy was a different breed of Boston Irishman. He may have been a Harvard-educated "lace curtain Irishman" from "Eastie," but he was also immensely rich, having made fortunes in banking, movies, and Wall Street speculation.[90] Joe Kennedy understood early on that the wealthy Brahmins who guarded the city's wealth would not let an Irish Catholic interloper enter their ranks, even a Harvard-educated one. So Joe went to New York City where his financial acumen triumphed over ethnicity and religion. Kennedy brought money made on Wall Street to Hollywood and made yet another fortune.[91] While these were perceived to be legitimate sources of income, rumors also abounded that Joe had financial interests in the lucrative demi-monde of Prohibition-era bootlegging—a charge disproved by Daniel Okrent in *Last Call*.[92] Poor boys John McCormack and Jim Curley had never dealt with a fellow Boston Irish Catholic as rich as Joe Kennedy. While John McCormack was uninterested in the accumulation of wealth, Jim Curley craved money and was undoubtedly impressed and intimidated by Joe Kennedy's financial success.

To break the deadlock, Curley and Kennedy sought out Hearst and McAdoo, Smith's old rival and enemy. Garner had carried the California primary on May 3 and with 44 delegate votes, it was the largest non-southern state delegation supporting the Garner candidacy.[93] If it could be dislodged from Garner's presidential campaign, a convention deadlock could be avoided. Curley knew Garner. They had served together in the House, and Garner had recently rewarded John McCormack, a young friend of Curley's, with an assignment to the Ways and Means Committee.

Jack Beatty's account of the contact with Hearst has Jim Curley failing to get a call through to the publisher's San Simeon mansion, but Joe Kennedy succeeding.[94] It was to prevent a convention deadlock and the presidential nomination of Hearst's enemy Newton D. Baker. It was this fear that moved the powerful and jingoistic publisher to contact McAdoo, the chairman of the California delegation, to shift its votes from Garner to Roosevelt.

Hearst would take Joe Kennedy's calls.[95] Hearst, Kennedy, and FDR had all graduated Harvard College, and none had been tapped for membership in Porcellian, Harvard's most exclusive club. While Teddy Roosevelt and other Roosevelts including James Roosevelt, FDR's father, made Porcellian, FDR did not in spite of being president of the *Harvard Crimson*. Even into his late thirties, FDR considered that rejection as "the greatest disappointment in his life."[96] Joe Kennedy also felt that sting. Biographer Thomas Maier writes, "For years later, Joe Kennedy remembered the day he didn't make the Porcellian Club, the most desired in his mind, realizing that none of the Catholics he knew at Harvard had been selected."[97] Hearst the Westerner, Kennedy the Catholic, and FDR the "mama's boy" were apparently deemed unworthy. Joe Kennedy had another valuable link to Hearst. Both traveled within the Hollywood orbit. Kennedy had become a movie producer at RKO-Pathe and was romantically involved with the glamorous movie star Gloria Swanson much as Hearst's mistress Marion Davies was also a movie star.

The deal was cut. Senator McAdoo moved the California delegation to FDR and Texas swiftly followed, guaranteeing him the nomination. FDR immediately named Cactus Jack to be his running mate.[98] The entire Massachusetts delegation with U.S. Representative John McCormack among it and two-thirds of New York's remained loyal to Al Smith through the fourth and final ballot, but the game was over. Alabama's John McDuffie, the House Democratic whip—Jack Garner's best friend and a future John McCormack sponsor—placed Garner's name in nomination for vice president. It was pro forma. Jack Garner was named by acclamation to be FDR's running mate and giving one of the seconding speeches for Garner was none other than Jim Curley—"Jaime Miguel Curleo, the delegate from Porto Rico."[99]

In typical U.S. House fashion, it was Curley and Garner's shared membership on the Foreign Affairs Committee twenty years earlier which was the centerpiece of Curley's speech. So it was Mayor Jim Curley and not Governor Ely who emerged from the convention as a winner. There would be no deadlock this time and only Al Smith and his most diehard loyalists, including most of those in the Massachusetts delegation, would leave the convention empty handed.

The Roosevelt-Garner ticket had completed the convention's primary mission: the nomination of a ticket which would win in November. The relatively early resolution of this conflict prevented the Democrats seizing defeat from victory yet again and placed them close to capturing the White House for what would be the first of five consecutive presidential victories.

Both Joe Kennedy and Jim Curley were active in the 1932 presidential campaign. Kennedy contributed ample funds (reportedly $50,000) to the Roosevelt effort, while Curley mounted a cross-country effort on FDR's behalf, chronicled in a book-length account, *On the Trail of the Forgotten Man: A Journal of the Roosevelt Presidential Campaign.*[100]

FDR's first presidential victory

After being chosen as vice president, the ever cynical Jack Garner told Roosevelt, "All you have to do is stay alive until Election Day. The people are not going to vote for you. They are going to vote against the depression."

And vote they did. In the nation itself, the 1932 Democratic victory was the largest landslide for the party since Andrew Jackson's reelection over Henry Clay in 1832. Democrats gained complete control over the Senate with a 13-seat surge bringing their total to 60 Senators to 35 for the Republicans, a 90-seat gain in the House—310 Democrats to 117 Republicans, and a majority of the nation's governorships.[101]

Following the Hoover defeat in November, the 72nd Congress reconvened in Washington and completed its work on two amendments to the Constitution—the 20th Amendment, "the lame duck amendment,"[102] and the 21st Amendment, which repealed the 18th Amendment's prohibition of alcohol consumption. The 20th Amendment changed the opening date for Congress from March 4 to January 3 of the year following an election and the inauguration date for presidents from March 4 to January 20.

Repealing the 18th Amendment had been a long-standing commitment of Democratic politicians for most of the 1920s.[103] Massachusetts, which was the 11th state to ratify the 18th Amendment, was the 8th to repeal it, while Rhode Island, which never ratified Prohibition, was the 3rd state to repeal it. With its repeal, alcoholic beverages could once again be manufactured, sold, transported, and consumed by Americans. It was on President Franklin Roosevelt's watch that ratification was completed and the "noble experiment" was now over.

With FDR's resounding 42-state victory over President Hoover, both Joe Kennedy and Jim Curley anticipated Cabinet appointments—Secretary of the Treasury for Kennedy and Secretary of the Navy for Curley. Both were passed over as FDR selected Republican industrialist William H. Woodin for Treasury and U.S. Senator Claude A. Swanson of Virginia for Navy. Upon Woodin's death in 1934, Joe Kennedy was passed over again in favor of FDR's Dutchess County neighbor Henry Morgenthau Jr. However, the New Deal's 73rd Congress under the legislative leadership of Sam Rayburn, chair of the House Interstate and Foreign Commerce Committee, had passed the Securities Act in 1933 and the Securities Exchanges Act of 1934 that would create a new independent regulatory commission to regulate the Wall Street speculation that had been blamed for the stock market Crash. Named to the new Securities and Exchanges Commission was Joe Kennedy, who would be chosen as its first chair by its members.[104]

Jim Curley continued to wait. After objections were raised to his appointment as secretary of the navy,[105] Curley next sought to be named Ambassador to Italy. Curley felt that he had a friendship with Benito Mussolini and hoped that he would lunch frequently with the Pope and drive Cardinal O'Connell mad with jealousy. Curley suspected that O'Connell, his great rival for power in the city, may have derailed his appointment while other rumors circulated in Boston that First Lady Eleanor Roosevelt had found the Curley style distasteful. Curley described her attitude toward him as "curt and frosty, with no trace of her gracious charm."[106]

However, there was an open appointment as Ambassador to Poland, a nation unfortunately caught between Nazi Germany and Soviet Russia, but Curley turned that one down.[107] His logic was impeccable, and his grasp of world affairs was surprisingly prescient: "I told President Roosevelt that he should have chosen a Republican enemy if he wished to put anyone on the spot between two nations who were daggers drawn, in an unprotected country that would soon inevitably be crushed under the heels of the oppressor." Once again, Joe Kennedy, a Harvard-educated "lace curtain Boston Irishman," had trumped Jim Curley, a "shanty Boston Irishman."

Back in Boston, John McCormack fended off another challenge from a Jewish Republican in his district. This time it was Bernard Ginsburg who received 25,995 votes (27.1%) to John McCormack's 69,994 votes (72.9%).[108] John's new friend David K. Niles knew that John exhibited none of the anti-Semitic tendencies that often emerged from Boston's other Irish Catholic politicians. Thanks to Niles, Jewish opposition to John faded away. "After 1932," Gerald Gamm pointed out, "McCormack would not again be opposed by a Jewish Republican and he fared well in succeeding elections among Jews."[109] This would lead to John's close association with Jewish voters earning him the label "Rabbi John"—a title highly esteemed in Jewish Mattapan, but less so in Irish South Boston.

Greater history was soon to be made in the 73rd Congress, and John McCormack would be there and the "hundred days" would begin.

Notes

1 The 1928 election resulted in a net loss of twenty-eight seats in the U.S. House from 195 to 167 and of seven seats in the U.S. Senate from 46 to 39. "Political Party Affiliations in Congress and the Presidency, 1789–1974," *CQ's Guide to U.S. Elections* (1975 ed.), p. 928.

2 Gordon, *John McCormack and the Roosevelt Era*, pp. 71–73. The percentages may be found in *CQ's Guide to U.S. Elections* (1975 ed.), p. 762.

3 "Disputes Box View on 'Smith Forces,'" *NYT*, January 29, 1929, p. 23.

4 Nick Longworth's most prominent biographer was his sister, Clara Longworth de Chambrun, who wrote *The Making of Nicholas Longworth: Annals of an American Family*, rpt (Freeport, NY: Books for Libraries, 1971), originally published in 1933.

5 Accounts of the Roosevelt-Longworth marriage are plentiful; see Alice's own memoirs, *Crowded Hours: Reminiscences of Alice Roosevelt Longworth*, rpt (New York: Arno Press, 1980), originally published in 1933. A contemporaneous account appears in Francis Parkinson Keyes, *Capital Kaleidoscope: The Story of a Washington Hostess* (New York: Harper and Brothers, 1937).

6 William "Fishbait" Miller with Frances Spatz Leighton, *Fishbait* (Englewood Cliffs, NJ: Prentice-Hall, 1977), pp. 103–04.

7 Carol Felsenthal, "A Love Affair with Borah," in *Alice Roosevelt Longworth* (New York: G.P. Putnam's Sons, 1988), pp. 135–62.

8 Longworth's personal dilemma and its electoral consequence are recounted in Manners, *TR and Will*, p. 290. The 1912 totals: Democrat Stanley E. Bowdie, 22,330 (42.0%); Republican Nicholas Longworth, 22,229 (41.8%); Progressive Millard F. Andrew, 5,771 (10.9%); and Socialist Lawrence A. Zitt, 2,553 (5.4%)—from *Guide to U.S. Elections* (1975 ed.), p. 721.

9 Contemporaneous accounts of Longworth's style appeared in popular magazines and include William Hard, "Nicholas Longworth," *Nation*, XXIII (January 1924), pp. 88–89; "Nicholas Longworth: A Contradictory Floor Leader of the House," *Current Opinion*, LXXVI (April 1924), pp. 414–16; Duff Gilfond, "Mr. Speaker," *American Mercury*, XI (August 1927), pp. 451–58; William Taylor Page, "Mr. Speaker Longworth," *Scribner's*, LXXXIII (March 1928), pp. 272–80; "The Speaker of the House," *Review of Reviews*, LXXVII (March 1928), pp. 320–21; and *Collier's*, "The Gentleman at the Keyhole. 'Nicked!'" (October 1929), p. 44.

10 As quoted in Jordan A. Schwarz, *The Interregnum of Despair: Hoover, Congress and the Depression* (Urbana: University of Illinois Press, 1970), p. 58. See also "You Can't Help Liking Nick," *Literary Digest*, XXI (November 1925), pp. 44–48.

11 Author's interview with the manager of the Hotel Washington, April 1996.

12 When John McCormack returned to Washington after Harriet's death, he returned to the Hotel Washington, but he never returned to Suite 820.

13 Coolidge's plight is vividly presented in Robert E. Gilbert, *The Tormented President: Calvin Coolidge, Death, and Clinical Depression* (Westport, CT: Praeger, 2003).

14 This story is recounted in John P. Roche's syndicated column following Speaker McCormack's death, "John McCormack, One of a Kind," *Columbus (Ind.) Republic*, December 1, 1980.

15 Gordon makes this point in his recounting of McCormack's career in the Massachusetts State Senate, *John McCormack and the Roosevelt Era*.

16 *House Journal*, 70th Congress, 2nd Session, December 12, 1928, p. 45.

17 "Guinn Williams," *BDUSC* (1989 ed.), p. 2056.

18 See the map of the 70th Congress in Kenneth C. Martis, *The Historical Atlas of United States Congressional Districts, 1789–1983* (New York: The Free Press, 1982), pp. 160–61.

19 Varying accounts of Sam Rayburn's ill-fated marriage to Metze Jones may be found in two of Alfred Steinberg's books. An unfavorable view of Rayburn appears in Steinberg's *Sam Johnson's Boy: A Close-Up of the President from Texas* (New York: Macmillan, 1968), p. 70, while a more sympathetic version appears in his *Sam Rayburn: A Biography* (New York: Hawthorn Books, 1975), pp. 78–81. Steinberg's source for the unflattering story was U.S. Senator Tom Connally of Texas (*Sam Rayburn: A Biography*, p. 357). The best and fullest account of this oft-ignored aspect of Rayburn's personal life is in D. B. Hardeman and Donald C. Bacon, *Rayburn: A Biography* (Austin: Texas Monthly Press, 1987), pp. 121–33.

20 "John William Wright Patman," *BDUSC* (1989 ed.), p. 1616. Patman's early House career is covered in Nancy Beck Young, *Wright Patman: Populism, Liberalism, and the American Dream* (Dallas, TX: Southern Methodist University, 2000), pp. 29–48.

21 Author's telephonic interview with the Hon. John W. McCormack, April 1977.

22 "Joseph Weldon Bailey," *BDUSC* (1989 ed.), p. 563. See also Sam H. Acheson, *Joe Bailey: The Last Democrat* (New York: Macmillan, 1932); and "Bailey to Lead No More," *NYT*, March 4, 1899, p. 2.

23 Champagne et al., *The Austin-Boston Connection*, pp. 38–40.

24 House Interstate and Foreign Commerce Committee, *House Journal*, 63rd Congress, 1st Session, June 3, 1913, p. 171.

25 On Rayburn's role in the Garrett-Garner caucus contest for minority leader, see Steinberg, *Sam Rayburn*, p. 73. Steinberg cites Senator Tom Connally as his source, *My Name Is Tom Connally* (New York, 1954), p. 139.

26 Steinberg, *Sam Rayburn*, p. 84.

27 The quote is from Hardeman and Bacon, *Rayburn: A Biography*, p. 136. See also Anthony Champagne, "John Nance Garner," in Roger H. Davidson, Susan Webb Hammond, and Raymond W. Smock, eds., *Masters of the House: Congressional Leadership over Two Centuries* (Boulder, CO: Westview Press, 1998), pp. 156–58.

28 Anthony Champagne, "Cactus Jack Garner," in Davidson, Hammond, and Smock, eds., *Masters of the House*, pp. 145–80.

29 Bascom N. Timmons, *Garner of Texas: A Personal History* (New York: Harper & Bros., 1948), p. 111.

30 Agricultural Marketing Act, approved June 15, 1929 (Public Law 70–10; 46 *Statutes* 11–19).

31 Three of the four largest Dow Jones percentage losses occurred during those nine days—October 28, 1929 (12.82%); October 29, 1929 (11.73%); and November 6, 1929 (9.92%); see "Dow Jones Industrial Average All-Time Largest One Day Gains and Losses." *The Wall Street Journal*, retrieved December 11, 2012. Among the more readable accounts of the Crash are John Kenneth Galbraith, *The Great Crash, 1929* (Boston: Houghton Mifflin, 1954); and Maury Klein, *Rainbow's End: The Crash of 1929* (New York: Oxford University Press, 2001).

32 John McCormack as quoted in "America: Today and Yesterday," *U.S. News and World Report* (July 27, 1970), p. 58.

33 Arthur W. Macmahon, "American Government and Politics: Second Session of the Seventy-First Congress, December 2, 1929 to July 3, 1930; Special Session of the Senate, July 7–21," *APSR*, XXIV (November 1930), pp. 913–46. E. E. Schattschneider, *Politics, Pressures and the Tariff: A Study of Free Private Enterprise in Pressure Politics, as Shown in the 1929-1930 Revision of the Tariff* (New York: Prentice-Hall, 1935).

34 Smoot-Hawley Tariff Act, approved June 17, 1930 (46 Stat. 590–763). See also Senator Smoot's biography, Milton R. Merrill, *Reed Smoot: Apostle in Politics* (Logan: Utah State Press, 1990), p. 340.

35 "'1,028 Economists Ask Hoover to Veto Pending Tariff Bill': Professors in 179 Colleges and Other Leaders Assail Rise in Rates as Harmful to Country and Sure to Bring Reprisals," *NYT*, May 5, 1930.

36 The full speech may be found in the *Congressional Record*, 70th Congress, Second Session, February 14, 1929, pp. 3472–77.

37 Veterans' Administration Act, approved July 3, 1930 (46 Stat. 991–1002).

38 Roger Daniels, *The Bonus March: An Episode of the Great Depression* (Westport, CT: Greenwood, 1971).

39 Adoption of National Anthem, approved March 3, 1931 (46 Stat. 1508). See the session-ending overview by Arthur W. Macmahon, "American Government and Politics: 71st

Congress, Third Session, December 1, 1930 to March 4, 1931," *APSR*, XXV (November 1931), pp. 932–55.

40   William G. Whittaker, *Davis-Bacon: The Act and the Literature*, Congressional Research Service, Report 94–908 (2007).

41   Among them were U.S. Representatives Charles A. Mooney (Dem-Ohio); Matthew V. O'Malley (Dem-NY); Samuel C. Major (Dem-Mo.); George S. Graham (Rep-Pa.); Bird J. Vincent (Rep-Mich.); Fletcher Hale (Rep-NH); Charles G. Edwards (Dem-Ga.); Ernest R. Ackerman (Rep-NJ); Harry W. Wirzbach (Rep-Tex.); James B. Aswell (Dem-La.); and Speaker Nicholas Longworth (Rep-Ohio). *House Journal*, 72nd Congress, First Session, December 7, 1931, pp. 6–7.

42   Drew Pearson and Robert S. Allen, *Washington Merry-Go-Round* (New York: Horace Liveright, 1931), p. 231.

43   On the House Republican succession problems, see "Party Perplexity after Longworth," *Literary Digest* (April 25, 1931), p. 11; and A.F.C., "Backstage in Washington," *Outlook and Independent* (April 22, 1931), p. 555. See "Snell Beats Tilson in Speakership Race," *NYT*, December 1, 1931, pp. 1 and 4.

44   Reconstruction Finance Corporation Act, approved January 22, 1932, (47 Stat. 5–12). A legislative overview of this session is E. Pendleton Herring, "Seventy-Second Congress, First Session, December 7, 1931 to July 16, 1932," *APSR*, XXVI (October 1932), pp. 846–74.

45   Glass-Steagall Act, approved February 27, 1932 (47 Stat. 56–57).

46   "Stock Market Crash Heralds Great Depression, October 29, 1929," from the MassMoments website, accessed July 25, 2014. See Tom Juravich, William F. Hartford, and James H. Green, *Commonwealth of Toil: Chapters in the History of Massachusetts Workers and Their Unions* (Amherst: University of Massachusetts Press, 1996). See also Charles H. Trout, *Boston, the Great Depression, and the New Deal* (New York: Oxford University Press, 1977).

47   It cannot be found in the 1,000-plus photographs among the Curley Papers at Holy Cross in Worcester, but it is located in the Charles H. Innes Papers at the Boston Public Library. Boston Republican boss Charlie Innes knew this photo might come in handy someday.

48   Garrison Nelson, "'A Mania for Anonymity' The Mysterious Presidential Aide, David K. Niles of Boston," a paper for the Annual Meeting of the New England Political Science Association in Portsmouth, NH, April 2012. Niles is listed as "a member of Curley's 'brain trust' and later an administrative assistant to Presidents Roosevelt and Truman," in Alfred Steinberg's chapter on "James Michael Curley: The Joyous Plague of Boston," *The Bosses* (New York: Macmillan, 1972), p. 178.

49   As Curley stated in his autobiography, "Among my 'brain trusters' were Professor Robert Rogers of M.I.T., Lothrop Withington, Edward A. Filene, Dean Archer of Suffolk Law School, Dr. Carl T. Compton, president of M.I.T., and David Niles, later a presidential adviser and strategist of Washington, D.C." (*I'd Do It Again: A Record of All My Uproarious Years* (Englewood Cliffs, NJ: Prentice-Hall, 1957), pp. 276–77.

50   "The 1930 House Elections," *Guide to U.S. Elections* (1975 ed.), p. 767.

51   See N. T. N. Robinson, "Democrats Claim House on Eve of New Congress," *Congressional Digest*, X (December 1931), pp. 289–90. On Garner's selection as the majority's nominee for the speakership, see "House Democrats as One Pick Garner," *NYT*, December 6, 1931, p. 2; and on his election to the speakership itself, see

"Cheering Democrats Organize House Under Garner as 72d Congress Opens; Party Leaders Are Ready for Big Job," *NYT*, December 8, 1931, pp. 1 and 16. An early forecast of a Garner speakership may be found in Ray T. Tucker, "Tiger from Texas," *Outlook and Independent*, XXVI (November 1930), p. 492.

52 Garner elected as Speaker, "House Democrats as One Pick Garner," *NYT*, December 6, 1931, p. 2.

53 See Robert A. Waller, *Rainey of Illinois: A Political Biography, 1903–34* (Urbana: University of Illinois Press, 1977), pp. 161–62.

54 Author's telephonic interview with the Hon. John W. McCormack, Boston, April 1977.

55 On McDuffie's Scottish ancestry, see his entry in the *National Cyclopedia of American Biography*, L, pp. 28–29.

56 The story of O'Connor's mistress was recounted to me by Professor Anthony Champagne of the University of Texas-Dallas in conjunction with his interview of Washington columnist Robert S. Allen who coauthored the syndicated column "Washington Merry-Go-Round" with Drew Pearson. The Allen interview was conducted by Professor Champagne on June 13, 1980, in Washington, DC and is on file at the Sam Rayburn Library in Bonham, Texas.

57 "Garner, John Nance," in *National Cyclopedia of American Biography*, Vol. D, p. 10.

58 Early maneuverings in the caucus may be found in *NYT*, November 24, 1931, p. 4; and *NYT*, November 26, 1931, p. 20.

59 On McDuffie's version of the 1931 majority leadership fight, see Ralph Neal Brannen, *John McDuffie: State Legislator, Congressman, Federal Judge, 1883–1950* (PhD dissertation, Auburn University, 1975), pp. 166–69. See also "The Failed Effort John McDuffie of Alabama," in Champagne et al., *The Austin-Boston Connection*, pp. 73–88.

60 *House Journal*, 71st Congress, 2nd Session, December 12, 1929, pp. 70–71.

61 "House Civil Service Committee, 72nd Congress," in Canon, Nelson, and Stewart, *Committees in the U.S. Congress, 1789–1946*, 1:388 and "Robert C. Ramspeck," *BDUSC* (1989 ed.) p. 1689.

62 Author's interview with Speaker John W. McCormack, Washington, DC, September 1968.

63 "William Patrick Connery, Jr.," in *BDUSC* (1989 ed.), p. 818.

64 Gordon, *John McCormack and the Roosevelt Era*, p. 95.

65 *Boston Globe*, December 6, 1931, cited in ibid.

66 See "House Democrats As One Pick Garner," *NYT*, December 6, 1931, p. 2.

67 *House Journal*, 72nd Congress, 1st Session, December 7, 1931, p. 6. Chosen in the three slots above McCormack were eight-term Christopher D. Sullivan of New York (age 61); six-term Morgan G. Sanders of Texas (age 53); and four-term Edward E. Eslick of Tennessee (age 59). The three members chosen after McCormack had returned to Congress in 1931 after losing previous bids: ten-term Clement C. Dickinson of Missouri (age 82); four-term David J. Lewis of Maryland (age 62); and four-term Fred M. Vinson of Kentucky (age 41). Computed from Congressional Quarterly, *American Leaders: A Biographical Summary, 1789–1991* (Washington, DC: Congressional Quarterly, 1991).

68 On Fred Vinson's career in Congress, see William W. Oliver, "Vinson in Congress," *Northwestern Law Review*, XLIX (March/April 1954), pp. 62–75.

69 Author's interview with the Hon. John W. McCormack in the Speaker's Office, Washington, DC, September 1968.

70 The most storied of the House committees, Ways and Means has been examined by John F. Manley, *The Politics of Finance: The House Committee on Ways and Means* (Boston: Little, Brown & Co., 1970) and in an updated version by Randall Strahan, *The New Ways and Means: Reform and Change in a Congressional Committee* (Chapel Hill: University of North Carolina Press, 1990). Ralph Nader's Study of Congress Project prepared a report by Richard Spohn and Charles McCollum, dirs., *The Revenue Committees: A Study of the House Ways and Means and Senate Finance Committees and the House and Senate Appropriations Committees* (New York: Grossman Publishers, 1975).

71 Quoted in George B. Galloway, *Congress at the Crossroads* (New York: Thomas Y. Crowell, Co., 1946), p. 90. Following Ways and Means on Eberhart's list of committee prestige were 2. Appropriations; 3. Rules; 4. Interstate and Foreign Commerce; 5. Judiciary; 6. Agriculture; 7. Foreign Affairs; 8. Naval Affairs; 9. Banking and Currency; 10. Rivers and Harbors; 11. Military Affairs; 12. Post Offices and Post Roads; and 13. Merchant Marine and Fisheries.

72 See the list of Ways and Means distinguished alumni in Donald R. Kennon and Rebecca M. Rogers, *The Committee on Ways and Means: A Bicentennial History, 1789–1989* (Washington, DC: U.S. House of Representatives, 1989), p. 391.

73 Lengthy accounts of the 1909–10 revolt include Charles R. Atkinson, *The Committee on Rules and the Overthrow of Speaker Cannon* (New York: Columbia University Press, 1911); William Rea Gwinn, *Uncle Joe Cannon, Archfoe of Insurgency: A History of the Rise and Fall of Cannonism* (New York: Bookman Associates, 1957); and James Holt, *Congressional Insurgents and the Party System, 1909–1916* (Cambridge, MA: Harvard University Press, 1967), chapter 2.

74 A brief account of Garner's 1932 campaign for the Democratic nomination may be found in Eugene H. Roseboom's *A History of Presidential Elections: From George Washington to Richard Nixon*, 3rd ed. (New York: Macmillan, 1970), pp. 436–38. Garner ran in only two primaries, winning in California with the support of William Gibbs McAdoo and William Randolph Hearst, and losing in Nebraska; see James W. Davis, *Presidential Primaries: The Road to the White House* (New York: Thomas Y. Crowell, 1967), p. 280. Sam Rayburn was Garner's floor manager at the 1932 convention. See Alfred Steinberg, *Sam Rayburn* (New York: Hawthorn Books, 1975), p. 96.

75 "Foreign Affairs Committee, 62nd Congress, 1911–13," Garner, the 3rd ranking majority Democrat was in his 4th term on the committee while Curley, the 8th-ranking Democrat, was in his first term, Canon, Nelson, and Stewart, *House Standing Committees*, 1, pp. 568–69. Garner left Foreign Affairs for Ways and Means in 1913, while Curley left the committee after his first election as Mayor of Boston in 1914.

76 "Primary Returns, 1932," Congressional Quarterly, *Presidential Elections, 1789–1992* (Washington, DC: Congressional Quarterly Inc., 1993), pp. 160–61.

77 Richard C. Bain and Judith H. Parris, *Convention Decisions and Voting Records*, 2nd ed. (Washington, DC: The Brookings Institution, 1973), pp. 234–39.

78 "1932: The Twentieth Republican Convention," in Bain and Parris, eds., 2nd ed., *Voting Decisions and Convention Records*, pp. 234–38.

79 John H. Bartlett, *The Bonus March and the New Deal* (Chicago: M.A. Donaghue & Co., 1937); and Roger Daniels, *The Bonus March: An Episode of the Great Depression* (Westport, CT: Greenwood, 1971).

80 The relative presidential success of governors is listed in Paul T. David, Ralph M. Goldman, and Richard C. Bain, *The Politics of National Nominating Conventions* (Washington, DC: The Brookings Institution, 1960), pp. 156–58.

81 Ralph Martin recounts an interview with Jim Farley asking Louis Howe to "be nice to Kennedy because he was a wealthy potential backer" (*Ballots & Bandwagons*, p. 257). See the wonderful account, "1932 Democratic Convention," in Ralph G. Martin, *Ballots & Bandwagons* (Chicago: Rand, McNally, 1964), pp. 250–371.

82 "The Roosevelt Bandwagon" in Dinneen, *The Purple Shamrock*, pp. 178–86.

83 Jack Beatty, *The Rascal King: The Life and Times of James Michael Curley (1874–1958)* (Reading, MA: Addison-Wesley, 1992), pp. 295–308.

84 "1932 Primaries," in Congressional Quarterly's *Presidential Elections, 1789–1992* (Washington, DC: Congressional Quarterly Inc., 1995), pp. 160–61.

85 *Cleveland Plain Dealer*, April 29, 1932, noted in Beatty, *The Rascal King*, p. 308.

86 "Jaime Miguel Curleo," in Dinneen, *The Purple Shamrock*, pp. 187–97; and in Beatty's *The Rascal King*, pp. 312–15 and 322.

87 "The 1932 Democratic Convention," in Bain and Parris, 2nd ed., *Convention Decisions and Voting Records*, Appendix C.

88 Bain and Parris, *Convention Decisions and Voting Records*, 2nd ed.; 1912, pp. 184–92; 1920, pp. 208–14; and 1924, pp. 218–26.

89 Hearst's machinations are well presented in Steve Neal's vivid recounting, *Happy Days Are Here Again: The 1932 Democratic Convention, the Emergence of FDR—and How America Was Changed Forever* (New York: HarperCollins, 2004), pp. 58–64.

90 Joe Kennedy is treated more favorably in the books about the larger Kennedy family like Joseph F. Dinneen's *The Kennedy Family* (Boston: Little, Brown, 1959); Doris Kearns Goodwin's *The Fitzgeralds and the Kennedys*; and Thomas Maier's, *The Kennedys: America's Emerald Kings* (New York: Basic Books, 2003). However, the books on Joe Kennedy himself are generally less favorable; see Richard J. Whalen, *The Founding Father: The Story of Joseph P. Kennedy* (New York: New American Library, 1965); Ralph G. Martin, *Seeds of Destruction: Joe Kennedy and His Sons* (New York: G.P. Putnam's Sons, 1995); Ronald Kessler, *The Sins of the Father: Joseph P. Kennedy and the Dynasty He Founded* (New York: Warner Books, 1996); and Ted Schwarz, *Joseph P. Kennedy: The Mogul, the Mob, the Statesman, and the Making of an American Myth* (Hoboken, NJ: John Wiley & Sons, 2003). The most complete and balanced treatment of this complex man is David Nasaw's *The Patriarch: The Remarkable Life and Turbulent Times of Joseph P. Kennedy* (New York: Penguin, 2012).

91 The fullest account of the movie-making phase of Joe Kennedy's life may be found in Cari Beauchamp, *Joseph P. Kennedy Presents: The Hollywood Years* (New York: Alfred A. Knopf, 2009).

92 Daniel Okrent, *Last Call: The Rise and Fall of Prohibition* (New York: Scribner's, 2010), pp. 366–71.

93 On the California primary results, see *Presidential Elections, 1789–1992*, p. 160.

94 Beatty, *The Rascal King*, p. 315.

95 "The Man Who Called Hearst," in Richard J. Whalen's comprehensive *The Founding Father: The Story of Joseph P. Kennedy* (New York: New American Library, 1964), pp. 117–29.

96 As quoted by FDR to Sheffield Cowles in Frances Richardson Keller, *Fictions of U.S. History: A Theory & Four Illustrations* (Bloomington: Indiana University Press, 2002), p. 116.

97 Thomas Maier, *The Kennedys: America's Emerald Kings* (New York: Basic Books, 2004), p. 72.

98 On the naming of Garner as vice president, see the colorful rendition in Ralph G. Martin's entertaining chapter: "Democratic National Convention of 1932," *Ballots and Bandwagons* (Chicago: Rand McNally, 1964), esp. pp. 361–71.

99	*Proceedings of the 1932 Democratic National Convention*, p. 355. Curley was introduced as "the representative of Porto Rico, Mayor James M. Curley of Boston." Curley opened with "Mr. Chairman and fellow-delegates, in conformity with an old Spanish custom, as one of the 'forgotten men,' I was admitted as a delegate from the beautiful island of Porto Rico. It has been my very great pleasure as a member of the Congress of the United States to serve for four years as a member of the Committee on Foreign Affairs with that distinguished, brilliant, and able son of Texas, John N. Garner."

100	James H. Guilfoyle, *On the Trail of the Forgotten Man: A Journal of the Roosevelt Presidential Campaign* (Boston: Peabody Master Printers, 1933).

101	The 1932 congressional data may be found in John F. Bibby, "Political Parties," in Donald C. Bacon, Roger H. Davidson, and Morton Keller, eds., *The Encyclopedia of the American Congress* (New York: Simon & Schuster, 1995), p. 1557.

102	Twentieth Amendment (Lame Duck Amendment), approved March 2, 1932, and ratified by the requisite number of states, January 23, 1933 (47 Stat. 745).

103	The 21st Amendment, which repealed the 18th (Prohibition) Amendment to the Constitution, was approved February 20, 1933, and ratified by the requisite number of states, December 5, 1933 (47 Stat 1625).

104	Despite some serious second thoughts by FDR, Kennedy was pushed for the SEC job by Raymond Moley, a Columbia University professor and FDR's original "Brains Truster"; see Michael R. Beschloss, *Kennedy and Roosevelt: The Uneasy Alliance* (New York: W. W. Norton, 1980), pp. 85–95.

105	"Almost Secretary of the Navy," Dinneen, *The Purple Shamrock*, pp. 198–210.

106	Curley, *I'd Do It Again*, p. 249.

107	Ibid., pp. 251–52.

108	"The 1932 House Elections," *Guide to U.S. Elections* (1975 ed.), p. 772.

109	Gerald H. Gamm, *The Making of New Deal Democrats: Voting Behavior and Realignment in Boston, 1920–1940* (Chicago: University of Chicago Press, 1989), pp. 61–62.

7

The New Deal and a National Stage

Franklin Roosevelt's First Congress

One of the twentieth century's more intriguing ironies is the fact that Franklin D. Roosevelt's presidency and Adolph Hitler's Third Reich existed conterminously. Hitler was named Chancellor of Germany on January 30, 1933, only 33 days before Roosevelt was inaugurated for his first term, and Hitler committed suicide on April 30, 1945, eighteen days after a cerebral hemorrhage ended FDR's life.

While both the United States and Germany experienced financial catastrophe and massive popular unrest, the United States chose to maintain its system of democratically electing government leaders while Germany succumbed to the authoritarian impulses of fascist dictatorship. The United States was not immune from those authoritarian impulses, and John McCormack was the person that Congress chose to expose these impulses and counter them with legislation. This was just one of the major tasks that McCormack was asked to undertake. By the end of the 1930s John McCormack had emerged from the backbenches of the House to the post of Majority Floor Leader, the House's second-ranking leadership post.

When Jack Garner left the House to become vice president, the speakership opened up once again. The 1933 contest would be a replay of the 1931 battle between Majority Leader Henry T. Rainey of Illinois and Garner's best friend, Democratic Whip John McDuffie of Alabama.[1] McDuffie was the second-highest ranking Democrat on the Rivers and Harbors Committee. This was the House committee that approved many of the government's largest spending projects and led to many friendships.[2]

McDuffie was also a key member of Garner's private drinking club in the Capitol. Originally called the "bureau of education," McDuffie's biographer Ralph Brannen credited him with renaming it "the board of education." It was where House members flaunted Prohibition and would "strike a blow for liberty" by drinking bourbon whiskey. Along with McDuffie and Sam Rayburn were James W. Collier of Mississippi, Charles A. Crisp of Georgia, Joseph W. Byrns of Tennessee, Lindsay C. Warren of North Carolina, Jacob L. Milligan of Missouri, Clifton A. Woodrum of Virginia, Anning S. Prall of New York, and Will Bankhead of Alabama.[3] While fellow 'board" members Byrns, Bankhead, and Rayburn would follow Garner as Speaker, Henry Rainey, Cactus Jack's immediate successor, was not included in the club.

Rainey would not need the "board" in his 1931 leadership battle or in his 1933 speakership bid, for he was able to count on the hardy band of Champ Clark loyalists and Democrats grateful for their Ways and Means–provided committee assignments to tilt elections in his favor.

After electing Rainey as Speaker, the House announced the election of its Ways and Means Committee. John McCormack was the seventh House member named that day.[4] Since 1911, Democratic members of Ways and Means were named first, so McCormack was in a position to shape the careers of the 100-plus incoming freshmen Democrats. The Ways and Means Committee that fused both policy impact and political influence for its Democratic members required an informal division of labor within its ranks.

As a non-homeowner, John McCormack was not a close student of the Revenue Code nor was he as attuned as others to the role that tax legislation plays in shaping the national economy. He was much more involved in the political mission of the committee: sizing up the new members and determining which committee assignments for them would best further the party's legislative agenda and their own personal ambitions. John McCormack would be the leadership's talent scout.

Jack Garner did not particularly enjoy his new role presiding over the stately Senate. He couldn't vote unless there was a tie, and the large Democratic majorities made those votes unnecessary. He couldn't prowl the floor pointing his cigar at the various Republican miscreants whom he happily bedeviled in the House. His reference to the office of the vice presidency as not worth more "than a pitcher of warm piss"[5] often gets cleaned up as "warm spit."

John McCormack and the South

John McCormack was already sympathetic to southerners. He firmly believed that "you needed the southerners if you were to succeed."[6] He was one of the few northern Democrats to support McDuffie in the 1931 and 1933 caucuses. When Garner departed, McCormack cast his votes for McDuffie of Alabama to be Speaker and for Bankhead of Alabama to be Majority Leader. The congressional southerners knew how to count the votes and they were well aware of who voted for them and who did not. The informal Garner ticket of McDuffie and Bankhead lost to the rival informal ticket of Henry Rainey of Illinois and Joseph W. Byrns of Tennessee. McCormack had supported Garner's men in both votes. The southerners had elected him to Ways and Means, and John loyally voted for Garner's associates and would continue to do so throughout the 1930s.

John was a pleasant anomaly to southerners who expected a hard-drinking, in-your-face Boston Irishman like Big Jim Gallivan. McCormack's courtliness, his sobriety, his religiosity, and his devotion to his wife were virtues that they had not expected to encounter in their stereotypical view of Boston Irishmen. After all, many of these members had served with Jim Gallivan and had been at Appropriations Committee hearings or on the House floor where Big Jim had often failed to appear. McCormack's dissimilarity from Gallivan got him a much fuller hearing from the southern hierarchy that ran the House than most other junior northerners received. As a Scots-Irishman, he was one of them, although he dared not admit it lest news of his altered ethnicity find its way back to South Boston and terminate his promising career.

A leading sponsor, John McDuffie of Alabama

As early as November 17, 1932, 40-year-old John McCormack was the subject of leadership speculation. John McDuffie, Jack Garner's chief lieutenant and Democratic whip, 1927–33, under both Speakers Garner and Rainey, wrote about McCormack to Eugene E. "Goober" Cox of Georgia[7]:

> The President is from the North and the Vice President, of course, comes from Texas, the far Southwest. My idea would be to have Mr. Rainey remain Chairman of the Ways and Means Committee and if possible, Floor Leader. It has occurred to me that it is also might be well to make John McCormack, by Caucus Resolution, Assistant Leader, then the Speakership to go to the South, without so much murmuring.

Rainey's 1933 election as Speaker prevented the selection of John McCormack as assistant leader, but John McDuffie was persistent and he would continue to champion McCormack's elevation to House leadership until his own appointment to the federal bench in 1935. McDuffie was from Alabama's south coastal city of Mobile, close to but not a part of Alabama's "black belt." He had a reputation for helping blacks unlike most, but not all, of Alabama's white Democrats. He was especially supportive of Arthur Wergs Mitchell, the son of slaves who was born in Lafayette, Alabama, along the state's eastern border with Georgia.[8]

Thanks to McDuffie's support, Mitchell and his wife were able to gain government employment when they moved from segregated Alabama to segregated Washington, DC. Mitchell, who had studied fitfully under Booker T. Washington at the Tuskegee Institute and picked up summer university courses at Columbia and Harvard, had acquired enough academic cachet to be seen as a credible challenger to Illinois Republican Oscar de Priest. De Priest was the first African American elected to Congress in the twentieth century, albeit the 23rd black Republican elected to Congress since the close of the Civil War. Moving to Chicago in 1931 and initially registered as a Republican, Mitchell sensed the shift in the national mood and with further encouragement from McDuffie and Postmaster General Jim Farley,[9] he ran as a Democrat in 1934 against de Priest, defeating him easily and becoming the Democratic Party's first ever African-American member of Congress.

Arthur Mitchell's only House committee assignment was Post Offices and Post Roads, a committee low in prestige but one that had sufficient "pork" to dole out and endear yourself both to constituents and colleagues. As one of the committee assigners on Ways and Means, John McCormack was well aware of Mitchell, and there is at least one written communication between the two men.[10]

McCormack was pleased to learn that John McDuffie helped a black junior House member. Having grown up in hierarchically defined Boston, a city painfully divided by religious, racial, ethnic, and social class prejudice where anti-immigrant, anti-Catholic, anti-Semitic, and racist sentiments were part of the city's daily discourse, John would have been greatly impressed by a powerful Deep South congressman making extraordinary efforts to help a black man. John abhorred bigotry and bigots. As he declared in a 1962 interview with *TIME* magazine[11]:

> A man's social origin means nothing to me; a person's name means nothing to me. A person's religion I respect. But what does mean everything to me is a person's mind. And when I meet a person with a bigoted mind, I am meeting a person I do not like, a person I have nothing but contempt for.

John McDuffie was a man John McCormack liked and trusted, and McDuffie regularly reminded fellow House members of John's suitability for chamber leadership.

Congress convenes and an early rival

The 20th Amendment made the 73rd Congress the last to be sworn on March 4, but rather than opening its 1st Session in December as in previous years President Roosevelt reconvened Congress on March 9 and within four hours the Emergency Banking Act was enacted. The nation's economic crisis was too severe to adhere to the traditional opening date of Congress.

John McCormack believed that FDR's New Deal had the potential to rid America of the horrendous specter of poverty, disease, and early death that had so dramatically decimated his own family back in South Boston.[12] He was delighted when he and four other House members were invited to the White House by FDR eighteen days after his March 4th inauguration. It was undoubtedly a happier meeting than John's initial White House visit with President Coolidge five years earlier.

Realizing that it was in America's urban places that the greatest expenditure of federal money would have to be allocated if recovery were to occur, FDR met with five members from Illinois, Massachusetts, and New York: third-termer Claude V. Parsons of Illinois newly named to the patronage-heavy Rivers and Harbors Committee; fourth-termer John McCormack, now 7th ranked on Ways and Means; sixth-termer John J. O'Connor of New York, now 3rd ranked on the Rules Committee; eighth-termer Tom Cullen of New York, now 4th ranked on Ways and Means; and fourteenth-termer Adolph J. Sabath of Illinois, now 4th ranked on Rules. Standing between McCormack and O'Connor was House Clerk H. V. Hesselman (Figure 7.1). While both McCormack and O'Connor were Massachusetts natives and Roman Catholics, they took an early dislike to one another. Tom Cullen shared McCormack's disdain for the arrogant and ambitious O'Connor and would unite with McCormack to scuttle O'Connor's frequent reaches for power in the House.

Later that year, John McCormack would have his first negative encounter with John J. O'Connor from New York City, Tammany Hall's man in the House. Born in Raynham, Massachusetts, a small town south of Boston, O'Connor graduated from Brown and Harvard Law and moved to New York upon graduation. A few years later, O'Connor's younger brother, Basil, a graduate of Dartmouth and Harvard Law, would follow him to New York. During the 1920s, Basil would become a law partner of

Figure 7.1 Newly inaugurated President Franklin D. Roosevelt meets with Democratic U.S. Representatives, from left, Claude Parsons of Illinois, John W. McCormack of Massachusetts, Committee Clerk H.V. Hesselman, John J. O'Connor of New York. Thomas H. Cullen of New York, and Adolph J. Sabath of Illinois, March 22, 1933 (Gotlieb Archival Research Center, Boston University).

Franklin Roosevelt during his political hiatus and would remain a close legal associate of FDR's until Roosevelt's death in 1945.

In 1923, O'Connor was elected to fill the vacancy of Tammany's greatest orator, W. Bourke Cockran, a native of Ireland's western County Sligo.[13] Cockran served seven nonconsecutive terms in the House and was especially close to Britain's Churchill family and was reputed to be one of Jennie Churchill's lovers. Jennie's son Winston considered Cockran to be his first political mentor and emulated his oratorical style. Cockran's were big shoes to fill, but John O'Connor had little doubt that he could fill them.

O'Connor's outsized ambitions first led him to contest the floor leadership of the House Democrats in December 1931, in spite of having served for only eight years. He withdrew from that contest but readied himself for the next one by attempting to line up northern urban votes. O'Connor tried to solicit the support of Mayor Frank Hague of Jersey City, who said he would not get involved until he knew "what the attitude of the President Elect is going to be, because after all he is the boss of the party and if I am to call myself an organization democrat I shall be expected to obey orders."[14] O'Connor also reached out to Jim Curley, an old Garner ally, and asked for help in getting the support of John McCormack. Curley offered to speak to McCormack and, in another letter, offered to meet with O'Connor and "to do anything I can in your behalf." However, a telephone memorandum in O'Connor's office reported that "Mayor Curley of Boston called Saturday afternoon, and asked that I tell you that he has seen Congressman McCormack upon two different occasions and he cannot be swayed from his support of Congressman McDuffie."[15] Under ordinary circumstances, John McCormack might have burned his bridges with the mercurial mayor, but to Jim Curley who had been the electoral beneficiary of John Fitzgerald's romantic peccadilloes, McCormack's knowledge of O'Connor's marital infidelities was explanation enough.

The 100 days

Backed by a House that opened with 311 Democrats and a Senate with 59, FDR had ample voting margins to pass his New Deal legislation. Before the first week was over, on March 9, 1933, Congress passed the Emergency Banking Relief Act in an effort to stop depositors from their stampeding run on banks. FDR declared a "bank holiday" and urged the passage of legislation requiring the licensing of Federal Reserve banks by the Treasury Department and denying operational rights to unlicensed ones.[16] A day later, the Economy Act was submitted to Congress, reducing federal employee salaries and cutting veterans benefits.[17] Although opposed by liberal Democrats, the bill passed each chamber and became law on March 20.

While awaiting the states to ratify the 21st Amendment repealing Prohibition, Congress passed the Beer-Wine Revenue Act legalizing wine, beer, lager beer, ale, and porter of 3.2% maximum alcoholic content by weight, or 4% by volume, and levied a tax of $5.00 per barrel of 31 gallons.[18] The states were given all regulatory and control measures, especially those relating to the sale and distribution of alcohol. It was approved March 22, 1933, barely eighteen days into FDR's first Congress.

Altogether, fifteen bills rocketed through Congress as FDR's New Deal left its indelible stamp on American political and economic life. The Civilian Conservation Corps (CCC), the Agricultural Adjustment Act (AAA),[19] the Federal Emergency Relief Act (FERA), Tennessee Valley Authority Act (TVA),[20] Federal Securities Act,[21] Gold Standard Repeal,[22] National Employment System Act, Home Owners' Loan Act,[23] Banking Act (Glass-Steagall Act),[24] National Industrial Recovery Act (NIRA),[25] Emergency Railroad Transportation Act,[26] and the Farm Credit Act of 1933 all became law by June 16, 1933.[27] Ultimately, the conservative-dominated Supreme Court would declare all or parts of four of these acts unconstitutional—the Economy Act in 1934, the NIRA, the Gold Standard Repeal in 1935, and AAA in 1936.[28]

On June 16, 1933, the closing day of the 1st Session of an exhausted 73rd Congress, the final act of the "100 days" was approved when President Roosevelt signed the Federal Credit Act of 1933 that consolidated the functions of all Federal units dealing with agricultural credit under the Farm Credit Administration.[29] Congress then adjourned for the remainder of the year. It was now the middle of June and summer was about to begin its annual heated assault on the non-air-conditioned Capitol. It was also the time for the members to return home and assess the voters' views of the legislative whirlwind that they had unleashed.

Most voters were already pleased with public officials as the repeal of the 12-year catastrophic reign of Prohibition decreed in the 18th Amendment went sailing through state ratifying conventions on a near record clip, reaching the magic number of 36 on December 5, 1933, less than ten months after it was originally submitted by Congress to the states. It certainly gave FDR's campaign song of "Happy Days Are Here Again" its extra lilt.

John McCormack had voted for every major piece of the president's legislative agenda and he returned to Boston as a "certified New Dealer."

A mysterious Boston ally: David K. Niles and FERA

Most immediately impacting urban unemployment was the Federal Emergency Relief Administration (FERA). Built upon an earlier and far more modest program of the Hoover Administration, FERA supplied low-skill jobs for the unemployed rather than handouts. Named to head the national FERA program was Harry Hopkins, an Iowa-born social worker from New York City, whom FDR had gotten to know during his time as New York's governor. Hopkins coordinated "priorities, production, political problems with allies, strategy—in short, with anything that might concern the president."[30] Named to run the Boston office was David K. Niles.[31] Niles was named to keep Jim Curley's greedy hands off the incoming federal funds.

Like his good friend John McCormack, Niles reinvented himself. He was born David Kohn Neyhus, the oldest son of Asher Neyhus, a tailor, and his wife Sophie Berlin in Beltrementz, a Polish port of Russia.[32] To escape Tsarist pogroms, the family left Russia and moved originally to Boston's North End, once the political domain of John Fitzgerald, and then to Roxbury, Jim Curley's turf. David took the birth date of his next oldest brother who had been born in Boston.[33] He attended but did not graduate from Boston's prestigious Latin School, then the major feeder to Harvard College. He dropped the Neyhus name a few years after he left Boston Latin, and he took on the surname of a WASP classmate, Nathaniel Niles who would win national championships in tennis and figure skating.[34]

One of his classmates was well aware of his reinvention and knew him both as David Neyhus and as David Niles. That person was Joseph P. Kennedy of the Boston Latin class of 1908 and the Harvard class of 1912. Niles may have left Latin without graduating, but he had met the entrance requirements for admission to Harvard. Archival records at Latin indicate that Kennedy and Neyhus were both enrolled in the early 1900s when the total number of students in all six years was 597.[35] According to Niles's FBI files, "in 1920 Niles entered the Motion Picture Industry as a protégé of Joseph P. Kennedy, who later became Ambassador to London under the Roosevelt Administration."[36] None of the Joe Kennedy biographies mention this relationship, and it is listed as "Unverified Information" in the FBI file.

Niles was very active in the 1924 Progressive Party campaign of U.S. Senators Robert La Follette of Wisconsin and Massachusetts-born Burton K. Wheeler of Montana. It was during that campaign that Niles made the acquaintance of Harold Ickes and Henry A. Wallace, FDR's future secretaries of the interior and agriculture respectively.[37] In 1928, he handled publicity for the Independents for Smith campaign. Niles was no stranger to national politics or national politicians.

Niles became a member of Jim Curley's third term "brain trust."[38] As the Boston head of FERA, Niles and fourth-term Congressman John McCormack began their 20-year relationship. The Niles Papers at the Harry S. Truman Library in Independence, Missouri, contain close to fifty separate relief requests made by Congressman McCormack to Director Niles, far and away the largest number of any of the state's House members.

Boston and the New Deal, Jim Curley's next moves

Jim Curley knew there would be no job in FDR's administration and statutorily prohibited from succeeding himself as mayor in 1933, he readied himself to run for governor in 1934. With incumbent Democratic Governor Joe Ely increasingly out of step with the pronounced liberalism of the Roosevelt Administration, he chose not to run. The open Democratic nomination for governor was won by Curley, and he went on to defeat Republican Gaspar G. Bacon in the general election with third-party candidate Frank A. Goodwin of the Equal Tax Party receiving the remainder of the vote. Boston legend is that Curley and Ely had a fist fight on the day of their transition, and it was reported that "both men were somewhat disheveled when the door was opened."[39]

But Curley's eyes were still on Washington, and he planned to use his governorship as a springboard to the U.S. Senate seat that would open up with the impending retirement of Democrat "silent" Marcus A. Coolidge. In 1936, Ely would join with Al Smith as former Democratic celebrities in the ultraconservative anti-FDR American Liberty League and campaign actively for the Republican nominee, Kansas Governor Alf Landon.[40]

As governor of Massachusetts, Curley continued to make life difficult for the federal bureaucrats. FDR's huge Works Progress Administration (WPA) tried to keep rapacious local politicians from grabbing federal monies to use as political patronage. Keeping Jim Curley away from this pile of federal money was no easy task. WPA's national director Harry Hopkins appointed Arthur Rotch to be the Massachusetts WPA administrator who quickly ran afoul of Governor Curley. Curley's persistence took its toll, and Rotch, who had come to believe that John McCormack would provide a counterweight to Curley, was visited by a WPA field representative who "told him to 'play ball' or resign."[41] Rotch resigned. Hopkins, unhappy with the Massachusetts situation, told Rotch's successor Paul Edwards to "take some bullet-proof vests along."

A Promise Fulfilled: Old Harbor Village: New Deal money was slow in coming to Boston. Most of the smaller funds for make-work projects from FERA were accepted and managed by David K. Niles with multiple requests coming from Congressman John McCormack. However, the larger multimillion dollar projects promoted by the Public Works Administration (PWA), run by Secretary of the Interior Harold Ickes, met major resistance from the fiscally conservative Governor Ely.[42] Part of the resistance was due to the funding ratio that required the state to cover 70% of the costs, but most resistance emanated from the anti-FDR sentiments of Joe Ely.

The 1934 election dramatically changed the political landscape. Jim Curley, then pro-FDR, was now governor of Massachusetts. Succeeding Curley as Boston's mayor was his antagonist, the Boston University–educated Catholic Democrat Fred Mansfield, but it was governors who had the larger say in the acquisition of federal funds. Curley's two pro-FDR allies had increased their influence. Now in his fifth House term, John McCormack had moved to a senior slot on the Ways and Means Committee and was being touted for House leadership, while David K. Niles had moved to Washington as deputy director under Harry Hopkins at the WPA.

John McCormack's childhood was spent in the squalid crowded tenements where disease and early death were constant companions, so housing that was clean, well-built, and affordable was his highest priority. When the PWA changed its funding ratio from a 70% state match to a 55% one, it was now possible for a multimillion dollar housing project to come to Boston. Jim Curley jumped at the opportunity and with the project to be built by Jim's favorite contractor, there was little doubt that New England's first federally funded housing project would be built in John's South Boston district.[43]

For many years, the project was the largest in New England, ultimately comprising 1,018 units. It would be called Old Harbor Village.[44] Started in 1936[45] and completed in 1938, its building and amenities were well described as uniquely family-friendly.[46]

On September 11, 1938, John McCormack spoke before a crowd of 10,000 to announce that Old Harbor Village was now open for occupancy. It was a very emotional moment for John since Old Harbor Village was barely five minutes away from the drafty and poorly built tenement at 47 Vinton Street where 24-year-old Patrick, his oldest brother, had died of tuberculosis in 1911 and his sainted mother Mary Ellen died two years later at the age of 52. On May 22, 1961, 23 years later, Old Harbor Village would be renamed the Mary Ellen McCormack Housing Project in honor of John's beloved mother.[47] John wept openly. Like Social Security before it, this project was yet another of the promises that John kept to the memory of his family and his South Boston neighbors.

However, Old Harbor Village was not the hoped-for salvation for Southie's poorest citizens. Its tenants were generally married couples with children and most were gainfully employed. Later South Boston projects like Old Colony and the D Street Project would be built to house the very poorest. Sadly, the Mary Ellen McCormack Housing Project was not racially integrated until 1988,[48] almost a quarter century after John had presided over the U.S. House when it passed the antidiscriminatory Civil Rights Act of 1964 and the Voting Rights Act of 1965. For a man who abhorred bigotry but loved his neighbors, one can only imagine the emotional wounds that these circumstances caused John.

Rabbi John, Mattapan, and Anti-Semitism: John McCormack's congressional district encompassed large neighborhoods of Boston's immigrants, not just the Irish of South Boston. Other ethnic groups populated the 12th District—Lithuanians in South Boston and the Jews in the Mattapan neighborhood of Dorchester. Before "white flight" took place in the 1960s, Mattapan was the largest Jewish enclave in the city.[49] Among some of the better-known natives of Mattapan were presidential chronicler Theodore H. White and jazz aficionado and columnist Nat Hentoff. John McCormack was sensitive to the Irish-Jewish tensions within his district and did what he could to ameliorate them. John was the first South Boston congressman to sponsor a young Jewish boy, Irving Mintz, for admission to West Point.[50]

Representing Jewish voters in Mattapan, many of whom had relatives in Germany, McCormack soon learned of anti-Semitic initiatives launched by the new Nazi government. In June 1933, less than five months after Hitler gained control of Germany, John went to the House floor and became the first New England Democrat to denounce the early signs of anti-Semitism in the Third Reich[51]:

> Mr. Speaker, I have watched with increasing anxiety developments in Germany since Adolf Hitler assumed controlling power. The time has come when I may no longer refrain from expressing my condemnation of the policy being pursued by the present German Government, particularly as it applies to a ruthless agonizing of the Jews.
>
> Christianity cannot ignore the debt she owes to Judaism. The tenets of toleration for all, peace among all, were sounded by the prophets of Israel long before Christ was born. These same principles of liberty, freedom and peace form the very bedrock of the Republic of the United States. Believing in them as I do, fighting for them as I always have and always will, the attempt of the Hitler regime to destroy them strikes a note of fear and repugnance with me.
>
> . . .
>
> I fervently trust that the efforts being made to bring an end to crime now perpetrated against the Jewish people in Germany will bear such successful fruition that racial persecution will forever be a thing of an unhappy past.

Although John defeated two Jewish Republicans—Samuel Abrams in 1930 and Bernard Ginsburg in 1932—he did not carry the Jewish vote in the ward.[52] It was John's early and courageous stand against the Nazis in 1933 that dissolved Jewish opposition to his subsequent reelection bids after 1934.[53]

The Second Session, 1934: In the days before air conditioning made tolerable the intense heat and sweltering humidity of Washington, Congress would often adjourn its first session in June and return later in December to conclude its legislative business in the second session. Often the second session convened after a November election had occurred ending the congressional careers of many members who were known as "lame ducks." Because the Constitution requires that presidential and vice presidential nominees have clear electoral vote majorities to be elected, it is Congress that determines the winners in cases where no majority exists. In accord with the 12th Amendment, the House, with each state having only one vote, chooses the president from among the top three contenders while the Senate chooses the vice president among the top two contenders. In two cases, it was "lame duck" members of the U.S. House who decided the winners of presidential elections in 1801 for Thomas Jefferson and in 1825 for John Quincy Adams. Lame-duck members of the Senate in 1837 decided that Democrat Richard M. Johnson was the vice presidential winner with Martin Van Buren. A large consensus emerged that it be the incoming Congress, not the outgoing one that should be entrusted with those fateful decisions.

It took less than eleven months from March 2, 1932, to January 23, 1933, to pass the 20th Amendment. Known as the "lame duck amendment," it changed the opening day of Congress to January 3rd and moved the date of quadrennial presidential inaugurations from March 4 to January 20. The 73rd Congress was the first impacted by the 20th Amendment, and its official conclusion was January 3, 1935. Thus, the nation's most productive Congress was also its shortest.

Congress returned to work on January 3, 1934. Six months had passed since "the hundred days" and slates of administrators were hired and bureaucracies put in place. But the agenda was still incomplete. In the months following the adjournment, FDR's men had put together another set of proposals and hoped that Congress would be as willing to pass them as they had been in the first session.[54] The first major legislative initiative of this session was the Gold Reserve Act of 1934, authorizing the president to set limits for devaluation of the dollar from 50 to 60 cents in relation to its gold content; to change the value within these limits from time to time, as deemed necessary by him; to impound in the Treasury the gold stocks held by the Federal Reserve banks; to assure to the government any profit that might accrue to the Treasury from an increase in the value of gold; and to use part of this profit to set up a fund (the Exchange Stabilization Fund) of $2 billion with which to stabilize the dollar.[55] The wealthiest Americans were horrified and declared FDR to be "a traitor to his class."[56]

Harbingers of hate

Throughout Europe, authoritarian parties emerged. Communist parties buoyed by the takeover of Russia became eager to redesign the European social structure in the wake of the collapse of the prewar aristocracy. These parties were countered by fascist parties whose nationalist impulses were fueled by the collapse of the Austro-Hungarian Empire and the redrawing of national lines along ethnic configurations.

The United States was not immune. Apprehension gripped its citizenry and fear-based political movements were not uncommon and some played a key role in national life. The anti-Masonic party of the 1830s that feared secret societies was the first political party to hold a national nominating convention.[57] The highly successful Know-Nothings of the 1850s had even elected a Speaker of the House in 1855, Nathaniel P. Banks of Massachusetts.[58] Also, the initial emergence of the Ku Klux Klan in the years following the Civil War shaped southern politics greatly during that period of social discontent and economic disarray.

The newer twentieth-century Klan also had a major political impact. The revival of the Ku Klux Klan in the years following World War I extended its reach beyond the South and broadened its targets to include Catholics and Jews, two religious groups whose numbers had been expanded by huge waves of non–Protestant European immigrants from Central and Eastern Europe in the decades before World War I.[59] The continuing economic dislocations of the Depression led to the increased fomenting of anti-Catholic and anti-Semitic sentiments. These newer Americans were now at risk.

The Special House Committee on Un-American Activities

The House member troubled most by anti-Semitism was Samuel Dickstein of New York, who feared that newly arrived Jews would be denoted as "communists." Dickstein was born in Vilna in Lithuania and had come to the United States with his parents in 1887 at the age of two. Educated at the College of the City of New York and the New York City Law School, Dickstein served primarily in appointive and minor elective posts until his electoral victory in 1922 over U.S. House Representative Socialist Meyer London.[60] As a House member, Dickstein's primary service was on the Immigration and Naturalization Committee which he chaired for seven Congresses (1931–45).

Dickstein pushed hard for the creation of a special committee to investigate Nazi activities in the United States and House Resolution 198 creating the committee was adopted on March 20, 1934. Its text was conventional[61]:

> *Resolved*, That the Speaker of the House of Representatives be, and he is hereby, authorized to appoint a special committee to be composed of seven Members for the purpose of conducting an investigation of (1) the extent, character, and objects of Nazi propaganda activities in the United States, (2) the diffusion within the United States of subversive propaganda that is instigated from foreign countries and attacks the principle of the form of government as guaranteed by our Constitution, and (3) all other questions in relation thereto that would aid Congress in any necessary remedial legislation.

Under conventional congressional practice, the member who successfully convinced the chamber to create a special or select committee was offered the chairmanship of it. On March 30, Speaker Rainey offered the chairmanship to Sam Dickstein. But since he already chaired a standing committee, Dickstein demurred and Rainey named John McCormack as the committee's chair with Sam Dickstein serving as vice chair.[62] McCormack was perceived as a comer in House circles and he had a sizable Jewish constituency within his Boston district. John's wholehearted embrace of the New Deal made him a leading FDR supporter in the House and gained him further positive attention from the House's Democratic hierarchs. John's early anti-Nazi stance and his growing stature on the House Ways and Means Committee made him an acceptable choice.[63] He was joined by Dickstein along with five others: freshmen Democrats

Carl M. Weideman of Michigan and Charles Kramer of California; and Republicans Thomas A. Jenkins of Ohio, its ranking minority member J. Will Taylor of Tennessee, and U.S. Guyer of Kansas[64] (Figure 7.2). Weideman, Kramer, and Taylor were fellow members of Dickstein's Immigration and Naturalizat ion Committee while Jenkins had served on it in the previous Congress.

John McCormack was in his third full term in the House and he had vivid memories of how Roman Catholics had been denounced as "un-American" as recently as the 1928 Hoover-Smith presidential election. He was particularly sensitive to issues focused on the nation's newest immigrants. Across both the Atlantic and Pacific oceans, antidemocratic impulses had seized much of the global agenda. Europe was awash in totalitarian politics. Russia was the first European nation to move in this direction; the 1917 collapse of Czarist Russia and the emergence of the Communist Party in control of the largest landmass on earth led to deep fears among conservatives on the Continent. Many Europeans were willing to put aside their hesitancy about antidemocratic movements and sought the protection of rightist authoritarian parties. Italy's Fascist party leader Benito Mussolini was the first beneficiary of this newfound acceptance of rightist authoritarianism after he was called to form a Cabinet following his "March on Rome" in October 1922. The strutting and sometimes buffoonish Mussolini seemed more comic than tragic. But to the north, a more serious threat to

Figure 7.2 McCormack-Dickstein House Select Committee to investigate Nazi Propaganda 1934, Samuel Dickstein (Dem-N.Y.), Ulysses S. Guyer (Rep-Kans.), John McCormack (Dem-Mass.), and Charles Kramer (Dem-Cal.) (Bettman, McCormack-Dickstein Committee, Photograph. Getty Images, Bettman Collection).

democracy arose when Germany's government was turned over to the insidious Adolf Hitler and his National Socialist Workers Party.[65]

Dickstein had mixed feelings about McCormack being named chair. In a favorable biography entitled *American Defender* authored by Dickstein devotee Dorothy Waring, she contended that the House "had . . . definitely decided [that] the chairman must be a Christian with a distinguishably Anglo-Saxon name."[66] In addition to misspelling John's surname, she missed the fact that it was not Anglo-Saxon but Celtic, but her dismissive account of John's appointment seems in accord with the sentiments of Dickstein himself. She contended that[67]

> when Representative MacCormack [*sic*] of Massachusetts finally became Chairman, heads of the various Nazi factions breathed easier. . . . Few believed, now that the Committee was in the hands of a Christian, there would be any investigation or hearings. Choosing to assume that the un-American activities Dickstein had reported on were figments of a Jewish imagination, it was inconceivable in the moronic minds of these destroyers of Government prestige that MacCormack [sic], a Christian, would be against them.

Dickstein was named as vice chair, and the committee was generally known as the McCormack-Dickstein or the Dickstein-McCormack Committee. John McCormack did not mind. He seldom opposed the self-promoting behaviors of his fellow House members whose ego needs for public approbation was greater than his own. John was learning how to function in the rooms of power, but safely in their shadows. That Sam Dickstein would later appear on the payroll of the Soviet government may have been suspected but not known until the release of internal documents, following the collapse of the Soviet Union.[68]

Public hearings were tense. On October 17, 1934, the *Times* reported that one public hearing in Manhattan was disrupted by Nazi sympathizers shouting "Heil Hitler" while someone cut microphone wires on the witness table. McCormack declared [69]: "The chair is aware that Anton Hegele, the New York leader of the Friends of the New Germany, urged members to come here today for the purpose of making a disturbance." "Why don't you examine Communists?" one woman asked—or "screamed," as *The Times* put it. "We are more American than you are."

General Butler and the "Businessman's Plot": It was this committee that first heard testimony from Major General Smedley Butler of the U.S. Marine Corps that some right-wing newspaper publishers and Wall Street financiers plotted to overthrow President Roosevelt and install a fascist form of government.[70] Butler told the committee that because he was a World War I hero and a two-time winner of the Congressional Medal of Honor, he was approached by a shadowy bond salesman by the name of Gerald P. MacGuire and told that he would be in line to assume the leadership of this coup d'etat once it succeeded in toppling Roosevelt.

Butler's testimony did not receive extensive attention in the national press, and it was dismissed as "a gigantic hoax" by the *New York Times*.[71] However, his allegations were prominently featured in the left-leaning *New Masses* magazine, where its lead reporter John L. Spivak published a lengthy two-part article in which Spivak refers to the panel as the "Dickstein Committee" and his only serious reference to John McCormack is of an aborted interview[72]: "I called upon the chairman, Congressman John W. McCormack. I had prepared a series of questions for the interview which he had agreed to give me. When I got to the sixth question which probed a little deeper into the suppression of evidence by his Committee, the Congressman became a little nervous."

Apparently, Spivak had obtained a copy of the committee's executive minutes and an agitated McCormack sought to cancel the interview. According to Spivak, John said, "I will not answer any more questions. It is obvious to me that they are cleverly arranged—all leading to one point—you want to hang me." Spivak's retort was, "No, I don't want to hang you. I think your committee has hanged itself."

McCormack was careful to contain the political damage that Butler's inflammatory tale might have wrought, and most subsequent treatments of Butler's testimony have treated it as a "cocktail *putsch*" in the words of New York Mayor Fiorello La Guardia.[73] Although McCormack contended that most of what General Butler had told the committee could be verified and publicly defended him, Butler felt that the committee had suppressed most of the evidence and had not sufficiently pursued the matter.[74]

Years later in an interview with Jules Archer, author of *The Plot to Seize the White House*, John said[75]:

> There was no doubt General Butler was telling the truth. . . . Millions were at stake when [Singer Sewing Machine heir Sterling] Clark got the [American] Legion to pass that resolution of the gold standard in 1933. When Roosevelt refused to be pressured by it, and went even further with the gold standard, those fellows got desperate and decided to look into European methods, with the idea of introducing them into America. They sent MacGuire to Europe to study the Fascist organization. . . . If General Butler had not been the patriot he was and if they had been able to maintain secrecy, the plot might very well have succeeded. . . . This was a threat to our very way of government by a bunch of rich men who wanted Fascism.

Despite the seemingly credible allegations, nothing actually occurred and the unexpected death of its leading plotter, Gerald C. MacGuire, led the committee to close its books decreeing that most of the claims were "hearsay" and redacted from the record. A subsequent confidential assessment stated[76]: "From the evidence in its record, the committee concluded that through strenuous efforts, progress had had been made in rooting Nazi ideology in the United States, but that the exposure of this activity by the committee had checked the progress and had, in addition, launched a disintegration of the movement furthering its advancement."

McCormack's chairmanship of the House's first Special Committee on Un-American Activities issued its report on February 15, 1935, and expired.[77] The one piece of legislation that emerged from the committee testimony was the McCormack Act of 1938 that required all foreign agents disseminating propaganda in the United States to be registered with the government.[78] Whether or not this act was the legislative precursor to the far more intrusive Alien Registration Act of 1940 (Smith Act) is debatable, but McCormack's longtime aide Martin Sweig contended that it was.[79] The committee's activities seemed neither to hurt nor help him in his congressional district, but McCormack's efforts to explore potential internal antidemocratic movements gave him a reputation in the House as both an ardent anti-Communist and an antifascist. It was during this time that he published three articles dealing with political extremism and how it should be addressed without violating the personal liberties of Americans.[80] John's management of the committee was deemed a success, enhancing his leadership prospects. According to Earl Latham's careful analysis of the committee's performance,[81]

> The procedures of the committee were a model of scrupulous conduct. Executive sessions were held before the public sessions, care was taken to see that extraneous names were not mentioned casually to the detriment of private reputations and witnesses succeeding each other supplied complementary information in a well-intentioned pattern.

Most importantly, John McCormack had performed his committee duties responsibly and carefully. They were the true test of one's ability to lead the House of Representatives.

Domestic Disturbers: While the McCormack-Dickstein committee focused on foreign influences fueling fascism, it did not deal with the growing antidemocratic threats of Louisiana's Senator Huey P. Long and the rabid anti-Semitic rants of Father Charles E. Coughlin, the Canadian-born radio priest broadcasting from the Church of the Little Flower in Royal Oak, Michigan. Long's "Share-the-Wealth" economic redistribution movement was especially attractive to those for whom the New Deal's legislative remedies were too slow.[82]

Huey Long's murder on September 8, 1935, in the Louisiana state capital may have ended the life of the best known of the demagogs eager to exploit Depression-induced economic anxieties, but there were others eager to parlay national economic unrest for political gain, including Father Coughlin, whose entry into John McCormack's life would await another election.

Another new Speaker and a renewed mandate

As the Second Session of the 73rd Congress drew to a close, some unfinished business was addressed. Gaining control over Wall Street was essential to the New Dealers, and to accomplish this goal, Congress initially passed the Federal Securities Act of 1933 that called for full disclosure to investors of new securities,[83] but it was the later act, the Securities Exchange Act of 1934, that gave it more teeth by establishing the Securities and Exchange Commission (SEC) and authorizing that unit to license stock exchanges.[84] Both bills had been drafted by FDR's team of Tommy "the Cork" Corcoran and Benjamin Cohen and shepherded through Congress by Sam Rayburn, the chair of the House Interstate and Foreign Commerce Committee. Heading the new SEC would be Boston-born New York financier Joseph P. Kennedy,[85] and for the first time in their respective careers, both Joe Kennedy and John McCormack would be conducting the public's business in the same city.

The Second Session closed on June 18, 1934, and most members went home to face the midterm election that would be a referendum on the New Deal and Congress' willingness to defer to President Roosevelt's ambitious and aggressive legislative agenda. Speaker Rainey, the oldest first-time Speaker of the House, was now dubbed "the legislative marshal of the New Deal." He feared that popular support for FDR's ambitious agenda had waned.[86] Approaching his 74th birthday, Rainey committed himself to an exhaustive national speaking schedule from Toronto, Canada, to Eureka Springs, Arkansas, in its support. It was an unwise move, and his 275-pound frame contributed to his fatal heart attack on August 19, 1934.[87]

The House Democrats had settled into a pattern of elevating the party's floor leader into the speakership when that office opened. That had been the case with Missouri's Champ Clark in 1911, Jack Garner in 1931, and Rainey in 1933. While Clark and Garner may have faced grumbling, neither faced floor opposition like Rainey did. But Joe Byrns who had bested Will Bankhead for floor leader in 1933 was not without enemies in the Democratic Caucus, and Bankhead contemplated a rematch. In the 1933 Byrns-Bankhead contest, John McCormack cast his vote for Bankhead, committing himself yet again to the leadership aspirations of the House's southern Democrats.[88] Opposition dissipated and Byrns won the speakership unopposed.[89]

The conflict shifted to the floor leadership and prominently mentioned were 49-year-old sixth-termer New Yorker John J. O'Connor of the Rules Committee and 43-year-old fourth-termer Bostonian John McCormack of Ways and Means. Neither was expected to be a serious threat to 60-year-old ninth-termer Will Bankhead of Alabama who chaired Rules, but it was a foreshadowing of their later conflicts. It was O'Connor's latest leadership attempt and despite his heavy courtship of Byrns, the future Speaker carefully avoided taking sides. The southerners took notice and were wary of O'Connor while John McCormack was becoming the South's favorite northerner.

With an anticipated landslide victory over his latest opponent, Republican Francis A. Pentoney, John McCormack continued to collect testimony for the Un-American Activities Committee in New York and Washington. His 1934 victory percentage of 82.8% was his highest to date. John McCormack was clearly safe and the House seat would be his for as long as he wished to run. Staying in Washington, far from the erratic machinations of Jim Curley who had just been elected governor and the vast array of Curley enemies, was a sensible course of action.

The congressional elections of 1934 had gone surprisingly well for the Democrats. In virtually every off-year contest in the two-party era of American politics, the president's congressional party had lost seats. But this time, it was different. Democrats actually increased the number of seats which they held in the House from 313 to 322 with an additional seven allies from the Wisconsin Progressives and three from the Minnesota Farmer-Labor Party. Their total in the Senate grew from 60 to 69. The national referendum on the New Deal was overwhelmingly positive.

Democratic success was especially evident in New England. In 1920, only two of New England's 32 House members were Democrats. By 1928, the number had slightly increased to four—three in Massachusetts, including McCormack, and one in Rhode Island. But by 1934, Democrats held a majority of New England's House seats—16 to 13. Reapportionment had cost New England three seats but the Depression had cost Republicans their regional majority. Treating the region as a single entity, which non–New Englanders do, meant that John McCormack led a region with numbers comparable to the House Democratic state delegations of California, Michigan, Illinois, and Ohio. The Democratic delegations of Texas and Pennsylvania were larger and with 29 Democratic members, New York's Tammany-dominated delegation was the largest of them all.

Containing the Tammany tiger

The American public continued its support of Franklin Roosevelt and the New Deal. But the Sachems of Tammany Hall remained philosophically loyal to Al Smith, one of their own. Their commitment to FDR was one of convenience and not conviction. However, by the early 1930s, Tammany Hall's vaunted place in Democratic circles was diminished.

The 1930 Census revealed that New York City had grown to 6,930,000 people and its population was greater than that of 46 states. Only the state of Pennsylvania had more residents than New York City. New York City wanted its due, but Tammany Hall was badly battered. Tammany's dapper bon vivant mayor Jimmy Walker had departed for England in 1931 with his second wife, British actress Betty Compton, following investigations by Judge Samuel Seabury into municipal corruption.[90] Tammany postponed the inevitable by successfully running the relatively clean John P. O'Brien to fill Walker's unexpired term in 1932, but it was not enough to forestall the election of the legendary Fusion candidate Fiorello La Guardia. La Guardia, the son of an Italian father and Jewish mother who was raised Episcopalian and was both a socialist and a Republican in his politics, personally embodied all of the non-Tammany elements of the city. La Guardia had served in the House for seven nonconsecutive terms until his defeat for reelection in 1932.[91] Jimmy Walker had defeated him for mayor in 1929, but by 1933, Walker was gone and neither the insurgent Democrat Joseph V. McKee nor the incumbent Tammany Democrat John P. O'Brien was a match for the energetic and charismatic La Guardia. For the next 12 years (1933–45), La Guardia ruled the city and broke all the rules of the wise-guy political pundits by becoming the first reform mayor of the city to be reelected.

With FDR secure in the White House and his ally Governor Herbert H. Lehman in the State House, Tammany was now shut out of the key centers of political power within the city and the state. FDR knew that Tammany was on the ropes, but as a master New York politician, FDR also knew that Tammany could not be safely ignored and he listened carefully to Postmaster General Jim Farley, Tammany's ambassador to the White House. However, even Tammany's Sachems knew that their claim to a place at the Democratic table was waning.

To restore their political influence, Tammany's Democrats targeted the U.S. House. They had enough seats to influence leadership contests and they had two prominent leaders with sufficient seniority to compete for these posts themselves—Tom Cullen of Brooklyn and John J. O'Connor of Manhattan.

Tom Cullen had entered the state assembly in 1896 and had an unbroken string of 48 years in public life, including 25 in the U.S. House (1919–44).[92] Cullen's rise to House prominence was slow. After serving on lesser committees, Cullen was named to the Appropriations Committee in 1925, his seventh year in the House,[93] where he would serve with future Speaker Joe Byrns and James A. Gallivan from the Massachusetts 12th District. In January 1930, his eleventh year in the House, Tom Cullen would leave the eighth slot on Appropriations for the tenth place on the Ways and Means Committee. Eleven months later, Cullen would begin his Ways and Means service with another Boston Democrat, John McCormack. Tom Cullen was the only Democrat to serve on committees with both Jim Gallivan and John McCormack.

Unlike Cullen, John J. O'Connor rocketed up the House committee hierarchy. He had the appropriate blend of ethnic origin and educational credentialing to make a major move in the Democratic politics of the time, and his major policy concerns were with immigration reform and child welfare, the two issues dearest to the heart of Governor Al Smith.[94]

For the Sachems of Tammany, bringing an Ivy League–educated lawyer into New York's House delegation was a coup, and John O'Connor quickly nudged Tom Cullen aside among the delegation's likely House leaders. On December 17, 1923, and only twelve days a member of the U.S. House, the 38-year-old John J. O'Connor was named as one of four minority Democrats to the prestigious Rules Committee.[95] It was a remarkable leap.

Although the Rules Committee is the smallest of the House's powerful standing committees, it is the one that sets the agenda for legislative business. The Rules Committee serves as the "traffic cop" of the House and determines whether a bill coming out of committee to the floor could be amended (an "open rule") or not (a "closed rule") and how much time would be allocated for floor debate. O'Connor emerged as an expert on legislative procedure, and for FDR, eager to continue his legislative successes, this should have been a man to placate, not stop.[96]

Serving with O'Connor on the Rules Committee in his initial Congress were Democrats Finis Garrett of Tennessee, a Sam Rayburn pal, the Democratic floor leader then in his tenth House term; and future rival Will Bankhead of Alabama, then in his fourth term. Although Bankhead was the son of a former U.S. Senator, it had taken him seven years to get to the Rules Committee while John O'Connor had ascended the House's committee hierarchy in less than two weeks. The Tammany pecking order had been set and John O'Connor was on top. O'Connor's rapid ascension made him a target of the anti-Tammany House Democrats who knew that if Tammany was to be stopped, John O'Connor had to be stopped.

John McCormack, the "Un-Tammany" Irishman: Although Cactus Jack Garner was now vice president and presiding over the Senate on the other end of the Capitol, Garner allies continued to promote John McCormack for a leadership role. None was more supportive than Garner's closest friend John McDuffie who was eager to put McCormack's name into play. Key southerners like McDuffie were very fearful of the

Tammany Hall Democrats of New York City and the stench of municipal corruption that emanated from them. The Democrats of Tammany Hall did not practice the deferential politics that the southern hierarchy had come to expect. But with the House Democrats extending their reach deeper into the north than ever before, a non–Tammany urban Catholic northerner was essential to block Tammany. The man selected by the anti-Tammany southerners was Boston's John McCormack.

Shortly after Speaker Rainey had been buried on August 29, 1934, John McDuffie wrote to Will Bankhead about John McCormack[97]:

> John McCormack is the most influential Congressman in New England. McCormack may be a candidate for Speaker or Leader. A combination with him would be helpful. He is strong in New England, but don't know his influence outside of that region. However, his ability and industry has undoubtedly impressed the House. His sense of fairness is very fine.

Other McDuffie letters followed. In a letter to Walter Chamblin, a friend of Sam Rayburn and a leading lobbyist for the Chesapeake and Ohio Railroad, McDuffie took his support for McCormack even further. In a postscript to his November 16, 1934, letter to Chamblin, McDuffie asserted,[98] "John McCormack is the best man outside the South or what is known as the South including the border states. I have an idea that both places [the speakership and the floor leadership] will hardly go to the South. A Speaker from the South and John McCormack from the North would make a good slate."

McDuffie, Bankhead, and their allies saw John McCormack as a key actor in their efforts to obtain eastern anti-Tammany urban votes. In a letter to John McCormack dated November 18, 1934, McDuffie's effusiveness is extraordinary as he writes[99]:

> If I had my way, John, you would be the next Majority Leader of the House of Representatives. You are undoubtedly the most capable, outstanding figure in the House outside of the South. Your big heart, liberality and tolerance for the other fellow's viewpoints, together with your keen intellect and superb ability make you qualified for any position in the House. It may be that my love for you makes me extravagant in my views about your qualifications. Whether my views are extravagant or not, they are sincere.
>
> My hope, during my fight, was to form an alignment with you. Mr. Bankhead had informed me he would be a candidate for Leader if I was not made Speaker, which prevented my making any alignment whatever.

The White House was also eager to limit the reach of Tammany Hall and it too had taken positive notice of McDuffie's efforts on McCormack's behalf. On November 21, 1934, Walter Chamblin responded to McDuffie[100]:

The President has not said anything publicly or privately but all of his henchmen are ready to go down the line for Rayburn for Speaker and McCormack as Leader.

Ed Flynn [FDR-backed leader of the Bronx and later Chairman of the Democratic National Committee] has told Sam that he and other leaders are satisfied with the Rayburn-McCormack ticket.

The White House maneuverings predated by six years the official pairing of the Sam Rayburn-John McCormack House leadership ticket. Although finally made official in 1940, this pairing was seen as sufficiently agreeable to the White House that FDR's operatives helped to increase the respective prominence and collective cooperation of these two key House players. Others brought into play on McCormack's behalf included Georgia's Gene Cox, who served on the Rules Committee with O'Connor and Bankhead. McDuffie wrote on December 10, 1934[101]: "I had a letter from John McCormack a short time ago, and I think if the leadership goes to the North he should get it. He is able, tolerant, kindly and a very positive character. He would have quite a following."

Cox continued the letter-writing campaign for McCormack in a letter to Bankhead on December 17, 1934, writing, "I had hoped that you would find it possible to form some sort of combination with someone from the East, preferably John McCormack that would insure your election."[102]

Under the House Democrats, the leadership selection system was two–tiered. There were generally no contests for the speakership. When the speakership came open as a result of a change in party control of the House, the sitting minority floor leader would move into the Speaker's chair unopposed.[103] And when the speakership came open as a consequence of the death or retirement of the sitting Democratic Speaker, the majority leader would move into the chair also unopposed.

On December 12, 1934, the Democratic Caucus selected Majority Floor Leader Joseph Wellington Byrns of Tennessee as their candidate for Speaker. Although Sam Rayburn considered challenging Byrns, he withdrew after Pennsylvania's Democrats announced for Byrns.[104] With Rayburn's challenge put aside, Byrns was chosen unanimously. However, the next tier office, that of majority leader, would be vigorously contested.

With Democrats holding 319 seats in the upcoming House, northern and western Democrats held a clear majority over the southern and border Democrats who had ruled the party for most of the past 40 years. It was time for the northern and western Democrats to contest for the House leadership. All they needed was a champion. If the northern and western Democrats united, they could topple the leader of the party's southern wing, Will Bankhead of Alabama. But they chose unwisely. John J. O'Connor would be the northern contender.

The Bankhead's were congressional royalty. Will's father John Hollis Bankhead had served in the House of Representatives for 20 years (1887–1907) and in the Senate for 13 years (1907–20) until his death.[105] John Hollis Bankhead had served as the state's senior Senator, while Oscar W. Underwood had served as its junior one. Will Bankhead's older brother, John Hollis II, gained the Senate seat in 1931.

Bankhead knew that his likeliest opponent would be O'Connor. Bankhead needed northern support and two stepped up.[106] One was Adolph Sabath, a Jewish Rules Committee member from Chicago, and the other was Boston's John McCormack. There were more differences than similarities between O'Connor and McCormack. Boston's John McCormack went home every evening to his devoted wife Harriet and New York's John O'Connor returned to the embraces of his mistress.[107] To the devout city Catholics among the Democrats, this was a crucial difference, and as John

McCormack had learned years ago in Boston, private virtue has public rewards. As he had in 1931 and 1933, John McCormack would not vote for O'Connor in this contest. This vote would alter John McCormack's House career forever.

The Democratic Caucus assembled on January 2, 1935, a day before the 74th Congress was to convene. Over three hundred Democrats assembled to cast their votes for majority leader. John McCormack was one of seven candidates on the first ballot. Since no one had a majority, a second ballot was needed. John McCormack, who had 21 votes on the first ballot, withdrew in favor of Will Bankhead, enabling Will to defeat John O'Connor in this crucial contest.[108]

Only six years in the House and 43-year-old Representative John McCormack had made his first formal challenge for the leadership. His vote total was unimpressive, but it helped to keep enough fellow northern Catholics from voting for John O'Connor to insure Will Bankhead's victory. His management of the Un-American Activities Committee had been commendable, and he had kept the volatile Sam Dickstein under control and the House out of the headlines. John McCormack had become a player in the House and he would start his fourth full term with more Democrats than had ever been seated in the House before. The new Floor Leader Will Bankhead quickly became one of the more effective southern spokesmen for the New Deal.[109] FDR had a genuine ally in the man from Jasper, Alabama, and he was aware of those members who had made it happen.

More good news would soon follow.

With the 74th Congress assembled, the first major piece of legislation passed was the Emergency Relief Appropriation Act of 1935, which began the withdrawal of the Federal Government from the arena of direct relief, which was left to the states and local communities, and provided for the establishment of a large-scale national work program for the employable jobless, who were required to meet a means test in order to qualify for work relief.[110] FERA was replaced by the WPA as the program's major agency and would ultimately employ millions of workers in construction projects that changed virtually every community in the United States.[111] Heading up the WPA would be the Iowa-born New York social worker Harry Hopkins, who would bring along as his chief deputy the Russian-born, Boston-raised pal of John McCormack, the shadowy David K. Niles.

Social Security Act of 1935

It was during the 74th Congress that John's Ways and Means Committee played a central role in the writing and passage of FDR's greatest New Deal legacy—the Social Security Act of 1935. This extraordinary act instituted a national system of social insurance, including old-age pensions. It created the Social Security Board as a general administrative agency and established a cooperative federal-state system of unemployment compensation and a tax for old-age and survivors' insurance to be levied upon employers and employees. It authorized grants to the states to help in meeting the cost of old-age pensions allowed under state law and to assist in relief of the destitute, blind, homeless, dependent and delinquent children, and in services such as public health, vocational rehabilitation, and maternity and infant care.[112] Now ranked sixth on Ways and Means, John's initial role on the committee was more of an expediter and a consensus builder than as a legislative draftsman.

Ranked just below John in the 7th slot on the Ways and Means Committee was David J. Lewis (Dem-Md.). Lewis joined Ways and Means in 1931 at the same time as John McCormack, but in spite of his six years of prior House service (1911–17), he was ranked 14th only above Fred Vinson of Kentucky. Lewis originally introduced the Social Security bill, but its Chair Robert L. (Muley) Doughton (Dem-NC) wanted to claim credit for the bill, and he had it introduced under his name so it would appear that he was the House author joining U.S. Senator Robert Wagner (Dem-NY) of the Senate Finance Committee. This was a time when FDR's power was at its peak, and Doughton wished to ingratiate himself with the President.

Thomas H. Eliot, the Harvard-educated scion of the "Cambridge Eliots," was one of the bill's draftsmen, and he observed that "McCormack took little part in the discussion, but his quick thinking saved an important section of the bill from temporary extinction."[113] Eliot recounted that McCormack held two proxies, Tom Cullen and Chris Sullivan of New York, when a rural committee member tried to eliminate "all provisions relating to unemployment compensation." With the proxies, John saved that portion of the bill. John knew how to count votes.

Tom Eliot was a quintessential Boston Brahmin and grandson to Charles W. Eliot who served as Harvard's president for 40 years (1869–1909). While the snobby Eliot gave Southie's John McCormack little credit for the passage of the 1935 Social Security Act, a closer observer, Edwin E. Witte, the executive director of the Committee on Economic Security, contended that John's commitment to the Roosevelt agenda was central to its passage. Witte, a PhD graduate of the University of Wisconsin who had studied under the legendary historian Frederick Jackson Turner and the almost as legendary economist John R. Commons, moved easily between the academy and policymaking.

Often described as "the father of Social Security," Witte's contemporaneous notes on the committee's role assigned a large role to John as he noted,[114] "Congressmen Cooper, McCormack, and Woodruff were very sympathetic with the bill. . . . Chairman Doughton and Congressmen Hill, Vinson, Cooper, and McCormack, who were, at all odds, the most important members of the committee, were anxious to carry out the President's wishes."

John was especially helpful in defusing a potential conflict with the National Catholic Welfare Conference. This was a time when Father Coughlin was excoriating FDR and urging Catholics to turn against the Roosevelt agenda. It was Coughlin's hope that he and fellow demagogue Huey Long could create a political party to topple FDR. Long's assassination in September 1935 ended that speculation, but Coughlin would create the anti-Roosevelt Union Party in 1936 with support from the nation's poorest and angriest Catholics. Boston's Irish Catholics were especially vulnerable, and the city was denoted "the most Coughlinite city in America." John had to move carefully with the Catholic Welfare Conference to keep their support for Social

Security in place. His actions were referred to as the "McCormack amendment" and described by Witte[115]:

> [The National Catholic Welfare Conference asked] that the requirement of the federal aid be dropped; also the requirement of state financial participation; further, they urged that this federal aid be limited to rural areas in which there are no adequate provisions for child welfare services. . . . The matter was not discussed in the congressional hearings at all, but when this particular provision was reached in the executive session of the Ways and Means Committee an amendment was offered by Congressman McCormack changing these sections in accord with the Catholic wishes. . . . The Ways and Means Committee wrangled for some time over what should be considered a rural area and adopted somewhat more restrictive language upon this point than provided for in the McCormack amendment. Thereafter, the amendment was adopted without objection.

While the act would pass with little opposition and FDR would sign it into law on August 14, 1935, the first monthly check would not be issued until January 1, 1940, almost four and one-half years later. Economic security for the working poor was on the horizon but not yet a reality of their lives.

In recent years, a spirited debate has emerged contending that the exclusion of farm workers and domestics who were disproportionately African American from Social Security coverage was due to southern congressional opposition to any legislation that would benefit their black constituents.[116] Contending that southerners on Ways and Means kept blacks from receiving benefits overlooks that other excluded groups included "the self-employed, seamen, and employees of churches, colleges, hospitals, and charities, not to mention all government employees."[117] It also overlooks that the majority of farm workers and domestics were white. The reason for their exclusion was simple as explained in testimony by Treasury Secretary Robert Morgenthau[118]:

> The bill in its present form imposes a burden upon the Treasury that it cannot guarantee adequately to meet. The national contributory old-age annuity system, as now proposed . . . means that every transient or casual laborer is included, that every domestic servant is covered, and that the large and shifting class of agricultural workers is covered. Now, even without the inclusion of these three classes of workers, the task of the Treasury in administering the contributory tax collections would be extremely formidable. If these three classes of workers are to be included, however, the task may prove insuperable—certainly, at the outset.

A close analysis of Morgenthau's testimony by Larry DeWitt, a public historian for the Social Security Administration, found that[119]

> no Southern member of the Ways and Means Committee spoke out either in favor of or against Morgenthau's proposal during his hearing testimony. In fact, the only

member who took a position on either side of the issue was John McCormack (D-MA), who worried and went on to explain, "if we do not get them in the bill, then you are going to have a lot of difficulty in the future getting them into the bill."

Furthermore, the four Ways and Means southerners were from the "outer south" states of Arkansas, North Carolina, Tennessee, and Texas, states with fewer black citizens and less antipathy toward them. Similarly, two border state members of the committee were McCormack allies, David Lewis of Maryland, the bill's original House draftsman and future Chief Justice Fred Vinson of Kentucky. There were many racist assemblages in Congress of this era; this was not one of them.[120]

John McCormack's worry in 1935 that there would be future difficulty in getting Social Security coverage for these excluded groups was prescient. It was not until 19 years later that the Social Security amendments of 1954 extended coverage to "farmers . . . additional farm and domestic workers."[121]

John McCormack was not the only Massachusetts member linked to significant legislation in the 74th Congress. John's best friend in the delegation, Billy Connery of the North Shore factory town of Lynn, chaired the Labor Committee, and partnering with U.S. Senator Robert F. Wagner (Dem-NY), they coauthored the Wagner-Connery Labor Relations Act of 1935. The act created the National Labor Relations Board (NLRB) and it gave federal protection to union organization throughout the nation. Often called "the Magna Carta of labor," the act guaranteed that the Democratic Party would now have troops of organized workers to mobilize working-class voters and their families to insure the continued electoral success of FDR and his ambitious legislative agenda. Billy's NLRB was a political triumph; John's Social Security was a humanitarian one.

John would continue his work on Social Security and his strenuous efforts on behalf of the Social Security Amendments in 1939 extended financial benefits to elderly wives, maritime workers, and persons obliged to be working after 65. As John moved up the committee ladder to fourth place on Ways and Means, his increased seniority gave him a more significant drafting role and made Social Security a "family protecting" policy.[122]

For John McCormack, the Social Security Act validated every reason that he had ever needed for entering public service. The blighted lives of his family, friends, and constituents back in the tenements of Southie now had hope for relief from a federal government that was at last sensitive to their dire needs.

Another speakership vacancy

As the 74th Congress came to a close, tragedy recurred in the speakership. Speaker Joseph W. Byrns died two weeks before the close of the second session. Byrns's speakership was unimpressive[123] and like Henry Rainey's, it was placed in the relative impotent "figurehead" category by Randall Ripley in his book *Party Leaders in the House of Representatives*.[124] This was the third death of a Speaker of the House in five years.[125] Perhaps placing elderly Representatives in the chair during periods of political tumult may have been unwise.

As expected, Will Bankhead, the Majority Floor Leader, was installed as Speaker of the House without opposition on June 4, 1936.[126] Although Rules Chair O'Connor attempted to lay claim to being the de facto majority leader, the floor leadership would remain vacant for the closing weeks of the session and for the remainder of the year. The succession was cloudy at this time and there was a need to get on with the business of renominating the Roosevelt-Garner ticket and continuing the Democrats' hold on the presidency and the Congress.

When the 74th Congress adjourned on June 20, 1936, its legislative record would have been very impressive, but coming after the "100 Days" of the prior Congress, the 74th represented a continuation of the New Deal's momentum.[127] That the momentum continued and did not flag was perhaps its most notable achievement. The passages of the Wagner-Connery Labor Relations Act and the Social Security Act were dramatic steps of a systematic movement on the part of the New Deal to protect organized labor and to federalize welfare. By shifting the burden of welfare benefits from the cities and the states to the federal government, the New Deal enhanced the power of congressional patronage.

On the political front, the federalization of welfare helped to create two political parties among the Democrats. One was the local Democratic Party built on old-fashioned patronage and personal contact. The other was the congressional Democratic Party. This party brought federal largesse home in the form of government building contracts, purchases of service, and entitlement programs such as Workmen's Compensation and Social Security. To succeed in this party, one needed placements on key congressional committees and a willingness to avoid blandishments for non-congressional offices.

With John McCormack on the Ways and Means Committee, fellow Massachusetts and New England Democrats could be placed on the House's most powerful committees. For McCormack, that meant that the region's governors, even James Michael Curley, would have to seek his favor for any access to federal funds. John McCormack was now in a position to parlay his safe district in Boston to internal power in Washington and to reflect that internal power back to his city, state, and region. John McCormack's reality far surpassed the hopes and dreams he had long ago.

As the two parties readied themselves for the upcoming nominating conventions and the November presidential election, the majority leader candidates of the South, Sam Rayburn of Texas, and of the cities, John O'Connor of New York, would await the results in anticipation that the balance of seats would tilt their way. John McCormack already knew how he would vote.

Notes

1   "Henry Thomas Rainey (1860–1934)," in Donald R. Kennon, ed., *The Speakers of the U.S. House of Representatives: A Bibliography, 1789–1984* (Baltimore: Johns Hopkins University Press, 1086), pp. 236–40. See also Robert A. Waller, *Rainey of Illinois: A Political Biography, 1903–34* (Urbana: University of Illinois Press, 1977).

2 Ralph Neal Brannen, *John McDuffie, State Legislator, Congressman, Federal Judge, 1883–1950*, unpublished PhD dissertation, Auburn (Ala.) University, 1975, p. 165.

3 Brannen, *John McDuffie*, p. 169; and Bascom Timmons, *Garner of Texas: A Personal History* (New York: Harper, 1948), p. 136.

4 *House Journal*, 73rd Congress, 1st Session, March 9, 1933, p. 9.

5 The quotation "[The Vice-Presidency] isn't worth a pitcher of warm piss" is attributed to Garner in A. Norman Jeffares and Martin Gray, eds., *A Dictionary of Quotations* (New York: Barnes and Noble, 1997), p. 272.

6 Author's telephonic interview with the Hon. John W. McCormack, Boston, April 1977.

7 John McDuffie to E. E. Cox, November 17, 1932, in the John McDuffie Papers, W.S. Hoole Special Collections, University of Alabama, Tuscaloosa, Alabama.

8 Dennis S. Nordin, The *New Deal's Black Congressman: A Life of Arthur Wergs Mitchell* (Columbia: University of Missouri Press, 1997), p. 30.

9 Ibid., chapter 3, pp. 55–56.

10 See Christopher Manning, *William L. Dawson and the Limits of Black Electoral Leadership* (DeKalb: Northern Illinois Press, 2009), p. 197, note 6.

11 John McCormack quoted in "Mr. Speaker," *TIME*, January 19, 1962.

12 The best treatment of this period in McCormack's life is Lester I. Gordon's PhD dissertation, "John McCormack and the Roosevelt Era" (Boston University, 1976).

13 James McGurrin, *Bourke Cockran, A Free Lance in American Politics* (New York: Charles Scribner's Sons, 1948).

14 Material supplied by Professor Anthony Champagne, Undated memorandum titled "re Speakership," Box 23, folder "John J. O'Connor Speakership—Dec. 1932–1935," John J. O'Connor papers, University of Indiana—Bloomington; and Frank Hague to John J. O'Connor, January 9, 1933, Box 23, folder "John J. O'Connor, Speakership—Dec. 1932–1935."

15 Undated 1933 telephone memorandum in John J. O'Connor Papers, Lilly Library, Indiana University, Bloomington, Indiana.

16 Emergency Banking Relief Act, approved March 9, 1933 (Public Law 73-1; 48 Stat. 1-7). The first item of Roosevelt's "New Deal" legislative program was the Emergency Banking Relief Act, which was introduced, passed, and approved during Roosevelt's first week in the White House. See "Fast—and Slow: The Emergency Banking Act of 1933," in Stephen K. Bailey and Howard D. Samuel, *Congress at Work* (New York: Henry Holt & Co., 1952), pp. 229–36. A summary of this Act may be found in Larry Schweikart's entry in Donald C. Bacon, Roger H. Davidson, and Morton Keller, eds., *The Encyclopedia of the United States Congress*, II (New York: Simon & Schuster, 1995), pp. 734–35.

17 Economy Act, approved March 20, 1933 (Public Law 73-2; 48 Stat. 8-16). Certain provisions of this Act were subsequently held unconstitutional in *Lynch v United States*, 292 U.S. 571 (1934). An assessment of this bill may be found in James E. Sargent, "Roosevelt's Economy Act: Fiscal Conservatism and the Early New Deal," *Congressional Studies*, VII (Winter 1980), pp. 33–52.

18 Beer-Wine Revenue Act was approved on March 22, 1933 (48 Stat. 16-20).

19 The Agricultural Adjustment Act was approved on May 12, 1933 (48 Stat. 31-54). Certain provisions of this Act were subsequently held unconstitutional in *United States v Butler*, 297 U.S. 1 (1936). This act was one which the Supreme Court contended had pushed the limits of congressional delegation to the president; see Henry W. Luedde, "New Limitations on the Power of Congress: The A.A.A. Decision," *St. Louis Law Review*, XXI (February 1936), pp. 149–60.

20 Tennessee Valley Authority was approved on May 18, 1933 (48 Stat. 58-72). Congress' willingness to delegate power to FDR is assessed in Henry C. Hart, "Legislative Abdication in Regional Development," *Journal of Politics*, XIII (August 1951), pp. 393–417. The tireless activities of Senator George W. Norris (Rep-Neb.) are recounted in "What One Man Can Do: Senator Norris and the Tennessee Valley Authority," in Bailey and Samuel, *Congress at Work*, pp. 194–228.

21 Federal Securities Act was approved on May 27, 1933 (48 Stat. 74-95). A history of this act by one of its key authors may be found in James M. Landis, "The Legislative History of the Securities Act of 1933," *George Washington Law Review*, XXVIII (1959), pp. 29–49. See also Michael E. Parrish, *Securities Regulation and the New Deal* (New Haven, CT: Yale University Press, 1970).

22 Repeal of the Gold Standard was approved on June 5, 1933 (48 Stat. 112-113). Certain provisions of this Act were subsequently held unconstitutional in *Perry v. United States*, 294 U.S. 330 (1935).

23 Home Owners Loan Act was approved on June 13, 1933 (48 Stat. 128-135). See Morton J. Schussbaum's entry, "Federal Housing Acts," in Bacon, Davidson, and Keller, eds., *The Encyclopedia of the United States Congress*, II, pp. 812–14; and Mark I. Gelfand, *A Nation of Cities: The Federal Government and Urban America, 1933–1965* (New York: Oxford University Press,1975).

24 Banking Act of 1933 (Glass-Steagall Act) was approved on June 16, 1933 (48 Stat. 162-195). A valuable summary of this act may be found in Larry Schweikart's entry in Bacon, Davidson, and Keller, eds., *The Encyclopedia of the United States Congress*, I, pp. 136–37. The conditions obtaining before the passage of the Act are recounted in Eugene N. White, "Before the Glass-Steagall Act: An Analysis of the Investment Banking Activities of National Banks," *Explorations in Economic History*, XXIII (January 1986), pp. 33–55. The Act's operations are explored in Franklin R. Edwards, "Banks and Securities Activities: Legal and Economic Perspectives on the Glass-Steagall Act," in Lawrence G. Goldberg and J. White, eds., *The Deregulation of the Banking and Security Industries* (Lexington, MA: Lexington Books, 1979), pp. 273–91; and a challenge to the Act's operations may be found in Thomas F. Huertas, "The Economic Brief against Glass-Steagall," *Journal of Bank Research*, XV (1984), pp. 148–59.

25 National Industrial Recovery Act was approved on June 16, 1933 (48 Stat. 195-211). Certain provisions of this Act were subsequently held unconstitutional in *Schechter Corp. v. United States*, 295 U.S. 495 (1935). See Bernard Bellush, *The Failure of the NRA* (New York: Norton, 1975); and Robert F. Himmelberg, *The Origins of the National Recovery Administration: Business, Government, and the Trade Association Issue, 1921–1933*, 2nd ed. (New York: Fordham University Press, 1976).

26 Emergency Railroad Transportation Act was approved on June 16, 1933 (48 Stat. 211-221). Problems with the Transportation Act of 1920 had been apparent early; see Thomas Reed Powell, "Commerce, Congress, and the Supreme Court, 1922-1925," *Columbia Law Review*, XXV (April–May 1926), pp. 396–431, 521–49.

27 A valuable list with the laws' key provisions may be found in Stathis, *Landmark Legislation*, pp. 201–203. See Pendleton Herring, "Seventy-Third Congress, First Session, March 9, 1933 to June 16, 1933," *APSR*, XXVIII (February 1934), pp. 65–83; and Joseph A. Imler, *The First One Hundred Days of the New Deal: The View from Capitol Hill*, unpublished PhD dissertation, Indiana University, 1975.

28 "Acts of Congress Held Unconstitutional in Whole or in Part by the Supreme Court of the United States," *The Constitution of the United States: Analysis and Interpretation*

(Washington, DC: U.S. Government Printing Office, 2004), pp. 2117–59, lists 158 cases of congressional acts ruled unconstitutional in whole or part. Those dealing with the New Deal are listed as Acts 58–64, 66–68, and 70.

29 Federal Credit Act of 1933 was approved on June 16, 1933. (48 Stat. 257-273).

30 Henry H. Adams, *Witness to Power: The Life of Fleet Admiral William D. Leahy* (Annapolis, MD: Naval Institute Press, 1985) p. 184.

31 Charles H. Trout, *Boston, the Great Depression, and the New Deal* (New York: Oxford University Press, 1977), pp. 135–42.

32 Abram L. Sachar, *The Redemption of the Unwanted: From the Liberation of the Death Camps to the Founding of Israel* (New York: St. Martin's/Marek, 1983), p. 192.

33 Two adjacent internet websites report David Niles's birth date as November 23, 1888 (Wikipedia.com) and November 26, 1890 (Conservapedia.com). The earlier date is the accurate one and was confirmed in the Boston Latin School records. The later date is that of his brother Asher Neyhus, who did not change his surname.

34 David Kohn Neyhus of 43 Compton is listed in Class III right above the name of Nathaniel William Niles, *Catalogue of the Public Latin School in Boston* (October 1903), p. 15.

35 From the Boston Latin archives, information found in the Boston Latin School Catalog of 1903 (published in the fall of the year): David Kohn Neyhus is listed in Class III (sophomore year), address 43 Compton (no additional details given). Joseph Patrick Kennedy is listed in Class IV (freshman year), address 165 Webster, East Boston. "The total number of students in all six years is listed as 597 . . . but as the two were only one year apart, they may still have known each other." Communication June 15, 2011.

36 FBI file on David K. Niles, 62-64769. This information is from a 1943 memorandum and listed as "Unverified Information."

37 Kenneth Campbell MacKay, *The Progressive Movement of 1924* (New York: Columbia University Press, 1947), p. 259.

38 Chapter 6, note 43, infra.

39 Dinneen, *The Purple Shamrock*, p. 225.

40 George Wolfskill, *The Revolt of the Conservatives: A History of the American Liberty League, 1934–1940* (Boston: Houghton Mifflin, 1962), p. 220.

41 Searle F. Charles, *Minister of Relief: Harry Hopkins and the Depression* (Syracuse, NY: Syracuse University Press, 1963), p. 185.

42 Trout, *Boston, the Great Depression and the New Deal*, pp. 149–54.

43 This point is made by South Boston native and Boston College history professor Thomas H. O'Connor in his *South Boston, My Home Town: The History of an Ethnic Neighborhood*, 2nd ed. (Boston: Northeastern University Press, 1994), p. 193.

44 The best account of its construction is in Lawrence J. Vale's *From the Puritans to the Projects: Public Housing and Public Neighbors* (Cambridge, MA: Harvard University Press, 2000), pp. 173–81.

45 Donald L. Willard, "1000 Homes Being Built by Uncle Sam on What Was South Boston Dump," *Boston Globe*, November 15, 1936, p. D2.

46 "Boston's First Public Housing Development: The Mary Ellen McCormack," *LP REEL NEWS*, Volume Four, Spring 2003, Lamont Productions, Inc., Washington, DC.

47 *Proceedings of the Boston City Council*, May 22, 1961, p. 119. "Name of Old Harbor Village Changed to Mary Ellen McCormack Project," in Vale, *From the Puritans to the Projects*, p. 431, note 38. Thanks to Ms. Frances Adams Francis of the South Boston Public Library for locating this item.

48 Allan R. Gold, "First Blacks Moving to Boston Project," *NYT*, July 2, 1988, p. 8.

49 See Hillel Levine and Lawrence Harmon, *The Death of an American Jewish Community: A Tragedy of Good Intentions* (New York: The Free Press, 1992); and Gerald Gamm, *Urban Exodus: Why the Jews Left Boston and the Catholics Stayed* (Cambridge, MA: Harvard University Press, 1999).

50 See Harry F. Greene's insightful Harvard honor's thesis, *The McCormacks of Massachusetts* (Cambridge, MA: Harvard University, 1963), p. 36.

51 "Persecution of the German Jewish People," *Congressional Record*, 72nd Congress, First Session (June 9, 1933), pp. 5441–42.

52 *Guide to U.S. Elections* (1975 ed.), p. 767 for 1930 and p. 772 for 1932. See Gerald H. Gamm, *The Making of New Deal Democrats: Voting Behavior and Realignment in Boston, 1920–1940* (Chicago: University of Chicago Press, 1989), pp. 61–62.

53 *Guide to U.S. Elections* (1975 ed.), p. 777 for 1934. See also Lawrence H. Fuchs, *The Political Behavior of American Jews* (Glencoe, IL: The Free Press, 1956), p. 138n.

54 An assessment of this session may be found in Edward P. Herring, "Second Session of the Seventy-Third Congress, January 3, 1934 to June 18, 1934," *APSR*, XXVIII (October 1934), pp. 852–66.

55 Gold Reserve Act of 1934 was approved January 30, 1934 (48 Stat. 337-344).

56 The fullest exposition of this charge may be found in H. W. Brands, *Traitor to His Class: The Privileged Life and Radical Presidency of Franklin Delano Roosevelt* (New York: Doubleday, 2008).

57 As described by Seymour Martin Lipset and Earl Rabb, in their *The Politics of Unreason: Right Wing Extremism in America, 1790–1970* (New York: Harper & Row, 1970), "The Anti-Masonic movement represented perhaps the first example in the United States of a preservatist antielitist mass movement based on the more provincial and traditional elements in the society; it was a sociological precursor of movements like the Ku Klux Klan and McCarthyism" (pp. 39–40).

58 The success of Know-Nothingism in pre–Civil War politics is recounted in Lipset and Rabb, *The Politics of Unreason*, pp. 53–59. Banks was elected Speaker in 1855 after two months and 133 ballots; see Edwin B. Morgan, "A Congressman's Letters on the Speaker Election in the Thirty-Fourth Congress," edited by Temple B. Hollcroft, *Mississippi Valley Historical Review*, XLIII (December 1956), pp. 444–58.

59 Lipset and Raab refer to "The Bigoted Twenties" in their *The Politics of Unreason*, pp. 110–49.

60 "Samuel Dickstein," *BDUSC* (1989 ed.), p. 909.

61 Text of House Resolution 198, 73rd Congress, contained in Report 153 to the U.S. House of Representatives, *Investigation of Nazi and Other Propaganda*, 74th Congress, 1st Session, February 15, 1935, p. 1. See Martin N. McGeary, "Congressional Investigations during Franklin D. Roosevelt's First Term," *APSR*, XXXI (August 1937), pp. 680–94.

62 On Dickstein's attitudes, see Walter Goodman, *The Committee: The Extraordinary Career of the House Committee on Un-American Activities* (New York: Farrar, Straus and Giroux, 1964), pp. 10–11.

63 House Resolution 198, 74th Congress, 1st Session, House Journal, March 20, 1934, pp. 289–90. The committee was named on April 5, 1934, p. 358.

64 "Investigate Nazi Propaganda Activities," in Canon, Nelson, and Stewart, *Committees in the U.S. Congress, 1789–1946*, 4, p. 402.

65 The role of despair is captured in Fritz Stern's *The Politics of Cultural Despair: A Study in the Rise of the Germanic Ideology* (New York: Anchor Books, 1965).

66 Dorothy Waring, *American Defender* (New York: Robert Speller, Inc., 1935), p. 186.

67 Ibid.

68 See "'Crook': A Soviet Agent in Congress," in Allen Weinstein and Alexander Vassiliev, *The Haunted Wood: Soviet Espionage in America—The Stalin Era* (New York: Random House, 1999), chapter 7. The documents were provided by Alexander Vassiliev and translated by Steve Shabad, reviewed and edited by Alexander Vassiliev and John Earl Haynes (2007). See John Earl Haynes and Harvey Klehr, eds., *Alexander Vassiliev's Notebooks: Provenance and Documentation of Soviet Intelligence Activities in the United States* (Washington, DC: Cold War International History Project, Woodrow Wilson Center, 2007).

69 Sam Tanenhaus, "Investigating Un-American Activities, Now and Then," *NYT*, March 9, 2011.

70 The first book-length treatment of the episode by Jules Archer, *The Plot to Seize the White House* (New York: Hawthorne Books, 1973), is lacking in documentation. A better-written and better-documented account of the plot may be found in Sally Denton, *The Plots against the President: FDR, A Nation in Crisis, and the Rise of the American Right* (New York: Bloomsbury, 2012).

71 "Inquiry Pressed in 'Facist Plot,'" *NYT*, November 22, 1934, p. 3.

72 John L. Spivak, "Wall Street's Fascist Conspiracy, Testimony that the Dickstein Committee Suppressed," *New Masses*, p. 10.

73 As quoted in Arthur M. Schlesinger's *The Politics of Upheaval, 1935–1936, The Age of Roosevelt*, Vol. III (Boston: Houghton, Mifflin, 1960), p. 83. See also Hans Schmidt, *Maverick Marine: General Smedley D. Butler and the Contradictions of American Military History* (Lexington: University of Kentucky Press, 1998), pp. 223–31.

74 Schmidt, *Maverick Marine*, p. 229.

75 Archer, *The Plot to Seize the White House*, excerpted from pp. 213–16. See also Nicholas Fox Weber's *The Clarks of Cooperstown: Their Singer Sewing Machine Fortune, Their Great and Influential Art Collections, Their Forty Year Feud* (New York: Alfred A. Knopf, 2007), pp. 185–205.

76 George P. Perros, "Introduction," *Preliminary Inventory of the Special House Committee on Un-American Activities Authorized to Investigate Nazi Propaganda and Certain Other Propaganda Activities Under the Authority of H. Res. 198, 73rd Congress*, p. 3. Undated memorandum, but internal references would seem to place it in the late 1940s.

77 *Investigation of Nazi and Other Propaganda*, House Report 74-153, February 15, 1935.

78 52 *Statutes* 631 (1938). However, that legislation is not included in the comprehensive compilation of Stathis, *Landmark Legislation*, for the 75th Congress (1937–39), pp. 209–12.

79 Author's telephonic interview with Dr. Martin Sweig, November 1971. The Smith Act "required all foreign nationals to register and be fingerprinted. Made it unlawful to advocate the forceful overthrow of the government, to teach such doctrine, or to organize of belong to any organization engaged in such activities" (Stathis, *Landmark Legislation*, p. 215). The Act was approved June 28, 1940, as Public Law 76-670, 54 *Statutes* 670-676.

80 The articles were: "Should Congress Enact a Federal Sedition Law?," *Congressional Digest*, XIV (October 1935), pp. 236–53; "Communism—Its Method," *National Republic*, XXIV (June 1936), p. 1; and "Personal Liberty," *Annals of the American Academy of Political and Social Science*, CLXXXV (May 1936), pp. 154–61.

81 Earl Latham, *The Communist Controversy in Washington: From the New Deal to McCarthy* (New York: Atheneum Press, 1969), originally published by the Harvard University Press in 1966. Latham's positive assessment of the committee appears on pp. 38–40 and the quotation on p. 39. Similar positive assessments of McCormack's chairmanship may be found in Sander Diamond, *The Nazi Movement in the United States, 1924–1941* (Ithaca, NY: Cornell University Press, 1974); Goodman, *The Committee*, pp. 10–14; and Schlesinger, Jr., *The Politics of Upheaval, 1935–36: The Age of Roosevelt*, Vol III, pp. 85–86. By contrast, Latham cites August Raymond Ogden, *The Dies Committee* (Washington, DC: The Catholic University of America Press, 1945), p. 34.

82 See Alan Brinkley's "Huey Long, the Share Our Wealth Movement and the Limits of Depression Dissidence," *Louisiana History*, XXII (Spring 1981), pp. 117–34; and *Voices of Protest: Huey Long, Father Coughlin, and the Great Depression* (New York: Vintage Books, 1984); and Terry L. Jones, "An Administration Under Fire: The Long-Farley Affair of 1935," *Louisiana History*, XXVIII (Winter 1987), pp. 5–17. In their excellent compilation, *Members of Congress: A Bibliography* (Washington, DC: Congressional Quarterly, 1996), Robert U. Goehlert, Fenton S. Martin, and John R. Sayre, list fifty items, including twenty books, about Huey Long (pp. 280–81).

83 Federal Securities Act of 1933 was approved May 22, 1933 (P.L. 73-22; 48 Stat. 74-95). See Stathis, *Landmark Legislation*, p. 202.

84 Securities Exchange Act of 1934 was approved on June 6, 1934 (48 Stat. 881-909). An overview of the SEC and its relationship to Congress may be found in J. Sinclair Armstrong, "Congress and the Securities and Exchange Commission," *Virginia Law Review*, XLV (October 1959), pp. 795–816.

85 Kennedy's appointment to chair the SEC, see David Nasaw's monumental, *The Patriarch: The Remarkable Life and Turbulent Times of Joseph P. Kennedy* (New York: Penguin Press, 2012), pp. 226–28.

86 Marvin W. Block, "Henry T. Rainey of Illinois," *Journal of the Illinois State Historical Society*, LXV (Summer 1972), pp. 142–57. The depiction of Rainey as "legislative marshal" came from the *Literary Digest*, 118 (1934), p. 6.

87 "Speaker H.T. Rainey Dies of Pneumonia and Heart Attack: End Comes Quickly," *NYT*, August 20, 1934, p. 1. See also, Waller, *Rainey of Illinois: A Political Biography, 1903–1934*, p. 203.

88 Author's telephonic interview with the Hon. John W. McCormack, Boston, April 1977.

89 "Speakership Won, Byrns Declares, Sufficient Votes Pledged to assure His Election in House, He Says; Mead Gains for Leader; Buffalo Member Seems to Have Better Chance than O'Connor or McCormack," *NYT*, November 25, 1934, p. 1.

90 Walker's career is favorably chronicled in Gene Fowler, *Beau James: The Life and Times of Jimmy Walker* (New York: Viking, 1949). The investigation by Judge Seabury into Walker's scandals is recounted in Herbert Mitgang's *The Man Who Rode the Tiger: The Life and Tines of Samuel Seabury* (Philadelphia: Lippincott, 1963).

91 Howard Zinn, *La Guardia in Congress* (Ithaca, NY: Cornell University Press, 1959).

92 "Thomas Henry Cullen," *BDUSC* (1989 ed.), p. 855.

93 Cullen's committee assignments may be found in Canon, Nelson, and Stewart, *Committees in the U.S. Congress, 1789–1946*, 3, pp. 252–53.

94 "John Joseph O'Connor," *BDUSC* (1989 ed.), p. 1583. See also James T. Patterson, *Congressional Conservatism and the New Deal: The Growth of the Conservative Coalition in Congress, 1933–1939* (Lexington, KY: University of Kentucky, 1967), pp. 278–90.

95 *House Journal*, 68th Congress, First Session, December 17, 1923, p. 112.

96 On O'Connor's legislative awareness, see his article, "Principal Legislation of the Seventy-Fourth Congress," *U.S. Law Review*, LXIX (September 1935), pp. 466–73.

97 Letter from John McDuffie to Will Bankhead, August 29, 1934, in Box 13, folder 12 of William B. Bankhead Papers, Alabama Department of Archives and History, Montgomery, Alabama.

98 John McDuffie to Walter Chamblin, November 16, 1934, in John McDuffie Papers, W. S. Hoole Special Collections, University of Alabama, Tuscaloosa, Alabama.

99 John McDuffie to John W. McCormack, November 18, 1934, John McDuffie Papers, W. S. Hoole Special Collections, University of Alabama, Tuscaloosa, Alabama.

100 Walter Chamblin to John McDuffie, November 21, 1934, in the McDuffie Papers.

101 John McDuffie to E. E. Cox, December 10, 1934, in John McDuffie Papers, W. S. Hoole Special Collections, University of Alabama, Tuscaloosa, Alabama.

102 John McDuffie to Will Bankhead in the William B. Bankhead Papers, Alabama Department of Archives and History, Montgomery, Alabama.

103 Garrison Nelson, "Partisan Patterns of House Leadership Change, 1789–1977," *APSR*, LXXI (September 1977), pp. 918–39.

104 Dorough, *Mr. Sam*, p. 253; and *NYT*, December 13, 1934, p. 17.

105 Bankhead family in the *BDUSC* (1989 ed.), p. 572.

106 "New Members Back Bankhead Drive in House; Dark Horse Chance Seen Better Due to Close Fight Impending," *NYT*, January 1, 1935, p. 10.

107 The story of O'Connor's mistress was recounted to me by Professor Anthony Champagne of the University of Texas-Dallas in conjunction with his interview of Washington columnist Robert S. Allen who coauthored the syndicated column "Washington Merry-Go-Round" with Drew Pearson. The Allen interview was conducted by Professor Champagne on June 13, 1980, in Washington, DC and is on file at the Sam Rayburn Library in Bonham, Texas.

108 "Democrats Select Byrns for Speaker," *NYT*, January 3, 1935, p. 16.

109 See Walter J. Heacock, "William B. Bankhead and the New Deal," *Journal of Southern History*, XXI (August 1955), pp. 347–59.

110 Emergency Relief Appropriation Act of 1935 was approved April 8, 1935 (49 Stat. 115-119).

111 Searle F. Charles, *Minister of Relief: Harry Hopkins and the Depression* (Syracuse, NY: Syracuse University Press, 1963), pp. 206–19; and George T. McJimsey, *Harry Hopkins: Ally of the Poor and Defender of Democracy* (Cambridge, MA: Harvard University Press 1987).

112 Public Law 74-271; 49 *Statutes*, 629-648 in Stathis, *Landmark Legislation*, pp. 206–207. On the Social Security Act of 1935, see "The Social Security Act, 1935," in Bernard B. Schwartz and Robert B. Stevens, eds., *Income Security*, Vol. 3 of *Statutory History of the United States* (New York: Chelsea House, 1970), p. 59–167.

113 Thomas H. Eliot, *Public and Personal*, edited by Frank O'Brien (St. Louis, MO: Washington University Press, 1971), p. 14. The story is repeated in Eliot's chapter on "The Social Security Act," in *Recollections of the New Deal: When People Mattered* (Boston: Northeastern University Press, 1992), pp. 108–109.

114 Edwin E. Witte, *The Development of the Social Security Act: A Memorandum on the History of the Committee on Economic Security and Drafting and Legislative History of the Social Security Act* (Madison: University of Wisconsin Press, 1963), p. 93.

115 Witte, *The Development of the Social Security Act* [of 1935] based on his contemporaneous notes, pp. 169–70.

116 Two books making this argument are Robert C. Lieberman, *Shifting the Color Line: Race and the American Welfare State* (Cambridge, MA: Harvard University Press, 1995); and Mary Poole, The *Segregated Origins of Social Security: African Americans and the Welfare State* (Chapel Hill: University of North Carolina Press, 2006).

117 Gareth Davies and Martha Derthick, "Race and Social Welfare Policy: The Social Security Act of 1935," *Political Science Quarterly*, CXII (Summer 1997), p. 226.

118 "Statements of Henry Morgenthau, Jr.," in Economic Security Act, Hearings of the House Ways and Means Committee, 74th Congress, 1st Session (1935), quoted in Larry DeWitt, "The Decision to Exclude Agricultural and Domestic Workers from the 1935 Social Security," *Social Security Bulletin*, LXX (2010), online, pp. 49–68, accessed April 17, 2015.

119 Ibid.

120 See chapter 5, "Jim Crow Congress," in Ira Katznelson's *Fear Itself: The New Deal and the Origins of Our Time* (New York: Liveright, 2013), pp. 156–94.

121 Wilbur J. Cohen, Robert M. Ball, and Robert J. Myers, "Social Security Act Amendments of 1954: A Summary and Legislative History," *Social Security Bulletin* (September 1954), pp. 3–18.

122 McCormack is mentioned primarily for his role in passing the Social Security Amendments of 1939, approved August 10, 1939 (Public Law 76-379; 53 *Statutes* 1360-1402, Part 2), in Schwartz and Stevens, *Income Security*, pp. 235–36.

123 J. M. Galloway, "Speaker Joseph W. Byrns: Party Leader in the New Deal," *Tennessee Historical Quarterly*, XXV (1966), pp. 63–76.

124 Randall B. Ripley, *Party Leaders in the House of Representatives* (Washington, DC: The Brookings Institution, 1967), p. 16.

125 "Congress: Reaper's Return," *TIME*, June 15, 1936, pp. 13–14.

126 "Speakers: Joe Byrns Dies and an Old Friend Gets His Job," *Newsweek*, June 13, 1936, p. 9.

127 See O. R. Altman, "'The Second Session of the Seventy-Fourth Congress,' (January 3, 1936 to June 20, 1936)," *APSR*, XXX (December 1936), pp. 1086–107.

8

The Problematic Landslide: Court-Packing and Purges

The 1936 presidential nomination and election

Even more than the 1934 congressional election, this would be a direct referendum on both the New Deal and President Roosevelt. The emergence of some curious allies gave Republicans hope for an electoral repudiation of the president and sufficient gains in Congress to reverse much of the New Deal's far-reaching legislation. The most visible was the Supreme Court that had challenged the constitutionality of a number of New Deal legislative measures, ultimately voiding eleven of them.[1] The Court's majority believed that President Roosevelt had convinced Congress to cede a number of powers that were intended to be beyond the scope of the executive branch and in its reach, state governments had lost much of their authority to the federal government.

The Court's attitude mattered little to the 1936 Democratic National Convention as it renominated President Franklin Roosevelt and Vice President John N. Garner by acclamation. John McCormack spent this summer on vacation in New Hampshire and chose not to attend. It would be the only convention between 1932 and 1968 that he would not attend. The biggest decision emanating from the 1936 convention was the Democratic Party's decision to abandon the "two-thirds rule," which had been in place since the Democrats' initial 1831 convention and thwarted many previous presidential aspirants in the past.[2] Leading the effort to overturn the rule was U.S. Senator Bennett Champ Clark (Dem-Mo.), son of former House Speaker Champ Clark whose 1912 majority tally in the convention balloting was blocked by the rule.[3]

In an effort to placate the white South that had lost this crucial veto over Democratic nominations, the convention created a "bonus" system, similar to that within the Republican Party, which would increase the delegate votes of those states which had been historically Democratic. It was half a loaf, but the southerners who were displeased did not have the votes or the public support to prevent the demise of this unique rule which had given them control over the party's nominees for a century. With Texan Jack Garner as vice president, the party's likeliest nominee four years hence, and bonus delegates added to their tallies, the South's need for keeping the two-thirds rule had passed.

Republicans nominated Governor Alfred M. Landon, "the Kansas Sunflower," with 984 votes to 19 for U.S. Senator William E. Borah, "the Idaho Stallion." The vice presidential nominee was Boston native Frank Knox, publisher of the *Chicago Daily New*,[4] and one of Teddy Roosevelt's "Rough Riders" during the Spanish-American War. Knox and Landon were less doctrinaire than most of their fellow partisans. Given FDR's presumed popularity the Republican convention quickly nominated Landon, who was the sole candidate, and confirmed Knox with no opposition. There was an air of "sacrificial lambs" to their candidacies.

Most of the anti-FDR sentiment emanated from the ultraconservative and well-funded American Liberty League that had lined up the last two former Democratic presidential nominees, John W. Davis and Al Smith, as well as John J. Raskob, the former national chair, and Massachusetts ex-Governor Joseph Ely to battle FDR's liberal agenda.[5] While most observers assumed a Roosevelt reelection, the pro-temperance *Literary Digest* conducted a postcard poll of 10,000,000 voters that contended that FDR would only capture fifteen states (including Massachusetts) and 43.0% of the popular vote. The poll had a relatively high response rate of 24% and had accurately forecast the winner in previous elections. The *Digest's* final preelection prediction of a 33-state Landon victory was naturally worrisome to Democrats.[6]

However, the *Literary Digest's* ten million postcards were sent out to names on lists of owners of automobiles and telephones. It was the nonowners of automobiles and telephones that had benefited most from the New Deal, and many were completely missed in the *Digest's* postcard poll.[7] The *Digest* disputed this assertion, but it appears to be the most plausible one.[8] Another unique predictor, Maine's September election—the first in the nation—had also given an edge to Landon. After all, "As Maine goes, so goes the Nation."

The election night results told a different story: FDR captured 46 states—31 more than the 15 the *Digest* had predicted—and a popular vote percentage of 60.8%—seventeen points higher than predicted—and an 11 million vote plurality over Governor Landon. The *Digest* was discredited and shuttered its doors very shortly afterward. Only the tiny Northern New England state of Vermont, with its three electoral votes, joined the five votes of Maine for Republican Alf Landon leading Jim Farley to revise that hoary chestnut to be "As Maine goes, so goes Vermont."

Congressional gains in the Roosevelt-Garner landslide swept 334 Democrats into the House and 76 in the Senate, the largest number of seats held by one party in either chamber in American history. Democrats occupied 77% of the House seats with the bulk of these new members coming from northern and western districts. As a result, the South's proportionate contribution to the Democratic majority had been reduced to only 32%—a sharp reduction from the 1928 results in which southern members held 62% of the Democratic seats. It was the closest election to a clear mandate the nation had seen, and FDR was eager to cash in on it.

The 1936 election in Boston, the "most Coughlinite city"

For John McCormack, the 1936 election was less easy than for other city Democrats. His difficulty was due to the political presence of Father Coughlin. Coughlin's message of religious devotion and economic populism was directed at the nation's growing substratum of poor urban Catholics, many still pained by the anti-Catholic attacks on Al Smith. Credit reform and the free coinage of silver were among his key economic proposals. Father Coughlin initially supported FDR's New Deal proposals, but when the president failed to credit Coughlin sufficiently for the size of his victory, their relations deteriorated. Ostensibly, the relationship broke over the Frazier-Lemke bill. Sponsored by North Dakota's Senator Lynn Frazier and Representative William Lemke, the bill was basically a three billion dollar issue of paper money to bail out American farmers. Two thousand farms were being foreclosed daily, but economic distress extended well beyond the nation's farmlands. The original version of the act was passed in 1934 but was voided by the Supreme Court.[9]

The revised version of the bill was blocked in the House Rules Committee by its chair, New York's John J. O'Connor. Coughlin denounced O'Connor as "a servant of the money changers." This troubled congressional Catholics, who were unnerved by the denunciations of a coreligionist from a priest with a microphone and a national audience. The McCormack-Dickstein committee was still meeting while the feud between Father Coughlin and Representative O'Connor boiled over. Early in 1935, an enraged John O'Connor threatened to "kick [Coughlin] all the way from the capitol to the White House with clerical garb and all the silver in your pockets which you got from speculating in Wall Street while I was voting for farm bills. Come on."[10] Given Tammany's unique interfaith alliance of Catholics and Jews, John O'Connor feared no electoral repercussions from his public encounter with Father Coughlin. The same could not be said of Boston's Catholic politicians.

Although Congress passed the Frazier-Lemke Farm Mortgage Moratorium Act in 1935,[11] it was not enough for Father Coughlin. His anti-FDR influence continued to grow. It was especially powerful in Boston in spite of the formidable opposition from William Cardinal O'Connell, the conservative leader of Boston's Catholics, who nevertheless was in FDR's camp. Governor James Michael Curley, then planning a run for the U.S. Senate, had to deal cautiously with the large number of Boston's Coughlinites. Curley's occasional Massachusetts Catholic ally, Joseph P. Kennedy, then head of the Securities and Exchanges Commission, carefully maintained a close relationship with Father Coughlin, whom he called "the Padre." Just after Senator Huey Long's murder in September 1935, Joe Kennedy, who was visiting Coughlin's home in Royal Oak, Michigan, called FDR. It was Joe Kennedy who drove Coughlin in his own Rolls Royce to Hyde Park, New York, to meet with President Roosevelt to defuse their growing animosity.[12] Unlike many other Boston Irish politicians, Congressman John McCormack abhorred anti-Semites and did not succumb to either the prejudice or political fearfulness of Father Coughlin's power.

In November 1934, Coughlin launched the Union for Social Justice that initially hoped to push FDR to support his economic reforms. If that failed, Coughlin intended to mobilize enough voters to throw FDR out of the White House in 1936. As it became clear that FDR had no intention of adopting Coughlin's economic agenda, Coughlin moved beyond a social movement to a political one and was named the first president of the National Union for Social Justice. As a native Canadian, he could not be nominated for President of the United States, but he could create a political party, the Union Party which ran in his stead colorless U.S. Representative William Lemke, a far cry from the Huey Long candidacy that would clearly have dented FDR's reelection bid. Lemke was a Minnesota farm boy with a Yale Law degree and had been elected with a joint nomination from North Dakota's Non-Partisan League and the Republican Party to the 73rd Congress in 1932. He was an economic populist and an early supporter of the New Deal. His break with FDR came over the failure of the president to fully support the Frazier-Lemke Farm Bankruptcy bill.[13]

Lemke's running mate was Boston Democrat Thomas C. O'Brien, a Catholic labor lawyer and the former district attorney for Suffolk County. O'Brien also chose to run for the U.S. Senate, a decision that would create tension between Coughlin and Massachusetts Governor Jim Curley, the Democratic nominee. Coughlin came to Boston in August 1935 leading Curley to call Boston "the most Coughlinite city in America."[14]

The long-standing feud between John Fitzgerald and Jim Curley had faded. Honey Fitz had become a spent force and his periodic efforts at electoral redemption through challenges for U.S. Senate nominations were embarrassing. Jim Curley, on the other hand, continued to be a major player in the state's politics. In 1936, after two years as governor, Curley chose not to run for reelection as governor but to challenge for the vacant U.S. Senate seat. His Republican opponent in the Senate contest would be 34-year-old State Representative Boston Brahmin Henry Cabot Lodge, Jr., the grandson of U.S. Senator Henry Cabot Lodge, who had defeated John Fitzgerald in 1916, the state's first ever popular election for the Senate. As was his style, Curley ridiculed Lodge as "Little Boy Blue—blue-blooded, handsome and a boy."[15]

Hoping that FDR's national landslide over Landon was on the horizon, Curley anticipated that the President's coattails would return him once again to Congress. One complicating factor in both races was the presence of Coughlin's Union Party candidates. It would be difficult enough for Curley to defeat Henry Cabot Lodge, Jr. without being undermined in the state's hard-nosed Irish Catholic neighborhoods by O'Brien. That is how it played out. Lodge received 48.5% of the vote to Curley's 41.0% and won with a solid plurality of 135,409 votes.[16] The fact that O'Brien's tally was 134,245 meant that a combined Curley-O'Brien vote would have come within 1,164 votes of Lodge's total. An aggravated Curley saw O'Brien as a "stalking horse."[17] Curley contended that he offered O'Brien $10,000 to leave the race but heard that the Republicans offered him $25,000 to remain in it. Jim was outbid. FDR rolled over Landon in Massachusetts by 174,103 votes, 51.2% to 41.8%.[18] Ticket-splitters allowed FDR to outpoll Jim Curley by 202,965 votes, but once again, the insertion of a competing Boston Irishman in a Curley contest had undermined James Michael's ambitions.

In the presidential contest, the Lemke-O'Brien ticket obtained 116,639 Massachusetts votes for 6.4% of the total and more than three times their national percentage of 2.0%. It was their highest vote total and their third highest percentage behind Lemke's represented state of North Dakota (13.4%) and his birth state of Minnesota (6.6%). In Michigan, headquarters of Coughlin's Shrine of the Little Flower, only 4.2% of the vote was reported for Lemke.[19] In Catholic Massachusetts and Rhode Island, the Union ticket had its best showing in the Northeast with percentages of 6.4 and 6.3 respectively. Nevertheless, America's Catholics had not followed the priestly advice of Father Coughlin to vote for the Union Party. Nor had many of them followed their old champion and 1928 presidential nominee Alfred Emanuel Smith into the Republican Party as he took his embittered "walk" from the Democratic Party of Franklin Roosevelt. There was some decline but FDR's alliance with Catholic America had withstood a major test.

The ethnic rivalry between Boston's Irish, Italian, and Jewish tribes heated up in the mid-1930s with each of the city's dominant wards varying in their commitment to FDR and the Democrats.[20] Boston's three most Irish wards—Charlestown Ward One, South Boston Ward Six, and South Boston/Dorchester Ward Seven—finished first, second, and third among the city's twenty-two wards in 1928 with Al Smith topping the ticket and with FDR as well in 1932. But in 1936, the three Irish wards had slipped to fourth, fifth, and sixth places respectively, while Ward fourteen, Mattapan, the city's most Jewish ward, was the city's most Democratic ward in 1936, 1940, and 1944. By 1948 with its left-liberal Henry Wallaceite wing removed from the Democratic Party it was the three Irish wards topping the list once again.[21]

Coughlinite and Townsend Plan candidacies appeared in five of Massachusetts's fifteen districts, but it was only in Republican George Bates's North Shore district and Democrat John McCormack's South Boston-Dorchester district that these candidacies gathered more than 30% of the vote. Republican Albert P. McCulloch, running on a ticket with Coughlinite support, held McCormack's electoral percentage to 68.7%—his lowest proportion ever.[22]

While his Boston constituents may have lowered McCormack's totals, John had clearly proved his worth in the House leadership. His successful management of the Un-American Activities Committee avoided much of the investigative abuses and individual name-calling which was to characterize the committee's later incarnations, especially those led by Martin Dies (Dem-Texas) and John Rankin (Dem-Miss.). But a precedent for naming such a committee had been established and the adverse consequences for the public's perception of the entire House itself as a result of those investigative abuses would linger for years.

When Father Coughlin's efforts to unseat FDR failed, he became even more strident and his anti-Semitism which was never fully veiled, intensified. Coughlin may have been relegated to a nuisance, but he was dangerous nevertheless. His tirades against the Jews had unfortunate resonance among the less well-educated Catholics upon whom the Democratic Party had come to rely for delivering the votes of America's cities. Anti-Semitism presented a dangerous fissure within the Democratic Party's efforts to consolidate its gains in urban America. As more Jews sought political refuge within the Democratic Party of Franklin Roosevelt, the long-simmering feud between Jews and Catholics, which had so deeply scarred the social landscape thousands of miles away in central and Eastern Europe, had resurfaced in Protestant America.

Catholic politicians who understood the divisive nature of the Catholic-Jewish conflict and knew what steps to take in diffusing it would be sought out by White

House operatives who knew that both sets of non-Protestants would be essential in keeping the Democratic Party on its positive trajectory. John McCormack was one of these select few and his ability to resist the Coughlinite inclinations of his fellow Bay State Democratic Irishmen gained him favorable notice among the keepers of FDR's electoral destiny.

Another leadership contest

Will Bankhead of Alabama was an unlikely figure to head the House of Representatives. Although his political pedigree was impressive—both his father and his brother were elected to the U.S. Senate—for Will, politics was a secondary calling. Will really wanted to be a stage actor. Early in his life, he ran off to Boston to take an acting job in a theater company, but a distraught letter from his mother back home in Jasper, Alabama, led him to abandon this career.[23] He returned to the law but never gave up his love of the theater, and he vowed that should any child of his seek an acting career he would be as supportive as possible. The proof of his commitment was his daughter Tallulah.

Will Bankhead's parental nurturance of and devotion to the acting career of his youngest daughter contributed greatly to her success. Tallulah Bankhead was arguably the most colorful, if not the most talented, of American actresses in the first half of this century. One of her favorite memories was Will's reading of scripts aloud in her dressing room, assuming as always the lead male role.[24]

Bankhead knew that he had a wonderful profile and was keenly aware that the camera would fasten on his handsome visage. The very public Bankhead was a clear contrast to Sam Rayburn and John McCormack, the two very private Democratic Speakers who would follow him to the chair.

Bankhead's ascension had left the majority leader's post vacant for months and this contest would be especially heated. With all the northerners elected in 1936, it was not surprising that a northerner would be a serious contender for the post that Bankhead had vacated when he became Speaker. Unfortunately for President Roosevelt, the northern candidate once again was John J. O'Connor of New York City, the chair of the Rules Committee.

The record number of newly elected northern and western Democrats in the House should have diminished the South's relative impact upon the selection process. Northern and western Democrats were hesitant about placing yet another southerner in the House leadership. O'Connor should have benefited from the northern increase but he was a staunch Tammany Hall Democrat committed to the conservative social agenda of Al Smith. Although O'Connor's brother Basil served FDR as the president's personal attorney, little love was lost between the president and Congressman O'Connor. O'Connor had been an opponent of the president back home in New York, and he was out of step with FDR's plans to reorient the Democratic Party as more uniformly liberal.

President Roosevelt wanted Sam Rayburn of Texas, the chair of the Interstate and Foreign Commerce Committee, to fill Will Bankhead's vacancy as floor leader. Roosevelt appreciated Rayburn's efforts in 1935, when he and Senator Burton Wheeler

(Dem-Mont.) joined forces to pass legislation intended to limit the nation's largest electrical utilities from consolidating their power through holding companies that controlled the rate-setting practices of hundreds of smaller utilities. Sam Rayburn was a New Dealer; John O'Connor was not. Sam Rayburn was three years older than O'Connor and had ten more years of House service, but his committee, Interstate and Foreign Commerce, was less well placed. O'Connor was in a position where he could do more harm to FDR than Rayburn. But O'Connor's prior failed contests made him many enemies, especially among the southerners.

John O'Connor lost out to Will Bankhead in the previous floor leader contest, so it was doubtful that Will wished to serve with a rival leading floor debates. And Cactus Jack Garner, from his vice presidential perch in the Senate, much preferred to have his fellow Texan Sam Rayburn directing the House Democrats. Was there anyone who could help? Yes, there was. It was John McCormack.

Boston Repays Austin: John McCormack was now a senior member of the appointment-making Ways and Means Committee and ideally positioned to help President Roosevelt, Vice President Garner, and Speaker Bankhead. He could do this by lobbying for Sam Rayburn among the newly elected northern Catholics, who had been socialized sufficiently to know that their committee assignments might hang in the balance. John McCormack also had a personal agenda. He disliked O'Connor personally and knew that he was cheating on his wife. O'Connor had mistreated McCormack earlier and John McCormack considered O'Connor to be "arrogant."[25] The social class differentials which marked the two men's backgrounds played no small part in how they regarded one another.

For those familiar with the politics of the Catholic Church in America, the long-standing disdain which existed between New York City's Francis Cardinal Spellman and Boston's Richard Cardinal Cushing mirrored this conflict. Both protégés of the imperious William Cardinal O'Connell, Spellman and Cushing were Massachusetts-born, Irish-descended churchmen, but Spellman's middle-class suburbanite sensibilities were offended by the ragged edges of Cushing's South Boston upbringing. Irishmen could and did discriminate against one another.

John McCormack's successful committee management gained him further stature in Washington. He grew increasingly powerful during the 1930s as he allied himself with southerners in the majority leadership contests by voting for Alabama's Will Bankhead over New York's John O'Connor in 1935 and for Commerce Committee Chair Sam Rayburn of Texas over O'Connor in 1937. It was the Rayburn-O'Connor fight of 1937 that had the greatest impact.[26] John's willingness to vote for a Texan against a fellow Massachusetts-born Catholic greatly impressed the House's southerners and pleased President Roosevelt who correctly regarded O'Connor as a major New Deal opponent.

John's 1937 vote for Sam Rayburn was especially important given the large number of non-southerners in the 75th Congress. John McCormack could now repay his debt to the Texans for their early recognition of his talents. When a number of non-southern Democrats followed his lead, Rayburn defeated O'Connor 184 to 127 on the first ballot in the Democratic Caucus.[27] When asked why he would not support a Catholic coreligionist like O'Connor, John McCormack was blunt: "Religion played no part in my decision."[28] John McCormack had repaid his debt to the Texans. He was now one of them.

McCormack's belief about O'Connor's arrogance derived from the fact that O'Connor was living openly with his mistress. While flamboyant New York Irish politicians like Congressman W. Bourke Cockran, Jennie Churchill's lover, and Mayor Jimmy "Beau James" Walker could flaunt their love lives, Boston's Irish politicians had learned the harsh lesson of Toodles and Honey Fitz. Jim Curley could and did steal, but he never cheated. The devoted husband John McCormack found O'Connor's public infidelities troubling and rallied many urban Catholic votes to Rayburn.[29]

Dean of the delegation

By 1937, John McCormack's role in the House had expanded, and his role in Massachusetts politics had become more central. For most of the 1930s, Billy Connery of Lynn, the dean of the Massachusetts House delegation, and U.S. Senator David I. Walsh of Fitchburg led the Massachusetts congressional Democratic Party. Both were old-style Irish Catholic Democrats who had allied with McCormack in his efforts to bring federal patronage to the Bay State. When Connery died in June 1937, it was John McCormack who succeeded him as head of the Massachusetts congressional Democratic Party. During the years of McCormack's management the party adopted a "southern strategy." McCormack was well aware of how important committee assignments were to members, and he was also aware of how important the seniority rule was to advancement on the committees. McCormack urged Massachusetts House members to make a career of their service in the House and serve long enough to obtain senior status on the committees. This had been, he reasoned, the key to the success of the South in the House.

Massachusetts members who took early to House service were rewarded with quality appointments. Members whose eyes seemed to lie elsewhere on the political landscape were not so fortunate. This was how John McCormack operated as "dean" of the Massachusetts House delegation. Given his high standing among the House Democrats, he was able to provide substantial patronage for his South Boston-Dorchester district. One need look no further than at the huge Old Harbor Housing Project which was constructed in South Boston and dedicated in 1937, the first federally funded public housing project in New England.

The cities and the South struggle for Democratic preeminence

The large Democratic victories of the 1930s were different from those of the Wilson era. Unlike the small margins of the Wilson Congresses, Democratic margins in the early Roosevelt era were enormous and regularly exceeded one hundred or more seats. The size of these majorities brought about their own problems. Large legislative majorities are far more difficult to manage than small ones. Individual members can wander away from party positions on many issues without having any material impact upon legislative victories or losses. Incentives for party loyalty evaporate in such super-majority circumstances.

For the House Democrats, there was an additional problem: the seniority system rewarded the noncompetitive districts of the party, placing those members of the Congress whose districts were the least attuned to changing circumstances in places of key leadership. Although long viewed as an anachronism by liberal critics of Congress, the "seniority rule" which names as standing committee chairs, the majority members with the longest continuous committee service was once viewed as a reformist gesture.[30] The rule was originally developed in the Senate in the aftermath of the Mexican War to avoid contentious intra-party battles over committee chairmanships between the various factions of the Whig and Democratic parties. As a more egalitarian body than the House, the Senate's use of seniority eliminated most chairmanship disputes. The fact that the Senate generally had many more committees than the House and that they had less importance also took much of the tension away from chairmanship selection.

However in the House, the Speaker Cannon era (1903–11) was a constant reminder of how chairman selection systems could be deeply politicized. Removing the chairman selection process from the Speaker was a key component of the House's reform surge in the 1909–10 revolt against Speaker Cannon. The two House parties may have differed in their means of choosing members for the committees, but both parties chose to use the "seniority system" to make their chairmanship selections. The major political consequence of the seniority system was to reward one-party regions of the nation. For Republicans this generally meant members from congressional districts in the rural northeast and in the farm states of the Midwest. For Democrats, the system advantaged members from the South and the products of the nation's large urban political machines. John McCormack benefited from the "seniority rule" which had become inviolable among House Democrats. With each new class of elected Democrats, John McCormack's safe South Boston-Dorchester district enabled him to move higher up the ranks of Democratic members.

The competitive districts of the nation located as they were in the north and the west may have provided congressional Democrats with their control over the respective chambers of the Congress, but they provided very few of its leaders. The two great wings of the Democratic Party were destined to collide. The southern and border States had provided a substantial base of members for the congressional Democratic Party. Those Democrats had survived a number of Republican landslides and had been the major source of the party's hierarchy, both elected floor leaders and committee chairs, for much of the first third of the twentieth century.[31]

The Democratic Party was created as a southern party. In 1796, when the nation's first two-party election pitted Vice President John Adams of Massachusetts against Thomas Jefferson of Virginia, regional divisions determined the vote. Jefferson received 54 of his 68 electoral votes from states south of the Mason-Dixon line, while Adams received 59 of his 71 votes from north of the line.[32] Jefferson lost the presidential portion of that contest, but in each of the subsequent ones, Jefferson's party—the Democratic-Republicans until 1824 and the Democrats after that—used their control of southern electoral votes to win twelve of the fifteen antebellum presidential elections between 1800 and 1856. It was the party of slavery with all of its elected presidents from Thomas Jefferson of Virginia to James K. Polk of Tennessee having owned slaves[33] and its two non-slaveholding presidents Franklin Pierce of New Hampshire and James Buchanan of Pennsylvania labeled as "doughfaces"—northern defenders of slavery.

The pre–Civil War arrival of millions of European immigrants jeopardized the political hegemony of the southern-dominated Democratic Party. European immigrants chose to avoid the South lest they be obliged to compete for low paid employment with unpaid slaves. As a result, the northern and western states and their cities grew more rapidly than did the South. This created an opportunity for the newly formed Republican Party, and it was one that they seized.

From 1860's election of Abraham Lincoln until the 1928 election of Herbert Hoover, Republicans won the presidency in fourteen of eighteen contests with eleven different nominees. During these 70 years, the Republican Party was clearly the party of the dominant demographic groups within the American electorate—white, native-born, Protestant, middle class, nonurban, and non-southern. The Democratic Party was the party of white native-born Protestant rural southerners. Social class distinctions mattered less in the South than did racial and religious ones. Had the nation remained this way, the Democratic Party would have existed only as a regional minority able to gain occasional power in Congress, but emerging victorious only in presidential contests when intra-party feuds within the Republican Party had divided its majority.

If the Democratic Party was to become a presidential majority party, it had to reach beyond the South to non-Protestant, non-native, non-rural, non-middle class, and nonwhite Americans. Accomplishing this broadening of the base without losing the electoral votes and congressional seats of white, rural Protestant southerners would be the ultimate test of the leaders of the Democratic Party.

The city constituencies

It was the cities that would have to be accommodated if Democrats were to become a majority, but there was serious resistance to that strategy. The North had cities; the South did not. In the years following the Civil War, Democrats had been able to gain political power in the mayoralty elections of a number of northern and western cities. Much of those urban gains were lost when the Democratic Party placed its presidential nomination thrice into the hands of William Jennings Bryan of Nebraska. Bryan, who was nominated for president in 1896, 1900, and 1908, was antiurban and anti-immigrant. The northern cities responded appropriately and Democrats lost the major urban areas of the nation. As they had been in antebellum times, the presidential Democrats were in conflict with the nation's changing demography.

Growing urbanization had no immediate impact upon presidential politics. In both of the post–Great War presidential elections, the Democratic tickets of James Cox-Franklin D. Roosevelt in 1920 and John Davis-Charles Bryan in 1924 failed to capture a plurality in any of the nation's twelve largest metropolises.[34] However, rural America felt threatened in the 1920s, and it chose to counter the growing urbanization of American life. A number of legislative measures were passed to limit urban America and the immigrant populations that rural America felt had accounted for much of their displacement. Among these was the 18th Amendment that limited the manufacture, transportation, and consumption of alcoholic beverages.

Twice during the 1920s in 1921 and 1924, Congress passed legislation limiting immigration to those whose countrymen were already situated in the United States.[35] But the needs and worries of urban American newcomers were seldom prioritized in the rural-dominated House of Representatives. An unappreciated aspect of the 73rd Congress elected in 1932 is that it was the first House chosen after a census-mandated reapportionment in 1912. Following the 1920 Census, it was revealed that for the first time in the nation's history, a majority of enumerated Americans lived in urban places. To protect the "rural yeoman character" of the nation's politics, rural congressmen successfully quashed legislation to reapportion the nation to reflect the shift of the population to the cities.[36]

The 1928 presidential election provided the quintessential urban-rural contest as it pitted the champion of urban America, the Irish-German Catholic New York City-born Al Smith against the Iowa-born Quaker Herbert Hoover of California. Al Smith's defeat amid the backdrop of anti-Catholicism and anti-urbanism cut the nation's urban Catholics deeply. In spite of the defeat, the choice represented an historic effort on the part of the Democrats to reach into non-Protestant and non-rural America for a candidate well beyond their southern base.

Following the 1930 Census, urbanizing industrial states gained new House seats led by California with nine and Michigan with four. Also exceeding national growth rates were the already large states of New York, Ohio, Texas, and New Jersey that accounted for the shift of 22 seats away from the smaller rural states.[37] Most new seats were located in the cities giving the House Democrats a more urban cast and assuring the legislative success of the New Deal in the 73rd Congress. It was hoped that the increased Democratic majorities of the 1934 contest would continue this legislative momentum. The Depression was far from over and FDR's advisors continued to develop new programs to deal with short-term economic dislocations and long-term economic security. The 74th Congress that convened on January 3, 1935, was less productive than the 73rd, but it is doubtful if any Congress could come close to the level of legislative productivity of that spirited majority.[38]

European tremors and neutrality

As Hitler and Mussolini flexed their muscles in Europe, Americans grew increasingly fearful of immersion in yet another international war. They were supported in this concern by the findings of the Senate Special Committee on Investigation of the Munitions Industry, chaired by U.S. Senator Gerald Nye (Rep-ND). The committee was named on April 12, 1934, a few weeks after the House had named the McCormack-Dickstein committee. Retired General Smedley Butler, the star of the McCormack-Dickstein Committee, was also a notable witness before the Nye committee.[39]

The Nye committee focused on war-profiteering by munitions companies and labeled its most egregious profiteers as "merchants of death." The committee continued its hearings into 1936 until it came to an abrupt halt when Nye, a staunch Republican, sought to implicate Democratic President Woodrow Wilson as withholding critical information from Congress during the debates on the war. At that moment, Senate Appropriations Chair Carter Glass of Virginia, who had served for thirteen months as Wilson's secretary of the treasury, exploded in a rage so violent that witnesses saw blood dripping from his knuckles as he pounded his desk.[40] Although the Nye committee closed up shop shortly afterward, its vivid stories of war-profiteering had taken their toll and infused American isolationists with enough information to prevent any American assistance to European nations facing the predations of Adolf Hitler.

Even after the Nye committee ceased its investigations, testimony presented before it touched a raw nerve among millions of Americans, who were fearful of the United States becoming involved yet again in the political morass that Europe had become in the 1930s. The consequence was that Congress would pass four Neutrality Acts in 1935, 1936, 1937, and 1939, each intended to keep America out of "foreign wars."[41] However, the complexity and diversity of the nation undermined the belief that American neutrality could ever be legislated.[42]

Neutrality Strained, the Spanish Civil War: The two early Neutrality Acts of 1935 and 1936 originated in the Senate and were passed in the House without roll calls, but the two later ones, of 1937 and 1939, spawned contentious battles that jeopardized the Roosevelt coalition of southerners, liberal intellectuals, and big-city Catholics.

The Spanish Civil War erupted in July 1936 as conservative Spanish generals sought to overthrow the elected Republican government of President Manuel Azaria. Spain was divided between the right-wing forces consolidated under the Falangist leadership of General Francisco Franco and the center-left forces loyal to the Spanish Republic.[43] Because the Roman Catholic Church of Spain had been allied with the right-wing and had accrued a great deal of wealth, the Spanish Republicans sought to appropriate much of that wealth and as a consequence were dubbed anticlerical, an echo of Spain's *liberales* movement early in the nineteenth century that was clearly anticlerical. Ultimately, Franco's forces would be aided with supplies from Hitler's Germany, Mussolini's Italy, and the conservative government of neighboring Portugal. Countering these fascist forces was support from the Soviet Union and idealistic left-wingers from the United States, organized under the aegis of the Abraham Lincoln and George Washington Brigades. In retrospect, the Spanish Civil War was seen as a rehearsal for World War II. It continues to hold fascination for those authors who believe that fascism could have been stopped had the United States intervened on behalf of the Spanish Republic. Those generally liberal contentions underestimate the depth and breadth of the Democratic Party's reliance on urban Catholics to deliver the electoral votes of the heavily Catholic large states. But as a native New Yorker, albeit a Protestant, FDR knew well of the sensibilities of America's Catholics regarding their coreligionists in other nations.[44]

In the United States, Catholics and conservatives rallied around Franco's Nationalists, while liberals and intellectuals rallied behind the Republican Loyalists and its American allies in the left-leaning Abraham Lincoln Brigade.[45] Massachusetts, the largest state with a Catholic majority, was clearly on Franco's side. Led by Cardinal O'Connell of Boston, U.S. Senator David I. Walsh, and U.S Representative John W. McCormack, Bay State Catholics challenged the efforts of First Lady Eleanor Roosevelt to bring 2000 Basque refugee children to the United States.[46] McCormack, as the House's leading anti-Communist liberal, even met with FDR to tell him that the group that Eleanor supported was "a Communist front."[47]

It was the Neutrality Acts that forbade official American government involvement in the conflict that kept these two wings at bay and stopped them from tearing apart the northern urban component of the Roosevelt coalition. FDR was warned that "[House Speaker] Bankhead and [Majority Leader] Rayburn told him in May 1938 that any move toward the Spanish Republicans would alienate the entire Roman Catholic population of the country . . . (The President's Roman Catholic allies, like [U.S. Senator] Robert Wagner and John McCormack and insiders like Corcoran, Farley, Flynn, and Missy LeHand presumably told him the same thing.)."[48]

John McCormack's commitment to the nationalist cause was strong enough to lead him to dissuade his longtime assistant Martin Sweig from writing a doctoral dissertation at Georgetown University on the Spanish Civil War. After Sweig became convinced that the Loyalist Republicans should have been supported, McCormack told Sweig that "you won't be writing that thesis in this office." Sweig got the message and changed his topic to the Boer War where both he, the son of German Jewish parents, and John McCormack could sympathize with the South African Boers against the British.[49]

The 1937 Neutrality Act addressed the issue in the midst of the Spanish Civil War while the 1939 Act was debated after the German invasion of Poland and the declaration of war by Great Britain and France against Germany. These two acts that caused political difficulty for FDR were unavoidable for John McCormack as he moved further up the House's leadership ladder.

The FDR-Joe Kennedy alliance

As John McCormack steadily ascended in the U.S. House, Joe Kennedy's administrative portfolios grew. After successfully directing the initial Securities and Exchanges Commission, he stepped aside for Harvard Law Dean James Landis and was named by FDR to head the newly created United States Maritime Commission, created by Congress in 1936 to replace the U.S. Shipping Board. Kennedy's experience running the Fore Fall River Shipyard in World War I was cited as a reason for his selection. That carried some irony, for it was in his management of that shipyard that Joe Kennedy and FDR had their first contentious encounter over payment for two Argentine warships.[50]

Joe Kennedy was also a key player in the 1936 presidential election as he declared to the nation that he was an FDR loyalist. Kennedy's 128-page book *I'm for Roosevelt* was a businessman's defense of the New Deal. Kennedy's opening chapter entitled "Which the Father of Nine Children Explains What He Thinks this Election Means to Them" contained one of the more disingenuous ambition disavowals ever printed on paper. On the third page of the book, Joe stated, "I have no political ambitions for myself or for my children."[51] This was a remarkable statement from a man who hoped to be nominated for president himself, prepped his oldest son for the post, and whose three later-born sons would each contend for the White House.

Joe Kennedy's greatest service to FDR during the first term was to use his considerable influence within the Roman Catholic hierarchy to rein in Father Coughlin. While John McCormack avoided Catholic Church politics, Joe Kennedy became increasingly involved. Kennedy was wary of Coughlin as early as December 1933, when he wrote to Felix Frankfurter stating that Coughlin "has the most terrific radio following that you can imagine and to my way of thinking he is becoming an out and out demagog [*sic*] with a rather superficial knowledge of fundamentals but a striking way of making attacks that pleases the masses, with a beautiful voice that stirs them frightfully."[52]

Coughlin's anticapitalist rants against bankers disturbed Joe Kennedy, a banker and a firm believer in capitalism. However, the most troubling aspect of Coughlin's message was that it had begun to estrange Catholics from the American mainstream. For a man like Joe Kennedy who had fought the battle for Catholic acceptance in multiple corners of American life, the Coughlin impact would potentially undo much of his life's work.

In order to undermine Coughlin, a religious strategy would be employed. Joe Kennedy's key Catholic ally was fellow Massachusetts native Francis Spellman, the very ambitious Auxiliary Bishop of Boston who served under the imperious William Henry Cardinal O'Connell, who had presided over Joe and Rose's wedding. O'Connell had no regard for Coughlin whom he characterized as a "speaker [who] begins to talk nonsense, or indulges in mere emotionalism or sensationalism he is stopped and that is the end of his talks."[53] Nor did he care much for his onetime protégé Francis Spellman, who he sent off to the Pontifical North American College where Spellman achieved the doctorate that O'Connell had not obtained. When Spellman left Boston to become Archbishop of New York, O'Connell said, "Francis is an example of what happens to a bookkeeper when you teach him how to read."[54]

The ambitious Spellman had made powerful friends in Rome—Pope Pius XI, Cardinal Eugenio Pacelli, the Vatican Secretary of State who would become Pope Pius XII, and Count Enrico Galeazzi, the Vatican architect and the Rome director of the Catholic men's fraternity the American-based Knights of Columbus. With Kennedy's urging and acting on the advice of Cardinal Pacelli and Count Galeazzi, the Vatican offered no support for Coughlin and as he became further isolated. Coughlin became more and more anti-Semitic and pro-Nazi in his broadcasts and publications, costing him to lose even more political influence.[55] Joe Kennedy had successfully contained Coughlin and risked alienating working-class Catholics, especially his fellow conservative Irishmen, on FDR's behalf. Father Charles Coughlin's influence would continue to decline at the brink of WWII, as he was forced off the air in 1939 after Nazis invaded Poland.

Now FDR truly owed Kennedy. He would not give him the cabinet post that he most craved, Secretary of the Treasury, and Kennedy would not accept the post that FDR offered him as ambassador to Ireland. That would be small potatoes. If Joe was to be named to a diplomatic post, he wanted one that he felt was commensurate with the support that he had rendered and the political risks that he had undertaken. The only one that seemed to meet Kennedy's vaunted expectations was that of the Court of St. James in London. Although he received the post, it was Kennedy's increasingly tone-deaf political conduct at the Court of St. James that would lead to his estrangement from FDR and his replacement by John McCormack as FDR's favorite Boston Irishman.

Mayor McCormack?

Failing in the 1936 Senate race, Jim Curley sought to return to City Hall in 1937. The four-year succession window had passed and he needed a victory. A number of the Brahmins led by State Representative Henry Lee Shattuck urged John McCormack to leave the House, return to Boston, and save the city from Curley.[56] John was disinclined. He was moving up in the national arena and the House Democratic hierarchy, and his South Boston barkeep brother Edward J. "Knocko" McCormack had become a key member of the Curley entourage. John was also well aware of the bare-knuckled approach to his opponents that Curley employed, and he respectfully declined. John's anxiety about the possible discovery of his reinvented past may have contributed to his decision not to challenge Curley. One can only imagine what Curley would have done to John had he found out that Joe McCormack, John's father, was not an Irish immigrant who had died when John was 13, but a Canadian Scot who had deserted the family when John was 13 and had died in Maine when John was 37.

It would be former Curley protégé, the tall, handsome, wavy-haired Maurice J. Tobin of Roxbury, who would take the challenge to defeat Jim Curley's fifth electoral onslaught on City Hall. Tobin was born in the Mission Hill neighborhood, the son of an Irish-born working-class carpenter. A Boston College graduate, Tobin represented that generation of Boston Irish-Americans transitioning from their "shanty Irish" roots to lace curtain and, perhaps, even more. His victory over Curley led the Great and General Court to remove the 1918 ban on successive mayoral reelections that it imposed upon the city following Curley's reelection close call in 1917.[57] The 36-year-old Maurice Tobin was the new Irish champion of the Boston Brahmins.[58] The Brahmins thought that Tobin's mayoral victory had rid them of Jim Curley. They would be mistaken.

Leverett Saltonstall, the craggy-faced descendant of Puritans, would stop Curley's 1938 comeback to the State House. Saltonstall had succeeded John McCormack in 1923 as Henry Shattuck's favorite protégé in the legislature. Saltonstall was a tenth-generation Harvard man and his Puritan ancestor Sir Richard Saltonstall had crossed the Atlantic with the legendary John Winthrop on the *Arbella* to establish their initial settlement in Salem and found the Massachusetts Bay Colony three centuries earlier. "Salty" was yet another quintessential Brahmin. Curley described Saltonstall as "a man with a South Boston face and a Back Bay name."[59]

Salty campaigned in South Boston, declaring, "I am proud of that South Boston face. It's not a double face."[60] He didn't carry Southie, but he easily defeated Jim Curley with a solid statewide victory—53.3% to 45.0%. It would be Jim Curley's last reach for state power. However, Curley was not yet through with Boston politics; nor was Honey Fitz, who would have one "last hurrah."

Packing the Supreme Court

Back in Washington, the 75th Congress opened on January 3, 1937, with Will Bankhead of Alabama newly elected as Speaker. The floor business of the Democrats was now entrusted to Sam Rayburn, the new majority leader, and Patrick Boland, the small, thin whip from Pennsylvania's coal country.[61]

Success does not always breed further success. The 1936 election provided huge Democratic majorities in both the House and Senate, a clear mandate. But this mandate differed from that of four years earlier. The 1936 mandate was one of thanks from a grateful nation to the president who had rescued it from an economic black hole. It was not necessarily a nation that wished the president to continue the massive restructuring of the federal government. The atmosphere had lightened and public optimism had rebounded.

FDR saw the 75th Congress as yet another one that he could handle easily. FDR's 46-state landslide in 1936 had also given the Democrats a 76 to 16 majority in the Senate with four like-minded allies from Minnesota, Wisconsin, and Nebraska. The House was almost as lopsided with a 334 Democratic majority with 13 other like-minded Progressive, Farmer-Labor, and Independent allies. Only 88 House Republicans had survived the landslide.

Unlike the two previous Congresses, FDR did not have an ambitious legislative agenda for the 75th. He was much more focused on protecting the congressional gains of his first term. Those gains were jeopardized by a Supreme Court disinclined to give the New Deal carte blanche to restructure the nation's governing and financial institutions. On March 9, 1937, FDR delivered his "Fireside Chat" on the Court, saying[62]:

> We have, therefore, reached the point as a nation where we must take action to save the Constitution from the Court and the Court from itself. We must find a way to take an appeal from the Supreme Court to the Constitution itself. We want a Supreme Court which will do justice under the Constitution and not over it. In our courts we want a government of laws and not of men.

With his popular vote mandate and enormous congressional majorities, FDR sought to tame the conservative Supreme Court that had declared eleven pieces of New Deal legislation to be unconstitutional.[63] FDR's plan would add a new justice to the Court for each justice over the age of seventy and six months who chose not to retire. The ultimate goal was to add six new Justices increasing the Court's size to fifteen. Critically referred to as "the Four Horsemen," conservative Justices James McReynolds, George Sutherland, Pierce Butler, and Willis Van Devanter were often joined by the two moderate conservatives Chief Justice Charles Evans Hughes and Owen Roberts, easily outvoting the three liberals on the Court—Louis D. Brandeis, Harlan Fiske Stone, and Benjamin N. Cardozo. With six new appointees of his own on the Court, FDR would no longer have to worry about the constitutionality of his congressional agenda. Would the public accept FDR's proposal?

Flush with newfound legitimacy in the wake of their successful prediction of FDR's 1936 reelection victory, the Gallup Poll conducted a number of public opinion surveys throughout the spring of 1937 to gauge the level of popular support and opposition to President Roosevelt's Court reorganization plan. While some retrospective treatments contend that the plan was overwhelmingly opposed, the data indicate a much closer division of opinion among the American people (Table 8.1). The question was most often posed as: "Are you in favor of President Roosevelt's proposal to reorganize the Supreme Court?"[64]

Although opposition remained steady, 64% of those polled in the April 7–12 survey agreed with the question, "Would you favor an amendment requiring Supreme Court justices to retire at some age between 70 and 75?" And in the April 21–26 survey, 61% agreed with the question, "Do you think the President will win his fight to enlarge the Supreme Court?"

While the public was marginally opposed, congressional opposition grew throughout the spring. Representative Hatton Sumners (Dem-Tex.), chair of the House Judiciary Committee and Sam Rayburn's best friend in the House, originally hoped to induce the more elderly justices to retire by creating the post of "retired Justice" with its attendant tax benefits, but his proposal never reached the House floor.[65] While Sumners understood FDR's frustrations with the Court, he felt that the proposal was

Table 8.1 Gallup Poll Responses to: "Are you in favor of President Roosevelt's proposal to reorganize the Supreme Court?" February 28 to May 23, 1937

Survey Date	Reported	Yes	No
February 17–22, 1937	February 28	47%	53%
March 3–8, 1937	March 25	47	53
March 17–22, 1937	March 28	48	52
April 1–6, 1937	April 11	49	51
April 21–26, 1937	May 2	47	53
May 5–10, 1937	May 23	46	54

Source: AIPO reported in George H. Gallup, *The Gallup Poll: Public Opinion, 1935-1971* (New York: Random House, 1972), pp. 50–59.

much too ambitious. After he and other congressional leaders met with the president on February 5, he declared to his colleagues, "Boys, here's where I cash in my chips."[66] Now aware of Sumners's opposition, House Majority Leader Rayburn urged that the legislation begin in the Senate.

The revolt among the congressional Democrats had begun. It would spread to the Senate where Majority Leader Joseph Robinson (Dem-Ark.), Al Smith's 1928 Protestant vice presidential running mate, was obliged to push himself hard against growing resistance in the Senate Judiciary Committee where Democrats held fourteen of the eighteen committee seats. But Senate Judiciary Chair Henry F. Ashurst (Dem-Ariz.) was secretly opposed to the plan and delayed the bill as long as he could. However, it was Joe Robinson's fatal heart attack on July 14 that sealed its fate. Eight days later on July 22, a motion to recommit the bill to the Judiciary Committee, effectively killing it, was passed overwhelmingly by a vote of 70 to 20.[67] Public opposition had grown as well and Gallup reported on September 12 that 68% of those polled said "No" to the question: "Would you like to have President Roosevelt continue his fight to enlarge the Supreme Court?"[68]

The Conservative Coalition and the failed purge

Congressional reaction to the Court proposal was so negative that it set in motion the counter–New Deal alliance, the "Conservative Coalition" of southern Democrats and Republicans that doomed much of FDR's later legislative agenda. In December 1937, Democratic U.S. Senator Josiah Bailey of North Carolina prepared what would generally be known as the "Conservative Manifesto."[69] Bailey had battled Harry Hopkins and the WPA earlier[70] but it was the failure of Court-packing and the 1937 recession that emboldened Bailey to draft a manifesto of conservative principles. It consisted of ten propositions from the conventional conservative agenda, some of which being lower taxes, states' rights, and less regulation. While a number of Senators from both parties participated in its drafting, it appeared to be more of a public anti-FDR venting than a guide to overall policymaking and its impact was minimal.

FDR still had influence as evidenced in the 1938 Fair Labor Standards Act, better known as the Wages and Hours bill. That bill's commitment to minimum wages and maximum hours had been a key plank in the 1936 Democratic Platform, and organized labor was eager to have the bill passed. FDR's key congressional allies were U.S. Senator Hugo L. Black of Alabama and John McCormack's friend Labor Committee Chair William P. Connery, Jr. Despite a successful vote in the Senate 56 to 28, the House version stalled within the Rules Committee, then chaired by FDR's Tammany Hall nemesis John J. O'Connor. Fourteen members sat on the committee: ten Democrats and four Republicans, but the five southern Democrats led by Gene Cox of Georgia joined with the four Republicans led by Joe Martin of Massachusetts to block the bill inside the committee. O'Connor, repeatedly rebuffed by House liberals in his leadership quests, was disinclined to help the president reward his liberal electoral allies in the labor movement.

These two bruising battles led FDR to let his hubris get the best of his generally astute political judgment, as the president launched his even more ill-fated "purge" of conservative Democrats.[71] FDR's first contest was an easy victory in the May 3, 1938, Florida Senate primary for New Deal supporter Claude Pepper which was followed by the House's liberals circulating a discharge petition to release the bill from the Rules Committee. The 218 votes—a majority of the House—were quickly rounded up and the bill was passed.

Further emboldened, FDR operatives organized "the elimination committee," comprised of key FDR loyalists. They were identified by Eleanor Roosevelt's Pulitzer Prize–winning biographer and close friend, Joseph P. Lash. Commerce Secretary Harry Hopkins was the leader of the group. Harold Ickes was also deeply involved. Others whom *TIME* magazine listed were "James Roosevelt, then serving as his father's secretary; Joseph Keenan, a Department of Justice official who had been part of the White House political staff in the Court fight, and David Niles, a Boston progressive and Hopkins's chief political adviser."[72] And in Lash's afterthought, "Corcoran and Cohen were there."

Susan Dunn's valuable account of the purge gave heavier weight to the role of Tommy Corcoran and Ben Cohen than did Lash, and she left out the names of Jimmy Roosevelt and David Niles.[73] While Jimmy Roosevelt would have been displeased by his omission, the mysterious David Niles would have had his "passion for anonymity" rewarded once again.

Gallup Polls in August 1938 indicated that only 39% of the Democrats agreed with the question: "Do you approve or disapprove of President Roosevelt's campaign to defeat Democrats who oppose his views?" A clear majority of Democrats—61%—disapproved.[74] But FDR's operatives continued in their quest.

Focusing primarily upon conservative southern dissidents, the purge backfired as "four of the purge's main targets sailed to renomination and reelection, easily brushing Roosevelt's onslaught aside: Walter George of Georgia, Cotton Ed Smith of South Carolina, Millard Tydings of Maryland, and Guy Gillette of Iowa."[75] Only FDR's Rules Committee nemesis New York's John O'Connor, who had successfully derailed FDR's executive branch reorganization bill in 1938, failed renomination.[76]

The purge launched a firestorm among the 75th Congress's few remaining Republicans and outraged the institutional sensibilities of numerous conservative southern Democrats. Linked together, this cross-party alliance would be known as the "Conservative Coalition," and it would dramatically limit FDR's efforts to extend the liberal legislative thrust of the New Deal into his second term.[77] While initially created to blunt the liberal surge of the New Deal, the institutional power of the Conservative Coalition would extend for decades.[78] James Patterson's excellent recounting of the coalition's emergence fastened upon the shared anti-metropolitan sentiments that joined these two groups together, dissimilar as they might have been regionally. They believed that the New Deal had been foisted upon them by the foreign forces of the cities, "our American Babylons with their slums and laboring masses in unions that exert pressures at the polls through their political action committees," in the words of J. Frederick Essary.[79]

The "switch in time"

FDR's efforts to "pack the Court" were undermined in April 1937, when the Court's two moderate conservatives, Hoover appointees Chief Justice Charles Evans Hughes and Owen Roberts, seemed to switch their votes in a pro–New Deal direction.[80] While Hughes had shown occasional sympathy for New Deal measures, it was Roberts's move to legitimate Washington State's minimum wage legislation in *West Coast Hotel v. Parrish*, 300 U.S. 379 (1937) that was called by Harvard Law Professor Thomas Reed Powell as "the switch in time that saved nine." This decision effectively ended the Court's staunch pro-business agenda that emanated from its 5–4 decision in *Lochner v. New York*, 198 U.S. 45 (1905). In that case, the Court ruled that a New York law attempting to limit the hours worked by bakers to sixty per week was an "unreasonable, unnecessary and arbitrary interference with the right and liberty of the individual to contract."

The post-*Parrish* Court became accepting of New Deal initiatives which remained untouched for the eight-year balance of FDR's presidency. With the opportunity to name eight new Justices and elevate Harlan Fiske Stone to Chief over that period the conflict abated. The Senate defeated none of his appointments with seven confirmed by voice vote and only Hugo Black (63 to 16) and William O. Douglas (62 to 4) faced nominal roll call opposition.[81] However, while FDR may have won the battle with the Court, he (and subsequent liberal presidents) would more often lose the war with the Congress. No further efforts were made by Congress to alter the size of the Court nor did the Court invalidate any further congressional legislation.

The 1938 midterm election

The House Democratic majority of the 75th Congress was much too large. It was a legislative majority too ideologically diverse and geographically extended to manage effectively, and it undermined whatever hopes FDR may have had for a united Democratic front to move the New Deal agenda forward.[82] His legislative program had stalled. Having won the substantive war (albeit losing the public relations battle) with the Supreme Court, FDR attempted a repeat of the 1934 congressional election by turning the 1938 congressional election into a philosophical mandate, if not a party one. It was a mistake.

The 1938 midterm election ended the New Deal thrust.[83] The 69 Senate Democrats and their four liberal allies held a 73 to 23 edge over the Republicans, but the willingness of conservative southerners to defect from FDR's agenda made this a relatively precarious philosophical majority. The House was in even worse shape; there were 262 Democratic seats left—a loss of 72 seats and only six allies instead of the prior thirteen. Republicans had virtually doubled their seats from 88 to 169. And an even greater concern for FDR was that the southern and border states now held a numeric majority among the remaining House Democrats, and many of the more conservative members had already withstood FDR's efforts to purge them.

With Europe lurching toward yet another full-scale war and the American economy sliding back into unemployment and recession, this would not be a happy time for

FDR. And if FDR were to follow the eight-year presidential precedent, this would be his last Congress and his presidential legacy would likely be less than that of his fifth cousin, the exuberant Teddy Roosevelt, whose career had long been a measuring stick for his own. The House Democrats knew that when they retained their leadership team of Speaker Will Bankhead, Majority Leader Sam Rayburn, and Majority Whip Patrick J. Boland of Pennsylvania. The only newcomer in the mix was John McCormack, who had reached the penultimate post of chair of the Democratic Caucus in 1939—only three steps from the speakership.

The 1938 "McCormack Act": Ideological cross-currents emerged in 1938 as both fascist and Communist activities increased in the United States. After the Friends of New Germany had been exposed by the McCormack-Dickstein Committee, the primary organization for this renewed effort was the German-American Bund led by their naturalized "fuehrer" Fritz Kuhn. Kuhn's large public rallies troubled American liberals and left-leaning politicians. Often accompanied with blatant anti-Semitic sentiments, these organizations impelled Representative Sam Dickstein, the Lithuanian-born Jewish Chair of the House Immigration and Naturalization Committee, to try to resuscitate the 1934–35 Special Committee on Un-American Activities. That earlier committee, chaired by John McCormack with Dickstein as its vice chair, focused primarily upon proto-fascist groups. But times had changed and the New Deal's popularity had diminished by 1938 in the wake of a 19% unemployment rate and increased labor unrest in the form of "sit-down strikes."

It was also at this time that Congress passed the Foreign Agents Registration Act (FARA) requiring that agents representing the interests of foreign powers in a "political or quasi-political capacity" disclose their relationship with the foreign government and information about related activities and finances.[84] Often referred to as the "McCormack Act," the act grew out of the McCormack-Dickstein Special Committee and was intended to investigate propagandists in the employ of foreign governments. Originally administered by the State Department, its authority was moved to the Department of Justice in 1942. Its most common current use is to keep tabs on Washington lobbyists for foreign governments. Although it has been on the books for over 70 years and amended a number of times, it only engendered 23 criminal prosecutions. It was not widely used and its most successful prosecution was that of the German-born pro-Nazi author George Sylvester Viereck. Although not always called the "McCormack Act," this was how it was identified during the prosecution of Viereck in 1941.[85]

While the act was intended to track the propagandizing activities of both fascists and Communists, it was clear that ultraconservatives in Congress had little interest in the activities of fascists, their focus was almost exclusively on Communists, using anti-Communism as a club to bash FDR and his left-leaning New Dealers.

The Dies Committee

Pushing for a resuscitation of the 1934–35 Special Committee that he and John had cochaired was Sam Dickstein, eager to expose increased Nazi activity (and to continue his payments from the Soviet Embassy). Seizing upon Dickstein's efforts was fellow Immigration Committee member, the increasingly conservative Democrat Martin Dies, Jr. who had broken with the New Deal to become a fervent anti-Communist.[86] In May of 1938, the House agreed to re-create the Un-American Activities Committee. McCormack who had been watching Dies for some time was convinced that Dies would train his fire almost exclusively upon the left-leaning New Deal liberals and progressives while ignoring right-wing activity. Despite John McCormack's efforts to confine these later investigations to the role of foreign governments, the House's conservatives were freely tossing "un-Americanism" and "subversive" charges at any number of domestic political entities with which they disagreed, most notably the labor unions affiliated with the Congress of Industrial Organization (CIO) as well as the artistic components of the WPA.[87]

In Michael Wreszin's essay on the Dies Committee, he contends, "Vice President Garner, who was beginning to make a sharp distinction between traditional Democrats and New Dealers, encouraged the young congressman."[88] Garner's increasing isolation from FDR convinced him that nefarious left-wingers had captured the White House. It was they who were blocking his 1940 presidential aspirations in spite of the fact that he was the leading preelection candidate to replace FDR. Garner was no favorite of the New Deal's labor allies who regarded him, in the words of United Mine Workers leader John L. Lewis, as a "a labor-baiting, poker-playing, whiskey-drinking, evil old man."[89]

The new seven-member Select Committee on Un-American Activities was created on May 25, 1938, by House Resolution 282, and Dies's first step was to deny Dickstein a seat on the committee.[90] Dies and fellow members of the committee believed that Dickstein had been corrupted by the Communists and they were right. As it turned out, Dies was justified in excluding Dickstein because he had become a paid agent of the Soviet Union.

This is clear in the following excerpts from former KGB officer Alexander Vassiliev's *White Notebooks* in which Dickstein, known as "C" for "Crook" because of his greedy requests from the Soviet Embassy, described what happened when he met with Speaker Bankhead and FBI Director Hoover[91]:

> On 7.06 the speaker of the Congress appointed a committee to investigate un-American activities. It consists of the following congressmen: Dies, chmn., Dem.; Healey, D.; Mason, D.; Starnes, D.; Dempsey, D.; Mosier, Rep.; Thomas, Rep.
>
> C. wasn't named. According to him, before appointing the committee the speaker invited in C. and Hoover (FBI) to discuss the membership of the committee. The speaker said that C. shouldn't be part of it for polit. reasons. His appointment could be taken as an anti-German gesture, which would complicate the committee's work. The speaker proposed that C. be an unofficial adviser to the committee. C. shares the speaker's motives. The rightwing press calls C. a Russian Jew and America's chief antifascist. (He was born in Russia and was brought to A. as a child.)

Without serving on the committee, Dickstein's effectiveness as a Soviet agent ended, and the Embassy that had tired of paying "Crook" removed him from its payroll.

Dies was now in the ascendancy and he was careful to begin his early public declarations with even-handed and moderate statements. McCormack's suspicions were soon confirmed as the committee quickly became a major public forum for the expression of rabid anti–New Deal sentiments and claims of vast Communist infiltration in the government and the entertainment industry.[92]

Thanks to Dies's ability to manipulate the media, the committee gained almost immediate notice and by February 1939, the Gallup Poll reported that 67% of those polled answered "Yes" to the question, "Have you heard or read about the Dies Committee—the special House Committee on Un-American Activities?" When asked what the committee's "area of investigation" should be, the respondents indicated: "War propaganda (42%); Nazi activities in U.S. (32%); and Communist activities in U.S. (26%)."[93] That was not how the committee would arrange its investigative priorities, as Dies made it unequivocally clear that internal Communist subversion was the greatest threat to the United States.[94] Congressional investigative warfare against FDR's New Deal had been declared by a fellow Democrat.

Joe Martin and the Conservative Coalition

Across the aisle, the Republicans had already installed Joseph W. Martin, Jr. of North Attleboro, Massachusetts, as their new floor leader. Like McCormack, Martin had served a state legislative apprenticeship in the Great and General Court, where he became a protégé of State Senator Calvin Coolidge of Northampton who rocketed from the Massachusetts State Senate to Lieutenant Governor to Governor to Vice President and to President of the United States in less than a single decade. Joe Martin succeeded Bertrand H. Snell of New York, who had become Republican floor leader in 1931 following the death of Republican Speaker Nicholas Longworth. With Republican House membership dwindling from 270 in the 71st Congress (1929–31) to only 88 Republicans in the 75th House (1937–39), a dispirited Bert Snell handed the leadership to his Assistant Floor Leader Joe Martin in 1938.

It was Martin's Rules Committee assignment that elevated him to national prominence as it placed him in regular contact with Georgia Democrat Gene Cox, John McCormack's best southern friend. Cox and Martin would be the key links of the nascent Conservative Coalition. As described by Martin, Cox was "the real leader of the southerners in the House."[95] The House Rules Committee was the smallest of the House's major committees and it then operated without subcommittees. Only relatively senior and electorally secure members were named to Rules, so the members got to know one another very well. Describing Gene Cox, Martin said: "He and I came to Congress the same year, and we became friends while serving together on the Rules Committee. After I was chosen leader he and I were the principal points of contact between the northern Republicans and the southern Democratic conservatives." This new "Conservative Coalition" gave the anti-FDR Democrats and Republicans a philosophical majority in the newly installed 76th Congress.

John McCormack elected Caucus Chair

John McCormack was returned to the House by his convincing 77.1% victory over his Yankee Republican challenger Henry J. Allen in 1938.[96] The 76th Congress would be philosophically much different from the 75th that had just adjourned. A combination of factors accounted for the change: Roosevelt's fatigue as he had overreached on the Court-packing proposal and the congressional purge, a sour economy with climbing unemployment numbers, and looming international crises. And if American history was a guide, this would be FDR's fourth and last Congress; FDR would be a lame duck.

As in years past, when Democrats lost northern and western seats in Congress, southern Democrats increased their proportionate holdings. The Democratic South ruled the 76th Congress, with the Senate led by Vice President Garner of Texas as its presiding officer and Kentucky's Alben Barkley as its majority leader; and the House of Representatives with Speaker Will Bankhead of Alabama and Majority Leader Sam Rayburn of Texas. Northerners held few leadership posts, the most notable were Pat Boland of Pennsylvania as Democratic whip and the 72-year-old Adolph J. Sabath of Illinois, chair of the House Rules Committee. John McCormack had been recommended for chair of the Democratic Caucus by his good friend Sam Rayburn, who presented John's name and watched it confirmed by voice vote.[97] In keeping with John's increased stature with the South, it was he who placed Will Bankhead's name into nomination as Speaker of the House for the 76th Congress.[98] John had supported both Bankhead and Rayburn in their earlier battles to attain House leadership and he was the one northerner whom they trusted implicitly.

With a much-diminished majority to work with, the Democrats of the 76th Congress knew that there would be no ambitious domestic agenda.[99] In the House, both Speaker Bankhead and Majority Leader Sam Rayburn were easily confirmed as the Democrat's key leaders. Rayburn and Martin would soon play large roles in the legislative life of John McCormack, but on this morning in January 1939, they were simply concerned with counting the heads of their respective legislative phalanxes. The New Deal was on the ropes and Europe was on the brink of war.

The 76th Congress had 261 House Democrats and 164 House Republicans, but the Conservative Coalition reduced the party margin of 97 to a minuscule philosophical one. In the Senate, Democrats held a 69 to 23 edge, but this was a collection of Democrats whose commitment to the president had been insufficient to implement his Court-packing proposal and whose independence from the White House had been rewarded in the failure of the 1938 purge. This was supposed to be President Franklin Roosevelt's final Congress and ending his presidency on a note of congressional resistance to his policy initiatives was not how FDR envisioned the closing of his executive career. It would be up to his diminished allies in the Congress to preserve the legacy of this most unique administration and Boston's John McCormack would be called on regularly to mobilize urban Catholics on the president's behalf.

FDR had long hoped for a reorganization of the executive branch and to routinizing the operations of the White House. Building on recommendations made by the Brownlow Committee,[100] Congress passed the Administrative Reorganization Act of

1939 that provided for executive reorganization subject to congressional veto within sixty days from submission.[101] The act also authorized the president to appoint six administrative assistants and David K. Niles, John McCormack's Boston Jewish ally, would be among the initial appointees. As a consequence of the reorganization plans approved by Congress, the Executive Office of the President, the Federal Security Agency, the Federal Works Agency, and the Federal Loan Agency were created.

Conservative members of Congress were troubled by suspected abuses within the staffing of administrative offices and sought to limit occupants of those offices from doing partisan work. They felt that FDR and his allies were using the WPA as the president's political arm. The legislative response was the Hatch Act authored by New Mexico Democrat Carl Hatch, which prohibited any person employed in any administrative position by the Federal Government, or by any department, independent agency, or other agency of the United States, to use his official authority for the purpose of interfering with or affecting the election or the nomination of any candidate for the office of President, Vice President, Presidential elector, Senator, Representative, and Delegate or Commissioner from Territories or insular possessions.[102] These same public officials were also prohibited from actively participating in political campaigns, soliciting or accepting contributions from work relief employees, and making use of official authority or favors in order to interfere with or influence the outcome of presidential or congressional elections. FDR signed it into law on August 2, 1939.

Promises kept, the 1939 Social Security Amendments

John McCormack's greatest legislative achievement of this Congress and his most long-lasting one was his fine-tuning of the Social Security Act of 1935. Because of the cumbersome nature of the original bill, payments to Social Security qualifiers had been delayed until 1943, eight years after the original act had passed. It had seemed like a hollow promise to America's workers. John was now the 4th-ranked member of Ways and Means, and he and fellow senior allies Chris Sullivan and Tom Cullen of New York along with Jere Cooper of Tennessee replaced average wages with total wages as the basis for computing old-age benefits.[103] Although Robert "Muley" Doughton of North Carolina still chaired Ways and Means, John emerged as the bill's de facto floor manager.

It was John McCormack's broadening of the bill in the Social Security Amendments of 1939 that provided for supplementary old-age benefits for aged wives and extended old-age insurance coverage to maritime workers, persons earning wages after they reached 65, and employees of Federal instrumentalities. The amendments increased the maximum federal grant for each aged or blind person from $15 to $20 a month and the federal contribution toward state aid to dependent children from one-third to one-half the amount granted to each person. And in an effort to gain business support, the act postponed the increased taxes to be paid by employers and employees until 1943. But most importantly, Social Security coverage was now extended beyond individual workers, and it would provide federal financial protection for families. This is the act that would have saved John's mother and siblings from the horrendous fate that destroyed the McCormack family earlier in the century.

European anxieties: Failed negotiations and fragile treaties

Munich, September 1938: While the 75th Congress meandered through its losing days, anxiety hung heavily in the European air with fears that the Continent was on the verge of yet another catastrophic conflagration. Joe Kennedy, now the U.S. ambassador to Great Britain, chose to insert himself into the mix in order to forestall the conflict. It was during this time that Joe became very friendly with Charles A. Lindbergh, whose heroic 1927 solo flight across the Atlantic had given him an iconic presence and a widespread belief that he was an expert on military aviation.[104] Lindbergh was impressed by the German *Luftwaffe* and had become a Germanophile. Joe Kennedy's increasing influence over British Prime Minister Neville Chamberlain was positively noted by Lindbergh in his journal. On the eve of the Munich meeting when Great Britain and France acceded to Hitler's demands that the Sudetenland of Czechoslovakia be annexed by Germany, Lindbergh noted in his *Wartime Journal* for Thursday, September 29, 1938[105]: "Went to see Ambassador Kennedy at 11:15. Everything is looking better, and Kennedy has taken a large part in bringing about the conference between Hitler, [British Prime Minister Neville] Chamberlain, Mussolini, and [French Premier Edouard] Daladier. The English like him and are saying that we have at last sent a real man to represent us."

That "Munich" would later become a synonym for the cowardly appeasement of dictators was not one of Joe Kennedy's greatest legacies[106] and it would later figure heavily in the estrangement of Kennedy from FDR, an estrangement that John McCormack would be called upon to heal.

With Great Britain and France now tamed, Hitler's western front was untroubled; he would then move to secure his eastern one with the Soviet Union.

Molotov-Von Ribbentrop Pact, August 1939: The most fateful occurrence of 1939 took place in Moscow on August 23 when the Molotov-Von Ribbentrop Pact was signed. This was to be a Treaty of Non-Aggression between Nazi Germany and the Soviet Union. Named after the Soviet Foreign Minister V. I. Molotov and the German Foreign Minister Joachim von Ribbentrop, this pact changed the dynamic of the European conflict by protecting Hitler's eastern flank as the Germans readied themselves to roll their tanks into Poland. The governments of Great Britain and France that had passively watched Hitler seize Sudetenland, Austria, and ultimately Czechoslovakia itself chose to commit to war if Poland was invaded.

Ambassador Joe Kennedy's hopes of keeping Britain out of the war were the first ones to be dashed. On September 1, 1939, Nazi tanks rolled into Poland and Great Britain and France issued ultimatums calling for their removal. Two days later, the ultimatums expired and both Britain and France issued declarations of war against Germany. Ambassador Joe Kennedy's reaction was immediate and dramatic, "It's the end of the world, the end of everything."[107]

Neutrality? On September 5 after the ultimatums had expired, the United States declared itself to be neutral in the conflict. It was obvious to anyone close to FDR that there was no neutrality in his personal attitudes toward Hitler and Nazi Germany, but Congress had committed itself to a policy of prohibiting the export of arms to belligerent nations in the Neutrality Act of 1935.[108] The Neutrality Act was renewed in both 1936 and 1937 and FDR was reluctantly obliged to uphold that law.

The Roosevelt administration increased its efforts to shore up the nations of Western Europe battling with the Axis powers. The president knew that there was serious public resistance to any major buildup of American military forces. Not since the end of the Great War in 1918 had there been a military draft. The steps, therefore, would have to be gradual ones. In Leroy Rieselbach's assessment of congressional voting in the 76th Congress, he identified members as 33.0% isolationist to 47.7% internationalist on foreign aid and 35.9% to 51.9% on foreign trade.[109] However, even the 76th Congress with its diminished New Deal agenda passed the Neutrality Act of 1939 in November that enabled belligerent nations to purchase American weapons provided they paid cash and transported the weapons on their own ships.[110] Known as "Cash and Carry," this policy would inch the nation closer to Lend-Lease.

With the conclusion of a cease-fire agreement with Imperial Japan on September 16, the Soviets joined in the dismemberment of Poland as they invaded Poland's eastern regions. For John McCormack, the increased likelihood of war in Europe became a philosophical turning point. He had favored the arms embargo early in the year but now he opposed it, stating on the House floor on November 1, 1939: "As Americans we should put our country in a position where the results of our law do not help the anti-God forces of the world and do not penalize those that stand for the existence and the permanence of religion, of Christianity, and of democracy."[111]

Many Americans hoped and prayed that we could stay out of the war and that the British and French could do a better job of containing German aggrandizement than they had a generation earlier. This time many also believed that America should not come to the rescue. But the armies of France and Britain were no match for the highly mechanized German troops, and it was clear to many observers, especially the president, that American isolationism would be an unfortunate and ultimately futile response to the Nazi threat. Hitler had come to believe that the United States with its unique ethnic and religious diversity was a "mongrel" nation and could never mount the type of unified commitment to a single goal that would be essential in thwarting his fantasy of world conquest.

In correspondence with FDR at that time, McCormack expressed the views and hopes of many of his constituents when he wrote that neutrality revision would "keep us out of war."[112] McCormack's anxiety increased in February 1940 when Stalin's Red Army forces pushed deeper into Finland's Mannerheim Line. Ever the anti-Communist, John sought to punish Russia by introducing an amendment to delete the $17,500 salary of American Ambassador Lawrence Steinhardt, but the House rejected it 108 to 105. As reported by historian David Porter, "Since anti-Soviet sentiments were widespread, the McCormack amendment was rejected 'only after the Administration had brought pressure to bear upon its supporters in Congress.' Majority Leader Sam Rayburn of Texas had warned that the McCormack proposal could provoke further Soviet aggression. 'The action here today,' Rayburn remarked, 'will not help Finland. It will not hurt Russia. It will make a more determined and a more irresistible Russia.'"[113] It would be the only public foreign policy disagreement between Rayburn and McCormack as the nation moved warily toward its inevitable involvement in the war.

The third and closing session of the 76th Congress met for a full year, but apart from the Smith Act in June and the Burke-Wadsworth Selective Service and Training Act in September, it was relatively unproductive as many Americans hoped to forestall the nation's involvement in yet another foreign conflict.[114] John McCormack continued to maneuver legislation on the floor and was deeply involved in helping to write and to pass the Alien Registration Act. Based upon the findings of the McCormack-Dickstein Committee and named for conservative Virginia Democrat Howard W. Smith, who would later become chair of the House Rules Committee, this act required all foreigners to register and to be fingerprinted.[115] It also made it unlawful to be a member of any organization that advocated the overthrow of the government by force or violence, or to advocate or conspire to advocate such overthrow. It was this act that gave the federal government much of its power to indict and imprison citizens whose activities were deemed to be "subversive." The excesses of the Smith Act became most pronounced during the anti-Communist eruptions of postwar America. But in 1940, a year heavy with national anxiety over international involvement, the act was seen as a sensible effort to prevent organized groups of "foreigners" from dragging a reluctant United States into war.

Notes

1   "Acts of Congress Held Unconstitutional in Whole or in Part by the Supreme Court of the United States," *The Constitution of the United States: Analysis and Interpretation* (Washington, DC: U.S. Government Printing Office, 2004), pp. 2117–59, lists 158 cases of congressional acts ruled unconstitutional in whole or part. Those dealing with the New Deal are listed as Acts 58–64, 66–68, and 70.

2   See "Twenty-Seventh Democratic Convention," in Bain and Parris, *Convention Decisions and Voting Records*, 2nd ed., pp. 247–50.

3   Democratic National Convention, *Proceedings, 1936*, p. 189.

4   See "Twenty-First Republican Convention," in Bain and Parris, *Convention Decisions and Voting Records*, 2nd ed., pp. 245–47.

5   George Wolfskill, *The Revolt of the Conservatives: A History of the American Liberty League, 1934–1940* (Boston: Houghton, Mifflin, 1962). See also Robert A. Slayton's essay "Al and Frank: The Great Smith-Roosevelt Feud," in David B. Woolner and Richard G. Kurial, eds., *FDR, the Vatican, and the Roman Catholic Church in America, 1933–1945* (New York: Palgrave Macmillan, 2003), pp. 55–66.

6   *The Literary Digest*, October 31, 1936, pp. 1–2. The *Digest's* projection for Massachusetts was 73.6% for Landon; 21.8% for Roosevelt; and 6.5% for Lemke. The actual vote indicated the enormity of their miscalculations as Landon received 41.8% of the vote; FDR 51.2%; and Lemke 6.5%. They got the Lemke vote right but missed Landon and FDR by more than thirty points.

7   Peverill Squire, "Why the 1936 Literary Digest Poll Failed," *Public Opinion Quarterly*, LII (1988), pp. 123–33.

8   The postelection issue was just as confused, "What Went Wrong With the Polls: None of Straw Votes Got Exactly the Right Answer—Why?" *The Literary Digest*, November 14, 1936, pp. 1–2.

9   The history of the various versions of the Frazier-Lemke Act are described in A. N. Diamond and Alfred Letzier, "The New Frazier-Lemke Act: A Study," *Columbia Law Review*, XXXVII (November 1937), pp. 1092–1135.

10   Tull, *Father Coughlin and the New Deal*, p. 109.

11   "Frazier-Lemke Farm Mortgage Moratorium Act (49 Stat., 803-863)," in Stathis, *Landmark Legislation*, p. 207.

12   See the account of the Kennedy-Coughlin meeting with President Roosevelt in Kenneth S. Davis, *F.D.R.: The New Deal Years, 1933–1937 A History* (New York: Random House, 1979), pp. 575 and 577.

13   Edward C. Blackorby, "William Lemke: Agrarian Radical and Union Party Presidential Candidate," *Mississippi Valley Historical Review*, XLIX (June 1962), pp. 67–84; and his book, *Prairie Rebel: The Public Life of William Lemke* (Lincoln: University of Nebraska Press, 1963); and *BDUSC* (1989 ed.), p. 1368.

14   The visit was reported by the *Boston Herald*, August 13, 1935. Sources vary on the Curley quotation with "the strongest Coughlinite city" in Beatty's *The Rascal King*, p. 395, and "the most Coughlinite city" in Brinkley's *Voices of Protest*, p. 206.

15   Hatch, *The Lodges of Massachusetts*, p. 200.

16   *CQ Guide to U.S. Elections* (1975 ed.), p. 494.

17   Curley, *I'd Do It Again!*, pp. 296–99. Curley noted, "The story seems plausible," p. 298.

18   Ibid., p. 494.

19   "1936 Presidential Election," in Congressional Quarterly, *Presidential Elections, 1789–1992*, p. 114.

20   John F. Stack, Jr., *International Conflict in an American City: Boston's Irish, Italians, and Jews, 1935–1944* (Westport, CT: Greenwood Press, 1979), chapter 2.

21   "Order of Boston Wards Most Heavily Democratic," in Samuel Lubell, *The Future of American Politics*, 3rd rev. ed. (New York: Harper Colophon, 1965), p. 202. It was first published in 1951.

22   *CQ Guide to U.S. Elections* (1975 ed.), p. 782, for the 1936 House results in Massachusetts.

23   See Tallulah's recounting of this event in *Tallulah: My Autobiography* (New York: Harper and Brothers, 1952), pp. 45–46.

24   Ibid., p. 46. See memories of her father in "My Life with Father," *Coronet*, XXXI (November 1951), pp. 56–60.

25   Author's telephonic interview with the Hon. John W. McCormack, Boston, MA, April 1977.

26   Champagne et al., *The Austin-Boston Connection*, pp. 102–18.

27   Rayburn defeated O'Connor, 184 to 127, on the first ballot, see *NYT*, January 5, 1937, pp. 1 and 15.

28 Author's telephonic interview with the Hon. John W. McCormack, Boston, MA, April 1977.

29 Champagne et al., *The Austin-Boston Connection*, pp. 115–16.

30 The earliest academic assessment of the seniority system was James K. Pollock's, "The Seniority Rule in Congress," *North American Review*, CCXXII (December 1925), pp. 235–45. The next major study was George Goodwin, "Seniority System in Congress," *APSR*, LIII (June 1959), pp. 412–36, which was followed by an eruption of findings in the late 1960s: Michael Abram and Joseph Cooper, "The Rise of the Seniority in the House of Representatives," *Polity*, I (Fall 1968), pp. 52–84; Nelson W. Polsby, Miriam Gallaher, and Barry S. Rundquist, "Growth of the Seniority System in the U.S. House of Representatives," *APSR*, LXIII (September 1969), pp. 787–807; and Barbara Hinckley, "Seniority in the Committee Leadership Selection of Congress," *American Journal of Political Science*, XIII (November 1969), pp. 613–30.

31 On the South's overrepresentation among congressional leaders, see Garrison Nelson, "Change and Continuity in the Recruitment of U.S. House Leaders, 1789–1975," in Norman J. Ornstein, ed., *Congress in Change: Evolution and Reform* (New York: Praeger, 1975), pp. 158–61.

32 Svend Petersen, *A Statistical History of the American Presidential Elections* (New York: Frederick Ungar, 1963), p. 12.

33 Robert Lopresti, a librarian at Western Washington University, found that 12 of our presidents owned slaves and eight of them owned slaves while serving as president. FactCheck.org.

34 See Samuel J. Eldersveld, "The Influence of Metropolitan Party Pluralities in Presidential Elections Since 1920: A Study of Twelve Key Cities," *APSR* (1949), pp. 1189–206.

35 Second Immigration Quota (National Origins) Act was approved May 26, 1924 (43 Stat. 153-169).

36 The argument propounded by rural state congressmen was that seasonally employed farm workers who should be counted were missing from their residences on January 1, 1920, and that the cities gaining population had large numbers of illegal aliens who should not be included in the reapportionment allocations; see *CQ Guide to the Congress of the United States* (Washington, DC: Congressional Quarterly, 1971), pp. 506–508.

37 Kennth C. Martis and Gregory A. Elmes, *The Historical Atlas of State Power in Congress, 1790-1990* (Washington, DC: Congressional Quarterly, 1993), pp. 86–93.

38 An academic assessment of this Congress may be found in E. Pendleton Herring, "First Session of the Seventy-Fourth Congress," *APSR*, XXIX (December 1935), pp. 985– 1005.

39 Smedley D. Butler, *War Is a Racket* (New York: Round Table Books, 1935).

40 U.S. Senate Historical Office, September 4, 1934, "Merchants of Death." See also James E. Palmer, *Carter Glass: Unreconstructed Rebel* (Roanoke, VA: Institute of American Biography, 1938).

41 The Neutrality Act of 1935, "Authorized the president to prohibit the export of arms and other implements of war to belligerent countries, prohibit American vessels from carrying munitions to these countries, and restrict travel by American citizens on belligerent ships in wartime. Established a National Munitions Control Board to regulate licensing and registration of persons engaged in the business of manufacturing, exporting, or importing arms, ammunition, and implements of war." Approved August

31, 1931 (Public Resolution 67; 49 Stat. 1081–85), from Stathis, *Landmark Legislation*, p. 207. The 1936 Neutrality Act extended the 1935 Act.

42 Robert A. Divine, *The Illusion of Neutrality* (Chicago: University of Chicago Press, 1962).

43 The definitive work on this conflict remains the magisterial book by Hugh Thomas, *The Spanish Civil War*, 3rd ed. (New York: Harper & Row, 1986). A revised edition was published by the Modern Library in 2001.

44 FDR's relationship with American Catholics was a mixed positive one and is captured in the essays in David B. Woolner and Richard G. Kurial, eds., *FDR, the Vatican, and the Roman Catholic Church in America, 1933–1945* (New York: Palgrave Macmillan, 2003), esp. Michael Barone, "Franklin D. Roosevelt: A Protestant Patrician in a Catholic Party," pp. 3–11; and Philip Chen, "Religious Liberty in American Foreign Policy, 1933–1941: Aspects of Public Argument Between FDR and American Roman Catholics," pp. 121–39.

45 The fullest treatment of how the Spanish Civil War impacted American politics may be found in Allen Guttman's excellent book, *The Wound in the Heart: America and the Spanish Civil War* (New York: The Free Press of Glencoe, 1962).

46 George Q. Flynn, *Roosevelt and Romanism: Catholics and American Diplomacy, 1937–1945* (Westport, CT: Greenwood Press, 1976), pp. 39–40.

47 Conrad Black, *Franklin Delano Roosevelt: Champion of Freedom* (New York: Public Affairs, 2003), p. 424. Black also recounted a strange tale of how Eleanor's brother Hall tried to get used American aircraft to the Loyalists only to be thwarted by the State Department (p. 449).

48 Ibid., p. 449.

49 Author's interview with Dr. Martin Sweig, Washington, DC, September 1968. The dissertation was accepted and Sweig received his doctorate.

50 The best book on the complex FDR-JPK relationship remains Michael R. Beschloss's *Kennedy and Roosevelt: The Uneasy Alliance* (New York: Norton, 1980).

51 Joseph P. Kennedy, *I'm for Roosevelt* (New York: Reynal & Hitchcock, 1936), p. 3.

52 Joseph P. Kennedy to Felix Frankfurter, December 5, 1933, in Smith, *Hostages to Fortune*, p. 122.

53 O'Toole, *Militant and Triumphant*, p. 138.

54 The O'Connell quote varies in different sources but the disdain toward Spellman is constant. This version is from John Cooney's *The American Pope: The Life and Times of Francis Cardinal Spellman* (New York: Dell, 1986), p. 112.

55 Ibid., pp. 100–102. Whalen's account is less ecclesiastical, *The Founding Father*, pp. 186–88.

56 Shattuck's efforts to recruit McCormack to run against Curley are recounted in John T. Galvin's *The Gentleman Mr. Shattuck: A Biography of Henry Lee Shattuck, 1870–1971* (Boston: Tontine Press, 1996), pp. 282–83; and Alan Lupo's *Liberty's Chosen Home: The Politics of Violence in Boston* (Boston: Little Brown, 1977), p. 81.

57 *Boston City Charter, Acts 1938*—Chapter 300, "An Act Providing that the Mayor of Boston Shall be Eligible for the Succeeding Term." Be it enacted, etc. as follows:

"SECTION 1. Section forty-five of chapter four hundred and eighty-six of the acts of nineteen hundred and nine, as most recently amended by section six of chapter four hundred and seventy-nine of the acts of nineteen hundred and twenty-four, is hereby further amended by striking out, in the *sixth and seventh lines, the words 'and shall not be eligible for election to the succeeding term'" (p. 24).

58 Tobin's life and career are well presented in Vincent A. Lapomarda, *The Boston Mayor Who Became Truman's Secretary of Labor: Maurice J. Tobin and the Democratic Party* (New York, Peter Lang Publishing, 1995). The 1937 mayoral results were 105,212 for Tobin; 80,376 for Curley, in Vincent A. Lapomarda, "Maurice Joseph Tobin," in Holli and Jones, *Big City Mayors*, p. 365.

59 Leverett Saltonstall, *Salty: Recollections of a Yankee in Politics*, as told to Edward Weeks (Boston: The Boston Globe, 1976), p. 63.

60 See Saltonstall's reminiscence of this campaign in his memoirs (ibid., pp. 61–65).

61 An overview of the opening session of the 75th Congress may be found in O. R. Altman, "First Session of the Seventy-Fifth Congress: January 5, 1937 to August 21, 1937," *APSR*, XXXI (December 1937), pp. 1071–93.

62 "Judicial Procedures Reform Bill," Fireside Chat, March 9, 1937.

63 See note 1 above.

64 Six surveys conducted between February and May 1937 and reported in George H. Gallup, *The Gallup Poll: Public Opinion, 1935–1971* (New York: Random House, 1972), pp. 50–59. The fullest set of Gallup Poll data may be found in Gregory A. Caldeira's superb article, "Public Opinion and the U.S. Supreme Court: FDR's Court-Packing Plan," *APSR*, LXXXI (December 1987), pp. 1139–53.

65 Sumners's proposal is described in Robert Shogan's *Backlash: The Killing of the New Deal* (Chicago: Ivan R. Dee, 2006), pp. 82–84.

66 Sumners's quotation may be found in the daily recounting of the battle in Joseph Alsop and Turner Catledge's *The 168 Days* (Garden City, NY: Doubleday, Doran, 1938), p. 67. See also the analysis of Sumners's crucial role in Anthony Champagne, "Hatton Sumners and the 1937 Court-Packing Plan," *East Texas Historical Journal*, 26 (Spring 1988), pp. 46–49.

67 *Congressional Record*, 75th Congress, 1st Session, July 22, 1937.

68 The last Gallup Poll on the Court's enlargement was conducted on August 25–30, 1937, and reported on September 12, 1937, *The Gallup Poll: Public Opinion, 1935–1971*, p. 69.

69 John Robert Moore, "Senator Josiah Bailey and the 'Conservative Manifesto' of 1937," *Journal of Southern History*, XXXI (February 1965), pp. 22–23, 27.

70 Ronald Marecello, "Senator Josiah Bailey, Harry Hopkins, and the WPA: A Prelude to the Conservative Coalition," *Southern Studies*, XXII (Winter 1983), pp. 321–29.

71 The best explication of FDR's failed efforts to transform the congressional Democrats may be found in Susan Dunn's *Roosevelt's Purge: How FDR Fought to Change the Democratic Party* (Cambridge, MA: The Belknap Press of Harvard University, 2010). See also Charles M. Price and Joseph Boskin, "The Roosevelt 'Purge': A Reappraisal," *Journal of Politics*, XXVIII (August 1966), pp. 660–70; and Thomas Philip Wolf, "The 1938 Purge: A Re-examination," in Thomas P. Wolf, William D. Pederson, and Byron W. Daynes, eds., *Franklin D. Roosevelt and Congress: The New Deal and Its Aftermath* (Armonk, NY: M.E. Sharpe, 2001), pp. 108–21.

72 Joseph P. Lash, *Dealers and Dreamers: A New Look at the New Deal* (New York: Doubleday, 1988), p. 305. Lash cites *TIME*, September 12, 1938, and Robert Jackson's interview at the Columbia Oral History Collection, p. 474n.

73 Dunn, *Roosevelt's Purge*, p. 26.

74 Gallup Poll released September 11, 1938, based on interviews with Democratic identifiers conducted from August 8 to 23 in Gallup, *The Gallup Poll: Public Opinion, 1935–1971*, Vol. 1, p. 117.

75   Dunn, *Roosevelt's Purge*, p. 215.

76   Charles W. Hurd, "House Rebels at Speed on Reorganization Bill; Vote Off Until Next Week; Foes are Hopeful; Leaders Defeated, 191 to 149, in Attempt to Force Quick Action; O'Connor Leads Battle, He Tells Congress of Letters Threatening 'Bloodshed' and 'Resort to Arms,'" *NYT*, April 1, 1938. See Richard Polenberg, "Franklin Roosevelt and the Purge of John O'Connor: The Impact of Urban Change on Political Parties," *New York History*, XLIX (July 1968), pp. 306–26.

77   See Robert Shogan, *Backlash: The Killing of the New Deal* (Chicago: Ivan R. Dee, 2005). See also David L. Porter, *Congress and the Waning of the New Deal* (Port Washington, NY: Kennikat Press, 1979). See also Sidney M. Milkis, "The Limits of Party Government: The 'Conservative Coalition' and the 'Purge' Campaign of 1938," *The President and the Parties: The Transformation of the American Party System since the New Deal* (New York: Oxford University Press, 1993), chapter 4, pp. 75–97.

78   The first academic analysis of the Conservative Coalition appears in James T. Patterson, "Conservative Coalition Forms in Congress: 1933–1939," *Journal of American History*, LII (March 1966), pp. 757–72. Two later expositions may be found in articles by John F. Manley, "The Conservative Coalition in Congress," *American Behavioral Scientist*, XVII (November–December 1973), pp. 223–47; and "The Conservative Coalition in Congress," in Lawrence C. Dodd and Bruce I. Oppenheimer, eds., *Congress Reconsidered* (New York: Praeger, 1977), pp. 75–95. The best full-length treatments are James T. Patterson, *Congressional Conservatism and the New Deal: The Growth of the Conservative Coalition in Congress, 1933–1939* (Lexington: University of Kentucky Press, 1967), during its early phase and Mack C. Shelley's *The Permanent Majority: The Conservative Coalition in Congress* (Tuscaloosa, AL: University of Alabama Press, 1983), in its later phase.

79   J. Frederick Essary, "The Split in the Democratic Party," *Atlantic Monthly*, CLX (December 1937), pp. 651–58, quoted in Patterson, *Congressional Conservatism and the New Deal*, p. 161.

80   Continuing reassessments include Michael Nelson, "The President and the Court: Reinterpreting the Court-packing Episode of 1937," *Political Science Quarterly*, CIII (Summer, 1988), pp. 267–93; William E. Leuchtenburg, "FDR's Court-Packing Plan: A Second Life, a Second Death," *Duke Law Journal* (June–September 1985), pp. 673–89; and William G. Ross, "When Did the Switch in Time Actually Occur?: Re-discovering the Supreme Court's Forgotten Decisions of 1936–37" (February 25, 2005), available at http://dx.doi.org/10.2139/ssrn.673983. However, the explanation that has generated the most debate is the one articulated by Yale's Bruce Ackerman in his book *We the People: Transformations* (Cambridge, MA: Harvard University Press, 1998) that contends the "switch in time" was the product of external liberalizing forces pressing on a conservative Court.

81   See "Confirmation Patterns in a Consensus Era, 1937–1967: Court Paths, Votes, Hearing Days, and Testimony," in Garrison Nelson, *Pathways to the U.S. Supreme Court: From the Arena to the Monastery* (New York: Palgrave Macmillan, 2013), p. 15.

82   Problems with the large legislative majority are recounted in O. R. Altman's accounts, "Second and Third Sessions of the Seventy-Fifth Congress, 1937–38," *APSR*, XXXI (December 1937), pp. 1071–93.

83   Milton Plesur, "Republican Congressional Comeback of 1938," *Review of Politics*, XXIV (October 1962), pp. 525–62.

84   See U.S. Code, Title 22, Subchapter II–Registration of Foreign Propagandists, Section 611.

85 *TIME* magazine's Frank McNaughton referred to it as the "McCormack Act."

86 Both Dies and Garner are negatively profiled in Allan A. Michie and Frank Ryhlick, *Dixie Demagogues* (New York: Vanguard Press, 1939). See also Dies's autobiography, *Martin Dies Story* (New York: Bookmailer, 1963).

87 August Raymond Ogden, *The Dies Committee: A Study of the Special House Committee for the Investigation of Un-American Activities, 1938–1944* (Washington, DC: Catholic University of America Press, 1945).

88 Michael Wreszin, "The Dies Committee 1938," in Arthur M. Schlesinger, Jr. and Roger Bruns, eds., *Congress Investigates: A Documented History, 1792–1974*, Vol. 4 (New York: Chelsea House in association with R. R. Bowker, 1975), p. 2927.

89 "At That Moment," *Times-Picayune*, October 31, 1976, p. 72.

90 The select committee's membership from May 25, 1938, to December 19, 1944, is listed in David T. Canon, Garrison Nelson, and Charles Stewart III, *Committees in the U.S. Congress, 1789–1946, Select Committees*, IV (Washington, DC: Congressional Quarterly Press, 2002), pp. 411–12. It became a standing committee on January 3, 1945, at the opening of the 79th Congress.

91 The account comes from the second White Notebook provided by Alexander Vassiliev and translated by Steve Shabad, reviewed and edited by Alexander Vassiliev and John Earl Haynes (2007). See John Earl Haynes and Harvey Klehr, eds., *Alexander Vassiliev's Notebooks: Provenance and Documentation of Soviet Intelligence Activities in the United States* (Washington, DC: Cold War International History Project, Woodrow Wilson Center, 2007).

92 The best treatment of the committee's activities may be found in Wreszin, "The Dies Committee 1938," in Schlesinger, Jr. and Bruns, eds., *Congress Investigates*, Vol. 4, pp. 2923–3112. Published in 1945, the first book on the subject is guarded; see Ogden, *The Dies Committee: A Study of the Special House Committee for the Investigation of Un-American Activities, 1938–1944*.

93 Gallup Poll released March 6, 1939, interviews conducted from February 18 to 23, 1939, in Gallup, *The Gallup Poll: Public Opinion, 1935–1971*, Vol. 1, pp. 143–44.

94 Martin Dies, *The Trojan Horse in America* (New York: Dodd, Mead, 1940).

95 Joseph W. Martin, Jr. as told to Robert J. Donovan, *My First Fifty Years in Politics* (New York: McGraw-Hill, 1960), p. 84. See also James J. Kenneally, *A Compassionate Conservative: A Political Biography of Joseph W. Martin, Jr., Speaker of the U.S. House of Representatives* (New York: Lexington Books, 2003), p. 47. Harold Ickes's *Diary* describes Gene Cox who is "often anti-Administration" but who turned out to treat Ickes with fairness, Vol. III, p. 130, February 11, 1940.

96 "1938 House Elections," in *Guide to U.S. Elections* (1975 ed.), p. 787.

97 House Democratic Caucus records for the 76th Congress, January 1939.

98 Robert C. Albright, "Study Election, New Deal Laws, Bankhead Urges; Re-nominated, He Says Modification May Be Necessary; Martin Minority Leader," *Washington Post*, January 3, 1939, p. 1; and "House Organizes with Old Officers; Bankhead Re-elected Speaker With 250 Votes to 167 for Martin, Republican," *NYT*, January 4, 1939, p. 9.

99 Accounts of the 76th Congress may be found in David L. Porter's *The Seventy-Sixth Congress and World War II, 1939–1940* (Columbia: University of Missouri Press, 1979); and Floyd M. Riddick, "American Government and Politics: First Session of the Seventy-Sixth Congress: January 3, 1939 to August 5, 1939," *APSR*, XXXIII (December 1939), pp. 1022–43.

100   A valuable retrospective on the Brownlow Committee was written by James W. Fesler, "The Brownlow Committee: Fifty Years Later," *Public Administration Review*, XLVII (August 1987), pp. 291–96.

101   Administrative Reorganization Act of 1939. Approved April 3, 1939 (53 Stat. 561-565).

102   Hatch Act. Approved August 2, 1939 (53 Stat. 1147-1149). See David L. Porter, "Senator Carl Hatch and the Hatch Act of 1939," *New Mexico Historical Review*, XLVIII (April 1973), pp. 151–64.

103   Social Security Amendments of 1939. Approved August 10, 1939 (53 Stat. 1360-1402). On John McCormack's role in the Social Security Amendments of 1939, see Bernard B. Schwartz and Robert B. Stevens, eds., *Income Security*, Vol. 3 of *Statutory History of the United States* (New York: Chelsea House, 1970), pp. 235–36.

104   Wayne S. Cole, *Charles A. Lindbergh and the Battle against American Intervention in World War Two* (New York: Harcourt Brace Jovanovich, 1974), pp. 49–50 and 53–56.

105   Charles A. Lindbergh, *The Wartime Journals of Charles A. Lindbergh* (New York: Harcourt Brace Jovanovich, 1970), September 29, 1938, p. 79.

106   See Wayne S. Cole's chapter 19, "Kennedy, Lindbergh, Roosevelt, and Munich," in his *Roosevelt & the Isolationists* (Lincoln: University of Nebraska Press, 1983), pp. 274–90.

107   As quoted in Robert Dallek, *Franklin D. Roosevelt and American Foreign Policy, 1932–1945* (New York: Oxford University Press, 1979), p. 198. On FDR's attitudes toward Kennedy's "defeatism," see Warren Kimball, *Forged in War: Roosevelt, Churchill, and the Second World War* (New York: William Morrow), pp. 15, 29, 37, 58, and 65.

108   The Neutrality Act of 1935 "Authorized the president to prohibit the export of arms and other implements of war to belligerent countries, prohibit American vessels from carrying munitions to those countries, and restrict travel by American citizens on belligerent ships in wartime." It was approved on August 31, 1935 (Public Resolution 74-67; 49 Stat. 1081-1085), from Stathis, *Landmark Legislation*, p. 207.

109   These numbers come from Leroy Rieselbach's careful analysis, *The Roots of Isolationism: Congressional Voting and Presidential Leadership in Foreign Policy* (Indianapolis, IN: Bobbs-Merrill, 1966), pp. 47–52.

110   Neutrality Act of 1939, approved November 4, 1939 (54 Stat. 4–12). Assessments of this act and the debates which it engendered may be found in Francis O. Wilcox, "The Neutrality Fight in Congress: 1939," *APSR*, XXXIII (October 1939), pp. 811–25; John C. Donovan, "Congressional Isolationists and the Roosevelt Foreign Policy," *World Politics*, III (April 1951), pp. 299–316; James T. Patterson, "Eating Humble Pie: A Note on Roosevelt, Congress, and Neutrality Revision in 1939," *Historian*, XXXI (May 1969), pp. 407–13; and Justus D. Doenecke, "Non-intervention of the Left: The Keep America Out of the War Congress, 1938-41," *Journal of Contemporary History*, XII (April 1977), pp. 221–36.

111   *Congressional Record*, 76th Congress, 1st Session (November 1, 1939), pp. 1168–70, for the full remarks; and quoted in Robert A. Divine's *The Illusion of Neutrality* (Chicago: University of Chicago Press, 1962), p. 328.

112   David L. Porter, *The Seventy-Sixth Congress and World War II* (Columbia: University of Missouri Pres, 1979), p. 55. Porter cites a letter from McCormack in FDR's President's Personal Files (PPF) 4057 in the Franklin D. Roosevelt Papers.

113   Porter, *The Seventy-Sixth Congress*, p. 116, cites the *Congressional Record*, February 1940, *NYT*, February 8, 1940, and David J. Dallin's *Soviet Foreign Policy, 1939–1942* (New Haven: Yale University Press, 1942), p. 179.

114 See two articles by Floyd M. Riddick, "House Versus the Senate in the Third Session of the Seventy-Sixth Congress," *South Atlantic Quarterly*, XL (April 1941), pp. 169–84; and "American Government and Politics: Third Session of the Seventy-Sixth Congress, January 3, 1940 to January 3, 1941," *American Political Science Review*, XXXV (April 1941), pp. 284–303.

115 Alien Registration Act (Smith Act). Approved June 28, 1940 (54 Stat. 670-676). A contemporaneous assessment of the act may be found in Harvey C. Mansfield, "Legislative Veto and the Deportation of Aliens," *Public Administration Review*, I (Spring 1941), pp. 281–86; and a later one in John C. Crow, "The Role of Congress and the Federal Judiciary in the Deportation of Aliens," *Missouri Law Review*, XXIII (November 1958), pp. 491–502.

9

FDR's Third Term, the Austin-Boston Connection, and the Brink of War

Early uncertainty

Early Uncertainty: The third and longest session of the 76th Congress convened on January 3, 1940. Americans were disquieted. Western Europe was staggered by Adolph Hitler's highly disciplined Nazi war machine as it roared through western Poland, defiantly ignoring the Franco-British ultimatum that Poland remains independent. The Fascists of Italy's Benito Mussolini had gained control of Abyssinia in East Africa while Imperial Japan continued its rapacious romp throughout the Pacific. Hitler's newly acquired ally the Soviet Union moved against neighboring Finland and prepared for their later incursion into the three Baltic states of Estonia, Latvia, and Lithuania. With the smaller countries overwhelmed by the superior military might of the ascendant dictatorships, the major Western democracies seemed incapable of stopping their advances or even defending themselves. Because fighting in Europe had yet to escalate to its eventual massive bloodletting, it was derided as "the phony war," but FDR was certain that it would not be contained for very long. Fearing that France and Britain would be next, FDR's January 3 annual budget request to Congress included $1.8 billion in defense requests.

With the European allies stumbling in their efforts against the armies of Germany and Italy, Congress found it difficult to focus on domestic legislation. Questions abounded in the House. While some were concerned about the precariousness of Speaker Will Bankhead's health, the larger question concerned President Franklin D. Roosevelt. Would he retire as a Hudson Valley country squire to his comfortable Hyde Park home along for a well-deserved retirement and his fabled stamp collection? Or would he seek a third term to lead the nation through yet another one of its crises?

Much of Congress had tired of FDR and his ambitious agenda but there were portents of a possible third-term run and debate ensued as to whether or not FDR would seek to continue his presidency in the upcoming November election, just ten months away.[1] With American history as a guide, this should have been the last year of the Franklin Roosevelt presidency. Only two prior ex-presidents had flirted with a third term, Presidents U.S. Grant in 1880 and Teddy Roosevelt in 1912. (Technically, Teddy had only been elected president once, in 1904, but he served as president for three years and six months of William McKinley's second term.)

Whatever qualms FDR might have had about seeking a third term ended when France fell to the Germans in June 1940.[2] His potential successors were a flawed lot. FDR favored Secretary of State Cordell Hull over Postmaster General Jim Farley but knew that Hull would be 69 on Election Day and was too old and too out of touch with the necessary mechanisms to rally, organize, and do political battle. FDR was no longer speaking to Vice President Jack Garner, who, in any event, was entirely incapable of comprehending how the European conflict would threaten America, and Jim Farley was an intellectual lightweight whom FDR had once dismissed, saying, "I have never heard Jim Farley make a constructive suggestion or even criticism regarding anything of importance to the country as a whole." While FDR would move both Louis McHenry Howe and Harry Hopkins into the White House's living quarters, Jim Farley was well aware that he never made the cut.[3] "Mrs. Eleanor Roosevelt once said, 'Franklin finds it hard to relax with people who aren't his social equals.' I took this remark to explain my being out of the infield." Jim Farley also was too much of a professional Irishman to work well with newly installed British Prime Minister Winston Churchill.

Harry Hopkins, an FDR favorite, newly named as secretary of commerce, left the Works Progress Administration for the Cabinet with "one old associate who moved with Hopkins into his new world . . . David K. Niles who had been his chief political adviser and campaign strategist."[4] It was Niles's task to determine if Hopkins was electable. Having never run for public office, Hopkins's early poll results were consistently discouraging and when Hopkins fell ill once again with ulcers, the campaign ceased.[5] It was the widespread reporting of a Hopkins quote from September 1938 that proved to be his ultimate undoing, "We shall tax and tax, and spend and spend, and elect and elect." The reporter who gave the quote its widest airing was Arthur Krock of the *New York Times*, who had his own horse in the race for the 1940 Democratic presidential nomination—Ambassador Joseph P. Kennedy, whom Krock described as "unmatched for competence, imagination, and courage in the areas of fiscal and monetary economics."[6]

Formal challenges to FDR's renomination came from Vice President John Nance Garner and Jim Farley. Farley who served as postmaster general and also chaired both the Democratic National Committee and New York's Democratic Party was an Irish-descended Roman Catholic often allied with Tammany Hall, the most powerful urban machine in the country. Farley chose to concentrate his efforts on Massachusetts, the only large northern industrial state to cast its 17 electoral votes for Democrats in the last three elections. Its predominantly Irish Catholic Democratic voters had rejected FDR's first nomination bid in 1932 in favor of Al Smith but now they were in a quandary. Many wanted FDR to run for a third term while others sought electable successors. According to the *Boston Globe*, House Democratic Caucus Chair John McCormack, believed to be the most loyal New Dealer in the delegation, "has been linked with the movement for Ambassador Joseph P. Kennedy in this state."[7] John was unaware of FDR's growing distrust of Kennedy and of the president's concern that Joe Kennedy had become much too close to Herbert von Dirksen, the German Reich's Ambassador to Great Britain.

When it became clear that Joe Kennedy would not be a presidential candidate in 1940, most of the state's leading Irish Democrats turned to the candidacy of Jim Farley, who had split with FDR over the "Court-packing" proposal of 1937.[8] But John still hoped for a third FDR candidacy and urged that the delegation remain uncommitted. However, according to Charles Trout, "With anti–New Deal Senator David I. Walsh in the vanguard, the initial objections of Congressman McCormack to a pledged delegation were overcome: twenty-eight of the thirty-four delegates to the national convention had committed themselves to Farley by the end of February."[9] John McCormack remained reluctant about Farley and announced: "I am pleased to accept the invitation extended to me by Chairman [William] Burke to run as a delegate-at-large, reserving to myself complete freedom of action in the event that President Roosevelt's' name is submitted to the national convention or if the convention drafts him."[10]

Six days after New Hampshire's March 12 primary voted to send an unpledged delegation to the convention, David Niles, John McCormack's White House contact, responded to a query from Maine-born and MIT-educated Oscar S. Cox of the Treasury Department about John. Niles assured Cox of McCormack's loyalty to FDR stating, "I think the Congressman will go along. He is one of my really close friends."[11]

FDR played his cards close to the vest with regard to a third term, while his operatives placed his name into the 1940 Democratic primaries and he won most of them with 71.7% of the total primary vote.[12] Massachusetts was one of only fourteen states to hold a presidential preference primary that year. Technically, the slate was "unpledged," but Farley's supporters won 69 of the 78 delegates.[13] As the senior-most Democratic member of the state's House delegation, John was named to chair the 72-member Massachusetts convention delegation with 12 at-large delegates with one-third votes and 60 district delegates with half-votes including Joseph P. Kennedy, Jr. of Cambridge.[14] FDR may have twice captured the Bay State's electoral votes but when confusion reigned, Massachusetts Democrats, like the increasingly isolationist U.S. Senator David I. Walsh, opted for Irishmen, much as they had in 1932 for Al Smith.

John McCormack had made it clear in a letter to Steve Early, the president's press secretary, that they had little to fear from the Massachusetts delegation.[15] There would be no Jim Curley–like embarrassment this time. In spite of the fact that Jim Farley had won the Massachusetts presidential primary and that the delegation was ostensibly pledged to him, John McCormack was emphatic and public in his declaration that FDR should remain in the White House. Following a private meeting with FDR on July 7,[16] John made his position known: "We urged him just as strongly as we could to be a candidate or consent to be drafted. I think it's absolutely indispensable that the President run."[17] John's most notable action during the convention was to prevent former Governor Joseph Ely from making a public statement announcing his decision to withdraw from the delegation.[18] Ely, who four years earlier had joined Al Smith in the 1936 "walk" in the American Liberty League's opposition to FDR, had become persona non grata to the FDR loyalists in Chicago.

The convention's temporary chair Speaker Will Bankhead opened the Democrats' twenty-eighth nominating convention on July 15. Shortly after, Will turned the gavel over to the convention's permanent chair, Alben Barkley of Kentucky, the Senate Majority Leader. Few knew that evening that this would be Will Bankhead's last major dance on the political stage. Two months later on September 15, Will Bankhead would be dead. His vacancy would be filled by Sam Rayburn and Rayburn's vacancy would be filled by John McCormack.

Senator Barkley read a message "at the specific request and authorization of the President." It was a subtle ploy.[19]

> The President has never had, and has not today, any desire or purpose to continue in the office of President, to be a candidate for that office, or to be nominated by the convention for that office.
>
> He wishes in all earnestness and sincerity to make it clear that all of the delegates to this convention are free to vote for any candidate.

After much of the Chicago crowd lapsed into feelings of disappointment and dismay, a voice on the loudspeaker blared out, "We Want Roosevelt." Calling out each state's delegation by name was the voice of Thomas D. Garry, the superintendent of Chicago's sewers, an ally of pro-FDR Chicago Mayor Edward Kelly.[20] The refrain was echoed by the crowd and before long a pro-Roosevelt stampede among the thousand-plus delegates had been launched by the infamous "voice from the sewers," which had bleated out FDR's actual wishes to the Democratic delegates. Formalities were performed and FDR's name was placed into nomination. The final tally was not even close. Roosevelt won 946 and 13/30 delegates to 72 and 9/10 for Jim Farley and 61 for Cactus Jack.[21] Most of Farley's votes came from his home state of New York with 29.5 and 12.5 from Massachusetts. FDR won easily, but there was no acclamation vote because a handful of Farley supporters, including Joe Kennedy, Jr., chose not to join the majority.

With Cactus Jack gone from the ticket, the vice presidential nomination was up for grabs. FDR's frustration with ideological ticket-balancing led him to support the candidacy of controversial Agriculture Secretary Henry A. Wallace of Iowa. It was a curious choice. The Wallace family was well known in agricultural circles as the publishers of *Wallace's Farmer*, and Henry's father, Henry C. Wallace, had served as secretary of agriculture in both the Harding and Coolidge Republican Administrations from 1921 until his death in 1924. Young Henry was more liberal than his father, and an effective defender of limiting farm production to raise prices. That policy was at the heart of the controversial Agricultural Adjustment Act and it was one of the earliest pieces of New Deal legislation ruled unconstitutional by the U.S. Supreme Court.[22]

Moderate southerners, who had reluctantly accepted the 1936 ending of the "two-thirds rule" in anticipation of Vice President Jack Garner being nominated in 1940, rallied around the candidacy of House Speaker Will Bankhead. Bankhead and many of the other southerners were stunned when Majority Leader Sam Rayburn, who had led a pro-Garner Texas delegation to the convention, turned aside a favorite son nomination of his own to rally the convention behind FDR's choice of Wallace. Bankhead was especially embittered when Rayburn, his second-in-command, announced[23], "I came here to second the nomination of another. Let me say that if I consulted my loyalty to friendship and my love, I would probably be seconding the nomination of [still] another, but under the circumstances I can do none other than follow what I believe to be the wish of our great leader."

The deal was sealed for Wallace when Mrs. Eleanor Roosevelt appeared before the convention to urge the delegates "to rise above considerations which are narrow and partisan. . . . This is no ordinary time."[24] The vote for Wallace was 626 ½ to 329 ⅔ for Bankhead. While Rayburn's Texas delegation cast all of its 46 votes for Bankhead, John McCormack's Massachusetts delegates followed FDR's lead as Wallace received 22 ⅔ of its 34 delegate allotment. And to prevent howls of dissent from reaching the nation's radio listeners, Henry Wallace was persuaded not to address the convention and the microphones were turned off.

Aiding Wallace's candidacy behind the scenes was John McCormack's mysterious ally, David K. Niles. Although Niles is seldom if at all mentioned in retellings of Wallace's vice presidential nomination,[25] it is clear that Wallace himself appreciated David's work on his behalf[26]:

Dear Dave:

I find myself groping for words to tell you in writing how grateful I am for the vastly effective work that you did in my behalf at Chicago.

Your influence and prestige among the delegates and your wide circle of friends were made manifest everywhere, and I feel that your help was not simply important but was pivotal.

Sincerely, H. A. Wallace

The Democratic Convention turned out better for FDR than he had hoped. He was easily renominated and the convention gave him the liberal secretary of agriculture, Henry A. Wallace of Iowa, as his vice presidential running mate. Choosing Henry Wallace from a Republican family would further FDR's long-term rearranging of American politics along ideological lines and not along party lines, and it rid him at last of the increasingly difficult Cactus Jack. Wallace was not a popular choice, and with the microphones shut off in the convention hall, Americans listening on their radios would not hear the deafening boos that erupted from the crowd once he was confirmed as the nominee.

The most disappointed vice presidential hopeful was Speaker Will Bankhead. He was especially bothered that his close ally, Majority Leader Sam Rayburn, had not supported his vice presidential candidacy but it was increasingly clear to most that Will Bankhead's health was declining. How much so would soon be evident.

Republican Nomination Politics: Republicans held their nominating convention before the Democrats, and while they were well aware of the fact that Democrats were wrestling with the third-term issue, they too had a nominating quandary. The June 1940 Republican National Convention meeting in Philadelphia had become deadlocked between the isolationist U.S. Senator Robert A. Taft of Ohio, the son of former President and Chief Justice William Howard Taft, and the 38-year-old Manhattan District Attorney Thomas E. Dewey, "the gangbuster" who had run a credible race for governor of New York two years earlier. Dewey was the overall winner of the Republican primaries and Taft was their best-known U.S. Senator, yet they chose as their nominee a utility executive who had never held public office. His name was Wendell Willkie, a native of Indiana and graduate of Indiana University.

Willkie had been a Democratic delegate from Ohio to the ill-fated 103-ballot convention in 1924. As the president of the private power conglomerate Commonwealth and Southern headquartered in New York City, Willkie's vocal opposition to the FDR-sponsored Tennessee Valley Administration made him a hero to the party's fiscal conservatives and his regular appearances on the popular radio quiz show "Information Please" had enhanced his public visibility.[27] He set off a firestorm of positive attention right before the Republican Convention, and the dazzled and perhaps dazed delegates gave him their nomination on the sixth ballot breaking the Dewey-Taft impasse. Willkie's candidacy had been championed by Russell Davenport, editor of *Fortune*, and sponsored by Henry Luce, the powerful publisher of *TIME, LIFE,* and *Fortune*.[28] Luce was an old Joe Kennedy pal and had written the foreword to Jack Kennedy's published Harvard honor's thesis "Why England Slept."[29] Luce hoped to use the growing estrangement between Joe Kennedy and FDR to topple the president. The fact that Luce's playwright wife Clare had cuckolded him with Joe Kennedy seemed not to matter, so eager was Henry Luce to end the Roosevelt presidency. Clare would successfully run for the U.S. House from Connecticut in 1942 in spite of Roosevelt's enjoyable on-target pun of her as "a Luce woman."[30]

Bankhead's Death and the Emergence of the Austin-Boston Connection: Following the conventions, the 76th Congress returned to work and passed the most important legislative act of that year, the Burke-Wadsworth Selective Service and Training Act of 1940. It was the nation's first ever peacetime draft and it called for all males between 21 and 35 to register and be eligible for one year of active duty and ten years in the reserves.[31] To accomplish this and other key pieces of preparedness legislation, FDR would need the full cooperation of congressional leaders Rayburn and McCormack in the House and Alben Barkley in the Senate. Uncertainty about FDR's third-term plans in 1939 and his election prospects in 1940 had made the passage of far-reaching laws problematic but it was finally approved on September 16, 1940.

France had already fallen before the Nazi thrust and Britain clearly was next. Passing this "peacetime" draft was a great accomplishment for the Democratic leaders of the Congress and one of John McCormack's prouder successes. But their joy was diminished, as only a day earlier the much-loved Speaker Will Bankhead collapsed and died.[32]

Will Bankhead's death was the third to befall Democratic House Speakers in six years. While Bankhead's body lay in state in the Hall of the House of Representatives in front of the dais, the House acted swiftly to replace him. John McCormack, chair of the Democratic Caucus, offered the resolution naming Majority Leader Sam Rayburn, who had served as Speaker pro tem during Bankhead's absence, as his successor.[33] McCormack's motion followed the announcement of Minority Leader Joe Martin that the Republicans would name no one from their side to contest the Rayburn selection. The solemnity of the occasion sped the succession.

While there was no contest for Speaker, there would be a spirited contest to fill Rayburn's vacancy as Majority Leader. The contesting sides for floor leadership took shape on the train carrying Speaker Bankhead's casket back to Alabama.[34] The leading contenders were 53-year-old Clifton Woodrum (Dem-Va.), a key member of the newly formed Conservative Coalition, and 48-year-old Caucus Chair John McCormack. Also in the running were Democratic Whip Patrick Boland of Pennsylvania, Tennessee's Jere Cooper, and Kent Keller of Illinois. Cooper joined the House in 1929 shortly after McCormack and also served on Ways and Means. The 60-year-old Boland and 47-year-old Cooper who entered the House in 1931 were hoping for a McCormack-Woodrum deadlock that would move them into serious contention. The 73-year-old Keller was clearly a long shot.

With conservative southerners in the ascendance, it was expected that the edge would go to Woodrum of Virginia, a nine-term member and third-ranking on Appropriations, the House's largest committee. Members supporting a delay in the voting pressured Lindsay Warren of North Carolina, who had been named acting Majority Leader when Rayburn became Speaker. Fresh from his successful management of the Transportation Act and just named Comptroller General of the General Accounting Office, Lindsay Warren was leaving the House and was presumed to be neutral in the Woodrum-McCormack contest.[35] Warren seemed to support a delay.

The White House did not. If a delay were not possible, perhaps a secret ballot would be used. The Woodrum forces hoped that a secret ballot would enable the South and much of the West to vote for Woodrum without incurring White House patronage wrath. After all, they contended that Sam Rayburn had successfully urged the 1937 Democratic Caucus to use a secret ballot in his contest against New York's John O'Connor. They eagerly awaited Rayburn's support in this matter.[36] But none came.

Times had changed for the House Democrats. The massive majorities of the 1930s had shrunk. While President Roosevelt's party majority in the House remained, his philosophical one had disappeared.[37] Democrats lost 72 seats in the 1938 election and southerners now held 41% of those presently occupied by the party. Many southern Democrats, notably Woodrum and Cox of Georgia, had allied themselves with Republicans in opposition to presidential policies. Woodrum was the first of the two major contenders to announce for the majority leadership post. He was then in his 18th year in the House and had a reputation as a "southern progressive," but his anti-WPA activities made the White House regard him as no ally of the administration.[38]

John McCormack, chair of the Democratic Caucus, would be Woodrum's chief opponent, but a man with six years less seniority in a chamber that valued experience. John McCormack served on Ways and Means. He had been a key talent scout, scouring the committee rooms for hard-working and loyal junior members whose requests for committee transfers he could either expedite or block. John was a good man to impress and he had more friends in the caucus room and the White House than was initially realized.

The White House was anxious about this contest. The failure of the 1938 purge indicated that there were limits to FDR's power to control congressional events. The nominating convention had gone well for the president, thanks in part to John McCormack, but there was a clear awareness in the White House that the upcoming 1940 reelection campaign would be far from the cakewalk that had occurred in 1936.

John McCormack had proved himself to the White House again when he outmaneuvered Jim Farley's forces on the president's behalf within the Massachusetts delegation at the 1940 convention. John's earlier efforts to scuttle the majority leadership candidacy of FDR nemesis John O'Connor of New York in 1937 had first brought him positive notice to FDR loyalists. The White House was fearful that an effort to postpone the choice of floor leader until after the election would hurt McCormack and help Woodrum. A continuing loss of electoral momentum among liberal members of the congressional party would further entrench the party's conservative wing. This fear led Interior Secretary Harold Ickes to work vigorously on McCormack's behalf with the Illinois delegation.

The South was not united for Woodrum. Georgia's Carl Vinson of Naval Affairs joined those pressuring Warren for a postponement of the vote until after the November election to further enhance Woodrum's prospects while fellow Georgian Gene Cox supported an immediate vote. The vote to delay was debated and defeated. Once the delay was defeated, Representatives Cooper, Boland, and John Rankin of Mississippi, also a member of the Conservative Coalition, withdrew from the balloting.[39] It had now become a two-man race.

Boston Joins Austin: On September 25, 1940, friendship trumped ideology. Rather than throwing his support to Woodrum, his fellow southern conservative, it was Gene Cox who placed John McCormack's name into nomination. The rout was on and John McCormack won handily on the first ballot, 141 to 67.[40] It was an even larger margin than had elected Sam Rayburn floor leader in 1937. McCormack became the first New Englander to lead the Democrats in the House[41] since Jeffersonian Ezekiel Bacon of Massachusetts chaired the Ways and Means Committee in 1811 in the early days of Henry Clay's speakership. When asked about his victory over Woodrum, John McCormack attributed his success to the fact that "I had a lot of friends in the South. You needed sixty to seventy votes from the South to win."[42]

The major actor in the floor leadership contest was Eugene Cox, the man Republican Floor Leader Joe Martin called "the real leader of the southerners in the House." Regarding Cox's role in his election, McCormack recounted, "Gene Cox and I were great pals. We voted just the opposite of each other. But he handled my fight in the caucus." Gene Cox was a poker-playing pal of McCormack's and in the former Speaker's own words, "If you're a poker pal, you're a damn good pal."

Cox had confounded his fellow conservative Democrats by presenting John McCormack's name to the Democratic Caucus. With the support of Cox and the other southern conservatives whose support he had cultivated over the years and whose committee assignments he had delivered, John McCormack's victory would help change the ways in which the House operated for more than a generation. Cox's efforts on McCormack's behalf divided the southerners in much the same way that McCormack had divided the northerners to elect Rayburn almost four years earlier.

A number of factors contributed to McCormack's success and are worth reviewing. His longtime service as a talent scout on the Ways and Means Committee enabled him to give junior members attractive committee assignments that they remembered. John also had allies in the White House who did not want the anti-WPA Woodrum in the post. Interior Secretary Harold Ickes was especially emphatic about it, as he recorded in his diary, "If [Woodrum] should be the majority leader, there would be nothing but trouble ahead for the President during his entire four years, if he is re-elected, and the President realizes this as strongly as anybody."[43] Multiple phone calls to House members from Ickes and Secretary of Commerce Harry Hopkins helped McCormack's candidacy and his old Boston pal David K. Niles worked with Ickes and Hopkins to move members into the McCormack column. As Harold Ickes confided to his diary[44]:

> Apparently several of us had been thinking along the same line and found that we favored Congressman John W. McCormack, of Massachusetts, for majority leader. McCormack is experienced and forceful, and is a sincere New Dealer. He would make a real leader. The fact that he is an Irish Catholic makes him all the more available at this time.

John McCormack tried to be as generous in victory as possible, but he felt that Carl Vinson had betrayed an earlier agreement by urging Lindsay Warren to delay the vote. For that and then not voting for him, McCormack placed Carl Vinson "in purgatory" for 12 years after the 1940 vote.[45] The Boston Irish, even those with Canadian Scot forebears, know how to hold a grudge. Years later, Vinson's biographer reported that his assessment of McCormack had improved. It was surprisingly complimentary.[46]

> McCormack possessed qualities Rayburn admired: loyalty, a desire to assume responsibility, and a willingness to work long hours. Moreover, the "fighting Irishman's" quick mind, acid tongue, and zest for a good fight superbly equipped him to advance his party in legislative combat. In time, this Texas-Massachusetts combination would become one of the most effective leadership teams in House history.

John McCormack had now joined Sam Rayburn in the top two leadership positions of the House Democratic Party. The "Austin-Boston Connection" of these two men was to last for more than 21 years from the closing days of Franklin Roosevelt's second term through the entirety of the Truman and Eisenhower Administrations. It ended with Rayburn's death in the first year of the Kennedy-Johnson administration, itself a product of the "Austin-Boston Connection." The Rayburn-McCormack combination never faced opposition in the Democratic Caucus and its impact upon House politics and the national agenda was profound. The "Austin-Boston Connection" would rule the Democratic Party in the House for the next half-century from 1940 to 1989. The moderate and liberal Democrats now had their own alliance to counter the Conservative Coalition.[47]

They were not quite the proverbial "Mutt and Jeff" team with the tall angular McCormack walking beside the shorter and stockier Rayburn, but the physical contrast between the two drew attention. Their most important feature was their extraordinary ability to work together. They had complementary personalities. In the phrasing of what social psychologists call "interaction process analysis," Rayburn was a "task leader" keeping the House Democrats focused on the agenda of President Roosevelt, while McCormack was a "social leader" whose responsibility was to keep the disparate elements of the Democratic Party together.[48]

One of the more insightful observations about how the two men operated came from a *TIME* magazine story after FDR endorsed the 1941 reelection campaign of New York City's Fusion Mayor Fiorello La Guardia over Tammany Democrat William O'Dwyer. As reported by *TIME*'s Frank McNaughton,[49] "President Roosevelt kicks someone in the rump and starts civil war again. This is why bald diplomatic Speaker Sam Rayburn spends considerable time biting his fingernails, [and] why tall glad-hand Majority Leader John W. McCormack is always busy soothing Democratic feathers."

For a major political figure, Sam Rayburn was surprisingly shy. He seldom bothered to learn the names of junior members of the House. Rayburn knew the names of the chairs and the Texans. Everyone else was just a vote. Let the whips and John McCormack learn their names. And John did. In the early days of his House career, John was very sociable especially to younger members. John and Harriet McCormack had no children of their own, and as a member of the House who had been elevated to prominence early, he enjoyed being "big brother" to the House's newcomers (Figure 9.1). As he aged, he became more of an uncle, listening to their troubles and offering counsel. John McCormack truly enjoyed the interpersonal aspects of the job. For McCormack, the House had become home.

Figure 9.1 John and Harriet return to Boston after his 1940 election as House Majority Floor Leader (Edward J. McCormack, Jr. Family Papers).

The third-term campaign of 1940 and the Catholic quandary

With the House leadership contest settled, the Democrats resumed their efforts to maintain control of the Congress and to reelect President Roosevelt. However, a troubling fissure emerged within the cobbled-together Democratic coalition. Many of the nation's urban Catholics had become disenchanted with the leftward tilt of FDR's second term and were seriously considering casting their votes for Wendell Willkie.

White House operatives worried that Farley's opposition and reports of Catholic defections among many isolationist bishops would lead to the desertion of this critical segment of the coalition.[50] Private polls conducted in New York City, the Democratic Party's urban anchor, showed serious Catholic slippage for the FDR-Henry Wallace ticket.[51] FDR had already lost many Italian Catholic voters after his widely reported graduation address at the University of Virginia on June 10, 1940, when he called Benito Mussolini's invasion of France "a stab in the back."[52] The poll indicated that while 80% of Italians had voted for FDR in 1936, he was now receiving only 30% of their vote to Willkie's 49%.

Among New York's Irish voters, the slippage was less severe but still pronounced. In 1936, New York's Irish-American voters had cast 83% of their votes for FDR in spite of the dual pressures of Al Smith's defection to the Republican Party and the broadcast pleas of Father Coughlin to vote for the Union Party. But by 1940, FDR's polled percentage of New York City Irish support had dropped to 51%.

FDR was not unmindful of Catholic sensibilities, and when ultraconservative Supreme Court Justice Pierce Butler, the Harding-appointed Minnesota Democratic Catholic, died in 1939, the President replaced him with Attorney General Frank Murphy, a Michigan Democratic Catholic in 1940. Murphy was the eightieth Justice to serve on the Supreme Court but only it's fifth Catholic. Justice Felix Frankfurter, the Court's third Jewish Justice, had already been appointed in 1939 to replace the deceased Justice Benjamin N. Cardozo. Thus, FDR had made sure that both the "Jewish" and the "Catholic" seats on the Supreme Court were appropriately filled. The fact that Catholics and Jews were equally represented on the Court despite the fact that Catholics vastly outnumbered Jews in both the American public and in the Democratic Party scarcely troubled an old-line Protestant like FDR.

FDR's First Meeting with Speaker Sam and Floor Leader John: On October 4, 1940, less than ten days after John was elected majority leader, FDR invited the House's new leaders to the White House for a private meeting.[53] It was clear that FDR was mulling what course of action the United States should take if the Axis powers reacted negatively to the shipment of warplanes to England. As FDR stated bluntly, "It's perfectly true that the Axis Powers—there's no question about it—they'd give anything in the world to have me licked on the fifth of November."

While discussing negative comments made by Alf Landon and Wendell Willkie, John McCormack interjected that Mrs. McCormack had recently said to him, "You know what Mr. Willkie [reminds] me of? . . . He reminds me of a carnival barker—one of those men who you know is [cheating] you, but wants to get you in. . . . You know he's not telling you the truth, in order to get your money in."

At this meeting, FDR discussed his electoral prospects in New England, among other things, contending that the polls will give "us New Hampshire. They're giving us Massachusetts, Rhode Island, and they'll probably put Connecticut at the bottom of the pile." The transcript then contains a fascinating exchange between McCormack and FDR about ethnic politics.

> Here John McCormack interrupted. He felt the President should focus on one underlying thought: the descendants of the early Anglo-Saxons—"They're great Americans, don't particularly love England, but they hate Hitler. [FDR: 'Yes.'] They're not voting for any other Democrat. [FDR: 'No.'] . . . We have cases of men who . . . are lifelong Republicans. They're declaring for the President on his foreign affairs [FDR: 'Yes, I know.'] because they know . . . that you're the expression of their views."
>
> The President then re-entered the conversation, picking up on "that old Anglo-Saxon element, composed most of the undergraduates of Harvard College, all through New England. I'm hoping they'll offset the Italian defection. . . . I'm speaking on the twelfth of October . . . about Columbus being an Italian—splendid nation which contributed so much to all of our civilization—prime stock, and so forth and so on, like the Latin Americans, the Spanish Americans, and I think [they'll] begin to come back."

Only a Harvard graduate like FDR could believe that Harvard men could numerically "offset" the defection of thousands of New England's Italian-descended voters.

While Harold Ickes may have confided to his diary that the selection of John McCormack as House Majority Leader may have helped the administration with Catholics, the visibility of that post to Catholics outside Washington and Boston was relatively low, and certainly not enough to overcome Catholic anxieties in New York, Chicago, or Detroit about an administration seen as increasingly insensitive to their fears of Communism abroad and socialism at home. It is the diary of Ambassador Joseph P. Kennedy that reveals more of what may have been occurring among Irish Catholic leaders.

The inconstant ambassador

Parked in London was the increasingly restive and ignored Joe Kennedy.[54] When the war erupted in September 1939, Joe sent most of the family back to the states, with the exception of daughter Rosemary, who needed special care. The move was not well received in Britain. With most of the family safe in America, Joe became concerned for his own safety and he moved from London to escape the "Blitz,"—the fusillade of Nazi bombs that the *Luftwaffe*, so highly admired by Kennedy's friend Charles Lindbergh, was now raining down from the London skies. In October, Joe's personal safety concerns and his eagerness to get involved in the closing days of the 1940 presidential election led him to depart England and not return.

While John McCormack's attitudes had changed, Joe Kennedy's had not. Roosevelt became increasingly suspicious of Kennedy's defeatism and new pro-German associates. Kennedy's freelance diplomatic activities in Britain were bothersome, and FDR had opened up a back channel to the new First Lord of the Admiralty Winston Churchill, whom FDR saw as far more resolute than Prime Minister Neville Chamberlain in confronting Hitler.[55] By May 1940, with French resistance to Hitler collapsing and the disappointing retreat of the British and a small French contingent at Dunkirk, Churchill became prime minister.

FDR's fears that Hitler would next move to invade Britain led him to increase his cabled communications with Churchill. Hundreds of their cables and other documents would be intercepted by Tyler Kent, an American cipher clerk of such ambiguous beliefs that he was alternately accused of being both a Soviet and Nazi agent. Kent's little-known sharing of these documents with those opposed to an Anglo-American alliance led him to be tried in violation of the British Official Secrets Act.[56] It was embarrassingly clear to Joe Kennedy that he had been deliberately left out of the FDR-Churchill loop, and he agreed to waive Kent's diplomatic immunity to permit him to be tried as a spy.

As FDR's distrust of Kennedy grew, the president became convinced that leaving Joe in London for most of his 1940 reelection campaign made sense. There was fear in the White House that Joe might climb onto the powerful isolationist America First bandwagon, much as Joe's friend the famous aviator Charles A. Lindbergh already had, and sway Irish Catholic voters to the Republican ticket.[57]

Joe Kennedy was delighted to finally leave the perils of London. In a memorable photograph of Churchill and Kennedy, as Churchill extended his hand, he deliberately averted Kennedy's gaze and it would appear as if Churchill was even more delighted to see the American ambassador leave. However, Joe's second daughter, the vivacious Kathleen "Kick," would return to England in 1943 to resume her ill-fated romance with the Anglican William Cavendish, Marquess of Hartington, the future Duke of Devonshire.

Joe and Rose returned to New York on October 27 and then onto Washington where "Missy" LeHand, the president's unofficial First Lady, greeted them at the White House.[58] Much of Washington was familiar with the rumors that Missy was FDR's mistress, so sending her to greet the Kennedys was FDR's one-upmanship touch. Rose Fitzgerald Kennedy also got the message. Twenty-seven years had passed since 1913 when a disenchanted Rose, the naïve and newly wed eldest Fitzgerald daughter, encountered her father's presumed infidelity with Toodles Ryan. She was now a worldly-wise woman who had become accustomed to the extra-marital privileges that alpha males like Joe and FDR had claimed for themselves.

Pressure from Henry Luce and pillow talk from his latest paramour Clare Boothe Luce had inclined Joe to endorse Wendell Willkie before the election. Days before the 1940 election, following a meeting with Justice Frank Murphy, Joe Kennedy confided to his diary on November 4 that he had been approached by Justices Murphy and William O. Douglas (over the objections of Felix Frankfurter) to make speeches for the Administration in order "to save the Catholic vote, which was rapidly leaving

Roosevelt." Joe Kennedy then went on to recount Murphy's qualms and his own about the increasing influence of Jews in the President's inner circle.[59]

> The picture as Murphy sees it, is a serious one. He said that Frankfurter is continually saying that he heard from England on the telephone—I imagine from [socialist intellectual Harold] Laski if he hears at all—and that it was Frankfurter and Ben Cohen who wrote the Attorney General's opinion on destroyers and bases. Murphy regards the Jewish influence as most dangerous. He said that after all, Hopkins' wife was a Jew; [Secretary of State Cordell] Hull's wife is a Jew; and Frankfurter and Cohen and that group are all Jews, and Jackson, Attorney General [who succeeded Murphy], is sympathetic with the Communists.
> Murphy said, "We can't have both Catholics and Communists—we must have one or the other." He regards Roosevelt as a tired man and thinks the element around him can do anything they want with him. Frankfurter, so Murphy says, engineered [Henry L.] Stimson's appointment [as Secretary of War].

It was Rose Fitzgerald Kennedy, a politician's daughter, who intervened on FDR's behalf. She greatly admired Eleanor Roosevelt, and as fellow survivors of marital infidelity, it was she who made sure that the two families would not become estranged. Knowing of how deeply invested Joe was in his sons' political advancement, FDR promised to help them achieve public office. Joe was skeptical, but Rose prevailed and much to the dismay of Henry and Clare Luce, Joe's radio address was a ringing endorsement of FDR's third term.[60]

FDR and Boston: As the 1940 campaign came to a close, FDR chose Boston to give his most memorable speech. As a graduate of the Groton School and Harvard University, FDR was no stranger to Boston, nor was his family as his sons James and John both married Boston women. FDR's daily link to Boston was the continual presence of Marguerite "Missy" LeHand, his private secretary and unofficial White House mistress, who was raised in Somerville, Massachusetts, the city that adjoined Cambridge. (David K. Niles had arranged for Frankfurter to rent Missy's sister's home upon his return visits to Harvard.)[61]

It was the most dramatic moment of the campaign when on October 30, days after Joe Kennedy's endorsement of his third term, FDR spoke movingly before an overflow crowd in the Boston Garden. Seated on the platform with President Roosevelt were the Bay State's Democratic dignitaries including Jim Curley and newly elected Majority Leader John McCormack, but only one was singled out for special attention: "I have been glad in the past two or three days to welcome back to the shores of America that Boston boy, beloved by all of Boston and a lot of other places, my Ambassador to the Court of St. James, Joe Kennedy."

To an anxious audience fearful about the possibility of yet another European war involving the United States, FDR then made the following promise[62]:

> And so I feel that, very simply and very honestly, I can give assurance to the mothers and fathers of America that each and every one of the boys in training will be well housed and well fed.

Throughout that year of training, there will be constant promotion of their health and well-being. And while I am talking to you mothers and fathers, I give you one more assurance.

I have said this before, but I shall say it again and again;

Your boys are not going to be sent into any foreign wars.

They are going into training to form a force so strong that, by its very existence, it will keep the threat of war far away from our shores.

The purpose of our defense is defense.

When the election results poured out of wire service teletypes that evening, it was clear that FDR had made history by becoming the nation's first ever three-term president. It was not as impressive as the 1936 victory over Kansas Governor Alf Landon when Roosevelt became the first Democratic nominee to win popular vote majorities in successive elections since Andrew Jackson in 1832, but it was impressive nonetheless. FDR carried thirty-eight states with 449 electoral votes and 54.7% of the popular vote as compared to 1936's forty-six states with 523 electoral votes and 60.8% of the popular vote. Willkie was defeated but not crushed.

Rather than exult in FDR's latest triumph, Joe Kennedy submitted his resignation as ambassador two days later and returned to Boston. His long-simmering frustrations erupted in an interview just four days after the election. Two reporters from the *St. Louis Post-Dispatch* were there, but it was reporter Louis Lyons of the *Boston Globe* whose reporting did the most damage. Among Joe's more memorable lines were[63]:

> KENNEDY: I'm willing to spend all I've got left to keep us out of the war. There's no sense in our getting in. We'd just be holding the bag. . . .
>
> People call me a pessimist. I say, "What is there to be gay about? Democracy is all done."
>
> INTERVIEWER: You mean in England or this country, too?
>
> KENNEDY: Well, I don't know. If we get into war it will be in this country, too.

In a parting shot at the official First Lady, Eleanor Roosevelt, Kennedy said,[64]

> She's another wonderful woman. And marvelously helpful and full of sympathy. Jim [Landis of the Harvard Law School] will tell you that she bothered us more on our jobs in Washington to take care of the poor little nobodies who hadn't any influence, than all the rest of the people down there together. She's always sending me a note to have some little Susie Glotz to tea at the Embassy.

Public and private outrage poured into the White House from multiple quarters, and even Joe Kennedy loyalists shrunk from his remarks. As criticism of Kennedy crested, FDR met with Joe in Hyde Park to hear personally the ambassador's thoughts on the European situation. In Michael Beschloss's evocative depiction[65]:

> The two men disappeared into the president's tiny study . . .
>
> Kennedy's vision of a vanquished Britain and an America adjusting to an authoritarian world was no more provocative than his conversations with Breckinridge Long . . . the Hollywood executives, William Randolph Hearst,

Herbert Hoover . . . But now the election had passed and Franklin Roosevelt was freer to indulge the frustrations that he had pent up for months.

Not ten minutes elapsed before Mrs. Roosevelt was called to the Big House. The President asked Kennedy to step out of the room. His wife had rarely seen him so angry. His face was drained, his voice almost tremulously restrained:

I never want to see that son of a bitch again as long as I live. Take his resignation and get him out of here!

The door to the Roosevelt White House was now closed to Joe Kennedy. Not fully realizing that he had burned his White House bridges and had forever lost the high regard that FDR once had for him, Joe returned to a place that had formerly held him in great esteem—Hollywood. No longer constrained by his status as an administration spokesman, he addressed his former colleagues, Harry Warner, Samuel Goldwyn, Louis B. Mayer, and others in the movie business, many of whom were Jewish émigrés from Eastern Europe who had anglicized their own names.[66] Kennedy told them that Adolf Hitler liked American movies but "you're going to have to get those Jewish names off the screen [and] stop making anti-Nazi pictures or using the film medium to promote or show sympathy to the cause of 'democracies' versus the 'dictators.'"[67]

Douglas Fairbanks, Jr., immediately relayed Kennedy's comments to FDR.[68] Joe blithely assumed that his November resignation was perfunctory and that he would soon return to England. However, when Joe arrived at the White House on December 1, FDR told him directly, "I don't want to send you back," adding "you've done enough."[69]

In February 1941, a month after his third inaugural, FDR wrote a letter about Joe to his son-in-law John Boettinger, the current husband of his only daughter Anna[70]:

The truth of the matter is that Joe is and always has been a temperamental Irish boy, terrifically spoiled at an early age by huge financial success; thoroughly patriotic, thoroughly selfish and thoroughly obsessed with the idea that he must leave each of his nine children with a million dollars (he has told me that often). He has a positive horror of any change in the present methods of life in America. To him the future of a small capitalistic class is safer under a Hitler than under a Churchill. This is subconscious on his part and he does not admit it. . . . Sometimes I think I am 200 years older than he is.

Joe Kennedy was now in eclipse while John McCormack was in the ascendancy.

"The Three of Us": On December 23, 1940, days before the 76th Congress would close shop, FDR wrote a "Personal and Confidential" letter to Sam Rayburn with its only copy sent to John. The letter referenced the defeat of a vote to override FDR's veto of the Walter-Logan bill that opened the door to lengthy litigation to delay the implementation of decisions issued by government regulatory agencies.[71] Derided by Representative Luther Patrick (Dem-Ala.) as "this lawyer's delight,"[72] FDR's veto was upheld. It was not a major victory but in this first post-purge Congress with FDR's third term barely four weeks away, any victory was appreciated. FDR's letter was one of exhortation and not congratulation[73]:

You and I and John McCormack are facing a very difficult session. On the success of that session will depend the future reputation of the President and the Speaker and the majority leader. It will not help any of the three to meet with a series of defeats in the next Congress.

That is especially true if the three of us, or any one of the three, accepts prospective defeat tamely. Therefore, I renew my ancient feeling that it is better to be defeated while going down fighting than it is to accept defeat without fighting.

Having received prior pep talks from FDR in the past, Sam thought the letter was condescending and complained to FDR that he should show more respect for Congress.[74] But for John McCormack, the letter was demonstrable proof that confirmed his place in the hierarchy of the Nation's Capital. John had just turned 49 and was now the president's chief legislative lieutenant. The remarkable ascent of John McCormack, the poor Irish-descended boy from the tenements of South Boston's Andrew Square, had been achieved and fully acknowledged by the most powerful man in the country, President Franklin D. Roosevelt. In less than ten years, John McCormack had risen from the backbenches of the House minority to the second-ranking post as the House's Majority Floor Leader.

1941: A year of peril and preparedness

Newly installed Majority Leader John McCormack returned to the House for his seventh full term from the 12th Massachusetts Congressional District as he again easily defeated his 1938 Yankee Republican challenger Henry J. Allen. He was now as safe a Democrat as any in the nation and ready to lead the House on the President's behalf.

John McCormack was well aware of the growing tensions between Catholics and Jews within the Democratic Party. With a substantial number of Jewish constituents in the Mattapan section of his South Boston-Dorchester district, John was quite mindful of anti-Semitic sentiments among many of the Irish-descended Catholics of South Boston.

In a letter to David K. Niles, who had become the president's key advisor on Jews and blacks in the Democratic Party, dated November 26, 1940, McCormack informed Niles about a radio license approval by the Federal Communications Commission for the owner of the *Lawrence (Mass) Tribune*. McCormack typed this letter himself, even though the newly elected Majority Leader of the U.S. House of Representatives certainly had staff to do such things. Apologizing for "the appearance of this letter, which I am typing myself," John maintained a private correspondence with Niles and no one needed to know of the depth of their friendship and political alliance.

John McCormack was David Niles's window into the House and Niles was McCormack's back door to the president. Their friendship and political alliance would play a central role in keeping Catholic-Jewish tensions within the Democratic Party at a low boil for most of the next 12 years. John McCormack knew full well that the only hope for maintaining the Democratic Party in power was to accommodate as many groups as possible and to finesse their differences through legislation, appointments, and appropriations. It was McCormack's awareness of the fluid nature of Democratic Party alliances that guided him throughout the entirety of his House leadership career that would last for more than 30 years and through all or part of six presidential administrations. You did what was necessary to keep the coalition together.

The Troubled Horizon: Although FDR's 1940 presidential victory was smaller than those of 1932 and 1936, he still carried thirty-eight states with a 449 to 82 margin in the Electoral College and 54.7% of the popular vote. In the 77th Congress, Democrats continued to hold the Senate 66 to 28 with one philosophical ally. Their prior 43-seat margin of 68 to 25 remained stable at 38, but the South's proportions always increased when Democrats lost seats. In the House, Democrats had gained five seats raising their margin to 105 seats (267–162) from their prior one of 93 (262–169). The House margin was large enough so that the newly elected Austin-Boston team of Speaker Sam Rayburn and Majority Leader John McCormack would still be able to produce pro-FDR majorities.

As American involvement in World War II became inevitable, the Roosevelt administration increased its efforts to shore up the nations of Western Europe battling with the Axis powers. The president knew that there was serious resistance to any major buildup of American military forces. The steps would have to be gradual ones and he would need the full cooperation of the congressional leadership.

On January 6, 1941, President Franklin D. Roosevelt appeared before a joint gathering in the Hall of the House of Representatives to address the 77th Congress. It would be his ninth State of the Union Address, the most ever for an American president. The members listened intently as the president spoke eloquently of the "Four Freedoms"—freedom of speech, freedom of religion, freedom from want, and freedom from fear.[75] Most of the world was now at war and the defense of these freedoms became paramount as the antidemocratic Axis armies of Nazi Germany, Fascist Italy, and Imperial Japan raged throughout Europe, Asia, and Africa. FDR hoped that the United States would become enmeshed in the efforts to protect our closest allies from their expansionist enemies.[76]

While Rayburn and McCormack attempted to shore up FDR's foreign policy proposals in the House, Joe Kennedy was almost as active in opposing them. No longer in the administration and with no White House portfolio to lose, Kennedy launched an isolationist crusade against FDR's foreign policy. On January 10, just days after FDR's "Four Freedoms" speech, Kennedy's isolationist sentiments were extolled in the *Washington Times Herald* and placed in the *Congressional Record* by U.S. Senators Republican Arthur Vandenberg of Michigan and Democrat Robert R. Reynolds of North Carolina, and his January 18, 1941, radio address was added by Republican Representative Francis Case of South Dakota.[77] There was no silencing of Joe Kennedy.

Joe Kennedy and John McCormack would each be affected by the war. Joe Kennedy would suffer the most as he would lose Joseph P. Kennedy, Jr., his first-born child and namesake, in a suicidal top secret bomber mission. Perhaps it was a foreshadowing of Joe Kennedy's greatest fears of American involvement as he continued to speak out in opposition to what he felt were FDR's efforts to bring the United States in on the side of the beleaguered Allies. On the other hand, John McCormack's reputation would be enhanced, located as he was at the congressional center of the most critical decisions that shaped American involvement in the war. As one of the three House leaders who authorized the funds for the building of the atomic bomb, he was in on the decision that would lead to the war's successful conclusion.

Lend-Lease Legislation: As the interventionists feared, "Cash and Carry" was not enough and the president submitted legislation to further circumvent the Neutrality Acts and to make American war matériel available to the beleaguered democracies. Conflict between Kennedy and McCormack came to a head over the Lend-Lease Act of 1941, a bill that authorized the President to "sell, transfer, exchange, lease, or lend" defense articles "to the government of any country whose defense the President [deemed] vital to the defense of the United States."[78] The Lend-Lease Act also made available to such nations the facilities of American shipyards. Opposition to the bill was heated, and on January 21, 1941, both Joe Kennedy and his isolationist ally Charles A. Lindbergh made impassioned pleas against the bill with Kennedy's oppositional testimony taking five-plus hours before the House Foreign Affairs Committee.[79]

Since most of the early financial aid was intended for Great Britain, British foreign policy became an issue. Trouble appeared among urban ethnic Democrats with immigrant constituents who abhorred the British, most notably the Irish whose hopes for a united Ireland were blocked by the British and to a lesser extent, the Jews who were frustrated by British foot-dragging in their commitment to a Palestinian homeland. Chicago-born Sol Bloom, the son of Polish Jewish immigrants and chair of the House Foreign Affairs Committee, represented New York City's "Silk Stocking" district.[80] Sol Bloom was considered emblematic of New York Jews much as John McCormack was considered emblematic of Boston's Irishmen. They were allies and Bloom, described in one account as the "supersalesman of patriotism," led the charge for Lend-Lease in the Foreign Affairs Committee.[81] As Majority Leader, John would manage the bill on the House floor. John McCormack's South Boston-Dorchester district was one of the Irish-American enclaves where anti-British antipathy was intense and there was no doubt that John's public support of Lend-Lease on the House floor would be crucial to its passage, support that involved a serious political risk for John back home.

While the voters within the districts of Bloom and McCormack may have been conflicted over this program to aid Great Britain, they personally were not. It was John McCormack who introduced Lend-Lease on the House floor under the bill number H.R. 1776 and it was Sol Bloom who rushed the bill through his committee back to the House floor for final passage. John McCormack deliberately chose the number 1776 for the bill.[82] It was a reminder to his Irish-American constituents in South Boston and Dorchester of the colonists' victory over the English Crown when British troops chose to evacuate the city of Boston on March 17, 1776, St. Patrick's Day. Historian Susan Dunn described the move favorably[83]:

> The revolutionary number had been the brainstorm of Massachusetts representative John McCormack who introduced the bill in the House. An imaginative politician, McCormack pitched the bill to his constituents in Boston as aiming to

rescue not Britain but the Catholic Church, . . . [even contending to a constituent] This is not a bill to save the English; this is a bill to save Catholicism.

John McCormack's unique role in deflecting Irish-American opposition to legislation aiding Britain was the subject of some congressional opponents of the legislation. In his account of the debate, the Irish author T. Ryle Dwyer noted that[84] when a Missouri Republican [Dewey Short] said, "'I never knew I would live to see the day that a good Irishman like John McCormack from Massachusetts would openly admit that Great Britain is our first line of defense.'"

Dwyer continued: "McCormack responded [the] next day, thanking the Congressman for paying him a great compliment by characterising him as an Irishman. 'There is,' McCormack added, 'one greater compliment that he could give me—by characterising me as "The American of Irish descent from Boston!"'" Given John's long-term concealment of his father's Canadian Scottish background, the distinction he made in that remark was as close to the truth as he could get.

Backers of the Lend-Lease program came up with an ingenious argument intended to gain isolationist support. By providing Britain with the military equipment to battle the Nazis, the British would thwart Hitler's expansion and enable the United States to remain far removed from the fray. It was disingenuous and FDR knew it, but he did not wish to get too far ahead of a reluctant public. John's arguments prevailed and the House easily passed the bill 260 to 165. The Senate passed it 60 to 31. Ultimately, the United States extended $50 billion in lend-lease aid to the countries that warred against the Axis Powers.

Even after Lend-Lease passed, Joe Kennedy kept up his verbal assault on FDR's policies. His next foray was the Commencement Address on May 24, 1941, at Oglethorpe University in Atlanta, Georgia. These remarks were also inserted in the *Congressional Record* by Democratic Senator Burton K. Wheeler of Montana and Republican U.S. Representative Robert F. Rich of Pennsylvania.[85] Kennedy's obsessional concern with American involvement in the war is revealed in his contention[86] that "although a British victory would be helpful from the standpoint of this country's foreign markets. It was 'nonsense' to say that an Axis victory spelled ruin. From 90 to 95% of our trade is internal. If worse comes to worse, we could gear ourselves to an intelligent self-contained national economy and still enjoy a fair degree of prosperity."

It did not matter. Americans had grown deaf to Joe Kennedy.

Congressional anti-Semitism

By late spring of 1941, the war in Europe had continued for more than twenty months and France and Britain appeared to be woefully inadequate opponents to the Nazi war machine. Many members of Congress were increasingly fearful that the United States would be drawn into the war with the isolationists among them convinced that it was the British and the Jews who were most eager to get the nation into the war.

John McCormack's immigrant Jewish allies, Sam Dickstein and Mike Edelstein of New York and Adolph Sabath of Chicago, grew increasingly fearful that the anti-Semitism that had driven them from their birthplaces in Eastern Europe would soon engulf the United States and once again relegate them to the status of a persecuted minority. Sol Bloom confided to Frank McNaughton of *TIME* his fears that congressional anti-Semitism was on the rise.[87] But it was in June of that year that its most dramatic manifestation occurred and Majority Leader John McCormack was in the middle of it.

The Death of Mike Edelstein: American prewar tensions escalated in the House. With the allies losing to the Axis powers early in the war, a number of the isolationist members took to the floor and attacked those they felt were pushing the United States into war to save the democracies. The most noxious of these was the small, fiery red-headed racist and anti-Semite John Rankin of Mississippi. On June 4, 1941, Rankin declaimed[88]:

> Mr. Speaker, Wall Street and a little group of our international Jewish brethren are still attempting to harass the President of the United States and the Congress of the United States into plunging into the European War unprepared; and at the same time the communistic elements throughout the country are fomenting strikes by harassing industry and slowing down our defense program.

Jumping up to challenge Rankin was second-term New York Congressman Michael Edelstein, a native of Meseritz, Poland, who had come to America with his parents at the age of three. An apoplectic and impassioned Mike Edelstein declared[89]:

> I deplore the idea that any time anything happens, whether it be for a war policy or against a war policy, men in the House and outside this House attempt to use the Jews as their scapegoat. I say it is unfair and I say it is un-American. As a Member of this House, I deplore such allegations, because we are living in a democracy. All men are created equal, regardless of race, creed, or color; and whether a man be Jew or Gentile he may think what he deems fit.

Applause filled the Hall of the House, but Mike Edelstein heard little of it. He left the floor of the House and headed to its lobby where, five minutes after his powerful and moving speech, he collapsed to the floor and died.[90] He was just 53.

An enraged John McCormack grabbed the puny John Rankin, lifted him off the ground, and shook him vigorously, bitterly denouncing Rankin's "damned infernal prejudice" that had led to Mike Edelstein's fatal heart attack. A vivid account of John's reaction was provided by his longtime Washington aide Judge Joseph Feeney[91]:

> The only time in his life that Judge [Joseph] Feeney ever remembers McCormack coming near physical violence was on a warm day in June, 1941. John Rankin was making one of his periodic attacks on Jews, asserting that "Wall Street and a little group of our international Jewish brethren" were attempting to plunge the United States into war. As Rankin concluded his remarks, a first-term Representative from New York City, M. Michael Edelstein, angrily rose from the floor. Edelstein was a

Jew, and had migrated from Poland with his parents when he was still very young in the 1890's. "Hitler started out by speaking about 'Jewish brethren,' Edelstein began his impassioned reply, but he did not get much further. After a little more than a minute he collapsed on the floor, and died five minutes later in the House lobby, apparently of a heart attack. The House was shocked, McCormack enraged. A big man of over six feet, he reportedly grabbed the five-and-a-half-foot Rankin roughly by his lapels, held him off the ground for a moment, and then pushed him away, bitterly denouncing him and his 'damned infernal prejudice.'"

The *New York Times* reported on page 24 that it was fellow Jewish immigrant Representative Sam Dickstein of New York who delivered the news to "a shocked House," but the *Congressional Record* moved quickly from the episode and apart from a handful of eulogies from those on the floor who witnessed it, Edelstein's death and John McCormack's rage is lost to history. The House quietly resumed its business with little recording of the event.

The Senate names the Truman Committee

During the two years when Europe was at war and the United States was not, the number of government contracts for war-related goods rose dramatically. In order to curtail the practices of unscrupulous contractors taking advantage of the government's urgent needs, Senator Harry S. Truman (Dem-Mo.) proposed an oversight committee. In February of 1941, he introduced Senate Resolution 71, which was amended and agreed to on March 1, 1941.[92] It gave a select Senate committee broad powers to investigate the national defense program and became one of the most important and powerful Senate investigative bodies, and the aggressive efforts of Truman gave it— and Truman—national recognition. Its official title was the Senate Special Committee to Investigate the National Defense Program, but to most people on Capitol Hill, it was known as the "Truman Committee." Ostensibly, the committee's mission was to oversee expenditures needed to fund the war and to avoid the financial abuses of wartime contractors that came to light during investigations of funding during World War I.

Vice President Henry A. Wallace named the original committee on March 8, 1941. Five Democrats and two Republicans were chosen. Senator Harry S. Truman of Missouri was appointed Chair and Senator Joseph H. Ball of Minnesota was the ranking minority member. Pursuant to Senate Resolution 175 of the 77th Congress, three additional members were appointed, bringing its size to ten: seven Democrats and three Republicans, a party ratio out of balance with the actual distribution of members in the Senate.

Then only in his second term, the committee's chair Senator Harry Truman was a product of the Kansas City machine run by Tom Pendergast and a man considered "reliable" by the Roosevelt administration. Truman's pre-Senate career had not been particularly distinguished, so there were those who questioned the choice of Senator Truman for this post. But it was Senator Truman who had introduced the motion creating the committee and the Senate generally rewarded the creators of select and special committees with the chairmanships of them.

Harry Truman was a small-town self-taught county judge from the Kansas City suburb of Independence and a World War I veteran. He found the more modest House members easier to deal with than his fellow U.S. Senators and became very close to Speaker Sam Rayburn. Rayburn's longtime aide and biographer D. B. Hardeman contended that Rayburn always loved Truman and Truman always loved Rayburn, "They were men who—both of them came from the soil."[93] Truman would become a frequent visitor to Sam Rayburn's Capitol Hill hideaway, "the Board of Education," where he would drink bourbon with Rayburn and play poker with John McCormack. Rayburn did not play poker but enjoyed his bourbon while John was a teetotaler but a serious poker player. John McCormack was close to both men. When asked who his "poker pals" were, McCormack named: "Gene Cox, Harry Truman, Fred Vinson, Mon Wallgren, and Warren Magnuson."

> INTERVIEWER: What about Sam Rayburn?
> McCORMACK: He didn't gamble. He made the sandwiches.[94]

The Truman Committee was considered to be a success. Unlike the ill-fated Civil War Committee on the Conduct of the War, which second-guessed President Lincoln throughout the conflict, Senator Truman's oversight committee was often cited as a model of probity and support.[95] It would be the Truman Committee investigators who would uncover Jim Curley's shady dealings and set the stage for the memorable 1947 clash between the two Bostonians, Minority Whip John McCormack and freshman U.S. Representative John F. Kennedy.

Domestic legislation virtually disappeared from the congressional agenda as the leaders of both parties in Congress maneuvered to prepare the nation for whatever action would be necessitated by the ongoing war.[96] The next piece of legislative business would be extremely problematic. The war in Europe continued to go badly for the Allies. The armies of Hitler and Mussolini were emboldened by the lack of major resistance in Western Europe and northern Africa. In late June of 1941, Hitler's army moved east against the Soviet Union. Hitler had abrogated the Molotov-Von Ribbentrop Treaty signed just two years earlier that had hastened the dismemberment of Poland. Calling his assault on the USSR "Operation Barbarossa," Hitler hoped to succeed where the vaunted Napoleon Bonaparte had failed early in the nineteenth century. Adolf Hitler's hubris was now at flood tide.

An unexpected uprising quelled

African Americans had benefited from the New Deal's bottom-up economic policies but questions remained regarding the unwillingness of FDR's Democrats in Congress to pass antilynching legislation, open up employment opportunities, and desegregate the armed forces. FDR was well aware that a sizable number of blacks had moved into the Democratic Party, as evidenced by the elections of Chicago's Clarence Mitchell in 1934 and William Dawson in 1938 to the U.S. House. Data on the 1936 election indicated that 71% of blacks had voted for FDR's reelection in 1936.[97] This was a far cry from his vice presidential candidacy in 1920 when the Cox-Roosevelt Democratic ticket garnered only 6% of "the Negro vote" in Chicago and only 3% of that vote in New York City.[98] While Chicago's black voters showed a slow trajectory—5% for Davis-Bryan in 1924, 29% for Smith-Robinson in 1928, 30% for Roosevelt-Garner in 1932, New York blacks voted 26% for the 1924 Davis-Bryan ticket, 41% for the 1928 Smith-Robinson ticket, and 58% for the 1932 Roosevelt-Garner ticket as urban blacks bid farewell to the party of Lincoln.[99]

The leading spokesman for black aspirations was the shrewd A. Philip Randolph who organized and led the Brotherhood of Sleeping Car Porters, an occupation that enabled blacks to intermingle with train-traveling affluent whites, albeit as their servants.[100] In an effort to get the nation's attention, Randolph organized the March on Washington movement.[101] When their initial demands failed to be met, the movement took shape and an anxious President Roosevelt sought to forestall the march by issuing Executive Order 8802 that created the first Fair Employment Practices Commission that ruled[102]:

> Now, Therefore, by virtue of the authority vested in me by the Constitution and the statutes, and as a prerequisite to the successful conduct of our national defense production effort, I do hereby reaffirm the policy of the United States that there shall be no discrimination in the employment of workers in defense industries or government because of race, creed, color, or national origin, and I do hereby declare that it is the duty of employers and of labor organizations, in furtherance of said policy and of this Order, to provide for the full and equitable participation of all workers in defense industries, without discrimination because of race, creed, color, or national origin.

While it was confined to defense industries and presumably would expire when the national exigencies had passed, it was a powerful first step. And as an executive order, it did not need congressional approval, so the southern Democratic segregationists could not block it. Speaker Sam Rayburn and Majority Leader John McCormack would not need to twist arms on this initiative. That would come later.

The 203–202 Selective Service Extension vote

Throughout the spring and summer of 1941, the Allies' position worsened as Greek and Yugoslav resistance to the onslaught of Hitler's forces collapsed. The *Luftwaffe*'s attacks on Britain and Northern Ireland intensified, and FDR's fears increased that Britain would be overtaken much as France had already been. More than ever, FDR needed extensive help from Congress and he needed a loyal John McCormack to maneuver bills through an increasingly wary House of Representatives. Although this was his first year as floor leader, this would be the ultimate test of McCormack's legislative skill.

It occurred during the bitter fight to extend the initial Burke-Wadsworth Draft Act that was intended to lengthen the commitment of the nation's first peacetime draftees from twelve months of active duty service to eighteen months.[103] Two votes concerning the bill were voted on August 12, 1941.[104] The first was a motion to recommit (roll call 105) and to kill the bill by sending it back to the Military Affairs Committee. That motion failed 190 to 215. The second vote was on final passage (roll call 106) and that vote on the Selective Service Extension Act in the House was as close as it could be—203 votes for to 202 votes against.[105] Of the 404 members who voted on both motions—201 supported the president's position by voting nay on recommitment and yea on final passage, while 188 voted to recommit and nay on final passage—a level of consistency of 96.3%. John worked the floor relentlessly rounding up votes while Sam Rayburn waited with gavel in hand to secure the bill's passage. In one account, McCormack is depicted as "scurr[y]ing about the chamber, foraging for support, and succeeded by a personal appeal in inducing three Democrats who were abstaining to agree to switch their votes to aye if the need should arise."[106]

Frank McNaughton, *TIME*'s congressional reporter, filed a story describing John's frantic moments to save the bill[107]:

> The bill appeared virtually dead. Frantically, McCormack buttonholes the 26 Democrats (he doesn't remember all of them). Made personal appeals, told them if they voted against the bill to slap [Chair of Military Affairs] Andy May, they would be "slapping John McCormack. You're hitting me. You're hitting the President. It's not Andy May you are hurting. You are hurting your House leaders."
>
> He won back six votes, enough to save the bill. . . .
>
> McCormack, frantically scurrying around during the roll call, had found three no votes, pleaded, begged with them, made a personal appeal. They agreed to sit in the front row. They were all democrats. If McCormack should need their votes—he hung over the tally like a cloud every minute of the roll call—these three Democrats had agreed to change their votes to aye at a wink from the Majority Leader.
>
> It was that close.

It was a narrow escape for first year Speaker Rayburn and Majority Leader McCormack. McCormack's energetic search for members who could be convinced to provide "live pairs" and not vote on the bill and Sam Rayburn's quick gavel made the difference. Isolationist Republican Dewey Short of Missouri who requested a recapitulation was gaveled out of order and Rayburn's testy response was noted by Michigan's Earl Michener[108]:

> Mr. MICHENER. Mr. Speaker, there is no use getting excited about this.
> The SPEAKER. The Chair trusts the gentleman from Michigan does not think the Chair is excited.
> Mr. MICHENER. The only thing that would make me think it was the speed with which the Speaker passed the bill and refused to recognize the gentleman from Missouri [Mr. SHORT], who was on the floor.
> The SPEAKER. The gentleman did not state for what purpose.

Mr. SHORT. Mr. Speaker, I did not have time. I wanted to move to reconsider the
vote by which the bill was passed.

The SPEAKER. The gentleman, in the first place is not eligible to make that motion.

Before the year was out, how much of a difference their efforts made would be evident
to all.

Aid for Russia: The president's foreign policy advisors, most notably Secretary of State
Cordell Hull, were convinced that Hitler would eventually mount an invasion against
Russia. In anticipation of that event, "Rayburn and McCormack received instructions
to push for a general clause which would not specify who would receive aid. . . . The bill
that Roosevelt finally signed on March 11, 1941, did not specifically exclude any nation
from aid."[109] That clause would open the Lend-Lease door for aid to Russia. For devoted
anti-Communists like John McCormack, this was a difficult step to take. Saving England
had been hard enough but being called upon to save the Communist-run Soviet Union
and its atheistic godless regime greatly tested the commitment of McCormack and his
fellow Catholics to the president's foreign policy agenda.[110] But John McCormack had
been a dutiful soldier in the Great War, and he was now a leader charged with the
responsibility of furthering the national war goals issued by his commander-in-chief.

Cordell Hull's prediction came true. Hitler's troops invaded Russia on June 22,
1941. There had been unofficial shipments of matériel to the Soviets following that
invasion, but now there was need for more formal action. The administration returned
to Congress and asked for the inclusion of the Soviet Union among the beneficiaries
of Lend-Lease.[111] The first informal pre–Lend-Lease American assistance to the Soviet
Union arrived in June.

Complicating the aid issue was the death of 83-year-old Appropriations Committee
Chair Edward T. Taylor of Colorado on September 3, 1941. Next in line to replace
him were the two most senior Democrats—Clarence Cannon of Missouri and Clifton
Woodrum of Virginia. Both men had begun serving in the House in 1923 and were
named to the Appropriations Committee the same day, November 11, 1929, but
Cannon got the chair on a technicality because he was listed above Woodrum as "C"
precedes "W" and Missouri precedes Virginia in the alphabet. Woodrum who had lost
to John McCormack for majority leader a year earlier had been thwarted once again
and the White House was pleased.[112]

The Einstein letter

FDR returned to a matter that had troubled him earlier. He had initially postponed
dealing with the matter because of his worries about Europe and his own 1940
presidential campaign. But with the campaign over and the Allies faltering, FDR could
now act on the disturbing letter that the émigré physicist Albert Einstein had sent to
him on August 2, 1939. Einstein's letter warned FDR that the Germans were making
great strides in converting uranium into fissionable material that could be turned into
atomic bombs.[113]

As recounted by Dr. Vannevar Bush of MIT, the lead original scientist on what would become the Manhattan Project, no one was exactly sure what to do about the letter[114]:

> Neither the President nor the Joint Chiefs of Staff understood a great deal of modern physics. What actually happened was that the scientists and engineers went ahead on their own, slowly at first, but with gradually increasing momentum, and were supported by the President who had confidence in them. They were also supported by Secretary Stimson for the same reason. Roosevelt did not attempt to delve into the subject, to balance one piece of advice against the other. As far as I know, he never discussed the subject with anyone besides M. Stimson, General Groves, and myself until it began to enter its final phases. But he certainly did understand, as we approached use, the implications for civilization.

With direct American involvement in the war more imminent, FDR acted on the Einstein letter. On June 28, 1941, five months before the war was officially declared, FDR signed Executive Order 8807 creating the Office of Scientific Research and Development (OSRD), with Dr. Vannevar Bush as its director. The office was empowered to engage in large engineering projects and research. Although creating atomic weapons was not mentioned in the Executive Order, which would be the eventual mission of the OSRD,[115] by October 9, 1941, the possibility of using fissionable uranium for weapons led to FDR meeting with Vice President Henry A. Wallace, Harry Hopkins, and Dr. Bush. This circle was expanded to create a Top Policy Group with the three of them to be joined by Secretary of War Henry L. Stimson, Army Chief of Staff George C. Marshall, and Dr. James B. Conant. Bush was a tall gangly "swamp Yankee" from Everett, Massachusetts. A graduate of Tufts and MIT, Bush quickly grasped how science could be linked to public policy. Like Bush, James B. Conant, the other academic in the group, was a Boston-area native having grown up in Dorchester, Massachusetts, the Boston neighborhood abutting John McCormack's Southie and one that John represented in the House. Conant, a respected chemist, held two Harvard degrees and was more socially aware and politically aggressive than his mild, lean, and bespectacled appearance might suggest. He would serve as Harvard's president from 1933 to 1953, and be a major player in postwar German reconstruction.

Even though the peacetime draft was now in place and Lend-Lease operated to make the United States "the arsenal of democracy," the Axis powers continued their triumphant assault throughout Eastern Europe, North Africa, and East Asia. It was clear to FDR that more had to be done.

The 1939 Neutrality Act had to be repealed in order to permit American merchant ships to be armed and to carry cargoes of arms and ammunition to the beleaguered nations. But congressional resistance had stiffened. At a White House meeting on November 5, Rayburn and McCormack urged FDR to make more of a push. FDR's letter for Rayburn and McCormack was read to their House colleagues (Figure 9.2). In it, FDR stated: "Failure to repeal these sections would, of course, cause rejoicing in the

Figure 9.2 Speaker Sam Rayburn and Majority Leader John McCormack reading a letter, November 13, 1941 (U.S. House Historian's Office).

Axis nation. Failure would bolster aggressive steps and intentions in Germany, and in the other well-known aggressor nations under the leadership of Hitler."[116]

Both houses of Congress narrowly passed the bill. President Roosevelt signed its repeal on November 17, 1941.[117] All the pieces were in place for full-scale American involvement. The last event occurred on December 7th at Honolulu's Pearl Harbor.

Notes

1 Among the many accounts of FDR's third-term decision include the earlier Bernard F. Donahue, *Private Plans and Public Dangers: The Story of FDR's Third Nomination* (Notre Dame, IN: University of Notre Dame Press, 1965); and the best-known Hebert S. Parmet and Marie B. Hecht, *Never Again: A President Runs for a Third Term* (New York: Macmillan, 1968). The two more recent accounts include Susan Dunn, *1940: FDR, Willkie, Lindbergh, Hitler—the Election and the Storm* (New Haven, CT: Yale University Press, 2013); and Richard Moe, *Roosevelt's Second Act: The Election of 1940 and the Politics of War* (New York: Oxford University Press, 2013).

2 Parmet and Hecht, *Never Again*, pp. 46–49.

3 Moe, *Roosevelt's Second Act*, pp. 86–87. The source is Farley's autobiography, *Jim Farley's Story: The Roosevelt Years* (New York: Whittlesey House, 1948), pp. 68–70.

4 Robert E. Sherwood, *Roosevelt and Hopkins: An Intimate History* (New York: Harper & Bros., 1938), p. 111.

5 See "Presidential Aspirations," in Searle F. Charles, *Minister of Relief: Harry Hopkins and the Depression* (Syracuse, NY: Syracuse University Press, 1963), pp. 206–19. Less helpful on this score is Henry H. Adams, *Harry Hopkins: A Biography* (New York: G.P. Putnam's Sons, 1977).

6   Michael R. Beschloss, *Kennedy and Roosevelt: The Uneasy Alliance* (New York: Norton, 1980), pp. 168–71. The quote is from Krock's *Memoirs; Sixty Years on the Firing Line* (New York: Funk & Wagnalls, 1968), p. 161.

7   "Slate for Farley Meets With Dissension in State: Walsh, Dever Prefer Group Unpledged, Others Would Wait Until Roosevelt Announces Move," *Boston Globe*, February 13, 1940, p. 1; and Charles H. Trout, *Boston: The Great Depression and the New Deal* (New York: Oxford University Press, 1977), p. 292.

8   "Hats in the Ring: Monsignor Jim," *New Republic*, CII (March 11, 1940), p. 334.

9   Trout, *Boston: The Great Depression and the New Deal*, p. 292.

10 John G. Harris, "Politics and Politicians," *Daily Boston Globe*, February 18, 1940, p. 18.

11 David K. Niles letter to Oscar S. Cox, March 18, 1940, Oscar Cox File, FDR Library and Museum, Hyde Park, NY.

12 A summary of the 1940 presidential primary results may be found in Congressional Quarterly, *Presidential Elections, 1789–1992*, pp. 164–65.

13 Congressional Quarterly reported that "sixty-nine James A. Farley delegates and nine unpledged delegates won in the Democratic primary, according to Kravitz, *NYT* of May 1, 1940, also reported that most Democratic delegates favored Farley." See Walter Kravitz, "Presidential Preference Primaries: Results, 1928–1956" (Washington, DC: Congressional Research Service, 1960), p. 10.

14 "Pledged for Farley: Walsh and McCormack to Be Delegates to National Convention," *NYT*, February 15, 1940, p. 10.

15 Letter from John McCormack to Steve Early, the President's Press Secretary, in Donahue, *Private Plans and Public Dangers*, p. 222, n. 88.

16 John G. Harris, "Politics and Politicians: 2 Bay State Men May Learn F.D.'s Third Term Stand," *Boston Globe*, July 7, 1940, p. B1.

17 Quoted in the *Baltimore Sun*, July 9, 1940, and cited in Donahue, *Private Plans and Public Dangers*, p. 226, 202n.

18 M. E. Hennessy, "Ely Quits Chicago, Undecided on 'Walk': "I Don't Know Willkie," He Says on Shift to G.O.P.," *Boston Globe*, July 19, 1940, p. 4.

19 FDR's statement from the *Official Proceedings of the 1940 Democratic National Convention*, p. 69.

20 Paul E. Boller, Jr., *Presidential Campaigns* (New York: Oxford University Press, 1984), p. 252.

21 "1940: The Twenty-Eighth Democratic Convention," in Bain and Parris, eds., *Convention Decisions and Voting Records*, 2nd ed., pp. 256–61.

22 Agricultural Adjustment Act, approved May 12, 1933 (Public Law 73-10; 48 Stat. 31-54), "Provided for farmers to be paid for limiting the production of seven basic commodities—wheat, cotton, corn, hogs, rice, tobacco, and dairy products" (Stathis, *Landmark Legislation*, p. 201). Many of its provisions were held unconstitutional in *United States v. Butler*, 297 U.S. 1 (1936).

23 *Official Proceedings of the 1940 Democratic National Convention*, July 18, 1940, p. 236.

24 Eleanor Roosevelt's remarks provided the title for Doris Kearns Goodwin's prize-winning book *No Ordinary Time: Franklin and Eleanor Roosevelt: The Home Front in World War II* (New York: Simon & Schuster, 1994).

25 Niles is missing from the lengthy biography by former U.S. Senator John C. Culver (Dem-Iowa) and John Hyde, *American Dreamer: The Life and Times of Henry A. Wallace* (New York: Norton, 2000), pp. 214–22, on the vice presidential selection.

26   Undated letter from Agriculture Secretary Henry A. Wallace to David Niles, Assistant
     Secretary of Commerce, Niles Papers, Truman Library.

27   Steve Neal, *Dark Horse: A Biography of Wendell Willkie* (Garden City, NY: Doubleday,
     1984), pp. 33–36 and 69–70.

28   Alan Brinkley, *The Publisher: Henry Luce and His American Century* (New York: Alfred
     A. Knopf, 2010).

29   John F. Kennedy, *Why England Slept* (New York: Wilfred Funk, 1940), foreword by
     Henry R. Luce, pp. xiii–xxii. Schwarz contends that Joe bought "thirty thousand to
     forty thousand copies" to guarantee that it would be a bestseller (*Joseph P. Kennedy*,
     pp. 293 and 453).

30   Jonathan Daniels, *White House Witness, 1942–1945: An Intimate Diary of the Years
     with F.D.R.* (Garden City, NY: Doubleday, 1975), p. 49.

31   Selective Training and Service Act of 1940, approved September 16, 1940 (P. Res. 783;
     54 Stat. 885-897) from Stathis, *Legislative Landmarks*, pp. 215–16.

32   News accounts include "The Speaker," *TIME*, September 23, 1940, pp. 16–17; and "The
     Congress: 'Mr. Will' Goes Home," *TIME*, September 30, 1940, p. 15.

33   "Rayburn Elected in House Tradition—Choice of Texan as Speaker Is Made by
     Acclamation before the Body of Bankhead," *NYT*, September 17, 1940, p. 19.

34   "Fight Over Voting for House Leader—McCormack, Whom President Is Said to Back,
     Has Odds if Balloting Is Open," *NYT*, September 18, 1940, p. 16.

35   See David L. Porter, "Representative Lindsay Warren, the Water Bloc, and the
     Transportation Act of 1940," *North Carolina Historical Review*, L (Summer 1973),
     pp. 273–88.

36   See varying accounts: Henry N. Dorris, "Push Plan to Defer House Leader Test," *NYT*,
     September 19, 1940, p. 15; and "Petition for a Caucus to Fill Rayburn Post," *NYT*,
     September 20, 1940, p. 15.

37   Among the books addressing the transformation, see Alan Brinkley, *The End of Reform:
     New Deal Liberalism in Recession and War* (New York: Alfred A. Knopf, 1995); and
     Steve Fraser and Gary Gerstle, eds., *The Rise and Fall of the New Deal Order* (Princeton,
     NJ: Princeton University Press, 1989); and Robert Shogan, *Backlash: The Killing of the
     New Deal* (Chicago: Ivan R. Dee, 2006).

38   See two articles by James E. Sargent, "Clifton A. Woodrum of Virginia: A Southern
     Progressive in Congress, 1923–1945," *Virginia Magazine of History and Biography*,
     LXXXIX (July 1981), pp. 341–64; and "Woodrum's Economy Bloc: The Attack on
     Roosevelt's WPA," *Virginia Magazine of History and Biography*, XCIII (April 1985),
     pp. 175–207.

39   On Rankin's activities, see Philip A. Grant, Jr., "The Mississippi Congressional
     Delegation and the Formation of the Conservative Coalition," *Journal of Mississippi
     History*, L (February 1988), pp. 21–28.

40   Totals from Henry N. Dorris, "House Democrats Name McCormack as Their Leader,"
     NYT, September 26, 1940, pp. 1 and 14.

41   Drew Pearson and Robert S. Allen, "Washington Merry Go-Round: John McCormack
     1st New Englander to Be Majority Leader in House," *Maryville (Mo.) Daily Forum*,
     October 5, 1940, p. 6.

42   This quotation and other direct ones come from the author's telephonic interview with
     the Hon. John W. McCormack, Boston, April 1977.

43   *The Secret Diary of Harold L. Ickes: The Lowering Clouds*, III, p. 332. The date was
     September 22, 1940.

44   Ibid.

45   Larry O'Brien recounts that John McCormack placed Carl Vinson "in purgatory" for twelve years "because many years ago he pledged to vote for me for majority leader and then went back on his word." in his *No Final Victories: A Life in Politics from John F. Kennedy to Watergate* (New York: Ballantine Books, 1975), pp. 118–19.

46   James F. Cook, *Carl Vinson: Patriarch of the Armed Forces* (Macon, GA: Mercer University Press, 2004), p. 162.

47   Champagne et al., *The Austin-Boston Connection*, pp. 251–61.

48   The classic "task leader-social leader" distinction is described in Robert F. Bales, "Task Roles and Social Roles in Problem-Solving Groups," in Eleanor E. Maccoby, Theodore M. Newcomb, and Eugene L. Hartley, eds., *Readings in Social Psychology*, 3rd ed. (New York: Holt, Rinehart and Winston, 1958), pp. 437–47. A political science application of this distinction using Chief Justices of the Supreme Court may be found in David J. Danelski, "Task Group and Social Group on the Supreme Court," in John H. Kessel, George F. Cole, and Robert G. Seddig, eds., *Micropolitics: Individual and Group Level Concepts* (New York: Holt, Rinehart and Winston, Inc., 1970), pp. 266–74.

49   Frank McNaughton, "Roosevelt Indorsement of La Guardia," a column filed with *TIME* on October 24, 1941, found in the Truman Library. La Guardia was the candidate of the Republican American Labor, Fusion, and United City parties and defeated O'Dwyer 52.4% to 46.6%, New York City elections.

50   George Q. Flynn, *Roosevelt and Romanism: Catholics and American Diplomacy, 1937–1945* (Westport, CT: Greenwood Press, 1976), pp. 123–26.

51   See the "Survey of Italian Voters in New York City," September 28 to October 3, 1940 in the David K. Niles Papers at the Farber Library at Brandeis University, Waltham, Massachusetts, in the Presidential Campaign, 1940 Box II. These papers are duplicates of those at the Harry S. Truman Presidential Library in Independence, Missouri.

52   Excerpted from FDR's graduation address to the University of Virginia, June 10, 1940: "The Government of Italy has now chosen to preserve what it terms its 'freedom of action' and to fulfill what it states are its promises to Germany. . . . On this tenth day of June, 1940, the hand that held the dagger has struck it into the back of its neighbor." Franklin Delano Roosevelt, "Stab in the Back" Speech, Miller Center for Public Affairs, the University of Virginia.

53   This was the transcription of a long-lost audiotape that was reproduced in *American Heritage* as "FDR Talks Frankly—About Foreign Policy, His Opponent, the Voters and the Polls," *American Heritage*, XXXIII (February/March 1982), accessed May 1, 2015.

54   The fullest account of their time in England, albeit soft on Joe Kennedy's anti-Semitism, is Will Swift's *The Kennedys amidst the Gathering Storm: A Thousand Days in London, 1938–1940* (Washington, DC: Smithsonian Books/New York: Collins, 2008).

55   Jon Meacham, *Franklin and Winston: An Intimate Portrait of an Epic Friendship* (New York: Random House, 2003); Joseph P. Lash, *Roosevelt and Churchill, 1939–1945: The Partnership That Saved the West* (New York: W. W. Norton, 1976). See their correspondence in Warren F. Kimball, ed., *Churchill and Roosevelt: The Complete Correspondence* (Princeton, NJ: Princeton University Press, 1984); and Francis L. Loewenheim, Harold D. Langley, and Manfred Jonas, *Roosevelt and Churchill: Their Secret Wartime Correspondence* (New York: Saturday Review Press, 1975).

56   Warren Kimball and Bruce Bartlett, "Roosevelt and Prewar Commitments to Churchill: The Tyler Kent Affair," *Diplomatic History*, V (Fall 1981), pp. 291–311.

See also Ray Bearse and Anthony Read, *Conspirator: The Untold Story of Tyler Kent* (New York: Doubleday, 1991); and Bryan Clough, *State Secrets: The Kent-Wolkoff Affair* (East Sussex, GB: Hideaway Publications Ltd., 2005).

57 See Albert Fried's assessment of Lindbergh's pro-German activities in his *FDR and His Enemies* (New York: St. Martins, 1999), pp. 173–207, with Joe Kennedy in apparent agreement on pp. 179–80.

58 Whalen, *The Founding Father*, p. 331. Senator James Byrnes (Dem-SC) and his wife were also there to greet Kennedy.

59 Joseph P. Kennedy: Diary entry for November 4, 1940, in Amanda Smith, ed., *Hostage to Fortune: The Private Letters of Joseph P. Kennedy* (New York: Viking, 2001), p. 491. It is clear in the correspondence that Justice Murphy shared Joe's anti-Semitism. As Kennedy noted, "[Murphy said] that it was Frankfurter and Ben Cohen who wrote the Attorney General's opinion on destroyers and bases. Murphy regards the Jewish influence as most dangerous. He said that after all, Hopkins' wife was a Jew; Hull's wife is a Jew; and Frankfurter and Cohen and that group are all Jews."

60 Swift, *The Kennedys amidst the Gathering Storm*, pp. 290–92.

61 David Niles Papers, Harry S. Truman Library in Independence, Missouri.

62 Campaign Address at Boston, Massachusetts, October 30, 1940, *Public Papers of the President: Franklin D. Roosevelt*, Document 127.

63 The Lyons interview was published in the *Boston Globe*, December 10, 1940, p. 1. Lyon's account of the interview appears in Louis M. Lyons, *Newspaper Story: One Hundred Years of the Boston Globe* (Cambridge, MA: Belknap Press of Harvard University Press, 1971), pp. 290–92. See also Whalen, *The Founding Father*, pp. 339–41.

64 Beschloss, *Kennedy and Roosevelt: The Uneasy Alliance*, p. 229.

65 Ibid.

66 Their reinventions are well depicted in Neal Gabler's book *An Empire of Their Own: How the Jews Invented Hollywood* (New York: Crown, 1988). Joe Kennedy is mentioned in passing on pp. 317 and 344. Wikipedia.com reports their birth names and places as follows: Harry Warner was born Hirsch Moses Wonsal in Krasnosielc, Poland, the son of Polish Jews as was Samuel Goldwyn who was born in Warsaw as Schmuel Gelbfisz, while Louis B. Mayer was born the son of Russian Jews in Minsk, Belarus, as Lazar Meir.

67 See Cari Beauchamp's marvelous book *Joseph Kennedy Presents: His Hollywood Years* (New York: Alfred A. Knopf, 2009), pp. 369–70. She cites correspondence between Douglas Fairbanks, Jr. and FDR, November 26, 1940, 468n.

68 Beauchamp, *Joseph Kennedy Presents.* Beauchamp also cites Ben Hecht, *A Child of the Century* (New York: Simon & Schuster, 1964), p. 520; and Douglas Fairbanks, Jr., *The Salad Days* (New York: Doubleday, 1988), p. 309.

69 As quoted in Kennedy's diary entry for December 1, 1940, and located in Smith, *Hostages to Fortune*, p. 496.

70 President Franklin D. Roosevelt in a February 1941 letter to John Boettinger as quoted in Doris Kearns Goodwin, *No Ordinary Time: Franklin and Eleanor Roosevelt, The Home Front in World War II* (New York: Simon & Schuster, 1995), pp. 211–12. Original in the FDR Library, Hyde Park, New York.

71 Conflict between the two old friends over the bill is recounted in David Porter, "The Battle of the Texas Giants: Hatton Sumners. Sam Rayburn. and the Logan-Walter Bill of 1939," *Texana*, XII (1974), pp. 349–81.

72 *Congressional Record*, 78th Congress, Third Session, December 18, 1940, p. 13948.

73 Mooney, *Roosevelt and Rayburn: A Political Partnership* (Philadelphia: J.P. Lippincott, 1971), p. 153. A valuable assessment of Sam Rayburn's dealings with presidents during his years as Speaker may be found in Lewis L. Gould and Nancy Beck Young, "The Speaker and the Presidents: Sam Rayburn, the White House, and the Legislative Process, 1941–1961," in Roger H. Davidson, Susan Webb Hammond, and Raymond W. Smock, eds., *Masters of the House: Congressional Leaders over Two Centuries* (Boulder, CO: Westview Press, 1998), pp. 181–221.

74 D. B. Hardeman and Donald C. Bacon, *Rayburn: A Biography* (Austin: Texas Monthly Press, 1987), p. 255.

75 FDR, "The Four Freedoms," *Congressional Record*, 77th Congress, First Session, January 6, 1941, pp. 46–47.

76 The two most recent accounts are Richard Moe, *Roosevelt's Second Act: The Election of 1940 and the Politics of War* (New York: Oxford University Press, 2013); and Lynne Olson, *Those Angry Days: Roosevelt, Lindbergh, and America's Fight Over World War II, 1939–1941* (New York: Random House, 2013).

77 "Views of Joseph P. Kennedy on Foreign Affairs," inserted by Senator Arthur Vandenberg (Rep-Mich.), *Congressional Record*, 77th Congress, First Session, January 10, 1941, pp. 92–93; Senator Robert R. Reynolds (Dem-NC), January 14, 1941, pp. A106–07; and U.S. Representative Francis Case (Rep-SD), January 20, 1941, pp. A196–98.

78 Lend-Lease Act approved March 11, 1941 (Public Law 77-11; 55 Stat. 31-33); and was extended on March 11, 1943 (Public Law 78-9; 57 Stat. 31-33); and again in 1944 on May 17, 1944 (Public Law 78-304; 58 Stat. 222-223). See accounts of this act in Wayne S. Cole, *Roosevelt and the Isolationists* (Lincoln: University of Nebraska Press, 1983); and Warren F. Kimball, *The Most Unsordid Act: Lend-Lease, 1939–1941* (Baltimore: The Johns Hopkins Press, 1969).

79 Testimony of the Hon. Joseph P. Kennedy, Ambassador Extraordinary and Plenipotentiary to Great Britain, *Lend-Lease Bill, Hearings before the Committee on Foreign Affairs, House of Representatives*, 77th Congress, 1st Session, January 21, 1941, pp. 221–315.

80 Sol Bloom, *The Autobiography of Sol Bloom* (New York: Putnam House, 1948).

81 See Hugh A. Bone's essay, "Sol Bloom: Supersalesman of Patriotism," in J. T. Salter, ed., *Public Men In and Out of Office* (Chapel Hill: University of North Carolina Press, 1946), pp. 225–39.

82 See Warren F. Kimball, "'1776': Lend-Lease Gets a Number," *New England Quarterly*, XLII (June 1969), pp. 260–67.

83 Susan Dunn, *1940: FDR, Willkie, Lindbergh, Hitler, the Election and the Storm* (New Haven, CT: Yale University Press, 2013), p. 278.

84 McCormack's role in deflecting Irish-American opposition to legislation aiding Britain may be found in T. Ryle Dwyer, *Irish Neutrality and the USA: 1939–1947* (Dublin: Gill and Macmillan, 1977), p. 39. See also Edward R. Stettinius, Jr., later to become secretary of state, who describes McCormack's role in his account, *Lend-Lease: Weapon for Victory* (New York: Macmillan, 1944) on pp. 68 and 70. McCormack's Irish-American connection is also made in Leon Martel, *Lend-Lease, Loans, and the Coming of the Cold War: A Study of the Implementation of Foreign Policy* (Boulder, CO: Westview, 1979), pp. 216–17.

85 "Address by Former Ambassador to Great Britain," inserted by Senator Burton K. Wheeler (Dem-Mont.), *Congressional Record*, 77th Congress, 1st Session, May 26, 1941, pp. A2510–12; and U.S. Representative Robert F. Rich (Rep-Penn.), May 26, 1941, pp. 4423 and A2492.

86 Ibid., p. A2492.

87 Frank McNaughton, "Anti-Semitism in Congress," a column filed with *TIME* on September 12, 1941, found in the Truman Library. His article names many members including John's closest Deep South friend, Gene Cox of Georgia and "the bitterest anti-Semite I have seen in years is Ted Wright, clerk to Speaker Sam Rayburn. He hates them all."

88 *Congressional Record*, 77th Congress, 1st Session, June 4, 1941, pp. 4726–27.

89 Ibid., p. 4727.

90 "Edelstein Dies after House Talk," *NYT*, June 5, 1941, p. 24.

91 The episode was described by McCormack aide Judge Joseph Feeney and recounted in Harry F. Greene's Harvard Honors thesis, *The McCormack's of Massachusetts* (Cambridge, MA: Harvard University, 1963), pp. 36–37.

92 The committee's official responsibilities were stated in Senate Resolution 71, 77th Congress, First Session, March 1, 1941: [Section 1] Resolved, That a special committee of seven Senators, to be appointed by the President of the Senate, is authorized and directed to make a full and complete study and investigation of the operation of the program for the procurement and construction of supplies, materials, munitions, vehicles, aircraft, vessels, plants, camps, and other articles and facilities in connection with the national defense . . .

93 Oral history with D. B. Hardeman conducted by D. Clayton Brown, August 1, 1969, Sam Rayburn Library and Museum, Bonham, Texas.

94 Author's interview with the Hon. John McCormack, April 1977. Fred Vinson of Kentucky, who served on Ways and Means with McCormack, later served as Secretary of the Treasury under Harry Truman and was named by Truman to be Chief Justice of the U.S. Supreme Court; Mon Wallgren and Warren Magnuson were the Democratic Senators from Washington State; and Gene "Goober" Cox was the segregationist Representative from Georgia.

95 Donald H. Riddle, *The Truman Committee: A Study in Congressional Responsibility* (New Brunswick, NJ: Rutgers University Press, 1964); see also Theodore Wilson, "The Truman Committee, 1941," in Arthur M. Schlesinger, Jr. and Roger Bruns, eds., *Congress Investigates: A Documentary History, 1792–1974*, Volume IV (New York: Chelsea House, 1975), pp. 3115–3262.

96 On the domestic side, see Floyd M. Riddick's assessment, "American Government and Politics: First Session of the Seventy-Seventh Congress: January 3, 1941 to January 2, 1942," *APSR*, XXXVI (April 1942), pp. 290–302.

97 "Blacks and the Democratic Party," FactCheck.org accessed November 11, 2014. The data came from the Joint Center for Political and Economic Studies.

98 These data may be found in David Burner's insightful *The Politics of Provincialism: The Democratic Party in Transition, 1916–1932* (New York: Alfred A. Knopf, 1968), chapter VIII, "The Composition of the 1928 Vote," pp. 217–43.

99 Best presented in Nancy J. Weiss, *Farewell to the Party of Lincoln: Black Politics in the Age of FDR* (Princeton, NJ: Princeton University Press, 1983).

100 Daniel S. Davis, *Mr. Black Labor: The Story of A. Philip Randolph, Father of the Civil Rights Movement* (New York: Dutton, 1972).

101　Herbert Garfinkel, *When Negroes March: The March on Washington Movement in the Organizational Politics for FEPC* (New York: Atheneum, 1969).

102　Franklin D. Roosevelt, "Executive Order 8802—Prohibition of Discrimination in the Defense Industry." See "President Orders an Even Break For Minorities in Defense Jobs; He Issues an Order That Defense Contract Holders Not Allow Discrimination against Negroes or Any Worker," *NYT*, June 26, 1941, p. 12.

103　See John Whiteclay Chambers II, *To Raise an Army: The Draft Comes to Modern America* (New York: Free Press, 1987); J. Garry Clifford and Samuel R. Spencer, Jr., *The First Peacetime Draft* (Lawrence: University Press of Kansas, 1986); George Q. Flynn, *The Draft, 1940–1973* (Lawrence: University Press of Kansas, 1993); and John O'Sullivan*, From Voluntarism to Conscription: Congress and Selective Service, 1940–1945* (New York: Garland, 1982).

104　See the fascinating analysis by J. Garry Clifford and Theodore A. Wilson, "Blundering on the Brink, 1941: FDR and the 203-202 Vote Reconsidered," in J. Garry Clifford and Theodore A. Wilson, eds., *Presidents, Diplomats, and Other Mortals: Essays Honoring Robert Ferrell* (Columbia: University of Missouri Press, 2007), pp. 99–115. My thanks to Professor Clifford for providing this essay.

105　Selective Service Extension of 1941, approved August 18, 1941 (Public Law 77-213; 55 Stat. 626-628). Both votes occurred on August 12, 1941, 77th Congress, 1st Session, *Congressional Record*, pp. 7073–75.

106　Thomas Parrish, *Roosevelt and Marshall: Partners in Politics and War* (New York: William Morrow, 1989), p. 180.

107　Frank McNaughton, "Congress Takes a Rest," story filed with *TIME*, undated, McNaughton Papers, Truman Library.

108　For Rayburn's successful management of the voting, see Hardeman and Bacon, *Rayburn: A Biography*, pp. 261–69.

109　Flynn's *Roosevelt and Romanism: Catholics and American Diplomacy, 1937–1945* (Westport, CTonn.: Greenwood Press, 1976), pp. 146–47.

110　See Flynn's chapter on Russia in ibid., pp. 137–83.

111　Most of the writing on Lend-Lease has dealt with aid to Russia; see Raymond H. Dawson, *The Decision to Aid Russia: Foreign Policy and Domestic Politics* (Chapel Hill: University of North Carolina Press, 1959); George C. Hening, *Aid to Russia, 1941–1946: Strategy, Diplomacy and the Origins of the Cold War* (New York: Columbia University Press, 1973); Robert Hudson Jones, *The Roads to Russia: United States Lend-Lease to the Soviet Union* (Norman: University of Oklahoma Press, 1969); Robert C. Lukas, *Eagles East: The Army Air Forces and the Soviet Union, 1941–1945* (Tallahassee: Florida State University Press, 1970); Leon Martel, *Lend-Lease, Loans and the Coming of the Cold War: A Study of the Implementation of Foreign Policy* (Boulder, CO: Westview Press, 1972); and Hubert P. Van Tuyll*, Feeding the Bear: American Aid to the Soviet Union* (Westport, CT: Greenwood Press, 1989).

112　Frank McNaughton, "House Appropriations' Committee Chairmanship," filed with *TIME*, September 4, 1941, in the Truman Library.

113　Einstein letter to FDR dated August 2, 1939, from atomicarchive.com.

114　Vannevar Bush, *Pieces of the Action* (New York: William Morrow, 1970), pp. 59–60.

115　Richard G. Hewlett and Oscar E. Anderson, "Roosevelt Makes a Decision," *The New World, A History of the Atomic Energy Commission, Volume 1, 1939/1946* (University Park, PA: Pennsylvania State University Press, 1962), pp. 41–49, Hewlett was the official historian of the Atomic Energy Commission.

116   FDR letter to Rayburn and McCormack, November 13, 1941, as cited in H. W. Brands, *Traitor to His Class: The Privileged Life and Radical Presidency of Franklin Delano Roosevelt* (New York: Doubleday, 2008), p. 217.

117   Repeal of Certain Sections of the Neutrality Act of 1939, approved November 17, 1941 (Public Law 77-294; 55 Stat. 764-765). See academic treatments of the issue in Robert A. Divine, *The Illusion of Neutrality* (Chicago: University of Chicago Press, 1962); Thomas N. Guinsberg, *The Pursuit of Isolationism in the United States Senate from Versailles to Pearl Harbor* (New York: Garland, 1982); and Manfred Jonas, *Isolationism in America, 1935–1941* (Ithaca, NY: Cornell University Press, 1966).

10

War Transforms the Nation

The bombing of Pearl Harbor

On December 7, 1941, twenty days after the Neutrality Act was effectively repealed, the high command of Imperial Japan launched a preemptive surprise attack on the American fleet at Pearl Harbor in Honolulu, Hawaii. Roaring out of the early morning sky were 353 Japanese warplanes, which, in two waves, proceeded to bomb and strafe virtually at will. The toll was devastating. Eleven warships, including four battleships were sunk or damaged, while on the ground 188 U.S. aircraft were destroyed, 2,042 men lost their lives, and another 1,282 were wounded. The War in the Pacific had begun. The shock to the nation was immediate and profound. An enraged President Roosevelt declared December 7, 1941, as "a day of infamy."

It was Majority Leader John McCormack who went to the floor of the House on December 8th and introduced the bill declaring a state of war with Japan[1] (Figure 10.1). The vote in the House was overwhelming 388 to 1 with the lone "Nay" coming from Representative Jeannette Rankin (Rep-Mont.) who also voted against American entry into World War I on April 5, 1917, when she was one of fifty opponents.[2] As recounted by Rayburn's assistant D. B. Hardeman[3]:

> With a cold stare, Rayburn cut her short. "There can be no objection," he said, signaling McCormack to continue. McCormack's resolution was identical to that passed in 1917, except for the substitution of the words "Imperial Government of Japan" for "Germany." The majority leader requested twenty seconds to speak in behalf of the resolution. "This," he said "is the time for action."

Three days later, John returned to the House floor and the state of war was extended to Japan's Axis allies, Germany and Italy.[4] Rankin voted "Present" on both votes as each passed unanimously. On the following day, Hitler declared war on the United States and World War II had begun. It would be a two-ocean war and different camps pushed an Asia-first or a Europe-first military effort. The once-powerful isolationist America First Committee dissolved days after the Pearl Harbor attack and most but not all of the congressional isolationists accepted interventionism.[5]

Figure 10.1 FDR signs Declaration of War against Japan, with Sam Rayburn and John McCormack in the background, December 8, 1941 (F.D. Roosevelt Library and Museum).

Executive expansion

Within days, Congress would pass the First War Powers Act and a new Selective Service Act. Under the legislative leadership of John McCormack, the First War Powers Act authorized the president "to redistribute functions, duties, and powers of executive departments, commissions, bureaus, agencies, governmental corporations, offices, or officers, and to enter into contracts without regard to designated provisions of law, and to investigate, regulate, or prohibit any transitions in foreign exchange, coins, exports, etc."[6] The new Selective Service Act required that all men between the ages of 18 and 65 register for the draft, and all men from 20 to 45 would be subject to training and service.[7]

During times of international military crisis, Congress would appropriate the funds but surrendered much of its authority to the executive branch.[8] Speaker Sam Rayburn and Senate Majority Leader Alben Barkley knew this having entered the House together in 1913 and served throughout World War I. They watched as their Democratic House Majority Leader Claude Kitchin regularly challenged President Wilson's foreign policy goals and defense policy. They understood better than most that Congress could not micromanage a war on an international scale. Rayburn and Barkley easily accepted a president-driven war policy agenda.

For two enlisted veterans of the Great War who had worn the uniform of the U.S. Army, like Representative John McCormack who had been a sergeant and U.S. Senator Harry Truman (Dem-Mo.) who had been a captain, accepting directives from a trusted commander-in-chief was the appropriate response to the national emergency.

Joe Kennedy seeks redemption and rebuffs John

Eager for a return to political relevance, Joe Kennedy immediately sent a telegram to the White House[9]:

> DEAR MR. PRESIDENT. IN THIS GREAT CRISIS ALL AMERICANS
> ARE WITH YOU. NAME THE BATTLE POST. I'M YOURS TO COMMAND.
>
> JOE KENNEDY

There would be no White House response. FDR told John McCormack that he never saw the telegram, but Steve Early, the president's press secretary, acknowledged it in a reply to Joe on December 9. Any hopes of Joe's return to power were dashed.

A month passed and as Joe became more despondent, Honey Fitz met with John McCormack to ask him to intercede with FDR on Joe's behalf. McCormack honored Fitzgerald's request and met with FDR at the close of a White House session with the congressional leaders. In Joe's diary, he wrote that John "was convinced that the real affection I had always for Roosevelt was still there and he thought the President needed me. The President at once replied that as far as he was concerned personally he had a great affection for me, but I was of course a tough Irishman and very stubborn."[10]

But Joe's arrogance and stubbornness intervened. On January 7, 1942, Joe wrote in his diary[11]:

> I left a memorandum with the girl in the [McCormack Washington] office in which I said that I appreciated Mr. McCormack's interest, also Mr. Fitzgerald's and I didn't want to appear ungrateful, but I definitely did not want McCormack to speak to the President about me—that I had already sent him a wire on the Sunday the Japs bombed Hawaii and had offered my services in any capacity he could use them. And since he knew my work, knew me, and knew I was available, the President was the one to decide as to whether or not he wanted me.

There was no way that Joe Kennedy, the Harvard-educated lace curtain Boston Irishman, was going to let a shanty Irishman from South Boston like John McCormack vouch for him to a fellow Harvard man like FDR. Kennedy would not find his way back into the good graces of FDR and grudgingly sat on the sidelines for the duration of the war. As far as FDR was concerned, Joe Kennedy was "yellow" and had forfeited any involvement in the war effort.

No one understood this better than Justice Felix Frankfurter (and David Niles's mentor) who Joe cultivated assiduously even though Kennedy's diary characterized Frankfurter as "a Jew chiseler." In Frankfurter's diary entry for May 12, 1943, he wrote that Kennedy[12]

> was not only venting his gorge against the New Deal but more particularly his personal resentment against Harry Hopkins and me, who he, in his foolish and

ignorant way, blames me for his exclusion from participation in the conduct of
the war. I don't suppose it ever enters the head of a Joe Kennedy that one who
was so hostile to the war effort as he was all over the lot, and so outspoken in his
foulmouthed hostility to the President himself, barred his own way to a responsible
share in the conduct of the war.

Domestic impact

Early in 1942, the 77th Congress continued to expand executive authority by
establishing the Emergency Office of Price Administration (OPA) which had the power
to fix price ceilings on all commodities (except farm products) and to control rents in
defense areas.[13] Clearly intended to prevent wartime shortages from leading to price
gouging and profiteering, the OPA regained regulatory power for the administration
that had been lost when the New Deal's initial thrust had receded. It was in the OPA
that a young Duke-educated lawyer from California, Richard M. Nixon, would first
enter government service. Nixon contended that it was his eight months at the OPA
that "had an enormous effect on the policies [he] later developed during my political
career" in that it made him cynical about governmental employees.[14]

On the West Coast of the United States, virulent anti-Japanese sentiment erupted
arising from fears that disloyal Japanese-descended citizens might aid and abet a
Japanese invasion of California. This led to Executive Order 9066 issued on February
12, 1942, calling for the internment and eventual forced relocation of thousands of
Japanese-American citizens from the coast.[15] Implementing the federal directive was
California's popular Republican Attorney General Earl Warren.

More power flowed to the executive when the Rayburn-McCormack team pushed
for the passage of the Second War Powers Act that authorized the president to allocate
materials and facilities as necessary for the defense of the United States.[16] The act
granted additional powers to several Federal agencies and covered a number of other
items, such as increasing penalties for priority violations and granting free postage for
soldiers. Before the 77th Congress ended, legislation was in place to control prices,
increase taxes, and permit women to serve in the armed forces. The United States was
now fully mobilized.

The war went badly for the Allies for most of 1942. In the Pacific, Manila fell to the
Japanese in January and American forces retreated to the Bataan Peninsula. The British
were forced to surrender Singapore in February and in March, American forces under
General Douglas MacArthur were ordered by FDR to leave the Philippines before
the onrushing Japanese. Declaring "I shall return," MacArthur relocated to Australia.
The "Bataan Death March" of 24,000 American and Filipino troops began in April.
Malaya, Java, Burma, and New Guinea soon fell before the Japanese onslaught. With
the American Pacific fleet decimated by the Pearl Harbor attack and American and
British forces immobilized, the Japanese were able to rampage freely throughout East
Asia for much of the summer. Japanese bombs fell on the Aleutian Islands of Alaska,

and the islands of Kiska and Attu were invaded in June as a diversion during the Battle of Midway. But that battle slowed the Japanese advance and by the end of the year, the successful defense of Guadalcanal in the Solomon Islands provided hope to the Allies that the Japanese thrust throughout Asia could be stopped.

Initially preoccupied with the Pacific war, American forces were involved later in the battlefields of Europe and Africa. For close to four years from 1940 to 1943, the battle for North Africa raged from Morocco to Egypt as the legendary commanders British Field Marshall Bernard Montgomery and German Field Marshall Erwin Rommel, "the desert fox," battled their way through desert sand storms and enervating heat for control of the south coast of the Mediterranean. American involvement in North Africa under Generals Dwight Eisenhower and Mark Clark began in mid-1942. With American reinforcements, the Allies were able to push the Axis forces out of their North African holdings by mid-1943; thereby opening up what Churchill called the "soft underbelly" of Europe for the Allied invasion of Sicily in July 1943 and the Italian mainland in September, with the main landing in Salerno.

In Eastern Europe, Hitler's hubris led him to attack the Soviet Union, his short-term ally, as he sought to accomplish what the French legend Napoleon Bonaparte failed to do: conquer Russia. As Hitler expanded the military theater in Eastern Europe and thinned the Nazi military war effort in the process, his domestic war on the Jews escalated as the "territorial solution" of deporting Jews from Germany and Austria shifted dramatically to the horrific "final solution" of exterminating them in Eastern Europe.[17] As Raul Hilberg wrote in his monumental *The Destruction of the European Jews*, during the later phase of the Final Solution, the victims were brought to the killers.[18] Sadly, the Allied war effort could not mobilize fast enough or effectively enough to prevent the Nazi slaughter of millions of Jews and others designated as "undesirables," their eradication an essential element in Hitler's racist Nazi policy.

The initial funding of the Manhattan Project

The most important business of the 77th Congress, however, took place in secret. The Manhattan Engineering District (MED) was created in August 1942 and Colonel Leslie Groves was promoted to brigadier general to manage what the world would later know as "the Manhattan Project." Finding congressional money to fund the development of the atomic bomb would be a major challenge for John McCormack and fellow congressional leaders and hiding it from anti-FDR members would be a greater one. The request had to go before the House Appropriations Committee chaired by the curmudgeonly Clarence Cannon of Missouri who believed at the time that it was some sort of "death ray." As described in Cannon's slim biography,[19] "In 1942, General Marshall and Secretary Stimson appeared before the House Appropriations Committee and asked for approximately one billion dollars for perfection of a 'secret weapon'. The vast sum was smuggled through the entire committee, then numbering 43 members, and through Congress, so cleverly disguised in obscure language that it escaped attention, or at least detection."

When more money was needed, Cannon met again with Stimson and Marshall for a third time. But after the third request a select bipartisan group of committee members went in secret to Oak Ridge, Tennessee, to see for themselves the progress to date, before voting more funds.

Appropriations Committee: The Constitution requires that all revenue bills originate in the House of Representatives and by custom, all spending bills also begin in the House. The job of the Appropriations Committee is to write the first versions of the regular appropriation bills each year, as well as any emergency funding measures that may be required. The full committee looks to its subcommittees to make most of the important decisions. The recommendations of these thirteen annual spending bills are generally accepted by the full committee without much change. The legendary power of the thirteen Appropriations subcommittee chairs has led them to be referred to as "the College of Cardinals."[20]

The Committee on Appropriations was created on March 2, 1865, as one of three committees carved out of the House Ways and Means Committee.[21] While Ways and Means kept its power over revenue legislation, the oversight function that accompanies each congressional allocation of funds fell within the domain of the new Appropriations Committee. The importance of the new committee can be attested to by the fact that Thaddeus Stevens (Rep-Penn.), the chair of Ways and Means during the 37th and 38th Congresses (1861–65), left that position to become the first chair of Appropriations. For most of the half century between the Civil War and the 1909–10 revolt against Speaker Cannon, the chairs of Appropriations joined the Speakers and the chairs of Ways and Means to be the majority triumvirate on the agenda-setting five- person House Rules Committee. The active role of the chairs who followed Stevens led Woodrow Wilson to conclude in his 1885 book *Congressional Government* that "all [other House chairmen] are subordinate to the chairman of the Committee on Appropriations."[22]

Shortly after Wilson's book appeared, opposition to Chairman Samuel J. Randall's (Dem-Penn.) autocratic exercise of power and to his high tariff policies led to the first major diminution in the legislative authority of the Appropriations Committee, and by 1885, the committee had lost control over half the federal budget. However, the House in 1921 chose to recentralize appropriations and the Appropriations Committee's exclusive right to approve appropriations bills. This was the authority that Clarence Cannon possessed and brought to the spending discussions regarding the Manhattan Project.

The Appropriations Committee is an "exclusive" one in that its members could not serve on others and it was the House's largest standing committee for most of the twentieth century. But what gave the committee a unique role was the high level of bipartisan philosophical commitment to cutting budgets, regardless of the party, ideology, or region of its members.[23] Given the cost, funding the secret and wide-ranging atom bomb program was a formidable challenge.

The two key actors on the committee, Clarence Cannon of Missouri and John Taber of New York, were fully aware of their historic responsibilities and the commitment to budget-cutting. Both men entered the House in 1923 with Taber placed on Appropriations as a freshman while Cannon joined the committee six years later after stints on three lesser committees.[24] However, Cannon had served earlier as a House clerk under Speaker James B. "Champ" Clark and had become the House Parliamentarian in 1913. Cannon was no newcomer to the ways of the House. The two men served on Appropriations until Taber's retirement in 1963 and Cannon's death months later. They served conterminously for 34 years (1929–63) and for 20 of those years (1943–63) they were its two senior members with Cannon chairing Appropriations for eight-plus Congresses and Taber chairing it for two. Apart from one colorful incident in 1945 when Cannon slugged Taber and busted his lip,[25] they were joint guardians of the public treasury and very hesitant about giving blank checks for any administrative proposal no matter how presumably worthy.

The narrow victory in the 1942 elections

With the war effort seemingly stymied, the congressional elections in November 1942 held a great deal of anxiety for FDR and the Democrats. The war had placed millions of voting-age Americans in combat far from local polling places. The reverses in the Pacific indicated that American preparedness to fight on two fronts was limited. Questions were raised that FDR and the Democrats were not well prepared for the inevitability of a war that was more than two years old before the Pearl Harbor attack.

This election would be no automatic ratification of the Democratic majority. Leading the House Democratic reelection campaign was young Sam Rayburn protégé Texas Congressman Lyndon B. Johnson, whose efforts to see FDR were often rebuffed. As seen by Kentucky-born Presidential Secretary Marvin McIntyre, Johnson was "one of those thin skinned Southern gentlemen."[26] McIntyre then went on to dismiss Rayburn who "like all other Speakers, had gotten swell-headed." The lack of White House-congressional coordination would take its toll. When the results came in, the Democrats barely held onto their House majority.[27] Tallying up voting results by congressional district separately indicated that more Americans had voted for Republican House candidates than they had for Democratic candidates.

The net loss of Democratic House seats totaled forty-five. The Democratic total had dropped from 267 in the 77th Congress to 222 in the 78th Congress and their margin over the House Republicans had shrunk from 105 seats to thirteen.[28] Had it not been for their regional base in the Solid South,[29] the House Democrats would have been swept out of the majority and President Roosevelt would have had to face the Axis powers with a government divided between the White House and the House of Representatives. In the Senate, Democratic seats dropped from 66 to 58 and the margin shrunk from 38 to 19, but the Senate remained relatively safe for the president and Senate Democratic Floor Leader Alben Barkley.

FDR's stalwarts in the House, Speaker Sam Rayburn and Majority Leader John McCormack, were not as well-off. Although reelected to their posts without opposition, they would have to limit the legislative agenda. Roland Young's statistical analysis documented the change. His research indicated that a majority of the 77th Congress Democrats were on the winning side of House roll calls—92% in 1941 and 87% in

1942 compared to 51% and 56% of Republicans in those years. In the 78th Congress, a majority of House Democrats were on the winning side, with 65% of the 1943 votes and 71% of the 1944 votes while Republicans dominated on the floor votes—83% in 1943 and 85% in 1944.[30] Furthermore, Young pointed out that "the ratio of House Democratic victories to Republican victories was 7:1 in 1941, 1:1 in 1942, 1:2 in 1943, 1:2 in 1944, and 3:1 in 1945."[31] As a consequence, no far-reaching social and economic reforms would be sped through the House in this Congress. This was particularly true of social legislation that might offend the white southern members who now held close to half of the Democratic seats in the House and whose commitment to FDR's domestic agenda was already in retreat.

The sinking of Congressman Joe Casey

Back in Boston, the 1942 congressional elections produced a political curiosity when both of the old lions, John F. "Honey Fitz" Fitzgerald and James Michael Curley, returned to the lists of congressional aspirants after a three-decade absence. The 79-year-old Fitzgerald mounted his Senate campaign with Joe Kennedy's money to topple freshman U.S. Senator Henry Cabot Lodge, Jr. This was a race in which John McCormack's name was floated as a likely candidate but it would be another FDR ally, the three-term Irish-descended Congressman Joseph E. Casey of Clinton, who would win the nomination.[32]

Seven years younger than John McCormack, the Boston University–educated Casey came from the central Massachusetts district that had produced David I. Walsh, the state's first Roman Catholic Governor and U.S. Senator.[33] Casey was presumed to be a Walsh protégé and served as an Al Smith delegate to the ill-fated Democratic National Convention in 1924. He was one of the 33 diehard loyalists who voted for Smith on 101 of that year's 103 nominating ballots. After the convention, a disappointed Joe Casey worked on the Progressive Party presidential campaign of Wisconsin's U.S. Senator Robert M. La Follette. David K. Niles, a man whose path would cross Casey's again, chaired the Massachusetts campaign, but Casey was unimpressed with Niles.[34]

With FDR's election in 1932 Joe Casey became an ardent New Dealer, and in 1934, he defeated Republican Frank Foss for the House seat. While in the House, Casey began a three-year stint on Naval Affairs in 1935. With John McCormack's help, late in 1937 Casey was named to replace John P. Higgins (Dem-Mass.) on the selective Appropriations Committee. In 1941, he replaced Arthur D. Healey (Dem-Mass.) on Martin Dies's reconstituted Select Committee on Un-American Activities. By 1940, Casey had broken with the isolationist foreign policy stands of his presumed mentor Senator Walsh and had become, in the assessment of William Shannon, author of *The American Irish*, "a valued and trusted friend of Roosevelt and one of the administration's half-dozen principal lieutenants on the House floor and in the Appropriations Committee."[35] According to Shannon, John McCormack was Joe Casey's "close friend."

In 1942, Joe Casey challenged one-term incumbent Senator Henry Cabot Lodge Jr. Casey came closer to defeating Lodge than Jim Curley in 1936.[36] Unbeknownst to

Casey, he had another foe, Joe Kennedy. During Joe Kennedy's wartime exile as he shuttled back and forth between Cape Cod's Hyannis Port and Florida's Palm Beach, he kept a watchful eye on Massachusetts's two U.S. Senate seats. In 1942, Kennedy took an active part in undermining Casey's U.S. Senate bid. Kennedy funded much of John Fitzgerald's campaign in the Democratic primary helping his 79-year-old father-in-law to a second-place finish in what would truly be the old man's last hurrah.[37] In the general election, Joe Kennedy ally Arthur Krock of the *New York Times* contended that Lodge was "substantially aided by Joe Kennedy."

To historian Thomas Whalen, Kennedy's opposition to the FDR-backed Joe Casey was related to his frustrations with FDR's indifference to his efforts to become involved in the war effort.[38] Another explanation would be that Joe Kennedy was disinclined to let a young, attractive Irish Democrat like Joe Casey gain the Senate seat that he hoped his namesake Joseph P. Kennedy Jr. would seek in 1948.[39] Had Joe Jr. survived the war, he would have been 33 and clearly eligible for the Senate. Displacing a Republican in a general election would make fewer enemies than trying to displace a fellow Democrat in a primary.

Lodge would leave the Senate in 1942 as an Army reservist to fight in Libya but was ordered back to Washington by Secretary of War Stimson. John McCormack, who was then supporting Joe Casey, erupted in public outrage and described Stimson's request to be an "unwarranted and perniciously political action."[40] Lodge's return preserved the seat for the Republicans much as McCormack had feared.

With the seat safely in Republican hands, Lodge formally resigned the Senate in 1944 to serve as a tank commander with the rank of lieutenant colonel. His open seat would be filled initially by Republican businessman and fellow Brahmin Sinclair Weeks, the son of John Weeks, secretary of war under both Presidents Harding and Coolidge. Weeks was appointed to the Lodge vacancy by Republican Governor Leverett Saltonstall, who would capture the seat for himself in 1944's special election. Upon the war's conclusion, Lodge returned to elective politics and defeated isolationist Democratic Senator Walsh in 1946, who had been discredited during the war after being linked to a homosexual brothel near the Brooklyn Navy Yard that had been an apparent Nazi spy nest.[41]

Joe Kennedy would eventually bring about Cabot Lodge's electoral demise and avenge the family defeat inflicted upon Honey Fitz in 1916 by Cabot's grandfather Senator Henry Cabot Lodge, but it would be in 1952 with PT-109 hero Jack, and not Joe, Jr.

After his defeat, the 43-year-old Joe Casey remained in Washington and assumed that FDR would support him for an upcoming run for governor of Massachusetts or for the chairmanship of the Democratic National Committee. FDR arranged for a meeting between Casey and Jonathan Daniels, an administrative assistant to the president and the son of Josephus Daniels of North Carolina, who served as Woodrow Wilson's secretary of the navy under whom FDR had served as undersecretary of the navy.

During the meeting at New York's St. Regis Hotel, Daniels noted that Casey was "a good-looking, intelligent seeming Irishman."[42] He listened closely to Casey's thinly veiled maneuverings for the DNC chairmanship but soon caught wind of what would doom Joe Casey's national dreams—anti-Semitism. Casey's most vituperative comments were directed at the mysterious Bostonian David K. Niles and his brother Eliot. Casey categorized Eliot Niles as a "brassy kike." Casey's impugning of the political acumen and reputation of Niles, the Harry Hopkins loyalist who had been FDR's key operative among the Jews and the blacks, cost him dearly. Joe Casey, like many anti-Semites, was oblivious to the fact that better-educated fellow Christians found anti-Semitic slurs offensive, if not counterproductive. The game was lost for Joe Casey but he never knew it.

The anti-Semites attack McCormack

"Rabbi" John McCormack, presumably Casey's "close friend," found anti-Semitism personally repulsive. John's Jewish constituents in Mattapan and his own experiences confronting anti-Catholicism heightened his sensitivity to religious prejudice. It was McCormack's vigorous defense of Jews against charges of war-profiteering and avoiding combat that led to the widespread dissemination in Boston of a lengthy anonymous anti-Semitic 13-stanza "poem" entitled "Ode to the Majority Leader." Its last two stanzas capture its derogatory tone[43]:

> "From head to toe, helmet to shoes,
>   The soldier is clothed by the fighting Jews.
> "So it goes to prove what McCormack said,
>   Without the Jews we would all be dead.

> "But it's the end of the story that gives me the blues,
>   The dead boys, you'll find will seldom be Jews
> "But McCormack still proves that the Jews are there,
>   If you look at the labels dead soldiers wear."

The *Boston Globe* traced the handout to "a civilian employee in the Navy Yard on October 4, 1943."[44] Anti-Semitism was riding high in Boston, with attacks upon Jews reported to an unsympathetic Boston Police Department in 1944.[45] As Edward Shapiro contended, "Modern American anti-Semitism peaked in 1944."[46]

Easily the least anti-Semitic northern Catholic in the House, John McCormack had Jews on his personal congressional staff and his closest northern allies in the House were Jewish—Sam Dickstein, Emanuel Celler, and Sol Bloom of New York City and Adolph Sabath of Chicago. As the northern urban anchor of the Austin-Boston Connection, McCormack realized that Catholics and Jews needed to remain united if they were to serve as an effective counterweight to the overwhelming southern Baptist affiliations of the Democratic Party's powerful southern wing.

According to Daniels, it was John McCormack and Sam Rayburn (along with David Niles) who blocked Joe Casey's appointment to direct the Democratic National Committee.[47] Never again would Casey come close to holding major power within the government or the Democratic Party. For a party that needed to reach into non-Protestant big-city America for the sizable electoral votes in the nation's largest states, anti-Semitism would not be tolerated.

Defending David Niles: As FDR's key contact with Jews, blacks, and the Left, David Niles consorted with more than a few Communists and would be denounced on the floor of the House both in 1940 and again in 1943 by ultraconservative Michigan Republican Frederick Bradley, who described him as "Harry Hopkins's brother-in-law."[48] That particular charge was easily refutable and it led to most of Bradley's other accusations being ignored.

The initial 1940 attack on Niles focused on the labor unions affiliated with the Congress of Industrial Organizations (CIO), namely, the United Mine Workers led by bushy-browed John L. Lewis and the National Maritime Union led by left-leaning Joseph Curran and its West Coast affiliate, the Maritime Federation of the Pacific led by the Australian radical Harry Bridges. Bradley recounted the tale of how Niles was able to elicit $450,000 from the UMW back in the 1936 campaign, and he was now turning control over shipping on both coasts to these two unions.

Bradley's assertions about Niles were challenged by Massachusetts Republican Representative George Bates of Salem and John McCormack. When Bates described Niles as coming from his state, Bradley backtracked and said, "I understand that he is a very fine man." After Bates pressed Bradley about the Communist allegation, Bradley retreated further: "I know nothing about his background in that particular." It was then that an obviously irritated John McCormack rose and ended the discussion by declaring: "So far as Mr. Niles is concerned, as I have already said, he is a fine gentleman, a very fine American, and equally a very fine public official. . . . We need more . . . of the type of Dave Niles in the service of the public."[49]

Bradley remained silent for the next three years, but when he learned from Cissy Patterson's conservative *Washington Times Herald* that Niles was presumed to play a major role in FDR's fourth-term reelection, he returned to the attack and promised that "I intend to delve into some of his activities to date in setting up the greatest political machine in all time in any nation."[50] To Bradley, this was a grandiose goal for a man with a minimal public profile. A week later he began with an apology stating that Niles was not Harry Hopkins's brother-in-law. This was the last courtesy that Bradley extended to Niles. Unlike his 1940 peroration, this time Bradley had genuine news[51]:

> I have been informed recently—and I think rather accurately—by close neighbors of his in the Roxbury district of Boston, Mass., about some of his personal background. They tell me that his real name was David K. Neyhus. His father's name was Asher S. Neyhus, a tailor by trade, while his mother's name is Sophia Neyhus, and she was born in Russia.

A child of Russian-born parents with a Jewish-sounding name who had renamed himself was a suspicious person. Had Bradley known of Niles's homosexual inclinations, Niles would have hit the security risk trifecta. Bradley avoided any anti-Semitic references, but linked Niles through Harvard to Supreme Court Justice Felix Frankfurter, the

Sacco-Vanzetti case, former SEC Chair James Landis, and that omnipresent arch-villain of American conservatives, Professor Harold Laski of the London School of Economics. Virtually breathless at this point, Bradley expounded[52]: "It is the purpose of the Frankfurter-Niles-Laski-Landis group to regiment every man, woman, and child in this country in one huge state—socialistic, communistic, or collectivist, or Fascist state, as you will—and it is strongly hinted that we are destined to become but one unit in an international world of the same general collectivist scheme."

The list went on and would eventually include radio commentator Elmer Davis, economists Eveline and Arthur Burns, John Kenneth Galbraith (then of the Office of Price Administration), and Wendell Willkie's onetime publicity director Gardner Cowles. The tool of this "diabolic program" would be the Office of Civil Defense and its immediate goal would be to reelect FDR to a fourth term en route to creating the aforementioned collectivist state.

All of this had become too much for second-term Democratic U.S. Representative Henry "Scoop" Jackson of Washington State, who pointed out that the governors of the various states, many of whom were Republicans, would name the state administrators of the Civil Defense offices. This mattered not to Bradley because Americans must defeat "this deadly peril" and "must be made aware of the true purpose of this stupendous, insidious political machine set up by the fourth-term undercover director David K. Niles." Bradley closed with the loud exhortation, "Wake up America!"

The source of the Boston news was troubling. It was not "close neighbors of his" that informed Representative Bradley about David Niles; it was the ambassador himself, Joseph P. Kennedy, who launched this tale.[53] Joe Kennedy was the one "Harvard" well aware of David's reinvention and knew him as David Neyhus when both were enrolled at Boston Latin in the early 1900s.[54] Kennedy had been a student at Latin two years behind David Neyhus.[55]

Anglicizing his surname was a high-risk strategy for David Neyhus, but he was well aware that foreign-born Jews wishing to succeed in American life would have to rename themselves. The name change occurred during the 1920s when according to Niles's FBI files, "in 1920 [when] Niles entered the Motion Picture Industry as a protégé of Joseph P. Kennedy, who later became Ambassador to London under the Roosevelt Administration."[56] Although, none of the Joe Kennedy biographies makes note of this assertion. Nevertheless, given Niles's later closeness with FDR and Kennedy's later animosity toward FDR, negative stories emanating from Boston sources concerning Niles's reinvention could be presumed to have Joe Kennedy's fingerprints on them.

After the Bradley barrage, Niles's original political mentor, the Massachusetts-born isolationist U.S. Senator Burton K. Wheeler of Montana, took Niles to lunch and exposed the Kennedy link to Bradley's defamatory remarks.[57] Niles conveyed the information to Frankfurter, whose diary reveals that Niles was concerned that "his aging mother who is an invalid with heart disease has to hear all this awful stuff about Dave." Frankfurter felt that Niles tried to shrug off the attacks as "occupational risks." However, "Dave does seem to be hurt and Harry Hopkins has not manifested the kind of friendship he should in the face of this assault upon Dave when in good truth it largely derives from or rather stems from Dave's devotion and service to Hopkins in the past."[58]

How galling it must have been to Joe Kennedy to realize that Felix Frankfurter and Harry Hopkins had placed his non-graduated Boston Latin classmate Neyhus, that poor jumped-up Jew from Roxbury, next to FDR's elbow while he could not get past the White House gates after all he had done for Roosevelt. Joe's self-pity and anger at his exclusion must have been torrential.

In spite of Bradley's hour-long harangue, David Niles continued in his post as a special assistant to the president for the next seven years under both Presidents Roosevelt and Truman. But how true were Bradley's charges? The public release of materials from the VENONA Project, the counterintelligence U.S.-U.K. World War II partnership that did cryptanalysis of Soviet communications, found that Niles was named as expediting transit visas to Mexico for a couple later identified as Soviet agents.[59] However, any cursory examination of Niles's papers at the Truman Library indicates that he was constantly besieged with requests for presidential favors, most of which he tried to accommodate. Two of the secondary accounts about VENONA indicate that bribes were paid to unnamed Niles's associates but none apparently to him, and one account mentions his homosexuality but does not link it with security being compromised. In fact, just the opposite, Niles apparently tried to blackmail a young Communist for sex rather than for secrets. Unbeknownst to the researchers, the young man in question was a longtime associate of Niles dating back to the late 1920s.[60] David Niles may have been gay but he was no "Red."

Jim Curley returns to the House

After losing the mayoralty again to Maurice Tobin in 1941,[61] Jim Curley sought electoral redemption in a 1942 race for the U.S. House. Curley's House candidacy presented a different problem for John McCormack than either Honey Fitz or Joe Casey, because he would win. In this election, Curley chose to avoid the statewide offices of U.S. Senator and governor which he had recently lost. Thirty years earlier, Curley had used the U.S. House as a waystation from 1911 through 1914 while he waited out Honey Fitz's second term as Boston's mayor. This time, Jim Curley just needed a victory. However, Curley could not run in his old 12th South Boston-Dorchester-Roxbury district, because that had become a safe haven for Majority Leader John McCormack. But Article One of the Constitution only requires that House candidates be residents of the state that you wish to represent and not the congressional district.

Seated in the adjacent 11th District was a freshman member, Thomas H. Eliot, a committed New Dealer who had worked in the Department of Labor and in 1935 had been the initial General Counsel of the newly formed Social Security Board.[62] Eliot challenged nine-term Republican and former Lieutenant Governor Robert Luce of Waltham in 1938 and narrowly lost by 1,801 votes. Two years later, he defeated Luce in the rematch.[63]

Eliot was a liberal Harvard professor and a Brahmin scion of the "Harvard Eliots" that had descended from the family's colonial origins in Beverly, a Puritan settlement that had been spun off from Salem. Among his ancestors was Samuel Atkins Eliot, a onetime mayor of Boston,[64] whose son was Charles W. Eliot, the reformist president of Harvard for 40 years. Charles's son was a cofounder of Washington University in St. Louis and among the St. Louis Eliot's was T. S. Eliot, the Nobel Prize–winning poet. With Harvard degrees peppered throughout the family lineage, representing Cambridge in Congress was a fulfillment of the family's fusion of education and public service. Eliot's progressivism and his article "In Defense of Congress" had earned him national notice.[65]

Eliot's battle with John McCormack occurred during the heated debate over the "Service Extension Act of 1941." This was the bill that passed the House, 203–202.[66] In the 77th Congress, Massachusetts had nine Republicans and six Democrats. The nine Republicans split 3 to 6 against the president's positions of nay to recommit and yea on final passage. The six Democrats split evenly 3 to 3 with Representatives Thomas Flaherty of Boston, Lawrence Connery of Lynn who had succeeded his deceased brother William, and Tom Eliot voting yea to recommit and nay on final passage while McCormack, Joe Casey, and Arthur Healey of Boston voted for the White House position. None of the three Democratic Bay State opponents returned in the 78th Congress. Connery died in 1941 while Flaherty was the odd man out in the delegation's loss of its fifteenth seat following the 1942 redistricting and was named to a minor municipal post. Healey who voted for the extension resigned the House in 1942 to become a federal district judge in Boston.

The Democratic defector who bothered McCormack the most was Tom Eliot. In an account of the 203–202 draft extension vote, J. Garry Clifford and Theodore A. Wilson contend that "John McCormack, who had not given his Massachusetts colleague preferred committee assignments, threatened political retaliation if Eliot voted incorrectly." Their account continues, "After the final tally [and Eliot's nay vote] McCormack cornered Eliot and snarled, 'I'll get you for this.'"[67] And he did.

As a key architect of the legal rules implementing Social Security, it is likely that Eliot expressed interest in a Ways and Means Committee assignment. But Democratic freshmen were not assigned to Ways and Means, the House's most important committee. Given its centrality in the careers of fellow Democrats, one had to be elected to Ways and Means by the Democratic Caucus.

Eliot was assigned to the Judiciary Committee, a good one for a freshman and far better than the ones that John was assigned to in his first Congress, but Eliot's Brahmin sense of entitlement would have irritated McCormack and the negative vote on the bill would have sealed Eliot's fate. As the recently elected Democratic floor leader, John would have considered it an affront for a freshman fellow Massachusetts Democrat to rebuff his personal appeal. John seldom forgot and on a vote of this importance, forgiveness would be in short supply.

Massachusetts lost its fifteenth House seat following the 1940 Census, and John played a role in the state's redistricting. The newly reapportioned 11th District lost Boston's multiethnic West End and Chelsea and picked up middle-income Irish Allston.[68] It was not redistricting that did in Professor Eliot; it was the presence of former Governor and Mayor James Michael Curley as his primary challenger. Curley was an electorally formidable foe who struck hard and efficiently. Ridicule was Curley's favorite weapon, and he contended that as a Unitarian, Eliot believed "that our Lord and Savior is a funny little man with a beard who runs around in his underclothes."[69] Curley knocked Eliot off in the September primary and would go on to win 69.3% of the vote in November. It would be his third term in the House and he was assigned to the powerful Appropriations Committee with help from John McCormack. Representative Eliot became Professor Eliot once again.[70]

The 78th Congress watches as the war continues

With the narrowest congressional margin of his presidency and preoccupied with the war, FDR's legislative agenda shriveled during the 78th Congress. As the war continued, congressional attention shifted away from the domestic agenda and the 78th Congress reflected that shift.[71] Congress began to plan for the postwar period, one in which the United States would play a major role. Debates about collective security led to the passage of a number of resolutions that would help guide the peace and protect the Allies from future threats.[72]

Key pieces of legislation in the increasingly conservative 78th Congress included the Smith-Connally Anti-Strike Act that broadened the president's power to place firms necessary to the war effort under the control of the government and made it illegal for a union to strike any war industry.[73] Coauthored by U.S. Representative Howard W. Smith (Dem-Va.) and Senator Tom Connally (Dem-Texas), this bill was directed at the United Mine Workers after its powerful and headstrong chief, John L. Lewis had ordered the union to shut down coal production. The Smith-Connally Act declared that in plants not essential to the war effort, unions had to observe a 30-day cooling-off period before they could call a strike. The Act then went on to outlaw monetary contributions by the unions to political campaigns and candidates. John McCormack, a longtime friend of Howard Smith, broke with him on this legislation believing quite correctly that this was an effort to use the war as an excuse to roll back the gains made by the labor movement through the Wagner-Connery Act.

For the Allies, 1943 held better news. The year opened with Soviet advances to reclaim Stalingrad and the announced breaking of the two-year German blockade of Leningrad. The siege of Leningrad would last another year, but the Soviets had opened up a land route for supplies to enter the besieged city and its million-plus residents. Churchill and Roosevelt met in Casablanca to discuss the opening of a new front in Sicily and Italy. Stalingrad was reclaimed in February by the Soviets and Guadalcanal was secured by the Americans. Both the advances of the Germans and the Japanese had been halted. But regaining the vast territories that their armies had conquered would take another sixteen months in Europe and nineteen in the Pacific. As the role of the American forces grew in Europe into the millions, an American general would be named the new overall commander of the Allied forces in Europe—General Dwight D. "Ike" Eisenhower.

The New York Times and other major American newspapers had run deeply troubling accounts of Jewish deaths in large numbers since the outbreak of the war in 1939. Even more troubling news arrived from Poland and its huge Jewish Warsaw Ghetto. Poland had the largest Jewish community in Europe and ultimately more than 440,000 Jews would be squeezed into its ghetto.[74] After realizing that approximately 265,000 residents of the Ghetto were sent to concentration camps for extermination and not for "forced labor," Jewish resistance to the Nazis erupted in January 1943 but by May the uprising would be crushed with another 13,000 dead and approximately 50,000 deported to the death camps.[75] Clearly, something larger and more systematic was in operation by the Nazis toward Europe's Jewish population than the "collateral damage" of world war.

The war in North Africa continued with the Allies led by Field Marshall Montgomery and American General George S. Patton ricocheting back and forth between Libya and Tunisia with Rommel's forces. By late spring, the Japanese had retreated from Attu and Kiska Islands in the Aleutians and their offensive thrust ended. In July, the pushback grew as Russian tanks defeated the Nazis in the Battle of Prokhorova and regained Kursk. The Allies moved on Sicily and their bombing of German cities escalated dramatically. Italy fell in September and Hitler allowed Mussolini to create a quasi-government to forestall the collapse of his regime. The momentum of the war had shifted in favor of the Allies.

In the Pacific, the Japanese and American forces engaged in a series of bloody island confrontations. Earlier news from the Pacific in early August was that a small patrol boat, PT-109, had been rammed by a Japanese destroyer and sunk off the Solomon Islands with no presumed survivors. It would be days before it was learned that the skipper of PT-109 was Lieutenant John F. Kennedy, the second son of former Ambassador Joseph P. Kennedy. Jack Kennedy, a varsity swimmer at Harvard, had rescued most of his crew. Much as the Battle of San Juan Hill had defined the military exploits of Teddy Roosevelt and hastened his arrival in the White House, so too would the accounts of Jack's heroism in the Solomon Islands open the door to his presidential aspirations.

Also on the political horizon during these turbulent but increasingly hopeful times for the Allies was the 1944 presidential election. This time there was little doubt that FDR would run again for his fourth term in order to bring the war to a successful conclusion. The growing loss of lives became more unsettling to the American public and FDR, less than a year away from the election, was well aware of that fact. Late in November 1943, FDR met in Cairo with Prime Minister Churchill and Chinese Generalissimo Chiang Kai-Shek to plan the final assault on Japan. Days later, FDR flew to Tehran, meeting at the Soviet Embassy with Churchill and Soviet Premier Joseph Stalin to plan the Allied invasion of Europe and the long promised "second front." It was FDR's first meeting with Stalin. It would be almost two more years before both the European and Pacific theaters would end with Allied victories but the plans to deliver victory were now in place.

FDR returned from Tehran to address the Congress (Figure 10.2). Anti-Communist members of the Congress were suspicious of Stalin and FDR's benign view of him did not put them at ease. But having John McCormack, one of the House's leading anti-Communists, defending the president's assessment lowered the anxiety level of enough members to forestall any efforts to slash Lend-Lease payments to the USSR which, after all and well appreciated by both Churchill and FDR, was doing the bulk of fighting and dying on the less-popularized Eastern Front. In his remarks welcoming the return of FDR, John declared, "Those conferences were not only for the purpose of the successful

Figure 10.2 FDR meets with congressional leaders to discuss Tehran meeting with British Prime Minister Churchill and Soviet Premier Stalin, December 1943. l-r Acting Senate Minority Leader Warren Austin (Rep-Vt.), House Majority Leader John W. McCormack (Dem-Mass.) Vice President Henry Wallace, and Speaker Sam Rayburn (Dem-Tex.) (F.D. Roosevelt Library and Museum).

conduct of the war, but after the war is over to try to establish conditions based upon the self-interest of nations and our own self-interest that will assure permanent peace in the future."[76] Whether these anxieties would manifest themselves in the upcoming 1944 presidential race was yet to be determined.

Later funding of the Manhattan Project

There was another race of far greater importance. As the war intensified, the race was on between the Allies and the Axis as to which set of nations would develop the ultimate weapon—the atomic bomb. Émigré physicists, predominantly Jewish, who had escaped from Hitler's Europe, were eager to develop this weapon before Hitler did. Although FDR had been impressed by Albert Einstein's two-page letter in 1939, he was not then in much of a position to act upon it. As the war's end drew nearer, the "atomic project" FDR had set in motion and which Congress had secretly funded had, over the years, made considerable progress, thanks to a tightly knit group of advisors and remarkably able scientists and engineers. Known as the Manhattan Engineering District (MED), it was to implement the plan with a minimum amount of governmental notice.

As General Groves recounted in his 1962 memoir of the project[77]:

For reasons of military security, we had always made a determined effort to withhold all information on the atomic bomb project from everyone, including members of the Executive Department, military personnel and members of Congress, except those who definitely needed it and who were authorized to receive it. As a result our methods of obtaining funds had always been rather unorthodox.

Early in the history of the project, funding needs were not great and were allocated through the War Department on an "as required" basis, but by 1944, the war had entered the endgame and bringing it to a conclusion with the minimal loss of American lives became the upper-most concern among the military. In spite of the low level of spending, word got out to Republican Representative Albert J. Engel of Michigan in late 1943 that construction had begun on a military facility at Oak Ridge, Tennessee. Representative Engel wished to see the site but was persuaded not to do so in the name of wartime secrecy. But the need for money to fund the project escalated in 1944, and a decision was made to involve key members of the congressional leadership in finding appropriations for the bomb. In General Groves's account[78]:

> [On] February 18, 1944, Secretary [of War Henry] Stimson, General [George C.] Marshall and Dr. [Vannevar] Bush (we all felt it would be better if I were not present) met in the Speaker's office in the Capitol, with Speaker Sam Rayburn, Majority Leader John W. McCormack and Minority Leader Joseph W. Martin, Jr. Mr. Stimson reviewed the general state of the project and discussed the financial situation, including expenditures, available monies and estimated future requirements. He gave them our general program of construction, talked of the various procurement efforts and indicated an appropriate schedule for the completion of our work. General Marshall talked of the project's relation to America's over-all strategic war plans, and Bush outlined the scientific background and explained the potentialities of the weapon.

The three visitors spoke solemnly and as John McCormack noted later, they "sat with their heads down in their chins."[79] The congressmen approved the plan "without reservation" and decided to finesse the amounts through the Appropriations Committee. Rayburn would be told what amounts would be necessary and he would then tell McCormack and Martin who would then meet with selected members of the Appropriations Committee so "these items should not be questioned." The House was now in play. While the Rayburn biographies add little to General Groves's account,[80] Joe Martin's autobiography is more illuminating, even though Dr. Bush's name is omitted.[81]

> One morning during the war Speaker Rayburn called and asked if I would come to his office. When I arrived I found that he was waiting with Secretary of War Henry L. Stimson, General George C. Marshall, the Chief of Staff of the Army, and Representative McCormack, the majority leader of the House. . . .
> Marshall described the design of the bomb in some technical detail. Stimson said that if the Germans got this weapon first, they would win the war overnight. They told us that they would need an additional $1,600,000,000 to manufacture the bomb. Because of the overriding necessity for secrecy, they made the unique

request that the money be provided without a trace of evidence as to how it would be spent. No more extraordinary request was ever made to the leaders of the House of Representatives, the trustees of the people's money.

Like Rayburn and McCormack, I agreed to use my influence to obtain an inscrutable appropriation. Since war funds generally lumped together so they could not be analyzed by the enemy, our problem was to get the sums requested by Marshall and Stimson through the House Appropriations Committee. While Rayburn and McCormack went to work on Representative Cannon, a Democrat from Missouri, who was chairman of the committee, I won the assent of John Taber, the ranking minority member. Together we all slid the appropriation through the House without any breach of secrecy. The Senate went along.

A similar strategy was employed for moving the money through the Senate. This time the meeting was with Senate Majority Leader Alben Barkley of Kentucky, Senate Minority Leader Wallace H. White of Maine, Elmer Thomas of Oklahoma, and Styles Bridges of New Hampshire, the chair and ranking minority of the Military Subcommittee of the Senate Appropriations Committee. These were to be the key congressional players in this drama. "Nevertheless," Groves observed, "most of the members of Congress remained completely in the dark about our work." Noticeably excluded was Senator Harry Truman, chair of the Senate Special Committee to Investigate the National Defense Program and the 11th-ranked member of the Appropriations Committee. But the Truman Committee had a mandate, and its efforts to uncover wasteful spending could very easily have jeopardized the success of the Manhattan Project. The two likeliest sites for investigation were Oak Ridge, Tennessee, where the bomb was built and Hanford, Washington, where the first plutonium reactor was tested.

Secretary Stimson and Senator Truman: Senator Truman knew that something was going on regarding these appropriations and he had committed his investigators to an all-out inquiry. As recounted in *Year of Decisions*, the first volume of his memoirs, "I had even sent investigators into Tennessee and the state of Washington with instructions to find out what certain enormous constructions were and what their purpose was."[82]

Secretary Stimson came to Truman's office and said, "Senator, I can't tell you what it is, but it is the greatest project in the history of the world. It is most top secret. Many of the people who are actually engaged in the work have no idea what it is, and we who do would appreciate your not going into those plants."[83]

General Groves, the project's director, indicated in his account that the Truman Committee "became interested in various aspects of the MED at an early date and we had some difficulty in keeping it from looking into the project." Finally, "Senator Truman, the chairman of the committee, agreed at Secretary Stimson's request to delay any investigation of the project as a whole until either security permitted it or the war was over. . . . Mr. Truman accepted the Secretary's decision in good grace."[84]

It appears that the Yale and Harvard Law–educated Stimson's patrician background and his high-level executive appointments made him dismissive of the plebeian members of Harry Truman's Senate committee, people who owed their offices to public approbation. Meeting the committee for the first time on April 15, 1941, Stimson saw the committee as simply seeking "political capital and publicity" and its members "as mild as milk."[85]

Harry Truman's pre-committee Senate career had been marked more by affability than hard work, and he was well accepted by the long-term residents of Capitol Hill, who were those directly informed by the president's people in this crucial matter, not the least of whom was his drinking buddy Sam Rayburn and his poker pal John McCormack. Sam Rayburn and Representative Clarence Cannon, the senior Democrat from Missouri and chair of the House Appropriations Committee, had known of the bomb's expenditures as early as 1942.[86] Stimson would make a formal appeal for more money to Rayburn and Floor Leaders McCormack and Martin 18 months before the bomb was dropped on Japan.

Former Army Captain Truman understood a command from above and called off the investigators and the sites were not visited by the Senate committee. Truman had some hint of the basic details of a huge secret project but Stimson made sure that Truman remained largely ignorant of the bomb's development.[87]

However, Truman's acquiescence did not endear him to Stimson who complained in his diary that Truman was "a nuisance and a pretty untrustworthy man [who] talks smoothly but acts meanly."[88] It would appear that Stimson's personal animus toward Truman may have been almost as much of a factor as national security was in concealing that information. That Stimson chose not to share this information with Truman as the chair of a Senate investigating committee may have made some sense at the time. Stimson's not sharing it with him after Truman's inauguration as vice president in January 1945, while faced with the discernible decline in FDR's health, would appear to support the personal animus explanation.[89]

There were others in Truman's political circle who knew of the bomb's existence and its expenditures; among them were Senate Floor Leaders Barkley and White as well as two senior members on his Senate Appropriations Committee, Thomas and Bridges, who were informed about the bomb days after Stimson informed the House leaders. But the likeliest scenario is that Senator Truman first learned about aspects of the bomb's existence from Rayburn and McCormack with whom he regularly socialized. As chair of the committee, Truman was ideally situated to keep his committee's members and investigators from uncovering this massive expenditure prematurely. Technically, such an inquiry would have been within the purview of the Truman Committee because of the MED's use of outside contractors and consultants. No inquiry was launched, and the silence of the Truman Committee on this critical matter was greatly appreciated and quietly acknowledged. Truman's greatest contribution may have been to keep his committee's investigators from learning about the atomic bomb and his silence in this matter undoubtedly contributed to Truman's vice presidential prospects among the key FDR loyalists in 1944. It is not too far fetched to see Harry as the piano player in the bordello, merrily playing the piano while deliberately unmindful of why various men were traipsing up and down the stairs.

While some Truman biographers contend that Harry had suspicions about the Manhattan Project,[90] most of the others accept Harry's contention that its existence was only revealed to him by Stimson after his swearing-in as president. However, the connection between the two events would suggest strongly that Senator Truman's selection as the Democratic vice presidential candidate in July 1944, five months after his close friends learned of the project's existence, appears to have been a reward for keeping his committee's investigators away from the atomic bomb. Seen in this light, the selection of Senator Truman seems less puzzling than is generally contained in conventional treatments of the topic, and John McCormack's role in connecting both of these events seems more central.

Ultimately, the expenditures for the atomic bomb and related items would swell to almost four billion dollars—an amount which would be very discernible in an overall federal budget of 90 billion dollars. Congress still had a number of "America Firsters," underground isolationists, and some pro-German sympathizers in its ranks. They would have seized upon this news and trumpeted it to America and to the world in an effort to alter the course of the war and to undermine President Roosevelt's conduct of it. Keeping much of Congress and the American public unaware of these expenditures was no small feat. It was a level of bipartisan congressional secrecy that speaks of a different era.

Months passed before the 78th Congress enacted any major legislation but early in 1944, electoral politics returned to the fore. In an effort to mobilize the votes of the millions of Americans in the armed forces, Congress amended the Soldier Vote Act of 1942. It authorized absentee voting in time of war by members of the land and naval forces, members of the merchant marines, and others absent from the place of their residence.[91] The original 1942 act mandated that the states make these ballots available to members of the armed forces but under the terms of the 1944 act, the U.S. War Ballot Commission was denied authority to subvert any state voting laws applicable to the voters involved. The echo of "states' rights" could be heard once again.

As General Dwight Eisenhower and the British allies prepared for the successful invasion of the European coast on June 6, D-Day, Congress geared up for the postwar travails of America's servicemen with the passage of the Servicemen's Readjustment Act of 1944, better known as "the GI Bill." This act granted authority to the Veterans Administration to assist veterans of World War II in adjusting to the conditions of civilian life through the provision of academic training, federal loans, employment programs, and medical assistance.[92]

With the war entering its final months, Congress addressed two other postwar concerns. The passage of the Surplus Property Act of 1944 established a three-member board to supervise the disposal of surplus government property through transfer or sale at fair market value, and assigned preferences in acquiring such property to other federal agencies, state and local governments, nonprofit educational institutions, veterans, and small businesses.[93] The last major legislative act of the 78th Congress was the War Mobilization and Reconversion Act. It centralized responsibility for contract settlement, surplus disposal, and reemployment programs in the office of War Mobilization and Reconversion.[94] Knowing that jobs for the returning veterans might be scarce, the act authorized interest-free loans or advances to state and local governments to help finance the planning of public works.

The war continued, as did presidential politics. It was a presidential election year and the major parties had nominees to select and campaigns to run. The 78th Congress may have been publicly uneventful but all of its House members would have to face the electorate once again. For the Democrats, it was clear who would top their ticket, but anxiety about the health of President Roosevelt hung heavily over the convention, the campaign, and the election.

Pre-Convention politics

Although Frank Walker, who succeeded Jim Farley as Postmaster General in 1940 and later became chair of the Democratic National Committee in 1943, was the ostensible man in charge of FDR's 1944 reelection campaign, some news accounts suggested that David K. Niles would be the key figure running the campaign from within the White House.[95] John O'Donnell's *Washington Daily News* "Capitol Stuff" reported[96]:

> But Niles, known on intimate terms only by the White House clique, a mysterious figure to the Democrats here except those from Massachusetts, is directing from behind the White House scenes the fourth term movements of political forces that go beyond the bounds of Democratic Party regularity.
>
> It was Niles, up in his native Massachusetts, who took over control of all Massachusetts appointments to WPA state jobs under delegated authority from Harry Hopkins, thereby arousing the fury of the Democratic faithful. And it is Niles, they will tell you on Capitol Hill today, whose power now reaches directly into the House of Representatives by his vote-getting influence in the South Boston district represented by Majority Leader John McCormack.

While David Niles was John McCormack's back channel to FDR's White House, John was Niles's source of information about the difficulty that FDR's congressional initiatives would face within the U.S. House from the southern Democrats.

FDR's Fourth Nomination and the Wary Democrats: Unlike the cloudy and uncertain nominating process in 1940, there was no doubt that FDR would be renominated in 1944. The Gallup Poll indicated that there was much less public resistance to a fourth term than there was to the third. However, there was some serious slippage among the nation's Catholics regarding FDR.

FDR won seven of that year's fourteen presidential preference primaries with five states, including Massachusetts, choosing unpledged delegates and two others, South Dakota and West Virginia, selecting favorite sons. No major named opponent surfaced and FDR captured 70.9% of the votes cast in the Democratic primary vote.[97] Shortly before the convention, FDR had made his announcement concerning renomination. The Democratic delegates assembled at the July 19–21 convention in Chicago quickly fell into line.

The success of the Allied troops following the D-Day invasion of Europe a scant six weeks earlier suggested that the war would end within a year. France had been invaded and the Nazi strongholds in Cherbourg and Caen had been liberated. Rome had fallen before the Allied assault and Italy's Benito Mussolini had been forced from office. In the Pacific, the Marshall and Admiralty Islands captured by the Japanese were now in American hands. And just before the opening of the convention, the Mariana Islands had been invaded. At last the war's end appeared in sight.

But an air of disquietude hung over the Democratic convention. The commander-in-chief did not look very well. His health seemed diminished. Smiles were fewer; distractions abounded. Some assumed it was the war that had taken its toll. Others assumed that years of battling pain had left him physically depleted. Regardless of what they stated publicly, most of those assembled in the Convention Hall knew privately that this would be FDR's last nomination. They prayed it would not be his last year.

Unbeknownst to the nation, the White House had already brought in outside physicians to examine the president—Dr. Frank Lahey, the founder of Boston's Lahey Clinic and a past president of the American Medical Association, was invited along with Dr. James Paullin of Atlanta, Georgia, by Vice Admiral Ross McIntire, the president's physician. On July 8, eleven days before the Democrats would gather in Chicago to renominate FDR, the three physicians examined the president.

Dr. Lahey was worried and stated in his memorandum to Admiral McIntire[98] "that I did not believe that, if Mr. Roosevelt were elected again, he had the physical capacity to complete a term. I told him that, as a result of activities in his trip to Russia he had been in a state which was, if not in heart failure, at least on the verge of it, that this was the result of high blood pressure he has now had for a long time, plus a question of coronary damage." And contained within the letter was a simple admonition, "If he does accept another term, he had a very serious responsibility concerning who is the Vice President." McIntire hid the memo and FDR pushed ahead with his renomination and the grueling reelection campaign against a vigorous 42-year-old opponent in New York Governor Tom Dewey.

The 1944 Democratic convention

Because national nominating conventions rely upon the rules of the House of Representatives, it is generally a senior congressional leader who is named permanent chair of the Convention, while the temporary chair is the person delivering the convention's keynote address. Senator Robert S. Kerr, the oil and gas baron of Oklahoma, who later would be dubbed the "uncrowned king of the Senate," gave the keynote address but in a curious move, it would be newly appointed U.S. Senator Samuel D. Jackson of Indiana who was named as permanent chair.

Sam Rayburn did not attend the 1944 convention even though his name was bandied about for the vice presidential nomination to replace Wallace.[99] Texas politics had become especially contentious and as anti-FDR feelings increased back home,

Rayburn was faced with a primary election challenge from the conservative white supremacist "Texas Regulars."[100] Sam's ally, Tom Connally, the flamboyant, bow-tied senior U.S. Senator, contended that had Rayburn been at the convention, he would have been nominated and his Austin-Boston pal John McCormack agreed. "If he had attended the Convention he would have won the nomination." In fact, McCormack continued, "I called him from Chicago to come up, but he said that he couldn't leave his District." McCormack even went so far as to line up the Massachusetts delegates in support of Rayburn.[101]

While Rayburn was not at the convention, John McCormack played a major role as cochair of the 1944 Resolutions Committee. Because the Resolutions Committee is the one that deals most directly with specific issues, the leadership of this committee is usually assigned to members of the party's congressional wing. These are the people whose job it will be to translate the campaign promises in the platform into legislation. And so it was in 1944, with John McCormack of Massachusetts cochairing the Resolutions Committee with U.S. Representative Mary T. Norton of New Jersey.[102] While John was well regarded in the House, Mrs. Norton was seen as the patronage-seeking ally of Jersey City's infamous Mayor "I am the law" Frank Hague.[103]

Once again John McCormack was in the room. Keeping troublesome planks out of the final platform was a skill that John had perfected during the past few years as Majority Floor Leader of the House. Controlling what comes to the floor is often much more important than mobilizing votes for a proposal once it has arrived there.

For the party out of presidential office, the role of the platform is to be as inclusive as possible of all the voting groups capable of returning your party to the White House. The role of the platform for the party holding the White House is to trumpet the successes of the incumbent administration and to promise even greater success in the future. Protecting an incumbent president from embarrassing platform proposals is the mark of a successful Platform Committee Chair. As usual, John McCormack delivered.

This Democratic convention was especially concerned about the civil rights issue. The growth of black voting representation in the nation's urban centers had exacerbated the conflict between the cities and the South. The presidential wing of the Democrats needed to mobilize black voters in the urban centers of Chicago, Detroit, St. Louis, Philadelphia, and Baltimore if it wished to gain the electoral votes of the key states of Illinois, Michigan, Missouri, Pennsylvania, and Maryland. But the congressional wing of the Democratic Party was still dominated by white rural southerners. With northern Democrats losing seats in 1942, the party's House margin had shrunk to only thirteen seats and the South regained its disproportionate share.

To reelect FDR in 1944, Democrats would need the electoral votes of the big states with their large numbers of urban ethnics, organized labor, and the votes of the black voters who had gained the right to vote only when they left the South. To hold the Congress, the white South had to be assured that Democratic national involvement in their affairs would be minimal. Resolutions Committee Chair John McCormack had to prepare the wording in the platform that would keep the South at bay on the ever-treacherous subject of civil rights.

Dueling platforms

Just three weeks earlier, the Republican convention met in Chicago and their 1944 platform issued a civil rights challenge with planks that were broad and specific. They appeared under three headings[104]:

Racial and Religious Intolerance
We unreservedly condemn the injection into American life of appeals to racial or religious prejudice.

We pledge an immediate Congressional inquiry to ascertain the extent to which mistreatment, segregation and discrimination against Negroes who are in our armed forces are impairing morale and efficiency, and the adoption of corrective legislation.

We pledge the establishment by Federal legislation of a permanent Fair Employment Practice Commission.

Anti-Poll Tax: The payment of any poll tax should not be a condition of voting in Federal elections and we favor immediate submission of a Constitutional amendment for its abolition.

Anti-Lynching: We favor legislation against lynching and pledge our sincere efforts in behalf of its early enactment.

By contrast, the 1944 Democratic Party platform was deafening in its silence. Chicago, the city holding the two conventions, may have been the same and the time span between the two events was less than a month, but decades seemed to separate the two parties in their responses to this critical social issue. Northern moderate Democrats were unfortunately well aware of how the mere mention of federal legislation to rid the nation of segregation, the poll tax, and even lynching set off the defenses of the segregated white South. The thought of a Federal Employment Practices Commission (FEPC) to limit job discrimination brought the white South close to apoplexy. So in the 1944 Democratic platform, the two sentences on civil rights were innocuous banalities with no new proposed legislation. Stated simply,[105]

"We believe that racial and religious minorities have the right to live, develop and vote equally with all citizens and share the rights that are guaranteed by our Constitution. Congress should exert its full constitutional powers to protect those rights."

With the platform adopted, the convention moved quickly to renominate President Roosevelt. The first ballot victory was impressive—1,086 votes for President Roosevelt; three delegations—Louisiana, Mississippi, and Virginia—gave 89 votes to conservative U.S. Senator Harry Flood Byrd (Dem-Va.), and one vote for Jim Farley, FDR's former Postmaster General.[106]

Anxiety about FDR's health was captured in the closing paragraphs of the 1944 Democratic Platform. Coauthored by John McCormack, it was a respectful paean to FDR, "Our beloved and matchless leader and President, Franklin Delano Roosevelt." The prayerful last sentence of the Platform was clear and unequivocal: "That God may keep him strong in body and in spirit to carry on his yet unfinished work is our hope and our prayer."[107]

The ending of the two-thirds rule in 1936 had diminished the South's century-long control over Democratic presidential and vice presidential nominations. Its immediate impact at the 1940 convention was to result in the dumping of two-term Vice President Jack Garner of Texas and his replacement by the Iowa liberal mystic, secretary of agriculture Henry A. Wallace. But 1944 was a different year.

Harry Truman replaces Henry Wallace

It was FDR's onetime hope that he could reorient American politics along a liberal-conservative axis, one that would let conservative rural southerners move into the Republican Party and would be more welcoming to the northern urban liberal and moderate Republicans of the Wendell Willkie stripe. In 1940, FDR's naming of the liberal Wallace, the son of a Republican former Cabinet member, to be his vice presidential nominee was a step in that direction. And in July 1944, FDR sent his Special Counsel Sam Rosenman to meet with Wendell Willkie in New York City in hopes of achieving that reorientation.[108] Willkie's premature death later ended that hope and the war changed FDR's plans.

The Iowa-born Henry Wallace never gained the support of the cities or the South where the Democratic power brokers resided. Iowa was a northern state and one with no major metropolis. How could he possibly relate to the Democrats' two core constituencies? With FDR's health preying heavily upon the minds of many delegates, even David K. Niles, whom Wallace had personally thanked for his 1940 vice presidential nomination, sensed that renominating Wallace was a lost cause. With these unspoken anxieties hovering around the convention, it was obvious that more than ever, the debates around this nomination had to be managed effectively. Dumping Wallace had to be done carefully lest the Republicans use it as proof that the Democrats feared that FDR would not complete a fourth term.

Vice President Wallace was aware that his renomination was in jeopardy. He gave a seconding speech for FDR declaring that Roosevelt was "the greatest liberal in the history of the United States . . . [and] Roosevelt is a greater liberal today than he has ever been."[109] And in a direct challenge to the South, Wallace declared[110]: "The future belongs to those who go down the line unswervingly for the liberal principles of both political and economic democracy regardless of race, color, or religion. In a political, educational, and economic sense there must be no inferior races. . . . The future must bring equal wages for equal work regardless of sex or race."

Maintaining ideological liberalism was not the primary goal of the 1944 Democratic National Convention; victory was. There were other major issues. Who would help FDR make the peace, and was Henry Wallace the man who could keep the broad-based Democratic Party together for this wartime election? For most of 1944's delegates, nominating a real Democrat for vice president was much more important than nominating a great liberal.

FDR was well aware of the shift in the party and knew that his political influence had waned. He sent conflicting messages to a number of people, from Vice President Wallace to a number of his likely rivals, Director of the War Mobilization Board Jimmy Byrnes, Supreme Court Justice William O. Douglas, and U.S. Senator Harry Truman (Dem-Mo.). His letter of endorsement of Henry Wallace's vice presidential renomination was nothing if not guarded.[111]

> I personally would vote for his renomination if I were a delegate to the Convention. At the same time, I do not wish to appear in any way as dictating to the Convention. Obviously, the Convention must do the deciding. And it should—and I am sure it will—give consideration to the pros and cons of its choice.

The party's power brokers of big-city Catholics and southerners had reluctantly accepted Henry Wallace in 1940. This time, they held the cards and Roosevelt's people suspected that they would be forced to cast Wallace adrift.

South Carolina's James F. Byrnes emerged as the leading replacement contender, with a likelier chance than had been the case in 1940.[112] Jimmy Byrnes's life and career were remarkably similar to those of John McCormack. Both of their mothers were Irish-descended and their fathers were gone early. Neither man received formal education after the eighth grade. Both apprenticed themselves to attorneys early in their adolescence and became lawyers at the age of 21 without having attended high school, college, or law school. Both men were married and neither had children. In many ways Byrnes was the southern analogue of John McCormack. While John took a legislative route to the U.S. House through the Massachusetts Constitutional Convention and the Great and General Court, Byrnes took a legal route as a court officer winning his first House contest in 1910 at the age of 26. John McCormack's career was defined by the 42 years that he served in the House. By contrast, Byrnes served in a number of governmental capacities: U.S. House, 1911–25; U.S. Senate, 1931–41; Associate Justice of the U.S. Supreme Court, 1941–42; Director of the Office of Economic Stabilization, 1942–43; Director of the Office of War Mobilization, 1943–45; Secretary of State, 1945–47; and Governor of South Carolina, 1951–55. During his time in the Roosevelt White House, Byrnes had become so indispensable to FDR that he was widely regarded as the "assistant President" in Washington. However, Jimmy Byrnes was both a southerner and had been born a Catholic.

Truman biographer Robert Ferrell contended that FDR's admonition that the Byrnes selection "be cleared with Sydney"—the CIO's Sidney Hillman—slowed its momentum[113] and opened the door to a blocking strategy by "Boss" Ed Flynn of the Bronx, the key Democratic power broker from FDR's New York. Flynn put those issues simply: "Byrnes who was the strongest candidate, wouldn't do because he had been raised a Catholic and had left the Church when he married, and the Catholics wouldn't stand for that; organized labor too, would not be for him; and since he came from South Carolina, the question of the Negro vote would be raised. For these reasons he would, as I said, hurt the President."[114]

Flynn and his fellow urban kingmakers also excluded House Speaker Sam Rayburn because "he was from Texas and couldn't be considered available."[115] Both Byrnes and

Rayburn got the message and pulled themselves out of the running. McCormack's mild civil rights platform would keep the South attached to the party. It was not necessary to also give them the vice presidency.

Attention then shifted to the electoral needs of the cities and black voters. Although Supreme Court Associate Justice William O. Douglas believed that he was FDR's choice,[116] Flynn contended that FDR reviewed the list of potential candidates and settled on Senator Harry Truman of Missouri. To Flynn, FDR knew that "Truman was the man who would hurt him the least" and urged him to get fellow Catholics Postmaster General Frank C. Walker of Pennsylvania and Mayor Ed Kelly of Chicago, along with the irrepressible George E. Allen of Mississippi (later to head the Reconstruction Finance Corporation), behind the selection. Both Flynn and Walker had chaired the Democratic National Committee during the Roosevelt presidency and they assigned their successor, the present National Chair Robert Hannegan, a fellow Missourian, to convince Senator Truman to run for the post.[117] As the grandson of a Confederate cavalryman and a product of Boss Tom Pendergast's Kansas City machine,[118] Harry Truman embodied both of the party's dominant wings.

Congressional supporters of Harry Truman included two of his well-placed pals— Sam Rayburn, the Speaker of the House, and John McCormack, the House Majority Leader and cochair of the Resolutions Committee. The close relationship can be seen in Figure 10.3, which pictures John and Harry in a semi-conspiratorial chat as they appear to be plotting the downfall of Vice President Wallace.

A dozen names were put into nomination, but the balloting quickly focused on the two-man contest between Vice President Wallace and Senator Truman. Wallace led Truman 429 ½ to 319 ½ on the initial ballot, but he still needed another 160 delegates

Figure 10.3 U.S. Senator Harry Truman (Dem-Mo.) and House Majority Leader John McCormack discussing the 1944 Democratic vice presidential nomination. (Truman Presidential Library and Museum).

of the 589 votes to be nominated. The balance of power lay in the 427 delegates who voted for neither man, 170 of which were held by the states of the Confederacy. With Jimmy Byrnes not in the running, Senator John Hollis Bankhead of Alabama, brother of the late Speaker Will Bankhead, was the recipient of most of those votes.

On the second ballot, Wallace moved to 473 votes, but Truman surged slightly ahead of him with 477½, with four-fifths of his gain provided by the southern delegations of Texas, Mississippi, South Carolina, and Virginia and the border state ones of Maryland, Oklahoma, and West Virginia. The momentum swung heavily toward Truman and by the end of the switches, Truman had defeated Wallace, 1,031 to 105.[119]

John McCormack's Massachusetts sent thirty-four delegates to the 1944 convention, the eighth-largest delegation. McCormack had been one of the twelve Massachusetts delegates to support Harry Truman throughout the balloting. John's loyalty had been beneficial and the new vice presidential nominee was his "poker pal" and a regular at Sam Rayburn's "Board of Education." Nominations were only half of the battle; elections still had to be won.

The 1944 Republican nomination

The Republicans nominated Thomas E. Dewey, the 42-year-old Governor of New York. Four years earlier, Dewey, then the District Attorney for New York City, had made a dramatic run for the 1940 nomination through the presidential primaries and had been blocked at the convention by the forces of U.S. Senator Robert Taft of Ohio leading to the nomination of Wendell Willkie.

By 1944 it was clear to the Republicans that FDR would be renominated with little opposition. Given that Senator Taft and Governor Dewey did not resume their former hostilities, the convention had little to do and adjourned after three days. Both men passed on that year's presidential preference primaries, which resulted in General Douglas MacArthur winning a plurality of the 2,271,605 votes cast.[120] General MacArthur remained steadfast at his post in the Pacific and there was little hesitancy in giving Dewey the 1944 Republican nomination. He received all but three of the 1,059 delegate votes.[121] To placate the Taft wing, John W. Bricker, the conservative three-term Governor of Ohio and Taft ally, was nominated for vice president, 1,057 to 2. Dewey would be the party's sacrificial lamb just as Kansas Governor Alf Landon had been in 1936. The hope of the Taft people was that Dewey's campaign would be as forlorn as that of Landon's. However, Governor Dewey saw this nomination as a way to place himself in the forefront as the nation's first post-Roosevelt president.

The lost prince, Joseph P. Kennedy, Jr.

Although political machinations continued stateside, the bloody battles in Europe and the Pacific raged on. It was clear that the Axis powers were on the defensive and the Allies stepped up their bombing raids over Europe to break its back. Navy Lieutenant Joseph P. Kennedy, Jr. was one of the more aggressive bomber pilots with 25 missions under his belt. While the conventions met, young Joe chose to volunteer for his riskiest mission ever. He was to fly a fully loaded bomber over France and then parachute to safety as the remote-controlled plane crashed into its target. Known as Operation Aphrodite, young Joe would be its first Navy pilot and on August 12, he and his copilot Lieutenant Wilford "Bud" Willy climbed aboard the PB-24 Liberator to carry out their latest and most dangerous mission.[122] Adding to the anxiety of the mission, President Roosevelt's second son, Colonel Elliott Roosevelt, was to fly behind Kennedy's Liberator and photograph its takeoff and flight over the Channel.

Prior to takeoff, Joe had been told by Earl Olsen, an electronics technician, that the remote control device might be faulty and the explosives on board could detonate early. Joe shrugged off the warning. Two minutes into the mission, the 25,000 pounds of bombs aboard exploded prematurely and young Joe and Willy were blasted to death with the plane's wreckage scattered near the English village of Blythburgh.[123] No remnant of either man was found.

The ambassador was devastated by the news and was disconsolate for months. Joe Jr. was the family prince, and it would be he who would fulfill Joe Kennedy's dream of a Catholic presidency. Much has been made of why young Joe would have undertaken this extraordinarily risky mission and some of that speculation has centered on Jack Kennedy's heroic exploits in the Pacific. Lieutenant John Kennedy's war was over a year earlier in 1943 as he returned to the states to recuperate from the rescuing of his crew on PT-109. Jack Kennedy's heroism led him to be awarded the Purple Heart and the Navy and Marine Corps Medal. Other medals would follow, including the Asiatic-Pacific Campaign Medal and the World War II Victory Medal. Most notably, Jack's heroism was feted in John Hersey's article "Survival" in the June 17, 1944, issue of the *New Yorker*.[124] The ambassador convinced the *Reader's Digest* to reprint a condensed version of the story and reportedly purchased 150,000 copies for Jack's first congressional campaign.[125] The *Digest* appeared on newsstands in August as Joe Jr. entered his last month on earth.

Biographers Ralph G. Martin and Nancy Clinch have speculated that the publicizing of Jack's exploits inspired sibling rivalry in his older brother that led to his unfortunate demise. To Martin, "[Joe's] death came almost exactly a year after his brother Jack's PT boat was sliced in half. The connection of events was tangible. Jack had never tried to be a hero, never really considered himself one. Joe was desperate to be one."[126] Others like Arthur Krock of the *New York Times*, a Joe Kennedy retainer, asserted that it was "to disprove a slander" and to show the British and the Roosevelts that the Kennedys were not "yellow" as it was alleged that the British believed and FDR had stated to associates.[127] With Elliott Roosevelt on hand to record the mission, this appears to be the most logical explanation. It certainly echoes what impelled the near-sighted and asthmatic Teddy Roosevelt to hurl himself up the San Juan Heights in the Spanish-American War of 1898.

Posthumously Joseph P. Kennedy, Jr. would be awarded the Navy Cross, the U.S. Navy's highest distinction and far more esteemed than Jack's Navy and Marine Corps Medal. Sadly, it was in his death that Joe Jr. finally finished ahead of Jack. Regardless of why it happened, it was now clear that Jack had to complete the Kennedy presidential mission that Joe Jr. was intended to accomplish.

FDR projects the war's end

By 1944, FDR was meeting with John McCormack in the White House every ten days, sometimes with Sam Rayburn; sometimes with Senate Leader Alben Barkley; and sometimes alone. In a late afternoon meeting in August, with his fourth nomination secured and the Willkie episode put aside, FDR called John into the office to discuss how he saw the war ending. FDR had no specific chore for John but apparently rambled on about the progress of the war. Two months had passed since the successful D-Day landing on June 6, and the Nazis were rapidly retreating eastward from their captured territories in France. FDR was optimistic about the European front; less so about the one in the Pacific. Presidential chronicler Jim Bishop noted that FDR told John, "Hitler can win every battle until he wins the Atlantic and he still hasn't won the war."[128]

However, FDR was far less sanguine about the war in Asia. John recalled FDR saying[129]:

> John, I have three plans before me regarding our campaign. Two regard invasions of Asia—the other is an invasion of Japan itself. I have to make a decision. If we go in, it is going to cost one million American casualties.

That number of "one million American casualties" led John to say that he wouldn't want to make that decision. Not surprisingly, that number would recur in Winston Churchill's assessment of why the atomic bombs had to be dropped on Japan and its source was likely FDR.

The 1944 campaign and the election

FDR waited until mid-September to campaign and was far less vigorous than in years past.[130] The most noted exchange of the campaign was the oft-repeated one surrounding the president's Scottish terrier, Fala. Republicans contended that Fala had been left behind on an Aleutian island and that the president had dispatched a destroyer to rescue his beloved pet at the cost of millions of dollars to American taxpayers. FDR had a field day and with mock indignation, he ridiculed the Republican attacks by saying that he had a right to "resent, to object to libelous statements about my dog."[131]

In September with the election just weeks away, the White House received opinion poll data to see where the American public stood on FDR's reelection. The poll indicated that FDR was in electoral trouble with American Catholics. FDR's pollster Hadley Cantril reported to David Niles that likely Catholic defections since 1940 represented a 10% drop for FDR or 730,000 voters, particularly among the 11% identified as upper income Catholics who reportedly dropped from 67% support of FDR to 49%.[132] Catholic defection rates were surprising given the fact that the tide of battle had turned in favor of the Allies, but it was Catholics (30%) who were far more fearful than Protestants (17%) that "Russia will take over a large part of Europe and try to spread Communism."

A postelection analysis of Boston's 22 wards by political analyst Sam Lubell confirmed Cantril's fears. Boston's Irish wards of Charlestown, South Boston, and Dorchester that had ranked 1st, 2nd, and 3rd in voting Democratic in both 1928 and 1932 dropped with Charlestown no longer among the top ten in 1944, John's two South Boston-Dorchester wards slid to 4th and 6th respectively and predominantly Italian East Boston that had ranked 3rd in 1936 also dropped out of the top ten.[133] In contrast, the two predominantly Jewish wards of Mattapan and David Niles Roxbury ranked 1st and 2nd in 1944.

The last victory

FDR's two-tiered strategy worked. He was reelected and the Democrats maintained their hold on both the House of Representatives and the Senate. FDR won the popular vote 53.4% to 45.9%. His 3.6 million vote margin fell below his 5 million vote margin over Willkie in 1940, but the 333 electoral vote margin (432–99) was as wide as ever. Dewey carried twelve states with 99 electoral votes, two more states and seventeen more electoral votes than Willkie, but it was far from enough to unseat the champ. Dewey added Wisconsin and Wyoming to the earlier Republican strongholds in the agricultural Plains states and the Northern New England enclaves of Maine and Vermont. The two Midwestern industrial states of Michigan and Ohio reversed their 1940 outcomes with Dewey's carrying Ohio, Taft and Bricker's state, and losing Michigan, his own native state.

In the 1944 congressional elections, the Democrats made a net gain of twenty-two House seats and only a net loss of two Senate seats. FDR's coattails were longer in 1944 than they had been in 1940 when the Democrats made only a net gain of seven House seats and a net loss of three Senate seats. In the upcoming 79th Congress, the Democratic seat margins would be larger—51 in the House (242–191)—and 19 in the Senate (57–38), but the South and the Border still held a clear regional plurality among the Democratic members of the Congress.

Democrats had extended their congressional majorities and FDR was returned once again to the White House. While his fourth inaugural was scheduled for January 20, 1945, politics was far from the nation's major concern. The war continued on both the European and Pacific fronts. The overarching question was: would FDR get to see the conclusion of this greatest war in human history or would fate intervene and deny him that triumph?

Notes

1   Declaration of a State of War with Japan, approved December 8, 1941 (Public Law 77-328; 55 Stat. 795). Roll call vote 130, *Congressional Record*, 77th Congress, 1st Session, pp. 9536–37.

2   *Congressional Record*, 66th Congress, 1st Session, April 5, 1917, pp. 412–13.

3   D. B. Hardeman and Donald C. Bacon, *Rayburn: A Biography* (Austin: Texas Monthly Press, 1987), p. 276. See also Lynne Olson, *Those Angry Days: Roosevelt, Lindbergh, and America's Fight over World War II, 1939–1941* (New York: Random House, 2013), p. 430.

4   Declaration of a State of War with Germany, approved December 11, 1941 (Public Law 77-331; 55 Stat. 796); and Declaration of a State of War with Italy, approved December 11, 1941 (Public Law 77-332; 55 Stat. 797) Roll call votes 131 and 132, *Congressional Record*, 77th Congress, 1st Session, pp. 9665–67.

5   Wayne S. Cole, *Roosevelt & the Isolationists* (Lincoln: University of Nebraska Press, 1983), chapter 32.

6   First War Powers Act, approved December 18, 1941 (Public Law 77-354; 55 Stat. 838-841).

7   Selective Training and Service Act Amendments, approved December 20, 1941 (Public Law 77-360; 55 Stat. 844-847).

8   See the full treatment presented in Roland A. Young's valuable *Congressional Politics in the Second World War* (New York: Columbia University Press, 1956).

9   Joseph P. Kennedy to Franklin Roosevelt, Telegram, December 7, 1941. Smith, ed., *Hostages to Fortune*, p. 533.

10   Smith, ed., *Hostages to Fortune*, p. 534.

11   Ibid.; Joe Kennedy diary entry for January 7, 1942, pp. 533–34.

12   Joseph P. Lash, ed., *From the Diaries of Felix Frankfurter* (New York: W. W. Norton, 1975), pp. 237–38. Frankfurter was reacting to a Joe Kennedy–orchestrated attack on David Niles by Michigan Representative Republican Frederick Bradley.

13   Emergency Price Control Act of 1942, approved January 30, 1942 (Public Law 77-421; 56 Stat. 23-37). See the overview of the 77th Congress in Floyd M. Riddick, "American Government and Politics: Second Session of the Seventy-Seventh Congress, January 6 to December 16, 1942," *APSR*, XXXVII (April 1943), pp. 290–305.

14   See Richard M. Nixon, *RN: The Memoirs of Richard Nixon* (New York: Touchstone, 1990), pp. 25–27. Originally published by Simon & Schuster in 1978.

15   See the thoughtful treatment of this event in Morton Grodzins, *Americans Betrayed: Politics and the Japanese Evacuation* (Chicago: University of Chicago Press, 1949).

16   Second War Powers Act, approved March 27, 1942 (Public Law 77-507; 56 Stat. 176-187).

17   The classic treatment remains Raul Hilberg, *The Destruction of the European Jews* (Chicago: Quadrangle Books, 1961). See also Christopher Browning, *The Origins of the Final Solution: The Evolution of Nazi Jewish Policy: September 1939–March 1942* (Lincoln: University of Nebraska Press, 2004).

18   Hilberg, *The Destruction of the European Jews*, rev. and definitive ed. (New York: Holmes & Meier, 1985), p. 273.

19   C. Herschel Schooley, "The Atomic Secret," in his *Missouri's Cannon in the House* (Marcelline, MO: Walsworth Publishing, 1977), pp. 65–70. Quote is on p. 66. Accompanying Cannon were fellow Appropriations Committee members John Taber (Rep-NY), the ranking minority member; George H. Mahon (Dem-Texas), the

12th ranking Democrat; and the chair and ranking member of the Military Services Subcommittee J. Buell Snyder (Dem-Penn.), and Albert J. Engel (Rep-Mich.). Clifton Woodrum of Virginia, the 2nd-ranking Democrat and John McCormack's 1940 rival for the majority leadership was not included.

20   Richard Munson, *The Cardinals of Capitol Hill: The Men and Women Who Control Government Spending* (New York: Grove Press, 1993).

21   The committee's history and its early operational systems may be found in U.S. House of Representatives, Committee on Appropriations, *A History of the Committee on Appropriations*, House of Representatives, H. Doc. 77-299, 77th Congress, 1st Session (1941); and in Charles Stewart III, *Budget Reform Politics: The Design of the Appropriations Process, 1865–1921* (Cambridge, UK: Cambridge University Press, 1989).

22   Woodrow Wilson, *Congressional Government: A Study in American Politics* (New York: Meridian Books, 1955), pp. 82–83.

23   This assessment is made most emphatically in Richard F. Fenno, Jr., "House Appropriations Committee as a Political System: The Problem of Integration," *APSR*, LVI (June 1962), pp. 310–24; and in his book-length classic, *The Power of the Purse: Appropriations Politics in Congress* (Boston: Little, Brown, 1966).

24   Canon, Nelson, and Stewart, *Committees in the U.S. Congress, 1789–1946, Members*, Vol. 3, p. 1019, for Taber and Vol. 3, p. 167, for Cannon.

25   As described by Taber, "I was able to keep myself under control when I was hit by the gentleman from Missouri, but I grabbed his wrist and held him down. . . . I had a cut lip and I went to the washroom and washed it off" (*Congressional Record*, 79th Congress, 1st Session May 30, 1945, pp. 5294–95). Cannon had taken exception to some newspaper comments that Taber had made about him.

26   Jonathan Daniels, *White House Diary*, October 15, 1942.

27   See John Harding, "The 1942 Congressional Elections," *APSR*, XXXVIII (February 1944), pp. 41–58; and Hadley Cantril and John Harding, "The 1942 Elections: A Case Study in Political Psychology," *Public Opinion Quarterly*, VII (Summer 1943), pp. 222–41.

28   The definitive list of party splits in Congress, 1860–2004 is in Congressional Quarterly, *CQ Guide to U.S. Elections*, 5th ed. (Washington, DC: Congressional Quarterly Press, 2005), Vol. 2, pp. 1635–37.

29   Cortez A. M. Ewing, *Congressional Elections, 1896–1944: The Sectional Basis of Political Democracy in the House of Representatives* (Norman: University of Oklahoma Press, 1947), pp. 88–92.

30   Young, *Congressional Politics in the Second World War*, p. 225.

31   Ibid.

32   William V. Shannon, *The American Irish*, rev ed. (New York: Macmillan, 1966), p. 357n. Shannon reports that Fitzgerald lost 18 of the city's 22 wards to Casey. The Elections Division of the Massachusetts Secretary of the Commonwealth records Casey with 40.1% of the vote, Fitzgerald with 29.8%, Fitz's nemesis Dan Coakley with 6.3%, and Joseph Lee with 12.0%.; others and blanks 11.8% in a telephone interview, May 10, 2011. McCormack is listed as a possible Senate contender in Alden Hatch's *The Lodges of Massachusetts* (New York: Hawthorn Books, 1973), p. 218.

33   Background material on Casey may be found in "Joseph Edward Casey," *BDUSC* (1989 ed.) p. 753; and in William V. Shannon's *The American Irish*, rev. ed. (New York: Macmillan, 1966), pp. 339–42.

34   According to Bernard F. Donahue, *Private Plans and Public Dangers: The Story of FDR's Third Nomination*, Niles "was not a Democrat himself, having headed the

La Follette-Wheeler campaign in Massachusetts in 1924 and the Progressives for Roosevelt in 1936" (p. 112). Donahue's source is a magazine article by Stanley High, "Whose Party Is It?," *Saturday Evening Post*, CCIX (February 6, 1937), pp. 10ff.

35 Shannon, *The American Irish*, p. 341.

36 *Congressional Quarterly*, *Guide to U.S. Elections* (1975 ed.), p. 494.

37 Joe's support for Fitzgerald is recounted in Joe's letter to William Randolph Hearst, September 16, 1942, and reported in his granddaughter's compilation, Smith, ed., *Hostage to Fortune*, p. 547. Less convinced about Joe's willingness to spend money to help Fitzgerald were Jack Kennedy aides Kenny O'Donnell and Dave Powers, in Kenneth P. O'Donnell and David F. Powers with Joe McCarthy, *Johnny, We Hardly Knew Ye* (Boston: Little. Brown, 1970), pp. 55–56.

38 Amanda Smith shares the anti-FDR interpretation of the Casey opposition as does Thomas J. Whalen, *Kennedy versus Lodge: The 1952 Massachusetts Senate Race* (Boston: Northeastern University Press, 2000), p. 10.

39 Kennedy biographer Arthur Schlesinger, Jr. favors this explanation; see his *Robert Kennedy and His Times* (Boston: Houghton Mifflin, 1978), pp. 48–49.

40 "Assails Stimson on Lodge Letter; McCormack Charges Secretary Took 'Pernicious Political Action' in Massachusetts Race," *NYT*, July 28, 1942, p. 9.

41 See David O'Toole, *Outing the Senator: Sex, Spies and Videotape* (privately published, 2005), p. 8. Apparently FDR was aware of Walsh's proclivities; see Thomas Fleming, *The New Dealers' War: F.D.R, and the War within World War II* (New York: Basic Books, 2001), p. 298.

42 Jonathan Daniels, *White House Witness 1942–1945: An Intimate Diary of the Years with F.D.R.* (Garden City, NY: Doubleday, 1975), pp. 104–109.

43 Anonymous, "Ode to the Majority Leader," Niles Papers, Brandeis University.

44 "McCormack Reviled in Anti-Semitic 'Ode,'" *Boston Globe*, November 23, 1943.

45 Jenny Goldstein, "Transcending Boundaries: Boston's Catholics and Jews, 1929–1965," a thesis presented to the Department of History, Brandeis University, Waltham, MA, 2001, p. 17. A defense of Boston by Dorothy G. Wayman, Cardinal O'Connell's biographer, appeared in the liberal Catholic weekly, *America*, "Journalist Refutes Charges of Anti-Semitism Laid to Boston," reprinted in Boston's Catholic newspaper *The Pilot*, October 14, 1944, cited in Goldstein, p. 7n104.

46 Edward S. Shapiro, *A Time for Healing: American Jewry since World War II* (Baltimore: Johns Hopkins University, 1992), p. 7.

47 Daniels, *White House Witness*, p. 138. Casey regularly called Daniels concerning any progress on a major post, but Daniels stalled him.

48 "Our Trojan Horse," a speech by Congressman Frederick Bradley (Rep-Mich.), May 13, 1940, *Congressional Record*, 76th Congress, 3rd Session, pp. 6011–17.

49 Ibid., May 13, 1940, pp. 6018–19.

50 "The Niles Political Machine" remarks by Representative Bradley, March 24, 1943, 78th Congress, 1st Session, p. 2412.

51 "Special Order," Bradley speech, April 1, 1943, *Congressional Record*, 78th Congress, 1st Session, p. 2818.

52 Ibid., p. 2820.

53 Beschloss, *Kennedy and Roosevelt: The Uneasy Alliance*, pp. 252 and 304n.

54 From the Boston Latin archives, "information found in the Boston Latin School Catalog of 1903 (published in the fall of the year): David Kohn Neyhus is listed in Class III (sophomore year), address 43 Compton (no additional details given). Joseph Patrick

Kennedy is listed in Class IV (freshman year), address 165 Webster, East Boston. The total number of students in all six year is listed as 597 . . . but as the two were only one year apart, they may still have known each other" (Communication June 15, 2011).

55   Joe Kennedy was well aware of David's famous classmate Nathaniel Niles (1886–1932) who was an extraordinary athlete, excelling in both figure skating and tennis. Nathaniel Niles competed in three Olympics (1920, 1924, and 1928), won three US Figure Skating championships in singles completion, and five national titles in ice dancing. As a tennis star, he won the US Championship in mixed doubles in 1908 and was the singles runner-up in 1917.

56   FBI file on David K. Niles, 62-64769. This information is from a 1943 memorandum and listed as "Unverified Information."

57   Joseph P. Lash, ed., *From the Diaries of Felix Frankfurter* (New York: W. W. Norton, 1975), pp. 237–38. Frankfurter was reacting to a Joe Kennedy–orchestrated attack on David Niles by Michigan Representative Frederick Bradley.

58   Lash, *From the Diaries of Felix Frankfurter*, p. 238.

59   John Earl Haynes and Harvey Klehr, *VENONA: Decoding Soviet Espionage in America* (New Haven, CT: Yale University Press, 1999), pp. 184–85; and Herbert Romerstein and Eric Breindel, *The VENONA Secrets: Exposing Soviet Espionage and America's Traitors* (Washington, DC: Regnery Publishing, 2000), pp. 180–81.

60   That account appears in Romerstein and Breindel, *The VENONA Secrets*, p. 181. The man was Matthew Silverman and had been arrested with Niles during a labor demonstration in Lawrence, Massachusetts. Representing Niles in court was Lindbergh's isolationist ally U.S. Senator Burton Wheeler.

61   The 1941 Mayoral results, 1941: 125,786 for Tobin; 116,430 votes for Curley. See also Vincent A. Lapomarda, "Maurice Joseph Tobin: The Decline of Bossism in Boston," *New England Quarterly*, XLIII (September 1970), pp. 355–81; and "A New Deal Democrat in Boston," *Essex Institute Historical Collections*, CVIII (April 1972), pp. 135–52.

62   See Eliot's two edited volumes of memoirs, *Public and Personal*, edited by Frank O'Brien (St. Louis, MO: Washington University Press, 1971); and *Recollections of the New Deal: When the People Mattered* (Boston: Northeastern University Press, 1992), edited and with an introduction by John Kenneth Galbraith.

63   *Congressional Quarterly*, *Guide to U.S. Elections* (1975 ed.), p. 787 for 1938, and p. 792 for 1940.

64   "Samuel Atkins Eliot," *BDUSC* (1989 ed.), p. 957.

65   Eliot was one of the members profiled in Richard L. Neuberger, "Progressives in Congress," *Common Sense*, XI (March 1942), pp. 83–86. See Thomas H. Eliot, "In Defense of Congress," *Common Sense*, X (December 10, 1941), pp. 372–73.

66   Selective Service Extension of 1941, approved August 18, 1941 (Public Law 77-213; 55 Stat. 626-628). Both votes occurred on August 12, 1941, 77th Congress, 1st Session, *Congressional Record*, pp. 7073–75.

67   The Eliot quote comes from J. Garry Clifford's February 1983 interview with Eliot, in J. Garry Clifford and Theodore A. Wilson, "Blundering on the Brink, 1941: FDR and the 203–202 Vote Reconsidered," in J. Garry Clifford and Theodore A. Wilson, eds., *Presidents, Diplomats, and Other Mortals: Essays Honoring Robert Ferrell* (Columbia: University of Missouri Press, 2007), pp. 99–115. My thanks to Professor Clifford for providing this essay.

68   Richard A. Hogarty and Garrison Nelson, "Redistricting on Beacon Hill and Political Power on Capitol Hill," *New England Journal of Public Policy*, XVII (Fall/Winter 2001–2002), pp. 91–104. The district shift of the Boston wards may be found in Kenneth

C. Martis, *The Historical Atlas of United States Congressional Districts, 1789–1983* (New York: The Free Press, 1982), pp. 238–39.

69   Beatty, *The Rascal King*, pp. 435–37.

70   Author's interview with the Hon. Thomas H. Eliot in Burlington, Vermont, November 1978. Eliot's defensiveness about his vote may be seen in a *New York Times* op-ed, "Did We Almost Lose the Army," on August 12, 1991, a half century later.

71   See the two overview articles prepared by Floyd M. Riddick, "American Government and Politics: The First Session of the Seventy-Eighth Congress," *APSR*, XXXVIII (April 1944), pp. 301–17; and "American Government and Politics; The Second Session of the Seventy-Eighth Congress," *APSR*, XXXIX (April 1945), pp. 317–36.

72   See Philip J. Briggs, "Congress and Collective Security: The Resolutions of 1943," *World Affairs*, CXXXII (March 1970), pp. 332–44.

73   Smith-Connally Anti-Strike Act, approved June 25, 1943 (Public Law 78-89; 57 Stat. 163-169).

74   *Warsaw Timeline of Events*, www.historyplace.com/worldwar2/timeline/warsaw.htm.

75   See the heart-wrenching tale of the ghetto's leader who was forced into compliance by the Nazis and would later commit suicide in Raul Hilberg, Stanislaw Staron, and Josef Kermisz, eds., *The Warsaw Diary of Adam Czerniakow: Prelude to Doom* (New York: Stein and Day, 1979).

76   *Congressional Record*, 78th Congress, 1st Session, December 17, 1943, p. 10826.

77   Leslie R. Groves, *Now It Can Be Told: The Story of the Manhattan Project* (New York: Harper & Row, 1962), p. 360. Most of this account and the quotes of Groves come from his chapter, "The MED and Congress" (pp. 359–66). See also Hewlett and Anderson, *The New World, 1939/1946: A History of the United States Atomic Energy Commission*, Vol. I, pp. 289–90.

78   Groves, *Now It Can Be Told*, p. 362.

79   John McCormack taped interview, Sam Rayburn Library, Bonham, Texas.

80   Rayburn's biographers provide confusing information on the meeting. Citing no sources, Dorough dates the meeting as fifteen months before the dropping of the bomb in August which would make the meeting in May 1944 and he includes the chair of Appropriations in the meeting and reports the sum requested as $800,000,000 in C. Dwight Dorough, *Mr. Sam* (New York: Random House, 1962), pp. 371–72. Both biographies, the lesser one by Alfred Steinberg, *Sam Rayburn: A Biography* (New York: Hawthorn Books, 1975), p. 212, and the better one by D. B. Hardeman and Donald C. Bacon, confine the meeting to Rayburn, McCormack, Martin, Stimson, Marshall, and Bush and also contend that the sum was $800,000,000 in their *Sam Rayburn: A Biography* (Austin: Texas Monthly Press, 1987), pp. 289–91. Hardeman and Bacon note that a John McCormack interview at the Sam Rayburn Library in Bonham, Texas, indicates that some meetings occurred as early as April 1943.

81   Joe Martin as told to Robert J. Donovan, *My First Fifty Years in Politics* (New York: McGraw-Hill, 1960), pp. 100–101.

82   Harry S. Truman, *Memoirs: Year of Decisions* (Garden City, NY: Doubleday, 1955), p. 10.

83   Ibid., pp. 10–11.

84   Groves, *Now It Can Be Told*, p. 365.

85   *Stimson Diaries*, April 15, 1941, from Reel 6: January 1939 to July 31, 1941, Volumes 29–34, at Yale University and as quoted in Wilson D. Miscamble, *The Most Controversial Decision: Truman, the Atomic Bombs, and the Defeat of Japan* (New York: Cambridge University Press, 2011), p. 22.

86   C. Herschel Schooley, "The Atomic Secret," *Missouri's Cannon in the House* (Marceline, MO: Walsworth Publishing Co., 1977), pp. 65–70.

87   Miscamble, *The Most Controversial Decision*, p. 24.

88   *Stimson Diaries*, March 13, 1944, from Reel 8 as quoted in ibid.

89   This is the assessment of Sean L. Malloy in *Atomic Tragedy: Henry L. Stimson and the Decision to Use the Atomic Bomb Against Japan* (Ithaca, NY: Cornell University Press, 2008), pp. 92–93. Hodgson's *The Colonel* devoted 68 pages to Stimson's decision-making regarding the bomb (pp. 274–332) while Stimson and Bundy give it only 22 pages; Henry L. Stimson and McGeorge Bundy, *On Active Service in Peace and War* (New York: Harper & Bros., 1947), pp. 612–33. Hodgson's account does not include Stimson's disparaging remarks and Truman is not mentioned at all in the Stimson-Bundy chapter.

90   Two Truman biographies indicate that Truman had some inkling about the bomb before Stimson's official briefing on April 12, 1945. See David McCulloch, *Truman* (New York: Simon & Schuster, 1992), pp. 289–90; and Robert Ferrell, *Harry S. Truman: A Life* (Columbia: University of Missouri Press, 1994), pp. 172 and 418, 37n.

91   Soldier Vote Act, approved April 1, 1944 (Public Law 78-277; 58 Stat. 136-149).

92   Servicemen's Readjustment Act of 1944 (GI Bill), approved June 22, 1944 (Public Law 78-346; 58 Stat. 284-301).

93   Surplus Property Act of 1944, approved October 3, 1944 (Public Law 78-457; 58 Stat. 765-784).

94   War Mobilization and Reconversion Act of 1944, approved October 3, 1944 (Public Law 78-458; 58 Stat. 785-792).

95   Thomas L. Storke, "Forced into the Open: Hopkins Protégé Directs 1944 Drive for F.D.," *Washington Daily News*, March 11, 1943, in the Niles Papers, Truman Library and Museum.

96   John O'Donnell, "Capitol Stuff," *Washington Daily News* March 22, 1943, Niles Papers.

97   "1944 Primaries," in *Congressional Quarterly, Presidential Elections, 1789–1992* (Washington, DC: CQ Press, 1995), pp. 166–67.

98   Dr. David Steinberg, "Dr. Lahey's Dilemma," *Boston Globe Sunday Magazine* (May 29, 2011). The original memo appeared in Carey Goldberg's article, "As Promised: Long-Lost Lahey Memo On FDR," *Boston Globe*, April 11, 2011. See also Robert H. Ferrell, *The Dying President: Franklin D. Roosevelt, 1944–45* (Columbia: University of Missouri Press, 1998); and Hugh E. Evans, M.D., *The Hidden Campaign: FDR's Health and the 1944 Election* (Armonk, NY: M.E. Sharpe, 2002).

99   Similar accounts of Rayburn's interest in the vice presidency may be found in biographies of both Wallace and Rayburn. On Rayburn, see Dorough, *Mr. Sam*, pp. 347–55; Steinberg, *Sam Rayburn: A Biography*, pp. 217–20; and Hardeman and Bacon, *Rayburn: A Biography*, pp. 291–301. On Rayburn's potential candidacy from the Wallace camp, see former U.S. Senator John C. Culver (Dem-Iowa) and John Hyde, *American Dreamer: The Life and Times of Henry A. Wallace* (New York: W. W. Norton, 2000), pp. 325 and 341.

100 The best treatment of this challenge to Rayburn is in Anthony Champagne's *Congressman Sam Rayburn* (New Brunswick, NJ: Rutgers University Press, 1984), pp. 104–18.

101 Hardeman and Bacon, *Sam Rayburn*, p. 296.

102 See "McCormack Asks Collaboration," *NYT*, July 10, 1944, p. 16; James A. Hagerty, "Wallace Backers in Chicago Gloomy . . . Brief Platform Sought—McCormack and Mrs. Norton Put It at 500 to 1,000 Words—Foreign Policy Stressed," *NYT*, July 15,

1944, p. 26; and "Foreign-Policy Day Set by Democrats—McCormack Says the Platform Makers Will Devote All of Wednesday to This Issue," *NYT*, July 17, 1944, p. 8.

103   Steinberg, "Frank Hague: I Am the Law," *The Bosses*, pp. 34–35.

104   "Republican Party Platform of 1944," in Kirk H. Porter and Donald B. Johnson, comps., *National Party Platforms, 1840–1968*, 4th ed. (Urbana: University of Illinois Press, 1970), p. 412.

105   "Democratic Party Platform of 1944," in Porter and Johnson, comps., *National Party Platforms, 1840–1968*, p. 404.

106   *Official Proceedings of the 1944 Democratic Convention*, p. 110.

107   "Democratic Party Platform of 1944," in Porter and Johnson, comps., *National Party Platforms, 1840–1968*, p. 404.

108   Donald Bruce Johnson, *The Republican Party and Wendell Willkie* (Urbana: University of Illinois Press, 1960), pp. 300–303. Rosenman's biographer Samuel B. Hand is less convinced of its seriousness in *Consent and Advise: A Political Biography of Samuel I. Rosenman* (New York: Garland, 1979), pp. 181–82. Hand cites an interview with Willkie's son, Philip, as dismissive of the new party contention, *NYT*, April 30, 1952.

109   "1944: Twenty-Ninth Democratic Convention," in Bain and Parris, eds., *Convention Decisions and Voting Records*, 2nd ed., p. 266.

110   Wallace's defiant address is reported in David M. Jordan, *FDR, Dewey, and the Election of 1944* (Bloomington: Indiana University Press, 2011), pp. 168–69.

111   *Official Proceedings of the 1944 Democratic National Nominating Convention*, p. 63.

112   The memoirs of Walter J. Brown, Byrnes's key assistant recounts the two vice presidential opportunities, chapter 6, "1940: Byrnes' First Near Miss for Vice President," and chapter 12, "Byrnes Almost the Vice President Again," in his book, *James F. Byrnes of South Carolina: A Remembrance* (Macon, GA: Mercer University Press, 1992). The highly variegated career of Byrnes is well recounted in David Robertson, *Sly and Able: A Political Biography of James F. Byrnes* (New York: W. W. Norton, 1994). See also his autobiography, *All in One Lifetime* (New York: Harper's, 1958).

113   Robert H. Ferrell, *Choosing Truman: The Democratic Convention of 1944* (Columbia: University of Missouri Press, 1994), pp. 39–45.

114   Edward J. Flynn, *You're the Boss: My Story of a Life in Practical Politics* (New York: Viking, 1947), p. 180.

115   Ibid., p. 181.

116   See "The Almost President," in Bruce Allen Murphy's enjoyable biography, *Wild Bill: The Legend and Life of William O. Douglas* (New York: Random House, 2003), pp. 212–32.

117   On Hannegan's role, see Robert H. Ferrell, *Choosing Truman: The Democratic Convention of 1944* (Columbia: University of Missouri Press, 1994), pp. 55–62.

118   A valuable depiction of Pendergast's Kansas City machine may be found in "Tom Pendergast: Missouri's Compromiser," in Steinberg, *The Bosses*, pp. 307–66.

119   Bain and Parris eds., *Convention Decisions and Voting Records*, p. 267.

120   Congressional Quarterly, "1944 Primaries," in *Presidential Elections, 1789–1992*, pp. 166–67.

121   "1944: The Twenty-Third Republican Convention," in Bain and Parris, 2nd ed., *Convention Decisions and Voting Records*, pp. 262–63.

122   Searls Hank, *The Lost Prince: Young Joe, The Forgotten Kennedy, The Story of the Oldest Brother* (New York: World, 1969), pp. 202–203.

123   See the account of Edward J. Renehan, Jr. in *The Kennedys at War, 1937–1945* (New York: Doubleday, 2002), pp. 300–305.

124   John Hersey, "Survival (A Reporter at Large)," *The New Yorker*, June 17, 1944, pp. 27–38. Amanda Smith recounts that Hersey married an old girlfriend of JFK's in April 1940 in *Hostages to Fortune*, p. 555n.

125   The *Reader's Digest* version of Hersey's story was entitled, "Survival: From a PT Base in the Solomons Comes This Nightmare Epic of the Will-to-Live," *Reader's Digest*, XLV (August 1944), pp. 75–80.

126   The sibling rivalry explanation of Joe Jr.'s fatal bombing mission appears in Ralph G. Martin's *Seeds of Destruction: Joe Kennedy and His Sons* (New York: G.P. Putnam's, 1995), p. 119. It gets its fullest treatment in the family psychobiography by Nancy Gager Clinch, *The Kennedy Neurosis* (New York: Grosset & Dunlap, 1973), pp. 96–97. She is dismissive of the family reputation thesis but does not mention that FDR's son Elliott was in the trailing plane.

127   Krock contended in his *Memoirs: Sixty Years on the Firing Line*, that Joe Jr. wanted to show that the Kennedys were not "yellow" (p. 324). Joe Jr.'s avoidance of appearing cowardly is also shared by Lawrence Leamer in *The Kennedy Men*, pp. 214–15.

128   Jim Bishop, *FDR's Last Year, April 1944–April 1945* (New York: William Morrow, 1974), p. 130. Bishop wrote a tribute to Jocko in his syndicated column, "He was a big guy with plenty of good stories," undated McCormack Family Papers.

129   Bishop, *FDR's Last Year*, p. 130.

130   A useful recapitulation of that campaign is recounted in Harold F. Gosnell, *Champion Campaigner: Franklin D. Roosevelt* (New York: Macmillan, 1952), and pp. 203–12. See also the academic analysis in David M. Jordan, *FDR, Dewey, and the Election of 1944* (Bloomington: Indiana University Press, 2011). David K. Niles is omitted from Jordan's account.

131   Paul F. Boller, Jr., *Presidential Campaigns* (New York: Oxford University Press, 1984), pp. 262–63.

132   The poll was conducted on September 7, 1944, by Dr. George Gallup's Office of Public Opinion Research at Princeton University and Hadley Cantril reported its results to David Niles on September 13, 1944. Middle-income Catholics (28%) dropped from 70% to 59% while lower income Catholics (61%) shifted slightly from 82% to 78%. (Niles Papers at the Truman Library).

133   "Order of Boston Wards Most Heavily Democratic," from Samuel Lubell, *The Future of American Politics*, 3rd rev. ed. (New York: Harper Colophon, 1965), p. 202.

FDR's Death and the Politics
of Postwar America

FDR's November victory over Governor Dewey meant that the old master had another four years to conclude the war and to lead the world into a postwar period of international peace and some semblance of economic stability. That was the hope.

Only six weeks had passed since FDR had won his fourth election and the confident Allies seemed to be moving quickly through France as German forces retreated eastward. But Hitler's manic hubris had only lain in wait. No mere counterattack as the Allies neared the German border, Hitler and his browbeat commanders had no intention of seeing the Nazi dreams of conquest dashed once again in the fields of France and Belgium. Allied forces were caught off-guard once again when in mid-December 1944 the Germans launched their last major counteroffensive, known as "the Battle of the Bulge," as they moved through the Ardennes Forest in an effort to recapture the Belgian port of Antwerp and split apart the Allied forces, Brits in the North from Americans in the South. It was their dramatic last gasp, and it would be the bloodiest battle of World War II. The fighting in the brutal cold and heavy snow was savage, and the losses on both sides were staggering.[1] While the U.S. Department of Defense later reported that American forces suffered 89,500 casualties, including 19,000 killed, 47,500 wounded, and 23,000 missing, the earlier official report by the U.S. Department of the Army listed 108,347 casualties, including 19,246 killed, 62,489 wounded, and 26,612 captured or missing. Those Allied troops captured were moved deep into Germany to serve as laborers and hostages, one of whom would later get PTSD-laced short stories from the horror (J. D. Salinger), another an oft-quoted novel of the Dresden firebombing, Kurt Vonnegut's *Slaughterhouse-Five*.

With the devastating tally of American losses, it was a somber 79th Congress that opened for business on January 3, 1945. It would be months before any major legislation was passed. Sam Rayburn and John McCormack were once again elected Speaker and Majority Floor Leader.[2] No opposition to their choices appeared in the Democratic Caucus and Rayburn's election as Speaker over Republican Joe Martin was the usual pro forma partisan one. As the year began, Congress was not the center of national attention; the wars in Europe and Asia were as American armed forces staggered through fatigue and fury toward their conclusions.

On January 20, 1945, Franklin Delano Roosevelt was sworn in as President of the United States for the fourth time. Unlike his previous inaugurations, FDR was sworn indoors at the White House rather than at the Capitol. It was a telling sign. The war was presented as an explanation. White House and Capitol Hill insiders knew that a public portrait of a president whose energy and intellect was waning would jeopardize the majesty of the presidential office, and perhaps have a negative effect upon both soldiers and civilians. But the impending military victory in the war was at hand, and no one wanted to discuss the fears that were clearly on American minds. The commander-in-chief was failing.

Yalta: With the war in Europe nearing its successful conclusion, "the Big Three" of President Roosevelt, Prime Minister Churchill, and Premier Stalin met in late February for the second and last time in the Crimean port city of Yalta on the shore of the Black Sea. FDR sat between Churchill and Stalin, who deeply distrusted one another. Both knew that without the enormous production of war matériel by American factories, victory would have not been possible. They both owed FDR.[3] FDR, who enjoyed irony, might have appreciated the fact that Churchill seated on his right knew the heavy toll on Britain's resources made it likely that the far-reaching multi-continent colonial empire of the United Kingdom would disintegrate after the war, while Stalin seated on his left knew that the war and the concessions of the Allies had guaranteed that there would be a postwar Soviet empire in most of Eastern Europe.

The weary and ailing FDR knew that the war in Europe was ending for Britain and the USSR. This was not the case for the United States. The Pacific War continued, and the warlords of Imperial Japan sought to halt the American advances by launching suicidal kamikaze attacks on American warships. A weapon vividly described by War Secretary Henry Stimson as "the war winner" was under clandestine development in Tennessee and New Mexico, but there was no guarantee that the weapon would be developed in time to end the Pacific conflict. Believing that an invasion of the Japanese mainland would cost "one million American lives," FDR accepted the promise of military support from the USSR to bring the war in the Pacific to a less costly conclusion.

On March 1, close to the midpoint between FDR's fourth inaugural and the end of his life, FDR spoke to a joint session of Congress about his meeting with the British and the Russians. The day before the meeting, FDR met with John McCormack to discuss his presentation. FDR believed that it might be an embarrassing request, but he wished to deliver the address seated, and asked John for advice.

John was initially shocked by FDR's request, but told the president[4],

> "Why Mr. President, there's nothing to it. We'll have a good sized chair ready and we'll keep the cameras out of the house until you're seated. No one is going to think anything about it. To us, what you have to say is important, and it doesn't matter whether you're standing, sitting, or lying down."

But John told Jim Bishop that he "left the White House feeling that he had been talking to a dead man. All the dynamism, the sparkle, the essence of life itself had left the outer shell of the man. What was left," McCormack said, "was a soft hollow voice, and eyes which seemed larger in the cavernous face."[5]

With Speaker Sam Rayburn out of town on that March day, it was Majority Leader John McCormack who would present FDR to that historic joint session of Congress. FDR opened his speech with an apology: "I hope that you will pardon me for this unusual posture of sitting down during the presentation of what I want to say, but I know that you will realize that it makes it a lot easier for me not to have to carry about ten pounds of steel around on the bottom of my legs; and also because I have just completed a fourteen-thousand-mile trip."[6]

The war had entered the endgame. So too had the president. Presidential aides shared their anxieties by comparing FDR's signatures on their most recent appointment letters. Administrative Assistant Jonathan Daniels was especially concerned when the president's scraggly signature "turned upward strangely showing that Roosevelt could not hold his wrist steady enough to move a pen in a straight line. It was a signature of a sort that marks many individuals who are terminally ill."[7]

A cerebral hemorrhage struck down the 63-year-old Franklin D. Roosevelt on April 12, 1945, less than three months into his fourth term. FDR would not get to see the successful conclusion of either war. Vice President Harry Truman had left his duties presiding over the Senate and was at Speaker Sam Rayburn's Capitol hideaway when the news was delivered.[8] Jim Bishop's version of what followed was[9]

> "Sam Rayburn was pouring drinks. House Parliamentarian Lew Deschler sat on a chair leaning against a wall; a correspondent of *The New York Times*, William S. White, a Texan, sat sipping. James M. Barnes, former Representative from Illinois, stood to shake hands."

Majority Leader John McCormack left the House floor to join them, as was their custom even though Harry now had become vice president. Although John contended in his 1977 oral history that he was in the room when the White House switchboard located Harry, no other accounts support that claim.[10] McCormack apparently arrived after the White House switchboard had called Harry and urged him to come to the White House at once. The fears had become real. FDR was gone.

Harry Truman later reflected on that April day, "I felt like the moon, the stars and all the planets had fallen on me," he told reporters on the afternoon that he was sworn in. One journalist said: "Good luck, Mr. President." Truman said: "I wish you didn't have to call me that."[11]

Later that evening, Sam Rayburn, John McCormack, and other key officials of the House and the administration gathered in the Cabinet Room for President Truman's swearing-in by Chief Justice Harlan Fiske Stone (Figure 11.1). Standing behind Truman were the sad-eyed members of FDR's cabinet, most of who would not serve for long in the Truman Administration. Standing behind Chief Justice Stone were four current House members: House Speaker Sam Rayburn of Texas, Minority Leader Joe Martin of Massachusetts, Democratic Whip Robert Ramspeck of Georgia, and Majority Leader John McCormack of Massachusetts. Standing with them was Fred Vinson of Kentucky, a former House member, then head of War Mobilization and Reconversion. Vinson, who was another of John McCormack's "poker pals," would first be named Secretary

Figure 11.1 Vice President Harry Truman sworn in as president, April 12, 1945, with the Cabinet arrayed on the left and House Leaders on the right (Truman Presidential Library and Museum).

of the Treasury by Harry Truman and later as Chief Justice of the US Supreme Court in 1946 to replace the deceased Stone. Missing from the photograph were any U.S. Senators. As Vice President, Harry Truman presided over the Senate and had served in that chamber for ten years, yet the Senate's omission from the swearing-in speaks volumes as to which of the two chambers of Congress Harry felt a greater affinity for.

Congress said goodbye to FDR on April 14, 1945. Chosen to open Congress' farewell was Majority Leader John McCormack, FDR's House floor general for the last five years of his presidency. FDR's people had helped John gain that post and he rewarded them with steadfast loyalty and legislative success. John's remarks were brief and heartfelt: "President Roosevelt was one of the great men of all time, a builder of human values. He loved the people. He will go down in history as the savior of democracy throughout the world. I have lost a dear friend."[12]

The final weeks of the European Front

As the Allies closed in on victory, both Benito Mussolini and Adolph Hitler would die violently within days of each other. Mussolini and his mistress Clara Petacci were captured by Partisans and shot to death on April 28. Mussolini's body was brought to Milan, where it was hanged by its heels in a public square. Two days later, on April 30,

Hitler, hoping to avoid Mussolini's fate, committed suicide in his Berlin bunker with his longtime mistress and wife of one day Eva Braun and the entire family of propaganda minister Joseph Goebbels. Their bodies were burned, though not beyond recognition. There would be no public display of Hitler's remains, portions of which were recovered by Soviet troops and taken by the KGB to Moscow.

Days later, the war in Europe came to a close on May 8, 1945, with the Allies' declaration of the surrender of the German forces. V-E Day—Victory in Europe—was celebrated in London, but the jubilation was muted in the United States as the nation continued to mourn FDR's passing. The beloved commander-in-chief had been the war's greatest American casualty.

Postwar Planning: Optimism filled the air as plans were formulated for a postwar international economic system. This one would prevent the disastrous financial dislocations of the post–World War I system which had fueled the rise of the dictatorships. In July 1944, over 700 delegates from 44 nations gathered at the Mount Washington Hotel in Bretton Woods, New Hampshire. At the Bretton Woods Conference, tensions between Britain's leading economist John Maynard Keynes and Assistant Secretary of the Treasury Harry Dexter White nearly derailed the meeting, but no agreement could be reached unless the U.S. Congress approved it.[13] This was the task assigned to the 79th Congress that gave final approval to the Bretton Woods Agreements Act on July 31, 1945. Guided through the House by Banking and Currency Chair Brent Spence of Kentucky, the Act provided for U.S. participation in the International Monetary Fund and the International Bank for Reconstruction and Development.[14] To administer the Fund, President Truman named Assistant Secretary White (nee Weit), a Boston-born son of Lithuanian Jews, whose background was similar to that of John's longtime ally David K. Niles. White would later be accused of passing secrets to the Soviets and the White case would bring John McCormack into conflict with another longtime ally, J. Edgar Hoover, director of the Federal Bureau of Investigation.

Ending the war in Asia

While V-E had been achieved; the war in the Pacific raged on. The Japanese Empire had been pushed out of its earlier conquests on the mainland of Asia and back to the islands. With no Hitler and Mussolini to occupy American forces in Europe and the eagerness of the Soviet Union to reap the Pacific spoils of the collapse of Japan's imperialist dreams, the warlords of Japan had entered an endgame of their own.

Reports of daily suicide missions troubled a public deeply fearful that Japan's death struggle would be a bitter and protracted one. The nation turned to new President Harry Truman with silent wishes that the closing months of this horrendous war with Japan would not lead to further loss of American lives.

With hopes high that Japan's surrender was imminent; the Senate debated the Ratification of the United Nations Charter. The Charter provided for membership in the United Nations, which was to consist of six major entities: a General Assembly, a Security Council, an Economic and Social Council, an International Court of Justice, a Trusteeship Council, and a Secretariat.[15] The Charter was concluded on June 26, 1945, and ratified by the Senate on July 28, 1945.

But Japan had yet to surrender. Speaker Sam Rayburn and Majority Leader John McCormack had known for more than a year that a weapon was available and close to completion. It could shorten the Pacific conflict without a mainland invasion. It was the "war winner"—the ultimate weapon of destruction—which they had secretly funded. It was the atomic bomb. Harry Truman knew enough about it not to ask. The question was not if it would be dropped; the question was when.

In the first volume of his memoirs *Year of Decisions*, President Truman contended that he first learned of the bomb's existence from Secretary of War Stimson shortly after he was sworn in: "It was the first bit of information that had come to me about the atomic bomb, but he gave me no details."[16]

Upon reading Truman's account, John McCormack was somewhat incredulous, as evident in his letter to Sam Rayburn of September 25, 1955[17]:

> I assume that you have read the first installment of Harry Truman's memoirs . . . apparently he does not know even now that some of us knew of the Manhattan Project sometime before F.D.R.'s death. As you remember the meeting in your office which "Joe" Martin and I with Henry Stimson, General Marshall and Professor Bush attended?
>
> I shall never forget it.

Sam Rayburn's response to John was even more skeptical[18]:

> When I read what Ex-President Truman said about his knowledge of what was going on with reference to the atomic bomb, it was the most amazing thing that I ever read. . . . If you remember, they said this was the greatest secret of the war and they needed 800 million dollars to carry on the project, and they could not go before a committee of 50 members and tell this story as it would no longer be a secret. The House Committee on Appropriations did give the money. Since the Congress did give the money, and Mr. Truman was Vice-President and sitting in the Cabinet, it becomes more and more amazing to me that he knew nothing about it.

But Truman might not have been dissembling. In a fascinating aside, the official CIA report on the VENONA Project that involved cryptanalysis of Soviet cables contended that "FBI Director [J. Edgar] Hoover allegedly knew nothing of the super-secret Manhattan Project before Steve Nelson had inadvertently informed him in the spring of 1943."

Steve Nelson (nee Stephen Mesarosh) was the Croatian-born longtime Communist Party (CPUSA) official and Spanish Civil War veteran of the antifascist but pro-Communist Abraham Lincoln Battalion (VALB). As described in Cecil Eby's fascinating *Comrades and Commissars: The Lincoln Battalion in the Spanish Civil War*, Nelson's comrade-in-arms was Joe Dallet, who was a martyr in that conflict and[19] through his close association with Joe Dallet's wife, Kitty, Nelson gained access to Kitty's fourth and final husband Robert Oppenheimer, who supported various VALB appeals on the West Coast at a time when Nelson was the major CP representative in the area and was attempting to gather data about the atomic bomb of the Los Alamos project.

Kitty Dallet's husband, J. Robert Oppenheimer, was generally known as the "father of the atomic bomb."[20] The fact that Nelson knew before Hoover supports Clarence Cannon's contention that "spies were in our plants."[21] It appears that J. Edgar Hoover needed a known Communist to tell him about the bomb. Harry Truman needed the secretary of war, who waited until Harry was president before sharing that information three years later.

One possible explanation for Truman's pleading relative ignorance about the atomic bombs, which devastated Hiroshima and Nagasaki, was that by 1955 when his memoir was published, a worldwide revulsion against American use of the bombs had emerged. Truman knew that he was blamed for unleashing the bomb. It may have been a simple case of retrospective ambivalence and national security concerns—or his unwillingness to re-create the context and actors that brought him to the decision he finally made and still felt was correct.

The atomic bombs are dropped

By July 1945 President Truman was certainly well aware of the bomb and its operation and implications when he met with British Prime Minister Winston Churchill and Soviet Premier Josef Stalin at Potsdam to discuss the fate of postwar Europe and a way to end the war with Japan. On July 26, a resolution calling for Japan's surrender was issued at the conference, but the Imperial Japanese government rejected it.

The growing fear among Americans that Japan would fight to the absolute death led President Truman to authorize the first use of atomic weapons against a mostly civilian population. Clarence Cannon, the tightfisted chair of House Appropriations, who authorized funding for the bomb, was similarly convinced that the American casualty figures would be astronomical. As his biographer quoted from a Cannon speech: "'Winston Churchill placed the figures at one million American lives saved, and 250,000 British boys saved, over the other option of direct attack on Japan, by frontal assaults such as those that were so costly at Iwo Jima and Okinawa, with casualties ranging as high as 50 percent of American troops used,' the Chairman told his listeners."[22]

There were only two operational bombs, nicknamed "Little Boy" and "Fat Man." "Little Boy" was dropped on Hiroshima on August 6, 1945, and "Fat Man" was dropped on Nagasaki on August 9. The death toll was staggering in both cities, with estimates ranging from 90,000 to 166,000 in Hiroshima and 60,000 to 80,000 killed in Nagasaki. Radiation effects increased the death tolls in both cities in the years that followed, but at the time it appeared that the bombs' immediate effect had tipped the balance with Japan's decision-makers. Japan accepted unconditional surrender on August 15—less than a week after the second bomb was dropped. While most Americans were jubilant about V-J Day and the ending of the war, others around the world were horrified by the destructive power of the bomb.

In an unusual meeting that would presage future discussions concerning American use of the bomb, Henry Luce, the powerful publisher of *TIME, LIFE,* and *Fortune,* joined with Joe Kennedy to meet with Joe's old beneficiary New York's Francis Cardinal Spellman after the first bomb was dropped. Earlier, Luce, who was born in China, visited the Pacific war zone, became convinced that Japan was on the verge of collapse, and arranged a meeting with Truman. It did not go well.[23] The three told Truman that enough devastation had been wreaked upon Japan and that further bombing should cease. Given Truman's negative attitudes toward this particular trio, and the fact that it was Truman who was ultimately responsible for ordering American forces to invade the Japanese mainland, their advice would go unheeded. The second bomb was dropped.

Highly charged debates continue to this day about the wisdom of dropping the bomb amid much speculation about its being a warning to the Soviet Union to limit its postwar expansionist reach.[24] But the bomb appeared to have ended the war in the Pacific and Americans were pleased as Truman scored an 87% approval rating in the Gallup Poll. That number would remain as the Gallup Poll's highest score for 46 years until President George H. W. Bush scored an 89% approval rating in 1991 following the successful conclusion of the First Gulf War liberating Kuwait.

With V-J Day declared, the United States, the world's sleeping giant, was the most powerful nation on earth, yet its vulnerabilities and insecurities could not be concealed. Harry Truman knew that the postwar euphoria was fleeting and domestic problems would soon overtake the national agenda. Writing to his wife Bess on September 17, 1945, barely a month after V-J Day, he expressed concern[25]:

> It's a lonesome place here today. Had [Labor Secretary Lewis] Schwellenbach over for lunch and heard all the pain in the labor camp. Hope to fix it tomorrow. Should have done it 60 days ago. [Director of War Mobilization and Reconversion John] Snyder is also having his troubles too. But I guess the country will run anyway in spite of all of us. Saw Rayburn, McCormack, Barkley, and McKellar on the state of Congress this morning—it's in a hell of a state according to all four.

In spite of the gloominess of the "big four" congressional leaders, Congress was eager to avoid the postwar ennui that had followed World War I and the rejection of the League of Nations. This time, the Senate committed the nation to the new United Nations. On December 20, 1945, the United Nations Participation Act would become law providing for the appointment of Representatives of the United States in the organs and agencies of the United Nations.[26]

A new House whip, John Sparkman of Northern Alabama

With the opening of the 2nd Session of the 79th Congress in 1946, Speaker Rayburn and Majority Leader McCormack replaced a key member of the leadership team when Majority Whip Robert C. W. Ramspeck left the House to become vice president of the Air Transport Association.[27] Unlike the Republicans who elected their whips, the Democratic leaders appointed theirs. It was a way of controlling the succession system to guarantee that factional feuds would not erupt over open contests for that post.[28] Ramspeck was the first whip named by the Rayburn-McCormack team. He represented the north Georgia district that contained the Atlanta-area counties of DeKalb and Fulton. Ramspeck was replaced by their next choice, 45-year-old fifth-termer John J. Sparkman of north Alabama, whose district abutted Tennessee.[29]

John Sparkman was a racial moderate, having come from the part of northern Alabama that lacked the rich fertile soil that permits cotton to grow and plantations to flourish. People from northern Alabama had socioeconomic conditions similar to those of the Tennessee residents living in Sam Rayburn's native area of the Cumberland Plateau. Farmers in northern Alabama did not have the need for slaves that existed in the more fertile areas of the state. As such, blacks did not play a large role in the economics nor the politics of northern Alabama.[30] In *Southern Politics*, Key pointed out that the politics of race were related to the proportions of blacks within geographical areas.[31] The greater the proportion of blacks within an area, the greater the anxiety of the local whites, and the greater the propensity of the whites to resort to suppression of black aspirations. Conversely, fewer blacks meant less white anxiety and less racial suppression. It was in districts such as these that southern moderates could survive and be elected without resorting to racist rhetoric.

Members from these districts like Oscar W. Underwood of Alabama's Jefferson County, who led the Democrats in both the House and the Senate, could be southerners without being racists. Underwood was the first House Majority Leader under whom Sam Rayburn served and Underwood joined with the forces of Al Smith in an unsuccessful effort to get the Ku Klux Klan condemned by name in the platform of the 1924 Democratic convention. From adjacent Walker County came Speaker Will Bankhead, a man whose father had served with Underwood in the U.S. Senate and like him, a man who had stood firm against the virulent racism of the South. Having served four years as floor leader under Bankhead, Sam Rayburn well knew the political propensities of the men of north Alabama, and he was comfortable knowing that John Sparkman was from Morgan County, one county to the north of Bankhead's residence. As described by Key, "Sparkman like [Jim] Folsom hailed from northern Alabama and expressed generally a progressive point of view."[32] Like his fellow north Alabamians Underwood and the Bankheads, John Sparkman was a southern segregationist but not a rabid racist.

For John McCormack, there was comfort in the arrival in the House leadership of yet another native of the southern Appalachians, for it was in these mountains that the original Scots-Irish settled in the 1750s. Although John spoke often of his friends among the southerners, it was the mountain southerners who were his closest friends and allies—Sam Rayburn of east Tennessee, Fred Vinson of Kentucky, Jere Cooper of Tennessee, Gene Cox of Georgia, Will Bankhead of north Alabama, and Alfred Bulwinkle of western North Carolina. Apart from Cox, none was an active racist. Unbeknownst to these Scots-Irishmen of the southern Appalachians, John McCormack shared their ethnic heritage as the son of a Canadian Scot father and an Irish-descended mother. John McCormack was one of them.

Further linking McCormack to these men was that Boston, of all the nation's largest metropolises, ranked near the bottom of the list with regard to the presence of African Americans residing in the city.[33] As a consequence, McCormack, who was remarkably free of both religious and racial prejudice, was not obligated to become a champion for civil rights legislation because there was little constituency pressure in Boston to push for it. Thus, the relative absence of blacks in their congressional districts enabled the men born in or representing those districts like Boston's McCormack and his protégé Cambridge's Tip O'Neill to join with moderate southerners in bridging the racial divide within the Democratic Party between its southern white, Protestant rural, and native-born wing and its northern, multiethnic, multireligious, and big-city wing.

Shifting the Agenda: The congressional agenda alternated between foreign and domestic policy. Economic dislocations besieged the nation almost immediately following the war greater than those of World War I. Defense industries and army bases had relocated people throughout the land. A nation that always had difficulty maintaining roots become even more rootless. The loss of the great father figure Franklin Roosevelt and the disappearance of a massive defining enemy in the Axis Powers left Americans in postwar anomie and without direction.

The First Session of the 79th Congress moved slowly as the war was too recently concluded for an effective shift of focus to occur.[34] Economic dislocation was the most troubling issue and on October 29, 1945, President Truman sent a letter to John McCormack urging that the Committee on Expenditures of the Executive Department report out with "the utmost urgency" and to pass the Full Employment bill that had already cleared the Senate.[35] With the passage of the Employment Act of 1946, Congress established the President's Council of Economic Advisors and the Joint (Congressional) Economic Committee.[36] The Act declared that it was the policy and responsibility of the federal government to use all practical means to assist industry, agriculture, labor, and state and local governments in promoting maximum employment, production, and purchasing power. In many ways, this act legitimated what the New Deal had accomplished.

"Iron Curtain" speech

Another source of anxiety was provided by an old friend, former British Prime Minister Winston Churchill. On March 5, 1946, barely seven months after V-J Day and the end of the war, and eight months before the midterm election would give control of Congress to the Republicans, Churchill traveled with President Truman to give a speech at tiny Westminster College in Fulton, Missouri. Fulton was a small town a hundred or so miles from Harry Truman's hometown of Independence. Seldom has a speech in a place so small had so large an impact. It was a speech entitled "Sinews of Peace," but its thrust was war-like containing as it did the chilling but prophetic words[37]:

> From Stettin in the Baltic to Trieste in the Adriatic an "iron curtain" has descended across the Continent. Behind that line lie all the capitals of the ancient states of Central and Eastern Europe. Warsaw, Berlin, Prague, Vienna, Budapest, Belgrade, Bucharest and Sofia; all these famous cities and the populations around them lie in what I must call the Soviet sphere.

Although Churchill had been voted out of office in July 1945, his stature among Americans remained high and his warning about the "Iron Curtain" that had descended over Eastern Europe resonated deeply in Congress, especially among the Republicans, few of whom had fully accepted the necessity of FDR's wartime alliance with Stalin's Soviet Union.

The Cold War had begun.

British Loan Act of 1946: Great Britain suffered massive postwar economic troubles and with new Labor Party Prime Minister Clement Attlee in office at 10 Downing Street, the British government requested that Congress provide a loan to float their economy. Three months of negotiations between Britain's John Maynard Keynes and McCormack "poker pal" Secretary of the Treasury Fred Vinson, and another five months of congressional consideration, would ensue before Congress passed the British Loan Act.[38] The Act authorized a loan of $3.75 billion to assist Great Britain in removing trade and currency exchange restrictions hampering postwar programs for economic reconstruction and trade liberalization.[39] It would not be an easy bill to sell. Many Americans had become less favorable to Britain as the Gallup Poll issued on September 28 showed that 30% of those polled indicated that their feelings were "less friendly toward Britain than they were a year ago."[40]

Once again, John McCormack was obliged to support the presumed enemies of his Boston Irish constituents. Working closely with the House Banking and Currency Committee chaired by Kentucky's Brett Spence, the committee favorably reported the joint resolution supporting the loan by a 20 to 5 vote.[41] Once the resolution arrived on the House floor, Spence yielded 30 minutes to John McCormack to make the final argument for its passage. It was a powerful statement linking pro-internationalism with anti-Soviet warnings, clearly a harbinger of the early Cold War rhetoric which would echo through Congress for decades to come. As John stated[42]:

> In other words, to abdicate our necessary role in world affairs—adopt the attitude of economic and political isolationism—the policy of appeasement and thereby leave practically all the other nations of the world, against their will and desires, subject to the influences, gravity and orbit of the Soviet Union . . .

> The Soviet Union of today is more than a government—so far as the force and power of government is concerned, it is a new civilization. As a civilization, it is the opposite of ours, with the state supreme and all-powerful. In addition it is challenging our civilization directly and other civilizations indirectly. It is a dynamic challenge, and can only be met by forward looking action on our part.

John's arguments held sway, and the House passed the British Loan Act on July 13 by a vote of 219–155.[43] The John McCormack of 1941 who had once vigorously pushed for Lend-Lease aid to the Soviet Union had reverted to the anti-Communist John McCormack of the prewar years. John's anti-Communist stance would remain in place for the remaining 24 years of his House career. This was one of the unwavering articles of his political faith.

The British Loan Act provided a window for the House of Representatives to play a major role in shaping foreign policy. The Constitution may have given the Senate the power to ratify treaties and to confirm ambassadors to foreign lands, but the House retained the primary role in allocating money through the appropriations process. As the world's wealthiest country, the United States and its Congress could use its formidable money power to affect the politics of other nations through the granting and denying of foreign aid. Holbert Carroll identified the British loan as well as the funding of the Export-Import Bank and the Bretton Woods Agreement as the Banking committee's "baptism in foreign affairs."[44] With Brent Spence as its senior Democrat from 1943 to 1963, with sixteen of these 20 years serving as its chair, and supported by both Speakers Sam Rayburn and John McCormack, the Banking committee gave the House financial leverage to impact foreign affairs.

Atomic Energy: Also on the agenda of the 79th Congress was the matter of atomic energy. The power of the atomic bomb to alter world history was a lesson not lost on Congress. Less than a year after the two atomic bombs brought the war in Asia to a conclusion, Congress passed the Atomic Energy Act, which transferred control over all aspects of atomic energy development from the War Department to a five-member civilian Atomic Energy Commission appointed by the president to administer research, production, control, and military application.[45] It also authorized a Joint Committee on Atomic Energy to be composed of nine members of the Senate to be appointed by the president of the Senate, and nine members of the House to be appointed by the Speaker of the House, to make continuing studies of the development, use, and control of atomic energy. While John McCormack facilitated the bill's passage through the House, it was not one in which he took personal interest.

Legislative Reorganization Act of 1946

First-time visitors to the imposing marble monument known as the U.S. Capitol are often disappointed when they view all the rows and rows of empty seats in the cavernous chamber of the U.S. House of Representatives. This is particularly true on morning visits, when members are performing their primary functions of writing and debating legislation in the House's vast array of committees and subcommittees. As Woodrow Wilson, the young John Hopkins University graduate student, observed in 1883, "Congress in session is Congress on public exhibition whilst Congress in its committee rooms is Congress at work."[46] Because the House's membership is now four and one-half times larger than the Senate, the House relies on its committees for legislation and not on floor debate. Strict time-limited floor debates prevent House members from engaging in the extensive diatribes that garner publicity for their compatriots in the U.S. Senate. Committees matter in the House, less so in the Senate.

The combination of the executive branch's explosive growth during the Depression and the massive expenditures required to respond to the enormous demands on the nation during World War II made it obvious that the oversight function assigned to the Congress by the Constitution and carried out by its committees was virtually incapable of monitoring the war effort. The existing committee structure with its overlapping jurisdictions and highly fragmented decision-making process was inadequate to deal with an ever-expanding executive branch and a world vastly shrunken by the events of the previous years. A postwar major revision of the congressional committee system was imperative.

Any adjustment to the committee system will create anxiety among members of Congress and this particular one, the Legislative Reorganization Act of 1946, was the most sweeping in congressional history. Seventy years later, most of it remains intact.

The reorganization was guided by Dr. George B. Galloway, the staff director of the Joint Committee on the Organization of Congress in 1946, who contended that "the business of Congress—once relatively limited in scope, small in volume, and simple in nature—has now become almost unlimited in subject matter, enormous in amount, and exceedingly complex in character."[47]

As the war entered its final phases in March 1945, Congress created the Joint Committee on the Organization of Congress to be cochaired by Senator Robert M. La Follette, Jr. (Prog-Wisc.) and Representative A. S. Mike Monroney (Dem-Okla.). With Galloway's scholarly input, the committee wrote the Legislative Reorganization Act of 1946.[48] It called for a substantial reduction in the number of standing committees, the development of more joint committees to expedite House and Senate business, and the expansion of committee staff and the Legislative Reference Service of the Library of Congress. It was arguably the most important and most debated internal legislative statute ever passed.[49]

The Act reduced the number of standing committees from 48 to 19 in the House and from 33 to 15 in the Senate.[50] It provided for the preparation of an annual legislative budget to complement the president's budget, and it raised the salaries of Senators and Representatives from $10,000 to $12,500. It provided for professional committee staffs and strengthened the Legislative Reference Service. It also included a separate title, the Federal Regulation of Lobbying Act, which required lobbyists to register and to report their lobbying expenses.

The Senate had undergone a major revision of its committee system in the 1920s, so the impact of the 1946 Act was less dramatic in the Senate than in the House. However, by shrinking the number of House standing committees to 19, the number of standing committee seats was reduced from 924 to 493. Six committees, four dealing with elections, were abolished outright. The new committee on House Administration took over the elections function as well as the legislative jurisdictions of six other committees. Six committees were also folded into the new committee on Public Lands, presently called the Committee on Natural Resources.

The 79th Congress adjourned on August 2, 1946. With the passage of the Legislative Reorganization Act, the Administrative Procedures Act, the Employment Act, the Hospital Survey and Construction Act (Hill-Burton Act), and the Atomic Energy Act, its second session had been one of the most important congressional sessions of the century.[51] However, there was no guarantee that the Reorganization Act would operate as designed, nor was there any certainty that the Democrats who had held the House since 1931 and the Senate since 1933 would even be in the majority to implement it.

Democratic disarray

Postwar euphoria disappeared rapidly. Returning veterans found jobs difficult to obtain, and consumer demand that had been put on hold erupted in the first year after the war's end. Industries were slow to return to produce consumer items and the few that were available rocketed in price. The Consumer Price Index measuring inflation moved from a stable 2.25% in January 1946 to hit a monumental 18.13% by December.[52] Efforts to maintain wartime price controls had failed, and labor unrest over the overall decline in real wages plagued the White House. As prices moved upward, President Harry Truman's popularity moved downward. With the 1946 congressional elections approaching, Truman's Gallup Poll popularity sunk 54 points to 33% in September 1946.[53] Harry Truman was no FDR, and Americans now feared that the "man from Missouri" was not up to the job. Democratic leaders were deeply apprehensive that their 16-year hold on the House was rapidly coming to a close.

Henry Wallace Exits Stage Left: Internecine war within the Democratic Party erupted as former Vice President Henry A. Wallace chose to challenge Harry Truman. Henry A. Wallace was the quintessential enigma in American political life. He had been an original member of the Roosevelt Cabinet and the major architect of its ambitious and controversial agricultural policy, most notably the unconstitutional Agricultural Adjustment Act. He had been a major lightning rod for conservative critics of the New Deal in Congress. He was surprised and delighted to have been chosen as vice president by FDR at the 1940 Democratic Convention. Although opposed by most of the Democratic organizational leaders, particularly those in Congress, Wallace's liberal followers and Mrs. Roosevelt were pleased by Wallace's selection to replace the always-cantankerous and difficult Cactus Jack Garner in the vice presidential spot. As always, David K. Niles was in on the planning.

Wallace's vice presidency had not been a success, and members of the Senate over which he desultorily presided became more anxious about him as they became more aware of intimations of FDR's mortality. It is doubtful if Wallace knew that his former sponsor, FDR's special assistant David K. Niles, was also working to torpedo his vice presidency. The Wallace vice presidency formally ended on January 20, 1945, with FDR's fourth inaugural and Harry Truman's swearing-in. Six weeks later in March, FDR offered Wallace the post of secretary of commerce as a consolation prize.

Upon FDR's death, less than one month after Henry Wallace was sworn as commerce secretary, he and his associates firmly believed that he should have been the man in the Oval Office, not Harry Truman. His repudiation at the convention eight months earlier stung even more. As an internationalist and a left-leaning intellectual, Wallace was disturbed by what he saw as the increasingly hard-line anti-Soviet stance taken by President Truman and Secretary of State James Byrnes of South Carolina. Wallace's private dismay became increasingly difficult to contain and in September 1946, he went public with his criticism of the Truman-Byrnes foreign policy. An angry President Truman called for Wallace's resignation and it was received.[54] Wallace remained publicly active, editing the opinion weekly the *New Republic* and authoring a bestseller *The Century of the Common Man* in 1948 while planning his return to presidential politics.

The Democratic Repudiation of 1946: The congressional Republicans fed on this combination of economic distress, international anxiety, and Democratic discord as they mounted a successful national strategy to gain control over both chambers of Congress for the first time since the 1928 Hoover election and the 71st Congress. Their strategy worked, and Republicans moved from 191 House seats to 246; and in the Senate, they made a net gain of 12 to hold 51 seats. It was an impressive victory, and as happened to President Wilson's Democrats in the 1918 midterm election, the congressional party of a war-winning president would lose control of Congress. No longer would the FDR mystique deprive the Republicans of their presumed rightful place as the nation's majority party.

At their homes in Bonham, Texas, and Dorchester, Massachusetts, Speaker Sam Rayburn and Majority Leader John McCormack awaited the election results anxiously. When the phone calls from the press arrived, their worst fears were confirmed. Fifty-five House seats had been lost to the Republicans as the GOP picked up seats throughout the three major non-southern regions, with losses especially deep in New York, Pennsylvania, and California. The 80th Congress of both the House and the Senate would be organized by the Republicans. The South remained solid for the congressional Democrats and it would be the South that would hold an overwhelming majority of Democratic seats.

For the first time since 1931, Sam Rayburn and John McCormack would be members of the minority party. For John McCormack, who had spent the entirety of his Massachusetts legislative career as a minority member, this new status was an unfortunate inconvenience but for Sam Rayburn, the loss of the speakership was devastating.

The 1946 election in Massachusetts

Back home in Massachusetts, John was preoccupied with the lieutenant governor primary contest of the Brahmin Democrat Roger Lowell Putnam, a scion of Boston's legendary Lowell family, whose mother was the younger sister of Abbott Lawrence

Lowell, president of Harvard; Percival Lowell, the noted astronomer; and Amy Lowell, the cigar-smoking feminist poet.[55] It was those Lowells who "talked only to the Cabots who talked only to God."[56] Roger Putnam was father-in-law to the son of Jim Fitzgerald, a Boston contractor and John's best friend. In spite of John's best efforts, Putnam lost to former Attorney General Paul Dever who would lose himself to Yankee Republican Arthur Coolidge.[57]

This was the race that Joseph P. Kennedy, Jr. was supposed to run. It was the 1946 lieutenant governor's race that ex-Ambassador Joe Kennedy intended to be the first step in his quest to produce the nation's first Catholic president upon Joe Jr's triumphant return from the war. But Joe Jr. did not return from the war.

It would have to be Jack, the second son, who would be obliged to achieve his father's goal of the first Catholic presidency. Fortunately for Jack, Joe's cousin, Joe Kane, a longtime shrewd Boston operative, convinced the Kennedys that 1946 was a Republican year and that Massachusetts Democrats would lose statewide contests in the postwar repudiation of the party. Joe Kane was right as Harvard-educated Republican Protestants captured the governorship with Pilgrim-descended Robert Bradford; the U.S. Senate seat with Puritan-descended Henry Cabot Lodge, Jr.; and the lieutenant governor's post with Maine-born Yankee Arthur Coolidge, fourth cousin to former President and Massachusetts Governor Calvin Coolidge. The Irish Catholic candidacies of Democratic incumbents Governor Maurice Tobin and U.S. Senator David I. Walsh were lost in the Republican tide as was the lieutenant governor candidacy of Paul A. Dever.

But there was a very winnable race available for Jack who had returned to Boston from his valiant service in the war and fresh from his father's comfortable and sunny Florida redoubt. It was the open seat in the 11th Congressional District after it had been vacated by Boston's "rascal king" James Michael Curley who had been encouraged to leave the seat for the mayoralty of Boston with a reported $100,000 inducement from Joe Kennedy.[58]

It is doubtful if John McCormack knew how much Joe Kennedy paid Jim Curley to leave his House seat open. That the open U.S. House seat was to be contended for by 29-year-old Jack Kennedy who had left Boston at the age of nine with no apprenticeship in the state legislature was an audacious move. John's eyebrows would have been further raised if he knew that there were questions concerning Jack's present residency in the city. Furthermore, John was well aware of Joe Kennedy's fractious relationship with FDR, one that he had tried unsuccessfully to ameliorate. Adding to John's wariness about Kennedy family aspirations was Joe Kennedy's sponsorship of Honey Fitz's 1942 Senate campaign against fellow Democratic Representative Joe Casey. Staying out of this race was the wisest course of action.

With his attention focused on the divisive Putnam-Dever contest for lieutenant governor, John McCormack made no effort to involve himself in the ten-member Democratic congressional primary in the adjacent 11th District. After all, it was a safe Democratic seat and whoever won the primary was its likeliest future House occupant. With John F. Cotter, a Jim Curley–linked candidate, running against the young Kennedy, there was little to be gained by John's involvement. Endorsing one of the ten would have made nine enemies and one likely ingrate. John avoided needless contests. Apart from sending Jack a congratulatory letter in July, there appears to be no formal contact between the two prior to the opening day of the 80th Congress.

The last great Brahmin triumph

Delighted as they were by Bradford's victory over Governor Tobin, Boston's Brahmins were also overjoyed by the successful return of former U.S. Senator Henry Cabot Lodge, Jr. to elective politics after his wartime service ended. Lodge ran against the isolationist incumbent Senator David I. Walsh and rolled up a massive 20-point victory (59.6% to 39.7%) and a 329,000 vote plurality. With the governorship in the safe hands of Pilgrim-descended Robert Bradford and both U.S. Senate seats held by Puritan descendants and Harvard graduates Leverett Saltonstall and Henry Cabot Lodge, it appeared that Boston's Brahmins had at last reasserted their political supremacy and put the Irish, both the lace curtain and shanty varieties, in their appropriate lesser places. Sadly, the unbridled exuberance that comes so easily with victory for ethnics seldom appears among those of Pilgrim and Puritan descent. Their joy was subdued.

While it would appear that Jim Curley's return to City Hall would have dampened their joy, they knew that Boston, the largest Puritan encampment, had been lost to them for more than a generation. Although the Brahmins and the Yankee Republicans conceded the city to the Irish interlopers, their continued control over the Great and General Court atop Beacon Hill enabled them to write legislation limiting the authority of Boston's City Hall occupants.

But Jim Curley would subtly benefit the Brahmins as they would benefit him. Curley's conviction for federal mail fraud earned him an 18-month jail term in the Federal Corrections Institution in Danbury, Connecticut.[59] But he remained mayor. With Curley serving simultaneously as Boston's mayor and as an inmate at the Danbury Federal Penitentiary, Governor Bradford's aides produced the "Curley law." That legislative sleight of hand "provided that Curley would remain as Mayor during his prison tenure; that he would continue to draw his full mayoral salary of $20,000 yearly; and that City Clerk John B. Hynes would serve as 'Temporary Mayor,' until Curley's return after which Hynes would enjoy lifetime service as City Clerk while Curley returned to the mayor's office."[60]

While some saw the gesture as a noble one by Governor Bradford, more cynical observers noted that Curley had absented himself from any endorsement of the 1946 reelection bids of fellow Irish Democrats U.S. Senator David I. Walsh and Governor Maurice Tobin. Those non-endorsements contributed to the Brahmin victories of Cabot Lodge in the Senate contest and Bradford in the gubernatorial one. Eschewing a Tobin endorsement was no surprise, given Curley's two defeats by Tobin in 1937 and 1941, nor was the non-endorsement of Senator Walsh whose conflicts with Curley had been of long standing.[61] Governor Bradford had apparently learned the lesson of prior Republican leader Charles H. Innes that Jim Curley could be useful when the Boston Irish needed to be divided.

Much as the mayoralty of Boston had slipped from the grasp of Boston's Protestants, so too had two of Boston's three seats in the U.S. House. John Fitzgerald's initial 1894 victory for one of the U.S. House seats had created a virtual Irish-American political fiefdom in Congress that was now in its sixth decade. This made Jack Kennedy's move to that contest a smart one. For the next few months, the overly thin and unhealthy-appearing Kennedy campaigned vigorously throughout the district. Jack gave the 1946 Fourth of July speech in Boston's historic Faneuil Hall, flanked on either side by the two original combatants in white linen jackets, his "lace curtain Irish" grandfather John F. Fitzgerald and the longtime chieftain of Boston's "shanty Irish" James Michael Curley. For Honey Fitz, the father of six, Jack was his namesake, the second oldest of his nineteen grandchildren, and the one he had once predicted would be elected president. Jack's candidacy had assured Fitz that his legacy would continue. This would not be the same for Jim Curley who had already buried five of his nine children. Only two would survive him and there were no Curley grandchildren. He was the end of his own family line.

To Boston's hard-eyed political pros, Kennedy's 1946 House victory was a clear harbinger of major contests to come. In December 1947, Clem Norton, a longtime political insider and John Fitzgerald pal, reported that President Truman wondered who would be the strongest man in Massachusetts to run for governor in 1948. Truman asked his assistant David K. Niles for an informed Boston perspective. Niles "replied without the slightest hesitation: 'Congressman John F. Kennedy.'"[62]

The congressional context of 1947

With Democratic President Harry S. Truman in the White House and Republicans in control of both the House and the Senate, divided government had returned to Washington. While it may not have elicited much public attention, the members were well aware that Congress had completely revamped its all-important standing committee system in the Legislative Reorganization Act. Most of this Congress' members had never served during divided government, and none had served in the new congressional arena that the Reorganization had created. Fears that many senior Democrats would be upset about the disappearance of their committee chairmanships through consolidation were rendered moot by the stunning victory of the Republicans in the 1946 elections. All of the Democratic chairs lost their posts through the party shift. This fact eased the transition to the new committee structure. A new congressional era had begun.

Republicans now had the votes to pass conservative legislation. Among the surviving Democrats, two groups stood out: the big-city machine Democrats who remained loyal to the most of the liberal agenda, and the safe district southerners many of whom had been allied with the Republicans since 1938. The White House was in disarray. FDR had been dead for almost two years, and Truman was a clear lame duck who would not survive the next presidential election. At last, the New Deal could be repealed. Jubilant Republicans eagerly awaited the opening of the 80th Congress.

Joe Martin, the Friendly Adversary, and the "Do-Nothing" 80th Congress: The new Speaker of the House was Republican Joseph W. Martin Jr. of North Attleboro from the 14th Massachusetts District tucked along the state's southeastern corner. He was the first Republican Speaker since Nick Longworth's death in 1930. For the eager House Republicans of 1947, the Roosevelt Democratic interregnum was over and the Grand Old Party's hegemony would be restored much as it had persisted for most of the 70 years following 1861 and the outbreak of the Civil War. They could not foresee that their control would be short-lived, and Joe Martin would be the only Republican Speaker between 1947 and 1994. Martin's Republican leadership from 1939 to 1959 would coincide with 20 years of the Democratic leadership of Sam Rayburn and John McCormack.

Known simply as Joe, Martin like Sam Rayburn and John McCormack was a "poor boy that made good." Martin's North Attleboro hometown was a classic New England overgrown village, but nearby were the larger urban ethnic enclaves of Portuguese-descended fishermen in Fall River and New Bedford. Martin's father, Joseph W. Martin Sr., was the son of a Plainfield, New Jersey, farmer who had relocated to Massachusetts to work as a blacksmith. His mother, Catherine Keating Martin, was an Irish immigrant whose ancestry helped him in the peculiar ethnic politics of his district.[63]

Ironically, Joe Martin's ancestry was closer to Ireland than that of John McCormack, neither of whose parents were born in Ireland. Like McCormack, Joe did not go to college. In true Horatio Alger–like fashion, it was Joe the oldest brother, working in his father's blacksmith shop and delivering newspapers, who would sacrifice his own education to provide for that of his younger brothers. Martin's visible role as a newsboy led to his discovery by a "wealthy banker and businessman named Edward R. Price."[64] Following graduation from high school in 1902, Martin became a reporter for the *North Attleboro Leader* and the *Attleboro Sun*. He then joined with others in purchasing the *North Attleboro Evening Chronicle*, became its editor and later the paper's sole proprietor.[65] Like many politicians of his day, Martin never married and long after his father's death, he continued to live at home in North Attleboro with his widowed mother.[66]

Republican Joe Martin and Democrat Sam Rayburn were similarly built, and apart from Martin's full head of dark brown hair and Rayburn's total absence of hair, the two men looked identical from the neck down. They were almost cast as salt and pepper shakers with Rayburn being salt and Martin being pepper. Other aspects of their lives were extraordinarily similar. Rayburn's short-lived marriage to Metze Jones had been long forgotten by the Capitol, and so he like Joe Martin was also assumed to be a bachelor. And like Martin, Rayburn's concerns for his mother's approval were a marked feature of his life. In a 1952 interview with Bela Kornitzer, Rayburn described his mother as "the stronger of the team. . . . She was very energetic and intelligent."[67]

Joe Martin began his political career in the state legislature. He was first elected to the Massachusetts House of Representatives in 1911 and then moved to the State Senate three years later. In 1917, Joe was defeated for reelection and resumed his publishing activities. It was while serving in the State Senate that Martin got to know State Senator Calvin Coolidge from the Connecticut River valley city of Northampton in Western

Massachusetts. Coolidge presided over the Senate chamber in 1914 and 1915 and was elected lieutenant governor from 1916 to 1918. Coolidge became an informal mentor to the young Joe Martin who would be named as the executive secretary of the Massachusetts Republican party in 1922.

As Executive Secretary, Joe Martin got to know the U.S. House Speaker, the Amherst and Harvard Law–educated Frederick Gillett of Springfield and the haughty patrician Senate Majority Leader Henry Cabot Lodge, who resided in the tony peninsula town of Nahant on Boston's upscale North Shore. With both houses of Congress led by men of the Bay State and its former Governor Calvin Coolidge seated as vice president, Massachusetts Republicans had clear command of the national agenda.

Joe was most comfortable with the Vermont Yankee Coolidge and well aware that Coolidge's ascendancy enhanced his own prospects relative to those of the Brahmins like Senator Lodge, who regarded the poor "swamp Yankees" and the "shanty Irish" of John McCormack's South Boston with almost equal disdain.[68] Joe Martin's ancestry and life circumstances were far less Boston Brahmin and more swamp Yankee and akin to those of Rayburn and McCormack, his friendly adversaries across the aisle.

In 1924, following the death of fourteen-term Yankee Representative William Stedman Greene and the decision of Robert M. Leach, Greene's immediate successor to forego life in Washington, Martin became the Republican nominee and easily defeated Democrat Arthur J. B. Cartier.[69] Like John McCormack, Joe Martin would win twenty-one consecutive elections to the U.S. House of Representatives, but unlike McCormack, Martin's career would end in a 1966 renomination defeat.

As Joe Martin began his congressional career in March 1925, Massachusetts Republicans were surrendering their control of the Congress. On November 4, 1924, Speaker Gillett would forsake the contentious House for the Senate. Five days later, on November 9, the legendary six-term U.S. Senator Henry Cabot Lodge, President Teddy Roosevelt's closest ally and President Woodrow Wilson's greatest nemesis, died after serving as Majority Floor Leader for six years.

Shortly after entering the House, Joe Martin received the 11th majority slot on Foreign Affairs, one of only two Republican freshmen on the committee along with Charles A. Eaton of New Jersey, who chaired Foreign Affairs during Martin's speakership. With an ethnically mixed district back home, this was an ideal assignment and he was fortunate to get it. But he did have a friend in the White House. In his second term Joe Martin moved to the House Rules Committee on December 20, 1928, placing him on the Republican leadership ladder.

The Rules Committee was Joe Martin's entrée to House leadership and the Republican with whom Sam Rayburn and John McCormack would most often deal during their leadership careers. Much of this was due to the unique legacy of the House Rules Committee. In 1880, the aggressive protectionist Democratic Speaker Samuel W. Randall of Philadelphia transformed the Rules Committee from a select committee with no continuing status into a five-member standing committee, retaining himself as chair and naming senior members of the Ways and Means and Appropriations Committees to serve with him as the three majority members.[70] The Rules Committee became the Speaker's committee establishing the sequence of bills to be debated on the floor and the conditions of debate relative to time and to amendments. It was Maine Republican Thomas B. Reed who's "Reed's Rules" linked the Rules Committee's power of agenda control with his existing authority over floor recognition and the naming of committee members that led him to earn the title of "Czar Reed," and rival the legendary Henry Clay as the nineteenth century's greatest Speaker of the House.[71]

Those speakership powers remained in place until 1909–10 when Reed's Appropriations Committee ally, the tobacco-chewing spittoon-missing Speaker Joseph G. Cannon's increasingly authoritarian ways led a coalition of Democrats and progressive Republicans to diminish the Speaker's power by removing him as chair of the Rules Committee ending his appointment power over the committees. The revolt diminished the speakership, but it did not diminish the Rules Committee. Although it is the smallest of the House's important committees, its seats have been filled often with members with floor leadership aspirations.

In early December 1928, just two weeks prior to Martin's naming to the Rules Committee, John McCormack entered the House to fill the vacancy of James A. Gallivan. Little did anyone know then how often the lives and House careers of Republican Joe Martin and Democrat John McCormack would be linked for the next 40 years.

When Joe Martin joined Rules, Bertrand Snell of upstate New York was its chair. Snell became minority leader in 1931 and named Joe "his unofficial assistant" in 1933.[72] Joe succeeded Snell as floor leader in 1939. Other leadership contenders on Joe's first Rules Committee included three Democratic colleagues—2nd-ranked Finis Garrett of Tennessee, the incumbent Democratic minority floor leader; 3rd-ranked William B. Bankhead of Alabama; and 4th-ranked John J. O'Connor of New York. After Garrett lost a 1928 Senate primary, rivals Bankhead and O'Connor positioned themselves for leadership contests in the 1930s.

FDR's 1938 failed "purge" of conservative Democrats provided an opening for Joe Martin. He was the leading Republican architect of the "Conservative Coalition," which united House Republicans with the disaffected Democrats. Martin's two key allies, Virginia's Clifton Woodrum and Georgia's Gene "Goober" Cox, whom he saw as the coalition's most talented member,[73] were both well known to John McCormack. Cox was John McCormack's best friend among the segregating southerners, while Woodrum was the man McCormack defeated in the 1940 Majority Leader contest.

In 1939, both Joe Martin and John McCormack gained formal leadership posts. Martin assumed the leadership of the House Minority that year, while John McCormack was elected chair of the Democratic Caucus, the party's fourth-ranking leadership slot. Joe replaced Bertrand Snell, who had suffered through four successive congressional elections (1930–36) in which the Republican Party shrunk from 267 seats in 1929 to 88 in 1937—its lowest proportion of the House since its founding in 1854. With Snell's retirement, Joe Martin easily won the leadership post[74] and was the beneficiary of the Republican Party's electoral comeback in 1938.

Joe Martin was a moderate conservative in his politics and had to weave a very difficult course between the Eastern internationalist wing of the party and the Midwestern isolationist wing.[75] Martin was more "Eastern" than "Midwestern" in his political philosophy. At the 1940 Convention, Joe Martin presided over the six-ballot nomination battle that resulted in Wendell Willkie's "dark horse" upset selection over both Ohio's Senator Robert A. Taft and the winner of that year's Republican primaries, the young New York City District Attorney Thomas E. Dewey.

Named chair of the Republican National Committee during Wendell Willkie's 1940 presidential campaign, Joe was asked by Willkie to head up his presidential bid. As Steve Neal reported, "When Martin took the chairmanship, Willkie said, 'I feel like the Northwest Mounted Police. I got my man.'"[76] Martin endeared himself to hard-core Republicans with his vigorous attacks on President Roosevelt, but FDR got even during his reelection campaign by ridiculing his Republican opponents with a political update of the nursery rhyme, "Winken, Blinken and Nod," by linking Martin's name with those of advertising executive and two-term Representative Bruce Barton (Rep-NY) and longtime isolationist U.S Representative Hamilton Fish (Rep-NY). It was a hit, and the president regularly regaled Democratic audiences with a recitation of all the gloomy predictions of the "firm of Martin, Barton and Fish."[77] While it always drew a derisive cheer from Democratic loyalists, FDR's ridicule solidified Joe Martin's hold on the House Republicans and his prominent place within the "Conservative Coalition."

In the House itself, Joe Martin was close to both Sam Rayburn and John McCormack, and it is likely that the two Democrats threw a victory at Martin every now and then as a way of keeping him on as Republican leader rather than have him replaced by some of the more strident conservative and less reasonable Midwestern House members such as Majority Leader Charles Halleck (Rep-Ind.) or Majority Whip Leslie Arends (Rep-Ill.).

The leadership's committee dilemma

With 431 fewer seats to allocate and the Democrats now in the minority, the ten remaining Democratic members of the House Ways and Means Committee who comprised the "committee on committees" were under serious pressure to accommodate the returning members who had survived the Republican landslide of 1946 and the arriving class of freshmen, many of whom were returning veterans having been battle-tested in the war.

Since the overthrow of Republican House Speaker Joseph G. Cannon, the "tyrant from Illinois," in 1909–10, the power to assign committee seats had been moved to each party's "committee on committees." For the Democrats, the assignment power was lodged in their party's elected members on the Ways and Means Committee.

John McCormack served on the Ways and Means Committee from 1931 to 1941 and had risen to its fourth slot by 1939.[78] Well aware of the importance of committee assignments, John became the committee's top talent scout. With thousands of appointments to House committees allocated in that decade, John had earned the loyalty of multiple Democratic members of the House. Those grateful members ensured his election as Caucus Chair in 1939 and as Majority Floor Leader in September 1940. But by January 1947, he was no longer on Ways and Means and had no confidence that he was to be retained in the House leadership.

For John McCormack and the others in the House leadership, the Legislative Reorganization Act was a mixed blessing. While it increased the efficiency of the Congress relative to the executive branch, the shrinkage in the number of committees cut down substantially on the mobility of members from committee to committee lessening the leadership's opportunity to make friends through the assignment process. Moreover, a more stable committee system would further entrench the committee chairs and make them more intractable than ever.

Joe Martin had waited a quarter-century to become Speaker of the United States' House of Representatives. With the 80th Congress opening on January 3, 1947, he would assume the Speaker's chair for the first time. Little did he know at the time that this would be only one of two Republican Congresses between 1931 and 1995 and that he would be the only Republican Speaker in those years. Joe Martin's time may have come, but not yet that of the House Republicans.

Notes

1 Sources consulted and cited in *Wikipedia* were Patrick Delaforce, *The Battle of the Bulge: Hitler's Final Gamble* (Pearson Higher Education, 2004); Donna Miles, *Battle of the Bulge Remembered 60 Years Later*, United States Department of Defense (December 14, 2004); "Army Battle Casualties and Nonbattle Deaths in World War II," Combined Arms Research Library, Department of the Army, June 25, 1953.

2 "Democrats Name Rayburn Speaker: Anderson of New Mexico Wins Contest for Ways and Means—Martin Minority Leader," *NYT*, January 3, 1945, p. 34.

3 One of the more objective treatments of the Yalta meeting may be found in David M. Kennedy's Pulitzer Prize–winning history, *Freedom from Fear: The American People in Depression and War, 1929–1945* (New York: Oxford University Press, 2005), pp. 799–809.

4 Bishop, *FDR's Last Year, April 1944–April 1945* (New York: William Morrow, 1973), p. 469.

5 Ibid., p. 469.

6 *Congressional Record*, 79th Congress, 1st Session, March 1, 1945, XCI, pp. 1618–22. The quote is on p. 1618.

7 Quoted in Robert H. Ferrell, *The Dying President: Franklin D. Roosevelt, 1944–1945* (Columbia: University of Missouri Press, 1998), p. 98.

8 Robert Donovan's version of that fateful afternoon has only Lewis Deschler, the House Parliamentarian, and James M. Barnes, a White House legislative liaison, in the room with Truman and Rayburn. Others were expected at the close of House business. See Robert J. Donovan, *Conflict and Crisis: The Presidency of Harry S. Truman, 1945–1948* (New York: W. W. Norton, 1977), pp. 3–5. See also President Truman's own recollection in Volume I of his memoirs, *Memoirs by Harry S. Truman, Year of Decisions* (Garden City, NY: Doubleday, 1955), p. 4; and David M. McCullough, *Truman* (New York: Simon & Schuster, 1995), p. 4 and p. 7, for the swearing-in.

9 Bishop, *FDR's Last Year*, p. 596.

10 John W. McCormack Oral History interview with Sheldon Stern, JFK Library, March 30, 1977, p. 36.

11 Harry S. Truman, *Memoirs by Harry S. Truman, Year of Decisions* (Garden City, NY: Doubleday, 1955), p. 19.

12 *Congressional Record*, 79th Congress, 1st Session, Vol. XCI, April 14, 1945, p. 3356.

13 The fullest account may be found in Benn Steil, *The Battle of Bretton Woods: John Maynard Keynes, Harry Dexter White, and the Making of a New World Order* (Princeton: Princeton University Press, 2013).

14 Bretton Woods Agreements Act, approved July 31, 1945 (Public Law 79-171; 59 Stat. 512-517). On Spence's central role, see Richard Hedlund, "Brent Spence and the Bretton Woods Legislation," *Register of the Kentucky Historical Society*, LXXIX (Winter 1981), pp. 40–56.

15 Ratification of the United Nations Charter, concluded June 26, 1945, and ratified by the Senate July 28, 1945 (Public Law 79-264; 59 Stat. 1031). Contemporaneous academic accounts of the UN debate in the Senate may be found in John F. Schmidt, "International Organization and the Senate," *Tennessee Law Review*, XIX (October 1945), pp. 29–39; and on the International Court itself may be found in Lawrence Preuss, "The International Court of Justice, the Senate, and Matters of Domestic Jurisdiction," *American Journal of International Law*, XL (October 1946), pp. 720–36.

16 Truman, *Year of Decisions*, p. 10.

17 Letter from John McCormack to Sam Rayburn, September 25, 1955, from the Sam Rayburn Library, Bonham, Texas.

18 Letter from Sam Rayburn to John McCormack, October 1, 1955, Center for American History, University of Texas, Austin, Texas.

19 On Steve Nelson's career, see Cecil D. Eby, *Comrades and Commissars: The Lincoln Battalion in the Spanish Civil War* (University Park: Pennsylvania State University Press, 2007), pp. 141–42, and the quotation appears on p. 429n.

20 On J. Robert Oppenheimer's life and involvement with the atomic bomb, see Kai Bird and Martin J. Sherwin, *American Prometheus: The Triumph and Tragedy of J. Robert Oppenheimer* (New York: Alfred Knopf, 2005); and James Kunetka, *The General and the Genius: Groves and Oppenheimer—The Unlikely Partnership That Built the Atom Bomb* (Washington, DC: Regnery History, 2015).

21 On Cannon's suspicions, see Schooley, *Missouri's Cannon in the House*, p. 67.

22 Ibid., p. 66.

23 Alan Brinkley, *The Publisher: Henry R. Luce and His American Century* (New York: Alfred A. Knopf, 2010), pp. 320–21.

24 Gar Alperovitz is the leading protagonist of the view that dropping the bomb was not to end the war but to send a strong message to the Soviet Union not to engage in postwar expansionist policies. His argument was first propounded in *Atomic Diplomacy: Hiroshima and Potsdam* (New York: Simon and Schuster, 1965) and reiterated in *The Decision to Use the Atomic Bomb and the Architecture of an American Myth* (New York: Alfred A. Knopf, 1995). The most recent challenges to the Alperovitz thesis come from the essayists in Robert James Maddox's edited volume, *Hiroshima in History: The Myths of Revisionism* (Columbia: University of Missouri Press, 2007).

25 Monte M. Poen, ed., *Letters Home by Harry Truman* (New York: G.P. Putnam's Sons, 19840), pp. 198–99.

26 United Nations Participation Act of 1945, approved December 20, 1945 (Public Law 79-264; Stat. 619-621).

27 "Robert C. Word Ramspeck," in *BDUSC* (1989 ed.), p. 1689.

28 See Garrison Nelson, "Partisan Patterns of House Leadership Change, 1789–1977," *APSR*, LXII (September 1977), pp. 918–39.

29 Ripley, "Party Whip Organizations in the United States House of Representatives," *APSR*, pp. 561–76.

30 See "Alabama: Planters, Populists, 'Big Mules'" in V. O. Key, Jr. with the assistance of Alexander Heard, *Southern Politics in State and Nation* (New York: Alfred A. Knopf, 1950), pp. 36–37. See also Key, *Southern Politics*, pp. 36–57.

31 "Southern Suffrage Restrictions: Bourbon Coup d'Etat," in Key, *Southern Politics*, pp. 533–54.

32 On Sparkman, see Key, *Southern Politics*, pp. 47–48; and Donald S. Strong's essay, "Alabama: Transition and Alienation," in William C. Havard, ed., *The Changing Politics of the South* (Baton Rouge: Louisiana State University Press, 1972), p. 458.

33 Regarding the proportion of blacks in the nation's historic fifteen largest cities, Boston ranked 13th in 1920 (2.2%) ahead of only San Francisco and Milwaukee; 14th in 1950 (5.0%) ahead of Milwaukee; and 13th again in 1970 (16.3%) once again ahead of only Milwaukee and San Francisco; see Melvin G. Holli and Peter d'A. Jones, eds., *Biographical Dictionary of American Mayors, 1820–1980: Big City Mayors* (Westport, CT: Greenwood Press, 1981), p. 440.

34 See Floyd M. Riddick's 1945 overview in "American Government and Politics: The First Session of the Seventy-Ninth Congress," *APSR*, XL (April 1946), pp. 256–71.

35 Letter from Truman to McCormack, October 29, 1945, reprinted in Harry S. Truman, *Memoirs: Volume One, Year of Decisions* (Garden City, NY: Doubleday, 1955), p. 492.

36. Employment Act of 1946 approved February 20, 1946 (Public Law 79-304, 60 Stat. 23-26). See Stephen K. Bailey's widely read case study, *Congress Makes a Law: The Story behind the Employment Act of 1946* (New York: Columbia University Press, 1950).

37 Winston Churchill, "The Sinews of Peace," Westminster College, Fulton, MO, March 5, 1946; reprinted in Robert Rhodes James, ed., *Winston S. Churchill: The Complete Speeches*, Vol. VII, 1943–1949 (New York: Chelsea House, 1974), pp. 7285–93. The quotation is on p. 7290.

38 An early assessment of the loan's intent was published in *Foreign Affairs*, the journal of the Council on Foreign Relations; Judd Polk and Gardner Patterson, "The British Loan," *Foreign Affairs*, XXIV (April 1946), pp. 429–40.

39 British Loan Act, approved July 15, 1946 (Public Law 79-509, 60 Stat. 535). A formal analysis of this Act appears in Richard P. Hedlund, "Congress and the British Loan, 1945–1946," PhD dissertation, University of Kentucky, 1976.

40 AIPO, *The Gallup Poll: Public Opinion, 1935–1971*, Volume I, 1935–48, p. 601.

41 Philip A. Grant, Jr., "President Harry S. Truman and the British Loan Act of 1946," *Presidential Studies Quarterly*, XXV (Summer 1995), pp. 489–96.

42 *Congressional Record*, 79th Congress, 2nd Session, July 12, 1946, pp. 8823–24.

43 Democrats supported the loan 157–22 while most Republicans opposed it 61–122 with Vito Marcantonio (ALP-NY) in favor; Congressional Quarterly, *Congress and the Nation, 1945–1964* (Washington, DC: Congressional Quarterly, 1965), pp. 42a–43a.

44 Holbert N. Carroll, *The House of Representatives and Foreign Affairs*, rev. ed. (Boston: Little, Brown, 1966), pp. 40–42.

45 Atomic Energy Act approved August 1, 1946. (Public Law 79-585, 60 Stat. 755-775). A summary of the legislative maneuvering which led to the passage of this act is contained in Bryon S. Miller, "A Law Is Passed: The Atomic Energy Act of 1946," *University of Chicago Law Review*, XV (Summer 1948), p. 799–821.

46 Woodrow Wilson, *Congressional Government: A Study in American Politics* (originally published in 1885; republished by Meridian Books of New York, 1956), p. 69.

47 George B. Galloway, *Congress at the Crossroads* (New York: Crowell, 1946), p. 49.

48 Two Senators who played an influential role in the Reorganization Act offered their views on the Act's intent; see Robert M. La Follette, Jr., "Congress Wins a Victory Over Congress: The Legislative Reorganization Act of 1946," *NYT Magazine*, August 4, 1946, pp. 11, 45–46; and Estes Kefauver, "Congressional Reorganization: Better Teamwork between the Legislative and Executive Branches of Government is Essential," *Journal of Politics*, IX (February 1947), pp. 96–107.

49 Assessments include John F. Reilly, "Is Congress Outmoded?: A Study of Proposals for Reorganization," *Georgetown Law Journal*, XXXIV (January 1946), pp. 201–19; Malcolm A. Hoffman, "Congress Streamlined," *Federal Bar Association Journal*, VII (July 1946), pp. 378–83; Joseph P. Harris, "The Reorganization of Congress," *Public Administration Review*, VI (Summer 1946), pp. 267–82; Aaron I. Ford, "The Legislative Reorganization Act of 1946," *American Bar Association Journal*, XXXII (November 1946), pp. 741–44; Charles W. Shull, "The Legislative Reorganization Act of 1946," *Temple Law Quarterly*, XX (January 1947), pp. 375–95; and Jack A. Rhodes, "Congressional Committee Reorganization in 1946," *Southwestern Social Science Quarterly*, XXVIII (June 1947), pp. 36–52.

50 Legislative Reorganization Act of 1946, approved August 2, 1946 (Public Law 79-601, Titles I and II: 60 Stat. 812-852).

51 See Floyd M. Riddick, "American Government and Politics: The Second Session of the Seventy-Ninth Congress," *APSR*, XLI (February 1947), pp. 12–27.

52 Consumer Price Index computed by the U.S. Bureau of Labor Statistics, U.S. Department of Labor, and accessed at InflationData.com.

53 Presidential Popularity—Harry S. Truman, "Gallup Opinion Index" (1976), pp. 32–34; and "Presidential Approval: Harry Truman," Roper Center Public Opinion Archives, University of Connecticut, accessed at rcweb@ropercenter.uconn.edu.

54 Wallace's firing from the Cabinet is described in Volume I of President Truman's *Memoirs, Volume One, Year of Decisions* (Garden City, NY: Doubleday, 1955), pp. 555–59.

55 Putnam's life and family history are recounted in his son's book, *A Yankee Image: The Life and Times of Roger Lowell Putnam* (West Kennebunk, ME: Published for the Lowell Observatory by Phoenix Publishers, 1991).

56 Cited in Cleveland Amory, *The Proper Bostonians* (New York: Dutton, 1947), p. 14.

57 Edwin Collins, "McCormack's Wards Give Vote to Dever Over Putnam," *BG*, June 19, 1946.

58 That Jim Curley-Joe Kennedy negotiations occurred, not everyone agrees on the conditions. Jack Beatty contends that Curley "needed somewhere in the neighborhood of $100,000 to make the run. He got it from Joseph P. Kennedy." Jack Beatty, *The Rascal King: The Life and Times of James Michael Curley (1874–1958)* (Reading, MA: Addison-Wesley, 1992), p. 456.

59 See Joseph F. Dinneen's account, "Five Months in Danbury," in *The Purple Shamrock: The Hon. James Michael Curley of Boston* (New York: W.W. Norton, 1949), pp. 299–313.

60 Reinhard H. Luthin, "James M. Curley: The Boston Brahmin-Baiter," in his *American Demagogues Twentieth Century* (Boston: Beacon Press, 1954), p. 41; and Dinneen's *The Purple Shamrock*, pp. 305–306.

61 Walsh's favorite biographer Dorothy G. Wayman recounts a few Curley-Walsh episodes in her book *David I. Walsh: Citizen-Patriot* (Milwaukee: Bruce Publishing, 1952), pp. 60 and 66.

62 "Clem Norton Says," a locally syndicated column in *Everett (Mass.) News-Gazette*, December 21, 1947, p. 1.

63 Joseph W. Martin, Jr., as told to Robert J. Donovan, *My First Fifty Years in Politics* (New York: McGraw-Hill, 1960), p. 21.

64 Martin, *My First Fifty Years in Politics*, pp. 23–25.

65 "Joseph William Martin, Jr." in Donald R. Kennon, ed., *The Speakers of the U.S. House of Representatives: A Bibliography, 1789–1984* (Baltimore, MD: The Johns Hopkins University Press, 1986), pp. 260–61.

66 Martin, *My First Fifty Years in Politics*, pp. 20–21; and James J. Kenneally, *A Compassionate Conservative: A Political Biography of Joseph W. Martin, Jr., Speaker of the U.S. House of Representatives* (Lanham, MD: Lexington Books, 2003), pp. 1–5.

67 Bela Kornitzer, *American Fathers and Sons* (New York: Hermitage House, 1952), p. 213.

68 Martin discusses the senior Lodge's awareness of his diminution in *My First Fifty Years in Politics*, pp. 41–42.

69 Congressional Quarterly, *Guide to U.S. Elections*, 6th ed. (Washington, DC: Congressional Quarterly, Inc., 2010), Vol. 2, p. 1174.

70 In addition to the official history, U.S. House of Representatives, Committee on Rules, *A History of the Committee on Rules, 1st to 97th Congress, 1789–1981*, House Committee Print, 97th Congress, 2nd Session (1983), there are reminiscence of a longtime member, Spark M. Matsunaga (Dem-Hai.) and Ping Chen, *Rulemakers of the House* (Urbana: University of Illinois Press, 1976). Other accounts include James A. Robinson, *The House Rules Committee* (Indianapolis: Bobbs-Merrill, 1963); Ted Siff and Alan Weil, *Ruling Congress: How the House and Senate Rules Govern the Legislative Process* (New York: Grossman, 1975); and Lewis J. Lapham, *Party Leadership and the House Committee on Rules* (New York: Garland, 1988).

71 Reed's location in the pantheon of the House Speakers is attested to as one of four Speakers profiled in Booth Mooney, *Mr. Speaker: Four Men Who Shaped the United States House of Representatives* (Chicago: Follett, 1964); one of nine profiled in Richard B. Cheney and Lynne V. Cheney updated volume, *Kings of the Hill: Power and Personality in the House of Representatives* (New York: Simon & Schuster, 1996); and one of the six with a separate chapter in Roger H. Davidson, Susan Webb Hammond, and Raymond W. Smock, *Masters of the House: Congressional Leadership Over Two Centuries* (Boulder, CO: Westview Press, 1998). Reed's speakership is prominently discussed in the two best books on the office: Mary Parker Follett's classic, *The Speaker of the House of Representatives* (New York: Longmans, Green, 1909); and the equally worthy volume, Ronald M. Peters's *The American Speakership: The Office in Historical Perspective*, 2nd ed. (Baltimore, MD: The Johns Hopkins University Press, 1997).

72 Kenneally, *A Compassionate Conservative*, pp. 17–21; and M. E. Hennessey, "Martin Rates High in G.O.P. Leadership: Reason for Success and Views on Campaign Revealed," *Boston Globe*, September 9, 1935.

73 Martin, *My First Fifty Years in Politics*, p. 84.

74 See ibid., pp. 81–82; and Kenneally, *A Compassionate Conservative*, pp. 32–36.

75 See the thoughtful assessment of Kenneally in *A Compassionate Conservative*, pp. ix–xii.

76 Steve Neal, *Dark Horse: A Biography of Wendell Willkie Wendell Willkie* (Garden City, NY: Doubleday, 1984), p. 124.

77 At a Madison Square Garden rally in October 1940, Roosevelt declared, "Great Britain would never have received an ounce of help from us—if this decision had been left to

Martin, Barton and Fish," in Frank S. Davis's account, "Sabotage Charged: Timidity, Weakness and Short-Sightedness Are Laid to Republicans," NYT, October 29, 1940, p. 12. The origin of the phrase "Martin, Barton and Fish" derived from conversations FDR had with his speechwriters, Judge Samuel I. Rosenman and the playwright Robert E. Sherwood. See William Safire, *Safire's New Political Dictionary: The Definitive Guide to the New Language of Politics* (New York: Random House, 1993), p. 439.

78 On McCormack's service on Ways and Means, see Canon, Nelson, and Stewart, *Committees in the U.S. Congress, 1789–1946*, pp. 937–39.

12

The Unhealed Early Wounds:
McCormack and Kennedy in the House

Setting the Stage: At noon on January 3, 1947, the 80th Congress opened in the dead of winter. Winter is ugly in Washington, DC—no cherry blossoms, no sunny reflections on the Tidal Basin, no soft breezes pushing boats along the Potomac. Its Januaries are cold, damp, and dreary.

On that dreary morning, two men elected from adjacent congressional districts in Boston would have their first formal encounter. The older man, 55-year-old John W. McCormack from the South Boston-Dorchester-Roxbury 12th District, with its nonintegrated enclaves of Irish, Jewish, and black residents, was beginning his 11th House term. A little over 6 feet tall, fit with the slightly stooped posture of a former first baseman, John McCormack was now one of the House's elders. In spite of a lung collapsed in his youth by tuberculosis, John continued to smoke cigars. He wore dark, pin-striped vested suits with starched white shirts and looked out over the House from his rimless glasses. Apart from the cigars, John gave off the appearance of a gray-haired Presbyterian minister, not surprising given his concealed Scots-Irish ancestry.

The handsome younger man, Jack Kennedy, was just 29, but his shock of brown hair and overly thin physique made him appear even younger. Jack Kennedy represented the 11th District, comprised of Boston's Italian North End and its polyglot West End, as well as hard-edged Irish Charlestown, suburban Allston, and parts of Cambridge. Jack was casually late for the opening Democratic Caucus. Unlike the ever-punctual John McCormack who had taken the train from Boston to Washington with his beloved wife of 26 years, Harriet, Jack Kennedy had flown up from his father's comfortable Florida redoubt in Palm Beach.

Although they were born a generation apart, Kennedy and McCormack were men from adjacent congressional districts with similar constituencies and identical party affiliations, religions, and presumed ethnic origins. They should act in concert. However, it was their differential social status and educational attainments that would lead them to clash with one another frequently and bitterly. They embodied that old bromide of Dr. Samuel Johnson: "The Irish are a fair people; they never speak well of one another." With the added contrast of the "lace curtain Irishman" Kennedy's birth in the leafy suburb of Brookline to that of the "shanty Irishman" McCormack's in the tough crowded tenements of South Boston, their conflict becomes more explicable.

That is much of the story but not its entirety. It is a tale that began early in the twentieth century and continued through most of the following six decades, through the foreign policy crises of two world wars, the dawn of the Atomic Age, the Cold War, and two East Asian conflicts; and the domestic policy crises of Prohibition, the stock market Crash, the Great Depression, and the civil rights revolution that attempted to undo the lingering effects of chattel slavery, the original sin of America's founding. It is a tale of the competing ambitions of two proud families united in party and religion, but vastly dissimilar in social class, education, and political ancestry.

A new Congress and a diminished role

For House longtimers like McCormack, the opening day of a new Congress is a time of hearty handshakes and warm embraces shared by the returning members. Gathered with old friends and allies, theirs is a spirit of renewal and hopeful optimism that this Congress will accomplish the positive changes that the previous one failed to do. It is also a time for reflection and sadness, as members ponder the fate of congressional friends and allies whose campaigns failed to return them to office and how lucky they were to escape that fate.

Now open for business, 429 members appeared for the 1947 swearing-in. This was a memorable Congress for a number of reasons. It was the first Congress with House Democrats in the minority since 1931, at the close of the 71st Congress, the midpoint of Herbert Hoover's ill-fated presidency. House Republicans gained 55 seats from the Democrats in the 1946 midterm election and would hold 246 seats to the 188 held by the Democrats—a 58-seat plurality. Democratic congressional casualties were greatest in the non-southern regions of the country. Those losses would come to increase the proportionate influence of Democratic members in the safe seats of the Solid South. The 11 states of the Confederacy provided 103 of the Democratic seats, and joined with 13 others from Kentucky and Oklahoma, the Greater South accounted for 61.7% of the Democrats in the 80th Congress.

This was not a happy homecoming for John McCormack. Since his party no longer controlled the House, John would no longer be its Majority Floor Leader, a post that he held for more than six years and one that he truly cherished. Also, with most of the Democratic survivors of the 1946 rout coming from the states of the South and the Border, there was no certainty that he would even be included in the House leadership. These concerns weighed heavily upon him as he sat in the Democratic Caucus room that morning, impatiently awaiting the arrival of Massachusetts's newest Democratic Representative, John Fitzgerald Kennedy.

The young veterans: Albert, Nixon, and Kennedy

As Sam Rayburn and John McCormack begrudgingly readied themselves for their new roles as members of the House minority, they would greet the new freshman class of 1946.[1] This was a unique one in that it included seventy or so young veterans who had survived the war and intended to alter the politics of the old order. Among the freshmen were three veterans, each of whom would leave a lasting legacy on American politics: Carl Albert, Richard M. Nixon, and John F. Kennedy. No prior or subsequent incoming House class had ever contained within it two future presidents and one future Speaker of the House. Only the 23rd Congress elected in 1832 comes close, with two of its freshmen serving as both the nation's 13th president Millard Fillmore, a Whig from New York, and its 14th president Franklin Pierce, a Democrat from New Hampshire.

The lives and careers of these three freshmen members would intersect with John McCormack's—Carl Albert of Oklahoma, his ally, who would be Majority Leader when McCormack was Speaker; Richard Nixon of California, his adversary, who was president when McCormack concluded his House career; and John F. Kennedy of Massachusetts, his Boston rival, whose successful quest for the White House would provide McCormack with his greatest political difficulties.

Meeting these freshmen on their 1947 arrival in the House was a very ambitious sixth-termer from Texas, Lyndon B. Johnson, who would leave the House shortly for the Senate en route to becoming Senate Majority Leader, Vice President, and President. Johnson's skill at becoming the protégé of powerful senior members like Sam Rayburn and Naval Affairs Committee Chair Carl Vinson of Georgia was one that a House "lifer" like Carl Albert would emulate. Nixon and Kennedy had no intention of remaining in the House for very long, and both eschewed the patient path of protégéship. Each would follow Johnson's path of escape from the House to the Senate in 1950 and 1952 respectively.

The impact of these 80th Congress Representatives cannot be overstated for Kennedy, Johnson, and Nixon would win the presidency four times and hold the White House for 14 consecutive years, 1961–74.[2] They would hold that office during the three great convulsions of the last half of the twentieth century—the Kennedy assassination, the military escalation and American defeat in the Vietnam War, and the pervasive Watergate scandal. However, none of this could have been foretold in January 1947.

Carl Albert: The oldest of the three notable freshmen was 38-year-old U.S. Army Lieutenant Colonel Carl Albert, the winner of a Bronze Star. Albert was elected from Oklahoma's Democratic 3rd District to replace former acting Governor Paul Stewart. Born in a corner of North McAlester, known as Bug Tussle, Albert attended a one-room schoolhouse.[3] His Missouri-born teacher placed the portrait of Missouri's U.S. House Speaker Champ Clark on the wall, inspiring young Carl to aim toward a career in the House that would eventuate in six years as its Speaker. Albert's brilliance as a high school orator led him to win a national championship and acceptance at the University of Oklahoma where his Phi Beta Kappa achievements and another oratorical championship were instrumental in his being named as a Rhodes Scholar and sent to study at Oxford University in England. This was a very talented young man for whom legislative distinction was on the near horizon.

Albert's "Little Dixie" district in Oklahoma's southeastern corner was reliably Democratic, and he would have the easiest time of the three to hold onto his seat, a feat that he accomplished fifteen times as he served from 1947 to 1977. Carl Albert's

Oklahoma district was just across the Red River from Rayburn's Texas 4th District. He understood and appreciated the geographical nature of Rayburn's relationship to him. It was that proximity that placed him on the House's leadership ladder as Democratic Whip in 1955, Majority Leader in 1962, and Speaker in 1971. Albert, the Rayburn protégé, would have his six-year speakership, 1971–77, sandwiched between the two Massachusetts Speakers: John McCormack who held the post for nine years and Thomas P. "Tip" O'Neill, Jr. of Cambridge who would hold it for ten years. These two House protégés, Albert and O'Neill, would extend the House's original Austin-Boston connection of Rayburn and McCormack, adding another 16 years to the 31 previously achieved by their mentors.[4]

Richard Nixon: The most controversial of the three notable freshmen was U.S. Navy Lieutenant Commander Richard M. Nixon, a 33-year-old Republican native of Yorba Linda, California, and a graduate of California's Whittier College and the Duke University Law School. After graduation, Nixon returned to California but moved to Washington in 1942 and was employed for eight months as an attorney in the Office of Price Administration (OPA) within the Office of Emergency Management. He was restless with bureaucratic work, according to one office contemporary, Thomas E. Harris[5]: "Nixon was uncomfortable among the liberals, the Eastern law-school graduates, the Jews he rubbed shoulders with on the job. No one thought of him as a right-winger in those days, but in style if not in politics he was thought of as a conservative. Because he lacked sophistication and big-city graces, he never quite fit in."

Nixon subsequently left Washington to enlist in the U.S. Navy and served on warships in the Pacific but saw minimal combat.[6] Recruited by local Republican businessmen from California's 12th District, Nixon defeated Yale-educated H. Jerry Voorhis, a five-term liberal incumbent, with a solid 56.0% of the 1946 vote.[7]

Voorhis was not a secure incumbent, and only twice in his previous five elections had he received more than 60% of the vote. Following the 1940 Census, California was awarded three more congressional districts, and the 1942 redistricting made the 12th District more competitive and Voorhis more vulnerable. One of the more curious aspects of Voorhis's time in the U.S. House was his four-year service on Martin Dies's Select Committee on Un-American Activities (1939–43). Wishing to spend time on the seven-member special committee with the regular anti-Semitic rants from Dies is perplexing, unless Speaker Rayburn and Leader McCormack hoped to rein it in by putting moderates and liberals like Voorhis and Joe Casey of Massachusetts on the committee. Voorhis even rose on the House floor on February 8, 1943, to declare that[8]:

> as a progressive in my political beliefs, I believe the committee has rendered a great service to the cause of true American progressives by exposing the methods used by Communists to attempt either to dominate, use, or destroy progressive organizations. I believe it has rendered a service to the labor movement by pointing out who the Communists in its ranks are. To a lesser extent the committee has rendered a service to sincere conservatives by pointing out how Nazi and Fascist individuals and philosophies have attempted to infiltrate into, to use, and if possible to dominate conservative organizations.

But the committee's blatant single-minded focus on Communism, a philosophy espoused by our wartime ally the Soviet Union, to the virtual exclusion of investigations of American Fascist and Nazi organizations, with philosophies espoused by America's wartime enemies Italy and Germany, led to Voorhis's 1943 departure from the committee having become "a minority of one."

After the Dies Committee expired in 1944, Mississippi's John Rankin, the House's most vocal racist, outmaneuvered Majority Leader McCormack on a parliamentary motion to make Un-American Activities (HUAC) a standing committee during the 1945 opening of the 79th Congress that enabled it to survive the 1946 committee reorganization.[9] Rankin's most memorable quote of 1946 defended the Ku Klux Klan from a HUAC investigation by contending, "After all, the KKK is an old American institution."[10] In any case, Voorhis's membership on the Un-American Activities Committee did not provide him sufficient cover to protect him from the conservative businessmen who advertised for a Republican candidate to defeat him.

The advertisement produced young lawyer Richard Nixon who rode the anti-Democratic wave into office.[11] Nixon's 1946 victory as an ardent anti-Communist and his HUAC assignment gave him the springboard for his meteoric rise that would propel him into the Senate four years later and the vice presidency two years after that and at the age of 40 to become the second youngest vice president in American history. Only 36-year-old John C. Breckinridge of Kentucky, President Buchanan's vice president, was younger.

No one watched Nixon's rocket-like trajectory up the political ladder from freshman Representative to Vice President in six years with more fascination and envy than the third House freshman, John F. Kennedy.[12] Nixon was a true provincial. He was not photogenic, he did not come from money, he did not marry money, his academic pedigree was pedestrian, he saw no wartime combat, he had yet to write a book, and dating beautiful Hollywood starlets was well out of his league. How Nixon made it so far so soon would be both a fascination and an inspiration for the princely Jack Kennedy with his good looks, quality education, and bottomless family funds.

Jack Kennedy: Twenty-nine-year-old U.S. Navy Lieutenant Commander John F. Kennedy from the 11th Massachusetts District was the youngest of these three freshmen. He would become the best-loved if not the longest serving of the three. A graduate of Choate and Harvard with other academic stints at Princeton, Stanford Business, and the London School of Economics, Kennedy was exceptionally well-educated for a House member. During his service in the Navy, Kennedy's heroic rescue of his PT-109 crew earned him the Navy and Marine Corps Medal as well as the Purple Heart, three Bronze Stars, and a host of other medals. Kennedy was also a published author with a best-selling book *Why England Slept*, explaining why it was that prewar England was unprepared for the outbreak of hostilities in 1939. As the son of the former Ambassador to Great Britain who also happened to be the nation's richest Catholic Democrat, Kennedy's route to the House was not like that of the other freshman, nor was he expected to remain there for very long.

Senator Harry Truman and Joe Kennedy: Unlike the families of Albert and Nixon, the Kennedys had history with Harry Truman, the present occupant of the White

House. Harry Truman and Joe Kennedy were not strangers to one another or to their respective reputations. On June 28, 1935, Harry wrote to his wife Bess that Byron "Pat" Harrison of Mississippi, chair of the powerful Senate Finance Committee, "invited me to a meeting at [Joseph P.] Kennedy's house at seven o'clock this evening. Kennedy runs the Securities Commission and I ought to know him."[13]

The letter to Bess was written just a few months into Harry's first year and it contained a revealing apology that "you have been married to a financial failure and the reason for that is that I have always believed in doing as I'd be done by, and to make money and keep it you must be a pirate or strike an oil well or a gold mine." And if anyone had a Washington reputation as a "pirate" when it came to making and keeping money, it was Joe Kennedy.

One fascinating and possibly apocryphal encounter between the two men occurred during a 1944 campaign visit to Boston by Harry Truman and Democratic National Chair Bob Hannegan, where they were accosted by a deeply embittered Joe Kennedy. Truman's presumed recollection of the encounter reads[14]:

> Old man Kennedy started throwing rocks at Roosevelt, saying he'd caused the war and so on. And then he said, 'Harry, what the hell are you doing campaigning for that crippled son of a bitch that killed my son Joe?
>
> I'd stood it just as long as I could, and I said, "If you say another word about Roosevelt, I'm going to throw you out that window."
>
> And Bob grabbed me by the arm and said, "Come out here. I'm gonna get ten thousand dollars out of the old son of a bitch for the Democratic Party." And he did.

Truman's confrontation with Joe Kennedy seems plausible given Truman's well-publicized remark during Jack Kennedy's 1960 pre-nomination campaign that "it's not the Pope I am afraid of, it's the pop."[15] However, the source of the Ritz-Carlton story was *Plain Speaking*, the best-selling book by journalist Merle Miller, who interviewed Truman for a television program that never aired. Miller's book contained a number of salty Truman quotes that were heatedly challenged by longtime Truman associates and historians.[16]

There are reports that Truman considered naming Joe Kennedy undersecretary of the navy. That nomination went to California businessman Edwin Pauley, but it was withdrawn after an irate Secretary of the Interior Harold Ickes resigned the Cabinet over the nomination. On June 3, 1946, Truman responded to John McCormack's request that Joe Kennedy be named to head up the newly created World Bank[17]: Neither appointment was made. According to the president's Day Calendar, the only public appearance of Joe Kennedy at the Truman White House was on September 29, 1947, with members of the Commission on Organization of the Executive Branch of Government chaired by former President Herbert Hoover.[18]

Buying a Vacancy: Jack Kennedy was initially invited to be the lieutenant governor running mate of Democratic Governor Maurice Tobin. It was the office that Joe Kennedy had originally sought for Joe, Jr.[19] Joe Kennedy's politically astute cousin Joe Kane advised Joe that the lieutenant governor's race would be problematic and there was no guarantee of victory. With data from a *Boston Post* poll, Kane contended that an easier target would be a U.S. House seat and word was out that U.S. Representative Jim Curley was planning his seventh run for mayor. The 11th Congressional District was a solidly Democratic one as it "sprawled across East Boston, the North and West End, and then over the Charles River into Charlestown, Cambridge, and parts of Somerville."[20] It was most of Honey Fitz's old U.S. House district, and it contained not only Fitz's North End, the birthplace of his mother, Rose Fitzgerald; East Boston, the bastion of his grandfather P. J. Kennedy and the birthplace of his father; but also parts of the city of Cambridge where his alma mater of Harvard was located. Even though Jack had not lived in Boston since he was nine, this was an ancestral homecoming.

Economically, the district was poor and primarily populated by the two warring Catholic tribes of Irishmen and Italians. It was presently occupied by Boston's former mayor and Massachusetts Governor James Michael Curley. Jim Curley had fallen on hard financial times and was facing a criminal trial for federal mail fraud. He had just paid off a $42,000 fine he had to the city, and he was strapped. Historically, Curley's major source of funding had come from sweetheart deals from Boston businesses who wished to continue functioning in the city, so he needed to restart his revenue flow by returning to City Hall as mayor in the 1945 contest. He had been victorious in 1913, 1921, and 1929 but had lost his two previous bids in 1937 and 1941 to Maurice Tobin. But Tobin had been elected governor and Curley's prospects improved. He needed money to wage a mayoral campaign and he had something to sell, namely his House seat. The ambassador was an eager buyer.

Jack Beatty's *The Rascal King* contends that Curley "needed somewhere in the neighborhood of $100,000 to make the run. He got it from Joseph P. Kennedy."[21] Using research from Nigel Hamilton's book *JFK: Reckless Youth*, Beatty continues "that sometime in 1944 Joseph Kennedy approached Curley with an offer to fund his inclinations: Kennedy would pay off Curley's debts, finance his campaign, and subsidize the salary of the former police commissioner Joseph Timilty . . . as his campaign manager. All Curley had to do was run for mayor—and resign his congressional seat if he won."[22]

> However, Hamilton's published account suggests a staggered settlement[23]:
> [Joe] Kennedy moved swiftly. Using ex-police commissioner [Joseph] Timilty as his emissary, he secretly sent Curley twelve thousand dollars in cash to pay off his longstanding debt, with the promise of significant campaign money and help if Curley would vacate his seat in congress and try for the mayoralty in the 1945 election. . . . Joe Kane later confessed to the scheme.

It was Jim Curley's seventh run and with 10% of the city claiming they knew Curley personally, it was his fourth and final victory for mayor of Boston.[24] Informally placed in charge of the inaugural festivities was John McCormack's irrepressible brother, Knocko.[25] However, Curley did not officially resign his House seat in spite of his self-serving autobiographical declaration that "I relinquished my seat in Congress early in 1946 and donated my Congressional salary of $10,000 to provide nursing care at

Boston City Hospital for those unable to pay, or for persons in need of specialized treatment."[26] While this was a noble sentiment, it was only financially possible if he hadn't resigned. Curley remained listed in the *Biographical Directory of the United States Congress* as serving through January 3, 1947, and as a member of the House Appropriations Committee through the end of that Congress.

Ultimately, ten eager Democrats aspirants contended for the open seat. Along with Jack Kennedy, there would be serious contenders like Mike Neville of Cambridge, a Tip O'Neill pal and former House minority leader of the Great and General Court; WAC Major Catherine Falvey of Somerville, who received the CIO labor endorsement; City Councilor Joseph Russo of East Boston; and John Cotter of Charlestown, Curley's secretary. Curley ignored Cotter's entreaties for an endorsement, having already made his quiet deal with the Kennedys.

Jack Kennedy loyalists Dave Powers and Kenny O'Donnell contend that Joe Kennedy played no major role in the campaign.[27] But Joe's money did—a $600,000 donation to Boston Archbishop Richard J. Cushing for a Home for Convalescent Children and a $250,000 altar in Joe, Jr.'s memory in Hyannis—photographed with grateful Catholic clerics beaming adoringly at the Kennedy donors, most often Jack and his mother or his best-looking sister Patricia.[28] Also, Joe's old pals at Henry Luce's empire published a favorable profile of Jack in *TIME* in its July 1, 1946, issue.[29] Jack was named chair of the welcoming committee for the massive 30,000-plus Veterans of Foreign Wars Convention in Boston. His media presence dwarfed that of his rivals, and when another unknown Joseph Russo was suspiciously induced to enter the race confusing and splitting the Italian vote for City Councilor Joseph Russo, Kennedy won the ten-person contest going away with 42% of the vote and 10,842 vote plurality over second-place finisher Mike Neville.[30] The November election against Republican Lester W. Bowen was won in an anticlimactic landslide—71.9% to 27.1%. Before the year was out, Jack would be named by the Junior Chamber of Commerce as one of America's "Ten Outstanding Young Men of the Year."[31]

A Dead-End Avoided: Sometimes it is better to be lucky than good. Jack's decision to run for the U.S. House and forego his father's wishes that he run for lieutenant governor was a wise one. That race was crowded. A number of potential candidates had already lined up for that contest, including two losing gubernatorial candidates: former Attorney General Paul A. Dever of Cambridge and Mayor Roger Lowell Putnam of Springfield, as well as John B. Carr of Somerville and Daniel O'Connell of Boston. Furthermore, House Majority Leader John McCormack had already weighed in with support for Putnam. Old-timers remembered that McCormack's support for U.S. Senate candidate Marcus A. Coolidge in 1930 had propelled him to a nomination for the Senate seat that he would win. As W. E. Mullins, the lead *Boston Herald* political columnist pointed out, "McCormack's political stature has grown and so his [*sic*] indorsement cannot be lightly brushed aside."[32]

With no horse in the race for the 11th and unopposed in his own 12th District, John McCormack focused his energies on gaining the lieutenant governor nomination for Roger Lowell Putnam. Roger Putnam was Boston-born, a former Republican and another of McCormack's Harvard-educated Brahmin friends. Putnam's daughter was married to the son of Boston contractor James Fitzgerald, McCormack's longtime best friend and John's companion on the fateful day in 1926 when they encountered the unconscious and drunk Congressman Jim "Chalk face" Gallivan on the floor of the men's room at the Boston Athletic Club.

Both Dever and Putnam had previously lost to the ultimate Brahmin Governor Leverett Saltonstall in 1940 and 1942 respectively. Each sought to use the lieutenant governor's race as their comeback. Dever's easy primary victory ended Putnam's career but it was a hollow one as he was defeated in the general election by Arthur W. Coolidge, a fourth cousin of President Calvin Coolidge. Governor Maurice Tobin lost to the ne plus ultra Brahmin Robert Bradford, a descendant of William Bradford, the second Pilgrim governor of Plymouth Plantation and a signer of the Mayflower Compact. Bradford's overwhelming victory by 148,409 votes (54.1% to 45.3%) over Tobin would not have been overcome by any amount of millions spent by Joe Kennedy. The all-Irish Walsh-Tobin-Dever Democratic ticket with its mix of BU and BC graduates was handily defeated by the all-WASP Harvard-educated triumvirate of Lodge-Bradford-Coolidge Republicans. Had Jack run in that race, his political career might have ended quickly and there would be no Kennedy legend to recount.

The initial encounter

The 80th Congress first placed Dick Nixon and Jack Kennedy on the national political stage.[33] Nixon and Kennedy were not the only ones among the group of able freshmen who had served in the war and had been newly elected. While Kennedy's wartime record had been feted, there were fellow young Democratic veterans whose service was as exemplary if not more so. Among them would be the 36-year-old Slovene-descended John Blatnik of Minnesota, an Army Air Corps officer who worked for the Office of Strategic Services behind enemy lines to mobilize Tito's Yugoslav partisans against the Nazis; the 34-year-old Robert Jones of Alabama, who had served as a U.S. Navy gunnery officer in both the Atlantic and Pacific oceans; the 33-year-old Marine Corps Major George A. Smathers of Florida, who would become Jack's closest congressional friend; and 38-year-old Carl Albert, whose wartime service in the Pacific earned him a Bronze Star as he moved rapidly up the ranks from private to lieutenant colonel. These were men unlikely to be intimidated by the ancient barons of the House, but they soon learned the painful lesson that the barons expected deference from the junior members, and insufficient respect would get one consigned to the dismal committees that would be fatal to your reelection bids.

But Jack Kennedy was a war hero with a major difference. His wartime exploits in the Pacific as a patrol boat commander had been published in two of the nation's leading magazines—*The New Yorker* and the *Reader's Digest*, the most read monthly magazine. It was the laudatory, lengthy article written by his friend and former *TIME* magazine reporter John Hersey for the *New Yorker*, entitled "Survival" and published in the June 17, 1944, issue,[34] that elevated Jack to preeminence among the many young heroes of the war.

Representatives John Blatnik, Bob Jones, and Carl Albert made careers of the House, with both Blatnik and Jones serving as chairs of the Public Works Committee while Carl Albert would become a protégé of the legendary House Speaker Sam Rayburn of Texas and eventually serve in the leadership for 22 years, moving from Democratic Whip in 1955 to Speaker of the House in 1971.

Senate Aspirations: The three most ambitious members of this class were Dick Nixon, George Smathers, and Jack Kennedy. None saw a future in the House, and each ran for the Senate as soon as they could with Nixon winning his California seat over Democratic Representative Helen Gahagan Douglas and Smathers winning his Florida nomination over incumbent fellow Democrat Claude Pepper in 1950. Neither Massachusetts Senate seat was up for grabs in 1950, so Kennedy had to wait two years to make his bid in 1952. When urged to remain in the House by his old Harvard Government Professor Sam Beer so that he could emulate the path of Henry Clay of Kentucky, the House's first great Speaker, Jack was direct and emphatic: "I no longer wish to be bored by John McCormack."[35] Asked by fellow Harvardman and combat veteran James MacGregor Burns to describe his House experience, Jack replied[36]:

> We were just worms over in the House—nobody pays much attention to us nationally. And I had come back from the service not as a Democratic wheelhorse who came up through the ranks—I came in sort of sideways. It was never drilled into me that I was responsible to some political boss in the Eleventh District. I can go it the hard way against the politically active people.

Early Tension: The McCormack-Kennedy enmity was mutual, but it was also consequential. Fourteen years after Jack Kennedy joined the House, he would be sworn in on January 20, 1961, as the nation's first Roman Catholic president, and a year after that, John McCormack would be chosen as the nation's first Roman Catholic Speaker of the U.S. House of Representatives. But on this 1947 morning, that was a future scenario that neither man could have foretold.

For the 55-year-old 11-termer John McCormack, rumors abounded of his imminent displacement as a party leader.[37] For the 29-year-old freshman Jack Kennedy who had never held elective office before, there was uncertainty about his committee assignments. While John McCormack had a long-standing friendship with Jack's grandfather John Fitzgerald and a lesser one with Jack's father, Ambassador Joseph P. Kennedy, his knowledge of Jack was limited.

Washington Arrivals: As was their custom, John and Harriet McCormack arrived in Washington early to resume their settled life in suite 820, their three-room suite in the Hotel Washington where they would live modestly for the entirety of John's 42 years in the House. In 1928, at the start of his House career, John and Harriet brought their furnishings, including a Persian rug, down from Boston and the room remained unchanged for the four-plus decades of their time there.[38]

Washington was a city well known to both of Jack Kennedy's families—the Fitzgeralds and the Kennedys. Jack's grandfather and namesake John F. "Honey Fitz" Fitzgerald had served in the U.S. House for six years, 1895–1901, before returning to

Boston to begin his quest for mayor of the city.[39] Jack's father, Joe, had been the initial chair of the Wall Street-regulating Securities and Exchange Commission in 1934–35 and later headed the U.S. Maritime Commission, 1936–38, before President Franklin D. Roosevelt named him Ambassador to the Court of St. James in London in 1938.[40] Three of Joe's children worked in Washington during the 1940s.[41] Jack, Harvard-graduated and newly commissioned, had served as an assistant in the office of Secretary of the Navy James Forrestal early in the war. Kathleen "Kick," Joe's vivacious second daughter, had worked for Cissy Patterson's conservative newspaper the *Washington Times Herald* prior to her departure for England to resume her romance with William Cavendish, the Marquess of Hartington, in 1943. Eunice, Joe's brainy third daughter, had served as the "dollar-a-year" executive secretary on Attorney General Tom Clark's National Conference on the Prevention of Juvenile Delinquency.[42]

Jack's first Washington stint in Navy Secretary Forrestal's office ended with a romantic entanglement with Kick's twice-divorced Danish blonde roommate Inga Arvad. With the FBI believing her to be a Nazi agent, Jack was quietly removed from the Navy Department and reassigned to a PT boat in the treacherous Pacific.[43] Jack survived and had returned from his near-fatal combat service as a wounded and decorated hero. His wartime exploits and his father's wealth had enabled the 29-year-old Jack Kennedy, a man with no prior elective service, to easily win a seat in the U.S. House. But returning to Washington was not a major life event for Jack. It was a city that had never impressed him. To Jack, Washington was a city of "northern charm and southern efficiency"—his oft-quoted sardonic dismissal of the nation's capital.

Since Kennedy knew Washington well, he chose not to arrive early after his 1946 election to set up his Washington apartment or his Capitol Hill office. Others were paid to do that so he could remain in Palm Beach as long as possible, relaxing and working on his Florida tan. Unlike most of the House newcomers, Jack did not move into a tiny cramped apartment near the Capitol. With financial support from his wealthy father, Jack and his sister Eunice, who was still employed by the Justice Department, were housed in a luxurious home once occupied by the Polish military attaché Austrian-born Prince Alexander Hohenlohe. It was a four-story townhouse replete with a baby grand piano, a mahogany-furnished dining room, a paneled library, and servants' quarters in the city's elegant Georgetown neighborhood miles away from the Capitol.[44]

Jack arrived on the morning of January 3 with a well-developed sense of entitlement. As recounted by Billy Sutton, his first key congressional aide, Jack arrived from Florida late for the Democratic Caucus. He walked into Washington's Statler Hotel "gleaming with his Florida tan, hair tousled, carrying a black cashmere overcoat and wearing a gray suit and a pair of brogues elegantly stretched by shoe trees."[45] Sutton told him that the committee assignments had already been made and that "you've got two pretty good committees: Labor and Education, District of Columbia." But there was a Democratic Caucus meeting that morning, and Joe Feeney from Democratic leader John McCormack's office, and the "unquestioned head of the Massachusetts delegation, had been calling for him all morning." Kennedy appeared unconcerned and settled in for some soft-boiled eggs and tea.

In Sutton's recollection,[46]

> "I said 'Mr. McCormack is quite anxious that you get up there.'"
> "[Jack] said: 'How long would you say Mr. McCormack was here?'"
> "I said 'Well evidently, I think as far as I know, he's been down here in
>   Washington, at least twenty-six years.'"
> "And he's eating his eggs, and he said to me. 'Well, I don't think Mr. McCormack
>   would mind waiting another ten minutes.'"

Had Sutton been correct, the 29-year-old Jack Kennedy would have been three years old at the time of John McCormack's entry in the House, but Sutton's guess was high by eight years. Jack was eleven when McCormack entered Congress in 1928.

Being stood up by a freshman Democrat in the Massachusetts delegation would not have impressed John McCormack, who had long ago learned the politics of congressional deference from the hard-nosed former Democratic Speaker John Nance "Cactus Jack" Garner of Texas. John McCormack would have minded and apparently did. But John McCormack had a greater concern on his mind, namely, his own place in the House Democratic hierarchy.

The January 3, 1947, meeting was their initial unpleasant encounter. It would not be their last and while both of their national careers originated in the U.S. House, their careers then diverged; until, that is, when Jack was president and John became Speaker of the House.

Who will be the minority leader?

With Republicans now controlling the House, Sam Rayburn of Texas, who had been House Speaker since September 1940, was slated to become Minority Floor Leader. It was a post he had never held and one that required debating skills and coalition building on the floor among the dispirited Democrats. Rayburn's natural shyness and reluctance to "glad hand" fellow politicians made this an unattractive post for him to hold. It was a clearly disappointed Rayburn who declared on November 6 that "I will not be minority leader. I don't desire to hold that post."[47]

Sam wired John McCormack of his intention to pass on the job of minority leader and offered his support to John, who was generally regarded as the Democrats' best partisan debater. When McCormack related this to John Sparkman of Alabama, whom Rayburn had appointed majority whip in 1946, he found that southern Democrats opposed him and that northern Democrats would not accept any southerner except Rayburn. Rayburn continued to resist in a November 21st statement,[48] and publicly urged the House Democrats to name McCormack to the post.[49] As the year came to an end, Rayburn remained adamant while conservative southern opposition to McCormack solidified.[50]

When J. Percy Priest of Tennessee was quoted in a newspaper saying that the party without Rayburn would "be torn apart internally,"[51] Rayburn replied that "I can be of more service to the country and the party by being free of the minority leadership, and taking the Floor when I feel it necessary on the larger issues. I feel this very deeply."[52] Rayburn encouraged Priest to support McCormack for Democratic floor leader, writing, "I think John McCormack should be elected and I hope you and others of my friends from the South will go along with me in this."[53] Similarly, Rayburn wrote to North Carolina's John H. Kerr, "I agree with you that it would be a mistake to attempt to defeat McCormack simply because he is a northerner as we cannot allow our party to be a sectional party. If we ever come into power again, we must have a great many northern votes."[54]

With just days to go before the opening of the 80th Congress, John Sparkman, who would lose his post as majority whip, pressured Rayburn to take on the minority leadership and President Truman, appalled at the thought that Rayburn might not be his right hand in Congress, also lobbied Rayburn.[55] According to Rayburn biographers D. B. Hardeman and Donald C. Bacon, "Truman weighed in . . . arguing that McCormack could not win and that Rayburn's refusal to serve would allow a reactionary southerner to step into a House leadership vacuum."[56] Indeed, the southerners led by John's longtime foe, the fiery reactionary John Rankin of Mississippi, continued in their efforts to stop McCormack's rise to leadership.[57] In an effort to induce Rayburn to accept a draft, some of the southerners floated the name of conservative fellow Texan Ewing Thomason of El Paso as leader. Even with Democratic losses in the north shifting the balance of power to the South and the overall ideology of the House Democratic Party to the right, Thomason was too conservative to lead the Democrats of the 80th Congress. Rayburn finally relented and agreed to be the minority Democrats' candidate for Speaker on January 3, thereby making him the Minority Leader.

While John McCormack's staff impatiently awaited the arrival of young Jack Kennedy at the opening caucus on January 3, it was John who nominated Rayburn as the party's candidate for Speaker. Four days later on January 7, Rayburn "prevailed upon my old friend and co-worker" McCormack "to accept the place of whip." Rayburn said that since "the majority passed to the other side and my colleagues on this side have imposed upon me the duty of the leadership, I am proud that I will have him as my consultant and co-worker in the leadership of the minority."[58]

Rayburn's reluctant acquiescence to the draft effort kept McCormack on the leadership ladder. Had Rayburn not accepted the minority leadership, McCormack would have had to compete against a southerner and would likely have lost. Had he lost, any claim to any party leadership position in the future would have disappeared. Rayburn's acceptance of the floor leader post preserved McCormack's career in the House leadership. As C. Dwight Dorough, Rayburn's early biographer, contended, Mr. Sam came to understand that "he had become, during his thirty-four years, a symbol of leadership for his Party in Congress, and as long as he was a member of the House of Representatives . . . he could not walk away from responsibility."[59] It was symbolic of Rayburn's role as a bridge between North and South that John McCormack nominated Rayburn for Speaker in the Caucus, and conservative racists Eugene Cox of Georgia and John Rankin of Mississippi made his seconding speeches.[60]

Southern Alliances: This was a wake-up call to John McCormack that he needed to have even better relationships with the South if he were ever to succeed Rayburn as Speaker. During the 1930s, McCormack had forged ties with many southerners allied with Speaker John Nance Garner of Texas. John had previously backed Garner's pal John McDuffie of Alabama for Speaker over Henry Rainey of Illinois and Will Bankhead of Alabama over Joseph Byrns of Tennessee for majority leader in 1933; and Bankhead for majority leader over John O'Connor of New York, a fellow Massachusetts-born Irish Catholic in 1935. It was McCormack's backing of Rayburn in the 1937 contest for majority leader over O'Connor that made the difference.[61] And in 1940 when McCormack ran for majority leader, he received strong southern support led by Eugene "Goober" Cox, a Georgia segregationist who placed McCormack's name in nomination. John attributed his victory to his southern friends contending that he won because "I had a lot of friends in the South. You needed sixty to seventy votes from the South to win."[62] While most southerners would accept John as the second-ranking Democrat, naming him to the top post was unacceptable. He was too urban, too northern, and too Catholic for their tastes.

John McCormack was undoubtedly humbled as he waited anxiously for four days to be named as Democratic whip. That anxiety could well have contributed to his irritation with the way that young Kennedy had treated him so cavalierly on the opening day of the Congress. Another potential indignity awaited McCormack as the standing committee assignments were formalized.

Committee seatmates, Jack Kennedy and Dick Nixon

Given the fact that the number of committees had been more than halved by the Legislative Reorganization Act of the previous year and that the Democrats were now in the minority for the first time in 16 years, Jack Kennedy's assignments were not bad. Of the 29 Democratic freshmen, Kennedy was one of only three to receive two assignments while the others received only one. Kennedy's first committee was Education and Labor, chaired by ten-term West Virginia Republican Fred Hartley. Hartley spent most of the 80th Congress writing the labor-limiting Taft-Hartley Labor Management Relations Act with Senate Republican powerhouse Robert Taft of Ohio. Hartley delivered the House version, and Jack Kennedy watched how well-motivated ideological Republicans can move legislation when they have the votes. Hartley's Senate partner Robert A. Taft, who had already lost one nomination battle for president (1940) and would go on to lose again twice (1948 and 1952), saw the labor-limiting legislation as his key signature policy initiative. It was intended to limit the reach of the 1935 Wagner-Connery National Labor Relations Act that had been described as the "Magna Carta of organized labor." Taft-Hartley outlawed the closed shop, jurisdictional strikes, and secondary boycotts, and provided for a 60-day moratorium on strikes called against industries engaged in interstate commerce.[63] President Truman vetoed the bill but it became an act when Congress overrode his veto.

The Education and Labor Committee would also be the battleground for federal funding of buses for parochial schoolchildren. As a Catholic with a huge parochial school population back in his Boston district, Kennedy was very sensitive to this issue as well, one that would end up before the Supreme Court.

Hartley was joined on the committee by a number of other conservatives, Clare Hoffman of Michigan and Democrats Graham Barden of North Carolina, and the rabid anti-Communist John S. Wood of Georgia who later chaired the Un-American Activities Committee. Jack Kennedy was one of the ten first-timers on the committee along with freshman Republican Richard M. Nixon, who had gained national attention by upsetting the well-known liberal U.S. Representative Jerry Voorhis.[64] This was the fellow committee member that most fascinated Kennedy.

In the initial Kennedy-Nixon encounter at the Washington Press Club on Fourteenth Street, Billy Sutton recounted in his oral history thus[65]:

> SUTTON: "There was this fellow over in the corner, a young fellow, very dapper dressed, from California, and he seemed to be the star of the show. [Jack] at that time was very—he was sort of taking things easy, and we pointed out that was Richard Nixon and McCormack. And then [Kennedy assistant Ted] Reardon . . . brought Mr. Nixon over and introduced him to [Jack]."
> HYNES: "This was the first time that they had met?"
> SUTTON: "Yes, and I was in the room that day. Jack was all aglow, you know. He was the man who had defeated Jerry Voorhis, I think which was just like you or I or Benny [Jacobson] here defeating John McCormack in Boston. It was a big thing to do and he did it, and [Jack] was quite elated over it, the surprise victory."

Chris Matthews's version in *Kennedy and Nixon* differs with Kennedy saying: "So you're the guy that beat Jerry Voorhis!" he said moving toward his new classmate, "That's like beating McCormack up in Massachusetts! How's it feel?" Nixon's response was typically awkward, "I suppose I'm elated!"[66]

Kennedy's second assignment was to the District of Columbia Committee; a committee then chaired by Illinois Republican Everett McKinley Dirksen who would leave the House in 1949 but return to Washington two years later as a newly elected U.S. Senator and would battle with the Democrats as Senate Minority Leader from 1959 to 1969. The District Committee had little to do but be the city council of the nation's capital. It was invariably filled with segregating southern Democrats who enjoyed ruling over the sizable black population as their own public plantation and with freshmen who were assigned there to learn the norms of congressional deference, summarized most succinctly in Sam Rayburn's phrase, "To get along, you have to go along." Once the norms were appropriately learned, more promising committee slots were found.

However, John Kennedy was the only Massachusetts Democrat assigned to the District Committee in the 86 years between John Keliher's one-year stint in 1908–1909 and the long overdue abolition of the committee in 1995. Jack Kennedy's initial brush-off of John McCormack in 1947 was not the cause of his being assigned to the District Committee. Kennedy's subsequent four years on it, however, were another matter. John McCormack knew that Joe Kennedy had paid Jim Curley to leave the seat open for his second son's political ascent and as the House's premier talent scout he did not see in young Kennedy the makings of a career House member. Young Kennedy would be gone soon and so McCormack saw no need to waste valuable seniority on him.

Nixon's second assignment was to the headline-hunting House Un-American Activities Committee. Known as HUAC, that committee generated more sensational news than any nine-member congressional committee had ever done in the two centuries of congressional history. In 1948, his second year on HUAC, Nixon would meet former Communist Whittaker Chambers whose credible accusations against high-ranking State Department official Alger Hiss placed Nixon on the national map and served as his launch pad to the Senate and beyond.[67]

More typical of the fate that awaited minority freshman was that of 1947's other Massachusetts Democrat, Harold Donohue of Worcester. He was assigned to Veterans Affairs where he had to endure the segregationist ravings of Mississippi's John Rankin, the committee's senior Democrat. But Donohue soon learned the deference game and was added to McCormack's own Expenditures in the Executive Departments in 1949 and was able to escape Veterans Affairs for the Judiciary Committee in 1951.[68] By contrast, Jack Kennedy was left to wither away on the contentious Education and Labor Committee and in the congressional purgatory of the District of Columbia Committee for all six of his years in the House. Jack had not played his House cards right, but deference to others he assessed as lesser intellects was not in his nature.

Using a simple metric of the proportion of freshmen on a committee as a measure of relative prestige, Education and Labor ranked 13th (32% freshmen) and District of Columbia (36% freshmen) ranked 14th among the nineteen standing committees of the House. Ten of the committees had no Democratic freshmen and only Minnesota's John Blatnik was assigned to a second-tier committee—Public Works. Ranked below both of Kennedy's committees in 15th place with 40% of freshmen members was the House Administration Committee that had consolidated the jurisdiction of twelve other minor committees in the Reorganization.[69] That was John McCormack's initial assignment in the 80th Congress. He left House Administration a few weeks later for the Committee on Expenditures in the Executive Departments that was ranked even lower in a tie for 17th place (44.5% freshmen). For those Washington outsiders who remembered that it was McCormack's long stint on Ways and Means, the House's most powerful committee, that had catapulted him into the leadership, and one that never had Democratic freshmen, this appeared to be a public embarrassment.

W. E. Mullins, the reigning political pundit of the *Boston Herald*, saw this assignment as a demotion for McCormack and contended that "Mr. McCormack has been done in by his foes . . . it could be humiliation by his associates." By contrast, Mullins pointed out that "the committee on labor and education to which young Kennedy has been appointed is one of primary importance."[70]

The 22nd Amendment

Scarcely five weeks in control of Congress the House Republicans sought to do to FDR in death what they were unable to do to him in life—limit presidents to two terms. They proposed a 22nd Amendment to the Constitution limiting the tenure of future Presidents of the United States to two terms; and prohibiting a person who had served as president, or acted as president, for more than two years of a term, from being elected president more than once. Ostensibly, it was an effort to restore some balance in executive-legislative relations, but to most Democrats it was clearly a rebuke to the memory of the departed Franklin Roosevelt who had bested Republican candidates in four successive elections.

Minority Whip John McCormack was assigned the task of rallying Democrats to challenge the amendment. "I simply believe," McCormack declared, "that a constitutional amendment would be imposing the dead hand of the past upon future generations of Americans."[71] Dead hand or not, the amendment moved through the House Judiciary Committee 20 to 5 and easily passed the House by a vote of 285 to 121 on February 5 with all 238 Republicans voting unanimously joined by 47 Democrats to vault the bill over the two-thirds vote required for constitutional amendments.[72] It would be ratified as the 22nd Amendment on February 27, 1951.

In spite of John McCormack's impassioned leadership on this vote, he failed to stop its passage. Of the 47 Democrats who voted for the amendment, only six were from northern and western states. It was the 41 southern and border state Democrats who gave the GOP the two-thirds necessary for the amendment's passage. Of the six non-southern Democrats supporting the amendment—two were fellow members of the Massachusetts delegation—the Harvard graduates third-termer Philip Philbin of Clinton and freshman John F. Kennedy of Boston. Jack had been in the House barely a month and he had already begun to challenge John McCormack on only the fourth roll call vote of his House career. In Kennedy's vote, there were echoes of the family feud between his father, Ambassador Joseph P. Kennedy and FDR who had slammed the White House door on Joe following the 1940 election. Jack undoubtedly remembered that FDR had shortened Joe Kennedy's ambassadorship at the Court of St. James in London amid multiple public accounts of Kennedy's defeatism during the London Blitz. Jack's defiance was already in evidence as he settled the first family score against FDR. The second was a few months away and it too would be a direct challenge to John McCormack. After his rebuff for floor leader by the South and the early disrespect shown him by young Kennedy, John McCormack needed some reassurance that he mattered. He would soon find a cause.

The Curley Petition

Boston Irish feuds persist for years. None more so than the Jim Curley and John Fitzgerald feud that began in 1913 with the infamous Elizabeth "Toodles" Ryan case that involved allegations of Fitzgerald's marital infidelity. While Curley went on to win four contests for mayor, one for governor, and two others for the U.S. House, Fitzgerald's career came to an abrupt and bitter end with the "Toodles" allegations and one from which he failed to recover. By 1947, it had apparently morphed into the Jack Kennedy-John McCormack feud with Fitzgerald's grandson and namesake challenging Jim Curley's South Boston protégé.

In 1947, 34 years after Fitzgerald's last year as mayor, Jim Curley would be spending his second term in prison concurrently with his 13th year as mayor. Joe Kennedy's reputed $100,000 contribution may have helped Curley return to City Hall but it could not protect him from the U.S. Justice Department. It was Missouri Senator Harry Truman's Special Committee to Investigate the National Defense Program that had discovered Curley's latest legal transgression. He had been convicted of using the U.S. mails to defraud in war contracts and had been sentenced to jail despite his plea to the judge that he was suffering from nine separate ailments, including an impending cerebral hemorrhage, the ailment that ended FDR's life.

Although Massachusetts's Republican Governor Robert Bradford had engineered legislation that enabled Curley to remain as mayor of Boston and to retain his salary while incarcerated,[73] Curley desperately wanted out of jail. Sitting in his cell at the federal penitentiary in Danbury, Connecticut, Curley pulled every possible wire to get out. As a federal crime where the prospects of an early parole would be unlikely, Curley would need a presidential pardon. He turned to John McCormack for help. John's brother, Edward J. (Knocko) McCormack, the brawny barkeep of South Boston's Wave Cottage was a longtime Curley ally and John McCormack was known to be close to President Harry Truman. John McCormack drew up a petition for the president with a very simple appeal for executive clemency.[74]

"We, the undersigned, who have served with Honorable James M. Curley in the Congress, and said James M. Curley having filed an application for Executive Clemency, because of his health and other extenuating circumstances, respectfully express the hope, and urge that early Executive Clemency be exercised on said application."

John McCormack always contended there were more than one hundred signatures on the petition, but the Truman Library's copy has only 88 names on the four-page petition from 85 members. Three signed it twice including the ever-anxious Thomas J. Lane of Lawrence. Seventy-four different Democrats (39%) and eleven Republicans (4.5%) signed. Members from all nineteen House standing committees, including thirteen from Ways and Means, John's old committee, and eight from Appropriations, Curley's most recent committee, signed it. Thirty states including every southern one, except Virginia, was represented on the petition.

Joining Lane and McCormack, Massachusetts Democrats Phil Philbin and Harold Donohue signed it but no Bay State Republicans did (contrary to the Jim Burns account). One Massachusetts Democrat refused to sign it—John Fitzgerald Kennedy, the grandson and namesake of Jim Curley's ancient rival.

Kennedy's initial explanation was disingenuous contending that he did not sign the petition because he had never served in the House with Curley. Jack's later account of the event appeared in an interview with Williams College Professor James MacGregor Burns, his first major biographer[75]:

"Spotting Kennedy on the floor of the House, McCormack handed him the petition. Would he sign? The two men eyed each other tensely.

"'Has anyone talked with the President or anything?'" Kennedy asked.

"'No,' said McCormack, 'if you don't want to sign, don't sign it.'"

"'Well, I'm not going to sign it,' Kennedy said. And he did not."

In spite of the fact that his key advisors, his father, his mother, and Boston Archbishop Richard Cushing, all urged him to do so, Jack refused to sign the petition. There was no formal explanation from Jack. One Kennedy biographer asserted that "Jack refused, for two reasons. First, Jack apparently checked with the U.S. surgeon general and other health officials, who convinced him that Curley was not seriously ill." "If I don't honestly believe he's sick and I don't honestly believe that he should be pardoned on the basis of what he said, do you think I should do it?" Jack asked a supporter. "It isn't worth being in Congress if I can't do what I feel." Jack had received many appeals from people asking his office to free loved ones from jail, some pathetically sad, and he'd had to refuse. So how could he sign the petition for Curley?[76]

The most plausible explanation appears in Michael O'Brien's lengthy Kennedy biography—"the primary reason he refused to sign stemmed from Honey Fitz's long-standing grievances against Curley. Jack felt loyalty to his grandfather. 'It would have been politically expedient not to have the Curley crowd against you,' said Sutton, 'It wasn't [Jack's] hatred for Curley. It was his love for his grandfather.'"

John McCormack had been puzzled by the Curley indictment. Unlike Kennedy, John accepted Jim Curley's personal explanation that there was very little hard evidence implicating him in the mail fraud case. In spite of reported efforts that the aristocratic Attorney General Francis Biddle, like FDR a graduate of both Groton and Harvard, was pushing to indict Curley, John hoped to quash the indictment. In Joe Dinneen's biography of Curley, he recounts that "McCormack went to the White House and talked with Roosevelt, who gave him one of his most charming smiles and told him to 'forget it,' that [Assistant Attorney General] Tom Clark would not ask for an indictment."[78] Hours after John reassured Curley, the Justice Department issued its indictment. Apparently, the White House and the Justice Department were not on the same page.

This may account for the certitude of Jack Kennedy's refusal to sign the petition. What did Kennedy know that McCormack did not? And how would Jack have learned of it? This leads to another possible explanation for Jack's adamant refusal. Jack's sister Eunice who was living at the Georgetown townhouse with him had worked in the Justice Department directly with Tom Clark, who replaced Biddle as attorney general. While speculative, it is possible that Eunice may have learned from junior Justice Department attorneys eager to impress the brainy young heiress that the criminal case against Curley was rock-solid and that Curley's claims of poor health were grossly exaggerated. Every Washington attorney with a Boston background or a Harvard, Boston University, or Boston College law degree was well aware of the Curley-Fitzgerald feud and keeping Jim Curley in jail was yet another way of accomplishing what Joe Kennedy is reputed to have declared, "Don't get mad; get even."

News accounts of Kennedy's decision reverberated throughout the state's newspapers far beyond his 11th District. One reported example came from the Western Massachusetts *Holyoke (Mass.) Transcript-Telegram* on July 9, 1947: "Kennedy's decision was a surprise to all Massachusetts congressmen especially because his district is in the heart of Curley's political stronghold in Boston."[78] Kennedy aide Ted Reardon told Kennedy biographer Michael O'Brien: "It was a courageous stand, but not taken without trepidation. As Jack walked into his office after making his final decision, he waved his hands and said. 'Well, I'm dead now. I'm politically dead, finished.' He told a supporter, 'I guess I'm going to be a one-term congressman.'"

"Currently the air is filled with threats of what the Curley group will do to Mr. Kennedy in the 1948 primary election," said the *Boston Herald*.[79] Several state newspapers praised Jack for exposing himself to political vengeance and for refusing to do something his conscience told him not to do but his stance had enabled him to distance himself from the tawdry politics of Irish Boston.

Would there be adverse consequences? Not in the 11th District. Jack was renominated and reelected in 1948 without opposition. Would it bother Kennedy? Jack's insouciance impressed Representative Bob Jones of Alabama, a former U.S. Navy gunnery officer who was also named to the District Committee as a freshman in 1947. Responding to questions about whether Jack was "ever concerned that his attitude might get him in serious trouble with the Democratic leadership in the House," Jones answered, "No, I never saw that. I don't think that I ever saw him when he was much of a worrier."[80] And to the interviewer's follow-up, "But you say he was never really concerned that by not getting on with McCormack this might harm him politically?" Jones replied: "No, I don't think so. I don't think he was ever fearful of that. As I say, he seemed to be of the mind that he would make his own political destinies."

The petition worked and President Truman eventually commuted Curley's prison term to the five months he had already served, and as Truman's official document stated,[81]

"Whereas on November twenty-sixth, 1947, I commuted the imprisonment sentence of the said James Michael Curley to expire at once; and

> Whereas it has been made to appear to me that it is fitting at this time that I extend further clemency to the said James M. Curley."

Curley went back to being the mayor of Boston and it is reported that President Truman said, "I did it for you, John."[82] Thanks to John McCormack's efforts and those of Postmaster General and National Democratic Chair Bob Hannegan, Jim Curley was released from prison and returned to Boston to serve out the balance of his fourth term as mayor (Figure 12.1). Curley would never forget that Jack, "the glaring exception," would not sign the petition.[83] Nor would John McCormack, the petition's author.

As Jim Burns observed, "It was not surprising that Kennedy could ignore the weak party leadership in his district. But how could he dare defy national party leaders like McCormack and Truman, who had the power to help or hurt a young man's national career?" Kennedy told Burns, "I never had the feeling I needed Truman."[84]

Burns also noted that "on other matters, however, Kennedy spoke and acted for his district. His votes against Western projects reflected not only opposition to the 'pork-barrel' aspects of this spending, but a Bostonian's lack of interest in such matters. His vote against federal aid for rural libraries suggested that his perspective was still from Boston and not even from that of the whole state, for rural central and western Massachusetts would have certainly benefited from the bill. His sponsorship of federal aid to parochial schools from 1947 to 1950 also was popular in his heavily Catholic district."[85]

Figure 12.1 Newly released from prison, Mayor James Michael Curley rides triumphantly through Boston with Edward J. (Knocko) McCormack, 1947 (Boston Globe).

"All you have talked about since you have been here is New England," a Midwestern Representative remarked during debate on an appropriations bill.

"Do you object to that?" Kennedy asked.

Jack Kennedy got enough credit to be reelected twice and his six mostly forgettable years in the House were not a total waste of time. He did get to meet some influential Republican members who would impact his later life, most notably Dick Nixon and Everett McKinley Dirksen. Nixon, with whom he served on Education and Labor, left the committee and the House when he defied the odds and upended liberal Democratic U.S. Representative Helen Gahagan Douglas to capture the open Senate seat in 1950.[86] The other key Republican with whom he served in the House and frequently encountered during his Senate and presidential careers was the grandiloquent Everett McKinley Dirksen of Illinois, his first chair on the dead-end Committee on the District of Columbia and Senate Minority Leader during his presidency.

Kennedy had spent his first year in the House "getting even" with President Franklin D. Roosevelt who had turned his father into a White House outcast by voting with Republicans and conservative southern Democrats for the "no third term" 22nd Amendment, correctly perceived as a posthumous rebuke of FDR. And he "got even" with Jim Curley for sabotaging his beloved grandfather's political career 35 years earlier, five years before he was born, as the only Massachusetts Democrat not to sign the petition requesting a pardon from President Truman. Kennedy's willingness to vote for the 22nd Amendment in spite of the fact that John McCormack was the floor leader marshaling votes against it, and Jack's refusal to sign the McCormack-drafted and circulated petition calling for a presidential pardon for Curley, made it clear to John McCormack that a young rebel had come to his House of Representatives. These two events coupled with Jack's irregular attendance on his assigned committees and on the House floor did not endear him to John McCormack.

Thus would begin the lengthy feud between Jack Kennedy, the first Irish Catholic President of the United States, and John McCormack, the first Irish Catholic Speaker of the U.S. House of Representatives. McCormack never forgot or forgave Kennedy's attitude and as is well known among the Boston Irish, it was a classic case of Irish Alzheimer's disease, where everything is forgotten but a grudge. It was a wound that never healed.

Notes

1 See William E. Leuchtenburg's recapitulation in "New Faces of 1946," *Smithsonian Magazine*, XXVII (November 2006), pp. 48–54.

2 Their 80th Congress intersections are described in Lance Morrow, *The Best Year of Their Lives: Kennedy, Johnson, and Nixon in 1948: Learning the Secrets of Power* (New York: Basic Books, 2005), while their presidential campaign intersections are presented in David Pietrusza, *1960—LBJ vs. JFK vs. Nixon: The Epic Campaign That Forged Three Presidencies* (New York: Union Square Press, 2008).

3 Carl Albert and Danney Goble, *Little Giant: The Life and Times of Speaker Carl Albert* (Norman: University of Oklahoma Press, 1990).

4 Champagne et al., *The Austin-Boston Connection*, chapters 6, 7, and 9.

5 Thomas E. Harris, later an AFL-CIO attorney, originally quoted in Milton Viorst, "Nixon of the O.P.A.," *NYT Magazine*, October 3, 1971, and reprinted in Stephen E. Ambrose, *Nixon: The Education of a Politician, 1913–1962* (New York: Simon & Schuster, 1987), p. 102.

6 Ambrose, *Nixon: The Education of a Politician*, pp. 105–11. See also Richard M. Nixon, *RN: The Memoirs of Richard Nixon* (New York: Grosset and Dunlap, 1978), pp. 27–29; and Herbert S. Parmet, *Richard Nixon and His America* (Boston: Little, Brown Co., 1990).

7 See his autobiography, Jerry Voorhis, *Confessions of a Congressman* (Garden City, NY: Doubleday, 1947) and reprinted in 1970 by the Greenwood Press of Westport, CT; and his biography by Paul Bullock, *Jerry Voorhis, The Idealist as Politician* (New York: Vantage, 1978). In Voorhis's 1972 book, *The Strange Case of Richard Milhous Nixon* (New York: Paul S. Eriksson, 1972), he stated that he avoided making comments about Nixon for twenty-two years, but his discussion of the contest is a relatively short eight-page non-illuminating summary of that 1946 election.

8 *Congressional Record*, 78th Congress, 1st Session, February 8, 1943, pp. 723–24, and later on February 10, 1943, p. 807.

9 The parliamentary maneuverings are well documented in Walter Goodman's chapter "1945–1946: Rankin's Coup," in his book *The Committee: The Extraordinary Career of the House Committee on Un-American Activities* (New York: Farrar, Straus and Giroux, 1968), pp. 175–99.

10 Michael Newton, *The Ku Klux Klan in Mississippi: A History* (Jefferson, NC: McFarland, 2010), p. 102.

11 The fairest treatment of that contest may be found in "Fifty-One Days in the Fall: Nixon Versus Douglas—Reality and Legend," in Irwin F. Gellman, *The Contender: Richard Nixon, the Congress Years, 1946–1952* (New York: The Free Press, 1999), pp. 319–43.

12   Kennedy's fascination with Nixon's early success is described in Christopher Matthews, *Kennedy & Nixon: The Rivalry That Shaped Postwar America* (New York: Simon & Schuster, 1996).

13   Harry Truman handwritten letter to Bess Truman about Joe Kennedy, June 28, 1935, in Family, Business, and Personal Affairs Papers, Truman Library.

14   Merle Miller, *Plain Speaking: An Oral Biography of Harry S. Truman* (New York: Berkley Publishing, 1973), pp. 186–87.

15   Reported in David McCullough's magisterial Pulitzer Prize–winning biography, *Truman* (New York: Simon & Schuster, 1992), p. 970. His source was the Merle Miller tapes at the LBJ Library, p. 1055n.

16   The most direct challenge to Miller's account is in Robert H. Ferrell and Francis H. Heller, "Plain Faking?" *American Heritage*, XLVI (May/June 1995), accessed June 11, 2015.

17   Truman note to John McCormack, June 3, 1946, in John McCormack file, Truman Library.

18   "The President's Day," September 20, 1947, Truman Library.

19   Nigel Hamilton, *JFK: Reckless Youth* (New York: Random House, 1992), pp. 737–41.

20   Whalen, *The Founding Father*, pp. 394–95.

21   Beatty, *The Rascal King*, p. 456.

22   Ibid. Hamilton's research is cited on p. 552, endnote 31.

23   Hamilton, *JFK: Reckless Youth*, p. 674. Hamilton's source is Joe Kane's interview in the Ralph Martin and Ed Plaut Papers at Boston University. This is the source cited in Ronald Kessler's *The Sins of the Father: Joseph P. Kennedy and the Dynasty He Founded* (New York: Warner Books, 1996), p. 291. Martin himself later made use of the Kane interview in his *Seeds of Destruction: Joe Kennedy and His Sons* (New York: G. P. Putnam & Sons, 1995), p. 133.

24   Jerome S. Bruner and Sheldon J. Korchin, "The Boss and the Vote; Case Study in City Politics," *Public Opinion Quarterly*, X (Spring 1946), p. 23.

25   Curley, *I'd Do It Again*, p. 320.

26   Ibid.

27   Kenneth P. O'Donnell, David F. Powers, and Joe McCarthy, *Johnny, We Hardly Knew Ye: Memories of John Fitzgerald Kennedy* (Boston: Little, Brown, 1972), pp. 61 and 72.

28   "Gift of $600,000 by Kennedy Tops Diocesan Record," *Boston Globe*, August 13, 1946, and "Honoring Son's Memory with Memorial Altar," *Lawrence (Mass.) Daily Eagle*, August 15, 1946, are representative of the multitude of articles acknowledging the Kennedy gifts.

29   "Political Notes: Promise Kept," *TIME*, XLVIII (July 1, 1946), p. 23.

30   O'Donnell, Powers, and McCarthy, *Johnny, We Hardly Knew Ye*, p. 79.

31   Associated Press, "Chamber of Commerce Names Union Leader on List of Greats," *Lawrence (Mass.) Tribune*, January 20, 1947. Named along with Kennedy was Arthur M. Schlesinger, Jr. who didn't vote for Kennedy in the primary but would serve him as a presidential assistant and wrote the Pulitzer Prize–winning biography, *A Thousand Days: John F. Kennedy in the White House* (Boston: Houghton Mifflin, 1965).

32   W. E. Mullins, "Dever Faces Tough Primary Test," *Boston Herald*, April 13, 1946.

33   Leuchtenburg's recapitulation in "New Faces of 1946," pp. 48–54.

34   John Hersey, "Survival (A Reporter at Large)," *The New Yorker*, June 17, 1944, pp. 27–38. Amanda Smith recounts that Hersey married an old girlfriend of JFK's in April 1940 in *Hostages to Fortune*, p. 555n.

35 Author's interview with Professor Samuel Beer, Philadelphia, Penn., September 2007.

36 James MacGregor Burns, *John Kennedy: A Political Profile* (New York: Harcourt, Brace and World, 1961 ed.), p. 93.

37 Charles S. Groves, "Southern Democrats Reported Seeking to Displace McCormack," *BG*, November 17, 1946, pp. 1–2.

38 Author's interview with the manager of the Hotel Washington, April 1997.

39 Books on John F. "Honey Fitz" Fitzgerald include Cutler's, *"Honey Fitz:" Three Steps to the White House*; and Doris Kearns Goodwin, *The Fitzgeralds and the Kennedys: An American Saga* (New York: Simon & Schuster, 1987).

40 Among the many books that focus on Joe Kennedy, the best and most balanced is the recent one by David Nasaw, *The Patriarch: The Remarkable Life and Turbulent Times of Joseph P. Kennedy* (New York: Penguin Press, 2012). The first of these books was Whalen, *The Founding Father*; Ralph G. Martin, *Seeds of Destruction: Joe Kennedy and His Sons* (New York: G.P. Putnam's Sons, 1995); Ronald Kessler, *The Sins of the Father: Joseph P. Kennedy and the Dynasty He Founded* (New York: Warner Books, 1996); Ted Schwarz, *Joseph P. Kennedy: The Mogul, the Mob, the Statesman, and the Making of an American Myth* (Hoboken, NJ: John Wiley & Sons, 2003). Extraordinarily valuable is the volume edited by Kennedy's granddaughter Smith, *Hostages to Fortune*.

41 Among the mammoth outpouring of books on the Kennedy family, three stand out: the first one by Joseph F. Dinneen, *The Kennedy Family* (Boston: Little, Brown, 1959, 1960); Doris Kearns Goodwin's, *The Fitzgeralds and the Kennedys: An American Saga*; and Thomas Maier's *The Kennedys: America's Emerald Kings: A Five Generation History of the Ultimate Irish-Catholic Family* (New York: Basic Books, 2003).

42 Watson Crews, Jr. "Eunice and the Kennedy Tradition," *The American Weekly*, a Sunday supplement to the *Lowell (Mass.) Sun* (July 31, 1947), originally published May 25, 1947.

43 The fullest depiction of this episode in Kennedy's life is in Nigel Hamilton's fascinating biography, *JFK: Reckless Youth* (New York: Random House, 1992), pp. 419–92.

44 The description of the Kennedy living quarters appeared in an Associated Press article. "Kennedy Has Sister as Capitol Hostess," *Concord (N.H.) Monitor and New Hampshire Patriot*, January 19, 1950. "It has an English basement with a large reception room plus servants' quarters. There's a paneled library upstairs, a large dining room complete with colonial mahogany furnishings and a kitchen. This floor leads [to] a fine flagstone terrace with a huge tree that serves as an awning in the summer and provides a cool spot for welcoming guests. The second floor boasts a green drawing room with baby grand piano and a guest room also in pale green. Two bedrooms and a deck porch make up the third floor."

45 This quotation is from Christopher Matthews's reconstruction of the Billy Sutton interview, in his *Kennedy and Nixon: The Rivalry That Shaped Postwar America* (New York: Simon & Schuster, 1996), p. 44. The Sutton interview is on file at the John F. Kennedy Library and Museum in Boston.

46 Oral history with William Sutton by Jack Hynes with Benjamin Jacobson, April 6, 1964, p. 6. On file at the John F. Kennedy Library and Museum, Dorchester, Mass.

47 Associated Press, "Rayburn to Shun Post as Minority Leader," *NYT*, November 7, 1946, p. 13.

48 "Refusal of Rayburn to Be Party Leader in House Opens Contest," *Boston Globe*, November 22, 1946, p. 3.

49   United Press, "Rayburn to Back McCormack for Minority leader," *Boston Globe*, November 28, 1946, p. 48.

50   William S. White, "Rayburn Rejects Leadership 'Draft': Southern Democrats Seek to Block McCormack for Post—Thomason Next Choice," *NYT*, December 31, 1946, p. 8.

51   This quotation was from a clipping entitled "Rayburn Draft Growing" from an unidentified newspaper, dated November 12, 1946; and quoted in D. B. Hardeman and Donald C. Bacon, *Rayburn: A Biography* (Austin: Texas Monthly Press, 1977), p. 324.

52   Sam Rayburn to J. Percy Priest, November 29, 1946, in H. G. Dulaney and Edward Hake Phillips, *"Speak, Mister Speaker"* (Bonham, TX: Sam Rayburn Foundation, 1978), p. 137.

53   Rayburn to Priest, November 29, 1946, in Dulaney and Phillips, *"Speak, Mister Speaker,"* p. 137.

54   Sam Rayburn to John H. Kerr, December 16, 1946, in Dulaney and Phillips, *"Speak, Mister Speaker,"* p. 137.

55   Steinberg, *Sam Rayburn*, p. 235.

56   Hardeman and Bacon, *Rayburn*, p. 324. C. Dwight Dorough claims that Truman "had nothing to do with the draft because there were rumors that he might have a Cabinet post for the Speaker" though he "naturally thought it a good idea to keep him in a position of legislative leadership" in *Mr. Sam* (New York: Random House, 1962), p. 388.

57   Rankin is reported to be "McCormack's most outspoken critic" in the United Press, "Rayburn to Back McCormack for Minority leader," *BG*, November 28, 1946, p. 48.

58   Sam Rayburn speech in Congress, January 7, 1947 in Dulaney and Philips, *"Speak, Mister Speaker,"* p. 139. See William S. White, "House GOP Selects Halleck; Democrats 'Draft' Rayburn," *NYT*, January 3, 1947, p. 1; and "McCormack in Whip Post," *NYT*, January 8, 1947, p. 14.

59   Dorough, *Mr. Sam*, p. 389.

60   Ibid., p. 388.

61   Anthony Champagne, Douglas B. Harris, James W. Riddlesperger, Jr., and Garrison Nelson, *The Austin-Boston Connection: Five Decades of House Democratic Leadership, 1937–1989* (College Station: Texas A&M University Press, 2009), pp. 121–24.

62   Author's interview with John McCormack, April 1977; and first presented in "The Matched Lives of House Leaders and the Policy Consequences of Continuity," at the Institute of Politics, John F. Kennedy School of Government, Harvard University, April 20, 1977, and "Congressional Race Politics and the End of the Austin-Boston Connection," at the New England Political Science Association, May 1990, pp. 27–35.

63   See Hartley's book *Our New National Labor Policy: The Taft-Hartley Act and the Next Steps* (New York: Funk and Wagnalls, 1948). An early use of roll call voting analysis on this bill may be found in Philip Ash, "The 'Liberalism' of Congressmen Voting for and against the Taft-Hartley Act," *Journal of Applied Psychology*, XXXII (December 1948), pp. 636–64.

64   See Paul Bullock, "Rabbits and Radicals: Richard Nixon's 1946 Campaign Against Jerry Voorhis," *Southern California Quarterly*, LV (Fall 1973), pp. 319–49. Voorhis was well known and well regarded. See Claudius O. Johnson's essay, "Jerry Voorhis," in John T. Salter, ed., *Public Men In and Out of Office* (Chapel Hill: University of North Carolina Press, 1946), pp. 322–43; and his autobiography, *Confessions of a Congressman* (Garden City, NY: Doubleday, 1947). His positive reputation remains; see the essay by former

U.S. Senator Paul H. Douglas (Dem-Ill.), "Three Saints in Politics," *American Scholar*, XL (Spring, 1971), pp. 223–32; and Paul Bullock, *Jerry Voorhis: The Idealist as Politician* (New York: Vantage, 1978).

65 William Sutton Oral History, p. 7. The Sutton interview is on file at the John F. Kennedy Library and Museum in Boston.

66 Christopher Matthews, *Kennedy and Nixon: The Rivalry That Shaped Postwar America* (New York: Simon & Schuster, 1996), p. 45.

67 The Nixon-Chambers encounter and its political impact are vividly presented in Morrow, *The Best Year of Their Lives: Kennedy, Johnson, and Nixon in 1948*, pp. 215–71.

68 On Donohue's committee assignments, see Garrison Nelson with Mary T. Mitchell and Clark H. Bensen, *Committees in the U.S. Congress: Committee Histories and Member Assignments*, Vol. 2 (Washington, DC: Congressional Quarterly, 1994), p. 246.

69 "House Administration Committee," in ibid., pp. 1005–1006.

70 W. E. Mullins, "This Is How I See It: Obscure Post for Veteran McCormack, Key Task for Freshman Kennedy Two X's of New Congress," *Boston Herald*, January 17, 1947.

71 "Limit on Tenure of a President Hit," *NYT*, February 2, 1947, p. 1.

72 The bill was favorably reported by a House Judiciary subcommittee, "Presidency Limit of 8 Years Asked," *NYT*, February 3, 1947, p. 18, and then passed by the House; see John D. Morris, "Limit of Two Terms for Any President Approved by House," *NYT*, February 6, 1947, p. 1. The House vote was 285–121, with Republicans voting 238 to 0 for it while Democrats voted against it 47 to 120 with Vito Marcontonio of American Labor Party voting nay as well; *CQ Almanac, 1947* (Washington, DC: Congressional Quarterly, 1948), III: 96–97. The Senate vote of March 12, 1947, was 46 to 0 favoring the amendment among the Republicans and 13 to 23 opposing it among the Democrats for a tally of 59 to 23, III, p. 93. Rayburn, McCormack, and Lyndon Johnson voted nay as did three of the five Massachusetts Democrats. Democrats John F. Kennedy and Philip Philbin joined the delegation's Republicans to support the measure.

73 Known as the "Curley Law," see Chapter 580, "An Act Relative to the Office of Mayor of the City of Boston and the Administration of the Affairs of Said City during the Present Emergency," *Acts and Resolves of the General Court of Massachusetts, 1947* (Boston: Secretary of the Commonwealth, 1947), approved June 26, 1947, pp. 593–94.

74 John McCormack file, Truman Library and Museum. It is possible that McCormack was right. Scattered news accounts mention the names of members who were presumed to have signed the petition but whose names are not listed on the four pages of the Truman Library copy.

75 The original account is from James MacGregor Burns, *John Kennedy: A Political Profile* (New York: Harcourt, Brace and World, 1959, 1960, 1961), pp. 92–93; and it is sourced as "The Kennedy-McCormack dialogue on the Curley petition is as Kennedy remembers it," p. 289n.

76 Michael O'Brien, *John F. Kennedy: A Biography* (New York: Thomas Dunne Books, 2005), pp. 212–13.

77 Dinneen, *The Purple Shamrock*, p. 288.

78 Other representative news accounts include "Rep. Kennedy Will Not Sign Curley Plea," *Boston Traveler*, July 8, 1947; "Kennedy is Hostile to Curley Bid," *Lynn (Mass.) Telegram-News*, July 9, 1947; "Kennedy Refuses to Aid Curley" *Worcester (Mass.) Gazette*, July 8, 1947; and "Kennedy Rebuffs Curley Petition," *New Bedford (Mass.) Standard-Times*, July 9, 1947 News clippings from the 1947 Kennedy Scrapbook at the Kennedy Library and Museum.

79   O'Brien, *John F. Kennedy*, p. 213. See also John A. Barnes, *John F. Kennedy on Leadership: The Lessons and Legacy of a President* (New York: AMACOM, 2005), p. 40.

80   Oral history of the Hon. Robert E. Jones, Jr. with John Stewart, May 21, 1968, Kennedy Library.

81   President Truman's statement of Executive Clemency, November 26, 1947. I thank Mr. Richard Dennis of Boston, Mayor Curley's stepson for a copy of this document.

82   The quotation was attributed to John McCormack; see Dinneen's biography of Curley, *The Purple Shamrock*, p. 307. Dinneen believed that outgoing Democratic National Chairman Robert Hannegan was the one to arrange the release.

83   Curley, *I'd Do It Again*, pp. 333–34. The general consensus is that the decision not to sign the petition was JFK's own and it countered his father's wishes.

84   Burns, *John Kennedy: A Political Profile*, pp. 92–93.

85   Ibid., p. 93.

86   A valuable account of that race by Ms. Douglas's biographer may be found in Ingrid W. Scobie, "Helen Gahagan Douglas and Her 1950 Senate Race with Richard M. Nixon," *Southern California Quarterly*, LVIII (Spring, 1976), pp. 113–26. See also Scobie's "Helen Gahagan Douglas: Broadway Star as California Politician," *California History*, LXVI (December 1987), pp. 242–61 and 310–413, as well as her full-length book, *Center Stage: The Life of Helen Gahagan Douglas* (New York: Oxford University Press, 1992). Also see Ms. Douglas's account in her autobiography, *A Full Life* (Garden City, NY: Doubleday, 1982), pp. 253–81.

13

A Republican Congress, a Vice Presidential Bid, and the Four-Way Election of 1948

The Displaced Democrats: Following the Democratic defeat in the 1946 congressional elections, Sam Rayburn was greatly distressed. It had been 16 years since Rayburn had served in the minority and he seriously considered surrendering the floor leadership to John McCormack, the party's ablest partisan debater. Rayburn was talked out of resigning by the returning congressional southerners,[1] so he put aside his hesitancy and accepted the minority leadership. He then promptly named John McCormack to be the minority whip. With the Democratic Party reduced to its minority status, southerners with their safe one-party districts had easily survived the 1946 congressional elections and they were once again in control of most of the Democratic seats in the House.

In the Senate, President Harry Truman's old Committee to Investigate the National Defense Program fell under the control of its first Republican Chair, Ralph Owen Brewster (Rep-Me.) with Carl A. Hatch (Dem-NM) serving as its ranking minority member. The 1946 Legislative Reorganization Act intended to eliminate select and special committees and to locate their investigative powers more clearly within the surviving standing committees. However, the Senate's newly ascendant Republicans narrowly overruled that sentiment and were eager to focus attention on the War Departments of Presidents Franklin Roosevelt and Harry Truman. The GOP won a narrow 49–43 victory on Senate Resolution 46, which reauthorized the committee on January 22, 1947, albeit with a somewhat limited mandate.[2] In the 80th Congress, the special committee was involved in several highly charged investigations of defense contracts made by Roosevelt's war departments. Howard Hughes, Henry Kaiser, and former Air Force Major General Bennett E. Meyers were a few of the better-known people who came under the scrutiny of the committee in its final year. The reconstituted committee failed in its efforts to embarrass Truman, and it went out of existence before any impact on the 1948 election was made.

Presidential Succession

Once the contentious debate over the 22nd amendment ended in early February, the next effort to restore greater balance to the legislative and executive branches was the final passage of the Presidential Succession Act of 1947. The 1947 Act was intended to place officials who had been publicly elected next in line to the vice president. Given the fact that Harry Truman took office only three months into the first year of FDR's fourth term, it meant that the nation would be without a vice president for forty-five months. However, with Republican Joe Martin serving as Speaker of the House and Republican Styles Bridges of New Hampshire serving as president pro tempore of the Senate, the fears that an assassin's bullet could reverse the results of an election returned to the debate. However, a Republican Congress felt that the nation's interests could be best served by having elected and not appointed leaders next in line.

This was the third Presidential Succession Act. The original 1792 act placed the Senate president pro tempore and the Speaker of the House after the vice president.[4] Although the nation had survived the 1841 succession of Vice President John Tyler who succeeded President William Henry Harrison after the latter's death one month into his term and served for 47 months, it was the 1881 assassination of President James A. Garfield that motivated the change. Garfield was murdered by the half-mad Charles Guiteau who had delusions of being named minister to France by a grateful Vice President Chester A. Arthur. Garfield's death in September of that year, with 42 months remaining in his term, led Congress to alter the line of succession lest assassination be used as a way to change the party control of the government. This was a realistic fear. From 1874 to 1896, divided government was a regular occurrence as neither major party had consistent control of the presidency and both branches of Congress. The Presidential Succession Act of 1886 replaced the 1792 act and removed the Senate president pro tem and the Speaker of the House from the line of presidential succession, replacing them with members of the Cabinet in the order of the dates of creation of the departments.[5] This would guarantee party control of the administration.

The 1947 Act undid the 1886 Act and restored the two congressional officers to the line of succession with the order reversed. The Speaker of the House would be next in line to the vice president and the Senate president pro tem followed the Speaker. Then it would be the Cabinet members in order of the dates of their department's creation.[6] The consequences of this change would be vividly demonstrated to the nation in November 1963 when the absence of a vice president placed Speaker John McCormack next in line for fourteen months after President Kennedy's murder.

While President Truman opposed the term-limiting 22nd Amendment, he was supportive of this statutory change in the line of succession and had originally proposed it to the Congress in 1945, but that was when the Democratic 79th Congress was in session and he would have been succeeded by Democratic Speaker of the House Sam Rayburn, his close friend. The bill narrowly passed the House Judiciary Committee 10 to 9, but it never moved much further.[7]

However, the Republican 80th Congress now sat in the Capitol, and to Harry Truman's credit, he renewed his call for a change in the succession law stating that the nation's interests could best be served by having elected and not appointed leaders next in line.[8] Although the Senate Democrats opposed the bill, voting 35 to 3 against, unanimous support among the 47 Republicans gave it a 50 to 35 approval. With the bill through the Senate, the House voted overwhelmingly in favor of it—365 to 11.[9] The Presidential Succession Act was approved on July 18, 1947, and it placed Republican Speaker Joe Martin next in line to President Truman and Republican Senate President pro tempore Arthur H. Vandenberg of Michigan behind Joe Martin. The Act caused little consternation at the time even though it would have changed party control of the presidency had anything happened to Truman.

There was a bifurcation of issues in the 80th Congress, with domestic policy issues generating high levels of contention and interparty hostility while foreign and defense policies took on a mostly bipartisan air.

The Education and Labor Committee, Taft-Hartley and Education Aid: The two key domestic issues of this Congress—the Taft-Hartley Labor Management Relations Act and federal aid to parochial schools—would be debated in the Education and Labor Committee before they could be voted on the House floor.

Republican Chair Fred Hartley of West Virginia was joined on the committee by a number of other conservatives, including the virulent America Firster Clare Hoffman of Michigan and Democrats Graham Barden of North Carolina and the rabid anti-Communist John S. Wood of Georgia, who later chaired the Un-American Activities Committee. Jack Kennedy was one of ten first-timers on the twenty-five-member committee, including eight freshmen—two Democrats and six Republicans. The last-named freshman Republican was California's Richard M. Nixon. The two freshmen Kennedy and Nixon observed one another closely.

The senior Democrat on the Education and Labor Committee in Kennedy's first term was staunch pro-labor Democrat John Lesinski from Dearborn, Michigan, and the United Auto Workers. A pro-labor ally listed fifth on the minority side was Adam Clayton Powell, Jr. of Harlem. Powell was the third black Democrat ever elected to the House and the first from the Northeast. Powell, who became chair of the committee in 1961 and was removed from it in 1967, would frequently intersect the lives of both Jack Kennedy and John McCormack over the next 20 years—not always positively, but always emphatically.

Taft-Hartley was intended by Republicans to counter many of the gains made by organized labor earlier. The act amended the Wagner-Connery National Labor Relations Act of 1935 and in the process, it outlawed the closed shop, jurisdictional strikes, and secondary boycotts; and provided for a 60-day moratorium before a strike could be called against industries engaged in interstate commerce.[10] It also required that union finances be made public, prohibited unions from contributing to political campaigns and Communists from holding union offices. The bill passed both houses easily with a 308 to 103 margin in the House and 68 to 24 in the Senate.[11] Both margins were clearly veto-proof and the June votes on the conference report were even more one-sided with the House 320–79 on June 4 and the Senate voting 54 to 17 on June 6.[12] The president wasted no time in vetoing the bill. Republicans and their Conservative Coalition Democratic allies in both Houses overturned the veto almost as quickly, with votes of 331 to 83 in the House on June 20 and 68 to 25 in the Senate on June 23.[13] Now more than ever, Harry Truman needed Rayburn and McCormack and met with them regularly as members of the "Big Four" with an ever-changing cast of Senate Democratic leaders. The First Session of the 80th Congress had left them reeling.[14]

Education issues were also vexing, with both religion and race issues complicating the funding of schools. The 79th Congress passed the Veterans Rehabilitation Act (P.L. 79–16) and the G.I. Bill of Rights (P.L. 79–346), committing the federal government to funding the higher education of thousands of returning GIs. Greatly aware that the present campus buildings and programs were not adequate to handle this initial flood, the President's Commission on Higher Education was named. Among its recommendations were a doubling of college enrollments by 1960 and extending free public education through the establishment of a network of community colleges.[15] Shortly afterward, the 79th Congress passed the National School Lunch Act. While expensive, these bills did not provoke serious opposition.

Conflict arose over the issue of reimbursing parents at private parochial schools and religious instruction in public schools. Two Supreme Court cases opened the debate. The first was *Everson v. Board of Education*, 330 U.S. 1 (1947), when Justice Hugo Black delivered a 5–4 ruling that a New Jersey law which allowed reimbursements of transportation costs to parents of children who rode public transportation to school, even if their children attended Catholic schools, did not violate the Establishment Clause of the First Amendment. The following year in the Illinois case of *McCollum v. Board of Education*, 333 U.S. 203 (1948), the Supreme Court ruled 7–2 with Black again writing the majority opinion that schools cannot permit "released time" during the school day which allows students to participate in religious education in their public school classrooms. This was a violation of the Establishment Clause.

While not wholly dormant, the issue of public funding for parochial schools would erupt most publicly in 1961 when the nation's first Roman Catholic President John F. Kennedy would face off against John McCormack, the nation's first Roman Catholic House Majority Leader.

Foreign and defense policy

Truman Doctrine: While domestic issues produced interparty contention, foreign and defense policy issues produced consensus. As Churchill's "Iron Curtain" prophecy became more evident, postwar concerns about the growth of Soviet influence in Eastern Europe and in the Mediterranean Basin led to the passage of two major bills, with leaders Sam Rayburn and John McCormack providing bipartisan Democratic support—the Greek-Turkish Aid Act that provided $400 million in financial and military aid to the governments of Greece and Turkey, both of which were then engaged in fending off heavy Soviet encroachments,[16] and the Foreign Relief Act that provided for $350 million in American economic assistance to several countries damaged by the effects of World War II and the severe winter of 1946–47.[17]

Department of Defense: Further preparation for the perilous postwar world included the passage of the National Security Act passed by voice votes in the Senate on July 9, 1947, and in the House on July 11 that replaced the War and Navy Departments with a National Military Establishment. It consisted of separately administered Departments of the Army, Navy, and Air Force under the general direction, authority, and control of a secretary of defense (but no Department of Defense); and designated the joint chiefs of staff as the "principle military advisers" to the president and the secretary and authorized a Joint Staff of hundred officers.[18] It also created a War Council, composed of the secretary of defense, the three service secretaries and the three chiefs of staff, to advise the secretary on matters of broad policy relating to the armed forces. The act also established the Central Intelligence Agency and the National Security Council. Unlike the years prior to World War II, Congress was readying the nation for a prolonged struggle with the Soviet Union, our onetime ally.

Marshall Plan: In June of 1947, Secretary of State George C. Marshall gave the Commencement Address at Harvard University. His call for an ambitious economic recovery program for Europe—a foreign "New Deal" as it were—led to the passage of the Economic Cooperation Act of 1948. This act created the European Recovery Program, implementing the Marshall Plan.[19] It established the Economic Cooperation Administration and authorized $5.3 billion for the first year of economic assistance to 16 European countries. It also provided $275 million for military aid to Greece and Turkey, $463 million for economic and military aid for China, and $60 million for a U.N. fund for children. While its overall impact was noble, it was the fear of growing Soviet influence that led the Congress to commit billions of American taxpayers' dollars to the resurrection of Europe's industrial infrastructure.

Germany and Japan had been crushed by the war, while Great Britain and France had been nearly bankrupted by it. Only the Soviet Union joined the United States to emerge from the war as a greater power than it was when the war began. American-Soviet relations took center stage in the nation's foreign policy debates.

Regardless of its prewar wishes, the U.S. Congress with its authority to appropriate more money than any other nation on earth would become inextricably linked to world issues. The belief that the two oceans spared Americans from foreign involvement disappeared with the 1941 attack on Pearl Harbor. John McCormack and his fellow congressmen realized that Congress and its "power of the purse" could impact the direction of postwar world affairs much as the 1941 Lend-Lease Act had impacted world affairs in the run-up to the war itself.

Vandenberg Resolution: Clearly conscious that a "divided government" of a Republican Congress and a Democratic president might embolden foreign adversaries to strike at the United States, U.S. Senator Arthur H. Vandenberg (Rep-Mich.), Chair of the Senate Foreign Relations Committee, expressed the bipartisan statement, "We must stop partisan politics at the water's edge."[20] That Vandenberg had been a prewar isolationist gave his words added meaning. Vandenberg's measure passed the Senate on June 11, 1948, by a vote of 64 to 4. Among its provisions were: a resolution advising the president to seek US and free world security through support of mutual defense arrangements that operated within the U.N. Charter but outside the Security Council, where the Soviet veto would thwart collective defense arrangements. Paragraph 3 of the resolution referred to issues of military assistance or alliance, encouraging "association by the United States, by constitutional process, with such regional and other collective arrangements as are based on continuous and effective self-help and mutual aid, and as effects its national security."[21] Later regional mutual defense pacts, such as the North Atlantic Treaty Organization (NATO) and the Southeast Asia Treaty Organization (SEATO), would derive their authority from this resolution.

Last, in an effort to avoid the difficulties of the prewar peacetime draft, Congress passed the Selective Service Act of 1948. This Act restored the Selective Service System providing for the registration of all men between 18 and 25 years of age, with induction restricted to those between 18 and 25, for up to 21 months.[22] Unlike 1941, John McCormack would not have to squeeze a one-vote majority from reluctant members, and Sam Rayburn would not need his quick gavel to pass this measure.

Another presidential election was on the horizon in November 1948 and serious doubts arose as to whether the dispirited Democrats could find a way to retain the White House and regain control of Congress. The coalition glue that was Franklin Roosevelt was gone, and Harry Truman was no FDR. A winning strategy had to be concocted.

Enter Clark Clifford

A native of racially segregated Fort Scott, Kansas, Clark Clifford was a tall, wavy-haired, movie-star handsome lawyer who had been educated at Washington University in St. Louis and had become a very successful attorney. He attained the rank of a Navy captain in the war and began his White House service as an assistant naval aide early in the Truman Administration. It was his Missouri connection that opened the doors for him, and he quickly became Truman's naval advisor. When Roosevelt's holdover Special Counsel Judge Sam "Sammy the Rose" Rosenman left the White House in 1946, the 39-year-old Clifford became special counsel and a key member of Truman's inner circle from 1946 to 1950. Clifford would eventually advise each of Harry Truman's three Democratic successors, Jack Kennedy, Lyndon Johnson, and Jimmy Carter, but it was as Truman's White House counsel from 1946 to 1948 that his legend as a political strategist was built. With Truman's popularity sagging badly and the Republican 80th Congress bent on overturning as many New Deal precedents as they could, the prospects for the upcoming 1948 presidential election looked very grim. The administration would be politically rescued by the legendary "Clifford memo."

It is contended that Jim Rowe, a Tommy Corcoran ally, actually prepared the initial draft of the memo and sent it to James Webb, Truman's director of the Bureau of the Budget.[23] Believing that Truman's antipathy toward "Tommy the Cork" would lead to Rowe's memo being unread, Clark Clifford redrafted a few paragraphs and submitted it to the president on November 19, 1947.[24] Now known as "the Clifford memo," it opened simply and then quickly picked up the pace:

> The title of this memorandum might well be "The Politics of 1948." The aim of the memorandum is to outline a course of political conduct for the Administration extending from November, 1947 to November, 1948. It is obvious that such an outline cannot encompass the details of a political course because they will depend upon interim developments. However, it is my conviction that we must chart a course at this time which will contain the basic elements of our policy . . .
>
> For instance, the basic premise of this memorandum—that the Democratic Party is an unhappy alliance of Southern conservatives, Western progressives and Big City labor—is very trite, but it is also very true. And it is equally true that the success or failure of the Democratic leadership can be precisely measured by its ability to lead enough members of these three misfit groups to the polls on the first Tuesday after the first Monday of November, 1948.

With Henry Wallace running as a Progressive and assembling supporters and funding, it was clear to Clifford that the best strategy for the Truman campaign was to tilt left and siphon off as much Wallace support as it could among moderate liberals. A leftward tilt made sense because tilting right would oblige Truman to fight for voters among the moderate conservatives, who would likely vote for New York Governor Tom Dewey, then making his third bid for the presidency. It was Dewey that the memo projected as the GOP nominee.

A key winnable region for Truman would be the West with its 71 electoral votes, 25 of which were California's. The West had benefited from the New Deal. Aiding Truman in this region was another Rayburn-McCormack ally, Clinton P. Anderson of New Mexico, a three-term House member who Truman named as secretary of agriculture in June 1945.[25] Truman could expect little help in the West from Harold Ickes, FDR's secretary of the interior who left the Cabinet on February 16, 1946, and initially leaned toward fellow FDR Cabinet member Henry Wallace.

Clifford then identified a number of the key demographic groups in the New Deal Coalition and how, if at all, they could be induced to turn out and vote for a Democratic nominee who was discernibly not Franklin D. Roosevelt.

Two groups in particular stood out: "the Negro" and "the Jew." Both were in the portfolio of Presidential Special Assistant for Minorities David K. Niles. Niles would be called upon to implement the Clifford strategies since he had greater access to Congress through his longtime back-channel links to John McCormack.[26]

The Negro Vote: Regarding African Americans, there had been a decline in their voting support for FDR and their level of identification with the Democratic Party between 1936 and 1944.[27] Much of this was due to the implacable resistance of white Democratic southerners in Congress to any form of civil rights legislation. Most troubling to blacks was southern Democratic opposition to anti-lynching bills. That came to a head in July 1946, when two young African-American couples were stopped at the Moore's Ford Bridge in Georgia by an angry white mob who pulled them out of a car, tied them to a tree, and fired sixty rounds at point-blank range killing all four.[28] That one of the men killed was a combat veteran and one of the women was pregnant sparked outrage in much of the nation. While the assailants were arrested, none was convicted. Once again, anti-lynching legislation in Congress was thwarted by the callous southern Democratic argument of "state's rights."

President Truman was personally horrified by this episode and other brutal attacks on returning black servicemen. On September 13, Truman's Appointments Secretary Matthew Connelly requested that David Niles arrange a meeting between the leaders of the upcoming American Crusade to End Lynching and President Truman.[29] The meeting took place on September 23.[30] Thousands of protestors gathered at the Lincoln Memorial one week later. Before the year was over, Truman would issue Executive Order 9808 on December 5, 1946, creating the President's Commission on Civil Rights. Niles had first suggested a similar committee in 1943 and along with his associate Philleo Nash, a Wisconsin-born academic with a PhD in anthropology from the University of Chicago, would be its staff members.[31] It was well known that "Niles and Nash were the two individuals that black leaders contacted if they wanted something from the Truman administration."[32]

Both Jim Rowe, the memo's original author, and Clark Clifford, its transmitter, knew that "the Negro" was not wholly committed to the Truman candidacy. A key phrase in the memo was: "A theory of many professional politicians is that the northern Negro voter today holds the balance of power in presidential elections for the simple arithmetical reason that the Negroes not only vote in a bloc but are geographically concentrated in the pivotal, large and closely contested electoral states such as New York, Illinois, Pennsylvania, Ohio and Michigan." The concern was "that the northern Negro is today ready to swing back to his traditional moorings—the Republican Party. Under the tutelage of Walter White, of the National Association for the Advancement of the Colored People, and other intelligent, educated and sophisticated leaders, the Negro voter has become a cynical, hardboiled trader."

Reaching out to Negro voters was Henry A. Wallace's Progressive Citizens campaign. His early speaking tours in the South with Broadway star Paul Robeson, who had led the anti-lynching delegation to the White House in 1946, made it clear that Wallace intended to gain black support for his candidacy. The NAACP's public relations director Henry Lee Moon published his influential book, *Balance of Power: the Negro Vote*.[33] It supported Clifford's contention that "the Negro vote" could sway elections in the electoral vote-rich states of New York, Illinois, Michigan, Pennsylvania, and Ohio.

Backed by his Committee on Civil Rights, Truman delivered an aggressive pro–civil rights special message to Congress on February 2, 1948. Among its ten calls for congressional action were:

1. Establishing a permanent Commission on Civil Rights, a Joint Congressional Committee on Civil Rights, and a Civil Rights Division in the Department of Justice;

2. Strengthening existing civil rights statutes;
3. Providing Federal protection against lynching;
4. Protecting more adequately the right to vote;
5. Establishing a Fair Employment Practice Commission to prevent unfair discrimination in employment;
6. Prohibiting discrimination in interstate transportation facilities;
7. Providing home rule and suffrage in Presidential elections for the residents of the District of Columbia;
8. Providing Statehood for Hawaii and Alaska and a greater measure of self-government for our island possessions;
9. Equalizing the opportunities for residents of the United States to become naturalized citizens;
10. Settling the evacuation claims of Japanese-Americans.[34]

It was a high-risk strategy and might have cost the ticket to southern voters, but Clifford (and Rowe) were convinced that the depth of southern commitment to the Democratic Party was sufficiently strong as to limit any electoral damage in that region. This was a projection that they would miss.

The South would react quickly and angrily. On April 8, 1948, Bill Colmer of Mississippi denounced Truman's speech on the House floor.[35] Colmer declared: "But now, for the first time in the history of the country, and the loyalty of my section to the Democratic Party, a President of the United States has asked the Congress to enact such a devastating, obnoxious, and repugnant program to the people of that section and their Jeffersonian conception of democracy as this so-called civil-rights program. No President, either Democrat or Republican, has ever seen fit heretofore to make such recommendations."

Caught between his two "poker pals," Harry Truman and Bill Colmer, John McCormack demurred and made no floor statements on either side for the remainder of 1948. As John knew well, a Democratic National Convention in Chicago would convene in mid-July, and it was imperative that the two sides remain somewhat united if the party was going to retain the presidency and regain the Congress.

David K. Niles and Phileo Nash

For John McCormack's mysterious White House ally David Niles, the situation had changed. Although it was Niles who was assigned to handle the July 1946 anti-lynching march in Washington that led to Truman's appointment of the Committee on Civil Rights, he had become so committed to securing the recognition of Israel that he offloaded the "Negro portfolio" to his capable associate Phileo Nash.

Niles subscribed wholeheartedly to the passion for anonymity and it bordered on the obsessive. Phileo Nash described it as "a mania for anonymity." According to Nash, Niles "was always gone from midweek to Monday mornings, attending board meetings of New York-based organizations that concerned his liaison duties, taking in a play on Thursday nights (he was an avid theatre-goer), and always returning home [to Boston] for a family dinner with his mother." On weekends he managed the Sunday night lectures at the Ford Hall Forum and would take an overnight train from Boston to Washington to begin the next week's activities. He would stay in hotels in both Washington and New York and was about as elusive as any Washington insider had ever been.[36]

With the Negro portfolio moved to Nash, Niles and Clifford could work together on the other demographic newcomer to the Democratic coalition, the Jews. There was a foreign policy link to domestic politics in the horrendous plight of Europe's thousands of "displaced persons" (DPs) and where to place them. Clifford (and Rowe) understood the link.

The Jewish Vote: As described in the Clifford memo:

(e) *The Jew*. The Jewish vote, insofar as it can be thought of as a bloc, is important only in New York. But (except for Wilson in 1916) no candidate since 1876 has lost New York and won the Presidency, and its 47 votes are naturally the first prize in any election. Centered in New York City, that vote is normally Democratic and, if large enough, is sufficient to counteract the upstate vote and deliver the state to President Truman. Today the Jewish bloc is interested primarily in Palestine and will continue to be an uncertain quantity right up to the time of election. Even though there is general approval among the Jewish people regarding the United Nations report on Palestine, the group is still torn with conflicting views and dissension. It will be extremely difficult to decide some of the vexing questions which will arise in the months to come on the basis of political expediency. In the long run, there is likely to be greater gain if the Palestine problem is approached on the basis of reaching decisions founded upon intrinsic merit.

Displaced Persons and the Palestine Solution: It had long been expected that America's preexisting economic and industrial resources would translate into world military might, but it was the war's unequivocal victories in both hemispheres that placed the United States at the center of world affairs. Initially locating the new United Nations Organization in San Francisco and then relocating it to New York City was its most logical and obvious manifestation.

Great Britain's Palestine Mandate would be problematic for American leaders, because it involved the territorial fate of the Jewish people, millions of whom now lived in the United States. Jewish immigrants had begun arriving in the 1890s to escape the European pogroms aimed at extinguishing them and their faith. For them the only remedy that made sense was to reestablish a Jewish homeland in Palestine.

The Palestine Mandate was created by the League of Nations in the aftermath of World War I from the remnants of the Ottoman Empire that had allied itself with the Central Powers of Germany, Austria-Hungary, and Bulgaria; the losing side in the Great War. Great Britain received the mandates over Palestine and Mesopotamia while

France received the mandates over Syria and Lebanon. Great Britain ended its mandate over Mesopotamia in 1932 when Iraq emerged as a separate nation, but it continued its Palestine Mandate. When the Nazi collaborationist Vichy government gained power in France in 1940, it allowed German forces to use Syria and Lebanon as staging areas to attack British-controlled Egypt. Operating from their bases in the Transjordan region of the Palestine Mandate, the British and their allies in the Arab Legion and the Iraqi Army pushed back and gained control over both Lebanon and Syria in 1941, which then were declared to be independent in 1943 and 1944 respectively.[37] Both new nations declared war on Germany and Japan in 1945, and France's Middle East mandates were no more.

Recognizing Israel: A bitter battle raged inside the Truman Administration over the DPs and the recognition of Israel. Leading the recognition effort were David Niles and Max Lowenthal. Lowenthal's official status was not as well acknowledged in the White House, but he, like Niles, had also worked for isolationist Senator Burton K. Wheeler of Montana and had been close to Felix Frankfurter.[38] The self-effacing Lowenthal, a Justice Brandeis protégé, drafted the legislation, while Niles worked Capitol Hill with John McCormack and the powerful senior Jewish triumvirate of Adolph Sabath of the Rules Committee, Manny Celler of Judiciary, and Sol Bloom of Foreign Affairs.

Truman confided to Oscar R. Ewing, a onetime senior official at the Democratic National Committee who would head up the Federal Security Administration, that "I have two Jewish assistants on my staff, David Niles and Max Lowenthal. Whenever I try to talk to them about Palestine, they soon burst into tears because they are so emotionally involved in the subject. So far I have not known what to do."[39]

Resisting the recognition of Israel were three very powerful men—the esteemed Secretary of State George C. Marshall; his Undersecretary, the aristocratic Robert A. Lovett, one of "the Wise Men"; and the brilliant but troubled Secretary of Defense James V. Forrestal. All three had been instrumental in bringing the war to a successful conclusion. All three feared that recognizing Israel would inflame Arab passions and lead the Arabs to ally with the Soviet Union.[40]

While Marshall and Lovett plied their craft at the State Department's sumptuous offices in Foggy Bottom and Forrestal did so at the Pentagon, a few miles from the White House, it was the two aides—Clifford and Niles—who saw Truman on a regular basis who would be the crucial influences in this matter. As a Kansas-born Protestant, Clifford relied on Niles and Lowenthal to keep him informed about Zionist political aims. Clifford's depiction of Niles was that he "was virtually unknown to the public. With outsiders, he cultivated an air of mystery, and insiders said his enigmatic style either masked real power or created a useful illusion of power."[41]

The First Session of the 80th Congress produced hearings but no legislation on the Displaced Persons bill. The bill slowly moved its way through Congress, but it was quickly overrun by events. On May 14, 1948, the United States recognized the new nation of Israel. The first person called by President Truman was John McCormack's mysterious Boston ally David K. Niles.[42] On June 22, three days before Truman issued his signing statement on the Displaced Persons Act, the United States had begun diplomatic

Figure 13.1 President Truman presenting the Medal for Merit to Special Assistant David K. Niles, 1947 (Truman Presidential Library and Museum).

relations with the Provisional Government of Israel by naming James G. McDonald of New York to be the Special Representative of the United States to head the Mission.

At last, the longtime dream of Zionists was a reality, and it would be a major component of Harry Truman's memorable legacy thanks in large part to the two reinvented Bostonians, John McCormack and David K. Niles (Figure 13.1). Although some accounts credit Harry Truman's former haberdashery partner Eddie Jacobson with pushing Truman to recognize Israel's existence,[43] it was David Niles's Zionist connections with Rabbi Steven Wise that mobilized political support for it to take place and John McCormack and his well-placed Jewish allies Sabath, Bloom, and Celler who guaranteed that the congressional anti-Semites would not stop it.

John McCormack had expedited the recognition decision when Eugene Kinnaly, his chief aide, informed him early in 1948 of a conversation that he had with Boston department store owner and leading Jewish philanthropist Lincoln Filene. Filene was approached by New York's Governor Tom Dewey and its former Senator John Foster Dulles, Dewey's key foreign policy advisor, and told of their plans to include the recognition of Israel in the 1948 Republican Party platform. Filene quietly listened but then informed Kinnaly, and it was McCormack who relayed the news to Niles who then put the plan into operation. The shrewd Filene, the onetime employer of both David Niles and John Roosevelt, FDR's youngest son, knew the appropriate back channel to Truman.

With President Truman's continued urging, Congress finally passed the Displaced Persons Act of 1948 in June; this authorized the admission into the United States of 200,000 European refugees displaced by the war, with an additional 3,000 orphans and another 2,000 Czechoslovakians eager to escape from a Communist coup in February 1948.[44] Since 205,000 of the displaced were Jewish, the debates gave off a noxious echo as anti-Semitism returned to the chambers of Congress.[45]

The House version passed on June 11, and it went to a conference committee. Truman considered the conference report to contain "the worst features of both the Senate and the House bills," but signed it anyway. Truman's signing statement expressed serious concern over the bill's dates determining who in the affected regions of Germany, Austria, and Italy was eligible for entry under the Act. He contended that the December 22, 1945 cutoff date in the bill "discriminates in callous fashion against displaced persons of the Jewish faith" because "more than 90 percent of the remaining Jewish displaced persons" arrived in those affected territories after that date.[46] He also contended that the date excluded anti-Communist Catholics.

> For all practical purposes, it must be frankly realized, therefore, that this bill excludes Jewish displaced persons, rather than accepting a fair proportion of them along with other faiths.
>
> The bill also excludes many displaced persons of the Catholic faith who deserve admission . . . [who] fled into the American zone after December 22, 1945, in order to escape persecution in countries dominated by a Communist form of government.

It was Truman's hope that remedial action would occur in subsequent amendments, but Republican lawmakers and conservative Democrats, like Nevada's Pat McCarran of the Senate Judiciary Committee, were disinclined to help.[47]

President Truman's popularity ratings were not encouraging. By April of 1948, his Gallup Poll approval ratings had dropped to 36% and remained below 40% throughout the preelection period.[48] Truman was unchallenged in the presidential primaries of that year, winning all seven primaries where his name was listed and gaining 63.9% of the total Democratic primary vote.[49] Unpledged slates won a few states, but there was no serious primary challenger to the president's nomination.

Summer arrived and Republicans were eager to leave Washington so they could campaign for the White House. President Truman barely survived the 80th Congress,[50] and Republican presidential prospects were brighter than they had been in 20 years. They already held both houses of Congress and for the first time since 1928 they would not have to face the reigning champion Franklin D. Roosevelt. Harry Truman's popularity had continued to plummet from the extraordinary heights of his war-ending V-E and V-J Day successes. An even more delightful Republican scenario emerged as the Democratic Party seemed to be cannibalizing itself.

Opposition to Truman

Henry Wallace's Progressive Party: As public opinion polls continued to show weakness in President Truman's popularity, Henry Wallace's Progressive Party presidential campaign gained support. Wallace's opposition to the anti-Soviet rhetoric emanating from the White House and his hopes of forging a friendlier association with our World War II ally made the Progressive Party a haven for left-leaning political activists. By choosing the name "progressive," Wallace's supporters hoped to tap into that root of credible third-party challenges mounted by former President Teddy Roosevelt and U.S. Senator Robert La Follette who led their followers under the Progressive Party banner in 1912 and 1924 respectively. Wallace's party was more ideological than either of these predecessor parties, and its more active adherents feared that a conflict—hot or cold—between the United States and the Soviet Union would undermine many of the social gains which had been made in the previous years under FDR.[51] However, Wallace's seemingly pro-Soviet stance appealed to harder left-leaners and a number of Communists were drawn to his party, a fact that dismayed non-Communist liberals, many of whom would eventually move back to Harry Truman.

The Republican Nomination: Republicans were ecstatic over the Wallace candidacy and hoped that Wallace's Progressives would undo the Democrats much as Teddy Roosevelt's Progressives had undone them in 1912. Despite their optimism, the 1948 Republican primary battles were relatively quiet. For years, successful Republican presidential nominees generally ignored the preference primaries, choosing instead to work the delegate count through top-down alliances with well-placed delegation leaders.

The two leading contenders, Ohio's staunch conservative U.S. Senator Robert A. Taft and New York's moderate Governor Thomas E. Dewey, mounted no serious challenge to one another in the primaries. Eight years before, their confrontation at the 1940 convention led to the upset nomination of the political amateur Wendell Willkie. Taft and Dewey knew each other well and harbored a serious dislike, if not hatred, for each other.[52]

Both Governor Dewey and Senator Taft were better positioned in 1948 than either had been earlier. In his 1946 reelection bid, Dewey had defeated his opponent U.S. Senator James M. Mead with 56.9% of the vote, a percentage higher than either Al Smith or Franklin D. Roosevelt had attained in their five victories for the governorship of New York.[53] Senator Taft was even better placed. The Republican victory in the 1946 congressional elections had elevated his status and public prominence. With that victory, Taft became chair of the Senate's Labor and Public Welfare Committee and the second-ranking member on the powerful tax-writing Finance Committee. He also continued to chair the party's Policy Committee. Although Maine's moderate Wallace H. White, Jr. was the Senate Republicans' Majority Floor Leader in the 80th Congress, it was Senator Taft who had been its driving legislative force.[54]

The convention battle was very closely contested.[55] After the first ballot, Dewey had 434 votes and needed another 114 delegates for nomination. On the second ballot, Dewey moved to 515 votes, only 33 short, and Taft moved to 274. After an adjournment, the delegates reconvened and Governor Dewey got his breakthrough thanks to California, which released its 53 delegates from Governor Earl Warren to Dewey. The victory was assured and Governor Dewey invited Governor Warren to join the ticket as vice president. Earl Warren was fast approaching legendary status as a vote-getter after racking up a nearly impossible 91.6% of the vote in his 1946 reelection bid. California's unique cross-filing system enabled Warren to be nominated on both the Republican and Democratic tickets, and he crushed his hapless Prohibition Party opponent, Henry R. Schmidt, 2,344,542 votes to 180,579.[56] The Dewey-Warren ticket was an impressive pairing and with hopes of a New York-California electoral vote total of 72 in their November column, the Republicans had more than one-quarter of the 266 needed to win the White House.

The 1948 Democratic convention

When the Democrats convened two weeks later, they already knew that Governors Dewey and Warren were arrayed against them on the other side. President Truman had moved successfully through the primaries with some opposition but not enough to worry the party's power brokers. It was the convention itself that would be troublesome, for it was here that the white South would mount its challenge. Fortunately for Truman, his allies were well placed at the Convention.[57] Senate Minority Leader and "Big Four" member Alben W. Barkley of Kentucky was named as the Convention's temporary chairman and gave a rousing defense of the New Deal and Harry Truman's commitment to continue it. Speaker Sam Rayburn, Barkley's longtime friend and another of the "Big Four," was chosen as permanent chair of the Convention. Sam would wield the gavel and direct the political momentum of the Convention toward an outcome he hoped would result in a presidential ticket to retain the White House and a party platform enabling the congressional Democrats to recapture Capitol Hill.

The Massachusetts Delegation: As Massachusetts Democrats prepared for the 1948 National Convention, Jim Curley overreached once again. In spite of his recent defeat for a fifth term as mayor of Boston, he sought to lead the Massachusetts delegation. Curley remained angry that Tom Clark, Truman's Attorney General and future Supreme Court Justice, would not drop the charges against him, so he had a notion of nominating General Douglas MacArthur for president in place of Harry Truman. That MacArthur was a presumed Republican did not bother Curley but it did bother John McCormack, and an infuriated McCormack threatened to leave the delegation if Curley headed it. Realizing that he had overreached, Curley backed down and John was named to head the delegation.[58]

McCormack for Vice President: At the 1948 convention, John was not chair of the platform-writing Resolutions Committee as he had been in 1944 and would be in 1952 and 1956. Had he been, the walkout of the South might have been prevented. While the South had blocked John from replacing Sam as the party's floor leader, other members of the House were eager to get him the nomination for vice president.

John McCormack's name was bruited about for vice president by Rep. John Fogarty of Rhode Island, who contended that he had conducted an informal poll "of Democratic Congressmen before adjournment and 93 out of nearly 100 who were queried said they liked McCormack for vice president."[59] Days later, Fogarty revised his numbers upward and said that "all but two" of 105 Democratic members of Congress were favorable to a McCormack vice presidential bid. Support also came from A. F. Whitney, head of the Brotherhood of Railroad Trainmen described in Clark Clifford's legendary memo as "the only [labor union] completely friendly to the Democrats." Rep. Clarence Cannon of Missouri, the crusty but all-powerful chair of the House Appropriations Committee, asserted that "if it were up to the members of the House of Representatives we would name him for Vice President tomorrow."[60]

When the topic of the vice presidency was broached in John's oral history for the Kennedy Library, he contended that[61]:

> I had about five hundred votes pledged to me without being a candidate. I got a call from Harry Truman, and in the course of it he mentioned Alben Barkley's name. I said, "Do you want Alben Barkley as the vice-president, Mr. President?" I wanted to get out, and I said, "If you do. . . . I am not a candidate."

When John was asked directly if he would have taken Truman's offer of the vice presidency, he said,[62] "I don't know whether I would or not, to be frank with you. . . . I'd have a lot of difficulty in saying no. I'll be frank with you; but I'd got myself so wedded to the House, and I knew the next step for me would be Speaker."

The McCormack boom ended quickly with Truman naming the 70-year-old Alben Barkley, who had led the Senate Democrats since 1937, to be his running mate.[63] A dispirited McCormack declared, "I recognize the importance of Senator Barkley as a pivotal man but what can anyone do in the circumstances." But later he stated wistfully that if Barkley refused Truman's offer, that "I had 75 chances out of 100 of winning the nomination."[64]

In the recollections of Truman aide Eben Ayers, an unenthusiastic Truman had said, "'You have to be cold-blooded about these things and as of now they can nominate Barkley and turn things over to him.' He indicated that he did not feel Barkley was the best candidate but that if the delegates wanted him, let them have him."[65] The 70-year-old Barkley described himself as a "warmed-over biscuit," and he prepared to battle the long odds decreed by the press regarding a Democratic presidential victory in November.[66]

Civil Rights and the 1948 Democratic Platform: The 1948 platform-writing Resolutions Committee would be chaired by Senate Democratic Whip Francis Myers of Pennsylvania, the only Democratic congressional party leader who was not included among the "Big Four." This was unlike 1944 when "Big Four" member John McCormack chaired the committee. Senator Myers did not have the strong relationships that McCormack had with the South, so he could not finesse the growing divisions between northern liberals and conservative southerners over the party's civil rights plank.

The most contentious battle was over civil rights and President Truman's proposal to resuscitate the Fair Employment Practices Commission (FEPC) that had expired on June 30, 1946. The two other competing parties had already spoken about civil rights. The 1948 Progressive Party Convention devoted thirteen paragraphs, eight of them racially focused, in their party platform's section entitled, "End Discrimination."[67] The civil rights commitment in the 1948 Republican Platform was less broad than the Progressives but it too focused upon opposition to the poll tax, lynching, and employment discrimination. It was clear to most of the assembled Democrats that the two mild sentences of John McCormack's 1944 convention platform would not suffice again.

Many northern moderate liberals were fearful that Henry Wallace's Progressive Party would siphon off enough Democratic votes from the big-city ethnics, especially

Jews and blacks, to cost them the White House. Since 1932, Democrats had come to rely on big-city voters to swing the electoral-vote-rich states of New York, Pennsylvania, Illinois, Ohio, Michigan, and Massachusetts into their column.[68] The Wallace candidacy jeopardized those prospects.

The southern delegations were another matter. The Mississippi state convention had committed its national delegation to walk out if a pro–civil rights plank was adopted by the convention. The Credentials Committee split on this issue. The majority report called for seating of all of the state delegations, but a substantial minority, led by New York and California, wished to deny Mississippi its seats until their offending state resolution was removed. Two key northern states, New Jersey and Massachusetts, joined with the majority and chose not to deny Mississippi its delegation seats. Once again, it was John McCormack who led the Massachusetts delegation's efforts to keep the anti–civil rights southerners connected to the Democratic Party.

But there was little McCormack could do to contain the battle over the platform. Initially, the civil rights plank emerging from the Resolutions Committee was almost as innocuous as that adopted in 1944 as it simply reaffirmed the two mild sentences of the McCormack-drafted resolution, but it prefaced those sentences with the declarations[69] "The Democratic Party is responsible for the great civil rights gains made in recent years in eliminating unfair and illegal discrimination based on race, creed or color. The Democratic Party commits itself to continuing its efforts to eradicate all racial, religious and economic discrimination."

Urban liberals were displeased by the lack of specificity in these statements and the southerners were displeased by the implicit criticism contained within them. The South offered the first three amendments. Governor Dan Moody of Texas presented an amendment which attempted to use states' rights as a buffer from federal civil rights legislation. Another resolution from Tennessee also reaffirmed states' rights, but it was the Mississippi resolution that was the most blatant[70]:

> And the party declares that the several states shall exercise, free from federal interference or encroachment by legislation, directive or otherwise, all the rights and powers reserved to them by the Constitution, among them being the power to provide by law for qualifications of electors, the conduct of elections, regulation of employment practices within the states, and define crimes within their borders and prescribe penalties therefore, except such crimes which under the grant of power by the Constitution to the federal government may be defined by it.

White Mississippi was asking the Democratic Party to defend its onerous practices of discriminatory poll taxes, race-based employment, segregation, and lynching; after all, this was the same party that refused to condemn the Ku Klux Klan at its 1924 convention. Neither the Tennessee nor the Mississippi resolutions went to a roll call vote; with the voice vote against the Mississippi resolution a resounding one. The Moody Resolution did go to a roll call and was voted down, 310 votes for to 924 votes against. All eleven states of the Confederacy voted unanimously for the Moody Resolution, providing it with 298 of its votes. The white South had lost.

The liberal resolution, authored by ex-U.S. Representative Andrew Biemiller (Dem-Wisc.) and Minneapolis Mayor Hubert H. Humphrey, then a candidate for the U.S. Senate, committed the party to a ringing support of President Truman's civil rights agenda with its declaration of "the right of full and equal political participation, the right of equal opportunity of employment, the right of security of persons, and the right of equal treatment in the service and defense of our Nation."[71]

Northerners had the votes and the resolution was passed in a close tally: 651 ½ to 582 ½. Joining the 298 southern delegates in opposition were 127 of the 134 delegates of the six states that bordered the Confederacy, including 60 from Harry Truman's Missouri and Alben Barkley's Kentucky delegations.

The 36 Massachusetts delegates voted unanimously against the Moody Resolution and for the Biemiller-Humphrey Resolution. The 50 Texas delegates voted unanimously the other way. Neither Sam Rayburn nor John McCormack spoke to either amendment. Rayburn, presiding over the Convention, was procedurally constrained; John McCormack, the ultimate "apostle of compromise," chose not to speak. Once again, John McCormack knew that his white southern allies in the House would forgive his votes for civil rights, but they would not forgive a speech critical of their discriminatory practices.

The southern delegates then rallied to the presidential candidacy of U.S. Senator Dick Russell of Georgia. Russell received 263 delegate votes, all but four from the Confederacy. President Truman opened with 926 votes and finished with 947 ½. Rayburn's Texas voted for Russell, but Mississippi chose not to vote. Its delegates made their dramatic exit from the convention, leaving Philadelphia empty-handed but with a plan in mind. Led by South Carolina Governor J. Strom Thurmond, they would prepare a strategy to force the Democratic Party to renounce its newfound aggressive commitment to civil rights for blacks.

The Dixiecrat strategy

Odds for the Truman-Barkley ticket got even longer as immediately following the convention many of the southerners gathered in Birmingham, Alabama, to nominate a ticket of South Carolina Governor J. Strom Thurmond for president and Mississippi Governor Fielding Wright for vice president.[72] The party was formally named the States' Rights Party but was generally known in news accounts as the "Dixiecrats." For the Dixiecrats, there was never any hope of gaining the White House. Their strategy was to win enough electoral votes to create a deadlock in the Electoral College and force the presidential election into the House of Representatives where they had enough votes to determine the presidential outcome.

Once in the House, the presidential game would change dramatically. With each state having only one vote, the large northern delegations of New York, Pennsylvania, Illinois, and Ohio would be reduced to the level of Wyoming, Vermont, and Delaware. The 17 convention delegations from the 11 states of the Confederacy and the six of the Border had voted against the Biemiller-Humphrey civil rights resolution—35.4% of the states. And within the House itself, all 11 southern congressional delegations and three of the Border ones had Democratic majorities. If the Dixiecrats could force the issue into the House, they had the votes to block anyone from becoming president who had a pro–civil rights agenda. The Dixiecrats may not have been able to restore antebellum chattel slavery to the United States, but they certainly would have made mincemeat of the 14th and 15th Amendments.

  "Turnip Day": Truman chose to ignore the Dixiecrats, but he snookered Republicans into the "Turnip Day" Session of Congress. In his acceptance speech at the convention, Truman told of how Missouri farmers had sown their turnips wet or dry on July 25, but since that date fell on a Sunday this year, the special session would begin on July 26. In the speech, he asked the Republican leaders of the Congress to address many of the issues that they had outlined in their platform, such as inflation, housing costs, national health insurance, civil rights, and an increase in the minimum wage. It was the first special session called by a president in an election year since 1856 and the first ever requested at a nominating convention.

  Governor Dewey and the congressional Republicans were caught off guard. The 80th Congress met, but its Republican leaders were split. Senator Arthur Vandenburg (Rep-Mich.) and Representative Hugh Scott (Rep-Pa.) were amenable to some of Truman's requests, but Senator Taft said, "I am not going to give that fellow anything."[73]

  As Truman recalled: "Just as I had predicted, the 'Turnip Day' session of the Congress came and went without any response to my demands for constructive legislation promised by the Republican Party platform. . . . After two weeks of doing nothing, the special session adjourned."[74]

  Minority Leader Sam Rayburn and Minority Whip John McCormack dutifully took their assigned responsibilities in the House and watched bemusedly as the Republican leadership sought to avoid any semblance of movement in the direction of the president's agenda. Although Labor Day, September 6, was to be the official opening day of the campaign, the congressional Republicans were well aware that the "Turnip Day" Special Session was Harry Truman's opening gambit. Truman now had demonstrable public proof of the "do-nothing 80th Congress."

Desegregation of the army

The Army Desegregated: While the Republican 80th Congress seemed to drift aimlessly, Truman acted decisively, and on July 26, 1948, the opening day of the Special Session and 12 days after the convention ended, he issued Executive Order 9981 entitled "Establishing the President's Committee on Equality of Treatment and Opportunity in the Armed Forces."[75] The order declared:

  It is hereby declared to be the policy of the president that there shall be equality of treatment and opportunity for all persons in the armed services without regard to race, color, religion or national origin. This policy shall be put into effect as rapidly as possible, having due regard to the time required to effectuate any necessary changes without impairing efficiency or morale.

Truman's message was clear and unequivocal. If Congress would not or could not act on his February civil rights message, then he would use the powers of his office and issue executive orders to implement civil rights policies. Desegregating the armed forces was not one of the ten original items, but as commander-in-chief of the military, it was the one that he could implement without congressional approval.

Congressional southerners exploded; none more so than U.S. Senators Burnet Maybank of South Carolina and Dick Russell of Georgia, who brought General Dwight D. Eisenhower before the Senate's Armed Services Committee. Both the Missouri-born Harry Truman and the Texas-born and Kansas-raised Eisenhower had grown up in states where racial segregation was a fact of daily life.[76] Ike had unhesitatingly commanded segregated armed troops throughout World War II and in April 1948 he testified before the Senate Armed Services Committee in support of the continuance of racial segregation in the armed forces.

While not as opposed to the plan as Arkansas-born General Douglas MacArthur and Missouri-born General Omar Bradley, his successor as army chief of staff, Ike expressed his opposition in widely circulated testimony before the Senate Armed Services Committee in April 1948[77]: "I do believe that if we attempt merely by passing a lot of laws to force someone to like someone else, we are just going to get into trouble."

It was not a particularly strong statement in opposition to President Truman's directive, but both Senators Russell and Maybank seized upon it and regularly repeated it in opposition to integration of the military.[78] The eventual desegregation of the armed forces was completed by April 1951 before Ike returned to active duty as the First Supreme Commander Allied Forces Europe (NATO) prior to launching his own successful presidential campaign in 1952.[79]

The 1948 election campaign

As the summer of 1948 drew to a close, the four presidential campaigns readied themselves for the intense two-month struggle. The campaigns differed in their geographical focus and in their allocation of time. More than ever, it was the campaign itineraries that revealed the depth of their commitments.[80]

Governor Thurmond remained in the South, while the others crisscrossed America. Governor Dewey was the most relaxed of the three other candidates. In the 63 days from September 1 through November 2, Dewey spent 27 days in Albany, nine in New York City, two at home in Pawling, and one day crossing the state from Buffalo after spending two days in his hometown of Oswasso, Michigan. He had begun to believe the polls that predicted an easy victory for him. After all, his friend Dr. George Gallup, the reigning guru of public opinion, conducted publicly disseminated polls that foretold of a Dewey victory. Dewey biographer Richard Norton Smith reported that "[Dewey] and George Gallup became close, and it was Gallup's numbers that finally convinced Dewey to make the gubernatorial race [in 1942]."[81] Governor Dewey campaigned as the incumbent, seeming to forget that it was Washington, and not Albany, where the Nation's Capital was located.

Henry Wallace focused on the large cities, knowing that was where the urban members of the New Deal coalition—organized labor, the newly arrived blacks, and the disaffected liberal intellectuals—could be mobilized. Wallace spent 16 days in New York City and six others in its environs; seven in Chicago; three in Philadelphia; two in Los Angeles and made one-day excursions to Baltimore, Pittsburgh, Milwaukee, Dallas, Houston, El Paso, San Francisco, Seattle, and Portland, Oregon. He spent only one day in Boston, September 18.[82]

That day was a microcosm of the 1948 campaign—the mystical Henry Wallace dropping into a major city for a one-day visit; the disengaged Tom Dewey trying to appear presidential as he governed his state from Albany; and the scrappy Harry Truman on board a railroad train as it moved through small towns, giving stump speeches to meet as many people as he could, whistle-stopping its way through 11 communities from Rock Island, Illinois, along the Mississippi River westward through Iowa and turning south to finish up in Polo, Missouri.

The Massachusetts Contest: Massachusetts was up for grabs. It was the only major industrial state to vote Democratic in the previous five elections, but it was now seen as a presidential battleground. Its four-time victor, the aristocratic Harvard-educated FDR, was dead. So too was Al Smith, the Catholic nominee who had first begun the lodging of the Bay State's electoral votes in the Democratic column. Harry Truman, the Baptist county judge from Independence, Missouri, was unlikely to extend the presidential Democratic hold on Massachusetts.

As the presidential campaign opened on Labor Day, it appeared that the clock had been turned back in Massachusetts. The Yankee Republican Brahmins had regained control of the Old Colony. Seated in the United States Senate were Puritan-descended Leverett Saltonstall and Henry Cabot Lodge, Jr, and presiding over the state from Beacon Hill was Governor Robert Bradford.[83] Harvard College had regained suzerainty over the state once again. Republicans occupied nine of the state's 14 U.S. House seats, and they held sway over both chambers of the state legislature, the General Court. It had been a struggle, but at last the Brahmins had banished the disruptive Irish interlopers from most of the seats of power. Or so they hoped.

The old Irish Democratic lions were in the winters of their lives. David I. Walsh, the state's first Catholic governor and U.S. Senator, died in June 1947, little more than seven months after his defeat in 1946 by Henry Cabot Lodge, Jr. John Fitzgerald, the state's first Catholic congressman and Boston's first native-born Irish-descended mayor, would finally dance off stage in 1950, living long enough to see his grandson and namesake John Fitzgerald Kennedy twice gain election to the U.S. House but not long enough to see him defeat Henry Cabot Lodge Jr., the grandson of his old nemesis. The hardiest of them all, Jim Curley, had barely survived. Even though he had won Boston's City Hall for the fourth time in 1946, he only got to occupy it after John McCormack interceded with President Truman to get him released from his second term in prison. By this time, the discredited Jim Curley had become more of a curious anachronism than a contemporary power broker.

John McCormack, who represented South Boston and Dorchester in the U.S. House, and Governor Maurice J. Tobin were the new Irish political elite of Boston. Tobin, from Jim Curley's Roxbury neighborhood, was once seen as a Curley protégé. He defeated

Jim twice for mayor and was elected governor in 1944 but was defeated for reelection in 1946. Sensing that 1948 would be a Democratic year, John and Truman's Appointments Secretary Matt Connelly, a Massachusetts native, sought to prevent a primary conflict between former Governor Tobin and former Attorney General Paul A. Dever. The conflict was avoided when Tobin was named Labor Secretary ad interim in August, replacing the deceased Lewis B. Schwellenbach, an old Senate pal of Harry Truman's.[84] Tobin was the first Massachusetts Democrat named to the Cabinet since 1895 when Richard Olney was selected secretary of state in President Grover Cleveland's second term.

It was not until the last week of the 1948 campaign that the two major party candidates came to Massachusetts. Truman was the first to arrive. Starting in Pittsfield on the western edge of Massachusetts, his train moved south to Thompsonville and Hartford in Connecticut then returned to Springfield, Massachusetts, and headed east through Worcester and Framingham en route to Boston. He was accompanied by House Minority Whip John McCormack and his newly appointed Secretary of Labor, Maurice Tobin.

President Truman's campaign stop in Boston was a triumph, thanks to assistance from an unlikely source—Archbishop Richard Cushing, the spiritual leader of the city's gigantic Roman Catholics archdiocese. Archbishop Cushing, successor to the imperious Cardinal William Henry O'Connell, had continued O'Connell's building projects and Boston, the city which had once scorned Catholics, emerged as the nation's second largest Roman Catholic archdiocese, next only to Chicago. Archbishop Cushing had a wonderful common touch.[85] He did not possess Cardinal O'Connell's lavish tastes or O'Connell's disdain for elected officials. Archbishop Cushing liked politics and politicians. A fellow "Southie" Cushing was especially fond of John McCormack. The archbishop's neighborhood was a cut above the Bayview numbered streets of John McCormack's neighborhood, but it was still "Southie."

Before addressing an overflow crowd in Boston Garden that evening, President Truman met privately with Archbishop Cushing. It was a successful meeting and as recounted by the *Boston Globe*'s John Robinson on Truman's 1973 passing, it would be one of many between these two humble men.[86]

Their 1948 meeting was especially eventful as Eben Ayers, the White House assistant press secretary who had once worked in Boston for the Associated Press, recalled[87]:

> Matt [Connelly] said there was a good quotation from the Archbishop, a line out of what he had said to the President, and he thought I might get it and give it out. When we went up to the President's room, he said the Archbishop told him that he thought the President was making the greatest fight in history in the interest of the people, and he was for him.

Ayers was skittish about using the quotation and wished for direct confirmation from the archbishop himself. He then recalled that "one of these Boston men finally called the Archbishop, called his residence, got him on the phone and the President talked with him and I stood next to the President when he talked with him. The President told him and asked him if it was all right to use it and he said it was."

Governor Dewey arrived in Boston the following day on October 27 and hoped that the newly empowered Republicans of Massachusetts would regain the state for the GOP, but the archbishop's endorsement of the president was a better story, and it trumped the Dewey visit. Even the embittered Jim Curley arrived at Boston Garden to take a seat on the stage behind the president.

Truman left Boston that morning to whistle-stop through southeastern Massachusetts, Rhode Island, and the coastal cities of Connecticut and then out of New England into New York City where two days were spent in the nation's largest political venue. Four days later would be election day, 1948. The public opinion polls and the newspaper editorialists all predicted a victory for Governor Dewey. But it was not to be.

Truman's national victory

Harry Truman's victory in the 1948 election was a legendary one.[88] As Clifford had hoped, Truman would carry the west, and with 10 of the 11 western states with 65 electoral votes in the Democratic column to only six votes of Oregon in the Republican one. Truman, the small-town Missouri Baptist, was saved by the popular votes of the big-city ethnics and blacks, whose numbers enabled Democrats to win many of the electoral vote-rich states of the Northeast and Midwest. Henry Wallace's Progressive Party received only 2.4% of the total vote and carried no states or electoral votes but his million-plus popular votes affected the electoral votes in New York State, Michigan, and Maryland. In those states, Governor Dewey's victorious plurality over President Truman was less than the total vote racked up by Henry Wallace costing the Democratic ticket 74 electoral votes. The Wallace candidacy could very well have been fatal to the Truman presidency had not the Biemiller-Humphrey civil rights plank worked to keep most of the moderate liberals and many urban blacks in the Democratic column.

The remnants of FDR's New Deal coalition were large enough to withstand the double defections of Henry Wallace's Progressive Party and J. Strom Thurmond's States' Rights Party, the "Dixiecrats." Political analyst Sam Lubell contended that it was because of the double defections that Truman won the 1948 contest.[89] To Lubell, the defection of the Henry Wallace Progressives took the hard left (and Communists) out of the Roosevelt coalition, making the party more appealing to moderate conservative voters, while the defection of Strom Thurmond's Dixiecrats made the party more appealing to its moderate liberals. The Democratic center had held.

The Truman victory was uneven in the South. Like the Wallace Progressives, the Thurmond-Wright Dixiecrat ticket also gained only a 2.4% share of the national popular vote but it carried four states: Alabama (79.7%), Mississippi (87.2%), South Carolina (72.0%), and Louisiana (49.1%). The Truman-Barkley ticket was left off the ballot in Alabama and the Thurmond-Wright ticket was designated the official Democratic one in the other three.[90] These four states gave Thurmond 38 electoral votes. A "faithless" Tennessee elector added one more to his overall tally. The rest of the South was relatively unmoved by the Dixiecrat candidacy—20.3% in Georgia; the teens in Arkansas (16.5%), Florida (15.5%), Tennessee (13.4%), and Virginia (10.4%); and single digits in Texas (9.1%) and North Carolina (8.8%).

With four Deep South states willing to abandon the Democratic Party over the issue of race politics, it was clear that a new era had arrived. After all, all four had voted for

Al Smith, the Roman Catholic presidential nominee, in 1928. Would they abandon their party over race when they hadn't over religion? The answer was an emphatic yes, and this new reality would have enormous ramifications for the legislative agenda of the congressional Democrats.

This election represented the start of the white South's disentangling itself from the Democratic presidential party. The disentangling was revealed when 90 of 422 (21.3%) congressional districts had party outcomes dissimilar from their presidential ones.[91]

Within the South, the most intense battles took place in the congressional primaries. Even Minority Leader Sam Rayburn, faced with serious opposition for the first time in a while, had to campaign as a segregationist. Rayburn was wise enough to know that this stance would end whatever presidential aspirations that he may have had; it was a painful realization.[92] Fellow Texan and Rayburn protégé Representative Lyndon B. Johnson, in his second Senate quest, campaigned against segregationist ex-Governor Coke Stevenson for the U.S. Senate nomination.[93] This spared Johnson from accumulating segregationist views—that unfortunate and likely fatal piece of political baggage.

The Swing Votes of Jews and Blacks: Truman's presidency was saved by the popular votes of the urban ethnics and blacks whose numbers enabled Democrats to win many of the electoral vote-rich states of the Northeast and Midwest. Reaching out to both groups helped Truman retain the White House, and in one of the more curious footnotes in American politics, each of these was opposed by two of the most important generals of World War II: former General George C. Marshall, Truman's secretary of state, almost resigned over the recognition of Israel; while the hero of the victory in Europe, General Dwight D. Eisenhower, saw little to be gained and much to be lost in the integration of the armed forces.

Both Jews and blacks were identified in the Jim Rowe/Clark Clifford memo outlining the victory strategy for 1948. Neither group had been historically affiliated with the Democratic Party.[94] Blacks had entered American electoral politics as Republicans, while Jews entered American politics as outsiders, often voting with the Socialist Party and the Progressive Party, oscillating between the two major parties depending upon changing circumstances.[95] Typical was Louis D. Brandeis, the first Jew named to the Supreme Court in 1916, a Teddy Roosevelt Progressive Republican who was chosen by Democratic President Woodrow Wilson.

Many Jews like David Niles who worked for Senator La Follette's Progressive Party in 1924 moved to Democrats Al Smith in 1928 and FDR in 1932. Their candidacies epitomized the politicization of the Jewish commitment to social justice. Niles never wavered in his commitment to the political goals of Zionism or to his friendships with Felix Frankfurter, its secular champion, and Rabbi Stephen Wise, its spiritual one. When Harry Truman became president in 1945, he only continued two FDR appointees: Special Counsel Sam Rosenman and Niles, who was especially skilled in the political nuances of urban ethnic politics.

Working together, Niles's White House efforts to get recognition for Israel and McCormack's congressional efforts to prevent anti-Semites in the House from derailing it contributed to Truman's solid support among the nation's Jewish voters.

It was different for American blacks. The Democratic Party had long been their adversary. Founded in 1793 by Virginia slaveholder Thomas Jefferson and renewed in 1825 by Tennessee slaveholder Andrew Jackson, the Democratic Party had defended slavery in the years before the Civil War and segregation in the years after it. It was Franklin D. Roosevelt and his wife Eleanor who opened the doors of the Democratic Party to American blacks.[96] Blacks were well aware that Harry Truman was not FDR and had Confederate soldiers among his ancestors. He was known to pepper his informal conversations with some poorly regarded depictions of blacks. Bess Truman, the president's wife, was suspected of holding segregationist views and in the words of U.S. Representative Adam Clayton Powell, "from now on, there is only one First Lady, Mrs. Roosevelt; Mrs. Truman is the last."[97]

But Truman's sponsorship of the FEPC and his pushing for the racial integration of the armed forces signaled his growing sensitivity to the plight of American blacks, and one that would have political dividends. This was apparent in an interview that Sam Lubell had with a Harlem editor: "After the Dixiecrats walked out of the Democratic convention, there was no question how Negroes would vote. Negroes felt if they didn't support Truman no other politician would ever defy the Southerners again."[98] Unsurprisingly, it was Niles's associate Philleo Nash who reported to President Truman after the election that "over the country as a whole, your majority in the Negro districts is the highest ever. The *average* will be above 80%."[99]

News from Massachusetts: The Bay State had remained loyal to the presidential Democrats. Harry Truman's plurality of 242,418 votes and his percentage of 54.7 were greater than any of those recorded by Al Smith and Franklin Roosevelt in the previous five contests. It was also his best showing among the northern industrial states.

Brahmin Republican Senator Saltonstall had survived the Truman tide, and only one of the nine House Republicans lost—Charles Clason, who was defeated by Foster Furcolo of East Longmeadow in Western Massachusetts. Furcolo would quickly become a favorite of John McCormack's among the young Democrats within the delegation. There was even better news in the state races. Paul A. Dever, the state's former attorney general, regained the State House for the Democrats by defeating Governor Bradford. Dever was also born in Southie before his family moved to Cambridge. South Boston was now providing Massachusetts with a governor, the Catholic Church with an archbishop, and the nation with a Majority Leader of the House of Representatives. Southie's civic pride was understandable, and its hubris, inevitable.

Both John McCormack and Jack Kennedy were reelected unopposed in this election and would resume their tense relationship early in 1949. John was not surprised about the election. He had been optimistic about the prospects of Massachusetts Democrats for months. After the national convention, he arranged a meeting with State Representative Thomas P. "Tip" O'Neill, Jr. of Cambridge. Then serving in his 12th year in the State House, Tip O'Neill and McCormack had never met. O'Neill had thwarted Jim Curley's efforts to remove him from the 1948 convention delegation, and McCormack was impressed.

As O'Neill recalled, McCormack told him that "you fellows put up a tremendous fight." The conversation continued for another three hours "as McCormack talked about everything under God's blue sky."[100] As he was wont to do, John McCormack took his time getting to his point: "Have you ever given any thought to making the state house Democratic?" "I certainly had not. It sounded like a ridiculous idea, but I listened politely as McCormack urged me to try to reverse the long history of Republican rule in Massachusetts."

O'Neill's initial reaction was "What a windbag," but an examination of Maurice Tobin's successful gubernatorial campaign in 1944 revealed that Tobin had carried 138 of the state's 240 legislative districts. It was possible, and John McCormack seemed to be more astute than O'Neill had initially assumed. McCormack raised $7,000 for the effort, Paul Dever added another $5,000, and Jack Kennedy and Jim Curley put a thousand each into the war chest.[101]

John McCormack was right. The Truman presidential victory and the Dever gubernatorial one had a positive spillover in the state legislative contests. Democrats gained four seats in the State Senate and 26 in the State House of Representatives.[102] In the Senate, the party split was 20–20 but in the House the split was 122 Democrats to 118 Republicans. For the first time since 1867, a Democrat was elected Speaker of the Massachusetts House— none other than the "doubting Thomas" himself, Mr. O'Neill of Cambridge. Tip O'Neill was now on his way up the political ladder that would eventually lead him to become John McCormack's most successful protégé and a Speaker of the U.S. House himself.

On January 20, 1949, U.S. Representative John W. McCormack, newly returned to his old post of House Majority Floor Leader, and U.S. Senator Carl Hayden of Arizona rode triumphantly with President Harry Truman in the Inaugural Parade (Figure 13.2). More than 14 years later, it would be the sight of these two men once

Figure 13.2 President Harry Truman with U.S. Representative John McCormack and U.S. Senator Carl Hayden, Inaugural Parade, January 20, 1949 (Truman Presidential Library and Museum).

again, John McCormack and Carl Hayden, seated behind President Lyndon B. Johnson on November 27, 1963, that would be troubling enough to launch a constitutional amendment.

Notes

1   See *NYT*, January 3, 1947, pp. 1 and 4; and January 8, 1947, p. 14.

2   Reauthorization of Committee to Investigate the National Defense Program, Senate Resolution 46 passed 49–43 on January 22, 1947.

3   The bill was favorably reported by a House Judiciary subcommittee, "Presidency Limit of 8 Years Asked," *NYT*, February 3, 1947, p. 18, and then passed by the House; see John D. Morris, "Limit of Two Terms for Any President Approved by House," *NYT*, February 6, 1947, p. 1. The House vote was 285–121, with Republicans voting 238 to 0 for it while Democrats voted against it 47 to 120; *CQ Almanac, 1947* (Washington, DC: Congressional Quarterly, 1948), III: 96–97. The Senate vote of March 12, 1947, was 46 to 0 favoring the amendment among the Republicans and 13 to 23 opposing it among the Democrats for a tally of 59 to 23, III, p. 93. Rayburn, McCormack, and Lyndon Johnson voted nay as did three of the five Massachusetts Democrats. Democrats John F. Kennedy and Philip Philbin joined the delegation's Republicans to support the measure.

4   Presidential Succession Act of 1792 approved March 1, 1792 (1 Stat. 239-241), in Stathis, *Landmark Legislation*, p. 14.

5   Presidential Succession Act of 1886 approved January 19, 1886 (24 Stat. 1-2), in Stathis, *Landmark Legislation*, p. 128.

6   Presidential Succession Act of 1947 approved July 18, 1947 (Public Law 80-199; 61 Stat. 389-381), in Stathis, *Legislative Landmarks*, p. 231. A contemporaneous scholarly assessment of the succession issue may be found in Ruth C. Silva's *Presidential Succession* (Ann Arbor: University of Michigan Press, 1951).

7   "Presidential Succession Bill Approved by House Committee," *NYT*, June 27, 1945, p. 1; and Arthur Krock, "In the Nation: No Action Yet on Presidential Succession," *NYT*, April 18, 1946, p. 26.

8   Arthur Krock, "In the Nation: Consistency by Mr. Truman That Is Also Fun," *NYT*, February 7, 1947, p. 22.

9   The Senate vote was 50 to 35 with Republicans in favor 47 to 0 and Democrats opposed 3 to 35, June 27, 1947; *CQ Almanac, 1947*, III, p. 334. The House vote on July 10, 1947, was 365 to 11 with Republicans in favor, 222 to 1; Democrats in favor, 149 to 10; and Vito Marcantonio (ALP-NY) opposed, pp. 500–501. Rayburn, McCormack, and Johnson voted yea while Kennedy's vote was recorded as "a general pair."

10 The Taft-Hartley Labor Management Relations Act was approved June 23, 1947 (61 Stat. 136-162). Academic analyses of voting on this bill may be found in Philip Ash, "The 'Liberalism' of Congressmen Voting For and Against the Taft-Hartley Act," *Journal of Applied Psychology*, XXXII (December 1948), pp. 636–40; Fred Witney, "Taft-Hartley and the Eighty-Third Congress," *Labor Law Journal*, V (January 1954), pp. 76–79; and Seymour Scher, "Politics of Agency Organization: The Taft-Hartley Congress and NLRB Bifurcation," *Western Political Quarterly*, XV (June 1962), pp. 328–44. Labor-sponsored congressional efforts to overturn Taft-Hartley are treated

in Gerald Pomper, "Labor and Congress: The Repeal of Taft-Hartley," *Labor History*, II (Fall 1961), pp. 323–43.

11   The Taft-Hartley vote in the House was 215 to 22 among the Republicans and 93 to 84 among the Democrats with Marcantonio voting nay, *CQ Almanac, 1947*, III, pp. 304–305. Rayburn, McCormack, and Kennedy all voted nay while Johnson joined fellow southerners and voted yea. In the Senate, the Republicans voted 47 to 3 while the Democrats split evenly 21 to 21 (ibid., p. 303).

12   The party split on the conference report in the House was Republicans in favor 217 to 12 and Democrats also in favor, 103 to 66, *CQ Almanac, 1947*, III, pp. 306–307. Marcantonio voted nay as did Rayburn and Kennedy while McCormack paired nay and Johnson voted yea. The Senate split was Republicans in favor 37 to 2 and Democrats slightly in favor 17 to 15 (ibid., p. 303).

13   The party split on the override vote in the House was Republicans, 225 to 11 in favor and Democrats 106 to 71 in favor, with Marcantonio joining Rayburn, McCormack, and Kennedy voting nay while Johnson voted to override, *CQ Almanac, 1947*, III, pp. 306–307. Senate Republicans voted 48 to 3 to override while Senate Democrats supported the veto 22 to 20 (ibid., p. 308).

14   For a summary of the First Session, see Floyd M. Riddick, "American Government and Politics: The First Session of the Eightieth Congress," *APSR*, XLII (August 1948), pp. 677–93.

15   *Higher Education for Democracy*: A Report of the President's Commission on Higher Education. Vol. 1, *Establishing the Goals* (New York: Harper & Brothers, 1947).

16   The Greek-Turkish Aid Act was approved in the Senate on April 22, 1947, by a vote of 67 to 23 with Republicans in favor, 35 to 16, and Democrats favoring it as well, 32 to 7. *CQ Almanac, 1947*, III, p. 270. The House vote on May 9, 1947, was similarly bipartisan as it passed 287 to 108 with Republicans in favor 127 to 94 and Democrats in favor 169 to 13. Rayburn, McCormack, Johnson, and Kennedy all supported the measure.

17   The Foreign Relief Act was approved May 31, 1947 (61 Stat. 125-128). The House vote on April 30, 1947, was 333 to 66 with Republicans in favor 181 to 45 and Democrats in favor 151 to 21; and Marcantonio (ALP-NY) in favor, *CQ Almanac, 1947*, III, pp. 272–73. The Senate vote on May 14, 1947, was 79 to 4 with Republicans in favor 42 to 2 and Democrats as well, 37 to 2; *CQ Almanac, 1947*, III, p. 271. Rayburn, McCormack, Johnson, and Kennedy all voted yea.

18   It was the House that changed the name from the National Security Council to the National Military Establishment and the Secretary of National Security to the Secretary of Defense. The National Security Act approved July 26, 1947 (61 Stat. 495-510). *CQ Almanac, 1947*, III, pp. 457–63.

19   Economic Cooperation Act of 1948 (Marshall Plan) approved April 3, 1948 (62 Stat. 137-159).

20   Hank Meier, "Hunting for the Middle Ground: Arthur Vandenberg and the Mackinac Charter, 1943," *Michigan Historical Review*, XIX (Fall 1993), pp. 1–21; James A. Gazell, "Arthur H. Vandenberg, Internationalism, and the United Nations," *Political Science Quarterly*, LXXXVIII (September 1973), pp. 375–94; and Thomas Michael Hill, "Senator Arthur H. Vandenberg, the Politics of Bipartisanship, and the Origins of Anti-Soviet Consensus, 1941–1946," *World Affairs*, CXXXVIII (Winter 1975–76), pp. 219–41.

21   The vote on the Vandenberg resolution, S. Res. 239, *Congressional Record*, 80th Congress, Second Session, June 11, 1948, p. 7846; and the party split 32–2 for

Republicans and 32–2 for Democrats, *CQ Almanac, 1948* (Washington, DC: CQ Press, 1949), p. 395.

22   Selective Service Act of 1948 was approved June 24, 1948 (62 Stat. 604-644).

23   Gary Donaldson, "Who Wrote the Clifford Memo? The Origins of Campaign Strategy in the Truman Administration," *Presidential Studies Quarterly*, XXIII (Fall 1993), pp. 747–54.

24   "Memorandum for the President," Clark Clifford to Harry S. Truman, November 19, 1947, Political File, Clifford Papers, Truman Library.

25   In Clinton P. Anderson's memoirs with Milton Viorst, *Outsider in the Senate: Senator Clinton Anderson's Memoirs* (New York: World Publishing, 1970), he recalled, "At the table [at the Wardman Park Hotel] I remember, were House Majority Leader John McCormack, Senate Majority Leader Scott Lucas, Congressman Gene Cox of Georgia, Congressman Bill Colmer of Mississippi, and several others" (p. 101).

26   Alfred Steinberg, "Mr. Truman's Mystery Man," *Saturday Evening Post*, CCII (December 14, 1949), pp. 24, 69ff. Not long ago, a Boston congressman telephoned Niles's secretary to ask what the K in "David K. Niles" stands for. "I haven't the slightest idea," she replied. "I guess," said the congressman, "that it must be K as in Kingmaker" (p. 24).

27   "Blacks and the Democratic Party," FactCheck.org, accessed November 12, 2014. Data in the article was prepared by the Joint Center for Political and Economic Studies.

28   Laura Weeden, *Fire in a Canebrake: The Last Mass Lynching in America* (New York: Scribner's, 2008).

29   M.J.C. [Matthew J. Connelly] memo to Niles, September 13, 1946, David Niles Papers, Truman Library.

30   Harry S. Truman, "The President's Day," September 23, 1946, Truman Library. Paul Robeson led the delegation and they met from 11:30 to 11:45.

31   Donald R. McCoy and Richard T. Ruetten, *Quest and Response: Minority Rights and the Truman Administration* (Lawrence: University Press of Kansas, 1973), pp. 48–50.

32   Jon E. Taylor, *Freedom to Serve: Truman, Civil Rights, and Executive Order 9981* (New York: Routledge, 2003), p. 75.

33   Henry Lee Moon, *Balance of Power: The Negro Vote* (Garden City, NY: Doubleday, 1948).

34   President Harry S. Truman, "Special Message to the Congress on Civil Rights," February 2, 1948.

35   *Congressional Record*, 80th Congress, 2nd Session, April 8, 1948.

36   Philleo Nash interview in Francis H. Heller, ed., *The Truman White House: The Administration of the Presidency, 1945-1953* (Lawrence: Regents Press of Kansas, 1980), pp. 51–56, esp. p. 53. Niles and Nash did not always get along as revealed in this exchange from the Nash Oral History at the Truman Library:

> HESS: Did you or Mr. Niles confer with Mr. Ross very often on civil rights matters?
> NASH: Dave Niles was not a man to confer with anybody very much. Dave Niles was a loner—he knew exactly what he intended to do and how and when and where, and he didn't confer much with other people because he found that if their views didn't coincide with his it just resulted in a conflict. So he operated very much on his own. I saw a good deal more of other people on the White House staff than Dave Niles did, and this, as a matter of fact, was the cause of some friction between us.
> HESS: Between you and Mr. Niles. Is that right?
> NASH: Yes.

37   Two recent books on the topic are Gideon Biger, *The Boundaries of Modern Palestine, 1840-1947* (London: Routledge, 2004) and Ilan Pappé, *A History of Modern Palestine: One Land, Two Peoples* (New York: Cambridge University Press, 2004).

38   On Lowenthal, see Michael J. Cohen, *Truman and Israel* (Berkeley: University of California Press, 1990), pp. 77–82; and Allis Radosh and Ronald Radosh, *A Safe Haven: Harry S. Truman and the Founding of Israel* (New York: Harper, 2009), p. 186.

39   Oscar R. Ewing, Oral History Interview at the Truman Library, May 2, 1969, p. 276. This comment is cited in Zvi Ganin, *Truman, American Jewry, and Israel, 1945–1948* (New York: Holmes and Meir, 1979), p. 157, and is used by Michael Medved to be dismissive of Niles's influence in *The Shadow Presidents: The Secret History of the Chief Executives and Their Top Aides* (New York: Times Books, 1979), p. 224.

40   See the chapter on "State Department Opposition," in Michael T. Benson, *Harry S. Truman and the Founding of Israel* (Westport, CT: Praeger, 1997), pp. 77–90.

41   Clark Clifford with Richard Holbrooke, *Counsel to the President: A Memoir* (New York: Random House, 1991), p. 7.

42   The role of David Niles in the recognition of Israel is documented in Abram L. Sachar's *The Redemption of the Unwanted*, pp. 190–224. See also Joseph W. Pika, "Interest Groups and the White House under Roosevelt and Truman," *Political Science Quarterly*, CII (Winter, 1987–88), pp. 647–68; and David Sachar, *David K. Niles and United States Foreign Policy Toward Palestine: A Case Study in American Foreign Policy*, senior honor's thesis, Department of History, Harvard University, 1960. Not all accounts credit Niles and his name is omitted in Herbert Druks, "Harry S. Truman and the Recognition of Israel," *Journal of Thought*, XVI (Winter 1981), pp. 15–16.

43   Jacobson is cited as pushing Truman toward recognition in Michael Beschloss's book *Presidential Courage: Brave Leaders and How They Changed America, 1789–1989* (New York: Simon & Schuster, 2007), pp. 217–19. Margaret Truman Daniel, the president's daughter, challenged the Jacobson influence in her book *Harry S. Truman* (New York: William Morrow, 1973) in which she dismisses Jacobson's special plea as a "myth . . . . The whole thing is absurd" (p. 387). However, when Clifford complained to Niles about Jacobson's frequent unannounced visits to the White House, all Niles could say was "I did not arrange it; Jacobson was seeing the President for years before we began seeing the President; the President will be seeing Jacobson for years after the present date and we can't stop it" (Benson, *Harry S. Truman and the Founding of Israel, p. 123*). Benson found the quotation in Jacobson's diary at the Truman Library.

44   The Senate vote on the bill was 63 to 13 with Republicans voting in favor 39 to 1 and Democrats in favor also, 24 to 12, *CQ Almanac, 1948*, IV, p. 215. The House vote on June 11, 1948, was 289 to 91 with Republicans in favor, 178 to 35; Democrats in favor, 109 to 56; and both Marcantonio and Isacson of the American Labor Party voting yea as well, IV, pp. 220–21. The Displaced Persons Act was approved June 25, 1948 (P.L. 80-774; 69 Stat. 1009-1014).

45   Leonard Dinnerstein, "Anti-Semitism in the Eightieth Congress: The Displaced Persons Act of 1948," *Capitol Studies*, VI (Fall 1978), pp. 11–26.

46   Presidential signing statement of June 25, 1948, *Public Papers of the President of the United States: Harry S. Truman, 1948* (Washington, DC: U.S. Government Printing Office, 1964), pp. 382–84. The quotation is on p. 383.

47   A valuable case study of McCarran's efforts to scuttle amendments to the Displaced Persons bill may be found in "Amendments to the Displaced Persons Act of 1948," in

Stephen K. Bailey and Howard D. Samuel, *Congress at Work* (New York: Henry Holt, 1952), pp. 236–67.

48 "Presidential Popularity—Harry S. Truman," *Gallup Opinion Index* (1976), pp. 31–34.

49 "1948 Primaries," in Congressional Quarterly, *Presidential Elections, 1789–1992*, pp. 168–69.

50 The most complete single-book treatment of this presidential-congressional conflict is Susan M. Hartman, *Truman and the 80th Congress* (Columbia: University of Missouri Press, 1971).

51 The Henry Wallace campaign has elicited much academic and popular interest; see Karl M. Schmidt, *Henry A. Wallace: Quixotic Crusade, 1948* (Syracuse, NY: Syracuse University Press, 1960); Allen Yarnell, *Democrats and Progressives: The 1948 Presidential Election as a Test of Post-War Liberalism* (Berkeley: University of California Press, 1974); and Richard J. Walton, *Henry Wallace, Harry Truman, and the Cold War* (New York: Viking, 1976).

52 Richard Norton Smith, *Thomas E. Dewey and His Times* (New York: Simon and Schuster, 1982), p. 34.

53 Congressional Quarterly, *Guide to U.S. Elections* (1975 ed.), p. 423.

54 Floyd M. Riddick, "The Second Session of the Eightieth Congress," *APSR*, XLIII (June 1949), pp. 483–92.

55 See the "1952: Twenty-Fourth Republican Convention," in Bain and Parris, 2nd ed., *Convention Decisions and Voting Records,* pp. 268–72.

56 Warren's 1946 vote total in *Congressional Quarterly's Guide to U.S. Elections* (1975 ed.), p. 400.

57 See the account, "1948: Thirtieth Democratic Convention," Bain and Parris, 2nd ed., *Convention Decisions and Voting Records*, pp. 272–77.

58 John G. Harris, "Curley Yields to McCormack: Steps Aside as Leader of Convention Slate When Congressman Objects to Support of MacArthur," March 19, 1948, *Boston Globe* files.

59 Among the stories were: "Vice Presidential Bid May Go to McCormack," *Boston Globe*, July 6, 1948; "Move Grows to Nominate McCormack Vice President," *Boston Globe*, July 8, 1948; "McCormack Sure His Religion Won't Hurt His Chances," *Boston Globe*, July 10, 1948; and Cornelius Owens, "Bay Staters to Vote McCormack to the End," United Press, July 11, 1948.

60 *Boston Globe* files, United Press story, July 12, 1948.

61 John W. McCormack Oral History interview with Sheldon Stern, March 30, 1977, p. 20.

62 Ibid., p. 21.

63 Cornelius Owens, "McCormack Too Late, Barkley Out in Front," *Boston Globe*, July 13, 1948, p. 1.

64 Cornelius Owens, "Rep. McCormack Quits Race for Vice President," *Boston Globe*, July 13, 1948.

65 Eben Ayers, Oral History Transcript, Truman Library, April 19, 1967.

66 See Alben Barkley's account in his *That Reminds Me: The Autobiography of the Veep* (Garden City, NY: Doubleday, 1954), pp. 200–204.

67 "Progressive Party Platform, 1948," in Kirk H. Porter and Donald Bruce Johnson, eds., *National Party Platforms, 1840–1968*, 4th ed. (Urbana: University of Illinois Press, 1970), pp. 441–42.

68   Samuel J. Eldersveld, "The Influence of Metropolitan Party Pluralities in Presidential Elections: A Study of Twelve Key Cities," APSR, XLIII (December 1949), pp. 1199–1206.

69   "Democratic Party Platform, 1948," in Porter and Johnson, eds. *National Party Platforms, 1840–1968*, 4th ed., pp. 430–36.

70   Democratic National Convention, *Proceedings, 1948*, p. 180.

71   Ibid., p. 181. For an analysis of Humphrey's role at the 1948 convention, see Irwin Ross, *The Loneliest Campaign: The Truman Victory of 1948* (New York: New American Library, 1968), pp. 121–26.

72   The first analytical assessment of the Dixiecrats was Sarah McCulloch Lemmon, "Ideology of the 'Dixiecrat' Movement," *Social Forces*, XXX (December 1951), pp. 162–71. Its origins and later implications may be found in Kari Frederickson, *The Dixiecrat Revolt and the End of the Solid South, 1932–1968* (Chapel Hill: University of North Carolina Press, 2001); and Scott Buchanan, "The Dixiecrat Rebellion: Long-Term Partisan Implications in the Deep South," *Politics and Policy*, XXXIII (2005), pp. 754–69.

73   This account of the "turnip session" comes from Clark Clifford's memoir with Richard Holbrooke, *Counsel to the President: A Memoir*, pp. 222–24.

74   Harry S. Truman, *Memoirs by Harry S. Truman, Years of Trial and Hope* (Garden City, NY: Doubleday, 1956), p. 208.

75   EXECUTIVE ORDER 9981 *Establishing the President's Committee on Equality of Treatment and Opportunity in the Armed Forces (July 26, 1948):* WHEREAS it is essential that there be maintained in the armed services of the United States the highest standards of democracy, with equality of treatment and opportunity for all those who serve in our country's defense: NOW THEREFORE, by virtue of the authority vested in me as President of the United States, by the Constitution and the statutes of the United States, and as Commander in Chief of the armed services, it is hereby ordered as follows: 1. It is hereby declared to be the policy of the President that there shall be equality of treatment and opportunity for all persons in the armed services without regard to race, color, religion or national origin. This policy shall be put into effect as rapidly as possible, having due regard to the time required to effectuate any necessary changes without impairing efficiency or morale.

76   See the fascinating chapter, "Ike and Harry on Race," in William Lee Miller's book, *Two Americans: Truman, Eisenhower, and a Dangerous World* (New York: Alfred A. Knopf, 2012). Ike's Senate testimony is described on pp. 322–23.

77   U.S. Senate Armed Services Committee *Hearings on Universal Military Training* (Washington, DC: U.S. Government Printing Office, 1948), p. 996.

78   Richard M. Dalfiume, *Desegregation of the U.S. Armed Forces: Fighting on Two Fronts* (Columbia: University of Missouri Press, 1969), p. 167. General Bradley's opposition appears on pp. 162 and 166–17 and MacArthur's on pp. 206 and 210. Bradley eventually apologized to President Truman when he realized that Truman was deeply committed to the desegregation policy and would not back down.

79   Rawn James, III, *The Double V: How Wars, Protest, and Harry Truman Desegregated America's Military* (New York: Bloomsbury, 2013); and Jon E. Taylor, *Freedom to Serve: Truman Civil Rights, and Executive Order 9981* (New York: Routledge, 2013).

80   See "Campaign Itineraries," Part IV of John H. Runyon, Jennifer Verdini, and Sally S. Runyon, eds., *Source Book of American Presidential Campaigns and Election Statistics, 1948–1968* (New York: Frederick Ungar Publishing, 1971), pp. 142–48 for the 1948 election.

81 Smith, *Thomas E. Dewey and His Times*, p. 263.

82 "Wallace in Boston Today; Socialists to Picket Garden Rally," *Boston Globe*, September 18, 1948, pp. 1 and 3; and Paul M. Kennedy, "6 Hecklers Ejected, Wallace Goes in Garden Back Door," *BG*, September 19, 1948, p. C21.

83 Cleveland Amory, a self-critical Brahmin, makes this point about Governor Bradford in *The Proper Bostonians* (New York: Dutton, 1947), p. 345.

84 "Tobin Accepts Cabinet Post; Drops from Race for Bay State Governor, Notifies Dever He'll Back Him in November," *BG*, August 12, 1948, p. 1.

85 Full-length biographies of Cushing include Joseph Dever, *Cushing of Boston: A Candid Portrait* (Boston: Brice Humphries, 1965); and John Henry Cutler, *Cardinal Cushing of Boston* (New York: Hawthorn Books, 1970). A recent assessment focusing upon Cushing's lack of anti-Semitism may be found in James Rudin, *Cushing, Spellman, and O'Connor: The Surprising Story of How Three American Cardinals Transformed Catholic-Jewish Relations* (Grand Rapids, MI: W.B. Eerdmans 2012).

86 John Robinson, "Among Friends, Truman Liked to Visit Boston," *BG*, December 23, 1973, p. 7.

87 The Boston episode appears on p. 280 and is quoted from an oral history interview of Eben Ayers with Jerry N. Hess, dated April 19, 1967, and on file at the Harry S. Truman Library and Museum, Independence, Mo. Quotations from his diary have been compiled in Robert H. Ferrell, ed., *Truman in the White House: The Diary of Eben A. Ayers* (Columbia: University of Missouri Press, 1991).

88 A sardonic view of this campaign may be found in Jules Abels, *Out of the Jaws of Victory* (New York: Holt, 1959). See also Irwin Ross, *The Loneliest Campaign: The Truman Victory of 1948* (New York: New American Library, 1968); and Zachary Karabell, *The Last Campaign: How Harry Truman Won the 1948 Election* (New York: Knopf, 2000).

89 Lubell, "The Man Who Bought Time," in *The Future of American Politics*, chapter 2, pp. 26–42.

90 V. O. Key, Jr., *Southern Politics in State and Nation* (New York: Alfred A. Knopf, 1949), pp. 329–44.

91 Data from Harold W. Stanley and Richard G. Niemi, eds., *Vital Statistics on American Politics*, 2nd ed. (Washington, DC: Congressional Quarterly, 1990), table 4–8, p. 133. The 1912 figure was 25.2% (84 of 333).

92 In the words of the most knowledgeable of the Rayburn scholars, Professor Anthony Champagne of the University of Texas-Dallas, "Yes, although there was a bit of a boomlet for Rayburn in 1952, but it never went anywhere. . . . But I think Rayburn realized a Southerner from his generation could never be President" (October 9, 2015).

93 John Connally with Mickey Herskowitz, *In History's Shadow: An American Odyssey* (New York: Hyperion, 1993), p. 114.

94 These data may be found in David Burner's remarkable book, *The Politics of Provincialism: The Democratic Party in Transition, 1918–1932* (New York: Alfred A. Knopf, 1968), pp. 233–43.

95 Matthew Rozsz, "The History of the Jewish Vote," in his *Risking Hemlock* blog, May 27, 2009, accessed September 20, 2014.

96 The best account remains Nancy J. Weiss, *Farewell to the Party of Lincoln: Black Politics in the Age of FDR* (Princeton, NJ: Princeton University Press, 1983).

97 Quotation from Adam Clayton Powell, Jr., *Adam by Adam: The Autobiography of Adam Clayton Powell, Jr.* (New York: Dial Press, 1971), p. 79.

98 Samuel Lubell, *The Future of American Politics*, 3rd ed. rev. (New York: Harper Colophon, 1965), p. 200. It was first published in 1951.

99 Nash to Truman, November 6, 1948, Clifford Papers, Truman Library as reported in John Acacia, *Clark Clifford: The Wise Man of Washington* (Frankfurt: University Press of Kentucky, 2009), p. 114.

100 Thomas P. O'Neill, Jr. with William Novak, *Man of the House: The Life and Political Memoirs of Speaker Tip O'Neill* (New York: Random House, 1987), p. 55.

101 Ibid., p. 56.

102 See "The Democratic Ascendancy," in Cornelius Dalton, John Wirkala, and Anne Thomas, *Leading the Way: A History of the Massachusetts General Court, 1629–1980* (Boston: Office of the Massachusetts Secretary of State, 1984), pp. 277–83.

The Lost Peace, Korea, and Anti-Communism

Harry Truman's improbable presidential victory enabled Democrats to regain control of both the House and the Senate in the 81st Congress, with a 75-seat gain in the House and a nine-seat gain in the Senate. The 263–171 party split in the House was their best since the 1940 election, and the 54–42 split in the Senate wiped out Republican gains in the previous election. Conditions looked good for a resuscitation of the New Deal or its Harry Truman variant, the Fair Deal. Sam Rayburn returned to the speakership in 1949, but it was a deceptive majority of Democrats over which he presided. Yet again, John McCormack was chosen as Majority Leader without opposition.[1]

In the Senate, Scott W. Lucas of Illinois, who had served as Democratic Whip under new Vice President Alben Barkley, moved into Barkley's old slot of Senate Majority Leader. Senator Francis J. Myers of Pennsylvania filled Lucas's job of Senate Majority Whip. Both Lucas and Myers had served in the House during the late 1930s when Rayburn was Majority Leader and McCormack was doling out committee assignments. Scott Lucas was a Senate heavyweight; Myers was not; neither would survive their 1950 reelection bids.

Having a former Senate Majority Leader serving as vice president presented the Democrats with a unique opportunity, so President Truman began to meet regularly with the top congressional Democrats, calling them "the Big Four," a term he first applied during his time as FDR's vice president.[2] Vice President Barkley and Majority Leader Lucas would present the Senate stance on issues while Speaker Rayburn and Majority Leader McCormack would present that of the House. Senate Whip Francis Myers did not make the cut.

The Southern Chair Phalanx: Liberals who voted for Truman over Wallace were dismayed to learn that the large Democratic majority of the 81st Congress was controlled philosophically by archconservatives from the South. It was they who survived the 1946 election and their unbroken seniority gave them committee chairmanships, Of the 19 House standing committees which remained after the 1946 Legislative Reorganization Act, 14 would have southern or border state chairs for all or part of the 81st Congress. Nine committees would begin 1949 chaired by southerners with two others from the border states. Before the 81st Congress ended two years later, four committee chairs would die, and three of them would shift their chairmanships from northerners to southern and border state members.[3]

These southern chairs may not have voted for Dixiecrat J. Strom Thurmond, but they seemed far more attuned to his policies than to those of the president. Protected by the seniority system, these southerners overwhelmingly dominated the roster of committee chairs. Columbia's Ira Katznelson used the term "Southern Cage" to describe the powerful grip that the South had over congressional policy in the 20 years between 1933 and 1952, when presumably liberal Democratic Presidents Franklin Roosevelt and Harry Truman held the White House.[4]

Among these committees were both of the House's major money committees—Ways and Means chaired by Robert L. "Muley" Doughton of North Carolina and Appropriations chaired by the crusty Clarence Cannon of Missouri. Mid-level committees such as Agriculture led by Harold Cooley of North Carolina, Armed Services led by Carl Vinson of Georgia, and Banking and Currency led by Brent Spence of Kentucky further extended southern and border state influence. Even the minor committees had southern and border state chairs—District of Columbia, Merchant Marine and Fisheries, Post Office and Civil Service, Un-American Activities, and Veterans Affairs.

Only six of the 19 House standing committees opened the 81st Congress chaired by northerners. It was 73-year-old Mrs. Mary T. Norton of New Jersey, who had cochaired the 1944 National Convention's Resolutions Committee with John McCormack, who chaired House Administration and Sam Rayburn's legislative copilot Robert Crosser of Ohio chaired Interstate and Foreign Commerce. The seniority system also rewarded ethnic minorities from safe congressional districts. McCormack's urban Jewish allies chaired three committees—Adolph Sabath of Chicago on Rules and Sol Bloom and Emanuel Celler of Brooklyn chaired Foreign Affairs and Judiciary respectively. Bloom's death in May 1949 shrank the number of northern chairs to five. These were not troublesome selections. Apart from a bizarre 1945 episode when Mississippi's anti-Semitic John Rankin had tried to put his fist in Manny Celler's face declaring that "the white Gentiles of this country also have some rights," religion had subsided as a point of Democratic divisiveness.[5] For John McCormack, it was further proof of the depth and breadth of Rankin's prejudices.

Racial balancing on the committees

While religious divisiveness had diminished, race remained. It was the incoming chair of Expenditures in the Executive Departments who presented a problem for a leadership bent on containing the racial divisions that had split the presidential Democrats in 1948. William L. Dawson of Chicago, a black Representative, was now the Expenditures Committee second-ranking Democrat behind John McCormack who was expected to leave that slot to resume the majority leadership. But would he be chair? Handling this matter required some delicacy on John McCormack's part, but first he had to pay some fealty to the South.

Remembering how close he had come to losing a spot in the House leadership two years earlier, John McCormack sought to cement himself further in southern esteem by permitting the return of his segregationist "poker pal" Mississippi's William M. Colmer to the agenda-setting House Rules Committee. Colmer had served on the committee previously from 1939 to 1947, but had lost his seat when the Democrats became the minority in 1947 and their seats were halved from eight to four.[6] Knowing of Colmer's segregationist politics, Sam Rayburn originally objected but reluctantly acceded to the prior commitment made by McCormack.[7] Rayburn and McCormack would come to regret this move as Colmer would consistently vote with fellow segregationist Howard W. Smith of Virginia.[8]

While southern segregationists may have been placated with Colmer's return to the Rules Committee, urban African-American Democrats were not. It was their votes in the large urban centers that contributed to Truman victories in the electoral vote-rich states of Illinois, Michigan, Missouri, and Maryland. Those four states provided the Truman-Barkley ticket with 70 electoral votes—23.1% of its 303 electoral vote total—easily overcoming the 38 electoral votes won by the Dixiecrats in Alabama, Louisiana, Mississippi, and South Carolina.

Dixiecrats may have failed to have the 1948 contest tossed into the House of Representatives, but they did have an impact on the politics of the House. Dixiecrat-supported Carl Elliott of Alabama defeated four-term Representative Carter Manasco, a longtime aide to late House Speaker Will Bankhead who filled Bankhead's seat after Will's 1940 death. In March 1944 during the 78th Congress and only in his second term, Manasco was elevated to the chairmanship of the Expenditures Committee. He had begun that Congress in the sixth majority slot, but as its more senior members moved to better committees or eschewed the Expenditures chairmanship, Manasco had become its chair. It was more of a testament to the committee's relative lack of importance than to Manasco's legislative skills. Earlier in that Congress, William L. Dawson of Chicago had begun his congressional committee career as the 12th and last ranking majority Democrat on Expenditures. Two years later, Dawson had become its sixth-ranking majority member.

Congressional African Americans: Bill Dawson was only the second black Democrat to serve in Congress. With Republicans then still known as the "party of Lincoln," all 23 blacks who served in Congress between 1870 and 1933 were Republicans.[9] The first blacks to serve in Congress were beneficiaries of the Reconstruction Era, with two Republicans serving in the Senate from Mississippi—Hiram R. Revels, 1870–71, and Blanche K. Bruce, 1875–81. Louisiana's P. B. S. Pinchback was elected to the Senate in 1875 but not seated. Twenty black Republicans served in the House—14 in the Reconstruction era, 1870–77, and six post-Reconstruction, 1877–1901. The 1900 defeat of North Carolina Republican George H. White ended black representation in Congress for a generation. Southern Jim Crow laws were legitimated by the U.S. Supreme Court in its unfortunate "separate but equal" *Plessy v. Ferguson* decision in 1896, making it easy for segregating white legislators to disenfranchise their states' black citizens.[10]

Although large numbers of southern blacks eager to escape segregation moved north to the major Midwestern metropolises of Chicago and Detroit, 28 years would pass before another African American would be elected to Congress. It was in Chicago that the first twentieth-century African-American congressman would be elected, Republican, Oscar S. De Priest, a native of Alabama and the son of former slaves.[11] In 1934, De Priest was defeated by Arthur W. Mitchell, the House's first African-American Democrat, a beneficiary of Alabama's John McDuffie, John McCormack's primary House mentor and leadership sponsor. Mitchell, the House's first ever black Democrat, was also a native of Alabama, a graduate of Alabama's Tuskegee Institute and a protégé of Booker T. Washington, who helped him gain admission to Columbia University. Chicago's growing reputation as a base for black politicians led him to relocate, and after a stint as a Republican, Mitchell ran as a Democrat in 1934 and defeated De Priest.[12]

In 1942, Mitchell was succeeded by Georgia native William Dawson, an alumnus of Fisk University and Northwestern University Law School.[13] Like Mitchell, Dawson began his career as a Republican but moved into the Democratic Party. As a Democrat, he easily won election to the House in 1942 and would serve for 28 years until his death in 1970. Like other pre-Reorganization junior members, Dawson served on a number of minor House committees until he received the sixth place on Expenditures in the Executive Departments in 1946.

McCormack Steps Aside: When Republicans gained control of the House in 1946, John McCormack's title had been diminished from House Majority Leader to House Minority Whip. As majority leader, John was not obliged to serve on any committees, but as minority whip he initially chose to serve on House Administration in the second slot behind ranking member Mary Norton which then had six freshmen among its 11 Democratic members. On February 26, 1947, John swapped seats with freshman Charles B. Deane (Dem-NC) and left House Administration for Expenditures in the Executive Departments.[14] Once again, he was placed in its second Democratic slot behind Carter Manasco and ahead of John J. Delaney of New York and Bill Dawson, who now ranked as the third and fourth minority members respectively. During Manasco's years as secretary to Will Bankhead, he and John got to know each other when John served as chair of the Democratic Caucus, the House Democrats' fourth-ranking post during Bankhead's last years as Speaker, 1939–40.

With Democrats regaining the House in 1948, John resumed his old post as Majority Leader but with Manasco's defeat, John was now also the ranking Democrat on Expenditures. It was certainly not as prestigious a committee as his former assignment to Ways and Means, but McCormack brought his prestige with him. John stepped aside to permit Bill Dawson to become the first black to ever chair a standing committee of Congress (Figure 14.1).

As John declared on January 1, 1949[15]:

> While I will remain on the Committee on Expenditures in the Executive Departments, I shall step aside as ranking member, which will enable Congressman William L. Dawson, of Illinois, to become chairman.
>
> It is a source of pleasure to me that Congressman Dawson will become chairman of this important committee. In addition, it will be a happening of great and pleasant significance.

John McCormack's willingness to serve under a black chair was not a surprise to those who knew of his friendly relationship with Dawson's predecessor Arthur Mitchell, the

Figure 14.1 U.S. Representative William L. Dawson (Dem-Ill.) (Wikimedia).

House's first ever black Democrat.[16] John's decision averted a nasty showdown and preserved the chairmanship for Dawson. John remained on the committee until he assumed the speakership 13 years later. Whether John McCormack was motivated by a desire to protect the seniority system or to prevent a loyal House member from being sandbagged by racism is immaterial. The fact is that John McCormack intervened on Dawson's behalf and made history.

Despite John's contention, the Expenditures Committee was not an important committee but it did have some power as the Legislative Reorganization Act gave it the "primary responsibility over: (A) Budget and accounting measures, other than appropriations. (B) Reorganizations in the executive branch of the Government."[17]

On July 3, 1952, the committee's name was changed to Government Operations. This was the only standing committee upon which John McCormack served from 1947 until his selection as Speaker pro tem in 1961. As the 81st Congress opened under Dawson as chair, McCormack settled into the sixth majority slot on the committee.

Ten ranks below him in the 16th slot was a talented freshman from Kansas City who would quickly become a favorite of Sam Rayburn's and later John McCormack's most scathing critic—Richard W. Bolling of Missouri.

William Dawson made relatively few waves as chair and was publicly deferential to white people. Dawson was so uncomfortable with the cool stares of whites that he regularly refused to sit in the "Members Only" dining room in the House. Dawson avoided the House Restaurant, determined not to encounter the same embarrassment visited upon Oscar De Priest when he learned that his membership in the U.S. House did not entitle him to the same privileges as the white members.[18] Unlike Harlem's Adam Clayton Powell, Jr., the only other sitting black member of the 81st Congress, Bill Dawson knew "his place." Powell was the second black House member to chair a congressional committee when he succeeded North Carolina's conservative Graham Barden as chair of Education and Labor in 1961. John McCormack's relationship to the self-aggrandizing and bumptious Powell was very dissimilar from his relationship with the unassuming Dawson.

Historian Christopher Manning described Dawson's attitude toward white legislators as seething with restrained hostility: "I won't break bread with them. They invite me to big dinners and the like. I won't go. Why should I? I know what they want from me. I don't need a meal from them, and I am not flattered by their company."[19] Manning also recounted Dawson's opinions of southern congressmen: "Sometimes if I am offered a cigarette—particularly from a white southerner—I'll take it. Then I'll stand there and make him light it."[20]

During Dawson's lengthy chairmanship, southern representation on the committee originally diminished but it did not disappear.[21] While there were six southerners among the 10 Democrats seated in the 80th Congress, 1947–49, when Manasco was ranking member, there were only three southerners among the 18 seated in the 81st Congress, 1949–51, when Dawson became chair. The percentage of southerners remained below their chamber average in the next two Congresses, but by 1955, the number had returned to six. With the heavy demands of their presence on the floor, majority leaders were disinclined to continue their committee assignments, but John McCormack knew how important it was that Dawson's chairmanship be unchallenged and he remained listed on the committee's roster until January 10, 1962, when he resigned to assume the speakership.

Because it was known that McCormack had a good memory and a penchant to limit the reach of disruptive ambitious members, Dawson's chairmanship of the committee was relatively untroubled. Having an opportunity to serve on the same committee with the majority leader was not one to be wasted. It appears that John McCormack's efforts that same year to return Bill Colmer of Mississippi to the Rules Committee was his way of convincing harder-nosed Democratic segregationists to accept the Dawson chairmanship (Figure 14.2). To John McCormack, the presidential wing of the Democratic Party had fumbled the race question at the 1948 convention with its strident civil rights platform. The Austin-Boston House leaders knew how to balance these divisive interests and to avoid walkouts.

Figure 14.2 U.S. Representative William Colmer (Dem-Miss.) (Wikimedia).

Kennedy for the Rules Committee?

While John McCormack returned to the House for his 11th full term, Jack Kennedy began only his second term. More than any of the other newcomers, Kennedy understood the media. His father's successful career in the movie business[22] and his own early years as a journalist made him sensitive to how print and broadcast coverage could create the illusion of power. In the case of the House, newsworthiness could compensate for lack of seniority. He witnessed this phenomenon first-hand as California Republican Dick Nixon who, like Jack in 1949, was the seventh-ranking member of his party on Education and Labor and used his committee membership on Un-American Activities to become a major media star.[23]

As media coverage of Nixon grew, Jack could not help but notice that that Nixon's internal stature grew as requests for external speaking engagements increased. It soon became clear to Jack that fellow second-termer Nixon had lost interest in the labor-management and parochial school funding issues that continued on the Education and Labor Committee's agenda. The cause of anti-Communism that Nixon had successfully used to defeat five-term incumbent Jerry Voorhis in 1946 had taken on a new urgency as Nixon deepened his involvement with Whittaker Chambers, the portly ex-Communist *TIME* magazine editor.[24] Chambers's riveting testimony before Nixon's House Un-American Activities Committee (HUAC) would take down former senior State Department official Alger Hiss, now the president of the Carnegie Endowment for World Peace. This was a huge coup for Nixon, who was well aware that this was his ticket out of the House into the Senate and, hopefully, beyond.[25]

Nixon's second committee assignment, Un-American Activities, was a media magnet while Jack's District of Columbia Committee was a media black hole which generated pointless meetings and no media attention whatsoever. To become the major national player that his father envisaged for him, Jack needed to escape the purgatory of these lesser assignments.

The 1948 election not only returned Democrats to power in the House, it also brought with it 95 House freshmen, most of whom were Democrats who would need majority seats on House committees. More than one hundred new majority slots opened up throughout the revamped committee system, as committee ratios shifted to accommodate their new majority. Democratic committee assignments were now in flux.

Jack Kennedy felt that he had served his apprenticeship on the Education and Labor and District of Columbia Committees. The Reorganization Act had combined the separate Education and Labor committees, with its Democratic members seeing themselves as legislative protectors of organized labor from the direct assaults emanating from the pro-business Republicans on the committee. Education and Labor was fast developing a reputation for being the most contentious committee in the House.[26] Kennedy's first Democratic chair in 1949 was the unimpressive John Lesinski of Michigan who often bragged about how ironic it was that a fourth grade–educated slug like himself could chair the education committee. This was not something that Kennedy, an honors graduate of Harvard, wished to have regularly echoing in his ears.

The District of Columbia Committee was also a poor choice and it got worse when Jack's first chair on the committee, the estimable and grandiloquent Republican Everett McKinley Dirksen of Illinois, left the House in 1949 to deal with eyesight issues. Dirksen and Kennedy would later cross swords in 1961–63 when Jack was in the White House and Dirksen was Senate Minority Leader. The District Committee's new chair was Democrat John L. "Johnny Mac" McMillan of South Carolina, who was a racist of a milder variety than Mississippi's John Rankin, but a racist nonetheless who treated the predominantly black residents of the District of Columbia as part of his own personal plantation.[27] Jack wanted out of these committees, but he needed help.

Kennedy had good reason to be hopeful. Most of the 95 new House members were Democrats from northern and western districts. The seat ratio would shift toward the Democrats since they were now the majority party. Those seats, plus those belonging to defeated and retiring members, easily brought the total to more than two hundred new assignments to be made. As with all young ambitious House members, Kennedy's attention focused on the "big three" standing committees of Ways and Means, Rules, and Appropriations. There were six majority vacancies on Ways and Means, five on Rules, and twelve on Appropriations. Electorally, Kennedy's unopposed 1948 reelection bid indicated that he had survived both crises of voting for the anti-FDR

22nd Amendment and not signing the Jim Curley petition. While they may have bothered John McCormack, neither issue seemed to have bothered the voters of the 11th Massachusetts District, who reelected him unopposed. Jack clearly had a safe seat, and it was now time to collect on that anticipated seniority.

Jere Cooper, Assignment Gatekeeper: The key players in making committee assignments for the Democrats were their 15 members on the House Ways and Means Committee.[28] It was the House's oldest standing committee, and the one charged with fulfilling the House's constitutionally mandated function of funding the national government, either through tariffs or through taxes. While the Ways and Means Committee got its power over federal income taxes in the 16th Amendment of 1913, its Democratic members got their power to name fellow Democrats to standing committees in 1911. This was in reaction to the arbitrary assignments issued by four-term Republican Speaker Joseph G. "Uncle Joe" Cannon of Illinois who had abused the power of assigning members to committees, a cherished prerogative of House Speakers since 1790.[29]

Democratic members on Ways and Means could not be appointed to the committee; they had to be elected to it by the Democratic Caucus. Consequently, there were never any Democratic freshmen on Ways and Means, and the Democratic member with the least seniority elected to the committee was John McCormack himself, who was elected to the committee in 1931 during his third year in the House.

Chairing the Ways and Means Committee in the 81st Congress was Robert Lee "Muley" Doughton of North Carolina, the son of a Confederate captain who was named for Confederate General Robert E. Lee.[30] Entering the House in 1911 two years before Sam Rayburn, Doughton first assumed the Chair of Ways and Means in 1933 as FDR launched the "hundred days" of the 73rd Congress. He chaired Ways and Means from 1933 to 1947 and again from 1949 to 1953—a total of 18 years. While Doughton attended to the revenue policy functions of Ways and Means, he assigned the political function of making standing committee assignments to its second-ranking member, Jere Cooper of Tennessee.[31]

Like Harry Truman, Jere Cooper had served as an Army captain in Europe during World War I. Cooper's 9th Tennessee District was in the northwestern corner of the state along the Mississippi River and adjacent to Kentucky, Missouri, and Arkansas. Tragedy befell Cooper when his young son died during his early years in the House. Consequently, Cooper, like John McCormack, was essentially childless, as were Speakers Sam Rayburn and Joe Martin and Senator Dick Russell of Georgia. For many childless politicians, the search for some semblance of family continuity leads to the identification and cultivation of younger politicians as protégés.[32] As the Ways and Means talent scout, Cooper was in a perfect place to act on that impulse.

Cooper was first elected to the House in 1928—the same year that John McCormack had won his first two House elections. After service on five minor committees, Cooper was elected to Ways and Means in July 1932 to replace deceased fellow Tennessean Edward Eslick, who had been elected to the committee with McCormack the previous year. Until John was elected Majority Leader in September 1940, Cooper and McCormack served together on the committee for eight-plus years, easily making thousands of assignments to the House's close to 50 pre-Reorganization standing committees. Needless to say, as the senior-most Democrat from Massachusetts, a former Ways and Means member, and the incoming Majority Leader, John McCormack's opinion regarding assignments for fellow Bay Staters carried a great deal of weight.

Having resumed the chairmanship of Rules, Adolph Sabath wanted reassurance from incoming Speaker Sam Rayburn that vacancies on Rules would be well filled. On November 15, 1948, Rayburn wrote Sabath, "I will see what can be done about not loading you down with people who will not work with Democrats."[33] Four days later on November 19, 1948, Cooper responded to a letter from Sam Rayburn regarding vacancies on the two most powerful House committees—Ways and Means and Rules— "and, to use your expression, be sure and see to it that only solid citizens are placed on them."[34] Cooper said that there were six vacancies on Ways and Means and five on Rules.

After listing the names of members who had been bumped off the committee in the 1946 contest and were likely to be reelected to Ways and Means, Cooper offered the names of three junior members who should be put up for election by the Caucus[35]:

> I would suggest [Edward] Hart of New Jersey, [Michael] Feighan of Ohio and [John] Kennedy of Mass., in the order named. Ed Hart is a good man anywhere but I seem to have some feint [*sic*] recollection that he probably voted for the Knutson Tax Reduction Bill. I do not have the record with me here and cannot check it and I may be wrong but that is my recollection about it. However, you know we can usually count on him. I think the same thing is true of Feighan and Kennedy.

Jere Cooper's letter cited their "reliability and regularity as observed during the apprenticeship."[36] Given the Rules Committee's responsibilities in managing the sequence of bills which came to the House floor, the leadership was always consulted in matters of this importance. With only twelve members—eight majority and four minority —it was the smallest major committee and regular attendance would be required. Kennedy's attendance record was unimpressive. He was also cited as a likely candidate for Ways and Means in Cooper's letter, but neither Kennedy nor the others mentioned by Cooper were so rewarded. Rayburn and McCormack ignored the Cooper suggestions. With the leadership blocking him, Kennedy would remain on both Education and Labor and the District of Columbia Committees for the next two Congresses, a total of six years in congressional purgatory.

This was not the springboard that the Kennedy family had hoped for when Joe purchased Jim Curley's seat. Kennedy family ambition was well known to Sam Rayburn, whose distrust of Ambassador Kennedy dated back to the 1932 convention when Rayburn served as Jack Garner's floor manager and Joe Kennedy and U.S. Senator William Gibbs McAdoo (Dem-Cal.) had convinced Garner to withdraw his presidential candidacy in favor of FDR and the vice presidential nomination. Furthermore, Sam sniffed "Senate fever" in young Jack and had no inclination of wasting years of prestigious seniority on someone who would abandon the House for "the other body." John McCormack, a longtime committee colleague of Cooper's, made no discernible effort. It appears that Sam Rayburn "got even" with Jack for supporting the anti-FDR 22nd Amendment, while John McCormack "got even" with Jack for not signing the Curley petition.

Cooper and his associates assessed the 11 desirable vacancies on Ways and Means and Rules and placed no Democratic first termers on either committee and only one two-termer on each—New York's James J. Delaney on Rules and Colorado's John A. Carroll on Ways and Means. The larger Appropriations Committee with its 45 total seats—27 majority slots and 18 minority ones—was the likeliest of the "big three" to accommodate junior members. While six of its 12 vacancies were filled by more senior members, only two second-termers and four Democratic freshmen were named to Appropriations, one of whom was Foster Furcolo of Massachusetts. Why had Furcolo been one of only four freshmen to be named to an exclusive committee, and how was he able to leapfrog Jack Kennedy? The answer to both questions was John W. McCormack.

Foster Furcolo and Larry O'Brien

The provincialism of Boston politicians like John McCormack led them to underestimate political talent from Western Massachusetts, but in 1949, two young men from Springfield, the state's third largest city, arrived in Washington to begin congressional careers that would impact McCormack for most of the next two decades. They were U.S. Representative Foster Furcolo and his key congressional aide Larry O'Brien.

Foster Furcolo was from the Springfield suburb of East Longmeadow, a small town in the Pioneer Valley of Western Massachusetts nestled in Hampden County, one of the state's least populated ones. Born in New Haven, Connecticut, in 1911, six years before Jack Kennedy, Furcolo was the son of immigrants: his father a doctor from Italy and his mother from Ireland. In Massachusetts, these are known as "mixed marriages" given the intense ethnic rivalry between these two Roman Catholic tribes. Attending public schools in New Haven, Furcolo would eventually go to Yale, where he attained his AB in 1933 and his law degree in 1936. He began his legal practice in Springfield in civil and criminal practice and moved his family to East Longmeadow.[37] During the war, he was a lieutenant (j.g.) in the Navy aboard the USS Kershaw that participated in the invasion of Okinawa.

In 1946, he was one of the returning veterans who chose to enter public life by running for the U.S. House, eschewing the earlier path to Capitol Hill through service in their state legislatures. Unlike the 1946 victors Carl Albert, Dick Nixon, and Jack Kennedy, Furcolo lost a close contest to five-term Republican incumbent Charles R. Clason, who served on the House Armed Services Committee.

In 1948, Furcolo rode Harry Truman's Massachusetts coattails and easily defeated Clason in the rematch by more than 14,000 votes. Furcolo's campaign manager in both contests was his good friend, the young Springfield lawyer, Lawrence F. "Larry" O'Brien.[38] So close were they that Furcolo had been best man at Larry's wedding to Elva Brassard in 1945. When Furcolo joined the House in 1949, O'Brien was named as his administrative assistant. Unlike Jack Kennedy who chose not to defer to House elders, O'Brien recalled that Furcolo "became a protégé of John McCormack," whom he described as the man "who ruled Massachusetts patronage with an iron hand and with McCormack's backing won appointment to the powerful Appropriations Committee."[39]

According to O'Brien's memoir, Foster Furcolo was "aggressive and had a knack for publicity."[40] Proof of O'Brien's contention was not difficult to find. Barely two weeks after being sworn in, Furcolo had impressed Congress with his proposal to have a "people's lobby" in their home districts to counter the influence of the paid lobbyists who swarm throughout the Capitol.[41] Even more remarkable was that Furcolo was granted a private meeting with President Truman at the White House on February 24, 1949, barely seven weeks after being sworn in.[42] With a powerful sponsor like John McCormack, doors opened for Foster Furcolo that remained shut for Jack Kennedy.

The power of the Appropriations Committee derives from its spending authority over the Federal Treasury. Many friends could be made with the judicious allocation of federal monies for other members' districts. A freshman member named to one of the House's "Big Three" committees was an accomplishment, and it was historic, making him the first Massachusetts Democratic freshman named to one of the House's exclusive committees. It was a distinction that marked Furcolo as a comer, much as John McCormack's third year election to Ways and Means had done for him 18 years earlier. McCormack's fondness for Furcolo was genuine, and he was always among the dozen or so House members to whom John regularly made personal campaign contributions.

O'Brien did not remain in Furcolo's Washington office for long. He returned to the local office in Springfield and in 1950, O'Brien helped Furcolo win reelection over Chester T. Skibinski, a Polish-American Republican who sought the votes of the district's large population of Poles and other Eastern Europeans. That was also the year when the Furcolo-O'Brien alliance ended unhappily. As noted by the *Boston Globe's* Mary McGrory[43]: "But in 1950 they fell out. Why, neither will say. It was a complete break and of such a serious nature that Larry O'Brien took an extraordinary step for a Bay State Irishman: he swore off politics."

However, O'Brien would not remain outside the arena for long. Larry had been introduced to U.S. Representative Jack Kennedy in 1947 by State Representative Edward P. Boland of Springfield, who would succeed Furcolo in that U.S. House seat in 1952.[44] Kennedy was impressed and in 1951, Larry O'Brien joined the Kennedy team to manage Western Massachusetts for Jack's 1952 U.S. Senate bid. Both Kennedy and O'Brien shared a disdain for Foster Furcolo.

O'Brien helped Jack win the 1960 presidential election and became best known to Washington as a charter member of JFK's "Irish Mafia." He served as Kennedy's key congressional liaison with fellow Irish-descended Speaker John McCormack and Senate Majority Leader Mike Mansfield of Montana. O'Brien was one of the very few Kennedy intimates to continue under President Lyndon Johnson and worked closely with McCormack on LBJ's House agenda until he was named as postmaster general in November 1965. O'Brien would later become chair of the Democratic National Committee and it was his Watergate Hotel office that was targeted in the 1972 ill-fated break-in that led to the 1974 resignation of President Richard Nixon.

The Patronage Battle: The other major source of McCormack-Furcolo-Kennedy tension was over Federal patronage. As all members of Congress have long known and political scientists were to learn from the writings of Richard Fenno and David Mayhew, patronage is crucial to the "credit-claiming" constituency services that members need to insure their reelections.[45] As dean of the Massachusetts Democratic delegation since Billy Connery's death in 1937 and the House Majority Leader for most of the 1940s on, John McCormack felt that he was entitled to control most of the state's patronage from Washington. With the 1950 Census on the horizon, there would be a need for hundreds of census takers in each Massachusetts district. John wanted to control their allocation. Jack Kennedy, operating from the adjacent House district, disagreed and brought the matter to President Truman's attention. Jack induced fellow junior members four-termer Philip Philbin of Clinton, second-termer Harold Donohue of Worcester, and freshman Foster Furcolo of East Longmeadow to join him. The meeting was scheduled for 11:00 a.m. on April 12, 1949, four years to the day that FDR had died and Harry Truman had become president.

President Truman's daily calendar, April 12, 1949

11:00 a.m.   Congressman John F. Kennedy, Mass.
Congressman Foster Furcolo, Mass.
Congressman Philip J. Philbin, Mass.
Congressman Harold D. Donohue, Mass.
(Congressman Kennedy asked Mr. Matthew Connelly to arrange—to discuss patronage situation)

5:20 p.m.   (The President left for the Capitol where he called on Speaker Sam Rayburn, off-the-record.)

In his oral history, Thomas P. "Tip" O'Neill, Jr., who succeeded Jack in the 11th Congressional District and became McCormack's favorite protégé, focused on the tensions between Kennedy and Foster Furcolo, his predecessor among John's Massachusetts protégés.[46]

There was never any love lost between Furcolo and Kennedy. And these are my opinions, and surely I don't want these ever to be printed until many, many years from now. But what happened was, when Jack was a member of Congress, the Massachusetts delegation was very much upset over the fact that they weren't getting a fair shake of the patronage, and they were accusing McCormack of dispersing the patronage as he felt like dispersing it . . . [Philip J.] Philbin and [Harold D.] Donohue and those fellows weren't particularly interested in patronage. But Jack, being the young fellow, had a real yen for patronage. He wanted to take care of this one; he wanted to take care of that one. So they had a meeting, and it was arranged that they would go to the White House to see Truman and complain about the patronage. When they got to the White House, Truman knew the purpose of their visit. He had talked to McCormack earlier that morning about it because McCormack had been over at a leaders' meeting. When they went to the White House, all Democratic members showed up but Furcolo. And Furcolo was one of the prime instigators, with Jack. They had come into Congress together, I guess, in '46 [*sic*] Well, I don't know whether they had come into Congress together or not, but they were both young members of Congress. And after the meeting—the President gave them no satisfaction whatsoever—Jack was furious at Foster because he felt that the President was well prepared and had his answers ready for them when they had arrived and that he already talked to McCormack about it. There could only be one leak, and the leak had to be Foster. And he accused Foster of leaking it to McCormack and not showing up himself after having helped instigate it. That was Jack's viewpoint of the thing. That was part of his ill feeling towards Furcolo.

O'Neill's account was not wholly accurate; Furcolo did attend the meeting, as revealed in a photograph of the four men leaving the White House that morning. U.S. Senator Leverett Saltonstall repeated a similar version of Furcolo's nonappearance in his reminiscences.[47] It would appear that it was Jack Kennedy needing a justifiable reason to dislike Furcolo, apart from personal disdain, who shared this version with both O'Neill and Saltonstall.

Harry Truman spent 10 years in the Senate and knew the rules of congressional deference. He advised the young Congressmen to leave well-enough alone. Later that day, the fourth anniversary of his becoming president, Truman went to the Hill to meet with Sam Rayburn and John McCormack, in the "Board of Education," where he was sitting on that fateful 1945 day before being summoned to the White House to learn of FDR's death. One can imagine how much the three of them enjoyed Jack Kennedy's discomfort and chortled at Jack's embarrassment in front of his Bay State colleagues.

Jack's House behavior worsened after that unsuccessful meeting with President Truman. Prior to the meeting, there were 44 roll call votes in the House from January 3 to April 12, 1949.[48] Jack voted on forty of them (90.9%). After the failed meeting, Jack voted on only 39 of the next 79 floor votes in 1949 (49.4%). Including reported positions taken as well as recorded floor votes, Jack's 1949 disagreements with John McCormack almost doubled from 11.9% (5/42) pre-visit to 22.4% (11/49) post-visit. Nothing bothered John more than Jack's repeated absenteeism from the floor and his assigned committees. On at least one occasion, McCormack could be seen "[looking] around elaborately for the absent Kennedy, [holding] aloft a Boston newspaper headlining a Kennedy demand for more housing, and asked: 'Where's Johnny? Where's Johnny?'"[49] Jack clearly had enough of John McCormack's leadership and was in the process of seceding emotionally from the House of Representatives.

Jack would soon hit the road to travel abroad and await the next opening to the U.S. Senate. While his ambitious contemporaries California's Dick Nixon and Florida's George Smathers had 1950 seats available for capture, Jack would have to wait three years before he could challenge Henry Cabot Lodge, Jr. in 1952.

The Fair Deal agenda

Having returned to their respective posts as Speaker and Majority Leader, Rayburn and McCormack sought to push Harry Truman's "Fair Deal" agenda that he outlined in his January 5, 1949, State of the Union Address. Truman knew that the Republican-dominated 80th Congress would not address many of these proposals.

Truman hoped that the Democratic-controlled 81st Congress would be different. His "Fait Deal" was ambitious.[50] Truman's proposed measures included a repeal of the Taft-Hartley Act, federal aid to education, aid to farmers, a tax cut for low-income earners, increase in the minimum wage from 40 to 75 cents an hour, expanded Social Security coverage, national health insurance, increased public housing, an immigration bill, new TVA-style public works projects, and a $4 billion tax increase to reduce the national debt and to finance these programs. On the civil rights front, Truman hoped for the abolition of poll taxes, an anti-lynching law, and a permanent Fair Employment Practices Commission. He received early help when Congress gave the White House some power to rearrange itself in the Executive Reorganization Act of 1949, subject to the disapproval of either House of Congress.[51]

While the 92 seat Democratic House advantage over Republicans (263–171) in the 81st Congress was the largest in eight years, Truman was not FDR, and the bitter racial tensions that the Dixiecrat revolt revealed between the Democratic Party's southern and northern wings could not be easily set aside.

In retrospect, two items stand out from Truman's address, health care and housing:

Health care: The present coverage of the social security laws is altogether inadequate; the benefit payments are too low. One-third of our workers are not covered. Those who receive old-age and survivors insurance benefits receive an average payment of only $25 a month. Many others who cannot work because they are physically disabled are left to the mercy of charity. We should expand our social security program, both as to the size of the benefits and the extent of coverage, against the economic hazards due to old age, sickness, and disability.

We must spare no effort to raise the general level of health in this country. In a nation as rich as ours, it is a shocking fact that tens of millions lack adequate medical care. We are short of doctors, hospitals, nurses. We must remedy these shortages. Moreover we need—and we must have without further delay—a system of prepaid medical insurance which will enable every American to afford good medical care.

Housing: The housing shortage continues to be acute. As an immediate step, the Congress should enact the provisions for low-rent public housing, slum clearance, farm housing, and housing research which I have repeatedly recommended. The number of low rent public housing units provided for in the legislation should be increased to 1 million units in the next 7 years. Even this number of units will not begin to meet our need for new housing.

Most of the houses we need will have to be built by private enterprise, without public subsidy. By producing too few rental units and too large a proportion of high-priced houses, the building industry is rapidly pricing itself out of the market. Building costs must be lowered.

Mixed Results: Housing issues took preeminence, and Speaker Rayburn and Majority Leader McCormack delivered with the Housing Act of 1949 which established a national housing objective and authorized Federal aid for slum clearance and low-rent public housing projects, and Federal assistance for the construction of decent, safe, and sanitary dwellings.[52] It made possible for the first time in U.S. history a comprehensive attack upon slum and blighted areas by local committees with the assistance of Federal loans and grants. It was the most ambitious public housing act ever. For John, it was an effort to replicate on a national scale what had been successfully achieved in South Boston with the Old Harbor and Old Colony housing projects. This was not the first public housing issue to come before the House during John's lengthy tenure, but it was the first major one that he managed on the House floor. It passed the House on June 29, 1949, by a vote of 227 to 186 with 192 Democrats, 34 Republicans, and American Laborite Vito Marcantonio in favor and 131 Republicans and 55 mostly southern Democrats in opposition.[53] Senate Republican leader Robert A. Taft of Ohio sponsored the Senate version of the bill, thus guaranteeing its passage and it was approved on July 15, 1949.

Truman's ambitious health care proposals were less successful but other items passed, notably the National Security Act Amendments of 1949.[54] These amendments renamed and reorganized the National Military Defense Establishment. The Departments of the Army, Navy, and Air Force would be folded into an executive Department of Defense with a deputy secretary, three assistant secretaries of defense, a nonvoting chairman of the Joint Chiefs of Staff, and an expanded joint staff of 210 officers. The vice president was added to the National Security Council. Harry Truman would make sure that future vice presidents would not be left in the dark on military matters, much as he had been by FDR.

The House Rules Committee and the 21-Day Rule

Getting bills to be voted on the House floor is the major responsibility of the leadership and it requires cooperation from the House Rules Committee, often characterized as "the traffic cop" of the House. In spite of the large Democratic House majority in the 81st Congress, this would be no easy task. At its opening on January 3, 1949, Majority Leader McCormack supported a motion by Rules Committee Chair Adolph J. Sabath (Dem-Ill.) to expedite legislation through the passage of the "21-day rule" that allowed chairs of bill reporting committees to bring bills directly to the House floor if the Rules Committee reported unfavorably on them or failed to report on them within 21 calendar days after its introduction. The large and heavily liberal Democratic majority voted 275–143 to close debate and vote on the resolution by Sabath which contained that rule amendment. With the backing of 225 Democrats, 49 Republicans, and Marcantonio, the rules change was adopted as 112 Republicans and 31 southern Democrats were outvoted.[55] It was not a long-lasting triumph and was eliminated at the start of the 82nd Congress in 1951.

Much of the problem was the discernible weakness of its 82-year-old Chair Adolph Sabath, a Jewish immigrant from Bohemia who came to the states at the age of 15 and settled in Chicago to become a Czech cog in the city's multiethnic Democratic machine. First elected to the House in 1907 during Teddy Roosevelt's presidency, Sabath had now become the House's "Dean," its longest serving member. Sabath was another one of John McCormack's urban Jewish allies, but unlike Manny Celler of the Judiciary Committee, Sabath had relatively little control over his committee. It was reported that Sabath would sometimes fall to the floor feigning a heart attack when the committee resisted his entreaties.[56]

The de facto leader of the Rules Committee was Georgia Democrat Eugene "Goober" Cox, who joined fellow southerners Howard W. Smith of Virginia and Bill Colmer of Mississippi to thwart progressive legislation.[57] Cox became the second-ranking Rules Committee Democrat in 1939 when FDR successfully purged John O'Connor from the House. It was then that Sabath became chair and Cox next in line. In June 1949, during floor debate on President Truman's ambitious Housing Act, the 69-year-old Cox started a fist fight with the 83-year-old Sabath. The two men apologized to the House, expressing their mutual admiration.[58] After 14 years in the second slot, Cox would have become chair in November 1952 when Sabath died at the age of 86, but Cox himself died five weeks later on Christmas Eve at age 72. Their deaths made Howard Smith the senior-most Democrat on the committee.

As the 81st Congress wore on, it became clear that Sam Rayburn was correct in his belief that returning Bill Colmer to the Rules Committee would be an obstructionist disaster for the Truman agenda. With only twelve members on the committee, the three southern Democrats needed only three Republican votes to stop legislation from reaching the floor. John McCormack presumably had some influence with the trio. Both Cox and Colmer were two of John's "poker pals." John agreed to return Bill Colmer to the committee in 1949 after the 1946 Republican victory had cost him a place on the committee, while Gene Cox had managed John's campaign for majority leader in 1940. Also, John and Howard Smith had worked together on prewar alien registration bills. The fourth southerner, John Lyle, a third termer from Texas, was linked to the powerful Parr family of Duval County and as a Texan on Rules, he was well aware that he owed his seat to Sam Rayburn.

The southerners had Republican allies—Leo E. Allen of Illinois, Clarence J. Brown of Ohio, and James W. Wadsworth, Jr. of New York—giving them the votes to block any legislation they opposed. The lone moderate Republican Christian A. Herter of Massachusetts left the Rules Committee in 1950 for a seat on Foreign Affairs en route to the governorship of Massachusetts in 1952. After two terms as governor, Herter joined the Eisenhower administration as undersecretary of state in 1957 and succeeded John Foster Dulles as President Eisenhower's second secretary of state in 1959.[59]

In James A. Robinson's insightful book *The House Rules Committee*, he tallied the number of bills that the committee refused to issue rules for. Examining the seven Congresses from 1947 to 1960, the 80th to the 86th Congresses, Robinson found that the Congresses varied in the committee's response to bills submitted to it with an average of 13.7 denied in the seven Congresses.[60] Rules Committee obstructionism peaked in the 81st Congress with 35 bills denied, a rate more than three times greater than the average of the six other Congresses. But thanks to the 21-day rule, Sam Rayburn and John McCormack were able to bring most of President Truman's ambitious agenda to the floor, including his highly contentious civil rights bills.

Civil rights battle, the poll tax, and the FEPC

It was the hope of the resurgent congressional liberals that Truman's commitment to civil rights could be fulfilled with anti-lynching legislation, a renewed FEPC, and the abolition of the poll tax that had been used by southern legislatures to limit if not altogether eliminate their states' black citizens from the voting rolls. Antilynching legislation never reached the House floor in the 81st Congress, but both the poll tax and the FEPC did, and both were voted upon with John marshaling the troops in favor of the bills. The key member in these battles was the staunch liberal Manny Celler, the chair of the House Judiciary Committee and another of John McCormack's urban Jewish allies. In July 1949, McCormack was able to bring an anti-poll tax vote to the floor.

With tempers fraying on two of the hottest days of the summer, July 25–26, nine votes were cast by the House in an effort to lift this onerous discriminatory burden from southern blacks. John stood his ground and fended off adjournment requests by Democrats Ed Gossett of Texas and Robert L. F. Sikes of Florida and a recommittal motion by Maine Republican Robert Hale to secure final passage of the bill by a solid majority, 273–116, with 151 Democrats joined by 121 Republicans and Vito Marcantonio voting for the measure and 92 Democrats and 22 Republicans opposed.[61]

Early in the second session, John brought the renewal of the FEPC to the floor in February 1950. Created by FDR's Executive Order 8802 on June 25, 1941, the original Fair Employment Practices Committee sought to limit discriminatory hiring practices in defense-related industries. With the war's end and the decommissioning of the troops, the original FEPC had expired on June 30, 1946. However, widespread reports of blatant job discrimination and violent attacks on returning black combat veterans led national civil rights organizations to pressure the Truman Administration to resurrect the FEPC, rechristened the Fair Employment Practices Commission, and legislate it into permanent existence.

This issue divided the Democrats at their 1948 National Convention. Led by Minneapolis Mayor Hubert H. Humphrey, northern and western liberals had been able to amend the 1948 platform to include a firm commitment to the renewal of the FEPC. It was that vote that led to the walkout of all the Mississippi and half of the Alabama delegates from the convention and the creation of the Dixiecrat revolt. Sam Rayburn was painfully aware that his fellow southerners would never accept the FEPC, a harsh reality that he first encountered in an angry April 1948 meeting.[62] But Harry Truman was insistent. The growing electoral clout of urban African-American voters could not be ignored by Truman strategists, who believed that black city votes outnumbered those of the white southern defectors.

With renewal of the FEPC a Truman priority, McCormack would once again marshal northern Democrats and enough sympathetic Republicans to pass the bill. The contentious battle raged for nine days, February 15–23, a relatively long period for a House floor vote. All told, there would be 16 votes on the bill, most of which were procedural delays to slow its passage or to kill it through a recommittal motion. The House passed the FEPC renewal on February 23, 1950, 240 to 177, thanks to a clear majority of Republicans who supported the FEPC 124 to 42 while the Democratic leadership could only deliver 116 votes for passage.[63] It was opposed by the southern phalanx that cast most of the 134 Democratic votes against it. Wanting an even stronger bill, the American Labor Party's Vito Marcantonio voted against the bill along with the House's most conservative members. The Conservative Coalition members in the House could not block the bill, but their allies in the Senate could. Senators had the ultimate legislative weapon—the filibuster.

The House had delivered for President Truman, but the Senate's entrenched and well-placed southerners were ready and eager to turn both bills to dust. And as sure as night follows day, that is what happened. Chairing the Senate's Judiciary Committee was the cigar-smoking avowed-segregationist James O. Eastland of rural Sunflower County, Mississippi, but it was the leadership of the courtly Georgian U.S. Senator Richard B. Russell, the Senate mentor to Sam Rayburn protégé Texas freshman Lyndon B. Johnson, who produced the southern filibusters to bury both bills.[64] Neither bill was voted on the Senate floor.

Without expressly admitting defeat, there would be no civil rights floor votes in the 81st Congress. The congressional segregationists had won, and African-American hopes for job protection had been dashed once again. There was one modest triumph for John in this Congress as an old favorite piece of legislation was revisited. The Social Security Amendments of 1950 extended and improved the Federal Old-Age and Survivors Insurance System and amended the public assistance and child welfare provisions of the Social Security Act.[65]

Although the president's civil rights agenda had been thwarted, with the passage of the session ending Fair Labor Standards Amendments on October 26 and the Agricultural Act of 1949 on October 31, the 1st Session of the 81st Congress had acquitted itself well. It would appear to be in fine shape for the following year and another election.[66] However, the high-profile conviction of Alger Hiss, the well-placed former State Department official on January 21, 1950, and the eruption of armed conflict on the Korean Peninsula in June would lead to the takeover of much of the congressional agenda by anti-Communist zealots.

The hovering cloud of anti-Communism

The 1945 defeat of the Axis Powers in Europe and the Pacific should have made the world a safer place, with the United States emerging as the most powerful nation on earth. The nation's responsibilities in the world had grown exponentially. For two men like Sam Rayburn and John McCormack, the world outside Washington and their hometowns of Bonham, Texas, and South Boston was a place with which neither was very familiar. Neither had traveled abroad, and John had yet to fly on an airplane. Both men were essentially provincials when it came to understanding the complexities of world geopolitics. So it also had been with their mutual friend President Harry Truman, but Truman had served in France during World War I and as FDR's presidential successor, he underwent a crash course in world politics.

Barely three months after becoming President Truman went to Potsdam, Germany, to meet with the USSR's Josef Stalin and both the outgoing Prime Minister of Great Britain Winston Churchill and his successor, the incoming Prime Minister Clement Attlee.[67] As the most seasoned and politically secure of the Potsdam conferees, Stalin was aggressive in his demands, as the Red Army moved in to occupy many smaller Eastern European nations. To counter Stalin, President Truman's implemented the "containment" policy proffered by the State Department's George F. Kennan with the Truman Doctrine to protect Greece and Turkey, the Marshall Plan to rebuild Europe's economic infrastructure, and the Berlin Blockade to airlift supplies to the encircled former capitol of Nazi Germany.[68]

While the overreach of the Soviets in Europe had been stopped, there was little that could be done in the Far East. China's warring factions, the Nationalists led by Generalissimo Chiang Kai-Shek and the People's Liberation Army led by Mao Tse-Tung, had postponed their long-standing civil war and united to defend China from Japanese incursions. Once the common foe was defeated, the fragile alliance fell apart and the civil war resumed. From 1946 until 1949, Mao Tse-Tung's Soviet-backed Communists and Chiang Kai-Shek's corrupt and badly organized Kuomintang forces rampaged through the countryside. A defeated Chaing retreated across the Straits of Formosa to the island of Taiwan. That the world's most populous country was now, it appeared, in the grasp of Communists heightened American fears.

To hard-line congressional anti-Communists, "Who Lost China" would be the new rallying cry. Two young Republican anti-Communists, 39-year-old Senator Joseph R. McCarthy of Wisconsin and 35-year-old California Representative Richard Nixon, saw this as a new postwar crusade with great political potential. Anti-Soviet anxiety increased when it was learned that the USSR had detonated its own atomic bomb in 1949. The question of how these presumably semi-primitive Russians gained this sophisticated knowledge fed widespread fears of internal subversion that must have included the passing of atomic secrets to our former ally and current adversary. The Cold War escalated on January 31, 1950, when President Truman ordered the development of the far more deadly hydrogen bomb. Much like 1941, rumors of war filled the airwaves. The armed forces had already been integrated in 1949 under a single Cabinet post, and the American military was far better prepared for war than it had been eight years earlier. Would there be another war barely five years after the previous one had ended? Yes, there would be another war, but not in Europe where most had anticipated but on the other side of the Pacific Ocean, on the Korean Peninsula, thousands of miles away.

Korean hostilities erupt

In June 1950, thousands of North Korean troops streamed across the 38th Parallel bisecting the Korean Peninsula. Later years would implicate the Soviet Union's Stalin as the one who encouraged this invasion, but to Americans, it was just another gruesome reminder of how a decade had forever altered the nation's place in the world. Only 10 years earlier, isolationists had controlled the nation's foreign policy agenda and noninvolvement was a national mantra. With decisive victories on two continents in less than four years, the United States was indisputably the world's most powerful nation. The price of this new role would be steep, and the Korean Peninsula would be the first place that it would cost American lives.

Korea was also a test of the new United Nations. Could the victors of World War II—Great Britain, France, the United States, and the Soviet Union—preserve the peace? The prospects were not encouraging. Already, one permanent member of the Security Council, China, had become a casualty of the postwar power shift. Although it was a civil war which had undermined Chiang Kai-Shek's Kuomintang, the fact that the communist ideology had motivated Mao Tse-Tung's victory upped the ante on the Security Council. The three Western victors were able to pressure the U.N. General Assembly to accept Chiang's Taiwanese government in exile as the "real China" and to preserve its seat on the Security Council.

The 81st Congress did not issue a declaration of war in Korea. Instead, the war was referred to as a "police action." The American public never fully supported the Korean War effort. But Korea had a major impact upon Congress as it chose to wage a two-front war, a foreign one and a domestic one, as legislation to strengthen foreign alliances were often joined with internal security legislation to root out America's supposed domestic enemies—Communists, radicals, and anyone else who could be labeled subversive.

Congress versus Communism—legislation and investigation

With anti-Communism rapidly moving to the top of the nation's anxieties, a fretful Congress was obliged to address the issue. Their efforts, many of which were misguided and sometimes demagogic may not have been able to allay most of the nation's fears, but it was through no want of energy. Two strategies emerged—legislation and investigation. Investigations may have generated more headlines and public awareness, but legislation had the longer-lasting impact as those efforts were codified into public laws.

Although the years from 1950 to 1954 are often designated as the "era of McCarthyism," assigning the blame or the credit for these troubling years to the junior U.S. Senator from Wisconsin Joseph R. McCarthy, it was Democratic U.S. Senator Pat McCarran of Nevada whose imprint was far more pronounced. While "Tailgunner Joe" may have grabbed more headlines than anyone else, Pat McCarran's power position as chair of the Senate's Judiciary Committee enabled him to create the Subcommittee on Internal Security. It became the Senate companion to the House's HUAC that thrived on investigation, but McCarran's committee produced legislation with far more long-term national impact.

The son of Irish immigrants who moved to Nevada far from the crowded East Coast tenements of their fellow displaced countrymen, McCarran entered the Senate in 1933 as FDR was inaugurated and worked his way up the committee ladder, culminating in his chairmanship of the Senate Judiciary Committee in 1943.[69] McCarran had little sympathy for FDR's New Deal and was generally ignored by fellow western Senators, who saw the New Deal's expansive programs as a way to develop the open lands of the West.

Legislating Anti-Communism, McCarran Internal Security Act of 1950: For congressional anti-Communists, the Korean conflict was a godsend that provided them with the justification they craved to toughen legislation against domestic "subversives," to grab the headlines and simultaneously keep their Democratic rivals off-balance. This renewed anti-Communist vigor manifested itself in the passage of the McCarran Internal Security Act of 1950. Drafted by Pat McCarran, then in his first term as chair of the Senate Judiciary Committee, the act established the Subversive Activities Control Board (SACB) to permit the U.S. attorney general to list organizations believed to be Communist and require that they register with the Justice Department and submit information concerning membership, finances, and activities.[70] It provided for registration of Communist and Communist-front organizations and for the internment of Communists during national emergencies and prohibited employment of Communists in national defense work. It further prohibited anyone who had been a member of a totalitarian party from entry into the United States.

President Truman was deeply bothered by the bill, contending that it would erode the Bill of Rights. He vetoed it on September 22, contending[71]: "The basic error of these sections is that they move in the direction of suppressing opinion and belief. . . . We need not fear the expression of ideas—we do need to fear their suppression."

Truman's veto did not even survive the day in which it was issued. With the Korean War going badly and American anxieties escalating, the House overrode his veto by an overwhelming vote of 286 to 48, and when the Senate voted to override the veto by the even wider margin of 57–10, the bill became Public Law 81-831. Among the 48 House votes opposing the override were 45 Democrats, two Republicans, and Vito Marcantonio. This was a vote that John McCormack missed, but five Massachusetts Democrats including Jack Kennedy and Foster Furcolo and six Massachusetts Republicans joined with 155 Democrats and 120 Republicans to put a thumb in Harry Truman's eye.[72] With Truman's approval rating among Americans continuing to slide, opposition to Truman among his fellow Democrats had become virtually cost-free, and John McCormack's job as floor leader became exponentially more difficult. McCarran's next move stirred John to action, because it touched his most passionate cause: immigration.

McCarran-Walter Immigration and Nationality Act of 1952: McCarran's 1950 act would be augmented in the next Congress as he moved to limit immigration on the same grounds of containing Communism. McCarran's xenophobia had already been on public display during his earlier efforts to stall and attempt to kill the Displaced

Persons Act of 1948.[73] In the 82nd Congress, McCarran allied himself with fellow conservative Democrat Representative Francis "Tad" Walter of Pennsylvania. Their alliance produced the McCarran-Walter Immigration and Nationality Act. This Act continued the original national origins quota system of 1924, but eliminated the exclusion of Asians.[74] It also tightened provisions for the exclusion of aliens believed to be dangerous to the country and facilitated the deportation of such immigrants. This was the first ideological test ever legislated to curtail immigration.

Francis "Tad" Walter: McCarran's House ally, Tad Walter, was a perfect fit. Like McCarran, Walter entered Congress in 1933 following FDR's first great landslide and had been somewhat supportive of early New Deal initiatives but became increasingly conservative. After paying his dues on four minor committees in the 73rd Congress, Walter was named to the House Judiciary Committee in 1935, an assignment that he held until his death in 1963. For almost 17 years, 1947–63, Walter was the second-ranking Democrat on Judiciary, having to reluctantly tolerate the strident liberalism of its long-time Chair Manny Celler, a McCormack ally. With little common cause between himself and Celler, Walter yoked himself to Senate Judiciary Chair McCarran through his chairmanship of the House Judiciary Subcommittee on Immigration and Nationality. Walter had succeeded Sam Dickstein in that slot. John had little fondness for Tad Walter, as Walter was the northern Democrat that the more conservative southern Democrats sought to replace John with as Majority Leader. Walter, who regularly voted against civil rights legislation, was a northern Democrat attuned to the southern ideological agenda.

Walter began his service on HUAC at the opening of the 81st Congress in 1949 as the senior-most of the four new Democrats added to fill the committee's openings, settling into the second-place slot vacated by John Rankin. He gained the chairmanship of HUAC in 1955 and held it for more than eight years until his death. Although Walter had backed Rayburn rival John O'Connor in earlier leadership contests, he became a sometime favorite of Speaker Sam Rayburn and might have replaced John McCormack as floor leader had he not overreached his authority by having HUAC hearings televised during one of their investigatory trips to San Francisco. Sam Rayburn was bothered by the televised showboating of senators in the committee hearings, arranged by Senators Estes Kefauver and Joe McCarthy, and was determined to keep cameras off the floor and out of the committee rooms of the House of Representatives. An angry Sam called Walter into his office, and the younger man reportedly left the meeting with Sam as a "thoroughly beaten man." Quoting a Rayburn aide, "I don't know what Mr. Rayburn said but when Mr. Walter emerged to the outer office, he was as white and shaken as I never saw him before or since. The old man had obviously pulled no punches."[75]

Unlike the 1950 act, John spoke forcefully to prevent the bill's passage. With barely six months left in his presidency, Harry Truman vetoed this bill, also declaring that it echoed the Sedition Act of 1798 and the National Origins Act of 1924[76]:

The idea behind this discriminatory policy, to put it baldly, [is] that Americans with English or Irish names were better people and better citizens than Americans with Italian or Greek or Polish names. It was thought that people of West

European origin made better citizens than Rumanians or Yugoslavs or Ukrainians or Hungarians or Balts or Austrians. Such a concept is utterly unworthy of our traditions and our ideals. It violates the great political doctrine of the Declaration of Independence that "all men are created equal." It denies the humanitarian creed inscribed beneath the Statue of Liberty proclaiming to all nations, "Give me your tired, your poor, your huddled masses yearning to breathe free."

For John McCormack, whose oldest nephew Jocko had married Lorna Izzo, a woman of Italian descent, and whose youngest nephew Eddie had married Emily Ruplis, a woman of Lithuanian descent, this onerous bill struck home. John's South Boston-Dorchester district may have been predominantly Irish Catholic, but with substantial pockets of Italians and Greeks from southern Europe; Poles and Hungarians from central Europe; and Lithuanians and Jews from Eastern Europe; he was well aware of the personal pain that would be visited upon these people who would be denigrated by this bill. As Harry Truman correctly pointed out, our NATO allies included the military forces of Italy, Greece, and Turkey.

On June 26, 1952, the 391 House members voted with 261 needed to override. The override passed 278 to 113 with 107 Democrats and 170 Republicans and one Independent, Frazier Reams of Ohio, voting to override.[77] There were only 113 votes to sustain the veto—90 Democrats and 23 Republicans. All six Massachusetts Democrats, including McCormack, Kennedy, and Furcolo, and two of its eight Republicans voted to sustain, but the override was successful and legislated xenophobia had sadly triumphed once again.

Niles Denied a Passport: David K. Niles, John McCormack's longtime White House ally and the longest serving special assistant to the president in American history, left the administration in 1951. Because the McCarran-Walter Act also limited travel abroad for presumed security risks, Niles was denied a visa to visit Israel. As he left the government after almost two decades of devoted and unwavering service to Presidents Roosevelt and Truman, Niles had at last come out as a gay man and was now living openly with his partner Boston businessman Louis Smith, a fact acknowledged by everyone who wrote to Niles in the last two years of his life. As happy as he seemed, cancer would infest his body and incapacitate him, but what took its greatest toll on David Niles and would deny him the capstone moment of his life was an internal FBI memo dated March 11, 1952, that quoted CIA Director Admiral Sidney W. Souers saying Niles was a security risk and nowhere as close to President Truman as most had believed. The FBI memo stated[78]:

Admiral Souers, advised that Niles was never close to President Truman, that he was a holdover from the Roosevelt Administration, that the only reason he had been retained was for political expediency in controlling the "New York Jewish crowd" and that President Truman had at one time stated he "turned the papers on my desk over when Niles comes into the office." Admiral Souers stated that this information is given "off the record" and should not be used in any reports.

With his status now compromised by the FBI, David Niles was prevented by the State Department from ever leaving the fearful country that he had served loyally. On September 28, 1952, David Niles died. This unobtrusive but powerful man, whose impoverished immigrant parents had carried their infant son thousands of miles across Europe and the Atlantic Ocean to escape Czarist pogroms, and who had served quietly at the elbow of two American presidents, succumbed to cancer without ever fulfilling his dream of visiting Israel, the new nation that his strenuous single-minded efforts had helped to create. Like Moses, David Niles never got to the Promised Land.

The Blair House Attack: With barely a week left to campaign as the 1950 midterm election wound to its conclusion, a frightening event occurred at the Blair House, where President Truman and his family were staying during a renovation of the White House. Two Puerto Rican nationalists from New York City, Griselio Torresola and Oscar Collazo, shot their way past the guard booths at the Blair House and got into a shoot-out with the Secret Service and the White House police. Collazo wounded one White House officer before he was shot in the chest by Secret Service agent Vincent Mroz. Torresola, the better shooter, shot three White House policemen, wounding two and killing Leslie W. Coffelt, whose return fire killed Torresola.[79]

The attempts of Puerto Rican nationalists to assassinate President Truman deeply colored the debate that became quite contentious. Truman supported a plebiscite on the new Puerto Rican constitution to determine how the Puerto Ricans wished to be governed. Congress passed legislation granting approval of the Constitution of the Commonwealth of Puerto Rico on July 3, 1952. This act provided approval of the new constitution drafted by Puerto Rico and elevated the status of the island to the status of a free Commonwealth voluntarily associated with the United States.[80] However, the new bill did not defuse the anger of the more militant nationalists who would storm into the House of Representatives in March 1954, firing pistols and wounding five House members and narrowly missing John McCormack.

The 1950 election and the 82nd Congress

The White House attack did little to enhance Truman's popularity as the continuing Korean conflict further weakened the congressional Democrats. President Truman's Gallup Poll approval ratings continued to slide as he registered a dismal 35% approval in early October with a 50% disapproval rate and 15% undecided.[81] It was a slide of 52 points from his June 1945 score of 87% in the immediate aftermath of the war's end in Europe.

As bad as the poll numbers were, the Democratic net loss of 29 seats was less than projected. While it reduced them to a 234–199 split in the House and a shrinking of their 92-seat plurality to a 35-seat plurality, they retained a nominal Democratic majority. The Senate results were much more troubling. The 12-seat Senate Democratic margin of 1948 (54–42) had been reduced to two seats (49–47). Both Senate Majority Leader Scott Lucas and Majority Whip Francis Myers lost their seats. Once again,

Figure 14.3 President Truman with Senate Majority Leader Ernest McFarland (Dem-Ariz.), Senate Democratic Whip Lyndon Johnson (Dem-Tex.), House Democratic Whip J. Percy Priest (Dem-Ky.), and House Majority Leader John W. McCormack (Dem-Mass.), 1951 (Truman Presidential Library and Museum).

seniority-protected southerners with their noncompetitive districts and stares regained philosophical control of Congress.

Arizona's Ernest McFarland succeeded Lucas. Myers's post as majority whip was filled by the Texas tornado, Lyndon B. Johnson, then only in his third year in the Senate (Figure 14.3). Having parlayed one mentor after another, including Sam Rayburn, in his quest for higher office, LBJ had placed himself on yet another threshold of power with a new mentor, U.S. Senator Richard B. Russell of Georgia.[82]

The Democratic majority in the House renewed their commitment to the Rayburn-McCormack leadership team, but their depleted numbers diminished their power.[83] When Democratic numbers ran low, legislative power shifted from the floor leadership to the committee chairs and the southerners who generally filled them. The Conservative Coalition's renewed momentum allowed it to eliminate the "21-day rule" from the previous Congress and to return the House Rules Committee to its obstructionist majority.[84] In this Congress and at this time, Speaker Rayburn and Majority Leader McCormack may have reigned, but they did not rule.

Anti-Communism: The investigative forays

The Korean stalemate, the emergence of "Red" China as a global power, and the realization that the USSR had the hydrogen bomb gnawed at the American psyche. This led to the scapegoating of the people presumed responsible for this all-too-sudden collapse of America's preeminent influence in the world. The most obvious manifestation of this sentiment was anti-Communism, and its chief congressional proponents were Senators Nixon, McCarthy, and McCarran and Representatives J. Parnell Thomas (Rep-NJ), Harold Velde (Rep-Ind.), and Francis E. Walter (Dem-Pa.) of the HUAC.

HUAC on the Attack: Members of Congress shared those anxieties, and sought to find the presumed culprits who they contended had made the United States vulnerable. Dominating the congressional stage was the House Special Committee on Un-American Activities. John McCormack was very familiar with the sentiment and the committee having chaired the committee's early incarnation in 1934–35, when most of its attention was focused on Nazi and fascist organizations.

When Texas Democrat Martin Dies resurrected the committee in 1938, John quickly realized that Dies intended to train the committee's fire on the Roosevelt Administration in order to dismantle the more egalitarian (i.e., "socialistic") programs of FDR's New Deal. John opposed its creation, but he was outvoted, and the Dies Committee came into existence. As John had correctly surmised, the Dies committee's energies were almost wholly directed toward the Roosevelt Administration. Because it was a special committee and had to be renewed at the start of each Congress, it was anticipated that it would disappear with Dies not running for reelection and the adjournment of the 78th Congress on December 19, 1944. John had underestimated his old bitter foe, Mississippi's racist anti-Semite John Rankin, who moved at the start of the 79th Congress on January 3, 1945, that the committee be reconstituted as a standing committee adding it to the permanent roster of House committees that did not have to be biennially renewed.

The Legislative Reorganization Act of 1946 abolished a number of long-standing House committees and consolidated others. Rankin's outmaneuvering of McCormack enabled HUAC to survive the reorganization and it was now listed in the House Rules as a standing congressional committee. With his friend Harry Truman in the White House, it was John's fear that HUAC and its zealous anti-Communist conservatives would use the committee to train their fire on highly placed members of the FDR-Truman Administrations. To no one's surprise, it happened, and the two most highly placed targets were Alger Hiss and Harry Dexter White.

Alger Hiss and Harry Dexter White: Alger Hiss, a graduate of Johns Hopkins and a Felix Frankfurter protégé at Harvard Law, had served in various capacities in FDR's Administration, culminating in his 1944 appointment as director of the Office of Special Political Affairs in the State Department, which was devoted to postwar planning. It was in that capacity that he accompanied Roosevelt to the Yalta Conference where FDR met in February 1945 for the final time with Churchill and Stalin. Out of that meeting came the strategy for ending the war and the hope that establishing the multinational United Nations would bring peace to the postwar world. Hiss served as secretary-general of the initial UN conference in 1945 and left government service to become president of the Carnegie Endowment for International Peace in 1946.

It was *TIME* magazine editor and former Soviet agent Whittaker Chambers who would bring the names of both Hiss and Harry Dexter White to the FBI. However, wartime exigencies and the fact that the Soviet Union was then our ally limited any further investigation of the two men. Elizabeth Bentley, another former Soviet agent, also submitted their names to the FBI and to HUAC. With national anti-Soviet anxiety rising, Dick Nixon and HUAC scored a major public relations coup on January 21, 1950, when Alger Hiss was indicted for perjury. Hiss had been labeled a Communist spy by Whittaker Chambers in testimony before HUAC in 1949. Nixon, who had taken a prominent role in the questioning of Chambers, became the greatest beneficiary of the case against Hiss and now, given the media attention as the consequence of his very public role with HUAC, had his ticket out of the House and into the Senate and perhaps beyond.

Harry Dexter White (nee Weit) was even more highly placed. An Ivy League–trained PhD academic economist with a book published by Harvard University Press,[85] White joined FDR's administration in 1934 and ultimately became a senior Treasury Department official and the link between the Departments of the Treasury and State. Much as Hiss had been involved in postwar political planning, White had been a key architect of postwar economic planning. He was a key figure along with Britain's famed economist John Maynard Keynes in the 1944 Bretton Woods Agreements that set up the World Bank and was named the first U.S. director of the International Monetary Fund. White went to Stanford, then Columbia, then Harvard. He was a good example of those "progressive" New Dealers who tried to circumvent archconservatives in both the government and the military—not least on the value of "helping" the Soviets who would, ultimately, do the World War II heavy-lifting against the Nazis.

While John McCormack did not know Hiss, he was well aware of Harry Dexter White. Like John's close friend David K. Niles, White was the son of Lithuanian Jewish immigrants who had initially settled in Boston's multiethnic West End, the political domain of "Mahatma" Martin Lomasney. Like Niles who had been born Neyhus, so too had White's surname been anglicized from Weit. White's initial foray into politics began with the 1924 Progressive Party candidacy of Wisconsin U.S Senator Robert "Fighting Bob" La Follette. Liberal Democrats were aghast at their party's nomination for president of former Woodrow Wilson Solicitor General John W. Davis of West Virginia, then a conservative corporate lawyer, and for vice president Nebraska Governor Charles W. Bryan, the younger brother of William Jennings Bryan.

Both White and Niles had worked on the 1924 La Follette campaign and each had been part of Professor Felix Frankfurter's Harvard circle, but there is no formal evidence that they interacted with one another. Neither of the two authors who have written about White came across any reference to Niles either in the La Follette campaign or in the Roosevelt Administration where both served as key Cabinet advisors—Niles as special assistant in the Commerce Department under Harry Hopkins, and White as undersecretary of the treasury under Henry Morgenthau., Jr., FDR's most trusted Cabinet secretaries[86]—two sons of Jewish immigrants, raised in Boston's North End, who both knew Felix Frankfurter, another son of Jewish immigrants. Four years younger than Niles, White was born in the West End, and then moved to a small house in the North End, Honey Fitz's turf, and ultimately to the nearby city of Everett. Unlike Niles's Boston Latin education, Everett High School was not a fast track to Harvard. White's diploma earned him a place at the Massachusetts Agricultural College, a public land grant college in the small western rural town of Amherst, now known as UMass-Amherst. White's obsession with obtaining a Harvard doctorate in economics was undoubtedly fueled by a sense of relative academic deprivation. It is not unreasonable to conclude that similar origins, career paths, high placements, and the lengths of time they served FDR made Niles and White aware of one another.

White would direct the independently funded Office of Monetary Research. With the United States entering the war following the Pearl Harbor attack in December 1941, White was named an assistant to Secretary Morgenthau to be a liaison between the Treasury and State Departments, a post where he knew better than anyone else the economic circumstances of the United States and its allies. This was what would have made him useful to Soviet agents. Early Whittaker Chambers' allegations about White were dismissed by Adolf Berle, FDR's assistant secretary of state[87] as well as FDR and J. Edgar Hoover.[88] It was the Elizabeth Bentley charges of 1945 that took hold. Bentley, who had been a courier for confidential documents, was seen as more credible by the FBI. Her charges against White were issued on November 7, 1945. The war had ended and Harry Truman was in his seventh month as the nation's new president and a new secretary of the treasury had been appointed to replace Morgenthau.

The new Treasury Secretary was Fred M. Vinson, a former House member from Kentucky, who left the House in 1938 to serve on the U.S. Circuit Court of Appeals for the DC Circuit. In 1943, FDR named Vinson to be director of the powerful Office of Economic Stabilization, which is where he was serving when Truman named him to be secretary of the treasury in July 1945. Fred Vinson and John McCormack were close friends, having both served on Ways and Means between 1931 and 1938. Fred and Harry were among John's "poker pals," and Fred lobbied for John's election as Majority Leader in the 1940 contest against Cliff Woodrum of Virginia.[89] Vinson distrusted Harry White and marginalized him within the Treasury Department.[90]

White's involvement with the USSR was known earlier than that of Hiss. The FBI's J. Edgar Hoover sent a memo in 1945 to Truman's Military Aide Harry Vaughn listing White's name along with others presumed to be providing critical information to the USSR. Despite the FBI warnings, Truman submitted White's name to the Senate for confirmation on January 23, 1946, as U.S. director of the International Monetary Fund created as part of the 45 nation Bretton Woods Conference in 1944. White was confirmed by the Senate on February 6 and Vinson had now offloaded him from Treasury. It was on June 19, 1947, when Attorney General Tom Clark opened a grand jury investigation into the Bentley charges that White resigned from the IMF.

FBI Director J. Edgar Hoover sent three incriminating reports about White to the Truman White House but the reports were apparently never read. Harry Truman disliked and mistrusted Hoover. Truman had developed a deep suspicion of J. Edgar Hoover, whom he considered to be an anti-Communist alarmist and as early as 1945, Truman complained how Hoover and his agents were "dabbling in sex life scandals and plain blackmail when they should be catching criminals." Truman believed that Hoover wanted to create an American internal security version of the NKVD and generally ignored Hoover's multiple reports of Communist infiltration.

Furthermore, there are questions whether or not Army General Omar Bradley, the chairman of the Joint Chiefs of Staff, withheld the VENONA reports from Truman.

VENONA was the name of a joint US-UK secret operation focused on Soviet communications with American citizens. U.S. Senator Daniel Patrick Moynihan (Dem-NY) contended in his book *Secrecy: The American Experience* that Bradley withheld the VENONA information from Truman, while Jerrold and Leona Schecter, based on interviews with Oliver Kirby, the deputy director of VENONA from 1946 to 1949, indicate in their book *Sacred Secrets: How Soviet Intelligence Operations Changed American History* that Truman was informed.[91]

Also, Hoover had so compromised the FBI with his covert support of New York's Republican Governor Thomas E. Dewey during the 1948 primaries and in the presidential election[92] that the White House understandably distrusted the FBI's warnings about the Treasury Department's Harry Dexter White and the State Department's Alger Hiss, the two most highly placed government officials named in these investigations.

HUAC Testimony: White was called before the HUAC to answer Bentley's charges on July 31, 1948. Two weeks later, White testified again before Richard Nixon's HUAC on August 13 and denied that he was a Communist. Within three days, the 58-year-old Harry Dexter White would be dead of a heart attack. Because White died so soon, while fellow accused Soviet agent Alger Hiss lived for 46 years after his 1950 conviction for perjury, White's case tends to be forgotten while Hiss's 1950 conviction continues to be debated. White was a far more important figure than Hiss, and Hiss contended that he was only collaterally targeted because of the White investigation.[93] White's motives in aiding the Soviets appear to be more pro-internationalist than pro-Communist. The length and depth of the Cold War has led most Americans to forget that the USSR was our major ally in World War II against Adolf Hitler, and its people suffered far more casualties, military and civilian, than all of the other allies combined.

While Hiss was formally convicted and jailed, Harry Dexter White's death closed that line of inquiry, but it would resurface early in the Eisenhower-Nixon Administration and it would involve John McCormack's one and only serious disagreement with FBI Director J. Edgar Hoover.

John McCormack and J. Edgar Hoover, a 34-year friendship

John McCormack was astute enough to know that the Republicans were using anti-Communism for political gain. But he had a unique perspective through his longtime friendship with J. Edgar Hoover. They first met at the March 1933 inaugural of FDR, when Hoover was able to gain seats on a reviewing stand for John and three colleagues. John apparently helped Hoover with FDR. In *Drew Pearson's Diaries, 1949–1959*, there is the following note: "Representative John McCormack of Massachusetts recalls how in 1933 when F.D.R. was about to fire Hoover because of his alleged membership in the Ku Klux Klan, McCormack and Congressman Oliver went to the White House twice to urge that Hoover be kept on."[94] Frank Oliver was a six-term Democratic Representative from the Bronx. While this an intriguing aside, there is nothing apart from the Pearson diary entry to confirm this story. However, both J. Edgar Hoover and Drew Pearson were past masters of leaking defamatory information. Pearson's victims only suffered embarrassment; Hoover's victims faced imprisonment. There appears to be no confirmation of the KKK link to Hoover that John was able to ameliorate with FDR.[95]

Hoover had been hired initially in 1917 by President Wilson's ambitious Attorney General, A. Mitchell Palmer, architect of the "Palmer Red raids." He moved up the ladder to the Justice Department's Alien Enemy Bureau, the General Intelligence Division (GID), and assistant to the attorney general. In 1921 when the GID was moved into the Bureau of Investigation, he was named Assistant Director. On May 10, 1924, Attorney General Harlan Fiske Stone appointed the 29-year-old Hoover acting director of the Bureau, and by the end of the year Hoover was named director. In 1935, the FBI would be formally created.

It was as director of the Bureau of Investigation that John McCormack came to know Hoover. Hoover and McCormack were fervent anti-Communists, which would explain their early bond. With the bulk of his early career serving under Republican presidents, Hoover needed Democratic allies in Congress to continue his appointed post under FDR. Representatives McCormack and Oliver were apparently instrumental in saving his job. Since John McCormack was on Ways and Means and widely regarded as a future leader and a person to whom FDR listened, Hoover saw John as a valuable ally and began to cultivate McCormack early in his tenure as director.

Their correspondence began in 1936 when John was addressed by Hoover as "My dear Congressman" and Hoover was addressed by John most commonly as "Dear Mr. Hoover" and infrequently as "My dear Director."[96] The first direct letter was sent by McCormack on December 17, 1936, in which McCormack remembers how kind Hoover was to John and his friends at the 1933 inaugural. It is double-spaced, has a semicolon, not a colon after Hoover's name and is signed "'John W. McCormack." McCormack sends "Compliments of the Season to you and your mother (and the doggie.), in whih [sic] Mrs. McCormack joins with me, I am Sincerely yours." Punctuation and typographical errors are the hallmarks of a personally typed John McCormack letter. It appears that John wished to keep some of his more confidential correspondence away from the prying eyes of his staff.

Hoover's first "Dear John" letter was written on March 27, 1946, thanking McCormack for introducing a bill to raise Hoover's salary.[97] Eight months later on November 13, 1946, John reciprocated with his first "Dear Edgar" letter to Hoover. It is a classic John McCormack letter—a short double-spaced letter thanking Hoover for congratulating John's 1946 reelection win and mentioning Mrs. McCormack, but it is signed "John McCormack." John occasionally signed his full name but most often, it will simply be "John." Hoover often signed his name but also used a stamp that said "Edgar" to close his letters to John. After 1946, the "John-Edgar" quality of their correspondence was now fixed and remained so until Hoover died in 1972. Occasionally noted on letters from Hoover's office was the following[98]:

> NOTE: Very cordial relations exist with Congressman McCormack who is known to the Director on a first-name basis. Letters of congratulations sent since 1942. Director signs letters to him "Edgar." Congressman McCormack is on the Special Correspondents' List.

Anti-Communism had never been a problem for John McCormack. As the first chair of the House Special Committee on Un-American Activities in 1934, John McCormack had listened intently to testimony about "un-American activities," which were then defined as domestic political actions linked to the furtherance of the international goals of foreign nations. Since both Adolf Hitler's Nazism and Stalin's Soviet Communism had international components that reached across the Atlantic, they had active adherents in the United States. McCormack's committee met for only a year and tried to counter both of these threats. By the 1950s, fascism was considered to be a vanquished force and only Communism remained as an international threat to the United States and its Western allies. As a devout Roman Catholic, McCormack was deeply opposed to Communism and had been one of Generalissimo Francisco Franco's most dedicated supporters during the Spanish Civil War of the late 1930s.

With Americans leading the U.N. forces battling Communism on the Korean Peninsula, House conservatives felt vindicated in their long-term hostility toward the Soviet Union. House liberals worried that their loyalty to the nation would be questioned, so they focused more upon preserving domestic gains than on promoting new programs or encouraging peaceful alternatives to the Cold War. Truman would suffer a further loss of public support in April 1951 when he removed General Douglas MacArthur from his commanding post of the United Nations troops in Korea. Truman suspected that MacArthur intended to exceed the UN mandate and roll back the Communist forces of China by invading its ally North Korea through his crossing of the Yalu River into Manchuria. After he was replaced by General Matthew Ridgway, MacArthur accepted an invitation to address a joint session of Congress. He concluded with the line, "Old soldiers never die. They just fade away." It was meant to be poignant, but it turned out to be true. MacArthur's political influence waned, but its damage to the Truman presidency and by extension, to the congressional Democrats, was irreversible.

82nd Congress, A Legislative Assessment: With the Conservative Coalition in control of much of the legislative agenda and President Harry Truman's popularity steadily dropping until it would ultimately land in the low 20s, the 82nd Congress did little to distinguish itself.[99]

The Second Session ended on July 7, 1952. It was the earliest close for a Congress since the 74th Congress convened in 1935; the first Congress seated after the passage of the "lame duck" 20th Amendment had closed on June 20, 1936. With only 111 legislative days in its second session, the 1952 session was one of the shortest sessions of the post-1935 Congresses. With presidential nominating conventions awaiting the parties, it was best to close the books on Congress and prepare for the nomination battles.

Time for a change

The internal divisions within the Democratic Party and the stalemate in Korea had taken their toll on 20 years of Democratic presidential control. Fatigue had set in, and few slogans have more appeal in such circumstances than "Time for a Change." President Truman's popularity had cratered, and with petty scandals rocking his administration, it was obvious that the Democrats seemed unable to get out of each other's way.

House Majority Leader John McCormack was well aware that the Democrats' narrow House majority was at risk, and he suspected that Massachusetts would be a featured battleground in 1952, but he did not yet know how and why.

Notes

1   Charles Hurd, "House Democrats Act to Free Bills From Rules Block; Caucus Votes 176-48 in Favor of Change to Force Measures to Floor When Stymied; Rayburn Again Speaker; McCormack Will Head Majority—Parley Avoids Decision on Un-American Group," *NYT*, January 2, 1949, p. 1.
2   Harry S. Truman, *Memoirs Year of Decisions. Volume One* (Garden City, NY: Doubleday, 1955), p. 56.
3   Graham Barden of North Carolina succeeded John Lesinski of Michigan as chair of Education and Labor; J. Hardin Peterson of Florida succeeded Andrew L. Somers of New York on Public Lands; and John Kee of West Virginia succeeded Sol Bloom as chair of Foreign Affairs.
4   "Southern Cage," Ira Katznelson, *Fear Itself: The New Deal and the Origins of Our Time* (New York: Liveright, 2013), esp. chapter 5, "Jim Crow Congress," pp. 156–94. Also Katznelson, Kim Geiger, and Daniel Kryder, "Limiting Liberalism: The Southern Veto in Congress," *Political Science Quarterly*, CVIII (Summer 1993), pp. 283–306.
5   "Rankin Shakes Fist at Celler in House," *NYT*, February 8, 1945, p. 17. Celler had learned that the American Dental Association "had urged that religious tests be required for entrance into dental colleges."
6   For Colmer's committee career, see Garrison Nelson, ed., *Committees in the U.S. Congress, 1947–1992; Committee Histories and Member Assignments, 1947–1992* (Washington, DC: Congressional Quarterly Press, 1994), vol. 2, p. 182.
7   Rayburn's opposition is stated in a letter to Jere Cooper (Dem-Tenn.), the senior Democrat on the House Ways and Means Committee, November 22, 1948, in the Rayburn Papers, Rayburn Library, 1948 files, Miscellaneous A-2, July–December as cited in James A. Robinson, *The House Rules Committee* (Indianapolis: Bobbs-Merrill Co., 1963), pp. 104–05.
8   Author's telephonic interview with Smith biographer Bruce J. Dierenfield, author of *Keeper of the Rules: Congressman Howard W. Smith of Virginia* (Charlottesville: University Press of Virginia, 1987).
9   The movement of blacks from the Republican to the Democratic Party is skillfully presented in Nancy J. Weiss, *Farewell to the Party of Lincoln: Black Politics in the Age of FDR* (Princeton, NJ: Princeton University Press, 1983).
10 *Plessy v. Ferguson*, 163 U.S. 537 (1896) in a 7–1 vote, the Court ruled that it was constitutional for white-only southern legislatures to write laws requiring the segregation of blacks in public places.
11 "Oscar De Priest," in *Black Americans in Congress* (Washington, DC: United States: Office of History and Preservation, Office of the Clerk, U.S. House of Representatives, 2009), pp. 278–85.
12 "Arthur Mitchell," in *Black Americans in Congress*, pp. 286–91.

13   "William Levi Dawson," in *Black Americans in Congress*, pp. 292–99. An insightful assessment of Dawson's career in Chicago and in the House may be found in Christopher Manning's biography, *William L. Dawson and the Limits of Black Electoral Leadership* (DeKalb, IL: Northern Illinois University Press, 2009).

14   John McCormack's committee assignments are listed in Nelson, ed., *Committee Assignments in the U.S. Congress, 1947–1992*, vol. 2, pp. 583–84.

15   "McCormack Aids Dawson: Steps Aside to Open Committee Chairmanship to Negro," *NYT*, January 1, 1949, p. 24.

16   See the letter from McCormack to Mitchell, March 16, 1936, in Doris E. Saunders, "Black Politics and Chicago: The Bill Dawson Story," in the Doris Saunders Papers, Vivian G. Harsh Research Collection, and Carter G. Woodson Library, Chicago, Illinois, cited by Manning, *William L. Dawson and the Limits of Black Electoral Leadership*, p. 197n.

17   "Expenditures in the Executive Departments," Legislative Reorganization Act of 1946, Section 121.

18   Elliott M. Rudwick, "Oscar De Priest and the Jim Crow Restaurant in the U.S. House of Representatives," *Journal of Negro Education*, XXXV (Winter 1966), pp. 77–82.

19   Manning, *William L. Dawson and the Limits of Black Electoral Leadership*, p. 93. Manning cites Christopher Robert Reed, *The Chicago NAACP and the Rise of Black Professional Leadership, 1910–1966* (Bloomington: Indiana University Press, 1997), p. 187.

20   Ibid. For this Dawson quotation, Manning cites Edward Clayton, *The Negro Politician* (Chicago: John Publishing, 1964), p. 56.

21   "Government Operations" in Nelson, *Committees in the U.S. Congress, 1947–1992*, vol. 1: *Committee Jurisdictions and Member Rosters*, pp. 511–18.

22   The fullest account is Cari Beauchamp, *Joseph P. Kennedy Presents: His Hollywood Years* (New York: Alfred A. Knopf, 2009).

23   A valuable assessment of the shared early years of Nixon and Kennedy in the U.S. House may be found in Christopher Matthews, *Kennedy & Nixon: The Rivalry that Shaped Postwar America* (New York, NY: Simon & Schuster, 1996).

24   Lance Morrow, *The Best Years of Their Lives: Kennedy, Johnson, and Nixon in 1948: Learning the Secrets of Power* (New York: Basic Books, 2005).

25   Irwin F. Gellman, *The Contender: Richard Nixon: The Congress Years, 1946–1952* (New York: :Free Press, 1999).

26   The House Education and Labor Committee had earned its reputation as the most disputatious committee in that chamber, according to Richard F. Fenno's classic *Congressmen in Committees* (Boston: Little, Brown, 1973), pp. 30–35.

27   Harry S. Jaffe and Tom Sherwood, *Dream City: Race, Power, and the Decline of Washington D.C.* (New York: Simon & Schuster, 1994), p. 62.

28   Nicholas A. Masters, "House Committee Assignments," *APSR* (June 1961), pp. 345–57. See also the sophisticated analysis of the process in Kenneth A. Shepsle, *The Giant Jigsaw Puzzle: Democratic Committee Assignments in the Modern House* (Chicago: University of Chicago Press, 1978); and a complementary book by Scott A. Frisch and Sean Q. Kelly, *Committee Assignment Politics in the U.S. House of Representatives* (Norman: University of Oklahoma Press, 2006).

29   Eric D. Lawrence, Forrest Maltzman, and Paul J. Wahlbeck, "The Politics of Speaker Cannon's Committee Assignments," *American Journal of Political Science*, XLV (July 2001), pp. 551–62; and Charles O. Jones, "Joseph G. Cannon and Howard W. Smith: An

Essay on the Limits of Leadership in the House of Representatives," *Journal of Politics*, XXX (August 1968), pp. 617–46.

30 "Robert Lee Doughton," *BDUSC* (1989 ed.) pp. 924–25.

31 "Jere Cooper," *BDUSC* (1989 ed.), p. 826.

32 This contention was presented in "The Matched Lives of House Leaders and the Policy Costs of Continuity," a lecture presented to the Institute of Politics, John F. Kennedy School of Government, Harvard University, April 20, 1977; and "The Matched Lives of U.S. House Leaders: An Exploration" was delivered to the 1978 Meeting of the American Political Science Association.

33 Rayburn to Sabath, November 15, 1948, Rayburn Papers, Rayburn Library, 1948 files, Miscellaneous A-2, July–December as cited by James A. Robinson, *The House Rules Committee* (Indianapolis: Bobbs-Merrill, 1963), pp 103–104.

34 Jere Cooper letter to Sam Rayburn, November 19, 1948, in the Sam Rayburn Library, Bonham, Texas.

35 Ibid.

36 See Robinson, *The House Rules Committee*, p. 104. Among the others mentioned by Cooper were: Edward Hart of New Jersey, Michael Feighan of Ohio, Mike Mansfield of Montana, Frank Karsten of Missouri, William Stigler of Oklahoma, Dr. Thomas Morgan of Pennsylvania, John Blatnik of Minnesota, Erland Hedrick of West Virginia, and Frank Buchanan of Pennsylvania. None of those listed, including Kennedy, were ever named to the Rules Committee; see Nelson, ed., *Committee Jurisdictions and Member Roster, 1947–1992*, vol. 2, pp. 674–85.

37 "Foster Furcolo," *BDUSC* (1989 ed.), p. 1035.

38 "Lawrence O'Brien," in William I. Hill and M. B. Schnapper, eds., *The New Frontiersmen; Profiles of the Men around Kennedy* (Washington, DC: Public Affairs Press, 1961), pp. 197–98.

39 O'Brien, *No Final Victories*, p. 14.

40 Ibid.

41 John G. Harris, "People's Lobby: Furcolo's Innovation Interests Congress," *Boston Globe*, January 16, 1949, p. c25.

42 White House calendar, February 24, 1949, Truman Library. According to the president's calendar for that day, "Congressman Foster Furcolo, Massachusetts (Wrote to the President and enclosed copy of his remarks from *Congressional Record* relative to his Federal Scholarship Plan. Asked if he might come up and discuss this with the President.)."

43 Mary McGrory, "The Right-Hand Men—Pierre Salinger, Lawrence O'Brien, and Kenneth P. O'Donnell," in Lester Tanzer, ed., *The Kennedy Circle* (Washington, DC: Luce Books, 1961), pp. 68–75. The quotation is on p. 69.

44 "Edward P. Boland," *BDUSC* (1989 ed.), p. 639.

45 These are the two most influential writers on the constituency links of the members. See Richard F. Fenno, *Home Style: House Members in Their Districts* (Boston: Little, Brown & Co., 1978); David R. Mayhew, *Congress: The Electoral Connection* (New Haven, CT: Yale University Press. 1974).

46 Thomas P. O'Neill, Jr., oral history interview with Charles T. Morrissey, May 18, 1966, pp. 50–52, John F. Kennedy Library and Museum.

47 Leverett Saltonstall as told to Edward Weeks, *Salty: Recollections of a Yankee in Politics* (Boston: The Boston Globe, 1976), p. 190.

48 House roll call data assembled from the *Congressional Quarterly Almanac, 1949* (Washington, DC: Congressional Quarterly Press, 1950), passim.

49 James MacGregor Burns, *John Kennedy: A Political Profile* (New York: Harcourt, Brace & World, Inc., 1959), p. 92.

50 President Harry S. Truman, "Annual Message to the Congress on the State of the Union," January 5, 1949.

51 Executive Reorganization Act of 1949, approved June 20, 1949 (63 Stat. 203-207).

52 Housing Act of 1949, approved July 15, 1949 (63 Stat. 413-464), Stathis, *Landmark Legislation*, p. 234.

53 Charles Hurd, "House Democrats Act to Free Bills From Rules Block; Caucus Votes 176-48 in Favor of Change to Force Measures to Floor When Stymied . . ." *NYT*, January 2, 1949, p. 1; and *Congressional Quarterly Almanac, 1949*, p. 518.

54 National Security Act Amendments of 1949, approved August 10, 1949 (63 Stat. 578-592), Stathis, *Landmark Legislation*, p. S234.

55 Robert C. Albright, "Truman Forces Win Significant Opening Battle: Rules Committee Curbed by House," *Washington Post*, January 4, 1949, p. 1.

56 This incident is described vividly in Neil MacNeil's classic history of the House, *Forge of Democracy: The House of Representatives* (New York: David McKay, 1963), p. 103.

57 The problem is well described in Eric Schickler and Kathryn Pearson, "Agenda Control, Majority Party Power, and the House Committee on Rules," *Legislative Studies Quarterly*, XXXIV (November 2009), pp. 455–91.

58 "Aged Fighters Bury Hatchet," *The Statesville (NC) Landmark*, June 3, 1949, p. 3.

59 See the biography by G. Bernard Noble, *Christian A. Herter* (New York: Cooper Square, 1970). This was volume 18 of the series on American Secretaries of State and Their Diplomacy.

60 James A. Robinson, *The House Rules Committee* (Indianapolis: Bobbs-Merrill, 1964). Rules denied by Congress: 1947–49, 80th (14); 1949–51, 81st (35); 1951–53, 82nd (8); 1953–55, 83rd (8); 1955–57, 84th (11); 1957–59, 85th (9); and 1959–61, 86th (11), pp. 25–30.

61 *CQ Almanac, 1949*, pp. 676, 678.

62 Rayburn's April 1948 meeting is recounted in Alfred Steinberg, *Sam Rayburn: A Biography* (New York: Hawthorn, 1973), pp. 239–40.

63 There were 16 FEPC House votes. It was passed on February 23, 1950, with Republicans voting 124 to 41 for the bill while the Democrats were split 116 to 134 with Vito Marcantonio joining the majority for a final vote tally of 241 to 177. Massachusetts Democrats voted 5 to 1 for the Bill with Kennedy the lone Democratic dissenter and its Republicans voted 6 to 1 with only Donald Nicholson of Wareham as its lone Republican dissenter. *CQ Almanac, 1950* (Congressional Quarterly, 1951), pp. 548–52.

64 See Keith M. Finley's superb analysis of Dick Russell's role in blocking Truman-era civil rights bills in his award-winning book, *Delaying the Dream: Southern Senators and the Fight against Civil Rights, 1938–1965* (Baton Rouge: LSU Press, 2008).

65 The Social Security Amendments were approved on August 28, 1950 (64 Stat. 477-561). Certain provisions of this Act were subsequently held unconstitutional in *Califano v. Goldfarb*, 430 U.S. 199 (1977), Stathis, *Landmark Legislation*, p. 235.

66 For a summary of the First Session, see Floyd M. Riddick, "The Eighty-First Congress: First and Second Sessions," *Western Political Quarterly*, IV (March 1951), pp. 48–66.

67 Harry S. Truman, *Memoirs: Year of Decisions* (Garden City, NY: Doubleday, 1955), pp. 333–412.

68 Kennan's influential memo was written under the pseudonym of X, "The Sources of Soviet Conduct," *Foreign Affairs*, XXV (July 1947), pp. 566–82. See John Lewis Gaddis, *Strategies of Containment: A Critical Appraisal of Postwar American National Security Policy* (New York, NY: Oxford University Press, 2005), originally published in 1982.

69 The McCarran saga is well told in the monumental book by Michael J. Ybarra, *Washington Gone Crazy: Senator Pat McCarran and the Great American Communist Hunt* (Hanover, NH: Steerforth Press, 2004).

70 McCarran Internal Security Act (including Subversive Activities Control Act of 1950), chapter 1024, 64 Stat. 987, 50 U.S.C. Certain provisions of this Act were subsequently held unconstitutional in *Aptheker v. Secretary of State*, 378 U.S. 500 (1964), *Albertson v. Subversive Activities Control Board*, 382 U.S. 70 (1955), and *United States v. Robel*, 389 U.S. 258 (1967); see Stathis, *Landmark Legislation*, p. 255.

71 President Harry S. Truman, "Veto of the Internal Security Bill, September 22, 1950," in *Public Papers of the President 1950*, pp. 645–53. The quotation is on pp. 649–50.

72 The veto override of the Internal Security Bill was voted on September 23, 1950—286 to 48 with 160 Democrats and 126 Republicans voting to override with only 45 Democrats, 2 Republicans and Marcantonio voting to sustain. Massachusetts Representatives voted to override 11-1-2 with seven Republicans and four Democrats including Kennedy and Furcolo voting to override while Democrat Phil Philbin voted to sustain while Democrat John McCormack and Republican Donald Nicholson were listed as "not voting" (September 22, 1950, *CQ Almanac, 1950*, pp. 54a–55a).

73 McCarran's anti-immigrant maneuverings are well covered in "Amendments to the Displaced Persons Act," in Stephen K. Bailey and Howard D. Samuel, *Congress at Work* (New York: Henry Holt, 1952), pp. 236–67.

74 McCarran-Walter Immigration and Nationality Act was approved June 27, 1952 (66 Stat. 163-282). Certain provisions of this Act were subsequently held unconstitutional in *Afroyim v. Rusk*, 387 U.S. 253 (1967), and *Schneider v. Rusk*, 377 U.S. 163 (1964) in Stathis, *Landmark Legislation*, p. 238.

75 Quoted in Hardeman and Bacon, *Rayburn: A Biography*, p. 425.

76 President Harry S. Truman, "Veto of Bill to Revise the Laws relating to Immigration, Naturalization, and Nationality, June 25, 1952," *Papers of the President*, pp. 441–47. The quotation is from p. 443.

77 Veto override vote, June 26, 1952.

78 FBI Memorandum to Mr. A. H. Belmont from V. P. Keay regarding David K. Niles, Estelle Friedrichs, Espionage, dated March 11, 1952. FBI files 62-69476 accessed under the Freedom of Information Act.

79 Stephen Hunter and John Bainbridge, Jr. "American Gunfight; A Little-Remembered Shootout near Lafayette Square Left President Harry Truman's Life Hanging in the Balance," *Washington Post Magazine*, October 9, 2005, pp. 16ff., from their book, *American Gunfight: The Plot to Kill Harry Truman—and the Shootout That Stopped It* (New York: Simon & Schuster, 2005). Collazo was tried and sentenced to death. Truman commuted the sentence to life imprisonment and President Jimmy Carter commuted his sentence to time served in 1979 and he was released and returned to Puerto Rico.

80 Approval of the Constitution of the Commonwealth of Puerto Rico, approved July 3, 1952 (66 Stat. 327-328).

81 AIPO, *Gallup Poll*, October 1–6, 1950.

82 John A. Goldsmith, *Colleagues: Richard B. Russell and His Apprentice, Lyndon B. Johnson* (Washington, DC: Seven Locks Press, 1993).

83 C. P. Trussell, "Close is Dramatic; Truman Gets Contracts Powers. And 20 Billion Is Granted for Arms; Faith in America Voiced; Peace Hope a Major Theme—Party Meetings Name Chiefs for 82d, Opening Today," *The New York Times*, January 3, 1951, p. 1.

84 U.S. House Historical Office, "Historical Highlights: The Repeal of the Twenty-One Day Rule, January 03, 1951," accessed June 12, 2015.

85 Harry Dexter White, *The French International Accounts, 1880–1913* (Cambridge, MA: Harvard University Press, 1933).

86 The two authors are R. Bruce Craig, *Treasonable Doubt: The Harry Dexter White Spy Case* (Lawrence: University Press of Kansas, 2004); and Benn Steil, *The Battle of Bretton Woods: John Maynard Keynes, Harry Dexter White, and the Making of a New World Order* (Princeton: Princeton University Press, 2013). Both authors were interviewed by phone, August 14, 2014.

87 John Earl Haynes and Harvey Klehr, *Venona: Decoding Soviet Espionage in America* (New Haven: Yale University Press, 1999), pp. 90–91.

88 Robert Skidelsky, *John Maynard Keynes: Fighting for Britain, 1937–1946* (London: Macmillan, 2000), p. 256.

89 Buster Hartley tape, Paul Wright Files, UMass-Boston Archives.

90 Craig, *Treasonable Doubt*, pp. 197–98.

91 U.S. Senator Daniel Patrick Moynihan, *Secrecy: The American Experience* (New Haven, CT: Yale University Press, 1998), pp. 70–73; Jerrold and Leona Schecter, *Sacred Secrets: How Soviet Intelligence Operations Changed American History* (Washington, DC: Brassey's, 2002), pp. 144–49.

92 Sullivan, *The Bureau*, pp. 41–45. See also, *J. Edgar Hoover: The Man and the Secrets* (New York: W. W. Norton, 1991), pp. 356–59.

93 This is a key point of Craig's book *Treasonable Doubt*.

94 Drew Pearson, *Drew Pearson's Diaries, 1949–1959* (New York: Holt, Rinehart and Winston, 1974), p. 284.

95 None of the Hoover biographies confirm this contention nor did a phone conversation with Ronald Kessler, author of *The Bureau: The Secret History of the FBI* (New York: St. Martin's Press, 2002).

96 An analysis of the salutations in 169 direct letters between the two men—99 from Hoover to McCormack and 70 from McCormack to Hoover. The first 28 letters from Hoover to McCormack from December 29, 1936, to January 24, 1946, had "My dear Congressman" as the salutation. The next 71 letters from Hoover between March 27, 1946, and May 20, 1970, all have "Dear John" as the salutation. John's first twenty letters to Hoover vary in their salutations—"Dear Mr. Hoover" (10) and "My dear Director" (10). Of the fifty later letters from McCormack to Hoover between November 13, 1946, and April 2, 1969, one has "Dear Mr. Hoover" as a salutation but all of the other forty-nine open with "Dear Edgar."

97 Hoover to McCormack, March 27, 1946.

98 Hoover to McCormack letter with salutation "Dear John" and signed "Edgar," November 7, 1962.

99 For a summary of the Second Session, see Floyd M. Riddick, "The Eighty-Second Congress: Second Session," *Western Political Quarterly* V (December 1952), pp. 619–34.

15

Rabbi John Rescues Kennedy and a Transformed Delegation

The Pre-Election Scramble of 1952: The desultory second session of the 82nd Congress in 1952 was overshadowed by the stalemate in Korea and the upcoming presidential election. Although the 1951 ratification of the 22nd "no third term" Amendment had "grandfathered" Harry Truman, making him eligible to run for president again, his Gallup Poll approval rating bottomed out at 22% in February,[1] ending any serious thought of his candidacy. When Truman formally renounced a renomination bid following his defeat by Senator Estes Kefauver (Dem-Tenn.) in the March New Hampshire primary, it was clear that the election of 1952 would be the first since 1928 with no presidential incumbent as a contender. Even in the 1928 contest, Republican Secretary of Commerce Herbert Hoover and Democratic New York Governor Al Smith were the prohibitive front-runners and each was nominated easily on the opening ballots of their respective conventions. In 1952, neither party knew who would be their respective nominees, making it the most wide-open nomination battle for both parties since 1920.

Adding to the uniqueness of the 1952 contest was a huge eruption of voting in the presidential primaries, from 4,805,120 in 1948 to a virtual trebling of 12,710,638 in 1952. Interest had grown with television coverage of Senate hearings. The House resisted television. Fearing televised grandstanding on the part of its more ambitious members, Democratic House leaders Sam Rayburn and John McCormack discouraged opening the House to television cameras either on the floor or in committee rooms. It was not until 1974 and the Watergate hearings of the House Judiciary Committee that the House was televised, four years after John McCormack's retirement.

The Senate was not camera-shy. Senator Kefauver was the first to grasp this opportunity. By launching his Senate Select Committee on Crime in 1950 and having it televised a few months later, the lanky, bespectacled 48-year-old Kefauver, then only in his second year in the Senate, established a national presence.[2] Ironically, like Harry Truman, whose elective career Kefauver would end, Kefauver used a Senate select oversight committee to create a national reputation much as Truman had done with his wartime Special Committee on Defense Expenditures. Senator Kefauver's committee uncovered massive levels of criminal activity in the big-city machines that were a major bulwark of the Democratic Party. Their leaders were irritated, but the public was impressed, and Senator Kefauver positioned himself for a presidential run.

Kefauver entered the New Hampshire presidential primary after the 1949 rule change that permitted candidates to accrue convention delegates in their own name. This was an effort on the state's part to increase turnout beyond the thirty-plus thousand-vote plateau upon which it was stuck. Without his consent, President Truman's operatives placed his name on the New Hampshire ballot, ignoring Kefauver's campaign and assuming that the national press would as well. But the national press was already in New Hampshire, thanks to Massachusetts Senator Henry Cabot Lodge, Jr., who had been successful in getting General Dwight D. Eisenhower (the nation's "most admired man") on the Republican ballot. Ike was in Europe presiding over the North Atlantic Treaty Organization (NATO) and his only serious opponent was the long-suffering U.S. Senator Robert A. Taft of Ohio, making his third run for the White House.

Both New Hampshire primaries made news. Turnout for the Republican primary more than tripled from 28,854 in 1948 to 92,530 in 1952 while on the Democratic side, the 1952 turnout of 35,995 was more than eight times the 1948 total.[3] Democratic voters chose Senator Kefauver over President Truman, 55.0% to 44.2%. Kefauver's plurality over Truman was 3,873 votes and the president dismissed the results as "eyewash." A week later in Minnesota's primary, President Truman received only 3,634 (2.8%) write-in votes, finishing third behind its favorite son Senator Hubert Humphrey and Senator Kefauver. On Saturday, March 29, eighteen days after the New Hampshire primary and eleven days after Minnesota's, President Truman withdrew from renomination consideration.[4] All told, Kefauver racked up 3,169,448 Democratic primary votes—64.3% of the total. Only FDR had obtained more primary votes, and no nonincumbent had ever scored that high a percentage. The Democrats southern and big-city anchors disliked insurgents, and their knives would be out for the young Mr. Kefauver, with no knife longer than that of President Harry Truman, who referred to the Senator privately as "Cowfever."[5] Truman pals Sam Rayburn, who would be the convention's permanent chair, and John McCormack, its resolutions chair, seemed not to mind.

General Eisenhower won New Hampshire with 50.4% of the vote to 38.7% for Senator Taft. Ike's chief supporter, three-term incumbent Senator Lodge, had emerged as a leader of the Republican Party's Eastern moderate internationalist wing in an ironic generational turnabout given the central role that his grandfather, the first Henry Cabot Lodge, had played in sinking President Woodrow Wilson's hopes of American involvement in the League of Nations. Young Lodge was joined in this effort by Minority Leader Joe Martin who had been an earlier backer of an Eisenhower candidacy when many, including Harry Truman, were uncertain of Ike's political propensities.

Both party's nominating conventions would meet in Chicago and televised to the nation. The Republicans met first. The early line was that Senator Taft, "Mr. Republican," would finally gain the long-sought nomination of his party. He had the support of the convention's managers and that the two men who had bested him for the previous nominations—Willkie in 1940 and Dewey in 1948—had lost to the Democrats was proof to them that a true conservative would have won either of these contests. But Eisenhower's national appeal and help from delegates committed to other candidates gave him a narrow lead on the first ballot, with 595 votes to 500 for Taft. Harold Stassen's 19 Minnesota delegates gave Ike the votes he needed for the victory.[6]

Named as the Republican vice presidential candidate was the 39-year-old junior Senator from California, Richard M. Nixon, then only in his second Senate year, but who had gained a fearsome reputation as an avowed anti-Communist. Nixon's eagerness to manipulate the political process for personal advancement was revealed during his positioning for the 1952 vice presidential selection. It was prophetic. Governor Warren, then running as California's favorite son contended that Nixon was "a traitor in our delegation. . . . He took the oath that he would vote for me, until such time as the delegation was released, but he has not paid attention to his oath and immediately upon being elected, started working for Eisenhower and has been doing so ever since."[7] Ironically, it was the effort to placate an angry Warren that would result in his being named Chief Justice of the United States Supreme Court[8] in 1953.

The Democratic selection

The Democrats met ten days later in Chicago with Speaker Sam Rayburn presiding as permanent chairman and Majority Leader John McCormack reprising his role as chair of the party's Resolutions Committee.[9] As a reward for Massachusetts's loyalty to the presidential Democrats, Governor Paul A. Dever was chosen to give the keynote address. Dever's distant cousin William E. Dever had been a one-term Democratic mayor of Chicago (1923–27) during the "roaring Twenties." Paul Dever was a protégé of the isolationist anti-Semitic U.S. Senator David I. Walsh. He was not close to John McCormack. But much like his tenuous relationship with Jack Kennedy, John chose to submerge his disagreements with Dever in the name of party unity.[10] Dever's address was intended to be a ringing defense of 20 years of the Roosevelt and Truman Administrations. It was not remembered that way. Paul Dever was a poor choice for the task. The glaring television lights, combined with the heat and humidity of late July, devastated the heavyset and jowly Dever who perspired profusely and appeared to melt on camera. Dever's raspy-voiced address to the nation was memorable more for his televised discomfort than for its verbal content.

Eager to avoid a repeat of the 1948 platform battle, the Democratic National Committee appointed John McCormack to chair a 21-member executive committee.[11] It served as a preliminary platform committee and met for five days before the convention assembled. McCormack appointed a nineteen-member drafting committee, drawn heavily from the party's congressional wing. John worked with Philip Perlman, President Truman's solicitor general, and his fellow "apostles of compromise"—Senator John Sparkman of Alabama, who was House Democratic Whip for ten months in 1946, Representative L. Brooks Hays of Arkansas, and African-American House Government Operations Chair William L. Dawson of Chicago, upon whose committee John McCormack served—to put together the platform and write gingerly around the issue of civil rights.[12]

Unlike the relatively spare 1944 Platform that John McCormack last supervised, the 1952 Platform was monstrously long (191 paragraphs) and tedious.[13] That was its intent. The final substantive issue discussed was civil rights, and it surfaced in the last six paragraphs of the platform. The defense of New Zealand appeared in the 46th paragraph, rural electrification in the 88th paragraph, and hunting and fishing licenses in the 135th. Burying civil rights under a mountain of triviality seemed to be the 1952 solution to this most contentious of the Democratic Party's issues. Times had changed, and the civil rights paragraphs provided more specificity than earlier Democratic Party platforms:

> We will continue our efforts to eradicate discrimination based on race, religion, or national origin.
>
> We know this task requires action, not just in one section of the Nation, but in all sections. It requires the cooperative efforts of individual citizens and action by State and local governments. It also requires Federal action. The Federal Government must live up to the ideals of the Declaration of Independence and must exercise the powers vested in it by the Constitution.
>
> We are proud of the progress that has been made in securing equality of treatment and opportunity in the Nation's armed forces and the civil service and all areas under Federal jurisdiction. The Department of Justice has taken an important part in successfully arguing in the courts for the elimination of many illegal discriminations, including those involving rights to own and use real property, to engage in gainful occupations and to enroll in publicly supported higher educational institutions. We are determined that the Federal Government shall continue such policies.
>
> At the same time, we favor Federal legislation effectively to secure these rights to everyone: (1) the right to equal opportunity for employment; (2) the right to security of persons; (3) the right to full and equal participation in the Nation's political life, free from arbitrary restraints. We also favor legislation to protect existing Federal civil rights statutes and to strengthen the administrative machinery for the protection of civil rights.

Segregation, the poll tax, antilynching laws, and the Fair Employment Practices Commission (FEPC) were not specifically mentioned, but the platform worked to keep the party together. There were no challenges on the convention floor and it was accepted by voice vote with only the Georgia and Mississippi delegations requesting that their objections to it be recorded. Most importantly, there were no walkouts from disgruntled delegates that would have been televised to the nation. John McCormack had delivered.

Although the NAACP's Walter White and the Leadership Conference on Civil Rights accepted the platform as an improvement over the amended one of 1948, Harlem Congressman Adam Clayton Powell formally denounced it. Powell, New York State's first African-American Congressman, was then committed to the candidacy of W. Averell Harriman Powell and was offended by the platform's lack of specific mention of the FEPC, and he targeted Congressman Dawson and Speaker Rayburn for his wrath. Powell called Dawson an "Uncle Tom" and asserted that "I am not saying that any money had to pass to Dawson, for there always have been men who for a slap on the back are willing to sell their people down the river."[14] And of Speaker Rayburn, Powell's disdain was palpable, "I charge now openly that Speaker Rayburn used every trick at his command to bring back into the convention the Dixiecrats who had been overwhelmingly put out. . . . It was an absolute disgrace."[15] John McCormack, the architect of the platform and Sam Rayburn's loyal lieutenant, escaped Powell's fury on this occasion. John's time would come.

The presidential nomination battle was a curious one. Senator Kefauver, who had successfully marched through the primaries, had a narrow first ballot lead of 340 votes to 273 for Illinois Governor Adlai E. Stevenson, 268 for Georgia Senator Richard Russell, 123 ½ for New York's Harriman, and 225 ½ votes scattered among ten other candidates. The required majority was 616, and it appeared a long way off. The 36 delegates of John McCormack's Massachusetts remained committed to Governor Dever. The 52 votes of Rayburn's Texas delegation belonged to Dick Russell throughout all three convention ballots.

For President Truman, whose first choice to succeed him was his and John McCormack's old "poker pal" Chief Justice Fred Vinson, the proceedings were less than riveting. Truman chose not to endorse his 75-year-old Vice President Alben Barkley, whose nomination was seconded by John McCormack. Truman shifted his support to Governor Stevenson whose initial reluctance to accept it mystified Truman.[16] Truman seemed more intent on denying Estes Kefauver the nomination than he was on Stevenson receiving it. As the lesser candidacies faded, the top three contenders gained votes on the second ballot: 362 ½ for Kefauver, 324 ½ for Stevenson, and 294 for Dick Russell. With Harriman's departure before the third ballot, the momentum shifted to Stevenson, and the major states of New York, Pennsylvania, Michigan, and Massachusetts provided Stevenson with his needed majority. It was the first multiple ballot nomination for president since the Democrats had overturned the two-thirds rule in 1936, and it would be the last.

For vice president, Governor Stevenson chose Senator John Sparkman of Alabama, of whom he knew little, having never served in Congress. Stevenson deferred to Harry Truman and to the Democratic congressional leadership on the choice of Sparkman, who had worked closely with John McCormack on this year's Resolutions Committee and had served as Democratic whip under Rayburn and McCormack in 1946, his last year in the House. Sparkman, the seventh of eleven children of a north Alabama politically active farmer, had the earmarks of a "poor boy." That appealed to Rayburn and McCormack who also were later-born sons in large families.[17] Sparkman was a voting segregationist and had initially supported Senator Russell's nomination bid, but he was not a raging racist and was generally viewed as a progressive back home in Alabama.[18] The big news about Sparkman's selection was that he was the first Deep South Democratic nominee since Herschel V. Johnson of Georgia was named as Stephen Douglas's vice presidential candidate in 1860. This was an olive branch extended by the national Democrats to those four southern states that had cast their electoral votes for the Dixiecrat ticket in 1948.

Race was not to be the defining feature of the 1952 presidential contest. Korea and anti-Communism were. General Eisenhower addressed the first issue by declaring, "I shall go to Korea." It brought hopes of a peaceful settlement to war-weary Americans who saw the Korean War as a hopeless military morass. Anti-Communism would be the domain of vice presidential nominee Nixon.

Governor Stevenson, the Democratic presidential nominee, was vulnerable on both issues. A graduate of the elite Choate School in Wallingford, Connecticut, and of Princeton University, he was the grandson and namesake of Grover Cleveland's second Vice President Adlai E. Stevenson. The Stevenson Democrats hoped to recapture much of the aristocratic FDR magic with a well-born, well-educated, and articulate "inheritor" as opposed to the grubby "climbers" represented by Harry Truman and Estes Kefauver.[19] Stevenson, who had never served in the military, was seen as much too effete to address the war issues and his extensive service in the State Department led him to be linked with Alger Hiss, a fellow Ivy Leaguer and the senior State Department official targeted in Richard Nixon's anti-Communist forays against the Truman Administration.

With Stevenson's acceptance speech and the usual photo of nominees holding joined hands aloft along the jam-packed platform, the 31st quadrennial convention of the Democratic Party had moved into history. Permanent Chair Sam Rayburn and Resolutions Chair John McCormack delivered a convention with an articulate nominee unburdened by the discernible tensions of the 1948 convention.

Sam Rayburn and John McCormack returned to their home states of Texas and Massachusetts somewhat unsure if the presidential ticket was strong enough to win the White House for a sixth consecutive time or more importantly, if that ticket would jeopardize the Democrats' narrow hold on the House of Representatives.

Massachusetts political upheaval

Massachusetts should have been safely lodged in the Democratic column, having voted Democratic in six previous elections, but change was in the air there as elsewhere. The 1952 election brought with it enormous personnel change with a new president, Dwight D. Eisenhower, the first Republican nominee to carry the state since ex-Governor Calvin Coolidge did in 1924; a new U.S. Senator, Democratic U.S. Representative John F. Kennedy who defeated the incumbent three-term Republican Henry Cabot Lodge, Jr.; a new governor, Republican U.S. Representative Christian A. Herter who defeated the incumbent two-term Democrat Paul A. Dever; and a new State Treasurer ex-U.S. Representative Foster Furcolo who would replace fellow Democrat John E. Hurley. Each of the three former Representatives would take even greater steps in political life, with Kennedy elected president in 1960; Herter named as Assistant Secretary of State in 1957 and as Eisenhower's second Secretary of State in 1959; and Furcolo, who succeeded Herter as Governor of Massachusetts for four years, 1957–61.

Taking their places in the House of 1953 were three new U.S. Representatives: Democrat Thomas P. "Tip" O'Neill, Jr. of Cambridge who took Kennedy's seat in the 11th District; Groton and Harvard-educated Brahmin Republican Laurence Curtis of Boston who took Herter's seat in the 10th District; and Democrat Edward P. Boland of Springfield who took Furcolo's seat in the 2nd District. Each of these three would serve out the decade.

Furcolo Quietly Departs the House: Foster Furcolo had been a beneficiary of John McCormack's help with an early appointment to the Appropriations Committee and a private meeting with President Truman. Later, knowing of likely opposition to Furcolo's reelection from the large Eastern European community in his district, John engineered the 1951 appointment of Furcolo to the seven-member Select Committee to Investigate and Study the Katyn Forest Massacre. The committee was chaired by Indiana's Ray Madden and Furcolo, listed third, was joined on the committee by Polish-Americans, Democrat Thaddeus Machrowicz of Michigan and Republican Alvin O'Konski of Wisconsin. The committee's mission was to investigate the presumed massacre of thousands of Polish officers by Soviet troops.[20] To some it seemed as if John's help for Furcolo was a way of irritating Jack Kennedy, intensifying the personal antagonism between the two that endured throughout the 1950s. In her oral history for the Kennedy Library, Mary Davis, Jack's first secretary in his House office, recounted the Kennedys' attitude toward Furcolo[21]:

> JOHNSON: Do you remember anything about the relationship between Kennedy and Furcolo, and between your office and Furcolo's office?
> DAVIS: It wasn't that close, really. And while there was a friendly association because, naturally, they were members of the same congressional delegation, there wasn't an overwhelming closeness. There wasn't a real warmth in the association between Jack and Foster Furcolo. And I think a lot of Jack's cronies and associates looked on Foster Furcolo as somebody who was rather new on the political scene and who could, in the future, possibly be a problem to Jack in his ascendancy. Because Foster was, here again, a nice, bright young man, new face, did a good job while he was here, and was ambitious. And I think they viewed Foster with jaundiced eyes somewhat.

Massachusetts newspapers in late 1952 were filled with stories of Ike's growing popularity in this staunch Democratic state and of the two high-profile contests for the U.S. Senate between Senator Lodge and Representative Kennedy, and the one for governor between incumbent Paul Dever and Representative Christian Herter. Barely noticed was Furcolo's appointment by Governor Dever on July 5, 1952, to be treasurer and receiver-general of the Commonwealth, replacing John E. Hurley who had become clerk of the Boston Municipal Court. One reporter speculated correctly that this was an effort on Furcolo's part to gain a statewide post in preparation for a later run for Governor or Senator.[22] Furcolo was named as the party's candidate for the full term in the primary in the hope that Italian voters could be induced to vote for another Democratic ticket albeit heavily weighted with the Irish names of Jack Kennedy and Paul Dever.

This was another career boost for Furcolo engineered by John McCormack. Foster Furcolo's driving ambition was to be a United States Senator. At this time in American history, only one Italian-descended American had been elected to the Senate—Rhode

Island's John O. Pastore, first elected in 1950, two years earlier. Pastore had vaulted into the Senate from the governorship of his state, and Furcolo hoped to do the same. Coming from the less-populated western part of Massachusetts, it was essential that Furcolo develop a statewide presence. The electoral needs of Furcolo and Governor Dever dovetailed. In seeking election to his third two-year term, Governor Dever wanted to diversify the ethnic base of the 1952 Democratic ticket by including the Italians who were seen as the swing vote between the Yankee Republicans and the Irish Democrats. Although John McCormack preferred that hard-working and legislatively talented members like Furcolo remain in the House, he understood Furcolo's larger ambitions and urged Dever to appoint Furcolo to fill the vacant office of state treasurer. This would diversify the Democratic ticket for Dever, fearful that yet another "all green" Irish ticket would upset the state's other minority voters. It was that same sentiment that led Joe Kennedy to support Italian-American Representative Michael LoPresti over the selection of Cambridge's Tip O'Neill, the Democratic nominee to succeed Jack in the 11th District.[23] Foster Furcolo won his contest, but Paul Dever lost his. A Boston Irishman was now gone from the corner office of the State House. The patronage pressure on John McCormack increased.

The Kennedy-Lodge contest

Not all of the changes were expected, but the most important one—the U.S. Senate victory for 35-year-old Jack Kennedy—was less expected. After Kennedy's thwarted quest for a better committee assignment and a failed White House meeting with President Truman in April 1949 to complain about John McCormack's monopoly of Massachusetts patronage, Kennedy lost interest in his House service. This appears to be the moment that Jack realized that John had blocked his advancement in the House and that his only solution was to run for the Senate. But there was no Massachusetts election for the Senate in 1950, so Jack would have to suffer for the next three years until he got his shot.

Jack continued to be assigned to the minor committees on Education and Labor and District of Columbia, although there is some evidence that he seldom if ever attended meetings of the District Committee. His floor attendance fell off as he chose to travel to Europe on "fact finding" trips with Torbert "Torby" Macdonald, his old Harvard roommate and former captain of its football team. Jack's womanizing on those trips was so pronounced that Torby described it as "like traveling with a bull." His speeches dwindled, and the number of roll calls on which his vote was recorded trailed off as well. Kennedy had emotionally seceded from the House of Representatives.

The Contrast with Kennedy: John McCormack loved working the House floor and as a successful defense attorney in Boston, he loved floor debate and the cut and parry of verbal competition. He was also able to talk a subject to death, drowning it with platitudinous homilies that often verged on the sanctimonious. While Sam Rayburn was often referred to as "untalkative"[24] and grunted his way through conversations, John McCormack's voluble personality filled with excessive verbiage was the perfect complement for Rayburn's taciturn one. Tip O'Neill, who first met McCormack after the 1948 national convention, initially found McCormack's wordiness to be tedious but soon realized that this was John's way of avoiding verbal commitments.

What mattered most to John McCormack was the committee service of the members, as he made clear in a 1968 oral history at the LBJ Library[25]:

> Well, they see [the member] in his devotion to his work in committee, which is vitally important, because for all practical purposes the committees of Congress are the heart of Congress. Either branch of Congress with very few exceptions cannot act unless a Bill is reported out of a committee. That happens practically 100 percent of the time. And how close they attend to their committee work, their presence on the floor of the House, the speeches that they make, the effectiveness of their speech, logical, sound, their contributions, their associations with their fellow colleagues, their personality.

This was a test that Jack Kennedy was not passing in the House as he shirked his committee duties. In the words of Dick Bolling of Missouri, Sam Rayburn's favorite young congressman, "I thought he was a third-rater. I don't mean second-rater, either. I mean third-rater."[26]

As accurately characterized in the favorable biography *Kennedy*, by Jack's major speech writer and Special Counsel Theodore Sorensen, "it was true that Congressman Kennedy's election to the Senate, after three elections to the House, had not inspired any predictions of greatness in the national press or in Democratic Party circles"[27] and "His performance in the House of Representatives had been considered by most observers to be largely undistinguished—except for a record of absenteeism which had been heightened by indifference as well as ill health and by unofficial as well as official travels."[28]

Kennedy looked longingly at the Senate. Fellow 1946 classmates Florida Democrat George Smathers, his closest congressional friend, and California Republican Dick Nixon, the one classmate who perturbed him the most, had Senate seats on the 1950 horizon. Jack did not. Smathers defeated incumbent liberal U.S. Senator Claude Pepper in the Democratic primary while Nixon defeated liberal U.S. Representative and movie actress Helen Gahagan Douglas for the open seat in the general election. Nixon labeled her the "pink lady," and in an era of anti-Communism she was doomed. Make of it what one will, listed among the many out-of-state conservative contributors to the Nixon campaign was Ambassador Joe Kennedy.[29]

Henry Cabot Lodge, Jr.: As Jack planned his escape from the House, he focused his energies on the Senate seat of Henry Cabot Lodge, Jr., the quintessential Boston Brahmin. It was an ambitious dream. Lodge had already beaten three previous successful Irish Democrats—Governor James Michael Curley in 1936, U.S. Representative Joe Casey in 1942, and after his return from the war, the incumbent U.S. Senator David I. Walsh in 1946. These victories had made Lodge overconfident when compared to Jack Kennedy who had faced minimal to no electoral opposition and whose House career was undistinguished. Also, it was increasingly obvious to most that Ike would sweep the nation and end Massachusetts's string of six consecutive Democratic presidential victories.

Even among Brahmins, Lodge stood out. Not only did he have the requisite Puritan ancestry, Harvard degree, and wartime heroism, Lodge was a "Brahmin's Brahmin." George Cabot, his great-great-great-grandfather, was a native of Salem, the first Puritan encampment, a graduate of Harvard and a U.S. Senator in the 2nd Congress serving from 1791 through the Washington Administration in 1796.[30] In 1798, fellow Harvard man President John Adams named Cabot to be the nation's first secretary of the navy, but he declined. Cabot who was originally interred in the Granary Burial Ground, that "holiest" of Brahmin resting places, was later reinterred at Mount Auburn in Cambridge.

George Cabot's great grandson was Henry Cabot Lodge of Nahant, yet another Harvard man who received Harvard's first doctorate in government and would serve in Congress for more than 37 years.[31] After the 1913 passage of the 17th Amendment, Lodge would be the state's first popularly elected U.S. Senator, dispatching Jack's beloved grandfather John F. Fitzgerald by 63,000 votes in 1916. As Chair of the Senate's powerful Foreign Relations Committee and as its Majority Leader, it was Lodge who would successfully scuttle President Woodrow Wilson's hope of American involvement in the nascent, but possibly vital, League of Nations. It was his grandson Henry Cabot Lodge, Jr. whom Jack would have to defeat to make good his escape from John McCormack's House of Representatives. However, the return of Joe Kennedy to public notice, with echoes from Joe's isolationist philosophy, threatened to derail Jack's candidacy.

Joe Kennedy's neo-isolationist and anti-Semitic remarks resurface

Joe Kennedy and Anti-Semitism: While Joe Kennedy's money in Jack's campaign was very welcome, his presence was not. During the closing months of his prewar ambassadorship in London, Joe then linked to the ultraconservative anti-Semitic "Cliveden Set," was seen as a "defeatist" and much too accepting of an inevitable Nazi victory in Europe.[32] In a letter to his isolationist (and suspected pro-Nazi) ally, the famous aviator Charles Lindbergh, Kennedy took pride in having convinced Chamberlain to bring French Premier Edouard Daladier to Munich for a meeting with Hitler and Mussolini to discuss the future of Czechoslovakia.[33] Convinced that offering up Czechoslovakia to Hitler would bring "peace in our time," Chamberlain returned to London in hollow triumph. FDR, well aware of Lindbergh's barely disguised pro-German tendencies, had the FBI closely monitor Lindbergh's activities and undoubtedly learned of Kennedy's role through the tapping of Lindbergh's phone.[34]

In 1944, Joe Kennedy made an effort to defuse the conjoined issues of defeatism and anti-Semitism[35] but it resurfaced with the publication of German documents. It did not endear the Ambassador to the voters in the Jewish wards of Boston and its suburbs leading to deep Jewish distrust of the Kennedys, both father and son.[36] In an effort to rehabilitate his own damaged image and to position Jack for higher office, Joe Kennedy engaged in public philanthropy as he donated thousands of dollars (and in some cases millions) to various charitable institutions in Massachusetts, careful to include Italian religious organizations and Jewish charities. Joe was also careful not to be the one delivering the checks. That responsibility was given to Jack and Patricia, Joe's fourth daughter and the family beauty. But Joe's penchant for publicity and controversy could not be contained.

At the invitation of his third son Bobby, then the president of the Law School Forum at the University of Virginia, Joe delivered a speech on December 12, 1950, entitled "Present Policy is Politically and Morally Bankrupt." It was a wide-ranging and hard-hitting attack on the Marshall Plan, NATO, and the United Nations. The clear target was President Truman and the policy of Soviet "containment" first outlined by State Department official George F. Kennan.

In Joe Kennedy's attacks on the Marshall Plan and the Truman Doctrine's aid to Greece and Turkey, he stated: "I naturally opposed Communism but I said if portions of Europe or Asia wish to go Communistic or even have Communism thrust upon them, we cannot stop them."[37] Much as he had in his 1941 anti–Lend-Lease testimony, Kennedy emphasized Americans' high standard of living that would be compromised by too great an involvement in trying to contain Soviet communism in Europe. Ex-President Herbert Hoover enthusiastically endorsed the speech and eight-term Republican Congressman Paul Shafer of Michigan fulsomely praised the speech and Joe Kennedy in the *Congressional Record*.[38]

Foster Furcolo was outraged and took a verbal swing at Shafer and a colleague's father. On February 14, 1951, he slammed the ambassador in remarks on the House floor reminding listeners of Joe Kennedy's greatest political faux pas: "I think if that Member is to use former Ambassador Kennedy's speech as an indication of what should or should not be done, perhaps he should also include in his remarks the stand former Ambassador Kennedy took in England when it was a question of whether England was going to try to resist Hitler."[39]

The appeasement charge against Joe Kennedy had returned. John McCormack was the floor manager of the Lend-Lease bill when Joe and his isolationist ally Colonel Charles A. Lindbergh testified vehemently against it before the House Foreign Affairs Committee. John remembered those attacks and seemed to agree with Furcolo when he added his own comment, "I appreciate the gentleman's remarks."[40] Jack was not on the floor to defend his father because he was away from the House once again that day. John was there that day and if there was any constant in John McCormack's personal ideology, it was an unequivocal hatred of "godless atheistic" Communism. Joe Kennedy's seemingly cavalier willingness to let the Soviets take over Europe was disturbing to John and may have created the seeds of disillusionment with Joe Kennedy, a man that he had once touted for president in 1940.[41]

The von Dirksen Cables: Another source of potential trouble for Jack's Senate candidacy surfaced when captured documents from the German Foreign Ministry had been translated into English by the U.S. Department of State and the British Foreign

Office. The documents were published in 1949 by the U.S. Government Printing Office and were now in the public domain. Most damning were a set of cables about Joe Kennedy sent from German ambassador to Great Britain Herbert von Dirksen to Ernst von Weizsacker, the state secretary in the German Foreign Ministry, which contained a number of observations about Joe Kennedy's attitudes toward American Jews[42]:

> *June 13, 1938*: "Although [Ambassador Kennedy] did not know Germany, he had learned from the most varied sources that the present Government had done great things for Germany and that the Germans were satisfied and enjoyed good living conditions."
>
> "The Ambassador then touched upon the Jewish question and stated that it was naturally of great importance to German-American relations. In this connection it was not so much the fact that we wanted to get rid of the Jews that was so harmful to us, but rather the loud clamor with which we accompanied this purpose."
>
> *October 13, 1938*: "[The Ambassador] would go to Germany only if he were certain of speaking to the Fuhrer. He intended explaining to the Fuhrer the position of the United States as regards both economics and the functioning of public opinion and in general wished to try to bring about a better understanding between the United States and Germany."
>
> "Today, too, as during former conversations, Kennedy mentioned that very strong anti-Semitic tendencies existed in the United States and that a large portion of the population had an understanding of the German attitude toward the Jews."
>
> "From his whole personality I believe that he will get on well with the Fuhrer."

The documents first gained public notice in 1949 and Senator Lodge hoped that they would undermine the Kennedy candidacy.[43] Joe Kennedy dismissed them as "poppycock," and they did not sink Jack Kennedy's Senate campaign as they would have in an earlier time. They had less impact than Lodge expected (or hoped). By 1952, the geopolitics of the world had changed. Our onetime ally the Soviet Union had become a postwar adversary and our former adversary Germany was now divided into four quadrants with the American, British, and French armed forces controlling three of them. West Germany had become a major buffer between Western Europe and the powerful Red Army poised in East Germany. Also, believing that de-Nazification was possible, a number of former Nazi-affiliated scientists were recruited by the Allies to turn their talents to contain the Soviets as the Cold War deepened. Most importantly, it was Jack Kennedy running for the U.S. Senate, not Joe Kennedy, and there was sufficient evidence to believe that Jack, unlike his deceased older brother Joe, Jr., was far less committed to his father's conservative and anti-Semitic beliefs.[44]

For a good Catholic like John McCormack and Massachusetts voters, Communism was a far greater threat to religion than fascism. There is little doubt that both the 1951 Virginia Law speech and the 1949 translations of the Kennedy-von Dirksen correspondence would have troubled John. He was both a fierce anti-Communist and an antifascist. Both McCormack and Furcolo were becoming disillusioned with the Kennedys. Furcolo was obviously dismayed over losing Larry O'Brien, his chief advisor, to an in-state rival and clearly aware that Jack Kennedy, who was six years younger and a less effective House member, would seek election to the U.S. Senate before he would. John McCormack the fervent anti-Communist could not have been pleased with Joe Kennedy's eagerness to surrender Western Europe to the Soviet Union nor with Jack's continuing absences from his committee responsibilities and floor votes.

While Jack's war-related health issues continued to impact his performance in the House, his progressive ambition took a greater toll. Having traveled extensively in Europe during his father's ambassadorship prior to World War II, Jack arranged for other European visits in 1951, presumably to acquire the patina of foreign policy expertise that he believed he would need to unseat Lodge. His eagerness to travel abroad to gain more foreign policy credibility was remarked upon negatively by other politicians, both in Washington and Boston.

John McCormack apparently became less circumspect in his irritation with Kennedy and his frequent absences from the floor and disinclination to do committee work. He was not alone. In a revealing oral history at the Kennedy Library with John Stewart, U.S. Representative Robert Jones of Alabama, who entered the House in 1947 along with Jack and also served with him on the District of Columbia Committee, remarked[45]:

> JONES: "I recall the time that I scolded him for the fact that he didn't take a greater interest."
>
> JONES: "And I think of one time in the second session when we had a fight on the floor in which Foster Furcolo took a great deal of interest. And that afternoon or that evening when we went back to the office we met, and I scolded him for the fact that he didn't take a greater interest, that he was equally as capable as Foster Furcolo and therefore, he should take a greater interest in discussion of issues on the floor, since he possessed the capabilities and the political acumen to make measurements of political affairs, and that he should be more interested."

Being compared unfavorably to Furcolo by a friend must have stung Jack deeply. Leaving the House for the Senate became even more imperative.

The Mackay episode

Yet another politician bothered by Jack's foreign travels and his indifference to his House responsibilities was John McCormack's Boston-based staff aide Charlie Mackay. The growing suspicion around Boston was that Jack was readying himself for a 1952 challenge to Republican U.S. Senator Henry Cabot Lodge, Jr. A major source of Lodge's strength was that he was widely recognized as an internationalist whose foreign policy bona fides were further enhanced when he returned to the Senate in 1947. Lodge was immediately assigned to the Senate's prestigious Foreign Relations Committee, where he served with Republican heavyweights, such as its Chair Arthur Vandenberg of Michigan, the Senate president pro tem and Wallace White of Maine, the Majority

Floor Leader. It was an auspicious return to the Senate for Lodge, who had resigned his seat in 1944 and served in the European Theatre. He was promoted to lieutenant colonel and decorated with the French Legion of Honor and Croix de Guerre with palm.[46] Lodge could easily match Jack's Pacific Theater heroism and clearly outdistanced him on foreign policy credentials.

The only solution for Jack was to hit the road and travel once again. But to do so meant a further shirking of his responsibilities to the House, its Democrats, and John McCormack its Majority Leader, who was responsible for cobbling together enough Democratic votes to pass the legislative program of President Truman. John's frustrations were undoubtedly shared in the office with the staff. In July 1951, Charlie Mackay's negative remarks caught the ear of Joe Kennedy's loyal associate John Ford. John Ford told Joe what he heard, and Joe wrote to John[47]:

> You may have heard of a man named John Ford who has been associated with me for over thirty years and who is the head of the theatre company in which I am interested in with Paramount here in New England. . . . I hold him in high esteem.
>
> In discussing a matter with your Mr. Mackey [sp], who he does not know except that at one time he got a job for his wife before he married her, Mr. Mackey, after discussing the subject at hand, brought up the question of Jack Kennedy. He said he was full of hot air; that he had gone to Europe and had come back with a lot of—I will omit the word—and was now planning to go to Korea to get a lot of stuff; and spoke very slightingly of Jack and his efforts. Now Mr. Mackey naturally is entitled to his opinion of Jack, and Mr. Mackey, as your secretary, is entitled to express his opinion of Jack if that meets with your approval; but Mr. Mackey is not entitled to talk about Jack in a derogatory manner if it does not meet with your approval, because when he speaks he speaks as Congressman McCormack's secretary.

John took notice immediately. Bob Healy, the esteemed longtime political reporter for the *Boston Globe*, once told me that "John McCormack had no regard for Jack Kennedy but was scared to death of Joe Kennedy."[48] This fear appeared clearly in John's anxious, handwritten, barely legible three-page response to the ambassador on his official House stationary, as he literally threw Charley Mackay "under the bus."[49]

> Dear "Joe:"
> "I received your letter and of course anything Mackay says does not represent my views. He speaks his own views. This is not the first time he has talked 'out of turn' to my embarrassment."
> "Confidentially, he has a very bad heart otherwise I would have acted definitely on him before. I have told him before he should keep his mouth shut if he has adverse or unfavorable views about anyone because the natural inference is that he expresses my views when it is not so."
> "As a matter of fact when I am in Boston I talk to him very seldom, as there is no occasion for me to do so."

"I am glad you wrote me because otherwise I would not know anything about what he said to John Ford. I shall call Mackay—talk with him—and to keep his loud mouth shut. You will hear from me shortly again on this matter."

Sincerely,

John

An apology was delivered on August 3 and Joe presumably closed the matter, by writing on August 8[50]:

Dear John:

I am very happy indeed over your two letters. Regardless of what Mr. Mackay says, my experience over 35 years with John Ford [the manager of Kennedy's New England film concerns] is the same as it would be with Eddie Moore—he just doesn't lie and he doesn't make mistakes.

However, that's neither here nor there; the important thing to me was that the observation did not come from your office and give credence to the fact that you were hostile to Jack. I have been around long enough to know that some people strike it off very well and some do not—which is against neither of them. As far as you and I are concerned, I have always held you in the greatest respect and affection and I have always had the greatest admiration for Mrs. McCormack, who has brought credit to everyone by her dignity and kindness all her life.

It's a strange thing that the only thing that even seems to disturb me is something said about my children. Nothing ever said about me has ever bothered me five minutes. I suppose that is the natural instinct of a parent who has always felt that the success of a family is estimated by their loyalty to one another.

You have achieved great heights in American politics. I have always felt a great pride in it because I was at the meeting that determined Rayburn for Speaker and McCormack for Leader, and I still feel that was one of the finest political moves that Roosevelt ever made. Jack is some years younger than you. He took up politics not because it was natural for him or that it was his desire, but because he felt that his brother, Joe, had made up his mind to dedicate his life to public service, and as the next oldest Jack took up a great many other obligations and desires of Joe's. I am sure there is nothing in Jack's hopes for the future that would ever conflict with your wishes. He may not follow your advice or suggestions as well as he should, but then, he doesn't follow mine and I assume that is a natural instinct. It's his responsibility and it's his future.

I have written you this way as a reason for ever written you in the first place. I would want somebody to write me if the positions were reversed. I am very grateful to you for your prompt response.

With my warmest regards to Mrs. McCormack and to you, I remain,

Very sincerely yours,

Joseph P. Kennedy

Joe's claim to John that he had been present when FDR helped put together the "Austin-Boston Connection" of Rayburn and McCormack stretched the truth. Kennedy was in England when the connection was made with Sam Rayburn elected Speaker on September 16, 1940, and John McCormack elected Majority Leader on September 25. It was a month later when Joe and Mrs. Kennedy returned home and were guests at the White House on October 27, 1940.[51] That Kennedy met with FDR from 6:55 to 10:20 p.m. and at 11:10 the other guests, Sam Rosenman, Harry Hopkins, and Robert Sherwood, left the White House.

John may not have known that particular sequence of events, but he did know that Joe claimed some credit for John's success and felt that he owed Joe Kennedy big time. Payment would come due the following year when Jack's challenge to Senator Lodge was jeopardized by evidence of Joe Kennedy's unfortunate anti-Semitic attitudes, oral and written.

Rabbi John: As noted earlier, religious and racial prejudices were especially bothersome to John McCormack. As he would state in 1962 interview: "A man's racial origin means nothing to me, and a person's name means nothing to me. A person's religion I respect. But what does mean everything to me is a person's mind. And when I meet a person with a bigoted mind, I am meeting a person I do not like, a person I have nothing but contempt for."[52]

No further proof would be needed than barely five months after Adolf Hitler had gained power, John was the first New England Democrat to publicly assail Hitler on the US House floor on June 9, 1933, for his abusive treatment of German Jews[53]:

Mr. Speaker, I have watched with increasing anxiety developments in Germany since Adolf Hitler assumed controlling power. The time has come when I may no longer refrain from expressing my condemnation of the policy being pursued by the present German Government, particularly as it applies to a ruthless agonizing of the Jews.

I fervently trust that the efforts being made to bring an end the crime now perpetrated against the Jewish people in Germany will bear such successful fruition that racial persecution will forever be a thing of an unhappy past.

An account by D. B. Hardeman, Sam Rayburn's aide and biographer, recalls an episode of McCormack's attitude toward anti-Semitism[54]:

McCormack was at a dinner meeting with a group of bankers in Boston. As McCormack was leaving, one of the men approached him in the lobby, "Tell me John, why do you always have a lot of Jews around you?" the man asked. McCormack turned and screamed, "You goddamn son of a bitch, you're one of those haters!" and pushed him hard in the chest, sending him sprawling across the floor.

The one item not widely known outside of Boston's Jewish neighborhoods was John's long-standing relationship with the mysterious David K. Niles. Although David K.

Niles has been discussed earlier in a number of connections with McCormack, it is important to remember Niles was one of FDR's first six presidential assistants and his portfolio was, in essence, the political link to blacks and Jews, ethnic newcomers to the Roosevelt coalition. Niles played the same role in Harry Truman's Administration and pushed Harry to recognize Israel and desegregate the armed forces in 1948 prior to that election.

The 1952 Lodge Campaign: Senator Lodge generally overlooked the Kennedy candidacy for much of 1952.[55] Having defeated three Irish Democrats who had flirted with anti-Semitism, Lodge was very confident that he could easily defeat Jack Kennedy whose only strength appeared to be his father's mammoth fortune, widely believed to be ill-gotten. Jack's desultory House record and Joe's rumored reputation as an anti-Semite should have made this an easy contest. Instead of shoring up his base, Cabot focused his considerable energy on behalf of Dwight Eisenhower's nomination and Ike's upcoming presidential campaign. The Stevenson-Sparkman ticket had elicited little enthusiasm among the Catholic Democrats of Massachusetts who were unlikely to support a divorced Princeton-educated Unitarian from the Midwest. Eisenhower's prospects continued to improve and Lodge was convinced that Massachusetts would once again easily return him to the Senate.

The state's newspapers had generally endorsed Lodge's prior candidacies with the major exception of Basil Brewer's *New Bedford Standard-Times*. Brewer was a Taft Republican who disdained Lodge's internationalism. That was expected. What was not expected was the surprising turnabout of the *Boston Post*'s eccentric publisher John Fox.[56] Like John McCormack, Fox was born in the numbered streets of South Boston's poor Bayview neighborhood, but with a Harvard Law degree and a knack for buying and selling securities, he became quite wealthy. Bored with his gentleman farmer life in Connecticut, Fox decided to buy the failing morning newspaper *The Boston Post* on June 17, 1952. It was often regarded in the city as "the Catholic paper." His goal was "to fight Communism," and he became an eager public supporter of Wisconsin's zealous anti-Communist Republican U.S. Senator Joe McCarthy. In the 1952 campaign, Fox's paper initially backed Protestant Republicans Christian Herter for governor and incumbent Henry Cabot Lodge, Jr. for the U.S. Senate, but it reversed field by endorsing two Catholic Democrats, Governor Paul Dever for reelection and the election of Jack Kennedy for the Senate. An explanation for Fox's change of heart would revolve around Joe Kennedy's $500,000 "loan" to Fox the day before the 1952 endorsement to save the *Post* from bankruptcy.[57] Joe Kennedy's rescue shifted the *Post*'s editorial loyalty to Jack Kennedy. As JFK recounted to Fletcher Knebel, "we had to buy that fucking paper." Years later, Bob Kennedy would recollect that "there was a connection between the two events"—the endorsement and the loan.[58]

The Wooing of the Jews: Recognizing that liberal Jewish Democrats would balk at Jack's candidacy, the Kennedy forces engaged in a multilevel offensive to assuage Jewish fears about the Kennedy family. Basing his research on the extensive oral histories in the Kennedy Library, biographer Herbert Parmet was able to reconstruct how the family went to work wooing Jewish leaders at a breakfast meeting at Boston's Parker House.[59] Multiple meetings were held, and Joe Kennedy himself even appeared to rebut the von Dirksen cables. As described by Parmet, "Some met with the Ambassador himself and heard his critique of the accuracy of what the German ambassador to Great Britain had actually informed Berlin and how his own diplomatic role, given the sensitivity of the situation, could easily have been distorted."[60] But it was a hard sell. Barely six years earlier, voters in Boston's Jewish Democratic wards had voted for Lodge and enthusiastically cheered Lodge's 1946 victory over Democratic Senator David I. Walsh.[61]

Blindsided by the *Post*'s surprise endorsement of Kennedy, Lodge attempted to appeal to Jewish voters who mistrusted the Kennedys, particularly Joe, and Jack by extension. To take advantage of this distrust, Senator Lodge brought three-term U.S. Representative Jacob Javits of New York to Boston's largest Jewish neighborhood, Mattapan. The meeting was held at the Elite Theatre on Blue Hill Avenue, Mattapan's major thoroughfare. Javits, a member of Jack's 1947 class, was there to support the gubernatorial candidacy of fellow Foreign Affairs Committee member Christian Herter but he also sought to help Lodge by implying that Jack was "the son of his father"[62] and that Joe Kennedy's prewar defeatist attitudes had led Jack to deny foreign aid to Israel.

Jack was clearly vulnerable on this issue. In August 1951, he had voted to cut $350,000,000 from the Mutual Security Act of 1951. The fiscally conservative Jack Kennedy was one of only 37 Democrats to join with 149 Republicans to reduce foreign aid to a number of Middle Eastern countries including Israel. The vote to reduce the size of the appropriation was close: 186 to 177 with John McCormack and the other Massachusetts Democrats, Philbin, Donohue, and Furcolo (as well as Republicans Heselton and Wigglesworth) voting against the cut. Jack was called out on this by Abe Michelson of the *Berkshire Eagle* and Jacob Javits drew the events together. The charges stung, placing the Senate campaign on the defensive, and they could easily have wiped away all of the Kennedy family's pro-Jewish efforts of the prior months.

There was only one Massachusetts Democratic voice that could convince Jewish voters to put aside their hesitancy about Jack Kennedy, and that voice was John McCormack's, "Rabbi John" himself. Joe Kennedy knew John had great cachet among the city's Jews and that he had none, so a panicked Joe Kennedy implored John to speak for Jack. It would be a way for John to atone for the unpleasantness of the previous year's Mackay episode.

Rabbi John to the Rescue: With the campaign winding down and the Javits charges still echoing in the city, Jack had to confront the issue of his father directly at a closed meeting of three hundred prominent Bostonians, most of whom were Jews. It was an all-star cast that accompanied Jack Kennedy to this gathering, with House Majority Leader John McCormack orchestrating the meeting. Well aware of the reverence that Jewish voters had for Franklin and Eleanor Roosevelt, John invited New York Representative Franklin D. Roosevelt, Jr. to speak on Jack's behalf. FDR, Jr. disdained Joe Kennedy whom he described as "one of the most evil, disgusting men I have ever known,"[63] but young Roosevelt knew that John McCormack was a loyal New Dealer and put aside the lingering Roosevelt-Kennedy family tensions. Further political star power was added with newly appointed State Treasurer Foster Furcolo, John's outgoing protégé, and Tip O'Neill, the 11th District nominee to succeed Jack in the House, who would become John's newest House protégé. Also in attendance was Eddie McCormack, the younger son of John's tough guy brother Knocko. Eddie, a recent cum laude graduate of the Boston University Law School, was then learning the political ropes and just a decade away from the most dramatic of the Kennedy-McCormack family showdowns.

Jack began his presentation with a litany of his positive votes supporting Jewish issues and turned to the crowd and asked: "What more do you want? Remember, I'm running for the Senate, not my father."[64] Here is when "Rabbi John" McCormack stepped to the podium. The speech was a tour de force.

As recalled by Tip O'Neill, John opened with[65]:

> Two nights ago, Jake Javits was here, and he told you about Jack Kennedy. I want to know that the story he told is not true. I want you to know there was a movement on foot in the Congress of the United States to strike out of the foreign aid bill all of the money for Israel. And I looked around the Congress for a man with courage and fortitude and stamina who would stand up. And I found young Jack Kennedy, and I gave him this amendment and I said, "Jack, offer this amendment. It will cut the budget some, but we will save the remainder for Israel." And by offering the amendment, he saved the remainder of the appropriations for Israel.

O'Neill contended that "the people of ward twelve and ward fourteen bought the McCormack theory and story in toto. Of course it was a figment of McCormack's imagination; it never happened that way."

An even more colorful rendition appears in Herbert Parmet's account based on his interview with Foster Furcolo, who was also present, remembering that McCormack, despite having been spurned by Kennedy earlier over the Curley petition, told them[66]:

> I want to tell you why you should all be for Jack Kennedy. He put his life right on the line for Israel and the Jewish people. I'll tell you about it. There was a bill to give Israel a hundred-million cut. They were going to eliminate the hundred million dollars. I went to Jack Kennedy. "Jack," McCormack quoted himself., "'we've got to save Israel.' He said, 'Are you willing to put your political life on the line for Israel?' I said, 'Yes, John, I am.' 'Then I want you to offer an amendment,' he said. Kennedy told him, 'If you cut this by fifty million dollars then you can get the fifty million dollars for Israel.' Jack Kennedy, McCormack declared emphatically, 'put his political life on the line for Israel.'"
>
> When it was over, McCormack asked Furcolo: "Well, what do you think?"
> "I'm a little sick to my stomach," said the other congressman. [State Treasurer]
> "Well, I know," said McCormack, "But you've got to go through for a Democrat."

McCormack's nephew Edward explained that "there was always the question of accuracy of the Speaker [sic] reporting of what happened, but in any event this was considered by the leaders of the Jewish community to be adequate."

McCormack was pleased with the help that he had provided to Kennedy that evening. John described his relationship with Boston's Jews in 1968[67]:

> In 1952 when he [Jack] was running for the Senate and Henry Cabot Lodge was up for re-election on the Republican side, and he was a very strong candidate, I played a very important part in that campaign. Because through some misunderstanding, the Americans of Jewish blood, our American friends of Jewish blood, had misjudged him, and I was one man in Massachusetts that they had tremendous confidence in, whom they would listen to, and I was able to, I think, bring them back on the line for the late President when he was a candidate for senator in 1952.

Although O'Neill contended that the Israel rescue story was completely fabricated, a closer examination of the House proceedings on May 23, 1952, on the vote for the Mutual Security Act of 1952 reveals that John may not have been quite as creative as Tip believed. As a fiscal conservative, Jack had made a number of requests to cut down foreign aid budgets, most notably to prevent American funds to find their way into dictators' pockets, particularly in Latin America. However, his 1951 vote to cut foreign aid in the Middle East had done collateral damage to Israel's funding and the public notice it drew was unfavorable. As the 1952 campaign gathered momentum, Jack sought to alter his stance and repair the damage. During the House debate on the Mutual Security Act of 1952, Democratic Representative Richard Chatham of North Carolina offered an amendment that would reduce that year's mutual security foreign aid appropriation for resettlements of $76,000,000 to Israel and $65,000,000 to the Arab countries to $50,000,000 apiece.[68] Chatham was challenged by New York Representatives Manny Celler and Franklin D. Roosevelt, Jr. and by John McCormack.

In a curious move, Jack spoke up in support of the $76,000,000 appropriation with three sentences of remarks accompanied by a speech that he had given "last Friday night to a group of Jewish war veterans in Boston." In the inserted speech, Jack spoke of traveling to Israel with Congressman FDR, Jr. the previous fall. Generally, such remarks are located in the *Extensions of Remarks* section of the *Congressional Record*, but Jack had them inserted in the *Record* as if he had spoken them on the floor. Chatham's amendment was defeated on a division of the House, 66 to 103, but since it was a standing division, no roll call was taken. The formal roll calls would occur after debate was closed and the question was called. On final passage, the 1952 Act was a full billion dollars less than the one passed in 1951. Altogether 77 members of the House partook of the debate on that long afternoon in May, and three roll calls were taken later that day on the two limiting amendments, both of which passed and the bill's final passage.[69] On those three votes, John McCormack, Foster Furcolo, and most of the other Democrats voted "Nay" on the two amendments limiting foreign aid funding and "Yea" on its final passage.

However, neither Congressmen Kennedy nor Chatham who had spoken earlier on the bill voted on any of the three final roll calls. Of the 77 participants in that day's debate, only Jack and Chatham, the author of the original limiting resolution, were not around for the roll calls. Jack had already left the building and was listed as "Not voting" on all three roll calls. Chatham's departure after his motion was defeated made some sense, but Jack's did not. It was this cavalier behavior of a grandstanding Kennedy speech and a disappearance at the crunch time of the roll call vote that had occurred much too frequently in the eyes of John McCormack.

But John McCormack's fabrication had delivered for Jack, and John had paid off his debt to Joe Kennedy by bringing FDR, Jr. to Boston and assembling the Jewish leaders as only "Rabbi John" could have done. After the event and in a later thank you note, John told young Roosevelt that his appearance had made the difference. Jack chose not to send FDR Jr. a thank you note. The earlier Joe Kennedy-Franklin Roosevelt family differences had apparently continued into the next generation.

While Jack may have forgotten the events of May 23, he never forgot the gesture, despite the many political differences he had had with McCormack over the years. "When the chips were down," Jack later told Tip O'Neill, "McCormack was in the line of fire for me because I was a Democrat. He did something I never would have done for him."[70]

Pat Jackson and the Notre Dame Petition

Another cloud on the Kennedy horizon was Republican Joe McCarthy of Wisconsin, a darling of Irish Boston's anti-Communists but openly disdained by Massachusetts liberals who saw him as an opportunistic "Red-baiter." Jack Kennedy needed the votes of both groups if he was to defeat Lodge. "Tail gunner" Joe McCarthy was elected to the Senate in 1946, the same year that Dick Nixon and Jack Kennedy would win their House seats, and he would be involved in both of their lives and political careers. For Kennedy, the family association with Joe McCarthy was especially problematic. McCarthy spent time with the Kennedys in Hyannis Port and even dated Jack's sisters, the brainy Eunice and the beauty Pat. McCarthy apparently considered coming to Boston to campaign for fellow Republican Lodge, but he was unsympathetic with the party's moderate eastern faction and with his wallet fattened by a Joe Kennedy campaign contribution, "Tail gunner Joe" made no appearance.[71] When Joe became chair of the Senate Committee on Government Operations in 1953, he would hire Jack's younger brother Robert F. Kennedy as a legal counsel. No issue bothered Democratic liberals more than Jack's association with Joe McCarthy.

Boston's liberal intellectuals had become very anxious following the 1950 suicide of Harvard's distinguished Professor of American Studies, F. O. Matthieson, who had seconded the nomination of former Vice President Henry Wallace at the 1948 Progressive Party convention and was targeted for investigation by the House Un-American Activities Committee (HUAC). Fearful that an inquiry into his politics would also discover his homosexuality, Matthieson plunged to his death from the window of Boston's Hotel Manger.[72] Boston's intellectuals, seldom known for fearlessness, become even more reticent.

In an effort to get liberal votes, longtime activist Gardner "Pat" Jackson was invited to Boston to join the campaign and prepare statements for liberal audiences. Jackson, an Amherst alumnus who served in World War I, became a *Boston Globe* reporter after the war. A classic WASP of wealth, connection, and Protestant guilt, Jackson was especially troubled by the Sacco-Vanzetti case and spent much of his time and fortune trying to clear the names of the two Italian immigrant anarchists who would be executed in 1927. During the 1930s, Jackson became involved with the Southern Tenant Farmers' Union (STFU) created by Norman Thomas, the perennial presidential candidate of the Socialist Party. Thomas was disturbed that FDR's Agricultural Adjustment Act (AAA) did little for the mostly black southern sharecroppers and Jackson was recruited to represent STFU with the Roosevelt Administration.[73]

Jackson got to know the Kennedys during the time he lived in Hyannis on Cape Cod. While Jack truly needed John McCormack to overcome Jewish suspicion about his candidacy, he also believed that he needed Pat Jackson to help him win liberal votes and to defuse the Joe McCarthy problem. As a staunch Roman Catholic anti-Communist, John McCormack would be of no help with the liberal voters.

Pat Jackson had become one of the anti-Communist liberals trying to rid the labor movement of Communist influences, then a major concern of the CIO, the Congress of Industrial Organizations. In 1959, Jackson was interviewed by Ed Plaut, the coauthor with Ralph G. Martin on the book *Front Runner, Dark Horse*.[74] Intended as an early take on the upcoming 1960 Democratic presidential nomination, the quotes from the Jackson interview would reverberate throughout the 1960 campaign and continue to be quoted to the present day. Martin was a newspaperman who had worked in Stevenson's 1952 and 1956 campaigns and got to know Kennedy well during his failed 1956 vice presidential bid. Kennedy was the "front runner" in the title, while Missouri's U.S. Senator Stuart Symington was the "dark horse."

In the interview, Jackson recounted a 1952 episode with Joe Kennedy that has been repeated in more than a dozen books about the Kennedys during the Lodge campaign. Then working for the CIO in Washington, Jackson's first stop in Boston was to the home of Supreme Court Justice Felix Frankfurter, his ally in the Sacco-Vanzetti case and whose wife had edited the letters of Sacco and Vanzetti with Jackson.[75] Jackson told Plaut that he and Frankfurter exchanged their views of Joe Kennedy:

> FRANKFURTER: Pat, isn't the most evil man you have ever met, the most evil of
> the entire lot Joe Kennedy.
> JACKSON: Yes because the man is amoral. He grew up with barflies and
> stewbums and he made his fortune but he never changed.

Jackson went on to say. "I always liked Jack, though. I knew him when he was in the House. He's a thinker. He was a thinker then, but he was just finding himself in those days." Jackson stayed at the Hotel Bellevue and was given a key to Jack's apartment at 122 Bowdoin. Jackson recalled: "Every morning, I let myself in his apartment before he was awake. And when he woke up, he and I would talk while he bathed and shaved."

> The first thing he wanted me to do was to get the open support of the ADA for
> him, and then of labor and other liberal groups. Believe me, that took some doing.
> His record was not a very liberal one. I forget who was the president of the Mass.

ADA at that time. I went to see Poppa Artie Schlesinger [of the Harvard history department] first. He has been one of my great friends since the Sacco-Vanzetti fight. It took some doing to get his support, and then we worked on others and I finally got Jack what he wanted and the ADA supported him openly. Then I went around to various labor leaders and persuaded them that they should support Jack instead of Lodge and that wasn't easy because Cabot had been a friend to labor. But we persuaded most of them . . . all but a few.

The Confrontation over the Notre Dame Petition: Jackson was convinced that there was one document that would insure liberal support for Jack and that was a petition drafted by faculty members at Notre Dame supporting Stevenson's candidacy. The document led to a dramatic confrontation between Jackson and Joe Kennedy. As Jackson recounted[76]:

Of course his father was in on the campaign. Joe Kennedy and his money were everywhere. He spent millions. One of the things I was determined that Jack should do was to make a statement about McCarthy. I talked to enough political leaders to be convinced that he had enough of a lead to do it. The best opinion was that he had the margin to do it. I prepared a newspaper ad. It was a very cautiously worded ad that simply quoted [unintelligible] and the 99 on the faculty of Notre Dame who issued a statement, "Communism and McCarthy: Both Wrong."

I discussed it with Jack many times and he said that he would sign the ad if I could get John McCormack to co-sign it with him. And I went to see McCormack and he finally agreed to sign it if Jack would. So I took it up to Jack's apartment the next morning and let myself in and the place was a hubbub of activity. Jack had on his coat and was about to leave and went dashing out just as I arrived. Sitting at a card table in the center of the living room were (Joe) Kennedy and three of his speechwriters . . . Jim Landis, John Harris and my old comrade-in-arms from the Sacco-Vanzetti fight, Joe Healey. Jim, of course, had been on Joe's payroll as one of his lawyers for many years. John was, and is, financial writer for the *Boston Globe* and I believe was playing a double role. I believe he was being paid by Joe in that campaign (I picked up the figure of $1000 somewhere). Joe Healey, who was later appointed Tax Commissioner by Gov [Foster] Furcolo may have been on a retain[er] to give tax advice to Joe Kennedy during the campaign but I don't know. The four of them were working on a speech. Joe Kennedy went over every word that Jack uttered in that campaign.

Well, I read them the ad at Jack's request and I had not gone two sentences when Joe Kennedy jumped to his feet with such force that he tilted the card table over against the others and he stood there shouting at me, one thing after another: "You're trying to ruin Jack," he said and over and over again, he'd say something about "You and your sheeny friends" and he said [Supreme Court Justice] Bill Douglas is a friend of mine and he kept saying, "I helped discover Adlai Stevenson" and he said, "Bill Douglas called me just the other day [unintelligible] . . . to go on a national television hookup and speak on behalf of Adlai Stevenson but I can't do it because he is too radical on foreign policy and too radical on labor . . ." and one thing after another in a rage.

Jackson had once suffered a beating that caused him to suffer the loss of an eye in the 1940s during his efforts to limit the influence of Communists in the labor movement,[77] but he was seriously taken aback by the intensity of Joe Kennedy's remarks:

> I have never had a working over like that in my life, no one has ever talked to me that way, shouted at me, in that way in my life. Then he left. I went into the little room in the back where I had my typewriter and did my work, and I had a telephone in there. I went in there and Joe Healy came in and put his arm around my shoulder and said "Don't worry about him; his bark is worse than his bite." And then Jim Landis came in and said something. The next morning I went to Jack's apartment as usual and let myself in and he heard me and he came into the room and said, "I hear you really had it yesterday, didn't you." And we talked about his father and Jack said something I have never forgotten and this is on the plus side and I've always remembered it. I asked him what made his father act this way about his children and Jack said, "My father's one motive that you can understand, Pat is love of family . . ." and then he paused, and added, ". . . although sometimes I think it's really pride," and he said it very quietly.

It was Jackson's hope that both Jack Kennedy and John McCormack would sign the ad but each said they would sign it only if the other one would do so first. Neither signed it. Having been burned when Jack had refused to sign the 1947 Curley petition, John McCormack had no intention of going it alone and risking his support among his fierce Irish-American anti-Communist constituents.

As graphic as the story is, there are flaws in the account. First, it was a pro-Stevenson petition with the professors exhorting one another to "work, vote, and pray" for the election of Governor Stevenson. It was not an anti–Joe McCarthy one. The key phrase that Jackson fastened on was:

> THIRD: We believe that he will be forthright and dauntless in combating the twin tyrannies—unchristian and anti-Christian—that threatens our democratic freedom and independence: on the one side, the vast and evil movement of Communism crawling over the face of the earth and, on the other, the menace of McCarthyism representing the awful appearance on the American scene of Fascism and Nazi primitivism.

Second, there never were "99 Notre Dame Professors" who signed the petition. There were four versions of the petition with 53 signatures on the first edition on October 27; 55 on the second on October 28; and 65 on the third and last one both issued on October 29.[78] Peter Lysy, the senior Notre Dame archivist, said that there had been a conference discussing legislative investigations with the possibility of 99 participants, but none of the petitions went beyond 65 signatories. There never was a real petition, only an ad that Jackson had drafted. Jackson continued, "There had been one previous discussion of an ad about McCarthy and that was at the advertising agency . . . yes, the Dowd Agency. Everyone there argued that it would be a terrible mistake. That it would cost many thousands of votes and the election. Dowd argued that and Landis said that he didn't like McCarthy but it would be a terrible mistake." The ad was never published and Jackson said that he tossed it into a "big box" in his attic. It is likely that it did not survive one of his many moves.

Jackson's final take on the event was that

I was there to woo the support of liberals, and it was some job. Jack already had the approval of conservatives, and that man craves the approval of liberal intellectuals. He needs it, craves it, the support of liberal intellectuals. A real craving. But I had to remain behind the scenes. No word was to leak out. The thing that has always bothered old Poppa Arthur Schlesinger Sr. was whether Jack has deep feelings about individual rights. He doesn't. There is no deep inner commitment to the rights of the individual. He feels none of this viscerally.

Jackson became disillusioned with Kennedy once he realized that Jack was not his kind of liberal. It was at that point, the account surfaced. Joe Kennedy denied Jackson's version of the incident in an interview with Irwin Ross[79]:

"Oh, Pat Jackson has been living off that story for years," he says, and then goes on to argue that Jackson was quite wrong in urging his son to attack McCarthy: it would have been suicide in the 1952 campaign.

The three named as witnesses [Landis, Harris, and Healey] to the scene maintain that they cannot recall it. But they agree that it could have occurred; it was in character for Joe. He often blew his top and he does use unfortunate ethnic epithets such as "micks" for Irish and "wops" for Italians. One speech writer added: "Jackson is an honorable guy and I don't see why he'd make it up."

James MacGregor Burns, Kennedy's first biographer, mentions the episode but omits "your sheeny friends."[80] In his notes, Burns states, "My account of the encounter in Kennedy's living room between Jackson and Joseph Kennedy is based on interviews with participants."[81]

The story took on a life of its own and has been retold a number of times, sometimes with "your sheeny friends" included and sometimes not. It is referred to in thirteen biographies[82] and omitted in fourteen.[83] Although loyal Democrats Burns and Martin left the "sheeny" quote out of their favorable 1960 biographies of Kennedy, all eleven accounts of the event surface after its initial print appearance in a five-part article in January 1961 by Irwin Ross in the *New York Post*. David Nasaw's definitive biography of Joe Kennedy follows the Burns model describing the incident, mentioning Jewish opposition, but not the "sheeny" remark.[84] In retrospect, it may be argued that Pat Jackson's palpable disdain for Joe Kennedy and his later disillusionment with Jack may have led him to embellish a real contretemps with the hateful slur as well as to miscount the signers of the Notre Dame petition.

Stevenson's 1952 defeat

Unsurprisingly, vice presidential nominee Senator John Sparkman's electoral impact on the ticket was minimal. The four Dixiecrat states of Alabama, Louisiana, Mississippi, and South Carolina returned to the Democratic fold, but their 37 electoral votes were more than canceled out by the loss of the 57 votes from the outer South states of Florida, Tennessee, Virginia, and Texas to the Republicans. The electoral vote map of the 1952 South was nearly identical to that of the 1928 Hoover-Smith contest with Stevenson capturing the same states as did Al Smith and Eisenhower capturing the same states as did Herbert Hoover. North Carolina cast its votes for both Hoover and Stevenson. It was the lone exception to this repeat of southern electoral history. With no electoral votes north of the Ohio River or west of Arkansas, the presidential map looked even worse than that of the 1920 election which sunk that year's ticket of James M. Cox and Franklin D. Roosevelt.

The congressional results were less disheartening. Eisenhower's popularity had not extended deep into the House and Senate races. The Democrats faced a net loss of two Senate seats and 23 in the House. With Oregon's mercurial Senator Wayne Morse leaving the Republicans to be an independent, the Senate was split: 48 Republicans to 47 Democrats. In the House, the Republicans held eight more seats than the Democrats (221–213) but there had been no massive repudiation of the congressional Democrats. It was also clear that the Democratic governors and Democratic state legislatures had limited the redistricting damage that the party might have faced following the post-1950 reapportionment.

Election night in Massachusetts

The loss of the House majority to the Republicans was painful enough for John McCormack, but the 1952 results in Massachusetts were more negative than positive. It was close to a double-digit presidential victory as Ike buried Governor Stevenson by almost 209,000 votes—54.2% to 45.5%—to capture Massachusetts electoral votes for the Republican Party for the first time since 1924. The vote for Stevenson was almost ten points below that for Harry Truman four years earlier. Unlike 1948 when John McCormack's South Boston neighbor, Archbishop Richard Cushing, sung Harry Truman's praises, Cushing was disinclined to issue a single word in support of Stevenson, a Princeton-educated, divorced Unitarian. Stevenson's Massachusetts defeat was foreordained.

Ike's victory had also helped Republican Congressman Christian Herter, the Paris-born Brahmin, defeat Democratic Governor Paul A. Dever by a narrow 14,500 vote margin (49.9% to 49.3%). Herter would serve two terms as governor and then be recalled to Washington in 1957 as undersecretary of state.

The year of 1952 had been unkind to Democratic Governor Paul Dever. It is reported that Dever did not wish to make this third gubernatorial run and that he flirted seriously with the chance to take on Senator Lodge, but Joe Kennedy's financial support for his campaign kept Dever in the governor's race and out of Jack's way to the Senate.

John McCormack won 82.2% of the vote in his contest and would return to the House for his 14th term. Ike's victory had helped Republicans recapture the House but their eight-vote margin (221–213) was too small to bother John, and he and Sam Rayburn both knew that the midterm election of 1954 would restore the Democrats to control of the House. Little did they know that the 1954 election victory would give Democrats control of the House for the next 40 years.

With the departures of Jack Kennedy and Foster Furcolo, two new Democrats were elected to the House from their open districts. They were Thomas P. "Tip" O'Neill, Jr. from Kennedy's 11th District and Edward P. Boland from Furcolo's 2nd District. They had served together in the Great and General Court and entering the House together, these two Irish-descended Boston College alums bonded immediately and agreed to share living quarters. Tip O'Neill and Eddie Boland were ideal protégé candidates for John McCormack. They were bright, conscientious, and electable. They worked hard on their committee responsibilities and seemed to have no ambitions beyond the House itself.

Both Eddie Boland and Tip O'Neill benefited from the fact that Massachusetts lost no House seats following the 1950 Census and both John McCormack and Joe Martin, respectively, the House's Majority and Minority Leaders, convinced the state legislature to leave all of the Massachusetts 14 Congressional Districts untouched.[85] So whatever Massachusetts population movement had occurred within the decade of the 1940s was not to be addressed until the 1960 Census and the 1962 redistricting. McCormack and Martin were trying to emulate the southern strategy of recruiting young men for U.S. House seats, gaining favorable committee assignments for them and then encouraging them to remain in the House to accrue seniority. The success of this bipartisan incumbent protection strategy would lead not only to committee chairmanships for Bay Staters, but also to three members from Massachusetts occupying the Speaker's chair for 23 of the 40 years between 1947 and 1986.

John McCormack and Sam Rayburn were less dismayed about their minority circumstances in the 83rd Congress than they had been about them in the 80th Congress. Rayburn was especially sanguine. Unlike his disappointment following the 1946 election, Sam Rayburn issued no threats to resign this time. Rayburn and McCormack looked disparagingly at the incoming band of zealous anti-Communist Republicans who seemed more obsessed with investigation than legislation, and correctly surmised that this latest Republican hold on the House would be short-lived.

There was some good news from Mississippi. The 83rd Congress would open without the violent segregationist John E. Rankin, who had failed of renomination and would no longer foul the House chamber with his racist and anti-Semitic rants. But there was sad news as well. Both of the senior Democratic members of the Rules Committee—Adolph Sabath in November and Gene Cox in December—died within a few weeks of one another.

Jack Escapes the House: In the Senate race, Jack defeated Henry Cabot Lodge, Jr. by over 70,000 votes (51.4% to 48.4%). The reluctant liberals and the Jews of Mattapan had come through for "Rabbi John" and for Jack. It is doubtful if John McCormack thought that Jack Kennedy would succeed in his quest for the Senate, but succeed he did. For John, the good news was that Jack was no longer in the House and in his stead; he would now have a real protégé—Tip O'Neill—in that seat.

The good news for Jack Kennedy was that after six years he had at last escaped John McCormack's House and could now continue his upward trajectory on the larger stage of the U.S. Senate.

Jack's initial reaction was curious. As the national returns were beamed on television, he saw smiling Republicans Eisenhower and Nixon with their hands joined and their arms aloft, and exclaimed, "Imagine that! Dick Nixon and I came into Congress together and now he's Vice President of the United States."[86] Another hurdle awaited Jack en route to completing the Kennedy family mission. John McCormack would be there also.

As the 83rd Congress opened in January 1953, John and Jack would ply their trade on opposite sides of Capitol Hill separated by the long marble corridor of the U.S. Capitol building. However, the real truth was that their escape from one another was illusory, and these two Bostonians would continue to butt heads for another decade. Less than nine years later in November 1961, Jack would be the 35th President of the United States and John was about to become the 45th man to serve as Speaker of the U.S. House of Representatives. It was not the first time in American history that the nation's two most powerful constitutional offices were filled by men from the same party and the same state, but never before had these two officers interacted as often or as contentiously as had the princely Jack Kennedy and the provincial John McCormack.

Notes

1   "Job Approval Lows" in "Presidential Approval Ratings—Gallup Historical Statistics and Trends," accessed August 4, 2014.

2   William Howard Moore, *The Kefauver Committee and the Politics of Crime, 1950–1952* (Columbia: University of Missouri Press, 1974).

3   Data are from the "1952 Primaries," Congressional Quarterly, *Presidential Elections, 1789–1992* (Washington, DC: Congressional Quarterly Press, 1995), p. 171.

4   Truman's withdrawal announcement made at a Jefferson-Jackson Day dinner in Washington caught most people by surprise; see David McCullough's Pulitzer Prize-winning biography, *Truman* (New York: Simon & Schuster, 1992), pp. 892–93.

5   Ibid., p. 889; and "it was only a week before the convention, his patience [with Stevenson] gone and resolved to do almost anything to stop Kefauver" (p. 903).

6   "1952: Twenty-Fifth Republican Convention," in Richard C. Bain and Judith H. Parris, eds., *Convention Decisions and Voting Records* (Washington, DC: The Brookings Institution, 1973), pp. 279–86.

7   Irwin F. Gellman, *The Contender: Richard Nixon, The Congress Years, 1946–1952* (New York: The Free Press, 1999), p. 433.

8   The Warren appointment by Eisenhower continues to fascinate; see Ed Cray, *Chief Justice: A Biography of Earl Warren* (New York: Simon & Schuster, 1997), p. 190; and Earl Warren's own recounting, *The Memoirs of Earl Warren* (New York: Doubleday & Co., 1977), p. 5. Another version appears in Stephen E. Ambrose's biography of Eisenhower as his biggest mistake was "the appointment of that dumb son of a bitch Earl Warren," in *Eisenhower: The President*, Vol. 2 (New York: Simon and Schuster, 1984), p. 190. A not wholly convincing argument to extricate Ike from these assertions is made by Michael A. Kahn, "Shattering the Myth about President Eisenhower's Supreme Court Appointments," *Presidential Studies Quarterly*, XXII (Winter 1992), pp. 47–56.

9   "1952: Thirty-First Democratic Convention," in Bain and Parris, eds., *Convention Decisions and Voting Records*, pp. 286–92.

10 McCormack had worked against Dever in the 1946 lieutenant governor's race by supporting Springfield Mayor Roger Lowell Putnam, a Brahmin and the father-in-law to the son of John's best friend James Fitzgerald, in the Harvard honor's thesis of George S. Abrams, *Paul A. Dever and the Democratic Party in Massachusetts: A Study in Personalized Politics* (Cambridge, MA: Harvard University Department of Government, 1954), pp. 78–79.

11 See Edward F. Cooke, "Drafting the 1952 Platforms," *Western Political Quarterly*, IX (September 1956), pp. 699–712; and Judith H. Parris, *The Convention Problem* (Washington, DC: The Brookings Institution, 1972), p. 118.

12 The phrase "apostles of compromise" comes from the careful assessment of the 1952 plank relative to the 1948 one found in Donald R. McCoy and Richard T. Ruetten, *Quest and Response: Minority Rights and the Truman Administration* (Lawrence: University Press of Kansas, 1973), pp. 322–26.

13 "Democratic Party Platform of 1952," in Kirk Porter and Donald B. Johnson, comps. *National Party Platforms, 1840–1968*, 4th ed. (Urbana: University of Illinois Press, 1970), pp. 473–87.

14 Charles V. Hamilton, *Adam Clayton Powell, Jr.: The Political Biography of an American Dilemma* (New York: Collier Books, 1991), p. 197.

15 Ibid.

16 McCullough, *Truman*, pp. 889–94.

17 "John J. Sparkman," in the online *Encyclopedia of Alabama*, accessed August 28, 2014.

18 See the chapter "Alabama: Planters, Populists, 'Big Mules'" in the classic volume by V. O. Key. Jr. with Alexander Heard, *Southern Politics in State and Nation* (New York: Allred A. Knopf, 1949), pp. 47–49, on Sparkman's areas of support.

19 The stylistic difference between "inheritors" and "climbers" are presented in Garrison Nelson, "White House Inheritors and Climbers: Presidential Kin, Class and Performance, 1789–2002," *New England Journal of Public Policy*, XVIII (Spring/Summer 2003), pp. 11–38.

20 From House Resolution 390, 82nd Congress, First Session, September 15, 1951, as amended by House Resolution 539, 82nd Congress, Second Session, March 11, 1952. The seven members—four Democrats and three Republicans—were named on September 24, 1951. Years later, Furcolo published a book on the brutal episode *Rendezvous at Katyn* (Boston: Marlborough House, 1973). See also "Polish Exiles Honor Katyn Investigators," *Boston Globe*, March 29, 1953.

21 Mary W. Davis oral history interview with E. William Johnson, April 21, 1976, p. 20. Ms. Davis had worked earlier for Republican Charles Eaton of New Jersey and was

recommended for the Kennedy post by Eugene Kinnaly, John McCormack's legislative assistant.

22 Ross Collins, "Furcolo Switch Seen as Stride to Governor's Chair or Senate," *Boston Globe*, July 6, 1952.

23 In an oral history at the Kennedy Library, Bob Griffin, a Kennedy aide, recalled that Joe Kennedy asked him who was going to win the primary in the 11th District. "He used to ask me about the LoPresti fight, and I kept telling him that I thought O'Neill was going to win. And his reaction was 'That doesn't help us. We need LoPresti on the ticket,'" in John A. Farrell's superb *Tip O'Neill and the Democratic Century: A Biography* (Boston: Little Brown, 2001), p. 126. Griffin speculated that Joe Kennedy had given money to the LoPresti campaign.

24 See the essay on "The 'Untalkative Speaker' Talks—About His Father," in Kornitzer, *American Fathers and Sons* (New York: Hermitage House, 1952), pp. 209–21.

25 John McCormack's interview with T. Harrison Baker of the University of Texas Oral History Project, LBJ Library, September 23, 1968, on the centrality of House committee work, pp. 2–3.

26 U.S. Representative Richard Bolling (Dem-Mo.) interview with Ed Plaut in the Ralph G. Martin Papers at the Howard Gotlieb Archival Research Center at Boston University. The interview was for Ralph G. Martin and Ed Plaut, *Front Runner, Dark Horse* (Garden City, NY: Doubleday, 1960).

27 Theodore C. Sorensen, *Kennedy* (New York: Harper & Row, 1965), p. 11.

28 Ibid., p. 27.

29 David Nasaw contends that Joe Kennedy "contributed $1000 to Nixon's campaign against Democrat Helen Gahagan Douglas whom he regarded as much too far to the left" in his exhaustive book, *The Patriarch: The Remarkable Life and Turbulent Times of Joseph P. Kennedy* (New York: The Penguin Press, 2012), p. 731.

30 "George Cabot," *BDUSC* (1989 ed.), p. 724.

31 The Lodge family history is recounted in Alden Hatch, *The Lodges of Massachusetts* (New York: Hawthorn, 1973).

32 Although these events are covered in the multiple books about the Kennedy family, the fullest account of their time in England, albeit soft on Joe Kennedy's anti-Semitism, is Will Swift's *The Kennedys amidst the Gathering Storm: A Thousand Days in London, 1938–1940* (Washington, DC: Smithsonian Books and New York: Collins, 2008).

33 The Joe Kennedy-Charles Lindbergh relationship may be found in Chapter 9, infra.

34 The debate continues, see the pro-Lindbergh and anti-FDR treatment in James P. Duffy, *Lindbergh vs. Roosevelt: The Rivalry That Divided America* (Washington, DC: Regnery, 2010). Duffy is challenged by Lynne Olson's *Those Angry Days: Roosevelt, Lindbergh, and America's Fight over World War II, 1939–1941* (New York: Random House, 2013).

35 In a May 1944 interview with an old friend, Joe Dinneen of the *Boston Globe*, Joe Kennedy acknowledged, when questioned about his alleged anti-Semitism: "It is true that I have a low opinion of some Jews in public office and in private life. That does not mean that I hate all Jews; that I believe they should be wiped off the face of the earth. . . . Other races have their own problems to solve. They're glad to give the Jews a lift and help them along the way toward tolerance, but they're not going to drop everything and solve the problems of the Jews for them. Jews who take an unfair advantage of the fact that theirs is a persecuted race do not help much." Kennedy's discussion of anti-Semitism was withheld from publication at the time by the editors of

the *Globe*, but in 1959 Dinneen sought to include a portion of it in a generally flattering book. Jack Kennedy, who understood how inflammatory his father's comments were, successfully urged Dinneen to delete the offending paragraphs. Richard J. Whalen, *The Founding Father: The Story of Joseph P. Kennedy* (New York: New American Library, 1964), pp. 387–90.

36   Joe Kennedy's anti-Semitism was long suspected; see "The Jewish Question," in Ronald Kessler's *The Sins of the Father: Joseph P. Kennedy and the Dynasty He Founded* (New York: Warner Books, 1996), pp. 161–76. It is also noted in the highly critical book, Nigel Hamilton, *JFK: Reckless Youth* (New York: Random House, 1992), pp. 108, 247, 512, and 669. As described by Seymour M. Hersh in *The Dark Side of Camelot* (Boston: Little, Brown, 1997), his critical assessment of the Kennedys, "There is no evidence that Ambassador Kennedy understood in the days before the war that stopping Hitler was a moral imperative." "Individual Jews are all right, Harvey," Kennedy told Harvey Klemmer, one of his few trusted aides in the American Embassy, "but as a race they stink. They spoil everything they touch. Look what they did to the movies." Klemmer, in an interview many years later made available for this book, recalled that Kennedy and his "entourage" generally referred to Jews as "kikes or sheenies" (p. 63). See also Edward Renehan's "Joseph Kennedy and the Jews" in the website of the History News Network for April 29, 2002. Renehan is the author of *The Kennedys at War, 1937–1945* (New York: Doubleday, 2002).

37   Joseph P. Kennedy, "Present Policy is Politically and Morally Bankrupt: United Nations Not a Vehicle to Enforce Peace," delivered at the University of Virginia Law Forum, Charlottesville, Virginia, December 12, 1950, from *Vital Speeches of the Day*, XVII (January 1951), pp. 170–74.

38   Paul M. Shafer (Rep-Mich.), "Credit due Joseph P. Kennedy for Part in the Great Debate." The formal publication of Shafer's remarks appeared in the *Appendix* to the *Congressional Record,* 82nd Congress, First Session on April 16, 1951, p. A2207.

39   Furcolo's remarks are reported in the *Congressional Record*, XCVII, *Congressional Record*, 82nd Congress, First Session, February 14, 1951, p. 1267.

40   John McCormack, *Congressional Record*, XCVII, Part 1, February 14, 1951, p. 1267.

41   Charles H. Trout, *Boston, the Great Depression, and the New Deal* (New York: Oxford University Press, 1977), p. 292.

42   The June 13, 1938 Cable No. 457 may be found *in Documents on German Foreign Policy, 1918–1945* from the Archives of the German Foreign Ministry (Washington, DC: Government Printing Office, 1951), Series D (1937–45), Volume I, *From Neurath to Ribbentrop (September 1937–September 1938)*, pp. 714–15. The October 13, 1938 Cable No. 498, Volume IV, *The Aftermath of Munich, October 1938–March 1939*, pp. 634 and 636. Interestingly, von Dirksen's memoir of his ambassadorial career in *Moscow, Tokyo, London: Twenty Years of German Foreign Policy* (Norman: University of Oklahoma Press, 1952) makes no mention of Joe Kennedy and only two paragraphs about Americans in the London portion of his memoir (pp. 188–234).

43   Parmet, *Jack: The Struggles of John F. Kennedy*, pp. 246–48.

44   Joe Jr.'s attitudes were much more similar to his father than were those of Jack. On Joe Jr.'s anti-Semitism, see Laurence Leamer, *The Kennedy Men, 1901–1963: The Laws of the Father* (New York: William Morrow, 2001), pp. 82–83, 122, and 137.

45   Representative Robert Jones (D-Ala.), oral history interview with John Stewart, May 21, 1968, JFK Library.

46   "Reservations," *TIME*, March 19, 1945.

47   Joseph P. Kennedy to the Hon. John W. McCormack, July 17, 1951, Joseph P. Kennedy Papers, JFK Library.

48   Author's telephonic interview with Bob Healy, July 1999.

49   McCormack to Joseph P. Kennedy, July 13, 1951, Joseph P. Kennedy Papers, JFK Library.

50   Joseph P. Kennedy to McCormack, August 8, 1951.

51   According to Bob Clark of the Franklin D. Roosevelt Presidential Library and Museum, as described in an interview with the author.

52   From Champ Clark, "Mr. Speaker," *TIME*, January 19, 1962, p. 21.

53   McCormack, "Persecution of the German Jewish People," *Congressional Record*, 73rd Congress, First Session, June 9, 1933, pp. 5441–42.

54   Clay Risen, *The Bill of the Century: The Epic Battle for the Civil Rights Act* (New York: Bloomsbury Press, 2014), p. 119; sourced from D. B. Hardeman interview with Raymond Wolfinger, September 13, 1965, box 22, David B. Filvaroff and Raymond E. Wolfinger, Civil Rights Act Papers, University of Buffalo Library.

55   The fullest depiction of that election is Thomas J. Whalen, *Kennedy versus Lodge: The 1952 Massachusetts Senate Contest* (Boston: Northeastern University Press, 2000).

56   A valuable short biography of John Fox appeared in his obituary prepared by the Associated Press and published in the *NYT*, January 25, 1985.

57   Nasaw, *The Patriarch*, p. 669.

58   Nasaw cites an interview with Robert Kennedy in Michael O'Brien's *John F. Kennedy: A Biography* (New York: Thomas Dunne/St. Martin's Press, 2005), p. 257.

59   Herbert S. Parmet, *Jack: The Struggles of John F. Kennedy* (New York: The Dial Press), p. 247.

60   Ibid.

61   Jewish dislike of Senator Walsh is described in Lawrence H. Fuchs, *The Political Behavior of American Jews* (Glencoe, IL: The Free Press, 1956), p. 138n.

62   "Cong. Javits Coming Here to Aid G.O.P.," *Boston Daily Globe*, October 13, 1952, p. 26. See also Tip O'Neill, *Man of the House*, p. 119.

63   Franklin D. Roosevelt, Jr. quoted in the Ralph G. Martin Papers at Boston University: "I think Jack's father is one of the most evil, disgusting men I have ever known."

64   The meeting is reported in Kessler, *The Sins of the Father*, p. 337.

65   Oral history of the Hon. Thomas P. O'Neill, Jr. with Charles T. Morrissey, May 18, 1966, JFK Library and Museum, pp. 74–75.

66   Parmet, *Jack*, pp. 247–48.

67   John McCormack's assistance to John Kennedy with Jewish voters is recounted in his interview with T. Harrison Baker of the University of Texas Oral History Project, LBJ Library, September 23, 1968, pp. 21–22. On John McCormack's electoral appeal to the voters of heavily Jewish Ward 14, see Lawrence H. Fuchs, *The Political Behavior of American Jews* (Glencoe, IL: The Free Press, 1956), p. 138n. The note also discusses Jewish dislike of Walsh.

68   *Congressional Record*, 82nd Congress, Second Session, May 23, 1952, pp. 5889 for Chapman; p. 5894 for Kennedy's remarks; and p. 5896 for the vote on the Chatham amendment.

69   *Congressional Record*, 82nd Congress, Second Session, May 23. 1952: House Roll Call Vote 84—221 Yeas; 137 Nays (Furcolo, McCormack, and Roosevelt); 73 Not Voting (Chatham and Kennedy), p. 5915; House Roll Call Vote 85–182 Yeas; 165 Nays (Furcolo, McCormack, and Roosevelt); 74 Not Voting (Chatham and Kennedy), p. 5916; House

Roll Call Vote 86–246 Yeas (Furcolo, McCormack, and Roosevelt), 109 Nays, Present 1, Not Voting (Chatham and Kennedy), p. 5917.

70   Thomas P. O'Neill, Jr. interview with Charles T. Morrissey, May 18, 1966, in the JFK Library, pp. 76–77.

71   Joe Kennedy contributed money for McCarthy's 1952 reelection campaign (Nasaw, *The Patriarch*, pp. 666–67).

72   Harry Levin, "The Private Life of F. O. Matthiessen," *New York Review of Books*, XXV (July 20, 1978), pp. 42–46.

73   Donald H. Grubbs, "Gardner Jackson, That 'Socialist' Tenant Farmers' Union and the New Deal," *Agricultural History*, XLII (April 1968), pp. 125–37. Two obituaries of Jackson capture his uniqueness: Arthur M. Schlesinger, Jr., "Gardner Jackson, 1897–1965," *New Republic*, May 1, 1965, p. 17; and James A. Wechsler, "Pat Jackson," *New York Post*, April 10, 1965. The fullest account of the New Deal and Fair Deal's reluctance to assist poor black agricultural workers is given in Ira Katznelon's compelling *When Affirmative Action Was White: An Untold History of Racial Inequality in Twentieth-Century America* (New York: W. W. Norton, 2006).

74   Ralph G. Martin, *Front Runner, Dark Horse* (Garden City, NY: Doubleday, 1960). The interview is located in the Ralph G. Martin Papers at the Howard Gotlieb Research Archive at Boston University. Martin wrote *Front Runner* while Plaut served as his lead interviewer. The book was intended to focus on the Jack Kennedy-Stuart Symington rivalry for the 1960 Democratic presidential nomination. The interviews appear to have occurred in 1958–59 although they are not dated.

75   Marion Denman Frankfurter and Gardner Jackson, *The Letters of Sacco and Vanzetti* (New York: Vanguard Press, 1930).

76   Martin, *Front Runner, Dark Horse*.

77   Biographical statement accompanying Jackson's Papers at Brandeis University in Waltham, Massachusetts, based on the obituaries prepared by Willard Clopton, "Stormy Career Ends for Gardner Jackson," *Washington Post*, April 18, 1965; and James A. Wechsler, "The Passionate Spirit of Gardner Jackson," *Boston Globe*, April 21, 1965. Ms. Sarah Shoemaker is an archivist at the Farber Archives at Brandeis University and prepared the Finding Guide for the Gardner (Pat) Jackson Papers.

78   My thanks to Mr. Peter Lysy, the Senior Archivist at the University of Notre Dame, who provided all four versions of the petition to me in 2011.

79   Irwin Ross, "The True Story of Joseph P. Kennedy," *New York Post*, Article IV, January 12, 1961.

80   James MacGregor Burns, *John Kennedy: A Political Profile* (New York: Harcourt, Brace & World, 1959, 1960), pp. 109–10.

81   Ibid., p. 290n.

82   I found it referred to in thirteen biographies and omitted in fourteen. While loyal Democrats James MacGregor Burns and Ralph G. Martin left the "sheeny" quote out of their favorable 1960 biographies of Kennedy, all eleven accounts after its initial print appearance in a five-part article in January 1961 by Irwin Ross in the *New York Post* reference to the remark. The accounts containing "your sheeny friends" include Irwin Ross, "The True Story of Joseph P. Kennedy," *New York Post*, Article IV, January 12, 1961; Victor Lasky, *J.F.K.: The Man and the Myth* (New York: Macmillan, 1963), pp. 140–41; Richard J. Whalen, *The Founding Father: The Story of Joseph P. Kennedy* (New York: New American Library, 1964), pp. 428–29; Herbert S. Parmet, *Jack: The Struggles of John F. Kennedy* (New York, Dial, 1980), p. 251; Ralph G. Martin, *A Hero*

for Our Time: An Intimate Story of the Kennedy Years (New York: Macmillan, 1983), pp. 63–64; David M. Oshinsky, *A Conspiracy So Immense: The World of Joe McCarthy* (New York: The Free Press, 1983), p. 241; Thomas C. Reeves, *A Question of Character: A Life of John F. Kennedy* (New York: The Free Press, 1991), pp. 101–02; Ralph G. Martin, *Seeds of Destruction: Joe Kennedy and His Sons* (New York: G.P. Putnam's Sons, 1995), pp. 169–70; Ronald Kessler, *The Sins of the Father: Joseph P. Kennedy and the Dynasty He Founded* (New York: Warner Books, 1996), pp. 343–44; Robert Dallek, *John F. Kennedy: An Unfinished Life, 1917–1963* (Boston: Little, Brown, 2003), pp. 170–71; and Michael O'Brien, *John F. Kennedy: A Biography* (New York: Thomas Dunne/St. Martin's Press, 2005), pp. 253–54.

83   The Jackson episode does not appear in Arthur M. Schlesinger, Jr., *A Thousand Days: John F. Kennedy in the White House* (Boston: Houghton Mifflin, 1965); Theodore C. Sorensen, *Kennedy: A Biography* (New York: Harper and Row, 1965); Joan and Clay Blair, Jr., *The Search for JFK* (New York: Berkley Publishing, 1976); Garry Wills, *The Kennedy Imprisonment: A Meditation on Power* (Boston: Little, Brown, 1981); Peter Collier and David Horowitz, *The Kennedys: An American Drama* (New York: Summit Books, 1984); John H. Davis, *The Kennedys: Dynasty and Disaster, 1848–1983* (New York: McGraw-Hill, 1984); Doris Kearns Goodwin, *The Fitzgeralds and the Kennedys: An American Saga* (New York: St. Martin's, 1987); Christopher Matthews, *Kennedy and Nixon: The Rivalry That Shaped America* (New York: Simon & Schuster, 1996); Seymour M. Hersh, *The Dark Side of Camelot* (Boston: Little, Brown, 1997); Laurence Leamer, *The Kennedy Men, 1901–1963: The Laws of the Father* (New York: William Morrow, 2001); Amanda Smith, ed., *Hostages to Fortune: The Letters of Joseph P. Kennedy* (New York: Viking, 2001); Geoffrey Perret, *Jack: A Life Like No Other* (New York: Random House, 2001); Ted Schwarz, *Joseph P. Kennedy: The Mogul, the Mob, the Statesman, and the Making of an American Myth* (Hoboken, NJ: John Wiley, 2003); and Thomas Maier, *The Kennedys: America's Emerald Kings: A Five-Generation History of the Ultimate Irish-Catholic Family* (New York: Basic Books, 2003).

84   Nasaw, *The Patriarch*, pp. 667–68.

85   Richard A. Hogarty and Garrison Nelson, "Redistricting on Beacon Hill and Political Power on Capitol Hill: Ancient Legacies and Present-Day Perils," *New England Journal of Public Policy*, XVII (Fall/Winter 2001–2002), pp. 91–104.

86   Perret, *Jack*, pp. 183–84.

16

Ike's Presidency, John's Partial Eclipse, and the Anti-Communism Crusade Fizzles

The Republican Interregnum: It was noon on January 20, 1953, and Republican Speaker Joe Martin of North Attleboro, Massachusetts, was delighted. Twenty-eight years had passed since March 4, 1925, when 40-year-old House freshman Joe Martin was sworn in on the same day that his good friend and political mentor Calvin Coolidge was formally sworn in again as president. Unlike the first time when Coolidge was sworn in by his father on an August 1923 evening at their family homestead in Plymouth Notch, Vermont, the 1925 swearing-in was a gala event with bunting everywhere, marching bands parading past the president and first lady, and celebratory inaugural balls scattered across the Capital city.

The 83rd Congress over which Joe Martin would preside as Speaker was only the second Republican Congress of the previous twelve since the stock market Crash of 1929 and the ensuing Great Depression had ended the Republican Party's long hegemony over American politics. Thanks to Dwight Eisenhower's landslide victory, Republicans had gained control of both houses of Congress and would open 1953 in charge of their second Congress since the Democrats launched the New Deal in 1933. However, neither chamber had a large Republican majority—221 to 213 in the House and 49 to 47 in the Senate.

Joe Martin, the friendly rival of Sam Rayburn and John McCormack, resumed the speakership with Majority Leader Charlie Halleck of Indiana covetously eyeing the Speaker's chair along with Republican Whip Leslie Arends of Illinois. On the Democratic side of the House, Sam Rayburn was elected minority leader on January 2 and reappointed John McCormack as minority whip.[1] The Austin-Boston team was named for the eighth time since their initial pairing in September 1940. The following day, John was removed from the honorary Joint Committee on Inaugural Ceremonies because it was Republican Eisenhower who had won the 1952 election. That John was replaced on the committee by the tall and genial Les Arends and not the stridently bumptious Charlie Halleck was perhaps its only saving grace. This was the first intimation that John's Washington stature was in decline.

John McCormack's eclipse

During the almost eight years of the Truman White House, John McCormack was listed on the President's Daily Calendar 238 times, most often as a member of the congressional "Big Four" with Harry Truman.[2] The contrast with the Eisenhower White House was striking, with John's presence mostly in large luncheon groups organized by Ike's masterful congressional liaison General Wilton Persons. John had only one late term meeting with Ike alone in the eight years that Eisenhower occupied the Oval Office, and that was after he had been named chair of the House Select Committee on Astronautics and Space Exploration.[3] Memoirs and historical accounts of the Truman presidency make frequent references to John McCormack, while he seldom if at all appears in the memoirs and historical accounts of the Eisenhower presidency.

Much of the reason for John's eclipse was that Ike perceived John to be too much of a partisan politician and as a career military man, Ike disdained partisan politicians. It was a sentiment not confined to Democrats. Republican House Speaker of the 83rd Congress Joe Martin was also shunned by Ike. Longtime U.S. Senator Leverett Saltonstall, then the senior Senator from Massachusetts, stated in his memoirs: "Eisenhower was never overly friendly with Joe Martin who was very political. Ike was so unpolitical that he had trouble dealing with politicians who were totally political."[4]

With John's prominent role in Washington diminished by the ascendancy of his two Texas Democratic allies, Sam Rayburn and newly elected Senate Democratic Leader Lyndon B. Johnson, John focused his energy on maintaining his shrinking control of Massachusetts Democratic politics. His occasional state competitor Governor Paul Dever was defeated by former Republican House member Christian A. Herter in the Eisenhower landslide and for the first time since 1931, John's third year in the House, he was without a Democratic executive ally either in the White House in Washington or in the State House in Boston. That was bad enough, but even more troubling was that seated at the other end of the Capitol was fellow Democrat 35-year-old U.S. Senator John F. Kennedy, who had a six-year term to build a personal statewide organization that could easily bypass the state's regular Democratic organization of which John was the titular head.

It was a genuine fear. With Joe Kennedy's ample fortune backing him and his own photogenic smile, eloquence, and charismatic appeal, Jack Kennedy was now a statewide office holder and a major force to be reckoned with. Most importantly, Jack was 25 years younger than John, a number that figured prominently in the calculus of the state's other ambitious politicians. Politics is future-oriented. It is not about "What have you done for me lately?" but "What will you do for me next?" or "What will you do to me if I don't do what you want next?" John McCormack was on the losing side of that generational calculus.

The Kennedy wing, led by former Ambassador Joe Kennedy, was eager to disentangle itself from Boston Irish politics in order to create a clean slate for newly elected U.S. Senator John F. Kennedy. The Kennedy organization operated outside of the Massachusetts Democratic Party and wished not to be tainted by it. Rather than relying upon state party operatives, the Kennedys created a statewide network of "Kennedy secretaries" whose commitment was to the family and not to the party.[5] This did not sit well with the state's organizational Democrats, who were ostensibly led by John McCormack. McCormack was not pleased by this development. Tip O'Neill, who had been elected to JFK's old House seat, tried to steer a course between the camps.

The congressional setting

Across the Capitol, the Senate Republicans hoped to begin the session with a slight 49–47 majority, but the postelection defection of the unpredictable Wayne Morse of Oregon reduced their margin to a single seat. They were led by the cerebral and humorless U.S. Senator Robert A. Taft of Ohio, thrice rejected by his party's nominating conventions in his pursuit of his father's path to the White House. Morse was punished for his defection from the Republican ranks and would eventually be coerced by Lyndon Johnson to become a Democrat in 1956.[6]

The Senate Ideologues: With control of all three elective branches of government, the most ideologically driven Republicans saw an opportunity to overturn the New Deal. The wedge would be anti-Communism. As they gazed at 39-year-old Richard Nixon, the successful alumnus of the House Un-American Activities Committee (HUAC) presiding over the Senate as vice president, they knew that it was a winning strategy. In the Senate, the anti-Communist charge would be led by Wisconsin's Joe McCarthy, now chair of the Senate's Government Operations Committee, and Indiana's William Jenner, who's Internal Security Subcommittee of Senate Judiciary rivaled McCarthy's in zeal and exceeded it in prestige. This was the Senate's version of HUAC, created and first chaired by ultraconservative anti-Communist Democrat Pat McCarran of Nevada.

Lyndon B. Johnson: Elected as minority leader of the Senate Democrats was the towering (6'3") 44-year-old Whip Lyndon B. Johnson of Texas. Only in his fifth year, Johnson was the youngest Senate leader of the twentieth century, having gained the post after both of his predecessors Scott Lucas of Illinois in 1950 and Ernest McFarland of Arizona in 1952 had met electoral defeat in the two prior elections. Johnson got to know both men who had defeated his predecessors. Everett McKinley Dirksen, who won Lucas's seat, would become Republican minority leader in 1959 and Barry M. Goldwater, who sent McFarland back to Arizona, would be LBJ's presidential opponent in 1964. While Johnson was young and junior in a chamber that cherished age and seniority, he had been well schooled in congressional procedure and politics by his two House mentors Sam Rayburn and John McCormack and in the Senate, by the courtly Dick Russell of Georgia. Russell was the likeliest of the Senators to assume floor leadership but he stepped aside to permit Johnson to fill that post and became LBJ's Senate mentor much as Sam Rayburn had been Johnson's House mentor. Both men were childless and[7] Johnson was a past master of understanding mentor-protégé relationships and the importance of becoming a "boy" to the powerful men he referred to as "like a daddy to me."[8] The fact that all three men—Rayburn, McCormack, and Russell—had no children was not lost on Lyndon Johnson.

Starting on Capitol Hill as a 22-year-old legislative secretary to wealthy U.S. Representative Richard Kleberg, owner of the King Ranch, then two years as the appointed head of Texas's National Youth Administration, Johnson would win the 1937 special election to the House in the seat held by James P. Buchanan. Johnson's predecessor "Buck" Buchanan was in his 13th term in the House at the time of his death and chaired the all-powerful House Appropriations Committee throughout FDR's first term, 1933–37. Buchanan's cousin Edward Pou of North Carolina was the senior Democrat on the House Rules Committee, chairing it for three Congresses until his death in 1934. Johnson's House mentors Sam Rayburn and John McCormack during these years were well acquainted with these powerhouse cousins.

The House Ideologues: The Republican takeover of the House in 1953 led to a new HUAC chair, ex-FBI agent Harold H. Velde of Illinois, who had no intention of being trumped by the Senate's investigative pair of McCarthy and Jenner. Always distrustful of the seemingly more sophisticated moderate northeastern Republicans, these men of the Midwest would demonstrate to the nation what "true patriotic Americans" believed. Velde broadened the scope of the committee into the government, the military, the clergy, and labor. It was his overreaching subpoena of ex-President Harry Truman that generated HUAC's most publicity.[9] After the Democrats regained the House in 1954 and he was no longer chair, Velde chose not to run for reelection in 1956.

The general and the Texans

Dwight D. "Ike" Eisenhower was born the third of seven boys in 1890 in Dennison, Texas, the county seat of Grayson County that was bordered on the north by the Red River separating Texas from Oklahoma and on the east by Fannin County, where Sam Rayburn's family had settled after leaving Tennessee in 1887 when Sam was five. Throughout Sam's House career, Grayson County was part of his 4th Texas Congressional District, and he often remarked that he had heard from Ike's Grayson County neighbors that Ike was a "good boy." Although the Eisenhowers relocated to Abilene, Kansas, when he was two and he considered himself to be more of Kansas than Texas, Ike's Texas roots provided an early valuable bond with the House's Sam Rayburn and the Senate's Lyndon Johnson. The two Texans were much less partisan and easier to work with than the highly partisan Senate Republican leaders, Ohio's Bob Taft and California's Bill Knowland. Nor did either of Massachusetts partisan House leaders, Republican Speaker Joe Martin and Democratic Whip John McCormack, find much favor in Ike's White House.

While Eisenhower was a newcomer to electoral politics, observers of his successes as commander of the Allied Forces in World War II knew of his great people skills and his ability to delegate responsibility effectively. Although it was anticipated that Ike would be most troubled by the Democratic congressional minority unused to a loss of legislative authority, it was Ike's fellow Republicans, like Senators McCarthy and Jenner, who would be the major source of his first-term difficulties. It was they who jeopardized the Eisenhower congressional agenda, fervently believing that the 20-year Roosevelt and Truman Administrations were filled with left-wingers who had usurped national authority and threatened the nation's security. They sought to overturn as much of its structure as they could, but their tool was not legislation but rather investigation. While some Senate Republicans wished that Eisenhower's legislative agenda was more conservatively ambitious,[10] Ike had made his peace with the New Deal and saw no political gain in trying to overturn it.[11]

Early in 1953, barely two months into his first year, Ike demonstrated his willingness to maintain the federal commitment to most of the New Deal's health and social welfare programs through the upgrading of the 1939-created Federal Security Agency, with its Truman-era enhancements, into the Cabinet-level Department of Health, Education, and Welfare (HEW). It was the first new Cabinet department created since the Labor Department was separated from Commerce in 1913 under President Woodrow Wilson. HEW's first secretary was Oveta Culp Hobby of Texas, the second woman named to head a Cabinet post. This was a major signal to the nation that this incoming Republican administration was committed to continuing many of the New Deal's "safety nets" and that there would be no return to the seeming heartlessness of the Republican-dominated 1920s that presaged the Depression.

Legislative Achievements: Among the legislative accomplishments in the 1st Session included the Submerged Lands Act of 1953 that gave coastal states ownership over the offshore natural resources within their boundaries, clearly a major boon to the oil-rich states of Texas and Louisiana, and the Refugee Relief Act of 1953. The most notable acts passed in the 2nd Session were the Housing Act of 1954, the Atomic Energy Act of 1954, and the Communist Control Act. That act augmented the McCarran-Walter Act of 1950 by declaring the Communist Party illegal, criminalizing its members who were already obliged to register under the Smith Act, thereby self-incriminating in violation of the Fifth Amendment.

The act that created the most tension among the New England members was the St. Lawrence Seaway Act of 1954 that authorized the U.S. government to work with the Canadian government to construct a deep water navigation system with locks, canals, and channels that would permit oceangoing vessels to move cargo from the Atlantic down the St. Lawrence River through the Great Lakes, originating in Montreal, Quebec, and traveling halfway across the continent to Duluth, Minnesota, on the western shore of Lake Superior. Given the fact that the St. Lawrence Seaway would divert vast numbers of oceangoing vessels from the Port of Boston, John McCormack rallied 11 of 13 voting Massachusetts members—six Republicans and five Democrats—against the bill.[12] While Massachusetts Republican U.S. Senator Leverett Saltonstall opposed the Seaway, the delegation's most vocal supporter of it was new U.S. Senator John F. Kennedy, eager to demonstrate that he had national aspirations beyond that of the region. Kennedy declared on January 14 that it was the "arbitrary refusal of many New Englanders to recognize the legitimate needs of other regions [which has] contributed to opposition to the needs of our own area, by representatives of other areas."[13]

Nine days later at the annual Jefferson-Jackson Day dinner at Boston's Sheraton Plaza, Jack was publicly rebuked by Jim Curley declaring that "the building of the St. Lawrence Seaway is the most destructive blow aimed at the North Atlantic Seaboard in its history. No more vicious blow against the welfare of New England has ever been attempted."[14] Kennedy rose to defend his vote, pointing out that seven of New England's eleven Senators had voted for the bill and received "a rousing cheer." Michigan Governor G. Mennen "Soapy" Williams, the evening's keynote speaker, declared that Kennedy's support was "an act of statesmanship." Jack Kennedy's national campaign had begun.

This was yet another risky move for Jack Kennedy, but he still had four years in office before he would next face the voters of Massachusetts. There was another issue that clouded Jack's reputation—his family's controversial relationship with the fiery but erratic Republican anti-Communist U.S. Senator Joe McCarthy of Wisconsin.

Joe McCarthy seizes center stage

Despite Representative Velde's efforts to place HUAC at the center of the anti-Communism crusade, it was Senator Joe McCarthy who took command of that agenda. McCarthy first burst on the stage with his February 9, 1950, claim in Wheeling, West Virginia, that he had the names of 205 Communists in the State Department. Later that year he gained more publicity by physically attacking syndicated columnist Drew Pearson in Washington's exclusive Sulgrave Club on DuPont Circle. The Senate responded to McCarthy's Wheeling charges with a special subcommittee of the Senate's Foreign Relations Committee led by Armed Services Chair Democratic Senator Millard Tydings of Maryland, a moderate conservative who was once a target of FDR's 1938 "purge." The Tydings's hearings were raucous and filled with multiple accusations pouring out of McCarthy's office highly critical of fellow Senators. When the Tydings subcommittee reported that most of the charges were false and denounced McCarthy for making them, McCarthy launched an attack on Tydings with doctored photographs indicating a friendly relationship between Tydings and Communist Party leader Earl Browder that led to the four-term Senator's defeat in 1950.[15]

Next in line for a McCarthy attack was Democratic U.S. Senator William Benton of Connecticut, a very successful Madison Avenue advertising executive and publisher of the *Encyclopedia Britannica*. Angered by the Tydings attack and McCarthy's continuing onslaught on the loyalty of government and military officials, including Secretaries of State General George C. Marshall and Dean Acheson, Benton introduced a resolution to expel McCarthy from the Senate.[16] The resolution failed and Benton would also meet electoral defeat in 1952. While Benton went down to defeat, McCarthy's vituperative attacks continued and won him reelection. With Republicans gaining control of Congress on Eisenhower's coattails, McCarthy became chair of the Senate's low prestige Government Operations Committee in 1953. As chair, McCarthy took command of its Permanent Subcommittee on Investigations that enabled him to traverse the country freely making charges with the full knowledge that he traveled under the legal umbrella of congressional immunity.

Shortly after McCarthy began his chairmanship in January, former Wisconsin Senator Robert M. La Follette, Jr., the Senate coauthor of the far-reaching Legislative Reorganization Act of 1946, who had lost his primary to McCarthy that year, fatally shot himself at his Washington home early in 1953. The reason most often cited was that La Follette feared a brutal McCarthy investigation into the loyalty of prior members of his congressional staff.[17] With McCarthy broadening his smear campaign to include homosexuals as well as Communists in government, homophobia rapidly engulfed Washington. Another Senate suicide occurred in June 1954 when Democratic U.S.

Senator Lester C. Hunt of Wyoming brought a rifle to his office and shot himself at his desk in the Senate Office Building. Hunt was being blackmailed by Joe McCarthy and his bullying allies Senators Styles Bridges of New Hampshire and Herman Welker of Idaho with the discovery of his son's conviction for homosexual solicitation.[18] This was the collateral damage of McCarthyism. The body count of anti-McCarthy Senators was rising, and the Eisenhower administration realized that McCarthy's uncontrolled antics were bringing disrepute to the newly installed Republican leadership.

A key Democratic supporter of McCarthy was Joe Kennedy, whose family had entertained him at Hyannis Port. McCarthy had dated two of Jack Kennedy's sisters, Eunice and Pat.[19] Joe Kennedy was eager to find high-profile Washington employment for his third son Robert, a 1951 graduate of the University of Virginia Law School. Bobby first worked in the Internal Security Section of the Justice Department and then was transferred to New York to prosecute financial fraud.[20] He left government service to manage Jack's successful 1952 campaign for the Senate. Following Jack's election, Bobby was named an assistant counsel on Joe McCarthy's Investigations Subcommittee. Bob Kennedy wanted the lead counsel's post on the subcommittee but McCarthy chose Roy Cohn. According to an interview with Harvey Matusow, a paid McCarthy informant who spent three years in jail for perjury, McCarthy apparently told Kennedy that he would be investigating "a lot of Jews" and wanted Cohn who was "discernibly Jewish" in that role.[21] After a short stint working with his father on the Hoover Commission to reorganize the government, Bobby returned to the committee and became its chief counsel when Democrats recaptured the Senate in 1954.

Moderate Republican Senators feared that McCarthy would discredit the party and the first Senate Republican to challenge him was Margaret Chase Smith of Maine. Her "Declaration of Conscience" on June 1, 1950, stated that "I don't want to see the Republican Party ride to victory on the four horsemen of calumny—fear, ignorance, bigotry and smear."[22] She was joined by six other moderate Republican Senators but little came of it.

The Eisenhower administration grew increasingly wary of McCarthy but his public feud with CBS newsman Edward R. Murrow heightened his visibility and fattened his ego. It was when McCarthy launched a televised attack on the U.S. Army and declared that the first year of the Eisenhower administration constituted "*twenty-one* years of treason" that the White House chose to take action. Eisenhower insiders Attorney General Herbert Brownell and UN Ambassador Henry Cabot Lodge sought to limit partisan damage from McCarthy's charges.

The televised Army-McCarthy hearings in the summer of 1954 sped McCarthy's downfall. McCarthy had launched an attack on Robert Stevens, the Secretary of the Army, contending that the army's drafting of G. David Schine, one of his investigators (and Roy Cohn's rumored gay lover) was in reprisal for McCarthy's investigations of suspected Communists in the armed services. In the course of the hearings, Joseph Welch of the Boston firm of Hale and Dorr, the Army's lead counsel, had obtained an original photograph of Schine and Stevens that was quite dissimilar from the doctored one presented by the committee that indicated personal closeness between the two men. When Welch facetiously suggested that perhaps it was a "pixie" that may have accounted for the dissimilarity, he was challenged by McCarthy to define the word "pixie."[23]

Welch responded, "Yes, I should say, Senator, that a pixie is a close relative of a *fairy*. Shall I proceed, sir? Have I enlightened you?" While McCarthy seemed not to know of that homophobic slur, Cohn, a closeted gay, panicked, and reached over to cover McCarthy's microphone. To knowledgeable observers, the reason for McCarthy and Cohn's badgering of the Army to get a discharge for Schine became quite clear.

It was Vermont's Ralph Flanders who introduced the successful formal resolution of censure against McCarthy on June 11, 1954. Six months later, on December 2, the censure motion carried 65 to 22 with all 42 voting Democrats, 22 Republicans, and Independent Wayne Morse supporting the motion and 22 Senate Republicans opposing it.[24] Jack Kennedy, then hospitalized for back troubles, was listed as "Not voting." He was the only Democratic Senator not to record an opinion on the matter. It was a non-vote that would haunt Kennedy's standing among liberals.[25]

The political fallout for the Republican Party led to Democrats regaining control of both houses of Congress in 1954. When Democrats regained the Senate, McCarthy lost his chairmanship and his Gallup Poll popularity plunged from 50% approval in January 1954 to 35% by November. His reputation was in tatters. McCarthy was now a spent force and his long-standing demons of alcohol abuse finished him off at the age of 48 on May 2, 1957.

John McCormack and the Harry Dexter White case

Given the anti-Communist zeal of his South Boston Catholic constituents, John McCormack was relieved that McCarthyism was a Senate matter. HUAC had clearly been overshadowed, but the passion of the anti-Communist crusade was hard to contain and it brushed up against John McCormack. While John's role during the Eisenhower Administration had diminished, the role of his old friend J. Edgar Hoover of the FBI expanded greatly. Hoover had been regularly ignored by Harry Truman, but now he had a major ally in Ike's Attorney General Herbert Brownell, a Nebraska-born Yale Law-educated corporate lawyer. Brownell was Tom Dewey's 1948 campaign manager when Hoover had made covert inquiries about help that he might render to that campaign. Hoover was eager to pursue the case of alleged Soviet spy Harry Dexter White, the Boston-born former Treasury Department undersecretary. It was Brownell who recognized the political power of anti-Communism that led him to urge that Richard Nixon's dogged pursuit of Alger Hiss made him the ideal vice presidential candidate for a Republican ticket focused on "Korea, Communism, and corruption."[26]

The similarity between Alger Hiss's post at the State Department and Harry White's in the Treasury Department made the pursuit of the 1946 appointment of White as the American head of the newly formed International Monetary Fund an ideal way to further tarnish the Truman Administration. White had died five years earlier in August 1948 of a heart attack, two days after facing a contentious HUAC hearing with

Nixon as one of his antagonists. That White was dead was irrelevant. The major target of these charges was former President Truman, who had placed White in that key post.[27] Investigation was to be the hammer that would be used to turn back the "twenty years of treason" of Democratic policies as initially decreed by Joe McCarthy.

Brownell supported Hoover's charges and when they went public, HUAC Chair Velde sought to subpoena President Truman to appear before the committee to answer them. John McCormack exploded. Velde was not worth bothering with, but John contacted Hoover requesting that he apologize to Harry Truman. It set in motion the only real disagreement between these old friends.

McCormack Challenges the FBI and Loses: Brownell publicly accused the Truman Administration of knowingly appointing White to the IMF in spite of multiple FBI security warnings about him. It was the partisan aspect of these accusations that bothered John the most. John met with Special Agent in Charge (SAC) J. J. Kelly to express his concerns and insist upon a Hoover apology to Truman.

In a fascinating irony, Kelly's report to Hoover of the tense meeting with McCormack was at the bottom of a December 18, 1953, birthday greeting from Hoover to John.[28]

> It will be recalled that SAC [J. J.] Kelly had lunch with Congressman McCormack on 11/27/53, at which time McCormack was critical of the Director's stand in the [Harry Dexter] White case and at which time McCormack indicated the Director had stepped on the toes of his friends in the Democratic Party. Kelly immediately took McCormack to task pointing out that the Director did not inject the Bureau into partisan politics and that it was ridiculous for McCormack to contend otherwise. By letter of 12/2/53 a detailed letter was directed to McCormack [GN—not in the file] in which the factors which made it necessary for the Director to testify were clearly explained to the Congressman. It was interesting to note that after McCormack's criticism of the Director, he evidently realized he had gone off half-cocked and made every possible attempt to ingratiate himself with Kelly.

J. Edgar Hoover's private files had just trumped John McCormack, one of his closest congressional friends. But this was a time when national security politics dominated the agenda, with its greatest beneficiary being the 39-year-old Richard M. Nixon, who rode Whittaker Chambers's accusations from the House to the Senate and to the vice presidency.

"The day we didn't go to war"

With anti-Communist speeches ricocheting throughout both chambers of Congress, the prospects for another war in Asia appeared on the near horizon. The French military was losing control of the war in their far-flung Southeast Asian possession of Indochina. A key counteroffensive developed by French commander Henry Navarre led to a seven-week battle in the early spring of 1954 centered on the village of Dien Bien

Phu in the hills of northwestern Vietnam. Although the Eisenhower Administration had committed $400 million in aid to their effort, later appeals made by French leaders to bring the United States into yet another direct military confrontation with Asian Communists were less successful. The Korean truce was less than a year old and the Eisenhower Administration demurred. James R. Arnold contends that it was John who made the strongest case against military involvement in that conflict[29]:

> Massachusetts Congressman John W. McCormack, already an influential Democratic leader in the House, wrote to the appropriate official in the federal government to say that he worried that if the Navarre Plan failed, the United States might feel obliged to send its own troops to Indochina. He saw support for the Navarre Plan as a calculated risk and hoped that the administration recognized it as such. No politician could challenge a national military hero, particularly one who had recently won overwhelming election. On a judgment of military risk, so McCormack, after expressing his concern, deferred to Eisenhower's desire.

It was John McCormack's declaration to *Washington Post* reporter Chalmers Roberts that April 4, 1954, was "the day we didn't go to war," an oft-quoted remark about a conflict that was avoided then and should have been avoided later.[30]

Change at the Supreme Court

On September 8, 1953, Supreme Court Chief Justice Fred M. Vinson, one of John McCormack's closest "poker pals," died. Eisenhower, who had been unimpressed with the overall quality of Harry Truman's four appointees to the Court—Vinson, Harold Burton, Tom C. Clark, and Sherman Minton—now had an opportunity to fill the Court's most important vacancy with his own selection. The Court's 1953 Term would begin in three weeks, but Ike chose to wait. In a note to Gabriel Hauge, his lead economic advisor, Ike wrote, "As for the Supreme Court vacancy, I have not yet decided whom I will nominate, but I have decided one thing—to make no mistakes in a hurry."[31] Yet in Ike's *Diary* entry of October 8, he wrote[32]:

> From the day of [Vinson's] death the name that figured most prominently in my search for his successor was that of Governor Earl Warren of California. Ever since last January, I had frankly hoped that one or two of the older men would soon retire from the Court, which would give me the chance to appoint people whose qualifications would more nearly meet my ideas of those that should be possessed by a Supreme Court Justice than were represented in some of the individuals now carrying that exalted title.
>
>   I was firmly convinced that the prestige of the Supreme Court had suffered severely in late years, and that the only way it could be restored was by the appointment to it of men of *nationwide reputation* for integrity, competence in the law, and in statesmanship.

Warren had been Tom Dewey's running mate in 1948 and Brownell as Dewey's campaign manager knew Warren well. Most displeased with Ike's likely choice of Warren was Edgar Eisenhower, Ike's conservative older brother, who told Ike that selecting Warren would be a "tragedy." But Ike wrote back to Edgar and made an extraordinarily strong case that Warren had the appropriate temperament, philosophy, and real-world political experience that he felt would make him an excellent Chief Justice, asserting "that a Governor with a *good* legal background just might be about the best type we could find—provided of course, that he had a successful record of administration and experience and was nationally known as a man of integrity and fairness."[33]

Ike later expressed in his correspondence with his younger and more liberal brother Milton, then at The John Hopkins University in Baltimore,[34] "[Earl Warren] has been very definitely a liberal-conservative; he represents the kind of political, economic, and social thinking that I believe we need on the Supreme Court.... He has a national name for integrity, uprightness, and courage that, again, I believe we need on the Court."

Two weeks later on October 5, 1953, Earl Warren was seated as the nation's 14th Chief Justice. Because the Senate was not in session, it was a recess appointment and it would be another five months before the Senate would confirm Warren by voice vote. No one knew at the time of the pro forma confirmation that never again would a Republican president name a Justice to the Court from a major public office.[35] It has been contended that Ike's Republican advisors had promised Governor Warren the next open seat on the Supreme Court as a way of mollifying him after then-U.S. Senator Richard Nixon had deliberately undermined Warren's "favorite son" presidential candidacy at the 1952 Republican convention.[36] There was no love lost between Warren and Nixon.

Brown v. Board of Education (1954): On the Court's docket was a set of five cases that would forever alter the course of American history; elevate Chief Justice Earl Warren to mythic status; and cause President Eisenhower his biggest political headache. On May 17, 1954, scarcely eleven weeks after the Senate's voice vote confirmation, Chief Justice Earl Warren, speaking for a unanimous 9–0 Supreme Court, delivered the most important decision of the twentieth century in the Kansas school desegregation case of *Oliver Brown. et al. v. Board of Education of Topeka, et al.*, 347 U.S. 483 (1954). The Court had at last overturned the onerous "separate but equal" doctrine enunciated in *Plessy v. Ferguson*, 163 U.S. 537 (1896) that had legitimized racial segregation throughout much of the United States, including Texas, where Ike was born, and Kansas, where he was raised.

Presidents Truman and Eisenhower came from the same part of America. Harry Truman, born and raised in the western Missouri town of Independence, and Eisenhower, raised in the eastern Kansas town of Abilene, grew up little more than 160 miles away from one another. Nearly equidistant between the two towns was Topeka, the state capital of Kansas and the locus of the desegregation decision. While Kansas and Missouri had not seceded from the Union, racial segregation was a daily fact of life in both states.[37] President Truman had become so horrified by violent racist attacks on returning black servicemen in the South that that he issued Executive Order 9981 on

July 28, 1948, that sought to end discrimination against military personnel on account of race, color, religion, or national origin. Ike was less concerned.

Integrating the armed forces was difficult, but the soldiers and sailors were grown men and could presumably defend themselves. But to Ike, schools were a different matter. These involved children and as the new president, Ike was anxious to know how the Court and its new Chief Justice would rule. After all he was now a grandfather of two—David born in 1948 and Susan born in 1951—who would be of school age during his presidency.

In *Super Chief*, Professor Bernard Schwartz's laudatory biography of Chief Justice Warren, he reports an encounter that Warren had with Ike at a White House dinner with guests including John W. Davis, President Woodrow Wilson's solicitor general and the 1924 Democratic nominee for president. Davis was the attorney for South Carolina in *Briggs v. Elliott* that had been one of five school segregation cases folded into the *Brown* case and would be the lead counsel for the defense when it reached the Court. *Brown* was on the Court's docket but months away from a decision.

During the dinner, Eisenhower told Warren at length what a great man John Davis was. Then, after dinner, taking Warren by the arm as they were walking to be served coffee, the President said, speaking of the South, "These are not bad people. All they are concerned about is to see that their sweet little girls are not required to sit in school alongside big black bucks."

Upon learning of this episode later, Thurgood Marshall, the Court's first African-American Justice who led the NAACP team of lawyers that argued for *Brown*, said in a 1977 oral history interview for Columbia University that "President Eisenhower was opposed to it, and was working against it, and even went so far as to try to convince Chief Justice Warren to vote the other way. That, in my mind, is the most despicable job that any president has done in my life."[38]

Ike was greatly displeased. As recalled in Warren's *Memoirs*, "Shortly thereafter the *Brown* case was decided, and with it went our cordial relations."[39] It has been widely contended that Ike said his appointment of Warren "was the biggest damn-fool thing I ever did." Jean Edward Smith, Ike's recent biographer, declared that he could locate no evidence of Ike's having made the remark.[40] However, it had become such a staple of Washington folklore that Warren felt certain enough of its validity to repeat it in his *Memoirs*[41]: "Even the fatherly President Eisenhower was widely quoted as having said that his appointment of me as Chief Justice 'was the biggest damn-fool thing I ever did.'"[42]

The Initial Congressional Reaction: While inflammatory racist speeches and local violence erupted in some of the segregating states, the negative reaction was less than anticipated because the Court had provided no timetable or guidance for implementing the decision. That would come the following year as an anxious nation awaited the next step in the second *Brown v. Board* decision, 349 U.S. 294 (1955) of May 31, 1955, in which the Court mandated that local public school boards come up with desegregation plans "with all deliberate speed." That is when all hell broke loose, with racist violence escalating, buildings burned and churches bombed in much of the South. The Confederate flag returned as a symbol of white resistance with Dick Russell's Georgia adding the "Stars and Bars" to its state flag.

House conservatives had a two-pronged attack. One was to offer constitutional amendments that would remove civil rights cases from the Supreme Court's appellate jurisdiction thus rendering it silent in these matters. But the amendment process was too lengthy and a legislative solution was proffered. Fastening on the fact that eight of the Justices voting in Brown were non-judges—former Governor Earl Warren, ex-U.S. Senators Hugo Black and Harold Burton, former Attorneys General Robert Jackson and Tom Clark, ex-Solicitor General Stanley Reed, former Securities and Exchanges Chair William O. Douglas, and Harvard Law Professor Felix Frankfurter. Therefore, these Justices were either unaware or disrespectful of judicial precedents and should have left *Plessy*'s "separate but equal" ruling remain the law of the land. The Warren Court had only one former federal judge in its ranks—Associate Justice Sherman Minton—but even he was a former Democratic U.S. Senator from Indiana. Over the next two years, a number of conservative southern Democratic House members dropped bills into the chamber's legislative hopper declaring that only former judges could serve on the U.S. Supreme Court.[43] However, with McCormack ally and staunch liberal Manny Celler chairing the Judiciary Committee, none of these bills ever reached the House floor.

The new protégés: Tip O'Neill and Eddie Boland

Joining the House for the first time in the 83rd Congress were two Democratic freshmen—Edward Boland of Springfield who had won State Treasurer Foster Furcolo's 2nd District seat and Thomas P. "Tip" O'Neill, Jr. of Cambridge who had captured the 11th District seat of U.S. Senator Jack Kennedy. Newly elected majority freshman Republican Laurence Curtis who won the Beacon Hill and Back Bay 9th seat was placed on the prestigious House Judiciary Committee while minority Democratic freshmen like Eddie Boland and Tip O'Neill were not so fortunate. As minority whip, John McCormack's assignment power was diminished. Consequently, Eddie Boland was named to the dead-end Post Office and Civil Service Committee while Tip was assigned to the equally undistinguished Committee on Merchant Marine and Fisheries, a committee that would help with his constituents but not one that would prepare him for House leadership.

John McCormack always enjoyed socializing new members to the norms and rituals of the House, and both Boland and O'Neill seemed eager to learn from him. This was quite a contrast from the cold indifference that he had encountered from freshman John F. Kennedy six years earlier.

As Kennedy left the House for the Senate, he took Tip aside and said,[44] "And I hope you won't mind if I give you some advice. Whatever you do, don't make the mistake I did. Be nice to John McCormack."

Tip listened. He recounted in his memoirs that John "was eager to take me under his wings."[45] O'Neill and Boland's responses to John were similar to that of Foster Furcolo whose House career had been positively impacted by John's interventions. While their willingness to listen made them different from Kennedy, their apparent willingness to remain in the House made them different from Furcolo. John now had two genuine House protégés.

Born a year apart, both the 41-year-old Boland and 40-year-old O'Neill were of Irish Catholic descent and came from struggling families, although neither family was as destitute as that of John McCormack's. Boland's father was from County Cork and worked on the railroads.[46] Boland graduated from Longmeadow's Bay Path Institute, and attended Boston College Law School. He enlisted as a private in the U.S. Army in 1942 and served until 1946 when he was discharged as a captain, O'Neill's father was a bricklayer and active in local politics as an elected Cambridge City Councilor, who later became superintendent of the city's sewers.[47] Tip's mother died when he was just nine months old and he was raised by a French Canadian housekeeper until his father remarried when Tip was eight. Tip went to parochial schools and graduated from Boston College.

Tip began his political career with a loss for the city council but then was elected to the Massachusetts House of Representatives in 1936 at the age of 24. He served in the Massachusetts House as its first ever Democratic Speaker, 1949–53, until his 1952 election to the U.S. House. Eddie also served in the Massachusetts House, 1939–40, until he was named Register of Deeds for Hampden County, a post he held when he was elected to the U.S. House in 1952. While neither Kennedy nor Furcolo had apprenticed in the Massachusetts Great and General Court, the fact that both Boland and O'Neill did created yet another bond between them and John McCormack.

For much of their time in the House, Eddie and Tip shared an apartment in Washington.[48] Eddie remained a bachelor until he wed in 1974 at the age of 62, while Tip's wife Millie chose to remain home in Cambridge raising their five children. Tip was a charter member of the "Tuesday-Thursday Club," flying into Washington on Tuesday mornings and flying out at the end of House business on Thursday evenings. They were the quintessential "odd couple" with the neat and fastidious longtime bachelor Boland cleaning up the apartment after the messy and cigar-stained O'Neill would go home every weekend.

In 1955, McCormack was able to move Tip onto the Rules Committee and Eddie on to Appropriations. These committee assignments mirrored their life choices. Eddie's 50-member Appropriations Committee was the House's largest one and it generated thousands of pages of monetary requests that required hours of homework to fully comprehend. By contrast, Tip's Rules Committee was its smallest major one and did most of its work en banc where its 12 (and later 15) members debated with one another as to which of the hundreds of bills on the committee's docket would be moved to the House floor, how long they would be debated, and whether or not they would be reported with an "open rule"—thereby subject to floor amendments—or with a "closed rule" and non-amendable.

Foster Furcolo's 1954 Senate Campaign: John McCormack's longtime control over Massachusetts patronage had been shrunken by the presence of Republican Eisenhower in the White House, Republican Herter in the State House, and Democratic rival Jack Kennedy holding a Senate seat for the next six years. The Kennedys had created their own statewide organization of loyalists easily outpacing the moribund allies of John McCormack.

John McCormack needed a Senate counterweight to Kennedy and one would emerge—Foster Furcolo, his first major House protégé and the incumbent State

Treasurer. McCormack was well aware that the state's Italian-descended citizens voted Democratic but had become restive watching Democrats continually nominate Irish-descended candidates for major offices. With two-term incumbent Brahmin Republican Leverett Saltonstall up for reelection in 1954, an opportunity to rectify this circumstance presented itself.

McCormack and Saltonstall knew each other well. Both had served in the Massachusetts House and each had been mentored by Henry Lee Shattuck. Saltonstall had won three elections as governor in 1938, 1940, and 1942. As governor in 1944, he won the special Senate election to fill Henry Cabot Lodge, Jr.'s vacancy with a 64.3% victory over Democrat John H. Corcoran. Salty repeated that outcome in 1948 with a 53.0% victory over John I. Fitzgerald (no relation to Honey Fitz) in spite of Harry Truman's overwhelming presidential triumph in Massachusetts. But Senate seats can be lost, and Lodge's defeat by Jack Kennedy two years earlier was instructive. Salty did not resent Kennedy's victory for they had bonded at a Harvard memorial service honoring Jack's brother Joe, Jr. and Saltonstall's son Peter, both casualties of the war.[49]

Early in 1954, Furcolo entered the senatorial fray against Saltonstall. If Furcolo was to succeed, he had to hope that his 1951 public shot at Joe Kennedy would be forgotten and that the Kennedys would provide some support for his candidacy. He should have known better. Furcolo easily won the September primary over two Irishmen with 59.1% of the vote to 22.7% for Joseph J. Murphy and 18.2% for John I. Fitzgerald.[50] Joe McCarthy was no longer a factor in the state's politics. Massachusetts upscale Republicans like the Harvard-educated Brahmins, Governor Herter and Senator Saltonstall, had steered clear of Joe McCarthy and his followers, assuming that they were working-class Catholic Democrats who wouldn't vote for them anyways. Following the 1954 election, Saltonstall would be one of 22 Senate Republicans voting for McCarthy's censure.[51]

As the Democratic nominee, Furcolo campaigned nonstop throughout the state. He anticipated little help from the Kennedys and he received little. Kenny O'Donnell contended that Jack's hiring of Larry O'Brien, Furcolo's former chief of staff to run Jack's Western Massachusetts organization, led Foster not to support Jack's 1952 Senate bid. "An empty suit" is what Jack considered Furcolo, according to the memoirs of Ted Sorensen, Kennedy's talented speech writer.[52] There also had been history between them in the House as Furcolo, with John McCormack's active assistance, had easily outshone Kennedy. There was little enthusiasm on Jack's part to share the Senate with Foster. According to O'Neill, Jack Kennedy regarded the Furcolo organization as "the enemy camp."[53]

It had been agreed that Kennedy would endorse Bob Murphy for governor and Furcolo for Senator in a televised appearance. Furcolo read the draft of Jack's remarks and was angered that the endorsement was not strong enough. Kennedy responded, "You've got a hell of a nerve, Foster. You're lucky you're here."[54] The chill between the two men was obvious, and newspapers reported the public unpleasantness the following day. Unbeknownst to Furcolo and his allies John McCormack and Paul Dever, Jack Kennedy had lent his key speechwriter and researcher Ted Sorensen to the Saltonstall campaign while Joe Kennedy sent it money.[55] This was suspected at the time, but it became well known by the time of the 1956 Democratic National Convention, and it would undermine Jack's Democratic vice presidential bid.

It was the public display of bipartisan cooperation between Senators Saltonstall and Kennedy that sent the strongest message. The Saltonstall-Kennedy Act (68 Stat. 376; 15 U.S.C. para. 713c-3) established a fund that supported fishery research and development projects, with funding awarded annually on a competitive basis.[56] It was signed into law by President Eisenhower on July 1, 1954. Given the centrality of fishing to the Massachusetts economy, this act provided ample evidence of each man's legislative ability. Kennedy had no interest in working against a legislative partner, especially a fellow Harvard man.

Furcolo's friends in Boston, most notably ex-Governor Paul Dever and John McCormack, urged him on. With their support and that of most of the organizational Democrats, Furcolo captured 927,899 votes to Saltonstall's 956,605 narrowing the gap to 28,706 votes in a close to two million vote contest.[57] He had lost by a mere 1.5 percentage points. While Furcolo expected no help from the Kennedys and received none, it would be later that he learned of their active opposition.

The quiet beginning of the longest era

The personal popularity of President Eisenhower continued its high level as the 1954 congressional election approached. Ike chose not to campaign directly for Republican control of the Congress. Instead, he let his ever-eager Vice President Richard Nixon engage in "party-building" activities. However, as Eisenhower White House insiders had feared, the tenuous Republican majorities of the 83rd Congress disappeared. Democrats already held a numeric majority in the Senate as a consequence of Wayne Morse's earlier defection and the 1953 death of Majority Leader Robert A. Taft, whose replacement by Ohio Democratic appointee Thomas A. Burke on November 10, 1953, had shifted the Senate's party balance to 48 Democrats, 47 Republicans, and the lone independent Morse.

In spite of Ike's popularity and Nixon's campaigning vigor, the Democrats were able to squeak out a narrow victory in both the House and the Senate. The House GOP's narrow margin was erased, as Democrats picked up 19 seats and a 29-vote majority, 232–203. In the Senate, the gain was only one seat, but it was enough to transfer control from the Republicans to the Democrats.

The Democratic victory in the 1954 midterm election was the first of 20 consecutive Democratic victories in House elections. This began the longest period of one-party dominance over a national institution ever recorded by a political party. The consequences of too many years in the majority would become apparent later, but for the newly installed majority Democrats of 1954, it was good to be back in power. Once again both Sam and John were reelected without opposition. It was their ninth consecutive Congress in the top two leadership posts of the House Democrats.

With John McCormack moving from minority whip to majority leader, a vacancy had opened up in the Democratic leadership team. As the new Congress opened, Sam and John learned that the lantern-jawed J. Percy Priest of Tennessee who had dutifully served as their appointed whip in the 81st and 82nd Congresses had passed on returning as whip to become chair of Sam's old Interstate and Foreign Commerce Committee. Given the decentralization of the 1950s House, it was the committee chairs that held most of the power.[58] Sam Rayburn and John McCormack, who once again occupied the two elected leadership posts, understood this fact of House life and were unsurprised by Priest's decision. Unlike the House Republicans, who had been electing their party whips for years, the Democrats appointed theirs. It was a way of containing internal party conflict by limiting the number of elected offices that could engender competition and disrupt the orderly management of the cobbled-together coalition that the House Democrats had become.[59]

The New Whip, Carl Albert: A new whip had to be chosen. Sam Rayburn chose 46-year-old Carl Albert of Oklahoma, newly elected to his fifth term in the House. Albert's 3rd Oklahoma District was in the southeastern corner of the state, and north of the Red River that divided Oklahoma from Texas. On the Texas side of the river were the districts of two powerhouses: The 1st District of Wright Patman Chair of the House's Select Committee on Small Business and the 4th District of Speaker Sam Rayburn. Rayburn, who still farmed his land, often crossed the Red River into Albert's district to purchase grain and farm implements. To Rayburn, Albert was a neighbor and represented a district and constituency similar to his own.[60]

With Sam's longtime protégé Lyndon Johnson now in the Senate, Carl Albert would fill that spot in the House. It would begin Albert's 22-year career as a House leader with seven years as whip, 1955–61; nine years as Majority Leader, 1962–71; and six years as Speaker of the House, 1971–77. Only Sam Rayburn with 25 years as leader, 1937–61, and John McCormack with 32, 1939–71, had longer consecutive service than Carl Albert in a House leadership post.

Although relatively diminutive in stature (5'4"), Albert's formidable speaking skills had won him oratorical contests and his brilliance as a student at the University of Oklahoma had earned him a Rhodes Scholarship at England's Oxford University.[61] In his first term in the House, 1947–49, Carl Albert had initially apprenticed on the forgettable House Post Office and Civil Service Committee which he left in August 1949 for the House Agriculture Committee.

Republican House Leadership: The peaceful leadership transition of the House Democrats contrasted with the restiveness of the House Republican team. Many House Republicans were embittered at their inability to use Ike's personal popularity to retain congressional power and their frustration was taken out on Joe Martin. Once again, Martin had to leave the speakership and resume the post of Minority Floor Leader.[62] Although his leadership post was renewed in the House Republican Conference, signs of disenchantment appeared in the discussion. Indiana's Charlie Halleck grudgingly stepped away from the majority floor leadership while Les Arends of Illinois remained solidly ensconced as the Republican whip holding that post regardless of the Republicans' majority or minority status. It appeared to some conservative Republicans that Joe Martin was much too chummy with Sam Rayburn and John McCormack whose 12th Massachusetts District was less than an hour's drive from Joe's 14th District. Sam even authorized that Joe receive a limousine to travel back and forth to the Capitol. It was during this time that Sam was invited to Massachusetts to campaign against Joe Martin, and Sam quickly retorted, "Well, if I lived there, I would work for him."[63]

Senate Leadership: With the Democrats back in control of the Senate, Lyndon Johnson of Texas was now majority leader and quickly emerged as the most powerful Senate leader in generations. Perhaps only the senior Henry Cabot Lodge of Massachusetts, who managed the Senate from 1919 to 1925, came close. Senate Republicans were in a different quandary. Joe McCarthy had been de-fanged and anti-Communism had run out of electoral steam. Their floor leader, William F. Knowland of California, who had succeeded the late Bob Taft in 1953, shared Taft's presidential dreams and would even let his name be floated in the 1956 presidential primaries which other Republican hopefuls had conceded to Eisenhower. Needless to say, Ike took note and limited Knowland's role in policy discussions.

The Anti-Communist Crusade Runs Aground: In the closing months of 1954, the anti-Communist crusade suffered a number of irrevocable losses. On September 28, 1954, Nevada Democrat Pat McCarran, the crusade's most effective legislative architect, died. In the November midterm elections, Republicans lost control of both Houses of Congress, thereby ending the committee chairmanships of Republican Senators Joe McCarthy on Government Operations and Bill Jenner's Subcommittee on Internal Security, and Harold Velde's chairmanship of the House Un-American Activities Committee. The final punctuation mark was Joe McCarthy's censure by the Senate in December. No longer could this trio use their committee chairmanships to venture forth from the Capitol to further the anti-Communist crusade. After five painful and fearful years of unfounded accusations, the anti-Communist storm had broken and American civil liberties were no longer endangered. Using anti-Communism to discredit the entirety of the Roosevelt and Truman Administrations to roll back the policy advances of the New Deal had failed. Investigative activities would no longer trump legislative business.

With Pat McCarran gone, the Senate's handful of Democratic anti-Communists lost their champion. The House's Democratic anti-Communists lost their most vocal spokesman when Mississippi voters finally bounced John Rankin from his seat. Pennsylvania's Francis "Tad" Walter picked up the banner, albeit with less drama. Walter soon became John McCormack's major headache among the House ideologues. A northerner who voted most often with conservative southerners, Walter was popular enough with his fellow Democrats to be elected three times as chair of the Democratic Caucus in 1949, 1961, and 1963.[64] Walter was ranking member of HUAC in the 83rd Congress and would serve as its chair from 1955 until his death in 1963. As the House coauthor of the McCarran-Walter bill that President Truman vetoed but was overridden by the Conservative Coalition of Republicans and southern Democratic allies, he was well aware that Majority Leader John McCormack led the fight against him.

John suspected that the more conservative House Democrats wanted him replaced as floor leader by Walter. While pro-immigration supporters like McCormack decried Walter's opposition to immigration, it was Walter's nine-year stint as HUAC chair that left major stains on the public reputation of the U.S. House that were very bothersome for Sam Rayburn and John McCormack.

Committee Upgrades: With their new majority in hand, Sam and John could now move some of their favorite junior members onto committees with greater prestige. Most affected was the 12-member House Rules Committee, now that its Democratic majority had been doubled from four seats to eight. Sam added six-termer Jim Trimble of Arkansas and four-termer Homer Thornberry of Texas to the committee while John McCormack expedited the return of New York's Jim Delaney to Rules. It was the last two new Democrats added to Rules who would have the most meaningful impact on the House and the nation. Sam moved Missouri's four-termer Dick Bolling from Banking and Currency where he had impressed Wright Patman, who had a key to Sam's Board of Education hideaway, while John moved sophomore Tip O'Neill from the dead-end Merchant Marine Committee to the eighth and last majority slot on Rules. As Dick Bolling once described it, he and Tip were to be "the eyes and ears of the leadership,"[65] keeping watch on the senior conservative duo of Virginia's Howard W. Smith, its chair, and Mississippi's Bill Colmer, his second-in-command. Smith and Colmer frequently allied themselves with the committee's four minority Republicans to vote 6–6 and prevent liberal legislation from coming to the House floor. They had become the Conservative Coalition's major House roadblock.

John McCormack's other new protégé Eddie Boland, who inherited Foster Furcolo's seat, would be moved from his dead-end assignment on Post Office and Civil Service to Furcolo's old slot on the powerful Appropriations Committee. John was building his own internal House machine.

The 84th Congress

The issues that engulfed the 83rd Congress had subsided. The hot war in Korea had ended with a tentative truce along the 38th Parallel between North and South Korea. It was less than a victory, but President Eisenhower had delivered on his campaign promise to end the fighting on that sad battle-scarred peninsula.

With the federal government divided between the president and the Congress for the second time in the five Congresses since the end of the war, Ike's legislative agenda stalled. Ike had to rely more on congressional Democrats to get his legislative agenda passed. This brought fellow Texans, Speaker Sam Rayburn and Senate Majority Leader Lyndon B. Johnson, into White House deliberations. For Eisenhower, who found party politics distasteful, getting along with moderate Texas Democrats like Rayburn and Johnson was not too difficult.

House Majority Leader John McCormack seldom joined Rayburn and Johnson in these meetings with Ike. For the first time in more than a decade, John was not "in the room" for most of these policymaking discussions. John McCormack, who gloried in the rough-and-tumble of the two-party politics of his native Massachusetts, was less influential with Ike than either of the Texans. Unlike Harry Truman, who found bipartisanship unsuited to his combative inclinations, Eisenhower found bipartisanship a welcome relief from narrow partisan debates and much more in keeping with his vision of a transcendent national politics removed from party bickering. Ike's antipathy toward partisanship impacted McCormack's fellow Bay Stater and intense Republican partisan Minority Leader Martin, who fared little better than John with President Eisenhower "viewing his legislative leader condescendingly as a typical politician and in Martin believing that president had little, if any, regard for the party."[66]

On a personal level, Rayburn took note of Ike's Texas birthplace often during his assessments of the president.[67] Rayburn protégé and future House Speaker Jim Wright recalled Sam's comments about Ike, "He's bound to be a good man. After all, he was born in my district. . . . And those who knew him say he was a good baby!" Rayburn genuinely liked President Eisenhower and found him far more preferable to the virulent Republican partisans who chafed at the relative nonpartisan character of the Eisenhower Administration and grew exasperated at Ike's unwillingness to overturn the social and economic policies of the New Deal.

The Southern Manifesto

A serious threat to Democratic presidential prospects in 1956 emerged from the South early in the year. In February, J. Strom Thurmond, the quixotic Democratic U.S. Senator from South Carolina who had carried four Deep South states against Harry Truman in 1948 as the States Rights/Dixiecrat candidate for president, launched a major petition drive in Congress. Intended to challenge the U.S. Supreme Court's pathbreaking ruling in the 1954 school desegregation case of *Brown v. Board of Education*, Thurmond's petition was formally entitled "The Declaration of Constitutional Principles," but was better known as the "Southern Manifesto."[68] The rabid segregationist Thurmond wrote the original draft, and the more polished and less rabid Dick Russell of Georgia prepared the final version. Rallying around the oft-ignored Tenth Amendment, the Manifesto accused the Court of a "clear abuse of judicial power" and called for a reversal of the Court's decision to bar racial segregation in publicly funded schools.

It was issued on the Senate floor on March 12, 1956, by the estimable six-term U.S. Senator Walter L. George of Georgia who had already announced his retirement. George was then Senate president pro tem and chair of the Foreign Relations Committee. It was his office that was the headquarters of the operation. The generally conservative George was ambivalent about the New Deal enough to be included on FDR's "purge" list in 1938, but he easily survived the renomination challenge.[69] At age 78, Senator George was the South's senior statesman. At its initial presentation, George contended that it was signed by "19 Senators, representing 11 States, and 77 House Members."[70] Later signers would push the total to 101; virtually all were Democrats, with only two Virginia Republicans Joel Broyhill and Richard Poff signing on. The Manifesto emphatically declared,[71]

> This unwarranted exercise of power by the Court, contrary to the Constitution, is creating chaos and confusion in the States principally affected. It is destroying the amicable relations between the white and Negro races that have been created

through 90 years of patient effort by the good people of both races. It has planted hatred and suspicion where there has been heretofore friendship and understanding.

The Senate's three nonsigners were Majority Leader Lyndon B. Johnson of Texas and Tennessee's Albert Gore and Estes Kefauver.[72] Technically, George had erroneously included eleven states among the Senate's signers overlooking Tennessee's demurral. All three nonsigners had national aspirations and were well aware of the growing political power of African-American Democratic voters in the electoral vote-rich states outside the South.

In the House, the results were mixed—78 initially signed and 28 did not. Notable among the House signers were nine chairs, half of the House's committee leaders: Tennessee's Jere Cooper of Ways and Means and Thomas Murray of Post Office and Civil Service, Virginia's Howard W. Smith of Rules, Georgia's Carl Vinson of Armed Services, North Carolina's Graham A. Barden of Education and Labor and Herbert Bonner of Merchant Marine and Fisheries, South Carolina's James P. Richards of Foreign Affairs and John L. McMillan of the District of Columbia, and Texas's Wright Patman of Select Small Business. Joining them were other members who would play a major role during John McCormack's speakership—Hale Boggs of Louisiana who would be John's whip throughout his nine years as Speaker, Wilbur Mills of Arkansas who would become the all-powerful chair of Ways and Means during the decade of the 1960s, Albert Rains of Alabama whom McCormack adversary Missouri's Dick Bolling recruited to block John's election as Speaker in 1962, and Phil Landrum of Georgia whose initial McCormack-backed effort to be elected to Ways and Means in 1963 would be thwarted by Bolling.[73]

Sam Rayburn did not sign the Southern Manifesto, and he was joined by 16 of his fellow Texas Democrats accounting for 17 of the 28 initial defectors. It was clearly a statement by the Texans that they no longer wished to be yoked to the South's segregationist past that made it virtually impossible for the national Democrats to nominate a presidential candidate from the Lone Star State. With the 1956 election looking grim, this was a foreshadowing of what Sam apparently hoped would happen in 1960. Lyndon Johnson had already cast his lot with the non-South, and Sam delivered the bulk of the House Texans as political cover. Having his own national ambitions hindered by campaigning as a segregationist against a Dixiecrat in 1948, Sam wanted to make sure that LBJ would be well positioned for the 1960 election.

While Washington settled into its stalemate, Massachusetts politics heated up. A presidential election was on the horizon and rumors abounded that two-term Republican Governor Christian Herter was being seriously considered as a vice presidential candidate by the "dump Nixon" forces who felt that the party's anti-Communism obsession that had gained Nixon the 1952 nomination cost the GOP control of Congress in 1954. It was no longer an issue that paid electoral dividends.

But Chris Herter was not the only Bay Stater who would be considered for a vice presidential nomination. The state's 39-year-old junior U.S. Senator John F. Kennedy was about to make his first major entrance onto the national political stage.

Notes

1   "Leaders of the New Congress," *NYT*, January 3, 1953, p. 8.

2   President's Truman's Daily Calendar website, Harry S. Truman Library and Museum, Independence, Missouri.

3   Information from Eisenhower appointment note cards provided by Mr. Kevin M. Bailey of the Eisenhower Library and Museum, Abilene, Kansas, March 8, 2015.

4   Leverett Saltonstall as told to Edward Weeks, *Salty: Recollections of a Yankee in Politics* (Boston: The Boston Globe, 1976), p. 156.

5   "The key to Kennedy's election that year was the campaign's designation of Kennedy 'secretaries' or political leaders, in virtually every community in the state, according to O'Brien" (Dan Ring, "John F. Kennedy Forged Strong Ties to Springfield in 1952 on His Way to the U.S. Senate," *Springfield (Mass.) Republican*, November 20, 2013).

6   See Ralph K. Huitt, "The Morse Committee Assignment Controversy: A Study in Senate Norms," *APSR*, LI (June 1957), pp. 313–29.

7   Their relationship is presented in John A. Goldsmith, *Colleagues, Richard B. Russell and His Apprentice Lyndon B. Johnson* (Macon, GA: Mercer University Press, 1998).

8   Three of the nine chapters titled in Alfred Steinberg's *Sam Johnson's Boy: A Close-Up of the President from Texas* (New York: Macmillan, 1968) have Johnson described as somebody's "boy"—Texan Alvin Wirtz, FDR, and Sam Rayburn.

9   Velde's House career is encapsulated in his obituary, *NYT*, September 8, 1985.

10 The failures of the 1950s Republican to overturn the New Deal are recounted in Edwin L. Dale, *Conservatives in Power: A Study in Frustration* (Garden City, NY: Doubleday, 1960).

11 See Charles C. Alexander, *Holding the Line: The Eisenhower Era, 1952–1961* (Bloomington: Indiana University Press, 1976); and Dominick Pratico, *Eisenhower and Social Security: The Origins of the Disability Program* (Bloomington, IN: Universe, 2001).

12 The House passed and amended bill on May 6, 1954, by a vote of 241 to 158 with Republicans voting 144 to 64 in favor while Democrats narrowly supported the bill 96 to 94. Frazier Reams of Ohio, the lone House Independent, supported the bill. *CQ Almanac, 1954* (Washington, DC: CQ Press, 1955), pp. 572–73. As Speaker, Joe Martin did not vote on the bill.

13 Senator John F. Kennedy speech on the St. Lawrence Seaway, *Congressional Record*, 83rd Congress, Second Session, January 14, 1954. New England Senate Republicans split 4–4 while its three Democrats Kennedy and both Rhode Island Senators John Pastore and Theodore Green voted for it. *CQ Almanac, 1954*, p. 565.

14 "Kennedy, Curley in Heated Clash on Seaway at Democratic Dinner," *Boston Globe*, January 24, 1954, pp. C1ff.

15 David M. Oshinsky, *A Conspiracy So Immense: The World of Joe McCarthy* (New York: Oxford University Press, 2005), pp. 110–13; and Richard M. Fried, *Nightmare in Red: The McCarthy Era in Perspective* (New York: Oxford University Press, 1990), pp. 124–25.

16 The Benton-McCarthy episode is vividly described in Sidney Hyman's biography, *The Lives of William Benton* (Chicago: University of Chicago Press, 1969), pp. 459–68.

17 McCarthy's attacks on La Follette's staff are recounted in Earl Latham, *The Communist Conspiracy in Washington: from the New Deal to McCarthy* (New York: Atheneum, 1969), pp. 121–23.

18   The story is recounted in Rodger McDaniel, *Dying for Joe McCarthy's Sins: The Suicide of Wyoming Senator Lester Hunt* (Cody, NY: WordsWorth, 2013).

19   Laurence Leamer, *The Kennedy Men, 1901–1963* (New York: William Morrow, 2001), pp. 301–10. On McCarthy's dating of the Kennedy sisters, see Thomas Reeves, *The Life and Times of Joe McCarthy: A Political Biography* (New York: Stein and Day, 1982), p. 203.

20   Robert Kennedy's employment by McCarthy in Leamer, *The Kennedy Men*, pp. 307–309.

21   Author's personal interview with Harvey Matusow in Burlington, Vermont, Summer 1993.

22   Senator Margaret Chase Smith, the speech is best known as "A Declaration of Conscience," but the title in the *Congressional Record* is "The Growing Confusion—Need for Patriotic Thinking," 81st Congress, Second Session, XCV, June 1, 1950, pp. 7894–95.

23   Emilio de Antonio and Daniel Talbot, *Point of Order!: A Documentary of the Army-McCarthy Hearings* (New York: W. W. Norton, 1964), p. 55.

24   There were eleven Senate floor votes regarding McCarthy's censure. Apart from supporting the August 2, 1954, vote on a Bill Knowland motion referring the censure motion to a select committee, Kennedy was listed as "not voting" on the ten subsequent votes between November 18 and the final censure vote on December 2, "Senate Votes: McCarthy Censure," *CQ Almanac, 1954*, pp. 472–73.

25   Even the generally favorable biography by James MacGregor Burns, *John Kennedy: A Political Profile* (New York: Harcourt, Brace, & World, 1961), refers to the episode in a full-length chapter ("McCarthyism: The Issue That Would Not Die," pp. 131–55).

26   Earl Mazo, *Richard Nixon: A Political & Personal Portrait* (New York: Harper, 1958), pp. 89 and 96.

27   See R. Bruce Craig, *Treasonable Doubt: The Harry Dexter White Spy Case* (Lawrence: University Press of Kansas, 2004); and Benn Stein, *The Battle of Bretton Woods, John Maynard Keynes, Harry Dexter White, and the Making of a New World Order* (Princeton, NJ: Princeton University Press, 2013).

28   J. Edgar Hoover letter to John McCormack, December 18, 1953, McCormack FBI File.

29   James R. Arnold, *The First Domino: Eisenhower, the Military, and America's Intervention in Vietnam* (New York: William Morrow, 1991), p. 125.

30   John's quote to Chalmers Roberts was reported in Melanie Billings-Yun, *Decision against War: Eisenhower and Dien Bien Phu, 1954* (New York: Columbia University Press, 1988), p. 92.

31   Eisenhower note to Gabriel Hauge, September 15, 1953, in Louis Galambos and Daun van Ee, eds., *The Papers of Dwight David Eisenhower, The Presidency: The Middle Way*, Vol. XIV (Baltimore: The Johns Hopkins Press, 1970), p. 522.

32   Eisenhower, *Diary* entry, October 8, 1953, in Galambos and van Ee, eds., *Eisenhower Papers*, Vol. XIV, p. 567. In Bernard Schwartz's magisterial biography, *Super Chief: Earl Warren and His Supreme Court: A Judicial Biography* (New York: New York University Press, 1983), he contends that liberal Justice William O. Douglas told him that "Vice President Richard M. Nixon called on Eisenhower to urge him to name Warren. According to Douglas, Nixon went to Ike saying something like, 'You must get Warren out of California, He has control of the Republican Party machinery and we can't do business with him'" (p. 4).

33   Eisenhower "Personal and confidential" letter to Edgar Newton Eisenhower, September 22, 1953, in Galambos and van Ee, *Eisenhower Papers*, XIV, p. 532.

34   Eisenhower "Personal and confidential" letter to Milton S. Eisenhower, October 9,
       1953, in Galambos and Daun van Ee, eds., *Eisenhower Papers*, XIV, p. 578.

35   Garrison Nelson, *Pathways to the U.S. Supreme Court: From the Arena to the Monastery*
       (New York: Palgrave Macmillan, 2013).

36   That speculation may be found in Ivan Hinderaker's article, "The 1952 Elections in
       California," *Western Political Quarterly*, VI (March 1953), pp. 102–107, see 105.
       See the accounts from the Warren side in G. Edward White, *Earl Warren: A Public
       Life* (New York: Oxford University Press, 1982), pp. 143–44. In Bernard Schwarz's
       magisterial *Super Chief: Earl Warren and His Supreme Court: A Judicial Biography*
       (New York: New York University Press, 1983), it is contended that Nixon pushed
       the nomination to get Warren out of California politics (pp. 4–5). The best recent
       rendering of the Warren-Eisenhower Court negotiations may be found in Yalof's
       Pursuit of Justices, pp. 44–51.

37   See the fascinating chapter, "Ike and Harry on Race" in William Lee Miller's recent
       book, *Two Americans: Truman, Eisenhower, and a Dangerous World* (New York: Alfred
       A. Knopf, 2012). Ike's Senate testimony is described on pp. 322–23.

38   Howard Kurtz, "Marshall Had Harsh Words about Eisenhower, RFK," *Washington
       Post*, January 31, 1993, p. A10.

39   Earl Warren, *The Memoirs of Earl Warren* (Garden City, NY: Doubleday, 1977), p. 292.

40   Jean Edward Smith, author of *Eisenhower in War and Peace* (New York: Random
       House, 2012) contends that "the problem is that Eisenhower never said that. I have no
       evidence that he ever made such a statement" (p. 603n).

41   The evidence seems mixed. Eisenhower's negative observation about Warren has been
       believed by most and challenged by a few. One lawyer contends that Ike had accepted
       Warren's liberal Court rulings on race; see Michael A. Kahn, "Shattering the Myth about
       President Eisenhower's Supreme Court Appointments," *Presidential Studies Quarterly*,
       XXII (Winter 1992), pp. 47–56. Kim Isaac Eisler's biography, *A Justice for All: William
       J. Brennan, Jr. and the Decisions That Transformed America* (New York: Simon &
       Schuster, 1993), contends that the papers of Justice Harold Burton indicate that Ike was
       disappointed by the national security decisions of Warren and Brennan. "It was those
       comments that later translated through the rumor mill to a statement that Eisenhower
       said: 'I have made two mistakes and they are sitting on the Court.' The truth was that
       Eisenhower didn't say it that way to Burton. But the thought was there" (p. 158).

42   Warren, *The Memoirs of Earl Warren*, p. 5.

43   Nelson, *Pathways*, p. 71.

44   Tip O'Neill with William Novak, *Man of the House: The Life and Political Memoirs of
       Speaker Tip O'Neill* (New York: Random House, 1987), p. 118. Tip's indebtedness to
       John McCormack was presented in a May 1981 *Reader's Digest* article as told to Mary
       McSherry ("Unforgettable John McCormack," pp. 123–27).

45   O'Neill, *Man of the House*, p. 120.

46   Background material on Eddie Boland derived from the *BDUSC* (1989 ed.), p. 639; and
       obituaries, most notably, Mark Feeney, "Longtime Congressman Edward Boland Dies,"
       Boston Globe, November 6, 2001; Myrna Oliver, "Rep. Edward Boland, 90; Opposed Aid
       to Contras," *Los Angeles Times*, November 6, 2001; and Scott Crass, "Men of the House:
       O'Neill's Roommate, JFK's Roommate, and Speaker McCormack," themoderatevoice.
       com, accessed October 20, 2014.

47   Among the Austin-Boston Speakers, book-length accounts of O'Neill's life and career
       are third in number to those of Sam Rayburn and Jim Wright. The two best are

O'Neill's best-selling autobiography with William Novak, *Man of the House: The Life and Political Memoirs of Speaker Tip O'Neill*; and the extensive biography by John A. Farrell, *Tip O'Neill and the Democratic Century* (Boston: Little, Brown & Co., 2001).

48 The Boland-O'Neill living arrangements are well described in Paul Clancy and Shirley Elder's *Tip: A Biography of Thomas P. O'Neill, Speaker of the House* (New York: Macmillan, 1980), pp. 81–82.

49 Saltonstall, *Salty*, p. 183.

50 Massachusetts Election Returns, 1954 Democratic Primary, Office of Massachusetts Secretary of State.

51 Saltonstall, *Salty*, pp. 168–73.

52 Theodore C. Sorensen, *Counselor: A Life at the Edge of History* (New York: Harper, 2000), pp. 127–28.

53 O'Neill, *Man of the House*, p. 83.

54 This account comes from Christopher Matthews book, *Jack Kennedy: Elusive Hero* (New York: Simon & Schuster, 2011), pp. 185–86. Matthews was provided access to the papers of Kenny O'Donnell by O'Donnell's daughter Helen.

55 On the loan of Sorensen to Saltonstall, see Matthews, *Elusive Hero*, p. 185. Joe Kennedy's campaign contributions are reported in the papers of Nigel Hamilton, Massachusetts Historical Society, Boston.

56 Saltonstall-Kennedy Act, *Congress and the Nation, 1945–1964*, p. 1069.

57 *CQ Guide to U.S. Elections* (1975 ed.), p. 424.

58 The House was committee-dominated in the 1950s. A typical assessment was that of John H. Fenton, *People and Parties in Politics: Unofficial Makers of Public Policy* (Glenview, IL: Scott, Foresman, 1966).

59 Randall B. Ripley, "Party Whip Organizations in the United States House of Representatives," *APSR*, LVIII (September 1964), pp. 561–76.

60 Carl Albert was well aware of the geographical factor. As he described this proximity in a 1971 interview with Elizabeth Drew of the Public Broadcasting Service:

> *Mrs. Drew*: And I think that I read that one of the first things you did when you were elected was to go across the Red River to—
> *Representative Albert*: Oh, yes.
> *Mrs. Drew*: Texas and see Speaker Rayburn.
> *Representative Albert*: His home was just about, oh 10 miles from my district line. And of course, he was—he was a legendary figure in the Southwest at that time. I had heard him speak many times. He'd been in my district and other places in Oklahoma.

61 Carl Albert with Danney Goble, *Little Giant: The Life and Times of Speaker Carl Albert* (Norman: University of Oklahoma Press, 1999).

62 See William A. Hasenfus, "Managing Partner: Joseph W. Martin, Jr., Republican Leader of the United States House of Representatives, 1939–1959," PhD dissertation, Boston College, 1986.

63 Alfred Steinberg, *Sam Rayburn: A Biography* (New York: Hawthorn, 1975), p. 192.

64 "Democratic Caucus Chairmen (1849 to present)," History Art & Archives, U.S. House of Representatives.

65 Author's interview with the Hon. Richard W. Bolling, Washington, DC, March 1988.

66 James J. Kenneally, *A Compassionate Conservative: A Political Biography of Joseph W. Marin, Jr., Speaker of the U.S. House of Representatives* (Lanham, MD: Lexington,

2003), p. 205. See also Joe Martin as told to Robert J. Donovan, *My First Fifty Years in Politics* (New York: McGraw-Hill, 1960), pp. 222–27.

67   Jim Wright, *Balance of Power: Presidents and Congress from the Era of McCarthy to the Age of Gingrich* (Atlanta: Turner Publishing, 1996) p. 36.

68   "The Southern Manifesto," *TIME*, March 26, 1956.

69   "Walter F. George," in the online *New Georgia Encyclopedia*, entry excerpted from Josephine Mellichamp, *Senators from Georgia* (Huntsville, GA: Strode Publishers, 1976).

70   "The Southern Manifesto," *Congressional Record*, 84th Congress, Second Session, March 12, 1956, Vol. 102, pp. 4515–16. See William S. White's contemporaneous account, "Manifesto Splits Democrats Again: Southern Pledge to Fight Integration Ends Truce on Civil Rights Issue," *NYT*, March 13, 1956. Academic assessments may be found in two articles in the *Arkansas Historical Quarterly*: Brent J. Austin, "The Southern Manifesto and Southern Opposition to Desegregation," LV (Summer 1996), pp. 173–93; and Tony Badger, "'The Forerunner of Our Opposition': Arkansas and the Southern Manifesto of 1956," LVI (Autumn 1997), pp. 353–60.

71   *Congressional Record*, 84th Congress, Second Session, March 12, 1956, pp. 4515–16.

72   Tony Badger, "Southerners Who Refused to Sign the Southern Manifesto," *The Historical Journal*, XLII (June 1999), pp. 517–34.

73   Richard W. Bolling, Defeating the Leadership's Nominee in the House Democratic Caucus (Syracuse, NY: Inter-university Case Program, 1965).

17

Political Positioning, 1956–60

The Contentious Year of 1956: Former President Harry Truman was the invited speaker for the annual Jefferson-Jackson Day Dinner on February 4, 1956. While the *Boston Globe* carried a photo of President Truman chatting amiably once again with Boston Archbishop Richard Cushing, the *Boston Traveler* printed a different photo the following day with the caption "Democratic Harmony."[1] Pictured in the photograph with Truman were Senator Kennedy, House Majority Leader McCormack, State Chair William "Onions" Burke, and ex-Governor Paul Dever. Harry Truman had done well in Massachusetts, carrying the state twice—in 1944 as Franklin D. Roosevelt's vice presidential running mate and in 1948 as FDR's presidential successor. It was a deceptive harmony that greeted him. Because these were Massachusetts Democrats, the various Irish clans who had gained control of the party over their ethnic rivals were involved to the hilt. The year of 1956 was one when local animosities played out on a national stage as the state's two most powerful clans, the McCormacks and the Kennedys, sought to position themselves for state control and national prominence.

Ironically, the catalyst was the presidential candidacy of a Democratic nominee who twice failed to capture the state's electoral votes—Adlai E. Stevenson of Illinois who lost to Republican Dwight D. Eisenhower in 1952 and 1956. While he may have united Democrats elsewhere, he was a divisive candidate in Massachusetts. A liberal Princeton-educated divorced Unitarian Midwesterner seeking support from the socially conservative Irish and Italian Catholics of Massachusetts, Stevenson was almost doomed from the start. However, twice he had the support of once-popular Paul A. Dever, the state's former two-term governor (1949–53).[2] Dever had lost his 1952 reelection bid in Eisenhower's landslide victory over Stevenson. His latest endorsement was seen as an effort to regain relevance after his disastrous appearance at the 1952 Democratic Convention.

In 1956, Stevenson's other ally was the state's junior U.S. Senator John F. Kennedy, the only other major Massachusetts Democrat to yoke himself to the campaign.[3] While Paul Dever's electoral career was over, Jack Kennedy's was relatively new with an anticipated high trajectory. Entering only his fourth year in the Senate, it was risky for the 38-year-old Kennedy to commit himself early to an unpopular presidential candidate. It was a less surprising alliance when their backgrounds were examined. Jack Kennedy's grandfather and namesake, John Fitzgerald, was a U.S. Representative in the 1890s when Stevenson's grandfather and namesake, former Postmaster General Adlai E. Stevenson, served as President Grover Cleveland's second vice president.

Both Stevenson and Kennedy had prepped at Choate and both began their collegiate careers at Princeton. Stevenson graduated from Princeton but Kennedy's freshman year ailments led him to return home and complete his education at Harvard, the alma mater of his grandfather, father, and older brother. Stevenson also attended Harvard as a law student but left Cambridge to return to Illinois and complete his legal training at Northwestern. Both Stevenson and Kennedy belonged to families that were similar to FDR's and they possessed political prominence and privilege ratified by their prep school and Ivy League educations. Most individuals with these backgrounds were conservative upper-class defenders of private privilege and corporate power. That these men were considered liberals made them "traitors to their class" yet they could be nominated and even elected.[4]

The state's organizational Democrats disliked Stevenson and didn't trust Kennedy due to their upscale credentials. In 1952, Stevenson was the first presidential Democrat to lose Massachusetts since John W. Davis lost to President and former Governor Calvin Coolidge in 1924 and his defeat led to a gubernatorial victory for Republican Christian Herter over Paul Dever. The fact that Kennedy had been able to capture a Senate seat from incumbent Republican Henry Cabot Lodge, Jr. in the wake of Stevenson's defeat puzzled as many people as it had impressed others.

Barely two months later, the long knives of Boston Irish politics would be unsheathed once again and internecine conflict would resume. Neither Dever nor Kennedy was a favorite of John McCormack. John had supported the candidacy of Springfield Mayor Roger Lowell Putnam, the father-in-law of his best friend James Fitzgerald's son, against Paul Dever's nomination as lieutenant governor in 1946,[5] while his issues with Jack Kennedy were even more recent and more public.

Leading the anti-Stevenson Massachusetts Democrats was returning State Chair William H. "Onions" Burke, Jr., a heavyset balding former tavern keeper and onion farmer from Hatfield in the sparsely populated western part of the state. Burke was a Jim Curley and John McCormack guy who chaired the state's Democrats from 1939 to 1944 during FDR's third and fourth nominations in 1940 and 1944.[6] He was rewarded in 1944 by FDR's naming him as Collector of Customs for the Port of Boston, a post he held from 1944 to 1952.[7] Burke was a quintessential patronage-hungry Irish conservative Democrat. He sought to resume the party chairmanship, and thanks to a favorable court order, Burke regained the chair ousting John Carr, a Paul Dever loyalist in 1956. However, this victory was temporary and he would have to face reelection in the early spring. Onions Burke and John McCormack were longtime allies and both were convinced that Stevenson would lose again in 1956. But there was more at stake for John and Onions than a presidential contest, and that was their continued control of the state party and along with it control of the state's delegation to the 1956 Democratic National Convention that would convene in Chicago later that summer.

While Stevenson was not favored by most of the state's Democrats, neither of his two major rivals, Tennessee Senator Estes Kefauver and New York Governor W. Averell Harriman, elicited much local enthusiasm. Burke's strategy to keep control of the state party was to mount a favorite son campaign for John McCormack in the upcoming April primary. It was a nonbinding advisory one and it would be conducted by write-in votes. Onions hoped to derail the Stevenson campaign and by extension embarrass Stevenson's key supporters Dever and Kennedy.

Enthusiastically backing John McCormack's candidacy was the *Boston Post*'s eccentric publisher John Fox. In the 1952 campaign, Fox's paper initially backed Protestant Republicans Christian Herter for governor and incumbent Henry Cabot Lodge, Jr. for the U.S. Senate, but it reversed field by endorsing two Catholic Democrats, Governor Paul Dever for reelection and Jack Kennedy for election to the Senate. However, by 1956, Fox changed course once again and soured on Jack. Jack Kennedy's first biographer James MacGregor Burns contended that Fox had become irritated as JFK had not agreed to Fox's demand that his fellow Harvard alumni withhold donations until the university had rid itself of left-wing faculty.[8]

A more plausible explanation for Fox's change of heart would revolve around Joe Kennedy's $500,000 "loan" to Fox the day before the 1952 endorsements to save the *Post* from bankruptcy. Fox's pro-Kennedy reversal helped Jack defeat Lodge, his prior favorite. Joe Kennedy treated the money as a loan, while Fox may have hoped that it was a gift. But once Jack was elected, Joe had little further need for Fox and collected all of the money with interest 60 days later.[9] With the *Post* struggling anew (it ceased publication in October 1956) and no Joe Kennedy rescue in the offing for 1956, Fox launched a month-long barrage of campaign articles extolling John McCormack, most of which appeared on the front page replete with cartoons and embellished personal accounts urging the *Post*'s readers to support McCormack's write-in campaign for president in the April 24 primary.[10]

The April Primary: The *Post* and other news outlets reported support for McCormack from Senate Majority Leader Lyndon Johnson's two most formidable allies—Senators Dick Russell of Georgia and Bob Kerr of Oklahoma.[11] Senator Kefauver got the hint and withdrew from the Massachusetts contest on April 12 and endorsed McCormack.[12]

The write-in results were devastating for Stevenson and Kennedy. John McCormack won easily with more than 26,000 votes, close to half of the total (47.9%), followed by Stevenson (34.9%), Kefauver (8.3%) and even Republican President Eisenhower (3.4%).[13] Jack Kennedy received only 949 votes (1.7%) and finished a very distant fifth behind McCormack. Jack's hopes of uniting with Stevenson to match Dick Nixon's 1952 success as a 39-year-old vice presidential nominee were fading fast.

The vote in Boston was particularly embarrassing for Kennedy. The *Post* was especially pleased to report that John McCormack had buried Kennedy in Boston with 12,838 votes for first-place John and only 283 for fifth-place Jack.[14] John was well aware of the *Post*'s role in his success and declared that "I am deeply grateful to every person who expressed his preference for me, to all who openly supported the movement and, in particular, I am most grateful to the *Boston Post*, the paper that started and conducted the write-in campaign for me."[15]

Having orchestrated the presidential primary triumph over Stevenson (and Kennedy), a cocky Onions Burke escalated his attacks, declaring that Stevenson's supporters should be at Princeton where former State Department official and convicted perjurer Alger Hiss had been invited to speak.[16] It was Hiss's first public appearance after serving three years and eight months of his five-year sentence.[17]

Onions declared that "anybody who's for Stevenson ought to be down at Princeton listening to Alger Hiss."[18] Stevenson, who had served with Hiss in the State Department, had given a deposition in 1949 attesting to Hiss's good character along with Supreme Court Justices Felix Frankfurter and Stanley Reed.[19] Seeing this as a JFK slam, young Kennedy supporters who had hopes of Jack's being named to the 1956 ticket with Stevenson were not pleased.

    John was surprised that Onions wanted to stay on as chair and tried to talk him out of running again, but Onions ignored John's advice. He had become too negatively obsessed with the Stevenson campaign to let go of the post and the huge primary victory for John McCormack let him put a thumb in the eyes of both Paul Dever, an ancient enemy, and Jack Kennedy, a new one. The final confrontation was a few weeks away.

    The Battle of the Bradford: There should not have been a McCormack-Kennedy confrontation but once sides were taken, the battle was unavoidable. The young Kennedy operatives, Kenny O'Donnell and Larry O'Brien, felt strongly that the public embarrassment of the write-in primary results had to be expunged if Jack was to be a major national figure. It was they who shifted their focus to gaining control of the state party organization and ridding it of Onions Burke. Much of this they did without Jack's notice and at one point Jack tried to defuse the impending conflict when he met with Onions for breakfast in the Western Massachusetts college town of Northampton and urged him to step aside for the good of the party.

    Burke refused Jack's request. An exasperated Kennedy told a reporter that he intended to remove Onions from the state committee. The war was on, and now John McCormack was obliged to make his pro-Burke stance publicly known, linking it directly to the outcome of the primary and making the vote about him[20]: "Chairman Burke was elected chairman only five months ago. It must be apparent to everyone that if he had not expressed himself in support of me in the 'write-in' vote for President, and in which I received a clear majority of the 'write-in' votes, he would have no opposition."

    John made a serious effort to dissuade Onions from running, and he even contacted Jack about it:

> I tried to talk him [Burke] out of it, but he persisted in being a candidate and I owed it to him. There were no marked differences between John Kennedy, then Senator Kennedy, and myself. At that time, the then candidate had made himself personally offensive to Senator Kennedy. And Senator Kennedy on at least two occasions sent word to me that he would support any man that I might suggest with the exception of Mr. Burke.
>
>   And if he persisted in running, why I couldn't see anything else but to support him. The only ones I contacted were those half-dozen members of the State Committee that they asked me to.[21]

As McCormack reflected on all of the Democratic candidacies supported by Onions Burke, including JFK's in 1952, he made special note of the 1954 Senate contest featuring his protégé Foster Furcolo, stating "Mr. Burke, as I did, vigorously supported the party nominees in 1954. It is through no fault of Burke or myself that Foster Furcolo was not elected United States Senator in 1954." It is doubtful if John knew that Joe Kennedy had sent money to the campaign of Republican incumbent U.S. Senator Leverett Saltonstall or that Jack had loaned his speechwriter Ted Sorensen to Salty, but Jack's public disdain toward Furcolo during that campaign was visible to all.

According to Larry O'Brien, Jack was not wholly pleased with their efforts, especially after the Boston newspapers designated it a Kennedy-McCormack fight.[22] "What the hell are you guys doing to me?" Kennedy kept asking his operatives.

While Kenny O'Donnell and others were urging JFK to get involved in the fight for control of Massachusetts, Joe Kennedy was not buying in. Joe Kennedy was displeased that O'Donnell and O'Brien had involved Jack in the tawdriness of Boston politics. The ambassador said: "Leave it alone & don't get in the gutter with those bums up there in Boston."[23] Kenny contended they had to keep their political activities concealed from the Kennedy family. To Joe Kennedy, Boston Irish politics were rife with tedious petty feuds and trivial penny-ante corruption, circumstances he unfortunately associated with his father-in-law John Fitzgerald, Jack's namesake. Boston Irishmen were best ignored but it was now too late. The Kennedys could not afford to lose two local battles to Onions Burke and his protector John McCormack.

The convention delegation had yet to be selected, so there was an opportunity to recoup some political leverage for Jack. But first they had to get rid of Burke.[24] They chose to meet at the Hotel Bradford further down the tawdry end of Tremont Street and a few blocks from the Parker House, where Boston's economic and political elite met to transact their business. The Bradford skirted Boston's "theater district." Later, that area would be merely a few blocks away from what would become known as "the Combat Zone," where vice and prostitution flourished. But during this time in the city's history, those activities were mostly confined to Scollay Square, where burlesque houses and hookers regularly separated sad-eyed sailors from their wages.

The Kennedy people backed John M. "Pat" Lynch, the mayor of nearby Somerville. Although not a particularly close Kennedy ally, the small-statured Lynch looked more like a fedora-wearing Boston pol than the tall lean Harvard types generally favored by the Kennedys. Lynch was a relatively new face and presumably free of the battalion of enemies that Onions Burke and his heavy-handed management style had created. Boos, yelling, and even fisticuffs erupted at the hotel.[25] After all, most of the attendees were burly, short-tempered Boston Irish Democrats. The Kennedys had two beefy policemen on their side. But leading the battle for Onions was Knocko McCormack, John's 300-pound brother, a former prize fighter who had no aversion to clocking any pro-Kennedy head within reach of his ham-handed fists.

JFK himself let his people know that Burke and McCormack had to be kept in the dark about their activities to "get (his) people on the state committee." But in the end it was Jack himself who told a news reporter that he was planning to remove Onions Burke from the state committee.

Reminiscences of the day vary. Kenny O'Donnell, Bob Kennedy's Harvard roommate, a key family operative, and their most protective ally, wrote: "Kennedy took command of the party in Massachusetts with a firm hand. He called a meeting of the delegation to the coming national convention & had himself elected as its leader."²⁶ Later, O'Donnell provided a more heroic version: "[the Jack Kennedy who] went into the pits & fought Onions Burke & John McCormack for the . . . control of the Democratic organization in Massachusetts . . . was much tougher & more sure of himself than the . . . JFK of 1952."

Jackie's Reminiscences: Jackie Kennedy, Jack's 26-year-old wife, remembered the day well. Her reminiscence was far less heroic than that of Kenny O'Donnell. The day of the state committee vote was especially stressful for Jack because Jean Ann Kennedy, the youngest of his five sisters and the shyest one, was to be married in New York City's majestic St. Patrick's Cathedral by Francis Cardinal Spellman to Stephen E. Smith, a handsome Georgetown-educated financier. Smith would eventually become the manager of the Kennedy family's various and sizable trust funds. Jean had met Steve Smith while she was a student at Manhattanville College, the school that had also educated two of her sisters-in-law, Ethel Skakel who had married Bob Kennedy in 1950 and Joan Bennett who would marry Ted Kennedy in 1958. As the oldest brother, Jack was to give Jean away that day, while also trying to keep abreast of political developments in Boston 220 miles away. While one account contends that Jack waited in an automobile while the battle raged, and learning of the victory then drove the four-plus hours to New York, others contend that Jack flew back and forth between the two cities trying to meet both his family obligations and his political aspirations. The most vivid recounting of Jack's stress level that day was provided in Jackie Kennedy's 1964 reminiscences with Jack's White House advisor and Pulitzer Prize–winning biographer Arthur M. Schlesinger, Jr.

Jackie misremembered some of the key details but her lengthy depiction of Jack's anxiety was quite telling²⁷:

> The worst fight in his life, which you should ask me about sometime, is when he got control of the Massachusetts legislature. That was to lead the Massachusetts delegation there, wasn't it? . . . Yes, against "Onions" Burke. Because that was the only time in all of the fights he's been through in his life when I'd really seen him nervous when he couldn't talk about anything else before. So that was the big thing of all the spring. I guess was, you know, to win that fight. And it really was on his mind all the time.
>
> . . . the vote, or whatever it was going to come up a few days later, and I remember thinking—the only time in my life I've ever thought that Jack was a little bit thoughtless. But I didn't really think that, because you could see how worried he was, because all that night, when everyone should have been making little toasts to Jean and things—which they were, and he made a touching one—he was talking to everybody at dinner about that fight. I mean, it was just on his mind, and I've never seen him like that—in the first Cuba, the second Cuba, any election—I mean, the election—the presidential election when I think of how calm he was that night—whether it would come out well or not, but still—but that was just all that spring.

With conflict continuing into the evening at the Bradford Hotel, Larry O'Brien, the best-known non-family member of Kennedy's "Irish Mafia," provided the most objective recounting of the episode in his autobiography[28]: "I called the Boston police commissioner. He arrived minutes later.

'I'm O'Brien. You've got to get these troublemakers out of here.'

'One more word out of you, O'Brien,' the commissioner replied, 'and I'll lock you up!'"

I hadn't known the commissioner was a McCormack man.

Both sides felt they had the votes, but the Kennedy forces won the day with a 47 to 31 tally and Pat Lynch became state chair.[29] The embittered supporters of Onions refused to make the vote unanimous and Burke himself threatened to run against Kennedy in 1958. But with the dawn and clearer heads, it was obvious that Onions had no campaign money and no political post from whence to run and so this threat was perceived by most as hot air from a politician who had just seen the end of his public relevance.

John McCormack congratulated Pat Lynch as the Kennedy camp emphatically denied that ridding the state party of Onions Burke had anything to do with their overall feelings of respect and friendship for John. Whether John believed them is debatable, but all the right things were said to mollify his loyalists and to paper over the differences that had emerged[30]:

> I don't say that apologetically—it was a secret ballot and a close vote. But the relationship between the then Senator Kennedy and myself was very pleasant, no disturbance, and as I say, on two occasions he sent word to me that he would support any one that I might suggest that had the stature, of course. And there's certainly nothing unfriendly about that.

In retrospect, this battle was surprisingly decisive. Had Kennedy suffered yet another embarrassing home state loss, his aspirations to be a major national-level player would have been postponed indefinitely if not ended altogether. The Kennedy wing avoided disaster that day but it had long-term consequences. The battle had not unified the state party, and it created deep wounds for the Kennedys among the McCormacks and the other Boston Irish with their long memories and short fuses.

In his 1977 oral history for the Kennedy Library, John contended that "this fight for the chairmanship between Burke and Lynch, so far as a fight between Kennedy and McCormack was completely exaggerated."[31]

The state conventions and the emergence of Eddie McCormack

With the presidential primary settled and the national convention delegation selected, it was time for the state's pre-primary endorsement conventions. While the conventions provided endorsements, the formal nominations occurred in the September primaries. In June, Massachusetts Democrats held the 1956 pre-primary convention in Worcester to select their preferred candidates for statewide offices. The governorship would come open with the announced departure of two-term Republican Governor Christian A. Herter who President Eisenhower appointed on February 21, 1957, as undersecretary of state to serve with Secretary of State John Foster Dulles. With Lieutenant Governor Sumner G. Whittier named as the Republican nominee for governor, two of the state's top offices were now open, but that was not the case for attorney general where Republican George Fingold chose to run for reelection.

Former Democratic Treasurer Foster Furcolo of East Longmeadow, narrowly defeated in the 1954 U.S. Senate contest by incumbent Senator Leverett Saltonstall, was named the party's endorsed candidate for governor and former House Minority Leader Bob Murphy of Malden, who had lost the governorship to Herter in 1954, was its candidate for lieutenant governor. Neither race was closely contested.

The most wide-open race was for the attorney general endorsement. It was a three-man contest with longtime State Representative Joseph D. Ward from Fitchburg in central Massachusetts hoping to fend off challenges from two newcomers to state office—the 36-year-old Endicott "Chub" Peabody of Cambridge and the 32-year-old Eddie McCormack of South Boston. Peabody was the quintessential Boston Brahmin. He was the grandson of the Reverend Endicott Peabody who had founded Groton School, FDR's prep school alma mater, and he had garnered All-American football honors at Harvard as a bruising tackler and called "the baby-faced assassin" by adoring sportswriters for whom both Harvard admittance and All-American football selections were fantasies. In one of those soap opera moments, it was during this time that Chub's twice-married sister Marietta Peabody Tree had broken off with her lover, the movie director John Huston, to begin her longtime affair with Adlai Stevenson.[32]

The other young contender for attorney general was Edward J. McCormack, Jr., the younger son of John's brother Edward "Knocko" McCormack. Knocko's best-known protégé was State Senator Bill Bulger, who would later become president of the State Senate and then president of the multicampus University of Massachusetts. Bulger was a native of the Old Harbor Housing Project and close childhood neighbor of U.S. Representative John Joseph "Joe" Moakley, who would gain John McCormack's House seat in 1972 and eventually chair the U.S. House Rules Committee. Sadly for Bill Bulger, his stellar political career was overshadowed by the criminal history of his oldest brother Jim, best known as "Whitey," whose notorious (and murderous) escapades took on mythic proportions. All of that was yet to come, but Bill Bulger's memoir *While the Music Lasts* has a vivid depiction of the younger McCormack brothers, John "Jocko" and Edward "Bubba." After describing Jocko as "a wild spirit," he devoted an adoring paragraph to Eddie[33]:

> Bubba, on the other hand, was graduated from the U.S. Naval Academy and Boston University Law School. It was at that juncture he discouraged further use of his nickname and announced that he was to be known henceforth as Eddie. That was more to distinguish himself from his father than because of any penchant for informality. Unlike his brother, Jocko, who was a pie in the face of society, Eddie was smart and debonair, a study in silk: very smooth, very smooth.

Young Eddie, described as "tall and handsome with dark blond hair," graduated from South Boston High School and began his undergraduate career at Colby College in Maine and transferred to the U.S. Naval Academy in 1947. With politics as the family business, Eddie chose a legal career and graduated from the Boston University Law School at the top of his class in 1952 and was the editor of the *BU Law Review.*

Upon graduating law school and beginning private practice, Eddie was elected to the Boston City Council to launch his political career. At the convention, there was support for Eddie to run for lieutenant governor, but he was determined to obtain the attorney general's endorsement. However, when Joe Ward bypassed Peabody on the second ballot and was the likely winner, the *Globe* reported that Eddie "stomped from the convention with his followers."[34] As Eddie left, further commotion occurred as "McCormack's walkout threw the convention into an uproar and brought his father, Edward J. 'Knocko' McCormack out of his seat to protest his son's action. The senior McCormack shouted: 'Don't be a sucker—you'll regret it as long as you live.'"

While Eddie failed to win the convention's endorsement, he successfully challenged Ward in the September 18 primary, winning easily by 40,993 votes (55.2% to 44.8%). For the first time in family history, a McCormack was now a serious statewide contender.

Joe Kennedy's Pre-Convention Plans: Former Ambassador Joseph P. Kennedy had once hoped that he would be the first Roman Catholic President of the United States. It was a hope shared by John McCormack who publicly declared his support of Joe's candidacy in 1940. But Joe Kennedy's financial success was hard-won, and he was sufficiently self-aware to know that a careful public scrutiny of the means by which he acquired his great fortune would doom his presidential prospects. The architects of the great American fortunes seldom ventured into the public realm. It was always safer to let the grandsons—be they Rockefellers, duPonts, Harrimans, or Danforths—carry the family standard into the public arena. Let the dust of the rapacious first generation settle; commit the next generation to charitable good works and philanthropy to expiate the family guilt; and then use the family's newly acquired good name to acquire elective political office and public approbation.

Joe Kennedy was not a patient man and he wanted to see the family triumph in his lifetime, so it would have to be one of his sons who would bear the Kennedy name into the White House. After amassing his fortune relatively early, the family settled into a comfortable but not opulent lifestyle. With his massive personal fortune in place, Joe Kennedy compressed the generational time clock and it was he who personally underwrote most of the family's charitable endeavors. Joe believed that he had put sufficient distance between the acquisition of his fortune and the achievement of a good name for his family. The ambassador's energetic efforts to further the political career of his eldest son Joseph P. Kennedy Jr. were well known. Joe Jr.'s tragic death over the troubled skies of war-ravaged Europe ended the life of the first bearer of the dream, but not the dream itself. His second son, John Fitzgerald Kennedy, named for Joe's difficult father-in-law, would be called upon to pick up the fallen lance.[35]

By the autumn of 1955, Jack Kennedy was only 38 and a U.S. Senator for less than three years. A reach for national office would seem presumptuous but presently seated as vice president was Richard Nixon who was named as Dwight Eisenhower's running mate in 1952 when he was only a year older than Jack and had been a Senator for a year less. If a Kennedy presidency was to occur in Joe's lifetime, the vice presidency would be the springboard. Clearly convinced that Adlai Stevenson was much too liberal to be elected in a nation gripped by the Cold War, Joe Kennedy looked for an alternative to Stevenson who would be amenable to accepting Kennedy funds in exchange for naming Jack as his running mate. He first settled on the 46-year-old Senate Majority Leader Lyndon Johnson of Texas. Kennedy was well aware that Johnson was a protégé of Speaker Sam Rayburn whose skilled floor management of the 1933 Securities Act and the 1934 Securities and Exchanges Act had created the Securities and Exchange Commission (SEC) that gave Joe, its initial chair, his first real taste of government power and national publicity. Both acts were written by FDR's legislative draftsmen Ben Cohen and Rhode Island–born Tommy "the Cork" Corcoran, protégés of Harvard Law professor and present Supreme Court Justice Felix Frankfurter. Although Tom Corcoran and Joe Kennedy eyed each other warily, they were both New England Irish Catholics and Tom's closeness to Rayburn made him an appropriate emissary to Lyndon.

Joe and Bobby met Corcoran in New York with a proposition of full Kennedy funding for a Johnson presidential campaign should Jack be named as LBJ's running mate. Johnson, who was recovering from a serious heart attack and knew that Ike's Gallup Poll favorability numbers were in the mid-sixties, correctly surmised that Joe intended for LBJ to wage a losing presidential battle that would leave the 1960 presidential field open for Jack. Corcoran's biographer says Johnson told Tommy "to politely decline Joe Kennedy's offer."[36] When he returned with Johnson's refusal, Corcoran remembered that Bobby exploded in a rage and "believed it was unforgivably discourteous to turn down his father's offer." Bobby may have seen himself as a scion of the richest and most powerful Catholic Democratic family in the country, while Lyndon Johnson saw him as a 29-year-old legal counsel on a relatively insignificant Senate committee. Although Jeff Shesol contends that this "affront" led to the lifelong feud between Bob Kennedy and Lyndon Johnson,[37] it appears that Joe was less offended and in a curious way even more appreciative of Johnson's political instincts.

There would no similar reach-out to New York Governor W. Averell Harriman. Harriman was also a multimillionaire and his key supporter, ex-President Harry Truman, intensely disliked Joe Kennedy and would later declare about Jack, "It's not the Pope I'm afraid of it's the Pop."[38]

Joe Kennedy resigned himself to another losing Stevenson nomination but still convinced that Stevenson's running mate would be ideally positioned for the 1960 nomination, he used his Chicago-based son-in-law R. Sargent Shriver, Eunice's husband, in a July reach-out to Stevenson about a possible vice presidential nod for Jack. Stevenson's negative response to Shriver cited three concerns—"rumors of John's poor health, Joseph Kennedy's public objections to his son's candidacy, and Kennedy's Catholicism."[39] Having failed twice to secure a vice presidential commitment for Jack, Joe went off to Europe to watch the convention's proceedings from afar.

National Convention anxieties

This would not be a happy convention for Speaker Sam Rayburn, yet again the permanent chair of the Democratic National Convention. He was unimpressed with both Stevenson and Kefauver and was fond of Republican President Eisenhower. Rayburn knew that national polls forecast yet another Stevenson defeat and for a while, he joined Harry Truman in supporting the nomination of Averell Harriman. Had a Stevenson ticket included a vice presidential nod for the Catholic Kennedy, Rayburn felt that the down-ballot Democratic candidates, most notably the southern House members whom he had induced not to sign the pro-segregation Southern Manifesto, would incur defeat.

The ubiquitous Arthur M. Schlesinger, Jr., a founder of the liberal Americans for Democratic Action (ADA) and Stevenson loyalist, met with Adlai on July 26 and recounted[40]:

> to me his discussions with Harry Truman, James A. Farley, Sam Rayburn and other party elders about the contenders—Kennedy, Estes Kefauver of Tennessee and Hubert Humphrey of Minnesota: HST thinks Humphrey "too radical"; dismisses Kennedy as a Catholic; has no use for Kefauver. Mentions [Albert] Gore [of Tennessee] and [George] Leader [of Pennsylvania].
>
> Farley told AES, "America is not ready for a Catholic yet."
>
> Rayburn: "Well, if we have to have a Catholic, I hope we don't have to take that little pissant Kennedy. How about John McCormack?"

According to D. B. Hardeman, Rayburn's longtime aide and his biographer, Sam was not impressed with Kennedy. In an oral history interview at the University of Texas Library, Hardeman recounted Rayburn's recollection of Kennedy in the House:[41]

> [Rayburn] said, "He was in the House here and he made absolutely no impression on us. A nice young man, but rumpled suits and hair hanging down in his face that needed cutting, spindly legs, and he had that yellow complexion like he had that Pacific fever. He was running around after the girls all night long. He just made no impression at all on us."

The 1956 Democratic Convention: In August, the Democrats would return to Chicago for their 1956 national nominating convention.[42] As the largest city in the Midwest and close to the nation's midpoint, Chicago had become a natural location for nominating conventions for both parties. As a north-south party, Democrats most often chose Baltimore as a more natural locus for their early conventions while Republicans as an east-west party more often chose Chicago. But Chicago conventions had been successful for the Democrats in that five of their previous seven Chicago nominations had been victorious—two for Grover Cleveland in 1884 and 1892 and three for Franklin D. Roosevelt in 1932, 1940, and 1944.

Both John and Jack were members of the Massachusetts delegation and both were assigned to prominent roles at the convention. At Harry Truman's behest, John McCormack was asked once again to chair the platform-writing Resolutions Committee, and Jack Kennedy was asked to narrate a long documentary film of highlights from American history stressing the positive role played by the Democratic Party in furthering American goals. Also serving on the delegation and attending his last convention was Jim Curley, whose last two defeats for mayor in 1949 and 1953 were more sadly pathetic than the glamorized "last hurrah" of Edwin O'Connor's Mayor Frank Skeffington in his acclaimed best-selling novel.[43]

Resolutions Committee: It was the third time that John McCormack had been chosen to chair the Resolutions Committee and to write the party's platform. He had also chaired the committee in 1944 and 1952. That John was not the committee's chair in 1948 was seen by many as accounting for the Dixiecrat walkout that year. Working with his good friend and committee beneficiary, Chicago African-American Representative William Dawson, they tried to keep the fractious Democrats from imploding once again (Figure 17.1). Dubbed the "apostles of compromise," in 1952,[44] McCormack and his committee wrote a civil rights plank that sought to be progressive enough to mollify liberals but not so liberal as to trouble the white South.[45]

The committee met with hundreds of witnesses; the most notable was the young African-American Baptist minister and doctorate holder from Boston University, the Reverend Martin Luther King, Jr., who in 1955 led a successful and well-publicized pro-integration boycott of the public buses in Montgomery, Alabama.[46]

Figure 17.1 Resolutions Committee, Democratic National Convention, Chicago, 1956; r-l: Chair John McCormack (Mass.), William L. Dawson (Ill.), and unidentified (U.S. House Historian's Office).

Staunch liberal Walter Reuther of the United Auto Workers AFL-CIO pushed for a stronger civil rights plank in support of the Supreme Court's *Brown v. Board of Education* ruling, but John feared public resistance from the South. John forestalled Georgia's Governor Marvin Griffin from challenging the platform from the segregationist side. As reported[47]:

> McCormack shrewdly allotted 30 minutes for debate: 20 minutes for his plank and only 10 minutes for the Reuther crowd. Georgia's Governor Marvin Griffin asked McCormack for permission to debate the South's point of view. "Hell no," retorted McCormack, "We need all our time to fight the boys who are trying to make the plank tougher." Griffin well understood. Said he affably: "Thank you, John. I'll just tell the boys that Yankee sonofabitch wouldn't give me any time."

The moderate platform passed and John had yet again contained a civil rights battle in the Resolutions Committee. There would be no walkouts from the South at this convention.

Stevenson's Nomination and the Vice Presidential Decision: It was clear to all but former President Harry Truman that Adlai Stevenson would be renominated. Truman, who had become deeply disenchanted with Stevenson, came to the convention to support the nomination of New York Governor Averell Harriman whom he had named as secretary of commerce in 1946 to replace Henry Wallace. Sam and John, who had hoped to avoid public displays of party disunity, dissuaded Harry from aggressively pushing the Harriman candidacy and Harry was reported as saying, "All right gentlemen, I'll do whatever my old friend John McCormack wants me to do."[48]

At the 1952 convention Stevenson needed three ballots to be nominated but only one to be renominated in 1956. In spite of Truman's opposition, Stevenson's first ballot count of 905.5 easily outdistanced the 210 for fellow patrician Harriman, the 80 for Texas Senator Lyndon Johnson, and 176.5 scattered votes.[49] Stevenson's easy first ballot victory should have emboldened him but the indecisiveness that hung over his every move manifested itself once again. This time it took the form of throwing the nomination for vice president open to the convention floor. It has been contended that this was the original Stevenson plan by deliberately providing a contrast of competition with the uncontested anointing of Dick Nixon by the Republicans for a second vice presidential nomination.[50]

For Speaker Sam Rayburn, who was presiding over his third consecutive Democratic National Convention, exasperation with Stevenson appeared once again. Rayburn was not delighted with the party's renomination of Stevenson. Stevenson was the first Protestant Democratic nominee to ever lose Rayburn's Texas. Al Smith's 1928 defeat in Texas could be explained by his Catholic religion while Stevenson's 1952 defeat was due to his poor campaign. Also, Stevenson's presidential defeat had cost the Democrats control of the 83rd Congress and it had been a struggle in 1954 to regain control of the House. So once again, it appeared that the congressional Democrats were put afloat upon Adlai Stevenson's leaky raft.

Now Stevenson wanted to jeopardize the party's chances even further by opening up the party's fractured nominating procedures to national television cameras. To the party's hierarchy, this display would be a disaster. How could a nation which saw a party unable to pick a vice presidential nominee trust that same party to act decisively in the face of a nuclear threat from the Soviet Union?[51]

JFK's Roles: Jack Kennedy's formal role at the convention was as chair of the 40-vote Massachusetts delegation, but his role was expanded when he was asked to narrate a film by Hollywood director Dore Schary extolling Democratic accomplishments. Jack's performance was well received and he was surprised and somewhat disappointed when the Stevenson forces asked him to give the major nominating speech for the former governor—the only U.S. Senator invited by the Stevenson camp to deliver a speech for him.[52] To Kennedy this was a signal that he would not be asked by Stevenson to join the ticket as a vice presidential nominee. The Kennedy family dream of the presidency would again be postponed.

Joe Kennedy's initial efforts to have either Lyndon Johnson or Adlai Stevenson commit to Jack being chosen vice president had fallen through and now wholly convinced that Stevenson would once again crash, Joe stayed in Europe. He made some transatlantic calls, but there was no major Joe Kennedy presence. However, to Joe Kennedy this was not the year to reach for the ring, as Kenny O'Donnell recounted[53]:

> The Ambassador's last words to Jack before he went to Europe were a stern warning not to accept the Vice-Presidential spot on the Stevenson ticket even if it were offered to him. The elder Kennedy was convinced, along with everybody else, that Eisenhower would beat Stevenson and that the defeat of the Democratic candidates would be blamed on Kennedy's Catholicism if Kennedy was Stevenson's running-mate, which was sound reasoning.

This was a thought shared by Sam Rayburn, who was rumored to oppose the Kennedy nomination at the convention for fear of southern reluctance toward a Roman Catholic candidate.[54] So these would become Bobby Kennedy's battles, first with his old roommate Kenny O'Donnell leading the charge against Onions Burke, and himself mounting the vice presidential campaign. Bobby had now supplanted his father as the Kennedy family member to whom Jack turned for political advice.

Bobby thought differently and was convinced that Jack's ten years of federal elective office in Washington made him ready for the big time. Richard Nixon, his former colleague on the House Education and Labor Committee, had vaulted into the vice presidency at age 39 after only four years in the House and two in the Senate. To the Kennedys, this made little sense. Dick Nixon lacked good looks, personal charm, family wealth, prestigious college degrees, and a beautiful wife, yet there Dick Nixon sat, only a heartbeat from the presidency. If Nixon could make it without any of these success-inducing accoutrements, how difficult could it be for 39-year-old Jack Kennedy who possessed all of those accoutrements to be elected vice president?

A Vice Presidential Quintet: Four vice presidential candidates emerged early from the ranks of the U.S. Senate: Estes Kefauver of Tennessee, Stevenson's major rival for the nomination in the primaries, John F. Kennedy of Massachusetts, Hubert H.

Humphrey of Minnesota, and Albert A. Gore of Tennessee who hoped to benefit from a Kennedy-Kefauver impasse. A late addition to the list was another northeastern urban Catholic, New York City Mayor Robert F. Wagner, Jr., the son of U.S. Senator Robert F. Wagner whose legislative coauthorship with John McCormack's close friend U.S. Representative William Connery of Massachusetts had produced the Wagner-Connery Labor Relations Act that had created the labor-protecting National Labor Relations Board.

Nominating and Seconding Speeches: Governor Abe Ribicoff of Connecticut made Kennedy's nominating speech. Ribicoff, the son of Polish Jewish immigrants, had served in the House with Jack, 1949–53, but had lost his 1952 Senate contest to financier Republican Prescott Bush, the father of President George H. W. Bush and grandfather of President George W. Bush. Ribicoff, who would later be named as JFK's first Secretary of Health, Education, and Welfare, made a vigorous nominating speech reciting Kennedy's name 11 times in four paragraphs.[55]

Next up was Protestant U.S. Senator George Smathers of Florida, JFK's best friend in the Senate and the only non-family groomsman at Jack's 1953 wedding to Jacqueline Bouvier. The tall, wavy-haired Smathers, sometimes referred to as "Smooch," rivaled Jack Kennedy and Lyndon Johnson in their Capitol Hill womanizing pursuits. Thinking he was the only nominator, Smathers intended to give a five-minute speech extolling Kennedy but soon felt Sam Rayburn's gavel poking him in the back and saying "McCormack." Smathers, like Ribicoff, lavished praise on Jack, stating, "Jack Kennedy's name is magic in Ohio—Cincinnati, Akron—California and other areas. It will be great for us to have him on the ticket." Kennedy's name was mentioned five times in the Smathers address.

In Smathers's recollection, "I found out later that Ted Sorensen had been working on McCormack, who had been a little reluctant, but I guess he finally decided he better not be left out. So I finished up fast and McCormack came on." In the account of Kenny O'Donnell, it was Bobby who "practically carried [John] to the platform."[56] As Ralph Martin noted, "One observer claimed that McCormack practically had to be pushed toward the platform."[57]

Announcing McCormack's arrival was Sam Rayburn, who forcefully declared, "Next I present for a seconding speech, a great leader, one of the greatest leaders that I have ever known in the House of Representatives, my beloved friend, my co-worker, that great Democrat and patriot, John W. McCormack."

Sam gave John a far more enthusiastic introduction than John was to give Jack. Final seconding speeches are intended to set off exuberant floor demonstrations, but John McCormack's seconding speech was lukewarm at best. "They are all good men," John declared, careful not to single out any one of the five contenders. The closing which should have launched a raucous demonstration was especially muted, as John McCormack mentioned Kennedy only once[58]:

I think this year, my colleagues of the Convention, that it is time to go East. Not just for the sake of all those great States alone, but because our selection of the Vice Presidential candidate will bring great strength to our Presidential nominee and to the Democratic Party and will bring great strength to the Congress, from all Congressional Districts throughout the country.

I am here to second the nomination of an experienced man, one to whom public office is a public trust. I am proud and happy to second the nomination of Senator John F. Kennedy. I hope he will be nominated.

John's lack of enthusiasm for Jack's nomination was obvious.

With a Jew making the nominating speech then seconded by a southern Protestant and a Roman Catholic, the Kennedy team put together an ecumenical lineup intended to defuse the religion issue and hopefully put further distance between Jack and his father's long-suspected anti-Semitism. Once again Joe Kennedy's advice was ignored: first in the Burke battle and now in the vice presidential fight.

The Balloting: Senator Kefauver led on the first ballot with 483.5 votes, well short of the 687 needed for victory. Kennedy followed with 304, Gore 178, Wagner 162.5, and Humphrey 134.5, with a scattering of votes for other contenders. Of the 334 southern delegates voting on the first ballot, Kennedy had received 105.5 votes (31.5%). There was little doubt that Kefauver was going to be punished for not signing the Southern Manifesto earlier in the year and the Kennedy candidacy would be their agent of retribution. As George Smathers contended, "The South is always more apt to go for a northerner who doesn't know any better than for a southerner who should know better but doesn't."[59]

On the second ballot, a dramatic movement toward Senator Kennedy materialized as one southern state after another—Alabama, Arkansas, Georgia, Louisiana, North Carolina, South Carolina, Virginia, and Texas, with both Lyndon Johnson and Sam Rayburn voting—ended up in Kennedy's column with John B. Connally, the delegation's spokesman, declaring: "Texas proudly casts its vote for the fighting Senator who wears the scars of battle, that fearless Senator, the next Vice President of the United States, John Kennedy of Massachusetts."[60] While the remark is often ascribed to Johnson, it was Connally who would later share the scars of the murderous attack on Kennedy who delivered it.

At one point in the balloting, Kennedy had 249.5 votes from the south—74.9% of the region's delegates. While some accounts contend that Jack was 38.5 votes from a majority,[61] a closer examination reveals that at his peak, Kennedy had 653.5 votes of 687 needed for the nomination—merely 33.5 votes away. Few anticipated a hotly contested vice presidential battle. No one knew what the real count was because the DNC only paid for an electronic tally board for the presidential nomination, so NBC's television broadcasters Chet Huntley and David Brinkley were seen on camera guessing as to how close the contest had become. At peak, 38.2% of Kennedy's delegate total came from the South.

At the podium stood Sam Rayburn who was obliged under the "unit rule" to vote for Kennedy once his fellow Texans supported Jack, but who wished to nip this thrust toward Kennedy before the party's march toward electoral suicide in the South continued much further. Using the quick gavel techniques that he had perfected over

12 years presiding over the House and the power to recognize friendly delegations, Sam made his move. Ruth Mehrtens of *TIME* magazine vividly set the scene[62]:

> At that point Kennedy stood with 648 votes—just 38½ short of nomination. Over at the Stock Yard Inn, Kennedy, lolling in a private room in his shorts, began dressing to make his triumphal convention appearance. But before he could get there, the Tennessee switch had changed the chemistry of the balloting. Kennedy's vote hung. Kefauver's began to surge. Oklahoma switched from Gore to Kefauver; Minnesota, which had been split between Kefauver and Humphrey, swung solidly behind Estes. Kennedy and Kefauver strained to go over the top, as, in a situation of total confusion, half a dozen standards waved high.

No one was more publicly vocal in his antipathy toward Kennedy than Missouri U.S. Senator Thomas C. Hennings, Jr., who, Sam Rayburn's aide and biographer D. B. Hardeman witnessed, "[was] up on a chair screaming at his delegation, saying, 'We can't go for him. We'll lose the whole state,' he said. 'Jack has voted against every farm bill since he has been in the Senate. We'll lose everything in Missouri if we back Jack.'"[63]

That is why Ruth Mehrtens account of John McCormack's apparent collusion with Hennings had such impact. According to her:

> Missouri's Hennings was seen whispering with Massachusetts' Representative John McCormack, who soon spun and came rushing through the crowd toward the chairman's platform. Yelled McCormack: "Sam! Sam! Missouri!" Sam Rayburn, who had been calmly watching the waving standards before deciding which state to recognize, called on Missouri. Tom Hennings announced a switch of 31½ votes from Humphrey to Kefauver—Estes was so close that it was all over but the shouting. By directing Rayburn's attention to Missouri, John McCormack had settled a score with Jack Kennedy, the rising young politician who last spring took control of the Massachusetts state organization away from McCormack and his old-guard friends.

Actually, Rayburn first selected Tennessee to announce its switch of 32 votes from its more favored son Senator Al Gore to its less favored one Estes Kefauver. And when Missouri moved 31 Humphrey votes, 2.5 Kennedy ones and a half vote for Gore, the 34-vote switch gave Kefauver a 16.5-vote lead (662 to 645.5). Kennedy's momentum was broken. It would take minor switches from another nine delegations before three Humphrey delegates from the District of Columbia gave Kefauver his winning total of 687.5. The final second ballot count was 755½ for Kefauver and 589 for Kennedy, who appeared in time to make the acclamation motion for Kefauver's nomination. Kefauver was now the nominee.

In retrospect, much of John's lack of enthusiasm for Jack had to do with Foster Furcolo's 1954 candidacy for the U.S. Senate. Jack's undermining of the Furcolo campaign had become known to a number of delegates, most likely informed by

John McCormack. In a 1969 interview with T. H. Baker, D. B. Hardeman recalled an encounter between former Democratic National Chairman Stephen Mitchell of Illinois and Jack Kennedy at the convention[64]:

> Well, I don't remember the details, but Foster Furcolo was the nominee for [senator] when Kennedy was running for re-election. He refused to be on a television with Furcolo or something like that. So Steve said, "Jack, would you like some fatherly advice?" He said, "I sure do, Steve." He said, "Go back to Massachusetts and try to get some Democrats elected besides yourself." He said, "That's damn good advice, Steve."
>
>   . . .
>
> Kennedy would have been nominated, in my opinion, had he not knifed Furcolo in Massachusetts. But if he'd do it to Furcolo in his own state, he'd do it to somebody else—that's the way a lot of the pros felt. And I think there was just enough in that very close situation to make the difference.

Sam Rayburn ended the Kennedy vice presidential boom that evening, but it would not deter the family. Rather, JFK's defeat would spur the family onto a "nationalization" of the Kennedy organization. Sam Rayburn would have to accept that reality four short years later. The fallout from the Kennedy defeat jeopardized Jack's relations with the congressional Democrats, who managed the convention and whose general disdain for Kennedy would slow his march to the presidency in 1960 and lessen his legislative success during it.

Further compounding the difficulty for John Kennedy at the convention was longtime family friend Frank Sinatra, the legendary crooner, whose Mafioso and Kennedy family connections often created difficulty for both of them. During one of the pauses in the balloting, Sam Rayburn asked Sinatra to sing that wonderful Texas anthem "The Yellow Rose of Texas." Rayburn's error was not to make the request but to touch Sinatra at the time of making it. "Take the hands off the suit, creep" was Sinatra's response.[65]

The *TIME* magazine account written by Ruth Mehrtens, its Boston-based reporter, put the blame for Kennedy's defeat on John McCormack, who she portrayed as petty and vindictive for settling "a score" with Kennedy. Mehrtens was an acquaintance and later wife of historian-journalist John Galvin of Boston's Dowd Agency, the advertising firm that handled Kennedy's Bay State public relations. Galvin was a golfing buddy of Jack's and a guest at Jack's wedding to Jackie.[66] It appeared as if Mehrtens had a dog in this fight. She also reported an incident between John and Georgia Governor Marvin Griffin that indicated a further lack of enthusiasm on McCormack's part for Kennedy's vice presidential quest.[67] The report of this incident led to even greater mistrust between the Kennedy and McCormack camps. McCormack felt compelled to send a telegram to *TIME* requesting an apology and Governor Griffin threatened legal action against the magazine for their story. The telegram read[68]:

I SENT YOU A TELEGRAM YESTERDAY ON THE FALSEHOOD CARRIED ON PAGE 18 OF YOUR PUBLICATION OF AUGUST 27TH QUOTING A

CONVERSATION WHICH YOUR MAGAZINE INDICATED TOOK PLACE BETWEEN GOVERNOR GRIFFIN OF GEORGIA AND MYSELF. I DID NOT NOTICE ANOTHER STATEMENT WHICH APPEARS ON PAGE 16 CHARGING CERTAIN ACTIONS ON MY PART IN CONNECTION WITH THE MISSOURI DELEGATION AND AFFECTING SENATOR KENNEDY. THAT STATEMENT IS ANOTHER FALSEHOOD. I NEVER TALKED OR YELLED TO SPEAKER RAYBURN ABOUT MISSOURI. I DID ABOUT KENTUCKY. YOU WILL NOTE THAT KENTUCKY SHIFTED TO KENNEDY. I DEMAND A PUBLIC RETRACTION AND APOLOGY FROM YOU.

Governor Griffin and Bob Kennedy also sent complaining telegrams to *TIME*. Bob Kennedy contended that[69] "from my own personal experience, I take issues with the implications of your statements regarding Congressman McCormack's activities during the balloting for the Democratic Vice-Presidential nominee. Congressman McCormack not only spoke seconding Senator Kennedy's nomination, but worked most vigorously during the first and second ballot on his behalf."

Days after the convention ended, and with Jack's Senate office overflowing with speaking engagement requests, he tried to contain the negative fallout, contending in a news interview that "those charges aren't true" and that "you must remember that Mr. McCormack seconded my nomination. That speaks for itself."[70] There was no point in recriminations; Jack's Senate reelection was two years away and the next presidential contest election was two short years after that. The Kennedys realized that they would need John McCormack working with them and not against them if they were to succeed. They had ceased to underestimate John's influence. It would begin a period of quiescence in the conflict between the two clans. An unstated Kennedy-McCormack truce had been established, if not publicly declared.

International crises

The closing months of the 1956 election were competing with two major international crises: first was the aborted Hungarian Revolution against the Communist-dominated Hungarian government, in which its heavily Catholic population hoped for American support in their efforts to liberate themselves. However, no support was forthcoming and the revolution was crushed when Soviet tanks rolled into Budapest. For many Eastern European Catholics, this was yet another betrayal of the West, adding to the dismemberment of Czechoslovakia in 1938 and the invasion of Poland in 1939. John McCormack and other members of Congress with large Eastern European Catholic constituencies were understandably dismayed by the inaction of the Eisenhower Administration.

Complicating the American response to Hungary was that the United States needed Russian support in the United Nations to force a rollback of the joint British-French-Israeli attack on the Suez Canal. In October and November, the Suez Canal had been closed for months, leading to tensions between the United States and Great Britain and

France, which sought to seize the canal from Egypt after its leader Gamal Abdul Nasser had nationalized it in July 1956 and denied Israeli ships passage through it.

Ike, deeply familiar with war-torn Europe, had no intention of provoking a confrontation with the Soviets at this time. With both nations possessing nuclear weapons, the United States and the Soviet Union had now entered the era of Mutually Assured Destruction (MAD).

A second Stevenson defeat

Stevenson's 1956 renomination brought little electoral success to the presidential Democrats.[71] He picked up the electoral votes of Missouri, but lost those of West Virginia, Kentucky, and Louisiana that he had won in 1952. Sam Rayburn had correctly surmised that this would be the presidential outcome, but this time, the congressional Democrats avoided Stevenson and gave him little help. The House and Senate remained Democratic, while the Stevenson-Kefauver ticket was left to crash on its own.

Stevenson's defeat in Massachusetts was especially dramatic. Stevenson's 40.4% of the state's vote was the lowest percentage received by a Democratic presidential nominee since John W. Davis in 1924, and his 208,800 vote plurality loss in 1952 was more than doubled in 1956 as Ike rolled to a 445,007 vote victory.[72]

As in 1952, the 1956 presidential election confirmed the personal popularity of President Dwight Eisenhower. However, in the 1956 election, Ike was unable to help Republicans regain control of the Congress. The congressional Democrats showed a net gain of one seat each in the House and the Senate. It was not their minuscule gain which was impressive; it was their ability to hold both houses of Congress in the face of an overwhelming landslide for the presidential candidate of the opposing party. Dwight Eisenhower was the first president since Whig General Zachary Taylor in 1848 to gain the White House while his party was unable to gain control of either chamber of Congress. To the voting analysts of the Survey Research Center at the University of Michigan, this election was decreed to be a "deviating" one—elections in which the nation's majority party continues to hold the party loyalty of the nation while losing the top spot to the minority party's nominee.[73]

The separation of the presidential and congressional Democrats that had begun in 1948 had worked. Later Republican presidents, such as Richard Nixon in 1968 and 1972 and George Bush in 1988 and even Democrat Bill Clinton in 1996, would find themselves in this plight of the muddled mandate of the American electorate.[74] But in 1956, it was news. It is not a distinction that helps presidents achieve the legislative successes which their administrations need to insure their presidential legacies.

With his impending inaugural on Monday, January 21, 1957, Dwight Eisenhower had become a presidential lame duck. The 22nd Amendment to the Constitution had foreclosed any reelection for Ike and the incoming 85th Congress knew that Ike no longer had to be seriously heeded. The countdown to 1960 had begun.

Although President Eisenhower was reelected and Massachusetts ended up once again in the Republican column, the House Democrats had won in spite of Ike's popularity. It turned out to be a better year for John McCormack than he anticipated. His protégé Foster Furcolo was now governor, Senator Jack Kennedy's ambition had been momentarily tamed, and the best news was that his nephew Edward J. McCormack, Jr. had emerged as a serious statewide contender. Now John McCormack had a reason to honor the family truce.

Foster Furcolo elected governor

Foster Furcolo made a successful comeback in the 1956 gubernatorial election. The departure of two-term Republican Governor Christian A. Herter led Republicans to nominate Lt. Governor Sumner G. Whittier; with a name combining two nineteenth-century Massachusetts luminaries, U.S. Senator Charles Sumner and the Essex County poet John Greenleaf Whittier, he was their choice. But Whittier was no Brahmin. His roots in rough-edged Everett and his degree from Boston University were tip-offs that he was really a swamp Yankee, that centuries-old tribe of poor Protestants who lived on the unfertile marshlands of the North and South Shores of Boston. Furcolo of East Longmeadow, the son of a surgeon, held two Yale University degrees and was better-credentialed in the status-dependent politics of 1950s Massachusetts.[75] Furcolo chose not to attend the national convention and there were no indications of a repeat of the Kennedy-Furcolo hostility this year as had occurred two years earlier, a sign that the post-convention undeclared truce between the Kennedys and the McCormacks was in place.

Lacking the Brahmin roots which Republicans held dear, Whittier was defeated by Furcolo, 1,234,618 votes to 1,096,759. Furcolo's 52.8% of the vote was impressive in light of President Eisenhower's 59.3% landslide over Adlai Stevenson; Furcolo ran 286,000 votes ahead of Stevenson. Avoiding Stevenson had been the right strategy. That had been the Democratic lesson. The Republican lesson from this election was that Whittier's loss reinforced the fears of many state Republicans that they had dipped too long in the Yankee pool. Since they were already running low on electable Brahmins, their fortunes would dwindle further if they continued to nominate only lesser-bred Yankee WASPs.

While John's protégé Furcolo had won the governorship, his nephew Eddie ran a very credible general election race with incumbent Republican Attorney General George Fingold, losing only by 39,243 votes (50.6% to 48.9%) of close to 2.8 million votes cast.[76] During the fall campaign, Fingold made charges that would later echo in Eddie's 1962 U.S. Senate primary contest with Edward M. Kennedy, Jack's youngest brother. As reported in the *Globe*,[77] "Fingold described his opponent as an untried and inexperienced lawyer of only four years who 'deludes himself into thinking he can ride into high office on the "Name's the Same" ticket'. Such a belief, said Fingold, 'can only be attributed to arrogance or ignorance.'"

For an initial statewide candidacy, Eddie's vote total impressed other Massachusetts politicians and indicated that the McCormacks had not suffered any serious loss of influence in their battles with the Kennedys. With John McCormack continuing as House Majority Leader, protégé Foster Furcolo as governor and nephew Eddie a serious comer in statewide politics, the two families had achieved a level of relative parity that made a truce desirable and open conflict subsided.

Ike's second inaugural

Every presidential inaugural is freighted with history and Dwight D. Eisenhower's second inaugural on January 21, 1957, was no exception. Ike was the first victorious Republican to be sworn in twice since William McKinley in 1901; the first Republican president ever to have been sworn in twice with the same vice president, and like Lincoln, he was sworn in by a Chief Justice he had appointed to the post. The major uniqueness of this event was that it had been 108 years since 1849 and only the second time that a president faced a Congress where both houses were controlled by the opposition party. The first and last time it had occurred was when fellow career military man Major General Zachary Taylor was sworn in at the midpoint of the nineteenth century.

On January 3, 1957, Sam Rayburn was elected Speaker of the House for the seventh time and was joined, once again for the seventh time, by Majority Leader John W. McCormack. Rayburn had surpassed Henry Clay's six speakerships, and John's beginning of his 14th year of service as House floor leader had surpassed the 12 years of New York Republican Sereno Payne's term as chair of Ways and Means, 1899–1911, then the de facto Majority Floor Leader.[78]

Thanks to the Democratic House victory of 1956, John returned to the Joint Inaugural Committee, a slight but welcome sign that he might have a larger role to play in the upcoming Congress than in the previous ones. President Eisenhower's appointment book records that on January 21, 1957, "McCormack escorts DDE and MDE to the Inauguration."[79] It is the only mention of John in the White House presence of President Eisenhower in the two years between June 8, 1956, and May 25, 1958. John had virtually disappeared from Ike's political consciousness.

While John had disappeared from Ike's world, Sam Rayburn was still a key part of it. Ike's second inaugural address was free of the triumphalism to which these speeches often succumbed. Ike's speech was a true "reach across the aisle," and much more inclusive than his first one in 1953. President Eisenhower told his aides of an unsolicited eruption of praise from Speaker Rayburn for his 1957 address. Eisenhower speechwriter Emmet John Hughes recalled that Ike told him that Sam had said, "I'd never say this publicly, and I'd never admit it to another Republican, but that was just the finest speech I've heard in forty-six years in this town."[80]

Civil Rights and the divided 85th Congress

The South's hopes that the Southern Manifesto of 1956 would quell integrationist sentiment in Congress were dashed in the election. Demographic analysis of the election revealed that a large number of blacks had voted for the Republican Party. The 52-point gap among African-American voters between Stevenson and Eisenhower in 1952 (76% to 24%) had shrunken to a 22-point gap in their 1956 rematch (61% to 39%).[81] It would be the highest percentage of African Americans voting Republican since the inception of the New Deal, thanks to Earl Warren's authorship of both the *Brown v. Board of Education* decisions of 1954 and 1955 and the endorsement of President Eisenhower by Harlem's mercurial and flamboyant Democratic U.S. Representative Adam Clayton Powell.[82] Blacks were seen as returning to their ancestral political home, the Republican Party.

Always sensitive to partisan electoral shifts in the Republican Party, Ike's shrewd Attorney General Herb Brownell had his Justice Department staff draft legislation that if passed, would be the first major piece of civil rights legislation since Reconstruction had ended 80 years earlier. Earlier efforts had failed but Ike's landslide that included a majority of southern electoral votes had given the Administration more political authority.

The Civil Rights Act of 1957 would be the most controversial piece of legislation coming before the 85th Congress. This act created the executive Commission on Civil Rights and established a Civil Rights Division in the Department of Justice.[83] It also empowered the attorney general to seek court injunctions against obstruction and deprivation of voting rights. If it was to be passed, two congressional obstacles had to be surmounted—the House Rules Committee and the Senate Judiciary Committee—both chaired by segregationists.

There would be relatively little difficulty in the House. Led by Manny Celler of New York and John McCormack, the bill easily passed through the House Judiciary Committee.[84] Difficulties that it might have encountered in the House Rules Committee, chaired by segregationist Howard W. Smith, were obviated by Republican Hugh D. Scott of Pennsylvania, who as National Party chair in 1948 had worked closely with Herb Brownell for the Tom Dewey-Earl Warren ticket. Scott and fellow moderate Henry J. Latham (Rep-NY) pushed the bill through the committee onto the House floor. In the initial June 18 House vote, the vote was 295–124. As the first civil rights bill to be passed since Reconstruction, southern resistance was virtually unanimous as 100 of the 101 southern Democrats voted "nay" and the 2 southern Republicans split 1–1. The lone Democratic exception was Florida's Dante Fascell, a northern-born native of Bridgehampton, New York, who had also refused to sign the Southern Manifesto. He was not punished for his vote as the voters of his Dade County district reelected him to 17 subsequent terms.[85] Although it was known that Texan Senator Lyndon Johnson was pushing hard for the 1957 Civil Rights Act, none of his fellow Texans in the House voted for the bill.

It was in the Senate where the bill would encounter serious problems, as segregationist Senate Judiciary Chair James Eastland of Mississippi awaited to eviscerate it. Well aware of Eastland's attitudes, Majority Leader Johnson chose not to submit the bill to the Judiciary Committee but brought the House bill directly to the Senate floor entrusting the floor management to longtime liberal U.S. Senator Hubert H. Humphrey (DFL-Minn.). The bill initially passed on August 7, but it was not until August 29, following the 24-hour and 18-minute filibuster of South Carolina's J. Strom

Thurmond, that the conference report was sent to the White House by a vote of 60–15 in the Senate.

Approved September 9, the Civil Rights Act of 1957 was a modest piece of legislation, focusing as it did wholly upon voting rights, but it was the first legislative breakthrough in civil rights since the previous century. Majority Leader Johnson with thinly disguised presidential ambitions needed a legislative triumph that would gain him favorable publicity beyond the South. This act accomplished that goal.

The McCormack-Kennedy truce

On August 30, 1957, the 1st Session of the 85th Congress concluded. It had been a tough session with lingering animosity over the Civil Rights Act, so while Washington would take its time to heal, so too would the McCormack and Kennedy clans. With the 1958 election on the horizon when John, Jack, and Foster would all seek reelection and young Eddie McCormack would renew his quest to be attorney general, it would be essential that there be no repeat of the 1956 public animosity among them all. To accomplish this end, it was announced on September 12 that there would be a November 16 testimonial dinner to "fete" Kennedy and McCormack.[86] The dinner was held in Boston's Commonwealth Armory, large enough to accommodate the thousands of dinner guests and the egos of these contentious Massachusetts politicians.

Key Kennedy operative Larry O'Brien addressed the public reconciliation in his memoir *No Final Victories*[87]:

> One obstacle we faced was the ill will of John McCormack and his followers as a result of the state committee fight. To try to smooth this over, we arranged for the state committee to hold a Kennedy-McCormack unity dinner, attended by some six thousand Democrats—the biggest dinner ever held in Massachusetts. The dinner didn't solve all our problems, but it gave the political columnists something positive to write about, instead of constant stories of a Kennedy-McCormack feud.

Sputnik panics the nation

The major news of this year occurred on October 4, 1957, when the Soviet Union launched "Sputnik 1," an earth-orbiting satellite. American reaction was immediate and intense, and the rush to catch up in the race for outer space was deeply felt in Congress. A month later, the anxiety of the American public grew greater with the successful launch of Sputnik 2, with a live dog named Laika inside. While some wits would dub the second satellite as "Muttnik," the Congress was not amused. Both Houses acted to create high-powered select and special committees on astronautics and space exploration.

On January 7, 1958, the first day of the 2nd Session of the 85th Congress, Representative Kenneth B. Keating (Rep-NY) introduced a resolution to create a joint committee of Congress on outer space. A month later, before action had been taken on

Keating's resolution, the Senate passed legislation creating a special Senate committee to study the same issues, making the joint committee proposal unlikely. Eager to insert himself at the forefront of this issue, Senate Majority Leader Lyndon Johnson announced the formation of the Senate Special Committee on Space and Astronautics on February 10, 1958, with 13 original members and himself as its chair.[88]

The House responded with the Select Committee on Astronautics and Space Exploration created by H. Res. 496 on March 5, 1958. Later that day Speaker Sam Rayburn named House Majority Leader John McCormack as its chair and House Minority Leader Joe Martin as its ranking minority member.[89] It passed without debate or controversy by voice vote on the day it was introduced and its 13 members were appointed immediately following its passage. Minority Whip Leslie C. Arends was named the second-ranking Republican on the committee. With high-level bipartisan support behind it, the House was committed to making the committee a standing one, and H. Res. 580 passed on July 21, 1958, did just that, effective at the opening of the 86th Congress. It was the first new standing committee in the House created since the passage of the Legislative Reorganization Act of 1946.

It is doubtful if any members of the House knew that John McCormack had yet to fly in an airplane, so his being named chairman of a committee dealing with space exploration was somewhat ironic. The party ratio was seven Democrats and six Republicans. Representative Kenneth B. Keating, who had worked hard for the establishment of the committee, was assigned to the fifth minority rank, just ahead of future House Minority Leader and President Gerald R. Ford, Jr. (Rep-Mich.). In addition, the select committee was given the authority to report legislation to the full House, a power normally reserved for the standing committees.

With Majority Leaders McCormack and Johnson chairing their respective space committees, it is no surprise that meaningful legislation passed quickly through the committees to the floors of the respective chambers where positive votes awaited them. The most notable of the acts passed were the Reorganization Plan No. 1 of 1958, which created the Office of Defense and Civil Mobilization;[90] the National Aeronautics and Space Act of 1958 which created a new civilian agency, the National Aeronautics and Space Administration (NASA), to direct the nation's scientific activities relating to all nonmilitary aspects of outer space;[91] and the Department of Defense Reorganization Act of 1958 which authorized the secretary of defense to consolidate common supply and service functions for the Army, Navy, and Air Force and to assign responsibility for development and operation of new weapon systems.[92]

The House's granting the Select Committee on Astronautics and Space Exploration authority to submit legislation directly to the Rules Committee was unprecedented for a select committee but with three floor leaders as members, it was not much of a stretch. John McCormack was at last able to create legislation rather than to just facilitate it. These are the triumphs for true legislators. Renamed as the standing committee on Science and Astronautics at the opening of the 86th Congress in 1959, John stepped aside as chair and was replaced by Overton Brooks (Dem-La.). John remained on the committee and took the second majority slot, while Joe Martin, the newly demoted minority leader, retained the ranking minority one.

More spending and admitting Alaska

The 85th Congress also did what it enjoys most: passing bills to spend federal monies in one another's districts. Early in 1958, Congress passed the Federal-Aid Highway Act of 1958, which authorized funding for a $3.26 billion Federal road-building program for fiscal years 1959–61.[93] The extraordinary activity of this "divided" government Congress was also evident in the legislation to add Alaska to the Union. This was the first new state admitted since Arizona in 1912 and the 46 years represented the longest gap ever between the admissions of states to the Union. Negative concerns about Alaska's "non-contiguity" with any of the other states were outweighed by the vastness of its mineral resources and its strategic location across the Bering Strait from the Soviet Union. Approved July 7, 1958, Alaska became the nation's 49th state.[94]

In its closing weeks, Congress also passed the Transportation Act of 1958 authorizing the Interstate Commerce Commission to operate a $500 million program of guaranteed loans to aid the Nation's railroads.[95] It also gave the ICC full authority to adjust interstate railroad rates and power, regardless of state law, and to permit railroads to discontinue interstate service if it found the service to be an "unduly burden."

Anxiety over Sputnik had domestic repercussions that would lead to the passage of one of the most far-reaching educational bills. This was the National Defense Education Act of 1958 that established a $1 billion program designed to improve the teaching of science, mathematics, and foreign languages.[96] Approved September 2, 1958, it authorized the U.S. Commissioner of Education to lend $295 million from fiscal 1959 through fiscal 1962 to university and college student loan funds to enable needy students to continue their education. It also provided grants to the states for public schools and 10-year loans to private schools for the purchase of equipment to be used in teaching science, mathematics, and foreign languages. The act authorized 5,500 three-year graduate fellowships, with preference to those students interested in teaching; $15 million a year for grants to state educational agencies; $32 million to colleges establishing advanced institutes for teaching modern foreign languages to train public school teachers; $18 million for federal grants for research into modern teaching aids; and $60 million in state grants for vocational education.

As the 85th Congress came to its conclusion, Sam and John pushed through legislation to provide financial assistance for their old friend Harry Truman. Entitled the Former Presidents Act, the legislation provided former presidents with a taxable annual pension of $25,000 and an annual allowance of up to $50,000 for an office staff.[97] Former Republican President Herbert Hoover also benefited from this legislation, which gave the act a bipartisan flavor, but Hoover's economic circumstances were far more comfortable and warranted less taxpayer assistance than did those of Harry Truman.

Attorney General Eddie McCormack

As in 1956, the pre-primary convention contest in 1958 for the Democratic endorsement for attorney general of Massachusetts was a bitter three-way brawl between Joe Ward,

Chub Peabody, and Eddie McCormack. It was a hard-fought battle but Eddie's close vote on the third ballot gave him the momentum for the endorsement.[98] While Peabody and ex-Rep. John Zamparelli of Medford were announced as Eddie's likely primary opponents,[99] everything changed on August 31, when Republican Attorney General George Fingold died in office.

Fingold was an energetic and politically ambitious lawyer who had been first elected in 1952 along with Republican Governor Christian A. Herter. Fingold, a Jewish Republican with a strong law and order record, was to be the Republicans' experiment in diversity. The Democratic Party, which had been almost an exclusive Irish Catholic enclave, had just nominated and elected the Italian-descended Foster Furcolo to the governorship in 1956. If Democrats could move beyond their ethnic base, why couldn't the Republicans? In their effort to open their party to non-Yankee leaders, George Fingold was an ideal choice. The Suffolk University–educated Fingold had a solid reputation and was a proven vote-getter. So he was tapped to thwart the 1958 reelection bid of Governor Foster Furcolo and to recapture the statehouse for the party.

Fingold's death ended that dream and ex-House Speaker Charles Gibbons of Stoneham, who planned a primary challenge to Fingold, was chosen as the party's candidate for governor. Gibbons was a tall, gray-haired, distinguished-looking legislator, but he was born in Kentucky, a graduate of Barbourville Baptist College and the owner of a delivery service.[100] He may have been a Protestant, but he wasn't even a swamp Yankee. Old-line Brahmins despaired. The Gibbons choice melted away Governor Furcolo's early worries and his quarter million vote plurality renewed his dreams of a seat in the U.S. Senate.

In September, Eddie was named as the interim attorney general by a joint panel of House and Senate members.[101] Governor Furcolo was pleased by the choice. Furcolo and John McCormack were longtime allies and helping Ed McCormack, the nephew and surrogate son of John McCormack, gain a post of power and promise was not a difficult decision. A few weeks later, Eddie would surprise Boston old-timers by creating a Civil Rights Division in the Office of Attorney General. He named Yale Law-educated Gerald A. Berlin of Cambridge for that post. It was Eddie's single-most important appointment as the McCormack-Berlin team pushed harder for civil rights than any previous attorney general team in Massachusetts, and their active partnership helped Eddie's office to acquire a national reputation.[102]

Eddie McCormack won the Democratic primary over Peabody and went on to victory in the November contest defeating Governor's Councilor Christian A. Herter, Jr.[103] However, little of this mattered to the national press as they prowled through the state speculating how well U.S. Senator Jack Kennedy would do in his reelection bid.

The 1958 midterm elections

It was not only Soviet satellites that troubled the American public in this election. A deep recession hit the economy and the Republican Party was blamed for it. The four months of March through June in 1958 saw high inflation at 3.6% in March and high unemployment of 7.4% in April.[104] The Eisenhower administration had seemingly lost control of the economy and the Gallup Poll of March 27 to April 1 reported Eisenhower's popularity below 50% for the first and only time.

The 1958 election shattered the near-parity between the parties that had existed in the Senate for eight years (1951–58). Democrats made a net gain of 15 seats and now held a 30-seat margin over the Senate Republicans (64–34)—their largest margin since the 1940 election. Similarly, the House Democrats picked up an additional 50 seats and now held a 130-seat margin over the House Republicans (283–153). President Eisenhower's congressional party had been soundly repudiated and his legislative agenda was in for a very rough ride.

Massachusetts Results: With Furcolo as governor and Eddie as attorney general, John's protégés now held statewide office with far more power than JFK's state Chair Pat Lynch ever did. It was very clear to the Kennedys that John's people were well-positioned to undermine his presidential bid should they choose to do so. It was essential that Jack not encounter a repeat of the monumental embarrassment of his fifth place showing in the 1956 presidential primary. If ever there was a time for a truce in the Kennedy-McCormack family feud, this was it. The key element was Eddie, John's surrogate son. While Jocko, Knocko's oldest son, once flirted with a political career, his enjoyment of the good life took precedence over the numbing grind and endless public scrutiny that accompanied a career in politics. So it would be Eddie, the studious younger nephew, who would follow John into political life.

With the truce in place, ex-President Harry Truman, who loved John McCormack and distrusted the Kennedys, made a return visit to Boston as part of the 1958 campaign. Two years earlier in February 1956, the Truman visit was followed by open warfare between the two clans in the primary and the state committee. With Jack, John, Foster, and Eddie all seeking reelection in November, harmony was essential and visible signs of conflict were plastered over.

Preelection forecasts predicted a large Democratic victory in 1958 and John, Foster, and Eddie appeared to be secure in their seats. So did Jack Kennedy, but his real opponent was not the hapless Republican attorney Vincent J. Celeste; it was the electoral expectations bar set for him as the national press swarmed through the state during those months. The electoral bar for Kennedy was set at different heights by the reporters who looked forward to a Kennedy presidential candidacy and by those who did not. It didn't matter. Jack defeated Celeste 73.2% to 26.2% with a plurality of 874,610 votes out of 1.86 million votes cast. Kennedy's plurality may have not been a million votes but his vote percentage was well beyond that of his likely rivals for the presidential nomination, and he would be tough to stop. The 1960 Kennedy campaign would not repeat the unfortunate mishaps of the 1956 Democratic Convention.

John was reelected once again as were his two House protégés Tip O'Neill and Eddie Boland. They would be joined by Jim Burke, whose South Shore congressional district was adjacent to John's. Burke had earlier tried for statewide posts but had run afoul of the pre-primary endorsement conventions. He would now join Tip and Eddie as John's most loyal lieutenants. To further insure Jim Burke's place in the House, John was able to get him elected to the House Ways and Means Committee, the very committee that had launched John's career in the House leadership. Jim Burke now joined O'Neill on Rules and Boland on Appropriations as McCormack loyalists in the House's three most important committees. John now had his own set of "eyes and ears" to keep him abreast of what was happening in the House's committee rooms. It would soon become clear why John would need those "eyes and ears."

Waiting for 1960

The contrast between the two "divided government" Congresses of the 85th and 86th could not have been clearer. The closely balanced 85th Congress worked well with President Eisenhower and produced an impressive legislative record. The overwhelmingly Democratic 86th Congress was the most one-sided congressional opposition faced by a president in the twentieth century and it took a legislative hiatus from the Eisenhower agenda.

Democrats were indifferent to the Eisenhower agenda. It was Ike's last Congress, not because he was ill like Woodrow Wilson in 1919, not because he was unpopular like Harry Truman in 1951, and not because he disdained the job like Calvin Coolidge in 1927, but because of the 22nd Amendment. That amendment, designed by Republicans to prevent another Franklin Roosevelt from serving in office for life, had claimed its first victim, and it was one of their own—the most popular Republican incumbent since Teddy Roosevelt. The irony was rich indeed. Compounding the difficulty was internecine hostilities within the Republican Party's Eastern moderate wing and its Midwestern conservative wing. Five of the past presidential nominations—Wendell Willkie in 1940, Thomas E. Dewey in 1944 and 1948, and Dwight Eisenhower in 1952 and 1956—had gone to these "Eastern Establishment" Republicans whose willingness to accept much of the New Deal's legislation had rendered them as "me too" nominees in the eyes of the party's staunch conservatives.

The 1958 election provided the "Eastern Establishment" Republicans with yet another champion—Nelson A. Rockefeller, grandson of both Standard Oil founder John D. Rockefeller and U.S. Senate Republican baron Nelson Aldrich of Rhode Island. Nelson Rockefeller had soundly defeated incumbent Democrat and fellow millionaire's son W. Averell Harriman in the 1958 race for governor of New York State, the nation's largest state, and for more than a century, the country's leading source of presidential nominees. Governor Rockefeller was now ready to assume the mantle of the Republican Party's presidential wing.

The congressional Republicans were not pleased believing that the presidential Republicans' "me too" philosophical agenda had failed them disastrously in the 1958 elections.[105] Internal bickering erupted within both the House and the Senate. The first victim of the conservative congressional Republicans was House Minority Leader Joe Martin. After 20 years of leading the House Republicans, four as Speaker of the House, the Republican Conference called Joe Martin's number. Cited by insiders was Martin's closeness to Sam Rayburn.[106] The contest within the Conference was closer than expected, but when the votes were tallied, Indiana's Charlie Halleck gained the minority leadership, 74 to 70.[107] Joe Martin hoped that the Eisenhower Administration would make some calls on his behalf. The calls never came, and Joe Martin was removed from his leadership post. After his defeat, the disconsolate Martin went to Sam's 77th birthday party and the two old party rivals and close personal friends were reportedly in tears as they embraced one another.[108] The surviving Republicans would be a diminished band but a more ferociously conservative one.

Joe did not return to his old assignment on the House Rules Committee but rather was named ranking minority member on the newly formed standing House Aeronautics and Space Exploration Committee. He served eight years on that committee until he was defeated for renomination in 1966 by fellow Republican Margaret Heckler. Joe Martin never again contended for a leadership post but his 20 years leading the House Republicans remains the longest stint ever in the House GOP's top leadership post.

The Senate Republicans also had a brutal leadership battle. A vacancy in the minority leadership occurred when California's Bill Knowland made his ill-considered run for the governorship. Knowland was badly beaten and returned to his publishing career with the *Oakland Tribune*. The leading contender was conservative Illinois Senator Everett McKinley Dirksen, who had been first elected assistant floor leader in 1957 and in 1959; he defeated the moderate John Sherman Cooper of Kentucky, 20–14. Dirksen had hoped to name his ally Karl Mundt of South Dakota as assistant leader. Had this occurred, both Senate Republican leadership posts would have been held by conservative Midwesterners. To many of the Eastern moderates, most notably Vermont's George Aiken, Dirksen was overreaching and upsetting the balance between the party's two major wings. Aiken threatened to walk out of the meeting if Dirksen succeeded. Not surprisingly, it was New Hampshire's manipulative Styles Bridges, an easterner by location but a conservative by inclination, who saved the day by promoting California's young moderate Thomas Kuchel for the assistant leader slot and Aiken did not walk.[109]

The 86th Congress opens

While Republicans cannibalized themselves, the House and Senate Democrats appeared to have no such problems. The afterglow of their success led to uncontested renominations of their leadership teams in both chambers.[110] In the House, Speaker Sam Rayburn and Majority Floor Leader John W. McCormack were reinstalled in their posts, and the Senate Democratic Majority Leader, Lyndon Johnson of Texas, and Majority Whip, Mike Mansfield of Montana, were reelected without opposition. Mansfield, like McCormack, was a Roman Catholic, now in his third year as second-in-command of the Senate Democrats, while John McCormack was now in his 19th year in second place. These were the leadership teams which were to present their party's legislative cases before the two chambers in 1959.

McCormack Blocks Khrushchev Capitol Speech: White House ambivalence toward John McCormack reappeared in March 1959 when the *New York Times* reported that "McCormack's name was omitted from the lists of two groups of Congressional leaders invited to the White House [last week] for briefings on the Berlin crisis. Mr. McCormack's colleagues wondered if he was being snubbed." He would later get a private invitation to the White House.[111]

In an effort to lessen Cold War tensions later in 1959, the Eisenhower Administration invited Soviet Premier Nikita Khrushchev to make a multiday visit to the United States highlighting a number of social and political events. Initially, a number of congressmen were hoping that Khrushchev would make a speech before a joint session of Congress. However, John McCormack and other Catholic congressmen, bitter over the crushing of the 1957 revolution in heavily Catholic Hungary, made a vocal and concerted effort to prevent Khrushchev from speaking before Congress. Although the move was endorsed by other Democratic leaders, such as Senate Majority Leader Lyndon B. Johnson, "House Democratic Leader John W. McCormack of Massachusetts said Mr. Eisenhower had made a mistake by inviting Khrushchev."[112] When it was announced that Khrushchev was intending to visit Congress, McCormack made his opinions clear[113]:

> The vocal opposition is led by House Majority Leader John W. McCormack (D-Mass.). In addition, Rep. Walter H. Judd (R-Minn.) and Senators Style Bridges (R-N.H.), Paul H. Douglas (D-Ill.) and Thomas J. Dodd (D-Conn.) have set up a Committee for Freedoms for All Peoples to counter some of the propaganda hay they figure Khrushchev will try to make on his trip.
>
> The group yesterday put out a statement calling on the public to demonstrate "solidarity with the victims of communism by a concerted manifestation of national mourning" during the Russian's visit. At one point, congressional sources said yesterday, a Khrushchev speech to a joint session was just about set. But McCormack's loud and bitter opposition seems to have been the key factor in killing the idea.

Drew Pearson's nationally syndicated column of August 22 identified the key actors in this drama as Congressman John McCormack, "considered the leading congressional spokesman for the Catholic hierarchy"; Senator Jack Kennedy, "foremost Catholic in Congress, does not share the McCormack-Dodd view of the Khrushchev visit"; and Secretary of State Christian Herter, "fearful that such a movement . . . may completely upset Eisenhower's hope that the Khrushchev visit may write a new chapter for peace."[114] That all three men represented adjacent Boston congressional districts for six years, 1947– 53, and that John's nephew Attorney General Eddie McCormack had defeated Herter's son the previous November and would later lose a Senate primary to Jack's brother in 1962 indicate the remarkable intersection of Massachusetts dynastic candidacies with national politics. The anti-Khrushchev protest exacerbated tensions between the Eisenhower White House and McCormack to such a degree that before the year would end, McCormack would pass on a personal invitation to a briefing of other congressional leaders with Eisenhower.[115] Clearly, neither man was impressed with the other.

In the closing months of 1959, the Soviets had launched Lunar 2 which hit the moon. Three weeks later on October 4, they launched Lunar 3 which orbited the

540   *John William McCormack*

moon and photographed most of its surface. The space gap was widening. A semi-rapprochement occurred early in 1960 when McCormack was invited six times to the Eisenhower White House, two of which were off-the-record meetings with Ike. The most important appears to have been the January 14 meeting when Ike and his advisor Bryce Harlow met with McCormack and fellow Space Committee members Brooks and Martin and the committee's lead scientific consultant Dr. T. Keith Glennan to address the widening gap between the American and Soviet space programs.[116] While the American space program would launch Tiros 1 and Discovery 14, a spy satellite, each nation was readying itself for the big news: the first launching of a man in space and a declaration of victory in this propaganda war between them. Ike now needed John's support.

The rise of the Democratic Study Group

Amateur Democrats: During the 1950s, a new breed of northern Democrats emerged who were better educated, wealthier, younger, and more suburban than the traditional city Democrats. Denoted by James Q. Wilson as the "amateur Democrat," these activists were much more ideological than the usual Democrats.[117] Wilson studied "club politics" in the nation's three largest cities—New York, Chicago, and Los Angeles—the former two of which had long-established political party machines, New York's Tammany Hall and Chicago's Kelly-Nash-Daley machine. He learned that these newer Democrats were far more interested in liberal philosophy and political reform than the patronage-hungry regular Democrats were. They could not be bought off nor did they appreciate the condescending tone of the regulars. These "amateur Democrats" represented a clear challenge to the existing big-city South alliance that had dominated Democratic politics for the previous quarter century and had been led by Sam Rayburn and John McCormack. Massachusetts had similar stirrings from its large number of politically active liberal intellectuals in their Commonwealth Organization of Democrats (COD) that was very sympathetic to Eddie McCormack's aspirations, if not necessarily to John's.[118]

It was the 1958 election when these young, liberal, well-educated Democratic candidates made their memorable congressional appearance with a net gain of 49 House seats throughout the North and the West. These new Democrats provided troops for the nascent congressional reform movement created by liberal U.S. Representatives Eugene McCarthy of Minnesota and Lee Metcalf of Montana.[119] While McCarthy gained election to the Senate in 1958 and Metcalf, the group's first chair, would follow in 1962, the sentiment they had generated in the House led to the formal creation of a reformist caucus, the Democratic Study Group (DSG). This massive influx of young well-educated Democrats was not linked to either the southern or big-city wings of the Democratic Party. They were pro-civil rights reformist liberals who were embarrassed by the party's segregationist wing and not as willing to defer to the southern hierarchy that chaired most standing committees and seemed to control the party's floor leaders. George Goodwin statistically confirmed the extent to which congressional southerners were protected by the seniority system.[120] Seniority became the target of the DSG liberals as they sought to change House rules to prevent senior southern Democrats from strangling the aspirations of African Americans. They were well aware that African-American voters had lessened their support of Democratic presidential candidate Adlai Stevenson in 1956 and were fearful that those voters would return to the Republican Party.

Sam Rayburn was always distrustful of large House majorities, feeling that they were much more difficult to control than smaller ones, so while he generally welcomed the newer members, he was well aware that their size and general cohesiveness might present a problem for his management of House business. As he closed on his 77th birthday, he was unsure if he had the energy to manage the bumptious new arrivals. John McCormack, who had even less cachet with them than Rayburn, was also anxious about what these newer members might do. It was John's linking of the big-city Democrats and the South that had given him power. He had minimal standing among these well-educated suburbanites who arrived on the House's doorstep in 1959. It was Dick Bolling of Missouri, a favorite of Sam Rayburn's, who would emerge as a leader of the DSG. Bolling, a native of New York City, was raised in northern Alabama and represented the Kansas City district where Harry Truman lived, so he had links to all three groups within the Democratic Party and saw himself as a future leader of the House. He and Rayburn had become quite close in the aftermath of Bolling's divorce, when the two would have dinner together twice a week with Sam sharing reminiscences and Dick recounting tales of House history that he had gleaned from his omnivorous reading.[121] Rayburn would introduce Bolling to his second wife Jim Grant, a Texas heiress and political activist.

These liberal Democrats met regularly to map out legislative proposals that would push the party's agenda in a more leftward direction. Before the next decade had ended, the DSG was the largest legislative service organization in the Congress and its agenda often took precedence over that of the party's reluctant floor leadership. However, the DSG's control over the House Democrats was a decade away. With the upcoming 1960 presidential election, the DSG was split between the candidacies of U.S. Senators Hubert Humphrey, their longtime hero and Minnesota ally of Gene McCarthy, and the more electable John F. Kennedy, as well as two-time nominee Adlai Stevenson, as their champion for the liberal reformist agenda.

The 1959 Legislative Output: The First Session of the 86th Congress was very sparse legislatively. One item of unfinished business was the admission of the State of Hawaii to the Union. The act of admission provided for the formal ratification of the state constitution adopted by the Hawaiians on November 7, 1950.

The debate over the admission of Hawaii was unique. Like Alaska, it was a territory not contiguous with any of the states within the Union. However unlike Alaska, it was not even part of the North American continent nor technically within the Western Hemisphere. Strategic considerations played a role in the Hawaii admission, much as they did with Alaska, but there was a strong undercurrent of racism in the debate. The Polynesian ancestry of many Hawaiian citizens, linked to Japan and China, troubled a number of congressmen, including Sam Rayburn. It was they who challenged the wisdom of admitting a state with a clear multiracial government.[122] So John

McCormack had to lead the House majority while a reluctant Sam Rayburn watched as the House passed the bill on March 12, 1959, by a 323–89 vote. House Democrats voted 203–65 for admission with all but two of the opposing Democrats coming from the states of the Confederacy. The Republicans voted 120–24 for the bill, with the seven southern Republicans casting three votes for and four votes against admission. A day earlier, the Senate had passed the bill 76–15, with Democrats splitting 46–14 and Republicans 30–1.

Labor Legislation: The continuing issue of labor union "racketeering" appeared on the legislative agenda and was passed as the Landrum-Griffin Labor Management Reporting and Disclosure Act of 1959. Its passage derived from testimony presented to the Senate Select Committee on Improper Activities in the Labor or Management Field that had been named on January 30, 1957. This committee consisted of eight members split evenly between Democrats and Republicans. Government Operations Chair John L. McClellan (Dem-Ark.), generally regarded as one of the Senate's leading racists,[123] chaired the select committee, but let the second-slotted Jack Kennedy and his brother Robert F. Kennedy, its lead counsel, monopolize the committee's televised public hearings. It was the two Kennedy brothers working in tandem that gained most of the committee's national visibility with its most dramatic moments occurring when Majority Counsel Robert Kennedy confronted Teamster boss Jimmy Hoffa.[124] It made great television and even greater politics for the Kennedy brothers, who were able to use these public confrontations as proof of their toughness and their willingness to challenge unsavory elements within the labor union movement that had been a longtime major component of the Democratic Party's presidential coalition.

The major bill emerging from these concerns was a House bill, named for its cosponsors, two mid-level members of the House Education and Labor Committee—Democrat Phillip M. Landrum of Georgia and Republican Robert P. Griffin of Michigan. The bill provided a "Bill of Rights" for union members, which included a guarantee that they would have regular elections, "equal rights and privileges" to nominate candidates, vote for union officials, participate in union meetings, and caucus with other members under "reasonable rules and regulations" established by the union.[125] Approved September 14, 1959, among other things, it required all union members to adopt constitutions and bylaws and to register them, and other information outlining their financial and organizational structure, with the secretary of labor. It also provided for a means of coping with union officials guilty of corruption to the use of union funds with Federal supervision of labor union elections.

Majority Leader Lyndon Johnson could not have been pleased that John McClellan, the ostensible chair of the select labor racketeering committee, let the Kennedy brothers get the lion's share of the media coverage. The coverage led to Jack Kennedy's running neck and neck with Adlai Stevenson in public opinion polls for the 1960 Democratic presidential nomination while Johnson trailed in single digits.[126] Johnson was undoubtedly aware that Bobby Kennedy's place on McClellan's Government Operations Committee had originally been paid for by Joe Kennedy's financial investment in a McClellan-linked bank in Arkansas.[127] Johnson should not have been surprised since he too had been a rumored beneficiary of Joe Kennedy's largesse when Jack was moved from the marginal Government Operations Committee to the prestigious Foreign Relations one in 1957. With the successful passage of the Landrum-Griffin Act, Jack Kennedy had demonstrated legislative ability that lessened the impact of Johnson's decision to take an "insider" strategy for the nomination and focus upon his undisputed floor leadership skills.

Civil Rights Act of 1960: Johnson's strategy was to get another civil rights bill passed. Much as the Kennedys had scored with the public by challenging corrupt labor unions, a Democratic constituency, Johnson anticipated scoring with the public by challenging his fellow southerners on civil rights. Once again, Johnson relied on the House team of Majority Leader John McCormack and the two civil rights stalwarts on House Judiciary, McCormack ally Chair Emanuel Celler and new Ranking Member Robert M. McCulloch of Ohio, to deliver a bill that he could push through the Senate.[128] This time the legislation was the Civil Rights Act of 1960 that authorized federal judges to appoint referees empowered to assist persons experiencing opposition in the exercise of the voting franchise.

To pass the 1960 bill through the House Rules Committee, McCormack sponsored a discharge petition to free the bill and on March 18, when 211 signatures (albeit seven shy of a majority) had been obtained, the Rules Committee felt obliged to release it for a floor vote. On March 23, the House initially passed the bill 295–124, with Democrats split 172–100 and Republicans 123–24.[129] The South split with 89 Democratic southerners and 5 Republican southerners voting against the bill. The remaining 11 Democratic opponents came from the border states of Kentucky (6), Oklahoma (3), and Missouri (2). Well aware that Johnson's presidential bid hung in the balance, LBJ's fellow Texans were more sympathetic to this bill than they were to the 1957 one. Among the seven Democrats voting "yea" were six Texans, including third-termer James C. Wright, Jr. of Fort Worth, who would later become Majority Leader in 1977 and Speaker in 1987. Jim Wright would be the last of the Austin-Boston Connection.

Despite multiple efforts to table the bill and recommit it to the Senate Judiciary Committee, where its segregationist Chair Jim Eastland would bury it, the Senate finally voted to approve it on April 8, 1960, on a vote of 71–18.[130] The bill returned to the House for final passage on April 21, 1960, on a vote of 288–95, with Democrats splitting 165–83 and Republicans 123–12. It was sent to President Eisenhower and was approved May 6; the act also provided criminal penalties for bombing, bomb-threats, and mob action designed to obstruct court orders.[131]

The conflict over civil rights had escalated dramatically throughout the nation. College students, both black and white, had begun sitting-in at lunch counters in segregated restaurants, leading to serious violence. The Reverend Martin Luther King, Jr. who successfully integrated the bus system of Montgomery, Alabama, through a boycott echoed back to the "nonviolent resistance" movement of India's Mahatma Gandhi. King's success was widely emulated throughout the South, and the entire panoply of segregationist practices which had been in place since the 1890s was in jeopardy. White southern law enforcement officials were charged with maintaining the peace, but for them maintaining the peace meant continued racial subjugation. There was no doubt that a federal remedy was necessary to interpose a superior legal authority between the southern law enforcement officials and the nation's black citizenry eager to shed their second-class status.

Senator Johnson went even further on his civil rights agenda that year when he was able to get presidential voting rights for the black-dominated District of Columbia. To accomplish this goal, it was necessary to amend the Constitution, and six weeks after the Civil Rights Act of 1960 was passed, the Congress accepted the 23rd Amendment. This amendment provided the citizens of the District of Columbia the right to vote for president and vice president, giving them three votes in the Electoral College.[132]

Contrasting strategies: Insider versus outsider

While Johnson's inside strategy required him to be on the Senate floor managing legislation, outsider candidate Jack Kennedy, less encumbered with legislative responsibilities, roamed freely throughout the country, contesting the presidential primaries and granting television and radio interviews. Clearly, this battle would be a test of two separate strategies to obtain a presidential nomination. Kennedy's decision to run this way was described by his initial biographer, James MacGregor Burns, as "running alone."[133] While Burns may have disliked the strategy, antiestablishment "outsider" strategies have been adopted by subsequent Democratic nomination campaigns, most notably those of South Dakota U.S. Senator George McGovern in 1972, Georgia Governor Jimmy Carter in 1976, Arkansas Governor Bill Clinton in 1992, and Illinois U.S. Senator Barack Obama in 2008.

Succinctly put, the strategy represents a fortuitous combination of cash, connection, and celebrity wherein the outsider candidate develops a pre-presidential persona replete with published books, multiple media appearances, an army of eager and tireless volunteers, and access to funds outside the traditional party sources. What made the Kennedy candidacy different was that much of the money came from his family's boundless wealth.

On June 29, McCormack and the fellow Democratic leaders agreed to recess Congress on July 2 and to call it back into session after the Democratic and Republican conventions ended. The original hopes that they could adjourn at that time were dashed when they realized how much unfinished business had been left undone. The passage of the 22nd Amendment meant that there would be no incumbent in contention for the nomination, so both of these conventions were truly open. While the Republican nomination seemed secure for Vice President Richard Nixon, the Democratic one appeared to be yet another free-for-all.

That Jack Kennedy had chosen to operate outside the existing Democratic power structure was no surprise to John McCormack. John had been witness to this Kennedy strategy for more than a dozen years and he had lost control of the Massachusetts state party as a consequence of it. John knew how the strategy operated, but could it gain for Kennedy the family's goal of the presidency, one that John himself had supported in 1940 twenty years earlier? The Kennedy-McCormack truce was still in place and John would go to the 1960 convention chairing a loyal pro-Kennedy state delegation.

Notes

1   "Democratic Harmony," *Boston Traveler*, February 5, 1956, p. 1.

2   John Harris, "Political Notebook: Adlai's Agent in State Seems to be Dever," *BG*, November 29, 1955, p. 4.

3   C. R. Owens, "Democratic Plight: Many Avoid Adlai but—Who Else Is There?" *BG*, January 15, 1956, p. C35.

4   H. W. Brand, *Traitor to His Class: The Privileged Life and Radical Presidency of Franklin Delano Roosevelt* (New York: Doubleday, 2008).

5   See the undergraduate honor's thesis by George S. Abrams, *Paul A. Dever and the Democratic Party in Massachusetts* (Cambridge, MA: Harvard University, 1954), p. 78.

6   "Democrats Elect Burke Chairman of State Committee," *BG*, September 17, 1939.

7   Samuel B. Cutler, "Burke Confirmed as Port Collector," *BG*, November 23, 1944.

8   James MacGregor Burns, *John F. Kennedy: A Political Profile* (New York: Harcourt, Brace & World, 1960), p. 177.

9   David Nasaw, *The Patriarch: The Remarkable Life and Turbulent Times of Joseph P. Kennedy* (New York: The Penguin Press, 2012), p. 669; and "Up from South Boston: The Rise & Fall of John Fox," *TIME*, July 7, 1958.

10 *Boston Post* stories by James G. Colbert in April 1956; "Strong Support Given McCormack in State" (April 4); "Labor Leaders Join in McCormack Boom" (April 5); "Boom for McCormack for President Grows" (April 6); "Foley Says McCormack 'Excellent Candidate'" (April 7); "Nation Will Notice Big McCormack Vote" (April 8); "Irish Societies Leaders' Back McCormack Drive" (April 9); "McCormack Acclaimed by Sen. Russell of Ga." (April 10); "50 Cent Raise in Pay Started McCormack on Political Career" (April 11); "Sen. Kerr Hails M'Cormack Candidacy" and "McCormack's Energy Brought Early Fame" (April 12); "Girl McCormack Married Always His inspiration" (April 13); "Honor to McCormack Paid Early by House" (April 14); "McCormack Delighted in Meeting Old Friends" and "McCormack Looms as Real 'Dark Horse'" (April 15); "McCormack Denounced Communism Very Early" (April 16); "McCormack Won Spurs as House Leader Early" (April 17); "McCormack Efforts Saved U.S. in Dark War Hours" (April 18); "Heavy Burdens Placed on McCormack by War II" (April 19); "Colleges and Universities Paid McCormack Honor" (April 20); "Labor Heads Hail McCormack" (April 21); "McCormack Is Slight Favorite over Adlai" (April 22); "Burke Scores ADA. Urges Large Write-In for McCormack" (April 23); "McCormack-Stevenson Fight Highlight of Today's Primary" (April 25).

11 Colbert on Russell's endorsement, April 10, and from the Associated Press, "House Cheers McCormack as Lane Hails Candidacy," *Boston Post*, April 11, and "Senator Kerr Hails M'Cormack Candidacy," *Boston Post*, April 12, 1956.

12 John Kelso, "Kefauver Concedes Bay State to McCormack, Quits Primary" *Boston Post*, April 13, 1956.

13 "1956 Primaries," in Congressional Quarterly, *Presidential Elections, 1789–1992* (Washington, DC: Congressional Quarterly Press, 1995), p. 172. Only write-ins were recorded in the April 24, 1956, Massachusetts primary.

14 James W. Colbert, "McCormack Halted Stampede to Adlai," *Boston Sunday Post*, April 25, 1956, pp. 1ff and "Vote of Boston," p. A4.

15 "M'Cormack Grateful to Voters and Post," *Boston Sunday Post*, April 25, 1956, p. A4.

16 Burns, *John F. Kennedy: A Political Profile*, p. 177.

17   Associated Press, "Hiss Will Give Address at Princeton April 26," *Washington Post and Times Herald*, April 7, 1956, p. 23 and "Princeton Backs Students on Plans for Hiss Speech," *Washington Post and Times Herald*, April 11, 1956, p. 10.

18   Matthews, *Kennedy and Nixon*, p. 107.

19   Stevenson's 1949 deposition for Alger Hiss is mentioned in Jeff Broadwater, *Adlai Stevenson and American Politics: The Odyssey of a Cold War Liberal* (New York: Twayne, 1994), p. 100.

20   "McCormack Statement on Democratic Hassle," *BG*, May 18, 1956, p. 6.

21   McCormack September 23, 1968 interview with T. Harrison Baker for the LBJ Oral History Collection, pp. 24–25.

22   Lawrence F. O'Brien, *No Final Victories: A Life in Politics from John F. Kennedy to Watergate* (New York: Ballantine Books, 1974), p. 49.

23   The Kennedy wing's efforts to gain control of the state party are fully described in the book "*Johnny, We Hardly Knew Ye*," *Memories of John Fitzgerald Kennedy* by Kenneth P. O'Donnell and David F. Powers with Joe McCarthy (Boston: Little, Brown, 1970). The Joe Kennedy quotation may be found on p. 119.

24   O'Donnell and Powers with McCarthy, *Johnny, We Hardly Knew Ye*, chapter 4, "Onions Burke and the 1956 Convention," pp. 106–44.

25   Interview with former Lynn (Mass.) Mayor Thomas Costin who was a young Kennedy delegate in attendance, Boston, April 1998.

26   O'Donnell and Powers with McCarthy, *Johnny, We Hardly Knew Ye*, p. 132.

27   *Jacqueline Kennedy: Historic Conversations on Life with John F. Kennedy*, interviews with Arthur M. Schlesinger, Jr. 1964 (New York: Hyperion, 2011), pp. 9–13.

28   O'Brien, *No Final Victories*, pp. 48–50.

29   William J. Lewis, "Kennedy's Forces Win, Democrats Pick Lynch; Burke Out as State Committee Chairman; Defeated 47–31 Says He'll Run against Senator," *BG*, May 20, 1956, pp. B1ff.

30   McCormack 1968 interview with T. Harrison Baker for the LBJ Library, p. 18.

31   John W. McCormack Oral History interview with Sheldon Stern, March 30, 1977, p. 23.

32   Caroline Seebohm, *No Regrets: The Life of Marietta Tree* (New York: Simon & Schuster, 1997), chapter 21.

33   William M. Bulger, *While the Music Lasts: My Life in Politics* (Boston: Faber and Faber, 1996), p. 91. Billy Bulger shared his reminiscences of South Boston politics with me while I was teaching classes at UMass-Boston, 1999–2001.

34   William J. Lewis, "Ward Wins; McCormack Walks Out, Councilor's Action Causes Uproar at Democratic Parley; Murphy Named," *BG*, June 10, 1956, p. B1.

35   One of the more thoughtful renderings is Francis Russell, "Joseph Patrick Kennedy: The Dynast from East Boston," in his *The President Makers: From Mark Hanna to Joseph P. Kennedy* (Boston: Little, Brown, 1976), pp. 325–92.

36   The fullest account of that request appears in David McKean's biography of Corcoran, *Peddling Influence: Thomas "Tommy the Cork" Corcoran and the Birth of Modern Lobbying* (Hanover, NH: Steerforth Press, 2004), pp. 230–31.

37   Jeff Shesol, "The Affront," in *Mutual Contempt: Lyndon Johnson, Robert Kennedy, and the Feud that Defined a Decade* (New York: W. W. Norton, 1997), pp. 41–60.

38   As quoted in Merle Miller's colorful but controversial *Plain Speaking: An Oral Biography of Harry S. Truman* (New York: Berkley Books, 1974), p. 199.

39   Described in Shaun A. Casey, *The Making of a Catholic President: Kennedy vs. Nixon, 1960* (New York: Oxford University Press, 2009), pp. 3–7.

40 Personal notes, Arthur M. Schlesinger, Jr., *Robert Kennedy and His Times* (Boston: Houghton Mifflin, 1978), p. 131.

41 D. B. Hardeman oral history interview with Michael L. Gillette, January 19, 1977, University of Texas Library, p. 64.

42 Among the accounts of that convention are "1956; Thirty-Second Democratic Convention," in Richard C. Bain and Judith H. Parris, *Convention Decisions and Voting Records*, 2nd ed. (Washington, DC: The Brookings Institution, 1973), pp. 293–98; the fullest treatment of the 1956 convention may be found in Ralph G. Martin's chapter, "Democratic National Convention of 1956," *Ballots and Bandwagons* (Chicago: Rand McNally, 1964), pp. 373–465.

43 Edwin O'Connor's *The Last Hurrah* (Boston: Little, Brown, 1956) was a wonderfully sanitized version of Jim Curley's mayoralty and it was a major best seller and a less successful 1958 movie with Oscar-winning Spencer Tracy in the role of Mayor Frank Skeffington. Jim Curley sued the filmmakers and reportedly pocketed $42,000 in an out-of-court settlement.

44 The phrase "apostles of compromise" comes from the careful assessment of the 1952 plank relative to the 1948 one found in Donald R. McCoy and Richard T. Ruetten, *Quest and Response: Minority Rights and the Truman Administration* (Lawrence: University Press of Kansas, 1973), pp. 322–26.

45 "Platform Builder; John William McCormack," *NYT*, August 7, 1956, p. 12; and John Harris, "Platform Drafters Search For Civil Rights Formula," *BG*, August 12, 1956, pp. B1ff.

46 King's first triumph over segregation is described in his book *Stride toward Freedom: The Montgomery Story* (New York: Ballantine Books, 1958).

47 "How Adlai Won: PLATFORMS: Something to Live With," *TIME* online archive, August 27, 1956.

48 "How Adlai Won: Harry's Bitter Week," *TIME* online archive, August 27, 1956.

49 Bain and Parris, eds., *Convention Decisions and Voting Records*, p. 297.

50 This is the Ralph G. Martin thesis in *Ballots and Bandwagons*. Martin contends that the open vote for vice president was an innovation and that without it Kennedy's 1960 presidential nomination would have been postponed for a decade.

51 Martin, *Ballots and Bandwagons*, p. 400.

52 "Party's Film Aids Kennedy's Drive; Senator, Star of Movie, Gets First Demonstration—Other 2d Place Seekers 'Gain,'" *NYT*, August 14, 1956, p. 13.

53 O'Donnell and Powers with McCarthy, *Johnny, We Hardly Knew Ye*, p. 135.

54 "Party's Film Aids Kennedy's Drive . . ." p. 13.

55 Ruth Aull and Dr. Daniel M. Ogden, eds., *Official Proceedings of the Democratic National Convention 1956* (Richmond, VA: Beacon Press, 1956), p. 435.

56 O'Donnell and Powers with McCarthy, *Johnny, We Hardly Knew Ye*, p. 139.

57 Martin, *Ballots and Bandwagons*, p. 424.

58 *Official Proceedings 1956*, p. 439.

59 Smathers interview in *Ballots and Bandwagons*, p. 411.

60 *Official Proceedings 1956*, p. 473.

61 In Theodore White's account of the balloting, "The 39-year old Boston Irish Catholic held a lead over Estes Kefauver. He came within 38 ½ votes of winning the nomination." White, *America in Search of Itself: The Making of the President, 1956–1980* (New York: Warner Books, 1982), pp. 82–85.

62 "National Affairs: The Wide-Open Winner," *TIME* online archive, August 27, 1956.

63   D. B. Hardeman interview with T. Harrison Baker, February 26, 1969, LBJ Archives, University of Texas Library, Austin, pp. 1–39.

64   Ibid.

65   Jonathan Alter, "The Power and the Glitz," *Newsweek*, CXXXI, May 25, 1998, p. 64B.

66   Paul Fay, Jr., *The Pleasure of His Company* (New York: Harper & Co., 1963), pp. 164–65. Fay served as Undersecretary of the Navy in the Kennedy administration under Lyndon Johnson's ally John B. Connally, later the Governor of Texas and the other occupant of the limousine when JFK was shot.

67   "National Affairs: The Wide-Open Winner," *TIME* online archive, August 27, 1956.

68   John W. McCormack telegram to *TIME* magazine, August 23, 1956, in Paul Wright Papers, University of Massachusetts-Boston. Herbert S. Parmet in the book *Jack: The Struggles of John F. Kennedy* (New York: The Dial Press, 1980), on p. 381, "Asked about the episode twenty-two years later, McCormack's recollection remained vivid: 'That was one of the rawest deals a man ever got, goddamn,' he replied. 'I didn't even know where Missouri was seated in that convention.' He insisted he merely wanted Rayburn to recognize Kentucky." John W. McCormack Oral History interview with Sheldon Stern, JFK Library, March 30, 1977, p. 25.

69   Robert F. Kennedy's telegram to John McCormack with his *TIME* magazine complaints, August 24, 1956, Paul Wright Papers, University of Massachusetts-Boston.

70   "McCormack Rift Denied by Kennedy," *Boston Post*, August 29, 1956.

71   See the election overview in Charles A. H. Thomson and Frances M. Shattuck, eds., *The 1956 Presidential Campaign* (Washington, DC: The Brookings Institution, 1960).

72   *CQ's Guide to U.S. Elections* (Washington, DC: Congressional Quarterly, 1975), pp. 294–95. See Lawrence Fuchs, "Presidential Politics in Boston: The Irish Response to Stevenson," *New England Quarterly*, XXX (December 1957), pp. 435–47.

73   "A Classification of the Presidential Elections," in Angus Campbell, Philip Converse, Warren Miller, and Donald E. Stokes, *Elections and the Political Order* (New York: John Wiley, 1966), pp. 63–78.

74   Garrison Nelson, "Sideshows and Strategic Separations: The Impact of Presidential Year Politics on Congressional Elections," in Harvey L. Schantz, ed., *Politics in an Era of Divided Government: Elections and Governance in the Second Clinton Administration* (New York: Routledge, 2001), pp. 105–27.

75   Massachusetts politics in the 1950s are best described by Duane Lockard, *New England State Politics* (Princeton, NJ: Princeton University Press, 1959); and Edgar Litt, *The Political Cultures of Massachusetts* (Cambridge, MA: MIT Press, 1965).

76   Election results from the Massachusetts Secretary of State's Office: Attorney General, September 18, 1956, Democratic Primary, Edward J. McCormack, Jr., 250,916 (55.2%) and Joseph D. Ward, 209,923 (44.8%). The November general election contest was even closer: with Eddie losing by only 39,433 votes of close to 2.8 million votes cast: George Fingold, 1,152,348 (50.6%) and Edward J. McCormack, Jr., 1,113,105 (48.9%).

77   William J. Lewis, "Aspirants All Slugging in State Political Fight," *BG*, October 11, 1956, p. 14.

78   C. P. Trussell, "Rayburn Elected as Speaker Again: Texan Is Named Record 8th Time as House Organizes—Urges Responsibility," *NYT*, January 4, 1957, p. 12.

79   Information from Eisenhower appointment note cards provided by Mr. Kevin M. Bailey of the Eisenhower Library and Museum, Abilene, Kansas, March 8, 2015. The initials referred to are—DDE is Dwight David Eisenhower while MDE is Mamie Dowd Eisenhower.

80 Emmet John Hughes, *The Ordeal of Power: A Political Memoir of the Eisenhower Years* (New York: Atheneum, 1962), pp. 231–32.

81 Data from "The Black Vote, 1936–2012," BlackDemographics.com, accessed March 5, 2014.

82 The fullest examination of Powell's 1956 endorsement of Eisenhower may be found in Charles V. Hamilton's definitive *Adam Clayton Powell, Jr.: The Political Biography of an American Dilemma* (New York: Collier, 1991), pp. 266–81. See also Powell's personal account in *Adam by Adam: The Autobiography of Adam Clayton Powell, Jr.* (New York: The Dial Press, 1971), pp. 129–31.

83 Civil Rights Act of 1957 was approved September 9, 1957 (71 Stat. 634-638).

84 A comprehensive analysis of the bill can be found in J. W. Anderson's *Eisenhower, Brownell, and the Congress: The Tangled Origins of the Civil Rights Bill of 1956–1957* (Tuscaloosa, AL: University of Alabama Press, 1964).

85 "Dante B. Fascell," *BDUSC* (1989 ed.), p. 985.

86 "Bay State Democrats To Fete Kennedy And McCormack," *BG*, September 12, 1957, p. 32.

87 O'Brien, *No Final Victories*, pp. 52–53.

88 Mark Nadel et al., "The House Science and Astronautics Committee and the Senate Aeronautical and Space Science Committee," in the Ralph Nader Congress Project, *The Environment Committees A Study of the House and Senate Interior, Agriculture, and Science Committees* (New York: Grossman, 1975), pp. 281–357.

89 The committee's history is recounted in U.S. Representative Ken Hechler's authoritative report, *Toward the Endless Frontier: History of the Committee on Science and Technology, 1959–1979*, House Committee Print (Washington, DC: Government Printing Office, 1980).

90 Reorganization Plan No. 1 of 1958 (Creation of the Office of Civil and Defense Mobilization). It was approved July 1, 1958 (72 Stat. 1799-1801). On August 26, 1958, legislation was enacted changing the name of the new agency to the Office of Civil and Defense Mobilization. (72 Stat. 861), Stathis, *Landmark Legislation*, pp. 248–49.

91 National Aeronautics and Space Act of 1958. It was approved July 29, 1958 (72 Stat. 426-438). Stathis, *Landmark Legislation*, p. 249.

92 Department of Defense Reorganization Act of 1958. It was approved August 6, 1958 (72 Stat. 514-522), Stathis, *Landmark Legislation*, p. 249.

93 The Federal-Aid Highway Act of 1958 was approved April 16, 1958 (72 Stat. 89-96).

94 Admission of the State of Alaska to the U.S. was approved July 7, 1958 (72 Stat. 339-352).

95 Transportation Act of 1958 was approved August 12, 1958 (72 Stat. 568-574).

96 National Defense Education Act of 1958 was approved September 2, 1958 (72 Stat. 1580-1605).

97 Former Presidents Act was approved August 25, 1958 (72 Stat. 838-839).

98 C. R. Owens, "[Eddie] McCormack Nears Win on Democrats' 3d Ballot: Lacks 9 Votes for Choice as Atty Gen. Sen Kennedy, Furcolo Win by Acclamation," *BG*, June 22, 1958, p. 1.

99 "No Big Fight in Primary Expected by [Eddie] McCormack," *BG*, June 29, 1958, p. 38.

100 On Gibbons background, see "Important Dates in Gibbons' Life," *BG*, September 3, 1958, p. 11.

101 William J. Lewis, "[Eddie] McCormack Picked for Interim Post: Legislators Select Boston Democrat, Party Nominee Will Finish Late Atty. Gen. Fingold's Term," *BG*, September 12, 1958, p. 1 ff.

102   "Berlin to Head Civil Rights Div. For [Eddie] McCormack," *BG*, October 28, 1958, p. 28.

103   John Harris, "[Eddie] McCormack Tops Herter by 30,000," *BG*, November 5, 1958, p. 1.

104   NPA Associates, the "U.S. Misery Index," from www.miseryindex.us.

105   James MacGregor Burns, *The Deadlock of Democracy: Four Party Politics in America* (Englewood Cliffs, NJ: Prentice-Hall, 1963), p. 283.

106   This version of the quote appears in James J. Kenneally, *A Compassionate Conservative: A Political Biography of Joseph W. Martin, Jr., Speaker of the U.S. House of Representatives* (Lanham, MD: Lexington Books, 2003), p. 48. The quotation is unattributed.

107   Allen Drury, "Hallek Unseats Martin as G.O.P. Leader in House: Congress to Open Today," *NYT*, January 7, 1959, pp. 1, 25.

108   Marie McNair, "'Mr. Sam' Shares 77th with Colleague," *Washington Post*, January 7, 1959, p. B27; and George Dixon, "Washington Scene: Sob Sisters May Get Revenge on 'Smart Halleck,'" *Washington Post*, January 20, 1959, p. A17.

109   Author's telephonic interview with the Hon. Thomas Kuchel (Rep-Cal.) in May 1981.

110   "List of Leaders for the 86th Congress," *NYT*, January 8, 1959, p. 15.

111   "A Breach Is Closed: McCormack Gets a Special Invitation to White House," *NYT*, March 12, 1959, p. 12.

112   "Congressmen Hopeful on Khrushchev Visit," *Washington Post*, August 4, 1959, p. A7.

113   "Bid for Khrushchev Capitol Speech Now Opposed by Supporters of Visit," *Washington Post*, September 3, 1959, p. A7.

114   Drew Pearson, "Washington Merry-Go-Round: 'Boycott' of K. Worries Officials," *Washington Post*, August 22, 1959, p. B15.

115   "McCormack Rejects Bid to Ike Briefing," *Washington Post*, November 12, 1959, p. A2.

116   Eisenhower Appointment Book, 1953–61, accessed in an email from Kevin Bailey of the Eisenhower Library, March 9, 2015.

117   James Q. Wilson, "The Goals of the Amateur," in *The Amateur Democrat: Club Politics in Three Cities* (Chicago: University of Chicago Press, 1961), pp. 126–63.

118   Litt, "Party Politics: The Reform Democrats," in *The Political Cultures of Massachusetts*, pp. 152–74.

119   "Liberal House Democrats Organize for Action," *CQWR*, January 8, 1960, p. 391. Two academic accounts of the DSG are Kenneth Kofmehl, "The Institutionalization of a Voting Bloc," *Western Political Quarterly*, XVII (June 1964), pp. 256–72; and Arthur G. Stevens, Jr., Arthur H. Miller, and Thomas E. Mann, "Mobilization of Liberal Strength in the House, 1955–1970: The Democratic Study Group," *APSR*, LXVIII (June 1964), pp. 667–81. The most recent assessment of the DSG appears in Julian E. Zelizer, "When Liberals Were Organized, "*The American Prospect* (Winter 2015).

120   George S. Goodwin, Jr., "The Seniority System in Congress," *APSR*, LIII (June 1959), pp. 412–36. Subsequent research confirmed and extended Goodwin's findings; see Michael Abram and Joseph Cooper, "The Rise of Seniority in the House of Representatives," *Polity*, I (Fall 1968), pp. 52–84; and Nelson W. Polsby, Miriam Gallagher, and Barry Spence Rundquist, "The Growth of the Seniority System in the U.S. House of Representatives," *APSR*, LXIII (September 1969), pp. 787–807.

121   Author's interview with the Hon. Richard W. Bolling, Washington, DC, April 1988.

122   Admission of the State of Hawaii to the Union was approved March 18, 1959 (73 Stat. 4-13). The congressional votes on admission may be found in *CQWR*, March 13, 1959, pp. 416–17, for the House and p. 418 for the Senate.

123   As noted in Capitol Hill in Black and White by Robert Parker with Richard Rashke (New York: Dodd, Mead, 1986), pp. 81 and 188.

124 The latest entry is James Neff's Vendetta: Bobby Kennedy versus Jimmy Hoffa (New York: Little, Brown, 2015).

125 Landrum-Griffin Labor Management Reporting and Disclosure Act of 1959. Approved September 14, 1959 (73 Stat. 519-546). Certain provisions of this Act were subsequently held unconstitutional in *United States v. Brown, 381 U.S. 437 (1965)*.

126 American Institute of Public Opinion, *The Gallup Poll, Public Opinion, 1935–1971* (New York: Random House, 1972), Vol. 3, 1959–71, passim.

127 Bobby Baker Oral History, Senate Historical Office, p. 82.

128 "Decision in the House," in Daniel M. Berman, *A Bill Becomes a Law: The Civil Rights Act of 1960* (New York: Macmillan, 1962), pp. 88–95.

129 *CQWR*, March 25, 1960, pp. 506–507.

130 *CQWR*, April 15, 1960, p. 653.

131 Civil Rights Act of 1960 was approved May 6, 1960 (74 Stat. 86-92).

132 The 23rd Amendment, approved June 16, 1960 (74 Stat. 1057) and ratified by the requisite number of states March 29, 1961 (75 Stat. 847-848).

133 James MacGregor Burns, *Running Alone: Presidential Leadership—From JFK to Bush II: Why It Has Failed and How We Can Fix It* (New York: Basic Books, 2006).

18

Transitions, 1960–61

An Ambitious Trio: House Majority Leader John McCormack knew that this day would eventually come. He may not have expected it so soon, but as an astute observer of political ambition, John knew that this was the inevitable conflict between three of the most ambitious young men he had ever encountered. He met the first in April 1937 when the 28-year-old Lyndon Johnson of Texas won a special House election. He met the other two 10 years later in January 1947, when California's 33-year-old Richard M. Nixon and Massachusetts's 29-year-old John F. Kennedy entered the national political arena as newly elected members of the U.S. House of Representatives and were placed together on the Education and Labor Committee. The younger two men watched each other closely and had taken each other's measure multiple times.[1] At last they appeared on the brink of their long-awaited contest against one another for the greatest prize of all—the presidency of the United States. In retrospect, given its remarkable closeness and the ultimate fate of its three major protagonists, each of whom became president— Jack Kennedy, Dick Nixon, and Lyndon Johnson—the 1960 contest would be the most discussed and closely analyzed election in recent American history.[2] John McCormack served as Speaker of the U.S. House with all three.

Lyndon Johnson was close to fellow congressional leaders Sam Rayburn and John McCormack, and was their preferred presidential choice. Neither Jack Kennedy nor Dick Nixon had impressed either of them. Rayburn, who once dismissed Kennedy as a "little pissant," was more forthcoming in his negative attitudes toward him while McCormack, once burned when Jack's powerful father Joe Kennedy learned of harsh assessments of Jack by John's staff, had to be more circumspect. Sam also had a Kennedy rival, Lyndon Johnson, in the upcoming nomination battle while John had an ambitious young nephew, Eddie, whose statewide career had just begun and needed Kennedy support if it was to succeed. Needless to say, both Sam and John were united in their intense disdain for Vice President Nixon, whose harsh criticisms of the Democratic Party generally and their close friend Harry Truman in particular they saw as defamatory and bordering on the demagogic.

Jack Kennedy's nomination

With the 1960 election on the near horizon, *The New York Times* published an article encapsulating the stereotypical demographic profile for successful presidential candidates. They were to be middle-aged, English-descended Protestant, small-town-born governors from large northern states with ideal marriages.[3] Jack Kennedy was well aware that as a 42-year-old big-city Irish-descended Catholic U.S. Senator, he was far from the stereotype. U.S. Representative William Jennings Bryan, 36 years old and the youngest Democratic nominee, had failed in his 1896 election bid as had the big-city Irish-German Catholic candidacy of New York Governor Al Smith in 1928. The only president elected directly from the U.S. Senate was the incompetent Republican Warren G. Harding of Ohio who won the White House in 1920. Kennedy was also aware that he had not impressed the Democratic Party's congressional establishment and even more troubling to him was the fact that many of the party's leading Catholic politicians, most notably Pennsylvania Governor David Lawrence and Congressman Bill Green, the head of Philadelphia's Democratic organization, were fearful that a Kennedy candidacy would reanimate the anti-Catholic prejudice that sank Al Smith.[4]

Knowing how much they had to overcome, the Kennedy presidential campaign was launched immediately after Jack's failed vice presidential bid at the 1956 Democratic convention. It generated ample public attention and Stevenson's landslide defeat could not be blamed on him. He was well positioned for a 1960 run, and the family's publicity team kicked into gear. His biography of eight U.S. Senators facing political crises, *Profiles in Courage*, became a best seller and led to his being named on April 11, 1956, as chair of the Special Committee on the Senate Reception Room to replace Lyndon Johnson, who had created the committee in 1955 to honor five outstanding U.S. Senators with their portraits.

Henry Luce, Joe Kennedy's powerful Republican ally in earlier political campaigns and the publisher of *TIME* and *LIFE*, featured the committee's report, "A Committee Nominates Five Immortals for U.S. Senate" in *LIFE* magazine's May 6, 1957, issue.[5] This was in addition to *LIFE*'s placing Jack on the cover of its March 11, 1957, issue prefaced by "the brilliant Massachusetts senator," with his article, "Where Democrats Should Go from Here"; publishing a favorable article on Bobby, "Young Man with Tough Questions: Bob Kennedy," in *LIFE*'s July 1, 1957, issue; and placing Jack on the cover of the December 2, 1957, issue of *TIME*, with a laudatory story entitled "Democrats' Man Out Front." The Kennedy presidential operation was well out of the gate before any of Jack's likely 1960 opponents had made their first phone call. Having seen the Kennedys operate back home in Massachusetts, John McCormack was unsurprised.

Jack's book was nominated for the 1956 Pulitzer Prize in biography and with Joe Kennedy's paid retainer, Arthur Krock, Washington Bureau chief of the *New York Times* and a longtime member of the Pulitzer panel lobbying for it, Jack's book was selected. When columnist Drew Pearson contended on television that Ted Sorensen, Kennedy's speechwriter, was its real author, Joe Kennedy's legal team led by Clark Clifford began preparing a multimillion dollar lawsuit. Pearson backed down but questions continued to linger. While it seemed not to bother Jack, who assigned a major share of the book's royalties to Sorensen, Jackie Kennedy felt that Sorensen had been unconvincing in his denials of authorship and marginalized Ted during their shared time in the White House.[6]

At the opening of the 85th Congress in 1957, Majority Leader Lyndon Johnson, chair of the Democratic Steering Committee that made committee assignments, moved Jack from the lesser Government Operations Committee to the highly prestigious Foreign Relations Committee as rumors of Joe Kennedy's largesse to LBJ circulated. Johnson, who had been approached in 1955 by Tommy Corcoran at the behest of Joe Kennedy to run for president with Jack as vice president, was well aware of Joe Kennedy's obsession with the White House.

Jack Kennedy launched an "outsider" campaign for the 1960 Democratic presidential nomination by using the polls and primaries to promote his candidacy.[7] Williams College Professor James MacGregor Burns[8] watched Jack ignore the state party organizations and pioneer a strategy of campaigning and governing that Burns would later call "running alone."[9] Burns, a fellow veteran and Harvard PhD, became close to Kennedy during his own losing 1958 House contest against moderate liberal Republican Silvio Conte, a Boston College pal of Tip O'Neill. Burns apparently chose not to resent that his masterful 1956 biography, *Roosevelt: The Lion and the Fox*, had been one of the finalists for the 1956 Pulitzer Prize in Biography that was won by Jack's *Profiles in Courage*. Getting the Kennedy biography contract may have been a consolation prize.

The Kennedy campaign knew there would be a number of rival candidacies: most notably liberal U.S. Senator Hubert Humphrey of Minnesota, U.S. Senator Stuart Symington of Missouri, Senate Majority Leader Lyndon B. Johnson of Texas, and two-time presidential nominee Adlai E. Stevenson of Illinois. Their best-connected rival, Lyndon Johnson, used an "insider" strategy built around endorsements from state party leaders and the heads of congressional delegations. Johnson's expectation that there would be a clear difference between popular opinion and the opinion of leaders within the Democratic Party organization was not borne out. The first part of the expectation was confirmed when Gallup Poll data from Democratic and Independent voter preferences for presidential candidates from January 1959 until May 1960 had Kennedy and Stevenson battling it out with Johnson never receiving more than 15% of the vote and averaging around 10% for most of the polling period.[10] Further disappointment for LBJ ensued when an October 1959 Gallup Poll of 1,454 Democratic county chairs indicated that Kennedy was not only the leader as their preferred choice 424 to 260 but also their "best guess" as the anticipated nominee 469 to 126.[11]

Johnson rebounded, and by June of 1960, with the convention little more than a month away, *Congressional Quarterly* polled 407 editors and 220 members of Congress and revealed that Johnson scored 43% of their votes as the likeliest presidential nominee to Stevenson's 30% and Kennedy's 21%. The pros saw a Johnson-Kennedy ticket as the likeliest Democratic choice and a Nixon-Rockefeller as the likeliest Republican one. Among the 407 editors, Kennedy was seen as the likelier vice presidential choice—65% to Johnson's 14%. Among the 220 congressional members interviewed, Johnson was the expected choice of 54% to Kennedy's 20%, while Kennedy was the expected vice presidential nominee—63% to LBJ's 7%.[12]

While Kennedy and Johnson would choose dissimilar nomination strategies, there was a clear consensus among knowledgeable Democratic Party professionals that the party's best hope for victory in 1960 would be a ticket that included both men. But would it be a Johnson-Kennedy ticket or a Kennedy-Johnson ticket? It was hoped that they would not so savage one another in the nomination phase that they would consider running together.

Knowing that both Jack and Lyndon would contend at the Los Angeles convention, it was Sam Rayburn who made it clear to Tip O'Neill that they each must abide by the desires of the convention should they place their names before it. O'Neill, whose link to John McCormack made him a regular at Rayburn's late afternoon Capitol hideaway "the Board of Education," would frequently spend early mornings in the Speaker's lobby reading daily papers with Rayburn. Neither had family responsibilities—Rayburn, single now for 30 years, and O'Neill's five children back in Cambridge being raised by his wife Millie. Many mornings, it would be just the two of them. Tip knew that Jack believed correctly that Sam disliked him and "[Jack] felt that . . . Rayburn had really hurt him in the '56 Kefauver struggle for the vice presidency; he had a feeling deep in his heart that Rayburn had pulled the rug on him."[13]

Tip and Sam had a candid chat on one of those mornings[14]:

> So this particular morning, I said to Sam Rayburn, "Mr. Speaker, supposing a candidate throws his hat into the ring and he can't win the nomination, but the convention wants him for the second spot. What do you think?" He said, "You mean a man who's a candidate for President of the United States, and the convention doesn't want him—they take another man—but they do want him for second spot? Well," he said, "to me, once a man puts his hat in the ring—he's a candidate at the convention—then he's obligated to the convention. If they don't want him for the presidency, but the fact that he got into the contest, he has no other obligation than to follow through with the wishes and the desires of the convention. And if they want him for second spot, he *must* take second spot." And he said, "There's no question about that in my mind whatsoever."

Rayburn knew full well that Tip held Jack's seat in the House and that this message would be relayed to Kennedy. Sam clearly anticipated a Johnson-Kennedy ticket emerging from the convention.

The Primaries: Kennedy's strategy was to demonstrate his electability through his standings in the polls and his four contested primary victories over Senators Hubert Humphrey of Minnesota and Wayne Morse of Oregon. Altogether, Kennedy's name appeared in 10 primaries. In four write-in primaries, he finished ahead of Stevenson in Illinois, Massachusetts, and Pennsylvania; and Symington in Nebraska. He was virtually unopposed in New Hampshire and Indiana. While Kennedy was victorious over Humphrey in Wisconsin and West Virginia and over Morse in Maryland and Morse's home state of Oregon, neither Humphrey nor Morse was a likely nominee.[15]

Though not an electoral heavyweight, Hubert Humphrey had become a factor in national liberal circles during the 1940s when he was able to reconfigure Minnesota politics through the creation of the Democratic Farmer-Labor Party and purge its more radical elements.[16] As mayor of Minneapolis, Humphrey sought election to the U.S. Senate in 1948. It was Humphrey and ex-Representative Andrew Biemiller of Wisconsin who authored the pro–civil rights planks at the 1948 Democratic convention that led to the southern walkout.

Senator Humphrey was first elected in 1948 and reelected in 1954. Lyndon Johnson, also first elected to the Senate in 1948, liked Humphrey's style and appreciated his solid ties to the nation's liberal establishment.[17] By preventing the newly elected Humphrey from being marginalized by the Senate's southern hierarchy, Johnson hoped to gain access to the liberal faction of the party. Humphrey's original committee assignments to Expenditures in the Executive Departments, Post Office and Civil Service, and the Select Committee on Small Business were not intended for a rising star within the party but were generally reserved for those whom the leaders saw as "one-term wonders." Johnson, who had been elected majority whip in 1951, got Humphrey on Agriculture and Forestry that year and onto Foreign Relations in 1953.[18] The Agriculture assignment would please Humphrey's Minnesota constituents and the Foreign Relations assignment would delight the national liberals. Humphrey owed Johnson for these interventions.

Kennedy's other opponent in the 1960 primaries was the erratic Wayne Morse of Oregon, nicknamed "the tiger of the Senate" because of his irascibility and penchant for time-consuming filibusters.[19] He was not a serious candidate. Morse had begun his Senate career in 1945 as a Republican and was reelected in 1950. On October 24, 1952, two weeks before Ike's victory enabled the Republicans to capture the new Congress, Morse chose to leave the Republican Party and to be seated as an Independent. Its impact was to shrink the GOP's margin in the Senate from two votes to one. If Morse's intent was to extract favors from the new Majority Leaders of the Republican Party, then it was a mistake. He was quickly voted off the Armed Services Committee where he was its third-ranked Republican and was sent to the purgatory of the District of Columbia Committee, generally reserved for freshmen, legislative nonentities, and troublesome members.[20] With Democrats returning to power in 1955, Johnson supported Morse for the prestigious Foreign Relations Committee as Morse chose to abandon his 26-month experiment in independence and became a Democrat.

Morse entered and lost the primary battles to Kennedy in Maryland and Oregon, his home state, following the collapse of the Humphrey campaign in the West Virginia primary. In retrospect, it appears as if the Morse presidential candidacy was a brake to slow the Kennedy steamroller. Morse owed Senate Majority Leader Johnson a large favor for his redemption. This would have been one way to pay his debt.

Kennedy faced surprising resistance from many fellow Catholic state leaders as well as other Democrats who were fearful of a repeat of Al Smith's 1928 debacle. Smith had carried only eight states in that campaign—the Catholic strongholds of Massachusetts and Rhode Island along with six Deep South Democratic ones. No Democratic candidate between the end of Reconstruction in 1877 and George McGovern's 1972 campaign had carried fewer states or electoral votes.

The other candidacy that threatened to undo Kennedy's march to the nomination was that of two-time nominee Adlai Stevenson, who still had the affection of the party's most liberal members. They felt that despite Adlai's two failures in 1952 and 1956 to defeat the beloved Eisenhower, he would be able to beat the far less beloved Dick Nixon. Nominating Stevenson a third time for president would not be a reach for the Democratic Party that had nominated Franklin Roosevelt four times; Grover Cleveland three times; and William Jennings Bryan three times. Three of those nominations had occurred after losing candidacies. Stevenson's fabled indecisiveness had made it difficult for any formal organized effort to rally around him and his support on the first ballot was more of a voted thank you than any real hope of a third nomination.

The Risk-Averse Lyndon Johnson: Kennedy's best-placed challenger Lyndon Johnson avoided direct primary competition with him. This was not unusual for Johnson. Johnson was always fearful of losing the office that he held en route to gaining the office that he sought. As a result, his efforts to advance his career were replete with a number of "safety nets" which limited the degree of rejection that he had to face. Johnson first ran for the U.S Senate in a 1941 special election and so he did not risk his House seat in this bid. Deprived of a Senate victory by dubious vote counting against him in that primary,[21] he was later victorious in 1948 with even more dubious vote counting in his favor. His 87-vote margin of a total vote of 988,295 earned him the sarcastic nickname of "Landslide Lyndon" and made it unlikely that he would ever again risk rejection.[22] When Johnson sought the presidential nomination in 1960, it was also the year when his Senate seat came up for its electoral renewal. A year earlier in the spring of 1959, Johnson, the risk-avoider, convinced the Texas Legislature to move the state's primaries earlier in the year and to permit a candidate to run for two national offices simultaneously.[23] This change in the law was the "safety net" that would allow him to contest for the presidency without giving up his Senate seat.

The rules of presidential nominating conventions are patterned on those of the Rules of the House, so the custom in both parties has been to have the highest-ranking House member preside over the convention and often a fellow House leader will chair its platform committee. This would not be the case in 1960. Neither Sam Rayburn, the permanent chair in 1948, 1952, and 1956, nor John McCormack, the resolutions chair in 1944, 1952, and 1956, would hold official party titles at the convention.[24] They were each chairing delegations committed to the two leading candidates with McCormack chairing Massachusetts pro-Kennedy delegation and Rayburn serving as Johnson's floor manager much as he had in 1932 and in 1940 when he served in that role for fellow Texan John "Cactus Jack" Garner. Instead, Florida Governor LeRoy Collins was chosen to be the permanent chair of the convention.[25]

Senator Kennedy asked John McCormack to lead his floor fight for the nomination, stunning most state insiders. As the *Boston Globe*'s C. R. Owens reported: "Majority Leader John W. McCormack, who was presiding at the caucus as chairman of the delegation, was informed by the senator that he, McCormack, will be director of all the Kennedy convention activities in Los Angeles."[26] In another column five days later, Owens contended that John had not intended to go to Los Angeles "until Kennedy made a personal appeal." Owens also reminded his readers[27]: "It will be recalled that four years ago there were post-convention claims that McCormack had not gone all out for Kennedy who saw his flourishing campaign for the Vice Presidential nomination collapse when the Congressman's very good friend Speaker Sam Rayburn recognized delegations which supported Estes Kefauver, the ultimate nominee."

John's five-member convention team in 1960 consisted of his three House protégés—Tip O'Neill, Eddie Boland, and Jim Burke—his nephew Eddie, and even longtime Kennedy rival Governor Foster Furcolo who was given convention work to keep "in touch with fellow governors and friends he had made while serving as a member of Congress."

Everyone knew that the real leader of JFK's team was his brother Bobby, who was frenetically working the phones with his usual single-minded devotion to Jack's presidential bid. To some the choice of John McCormack for this role seemed more out of deference than need. More knowledgeable observers were aware that McCormack could help Kennedy mollify Sam Rayburn, Lyndon Johnson's mentor, and to remind other congressional Democrats on the convention floor that Jack Kennedy was an alumnus of both chambers and had not burned his bridges to the House's leadership in his quest for the presidency. Naming John McCormack as floor manager served two purposes. It prevented McCormack from presiding over the convention where his control of the gavel and power of recognition could affect the outcome of the vote, much as the Kennedys felt that Rayburn had done to sink Jack's vice presidential bid in 1956. More importantly, if Jack wished to reach out to LBJ as his vice presidential choice, he would need to get past Sam Rayburn's opposition and the only Massachusetts man trusted by Rayburn was John McCormack. If Jack Kennedy should succeed in gaining the presidency, an amiable working relationship with the leaders of the House would be essential. There were limits to Kennedy's "outsider" strategy and he knew what they were.

There was a whiff of Joe Kennedy in the air. When Sam Rayburn was asked about Joe, he said, "I haven't seen him, but he's in the bushes around here."[28] Unlike 1956, Joe chose to attend the 1960 convention. He got a private box for himself and family members and invited his old friends Henry and Clare Boothe Luce to join him to watch the convention's drama unfold. Joe had always wanted a ticket with Lyndon Johnson and Jack running together, but had failed to convince Lyndon in 1955 and asked John McCormack for help after being told, "Well, he won't take the nomination." Joe then asked John to contact fellow Catholic heavyweights Pat Brown, Governor of California, Charley Buckley of the Bronx, and Bill Green of Philadelphia to gauge the level of support that they would provide for Jack.

In John McCormack's 1977 oral history, he recounted his report to Joe Kennedy[29]:

> Joe called me up about talking to these three members, these three persons, and making a report to him And then I told him I thought Lyndon Johnson was the best man to be the running mate for John, when John's nominated. And he said, "Well Lyndon's campaigning throughout the country, he and Sam Rayburn, telling the whole country that he won't take the nomination." I said, "Of course they are telling them that . . . but when you talk about Lyndon Johnson and Sam Rayburn, you're talking about two men who are responsible men, Joe. And one thing is certain. A responsible man makes the responsible decision at the right time. And they mean what they say, that they'll not take the nomination today. But if John offers it to them, Lyndon Johnson and Sam Rayburn are such responsible men, they'll realize the duty to the party is such, and they'll accept."

John and the Vice Presidential Selection: Just before the formal balloting, Tip O'Neill brought a page of the delegate counts to the suite where the Massachusetts delegates met and found delegation chair John McCormack meeting with Sam Rayburn and Wright Patman, chair of the House Banking Committee. Rayburn glanced over the totals and correctly concluded that Kennedy had enough votes for a first ballot victory. If Jack wanted Lyndon to run with him, Jack should call Sam first and he would speak to LBJ about the overwhelming importance of keeping the hated Dick Nixon out of the White House.[30] John McCormack may not have brokered this historic arrangement, but as always he was "in the room" when it occurred.

Once the voting began, the totals came in as expected and as recounted in Richard Bain and Judith Parris's *Convention Decisions and Voting Records*[31]:

> When the roll call had been completed amid a demonstration by jubilant Kennedy supporters, the nominee had 806 votes to 409 for Johnson, 86 for Symington, 79 ½ for Stevenson, and 140 ½ for the favorite sons. The nomination was made unanimous by voice vote. The cheers continued until Kennedy appeared on the podium to acknowledge them briefly.

O'Neill returned to the Kennedy suite with the news but before the call could be made, Bobby Kennedy had to be sent off on wild goose chases throughout the hall. With Bobby gone, the call was made. Whether it was a courtesy call with the anticipation that LBJ would refuse it or if it was a sincere offer from JFK has been debated for years. Much to everyone's surprise and Robert Kennedy's dismay, LBJ accepted the offer.[32]

This dramatic generational shift within the Democratic Party, the nation's oldest political party, was achieved through the efforts of three of the party's oldest lions— the 78-year-old Sam Rayburn, Lyndon Johnson's political father; the 71-year-old Joe Kennedy, Jack Kennedy's father whose fabulous wealth made much of this possible; and 68-year-old John McCormack, the one man who had known them both for more than 30 years and was in the room when the crucial arrangement was made. Youth may have been served but it would not have occurred without the involvement of these three elders. As recounted by Larry O'Brien, second-in-command of the Kennedy campaign: "I don't like the word older, but I will single out the efforts of our own Massachusetts congressman, John McCormack, who is chairman of the Massachusetts delegation and majority floor leader of the House of Representatives. He, and men like him, have been invaluable."[33]

The Johnson vice presidential nomination was submitted to the convention by Pennsylvania Governor David Lawrence, the Catholic leader most fearful about a Kennedy candidacy. As Lawrence concluded and a Johnson rally ensued, John McCormack rose and called Permanent Chair LeRoy Collins to suspend the rules, close the nominations, and declare the Johnson choice by acclamation.[34] McCormack's move set off another rally for Johnson but it also caused a shouting firestorm among the liberal Democrats in the California and Michigan delegations.[35] Michigan's Governor G. Mennen (Soapy) Williams was photographed rebuking McCormack with his fingers in John's face. It didn't matter. When the booing, cheering, and the shouting subsided, the Democrats now had their 1960 ticket.

Johnson's Senate seat in Texas had been protected by the Texas Legislature so he would not lose his seat should the Kennedy-Johnson ticket fail in November. Should the ticket fail, LBJ could rightly contend to the liberals that he had helped it as much as he could and be well positioned for his own 1964 presidential bid. Should the ticket win, Johnson would be seated in the vice presidential chair presiding over the Senate and he would just ask his fellow Senate Democrats if he could attend their caucus. Johnson assumed that Washington insiders would give him the credit for any of Kennedy's legislative successes much as they had given him most of the credit for the legislative successes in his six years as Senate majority leader during the Eisenhower Administration.

Richard Nixon's Nomination: Vice President Nixon's nomination was easy. His eight years as the Republican Party's attack dog had won him the loyalty of most Republican operatives, even though it may have occasionally dismayed President Eisenhower. Knowing of the power of the party's Eastern establishment, Nixon met with New York Governor Nelson Rockefeller to work out a platform that was more philosophically moderate than the one drafted by Platform Chair Charles Percy, President of Bell and Howell. The revised platform, known disparagingly as the "Treaty of Fifth Avenue," angered the party's deep-died conservatives who were determined to deny Nixon a unanimous convention vote.[36] Ultimately only ten of them—all from Louisiana—voted for conservative U.S. Senator Barry M. Goldwater of Arizona. With the nomination in hand, Nixon chose another Eastern establishment figure, United Nations Ambassador Henry Cabot Lodge, Jr. of Massachusetts, to be his vice presidential running mate. It was a curious choice given the fact that Lodge had lost his own Senate seat to Jack Kennedy in 1952, but Lodge was a good-looking, articulate defender of American interests at the UN, and his foreign policy experience would clearly outdistance that of any Democratic vice presidential contenders. Lodge, unlike Nixon, was unanimously confirmed.

The post-recess session, 1960

On July 3, the 86th Congress voted a five-week recess to nominate the presidential candidates but returned to work after the convention. The Senate met first and all eyes were on it as Vice President Richard Nixon, the Republican presidential nominee, presided over the Senate; Senate Majority Leader Lyndon B. Johnson, the Democratic vice presidential nominee, managed the majority's position on the floor; Senator John F. Kennedy, the Democratic presidential nominee, debated Social Security, the minimum wage, and national security; while Thruston Morton of Kentucky, the chair of the Republican National Committee, and Henry M. "Scoop" Jackson of Washington State, the chair of the Democratic National Committee, tried to tilt the debate toward their party's respective positions.

The postconvention session was not adjudged to be a success for the majority Democrats. While attention fastened on the Senate, the House Rules Committee continued its obstructionist policies derailing major bills that the Rayburn-McCormack-led House Democrats wanted for the upcoming campaign. As described in the *New York Times*, "A higher minimum wage, Federal aid for school construction, a Social Security system of medical insurance for the aged and liberalized housing programs all became casualties of conservative Democratic-Republican alliances."[37]

Washington insiders were well aware that the overwhelming House Democratic victory of 1958 with its northern and western liberal newcomers had been philosophically voided by the House Rules Committee. Upon being chosen minority leader in 1959, Charlie Halleck committed himself to a resuscitation of the Conservative Coalition with like-minded southerners.[38] The opening gambit for Halleck was to fill the two Republican Rules Committee vacancies of relative moderates Henry J. Latham of New York and Hugh D. Scott of Pennsylvania with conservative B. Carroll Reece of Tennessee and ultraconservative Hamer Budge of Idaho. While the Reece change was minor, the replacement of Scott by Budge was an answered prayer for segregationist Democrats Howard W. Smith of Virginia and Bill Colmer of Mississippi, who now had four Republican votes to join them in 6–6 votes to stop liberal legislation from reaching the House floor. The other six Democrats were split evenly between three Rayburn allies and three McCormack ones.

As O'Neill recounted in his Oral History[39]:

> Well, all the time that I was on the committee, rare was the occasion when Sam Rayburn ever asked me anything. I was always considered to be left of John McCormack. [James J.] Jim Delaney, [Ray J.] Madden, myself: we were McCormack people on the committee. [Richard] Bolling and [Homer] Thornberry and [James W.] Trimble: they were considered to be Rayburn people. And so if Rayburn had a problem on the committee, he would contact his men; while McCormack, [when] the leadership had a problem on the committee, McCormack always talked to Madden, Delaney, and myself.

The taming of the Rules Committee would have to await the presidential election and the philosophical composition of the incoming 87th Congress.

International tension and the CIA

One of the undercurrents of the 1960 campaign was the growing international tension between the United States and the Soviet Union. Exacerbated by the May 1st capture of the U-2 spy plane flown over the Soviet Union, questions were raised about the efficacy of America's intelligence gathering agencies, most notably the Central Intelligence Agency (CIA) that had authorized the U-2 flight.

Not widely known was John's role in helping to create the CIA during his time on the Expenditures Committee in the years following World War II. As described in David M. Barrett's book *The CIA and Congress*[40]:

> The Massachusetts representative [House Democratic Majority Leader John McCormack] was a leading member of the Executive Expenditures Committee

and had helped create the Central Intelligence Agency. Despite his skeletal, pale face and white head of hair, McCormack was energetic and a quick study. The CIA was a vital asset in the Cold War, he believed. Though a whole-hearted Catholic and probably horrified at the thought of homosexuality, McCormack was not one to lead campaigns against them.

John's continuing involvement enabled him to learn about the U-2 episode, while Sam Rayburn had no interest.[41] "Rayburn's ignorance of the U-2 was partly his own fault: unlike House majority leader John McCormack, who had always liked having private lunches with DCIs [Directors of Central Intelligence] every year or so, the Speaker had not seemed 'desirous' of briefings, in the words of a CIA official."

As the presidential campaign was to begin its September kickoff, troubling news reached John McCormack when Drew Pearson broke a story concerning two National Security Administration analysts who had gone missing.[42] John followed up on the story and learned that the two men, Bernon Mitchell and William Martin, were NSA cryptologists and suspected gay lovers who went missing in Mexico en route to Cuba and later to the Soviet Union. The case seemed similar to the infamous 1951 Guy Burgess-Donald MacLean-Kim Philby episode in Great Britain. A turf battle emerged between two of John's less well-regarded committee chairs, Tad Walter of House Un-American Activities Committee (HUAC) and Carl Vinson of Armed Services, and John assigned the investigation to Walter.[43] While the Defense Department contended that the two men "had been employed in 'limited areas of communications statistical work,'" John disagreed.

The defection of Mitchell and Martin troubled him personally. John declared that the loss of the code information "[was] far more serious than any official [had] publicly admitted," and took to the House floor and denounced this circumstance as "one of the worst security breaches" in American history.[44] Despite John's public pronouncements, the case slipped off the national radar shortly afterward.

The religious factor

There was no escape from the religious question and Kennedy's Catholicism. Placards, both pro and con, appeared at virtually every Kennedy rally and it became a regular feature of Protestant sermons on Sundays. The more fearful Protestant ministers believed that Kennedy's election would enable the Pope to gain control of the United States, while other more enlightened ministers accepted Kennedy's oft-repeated declarations that his religion would not dictate his policies.[45]

The one issue that seemed to recur was public funding for parochial schools. The Supreme Court in the New Jersey case of *Everson v. Board of Education*, 330 U.S. 1 (1947) ruled that public money to reimburse bus fares for parents whose children attended private parochial schools did not violate the Constitution's "wall of separation between Church and State" because the money went to the parents and not to the schools themselves. As a postwar House member from Massachusetts, the nation's second most

Catholic state, Congressman Kennedy had supported federal aid to parochial schools.[46] His stance changed as his constituency grew and Catholic proportions shrunk. Senator Kennedy's campaign stance on parochial school funding was materially different from that of Representative Kennedy. Following his August nomination, Kennedy gave a major speech to the Greater Houston Ministerial Association on September 12, 1960, in which he stated emphatically, "Contrary to common newspaper usage, I am not the Catholic candidate for President. I am the Democratic Party's candidate for President who happens also to be a Catholic."[47] He was quite explicit in his comments:

> I believe in an America where the separation of church and state is absolute; where no Catholic prelate would tell the President—should he be Catholic—how to act, and no Protestant minister would tell his parishioners for whom to vote; where no church or church school is granted any public funds or political preference, and where no man is denied public office merely because his religion differs from the President who might appoint him, or the people who might elect him.
>
> I ask you tonight to follow in that tradition—to judge me on the basis of 14 years in the Congress, on my declared stands against an Ambassador to the Vatican, against unconstitutional aid to parochial schools, and against any boycott of the public schools—which I attended myself.

It was a powerful statement and it defused enough anti-Catholic Protestant votes for Kennedy that it enabled him to carry the same proportion of Protestants that Stevenson had carried four years earlier—38%.[48] But it came at a cost and the cost was that many of the well-placed Catholic clergy were enraged. Realizing that Kennedy was serious about not favoring funds for parochial schools or naming an American ambassador to the Vatican, many senior Catholic clergymen supported the candidacy of Republican Richard Nixon, a Quaker. No one was more adamant than the powerful Francis Cardinal Spellman of New York City, sometimes described as "the American Pope."[49] Spellman and Joe Kennedy had worked closely in the 1930s to undermine the influence of the anti-Semitic FDR opponent Father Charles Coughlin. Kennedy-Spellman ties were once so close that Cardinal Spellman had performed wedding ceremonies for four of the Kennedy children—Eunice, Bob, Jean, and Ted—while Jack's service was conducted by Spellman's church rival, Boston's Archbishop Richard J. Cushing and Patricia's by the Reverend John J. Cavanaugh, former president of Notre Dame University. Kathleen, the defiant second daughter, was married in a civil ceremony to an English aristocrat.

Well known in Boston Catholic Church circles was the long-standing rivalry between Cardinals Spellman and Cushing. When Spellman became Archbishop of New York in 1939, Cushing, who was six years younger, succeeded him as Auxiliary Bishop of Boston under the imperious William Henry Cardinal O'Connell. While Spellman's grandfather was an Irish immigrant, he was a middle-class grocer's son from Whitman in central Massachusetts while both of Cushing's parents were "off the boat" and his father was a South Boston blacksmith. While Spellman graduated from Fordham and the Pontifical North American College in Rome, Cushing dropped out of Boston College and studied for the priesthood at St. John's Seminary in nearby Brighton. Spellman became a Cardinal in 1946 after seven years as Archbishop of New York while Cushing had to wait for 14 years after being named Archbishop of the larger Diocese of Boston in 1944. Cushing was named a Cardinal in 1958 by Pope John XXIII after being bypassed for years by Pius XII, a Spellman ally.

Like his dear friend and fellow "Southie" John McCormack, Cushing was without prejudice having joined the NAACP and he was very close to his Jewish brother-in-law. As friends and allies who communicated regularly, neither Cushing nor McCormack distanced themselves from their roots in Boston's Irish ghetto and never forgot where they came from.

As the 1960 election came to a close, the *New York Herald-Tribune*'s John Crosby reported that Spellman had favored Nixon over Kennedy which Crosby linked to an ongoing rivalry between the two prelates. Needless to say, the rift was emphatically denied and the article was declared to be "a complete fabrication."[50] However, one powerful Catholic layman who had informants throughout the Church believed the accounts—Joseph P. Kennedy.

The willingness of Spellman and many conservative bishops to abandon the Kennedy candidacy led to a furious encounter with Joe Kennedy just before the election in October when Joe stormed into the Cardinal's residence located behind St. Patrick's Church and known as "the Powerhouse." As described by Spellman aide Monsignor Eugene Clark,[51] "He [Joe] blew his cork. He was in a foul mood, but he didn't blow his cork at the Cardinal. No one ever dared do that. He didn't take the Cardinal head-on. He spoke about the bishops not supporting his son, but Cardinal Spellman didn't give an inch."

Monsignor Clark also recalled an angry phone call between the two in which Spellman hung up on Joe Kennedy, declaring, "That is a truly evil man."[52]

But Spellman and the bishops could not keep Kennedy from receiving the highest Catholic vote in the past 16 presidential elections, 1948–2012. Gallup contended that 78% of Catholics voted for Kennedy while the National Election Studies at the University of Michigan credited Kennedy with 82%.[53] Gallup's numbers represented a 27-point improvement over Stevenson's 1956 proportion of 51% while the Michigan data represented a 36-point improvement over Stevenson's 46%.

The twentieth century's closest popular vote election

It was the youngest election face-off between two major political party candidates in American history, with 43-year-old Democrat Jack Kennedy confronting 47-year-old Dick Nixon. Whoever won this race would succeed the then-oldest occupant of the White House, 70-year-old Dwight D. Eisenhower. One of the more distinctive characteristics of this race was that the two men had served in the House together on the same committee and each had served in the Senate. While some characteristics were similar, it was their dissimilarities that gave this particular contest legendary status: the Quaker poor boy of modest means from the West Coast against the well-born, well-educated, and wealthy Catholic from the East Coast. It was a classic contest between a climber and an inheritor.

They chose different strategies. Nixon chose to campaign in all 50 states, even in the South, those historic Democratic bastions. His was a national campaign, while Kennedy's was a more focused one. Kennedy concentrated his energy on urban centers and their neighboring suburbs. This was where his media-sensitive campaign would have its greatest impact; Kennedy was well aware of how telegenic he was, and he parlayed it to voters looking for a change from the gray years of the Eisenhower presidency. Nixon was every bit as energetic as Jack, but his multiple detours into states that had no media presence were part of an ill-considered strategy. It would later come home to roost at the time of the first televised debate.

Since this was the first election where television, a relatively new medium from the start of the decade, was now virtually universal throughout the nation and with no incumbent entered in the contest, it made sense to arrange televised debates between the two men. Television executives were ecstatic over the prospect and the networks held lengthy negotiations with the two campaigns as to which format would be adopted, which topics would be discussed, and how might the questions be posed to the candidates. They ultimately agreed on four debates, and the two camps negotiated topics. Nixon's 1952 vice presidential candidacy had been rescued by his televised defense of his receiving money from wealthy backers, now known as the "Checkers speech." His tour de force television performance that evening convinced him that television was a successful medium for him. It was that performance, the televised 1959 "kitchen debate" with Soviet Premier Khrushchev at the World's Fair in Moscow, and his collegiate debate experience that gave him the confidence that he could easily dispatch Kennedy in these televised debates. It was an unfortunate hubris that would not prepare him for what would be the general assessment of his performance.

It was popular urban legend that radio listeners and television viewers had adjudicated the debate differently, with Nixon's style popular among radio listeners and Kennedy's style of speaking directly to the television cameras giving him an edge among the viewers. Nixon's belief that his experience as vice president would trump that of Kennedy's Senate experience was lost in the aftermath. The later debates generated less interest, but the perception now was that Kennedy was Nixon's equal, thereby canceling out Nixon's presumed edge of experience.

When the votes came in on election night, starting on the East Coast, Kennedy jumped to an early and sizable lead. He captured nine of the twelve states of the Northeast, losing only Maine, New Hampshire, and Vermont. The Midwest results were mixed with Jack winning the industrial Midwest of Illinois, Michigan, Minnesota, and Missouri but losing the farm states of Iowa, Kansas, Nebraska, and the Dakotas, as well as the conservative industrial states of Ohio and Indiana. As results crossed the Missouri River, Kennedy's popular vote lead disappeared. He lost all of the Mountain states, apart from Nevada and New Mexico, and the West Coast. The new states of Alaska and Hawaii split, with Nixon carrying Alaska and Kennedy carrying Hawaii. The most fascinating results were in the South, where Kennedy carried six of the eleven Confederate states, losing the outer South states of Tennessee, Virginia, and Florida.

Lyndon Johnson's impact on the ticket was obvious, as Kennedy won the 38 electoral votes of Texas, Louisiana, and neighboring New Mexico that had failed to support Adlai Stevenson in 1956. These states joined Arkansas, Georgia, and the Carolinas in the Kennedy column. Mississippi and Alabama cast 14 of their 19 electoral votes for slates of independent electors that would eventually vote for conservative U.S. Senators Democrat Harry F. Byrd of Virginia and Republican Barry M. Goldwater of Arizona. Kennedy's targeted campaign captured four fewer states than Nixon's did, but with victories in seven of the ten largest ones, the Electoral College majority was won.[54]

Kennedy and Johnson carried Massachusetts and Texas as well as most of the Northeast and the South. Their inter-regional strategy had worked. With 113,000 total votes of the close to 69,000,000 cast separating Kennedy and Nixon, it was the closest popular vote election of the twentieth century. Ambassador Joe Kennedy's dream had been realized, and the nation's first Catholic president was of Boston Irish descent. The Austin-Boston connection that Sam Rayburn and John McCormack had embodied for the previous 20 years to bring party unity to the U.S. House of Representatives had now been extended to the White House.

The Kennedy-Johnson ticket captured 76 votes in the six Confederate states of Arkansas, Georgia, Louisiana, North Carolina, and South Carolina, and Texas while Nixon captured the 33 electoral votes of Florida, Tennessee, and Virginia. The five border states split between Kennedy victories in Maryland, Missouri, and West Virginia with 30 electoral votes and Nixon winning 18 of Kentucky and Oklahoma's 19 electoral votes losing a "faithless" Oklahoma elector to Virginia Senator Harry F. Byrd of Virginia.

One of the more intriguing aspects of that contest, apart from its closeness, was the vote in Alabama. Segregationist Democrats in the South, but most notably in Mississippi and Alabama, sought to repeat their 1948 strategy of denying votes to the Democratic nominee in order to push the selection into the House of Representatives where the sixteen southern and border state House delegations could cast their state's vote for the presidential candidate most willing to accede to their requests for a slowdown if not a total rejection of the civil rights thrust emanating from Congress. Mississippi's eight electors were unpledged but the Democratic primary for Alabama's eleven electoral votes were split—five loyalists for Kennedy and six "Free" or unpledged. The popular vote totals were allocated by the highest vote total of the respective campaigns with Kennedy awarded 318,303 votes and 324,050 unpledged votes for Governor Frank M. Dixon.[55] Overall, the southern and border states gave Kennedy a 106 to 51 winning vote edge and adding Alabama's disputed five votes gave Kennedy a total of 111 electoral votes without which he still finished ahead of Nixon 192 to 168. However, that total would have kicked the contest into the House of Representatives where it was clear from their signatures on the 1956 Southern Manifesto and their floor votes on the Civil Rights bills of 1957 and 1960 that the numbers were on the segregationist side. While Kennedy won nine southern and border states to Nixon's five, removing them from their overall state split of 22 for Kennedy and 26 for Nixon would have left Kennedy with only 13 states to Nixon's 21. Had this been the outcome, the congressional segregationists would have easily been able to dictate terms of surrender on civil rights initiatives.

.

The Kennedy-Johnson ticket's Electoral College victory of 303–219 was the same number of electoral votes that Harry Truman had captured in 1948, and it was higher than the 277 electoral votes carried by Woodrow Wilson's reelection bid in 1916. It was far from a mandate, and the loss of 21 Democratic seats in the House indicated that Kennedy would have far fewer congressional Democrats to help him push his program. The challenge for Sam Rayburn and John McCormack to move the Kennedy agenda through the House had gotten more difficult.

Inauguration days

At his March 4, 1797, inaugural in Philadelphia, John Adams of Massachusetts, Washington's vice president and the Harvard-educated son of a Puritan deacon, began a tradition as he was sworn in by Yale-educated Chief Justice Oliver Ellsworth of Connecticut thus joining the ceremonial leaders of the second and third of the nation's three branches of government in the building that housed the Congress of the United States, the first constitutional branch of the new government. The precedent was now established.

The 44th presidential inaugural occurred on January 20, 1961, when 43-year-old John Fitzgerald Kennedy of Massachusetts was sworn as the nation's 35th President by Chief Justice Earl Warren. This presidential inaugural was unusual for a number of reasons. It was the fifth one in the twentieth century where an electoral shift in party control had occurred. That these interparty transfers occurred without street riots and heavily armed soldiers lined along the parade routes is remarkable for any nation, especially one as large and diverse as the United States. Adding to its uniqueness was the 27-year contrast between the outgoing 70-year-old President Eisenhower and the incoming 43-year-old John Kennedy, making it clear that this was not just a party transfer of power but a generational one as well.

Arrangements at the Capitol had been made once again by the Joint Congressional Committee on Inaugural Ceremonies. This had been the formal title given to the committee in 1901 at the time of President William McKinley's second inauguration. Because the event takes place on congressional turf, the Congress assigns this ceremonial function to a six-member committee with three senior members from each chamber—two from the majority party and one from the minority. House Majority Leader John McCormack of Massachusetts was once more listed on the Joint Inaugural Committee. This would be John's third time, having served on it for Harry Truman's inaugural in 1949, Dwight Eisenhower's second in 1957, and now this one for Jack Kennedy, a man with whom he had clashed earlier and would again before the year ended. John McCormack would later serve on the committee twice more for both Lyndon Johnson's inauguration in 1965 and Richard Nixon's first one in 1969.

While it is hard to locate John McCormack in the crowd on the stand at the Capitol, Speaker Sam Rayburn's glistening bald head was clearly visible. Sam Rayburn would have the enjoyable job of swearing in his dearest protégé, former U.S. Senator Lyndon B. Johnson, as vice president. It would be the first time that a House Speaker would administer the vice presidential oath. After all, the vice president would now become president of the Senate, but this choice was a testament to the unique father-son relationship between Rayburn and Johnson, the two Texas Democrats who held the party's congressional reins throughout the eight Eisenhower years.

Memories of this event fasten on the subfreezing cold that Friday morning and the difficulty that the 86-year-old white-haired Robert Frost, the California-born Harvard dropout and now the patron saint of Northern New England poetry, had in reading his own poem. Jack Kennedy's gracious gesture of shielding the glare from the sun and the snow that bothered Frost so that he could complete the poem's reading touched the hearts of American intellectuals, real and self-declared. Kennedy's inaugural address announced the nation's generational change in American leadership, with its oft-quoted lines imploring American citizens to "ask not what your country can do for you but what you can do for your country" and to recognize[56]

[that] the torch has been passed to a new generation of Americans—born in this century, tempered by war, disciplined by a hard and bitter peace, proud of our ancient heritage—and unwilling to witness or permit the slow undoing of those human rights to which this nation has always been committed, and to which we are committed today at home and around the world.

This speech repeated to this day has joined Abraham Lincoln's second inaugural address in 1865 and FDR's first in 1933 as one of the three most memorable in American presidential history. The service then ended, the parade began, and the parties roared through the evening.

The first order of business for a new president is the naming of the Cabinet. Kennedy named ten white men to his Cabinet. Three governors were selected—Orville Freeman of Minnesota as secretary of agriculture, Luther Hodges of North Carolina as secretary of commerce, and Abraham Ribicoff of Connecticut as secretary of health, education, and welfare. Others with governmental experience included Stewart Udall of Arizona, a fourth-term House member as secretary of the interior along with Dean Rusk and C. Douglas Dillon, the new secretaries of state and treasury, both of whom had State Department experience. From the private sector came Ford Motor executive Robert McNamara, the new secretary of defense; United Steel Workers attorney Arthur Goldberg, the secretary of labor; and Postmaster General Edward Day. Two unique features of the Kennedy cabinet stand out. Kennedy named two Jews to the Cabinet: his longtime friend and ally Abraham Ribicoff and Adlai Stevenson ally Arthur Goldberg of Illinois. It was the first time two Jewish Cabinet officers had been named and it was an extension of Kennedy's own triumph over religious prejudice and a surprise to those well aware of Jack Kennedy's father's unfortunate anti-Semitic tendencies.

But Joe Kennedy would be served as his third son, Robert F. Kennedy, the legal counsel on the Senate's Government Operations Committee, would be named attorney general. Apart from being the president's brother, this was a hard one to sell to the Senate given that Bob Kennedy was only 35, the youngest selectee, and chief counsel on one of the Senate's lesser committees. He was not a popular choice. A number of major newspapers decried the selection and the new administration would have suffered greatly had the nomination been rejected by the Democratic Senate.[57]

Sources close to Lyndon Johnson contend that Jack did not wish to name Bobby as attorney general. Tyler Abell, stepson of insider political columnist Drew Pearson and the husband of Bess Clements Abell, Lady Bird Johnson's social secretary, recalled a conversation with longtime Washington Democratic heavyweight Clark Clifford, who was asked by Jack to call his father about the selection.[58] Before Clifford could complete his sentence, Joe Kennedy declared, "Bobby's Attorney General" and abruptly hung up. A similar account involving Clifford appears in the Senate Historical Office's oral history of Bobby Baker, the disgraced Senate Majority Secretary and close protégé of Lyndon Johnson, who shared LBJ's disdain for Bob Kennedy. In Baker's account, Clifford tried to meet with Joe Kennedy in New York and was told by Joe, "Bobby's going to be the Attorney General. Get out of here."[59] While the Baker account is more dramatic than Abell's, Joe Kennedy would be more likely to hang up on a telephone call than to order Clifford out of his apartment. A major power broker like Clifford would take less offense at a terminated phone call than being ordered to leave someone's premises.

In Baker's account, LBJ was fearful that Bobby Kennedy would have been voted down by the Senate's Republicans and southern Democrats, most of whom were LBJ allies. The leader of the southern Democrats was the courtly Dick Russell of Georgia, who was LBJ's Senate mentor and whose staunch support for Johnson enabled him to become the Senate's youngest floor leader in 1953.[60] As recounted by Baker[61]:

> So the President had said, "Lyndon, I need your help," because Senator Russell and the Republicans were solid against Bobby being Attorney General. He had really no legal experience. Johnson said "Bobby [Baker], if the President is defeated by my supporters, it's a terrible, terrible can't do situation for me." He said, "See what you can do with our mutual friend Senator Russell, because if you get enough bourbon in him, he gets more reasonable."

Russell agreed to a voice vote for the nomination and with the cooperation of Senate Minority Leader Everett Dirksen of Illinois, Bob Kennedy won approval from a very hesitant Senate. Had it been a recorded roll call vote, Baker contended, "[Bob Kennedy] would have been lucky to get 40 votes."[62]

The Vacant Senate Seat: With two of the three surviving Kennedy brothers now serving as president and attorney general, former Ambassador Joseph P. Kennedy was busily planning to launch his youngest son Edward, better known as Teddy, into the Senate to fill the seat that Jack had vacated on December 22, 1960. Jack had only held the seat for less than eight years but it had already been declared as family property. Joe would reportedly exclaim, "Look, I paid for [it]. It belongs to the family."[63] Since Teddy was only 28 and constitutionally ineligible, a two-year fill-in was necessary to prevent others from claiming the vacancy.

Speculation focused most notably on two-term Massachusetts Governor Foster Furcolo, a frequent beneficiary of John McCormack's goodwill, who had the constitutional authority to appoint a replacement but not the political temerity to arrange his own appointment to the seat. State governors have the authority to fill Senate vacancies with appointees and Furcolo clearly wanted the seat. Furcolo had first contended for the Senate in 1954, losing a close race to Republican U.S. Senator Leverett Saltonstall, and hoped to ride JFK's coattails to victory in a 1960 rematch. However, Furcolo's unpopularity led to his defeat in the Senate primary by Springfield Mayor Thomas O'Connor.[64] Jack carried 60.2% of the Massachusetts vote but his coattails failed to elect O'Connor over incumbent Senator Saltonstall or gubernatorial contender Democrat Joe Ward over Republican John A. Volpe.[65] After the election, it was speculated that Furcolo would resign the governorship and let Lieutenant Governor Robert F. Murphy who also suffered a primary defeat name him to Jack's vacant seat. Never popular with the Kennedys, Furcolo wisely passed on that scenario.

Furcolo appointed one of Jack's congenial Harvard College roommates, Benjamin Smith II, to keep the seat warm for the next two years.[66] Smith, who had ushered at Kennedy's 1954 wedding to Ms. Jacqueline Bouvier, was the former mayor of Gloucester. The Smith appointment puzzled only those who underestimated the determination of Joe Kennedy to obtain as much public approbation as possible for his three sons.

Most puzzled and disappointed was the state's recently reelected Attorney General Eddie McCormack, a Furcolo ally and John McCormack's nephew. The 37-year-old attorney general was a likelier choice for the Senate. A 1947 graduate of the U.S. Naval Academy, who had topped his class at Boston University Law School and edited its law review, Eddie was a two-time statewide winner and a well-regarded state attorney general. With 58.8% of the vote for his 1960 reelection, Eddie was the second-highest vote-getter among the statewide officeholders[67] and he was even singled out for special mention a few weeks earlier at Kennedy's Boston Garden election eve speech when Jack declared,[68] "The candidate for attorney general has done an outstanding job. He is a nephew of our beloved friend John McCormack, and in his own right deserves to be re-elected attorney general of the State of Massachusetts. [Applause]"

Eddie was the only statewide Democratic incumbent on the stage that night and hoped that his combination of political success and family connections would give him the inside track for the Senate seat. Eddie also apparently believed that John's help with Sam Rayburn in convincing Lyndon Johnson to accept the vice presidential nomination meant that the family truce was still in place, but Joe Kennedy had different plans. Eddie's palpable disappointment would soon lead to the most visible and bitter of the Kennedy-McCormack battles.

The opening of the 87th Congress

Jack Kennedy's major problems with Congress were in large part of his own making. His six years in the House and eight years in the Senate accounted for more pre-presidential congressional experience than any president since Republican James A. Garfield of Ohio who was elected in 1880. However, repeating the words of Dick Bolling, who would later chair the Rules Committee, Kennedy was "a third rater, not a second rater" in the House.[69]

Bobby Baker also contended that Sam Rayburn was unimpressed by Kennedy[70]:

> [Rayburn] just said, you know, that he was never around when you had a key vote. He just said that basically he's a lazy Congressman. Because it's very easy if you're from the East Coast to work Wednesday and Thursday and be gone. He was very seldom on the House floor and the Speaker was very astute about the work dogs and the show dogs. He thought Congressman Kennedy was a show dog.

Elected to the Senate in 1952, Kennedy's legislative performance improved but his eye was on the White House, as evidenced by his failed bid for the 1956 vice presidential nomination in the middle of his fourth year in the Senate.[71] Baker contended that Senator Kennedy felt that "this was a boring job, being a Senator and keeping up with all the things that didn't have any appeal to him."[72] In the Senate, Kennedy was publicly visible but still deficient in his committee work. These were the Senators Lyndon Johnson would characterize as more "minnow" than "whale."

Regardless of JFK's mixed Capitol Hill experience, he was well aware that presidential reputations are heavily dependent upon congressional success. It was here that Kennedy would need the support of congressional southern Democrats who heeded the advice of Texans House Speaker Sam Rayburn and Vice President Lyndon Johnson as well as the southerners' favorite northerner House Majority Leader John McCormack, none of whom held Jack in great esteem. In spite of their personal feelings, Kennedy was the president of their party and their political fate was now inextricably linked with him. Much to their shock, the public's enthusiasm for the young and attractive Kennedy family exploded into record high Gallup Poll approval ratings reaching a high of 83% in the aftermath of early April's Bay of Pigs fiasco.[73] It would be best for all concerned to accommodate one another and not let old wounds undermine the agenda of either the Democratic president or the Democratic Congress.

Changing congressional demographics

While Democrats had retained nominal control over both houses of Congress in the 1960 election, Jack Kennedy's narrow victory had no national coattails and the House Democrats lost 21 seats, most of which were outside the South, shrinking their number from 283 to 262 and their margin over the Republicans from 130 in the 86th Congress to 87 in the 87th Congress. Astute observers often noted that when Democratic congressional margins were small the almost monolithic southern and border state Democratic phalanx loomed large. There were only 131 non-southern and border Democrats in the House and only 37 in the Senate. Moreover, southerners controlled the major House committees of Rules, Ways and Means, Armed Services, and Interstate and Foreign Commerce as well as the Senate committees on Armed Services, Finance, Foreign Relations, and Judiciary. The 1960 election enhanced the power of the Conservative Coalition's Republican-Southern Democratic alliance as they continued their philosophic control if not party control of each congressional chamber. Kennedy's victory had serious portents of a hollow one—all prestige and no power, or in the more cynical version of his best-selling book, leaving him with "all profile and no courage," a quotation attributed to Eleanor Roosevelt.

But a liberal counterweight had emerged—the Democratic Study Group (DSG). Formed in 1959 following the huge 49-seat Democratic House gain in the 1958 midterm elections, the DSG was committed to a liberal legislative agenda and a fervent desire to eliminate the procedural roadblocks that prevented their passage, namely, the seniority system and the obstructionist Rules Committee. While DSG members were generally deferential to Speaker Sam Rayburn, there was less trust in Majority Leader John McCormack whom many saw as much too accommodating of the southern members. Most of these newer Democrats came from the nation's suburbs, districts that were regionally and demographically distinct from the South–big-city alliance that had propelled the "Austin-Boston connection" to power. These districts were created as an unintended consequence of the construction of the Eisenhower Interstate Highway System. Originally intended to provide escape routes from the nation's large cities should Soviet missiles rain down on the United States, these interstate highways provided escape routes of a different sort for mostly white families with young children who wished to leave the cities. As the affluence of the 1950s grew, middle- and upper-middle-class families who had the financial wherewithal to own private automobiles and enough credit to obtain mortgages sought refuge in their single family homes with ample lawns and two-car garages in the leafy suburbs.

The Kennedy campaign paid great attention to the suburbs as Jack and his advisors were schooled in the new politics of the suburbs by MIT Professor Robert C. Wood, whose pioneering 1958 book *Suburbia: Its People and Their Politics* was the first to illuminate the demographic changes wrought by out-migration from the nation's large cities.[74] Bob Wood would later put theory into practice during his time formulating the new Department of Housing and Urban Development in the Johnson Administration.

Thanks to the Servicemen's Readjustment Act of 1944, better known as the G.I. Bill of Rights, returning World War II veterans received a wide range of congressionally approved benefits that included low-cost mortgages, low-interest loans to start a business, cash payments of tuition and living expenses to attend college, high school or vocational education.[75] Consequently, these young congressmen who benefited from these programs were better educated and more professionally employed than the congressional old-timers whose power had been grandfathered by the seniority system. Furthermore, they were well aware of how their lives were positively impacted by the federal government.

Although their 1958 numbers had been diminished by the 1960 election, the DSG members who had been reelected developed staying power and they too would eventually benefit from the seniority system. The best news for the DSG was Jack Kennedy's election. Technically, he was not one of them, but his nomination victory over the Democratic establishment and election victory over the Republicans closely mirrored their own nascent political careers. However, the DSG's congressional power was a few years away, so they could only pressure the hierarchs; they could not yet replace them.

Expanding the Rules Committee, Mr. Sam's last fight

This year would be the 79-year-old Sam Rayburn's last year on earth but he had enough energy to deliver the Kennedy Administration's first major procedural victory—the successful expansion of the House Rules Committee.

The Kennedy-Johnson ticket was helped to victory by a strong showing among black voters in the North's large cities that swayed electoral votes in the large states for the Democratic ticket. JFK's efforts on behalf of Martin Luther King Jr. had helped him with black voters, even winning over "Daddy" King who was going to vote against Kennedy because of JFK's Catholicism. When Kennedy learned of "Daddy King's" initial hesitance, he remarked to Arthur Schlesinger, Jr., "Imagine, Martin Luther King having a bigot for a father. . . . Well, we all have fathers, don't we?"[76]

However as long as the twelve-member House Rules Committee regularly blocked liberal civil rights bills, American blacks would remain second-class citizens. Rules had been chaired since 1955 by the 77-year-old Judge Howard W. Smith of Virginia, a soft-spoken but tough-minded opponent of racial integration who declared in 1957, "The Southern people have never accepted the colored race as a race of people who had equal intelligence . . . as the white people of the South."[77] Smith had become the senior Democrat on Rules late in 1952 when two of John McCormack's close friends and allies—its longtime chair, the Bohemia-born Adolph J. Sabath of Chicago[78] and Eugene "Goober" Cox of Georgia—passed away within weeks of one another, and thus Smith became chair in 1955 when Democrats regained the House. Obstructionism in the House Rules Committee was not new. In 1949, the newly elected 81st Congress led by Speaker Rayburn and Majority Leader McCormack enacted a "twenty-one-day rule" to get bills discharged from the Rules Committee that had not been scheduled for floor action three weeks after arriving in the committee. However, the rule did not survive the 1950 congressional election and it was easily repealed at the start of the 82nd Congress by a vote of 243–180 on January 3, 1951.[79]

The Rules Committee greeting President Kennedy in 1961 had eight Democrats and four Republicans, but with Howard Smith and Mississippi's Bill Colmer voting with the four Republicans, committee conservatives stopped liberal legislation from reaching the floor with 6–6 votes. The six other Democrats were loyal to the leadership with Jim Trimble of Arkansas, Homer Thornberry of Texas, and Dick Bolling of Missouri seen as Sam Rayburn's men while Jim Delaney of New York, Ray Madden of Indiana, and Thomas P. "Tip" O'Neill, Jr. of Massachusetts being considered John McCormack's. Both Dick Bolling and Tip O'Neill would figure prominently in the speakership of John McCormack. Thanks to McCormack's mentorship, O'Neill would be placed on the "leadership ladder" as Democratic whip in 1971, becoming floor leader in

1973 and Speaker for ten years, 1977–87, while Bolling, the hard-edged liberal who despised McCormack and regularly sought to undermine him, would take over the chairmanship of the Rules Committee in 1979.

The initial plan offered by Rayburn to Judge Smith was an expansion to fifteen members, but Smith refused. Three DSG heavyweights Chet Holifeld of California, John Blatnik of Minnesota, and Frank Thompson, Jr. of New Jersey urged Rayburn to alter the Rules Committee by removing Bill Colmer and replacing him with a liberal.[80] Rayburn, always sensitive to House precedents and not wishing to anger his fellow southerners, voided that idea. The original plan reemerged—increase the committee's membership to fifteen. It was Sam Rayburn's hope that expanding the committee's size to fifteen with its traditional two-to-one party ratio would lead to a 10 to 5 Democratic split that would provide an 8 to 7 nonconservative majority if not a liberal one. The battle was intense, and on January 31, eleven days after Kennedy was inaugurated, the Rules Committee was expanded to fifteen in a very close vote, 217 to 212.[81]

Vote tallies indicated that the party split was 195 Democrats and 22 Republicans supporting the expansion and 148 Republicans and 64 Democrats opposing it.[82] Among the 99 Democrats from the eleven Confederate states, the split was 36 for to 63 against with only Paul C. Jones of Missouri, the lone non-southern Democrat, in opposition. All six southern Republicans voted against the expansion. But the change occurred thanks to pro-expansion margins among southerners in Texas (14 to 6), Louisiana (5 to 3), Arkansas (4 to 2), and Tennessee (4 to 3). Sam Rayburn and Georgia's Carl Vinson, a longtime McCormack nemesis, had delivered a sharp defeat to Judge Smith. A week later, the relatively moderate Carl A. Elliott of Georgia and the Texas-born semi-liberal B. F. "Bernie" Sisk of California were named to the two new Democratic slots on the committee along with Republican Katherine St. George of New York.[83] With two nonconservatives among the three new members added to the committee, it was now possible to fashion an 8–7 majority to move civil rights legislation through the committee and fulfill the promises made to those African-American voters in Chicago and Detroit who had helped deliver crucial victories to the Kennedy-Johnson ticket. However, this was a temporary change, good only for the 87th Congress. It would have to be renewed in 1963, the next time with John McCormack as Speaker and no powerful Sam Rayburn to guide it through.

Moving the Kennedy agenda

The House Rules Committee was now relatively tame and Kennedy moved quickly to fulfill the liberal promises made during the campaign. On March 1, 1961, he issued Executive Order 10924 establishing the Peace Corps and asked for congressional support. Ostensibly, the Corps was to assist people in underdeveloped lands, but it also served the Cold War purpose of preventing people in these mostly unaligned nations from drifting into the Soviet orbit. Shortly afterward, Kennedy got congressional approval for an Arms Control and Disarmament Agency, and on March 14, he announced the Alliance for Progress with financial assistance for Latin American countries to push for political stability and democratization in hopes of preventing them from following Cuba's pro-Soviet example.

The charter for the Alliance was signed at an inter-American conference at Punta del Este, Uruguay, in August 1961.[84] During the following month, both the Peace Corps and the Arms Control and Disarmament Agency would move through Congress and be signed by President Kennedy. The Peace Corps Act was signed on September 21, 1961, and the Arms Control and Disarmament Act five days later on September 26, 1961. While these three initiatives constituted fulfilled promises, not all of the Kennedy agenda was as successful.

The Bay of Pigs fiasco

In December 1960, a few weeks before Jack's inauguration, Cuba's Fidel Castro established strong diplomatic and trade relations with the Soviet Union. Barely two years earlier, Castro was feted in the American press as a hero for overthrowing the Cuban tyrant Fulgencio Batista. However, American-Cuban relations quickly deteriorated as Castro's leftist politics became more apparent and the Eisenhower Administration feared that Castro's sentiments posed a danger to American hemispheric hegemony. During the closing months of Ike's presidency, the CIA began meeting with anti-Castro Cuban refugees to outline a plan that would destabilize the Castro regime and cause it to collapse.

After Kennedy took office, he was informed of the CIA's plans to overthrow Castro. One of the plans involved landing well-armed anti-Castro refugees on the southeastern coast of Cuba, miles away from Havana. The hope was that this anti-Castro guerilla force would rally disillusioned Cubans to join them and march into Havana and topple Castro. However, Castro's newly established alliance with the USSR represented an extension of the simmering Cold War into the Western Hemisphere and limited the options available to the new Kennedy Administration. With the CIA convinced by unreliable refugees that the plan would work, the 1,500 members of the brigade found themselves encircled by Castro's forces. Over a hundred were killed, and the remainder were captured.

Irving L. Janis, in his excellent dissection of the Bay of Pigs crisis, recalls White House Counsel Ted Sorensen's reflections[85]: "How could I have been so stupid to let them go ahead?" [Kennedy] asked. Sorensen wrote, "His anguish was doubly deepened by the knowledge that the rest of the world was asking the same question."

The Soviets chortled over the public ineptitude of the new Kennedy Administration and rejoiced in their own triumph as they were able to successfully launch the first earth-orbiting space ship on April 12 with Yuri Gagarin aboard. Ten months later, the United States would replicate that feat with John Glenn in February of 1962. At this point, the Soviets were well ahead in the space race.

Continuing issues

Every Congress has to deal with issues concerning farmers and labor unions and the 87th Congress was no exception. The needs of farmers, almost always the most politically volatile of constituencies, were addressed with the Emergency Feed Grain Program of 1961 (Public Law 87–5), which sought to limit the overproduction of feed grains, passed in the House 209 to 202. This bill signed into law on March 9, 1961, would be Kennedy's first policy victory in the House, with the Rayburn-McCormack team delivering 205 Democratic votes for its passage.[86]

It had become more obvious that Rayburn's health had taken a turn for the worse but he continued to push the Kennedy agenda. On May 1, the Area Redevelopment Act intended to help economically depressed areas; a bill that had been twice vetoed by President Eisenhower was signed by President Kennedy "with great pleasure," authorizing the president to appoint an Area Redevelopment administrator under the secretary of commerce with authority to borrow $300 million from the Treasury for a revolving fund to finance industrial and rural redevelopment loans and public facility loans.[87] The act limited Federal participation to a maximum of 65% of redevelopment project costs, but permitted 100% loans for public facilities. While the original House support for the bill on March 29 was solid (251–167), the April 26 vote on the conference report was much closer (224–193). As McCormack noted, almost all who voted against the conference report had voted against the appropriations portion of the original bill. Kennedy-backed legislation was now moving steadily through the 87th Congress. The vote margins may not have been large, but they were sufficient.

In its initial effort to reward the electoral efforts of organized labor on its behalf, the Kennedy Administration sought to raise the minimum wage to $1.25, with expanded coverage, while opponents rallied around the substitute offered by William Ayres (Rep.-Ohio) and A. Paul Kitchin (Dem.-NC) of a $1.15 minimum wage with more narrow coverage. The key vote was on a substitute sponsored by Majority Whip Carl Albert that reduced the number of workers covered to win over conservative support. Despite his efforts, the Albert bill was rejected by one vote, 185–186.[88] Receiving much of the blame for its defeat was John McCormack, as questions were raised about his relationship with the Kennedy Administration, evidenced by headlines such as "House Wage Bill Defeat Lands McCormack in Kennedy Doghouse."[89]

The House Ayres-Kitchin version went to conference and with Senate language supporting the bill changes, it passed relatively easily in the House en route to its presidential signing on May 5 as the Fair Labor Standards Amendments of 1961. This act raised the minimum wage in stages from $1 an hour to $1.25 an hour but most importantly, it extended full wage and hour coverage in stages to about 3,624,000 previously exempt workers, two-thirds of them in the retail and service trades. It was the first coverage extension of workers' hours and wages since 1938, the last year before the Conservative Coalition took philosophical control of Congress from Roosevelt's New Dealers.[90] That it was the Senate version and not the House one raised public concerns about Rayburn's age and John McCormack's legislative skill, as noted by the *Boston Herald's* Leslie Carpenter speculating that "McCormack May Miss Speakership."[91]

With yet another sweltering Washington summer on the horizon, Congress moved quickly on two favorite bills. The Republican favorite was the Interstate Highway System with the passage of the Federal-Aid Highway Act of 1961 authorizing an additional $900 million a year for a total of $9.7 billion through fiscal 1972. The bill passed both chambers by voice vote and was signed by President Kennedy on June 29, 1961.[92] The Democratic favorite, the Social Security Amendments of 1961 were approved a day later increasing both Social Security benefits and taxes.[93]

While both the highway and the Social Security Amendments passed easily, controversy surrounded a key piece of domestic legislation when Congress agreed to pass the Housing Act of 1961. Approved June 30, 1961, this act authorized $2 billion in new funds for urban renewal, $55 million for urban planning, and special grants and loan funds for development of mass transit facilities and "open spaces" in cities.

While Kennedy's first five months in office had seen a surprisingly large number of congressional triumphs with his domestic agenda, his foreign policy initiatives had been disastrous, beginning with the CIA's poorly planned and ill-executed Bay of Pigs invasion Compounding this disaster was Kennedy's unfortunate meeting seven weeks later on June 4 with USSR President Nikita Khrushchev in Vienna, Austria. It was at this meeting that a clearly unimpressed Khrushchev concluded that Kennedy was over his head in foreign policy and that the United States was either unwilling or incapable of stopping Soviet aggression. Kennedy would later say of Khrushchev, "He beat the hell out of me," telling James "Scotty" Reston of the *New York Times*, "It was the worst thing in my life. He savaged me."[94] Two months later in August, an emboldened Khrushchev would soon put Berlin into play on the Cold War chessboard by constructing a wall separating East Berlin from the three western sectors.

The hot summer of 1961: Freedom Riders and firebombs

Hanging heavily over the new administration was the longest and most vexing issue that the nation had to confront—civil rights. This was the domestic issue that had dominated the national agenda from the first arrival of slaves in 1619 Virginia. Civil rights threatened the Democratic Party more than the Republican Party. Historically linked to slavery and segregation, it was a party that had difficulty with its racial mix. This was especially true of the contemporary Democratic Party, with its fragile alliance between northern urban liberals and their black allies who often found themselves in regular conflict with the rural southern segregationist whites who shared their partisan affiliation but not their philosophical commitments.[95]

This was where the Austin-Boston connection of Sam Rayburn and John McCormack should have been well positioned to offer help. Up to this point, neither Sam Rayburn's Texas or John McCormack's Boston were rife with race politics. Texas was the largest southern state with the smallest black population and Boston's black proportion ranked next-to-last among the nation's largest metropolitan areas. Neither man had to play race politics to hold office.[96]

John's longtime aide Martin Sweig contended that "John McCormack never made a civil rights speech, but he always voted for civil rights bills."[97] John McCormack's Boston district, the Massachusetts 12th, had only a 7% proportion of blacks in the 1950 Census and not much more in the 1960 Census.[98] Of the twelve largest Standard Metropolitan Statistical Areas (SMSAs) in the country, Boston ranked 12th in the 1960 Census and 11th in the 1970 Census with regard to the proportion of blacks in the SMSAs' "core city." In 1960, Boston's 9.1% proportion of blacks fell 15.5 points below the 24.6 median for these twelve urban places. In 1970, Boston's 16.3% was 16.9 points below that year's median for black populations in the core cities of the twelve largest SMSAs.[99] As a result, McCormack was not as vocal a champion of civil rights as fellow big-city Democrats in New York, Philadelphia, Detroit, and Chicago, who had become very attentive to the growing voting power of their black constituents.

By always voting for civil rights bills, McCormack maintained his liberal credentials, but to give a civil rights speech was another matter. A speech would be regarded as a direct verbal affront to those peculiar southern laws and mores that had kept racial segregation intact and blacks at the bottom of southern society. John McCormack's southern friends were too numerous and too important, and black voters and legislators too few in number, to make speeches offensive to the largest segment of congressional Democrats. John McCormack knew how to count votes and keep friends. But the race crisis loomed large on the congressional horizon.

Seven years had passed since the Supreme Court had ruled against racial segregation in *Brown v. Board of Education*, and little progress had been made. By 1961, civil rights for African Americans could no longer be postponed or contained. Early in 1960, young African-American college students in North Carolina and Tennessee had engaged in a number of "sit-ins" at segregated lunch counters to push the federal government to move against racial discrimination in places of public accommodation like restaurants. Violent opposition to their peaceful presence increased public awareness and sympathy for their plight. With growing public sympathy, civil rights pioneers began to push for the integration of public transportation, most notably on commercial buses driving along federally financed interstate highways in the South.

The law was on their side. Twice before the U.S. Supreme Court had ruled that racial discrimination in interstate bus travel was unconstitutional—*Irene Morgan v. the Commonwealth of Virginia*, 328 U.S. 373 (1946) and *Boynton v. Virginia*, 364 U.S. 454 (1960)—yet it was well known to African Americans that major interstate bus companies Greyhound and Trailways felt compelled to follow the segregating mores when traveling through the South. Furthermore, the Interstate Commerce Commission had ruled in *Sarah Keys v. Carolina Coach Company*, 64 MCC 769 (1955) that there should be no racial discrimination in restaurants serving interstate travelers.

Calling themselves "Freedom Riders," the first 13 riders—seven blacks and six whites—split into two groups: one on a Greyhound bus, the other on a Trailways bus. They began their historic journey in Washington, DC on May 4 and planned to ride through the southeastern states of Virginia, the Carolinas, and Georgia and into the perilous Gulf States of Alabama and Mississippi, intending to reach New Orleans where a rally was planned. It did not go well. A number of arrests occurred, but it was the rampant mob violence that greeted their arrival in the Alabama cities of Anniston and Birmingham that captured national and international attention. Local law enforcement authorities let racist goons, many of whom were white-robed members of the Ku Klux Klan, viciously attack the riders. The Greyhound bus was firebombed in Anniston and the mob pushed against its doors to keep the riders inside before an explosion caused the mob to back off and the riders were able to leap from the bus and escape a fiery death.[100]

Much the same occurred in Birmingham where the infamous Police Commissioner Eugene "Bull" Connor stepped aside and let violent Klansmen attack the riders with baseball bats, chains, and iron pipes, sending many to local hospitals where treatment was often denied. As the outrages grew, the nation impatiently waited for the two Kennedy brothers in the White House and the Justice Department to respond to these violent attacks on American citizens. Neither Jack's fabled charm nor Bobby's steadfast determination could any longer ignore or finesse the horrific reality that filled the nation's newspapers and television screens every day.

Attorney General Kennedy offered the original riders safe passage to the state capital of Montgomery. There too, violent mobs awaited the buses, attacking not only the riders but also the reporters and cameramen who sent these grotesque images to the nation and the world. Kennedy's personal Justice Department representative John Siegenthaler was beaten unconscious in Montgomery. Only the threat of federal troops persuaded Alabama Governor John Patterson to reluctantly employ the Alabama National Guard to bring some order to the city.

As scions of northern white privilege, the Kennedy brothers were relative latecomers to the civil rights struggle.[101] Blacks seldom served in the households of wealthy white northerners while black servants as nannies, cooks, footmen, and drivers were a very common presence in the homes of wealthy white southerners. It was remarked that the Kennedys never treated blacks as fully equal. However, that did not stop them from seeking a peaceful solution to the Freedom Rider crisis.[102]

Jack Kennedy was in a difficult political bind. In order to get his legislation passed, he had to placate the aging southern hierarchs who chaired most committees in both chambers of Congress. He could not be critical of the South. However, that was becoming more difficult with the regularly televised beatings of African Americans and their white allies in the southern cities. With the fateful Vienna meeting with Premier Khrushchev just a few weeks away, the Kennedy brothers grew impatient with the riders, and even questioned the patriotism of the riders hoping that they would cease their push. The White House issued a statement that sought to take neither side in the dispute. The request for a slowdown was ignored as James Farmer of the Congress of Racial Equality (CORE) continued to fill buses with antisegregation protestors. How much of Kennedy's stature was weakened by the riders is debatable, but combined with the Bay of Pigs fiasco, the young president had a seriously weakened international position.

Kennedy's failed education bill

Congress slows down during the summer as Washington's excessive heat and humidity take their toll on elderly legislators that no amount of air conditioning can fully counter. With Kennedy's first presidential summer came the realization that Speaker Sam Rayburn's health was deteriorating. The thyroid cancer that would claim Sam's life in November was already sapping his strength and with it, his control over the House. Majority Leader John McCormack assumed a larger role in House deliberation. If there was one issue that would divide Kennedy and McCormack, the nation's two most politically powerful Catholics, it would be federal aid to parochial schools.

The conflict was inevitable, and Washington insiders saw it as an extension of the presumed feud between the Kennedy and McCormack camps. Drew Pearson documented the mistrust in his June 14, 1961, article "Potent McCormack Pokes Finger," stating, "John McCormack . . . has referred to his chief in the White House as 'anti-clerical,' while the President has referred to John as the 'Archbishop of Boston.'"[103] Introducing the Kennedy version of the bill to the Rules Committee, with no aid to parochial schools, was Dick Bolling, described by Pearson as "a Democrat, who may become [the] next speaker of the House."[104]

With Rayburn's diminished control of the House, McCormack had pushed heavily for federal aid to parochial schools. Kennedy, who was always fearful of anti-Catholic attacks on his administration, was disinclined to support the legislation.[105] It was not the first nor would it be the last major confrontation between the nation's first Catholic president and the man who would become the nation's first Catholic Speaker of the House.

Education mattered to Kennedy, and his most ambitious domestic proposal was the $2.5 billion request for education. Throughout much of the 1960 campaign, Kennedy had stressed the need for federal aid to education for school construction and increases in the salaries of teachers. Once inaugurated, the administration submitted a bill on February 20 that Kennedy described as "probably the most important piece of domestic legislation of the year."[106] In Ted Sorensen's biography *Kennedy*, he contended[107]: "The one domestic subject that mattered most to John Kennedy [was] education. Throughout his campaign and throughout his Presidency, he devoted more time and talks to this single topic than to any other domestic issue."

Predictable opposition occurred from southern members fearful that federal intrusion in an area historically linked to the communities and the states would expedite the racial integration of that region's public schools. Less predictable was the opposition from the Catholic bishops who were angered that JFK was unwilling to include parochial and private schools in the bill.

President Kennedy reiterated the position taken by candidate Kennedy at a March 1, 1961, press conference antagonizing the American Catholic hierarchy once again as he renewed his commitment to the *Everson v. Township* position[108]:

[The] Constitution clearly prohibits aid to the school, to parochial schools. I don't think there's any doubt of that.

The *Everson* case, which is probably the most celebrated case, provided only by a 5 to 4 decision was it possible for a local community to provide bus rides to nonpublic school children. But all through the majority and minority statements on that particular question there was a very clear prohibition against aid to the school direct. The Supreme Court made its decision in the *Everson* case by determining that the aid was to the child, not the school. Aid to the school is—there isn't any room for debate on that subject. It is prohibited by the Constitution, the Supreme Court has made that very clear. And therefore there would be no possibility of our recommending it.

The National Catholic Welfare Conference, representing the full hierarchy in America with its collection of cardinals, bishops, and archbishops, issued a statement on March 2 calling for the education bill's defeat should it not include funding for parochial and private schools. Among the cardinals was onetime Joe Kennedy ally Francis Cardinal Spellman of New York City and John McCormack's dear friend (and confessor) Richard Cardinal Cushing of Boston.[109] At his March 8 press conference, Kennedy reiterated his belief that "across the board" loans as well as grants to private schools were unconstitutional.[110]

The Senate chose to ignore the bishops and passed the bill relatively easily on May 25 by a vote of 49 to 34 with eight Republicans joining 41 Democrats in support of the bill while twelve Democrats, nine southerners and three Catholic northerners—Thomas Dodd of Connecticut, Frank Lausche of Ohio, and John J. Hickey of Wyoming—joined 22 Republicans in opposition.[111]

The House was another matter. There were 88 Catholics in the House and with congressional districts far less demographically diverse than the states represented by Senators, they were more vulnerable to organized Catholic Church pressure. The bishops had a key ally, Majority Leader John W. McCormack labeled "the Bishop of Boston" for his unfailing support of the Church's legislative positions. Now that the education bill achieved engrossed status thanks to its passage in the Senate, the bill was successfully reported out of the House Education and Labor Committee on June 1 due to the efforts of New Jersey's Frank Thompson, a Dick Bolling ally. The Rules Committee was its next stop and there it would die.

Awaiting the bill in the Rules Committee were ten Democrats and five Republicans. An ambush appeared to be in the air. It was correctly anticipated that all five Republicans and the two conservative Democrats, Smith and Colmer, would not let the bill get to the House floor. Its only hope was that the eight nonconservative Democrats would remain committed to the Kennedy agenda. Attention quickly focused on the three nonconservative Democrats who were Roman Catholic, each of whom had graduated from Catholic colleges. The senior Catholic Democrat on the committee was Ray J. Madden of Indiana, a native of Waseca, Minnesota, a graduate of Waseca's Sacred Heart Academy and legally trained at the Jesuit-run Creighton University. In 1961, Madden was 69 years old and in his ninth term in the House and sixth term on Rules. The next ranking Democratic Catholic was James J. Delaney from Queens in New York City, a graduate of the public schools and the law department of St. Johns College run by the Vincentian Society. He was 58 years old and serving in his eighth term in the House and his fifth nonconsecutive term on the committee. The junior-most Democratic Catholic on Rules was Tip O'Neill of Cambridge, Massachusetts, who attended parochial schools and graduated from Jesuit-run Boston College. Tip was then 48 years old and in his fifth term in the House and fourth on Rules.

There was little doubt that O'Neill was the most heavily cross-pressured of the three. He was a John McCormack protégé who owed his seat on the Rules Committee to John but who also was holding the Boston-Cambridge House seat of Jack Kennedy. Madden supported the Kennedy position of excluding parochial and private schools from the bill, while Delaney joined the bill's seven opponents to sink it.[112] O'Neill vacillated; first opposing the bill (the McCormack position) then agreeing to send it to the House floor (the Kennedy position). After O'Neill's initial vote, Madden wryly observed, "I never thought I'd see the day when Jim and Tip would join the coalition of Republicans and Dixiecrats."[113] O'Neill's quandary became moot once Delaney cast the eighth vote against moving the bill from the committee to the floor. As Dick Bolling contended in a Kennedy Library Oral History: "I knew it way in advance that unless we had a miracle, Delaney was going to vote his conviction. He wasn't voting his religion, he was voting his conviction, and that's fair enough."

Jim Delaney was a regular member of McCormack's luncheon group, and Dick Bolling was bothered that McCormack would not lean on Delaney to support the bill. However, he was careful not to chastise Delaney, knowing that he would need his vote on later less personal issues.

In a conversation with Kennedy recalled by Wilbur Cohen, the assistant secretary for legislation of health, education, and welfare,[114] "When news of the butchery in Rules reached the White House, Kennedy called Wilbur Cohen into the Oval Office and inquired, 'Wilbur, why couldn't you get one more Republican on the Rules Committee to vote with us?' Cohen recalls his response: 'Impetuously and somewhat annoyed, I retorted: "Mr. President, why can't you get one more Catholic?"'"

In a last-ditch effort, a Calendar Wednesday maneuver was attempted to circumvent the Rules Committee with a watered-down $325 million version of the original bill. Calendar Wednesday was a House procedure during which standing committees may bring up for consideration any bill that has been reported on the floor on or before the previous day. It was yet another reform outgrowth of the 1909–10 session that prevented the tyrannical Republican House Speaker "Uncle Joe" Cannon from using his chairmanship of Rules to kill progressive bills. The procedure is not often used nor widely supported, and this effort to circumvent the Rules Committee was soundly defeated on August 30 by a vote of 170–242.[115] Ironically, it was still regarded as a vote in favor of the president's position. McCormack and Delaney voted for it and both Madden and O'Neill reported pairs for it. Questions were raised that McCormack and Rayburn were in conflict. Dick Bolling's second wife, Jim Grant Bolling, was assigned by HEW to monitor the bill's progress in the House. In her Oral History for the Kennedy Library, she remarked[116]:

GRELE: At one time in the deliberations on the first bill, a reported conflict between Speaker Rayburn and Majority Leader McCormack reached the newspapers. Was there any substance to this?

J. G. BOLLING: I believe there was. You have the vote of Delaney and O'Neill [Thomas P. "Tip" O'Neill, Jr.], when they tried to force the hearing on the bill, which would indicate to me that the present speaker was opposed to the bill. I would think that that was valid.

GRELE: Majority Leader at the time McCormack denied that he had challenged Speaker Rayburn's leadership or his power to schedule or that he [led] a "Catholic Bloc." Was there any substance to any one of those charges?

J. G. BOLLING: No, I don't think that he has challenged his leadership. I think that he had. . . . And I don't think that he strongly opposed the bill. I think he just was opposed to it. I don't think there was a great stir over it, but I do think this would be reflected on O'Neill's and Delaney's vote on the Rules Committee.

GRELE: Does this conflict mean that by that time Speaker Rayburn had come around to support of the bill?

J. G. BOLLING: It's difficult to say what he had decided about teachers' salaries, but I think that it was in the nature of Speaker Rayburn to support the Administration's bill. And I think that by this time, if we were getting around to construction and to teachers' salaries, I would think that surely he was supporting the bill.

As political scientist Dick Fenno noted, "It suffered the most lop-sided defeat in the history of federal aid."[117] Ray Madden said that Rayburn told Kennedy that aid to education was "dead as slavery."[118]

In retrospect, it appears that Kennedy's push for education was short-lived. As Hugh Davis Graham contends[119]:

Myer [Mike] Feldman, Sorensen's chief lieutenant, concluded more recently that Kennedy had no deep personal concern for public education—save for the training of the mentally retarded, which was related to the circumstance that had touched his family with tragedy—and that Kennedy's accelerating commitment to federal aid as a presidential candidate and as president owed far more to practical politics than to the kind of bedrock emotional commitment that drove former schoolteacher Lyndon Johnson.

While Kennedy expressed disappointment, a number of the liberal DSG Democrats were enraged, none more so than Frank J. Thompson, Jr. of New Jersey. "Thompy" as he was known, was a native of Trenton and a graduate of its public schools and Wake Forest University. Having fought at Iwo Jima and Guadalcanal he had a reputation as a tough Jersey guy.[120] He was a key mover of the bill on the Education and Labor Committee and was very vocal in his denunciation of his fellow Catholics who had sunk it. He was especially angered at John McCormack and would soon join forces with Dick Bolling in seeking ways to undermine John and remove him from the House leadership. Dick Bolling's anger was personal. It was his second wife Jim, a staff member of the Department of Health, Education, and Welfare, who was tasked with monitoring the Kennedy bill as it moved through the Education and Labor Committee. She seemed more attuned to how the Rules Committee would react than her husband, who was undoubtedly embarrassed when he could not get it through his committee.[121] It was the personal aspect that most stung Bolling. It is doubtful if John McCormack was aware of Mrs. Bolling's role in the bill, but his commitment to federal funding for parochial schools trumped all other concerns. Whether intended or not, McCormack's passivity in the face of organized Catholic resistance to this bill led to an unfortunate defeat for the Kennedy Administration that jeopardized the truce between the two families.

Berlin Wall: While Americans were preoccupied with the escalating racial tensions in the South, Europeans were captivated by events in Berlin. It was a city filled with people running from one end of the city to the other carrying as many of their personal belongings as they could. These scenes were captured on television cameras as the world took note of the widespread defections of citizens from Soviet-controlled dreary East Berlin to the vibrant western sectors of the city. To avoid further international chagrin, the Soviet Union would act swiftly and decisively to stanch the outward flow of thousands of unhappy East Berliners.

On August 13, barriers were built along the sectional border between East and West Berlin.[122] A day later, the city's historic Brandenburg Gate was closed and by August 26, the city's crossing points were closed to all West Berlin citizens. Unsurprisingly, it would increase the USSR's international embarrassment, but it would demonstrate the drastic lengths to which the Soviets would go to preserve control over Eastern Europe.

The Soviets were embarrassed by the obvious popular disenchantment of communist regimes in their Eastern European satellites of Czechoslovakia, Hungary, Poland, and the Baltic Nations. Khrushchev, who had taken Kennedy's measure in an earlier Vienna meeting, was sure that there would be no adverse American reaction to the construction of the wall or to placing Soviet missiles on the island of Cuba, preventing another American invasion. With domestic policy issues overshadowing foreign policy ones, Khrushchev was right. The Berlin Wall as it was called would provide the dramatic backdrop for President Kennedy's most famous European speech, declaring "Ich bin ein Berliner" on June 26, 1963, but it would remain in place for another 26 years until 1989 as the unfortunate monument to Soviet resolve and fear.

Assessing Kennedy's First Session: The assessments of President Kennedy's first congressional session were generally but not wholly positive.[123] As the pundits weighed in, there was an air of disquietude hanging over Washington during its closing days. Sam Rayburn, the 17-year Speaker of the U.S. House, a member since 1913 when Woodrow Wilson first assumed the presidency, was looking very tired and very sickly. Mr. Sam had been the rock of the U.S. House since FDR's second term when he first became Majority Leader in 1937. He had been the steadying influence for a Democratic Party that was transformed from a sleepy white-only rural native-born southern Protestant-dominated minority party to the nation's majority party with a large number of members who were now urban, Catholic, Jewish, and black. The Democratic Party became more diverse under Mr. Sam's watch, and he was able to keep it together through the presidencies of Franklin D. Roosevelt, Harry Truman, and Dwight Eisenhower. Had he the time, he would have kept the House Democrats together throughout a Kennedy presidency. But he did not have the time.

Mister Sam says goodbye

Sam Rayburn had been unimpressed with Jack Kennedy during his six desultory years in the House but it was Sam who put aside his earlier qualms and urged LBJ to take the vice presidency as a way of preventing Richard Nixon from gaining the White House. Without Sam pushing for the expansion of the Rules Committee in January of 1961, very little of Jack Kennedy's ambitious congressional agenda would have reached the House floor.

On August 31, 1961, a weakened Sam left Washington to return to his hometown of Bonham and never again graced the halls of Congress. A prophetic earlier photo from March 23 shows Rayburn shaking President Kennedy's hand as he leaves a meeting of Vice President Johnson and the entire array of congressional leaders, both Democrats and Republicans from the House and the Senate. Curiously, Majority Leader John McCormack, Sam's second-in-command for 21 years and his putative successor as Speaker, was tucked away in the back of the photo at the furthest distance from Sam (Figure 18.1). One may speculate why that was so. Was it due to their upcoming

Figure 18.1 An ailing Sam Rayburn leaves a meeting with President Kennedy and the congressional leadership with John McCormack (back row) (John F. Kennedy Library and Museum).

estrangement over Kennedy's failed education bill, or to John's not wishing to appear too eager to succeed Sam, or to John's general self-effacing personal style?

The First Session of the 87th Congress adjourned on September 27 with John McCormack now seated as Speaker pro tem. Twelve days later, President Kennedy made an unscheduled trip to the Baylor Medical Center in Dallas to visit Sam Rayburn in Room 729 who was then undergoing another round of chemotherapy to slow the spread of thyroid cancer in his 79-year-old body. As recounted by Alan Peppard of the *Dallas Morning News*[124]:

> At Baylor, with only a nurse present, Rayburn and Kennedy had their final tête-à-tête. The handsome millionaire president and the dying bachelor from Bonham conversed about their common interest: politics. They hoped for some FDR magic in the 1962 midterms. Press secretary Pierre Salinger said that the two men talked about 1934, Franklin Roosevelt's first midterm election, when the Democrats beat the odds to pick up seats.
>
> Walking out of Baylor a few minutes later, the grim-faced president hurried past reporters, then paused at the door of his car. "He's sick, of course," he said in a low voice, "but I was glad I could be with him. He showed enough courage for anybody."
>
> Air Force One had arrived at 3:42 p.m. and was back in the air at 5:01 p.m.

Two days later, Rayburn was in a coma. The legendary Mr. Sam, the master of the House of Representatives, died on November 16, 1961. Few mourned his loss more than those executive leaders of the nation who had become dependent upon his legislative skills to expedite their proposals through the labyrinth of the House. Sam's funeral in Bonham brought together Presidents Truman, Eisenhower, and Kennedy and Vice President Johnson, Rayburn's closest protégé, all of whom stood in the front row at the service.

The trip to Dallas for the funeral in Bonham was John McCormack's first airplane trip, somewhat ironic for the man who had been the first chair of the House Select Committee on Aeronautics and Space. Mrs. McCormack was fearful of flying, and John would not travel without her. But John had greater fears to face. Was he up to filling Sam's shoes? That debate had already begun.[125]

Also in attendance that sad day in Bonham was Rayburn protégé and future McCormack enemy, Dick Bolling, who dined with Rayburn twice a week during the end of his troubled first marriage to Barbara Stratton. The quick-witted but abrasive Bolling was steeped in the history of the House, and he would share those tales with Sam, a man who made more House history than anyone else. Bolling had accompanied the most famous constituent of his Missouri 5th District to the funeral, the 77-year-old ex-President Harry S. Truman who sent a cordial note to Bolling on December 13: "The trip to Bonham was a sad one but I was happy you could be with me." And in a handwritten note, "In fact, I'm always glad to have you around."[126]

Harry, Sam, and John were well acquainted with Dick's tumultuous personal life. It was Sam who would introduce Dick to his second wife, a well-connected Texas lady and as described by Bolling: "Her name was Jim—James Grant Aiken Bolling.

She was a politician and she worked for the Kennedy administration representing HEW."[127] Dick's divorce and his and Jim's wedding bothered Harry Truman, arguably the single-most faithful occupant of the White House.[128] And given the multiple gossip mongers of Capitol Hill, this well-traveled story would have been equally as bothersome to John McCormack, arguably the most faithful occupant of the speakership.

Because of his closeness with Rayburn, Bolling had come to believe that he was the true carrier of the Rayburn tradition and that he should be elected Speaker of the House instead of John McCormack.[129] However, there was a long-standing tradition of party floor leaders becoming Speaker when the office came open. This had been true in the case of minority floor leaders who gained the speakership when their party gained majority control of the House like Jack Garner in 1931, Joe Martin in 1947 and 1953, and Sam Rayburn in 1949 and 1955. It had also been true for those majority floor leaders that moved up when the speakership became vacant through retirement or death as in the cases of Nick Longworth in 1925, Henry T. Rainey in 1933, Joe Byrns in 1934, Will Bankhead in 1936, and Sam Rayburn in 1940. Each of the previous seven Speakers of the House had moved to the chair from the floor leadership post.[130] The elevation from floor leader to Speaker was virtually automatic, and it was a tradition that John McCormack hoped would continue.

There were some parallels between Majority Leader Sam Rayburn's succession as Speaker following Will Bankhead's fatal heart attack in 1940 and John's succession of the deceased Rayburn in 1961. Congress was still in session when Bankhead died on September 15, 1940, and would remain in session until January 3, 1941. With Bankhead's casket resting on the House floor, Rayburn was elected Speaker on the following day by acclamation with support from both Democrats and Republicans. He served out the three-plus month remainder of the 3rd Session of the 76th Congress. The 87th Congress was not in session when Sam died in November, but John had already been named Speaker pro tem on August 31 when Sam left the House to die in Texas.

Speaker pro tem: There would be no acclamation for John McCormack. That there was opposition was no surprise. Many in Washington believed that John was only effective as a second-in-command and would have difficulty as first-in-command.[131] John appeared to lack Sam Rayburn's unique combination of interpersonal skill and intellectual toughness to control the increasingly contentious House and he wasn't a southerner. Many also feared that John's long-standing conflicts with the Kennedys would jeopardize the president's second year agenda.[132]

Some of the opposition to McCormack was based on religion. With John F. Kennedy, a Roman Catholic president, and U.S. Senator Mike Mansfield (Dem-Mont.) another Roman Catholic as Senate Majority Leader, the prospect of John McCormack, the most devout Roman Catholic of them all, as Speaker of the House was troubling to many southern Protestants, most of whom were Baptists and traditionally fearful of Catholic influence.[133] The lobbying group Protestants and Other Americans United for Separation of Church and State formally declared that John "has been for many years the foremost champion on Capitol Hill of the Catholic bishops' position on church and state."[134] This was a sentiment shared by Bobby Baker: "Anytime [McCormack] had a bill for the Catholic Church, he was the best spokesperson they ever had."[135]

A plot was hatched to prevent John from becoming Speaker. It was a curious alliance of southern conservatives and staunch DSG liberals like Dick Bolling and Frank Thompson still fuming over McCormack's role in sinking Kennedy's education bill. An informal ticket emerged with Albert Rains of Alabama as the candidate to challenge John McCormack for Speaker and Dick Bolling as the candidate to challenge Carl Albert for Majority Leader. Ostensibly, this was a challenge to the "automatic" rule that elevated floor leaders to Speakers and whips to floor leaders.[136]

It seemed to be a curious match. Rains was then in his ninth term in the House and a senior member of the mid-level Banking and Currency Committee but had evinced little in the way of leadership ambition. Rains was born in north Alabama's DeKalb County, one county separating him from Madison County where U.S. Senator John Sparkman resided and where Dick Bolling spent much of his adolescence. However, he impressed a number of members with his successful floor management of Kennedy's housing bill. A short five years earlier, Rains had signed the pro-segregation Southern Manifesto drafted by South Carolina's Strom Thurmond. On the other hand, Rains was one of the four Alabamians to vote for expanding the Rules Committee earlier in the year. Had Rains and Bolling blocked McCormack and Albert from the leadership, it is hard to fathom how long this cabal of conservative southern Protestants and pro-Kennedy DSG northern liberals would have lasted after thwarting McCormack's long-awaited speakership. The challenge to John became moot when on December 28, it was reported "240 Votes Pledged to McCormack as Speaker."[137] It is doubtful if John had any real awareness of the disdain with which he was held in some quarters of the House. Any hope the plotters had of gaining a majority of southern Democrats was undermined when Rules Committee Chair Howard Smith endorsed McCormack's elevation to Speaker.[138]

The greatest disappointment suffered by the plotters was the absence of support from the Kennedy White House, since it was well known in Washington that Kennedy and McCormack held each other in "minimum high regard." However, few outside Boston were aware of the post-1956 truce that existed between the families. The plotters would get no help from the Kennedys since the president and his brother Bobby were preoccupied with getting their youngest brother Teddy the U.S. Senate nomination from Massachusetts. The Kennedy brothers correctly surmised that John's nephew, State Attorney General Eddie McCormack, would be Ted's likeliest rival. Consequently, there was no need to anger John McCormack at this point, given their hope that John could convince Eddie not to challenge Teddy. Lacking White House support and with nothing binding them together but their dislike of John McCormack, the strange bedfellows backing Albert Rains ended their campaign and grudgingly voted for John McCormack in the Democratic Caucus and on the floor when John was elected Speaker over Minority Leader Charlie Halleck, the Republican nominee.

The Arrival: John McCormack, the grammar school–educated poor kid from the mean streets of South Boston's Irish ghetto, was now poised to become the 53rd Speaker of the U.S. House of Representatives, its seventh from Massachusetts, and at 70 years of age, its second-oldest occupant and second-in-line to the presidency. McCormack had survived the abandonment of his family by his alcoholic father when he was 13 and had seen grinding poverty and tuberculosis send five of his eight young siblings to early graves. Few people in American political life have traveled as far as John McCormack, and while the scars from his earlier wounds may have been concealed, they never fully vanished. Deeper and more painful wounds would be inflicted before his speakership would end.

Notes

1   Christopher Matthews, *Kennedy & Nixon: The Rivalry That Shaped the Nation* (New York: Simon & Schuster, 1998).
2   Theodore H. White's enormously successful *The Making of the President 1960* (New York: Atheneum, 1961) set the bar. A best seller and a Pulitzer Prize winner, its idolatrous take on Kennedy helped create the "Camelot myth" that continues to color most assessments of the 1960 campaign and the Kennedy presidency. With the 50th anniversary of the election occurring in 2010, at least five books presented a retrospective assessment of both the 1960 election and White's book. In chronological order, they are: Gary A. Donaldson, *The First Modern Campaign: Kennedy, Nixon, and the Election of 1960* (Lanham, MD: Rowman & Littlefield, 2007); David Pietrusza's solid *1960 LBJ vs. JFK vs. Nixon: The Epic Campaign That Forged Three Presidencies* (New York: Union Square, 2008), which is the most detailed of the four retrospectives; W. R. Rorabaugh's, excellent *The Real Making of the President: Kennedy, Nixon and the 1960 Election* (Lawrence: University of Kansas Press, 2009), which is the most succinct and has the clearest narrative; Shaun A. Casey's *The Making of a Catholic President: Kennedy v. Nixon 1960* (New York: Oxford University Press, 2009) deals extensively with Protestant resistance to JFK but skips over Kennedy family links to Joe McCarthy that led to liberal distrust of Kennedy; and Edmund F. Kallina Jr.'s *Kennedy v. Nixon: The Presidential Election of 1960* (Gainesville, FL: University of Florida Press, 2010) is the account most in conflict with the Teddy White version and appears to have longed for a Nixon victory.
3   Sidney Hyman, "Nine Tests for the Presidential Hopeful," *NYT Magazine*, January 4, 1959, pp. 11ff.
4   Tip O'Neill oral history with Charles T. Morrissey, May 18, 1966, John F. Kennedy Library and Museum, pp. 15–17.
5   LIFE placed JFK on its March 11, 1957 cover prefaced by "the Brilliant Massachusetts Senator" with his article, "Where Democrats Should Go From Here," *LIFE*, XLII, pp. 164–66, 171–79. In its May 6, 1957 issue, JFK was listed again with "A Committee Nominates Five Immortals for U.S. Senate," XLII, pp. 73–74 in LIFE magazine's May 6, 1957. LIFE's July 1, 1957 published a feature article on Bob Kennedy, "Young Man with Tough Questions: Bob Kennedy," XLIII, pp. 81–82, 84; and TIME placed Jack on the cover of its December 2, 1957, issue with a feature story entitled "Democrats' Man Out Front." LXX, pp. 17–21.
6   Ted Sorensen, "My Role in *Profiles in Courage*," from *Counselor: A Life at the Edge of History* (New York: Harper, 2008), pp. 145–66; and Jacqueline Kennedy, *Historic Conversations on Life with John F. Kennedy*, interviews with Arthur M. Schlesinger, Jr. (New York: Hyperion, 2011), pp. 279–80.

7   William H. Lucy, "Polls, Primaries, and Presidential Nominations," *Journal of Politics*, XXXV (November 1973), pp. 830–48.

8   James MacGregor Burns, *John Kennedy: A Political Profile* (New York: Harcourt, Brace, 1959). The page references are from the 1961 printing.

9   James MacGregor Burns, *Running Alone: Presidential Leadership—from JFK to Bush II: Why It Has Failed and How We Can Fix It* (New York: Basic Books, 2006).

10 Dr. George H. Gallup, *Gallup Poll: Public Opinion 1935–1971*, Vol. III (New York: Random House, 1972), passim.

11 Gallup Poll, release date of October 19, 1959, for "personal preference and October 21, 1959 for 'best guess'" of likely nominee, Vol. III, pp. 1633–34.

12 "Johnson, Nixon 'Strongest' Candidates to Editors and Members of Congress in CQ Poll," *CQWR*, July 1, 1960, pp. 1133–35.

13 O'Neill Oral History, May 18, 1966, p. 18.

14 Ibid., pp. 21–22.

15 "1960 Primaries," *CQ's Guide to U.S. Elections* (Washington, DC: CQ Press, 1975), pp. 338–39.

16 For a fuller account of Humphrey's background, read either Hubert H. Humphrey, *The Education of a Public Man: My Life and Politics* (Garden City, NY: Doubleday, 1976); or Timothy N. Thurber's *The Politics of Equality: Hubert H Humphrey and the African American Freedom Struggle* (New York City: Columbia University Press, 1999), p. 352.

17 The personal closeness between Humphrey and Johnson is described in Robert A. Caro, *The Years of Lyndon Johnson: Master of the Senate* (New York: Alfred A. Knopf, 2002), pp. 458–59.

18 Hubert Humphrey's committee assignments in the U.S. Senate may be found in Nelson with Bensen and Mitchell, *Committees of the U.S. Congress, 1947–1992*, Vol. 2 pp. 437–38.

19 See Arthur Smith, *Tiger in the Senate: The Biography of Wayne Morse* (Garden City, NY: Doubleday, 1962); and Lee Wilkins, *Wayne Morse: A Bio-Bibliography* (Westport, CT: Greenwood Press, 1985).

20 See Ralph K. Huitt, "The Morse Committee Assignment Controversy: A Study in Senate Norms," *APSR*, LI (June 1957), pp. 313–29.

21 Johnson's 1941 Senate primary loss to W. Lee "Pappy" O'Daniel is recounted in Robert Dallek, *Lone Star Rising; Lyndon Johnson and His Times, 1908–1960* (New York: Oxford University Press, 1991); and in Robert A. Caro's critical, *The Years of Lyndon Johnson: The Path to Power* (New York: Alfred A. Knopf, 1982), Chapter 34.

22 Johnson's controversial victory in the 1948 Senate primary against former Governor Coke Stevenson is elaborately recounted in Dallek, *Lone Star Rising*, chapter 10; and in Caro's second (and even more critical) volume, *The Years of Lyndon Johnson: Means of Ascent* (New York: Alfred A. Knopf, 1990), esp. chapters 13, "The Stealing," and 14, "Lists of Names."

23 See Dallek, *Lone Star Rising*, pp. 546 and 691n.

24 "14-Member Democratic Committee Seeks to Fill Top Convention Posts," *Washington Post, Times Herald*, April 19, 1960, p. A2.

25 "Floridian with Gavel: LeRoy Collins," *The New York Times*, July 15, 1960, p. 19.

26 C. R. Owens, "Jack's Pep Talk Revives Orphaned Bay State Bloc," *Boston Globe*, July 12, 1960, p. 14.

27 C. R. Owens. "Politics' New Look: Old Pros Pulled Their Weight on the Convention Floor, but Ivy Leaguers, the Status seekers, were Tops," *Boston Globe*, July 17, 1960, p. 63.

28 Rorabaugh quotes Alfred Steinberg's *Sam Rayburn: A Biography* (New York: Hawthorn, 1975), p. 238, in his *The Real Making of the President*, p. 75.

29 John W. McCormack Oral History interview with Sheldon Stern, JFK Library, March 30, 1977, p. 29.

30 Tip O'Neill, Oral History, May 18, 1966, JFK Library, pp. 26–29.

31 Richard C. Bain and Judith H. Parris, eds., *Convention Decisions and Voting Records* (Washington, DC: The Brookings Institute, 1973), p. 305.

32 The narrow success of the Kennedy-Johnson ticket has led many to take credit for putting it together. Even though John McCormack was named by Kennedy to be his convention floor manager, he is most often left out of accounts that focus on decision-making within the Kennedy camp. See Arthur M. Schlesinger, Jr., *A Thousand Days: John F. Kennedy in the White House* (Boston: Houghton, Mifflin, 1965), pp. 50–57; Jules Witcover, *Crapshoot: Rolling the Dice on the Vice Presidency* (New York: Crown, 1992), pp. 140–63; John McCormack's role, if acknowledged, was presumably to convince his good friend Sam Rayburn, Johnson's floor manager, that John Kennedy was offering the vice presidency to Lyndon Johnson in good faith and not as an empty gesture with the assumption that the offer would be rejected. See John McCormack's oral history with T. Harrison Baker for the University of Texas, LBJ Library, September 23, 1968, pp. 13–17. See also Robert Dallek, *Lone Star Rising; Lyndon Johnson and His Times*, pp. 574–82.

33 "O'Brien Puts Oil in Kennedy Machine," *Los Angeles Times*, July 13, 1960, p. A1.

34 "Lone Star Flag Leads Parade: Johnson's Nomination Touches off Jubilant Demonstration," *Los Angeles Time*, July 15, 1960, p. A.

35 "Johnson Victory Snuffs Out California Delegate Revolt," *Los Angeles Times*, July 15, 1960, p. 2.

36 On the 1960 Republican convention, see Theodore H. White's oft-cited "The Republicans from the Summit to Chicago," *The Making of the President 1960* (New York: Atheneum, 1961), chapter 7.

37 John D. Morris, "Upper Hand Held by Conservatives: Key Goals Eluded Kennedy and Johnson during the Post-Convention Session," *NYT*, September 1, 1960, p. 10.

38 Robert C. Albright, "Halleck Plans a Big Bridge across Aisle," *Washington Post*, January 25, 1959.

39 Tip O'Neill, Oral History, May 18, 1966, JFK Library, p. 143.

40 David M. Barrett, *The CIA and Congress: The Untold Story from Truman to Kennedy* (Lawrence, KS: University Press of Kansas, 2005), p. 75.

41 Barrett, *The CIA and Congress*, p. 393.

42 Drew Pearson, "Washington Merry-Go-Round: Missing NSA Aides Know Codes," *Washington Post*, August 17, 1960, p. B25.

43 Betty Prior, "McCormack Says Missing NSA Pair Took Valuable Code Secrets to Soviet," *Washington Post*, August 31, 1960, p. A19.

44 "Anatomy of a Traitor: What Makes Americans Defect?" *Newsweek*, September 19, 1960, pp. 33–37.

45 The ongoing debate within church circles is presented in Shaun A. Casey's *The Making of a Catholic President: Kennedy vs. Nixon 1960*.

46 Lawrence J. McAndrews, "The Avoidable Conflict: Kennedy, the Bishops, and Federal Aid to Education," *Catholic Historical Review*, LXXV (April 1990), pp. 278–93, esp. p. 279.

47 John F. Kennedy: "Speech of Senator John F. Kennedy, Greater Houston Ministerial Association, Rice Hotel, Houston, TX," September 12, 1960. Online by Gerhard Peters and John T. Woolley, *The American Presidency Project*, accessed June 16, 2015.

48 *Gallup Poll*, III, p. 1684.

49 John Cooney, *The American Pope: The Life and Times of Francis Cardinal Spellman* (New York: Dell, 1984), pp. 337–46.

50 "Spellman Denies Political Report, He and Cushing Call Rivalry a 'Fabrication'— Backing of Nixon Disclaimed," *NYT*, November 5, 1960, p. 9.

51 Cooney, *The American Pope*, p. 338.

52 Ibid., p. 337.

53 Data from CARA, the Georgetown University-based Center for Applied Research in the Apostolate, accessed May 12, 2015. Gallup numbers are from the final preelection poll while the University of Michigan's National Election Study data are postelection.

54 The classic account remains Theodore H. White's *The Making of the President, 1960.* An academic rendition of the 1960 election by notable political scientists including V. O. Key, Jr., Paul Tillett, and Stanley Kelley, Jr. may be found in Paul T. David, ed., *The Presidential Election and Transition, 1960–1961* (Washington, DC: The Brookings Institution, 1961).

55 Source for Popular Vote data: State of Alabama Department of Archives and History, "Statement and Tabulations of General Election, November 8, 1960," *Alabama Official and Statistical Register 1963* (Montgomery: Walker Printing Co., 1963), accessed May 12, 2016.

56 John F. Kennedy, "Inaugural Address: January 20, 1961," accessed from the American Presidency Project at www.presidency.ucsb.edu on February 7, 2014.

57 Newspaper opposition to RFK as attorney general as reported in *NYT* and *New Republic* in Arthur M. Schlesinger, Jr.'s book, *Robert Kennedy and His Times* (Boston: Houghton Mifflin, 1978). Interestingly, the *Wall Street Journal* seemed pleased with Bob Kennedy's selection; see William Beecher, "Crime Crackdown: Robert Kennedy Plans Multi-Agency Drive against Top Racketeer; He'll Stress Size of Cases, Not Quantity; His Tie to President Will Be an Aid But He Faces Old Hurdles," *Wall Street Journal*, January 23, 1961, p. 1. The Senate questioning was less contentious than anticipated, see "Excerpts from the Testimony of Robert Kennedy before Senate Panel," *NYT*, January 14, 1961, p. 8.

58 Author's telephonic interview with Mr. Tyler Abell, May 2014.

59 Oral History interview with Robert G. Baker, May 4, 2010, Senate Historical Office, p. 203.

60 The Johnson and Russell relationship is described in John A. Goldsmith's *Colleagues: Richard B. Russell and His Apprentice, Lyndon B. Johnson* (Macon, GA: Mercer University Press, 1993).

61 Bobby Baker Oral History, U.S. Senate Historical Office, p. 203.

62 Ibid., p. 204.

63 An unsourced quote in David Burner and Thomas R, West, *The Torch Is Passed: The Kennedy Brothers and American Liberalism* (New York: Athenaeum, 1984), p. 230.

64 John P. Mallan and George Blackwood, "The Tax That Beat a Governor: The Ordeal of Massachusetts," in Alan Westin, ed., *The Uses of Power: 7 Cases in American Politics* (New York: Harcourt, Brace & World, 1962), pp. 285–322.

65   The baroque nature of Massachusetts state politics in the 1960 election is well captured in Murray B. Levin with George Blackwood, *The Compleat Politician: Political Strategy in Massachusetts* (Indianapolis: Bobbs-Merrill, 1962).

66   "Benjamin Smith II, 75, U.S. Senator in 1960's," obituary in *NYT*, September 28, 1991.

67   See Kevin White, Secretary of the Commonwealth, *Election Statistics: The Commonwealth of Massachusetts 1960* (Boston: Office of the Secretary of State, 1961), p. 7.

68   "Speech of Senator John F. Kennedy, Boston Garden, Boston, Mass., November 7, 1960," in The American Presidency Project, www.presidency.ucsb.edu, accessed June 10, 2014.

69   Chapter 15; note 28.

70   Bobby Baker Oral History, U.S. Senate Historical Office, p. 81.

71   Jack Kennedy's eight years in the Senate have been recently and favorably recounted in the valuable book by John T. Shaw, *JFK in the Senate: Pathway to the Presidency* (New York: Palgrave Macmillan, 2013).

72   Bobby Baker U.S. Senate Oral History, p. 82.

73   AIPO, release date, May 5, *The Gallup Poll*, III, p. 1717.

74   Robert C. Wood, *Suburbia: Its People and Their Politics* (Boston: Houghton Mifflin, 1958).

75   Stathis, *Landmark Legislation*, p. 224.

76   Pietrusza, *1960: LBJ vs. JFK vs. Nixon*, p. 298.

77   Bruce J. Dierenfield, *Keeper of the Rules: Congressman Howard W. Smith of Virginia* (Charlottesville; University Press of Virginia, 1987).

78   See two articles by Burton A. Boxerman, "Adolph Joachim Sabath in Congress: The Early Years, 1907–1932," *Journal of the Illinois State Historical Society* 66 (Autumn 1973), pp. 327–430; and "Adolph Joachim Sabath in Congress: The Roosevelt and Truman Years," *Journal of the Illinois State Historical Society*, LXVI (Winter 1973), pp. 428–43.

79   *Congressional Quarterly Almanac, 1951* (Washington, DC: Congressional Quarterly, 1952), pp. 400–401.

80   An assessment of this battle may be found in Milton C. Cummings, Jr. and Robert L. Peabody, "The Decision to Enlarge the Committee on Rules: An Analysis of the 1961 Vote," in Robert L. Peabody and Nelson W. Polsby, eds., *New Perspectives on the House of Representatives* (Chicago: Rand, McNally, 1963), pp. 167–94. See also "Packing the Committee" in James A. Robinson's *The House Rules Committee* (Indianapolis: The Bobbs-Merrill Company, Inc., 1963), pp. 71–81.

81   *CQWR*, February 3, 1961, pp. 172–73.

82   Congressional Quarterly, *Congress and the Nation, 1945–1964: A Review of Government and Politics in the Postwar Years* (Washington, DC: Congressional Quarterly Service, 1965), pp. 88a–89a.

83   See Rules Committee listings in Nelson, *Committees in the U.S. Congress, 1947–1992*, Vol. 1: p. 678, for the 87th Congress.

84   Retrospectives on the Alliance, L. Ronald Scheman, *The Alliance for Progress: A Retrospective* (New York: Praeger, 1988), pp. 10–11; Tony Smith, "The Alliance for Progress: The 1960s," in Abraham F. Lowenthal's *Exporting Democracy: The United States and Latin America* (Baltimore: Johns Hopkins University Press, 1991), p. 72.

85   Irving L. Janis, "Fiascoes: A Perfect Failure," in *Groupthink: Psychological Studies of Policy Decisions and Fiascoes* (Boston: Houghton Mifflin, 1983), p. 16. The Sorensen reference is from Theodore C. Sorensen's book *Kennedy* (New York: Bantam, 1966), p. 394.

86   *Congress and the Nation, 1945–1964*, pp. 711–12.

87   Ibid.., pp. 375–76.

88   "President Suffers Defeat in House Minimum Wage Report," *CQWR*, March 31, 1961, p. 519.

89   J. F. Ter Horst, "House Wage Bill Defeat Lands McCormack in Kennedy Doghouse," *Boston Globe Files*, March 28, 1961, pp. 1, 7.

90   Fair Labor Standards Amendments of 1961, approved May 5, 1961 (5 Stat. 65-75), *Congress and the Nation*, pp. 645–48.

91   Leslie Carpenter, "McCormack May Miss Speakership," *Boston Herald*, June 35, 1961, pp. 1, 34.

92   Federal-Aid Highway Act of 1961, approved June 29, 1961 (75 Stat. 122-129), pp. 534–35.

93   Social Security Amendments of 1961, approved June 30, 1961 (75 Stat. 131-143).

94   The authoritative account of the Vienna confrontation between Kennedy and Khrushchev may be found in Frederick Kempe's masterful *Berlin 1961: Kennedy, Khrushchev, and the Most Dangerous Place on Earth* (New York: G. P. Putnam's Sons, 2011), pp. 209–38. Quotation is on pp. 257–58.

95   The fullest description of the impact of race in Democratic politics can be found in Bruce Bartlett's *Wrong on Race: the Democratic Party's Buried Past* (New York: Palgrave Macmillan, 2008).

96   The Austin-Boston connection's to race politics is described in Anthony Champagne, Douglas B. Harris, James W. Riddlesperger, Jr., and Garrison Nelson, *The Austin-Boston Connection: Five Decades of House Leadership, 1937–1989* (College Station: Texas A&M University Press, 2009), pp. 9–11.

97   Author's telephonic interview with Dr. Martin Sweig, February 6, 1996.

98   U.S. Department of Commerce, *Congressional District Data Book* (Washington, DC: U.S. Government Printing Office. 1961), p. 30.

99   Data for SMSA city comparisons from Melvin G. Holli and Peter d'A. Jones, eds, *Biographical Dictionary of American Mayors, 1820–1980* (Westport, CT: Greenwood, 1981), pp. 433–41.

100 A fuller account of the Freedom Riders can be found in Raymond Arsenault's *Freedom Riders: 1961 and the Struggle for Racial Justice* (Oxford: Oxford University Press, 2006).

101 A book-length discussion of the Kennedys' relationship with race is Nick Bryant's *The Bystander: John F. Kennedy and the Struggle for Black Equality* (New York: Basic Books, 2006).

102 For a discussion of the Kennedys' relationship to race in terms of policy, see Chapter V, "Tough Guy," of Kenneth O'Reilly's *Nixon's Piano: Presidents and Racial Politics from Washington to Clinton* (New York: Free Press, 1995), pp. 189–238.

103 Drew Pearson, "Potent McCormack Pokes Finger," *Washington Post*, June 14, 1961, p. C23.

104 Drew Pearson, "Odd Alliance Delays School Bill: Backstage Factor Strange Alignment," *Washington Post*, June 26, 1961, p. B19.

105 See Hugh Douglas Price, "Race, Religion, and the Rules Committee: The Kennedy Aid-to-Education Bills," in Alan F. Westin, ed., *The Uses of Power: 7 Cases in American Politics* (New York: Harcourt, Brace & World, 1962), pp. 1–71; or Drew Pearson, "Why Kennedy Hedged School Stand: An Important Record," *Washington Post*, June 27, 1961, p. B23.

106 *Congress and the Nation, 1945–1964*, p. 1210.

107 Theodore C. Sorensen, *Kennedy* (New York: Harper & Row, 1965), p. 358.

108 "Presidential Press Conference, March 1, 1961," in *The Kennedy Presidential Press Conferences* (New York: Coleman Enterprises, 1978), p. 49.

109 Lawrence J. McAndrews, "The Avoidable Conflict: Kennedy, the Bishops, and Federal Aid to Education," *Catholic Historical Review*, LXXV (April 1990), pp. 278–93, esp. p. 279.

110 *CQWR*, March 10, 1961, p. 398–99. See also Robert Healy, "Kennedy Won't Budge on School Aid Issue: Holds Firm Despite Church Opposition," *Boston Globe*, March 12, 1961, p. A3. Kennedy addressed the issue in his March 1, 1961, press conference and he relied upon the *Everson* ruling to justify his nonsupport of federal aid to parochial schools.

111 *CQWR*, May 26, 1961, p. 903.

112 See O'Neill's brief account in Thomas P. O'Neill, Jr. with William Novak, *Man of the House: The Life and Political Memoirs of Speaker Tip O'Neill* (New York: Random House, 1967), pp. 167–69; and the fuller treatment in John A. Farrell's marvelous biography, *Tip O'Neill and the Democratic Century* (Boston: Little, Brown, 2001), pp. 185–89.

113 Farrell, *Tip O'Neill and the Democratic Century*, p. 187.

114 This account is documented in Hugh Davis Graham's *The Uncertain Triumph: Federal Education Policy in the Kennedy and Johnson Years* (Chapel Hill: The University of North Carolina Press, 1984), pp. 22–23. The Wilbur Cohen remarks are from an interview with Graham, April 20, 1981.

115 "House Rejects Compromise Education Bill," *CQ Weekly Report*, XIX (September 1, 1961), p. 1507.

116 Jim Grant Bolling, Oral History Interview with Ronald J. Grele, JFK Library, March 1, 1966, pp. 53–55.

117 Richard F. Fenno, Jr., "The House of Representatives and Federal Aid to Education," in Robert L. Peabody and Nelson W. Polsby, eds., "*New Perspectives on the House of Representatives*," 2nd ed. (Chicago: Rand, McNally, 1969), pp. 283–323; the quotation is on p. 321. The chapter was derived from Frank J. Munger and Richard F. Fenno, Jr., *National Politics in Federal Aid to Education* (Syracuse, NY: Syracuse University Press, 1962). See also Hugh Douglas Price, "Race. Religion, and the Rules Committee," in Westin, *The Uses of Power: 7 Cases in American Politics*, pp. 2–71.

118 Farrell, *Tip O'Neill*, p. 187.

119 Graham, *The Uncertain Triumph*, p. 3.

120 See Augusta E. Wilson's flattering and short biography of Thompson, *Liberal Leader in the House, Frank Thompson, Jr. if New Jersey* (Washington: Acropolis Cooks, 1968).

121 Richard W. Bolling Oral History, JFK Library, p. 46.

122 For a fuller discussion of the Berlin conflict, see Frederick Kempe's masterful *Berlin 1961: Kennedy, Khrushchev, and the Most Dangerous Place on Earth* (New York: G. P. Putnam's Sons, 2011).

123 An objective assessment of Kennedy's first year in office can be found in Helen Fuller's *Year of Trial: Kennedy's Crucial Decisions* (New York: Harcourt, Brace & World, Inc., 1962).

124 Alan Peppard, "JFK Traveled to Sam Rayburn's Side in Final Hours," *Dallas Morning News* online archive, updated December 22, 2010.

125   Richard L. Lyons, "The Next Speaker; McCormack is Next in Line Is Last of Passing Breed," *Washington Post*, December 5, 1961, p. A13.

126   President Harry Truman to U.S. Representative Dick Bolling, December 12, 1961, in the Bolling Papers, University of Missouri-Kansas City Library.

127   Richard W. Bolling interview with Ronald J. Grele, November 1, 1965, JFK Library.

128   Interview with a former Rules Committee staffer, March 1981.

129   Edward F. Woods, "Rep. Bolling Being Mentioned as Successor to Rayburn: Believed to be Choice of House but Many Feel McCormack Has Inside Track," *St. Louis Post-Dispatch*, September 6, 1961, p. 1. Also contemporary magazines articles discussing Bolling as a possible speakership successor to Rayburn appeared in William S. White, "The Invisible Gentleman from Kansas City," *Harpers* (May 1961) and in "Retirement for Rayburn," *TIME*, May 5, 1961, accessed May 4, 2015.

130   Garrison Nelson, "Leadership Position-Holding in the United States House of Representatives," *Capitol Studies*, IV (Fall 1976), pp. 11–36; and "Partisan Patterns of House Leadership Change, 1789–1977," *APSR*, LXII (September 1977), pp. 918–39.

131   A recounting of John McCormack's real and perceived inadequacies were catalogued in Nelson W. Polsby's last book, *How Congress Evolves: Social Bases of Institutional Change* (New York: Oxford University Press, 2004), pp. 36–40. In the University of Missouri-Kansas City Library archives containing the papers of McCormack critic Dick Bolling, it is clear that the two had become very close. In personal conversations and in this book, Polsby expressed a great deal of interest in my "fascinating evidence that McCormack routinely misrepresented important details of his background in interviews in order to conform his personal history to the Horatio Alger norms presumed to be attractive to his South Boston constituency" (p. 193 n4).

132   Drew Pearson, "Kennedy Has Three Reasons for Sidetracking McCormack," *Charleston (S.C.) Gazette*, October 11, 1961, p. 16; see "Kennedy-McCormack Donnybrook Brews," *CQ Weekly Report*, October 13, 1961, pp. 1732–34; and the syndicated columns of Mary McGrory, "Pair of Contrasting Bostonians," *Hammond (Ind,.) Times*, October 12, 1961; and Drew Pearson, "Old Feud Mars Speaker Race," *Charleston (S.C.) Gazette*, October 13, 1961, p. 18.

133   William F. Arbogast, "Religious Dispute Lurks in House Speaker's Race," *Indiana Evening Gazette*, November 21, 1961, p. 5.

134   United Press International, "Church-State Separatists Don't Want McCormack," *BG*, November 21, 1961, p. C1 ff. Associated Press, "Promise You Won't Scuttle School Aid, McCormack Urged," *BG*, November 27, 1961, p. 8.

135   Bobby Baker, Oral History Interview, U.S. Senate Historical Office, p. 71.

136   Mary McGrory, "Strange Coalition Behind Scenes Hopes to Beat [McCormack]," *BG*, December 3, 1961, p. 53; and "Unusual Coalition Eyes Rains for Speaker," *CQWR*, December 8, 1961, p. 1933.

137   "240 Votes Pledged to McCormack as Speaker," *BG*, December 28, 1961, p. 5.

138   On Howard Smith's endorsement of McCormack, see Drew Pearson," Washington Merry-Go-Round: McCormack-Smith Pact Reported," *Washington Post*, December 29, 1961, p. B19.

19

The Tenuous Partnership, 1962

President Kennedy's first year was regarded as a mixed one, with more success in the domestic policy realm than in the foreign policy one. Writing for *TIME* magazine, Neil McNeil, its longtime congressional reporter, prepared a surprisingly positive assessment in August 1961[1]:

> We must remember in judging the performance that the 87th Congress felt hostility toward Kennedy's program. . . . And, despite that hostility, the Congress has passed a large part of his program . . . unmatched since FDR's 1933 session. This has been done . . . at a time when President Kennedy was suffering continuing failures in foreign policy and in his military adventure in Cuba, a record of failure that could only make it more difficult, not less, to pass a domestic program through a reluctant Congress.
>
> We think it fair to say that the Kennedy success with his program on Capitol Hill has been the one major bright spot in his Administration's career to date.

In the First Session Kennedy was aided by Speaker Sam Rayburn, as motivated by his desire to help his protégé Lyndon Johnson as he was to enhance Kennedy's reputation. The most loyal of Democrats, Rayburn understood that they must swim together or sink together. However, Kennedy's second year would open with the House speakership held by the man in Congress with whom Jack was most familiar: John W. McCormack of South Boston. The informal truce between the families had suffered during the 1st Session, most notably on the issue of federal aid to parochial schools and public speculation that the Kennedy Administration might block John's ascension to the speakership. Also lurking on the year's agenda was the most direct conflict between the two families, the battle over the remaining two years of Jack's U.S. Senate seat.

As the Kennedy Administration prepared for the 2nd Session of the 87th Congress, the Administration congratulated itself on moving the nation forward declaring, "In 1961, the American people awakened as never before to a sober realization of the perils that beset our nation."[2] However, *New York Times* men Russell Baker and Tom Wicker forecast that smooth sailing would not be on the horizon for the upcoming year. The droll Baker touch in the opening paragraph is obvious.[3]

> The President has set his strategy, called his captains to council, listened to his scouts and given the pre-battle exhortations to hearten the legions. In these

hortatory remarks, he has sounded partly like Caesar before facing the Belgae and partly like Lyndon B. Johnson selling one of his half-a-loaf compromises in the old Senate days.

. . .

Structurally, Congress opposes the President with still other obstacles. There are the conservative Southerners ready to oppose him. Pivotal committee members of his own party are against him on key measures. Finally, leadership of the House has passed from the incomparable Sam Rayburn to a collective group of uncertain ability, with the prospect that power will ultimately fragment into a dozen committee baronies. In all, the Congressional prospect is not one to encourage a President with high hopes.

The speakership succession

As 1962 began, most observers focused on John McCormack, who, for 21 years, had served loyally as Sam Rayburn's chief deputy—17 as Majority Leader when Sam was Speaker and 4 years as Minority Whip when Sam was Minority Leader. It was the longest political apprenticeship in American history. At last the formal vote would take place on January 10, 1962. The anti-McCormack cabal had collapsed and there were no dissenting votes in the caucus, nor were there any dissenting votes among the Democrats who voted for Speaker on the opening day of the 2nd Session.[4] At last, John's 33 years of paying dues in the House were acknowledged.

John McCormack was the first Massachusetts Democrat to gain the chair. In 1977, his protégé Thomas P. "Tip" O'Neill, Jr. would be the next. Six prior Speakers from Massachusetts had come from five different political parties.[5] John McCormack held the speakership for nine years, the longest period of consecutive years in the office until Tip O'Neill served for a full decade. Throughout that time, there were two Democratic House members who served conterminously with him and represented polar positions concerning John and his management of the office—Carl Albert and Dick Bolling.

Dueling Rayburn protégés, Carl Albert and Dick Bolling

Because the succession from floor leader to Speaker had become virtually automatic, it was the open contests for floor leaders that were the most contentious.[6] While McCormack was chosen Speaker without voted opposition, a contest emerged for Majority Floor Leader. The two contenders were Albert of Oklahoma and Bolling of Missouri.[7] Carl Albert, who had served as Democratic whip since 1955 and had been sponsored in his career by Sam Rayburn, was the "insider" candidate for the majority leadership. Albert's 3rd Oklahoma District and Rayburn's 4th Texas District were adjacent to one another, separated only by the Red River. However, a likely challenge to Albert's election appeared in the candidacy of Dick Bolling, the "outsider" candidate who was also a Rayburn protégé.[8]

There were more similarities than differences in the backgrounds and House locations of both men. Their seniority was similar: Albert was first elected to the House in 1946 along with Kennedy and Nixon, while Dick Bolling was elected to the House in 1948. Each was well placed in the House: Albert was ranked 7th of 22 on Agriculture, while Bolling ranked 7th of 8 on Rules. Neither was close to chairing a committee. Bolling's Rules Committee was higher ranked given its centrality in setting the legislative agenda of the House, but Albert's Agriculture Committee had developed a unique reputation as a committee where favors could be done for fellow members and coalitions could be built.

In the years following World War II, the House Agriculture Committee had become a mini-Congress, filled with supporters of various commodities—including wheat, corn, rice, sugar, cotton, tobacco, apples, and dairy—that contended for protection from the government.[9] The New Deal's federalization of agricultural programs made Washington's role more important than ever in the lives of the farmers. Since every region had commodities impacted by government regulation, the committee had reach beyond the nation's farm states. There were more friends to be made on Agriculture than Rules. John McCormack well understood this and his coalition-building style led him to be the only northeastern Democrat to vote consistently for farm bills. He contended that he was called "the urban farmer."[10]

Unlike John McCormack, Albert and Bolling were well educated and well traveled. Albert was a Phi Beta Kappa graduate of the University of Oklahoma and a Rhodes Scholar who received a Bachelor of Arts in Laws and a Bachelor of Civil Laws from Oxford while Dick Bolling held two degrees—a BA and MA in literature and French from the University of the South in Sewanee, Tennessee.

Both were army veterans who served in World War II. Albert began as an army private in 1941 and served briefly in the Third Armored Division. He applied for and received an officer's commission and was offered a new assignment in the U.S. Army Air Corps' judge advocate general's (JAG) office. As the war progressed, he was transferred to the Pacific Theater to serve in General Douglas MacArthur's JAG office. Albert returned home in 1946 as a lieutenant colonel with a Bronze Star. Bolling also entered the army in 1941 as a private and served until discharged as a lieutenant colonel in July 1946, with four years overseas service as assistant to the chief of staff to General MacArthur in Australia, New Guinea, the Philippines, and Japan. He was awarded the Legion of Merit and the Bronze Star as well.

While Albert and Bolling disagreed about the virtues of John McCormack, they respected one another. It was their similarity that enabled them to work together on many key issues. However, it was their differences that accounted for their dissimilar House careers.[11]

Carl Albert, John McCormack's Ally, "The Little Giant": Carl Albert, like John McCormack, was a "poor boy who had made good." His father was a coal miner and farmer and he had been raised in a log cabin in Bug Tussle, Oklahoma, receiving much of his early schooling in a one-room schoolhouse.[12] Albert's most distinctive feature was his height. At 5'4," he was far shorter than virtually all of the men and many of the women with whom he served. He was genuinely humble and well regarded by his colleagues as a result. It was those qualities and his intelligence that led Speaker Sam Rayburn and Majority Leader John McCormack to name Albert as whip when Democrats regained control of the House in 1955.[13] Unlike the Republicans, House Democrats appointed their whips as a way of controlling the leadership succession and to contain the party fissures that often accompanied open leadership contests.[14]

A major factor in Carl Albert's appointment was that his 3rd District in southeastern Oklahoma was across the Red River from Rayburn's 4th Texas District, and also adjacent to Banking Committee Chair Wright Patman's 1st Texas District in the state's northeastern corner. Sam frequently crossed the Red River to get agricultural supplies for his small family farm. Both Sam and Carl had come from struggling agricultural backgrounds. In Rayburn's case, his father left east Tennessee's Roane County, an iron-rich county better suited for mining, in search of more fertile fields in northeast Texas while Albert's father became a coal miner to keep his family farm solvent. Rayburn and Albert represented the traditional southern small farmer base of the Democratic Party. While Albert grew up in Oklahoma's "Little Dixie," Rayburn's Roane County was pro-Union throughout the Civil War.

Dick Bolling, John McCormack's Liberal Nemesis: Dick Bolling was of a different breed. He was a handsome, wavy-haired, strongly built college football player who was well educated and well read. Like Jack Kennedy, Bolling's educational attainments and life experiences made him disdainful of the poorly educated urban provincial John McCormack. It was a disdain that he concealed early in his House career, but later it would erupt into open warfare.

Richard Walker Bolling was born in New York City in 1916. His father was a successful surgeon and his mother came from a prominent southern family. They enrolled him at New England's prestigious prep school, Phillips Exeter Academy in New Hampshire, alma mater of Daniel Webster. Dick was 15 when his father died and his mother returned to Huntsville in the native northern Alabama of the Walker family. Bolling's grandmother was a Walker and her great-grandfather John Williams Walker was one of Alabama's first two U.S. Senators in 1819.[15] Returning to northern Alabama, Dick Bolling was schooled in the Walker family tradition of public service.

Located in the southern foothills of the Appalachian Mountain chain, northern Alabama was the one part of the state where little cotton could be grown. This was iron ore country. With little cotton, there were no plantations and with no plantations, slavery was not a major factor.[16] None of the northern counties exceeded Alabama's statewide average black population and many of them, including Walker County, birthplace of Speaker Will Bankhead and named for Bolling's senatorial ancestor, fell below the national average for black citizens. With few blacks among their county residents, racial segregation had less meaning in north Alabama and the blacks in that region were less quiescent than those in Alabama's "black belt." That fact would account for the brutal eruptions of racial violence that later occurred in Birmingham, northern Alabama's largest city. Thus it was possible for leaders from these counties to reach out beyond the South to the Representatives from the northern cities with their religious and racially diverse constituencies. It is not surprising that these counties provided Alabama's national Democratic leaders, including the Bankhead clan, U.S.

Senators Oscar Underwood and John Sparkman, and Supreme Court Justice Hugo L. Black. Sam Rayburn from the southern Appalachian mountains of east Tennessee was well acquainted with the men of north Alabama. Oscar Underwood had been Rayburn's first floor leader in the House and as the senior member of Ways and Means, he assigned Sam to his first and only committee; Will Bankhead was Speaker when Rayburn was Majority Leader; and John Sparkman was named by Rayburn and McCormack to be Democratic Whip in 1946. Dick Bolling's formative years in this part of the South gave him and Rayburn a common bond.

After the war, Bolling relocated to Kansas City, Missouri, as the veterans' advisor at the University of Kansas City and was elected in Harry Truman's upset win in 1948. Truman's Jackson County encompassed Bolling's district and the president took a serious interest in Bolling's career. Ironically, Bolling's initial committee assignment was on Expenditures in the Executive Departments where he served with Majority Leader John McCormack, who had remained on the committee to validate the chairmanship of Chicago's William Dawson, the first African-American committee chair. It was Bolling's next assignment to Banking and Currency that would prove crucial to his advancement in the House. On that committee, he made the acquaintance of Wright Patman of Texas who had a key to Rayburn's Capitol hideaway, "the Board of Education." Patman's sponsorship of Bolling brought him to Rayburn's attention.

With his bona fides vouched for by Harry Truman and Wright Patman, there is little wonder that Rayburn took young Dick Bolling on as a protégé. When the Democrats regained control of the House in 1954, Rayburn urged Bolling to run for a seat on Ways and Means. However, there was a catch. In order to be sponsored for Ways and Means, Bolling would have to support the oil depletion allowance—a tax loophole that had protected the fortunes of the oil and gas magnates of Texas and Louisiana. Bolling turned it down and Rayburn had him assigned to one of the four new vacancies that had opened up on the Rules Committee.[17] Named to one of the other new vacancies was John McCormack's protégé, Tip O'Neill. For the next 32 years from 1955 to 1987, Bolling and O'Neill would move steadily into greater positions of House power, and work mostly, but not always, in concert.

Knowing of Bolling's strong link to his old poker pal, John wrote a fan letter to former President Truman following the successful passage of the 1957 Civil Rights Act. Its opening paragraph contains John's high praise for Bolling:[18] "Dear Mr. President:

> I know of the high regard you have for Dick Bolling. In my book he is 'the tops'.
>
> His ability and loyalty have always been outstanding but even more noticeably during the past session."

The feelings were not mutually shared, as Bolling was one of the cabal leaders who tried and failed to block McCormack's replacement of Rayburn as Speaker in 1961. Having determined that he could not topple McCormack, Bolling set his sights on the post of Majority Leader. He contended that he had no major argument with Carl Albert but was troubled by the House Democrats' "automatic succession system" of whip to leader to Speaker. While the succession system had contained intra-party conflict among the House's fractious Democrats, it had also thwarted leadership ambitions among talented junior House members that often led them to depart the House for the Senate or their states' governorships. However, if Bolling were to become Majority Leader, he would be in a position to undermine Speaker McCormack and provide support for Kennedy Administration initiatives. It was that belief that led Bolling to hope that Kennedy would push for his selection over Carl Albert.

Bolling and Kennedy shared similar characteristics of prep schools and wealthy and powerful families and were more similar to one another than either was to McCormack and Albert. However, Kennedy had a charming self-deprecating wit while Bolling's wit tended to be caustic and directed at others. This was a style similar to that of the Gilded Age Speaker Republican Thomas Brackett "Czar" Reed of Maine to whom Dick dedicated his 1967 book, *Power in the House*.[19] Reed who once declared that "the Senate is where good Representatives go to die" had a snarky wit that cost him the 1896 Republican nomination that went to William McKinley. Bolling tended to be an intellectual snob, making him respected but not well liked.

Two other rivals, Albert Rains of Alabama and House Un-American Activities Committee (HUAC) Chair Tad Walter of Pennsylvania, were unlikely to receive White House support. Neither Rains nor Walter were perceived as liberals, and it was the liberals who were most anxious about a McCormack speakership. Bolling was much fonder of Albert than he was of McCormack, but as an historian of the House, Bolling knew that tradition would hold and McCormack would gain the speakership. White House interventions in congressional leadership contests were infrequent, and presidents could choose to intervene or not. In 1937, FDR had tilted the Senate leadership battle between Alben Barkley of Kentucky and the conservative Byron "Pat" Harrison of Mississippi toward Barkley, while Eisenhower had offered no support to the embattled Minority Leader Joe Martin in his 1959 contest with Charles Halleck. Kennedy chose the Eisenhower strategy. There may have been two reasons not to intervene in the McCormack case: first, the Roman Catholic hierarchy, already disappointed in Kennedy's noninclusion of aid to parochial schools in his education bill, would have been further dismayed by his blocking of John McCormack, their most loyal and active champion. The other reason according to Arthur Krock was that[20]

the President and Representative McCormack have been on opposite sides of Democratic Party contests in Massachusetts for nomination and for state leadership. Currently there is a prospect that McCormack's nephew, whom he and his wife have reared as their son, and Edward Kennedy, the President's youngest brother, will be rivals for the Democratic nomination for Senator in 1962. If Mr. Kennedy had openly or covertly moved to prevent Representative McCormack's logical promotion, he would have incurred the charge of using the House to pursue a personal and political local feud.

. . .

By refraining from any activity in the choice of a Speaker, the President is freer to influence the choice of the majority leader; and get more help from a grateful than a resentful Speaker for the legislation the House has obstructed, and for enlarging the majority leader's authority.

Meanwhile, Bolling spoke to Attorney General Robert Kennedy about his run and even elicited a public endorsement from former House member and Kennedy Interior Secretary Stewart Udall.[21] But the big blow to the Bolling candidacy occurred when on October 29, 1961, President Kennedy went to Big Cedar, Oklahoma to dedicate a road and delivered a speech with fulsome praise for Carl Albert. When asked by Oklahoma Governor Howard Edmondson, "Why in the hell are you going to a little town in Oklahoma to dedicate a road that goes to nowhere?" President Kennedy replied that he was not going to dedicate a road. "I'm going to Oklahoma to kiss Bob Kerr's ass."[22] U.S. Senator Bob Kerr of Oklahoma was the founder of the Kerr-McGee Oil Company and the richest self-made millionaire in the Senate. As Chair of the powerful tax-writing Senate Finance Committee, Kerr was informally known as "the uncrowned king of the Senate."[23] Much of that was due to Kerr's giving "loans" to fellow Senators and then not asking for repayment.[24] This was a man that Kennedy chose not to offend.

Dick Bolling did not get the message immediately and his campaign manager, the New Jersey tough guy Frank Thompson, continued to issue optimistic pronouncements. They hoped for Kennedy Administration help, but as the *Times*'s John D. Morris speculated,[25]

> "The President would have preferred Mr. Bolling as Speaker, or failing that as majority leader, but the White House took no part in maneuvering for either job. The hands-off policy reflected the belief of Presidential advisors that White House intervention would be ineffective and therefore unwise."

Days before the 2nd Session of the 87th Congress convened, Bolling withdrew his candidacy "because developments in the last few days convinced me that I do not have a chance to win."[26] He acknowledged that the White House was "very wise in staying out" of the majority leadership race.

What Bolling did not know was that the Kennedy brothers were busily responding to a higher authority, their father Joseph P. Kennedy the ambassador, who was determined to get Jack's Senate seat for Teddy, his youngest son. Arthur Krock, the longtime Washington columnist for the *Times* and a well-paid retainer of Joe Kennedy's,[27] signaled the family's approval of the Albert selection in his January 5 column on "The Function of Leadership in Congress," wherein he contended that[28]

> the Democratic split on certain legislation desired by Mr. Kennedy—a split reflected in the Senate, too, but not with the nullifying force it acquired in the House in 1961—requires the majority leader to keep the President accurately and objectively informed of its obstructive potential, unpopular as this information may be. And the prospect of this . . . apparently was estimated to be more attainable under Albert's leadership than Bolling's.[29]

The Kennedys correctly surmised that Massachusetts Attorney General Edward J. McCormack, Jr., Knocko's son and John's nephew, would be their major opponent in the upcoming Senate primary. Eddie had already won two statewide contests and was far better regarded in liberal circles than Uncle John. They hoped that the Kennedy-McCormack truce was still in place and they would do nothing to antagonize John McCormack in the hope that he might dissuade Eddie from making the Senate run.

Dick Bolling would then seek out a different audience—academic students of Congress. Bolling, who had been employed as an academic after returning from the war, was especially solicitous of young political scientists and was readily available for interviews during the period of the 1960s when the American Political Science Association (APSA) launched its ambitious multivolume Study of Congress Project. While the two major congressional liaisons for the project were Representatives Chet Holifield, Democrat of California, and Thomas B. Curtis, Republican of Missouri, Bolling's cooperation with the project led to his being acknowledged frequently in the books produced by the APSA study.

Hale Boggs, the New Whip: With the collapse of the Bolling candidacy, McCormack and Albert appointed the Mississippi-born New Orleans Congressman Hale Boggs as Democratic Whip.[30] The good-looking, ruddy-faced Boggs was an immensely talented legislator. However, he had aroused Sam Rayburn's suspicions earlier in his House career when as a relatively new member of Ways and Means, he ran and lost a 1952 primary for Governor of Louisiana. Rayburn, the consummate House loyalist, did not like to reward anyone who saw the House as a stepping-stone for other offices. His hesitancy about Boggs was not irreversible. Louisiana was a state that Texans eyed warily. It was adjacent geographically but far from similar politically. The continuing dominance of the Long family made other southern Democrats uncertain of where Louisianans would land. It was also the only southern state where Catholics regularly won office. Boggs understood that Rayburn was reluctant about him and using the extraordinary charm of his lovely wife, Lindy, and multiple home-cooked meals, Boggs was able to convince Rayburn that he would be the Speaker's man in the Bayou State.[31]

Lindy Boggs was not only beautiful and well-educated. She was a Claiborne, and as such, she was congressional royalty. Marie Corinne Claiborne Boggs was descended from six antebellum members of Congress.[32] Her first ancestor to serve in the Congress was Thomas Claiborne who served in the House as a Jeffersonian Republican from Virginia for ten years—six years during the Washington and John Adams Administrations (1793–99) and four years during Thomas Jefferson's presidency (1801–1805). Lindy was even connected to a sitting member of the Senate in the person of her distant cousin, Rhode Island's patrician Claiborne Pell, a close friend of the Kennedys who served in the Senate from 1961 to 1997.

Lindy's sparkling nature made her the First Lady of the House of Representatives. Rayburn's three-month marriage had collapsed years before, Harriet McCormack had become a recluse, and Carl Albert's wife Mary was uncomfortable with the social demands of the Capitol. There is little question that Lindy had softened the rougher edges of Hale Boggs and purchased forgiveness for him from those in the House hierarchy who were discomfited by aspects of his hard-drinking "good old boy" persona. Sam Rayburn was taken with Lindy Boggs, as he was with other talented and beautiful women. His marital collapse in 1927 had not lessened his fascination with the women of Washington.[33]

John McCormack was unfailingly polite to the powerful women of Washington, but as a more traditional politician, he was less comfortable with those who had ambitions of their own. But Lindy Boggs was special, and her presence took pressure off John's increasingly frail and retiring Harriet who was nearing her 80th birthday. Hale Boggs was an elected urban Catholic from New Orleans and almost as important to John McCormack and Carl Albert, Hale was another "poor boy that had made good" (Figure 19.1). Boggs had been born the son of a bank teller in rural Mississippi where Catholics were few and hardships plentiful. It was at Tulane University that Boggs made his mark, enabling him to overcome economic adversity and religious prejudice. And it was at Tulane where he met Lindy Claiborne, a marriage that would truly transform his life. New Orleans Catholics were not as doctrinally conservative as the Boston Irish Catholics, but John McCormack valued background more than aspiration. He was much more interested in where you were from than where you wanted to go. The past was certain; the future was not.

With the appointment of Hale Boggs to the post of House Majority Whip, Roman Catholics appeared to control Washington. Catholics now held the presidency—John F. Kennedy; the Senate Majority Leadership—Montana's Mike Mansfield; the House

Figure 19.1 U.S. House Democratic Leaders: Majority Whip T. Hale Boggs, Floor Leader Carl Albert, and Speaker John McCormack (Carl Albert Congressional Research Center, University of Oklahoma).

Speakership—John McCormack; and now the House Majority Whip post—Hale Boggs. Anti-Catholic groups were horrified and the lobbying group Protestants and Other Americans United for Separation of Church and State was near apoplexy.[34] That did not seem to matter to the House, and the leadership trio of Speaker McCormack, Majority Leader Albert, and Majority Whip Boggs served together for nine years, 1962–71, the longest period that any leadership team held power in the U.S. House.

The House team of McCormack-Albert-Boggs was now in place, but all three had reputations as collegial and not commanding. Each fell into the category of "social leader" as none of them had chaired a standing committee and little legislation bore their names. None was perceived as Sam Rayburn was, a forceful and effective "task leader." That commanding House presence had ended with the death of Sam Rayburn. As a result, news articles speculated that President Kennedy's second year might be even less successful than his first one. Typical of these articles was Drew Pearson's March 17, 1962, *Washington Post* piece, "The House Misses Mister Sam," in which he listed a number of legislative items where John had been outfoxed by House Minority Leader Charlie Halleck.[35]

The personal contrast, the Sybarite and the Ascetic

It was the personal lifestyle contrast between President Jack Kennedy and Speaker John McCormack that proved to be the greatest impediment to their working together. Kennedy's barely concealed infidelities with an array of beautiful women greatly troubled John, arguably the most faithful husband in the two-century history of the U.S. House.

While Jack Kennedy's personal lifestyle choices and his family's comfortable upper-class existence on Cape Cod and Palm Beach were feted countless times, John McCormack's lifestyle choices and living circumstances received less attention. One of these rare portrayals appeared in a 1964 article in the widely read *Saturday Evening Post*[36]:

> Curiously, despite his 35 years in Congress almost nobody in the capital really knows McCormack at all well as a person. He long ago drew a curtain around his private affairs, keeping out the curious eyes of official Washington.
>
> Few of even his most intimate friends in Congress have ever set foot in the modest three-room suite in the Hotel Washington overlooking the U.S. Treasury, where the childless McCormacks have lived since 1928. There, each day after work, the white-maned Speaker has dinner alone with his devoted wife Harriet, before retiring to write letter after letter in his angular, laborious script to the families of deceased constituents in his Boston wards.
>
> He and his wife have dined together every evening since their marriage in June of 1920, which probably sets a record for devotion. McCormack always cuts the meat on his wife's plate, a custom which began early in their married life and

continues for sentimental reasons. If some rare political or civic banquet proves to be inescapable, McCormack will make an appearance but ignore the food, saving his appetite for his usual room-service meal at home with Harriet. Some months ago the Massachusetts Knights of Columbus planned to honor him with its highest award at a traditional stag dinner attended by political and church leaders, prominent businessmen and entertainment figures. McCormack agreed to appear only if his wife were by his side. She was the only woman there.

The McCormacks seldom entertain, and appear at Washington social events so rarely that it rates headlines whenever they do. For years their idea of recreation has been a solitary walk together or, more recently, an excursion in the chauffeur-driven Speaker's limousine, perhaps with a stop for milk and ice cream.

While Jack Kennedy and John McCormack may have both been sons of Boston-born Irish-descended mothers, they clearly operated in parallel universes and it was only their shared commitment to national politics that obliged them to interact with one another.

The tenuous policy partnership, 1962

James Sundquist's assessment of policymaking in those years borrowed a term from an insider who described the year 1962 as the "shakedown cruise."[37] President Kennedy's popularity remained high and Speaker McCormack and Senate Majority Leader Mansfield worked hard to move legislation through the 2nd Session of the 87th Congress. Still recovering from his aborted bid for the majority leadership, Dick Bolling sought to insert himself into the leadership's decision-making with the Democratic Study Group (DSG) sponsored creation of a Democratic House Policy Committee that would give liberals a greater voice in leadership decisions.[38] Needless to say, John McCormack was no fan of the proposal.

While some observers contended that John McCormack had little influence over southern members,[39] it was the House's southerners that protected John's speakership from some of the more zealous members of the DSG. One need go no further than Larry O'Brien's recollections in *No Final Victories* of hearing South Carolina's L. Mendel Rivers, future chair of Armed Services, describe his loyalty to Speaker McCormack[40]:

> "One of the most conservative of the Southerners, Mendel Rivers of South Carolina, used to say, 'I'm not a Democrat, I'm a McCormacrat,' and from time to time, on close issues, McCormack would say to him, 'Well, Mendel, it's time for you to prove you're a McCormacrat,' and he could sometimes swing Rivers' vote."

With the Kennedy-McCormack partnership in place, the first major piece of legislation in the 2nd Session was the Manpower Development and Training Act of 1962.

Approved March 15, 1962, this act authorized a new federal program to train workers to help alleviate unemployment and to provide skilled personnel in certain industries.[41] Under this program the secretary of labor and the states were responsible for helping to determine manpower needs, selecting candidates for training and placing trained persons. This act was one of only three out of the 11 Kennedy legislative proposals that passed through Congress and was enacted.[42]

Kennedy-sponsored revisions to the tax code initiated in 1961 finally reached the House floor on March 29.[43] McCormack ally Tip O'Neill successfully got the House to end debate over a closed rule that allowed the act to proceed without Republican amendments. The vote on final passage was 219–160, and the *Boston Globe* reported that the Kennedy Administration publicly appreciated the McCormack and O'Neill efforts[44]:

> As late as the night before the vote, the White House aides were convinced they didn't have the House votes. But they were overlooking McCormack. "It was the Speaker who won that fight for the administration," an aide points out, "and don't forget it. He put together a solid 225 votes, more Democratic votes than you can usually round up to support adjournment."

Controversy nearly swallowed up the Public Welfare Amendments of 1962 that broadened welfare aid to those people considered to be the neediest, while undertaking a campaign to reduce the need for aid through programs of rehabilitation, training, and self-care for the needy.[45] Approved July 25, 1962, the amendments increased federal reimbursements to the states for rehabilitative services to public assistance clients from 50 to 75% of the total cost. They also authorized appointment by the secretary of health, education, and welfare of a 12-member Advisory Council on Public Welfare. Once the shouting had abated, the House voted 357–34 and Congress adopted the conference report on the Public Welfare Amendments.[46]

Getting Teddy ready

Early in 1961 Ambassador Joseph P. Kennedy basked in wonderful familial glory. One son was now President of the United States and another was Attorney General. What about Teddy, the youngest and most charming of the boys, the most natural politician among them and the one who most resembled Joe Jr., his namesake and the family's lost prince? The answer was obvious: Ted would run in the November 1962 special election to complete the two years remaining in Jack's Senate term that would expire on January 3, 1965. After all, Joe Kennedy reportedly declared, "It is our seat. I paid for it." Sadly for Joe Kennedy, this would be his last good year before his disabling stroke in late December.

Jack's Senate seat was then held by Ben Smith, an old Harvard roommate, but it was widely anticipated that Smith would step aside once Ted became eligible. On February 22, 1962, Edward Moore Kennedy reached the constitutional age of 30 for a seat in the United States Senate. Speculation that had been brewing for months was now out in the open: Teddy was running for the remainder of that Senate term.

Massachusetts politics had to be managed if the Kennedys were to gain and keep public office. The Kennedys may have lived elsewhere and had business dealings in the far larger states of New York, Illinois, and California, but political careers require a geographical base and Massachusetts was their base. It may have been a political swamp, but it was their swamp.

There was a concern that this additional Kennedy reach would upset the tenuous Kennedy-McCormack congressional partnership. Jack and Bobby were initially hesitant about helping Ted obtain the Senate seat. Ted himself had questions about their commitment. In his excerpt, "the Youngest Brother," from the *Globe*'s 2009 multipart series, *Ted Kennedy*, Neil Swidey wrote[47]:

> In the summer of 1961, Ted wrote to inform his father that Edward McCormack, the popular Massachusetts attorney general and a certain candidate for the Senate, had told a mutual friend he doubted Ted was going to run for the seat. That's because at a luncheon in Washington, Bobby had publicly showered McCormack with praise. "When I heard this, I ran down brother Bob and he said, 'What's so bad about that?'—he would say some nice things about me, too," Ted wrote. "So you can see what I am up against here, Dad."

The Kennedy brothers knew that there were two key problems. The first, that of nepotism and family power grabs, may have bothered the national Democrats and the state's liberals, but the voters of Massachusetts couldn't seem to get enough of the Kennedy brothers. Their only regret was that there was only one more left whom they could place into high public office. The other problem was more potentially damaging. During his freshman year at Harvard in 1951, Teddy had asked a classmate, William Frate, to take two Spanish-language exams for him. The deception was uncovered and both boys were asked to withdraw. Harvard's capacity to forgive the sins of children of its generous donors has long been suspected in the city of Boston, and Ted was not summarily dismissed. He was given an opportunity to reapply later. After two years serving in Paris as a guard at SHAPE (Supreme Headquarters Allied Powers Europe) with the U.S. Army, he returned to Harvard and graduated in 1956. In a city which seemed to venerate education, this incident had the earmarks of serious danger.

So Jack and Bob turned for advice to one of the great Washington Democratic operatives, the handsome and dashing Clark M. Clifford. Unlike many of his contemporaries, Clifford did not operate in the shadows. He enjoyed his fame. His work on President Truman's 1948 election campaign as the president's White House counsel was well known in the capital city and he had a reputation of offering sage advice.[48] The Kennedys had used him to help them through the difficulties of the 1960–61 presidential transition, and he would be called upon to help them troubleshoot problems. Initially, Bob and Jack asked Clifford to call their father Joe to express their concerns. Reportedly, on a phone call with Clifford, Joe declared, "Teddy's in the

Senate," and slammed the phone down. This anecdote is remarkably similar to one about Bobby's appointment as attorney general in 1961.

In September 1961, five months before Ted would meet the Constitution's 30-year minimum age requirement for the Senate, the brothers met with Clifford in the White House three times to obtain advice on how to defuse the cheating scandal.[49] They anticipated that Eddie McCormack would be Ted's major rival and they wished to have this piece of unpleasantness behind them before the campaign began. Clifford's advice was simple: find a friendly reporter to release the story soon after the announcement of candidacy and put your own interpretation on it before others get to it first. Bob Healy of the *Boston Globe*, who was regularly called by the ambassador, would write the story and it appeared in the *Globe* on March 30, 1962.[50] In his book *President Kennedy: Profiles of Power*, Richard Reeves recounts the incident in greater detail[51]:

> The President had already done a bit of staffwork for his brother, meeting with *Boston Globe* editors and reporters who had allowed him to do some editing on the most dangerous story of his brother's campaign. The *Globe* had investigated a campaign rumor that had turned out to be true: The youngest Kennedy had been thrown out of Harvard for cheating. The editors had told the President what they had and negotiated back and forth with him for a couple of days. "We haven't spent as much fucking time on anything since Cuba," Kennedy joked after a long session with the *Globe*'s Washington bureau chief, Robert Healy.

Included in the *Globe*'s 2010 obituary of Healy is a recounting of the involvement of the Kennedy White House in spinning the story:[52] "The upshot was the Kennedys would cooperate if the story was played below the fold on Page One (that is, on the lower half of the front page). Furthermore, it ran with the innocuous headline, 'Ted Kennedy Tells about Harvard Examination Incident.'"

As anticipated, Attorney General Edward J. McCormack, Jr. also wanted the Senate seat. Eddie McCormack had passed on a 1960 bid for governor and wished to join his uncle John in Washington.[53] John and Eddie were especially close, with multiple news accounts describing the relationship between the two with Eddie having been raised as a son by the childless Speaker and his wife, Harriet.

There were two major hurdles confronting Teddy and Eddie en route to the nomination: the June Democratic State Convention in Springfield that had the power of endorsement, and the September Democratic Primary where the formal establishment of candidacy would occur.

Neither the Kennedy brothers nor John McCormack wanted this contest. With two powerful Irish families going head-to-head, it would be contentious at best and ugly at worst. Fallout from the contest could undermine Jack's presidency by angering the newly elected Speaker who had allies among many of the House's southern committee chairs and it could also unsettle Kennedy loyalists in the House that John's irritation would weaken the party's hold on the White House and the Congress. The easiest way out was to induce Eddie not to challenge Ted. Kennedy operatives tried to convince Eddie to stay out of the race with offers of a lucrative law partnership in New York City as a way of clearing up some of Eddie's financial indebtedness or an administrative post in the Department of the Navy, given that Eddie was a graduate of the U.S. Naval Academy in Annapolis.[54]

The one offer that appeared to come directly from Joe Kennedy to John and would truly have changed history was that of Kennedy support for Eddie to run for governor against the incumbent Republican John A. Volpe in 1962. In a 1968 interview for the Johnson Library, John McCormack recalled that Ambassador Kennedy approached him with an intriguing proposition.[55] He informed John that Teddy would run for Jack's seat when he turned thirty in 1962 and that Eddie McCormack should run for governor. The implication was that Joe would help with Eddie's campaign funding. John McCormack was now acting Speaker of the House as Sam Rayburn's health deteriorated and with Jack as president, it was essential in Joe's eyes that the two families work together. This was the proposition that John most favored.[56] Joe McGinniss corroborates the proposal[57]: "[Joe Kennedy] offered to back McCormack's candidacy for governor and pledged full financial support. In case of an unexpected defeat, there would be a fallback position as assistant secretary of the navy, a coveted plum for any Annapolis graduate.

No, said Eddie McCormack. He planned to be the next United States senator from Massachusetts."

A Kennedy-McCormack ticket would protect the national Democratic agenda and it would enable the two families to extend their control over the state's political fortunes into the next generation. The speculation was simple: Teddy would get Jack's seat in 1962 and be positioned for the 1964 election to the next full term. And Eddie would win the governorship in 1962 over Volpe, be reelected in 1964 when Jack would triumphantly renew his presidency and Eddie would then be positioned to fill the Senate seat of a retiring Republican Leverett Saltonstall in 1966. By 1967, it would be both Teddy and Eddie in the Senate. It was a wonderful plan but it was not to be. Eddie had spurned an earlier opportunity to run for governor in 1960 when Governor Furcolo made his unsuccessful second run for Saltonstall's Senate seat. With two young sons Edward III and John at home in Boston and a gubernatorial term of only two years available to him, Eddie chose to pass on the race for governor.[58] Having already run two biennial statewide races in 1958 and 1960, Eddie was well aware of how grueling these two-year terms could be. A six-year term in Washington was far more appealing. Eddie would eventually run unsuccessfully for governor against Volpe in 1966 after the terms for statewide officeholders had been lengthened to four years.

The potential deal was voided when Ambassador Kennedy collapsed while playing golf in Palm Beach shortly before Christmas of 1961. Diagnosed as a debilitating stroke, Kennedy lost much of his ability to move and to speak. Although he was to die eight years later in 1969, he never fully recovered his faculties.[59] Only Joe Kennedy could sign the checks and extend the family's financial largesse to people beyond the family, and without his consent, money for an Ed McCormack gubernatorial candidacy would not be forthcoming from Kennedy coffers.

Contrasting styles

Syndicated columnist Doris Fleeson observed that "Rep. John W. McCormack of Massachusetts often complained that much of the Washington press disliked him and treated him unfairly."[60] It was that sentiment that made John painfully aware of how his eighth grade education and dirt poor South Boston upbringing would be contrasted with Jack's prep school and Harvard education and his wealthy upbringing in Brookline, Hyannis Port, and Palm Beach. The 25-year gap between the elderly, tall, gaunt, pale-faced John McCormack and the well-tanned, young, vibrant, and handsome Jack Kennedy was obvious to all. Teddy White, whose gushing prose about the Kennedys had helped create the Camelot myth, later confessed that he and many fellow reporters had fallen completely under the Kennedy spell.[61] Unlike Arthur Krock, White did not have to be paid to sing the family's praises. He was simply smitten. In spite of John McCormack's meritorious life, reporters were not smitten. John had been a successful Boston attorney and had a 40-year public career of distinction but John was less open with reporters than others. John's reinvented family history had been long concealed and too great a public presence would have led prying reporters to uncover it. So John surrendered center stage to Presidents Roosevelt, Truman, Kennedy, and Johnson and to his dear friend and ally Sam Rayburn whose career overshadowed his for the prior 21 years.

The greater contrast occurred between the fathers of Teddy and Eddie. While Teddy's father Joe Kennedy was often referred to by the glamorous title of "the Ambassador," a title that he never relinquished, Eddie's father Edward McCormack, Sr. was almost always referred to as "Knocko." Eddie's barely educated father with his 300-pound beefy frame and his career as a South Boston barkeep could not be avoided. Even their scandals were dissimilar, as tales of the married Joe adulterously bedding movie stars and high-end alcohol trafficking were far more glamorous than Knocko's local book-making and small-time gambling at his Wave Cottage on South Boston's P Street, a world away from London's Court of St. James. While Joe consorted with FDR, British Prime Minister Neville Chamberlain, and England's Cliveden Set, Knocko hung out with twice-jailed Boston Mayor Jim Curley and the hard-edged shanty Irish of Southie.

Eddie's academic record at Colby, the Naval Academy, and BU Law was far superior to Teddy's Harvard cheating and his reputed mediocre law school record at the University of Virginia. It did not matter. This would not be a fair fight, and John McCormack knew that better than anyone else involved. John's fears were twofold, a Kennedy defeat in his home state by a McCormack would undermine the political effectiveness of both families and he was fearful that the reputation of the McCormacks would be irrevocably stained by this contest. As John declared emphatically in his 1968 oral history with T. Harrison Baker for the University of Texas,[62] "This is for the historians of tomorrow. I didn't want my nephew to run for the Senate."

Despite their closeness, Eddie seldom turned to John for advice in these matters and made this decision without consulting him, just as he had not when he ran for the Boston City Council.[63] The U.S. Senate was where Eddie wanted to be, and he was determined to make this reach. Eddie simply could not believe that the hundreds of thousands of Massachusetts voters, who had twice elected him to be their attorney general, would reject this bid. How could the voters possibly select this callow and shallow young man over him? John was unsurprised. He had witnessed the Kennedy operation up close for more than 15 years and was well aware what Eddie's fate would likely be.

The Kennedy camp proposed to Eddie's camp the use of a poll to determine who the most electable candidate was. If Eddie won the poll, then Teddy would withdraw from the race; and if Teddy won, Eddie would withdraw and campaign for governor. Never leaving anything to chance, the Kennedys had already run a poll and learned that Teddy would easily win that contest.[64] A public poll indicated that Teddy would still win, but the margin would be closer.[65] In any case, with his heart set on a Senate seat, Eddie McCormack dismissed any discussion of polls.

At the Springfield convention in June, any hopes of an Eddie victory were dashed when the key player at the convention, Springfield's own U.S. Representative Eddie Boland who John McCormack had placed on the powerful House Appropriations Committee, gave the nominating speech for Teddy at the convention. Boland's roommate Tip O'Neill, who held Jack's seat in the House and John's favorite protégé, tried to remain as neutral as possible in this contest between the scions of the nation's two most powerful Democrats. Teddy emerged from the convention with a solid victory, and now the three-month campaign for the primary had begun.

Throughout the summer, news articles appeared contending that the Kennedy agenda would be seriously undermined in the House by the Teddy-Eddie battle, but John made strenuous efforts to prevent that from happening. Larry O'Brien, Jack's congressional liaison, who came to Washington in 1949 as the administrative assistant of Foster Furcolo, John's first major protégé in the Massachusetts delegation, was very pleased that McCormack was so willing to work with Kennedy. As O'Brien recalled in his memoirs[66]:

> As majority leader, McCormack could not have been more kind and cooperative with me and I soon came to regard him with the highest degree of affection. This warm relationship would continue throughout his years as Speaker. In Massachusetts politics, in earlier years, I had regarded him as a symbol of the Old Guard, and we Kennedy men had seen ourselves as the Young Turks of the state's politics. But in Washington I came to appreciate just what a skillful and valuable politician John McCormack was. He was a man with an almost perfect liberal voting record, yet he was widely admired by the southern conservatives and, upon Rayburn's death, could command their strong support for the speakership.

Legislation awaited

While the events of Massachusetts may have concerned both the President and the Speaker, their primary responsibilities were to address the nation's needs. Perhaps the most frustrating public embarrassment of the 87th Congress occurred over an appropriations bill that got stuck in mid-July in a feud between 83-year-old Clarence Cannon of Missouri, chair of the House Appropriations Committee, and 84-year-old Carl Hayden of Arizona, chair of the Senate Appropriations Committee.[67]

Ostensibly, the conflict was over which chamber's Appropriations Committee could initiate legislation. When the Constitutional Convention lodged the revenue power in the House and the House lodged that authority in its Ways and Means Committee, both revenue and spending bills originated in the House but the demands on Ways and Means during the Civil War were so overwhelming that the two functions were separated and a new Appropriations Committee was created. It was initially chaired by the legendary Thaddeus Stevens of Pennsylvania, who left the chairmanship of Ways and Means to chair Appropriations in 1865. The Senate followed suit in 1867, creating its own Appropriations Committee to serve along with its tax-writing Finance Committee. While Ways and Means retained its power to initiate revenue bills, it was not clear if House Appropriations had similar initiation authority. Also, if the two spending committees met in joint session during a conference, which chair would preside? And in which chamber's room would the meeting occur? As a frustrated John McCormack pleaded with Cannon to back off his demands, a month-long deadlock ensued and payments for government employees were embargoed by the feuding octogenarians.[68] Ultimately, a room in the Capitol was located equidistant between each chamber's rostra and the two chairs agreed to alternate the initiation of spending bills and to take turns chairing their joint session. Cannon was one of John's least favorite chairs and Appropriations was one of his less favored committees. In a 1961 interview with Richard Fenno for his classic *The Power of the Purse*, John described the committee and explained how it operated[69]:

> They are a dedicated committee, a powerful committee, and a tireless committee. They are the hardest workers in the Congress. They get no glamour, no fanfare and nobody even knows what they are doing until it gets to the floor. They sit morning and afternoon, and sometimes at night—plodding, plodding, and figuring. I could never do it. Appropriations is the last committee I would ever want to go on.
> . . .
> The Committee likes to grasp for power (he kept cupping his fingers in a grasping motion at the time). They like to reach out and concentrate. They want this single budget. That would give two or three people all the power in conference. It's that tendency to concentrate. It's bad. . . . They're a tremendously powerful committee, but sometimes they go a little too far.

The Cannon-Hayden conflict did little to enhance the reputations of Congress generally or John McCormack particularly. John's initial year as Speaker was not going well.

The summer of 1962 contained other unfinished business, most notably the Foreign Assistance Act. It was imperative that the 87th Congress have a positive legislative record going into the 1962 midterm election, so that the Democrats could retain both houses of Congress.

The failed "Bay of Pigs" invasion of Cuba in the previous year continued to bother the Kennedy Administration, and in an effort to further isolate Cuba and to limit resupply from its major sponsor and protector, the Soviet Union, Congress passed the Foreign Assistance Act of 1962. On July 12, the House had passed an engrossed bill on a roll call vote of 250–164 over the united opposition of the Conservative Coalition, and President Kennedy signed it August 1, 1962 (PL 87-565). This act amended the Foreign Assistance Act of 1961 to prohibit aid to Communist nations (which were cited for the first time by name), those countries providing items of strategic value to Cuba, and those countries which permitted ships under their registry to carry economic aid to Cuba, unless the president determined, among other things, that such aid was vital to U.S. security.[70] It authorized appropriations totaling $4,572,000,000 including $600 million for the Alliance for Progress in each of the fiscal years 1963–66, but stipulated that no funds, except $100 million in fiscal 1963, could be used for anything other than dollar-payable loans.[71]

For the civil rights movement that had been hoping for more from the Kennedy Administration, a long-standing political irritant was removed with the passage of the 24th Amendment to the Constitution. Approved August 27, 1962, and ratified by the requisite number of states on January 23, 1964, the amendment provided that no citizen would be denied the right to vote by reason of failure to pay any poll tax or other tax.[72]

Satellite technology had advanced to a point where corporate America wanted in on the potential profits. Congress tried to address their concerns with the passage of the Communications Satellite Act of 1962. Approved August 31, 1962, this act authorized the president to name a group of incorporators to establish the Communications Satellite Corporation (COMSAT), a private commercial communication system, and to arrange for an initial stock offering.[73] It provided for the subsequent choice of 15 directors—three by the president, and six each year to be elected annually by public stockholders and by communication carriers. It also gave the president broad responsibility for aiding corporations in the rapid development of a satellite system and for supervising its international activities.

Questions concerning long-term unemployment were addressed by the Public Works Acceleration Act, approved September 14, 1962, that authorized an appropriation of $900 million for immediate acceleration of job-creating federal and local public works projects in areas with long-term high unemployment.[74] As each of these pieces of legislation passed through Congress to the president's desk, all eyes turned once again to Massachusetts.

The Teddy-Eddie primary

Throughout the summer of 1962, the Kennedy and McCormack camps tossed charges at one another. It was feared that the tenuous relationship between President Kennedy and Speaker McCormack would be jeopardized in spite of their promises that this would not occur. Liberal academics, a substantial portion of the Massachusetts electorate, rallied behind Eddie McCormack. This confused many outside observers because of the presence of H. Stuart Hughes, the grandson of former Chief Justice Charles Evans Hughes who had also been a two-term governor of New York and the 1916 Republican presidential candidate. Now at Harvard, Professor H. Stuart Hughes was the candidate of antiwar liberals who were deeply fearful of growing tensions between the United States and the Soviet Union and had hoped for a rapprochement between the two nations that would lead to nuclear disarmament.

Liberals and academics first rallied behind Eddie during his campaign for election as attorney general in 1958. He promised to create an active Division of Civil Rights and Civil Liberties and upon his election, he appointed Yale-educated Gerald A. Berlin to be his assistant attorney general for that division.[75] The office was a success and its reputation was nationwide. In 1961, along with Minnesota Attorney General Walter F. Mondale, Eddie McCormack entered an amicus curiae brief as a "friend of the court" in what would be known as the U.S. Supreme Court case of *Gideon v. Wainwright*.[76] This case involved the rights of an indigent petty criminal from Florida, Clarence Earl Gideon. It established the right under the 14th Amendment's "equal protection clause" to obtain legal counsel for all criminal defendants, not just those whose offenses warranted the death penalty as was the case in *Powell v. Alabama*, 287 U.S. 45 (1932). Anthony Lewis, a *New York Times* reporter, wrote up the case in his book *Gideon's Trumpet* that became a surprising best seller and was made into a television movie.[77] By siding with Gideon, Ed McCormack and Walter Mondale had broken with many of their fellow states attorneys general and placed themselves high in the liberal pantheon. That Walter Mondale, a Hubert Humphrey protégé, would do this was not surprising, but that Edward McCormack, John McCormack's nephew, would also do this represented a clear act of courage.

Eddie, a life member of the NAACP, had earned his liberal credentials and his two elections to the office of attorney general in 1958 and 1960 demonstrated that he had statewide vote-getting appeal. Most academics lined up behind Eddie McCormack and not Harvard Professor H. Stuart Hughes nor Harvard alum Ted Kennedy. The leading academic on Eddie's behalf was Harvard Law's brilliant Mark DeWolfe Howe, a foremost authority on Justice Oliver Wendell Holmes, Jr. During the campaign, Professor Howe appeared on the television program "The Open Mind" and spoke of Ted Kennedy's candidacy[78]:

> I don't think there's any question but that on any achievement of his own, Ted Kennedy, at the age of thirty, is not qualified to seek such a high office as he is seeking . . . whatever his native gifts may be, and perhaps they are considerable, nothing has yet happened to show that he has those gifts. Without the affiliations, without the name, his candidacy would have been, as it continues to be, in my judgement, wholly preposterous.
>
> Beyond that I think it is not only preposterous but outrageous. Seeking an office in the United States Senate, while his brother is in the White House, seems to me to represent a total misunderstanding of the responsibilities of a United States Senator. To have a rubber stamp senator is to me an offense against the whole tradition that there should be a separation of powers in our government.

Eddie entered the fray anticipating liberal and organizational support. Some, like Harvard's Young Democrats, joined up. Other hoped-for endorsements never materialized and organizational Democrats disliked being placed in a position where they were bound to offend one side or the other. Both of the families were powerful and both were Irish. No matter which choice was made, forgiveness would be slow in coming from the side not taken. Lasting enemies would be made. Massachusetts's liberals, mostly Jewish and un-churched Protestant intellectuals, had little awareness of the dangerous path upon which they had just placed Ed McCormack. Their animosities were short-lived. Irish Catholic feuds that transcended generations were beyond their comprehension.

The camps agreed that two debates should be held, one in South Boston on August 27 and the other in the Western Massachusetts city of Holyoke on September 5. The choice of South Boston High School was a curious one given that it was Eddie's high school alma mater. Boston University Professor Murray Levin contended that Kennedy's manager believed, "Psychologically, we purposely put [Ted] in a box. That's why the debate was held in South Boston. So that we would be somewhat cast in the role of the stranger, or the visitor, or the underdog, or call it what you will."[79] Making a multimillionaire's son an underdog was no small feat but it paid off for Kennedy.

The high school auditorium was packed to overflowing with national and even international news reporters covering the event. It was clear early on that Eddie was deeply irritated with Teddy's candidacy and in the closing minutes, Eddie issued the declaration that would seal his fate. Turning toward Ted, pointing his finger, Eddie uttered the deathless phrase, "If his name was Edward Moore, with his qualifications, with your qualifications, Teddy, if it was Edward Moore, your candidacy would be a joke, but nobody's laughing because his name is not Edward Moore. It's Edward Moore Kennedy"[80] (Figure 19.2). The unsheathed anger of the attack initially stunned the crowd into silence, but soon McCormack's followers, the working-class Irishmen who had long chafed at the disrespect that they had endured from their "lace curtain Irish" cousins,

Figure 19.2 U.S. Senate primary debate between Edward M. Kennedy and Attorney General Edward J. McCormack, Jr., September 1962 (Getty Images).

would bring down the house in South Boston High School. It also brought Teddy to near tears as he stammered through his closing remarks.

Informal tracking polls done by Murray Levin had McCormack ten points behind prior to the debate and forty points behind after it.[81] The women voters of Massachusetts rose up and soundly smote Eddie McCormack, a man who had "ridiculed a name that [Teddy's] mother had given him" in the words of one Dorchester female interviewee. This sentiment was reiterated in David Farrell's *Boston Herald* column, "[Eddie's] assault on Kennedy and the latter's refusal to be drawn into an army base brawl, apparently created unfavorable reaction to the Attorney General among many viewers, especially women."[82] Another debate remained a week later but lacking any drama the contest ended on the first night.[83]

Teddy romped to victory over Eddie on September 10 with 569,030 votes to Eddie's 247,403—69.3% to 30.7% and a 311,900 vote plurality.[84] Two days later John visited the Oval Office to offer congratulations and to assure the president of the House's commitment to the success of the Kennedy agenda (Figure 19.3).

The general election on November 6 was anticlimactic, as Ted defeated Republican George Cabot Lodge, 1,162,611 (55.4%) to Lodge's 877,963 (41.9%) and Hughes's 50,013 (2.4%).[85] Its only curiosity was that Ted's opponent was George Lodge, son of Henry Cabot Lodge, Jr., who had been defeated by Jack in the 1952 U.S. Senate race and again in 1960 when the Kennedy-Johnson ticket was victorious over the Nixon-Lodge one. The only Lodge family victory over the Fitzgerald-Kennedy clan came in

Figure 19.3 Post-primary meeting: President John Kennedy and U.S. House Speaker John McCormack, September 1962 (John F. Kennedy Library and Museum).

1916 when George Lodge's grandfather U.S. Senator Henry Cabot Lodge, Sr. defeated Ted's grandfather John F. "Honey Fitz" Fitzgerald in the state's first ever popular election for the U.S. Senate. Defeating a Lodge for the third time was no longer news but by defeating both a McCormack and a Lodge in the same year, Ted Kennedy had completed a dynastic double play that would consolidate Kennedy political fortunes in Massachusetts for the next 40 years.[86]

The most unique perspective of the Kennedy-McCormack relationship during this time came from none other than the Kennedy family matriarch, Rose Fitzgerald Kennedy, the daughter of John Fitzgerald, twice Mayor of Boston and three-time Member of the U.S. House and wife of the U.S. Ambassador to Great Britain. She would become mother to a President, an Attorney General, three U.S. Senators, an Ambassador to Ireland, and one daughter's husband was the Ambassador to France. She was grandmother to an additional two U.S. Representatives, an Ambassador to Japan, and the Lieutenant Governor of Maryland, while one granddaughter was married to the Governor of California and another was divorced from a future Governor of New York. Sitting in the U.S. House today is her great grandson Joseph P. Kennedy IIII extending the family's political reach in the House from 1894 to 2016. In her memoirs, Rose Kennedy recalled[87]:

> Teddy's opponent for the Democratic endorsement, at the state convention, was Eddie McCormack, who not only was attorney general of Massachusetts but was the nephew and protégé of John W. McCormack, the Speaker of the U.S. House of Representatives, who of course was backing him with all the influence at his command. (The Fitzgeralds, Kennedys, and McCormacks had had many encounters in Massachusetts' political life: usually as friends, sometimes as foes, sometimes friendly enemies.)

The relationship between the two families was long-standing. John had sponsored Joe Kennedy's nomination for president in 1940 before he sensed that FDR would run for a third term and John had been urged by Rose's father, John Fitzgerald, to intercede with FDR on Joe's behalf early in 1942 after the two had become seriously estranged. Thomas C. Reeves, in his critical biography of JFK, *A Question of Character*, attributed Jack's 1947 selection to "the more prestigious House Committee on Education and Labor (perhaps because of the friendship between Rose and minority whip John McCormack)."[88] Robert Kennedy, in an interview about Jack's first election to the Senate in 1952, remarked[89]:

STEWART: Was the President at all fearful of damaging his relationship with McCormack—of totally damaging his relationship with McCormack?
R. KENNEDY: There was some concern about that, but I don't think that he thought that had been a very warm relationship in any case.
STEWART: It hadn't been, even up until that time?
R. KENNEDY: No. It was with my father and my mother, but not particularly with us.

In many ways, the Teddy-Eddie battle of 1962 brought closure to the feud. The Kennedys had won and John behaved cordially to Ted and deferentially to Jack much as he had to Jack's two Democratic presidential predecessors, Franklin Roosevelt and Harry Truman.

Integrating "Ole Miss"

Ted's triumphs were among the few happy moments for the president in the fall of 1962, a time in which civil rights violence at the University of Mississippi in late September and the god-awful confrontation with the Soviet Union the following month over nuclear missiles in Cuba would place the world's survival in peril.

As September ended, James Meredith, an African-American Mississippi native, wished to enroll at the taxpayer-supported university of his home state and faced massive resistance from the state's vehement segregationist Democratic Governor Ross Barnett who defiantly declared, "I have said in every county in Mississippi that no school in our state will be integrated while I am your Governor."[90] Led by white students and armed angry townspeople, violent rioting broke out on the campus. Attorney General Robert Kennedy sent hundreds of U.S. Marshals to facilitate the enrollment, but as rioting escalated, thousands of U.S. troops and the federalized Mississippi National Guard were needed to bring order to the campus.[91] Hundreds of marshals were injured in the melee and two lives were tragically lost, including that of French journalist Paul Guihard. With the rioting quelled, Meredith was admitted on October 1 and a Deep South state university was finally integrated.[92]

It was a pivotal moment in the civil rights struggle and for the Kennedy brothers, who were seen as relatively passive during these racial troubles.[93] Jack would introduce far-reaching legislation in the following year pushing for greater federal involvement in securing rights for African Americans living in the South. It was also the beginning of begrudging liberal admiration for Bob Kennedy, whose prior links to Joe McCarthy had long denied him their support.[94]

The 87th Congress wraps up

The foreign policy issue generating the most congressional controversy was an old battle over the United Nations. This time it was the United Nations Loan, approved October 2, 1962, which authorized a $100 million loan to the financially troubled UN.[95] To placate its critics on long-term financing, the act further provided that the United States should use every effort to promote a pattern of United Nations financing (including a vigorous program for collection of delinquencies on annual assessments on a current basis) that would avoid any future large-scale defects. It also instructed the Department of State to submit to Congress not later than January 31, 1963, a report on the steps taken by the United Nations General Assembly. Despite the controversy, in a

September 11 letter to John McCormack, President Kennedy described the House bill as "wholly satisfactory."[96]

Congress closed out the second session with a minor flurry. Passed in the closing days were the Drug Amendments of 1962, approved October 10, 1962, which amended the Federal Food, Drug, and Cosmetic Act to sharply strengthen federal safety controls on drugs, authorized the standardization of drug names, and clarified and strengthened existing inspection authority.[97] The House passed the bill unanimously 347–0.

A day later the Trade Expansion Act of 1962 was approved. This act authorized the president to reduce duties by 50% between July 1, 1962, and June 30, 1967; to remove duties on entire categories of goods when the United States and members of the European Economic Community (at the time of negotiations) together accounted for 80% or more of the total free world trade; to cut or remove tariffs on agricultural products not meeting the 80% rule if necessary to maintain or expend United States farm exports; and to eliminate tariffs on products currently dutiable at a rate of 5% or less.[98] Approved October 11, 1962, it also authorized the president to withdraw concessions to any country maintaining "unreasonable" restrictions against U.S. exports including agricultural ones; to restrict imports if they threatened national security; and to raise tariffs in those instances where American workers and businesses might be injured.

Last, highway construction lobbies were rewarded with the Federal-Aid Highway Act of 1962 that authorized $1,118,550,000 for federal-aid highways in fiscal 1964 and $1,165,000,000 for fiscal 1965.[99] Approved by the president on October 23, 1962, the act authorized supplemental funds for fiscal 1963 of $10 million for forest roads and $6 million for public lands highways authorized for fiscal 1964 only, $850,000 to complete construction of Nicaragua's Rama Road, $32 million to complete construction of the Inter-American Highway, and $800,000 for an Alaska highway study.

The final piece of business on October 13 was the appropriations bill that had caused so much earlier tension between Senate Appropriations Chair Carl Hayden and House Appropriations Chair Clarence Cannon. Having heard that a Senator had insulted the House and that the House leaders were willing to accept most of the Senate version, the 85-year-old Cannon exploded and declared: "At the end of these long months, the longest peacetime session Congress has had—and with no visible reason—I honor the high office they hold but I cannot endorse the quality of leadership."[100]

And with a final flourish from a man whose House career began in 1911 as a secretary to then Minority Leader Champ Clark, Cannon excoriated McCormack and Albert: "I have sat under 10 Speakers—but I have never seen such biased and inept leadership."

87th Congress postmortem

The 87th Congress concluded its business on October 13 and its members returned home with most preparing for yet another election in three weeks. John was unopposed for reelection once again so he intended to relax and recharge himself for the upcoming Congress with the hope that Democratic losses in the midterm election would not be severe. John was unprepared for the crisis that would soon occupy Washington and the world three days later.

President Kennedy's popularity remained high but how successful was he with Congress, and how could it be measured? President Kennedy's first full Congress was a relative legislative success. *Congressional Quarterly* gave the president high marks for his legislative agenda and reported that he had achieved an 85.4% success rate with Congress.[101] The weekly *Congressional Quarterly* had been calculating rates of floor success since 1953, Eisenhower's first year in office. The measure was based on the percentage of bills that reached the floor and on which the president had announced a position. Consequently, bills that failed to escape the House Rules Committee were not included since there were no floor votes to report.

Ike's House floor voting success with fellow Republican Joe Martin as Speaker was a robust 91.2% in 1953. The Democratic takeover of the House in the 1954 midterm elections lowered Ike's 1955 success rate with Democrat Sam Rayburn as Speaker to 63.4%. The six sessions of "divided government" 1955–60 for Eisenhower's success in the House averaged 65.0% with a high of 74.0% in 1958 and a low of 55.5% in 1959. Ike's popularity had remained steady with the American public. So too had his relative success with the Democratic U.S. House.

How would President Kennedy do? The first session in 1961 had Sam Rayburn presiding over the House and Kennedy's success rate that year was a solid 83.1%. John McCormack's presiding over the 2nd Session of the 87th Congress in 1962 produced a success rate of 85.0%—no discernible difference from that of Rayburn in the prior session. McCormack's pledge to Kennedy that the Teddy-Eddie unpleasantness would not diminish his commitment to the Kennedy agenda was honored (Figure 19.4).

Contemporaneous assessments of the 87th Congress were on the mixed positive side, as summarized by John D. Morris of the *New York Times*, "The two-year term was marked by several major victories, a number of defeats and many compromises for Mr. Kennedy," citing the foreign trade bill as its greatest success and the failure of Medicare as its biggest failure.[102] Drew Pearson and the Americans for Democratic Action (ADA) complained about the domination of Congress by its elderly members, leading Pearson to declare, "History will probably brand the 87th Congress as the 'Congress of the Old Men.'"[103] The ADA remarked: "If a medical diagnosis were appropriate, the Congress could be described as anemic, suffering, in the parlance of TV commercials, from 'tired blood.'"[104] Others, such as the A.F.L.-C.I.O. department of legislation, believed that the 87th Congress's "accomplishments outweighed its unfinished business."[105] The syndicated columnist and JFK pal Charles Bartlett, the man credited with introducing Jack to Jackie, was more sanguine about the 87th Congress in his article "End's Well—So All's Well: Congress and President Are Happy: Session Ends on a Note of Harmony."[106] The emergence of the Cuban Missile Crisis and the general tendency of Americans to rally around the president in times of crisis, the so-called "rally 'round the flag effect'," made moot the assessments of Congress as the crisis passed and the midterm election awaited.[107]

Figure 19.4 President Kennedy, Vice President Johnson, and the Congressional Leadership. Senate Majority Leader Mike Mansfield, Senate Majority Whip Hubert Humphrey, House Majority Whip Hale Boggs, House Majority Leader Carl Albert, Vice President Johnson, and House Speaker John McCormack, September 25, 1962 (John F. Kennedy Library and Museum).

Cuban Missile Crisis

Just days after the adjournment came alarming news. Cuba's Fidel Castro, fearful of another American invasion, urged the USSR's Khrushchev to locate missiles with atomic warheads on the Cuban mainland. These deployments were discovered by aerial reconnaissance over Cuba. There was little question that the Soviet Union was deploying these missiles in order to regain the balance of power in the continuing agony of the Cold War. The first of the thirteen days of the missile crisis was October 16—only three days after the 87th Congress had ended and its members returned home to campaign.

Once discovered, the Kennedy Administration brought all of the key Cabinet members and congressional leaders back to Washington to work out a feasible strategy to defuse this troublesome circumstance. Summoned to the White House from Boston was John McCormack much as he had been 21 years earlier in December 1941, when Pearl Harbor was bombed.[108] A day after the Pearl Harbor attack Majority Leader John McCormack issued a Declaration of War against the Imperial government of Japan. Was another declaration of war forthcoming? If so, against whom?

All told, 20 members of Congress had been brought to the White House on October 22. In their 1997 study of the White House tapes, Ernest R. May and Philip

D. Zelikow identify thirteen names consisting of floor leaders and senior committee members.[109] The Democratic Senators were Mike Mansfield of Montana, Hubert H. Humphrey of Minnesota, J. William Fulbright of Arkansas, Richard B. Russell of Georgia, and Jack's good friend George A. Smathers of Florida, who had a strong interest in Cuba barely ninety miles from Florida's Key West. Republican Senators included Everett McKinley Dirksen of Illinois, Bourke B. Hickenlooper of Iowa, and Jack's longtime Senate colleague Leverett Saltonstall of Massachusetts. Among the House members brought to the White House were Democratic Representatives Hale Boggs of Louisiana, Carl Vinson of Georgia and Republicans Charles A. Halleck of Indiana and John Taber of New York.

Last, May and Zelikow included "John W. McCormack (D., Mass.), who had become Speaker of the House in November, 1961, following the death of Sam Rayburn, was listed as among those present but said nothing."[110] Surrounded by his fellow congressional leaders and Kennedy's national security advisors denoted by David Halberstam as "the best and the brightest,"[111] John kept his opinions to himself, one of the very few times that John's insecurity about his eighth grade education manifested itself.

In 1994 Brassey's published the CIA's declassified *The Secret Cuban Missile Documents* with an introduction by Harvard's Graham T. Allison who had studied the crisis with enormous care.[112] The book opened with six pages of 81 names of "persons mentioned." Listed also were the names of five journalists: syndicated columnists Joseph and Stewart Alsop; David Lawrence of *U.S. News & World Report*; Paul Scott of the syndicated Allen-Scott Report; and unsurprisingly, the *New York Times*'s Arthur Krock, the "eyes and ears" of Joe Kennedy.

An additional three congressional names are listed in Allison's volume but not in the May-Zelikow compilation. These included the feuding Democrats Clarence Cannon of Missouri and Carl Hayden of Arizona as well as Republican Senator Kenneth B. Keating of New York who was the first member of Congress to warn of the Soviet missiles in Cuba. There were now sixteen members of Congress identified and as May and Zelikow noted, John McCormack was not among those who spoke. Yet again, John was "in the room" as a presence but not as a participant.

The Kennedy Administration acted swiftly to pressure the Soviets to remove the missiles and not to destabilize any further a world perilously close to nuclear annihilation. Soviet leader Nikita Khrushchev acted rationally and the Soviet missiles were removed and less widely known, Soviet-targeted American missiles were removed from Turkey. The nation breathed a major sigh of relief and politics resumed. The 1962 congressional elections were a week away and the need to campaign apparently took precedence over national survival.

Ironically, the Senator who brought the missile issue to the fore, New York Republican Kenneth Keating, would be defeated for reelection in 1964 by Attorney General Robert F. Kennedy whose memoir *Thirteen Days* became the most widely read account of the missile crisis.[113] Most likely intended to be Bob Kennedy's pre-presidential *Profiles in Courage*, his version of those days gave himself a central role in that event, one that has since been challenged by the Kennedy Library's own in-house historian, Sheldon M. Stern.[114]

The 1962 midterm election

Midterm elections are clearly dissimilar from presidential elections. Percentages of voter turnout drop from the high and mid-fifties to the high and mid-thirties as only the most partisan and most committed voters show up to the polls. These alternating waves of high turnout presidential contests followed by low turnout congressional ones were described by the prescient Angus Campbell of the University of Michigan as "surge and decline."[115] The electoral consequence of presidential "surges" has been to provide the newly elected presidents with sympathetic congressional majorities eager to fulfill the promises made by the successful nominee. These are the presumed "coattails" that presidents hope for when they declare their "mandates" in inaugural addresses.

The midterm congressional elections are where the "declines" occur and are often declared to be referenda on the incumbent president. Postelection analyses of midterm congressional elections are almost always focused on the likely outcome of the following presidential election, particularly if the incumbent president is likely to seek reelection. Since midterm congressional seat losses are near-universal, success is relative with lesser seat losses than the average considered successful while higher than expected seat losses are considered disastrous. This is most often true when a president's party loses majority control of either or both houses of Congress.

Expectations concerning the 1962 election varied greatly. Larry O'Brien, Kennedy's congressional liaison, a charter member of the Irish Mafia, and its best vote counter, initially forecasted a pessimistic scenario[116]:

> Over the years, the party in power had lost an average of forty-four House seats and five Senate seats in the off-year elections. After all the 1962 results were in, our party lost only five seats in the House and actually gained two seats in the Senate. As far as history was concerned, we had won a victory; but as far as our legislative prospects for 1963–64 were concerned, we faced two more years of the same tough struggle.

The net loss of only five House seats from 263 to 258 and Senate Democrats' gain of two seats from 65 to 67 was the best showing for a new president at his first midterm since Franklin Roosevelt in 1934. Kennedy and the congressional Democrats were quite pleased at the outcome. While conservative Republicans suspected that the Cuban Missile Crisis had been overblown to give Democrats an electoral edge, it was Angus Campbell's thesis that was borne out. Kennedy's presidential victory in 1960 had no coattails as Democrats lost 21 House seats. Since there was no "surge" in 1960, there was no "decline" in 1962. But what would 1963 hold?

Notes

1   As quoted in Lawrence F. O'Brien, *No Final Victories: A Life in Politics from John F. Kennedy to Watergate* (New York: Ballantine Books, 1974), p. 132.

2   As recounted in "U.S. Moving Again, Kennedy Asserts: He Says His Talks in 1961 'Awakened' the Nation," *NYT*, December 24, 1961, p. 18. The excerpt comes from the introduction to Kennedy's book, John Gardner, ed., *To Turn the Tide: A Selection from President Kennedy's Public Statements* (New York: Harper, 1962).

3   Russell Baker and Tom Wicker, "Kennedy and the Congress: Some Major Duels Are Forecast; President Has Modified Many of His Earlier Goals but Conservatives Are Expected to Fight Hard against Trade and Medical Care Bills," *NYT*, January 7, 1962, p. 171.

4   Wilfrid C. Rodgers, "McCormack Romps to Speaker Victory: Formal Vote Today Paves Way for Firm Reign," *BG*, January 10, 1962, p. 1, and McCormack chosen "unanimously," *NYT*, January 10, 1962, p. 1; and Jeffrey A. Jenkins and Charles Stewart III, *Fighting for the Speakership: The House and the Rise of Party Government* (Princeton, NJ: Princeton University Press, 2013), p. 415.

5   For information on the seven Massachusetts Speakers, including the seventh Speaker Democrat Thomas P. (Tip) O'Neill, Jr., who served from 1977 to 1987, the best source is Donald R. Kennon, *Speakers of the U.S. House of Representatives: A Bibliography, 1789–1984* (Baltimore, MD: Johns Hopkins University Press, 1986). It is a major update over the 1928 publication, William Henry Smith, *Speakers of the House of Representatives of the United States* (New York: AMS Press, reprint 1971).

6   Robert L. Peabody, "Party Leadership Change in the United States House of Representatives," *APSR*, LXI (September 1961), pp. 675–93; Barbara Hinckley, "Congressional Leadership Selection and Support: A Comparative Analysis," *Journal of Politics*, XXXII (May 1970), pp. 268–87; and Garrison Nelson, "Partisan Patterns of House Leadership Change, 1789–1977," *APSR*, LXXI (September 1977), pp. 918–39.

7   Robert C. Albright, "Democratic Floor Leader Contest Beginning to Boil," *Washington Post*, December 4, 1961, p. A2; and Marquis Childs, "The High Stakes in House Battle," *Washington Post*, December 29, 1961, p. A12.

8   See Nelson W. Polsby, "Two Strategies of Influence: Choosing a Majority Leader, 1962," in Peabody and Polsby, eds., *New Perspectives on the House of Representatives*, pp. 237–70.

9   On the uniqueness of the Agriculture Committee's internal structure, see Charles O. Jones, "Representation in Congress: The Case of the House Agriculture Committee," *APSR*, LV (June 1961), pp. 358–67.

10 Author's telephonic interview with the Hon. John McCormack, April 1977.

11 "Sam Rayburn's Boys: Who Will Lead?," in Anthony Champagne et al., *The Austin-Boston Connection: Five Decades of House Democratic Leadership, 1937–1989* (College Station: Texas A+M University Press, 2009), pp. 148–87.

12 Albert's autobiography with Danney Goble is entitled *Little Giant; The Life and Times of Speaker Carl Albert* (Norman: University of Oklahoma Press, 1990).

13 Chapter 17, infra.

14 Randall B. Ripley, "Party Whip Organizations in the United States House of Representatives," *APSR*, LVIII (September 1964), pp. 561–76.

15 "Richard Walker Bolling," *BDUSC* (1989 ed.), pp. 639–40.

16 As described by James W. Loewen, "It is also true that, in areas with few slaves, most white Southerners did not support secession. West Virginia seceded from Virginia to stay with the Union, and Confederate troops had to occupy parts of eastern Tennessee and northern Alabama to hold them in line." In his *Washington Post* op-ed, "Five Myths about Why the South Seceded," February 26, 2011.

17 Author's interview with the Hon. Richard Bolling (Dem-Mo.), Washington, DC, April 1984.

18 The letter dated September 4, 1957, may be found in the Bolling Papers in the archives at the University of Missouri-Kansas City.

19 Richard W. Bolling, *Power in the House: A History of the Leadership of the House of Representatives* (New York: E.P. Dutton, 1968).

20 Arthur Krock, "Rayburn's Successor: Absence of Intervention by Kennedy Makes McCormack Likely Choice," *NYT*, November 19, 1961, p. E9.

21 Correspondence with Professor Anthony Champagne of the University of Texas at Dallas provided this information, November 10, 1999.

22 This is a version from Champagne et al., *The Austin Boston Connection*, pp. 155–56. A similar version available is in Anne Hodges Morgan, *Robert S. Kerr: The Senate Years* (Norman, OK: University of Oklahoma Press, 1977), p. 225. She cites an Edmondson interview with William R. Reynolds of the *Oklahoma City Times*, p. 301 n121.

23 Anne Hodges Morgan, "Robert Samuel Kerr (1896–1963)," online *Encyclopedia of Oklahoma History and Culture*, accessed January 5, 2014.

24 Bobby Baker Oral History, U.S. Senate Historical Office, pp. 98–100.

25 John D. Morris, "Albert Assured of Leader's Post, Rep. Bolling Formally Quits House Democratic Race," *NYT*, January 4, 1962, p. 22.

26 Richard L. Lyons, "Rep. Bolling Quits Race for Leader," *Washington Post*, January 4, 1962, p. A1.

27 Arthur Krock, *Memoirs: Sixty Years on the Firing Line* (New York: Popular Library, 1968), p. 332. Krock candidly admits that "my life was greatly enriched by my association with the Kennedys—in Washington, at Joe's country house, Marwood nearby, at Palm Beach and at Hyannis Port," pp. 309–10.

28 Arthur Krock, "In the Nation: The Function of Leadership in Congress," *NYT*, January 5, 1962, p. 28.

29 Ibid.

30 "Thomas Hale Boggs, Sr.," *BDUSC* (1989 ed.) p. 638; and Patrick J. Maney, "Hale Boggs: The Southerner as National Democrat," in Roger H. Davidson, Susan Webb Hammond, and Raymond M. Smock, eds., *Masters of the House; Congressional Leaders over Two Centuries* (Boulder, CO: Westview Press, 1998), pp. 223–58.

31 Among the sources Maney cites for this observation are Neil McNeil's wonderful *Forge of Democracy: The House of Representatives* (New York: David McKay, 1963), pp. 81–83; Albert, *Little Giant*, p. 171; and Lindy Boggs's own book, *Washington through a Purple Veil: Memoirs of a Southern Woman* (New York: Harcourt, Brace, 1994), pp. 139–41.

32 "Corinne Claiborne Boggs, (Lindy)," *BDUSC* (1989 ed.) pp. 637–38.

33 This is a point made frequently in the book *Rayburn: A Biography* (Austin, TX: Texas Monthly Press, 1987) coauthored by Rayburn's longtime assistant D. B. Hardeman and Donald C. Bacon.

34 For an account, see: "'Anxiety' Is Voiced on M'Cormack View," *NYT*, November 18, 1961, p. 56.

35 Drew Pearson. "The House Misses Mister Sam," *Washington Post*, March 17, 1962, p. D23.

36 Don Oberdorfer, "The Job John McCormack Dreads," *Saturday Evening Post*, March 21, 1964, pp. 66–68.

37 James L. Sundquist, *Politics and Policy: The Eisenhower, Kennedy, and Johnson Years* (Washington, DC: The Brookings Institution, 1968), p. 483.

38   *CQWR*, January 5, 1962, p. 29.

39   Richard Reeves, *President Kennedy: Profile of Power* (New York: Simon & Schuster, 1993), p. 270. The quotation referred to is: "The new Speaker, John McCormack, was from Massachusetts, but he was not particularly close to the Kennedys, nor did he have much sway over the southerners."

40   Lawrence F. O'Brien, *No Final Victories: A Life in Politics—from John F. Kennedy to Watergate* (Garden City, NY: Doubleday & Company, Inc., 1974), pp. 115–16.

41   Manpower Development and Training Act of 1962, approved March 15, 1962 (76 Stat. 23-33). See also: "Congress Approves Manpower Retraining Bill," *CQWR*, March 16, 1962, pp. 423–25.

42   Sundquist, *Politics and Policy*, pp. 475–76.

43   *CQWR*, "House Passes Administration Tax Bill, 219-196," March 30, 1962, pp. 492–93.

44   Wilfrid Rodgers, "White House Sings Praise of 'Old Pro' McCormack," *Boston Globe*, April 8, 1962, p. A4.

45   Public Welfare Amendments of 1962, approved July 25, 1962 (76 Stat. 172-208).

46   "Congress Clears Welfare Revisions Bill," *CQWR*, July 27, 1962, pp. 1249–51.

47   Neil Swidey, "Chapter 2: The Youngest Brother," from *Globe* Staff, *Ted Kennedy*, February 16, 2009.

48   The most valuable accounts of Clark Clark's remarks, life, and career can be found in his memoirs, Clark M. Clifford with Richard Holbrooke *Counsel to the President* (New York: Random House, 1991); and John Acacia's biography *Clark Clifford: The Wise Man of Washington* (Lexington, KY: University Press of Kentucky, 2009).

49   See Clifford with Holbrooke, "A Crisis for Edward M. Kennedy," in *Counsel to the President: A Memoir*, pp. 368–71.

50   Robert Healy, "Ted Kennedy Tells about Harvard Examination Incident," *Boston Globe*, March 30, 1962, pp. 1, 6. Healy told me of how frequently he heard from Joe Kennedy in a telephonic interview in July 1999.

51   Reeves, *President Kennedy*, p. 324.

52   Mark Feeney, "Robert L. Healy, at 84; Globe editor, columnist, political insider," *Boston Globe*, June 7, 2010.

53   "McCormick [*sic*] Announces for Senate; Won't Defer to Anyone," *Boston Globe*, March 6, 1962, p. 31.

54   Joe McGinniss, *The Last Brother* (New York: Simon & Schuster, 1993), pp. 255–56.

55   See John McCormack's interview with T. Harrison Baker, LBJ Library, September 23, 1968, pp. 24–25.

56   Ibid.

57   McGinniss, *The Last Brother*, p. 256.

58   Author's interviews with Eddie's son Edward J. McCormack III, August 2015 and with the Hon. Francis X. Bellotti, former attorney general of Massachusetts, April 2015.

59   The most sympathetic account of Joe's condition can be found in David Nasaw's *The Patriarch* (New York: Penguin Press, 2012), pp. 775–87.

60   Doris Fleeson, "McCormack Rescuing His State or His Nephew? Bill to Hike Membership," *BG*, February 14, 1962, p. 15.

61   Theodore H. White, *In Search of History: A Personal Adventure* (New York: Harper & Row, 1978), pp. 518–25.

62   "John W. McCormack Interview" with T. Harrison Baker, LBJ Library, September 23, 1968, p. 28.

63 "Thomas P. O'Neill Interview" with John F. Stewart for the JFK Library, December 6, 1967, pp. 161–62.

64 "O'Neill Interview," pp. 157–61.

65 Robert Healy, "The Political Circuit: How Ted Fared in State Poll," *BG*, July 15, 1962, p. 21.

66 O'Brien, *No Final Victories*, p. 115.

67 Jeffrey Pressman, *House vs. Senate: Conflict in the Appropriations Process* (New Haven, CT: Yale University Press, 1966).

68 On McCormack's role, see Drew Pearson, "The Washington Merry-Go-Round: Cannon Still Blasts Sen. Hayden," *Washington Post*, July 15, 1962, p. E7.

69 Richard F. Fenno, Jr., "Interview with John W. McCormack (D-MA)," January 1961 for the Center for Legislative Archives, p. 1. While John's sentiment appeared in the book, the interview did not, Richard F. Fenno, Jr., *The Power of the Purse: Appropriation Politics in Congress* (Boston: Little, Brown, 1966).

70 Foreign Assistance Act of 1962, approved August 1, 1962 (76 Stat. 255-263).

71 *CQWR*, "House Passes Foreign Aid Authorization," July 13, 1962, pp. 1159–60.

72 The 24th Amendment, approved August 27, 1962. Ratified by the requisite number of States January 23, 1964 (76 Stat. 1259).

73 Communications Satellite Act of 1962, approved August 31, 1962 (76 Stat. 419-427). "Communications Satellites," *CQWR*, May 4, 1962, p. 752. "Senate Passes Communications Satellite Bill," *CQWR*, August 24, 1962, pp. 1401–403.

74 Public Works Acceleration Act, approved September 14, 1962 (76 Stat. 541-544). "Accelerated Public Works," *CQWR*, September 14, 1962, p. 1524.

75 Robert Morgan, "State Moves to Strengthen Civil Rights," *Boston Globe*, February 5, 1959, p. 1. Author's telephonic interview with Gerald A. Berlin, Esq., July 1999.

76 372 U.S. 335 (1963). The case was originally brought to the Court as *Clarence Earl Gideon v. H.G. Cochran, Jr., Director, Division of Corrections*.

77 Anthony Lewis, *Gideon's Trumpet* (New York: Alfred A. Knopf, 1964). The page references are from the 1964 Vintage Books edition.

78 Murray B. Levin, *Kennedy Campaigning: The System and the Style as Practiced by Senator Edward Kennedy* (Boston: Beacon Press, 1966), p. 145.

79 Ibid., p. 190. Levin does not identify the author of the remark but it was most likely Gerry Doherty who was interviewed, October 2015.

80 Ibid., p. 210.

81 Author's discussions with Professor Murray Levin, September 1962.

82 As quoted in Levin, *Kennedy Campaigning*, p. 218.

83 Arthur Siegel, "Combatants Swap Punches for Pillows," *BG*, September 6, 1962, p. 6.

84 Massachusetts Secretary of State, Democratic Special Senate Primary, September 10, 1962.

85 Congressional Quarterly, *Guide to U.S. Elections* (1975 ed.), p. 494.

86 Ted Kennedy's assessment of the 1962 contest in his *True Compass: A Memoir* (New York: Twelve, 2009), pp. 184–86.

87 Rose Fitzgerald Kennedy, *Times to Remember* (Garden City, NY: Doubleday & Company, 1974), p. 428.

88 Thomas C. Reeves, *A Question of Character: A Life of John F. Kennedy* (New York: Macmillan, Inc., The Free Press, 1991), p. 86.

89 Edwin O. Guthman and Jeffrey Shulman, eds., *Robert Kennedy: In His Own Words, the Unpublished Recollections of the Kennedy Years* (Toronto: Bantam Books, 1988), p. 452.

90   Ross Barnett speech, September 13, 1962, "Integrating Ole Miss: The Controversy,"
     JFK Library.

91   Retrospective on the event may be found in William Doyle. *An American Insurrection:
     The Battle of Oxford, Mississippi, 1962* (New York: Doubleday, 2001); and Charles W.
     Eagles, *The Price of Defiance: James Meredith and the Integration of Ole Miss* (Chapel
     Hill: University of North Carolina Press, 2009). See also Taylor Branch, *Parting the
     Waters: America in the King Years, 1954–63* (New York: Simon and Schuster, 1988),
     p. 653.

92   Meredith's own account may be found in his memoir, *Three Years in Mississippi*
     (Bloomington: Indiana University Press, 1966). Meredith's years at Ole Miss were
     recounted in Nadine Cohodas, *And the Band Played Dixie; Race and the Liberal
     Conscience of Ole Miss* (New York: Free Press, 1999).

93   Nick Bryant, *The Bystander: John F. Kennedy and the Struggle for Black Equality*
     (New York: Basic Books, 2006).

94   Arthur M. Schlesinger, Jr., *Robert Kennedy and His Times* (New York: 1978),
     pp. 325–35.

95   United Nations Loan, approved October 2, 1962 (76 Stat. 695-696).

96   "United Nations Loan," *CQWR*, September 21, 1962, pp. 1561–62.

97   Drug Amendments of 1962, approved October 10, 1962 (76 Stat. 780-796); and "Drug
     Bill," *CQWR*, October 5, 1962, pp. 1791–92.

98   Trade Expansion Act of 1962, approved October 11, 1962 (76 Stat. 872-903); and
     "Congress Votes $3.9 Billion in Foreign Aid," *CQWR*, October 11, 1962, pp. 1887–89.

99   Federal-Aid Highway Act of 1962, approved October 23, 1962 (76 Stat. 1145-1149);
     and "Highway Authorizations," *CQWR*, October 19, 1962, pp. 1957–58.

100 *Congressional Record*, 87th Congress, 2nd Session, October 13, 1962, CVII, p. 23486.

101 *CQWR*, "Congress Backs President on 85.4% of Tests in 1962," October 26, 1962,
     pp. 2035–37.

102 John D. Morris, "Congress Ends Longest Session Since Korea War: Battle over
     Appropriations Brings Attack on Leaders by Cannon of Missouri; Return Set for Jan.
     9; Kennedy Won a Few Major Battles, Lost Others and Made Compromises," *NYT*,
     October 14, 1962, p. 1.

103 Drew Pearson, "Washington Merry-Go-Round: Exit 'Congress of the Old Men,'"
     Washington Post, October 15, 1962, p. B19.

104 "National and World Challenges Ignored by 1962 Session," *ADA World*, October
     1962, Congressional Supplement.

105 Robert E. Walsh, "Labor Notebook: 87th Congress Did More Than It Didn't,
     AFL-CIO Dept. Finds," *BG*, October 21, 1962, p. 60.

106 Charles Bartlett, "End's Well—So All's Well: Congress and President Are Happy:
     Session Ends on a Note of Harmony," *BG*, October 8, 1962, p. 18.

107 Vince J. Burke, "Question in House Elections: 88th Be Friendlier to Kennedy?"
     Washington Post, October 31, 1962, p. A2.

108 David Detzer, *The Brink: Cuban Missile Crisis, 1962* (New York: Thomas Y. Crowell,
     1970), p. 180.

109 The list is according to: "Meeting with the Congressional Leadership on the Cuban
     Missile Crisis on 22 October 1962," tapes 33.2 and 33A.1, John F. Kennedy Library,
     President's Office Files, Presidential Recordings Collection, *Presidential Recordings
     Digital Edition*, ed. David G. Coleman, Kent B. Germany, Ken Hughes, Guian A.

McKee, and Marc J. Selverstone (Charlottesville: University of Virginia Press, 2014). URL: http://prde.upress.virginia.edu/conversations/8030006. See also Ernest R. May and Philip D. Zelikow, *The Kennedy Tapes: Inside the White House during the Cuban Missile Crisis* (Cambridge, MA: The Belknap Press of Harvard University Press, 1997), p. 246.

110   Ibid.
111   See David Halberstam's portraits of the architects of American foreign policy from 1961 to 1969 in his *The Best and the Brightest* (New York: Random House, 1972).
112   Central Intelligence Agency, *The Secret Cuban Missile Documents* (New York: Brassey's, 1994). Graham T. Allison, *Essence of Decision: Explaining the Cuban Missile Crisis* (Boston: Little, Brown, 1971) and its 2nd edition with Philip D. Zelikow, published by Longman of New York City in 1999.
113   Robert F. Kennedy, *Thirteen Days: A Memoir of the Cuban Missile Crisis* (New York: W. W. Norton, 1969).
114   Stern's books on the missile crisis include *Averting "The Final Failure": John F. Kennedy and the Secret Cuban Missile Crisis Meetings* (Stanford, CA: Stanford University Press, 2003); *The Week the World Stood Still; Inside the Secret Cuban Missile Crisis* (Stanford, CA: Stanford University Press, 2005); and *The Cuban Missile Crisis in American Memory: Myths versus Reality* (Stanford, CA: Stanford University Press, 2012). Stern also challenges some of the content in the published transcripts issued by Allison, May, and Zelikow.
115   Angus Campbell, "Surge and Decline: A Study of Electoral Change," *Public Opinion Quarterly*, XXIV (Autumn 1960), pp. 397–418.
116   O'Brien, *No Final Victories*, p. 141. See also Thomas G. Paterson and William J. Brophy, "October Missiles and November Elections: The Cuban Missile Crisis and American Politics, 1962," *Journal of American History*, LXXIII (June 1986), pp. 87–119.

20

The Fateful Year of 1963

The 88th Congress opened on January 9, 1963, with Speaker John W. McCormack presiding in the chair after his first election to a full term.[1] He was joined once again with Majority Leader Carl Albert, who was reelected, and Hale Boggs, the Majority Whip, who he and Albert had reappointed. The House Republicans would be led once again by Indiana's Charlie Halleck, then serving in his third (and what would be his final) term as minority leader; and Les Arends of central Illinois, the ultimate survivor whose leadership service as minority whip, like that of John McCormack's, dated back to the 1940s.

Across the Capitol, the Senate Democrats were once again led by the unique combination of LBJ loyalists, the quiet and unassuming Mike Mansfield of Montana as majority leader and his chief ally, the voluble and energetic Hubert H. Humphrey, Jr. of Minnesota, the majority whip. The Senate Republicans were led by an even less likely pairing of the effusive conservative Everett McKinley Dirksen of Pekin, Illinois, as minority leader and California's moderate and modest Thomas H. Kuchel as minority whip. These two Republican Senators would play a large role in the debate on civil rights, but now they, like most Americans, were pleased to have survived the Cuban Missile Crisis.

With the Teddy-Eddie contest settled and the Cuban Missile Crisis passed, attention focused once again on the Kennedy-McCormack relationship. While Wilfrid C. Rogers of the *Boston Globe* saw John working closely to get Kennedy's programs through the House, James "Scotty" Reston of the *New York Times* was less sure and contended that their relationship was "a mystery" and that "on some critical questions, the Speaker plays an oddly ambiguous role."[2]

The early concerns focused on the committees of Rules and Ways and Means. The 1961 Rules Committee expansion from 12 to 15 was a temporary one and had to be voted on again if it was to continue. It was anticipated to be a "bitter and close fight," while the Ways and Means concern was a policy one, regarding its role in shaping the president's commitment to medical care for the aged.

Bob Kerr, Wilbur Mills, and Medicare: An important change had occurred in the battle for Medicare. On New Year's Day, 1963, the self-made oil millionaire U.S. Senator Bob Kerr of Oklahoma died of a heart attack. His penchant for providing unsecured loans to cash-strapped Senators with no requests for repayment had put a number of them in his pocket and made him a very powerful man. He opposed Medicare and had even purchased a Senator's vote against it. Kerr was especially close to LBJ, and as a senior member of the Senate's tax-writing Finance Committee, he played a major role in shaping revenue policy. Arch-conservative Harry Flood Byrd of Virginia, who nominally chaired Finance, and Russell B. Long of Louisiana, who succeeded the ailing Byrd as chair in 1965, were no match for the influence of Bob Kerr.

In 1960, Congress passed a bill coauthored by Kerr and new Ways and Means Chair Wilbur D. Mills of Arkansas that provided some medical help through state-federal matching grants for indigent seniors but as John Manley contended, "it satisfied no one."[3] Kerr's death provided an opportunity for the relatively young Mills to become the major fiscal player in Congress. Mills, the son of a school superintendent in Kensett, Arkansas, graduated from Hendrix College and the Harvard Law School, studying under future Supreme Court Justice Felix Frankfurter. Mills had a childhood ambition to become a member of the Ways and Means Committee, inspired by the district visit of William Oldfield, then minority whip and member of Ways and Means who hired seven-year-old Wilbur Mills for a nickel to precede him into the various shops and identify the townspeople.[4] He began his House career in 1939 at the age of 29 and was elected to Ways and Means in October 1942. Mills fulfilled his childhood ambition at the age of 33.

John McCormack had a great fondness for the Ways and Means Committee. It was Speaker Jack Garner's sponsorship that got him elected to the committee in 1931, his first placement inside the House's inner power circle. His ten years on the committee during the 1930s permitted John to become its talent scout and to deliver a few thousand committee assignments to the hundreds of new Democrats elected in that tumultuous decade, making him a popular and powerful member. When John left the committee in 1940 to become majority leader, Tennessee's Jere Cooper succeeded him and it was Cooper's death in October 1957 that opened the chairmanship for the 48-year-old Wilbur Mills.

Mills served as chair for 17 years, 1958–75, until his ill-fated 1972 presidential bid exposed some of the personal demons that were hidden from public view. Mills was the only chair of Ways and Means during John's speakership and given John's difficulties with the chairs of the other House's "big three" committees—Clarence Cannon of Appropriations and Howard W. Smith of Rules—dealing with Mills was far more enjoyable. John McCormack would eventually outlive Cannon, who died in May 1964, and outlast Smith, who lost his 1966 renomination.

Under Mills's leadership, the 25-member Ways and Means Committee had no subcommittees and Mills's closeness with senior Republican John W. Byrnes of Wisconsin enabled the committee's leaders to control its legislative output.[5] Ways and Means also submitted the vast bulk of its bills to the House floor under closed rules where no amendments could be added, thus limiting debate and guaranteeing their relatively easy passage. There is no question that Wilbur Mills was the dominant legislator during John's nine-year speakership.

Mills was much more sympathetic than Bob Kerr to Kennedy's Medicare agenda and to JFK's plan to overhaul the nation's cumbersome and complicated tax code. McCormack's lifelong commitment to government-funded health care dating back to his early days in the Massachusetts House led him to urge the placement of Medicare supporters on Ways and Means. As described by John Manley, leadership intervention on the committee on behalf of Medicare was evident when[6]

> at least two members were asked by Speaker McCormack about medicare and all but two of the replacements were well-known supporters of medicare, it seems clear that the opinion of most that no anti-medicare Democrat could win a Ways and Means seat after 1960 was correct. Such a rule could not have operated without clear-cut leadership endorsement; without such a rule the conservative coalition on Ways and Means might not have been broken on Ways and Means.

Committee membership headaches

While John McCormack faced no voted Democratic opposition in the caucus or on the House floor, there were visible signs of discontent regarding three House committees: Rules, Ways and Means, and District of Columbia. To make the Rules Committee expansion permanent, the House rules had to be amended. The late powerful Sam Rayburn had expended a great deal of political capital to get the House to accept the expansion by the narrow vote of 217 to 212. This would be difficult to repeat. House Republicans were ready to ally themselves with southern Democrats to block the expansion.[7] John McCormack was well aware that the Democrats had lost five seats in the 1962 election and that he did not enjoy the same esteem as Mr. Sam.

A deal was cut. In exchange for Georgia's 10 votes for the expansion, the House leadership would sponsor Georgia's Phil Landrum for one of the two vacancies on Ways and Means. Since the Ways and Means Democrats made all of the Democratic assignments to the other House committees, one had to be elected to it by the caucus. However, Georgia's votes were unnecessary as the vote to make the Rules Committee expansion permanent was surprisingly easy, 235 to 196. It carried with the votes of 28 Republicans and a majority of southern Democrats. Initially, the vote was seen as "a big victory for the new House leadership team which won the fight on its own out from under the shadow of the late Speaker Sam Rayburn."[8]

The expected leadership sponsorship of Phil Landrum's Ways and Means candidacy for one of the two seats opened up by the 1962 retirement of 6th-ranked Burr P. Harrison of Virginia and the defeat of 11th-ranked James B. Frazier, Jr. of Tennessee. Landrum was opposed by DSG liberals because of his coauthorship of the 1959 Landrum-Griffin Act that limited the political activities of organized labor. When the votes of the caucus came in, five-termer Ross Bass of Tennessee received 169 votes; five-termer W. Pat Jennings of Virginia, 161 votes; and six-termer Phil Landrum finished out of the running with the embarrassing total of 126 votes.[9] To liberals, Georgia's votes were unnecessary and the leadership's sponsorship of Landrum for Ways and Means was a needless commitment to obtain them.

Praise for John quickly faded as the *Washington Post* editorialized on January 16 that the seating of Bass and Jennings was a victory for the Kennedy Administration but it "disclosed the essential weakness of the House leadership on which the Administration must depend" and "the repudiation of Speaker McCormack again spotlights the decentralization of power in the House. Speaker McCormack holds only half a rein on a headless horse and Congress will keep bolting from the track until more effective instruments of party leadership are provided."[10]

Most cheered by McCormack's miscalculation was his Missouri adversary Dick Bolling who prepared a congratulatory 13-page pamphlet for the Inter-University Case Program at Syracuse University entitled *Defeating the Leadership's Nominee in the House Democratic Caucus*.[11] This would be the first but not the last of Bolling's published attacks on John's leadership of the House.

The other committee issue was over the poorly regarded District of Columbia Committee then chaired by South Carolina segregationist John "Johnny Mac" McMillan, who treated the district like his personal plantation. It was hoped that the McCormack-backed slate of African-American Charles C. Diggs, Jr. of Michigan, Edith Green of Oregon, and Carlton R. Sickles of Maryland would be able to tilt the District Committee in the direction of permitting home rule. But when the Ways and Means Committee issued committee membership lists, neither Green nor Sickles were named to the committee. Instead, the more conservative James W. Trimble of Arkansas and Texas-born B. F. "Bernie" Sisk of California were named. Since Trimble and Sisk were both Rules Committee members, supporters of home rule were fearful that Rules Committee Chair Howard Smith of Virginia, an avowed opponent of home rule, now had the votes to prevent any measure supporting it to emerge from the committee. John McCormack was blamed once again as it was contended that "although McCormack was anxious to do something about the District Committee, he was unwilling to tangle with the Southerners over this matter."[12] And a subsequent *Post* editorial stated, "the outcome was a victory for the Ways and Means Committee at the expense of Speaker McCormack."[13]

Barely a month into his first full term as Speaker, John McCormack's leadership of the House was already seen as lacking. Unflattering comparisons of John's equivocations to Sam Rayburn's steadfast determination were common and John's willingness to accommodate senior southern hard-liners was regularly cited as evidence of his unawareness of how much the demography of the House Democrats was changing. Sadly for John McCormack, this was a narrative that would bedevil his speakership for all of its nine years.

Southern Committee Chairs: McCormack's major problem of trying to direct the House's legislative agenda was simply due to the predominance of southern and border state committee chairs. During John's nine years as Speaker, 17 of the 21 House standing committees, including Select Small Business which functioned as a standing committee, had at least one southern or border state chair. All "Big Three" House committees were southern-controlled with the relatively young and legislatively talented Wilbur Mills of Arkansas chairing Ways and Means for all nine years; the curmudgeonly Clarence Cannon of Missouri chairing Appropriations' until his death on May 12, 1964, to be succeeded by the far more congenial George H. Mahon of Texas; and most notably the Rules Committee chaired first by Howard W. Smith of Virginia until his renomination defeat in 1966 when he was succeeded by William M. Colmer of Mississippi. McCormack knew the two Rules chairs well. He relied on Smith to insure his speakership election in 1962 and he had placed Colmer on Rules over Sam Rayburn's objections in 1949. And barely a half-step below the "Big Three" was the Armed Services Committee initially chaired by a McCormack skeptic, Carl Vinson of Georgia, the House's senior-most member in the 87th and 88th Congresses who was succeeded in 1965 by John's friend, the patronage-hungry L. Mendel Rivers of South Carolina.

The only committees without southern or border chairs during McCormack's speakership were Foreign Affairs, chaired by Thomas E. "Doc" Morgan of Pennsylvania; Interior and Insular Affairs, chaired by Colorado's Wayne Aspinall; and the two chaired by his good friend African-American William L. Dawson of Chicago on Government Operations and his ally, Brooklyn's Emanuel Celler on Judiciary. Apart from Judiciary that had a moderately high rating, the other three were among the House's lesser committees.

John had chaired two short-lived select committees a quarter-century apart, Un-American Activities in 1934–35 and Astronautics and Space Exploration in 1958, but had never managed a full standing committee nor had either of his two key lieutenants, Majority Leader Carl Albert and Majority Whip Hale Boggs. Consequently, the chairs of the committee-dominated House of the 1960s paid them relatively little heed. Drew Pearson described the different roles of the trio thus[14]: "McCormack, for instance, works with Northern big city Democrats, Boggs with the South and Carl Albert with the Democrats in between. At times, they cut across geographic lines . . . and there is no man more persuasive in talking to Judge Howard Smith, the Dixiecrat Congressman from Virginia than Carl."

Sadly, even with their talents combined, they could not match Mr. Sam's powerful grasp of the House. It would prove particularly problematic in the tense year of 1963.

Civil Rights and the resistant South

Civil rights for all Americans has been the nation's longest and most contentious issue since the Constitutional Convention decreed on July 12, 1787, that Article 1, Section 2, Paragraph 3 of the Constitution should contain the following paragraph:

> Representatives and direct Taxes shall be apportioned among the several States which may be included within this Union, according to their respective Numbers, which shall be determined by adding to the whole Number of free Persons, including those bound to Service for a Term of Years, and excluding Indians not taxed, *three fifths of all other Persons.*

It was well known to the nation's Founding Fathers that "all other persons" referred exclusively to African-descended slaves. They were technically not property because they could be enumerated but they were not full persons either. The "three-fifths" compromise may have saved the Constitutional Convention from collapsing, but it placed one-fifth of the persons then residing in the United States into a subordinate status that was lifted only partially with the nation's Civil War and the deaths of 630,000 Americans.

Civil rights was the domestic issue that dominated the national agenda of the 1960s and threatened the Democratic Party, a party that had its origins deep in the antebellum South. Democrats had defended slavery before the Civil War and segregation after it.

While two civil rights bills in 1957 and 1960 had addressed the voting rights of African Americans in states that had systematically denied them, the far more intractable issue of blatant racial discrimination in employment, education, housing, and public accommodations had remained unaddressed by Congress since 1877. Cascading violence on the racial front could be ignored no longer and it was time for President Kennedy to act.

Throughout the thousand days of the Kennedy presidency, it was believed that the president and his brother, the attorney general, would move the race relations agenda toward greater equity for the black citizens of the nation. Pressure was put on the Kennedy Administration through hundreds of civil rights demonstrations. Most demonstrations were small, peaceful, and relatively private. But the pressure was relentless and it was applied daily throughout the South and the North.

In May 1961 the large public and violent demonstrations began. The early demonstrations were lunch counter sit-ins at segregated restaurants. Referring to themselves as Freedom Riders, black and white demonstrators next moved to integrate interstate buses. Racial tension escalated as the riders were brutally attacked by segregationist mobs when the buses entered the Deep South.

On February 28, 1963, President Kennedy submitted a relatively modest civil rights package, expanding already existing laws on voting rights; providing help to schools undergoing desegregation; and extending by four years the life of the federal Civil Rights Commission. Positive steps perhaps, but small ones nevertheless. Small steps would not prevent the traumas of this year, for 1963 was the year when all hell broke loose.

Birmingham, May 1963: William L. Moore, a pro-civil rights white man from Baltimore walking from Tennessee to Mississippi, was shot to death in northeast Alabama in April. Six weeks later on June 12, a sniper killed Medgar Evers, Mississippi state chairman of the NAACP. Two days later on June 14, riots spilled over into Cambridge, Maryland. And before the year was out, civil rights demonstrations erupted in the North, challenging discrimination in the white-dominated construction unions of New York, Chicago, Philadelphia, and Trenton and Newark, New Jersey.

Southern Democratic governors, most notably Ross R. Barnett of Mississippi and George C. Wallace of Alabama, fanned the flames of racial conflict. While the 65-year-old Ross Barnett could be easily dismissed as a doddering relic of old-time racism and was characterized as such in contemporary cartoons, Wallace was different. Two years younger than Jack Kennedy, Wallace's pugnacious style and his flair for the dramatic made him a far more dangerous adversary. Wallace was the new and more troubling face of segregation as he defiantly declared in his 1963 inaugural address: "Segregation now, segregation tomorrow, and segregation forever!" While Barnett relied on various legal stratagems to prevent the integration of the University of Mississippi, Wallace created a dramatic televised encounter as he chose to stand in the doorway of the University of Alabama to prevent its integration by two black students, Vivian Malone and James Hood. Attorney General Kennedy sent his high-ranking Deputy Attorney General Nicholas deB. Katzenbach to Tuscaloosa to escort the students through the governor's protest. Wallace immediately became a hero to the white South, while the Kennedy brothers became demonized. The gloves were off. It was June 11, 1963.

With Governor George Wallace's defiance garnering national attention, Alabama replaced Mississippi as the epicenter of white resistance to federal efforts at desegregation. It was in Alabama's largest city of Birmingham that the most violent confrontations occurred in May 1963. Business leaders had hoped to defuse racial conflict in the "Birmingham Truce Agreement" that provided partial desegregation, but Eugene "Bull" Connor, the city's commissioner of public safety, attacked the agreement and made it clear that he would not enforce it. Bombings at the home of the Reverend A. D. King, Martin Luther King's younger brother, and at the Gaston Motel where he and his family had fled for safety made it clear those segregationist white members of the community, including its white-only police, were part of this murderous attack on the leaders of the Birmingham Project.

Initially, the Kennedy response was a "plague on both houses," blaming the black protestors as well as the white police for the violence. As Nick Bryant's *The Bystander* contended, the Kennedy Administration's uncertainty on how to deal with the Birmingham conflict was evidenced in Kennedy's initial reaction to an AP photograph of a police dog trying to bite a baby in the middle of the riots, and his later shift in attitude:[15]

> Kennedy offered up no new concrete policy measures in response to the extraordinary violence in Birmingham. The AP photograph had clearly unsettled him, but his immediate response reflected deep confusion rather than enhanced resolve.
>
> The Birmingham protests—and the photograph that encapsulated them—were not a watershed moment in Kennedy's presidency. Kennedy did not take an aggressive stance with regard to new legislation or make a public address. As Andrew Hatcher told reporters after the May 4 meeting finished, the president "continues to hope that the situation can be resolved by the people of Birmingham themselves."
>
> The administration did, however, subtly shift its tactics and moved from conflict management into conflict resolution. In Albany, Kennedy had sought to encourage a dialogue between black demonstrators and white civic leaders. Now, in Birmingham, he worked actively to bring dialogue about.

Burke Marshall, a key Justice Department official, recalled to Wyatt T. Walker, a prominent civil rights activist and close associate of King, that "Robert Kennedy himself opposed the demonstrations as an 'ill-timed' ambush on a reform city government that was not yet in office."[16] Finally, with Jack Kennedy's reputation taking a beating among liberal newspaper editors and the international press, he realized that bolder steps had to be taken.

Larry O'Brien, in his memoirs, recalls the strategy behind Kennedy's hesitancy toward advancing civil rights legislation[17]:

> It is a well-known fact that Kennedy, having promised civil rights action in his 1960 campaign, did little with the Congress in this area during his presidency. He took certain executive actions, and his Justice Department was vigorous in promoting voter rights and school desegregation in the South (the locus of most civil rights activity in those simpler days) but he didn't introduce substantial civil rights legislation until the summer of 1963. The reason was simple. The Rules Committee fight had shown us how precarious our congressional majority was. We needed the Southerners to have any majority at all, and we would lose them if we pushed for a civil rights bill; so Kennedy did what he could by executive action, and by his public statements, and waited for the proper time to go to the Congress.

While the violence subsided, the anger remained, and it was clear that the Kennedy brothers' standoffishness could not contain the crisis. Since there was no guarantee that an immediate solution was at hand, the president realized that his initial civil rights bill was inadequate. The next step would be to broaden and toughen legislation that would deal at last with this long-festering sore of the American body politic.

Monday, June 10 and Tuesday, June 11, described by Canadian author Andrew Cohen, were the "two days in June" that would dramatically transform the nation and profoundly impact the legacy of President John F. Kennedy.[18] Earlier in the day of June 11, Governor Wallace had "stood in the schoolhouse door" to prevent the integration of the University of Alabama. Kennedy needed to counter Wallace's dramatized resistance and that evening he addressed the nation in a televised appearance. "We are confronted primarily with a moral issue. . . . The fires of frustration and discord are burning in every city, North and South, where legal remedies are not at hand," he said. "Redress is sought in the streets, in demonstrations, parades and protests which create tensions and threaten violence and threaten lives."[19]

After watching the speech, Martin Luther King, Jr., reportedly "leapt to his feet and cried, 'Walter [Fauntroy], can you believe that white man not only stepped up to the plate, he hit it over the fence!' King was staggered by the president's words."[20]

The words were eloquent and well chosen. But Kennedy's accent was the clipped one of Irish Boston by way of Harvard University. Would the white South listen? Or would they ignore Kennedy's entreaties much as they had the equally eloquent pleas from John Quincy Adams and Senator Charles Sumner, the great abolitionist orators of Yankee Boston? These were names Jack knew well and both had challenged slavery. Adams had earned a chapter in *Profiles in Courage* and had been silenced on the House floor by a "gag rule" against debating slavery, while Sumner was nearly beaten to death on the Senate floor by a South Carolina Representative for challenging pro-slavery incursions into Kansas. The tunnel named for Sumner under Boston Harbor joined the East Boston of Jack's paternal grandfather P. J. Kennedy to the North End of his maternal one John Fitzgerald. However, the voices of Boston often rang deaf in southern ears. The well-educated natives of the "City on a Hill" often brought condescension as well as righteousness to their Capitol Hill speeches and to others there was also more than a touch of hypocrisy.[21]

The white South was unmoved and their elected leaders in Congress awaited the next step as they sought to assess how sincere the Kennedy brothers were in pushing their civil rights agenda. The June 11 speech was rhetoric; legislation was real. The revised bill designed to eradicate as much racial discrimination as possible was introduced on June 19. However, the white South in both chambers chose to stall massive parts of the Kennedy program through postponements and multiple committee hearings. Most of them had been elected by all-white or nearly all-white electorates in their states and congressional districts. They were clearly fearful of even more bigoted primary opponents challenging their reelections. This had happened earlier during the 1948 Dixiecrat eruption and those memories returned to haunt them. While the Kennedy brothers were sincere in their commitment, the consequence for them was *immobolisme* in the parlance of France's Fourth Republic.

An Immobilized Congress: The civil rights struggle led the 88th Congress to move at a snail's pace throughout most of 1963. In spite of minimal House losses and two Senate seats gained for the Democrats in the 1962 congressional elections, the 88th Congress ground to a near halt. White southern committee chairs who controlled the legislative levers of the House and the Senate immobilized Congress. Only a few legislative items made it through the congressional gauntlet.

An indication of how badly the House stalled legislation may be seen in the small number of substantive roll calls voted on in 1963.[22] In 1961 and 1962, the House had its 50th substantive roll call on June 28 but in 1963, it occurred more than a month later on July 31. The First Session of the 87th Congress had its final substantive roll call, number 116 on September 26 as compared to only 69 on the same date in 1963. On November 20, 1963, the day before Kennedy made his ill-fated trip to Texas, the 88th Congress had only cast 95 substantive roll-call votes. The passive resistance of the civil rights demonstrators was being thwarted by the collective passive aggression of the 88th Congress.

As the body count of murdered civil rights activists grew in June, the Congress passed by voice votes in each chamber the Equal Pay Act of 1963 which provided that no employer subject to the Fair Labor Standards Act could discriminate on the basis of sex in payment of wages for jobs requiring equal skill, effort, and responsibility.[23] The women of America were pleased but civil rights legislation remained locked up.

In spite of the presumably positive numbers of Democrats in the 88th Congress, the legislative output was dramatically sparse. Apart from the Equal Pay Act, only two other pieces of legislation were worthy of note, the Department of Defense Appropriations Act (PL 88-149) and the Community Mental Health Centers Act which contained the Mental Retardation Facilities Construction Act. For Kennedy, this bill had personal resonance. His oldest sister Rosemary who was already intellectually challenged was further impaired as a consequence of a failed lobotomy when she was 25 and she was sequestered in St. Coletta's School for Exceptional Children in Jefferson, Wisconsin, for the remaining 60 years of her life.[24]

Both bills became law in October but the list of unfinished items on the agenda of the 88th Congress was especially long. Awaiting congressional action and sharing equal time with civil rights was Kennedy's 10.4 billion tax cut to jumpstart the economy that seemed to have been stuck with an unemployment rate in the 5.70–5.90% range for the previous two years. This rate was not as high as the 7.10 reported by the Bureau of Labor Statistics in May 1961 but the downward pace of 1961 had stalled.[25] Reporters questioned John McCormack concerning which bill had greater priority leading him to refuse "to assign No.1 and No. 2 labels to taxes and civil rights."[26] The Kennedys' nonreliance on John McCormack was evident in the secret White House recordings prepared by Ted Widmer in his fascinating book *Listening In* that includes not a single reference to Speaker McCormack, ostensibly, the second-most important of the nation's public officials.[27]

With both the civil rights and tax cuts bills in committee, President Kennedy turned once again to foreign policy. The nuclear disaster that the nation had so narrowly escaped in the Cuban Missile Crisis preyed heavily upon the Kennedy Administration. On April 5, American and Soviet representatives agreed to set up a direct telecommunication link. On June 20, the "hot line" agreement was signed. While direct negotiations continued, Senate Democrats led by Hubert Humphrey (DFL-Minn.) and Thomas Dodd (Dem-Conn.) sought to gain approval of a treaty limiting nuclear weapon tests in the atmosphere. The treaty was concluded on August 5, 1963, and with much of the summer spent on debate, the Senate consented to ratify the Treaty of Moscow by 80 to 19 on September 24.[28] So was passed the Nuclear Test Ban Treaty, the greatest foreign policy triumph of the Kennedy Administration.

The treaty bound the signatories, which included the United States, the U.S.S.R., and more than a hundred other nations, "to prohibit, to prevent, and not to carry out any nuclear weapon test explosion, or any other nuclear explosion at any place under its jurisdiction or control (a) in the atmosphere, beyond its units including outer space, or underwater, including territorial water or high seas, or (b) in any other environment if such explosion causes radioactive debris to be present outside the territorial units of the state under whose jurisdiction or control such explosion is conducted." The signatories also pledged to refrain from causing, encouraging, or in any way participating in any nuclear test anywhere else. France and China did not sign.

A new headache for John McCormack emerged in August when Rules Committee member Homer Thornberry of Texas was appointed to the federal bench. Thornberry was a Johnson confidant and as young men they had met on the grounds of the Texas State Capitol in Austin where Thornberry was a page and Lyndon's father served as a State Representative.[29] Thornberry was one of Sam Rayburn's appointees to the committee and his departure shifted the committee ratio from a narrow 8–7 liberal-majority to a 7–7 philosophical deadlock. The Texans wanted John Young of Corpus Christi to replace Thornberry while the DSG wanted Michigan's James O'Hara for the slot. McCormack sided with Young, and as Rowland Evans and Robert Novak contended correctly,[30] "[No] politician hates the spilling of intraparty blood any more than John McCormack. Thus, he conceivably could decide that ignoring the liberals might turn out to be more troublesome than agreeing to their demands."

The Revised 1963 Civil Rights Bill: The Kennedy Administration expanded its original civil rights package to include provisions regarding access to public accommodations, legal authority to desegregate the schools and to shut off federal funding in areas of persistent discrimination, and to support existing legislation regarding fair employment practices. As *Congressional Quarterly* reported, "In contrast to its relative inactivity in the legislative field, the Kennedy Administration, through executive action, took new steps in the areas of voting rights, employment, transportation and education."[31] It would take more than seven months to move the Kennedy civil rights bill from the legislative hopper through the House Rules Committee. By the time that the legislation finally arrived on the House floor on January 30, 1964, President John Kennedy had been dead for more than two months.

But progress was being made. On August 18, 1963, James Meredith, the black student whose admission to the University of Mississippi had led to violent riots and two deaths ten months earlier, received his degree without incident. On August 28, more than a quarter-million citizens gathered peacefully at the Lincoln Memorial in Washington to hear the Reverend Martin Luther King, Jr. deliver his riveting "I Have a Dream" speech to the marchers, to the nation, and to the world. Later that day, having watched the March on television, an impressed Kennedy met with ten of its leaders in the White House.[32]

"Fearing violence and controversy, Jack chose not to attend the March"[33] in the words of Thomas C. Reeves, a critical biographer. Richard Reeves, a more favorable biographer, contended that Kennedy "refused to meet with [A. Philip Randolph], King, and Roy Wilkins before the March to avoid photographs that would make him look bad if there was trouble in the streets."[34] Kennedy watched the March on television and was especially impressed by King's speech. Kennedy's post-March meeting was less productive than hoped because he chose to encourage black leaders to follow the Jewish example of greater education as a means of guaranteeing full acceptance. The fact that there were no laws prohibiting Jews from voting or participating in the social and political life of the states in which they resided nor were Jews lynched from southern trees as were blacks—the "strange fruit" in Billie Holliday's haunting song—indicated that Kennedy was still somewhat clueless about the full dimensions of race prejudice.

The white South remained implacably resistant to black gains and little more than a week after King's memorable speech, Governor Wallace contended on September 5 that "the society is coming apart at the seams. What good is it doing to force these situations when white people nowhere in the South want integration? What this country needs is a few first-class funerals."[35]

Ten days later, another bombing in Birmingham took place. This time it was the 16th Street Baptist Church, which Dr. King and the SCLC had used as a meeting place for their efforts to lessen the grasp of segregation in Birmingham. On Sunday, September 15, the Ku Klux Klan planted 15 sticks of dynamite at the church, and when the sticks exploded, four young girls were killed. No single action turned as much of America and the world against white racism than this event. Three of the girls were 14 years old, and the other only 11. Governor Wallace's Alabama had revealed itself to the nation and the world as a hateful place, and Wallace intended to use this fact of life to buoy a presidential candidacy in 1964 and subsequent ones in 1968, 1972, and 1976. The "first-class funerals" would occur days later. It was clear the white South would not surrender its prerogatives peacefully.

The stress confronting Jack Kennedy and John McCormack as Congress wrestled fitfully with the civil rights bill was exacerbated when tragedy entered both men's lives. With the death of Jack's two-day-old baby boy Patrick in early August, and the diagnosis of cancer for John's brother Edward (Knocko), both men had to confront personal loss at this time of political upheaval. It has been contended that the death of baby Patrick and Jackie's painful reaction to it led Jack to reassess his personal priorities and recommit himself to his marriage. One sympathetic author stated that this period of time was the last and most important 100 days of JFK's life.[36]

Kennedy-Johnson tension

Electoral politics cannot be postponed indefinitely. The election of 1964 was on the horizon and Kennedy was well aware of how narrow his victory was in the 1960 election and of Lyndon Johnson's important role in guaranteeing its success. Speculation centered on the Kennedy-Johnson relationship. While most agreed that Lyndon Johnson's place on the ticket had ensured Kennedy's election in 1960, questions arose as to whether his presence would be necessary for Kennedy's reelection. While rumors of Johnson's displacement by U.S. Senators Stuart Symington of Missouri, Henry Jackson of Washington State, and North Carolina's Governor Terry Sanford abounded, Larry O'Brien, the best vote counter among Kennedy's intimates, said that the ticket would be Jack and Lyndon again.

Johnson's own anxiety about his remaining on the ticket was clear to the White House. In a conversation days before the Texas trip with his secretary Evelyn Lincoln, President Kennedy remarked, "The only thing Mr. Johnson is afraid of is that I will not put him on the ticket in 1964."[37] Most insiders were well aware of the general disdain that Vice President Johnson and Attorney General Robert Kennedy had for one another, but it was the president's brother and not the president himself who held that disdain. Furthermore, prior presidential tickets had survived similar difficulty.

One of the more poignant comments was recalled by the well-connected Bess Abell, daughter of U.S. Senator Earle C. Clements of Kentucky, LBJ's whip during his early years as Majority Leader and the daughter-in-law of syndicated columnist Drew Pearson. Mrs. Abell, who worked at the home of vice president and Mrs. Johnson as Lady Bird's social secretary, frequently arranged guest lists and parties for them. While arranging a party for president and Mrs. Kennedy and several of their friends and staff, Bess was told by the vice president: "There's only one person at the White House who likes me and fortunately his name is Jack Kennedy."[38]

As the fall of 1963 opened, President Kennedy's approval rating had dipped to 59% in the Gallup Poll.[39] It was a drop of 24 points from his high rating of 83% in April 1961;

17 points from the 76% in the first poll of 1963, and 11 points below his average score of 70%. The civil rights struggle was costing Kennedy valuable popularity and he could ill afford to remove LBJ from the ticket. Texas was the largest state in the South and there was little guarantee that anyone beside Lyndon Johnson could deliver those 25 electoral votes to the ticket. Liberal hopes and expectations about Kennedy dropping Johnson from the 1964 ticket would not be fulfilled. A desultory congressional session had not helped matters.

In 1963, Kennedy scored a high of 83.1% success rate on bills that escaped the Rules Committee to arrive on the House floor.[40] However, the overall success of Kennedy proposals in 1963 was dismal—27.2%, easily the lowest of the twelve scores calculated by *Congressional Quarterly*. It was even lower than Ike's last lame-duck year as president in 1960 when he had to face a divided government with Democratic majorities in both houses of Congress. *CQ* produced a simple chart of legislative success for the dozen years from 1953 to 1964 and JFK's lack of success in 1963's 1st Session of the 88th Congress is striking.[41] It is clear that the deliberate delay of Congress' southern chairs was a harsh message to Kennedy that his overall legislative agenda was to be held hostage to his civil rights proposals.

President	Congress	Year	Proposals Submitted	Approved By Congress	Approval Score (%)
Eisenhower	83rd 1st	1953	44	32	72.7
Eisenhower	83rd 2nd	1954	232	150	64.7
Eisenhower	84th 1st	1955	207	96	46.3
Eisenhower	84th 2nd	1956	225	103	45.7
Eisenhower	85th 1st	1957	206	76	36.9
Eisenhower	85th 2nd	1958	234	110	47.0
Eisenhower	86th 1st	1959	228	93	40.8
Eisenhower	86th 2nd	1960	183	56	30.6
Kennedy	87th 1st	1961	355	172	48.4
Kennedy	87th 2nd	1962	298	133	44.6
Kennedy	88th 1st	1963	401	109	27.2
Johnson	88th 2nd	1964	217	125	57.6

Scathing reviews

The frayed relationship between the Democratic president and the Democratic Congress elicited much negative commentary. *The New York Times*, in an effort to paper over the conflict, published a pictorial in its October 27, 1963, issue entitled "How the President Persuades Congress."[42] However, the overall assessments of this session were decidedly critical.

The esteemed Capitol Hill insider Stewart Alsop correctly identified the problem confronting Kennedy as the domination of both houses of Congress by seniority-protected southern committee chairs, clearly disturbed over what they perceived as the Kennedy brothers' aggressive civil rights program. As Alsop observed[43]:

> But the real trouble with Congress is deeper and more permanent than Mike Mansfield's excessive amiability or Bobby Baker's slickness. Representative Bolling, a Democrat and foremost student of congressional history in the House, went to the heart of the matter in one sentence: "The trouble with Congress is not Congress but the Democratic Party in Congress."
>
> . . .
>
> There are two parties in Congress. But in reality they are not the Democratic and Republican parties. They are the generally liberal Presidential Party and the generally conservative Party of the Congressional Establishment. . . . The Establishment, which has also been called the Club, the Inner Club, includes most of the Southerners. It also includes most senior Republicans and a scattering of conservative Democrats from outside the South. But the Southerners dominate it. Since the Establishment controls the machinery, the Southerners representing less than a sixth of the voting population dominate both Houses of Congress.
>
> . . .
>
> When the civil-rights bill was introduced last summer, the Southerners reacted like Samson in the temple. To defeat civil rights they risk bringing the whole structure of the congressional institution crashing about their ears. No Southerner will admit it for the record, but the southern strategy is to delay not only the civil-rights bill itself but anything else that can be delayed.

Other reporters at the time, such as Robert J. Donovan writing for the *Boston Globe*, also theorized about the legislative backlog. In a September 2, 1963, article assessing seven reasons why the 1st Session of the 88th Congress was largely unmoving, Donovan cited two of those reasons to be conservative and southern blockers:[44] "Congress, responsive to pressure groups at home, is still more conservative than the President and is thereby unreceptive to programs that smack of the welfare state.

. . .

Powerful Southerners in the Senate have used their position and their skill to bring about delay, particularly in consideration of civil rights legislation."

It was this fact of Congressional life that was at the heart of James MacGregor Burns's prescient analysis, *The Deadlock of Democracy: Four-Party Politics in America.*[45] Coming as this did from Jack Kennedy's biographer, one can easily imagine how deeply these views were held in the White House.

As the year wore on, the House Judiciary Committee, headed by two pro-civil rights champions—its Democratic Chair Manny Celler of New York and its Republican ranking minority member William McCulloch of Ohio—pushed hard for strong enforcement of the civil rights bill's provisions. Kennedy intimate Charles Bartlett of the *Chattanooga Times*, in his syndicated column, may have been speaking for the White House when he contended that the "[House] civil rights bill may be too strong."[46]

Bobby Baker Scandal: However, there was a very ominous cloud hovering over Vice President Johnson and that was the plight of his longtime protégé Secretary of the Senate Bobby Baker of Pickens, South Carolina, a man LBJ once spoke of: "I have two daughters. If I had a son this would be the boy."[47] The energetic and ambitious Baker was a young man in a hurry and at the age of 14, he became a page for U.S. Senator Burnet Maybank of South Carolina. He learned quickly that doing favors for powerful (and not so powerful) U.S. Senators would make him invaluable and soon found himself allied with another young man in a hurry—the new U.S. Senator from Texas—Lyndon Johnson. That some of these favors bordered on the illegal and the immoral made him even more indispensable. Baker's 1978 autobiography *Wheeling and Dealing* depicts some of his more ethically challenged favors for Senators but it is his 200-plus page oral history for the U.S. Senate Historical Office that fully captures how far he was willing to go to endear himself to members of "the world's greatest deliberative body."[48]

John McCormack knew Baker very well and during the 1956 Democratic Convention when McCormack chaired the Resolutions Committee, Baker served as his key staff person. Baker spoke well of McCormack, whom he described as "my wonderful friend."[49] Needless to say, John was totally unaware of Baker's other activities and would have been horrified to learn of them.

It was Baker's link to the Quorum Club, a watering hole in the Carroll Arms Hotel next to the then called new Senate Office Building where Senators and lobbyists met to relax and do business in the company of young, beautiful, and available women, that enabled him to gain information that he could use to further legislation and to line his own pockets. It was a scam to provide vending machines in companies that relied on federal grants that was his undoing. Baker's commingling of politics and personal enrichment led the Senate Rules and Administration Committee to open an investigation of him that resulted in his resignation as secretary of the Senate on October 7, 1963.

There was speculation that Attorney General Robert Kennedy was using the Baker scandal to push LBJ off the 1964 ticket. However, one of the men making use of Baker's female procurements was President Kennedy himself. The woman's name was Ellen Rometsch and much like Jack's dangerous prewar dalliances with Inga Arvid, a Danish woman with supposed Nazi ties, Rometsch was an East German woman with Communist connections. Knowing full well that LBJ's presumed financial links to Baker were far less politically damning than Jack's adulterous behavior with an alleged Communist spy, Bobby Kennedy got her deported quickly and the Justice Department did not pursue the Baker case further. Kennedy's assassination ended the Senate's investigation of Johnson. For its help in burying this matter, the FBI's J. Edgar Hoover got permission from Attorney General Kennedy to wiretap the telephones of Martin Luther King and his associates.[50]

Vietnam crisis

Half a world away in South Vietnam, the festering problem of Vietnam intensified. The Diem regime of President Ngo Dinh Diem and his brother Ngo Dinh Nhu, the secret police chief, had lost control of the army and plots to kill them both hung in the air. On November 1, 1963, the government was overthrown and the two brothers were murdered. Hopes that a new government would be more successful in fighting the Communist-backed Viet Cong were short-lived. Vietnam's woes moved closer to the American mainland.

In the midst of these developments, President Kennedy returned to the political part of his job and began serious planning for his upcoming renomination and reelection in 1964. The election was now only a year away. Kennedy saw no serious internal threat to his renomination on the horizon. Conservative Democrats muttered about him but none were likely to challenge a president of their own party who had just steered the nation through one of its most fearful foreign policy crises. The Republicans were another matter, and it was in Kennedy's interest to shore up those states that had supported him in 1960 but might be problematic in 1964. While the religious issues surrounding his Catholicism had abated, racial tension had reached its boiling point.

Prepping for 1964

Kennedy correctly regarded the South as an area of serious political concern. In 1960, the Kennedy-Johnson ticket had carried six southern states with 71 electoral votes, almost one-quarter of his total of 303. Like Al Smith before him, Kennedy's Catholicism apparently cost him the "outer south" states of Kentucky, Tennessee, Virginia, Florida, and Oklahoma. The Smith-Robinson ticket of 1928 had held six southern states—Alabama, Arkansas, Georgia, Louisiana, Mississippi, and South Carolina. Kennedy had won four of these and five electoral votes of Alabama's eleven. The balance of Alabama's votes and all eight of Mississippi were cast for "independent electors." Neither of those states appeared winnable.

On the positive side, the Kennedy Administration had not flown in the Pope from the Vatican to take the reins of government, and some of the anti-Catholic fears which had cost the ticket in the outer South may have diminished sufficiently to return them to the Democratic presidential column. However, for the more virulent anti-Catholics, this was a federal government with an array of powerful Catholics holding the key posts of President, Attorney General, Speaker of the U.S. House, House Majority Whip, and Senate Majority Leader.

Two southern states were in the balance: North Carolina and Texas. North Carolina was the region's most progressive state and was home to the South's best-regarded universities—Duke and the University of North Carolina at Chapel Hill. Kennedy had placed its former Governor Luther Hodges in his Cabinet and its incumbent Governor Terry Sanford was committed to containing interracial conflict. North Carolina appeared safe. In fact, there were rumors that Kennedy was considering Terry Sanford as a replacement for LBJ.[51] Texas was another matter. Throughout the twentieth century, Texas had been the largest of all the southern states and its 25 electoral votes placed it sixth among the big states in the nation and of those big states, it had the longest tradition of supporting Democratic nominees. In fact, no successful Democratic presidential nominee from the Civil War until 1992 had won the election without carrying Texas.

A "nonpolitical" trip to Texas was arranged for President Kennedy and the First Lady in late November. Jackie was still recovering from the death of baby Patrick but she was well aware of how important Texas was in the calculus of electoral votes. So she put aside her personal concerns to join Jack on this important political trip.

The death of Knocko

With Congress adjourned and the Cuban Missile Crisis presently, if not completely, resolved, John and Harriet remained in Washington but troubling family news came from Boston. His legendary younger brother, Edward J. "Knocko" McCormack, Sr., had become seriously ill with cancer. A first operation had been unable to contain its spread. A second operation was scheduled at the Veterans Hospital in nearby Jamaica Plain, but it was too late. On Sunday, November 17, Knocko passed away leaving John with only one remaining sibling, Donald, known within the family as "Buttons," who lived in Texas.[52]

The funeral was a grand event held at St. Brigid's on West Broadway in South Boston. It was estimated that more than 2,000 people attended the funeral mass, nearly matching the turnout for the funeral of Knocko's close friend and political ally, four-term Mayor and Governor James Michael Curley.[53] John brought three members of the House delegation with him to the services—Phil Philbin, Jim Burke, and his closest protégé, Tip O'Neill. In attendance were Governor Endicott Peabody, Speaker of the Massachusetts House John Thompson, and fellow Southie, Senate President John Powers. The Final Absolution was delivered by John's close friend and confessor Richard Cardinal Cushing, yet another of South Boston's most distinguished sons. Sadly, McCormack's and Cushing's roles as mourners and eulogists would be reprised on a very much larger stage a week later.

November 22, 1963

Political trouble awaited President Kennedy upon his arrival in San Antonio on November 21. The Democrats of Texas were embroiled once again in factional feuding.[54] Their internal battles had already cost them Lyndon Johnson's Senate seat, which was won by Republican John Tower in a 1961 special election, the first ever Republican victory for a Texas U.S. Senate seat. An ideological rift between the two wings of the Texas Democratic Party had erupted between the liberals led by U.S. Senator Ralph Yarborough and the conservatives led by Governor John Connally, a longtime protégé of Johnson. JFK knew that to keep Texas and its 25 electoral votes in his column the following November he had to mediate the Yarborough-Connally feud.

Landing first in San Antonio on Thursday, November 21, president and Mrs. Kennedy met enthusiastic and favorable crowds from the Texas city with the largest Hispanic population. They next flew on to Houston to honor longtime Representative Albert Thomas, a close Rayburn-McCormack ally, and once again were impressed with another warm welcome. After a day in San Antonio and Houston, the presidential party flew north. An overnight stay at the Hotel Texas in Fort Worth was arranged and the following morning, Jim Wright, a Sam Rayburn protégé and future Speaker of the House then in his 5th term as Fort Worth's Representative in Congress, brought them to breakfast with continued warmth from the Texans. Fort Worth was the more rugged, more Democratic, and more westerly of north Texas's two major metropolises. Then they went to Dallas, a few miles to the east but far removed from Fort Worth in terms of political philosophy. Dallas had emerged as the most conservative of the new South's major cities. It was anticipated that its welcome for the president and the first lady would be relatively tepid. It was a short flight from Fort Worth to Dallas and the seating in the motorcade was arranged to gloss over the factional feuding within the state party.

When they arrived in Dallas, president and Mrs. Kennedy sat in the backseat of an open car with Governor John Connally and Mrs. Connally seated in front of them while Senator Yarborough rode with Vice President Johnson. Huge crowds lined the streets to watch the motorcade pass. Their enthusiasm and warmth belied the earlier expectations. It was going very well.

Echoing through the underpass in Dealey Plaza were three rifle shots that hit their mark. President John Fitzgerald Kennedy was mortally wounded and would be dead within the hour.

Notes

1   "Major Officials Named For the 88th Congress," *NYT*, January 10, 1963, p. 4. The *Times* listed Carl Albert's home state as Colorado, not Oklahoma, but it indicated that none of the leaders named faced caucus challenges. Robert C. Albright, "88th Congress Set for Battle at Bang of Gavel," *Washington Post*, January 6, 1963, p. E1.

2   Wilfrid C. Rodgers, "McCormack Pitches for JFK's Programs," *BG*, January 6, 1963, p. A4; and James Reston, "Washington: Who Runs the Democrats? Kennedy or McCormack," *NYT*, April 28, 1963, p. 185.

3   John F. Manley, *The Politics of Finance: The House Committee on Ways and Means* (Boston: Little, Brown, 1970), p. 340.

4   Marshall Frady, "Wilbur Mills," *LIFE*, LXXI (July 16, 1971), pp. 52 ff. The full story of the Oldfield relationship was told to the author by Mr. Mills in December 1971.

5   Mills's centrality in the House during this time is well captured in the superb works of John F. Manley, "The House Committee on Ways and Means: Conflict Management in a Congressional Committee," *APSR*, LIX (December 1964), pp. 927–39; "Wilbur D. Mills: A Study in Congressional Influence," *APSR*, LXII (June 1969), pp. 442–64; and his book *The Politics of Finance: The House Committee on Ways and Means* (Boston: Little, Brown, 1970); and Julian E. Zelizer, *Taxing America: Wilbur D. Mills, Congress, and the State, 1945–1975* (New York: Cambridge University Press, 1998).

6   Manley, *The Politics of Finance*, p. 29.

7   Richard L. Lyons, "GOP Leaders Join Democrats of South in Rules Unit Battle," *Washington Post*, January 8, 1963, p. A2.

8   Richard L. Lyons, "28 Republicans Join in Backing Administration," *Washington Post*, January 10, 1963, pp. A1 and A7.

9   Richard L. Lyons, "2 Proven Supporters of Kennedy Named to Ways and Means Committee," *Washington Post*, January 15, 1963, p, A1.

10 "Means and Ways," *Washington Post*, January 16, 1963, p. A18.

11 Richard W. Bolling, *Defeating the Leadership's Nominee in the House Democratic Caucus* (Syracuse, NY: Inter-University Case Program, 1965).

12 Elsie Carper, "Fear of Home Rule by Southerners Seen in Naming District Committee; Local Leaders Sense Double-Cross," *Washington Post*, January 31, 1963, pp. A1 and A11.

13 "Question of Leadership," *Washington Post*, February 4, 1963, p. A14.

14 Drew Pearson, "Washington Merry-Go-Round: Albert's in Middle of House Troika," *Washington Post*, February 19, 1963, p. B21.

15 Nick Bryant, *The Bystander: John F. Kennedy and the Struggle for Black Equality* (New York: Basic Books, Perseus Book Group, 2006), p. 389.

16 Taylor Branch, *Parting the Waters: America in the King Years, 1954–1963* (New York: Touchstone, Simon & Schuster, 1988), p. 711.

17 O'Brien, *No Final Victories*, pp. 145–46.

18 Andrew Cohen, *Two Days in June: John F. Kennedy and the 48 Hours That Made History* (Toronto: Signal, McClelland & Stewart, 2014).

19 President John F. Kennedy, *Public Papers of the Presidents of the United States, 1963* (Washington, DC: U.S. Government Printing Office, 1964), pp. 468–71.

20 Cohen, *Two Days in June*, p. 339.

21 Jason Sokol, *All Eyes Are Upon Us: Race and Politics from Boston to Brooklyn* (New York: Basic Books, 2014).

22 Data derived from the 1961, 1962, and 1963 annual editions of the *Congressional Quarterly Almanac*.

23 Equal Pay Act of 1963, approved June 10, 1963 (77 Stat. 56-57). *Congress and the Nation, 1945–1964*, p. 640.

24 Kate Clifford Larson, *Rosemary: The Hidden Kennedy Daughter* (Boston: Houghton, Mifflin, 2015).

25 U.S. Misery Index.com, accessed January 19, 2015.

26 Congressional Quarterly, "Rights, Tax Bills Share Top Priority," *Washington Post*, July 10, 1963, p. B2.

27 Ted Wismer, *Listening In: The Secret White House Recordings of John F. Kennedy* (New York: Hyperion, 2012).

28 *Congress and the Nation, 1945–1964*, pp. 134–35. The Nuclear Test Ban Treaty. Concluded August 5, 1963 and approved by the Senate, September 24, 1963 (14 UST. 1313-1387).

29 Alfred Steinberg, *Sam Johnson's Boy: A Close-Up of the President from Texas* (New York: Macmillan, 1968), pp. 29–30.

30 Rowland Evans and Robert Novak, "Inside Report: Pressuring the Speaker," *Washington Post*, August 9, 1963, p. A17.

31 *Congress and the Nation, 1945–1964*, p. 1598.

32 Accounts of the meeting included Taylor Branch, *Parting the Waters: America in the King Years, 1954–1963* (New York: Touchstone, Simon & Schuster, 1988), pp. 883–87; Lucy C. Barber, *Marching on Washington: The Forging of an American Tradition* (Berkeley: University of California Press, 2002), p. 173, with a photo.

33 Thomas C. Reeves, *A Question of Character: A Life of John F. Kennedy* (New York: The Free Press, 1991), p. 359.

34 Richard Reeves, *President Kennedy: Profile of Power* (New York: Simon & Schuster, 1993), p. 581.

35 John Herbers, "Wallace Urges Racial 'Reality'; Scores the Advice of 'Theorists,'" *NYT*, September 6, 1963, p. 14.

36 Thurston Clarke, *JFK's Last Hundred Days: The Transformation of a Man and the Emergence of a Great President* (New York: Penguin, 2013).

37 Evelyn Lincoln, *Kennedy and Johnson* (New York: Holt, Rinehart and Winston, 1968), p. 191.

38 Tyler Abell, email to author, July 2, 2015.

39 *The Gallup Poll: Public Opinion 1935–1971* (New York: Random House, 1972); Gallup Poll release date January 19, 1963, on p. 1800; and release date November 10, 1963, on p. 1850.

40 *CQWR* initially reported a floor success rate of 87.1% for Kennedy but in subsequent accounts, that number was lowered to 83.1%. See "Presidential Victories on Votes in Congress, 1953–2007," in Norman J. Ornstein, Thomas E. Mann, and Michael J. Malbin, eds., *Vital Statistics on Congress, 2008* (Washington, DC: The Brookings Institution, CQ Press, 2008), pp. 144–45, and updated with annual *Congressional Quarterly Almanacs*.

41 *CQWR*, October 23, 1964, p. 2569.

42 "How the President Persuades Congress," *NYT*, October 27, 1963, p. 207.

43 Stewart Alsop, "The Failure of Congress," *The Saturday Evening Post*, December 7, 1963, pp. 23–25. Quotation is from p. 24.

44 Robert J. Donovan, "Dilatory Congress May Have to Stay after School," *BG*, September 2, 1963, p. 34.

45 James MacGregor Burns, *The Deadlock of Democracy: Four-Party Politics in America* (Englewood Cliffs, NJ: Prentice-Hall, 1963).

46 Charles Bartlett, "Civil Rights Bill May be Too Strong," *Boston Globe*, October 6, 1963, p. 68.

47 Jeff Shesol, *Mutual Contempt: Lyndon Johnson, Robert Kennedy, and the Feud That Defined a Decade* (New York: W. W. Norton, 1997), p. 146.

48 Bobby Baker with Larry L. King, *Wheeling and Dealing: Confessions of a Capitol Hill Operator* (New York: W. W. Norton, 1978) and his oral history with the U.S. Senate Historical Office. Todd S. Purdum's "Sex in the Senate: Bobby Baker's Salacious Secret History of Capitol Hill," in *POLITICO* (November 19, 2013) encapsulated some of the more noteworthy episodes from Baker's oral history.

49 Robert G. Baker oral history interview with Donald Ritchie, U.S. Senate Historical Office, June 1, 2009, p. 71.

50 David J. Garrow, "The FBI and Martin Luther King," *The Atlantic*.com (July/August 2002).

51 Evelyn Lincoln, *Kennedy and Johnson* (New York: Holt, Reinhart and Winston, 1968), p. 205.

52 "Knocko McCormack Dies, Ending an Era; Politician was 67," *BG*, November 18, 1983, pp. 1, 24.

53 "2000 Pay Last Tribute to Edw. M'Cormack Sr.," *BG*, November 21, 1963, p. 44.

54 Ronnie Dugger, "Squabbling in Democratic Party Clouds Kennedy Tour of Texas," *Washington Post*, November 20, 1963, p. A2; and Edward T. Folliard, "Texas Feud to Test Kennedy's Political Skill during Visit," *Washington Post*, November 21, 1963, p. A9.

21

A Legislative Legacy Built upon a Tragedy

In the evening of November 22, Air Force One returned to Andrews Air Force Base with Lyndon B. Johnson, the 36th President of the United States, a new First Lady, and a bronze casket containing the body of John F. Kennedy, the 35th President, accompanied by his 34-year-old widow. A visibly shaken Lyndon Johnson took the oath of office on Air Force One as it flew back to Washington with President Kennedy's casket on board. Johnson was now president. The world had turned upside down.

Speaker John McCormack had just returned to Washington the day before following the burial of his brother Edward in Boston the previous week. John received the news from a reporter while he had lunch in the House dining room with two key aides, Dr. Martin T. Sweig and Edward Fitzgerald. He was unsteady and in one eyewitness account[1]: "[John] suffered a severe attack of dizziness. He started to rise, reeled, and began to lose consciousness. He raised a hand to his eyes, sank back in his seat and sat trembling." He then declaimed, "My God . . . My God. What are we coming to?"[2] John realized immediately that he was now next in line to the presidency.[3] Among other security concerns, it became a "burning issue of whether or not Speaker of the House McCormack [would be] receiving Secret Service protection as the constitutional successor to Lyndon Johnson."[4] John wanted no such protection, but would the choice be his?

Next in line

John returned to his office and met with Majority Leader Carl Albert and Armed Services Chair Carl Vinson of Georgia, who had succeeded Sam Rayburn as the dean of the House, the chamber's senior-most member. Albert and fellow Oklahoman U.S. Representative Ed Edmondson, a former FBI agent, contacted the FBI's Cartha DeLoach in hopes of obtaining protection for John. In their initial request, they described that "utter confusion and hysteria reigned" in John's office. Edmondson then called Jim Rowley, the chief of the U.S. Secret Service, to gain protection for John. Dr. Martin Sweig, John's administrative assistant, had already contacted the FBI requesting assistance, but it was the Secret Service and not the FBI that was responsible for protection. Later that afternoon, two men knocked on John McCormack's door on the 8th floor at the Hotel Washington. They identified themselves as Secret Service men, and since he was now next in line to the presidency, he would receive their protection. Having voted for the Presidential Succession Act of 1947, John was very well aware of where the House Speaker was in the line of succession. As described by journalist Jim Bishop[5]:

The Speaker refused to admit the two men. He was brusque. It was not necessary for them to tell him he was the next man. He and Mrs. McCormack were averse to altering their private lives in the shadow of the Secret Service. He would not have these men accompany him in an automobile or stand over Mrs. McCormack in the shops. "Please," he said softly as he could, "get out of the hall."

John was driven to Andrews Air Force Base along with a motorcade of House members to await the arrival of Air Force One. He joined fellow dignitaries who assembled at Andrews to meet the plane with its tragic cargo. The most distressed of those assembled was Attorney General Robert F. Kennedy, who bolted up the stairs to comfort his sister-in-law, the newly widowed Jacqueline Kennedy. Accounts vary, but it is reported that Bob Kennedy barely looked at the new president and brushed past him in his effort to console Jackie. For two men like Lyndon Johnson and Bob Kennedy who had a long history of distrust and acrimony, this moment was the exclamation point.

The crisis would have been worse had the early reports of Vice President Lyndon Johnson suffering a heart attack been true. While that rumor was untrue, there was a troubling account by Gerald Blaine, a member of the Secret Service's "Kennedy Detail," who described an incident outside Johnson's Washington residence early on the morning of November 23. Johnson, who had a tendency to urinate whenever and wherever the call of nature occurred, was nearly shot to death by an anxious Blaine who had his Thompson submachine gun at the ready when he heard a suspicious rustling sound outside the house.[6] Johnson emerged and no shot was fired. As described in his book: "Blaine struggled to regain his composure as the reality of what had just happened washed over him. Fourteen hours after losing a president, the nation had come chillingly close to losing another one." Although John McCormack's name is not mentioned in the book, a few news stories about the book correctly pointed out that John would have become president had Agent Blaine pulled the trigger.[7]

Kennedy was the first president to be killed while under Secret Service protection, and anxiety levels within the agency grew as public dismay about their inability to protect Kennedy led to heightened criticism.[8] Not helping matters was that next in line Speaker John McCormack sought to cancel Secret Service protection as a violation of his and Mrs. McCormack's personal privacy. While McCormack aide Martin Sweig immediately requested FBI protection for John, a problem developed.

The FBI memo states[9]:

Both men, armed, reported to Dr. Sweig at approximately 4:35. I additionally issued appropriate instructions to SAC Gillies of the Washington Field Office that there should be an around-the-clock surveillance of the Speaker until further notice. . . . I told Agents—and—and SAC Gillies that if our Agents are challenged at any time by Secret service men they should exhibit their credentials and explain to the Secret service men that our Agents were present at the specific request of the Speaker's Office.

The surveillance did not last long. The following day, DeLoach sent another memo to Mr. Mohr[10]:

At 11 a.m. this morning, SAC Gillies of the Washington Field Office advised me that our Agents are having a somewhat difficult time in carrying out their responsibilities. Mrs. McCormack found out through hotel authorities that Metropolitan police were maintaining a room down the hall from the Speaker's suite in the Washington Hotel . . .

At 3 a.m. this morning, the Speaker, wearing only his pajama pants and an undershirt, visited a public bathroom at the end of the corridor. At approximately 7:45 a.m. this morning, the Speaker, after having breakfast in his suite, pushed the breakfast cart down the hotel corridor to the room in which the police officer and our Agents were sitting. The Speaker suddenly crashed open the door which had been left slightly ajar. He confronted our Agents and the police officer and asked them to identify themselves.

The Agents, acting under our instructions, fully identified themselves and advised the Speaker that his office had specifically requested this action. The Speaker indicated his appreciation in a very cordial manner. He was very firm, however, in insisting that no protection be afforded him.

Declaring that "the Nation's Capital is full of fear and hysteria and he did not want to give rise to further feelings in this regard," John countermanded the request the following day. John valued his privacy, and with his increasingly frail 80-year-old wife, he wished to minimize any disruptions in the well-ordered life he and Harriet had spent in Washington for 35 years. He refused the security detail. Another account of the Secret Service's efforts to protect John was shared by former House Speaker Jim Wright, who told of how members of the Secret Service dressed as priests tried to follow McCormack in those vestments. When John continued to encounter the same "priest," he discerned the ruse and exploded once again, accusing the Secret Service of desecrating priestly garb.[11]

John McCormack was a tough guy, but none of his childhood hardships in the Irish tenements of Boston's Andrew Square prepared him to be a heartbeat away from the White House. It deeply humbled him. No American in the twentieth century had traveled as far as John McCormack. Having overcome enormous obstacles to gain his prestigious post, John had no intention of surrendering to fear at this time in his life.

Lingering questions

The murder of President Kennedy more than a half century ago continues to haunt the nation with each year producing new accusations labeling presumed perpetrators.[12] Was it the Russians, embarrassed over the Cuban Missile Crisis? Or was it Fidel Castro's Cubans fearful of another attempted invasion of the island? Was it southern white racists infuriated at the civil rights thrust of the Kennedy Administration? Or was it the mob and the Mafia that wished to return to their corrupt haven in Havana and stop criminal prosecutions launched by the Kennedy Justice Department? The most insidious accusations link the murder to the government itself. Was it the Central Intelligence Agency still smarting over the rebuke of their failed Bay of Pigs scheme?

Or was it the FBI, who's Director J. Edgar Hoover had long hated the Kennedy brothers? Or the most insidious of all, was it conservative wealthy Texans loyal to Vice President Lyndon B. Johnson who feared that LBJ would be removed from the 1964 Democratic ticket? That the likeliest assassin was a young misfit veteran with a Russian-born wife and a 20-dollar mail-order rifle was much too banal an explanation to accept. Since this was an event of world-altering importance, the presumed villains had to be of comparable stature. But that was not the case.

Funeral arrangements

William Manchester's monumental but controversial opus *The Death of a President* vividly captured the tension surrounding the memorial service in the Capitol. Jackie's brother-in-law Sargent Shriver announced, "Jackie's decided about tomorrow. She wants [Senate Majority Leader Mike] Mansfield to deliver the eulogy in the rotunda."[13] Mrs. Kennedy's desires that there be only one eulogist, and the Senate leader at that, would have excluded the House and its Speaker John McCormack from participating in the service. House Doorkeeper William "Fishbait" Miller "flatly told Shriver that Mrs. Kennedy would have to withdraw her request or settle for a compromise." The reason was simple, as Fishbait explained[14]:

> That part of the Capitol is under the jurisdiction of the House. It belongs to the Speaker. . . . If you have any request concerning the rotunda, it will have to be made to the Speaker. . . . That's going to [be] the Congressional part of the funeral, and you can't just walk in and say Mike Mansfield's going to speak, whatever Jackie's wish. You might hurt the Speaker's feelings.

It is doubtful if Jackie cared one whit about John McCormack's feelings, but she backed off. Whether her original request was because Mrs. Kennedy wanted no eulogy from John McCormack, the factional leader of Jack's home state rivals, or because she was simply unmindful of Capitol protocol did not matter. John McCormack, the Speaker of the House, would be one of the eulogists.

Two days after the assassination, the nation's major leaders—House Speaker John McCormack, Senate Majority Leader Mike Mansfield, and Chief Justice Earl Warren—gathered in the Rotunda of the Capitol to eulogize the fallen leader. The speeches produced different reactions. Mansfield spoke first, then Warren, and then McCormack. Manchester's book took the measure of the three speeches and reactions to them. Both Mansfield and Warren's speeches elicited comment[15]:

> No one criticized McCormack, because he did not say anything, but the Chief Justice's strong denunciation of hatemongering had a mixed reception. . . . Mike Mansfield, however was by far the most controversial of the three. Like Warren, he grasped the essence of the Dallas crime—"the bigotry, the hatred, prejudice, and the arrogance which converged in that moment of horror to strike him down"—but

in its imagery and high diction his address was altogether different. It was, indeed, an authentic masterpiece.

Mansfield's was the speech that most moved Jackie.

On Tuesday, November 26, the president's casket was laid to rest in the Arlington National Cemetery. Presiding over the religious portion of the service was Boston's Richard Cardinal Cushing, John McCormack's fellow Southie and his confessor.

A photograph and its impact

The 88th Congress was still in session and the nation's business had to get done. On November 27, 1963, following five days of official mourning, new President Lyndon B. Johnson appeared before a joint session of Congress in the Hall of the U.S. House of Representatives where he had once served for 12 years and where Jack Kennedy had served for six.

It was then that the fateful photograph of soon-to-be 72-year-old Speaker of the House of Representatives John McCormack of Massachusetts and 86-year-old Carl Hayden of Arizona, the president pro tempore of the Senate, was taken. It was a disquieting image. The Presidential Succession Act of 1947 had placed the Speaker of the House next in line to the president when the vice presidency fell vacant, and the Senate's president pro tempore was next in line to the Speaker. The intent of the law was to guarantee that elected officials and not appointed ones would fill the vacancies created by the departures of the executive officers.[16]

Many Americans were aware that President Johnson had a heart condition that had kept him out of the 1956 nomination battle and its recurrence had been widely rumored at the time of Kennedy's assassination. For a nation barely recovering from the abrupt loss of its vibrant, youngest elected president, the sight of the McCormack-Hayden tandem was deeply disturbing. As described by Michael Beschloss in his compilation of President Johnson's tape recordings, "Many Americans were frightened at the sight of the two elderly men next in line for the presidency behind LBJ, who had once suffered a massive heart attack."[17]

President Johnson was deeply concerned as well, and on December 23, 1963, he sent a two-page letter to be cosigned by John McCormack focusing on the procedures to be followed "in the event of my inability to exercise the powers and duties of the Presidency."[18] Should that occur, Johnson said that "the Speaker of the House would serve as Acting President, exercising the powers and duties of the Office until the inability had ended."

The photograph had a lasting effect upon the Constitution. It led to a successful effort initiated by Kennedy loyalist Senator Birch Bayh (Dem-Ind.) to gain passage of the 25th Amendment to the Constitution, the "Presidential Succession and Disability Amendment."[19] Bayh's proposed amendment allowed the Congress to fill the vice presidency if it became vacant and limited the operation of the 1947 Presidential Succession Act. It also provided guidelines for dealing with presidential infirmities should they occur. LBJ was fearful that his support for the amendment might be seen as a "slap at McCormack."[20] While John McCormack appreciated the passage of the amendment lifting the burden from his shoulders, he did not appreciate the references to his age that aided in its passage.[21]

The Warren Commission: While the nation held its collective breath over seeing these apparent relics of Congress Past next in line, Johnson first called John McCormack on November 29 to assemble the members of the commission to investigate the assassination.[22] Chief Justice Warren would be the chair. McCormack had just told LBJ that Majority Whip Hale Boggs was planning on conducting his own investigation. Johnson wished to forestall this and agreed to include Boggs on the panel. McCormack was concerned that three southerners would be on the commission: Senator Dick Russell of Georgia, Republican Senator John Sherman Cooper of Kentucky, and Hale Boggs of Louisiana. To Texan LBJ, Kentucky was not a southern state. They both agreed that Gerald Ford's home state of Michigan was a northern state, and the two later additions, former CIA director Allen Dulles of New York and former World Bank President John J. McCloy from Philadelphia, provided sufficient regional balance.

The lasting friendship

Speaker John McCormack was far more comfortable with President Johnson, the protégé of his dear friend Sam Rayburn, than he was with the youthful and brash Kennedy entourage. To non-Bostonians, it appeared that Jack Kennedy and John McCormack shared religion, ethnic origins, and birthplaces. To the more knowledgeable Boston Irish, it was their different social and educational experiences that characterized them, not their similarities. In Lyndon Johnson, another "poor boy made good," McCormack perceived a political soul mate. Their formal correspondence began in 1940 when John responded to the gift of a box of pecans that Johnson, always eager to please those in higher places, had given to John after his election as Majority Floor Leader. The earliest record of correspondence between the two men in the LBJ Library is a letter from McCormack thanking Johnson for his thoughtfulness[23]:

> Dear Lyndon;—
>   It was great of you to think of Mrs. McCormack and myself and we will both enjoy eating the Pecan's, and when we are, we will be thinking of you.
>
> > Cordially yours,
> > *John*

Their interactions over the next 30 years would be those of mutual admiration and affection with frequent communication between the two men and their wives, Harriet and Lady Bird. Less than a month after Johnson had taken office, he and Harriet McCormack shared a pleasant exchange in which Harriet remarked, "You're doing a beautiful piece of work, and when it's over, you're going to be the finest president that ever was here . . . and I hope God will be good to you."[24]

Their shared affection for Speaker Rayburn continued to bind them together, and neither John McCormack nor President Johnson ever forgot the significant role that Mr. Sam played in their personal and professional lives. This sentiment was evident in this 1968 letter from Johnson to McCormack responding to a personal gift[25]:

> Dear Mr. Speaker and Miss Harriet:
>
> There have been many days in my life when I have been deeply touched by your generous gifts of heart.
>
> But today outshines them all. Your gift of the Remington sculpture—which I will always think of as the Rayburn-Remington sculpture—sets in bronze the goodness and great loyalty that you both have always brought me.
>
> I am doubly delighted with your gift because it links us all to our dear friend, Mr. Sam. It is a beautiful reminder of our common debt to his leadership and friendship—even though he did think this piece showed "an ugly Indian and even uglier horse."
>
> Just as Sam Rayburn kept this sculpture near, where you could come by and rub it up once in a while, I will keep it beside me—where I hope you will come to share it with me, together with the treasure of our affection.
>
> Lady Bird cannot wait to pick out a piece of honor for your gift. She is as thrilled as I am to possess it, and to know that our families will always be joined through this gem of American art and history.
>
> God bless you both, dear friends.
>
> Sincerely,
> *LBJ*

Even outside of their Rayburn connection, the two men were close, a stark contrast to McCormack's relationship with President Kennedy. Their personal friendship also appears in a letter from President Johnson to John McCormack on his 76th birthday, lauding him for his lifetime of public service and professional counsel[26]:

> There comes a time at least once a year when every fellow asks himself what he has done to justify his being here this year. On your birthday, you have more reasons for being here than nearly any one I know. Your wise and seasoned judgments, your progressive and compassionate principles, and your fearless loyalty to all that are worthy of it must give you the satisfaction that comes to few men. Lady Bird and Luci and I and all the other little Johnsons will always be grateful that you came our way.

Reporter Tom McNamara, writing on the House of Representatives for Drew Pearson, also remarked on the warm relationship between John and Lyndon midway through the Johnson presidency[27]:

Yet these two men, of different backgrounds, different religion, different upbringing, have worked as a team in putting across some of the most important legislation of any Congress in history. There are various reasons for this, not all known to the public. One is that the Speaker is a team player and a very loyal one. Almost every Saturday he meets with some of the extreme right wing, men opposed to much that Lyndon Johnson stands for. But when it comes to loyalty, Mr. Johnson comes first.

There may have been times when John made an unwise decision, as when he opposed the President's request to let Congress adjourn for the White House reception instead of holding its feet to the beautification bill. But never has John made a disloyal decision.

It was the deep and long-standing affection between LBJ and John that guaranteed that there would be no support from the Johnson White House for any Dick Bolling-Frank Thompson efforts to remove John from the speakership. Lyndon watched John's back.

The dual crises

In the immediate aftermath of Kennedy's assassination and Lyndon Johnson's succession, two crises transcended all other concerns. The first was the centrality of civil rights, the issue that Kennedy's assassination would not detour. Anthony Lewis, the author of *Gideon's Trumpet*, writing in the *New York Times*, emphasized how civil rights would define the legacy of Jack Kennedy and the presidency of Lyndon Johnson[28]:

> For Lyndon Johnson as for John Kennedy, the great challenge within the country is the cry for justice in race relations. History will judge the Johnson Administration, domestically, by its success in answering the cry. The fact is that the United States is in the midst of a revolution in race relations. It is a revolution of rising Negro impatience and expectations, of growing white guilt and emerging white fear.

Lewis's hope was that Johnson's southern roots would impel those committee chairs whose blatant resistance to the Kennedy Administration might be overcome. A similar theme was stressed by Roscoe Drummond of the *New York Herald-Tribune* in a syndicated column for the *Boston Globe*. Drummond wrote[29]:

> The only good thing to come in the wake of the act of hideousness by which an assassin's bullet took the life of President John F. Kennedy is the succession of Lyndon Johnson.
>
>   . . .
>
> My judgment is that there will be a great revulsion from this act of hideousness and that the movement through Congress of legislation to expand the boundaries of civil rights will proceed even more rapidly.

It was clear that well-meaning Americans had no intention of letting the Kennedy murder kill the quest for racial justice.

The second issue was the inability of the 88th Congress to address any meaningful legislation leading Walter Lippmann, the dean of American political analysts, to declare, "This has been a bad Congress and the country needs and deserves to have a better one than it has had."[30] This was a crisis of governance. It is not without irony that the two men whose work together would break through this latest governmental crisis and provide meaningful legislative change to the nation were the Austin-Boston connection of Texas-born President Lyndon Johnson and Boston-born Speaker John McCormack.

Early days

Now together in the nation's two most powerful posts, Speaker McCormack and President Johnson had the first test of their joint leadership in the closing days of the 1st Session of the 88th Congress. The Clean Air Act and the Vocational Education Act of 1963, both introduced by the Kennedy Administration, were quickly passed. The Clean Air Act was signed into law on December 17, 1963, and the Vocational Education Act on December 18.[31] Neither bill was a test of their leadership. The test was a nettlesome Kennedy Administration bill involving the sale of $250 million worth of wheat to the Soviet Union. It intended to alleviate the tensions of the Cold War that had brought the world to the edge of destruction just thirteen months earlier in the Cuban Missile Crisis.

Senator Karl Mundt (Rep-SD), an ally of the late Senator Joe McCarthy and a deeply committed Cold Warrior himself, attached an amendment to the agricultural appropriations bill preventing the Export-Import Bank from extending credit to the Soviet Union, thus blocking the Soviets from receiving American grain.[32] Johnson and Larry O'Brien, President Kennedy's congressional liaison, worked to get the amendment defeated in the Senate. O'Brien, unlike most of the Kennedy loyalists, remained in the Johnson Administration. Just four days after the Kennedy assassination, the Mundt amendment was defeated by a roll call vote of 57–35. Managing the Senate had never been a major problem for Lyndon Johnson.

The House was another matter. Iowa Republican Ben Jensen introduced an amendment similar to Mundt's in the House three weeks later. The amendment was passed and added to the House's version. This shifted the battle to the joint House-Senate conference committee. It had been 14 years since Johnson left the House and he was not one of its leaders as he had been in the Senate. This was a House led by John McCormack and Carl Albert, two close friends of his, but their commitment to Johnson's success was far less than that of LBJ's mentor, Sam Rayburn.

Johnson, working with McCormack and Albert, called the House back into a special session just days before Christmas and pushed them into accepting a second conference report without the Jensen amendment. At 7 in the morning on December 24, the House convened and a new conference report was accepted by a weary set of Representatives. The Senate accepted the conference report on December 30.

Figure 21.1 LBJ Aide Larry O'Brien with House Speaker John McCormack, Majority Leader Carl Albert and Majority Whip Hale Boggs, 1964 (Carl Albert Congressional Research Center).

To Lyndon Johnson, it meant, "At that moment, the power of the federal government began flowing back to the White House."[33] It is doubtful if Larry O'Brien appreciated LBJ's dismissal of Kennedy's Capitol Hill initiatives, but he alone of Kennedy's intimates understood that it was Johnson's insecurities which led him to make those self-aggrandizing claims which elevated him at the expense of others. To Members of Congress, the message was different. The mourning period for Jack Kennedy was clearly over and no holidays, no matter how sacred, would ever stand in the way of legislation desired by Lyndon Johnson. They were now on notice as to what was coming and when the whirlwind arrived, they had to hold on to their hats. There was a new sheriff in town. The legislative presidency of Lyndon Johnson had begun (Figure 21.1).

Second Session, 1964

"*Out-Roosevelting Roosevelt*": Johnson delivered his first State of the Union Address on January 8, 1964. After listening to it, Republican presidential hopeful Barry Goldwater declared to a Manchester, New Hampshire, audience, "I don't want to comment in detail until I have read the message . . . but from what I heard on the radio, it's my impression that he had out-Rooseveltled Roosevelt, out-Kennedyed Kennedy and made Truman look like some kind of a piker." He later commented, "I think he's out liberaled every liberal since 1932." Ironically, this statement frequently believed to have been said by LBJ himself was actually an insult delivered by his 1964 opponent on the campaign trail.[34]

When the Second Session of the 88th Congress opened on January 7, 1964, it had much unfinished business. The apparent deliberate dawdling of the mostly southern committee chairs in the Kennedy-led 1st Session would not be countenanced by Lyndon Johnson. This time, with a fellow southerner in the White House, the mostly southern chairs were less inclined to embarrass a president who was one of their own. President Johnson knew that he had a window of opportunity with this Congress. A grieving nation had reposed its trust in him and many Americans hoped that his fabled legislative skills would give the martyred President John Kennedy a legacy for historians to judge him worthy. Johnson also understood intellectually but did not wholly accept emotionally that he would never gain the personal popularity enjoyed by Kennedy. But he could fashion a legislative legacy that would well serve both Kennedy's memory and his own political future.

John McCormack turned 72 in December 1963 and serious concerns were raised about his age. It had been barely 15 months since the near-disastrous Cuban Missile Crisis that had been so adroitly handled by President Kennedy.[35] While the majority of Americans were clearly saddened by Kennedy's death, most seemed comforted by the presence of Lyndon Johnson in the White House. None of the other seven vice presidents who succeeded their deceased predecessor, including McKinley's successor Teddy Roosevelt or FDR's successor Harry Truman, had as much governmental experience as did Johnson. While Johnson's presence was reassuring, John McCormack's presence as the next in line was less so. Critical editorials included one from the western corner of Massachusetts. *The Berkshire Eagle* ran an editorial speculating that "it would not seem amiss for Mr. McCormack to recognize the incongruity of his present situation by stepping down as Speaker of the House so that a younger man can be elevated to the post which is now, in effect, the Vice Presidency."[36] At a Boston College event, Paul Scott of the Allen-Scott Report charged that "a small but powerful group of far-left labor leaders were behind the campaign to oust McCormack . . . an unofficial group in the House headed by [Representative Dick] Bolling."[37] Though John McCormack was not as beloved by Democrats in Congress as the late Speaker Rayburn, they did not dislike him enough to push him out, especially since as Rowland Evans and Robert Novak reported, Bolling was not very well liked either[38]:

The fact that Richard Bolling heads the new [policy] committee [cannot] be ignored. . . . But brilliant and articulate though he is, Bolling is not greatly beloved in the House. Indeed, some members of the new committee express deep concern over Bolling's role. Because of this, some have considered quitting.

Despite failing to block McCormack's becoming Speaker in 1961 and ousting him in 1963, Bolling's obsession with removing John from the speakership would continue throughout the decade.

As the desultory First Session of the 88th Congress came to a close, John McCormack reached out to Minority Leader Charlie Halleck in an effort to move legislation, and as reported by the *Post*'s Chalmers Roberts[39]:

[He] did something the late Speaker Sam Rayburn would have never thought of doing: He took the floor to detail his and Albert's efforts to strike a deal with Halleck. It all sounded very unseemly out in the open though everybody, including the reporters hanging out in the cloakrooms, was aware of what was going on through the long, weary hours.

Knowing that John McCormack had no intention of surrendering the speakership, Johnson went to work with John and Senate Leader Mansfield. Within a few weeks a number of bills that had been buried in committee now came to the floor.

The Revenue Act: First among these was the Revenue Act of 1964, a major Kennedy-supported overhaul of the existing tax code. Shepherded by the increasingly powerful Ways and Means Chair Wilbur Mills, the bill passed the House in September 1963 but it was stalled in the Senate. Julian Zelizer contended that Mills filled a "power vacuum" created by "Rayburn's death, his replacement by a politically timid John McCormack, and the reform of Howard Smith's powerful Rules Committee."[40] Renewed prosperity had given the new president an opportunity to reduce taxes. The Revenue Act reduced the existing 20-to-91% tax rates to 14-to-70% tax rates by 1965; reduced the 18% withholding tax to 14%; and corporate tax rates from 52% to 48%.[41] Among other provisions, the act tightened tax rules governing the operation of stock option plans and sick pay exclusions, and provided stricter limits on tax deductions resulting from casualty and theft losses. It increased taxes on sales resulting from "accelerated" depreciation practices and reduced the capital gains tax on taxpayers 65 and older, and it created a new deduction for moving expenses, liberalized child-care deductions, broadened investment tax credits, and provided a minimum standard deduction. The Revenue Act of 1964 was a major fiscal overhaul, and it became law on February 26, 1964.

Civil rights

The House resumed work on President Kennedy's civil rights package. Howard Smith had already told Johnson that there would be no action on the bill before the year's end and LBJ and John considered a discharge petition—an infrequently used procedure to move legislation to the House floor that had been bottled up in a committee. At a leadership breakfast on December 3, John told LBJ that "the congressional leadership did not like the idea of a discharge petition because that had wider implications. Whatever the merits of the bill, a discharge petition could undermine not just Smith but the entire committee system which gave chairmen such power."[42] He further added that "he never signed discharge petitions but assured Johnson he would sign this mighty damn quick."

The bill now known as HR 7152 moved through the Rules Committee on January 30, 1964. Despite Johnson's commitment to action and the willingness of congressional leaders to work with him, the legislative agenda got bogged down once again even though the House Rules Committee had been relatively tamed.[43] Following nine days of animated floor debate, the bill passed the House handily 290–130.[44] While 141 northern Democrats, 11 southern Democrats, and 138 Republicans voted for the bill, those opposing it were 4 northern Democrats, 92 southern Democrats, and 34 Republicans.[45] After the vote, Johnson called McCormack's office while John was meeting with Harriet and Manny Celler. Johnson said, "Congratulations, I'm proud of you . . . you had great leadership. I am going to put out a statement commending you." Later, McCormack said, "And it helped the cause throughout the country . . . it didn't bring any bitterness around, which is important in the South, as I see it, next fall."[46] Speaker John McCormack and the House leadership had delivered for the Kennedy legacy and the Johnson presidency. Sadly, John's hopeful assumption that southern bitterness would not arise was dashed before the year was out.

John McCormack was always very careful with civil rights legislation. He always voted for civil rights bills but did not speak for them. He maintained a delicate balancing act between his conservative southern allies and northern African Americans and Jews. Racial and religious prejudice was not part of his life's baggage.

During the debate over the civil rights bill, D. B. Hardeman, Sam Rayburn's onetime aide and biographer, had been working for Democratic Whip Hale Boggs. When a question was raised about John McCormack's lack of prejudice and his depth of commitment to the bill, Hardeman vividly recounted an episode that John had with an anti-Semite in Boston that led McCormack to knock the antagonist "sprawling across the floor."[47]

More than most big-city Democrats, John McCormack knew the perils of playing "us-them" politics. His success in Boston had been built around coalitions of Irish, Italian, and Eastern European Catholics and Jews. Given the size of his pluralities back home, even Yankee Protestants frequently cast their votes for John McCormack. Us-them politics may deepen the electoral commitment of supporters to your candidacy, but the downside of that strategy limits your ability to govern effectively. Compromise is difficult when the immutable aspects of your opponent's race, religion, and even social class are used to drive a wedge between you and them. John McCormack, the son of a Canadian Scot whose ethnic identity was unknown to his constituents, also had personal reasons to fear the divisiveness of us-them politics.

Senate Resistance: It would be in the Senate where the knives would be the longest.[48] Mississippi's James O. Eastland ensnared Kennedy's original civil rights bill in the Senate Judiciary Committee. Eastland was a genial but determined segregationist who would not let the bill leave the committee in its present form. Intense pressure from northern Democrats and many Republicans got the bill out of the Judiciary Committee and onto the Senate floor. There another hazard awaited—the filibuster, the preferred tool of the Senate's segregationists.

Southern Democrats knew how to work the Senate filibuster to perfection. Once the floor had been gained, a Senator possessed the right to recognize those who wished to speak next. Southern Senators would only recognize one another. The consequence was that the filibuster went on for weeks. It was not a happy picture that the Senate presented to the nation and to the world. No one knew this better than President Lyndon Johnson, who as Senate leader had tried to break their civil rights filibusters in 1957 and 1960.

From 1917 through 1963, 28 votes had been cast in the Senate to bring an end to a filibuster through cloture. Of those 28 votes, eleven had dealt with civil rights bills—two antilynching bills in 1938; three anti-poll tax bills in 1942, 1944, and 1946; three FEPC bills, one in 1946 and two in 1950; two literacy test bills in 1962; and the Civil Rights Act of 1960. All eleven votes had failed and in only three cases had the pro-civil rights forces been able to gain a simple majority, not even close to the extraordinary two-thirds one required for cloture.[49] The prospects looked poor.

The Senate leadership was committed to the bill, but the Senate leadership differed from that of the House. Senate Leader Mike Mansfield was very different from Johnson.[50] An Irish-descended pipe-smoking Catholic from the coal mining towns of Montana, Mansfield, was steeped in the mountain state tradition of individualism and preferred not to impose his will upon his fellow Senators. Second-in-command to Mansfield and the floor manager of the Civil Rights Bill was Minnesota Senator Hubert Humphrey, whose 1948 civil rights resolution had led to the walkout of southern Democrats from the presidential party. An old adversary confronted Humphrey on the Senate floor—J. Strom Thurmond of South Carolina, the "Dixiecrats" presidential nominee in 1948. Once again, a success of Hubert Humphrey's would drive him from the Democratic Party. The 1948 defection was temporary, but before this year was out, the dyspeptic Strom Thurmond would join the Republican Party on September 16, 1964, in support of Republican presidential nominee Barry Goldwater, and would remain a Republican until his death in 2003.

Dick Russell, leader of the resistance

The leader of the southern opposition was Georgia's wily Senator Richard Brevard Russell, Jr., who rarely raised his voice. Dick Russell was sworn in as Senator on January 12, 1933, following a special election to replace the late William J. Harris, a subcabinet member of Woodrow Wilson's Administration[51] where he served with FDR. Dick Russell entered the Senate a few weeks before FDR's New Deal's 100 Days. Although Russell was only 35 at the time, he had already served as the Speaker of the Georgia House (1927–31) and as the state's Governor (1931–33).[52] Dick Russell was a political prodigy and it was widely believed that with enough accrued seniority, he would eventually move to the top of the Senate's power structure. When the 30-year-old Ted Kennedy first arrived in the Senate in 1963, he made a courtesy call to Dick Russell's office in the hopes of charming the skeptical Russell. Russell's reaction was, indeed, skeptical[53]: "When the delicate subject of Kennedy's age came up, the young senator mentioned that the Georgian too had been a very young man when he had first come to the Senate. 'That's true, son,' Russell is alleged to have remarked, 'but you have to keep in mind that I'd already been governor of my state.'"

Russell chaired the Immigration Committee from 1937 to 1947 but it was folded into the Judiciary Committee by the Legislative Reorganization Act of 1946, so Russell had to wait another five years until he could resume chairing a standing committee. That committee was Armed Services, and he held that post for 16 years (1951–53, 1955–69), ten of which were served with Lyndon Johnson.[54] In 1969, Russell succeeded his friend, Louisiana's late Senator Allen Ellender, as chair of the powerful Senate

Appropriations Committee also becoming Senate president pro tempore. These were the posts he held at the time of his death in January 1971.

Russell flirted with presidential politics in 1948 and 1952. In 1948, Russell mounted the most serious challenge on the convention floor to President Harry Truman. He received 263 votes at that year's fragmented convention, all of which came from the states of the Confederacy.[55] President Truman received his only Confederate state votes from North Carolina. Unlike Governors Strom Thurmond of South Carolina and Fielding Wright of Mississippi, Russell remained within the Democratic Party. He did not join the Dixiecrat walkout. Dick Russell was a pragmatic ideologue. Leaving the party in the hands of your enemies was not smart politics, and Dick Russell was a very smart politician.

Despite its surface glamour and conviviality, Washington can be a very lonely city. For leaders of the Congress like Dick Russell whose seniority was achieved because many of those with whom they served had either died, been defeated, or retired, peer companionship was difficult to find as time passed. This led many to seek out the companionship of younger members of the chamber, and a sagacious junior member will provide a senior member with companionship and an opportunity to develop a mentor-protégé relationship.

LBJ, a professional protégé

Lyndon Johnson's quest for politically connected "daddies" led him to Dick Russell when he entered the Senate. Johnson was especially successful with men who had no sons. Johnson's relationship with Alvin Wirtz, the Texan power broker who sponsored him early in his career, was explained by one of Johnson's biographers[56]: "Texas regulars continued to find Wirtz a thorn under the saddle and a major mystery. One question that bothered them was his untiring effort to promote Johnson. Some said it was the result of having only daughter Ida Mae at home, and no sons."

After serving as "Rayburn's boy" to the childless Speaker of the House, Johnson moved to the Senate in 1949 and to the lifelong bachelor Dick Russell. Johnson and his wife Lady Bird opened their house on Sunday afternoons to Russell, and he rewarded Lyndon with an inside track to the Senate leadership.[57] Russell knew that the post-1948 Democratic presidential party would have to accommodate the aspirations of northern urban blacks. He also knew that he had too much racial baggage to lead the Democrats in the Senate, so in 1952, he opted out of the leadership race and urged his fellow southerners to support Lyndon Johnson, one of the very few southern Democrats who was elected in 1948 on a platform less racist than his opponent.

Russell knew that the Civil Rights bill would pass, but he organized one of the most successful filibusters in the history of Congress to thwart it. All told, the 1964 southern filibuster lasted 57 days over a 73-day period. Ultimately, the Senate voted 71–29 to invoke cloture for the very first time on a civil rights bill. With the breaking of the filibuster on June 10, 1964, the Civil Rights Act of 1964 was passed with a vote of 73–27 on June 19. Northern Democrats voted for the bill 43–1, and while only three of

23 southern Democrats voted for it, Republican support for the bill was 27–6, with the most notable dissenter being Senator Barry Goldwater of Arizona, whose victory in the June 2 California primary over New York Governor Nelson Rockefeller guaranteed him the Republican presidential nomination.

The passage of the bill made no difference in parts of the rural South. On June 21, three civil rights activists—New Yorkers Michael Schwerner and Andrew Goodman and Mississippi African-American James Chaney went missing. In his call to John McCormack that afternoon, Johnson was fearful about their fate. He then called J. Edgar Hoover, no fan of civil rights, pushing him into a massive FBI presence that eventually broke the case. On August 4, a shallow grave revealed that all three men had been shot and burned by the Mississippi Klan. This was a painful reminder of the fearful cost of racism in America.

Johnson wanted the bill passed before the Republican nominating convention in mid-July and McCormack was able to get the conference report adopted without being held up by Howard Smith's Rules Committee. However, Smith successfully moved that an amendment adding "sex" as a protected class under the bill would prevent white women from being discriminated against in its enforcement. Whether Smith was truly sincere about protecting women or was trying to scuttle the bill has been debated for years but its addition has had long-term implications for the implementation of affirmative action programs.[58]

When Johnson signed the bill on July 2, he presented one of the pens to the Reverend Martin Luther King, Jr., who was featured prominently in the official photograph of the bill's signing. Over Johnson's left shoulder was House Judiciary Committee Chair Emanuel Celler, who drafted the bill, and standing beside him was John McCormack, who as Speaker had helped facilitate its passage through the U.S. House of Representatives. It would be one of many triumphs that Lyndon Johnson and John McCormack would enjoy as the two worked closely to complete the unfinished goals of Franklin Roosevelt's New Deal (Figure 21.2).

The act expanded federal powers to protect voting rights. It granted authority to the Justice Department to participate in a lawsuit involving the failures of state or local authorities to desegregate public accommodations, public facilities, and public schools.[59] Approved July 2, 1964, it outlawed discrimination in federally funded projects, and the denial of equal job opportunities in businesses and unions with more than 25 members. It also created a Community Relations Service and an Equal Opportunity Commission to end employment discrimination. Once the Civil Rights Act was passed, Congress moved swiftly to deal with its other delayed issues. After all, a presidential election awaited their parties and their own congressional elections might be somewhat dicey as a consequence of the public's reaction to the Civil Rights Act. The energy level in Congress subsided after the months of wrangling over the Civil Rights bill. President Johnson and Speaker McCormack put aside a number of other measures, most notably antipoverty legislation in the following Congress with the hope that the 1964 election would continue the Democratic majority and the maintenance of their respective posts. Awaiting them was the nominating convention that each hoped would be free of contention.

Figure 21.2 President Johnson signs the Civil Rights Act of 1964 into law (Lyndon B. Johnson Library and Museum).

The 1964 Republican Convention

Less than a month after the most far-reaching Civil Rights bill in history had been signed, the Republican Party—the party of Abraham Lincoln, the party that preserved the Union, and the party that freed the slaves—met in San Francisco to nominate as its presidential candidate, Barry Goldwater, who was one of only six Republican Senators to vote against the bill. A bitterly divided Republican party had rebuffed Nelson Rockefeller, the candidate of the party's "Eastern establishment," and nominated Goldwater for president and New York U.S. Representative and Republican National Chair William E. Miller for vice president.[60] In that convention, Senator Goldwater uttered his most defiant defense of his political philosophy by declaring, "Extremism in the defense of liberty is no vice. . . . Moderation in the pursuit of justice is no virtue."[61] Disgruntled Republicans remained in their seats but there was little Republican love for Goldwater east of the Alleghenies. A billboard at the Republican Convention that declared Goldwater's slogan, "In Your Heart, You Know He's Right," was challenged by a smaller sign with the slogan, "In Your Guts, You Know He's Nuts."

The 1964 Democratic Nomination

Johnson's Preconvention Campaign: For a successful politician, Lyndon Johnson was curiously skeptical about elections in general and primaries in particular. His tainted 1941 defeat to W. Lee "Pappy" O'Daniel in that year's special Senate primary was the source of that sentiment and was reaffirmed in his similarly tainted 87 vote victory in the 1948 Senate primary victory over former Texas Governor Coke Stevenson. Allegations of vote fraud in that contest left him saddled with the sarcastic sobriquet "Landslide Lyndon."[62] To protect himself in his 1960 presidential quest he got the Texas legislature to pass a law enabling him to run simultaneously for president and for reelection to the Senate. However, his avoiding the presidential primaries that year against JFK likely cost him the nomination.

After Johnson became president in 1963, one would assume that his risk-averse behavior would diminish. Despite strong showings of 70% plus approval in the public opinion polls, Johnson's risk-avoidance increased. Rather than competing himself in the preconvention primaries of 1964, Johnson had "surrogates,"—Wisconsin Governor John W. Reynolds, Indiana Governor Matthew E. Welsh, and Senator Daniel Brewster of Maryland—run for him so that he could avoid the electoral ambushes of Alabama's segregationist Governor George Wallace, who had parlayed his strident racist stances into national prominence.

John McCormack Presiding: The 1964 Democratic Convention met in Atlantic City, New Jersey. It would be the only one ever presided over by Speaker John McCormack in his stint as permanent chair. In the previous conventions in which he was an officer, he had maneuvered behind the scenes as the chairman of the platform-writing Resolutions Committee to iron out difficulties within the committee before they came to the convention floor for a divisive debate. John McCormack's role at Democratic conventions was very similar to his role in the U.S. House—an unpublicized consensus-builder and dissipater of conflict. McCormack liked a conflict-free Democratic convention and a conflict-contained House floor.

Drama appeared at the 1964 Democratic convention with the battle over the seating of the Mississippi delegation. Two delegations appeared to be seated: the regular one filled with the usual white-only faces of years past and a Mississippi Freedom Democratic Party (MFDP) delegation led by Fannie Lou Hamer and filled with the darker faces of Mississippi's long-oppressed black citizenry.[63] At his uncle John's elbow was Eddie McCormack, eager to resuscitate his political career after his shellacking in the 1962 Massachusetts Senate primary. There was tension within the Massachusetts delegation as liberal Ted Kennedy loyalists wanted the MFDP to be seated and the Mississippi regulars to be ousted, but LBJ wanted to minimize any public display of party disunity and John made sure that Johnson's wishes would be obeyed.[64]

At his uncle's behest, Eddie kept John apprised of efforts made by Hubert Humphrey's representative, Credentials Committee member Walter F. Mondale, his ally from the *Gideon v. Wainwright* case, to defuse this explosive situation. It was an ironic echo of the 1948 convention when then-U.S. Senate candidate Minneapolis Mayor Hubert Humphrey's strengthening of the FEPC plank spawned the Dixiecrat walkout. With a likely vice presidential bid on the horizon, Humphrey's people wanted to minimize the drama.

In the hope that neither delegation would storm out of the convention, a small compromise was arranged with two at-large seats assigned to the MFDP and most of the seats assigned to the white-only regulars. Neither delegation was satisfied. Most of Mississippi's regulars walked out. An effort by some MFDP members to sit in their vacated seats was thwarted by the convention organizers who removed the chairs. While the events had echoes of the 1948 walkout, most of the other southern delegates remained seated as the MFDP led a public march outside the hall. On balance, Permanent Chair John McCormack, Credentials Chair David Lawrence, and the Humphrey team had contained a conflict that had the potential for a public relations disaster. For the fourth time since 1944, John McCormack had delivered a relatively conflict-free Democratic convention.

In the aftermath of the 1964 Convention, the *Boston Globe* contended that John McCormack had emerged as the most powerful Democrat in Massachusetts, taking control back from the Kennedys, to whom he had lost power eight years earlier[65]:

> The specter of political power—especially in the Federal patronage department—in the Democratic Party of Massachusetts, passed from the hands of the Kennedys to President Johnson via the McCormacks. The effort was clear to TV viewers last week when they so often saw House Speaker John W. McCormack wielding the convention gavel, and his favorite nephew, Edward J. McCormack, standing close by on the speaker's platform.

As his running mate, President Johnson chose U.S. Senator Hubert H. Humphrey of Minnesota, the present Senate Majority Whip.[66] Humphrey stirred the convention by reciting a number of popular legislative measures that Goldwater had voted against and concluding each of them with the refrain, "But not Senator Goldwater."[67] The refrain was soon picked up by the delegates and resounded mightily throughout the convention hall. Much like FDR's 1936 renomination, Johnson insisted that both he and Senator Humphrey would be nominated by acclamation, so that no delegate votes would be recorded against the ticket. This was to be a stark contrast to the contentious Republican nomination battle in San Francisco.

The Gulf of Tonkin Resolution

As members of Congress returned to work after the conventions to close out the year and ready themselves for the upcoming election came news that American warships had been fired upon by North Vietnamese forces. Coming as it did during the season of the two national nominating conventions, there was no way to prevent the congressional response from being colored by partisan considerations. Congress chose to pass the Tonkin Gulf Resolution, approved August 10, 1964, that declared support for "the determination of the President, as Commander-In-Chief, to take all necessary measures to repel any armed attack against the forces of the United States and to prevent further aggression in Vietnam."[68] It affirmed the United States' commitment to assist any member of the protocol State of the Southeast

Asia Collective Defense Treaty which requested aid in defense of its freedom. Congressional support for the bill was unanimous, 414–0, in the House and nearly so in the Senate, 88–2, opposed only by Democratic Senators Wayne Morse of Oregon and Ernest Gruening of Alaska.[69]

In the absence of a formal declaration of war, both chambers supported LBJ's contentions about what happened in the Gulf of Tonkin, and President Johnson was able to use this particular resolution again and again to justify the massive troop buildup in South Vietnam. Little did Johnson realize that this buildup would lead to the horrible "Americanization" of a war which would end his dreams of a Great Society and deny him an exalted place in the pantheon of America's great presidents.

The 88th Congress concludes

Vietnamese troubles were more of a nuisance than a major focus and Congress moved on to other items. Apart from civil rights, the most ambitious of Johnson's legislative achievements of this year was the passage of the Economic Opportunity Act of 1964. Approved August 20, 1964, this act authorized ten separate programs under the supervision of the Director of the Office of Economic Opportunity designed to make a coordinated attack on the multiple causes of poverty.[70] Together these programs were designed to alleviate the combined problems of illiteracy, unemployment, and lack of public services that, according to the statistics of the Johnson Administration, left one-fifth of the nation's population impoverished. Poverty issues continued to be addressed by this Congress, and in that spirit it passed the Food Stamp Act of 1964 that provided for a permanent food stamp program financed by the Federal Government authorizing a $375 million appropriation to cover the federal costs of the program for the first three years (fiscal 1965–67). As enacted, the program was intended to aid low-income families to improve their diets.[71]

With Ways and Means Chair Wilbur Mills leading the way, additional revenue needs were met in part with the Interest Equalization Tax, approved September 2, 1964, that imposed a tax of 15% of value on new issues of foreign stock and a similar tax on bonds geared to their maturity, generally effective July 19, 1963, and continuing to the end of 1965.[72]

Kennedy holdover Interior Secretary Stewart Udall, a former House member, successfully convinced Congress to pass both the Wilderness Act of 1964 providing a National Wilderness Preservation System for land, water, mineral, and wildlife conservation purposes and the Land and Water Conservation Fund Act, approved September 3, 1964.[73]

The 88th Congress closed with the National Defense Education Act Amendments extending the provisions of the 1958 National Defense Education Act to June 30, 1968.[74] Approved October 16, 1964, it broadened the act to cover important new academic objectives, extended school aid programs to "federally impacted" areas for one year, and enacted an expanded library-services program. It also raised NDEA student loans from the existing \$135 million to \$195 million by 1968, and fellowships from 1,500 to 7,500 by 1968.

Nearing its close, the 88th Congress received a remarkable glowing review from the *Post*'s Robert Albright[75]:

> In one of history's classic ironies, the 88th Congress, once accused of dawdling and showing a slight taint of scandal, is emerging as one of the top legislative performers of our time. In quantity and quality, its actions, ranging from ratification of the nuclear test-ban treaty to a sweeping civil rights manifesto, top the records of its run-of-mine predecessors.
>
> Its across-the-board achievements in nearly every field stack up favorably with the near sweep registered by Franklin D. Roosevelt in his initial 73rd Congress. But there is one clear line of difference. It can never be said of the 88th that it 'rubber-stamped' anything. Nearly every Administration bill rolled out for action has been the subject of a swift and often roughneck rumpus . . .
>
> . . .
>
> The men who actually ran the 88th were described by all hands as the "second team." Speaker John W. McCormack (D-Mass.) and Rep. Carl Albert (D-Okla.) were installed to fill the vacuum left by the death of savvy old 'Mr. Sam' Rayburn. Earlier, Sens. Mansfield and Humphrey had inherited the Senate leadership mantle from that worker of legislative miracles, Lyndon Johnson, then No. 2 man in the Kennedy hierarchy.
>
> In the beginning there were costly tactical misjudgments. But somewhere along the line the pinch-hitters found that with a little GOP help they could bat the ball out of the park. Mostly, they've been playing in big league form ever since.

Congress adjourned late for the 1964 elections. Public opinion polls predicted a huge victory for President Johnson and the congressional Democrats. The strategy of keeping Congress in session so that it could produce an impressive legislative record to ensure John F. Kennedy's legacy and Lyndon B. Johnson's future success was put to the test. It worked.

"Landslide Lyndon's" real landslide

Johnson's campaign pounded home the extremism message about Goldwater through two television commercials, each of which was only aired once. One focused upon a young girl picking daisy petals to the accompaniment of a countdown on a nuclear bomb blast.[76] The other advertisement had a young girl licking an ice cream cone while a man deeply intoned the voice-over which discussed the lethal consequences of atomic bomb testing in the atmosphere, which would return to the earth in raindrops and land upon grass eaten by cows and turned into milk for ice cream. The TV spots were blatantly unfair but devastatingly effective. Given the size of President Johnson's lead in the preelection polls, they were unnecessary. In an expression common at that time, the spots "overkilled" the Goldwater-Miller ticket.

President Johnson carried 44 states and the District of Columbia with 486 electoral votes over Senator Goldwater. At the time, it was the second highest total of electoral votes ever, trailing only Franklin Roosevelt's 46-state 1936 landslide with 523 electoral votes. LBJ had outpolled FDR with the American public—61.1% for Johnson to 60.8% for Roosevelt.[77] The congressional elections gave Johnson a legislative majority of 295 seats in the House and a 155-seat margin over the Republicans. Senate Democrats held a 68 to 32 seat advantage.[78] Not only did LBJ's landslide victory gave him a higher vote percentage than FDR had received in 1936, but he became the first Democrat ever to win the entirety of New England's electoral votes. FDR in 1936, Woodrow Wilson in 1912, and even James Monroe in 1820's "Era of Good Feelings" election had failed to accomplish that feat. The number of elected House and Senate Democrats was the highest since FDR's 1936 reelection and LBJ was eager to cash in on it.

The American public's overwhelming rejection of Barry Goldwater gave LBJ something which he had never really had—a clear victory and a clear mandate. However, not wholly appreciated at the time was that Goldwater's home state victory in Arizona was joined by victories in five Deep South states—Alabama, Georgia, Louisiana, Mississippi, and South Carolina. These five states had voted for Catholic Democrat Al Smith of New York in 1928 but not for an apostate fellow southern Democrat like Lyndon Johnson of Texas.[79] The kernel of what would become the "Southern Strategy" for Republicans was now in evidence.

Johnson got a guilt-ridden Congress to pass Kennedy's stalled far-reaching civil rights bill, and his overall success was affirmed as Congress passed 57.6% of the measures that he submitted and a 88.2% success rate on those votes that got to the floor. These numbers were demonstrably higher than any of JFK's three years.[80] LBJ's 44-state landslide, none of which came from the Deep South, convinced many liberal Democrats that the party could win presidential contests and hold Congress without being beholden to the South. That hubris would haunt them.

The Great Society 89th Congress

Without stating it, Johnson treated the legislative accomplishments of the 88th Congress as the completion of Kennedy's legacy. From now on, any accomplishments would be his. Everywhere Lyndon Johnson looked in the 89th Congress that convened on January 3, 1965, there were friends and allies in key leadership posts. In the Senate, Hubert Humphrey presided as Vice President and Majority Leader Mike Mansfield (Dem-Mont.) and Majority Whip Russell Long (Dem-La.) ran the floor. In the House, Sam Rayburn's friend John McCormack presided, and Rayburn's protégé Majority Leader Carl Albert (Dem-Okla.) and his own pal Majority Whip Hale Boggs (Dem-La.) ran that floor. When he delivered his constitutionally mandated State of the Union Address on January 4, 1965, proclaimed as his "Great Society" speech, Johnson committed himself to a completion of the New Deal.

Even the House Republicans would be less contentious in this Congress as the relatively moderate Conference Chair Gerald R. Ford, Jr. of Michigan toppled the far more adversarial Charlie Halleck of Indiana for the post of minority leader.[81] Halleck, the beneficiary of the House Republicans defeat in 1958, was now the victim of the 1964 electoral debacle.

The liberal House Democrats sought to distance themselves further from the South by punishing two southern conservatives who had publicly supported Barry Goldwater—John Bell Williams of Mississippi and Albert Watson of South Carolina.[82] Both were stripped of committee seniority on a caucus vote of 157–115. Leading the charge against them was Dick Bolling ally and DSG leader Frank Thompson of New Jersey. Williams lost 18 years of seniority and the second spot on Interstate and Foreign Commerce while Watson lost only two years. Williams left the House in 1968 for the governorship of Mississippi. While Williams remained a Democrat, Watson left the Democratic Party and became a Republican, a path that would be later followed by more than 20 southern Democratic members of Congress as politics became ideologically fused with regionalism.

Seating Mississippi

The DSG next sought to expel the five-member Mississippi delegation from the House.[83] This was an extension of the MFDP's effort to gain seats at the 1964 Democratic Convention. The argument was that no members of the MFDP had their names listed on Mississippi's 1964 congressional ballots. The five Mississippi members were well placed on House committees with Democrats Bill Colmer, 2nd-ranking on Rules; Jamie Whitten, 4th-ranked on Appropriations; John Bell Williams, then 2nd on Interstate and Foreign Commerce; and Thomas Abernethy, 2nd on District of Columbia and 5th on Agriculture. Prentiss Walker, the delegation's lone Republican, was in the last minority slot on Agriculture and left the House in 1966 for a failed U.S. Senate bid.

On January 4, 1965, Majority Leader Carl Albert submitted a previous question motion, ending debate and authorizing Speaker McCormack to administer the oath of office to the five members-elect from Mississippi. The motion carried 276 to 149. Manhattan's William Fitts Ryan was the primary mover and DSG head John Blatnik of Minnesota was in charge of rounding up votes. Of the 149 opposing the motion were 123 northern Democrats, 24 Republicans, and 2 southern Democrats—one-termer Charles Farnsley of Kentucky and third-termer Henry Gonzalez of Texas, the state's first Latino member.[84]

Despite a *Washington Post* editorial urging that Mississippi not be seated, 66 northern Democrats accepted the leadership's position.[85] Among Democrats accepting the seating of the Mississippi Five were Judiciary Chair Manny Celler of New York, House author of both the 1964 Civil Rights Act and the 1965 Voting Rights Act, as well as six of John McCormack's fellow Irish-descended members from New York—Edna Kelly, John Rooney, Hugh Carey, Eugene Keogh, John M. Murphy, and Jim Delaney—

and John's "own "Irish Mafia" from Massachusetts—Eddie Boland, Jim Burke, Harold Donohue, Phil Philbin, and Tip O'Neill. The names read like the ensemble listed in the jaunty "McNamara's Band." Two surprising votes in support of the leadership's position on seating Mississippi were DSG leaders Dick Bolling and Frank Thompson. They would save their opposition for another day.

Syndicated columnist Drew Pearson who wrote about the DSG's strategy in January was bothered by John McCormack's role and contended in a May column that the seating of Mississippi's members was not only prearranged by John, but he had apparently given them assurances that they would be able to avoid future threats to unseat them.[86] Pearson expected that "John will probably smite his bosom and issue an indignant denial calling Drew Pearson a liar after this is published." As anticipated, John sent a scathing letter the following day on May 21 to Pearson[87]:

> Dear Drew:
>
> It is not necessary for anyone to call you a liar because everyone, including yourself, knows that you are a liar.
>
> In addition, you are my "INGRATE number 1." For, many years ago, at your request, through Tom McNamara, when you were under fire, I made a public statement defending you.
>
> Very truly yours,
> *John W. McCormack*

Inaugural Day January 20, 1965

On the morning of January 20, 1965, Lyndon Johnson finally achieved his long-sought dream of being formally inaugurated as president before a national and international audience.[88] This was far different from being sworn inside the sad and cramped quarters of Air Force One on November 22, 1963. Chief Justice Earl Warren administered the oath to President Johnson. This was the third time that Warren would swear in a president, with Dwight Eisenhower in 1957, Jack Kennedy in 1961, and now Lyndon Johnson in 1965. Warren's fourth and last swearing-in would be of his old adversary, Richard Nixon in 1969.

The best moment for John McCormack on Inaugural Day 1965 was his personal swearing in of Hubert Humphrey as the new vice president, ending his 14 months as next in line to President Johnson. It was only the second time that a Speaker had sworn in a vice president, but there was a precedent. Four years earlier on January 20, 1961, Lyndon Johnson had been sworn in as vice president by his beloved mentor, Speaker Sam Rayburn. For John McCormack, who had been a frequent member of the Joint Committee on Inaugural Ceremonies, this would be the first time that he would participate in the swearing-in. John was clearly relieved at the shedding of his burden as next in line. However, his enjoyment was short-lived as he became the target of a major published rebuke.

Bolling's *House Out of Order*

In February 1965, John's liberal nemesis Dick Bolling published a book entitled *House Out of Order* and it contained a highly critical analysis of how the House operated during John's tenure as Speaker.[89] Bolling's insider critique was similar in tone to 1963's *The Senate Establishment* by fellow liberal Democrat U.S. Senator Joe Clark of Pennsylvania,[90] in that it focused on the crippling effects of the seniority system and control of the congressional agenda by long-serving members from noncompetitive states and districts. Clark's book had a more contemporaneous quality while Bolling's provided a valuable historical assessment of how the House had operated in previous years under different Speakers. In many ways, Bolling's book could be seen as updating Woodrow Wilson's classic 1885 book *Congressional Government*.[91]

Other books on the House at this time included the superb *Forge of Democracy: The House of Representatives* in 1963 by *TIME* magazine's congressional reporter Neil MacNeil[92] and *Home Place: The Story of the House of Representatives* in 1965 by Texas-born William S. White, a Pulitzer Prize–winning former congressional reporter for the *New York Times* and syndicated journalist with close links to both Sam Rayburn and LBJ.[93] White's book was less than 180 pages long, and it was a condescending look at the House by an author who was far more enamored of the Senate as revealed in his laudatory 1957 tome, *Citadel: The Story of the U.S. Senate*.[94]

Bolling made an unusual admission in the book's acknowledgment, saying that he had prepared two early drafts of the manuscript but the final publishable version was written by journalist Wes Barthelmes, who would serve as press secretary for Representative Edith Green of Oregon and U.S. Senators Bob Kennedy and Joe Biden. Bolling's open acknowledgment of Barthelmes's role was apparently intended to avoid the Jack Kennedy-Ted Sorensen messiness of who really wrote *Profiles in Courage*.

Bolling's personal closeness to Sam Rayburn led him to believe that he would succeed Rayburn as Speaker upon Sam's death, a belief that was openly discussed in a September 6, 1961, article for the *St. Louis Post-Dispatch*.[95] Bolling was well down the seniority list among the House's Democrats in an institution that he ruefully knew regularly deferred to seniority. In 1962, Bolling was in a 37th place tie with 19 others and was junior to 80 House Democrats,[96] but his hubris would lead him to make an abortive and quickly collapsed challenge to Majority Whip Carl Albert's elevation to Majority Leader in 1962.

Bolling's suggestion that the House return to a seniority-avoiding Speaker-dominated committee system was a throwback to the Czar Tom Reed and Uncle Joe Cannon speakerships of the late nineteenth and early twentieth centuries.[97] The three Reed Houses had a first-term member average of 45.5% and the four Cannon Houses had a first-term member average of 28.2%.[98] Both numbers were far higher than the five post-1950 Rayburn House first-term member average of 15.7% and the four McCormack Houses of 16.4%. The high turnover and short careers of House members in the Reed and Cannon speakerships were quite dissimilar from the low turnover and lengthy career members of the Rayburn and McCormack Congresses. It is doubtful that many of the members then serving with Bolling would surrender their hard-earned seniority prerogatives and willingly return to a Speaker-dominated committee assignment process, but it made for an interesting debate.

In the book, Bolling shared his perception of the differences between Rayburn and McCormack, but he seemed puzzled about the closeness of their relationship[99]:

> Between McCormack and Rayburn there was a marked contrast, temperamentally and physically:
>
> Rayburn—small stocky, and controlled; McCormack—tall, thin, volatile, and unlike Rayburn, anxious to take immediate partisan advantage of legislative situations. However, they usually worked in harmony. McCormack tended increasingly to defer to Rayburn's judgment, but Rayburn was unstinting in his praise for McCormack's skill in respect to a matter almost foremost in his mind— the potential irremediable split in the Democratic Party.

Had Bolling's fabled grasp of House history focused on the 1930s and the strong bond that McCormack had established with the Texans at that time and FDR's role in helping to cobble together the "Austin-Boston connection" as the counterweight to the emergent Conservative Coalition, he would have been less surprised about the Rayburn-McCormack alliance and might have been less willing to continue his decade-long vendetta against John's speakership.

The Selma to Montgomery March

Although Congress had passed the Civil Rights Act of 1964, activists were well aware that as long as blacks were excluded from voting booths, there was no way to protect the gains that had been made. White-only southern legislators would find new and creative methods of flaunting the law. Making these legislators subject to the voting power of their states' African-American citizens would go a long way to eliminating the last vestiges of racial discrimination. Well aware that the 89th Congress had a sizable majority of northern and western Democrats, the strategy would be to find a way to prod Congress into passing a strong voting rights bill. This should not have been a problem in the House with the Judiciary Committee led by its Chair, McCormack ally Emanuel Celler, but William McCulloch of Ohio, so instrumental in the passage of the 1964 act, had become hesitant about passing yet another far-reaching civil rights bill.

As a way of prodding the Congress, the Reverend Martin Luther King, Jr.'s Southern Christian Leadership Conference (SCLC) and the Student Non-Violent Coordinating Committee (SNCC) organized a 54-mile march from Selma in central Alabama to the state capital in Montgomery where its segregationist Governor George C. Wallace still held sway. King was careful to let the White House know of his strategy in hopes that federal troops might be called upon to protect the marchers. As had happened in earlier demonstrations, violence erupted and two activists were murdered—black activist Jimmie Lee Jackson shot by a white state trooper and James Reeb, a 38-year-old white Unitarian-Universalist minister from Boston, beaten to death by a white mob.

As in Birmingham, Selma's local law enforcement officers behaved atrociously and let white mobs attack the marchers at the Edmund Pettus Bridge in what would be known as "Bloody Sunday." Governor Wallace refused to protect the marchers and the federal government stepped in once again with U.S. Army troops and the federalized Alabama National Guard. Ultimately, there would be 25,000 marchers by the time the State Capital Building was reached on March 25.[100]

Civil rights legislation, the next round

Speaker McCormack and the congressional leaders of both parties met with President Johnson to fashion a new strategy. Perhaps remembering that Kennedy's powerful June 1963 speech had caused a legislative backlash in Congress that immobilized it for months, Senators Mansfield and Dirksen urged Johnson to send the voting rights bill to the Hill with no public presentation. "This is a deliberate government," Dirksen contended. "Don't let these people say we scared him into it. Don't circumvent the Congress."[101]

Johnson was conflicted. In his memoir *The Vantage Point*, it is not clear if he wished to avoid taking the civil rights message to the airwaves as had the telegenic Kennedy two years earlier. The inevitable comparisons would be hurtful. But his memoir indicates serious concern that if he went to a joint session of Congress to address it and failed, it could very well jeopardize his political capital much too early in his administration[102]:

> I understood their hesitation. It is sometimes risky for the President to "go to the people" in support of a bill. If Congress does not support the public appeal, the move can completely backfire. Yet in this case I felt I had to reassure the people that we were moving as far and as fast as we could. I knew this reassurance would not be provided by the cold words of a written message. But if my congressional leaders were against it, I certainly had to weigh their counsel.

It was John McCormack who convinced Johnson to address the Congress directly. As Johnson recalled:

> At that point Speaker McCormack said: "I disagree. I strongly recommend that the President go to Congress and present the bill to a Joint Session. I suggest that he tell the Congress and the entire nation about the bill. Such a speech would show bipartisanship . . . it would show the world that action is being taken."
>
> He spoke with intense conviction. His words, and the decades of experience behind them, had an immediate impact on the rest of the leadership. I could see the tide beginning to shift. Majority Leader Albert supported the Speaker. "I agree," he said. "I don't think your coming before the Congress would be a sign of panic. I think it would help."

For Lyndon Johnson, listening to congressional seniors had long been his key to success, and once again he acted on the advice of John McCormack, the most senior of them all and the longtime comrade-in-arms of his beloved mentor Sam Rayburn. John

McCormack knew without saying that the white South would listen to the intonation and inflections of a man of the South. Lyndon Johnson was the first southern-born and raised president since Virginia-born Woodrow Wilson left office in 1921 and the first president elected from a southern state since Zachary Taylor of Louisiana, who won the office in 1848. This would not be the voice of Bostonian moral superiority.

The words would be well chosen and the sentences well crafted. Dick Goodwin, the president's speechwriter, would make sure of that.[103] The tone of delivery would be that of the Texas hill country, the tones of rural southern people, the tones of those who had lived with black people and who understood their pain and their dreams. The written words were Goodwin's. The intoned speech was Johnson's.

John McCormack also knew that most of those seated in the House chamber for that joint session of Congress would be the 260 House members who had voted for the bill. Their sheer numbers would guarantee a favorable majority for the speech and perhaps induce wavering Senators to join in its passage.

Johnson's commitment was evident throughout the speech, as the following excerpts indicate[104]:

> But even if we pass this bill, the battle will not be over. What happened in Selma is part of a far larger movement which reaches into every section and State of America. It is the effort of American Negroes to secure for themselves the full blessings of American life.
>
> Their cause must be our cause too. Because it is not just Negroes, but really it is all of us, who must overcome the crippling legacy of bigotry and injustice. And we shall overcome.
>
> As a man whose roots go deeply into Southern soil, I know how agonizing racial feelings are.
>
> . . .
>
> And so at the request of your beloved Speaker and the Senator from Montana; the majority leader, the Senator from Illinois; the minority leader, Mr. McCulloch, and other Members of both parties, I came here tonight—not as President Roosevelt came down one time in person to veto a bonus bill, not as President Truman came down one time to urge the passage of a railroad bill—but I came down here to ask you to share this task with me and to share it with the people that we both work for. I want this to be the Congress, Republicans and Democrats alike, which did all these things for all these people.

Four times in this speech, Lyndon Johnson used the word "overcome" to highlight the importance of this bill, echoing the civil rights anthem of "We Shall Overcome." The reference held enormous meaning for African Americans and their allies who had fought for this legislation. The power of the moment was caught vividly in Randall B. Woods's description of the speech[105]:

> And then, the president of the United States, remarkably, raised his arms over his head and proclaimed slowly, deliberately, "We—shall—overcome!" The assembled

throng rose almost as one and delivered a roaring, prolonged ovation. In the galleries and on the floor, long-time laborers in the vineyard of civil rights wept openly. Watching from their homes, stunned black Americans dared to hope that at last their dream of full citizenship might actually come true.

The civil rights disconnect of 1963 was replaced in 1965 by the very real engagement of Congress in expanding the voting opportunities of southern blacks. Unlike the 1964 Civil Rights Act, the Senate acted first and the Senate's southerners led by Judiciary Chair Jim Eastland were outmaneuvered by Majority Leader Mansfield. Southern amendments to the bill were voted down and a May 25 vote of 70 to 30 for cloture ended any filibuster threat. A day later, it passed the Senate 77 to 19. In the House, there was some difficulty as William McCulloch, the ranking Republican on House Judiciary who had been so supportive of the 1964 act, opposed the breadth of the coverage requirement and the poll tax ban in state elections, as the 24th Amendment had banned poll taxes in federal elections. Agreeing with the White House, John McCormack supported both provisions, and after the McCulloch alternative was defeated, the House passed the Voting Rights Act with an overwhelming 333 to 85 vote on July 9.[106]

With support from Martin Luther King, Jr. and the Justice Department, most of it survived the conference report and it was approved August 6, 1965. The passage of the Voting Rights Act of 1965 provided for direct federal action enabling black Americans to register and vote, rather than the often-prolonged individual legal suits required by previous acts. It suspended the use of literacy tests or similar voter qualification devices and authorized appointment of federal voting examiners to order registration of blacks in states and counties in which voter activity had fallen below certain specific levels. Other provisions established criminal penalties for interference with voter rights, outlined a judicial recourse for delinquent state and local governments, and directed the attorney general to institute proceedings against the use of poll taxes.

In one of those little-noticed civil rights victories, John declared that the House Barbershop that had been denying black employees of the House service for years now must accommodate the tonsorial requests of all of its employees, not just the white ones. The date of this order was October 14, 1965, more than a century after the Civil War had concluded and blacks were first emancipated.[107]

Moving other legislation

The good news for the liberals, if not necessarily for John McCormack, was the House's restoration of the "21-day rule" by a vote of 224 to 201.[108] Last accepted in the 81st Congress (1949–51), this legislative provision had been a longtime favorite of Democratic liberals. It allowed a bill to be called for floor consideration if the Rules Committee had not granted a rule on the bill within 21 days, allowing the leadership to circumvent the often obstructionist Rules Committee.

Humphrey's Mission: Throughout 1964 and the opening months of 1965, LBJ made frequent phone calls to John McCormack but they dwindled after March.[109] Coincidentally, it was on March 6, 1965, that LBJ gave marching orders to Vice President Hubert Humphrey declaring[110]:

> your number one responsibility in my administration comes even ahead of McCormack, Mansfield—anybody else. I expect you to be my liaison with both of them. . . . I think the Vice President is peculiarly equipped because . . . he has the legislative training, he has the contacts, he has the power to make a speech for them, he's on the ticket, he's only one of two elected. He's there with them. The President can't go see them.

Johnson continued his exhortation broadly exaggerating the role of fellow Texan Vice President John Nance Garner in the Roosevelt Administration and telling Humphrey what he expected: "You just get you a chart. Get those 104 [Great Society] bills and you just watch them like a hawk, because if you're successful . . . you will be a successful Vice President. . . . Garner could run the Senate. . . . He could talk to Rayburn and run the House. And he did. And Roosevelt passed all of his stuff."[111]

LBJ warned Humphrey of what he encountered during the Kennedy Administration, "Now Kennedy felt if I did it, then . . . they'd say I was the master craftsman. . . . He told the Catholics—Mike and them—to pay no attention to me and come down here. Now, they don't have to do that. You can negotiate with Mike, you can negotiate with Russell Long, you can negotiate with McCormack. . . . Now let them know that you are speaking for the President."[112]

For the self-effacing Senate Majority Leader Mike Mansfield and the highly private Speaker of the House John McCormack, that Johnson got the public credit and not they was not very bothersome. Johnson often lumped the two men together as "the Catholics." Both men knew Lyndon Johnson well and understood that his insecurities had to be met if LBJ was to remain a contented man. Also, both Mansfield and McCormack had been socialized into the post–New Deal sensibility that the Congress was not the engine of social change, the presidency was, and they took their secondary role with equanimity and some pride that they had served their president and their party well. Not surprisingly, the many useful accounts of the Johnson Great Society legislative agenda refer to John McCormack in passing and seldom as a central figure.[113] It was quite a contrast from John's service in the Truman Administration when he and Sam Rayburn were deeply involved in crafting as well as passing Truman's legislation. No longer energetically working the House floor as he had for two decades, John presided from the Speaker's chair and watched others do the work that he most enjoyed while he held the title but not the power.

The first major bill passed was the Appalachian Regional Development Act of 1965, authorizing $1,092,400,000 for development of the economically depressed 12-State Appalachian region.[114] Approved March 9, 1965, this act created a federal-state regional commission to help draw up coordinated regional economic development plans for the area.

A month later, the Elementary and Secondary Education Act of 1965 was passed. It provided an estimated $1.4 billion for the nation's elementary and secondary schools.[115] Approved April 11, 1965, it also made federal grants available to the states for purchasing textbooks and other library materials, for supplementary community-wide educational center, for new research and training centers, and to strengthen state departments of education. Unlike the 1961 education bill battle over aid to parochial schools when John did little to move the bill through the House, John readjusted the committee ratio on Education and Labor and placed liberals on Rules to guarantee the successful passage of this year's far-reaching education legislation.[116]

LBJ's legislative allies gave the Republicans something to cheer about when the Congress passed the Excise Tax Reduction Act of 1965, approved June 21, 1965, which repealed a variety of excise taxes resulting in $4.7 billion cut in federal excise taxes between June 22, 1965, and January 1, 1969.[117]

The summer of 1965 was extraordinarily productive. The 1963 photograph of septuagenarian Speaker John McCormack and octogenarian Senate President pro tem Carl Hayden seated behind President Lyndon Johnson five days after President Kennedy's assassination had led to the passage of a constitutional amendment enabling Congress to fill the vice presidency when it became vacant. It worked. Known officially as the Presidential Succession and Disability Amendment, the 25th Amendment provided that the vice president should become acting president under either of two circumstances[118]: (1) If the president informed Congress that he was unable to perform his duties, the vice president would become acting president until the president could resume his responsibilities; or (2) if the vice president and a majority of the Cabinet or such other body as Congress by law find the president to be incapacitated, the vice president would become acting president until the president informed Congress that his disability had ended. Congress had 21 days to resolve any dispute over the president's disability. Whenever a vacancy occurred in the office of the vice president, either by death, succession to the presidency, or resignation, the president was to nominate a vice president to be confirmed by a majority of both Houses of Congress. It was approved July 6, 1965, and ratified by the requisite number of states on February 25, 1967, one year and ten months after Congress had approved it and sent it to the states for ratification. The time it took to move though the state legislatures was close to the median of other Constitutional amendments. The 1963 photograph had alerted the nation, but it had not panicked it.

A week later, the Democratic majorities concluded their work on the Older Americans Act authorizing a five-year program, designed to develop and improve programs to help older persons through grants to the states for community planning and services, and established an Administration on Aging within the Department of Health, Education and Welfare.[119] Approved July 14, 1965, it authorized federal grants totaling $17.5 million in fiscal 1966 and 1967 to states and to public and private nonprofit organizations for developing programs for the elderly. It also created an Administration on Aging in the Department of Health, Education and Welfare, directed by a Commissioner on Aging appointed by the president and confirmed by the Senate.

The importance of this constituency was so valued that both the House and the Senate set up their own committees to deal specifically with aging. In the House, it was called the Select Committee on Aging and in the Senate, the Special Committee on Aging.[120] Both committees grew rapidly in the years to come, reflecting the political capital to be derived from protecting the benefits of an expanding political subgroup that had a higher-than-average turnout rate.

As the drug culture of the 1960s grew to epidemic proportions, Congress passed the Drug Abuse Control Amendments of 1965. Approved on July 15, 1965, these amendments expanded federal control over depressant and stimulant drugs to reduce illegal distribution and use of barbiturates and drugs affecting the central nervous system or producing hallucinogenic effects.[121] They also strengthened the powers of federal inspectors and enforcement agents, and limited prescription refills.

The most far-reaching pieces of legislation passed by the 89th Congress were the Social Security Amendments of 1965. One set provided Medicare for the Aged, which was a federally supported hospital insurance program for about 19 million under the Social Security Act with a supplementary medical benefits program and an expanded program of medical insurance, to increase benefits under the Old-Age, Survivors, and Disability Insurance System.[122] Led in the House by Wilbur Mills of Ways and Means, it was approved July 30, 1965.

In President Johnson's memoirs, he reflected on John McCormack's pivotal role in the legislative efforts to pass Medicare through the House[123]:

> If the ratio on the Ways and Means Committee were to be made on the same basis at this time, the memo pointed out, the ratio would have to be 17 to 8 in favor of the Democrats. That, along with the fact that three Republican diehard opponents on the committee had just been defeated, provided reasonable assurance that Medicare would be reported out. Clearly a readjustment on the committee was called for. The memo noted that the attitude of Speaker McCormack, who was a former member of the Ways and Means Committee, would be a major factor in this effort. Speaker McCormack's attitude was, for that matter, a key to the enactment of our entire program. He had been a force for progressive legislation in Congress for more than thirty-five years. No man understood better how to convert dreams into programs and no man cared more about accomplishing such goals.

The other set of amendments produced Medicaid for the Medically Needy that provided for medical care for the indigent through a system of federal reimbursements to the states for medical aid outlays.[124] Approved July 30, 1965, it extended the Medical Assistance Program for the Aged to needy persons under the dependent children, blind, and permanently disabled programs (Figure 21.3).

Inner city race riots and an urban policy

A new crisis confronted the nation as northern cities erupted in flames and the black residents of the urban ghettoes exploded in rage.[125] White citizens in the American cities of the North such as New York, Newark, Cleveland, and Detroit, which had been

Figure 21.3 Congressional leaders at the White House, July 27, 1965 (Lyndon B. Johnson Library and Museum) l.-r. House Majority Leader Carl Albert, Vice President Hubert Humphrey, House Speaker John McCormack, House Majority Whip Hale Boggs, U.S. Senator George Smathers, and Senate Majority Leader Mike Mansfield.

relatively isolated from this trauma of race warfare, now saw their smug superiority toward the benighted South fall away before their own fears.

As he had always done, President Lyndon Johnson sought a legislative solution to the nation's ills. The first of these was to urge the passage of the Housing and Urban Development Act of 1965, which authorized an estimated $7.8 billion to fund a variety of new housing and urban development programs and extended and broadened existing ones.[126] Approved August 10, 1965, it provided federal rent supplements for families or individuals unable to afford standard private housing and grants to local public bodies for urban beautification and improvement programs.

A month later, the Johnson Administration succeeded where the Kennedy Administration had failed with the passage of the Department of Housing and Urban Development Act. Named as the initial secretary of HUD was Robert C. Weaver, the nation's first African-American cabinet member. Approved September 9, 1965, this act established a Cabinet-level Department of Housing and Urban Development under a secretary of HUD, appointed by the president with Senate confirmation.[127] It gave to the secretary all powers, functions, and duties of the Housing and Home Finance Agency (HHFA) including the Federal Housing Administration, Public Housing Administration, the Federal National Mortgage Association, the Community Facilities Administration, and the Urban Renewal Administration.

Continuing the legislative push

One of the stranger consequences of the Kennedy assassination was discovering that murdering a president was not a federal crime. It was particularly painful in the

Kennedy case because of the incompetence of the Dallas police. The Texas authorities who arrested Lee Harvey Oswald, the alleged assassin of the president, held a press briefing announcing to the nation when Oswald would be leaving the police hall and which exit he would be using. Awaiting Oswald in the doorway was Jack Ruby, a somewhat disreputable nightclub owner, who fired shots point-blank into Oswald, killing him immediately. The lack of a trial for Oswald and the lack of an opportunity to establish his guilt once and for all continue to haunt American politics.

Congress made an effort to deal with the federal-state jurisdictional matters by passing the President and Vice President Assassination Penalties, approved August 28, 1965, which amended the U.S. Code, making it a federal crime to kill, kidnap, or assault the president or any other federal official and prescribed penalties for violation of this law.[128] Whether federal protection might have guaranteed Lee Harvey Oswald's life and his eventual trial can only be speculated, but it might have spared much of the nation's subsequent anguish and lessened the proliferation of multiple conspiracy theories poisoning the attitudes of many Americans toward their government.

An underappreciated demographic change that first appeared in 1965 was the arrival in the nation's workforce of the first "baby boomers" to reach employable adolescence. Their arrival enhanced job opportunities and increased disposable income. The Kennedy Administration's fiscal adjustments had helped the nation recover from the unfortunate recession of 1958, but this new major influx opened the door to an era of sustained prosperity. Lyndon Johnson, who studied the numbers carefully, saw this new money in the federal budget as an opportunity to ingratiate himself with a key Kennedy constituency which had felt the loss of the young president quite deeply—the intellectuals and the arts community. In an effort to reach out to this community in the only way he understood, President Johnson urged the passage of legislation and federal money appropriated for the arts and humanities.

Congress passed the National Foundation on the Arts and the Humanities Act of 1965 that established a National Foundation on the Arts and the Humanities consisting of two autonomous subdivisions, a National Endowment for the Arts and a National Endowment for the Humanities.[129] The operations of the Foundation were to be coordinated by a federal council on the Arts and the Humanities, composed of nine federal officials headed by the secretary of the Smithsonian Institution. Approved September 29, 1965, it provided $20 million in fiscal 1966 to be granted to organizations and to individuals engaged in creative and performing arts, and to be granted or loaned for scholarships and research in the humanities. In President Johnson's eyes, this act would please the nation's intelligentsia and dismiss forever his feelings of unworthiness in their eyes. He hoped that the cornpone image of him as the Texas "bumpkin" would be banished from their collective assessment. It was not the only assessment that Johnson would misjudge.

John McCormack's long-realized goal

On October 3, 1965, President Johnson traveled to Ellis Island in the harbor of New York City to sign into law the Immigration and Nationality Act of 1965.[130] This act abolished the national origins quota system and introduced a new ceiling of 170,000 non-Western Hemisphere immigrants allowed into the United States per year, with no more than 20,000 coming from the same source country, and placed the first ceiling on immigrants from the Western Hemisphere at 120,000. When John McCormack first entered Congress in 1928 as a 37-year-old freshman, it was his goal to do away with the national origins requirement of the Immigration Act of 1924, which he addressed in his maiden speech to the House of Representatives. That he would be in the Speaker's chair at the time of its abolition must have been a deeply gratifying moment. The act had long punished immigrants and their children, and as the grandson of Irish immigrants and the son of a Canadian immigrant, John truly understood how immigrants had been stigmatized by the 1921 and 1924 Immigration Acts. This act, along with the Social Security Act of 1935, its amendments in 1939, and the recently passed Medicare Act was yet another of the promises kept by John McCormack to the memory of his family and his constituents in South Boston.

A further reach on Johnson's part and one with his wife, Lady Bird, firmly in mind was his encouragement of the Highway Beautification Act of 1965. Approved October 22, 1965, the act authorized a new program for the scenic development and beautification of the nation's federal-aid highway system through removal of junkyards and landscaping of areas adjacent to the highways.[131] Congress humored the then-popular president by passing the legislation, but then in each of the three subsequent years, 1966, 1967, and 1968, it refused to authorize or appropriate funds to implement the provisions of the act.

Congress closed out the extraordinary 1st Session of the 89th Congress with a major environmental regulatory act and a major education funding one. The environmental regulatory act was the Water Quality Act of 1965 that required the States to establish and enforce water quality standards for all interstate waters within their boundaries and authorized the federal government to take such action if the states did not.[132] Approved October 2, 1965, it established a Federal Water Pollution Control Administration, to provide grants for research and development, to increase grants for construction of sewage treatment works, and to require establishment of water quality criteria. It also authorized appropriations of $20 million a year in fiscal years 1966–69 for federal matching grants to states, municipalities, and interstate or inter-municipal agencies for projects to help develop improved methods of preventing untreated sewage and wastes from being discharged into bays, rivers, etc.

The major education bill passed in the closing weeks was the Higher Education Act of 1965 that appropriated $840 million for extensive aid for poor and middle-class students who wished to attend college and new programs of graduate study for public school teachers.[133] Approved November 8, 1965, it also authorized a National Teachers Corps designed to improve elementary and secondary education in city slums and impoverished rural areas by sending in teams of experienced teachers and several young graduate students to strengthen local school programs. It authorized funds for community service programs focusing on urban problems to be conducted by colleges and universities, grants to improve college libraries and train librarians, a program to raise the academic quality of developing institutions, and equipment grants to improve classroom instruction in the sciences, humanities, arts, and education.

It was an extraordinarily productive year and it rivaled FDR's New Deal successes of 1933. President Johnson had kept constant pressure on the Congress and it had delivered. However, the congressional leadership teams of Mansfield and Long in the Senate and McCormack-Albert-Boggs in the House got relatively little credit for this legislative outpouring. The Johnson White House took almost total command of Congress.

Tom Foley of Washington State who served as whip from 1981 to 1987 and as Speaker after Jim Wright's 1989 resignation, entered the House in 1965 and recalled that "Speaker John McCormack made only marginally more use of the Whip [than Rayburn] and the White House congressional liaison staff performed most of the vote-counting function during the Kennedy and Johnson Administrations."[134] This was a function that had always been held by the congressional leaders but no longer.

As for President Johnson, despite Barry Goldwater's 1964 canard, he had not "out-Rooseveleted Roosevelt." After all, FDR confronted a major national economic crisis and had a relatively blank slate upon which to initiate his programs and create federal agencies. Johnson inherited a well-entrenched bureaucracy and a bustling economy. The domestic crises of his administration were in the future and not in the past. Many have also contended that Johnson's expansive legislation created problems rather than solved them.[135]

With a huge majority and procedural changes strengthening the floor leadership, Johnson was able to amass a record of tremendous congressional success. *Congressional Quarterly*'s box score comparing presidential legislative success with Congress from 1953 to 1965, Johnson's 1965 score reached 68.4%, more than doubling Kennedy's 1963 session.[136] In 1965, *Congressional Quarterly* calculated his floor voting success rate at the nearly miraculous support level of 93% overall and 94% in the House alone.[137]

Reviewing the First Session of the 89th Congress, longtime syndicated columnist Drew Pearson wrote[138]:

> Shortly after Labor Day, as Congress began to stumble toward its close, Lyndon Johnson confided to a friend that he had watched Franklin Roosevelt's famous New Deal Congress pass a record of major pieces of legislation by 1936. With some pride, the President added that the 89th Congress had passed 65 major pieces of legislation by Labor Day.
>
> Without arguing the exact number and importance of these bills, I can report that I have watched every President since Warren Harding and no congress in that time achieved a record equal to the 89th Congress.

CQ also reported that the "back of the 'conservative coalition' [was] broken," and that during the five years of the Kennedy-Johnson Administrations, the Conservative Coalition had appeared on 19.6% of roll calls, with a high of 28% in 1961 and a low of 14% in 1962.[139] The victories won by the Conservative Coalition varied as well, particularly in the House, ranging from a high of 74% in 1961, when the House was still led by Sam Rayburn, to a low of 25% in the 1965 House led by John McCormack.

Johnson's successful efforts to enhance education, the environment, civil rights, urban life, and the arts made it possible for him to "out-Kennedy Kennedy." In retrospect, that really seems to be the intent of his ambitious legislative thrust in 1964 and 1965. Speaker John McCormack sat off to the side and basked in the reflected glow of LBJ's congressional triumphs, but personal news from Texas had a sobering impact upon him. His youngest brother Donald, known also as Danny or "Buttons," had died in a Veterans Hospital in Temple, Texas. John was with LBJ in the White House when word reached him of the tragedy. When apprised of the news, John McCormack could only say, "That's that."[140]

Buttons's Death and a Tombstone: John was now the last of the McCormacks. He would have the remains of his brother flown to Boston. The funeral service for Buttons was well attended, more in deference to John's prominence that to any knowledge of a man who had departed Boston years earlier and seldom returned. John would have him buried in the same grave as his mother Mary Ellen, his older sister Catherine, and his oldest brother Patrick.[141] All four would be rejoined in the Mount Benedict family plot in West Roxbury. Knocko had already been buried in Boston's New Calvary Cemetery; there was one space remaining in the Mount Benedict Cemetery, and that space would be filled by Buttons. All John would need now is a tombstone.

John now had the money to pay for a tombstone for his deceased relatives. He knew there were four buried there, though the tombstone only had the names of Mary Ellen and Donald. This moment, at the peak of John's power as Speaker of the House where he had overseen the most ambitious legislative agenda since FDR's earliest Congress three decades earlier, he still had to conceal the family history. Buried there with his mother were 19-year-old Catherine and 24-year-old Patrick with their father's Canadian ancestry on their death certificates. They had not died as infants, despite what he had told his South Boston constituents and led the powerful Irish gatekeepers of Boston to believe. One can only imagine the personal pain this must have caused him, this most moral man, but without this reinvention, he never could have provided to the nation's poor, destitute, and racially diverse citizens the enormous good he did. In this case, the end justified the means.

Legislative output continued

When the Second Session of the 89th Congress convened on January 10, 1966, President Johnson and the congressional Democrats looked forward to a continuation of the legislative triumphs of 1965. But events intervened.

Retrospective analysis of this time has been critical. In James T. Patterson's prescient analysis, *The Eve of Destruction: How 1965 Transformed America*,[142] this year of massive liberal legislative triumphalism would soon be followed by the inability of the American military to successfully extricate itself from the hopeless morass of the endless Vietnam War in spite of its massive troop infusions. The Vietnam War escalated beyond all expectations and week after week, its toll on America's young men mounted. The blindly optimistic pronouncements of the generals in the field and the leaders in Washington came to be more and more resented in the face of the grim and continuing reality of what would become the nation's longest armed conflict. A "credibility gap" had emerged between the leaders and the led.

Combined with the rampant destruction of American inner cities as the long-awaited promise of legislated racial equality failed to liberate the nation's African Americans from centuries of social and economic despair, these events would lead to the disappearance of white male voters from the Democratic Party's fragile coalition and five victories in the next six presidential elections for Republicans who harnessed these failings into electoral success.

As if suffering from collective exhaustion from the previous year, Congress got off to a relatively slow start in 1966.[143] It was not until the summer that new legislation emerged from the committees and found its way to the chamber floors. By then new domestic crises had emerged as more American cities erupted in flames and ugly confrontations between predominantly black ghetto dwellers and predominantly white municipal police forces filled the nightly news.

Ironically, it was the news media which was the initial beneficiary of 1966's new legislation. The Freedom of Information Act, approved July 4, 1966, required the federal government and its agencies to make available to citizens, upon request, all documents and records excepting those which fit in one of nine exempt categories.[144] Among the exempted materials were documents relating to national security and foreign policy and internal personnel practices. John Moss of California, backed by Majority Leader John McCormack and Government Operations Chair Bill Dawson, was the moving force for this eleven-year crusade for greater transparency from government agencies.[145]

Congress also moved on a two-pronged solution to the nation's transportation problems. The first was to deal with the Urban Mass Transportation Act of 1966 that continued and expanded programs begun under the Urban Mass Transportation Act of 1964.[146] Approved September 8, 1966, it authorized annual appropriations of $150 million in fiscal 1968 and 1969 for the program. It also expanded the 1964 Act by authorizing use of grants for three new purposes: technical studies, research, and training in urban transportation problems. The second was to deal with highway safety addressed in the Highway Safety Act of 1966, approved September 9, 1966, which required that each state establish a highway safety program in accordance with uniform government standards for driver education, accident investigation, and highway design and maintenance.[147]

The next logical step for Congress was to create a new Cabinet-level department, and a month later in October, Congress passed the Department of Transportation Act, which established it as the twelfth Cabinet-level department.[148] Approved October 15, 1966, it placed some 34 federal agencies under the direct control of the new secretary of transportation. Excluded from the Department were all economic regulatory and rate-setting activities of existing agencies. Within less than three years, President Johnson had added two new Cabinet departments. Even FDR hadn't been able to do that. Not since George Washington had a president created more than one Cabinet Department, more evidence of LBJ's obsession with grandiosity.

Organized labor, which had emerged as the Democratic Party's major power broker, was attended to with the passage of the Fair Labor Standards Amendments of 1966, approved September 23, 1966, substantially broadening federal minimum wage and overtime pay protection and increasing the minimum wage from $1.25 to $1.60 and extended minimum coverage to an estimated 9.1 million additional employees, including for the first time some agricultural employees.[149]

Environmentalism: Interior Secretary Stewart Udall was one of three original Kennedy Cabinet appointees to last throughout the Kennedy-Johnson years. The others were Secretary of State Dean Rusk, who JFK did not know before his appointment to that post, and secretary of agriculture W. Orville Freeman, the former Governor of Minnesota and a longtime ally of Vice President Hubert Humphrey. Secretary Udall was the last surviving "congressional" in Johnson's cabinet and the closest of the three holdovers to Kennedy. Udall's continued survival in that post was largely attributable to the high level of energy he brought to the environmentalist and conservationist agenda. Stewart Udall was also the older brother of the fast-rising U.S. Representative Morris Udall, who in 1969 would contest Speaker John McCormack in the first intra-party challenge to a sitting Speaker since 1923.

Stewart Udall pushed Congress for legislation protecting the natural environment. He was very successful with key legislation passed in the closing days of the 89th Congress. One was the National Wildlife Refuge System Administration Act that directed the secretary of the interior to take special actions to protect some 35 species of mammals and 30–40 species of birds which conservationists believed would otherwise become extinct.[150] Approved October 15, 1966, it also declared that the secretaries of interior, agriculture, and defense and their departments should seek to protect endangered fish and wildlife species, including migratory birds. Also passed was the Clean Water Restoration Act of 1966, which provided substantial amounts of money to help communities pay the costs of abiding by the purity standards stipulated in the Water Control Act of 1965.[151]

Last Minute Laws: In the preelection rush to adjourn in 1966, a little-noticed act was passed, the Financial Institution Supervisory Act of 1966 that would have later ramifications for the American economy. This act gave federal bank regulatory agencies temporary new powers to stop or correct unsound financial practices, approved October 16, 1966.[152] It raised the amount of federal insurance on insured banks and savings and loan accounts from $10,000 to $15,000 per account. It also empowered agencies to issue cease-and-desist orders against unsound practices at financial institutions and to remove bank and saving and loan association officials engaged in such practices.

The 1966 congressional election was days away when the 89th Congress passed the Demonstration Cities and Metropolitan Development Act of 1966, approved November 3, 1966, designed to rebuild entire urban areas by tying together the wide array of existing federal and local programs and new innovations by the participating communities for a coordinated attack on blight.[153] The program was later renamed "model cities."

As the drug crisis worsened, the 89th Congress decided to focus more on rehabilitation than punishment with the passage of the Narcotic Addict Rehabilitation Act of 1966. Approved November 3, 1966, this act authorized the commitment to institutional treatment and intensive follow-up care for three classes of addicts: those accused of a federal crime, other than a crime of violence; those convicted of a federal crime; and those charged with or convicted of no federal crime, if the addict or a "related individual" requested such treatment.

Eddie McCormack's last hurrah

Back in Boston, the voters of Massachusetts had approved a long-delayed change in the length of gubernatorial terms. Like most New England states with their colonial-era distrust of gubernatorial power, Massachusetts historically had the shortest fixed-term length of any major state. It was the Constitutional Convention of 1917–18 that had lengthened the term of the state's constitutional offices from one year to two years. As a member of that Convention, 25-year-old John McCormack supported lengthening the term to two years, and now the voters had chosen to lengthen the term to four years. This mattered to John because his nephew Eddie intended to make a political comeback in this contest. Eddie's career had rebounded from the embarrassing Senate primary defeat to Ted Kennedy in 1962 as a result of his help with the MFDP compromise at the 1964 Democratic Convention.

Eddie's fellow state attorney generals who joined him in the *Gideon* case had moved up. Minnesota's Walter Mondale was appointed to fill Vice President Humphrey's vacant Senate seat in December of 1964 and Missouri's Tom Eagleton had already been elected lieutenant governor and he too cast his eyes on a Senate seat that he would win in 1966. With 34-year-old Democrat Ted Kennedy holding one Senate seat and venerable Republican Leverett Saltonstall holding the other, Eddie chose the race for governor, one that was well within his grasp in 1962 but that he had chosen to ignore.

Republican Governor John A. Volpe saw himself as the vice presidential choice of the 1968 presidential nominee and vacillated between positioning himself as the incumbent governor for the first four-year term or waiting for Senator Saltonstall's seat. Volpe had been defeated for reelection as governor in 1962 by longtime Ed McCormack rival Endicott "Chub" Peabody of Cambridge, so there was no guarantee that he would retain the governorship. Peabody, who had lost his own renomination bid in 1964 to Lieutenant Governor Frank Bellotti, was also on the comeback trail, and he would seek the U.S. Senate nomination. Once Senator Saltonstall chose not to run, Edward Brooke, the state's popular attorney general and the nation's highest-placed elected African-American state official, would run to replace Salty.

It was anticipated that the Democrats vying for the gubernatorial nomination would be two-term former Attorney General Eddie McCormack and State Senate President Maurice A. Donahue from the western city of Holyoke. Much to the great surprise of many Massachusetts observers, a new name surfaced—Kenneth P. O'Donnell, the most loyal member of JFK's "Irish Mafia," who had served as Jack's only appointments secretary during his presidential term. O'Donnell had been Bob Kennedy's roommate at Harvard and had been long rumored to be Joe Kennedy's man in the Kennedy White House. Jackie Kennedy remarked that when Kenny appeared, they all had to get back to work. Kenny's candidacy caught people off guard. He had never held elective office and with his pal Bob Kennedy in New York State surrounded by a new entourage, he seemed adrift.

The Kennedy brothers now serving in the U.S. Senate from Massachusetts and New York and their associates, U.S. Senator John C. Culver of Iowa, Ted's Harvard roommate, and U.S. Senator John Tunney of California, Ted's roommate at the University of Virginia Law School, eschewed the drudgery and limited glamour of gubernatorial offices for the far more exciting ones in the U.S. Senate. While both Kennedy brothers held Senate seats, they were very junior members of a body that revered seniority, and their brother Jack was no longer president. Now in the White House was Lyndon B. Johnson, a man Bob despised and Ted tolerated. The one Massachusetts man most beloved by Lyndon Johnson was John McCormack, who had known Lyndon since 1937 and who shared a deep-seated adoration for the legendary Sam Rayburn. Unlike 1962, it was the McCormacks of 1966 who were better placed than the Kennedys, and if a presidential intervention would occur, it would benefit Eddie McCormack and not Kenny O'Donnell, the closest ally of Bob Kennedy, who remained convinced that LBJ was somehow complicit in Jack Kennedy's death.

There were portents of Bobby-Teddy tension as one photograph caught the Kennedy brothers seated together with hands shielding their faces from one another. Politically, Massachusetts was not Bob Kennedy's state and he was not conflicted about supporting his closest pal Kenny O'Donnell for governor. On the other hand, Ted was caught in a dreadful quandary. This was his state, and he had made serious efforts to reach out to the McCormacks and was fearful that a Kenny-Eddie contest would resurface the painful memories of the bitter 1962 Senate race. John McCormack had already reached out to Ted and had even testified publicly in the U.S. Senate on behalf of Ted's barely qualified federal judge candidate Francis X. Morrissey, widely seen as Joe Kennedy's most loyal and obsequious retainer.

The unusual nature of McCormack's gesture did not go unnoticed by national columnists Rowland Evans and Robert Novak[154]:

> Speaker John McCormack, the foxy grandpa of Massachusetts Democratic politics, deposited another valuable chit in his bank last week with one simple act: testifying fervently for Senate confirmation of Francis X. Morrissey as a district judge in Massachusetts. It is unusual for the Speaker of the House to testify before a Senate committee. Considering McCormack's long simmering feud with the Kennedy clan, it would seem doubly unusual to support Morrissey—whose chief qualification for the bench seems to be long and loyal service as a political servant for the Kennedys.
>
> But the Speaker's main political ambition today is to nominate nephew Edward McCormack for governor of Massachusetts next year. That ambition would be shattered if Sen. Edward (Ted) Kennedy comes out for Edward McCormack's chief rival: Kenny O'Donnell, an aide of John F. Kennedy. Consequently, Speaker McCormack is bending over backwards to be nice to Teddy Kennedy and keep him neutral—maybe even pro-McCormack. He opposed President Johnson earlier in supporting Kennedy's anti-poll tax amendment.

At the prenomination state convention on June 10, Eddie bested Donahue with help from "enough of [Kenny's] handful of delegates at the last minute to put McCormack over and knock Donahue out of contention."[155] Peabody easily won the nod for the Senate nomination. Eddie and Chub, who had bitterly contested for the attorney general nomination in 1956 and 1958, were now the anticipated nominees for the upcoming November election as governor and U.S. Senator respectively. However, each would have to prevail in the September primaries if they would be able to challenge the likely Republican candidates, Governor John Volpe and Senate candidate Edward Brooke.

Suspecting that this might be Eddie's best shot at electoral redemption, John came up from Washington to campaign on Eddie's behalf. He even made an unprecedented appearance at the state convention and made himself available throughout the summer in support of Eddie's nomination.

Eddie defeated Kenny O'Donnell in the Democratic primary.[156] In Helen O'Donnell's surprisingly candid book *A Common Good*, describing the relationship between her father and Robert Kennedy, she devoted only six pages to her father's failed gubernatorial bid and chose not to mention the name of Edward McCormack, who defeated him in that contest.[157] She quoted family friend Paul Kirk, who would later become chair of the Democratic National Committee and was appointed to fill Ted's Senate vacancy in 2009, contending that the motivation for Kenny's run was more therapeutic than political[158]:"Kenny was at once a private man who, by 1966, I believe, wished to continue to be a public personality. Running for governor in 1966 was the right thing for him to do, and . . . he needed to satisfy his public and professional day-to-day activities . . . [to] fill the void."

Election prospects looked good for Eddie as he traveled to Washington and was photographed with both Kennedy brothers. LBJ wrote a congenial letter of congratulations to him on his gubernatorial nomination[159]:

Dear Ed:

Warm congratulations on your nomination as the Democratic candidate for Governor.

I have watched with much interest your public career, especially as a conscientious and effective Attorney General for the people of Massachusetts and as my personal representative to the United Nations Conference in the World Food Program in Rome.

Judging from these achievements, and having known you for so many years, I am confident of the type of progressive, meaningful record you will write for Massachusetts as its next Governor.

All good wishes in your campaign.

Sincerely,
LBJ

With Eddie now nominated, former rival Ted Kennedy happily backed his gubernatorial campaign[160]:

The Kennedy and McCormack dynasties held an ostentatious "unity" session on Capitol Hill Monday as it became clear that Sen. Edward M. Kennedy was assuming the role of strong party leader among Massachusetts Democrats.

. . .

Kennedy announced that he would "campaign in all parts of the state with the candidates," singularly and collectively. "I hope to appear with all of them on television discussing the issues relating to their offices and programs they will offer to the people," he added.

Despite Teddy's help, the election year of 1966 was a bad year for Democrats and Eddie McCormack would be yet another casualty of the resurgent Republicans, losing badly to incumbent Republican Governor John A. Volpe in the general election, 62.6% to 36.9%.[161] Eddie gave up electoral politics and he and Stan Bregman established a Washington-based law firm.[162] They would be joined in 1969 by Tyler Abell, assistant postmaster general, the stepson of syndicated insider columnist Drew Pearson and the husband of Bess Abell, Lady Bird Johnson's social secretary.

The Americanization of the Vietnam War

In 1961, Jack Kennedy's first year in office, American troop strength in Vietnam was 3,205. It was a trebling of the 900 troops in Eisenhower's last year, 1960, and the pace of American involvement grew rapidly—11,300 American troops in 1962, and 16,300 in 1963. In Lyndon Johnson's first full year, the number had risen to 23,300 and by 1965 the troop levels had exploded to 184,300 with no end in sight. The rising troop levels were taking their toll on Lyndon Johnson's popularity as his Gallup Poll numbers began to sink. As more than 300,000 American soldiers, now half a world away, trudged through the dangerous snake-infested jungles and swamps of Southeast Asia, there is little question that the Americanization of the war would have a catastrophic impact on the Johnson presidency. It was a war with no escape for LBJ.

LBJ's ambitious domestic agenda got mired in the Vietnam morass and his support level in the Congress for 1966 dropped to 79%[163]—a respectable number, but a clear fall from 1965's triumphant 93%. Speaker John McCormack steadfastly defended President Johnson's conduct of the war. To McCormack, the defense of a Catholic anti-Communist regime came naturally.[164] Geopolitical considerations aside, there were coreligionists to protect and a faith to be defended.

McCormack subscribed totally to the "domino theory" then prevalent among Johnson Administration spokesmen. Should we fail to defend South Vietnam, the Philippines would be next, and then Hawaii and Alaska. His was the most elaborate of the domino theories. Most of the others confined their fears to the nations of Indochina and their neighbors. McCormack's fears wandered far from Southeast Asia. Few others with power as great as McCormack saw the Viet Cong reaching the Aleutians or Honolulu.

John McCormack's foreign policy perspective was shaped by the 1930s. Hitler's reach into the Saar, the *Anchluss* with Austria, and the seizure of the Sudetenland all replayed themselves again and again when he discussed Vietnam. Differences in degree and context could not shake John McCormack's belief that communism unchecked in South Vietnam would jeopardize all American interests in the Pacific. The Vietnam War devoured President Johnson's Great Society vision. Skeptical liberals, emboldened by Senate Foreign Relations Chair J. William Fulbright's antiwar challenge to the president, began to distance themselves from Lyndon Johnson.

The 89th Congress came to a close on October 22, 1966. Clearly, it had been one of the most legislatively productive Congresses in the nation's history, but most of its legacy rested on the remarkable gains of 1965's 1st Session. In a striking graphic in Jeffrey Cohen's sophisticated analysis of *The President's Legislative Policy Agenda, 1789–2002*,[165] the 89th Congress's response to LBJ's policy initiatives easily towers over all of the 107 Congresses charted from that of George Washington 1st Congress to the 107th Congress of George W. Bush.

Speaker John McCormack, writing a review of the 2nd Session for the *Boston Globe*, remarked[166]:

> The great accomplishments of this session coupled with the unequaled record of the first session again remind all Americans that the 89th Congress has truly earned the title of the Congress of fulfillment. This Congress took dead aim at the major problems plaguing the nation—and it did not miss the mark.
>
> . . .
>
> Through the work of this Congress, the Democratic Party has built a lasting foundation for a great society, and through the work of this Congress our party has rededicated itself to being the party of progress, the party of vision, the party of principles and the party of the people.

Foreshadowing: The Gulf of Tonkin Resolution of 1964 that LBJ treated as a de facto declaration of war led to a 23-fold expansion of American forces in Vietnam from 16,300 in 1963 to 385,300 in 1966. American support for the war began its inexorable erosion. This was compounded by the regular summer eruptions of 1964–66 in the black ghettoes of American cities: Rochester, New York, Harlem in New York City, Philadelphia, Watts in Los Angeles, and Hough in Cleveland. These riots led to disenchantment with the expansive social agenda of the 89th Congress.

Despite John McCormack's glowing review, the 2nd Session was less than positive. On December 4, 1966, Gallup released a poll indicating that LBJ's popularity had fallen to 48%. It was 31 points below the 79% that he had received in the first poll of his presidency released on December 22, 1963, and 32 points below his high of 80% of January 15, 1964. The first poll of the 89th Congress on February 3, 1965, gave LBJ a 71% approval rating and 15% disapproving, but by December 1966, Johnson's positives had dropped by 23 points and his negatives had risen by 22 points to 37%, but he still held a plurality of Americans in his corner. His Vietnam policy was slightly favored 43% to 40%, but the Great Society program had run aground with only 32% of polled

Americans favoring it and 44% finding it unfavorable.[167] Like Franklin Roosevelt's New Deal in 1938, a sizable number of Americans believed that Johnson's Great Society had overreached. The 1966 midterm election was the public's way of signaling the need for retrenchment. Much as FDR had encountered in the years after 1938, it would be a rejuvenated Conservative Coalition that would take philosophical control of the congressional agenda.

The 1966 Midterm election

The 1966 congressional elections brought the Democrats back to earth and to the loss of 47 Democratic seats in the House. Democrats held 248 seats and continued to organize the House with John McCormack remaining as Speaker, but the loss of northern and western seats placed control of the legislative agenda back in the hands of the Conservative Coalition. This was the unhappy prospect greeting the Democratic leaders as they opened the 90th Congress in 1967.

For John McCormack, this election saw the departure of two members who had played major roles in his congressional life. The best known of these was 42-year veteran House Republican Joe Martin of North Attleboro who had served as Republican floor leader for 16 years (1939–47, 1949–53, 1955–59) and Speaker for two terms (1947–49 and 1953–55). Martin's speakerships were bookended by Sam Rayburn's and his 20-year leadership career had been conterminous with John's until his 1959 ouster by Charlie Halleck in the wake of widespread Republican defeats in 1958. Joe would lose to the feisty Margaret Heckler in the 1966 Republican primary. She was 46 years younger than Joe. Her later defeat in 1982 by Democratic Representative Barney Frank who had been placed in the same district led to her being named Secretary of Health and Human Services by President Reagan.[168] Another renomination loser in 1966 was Rules Committee Chair Howard W. Smith of Virginia who had served in the House for 36 years with John (1931–67) and 12 years as Rules chair (1955–67). Theirs was a relationship intermittently friendly and adversarial.[169]

In spite of the seat loss, the *Boston Globe* declared on John's 75th birthday, December 21, 1966[170]:

> McCormack is undisputed kingpin of the House of Representatives, five years after succeeding the late Speaker Sam Rayburn. He is the acknowledged leader not only of 248 House Democrats but of the entire body. Earlier doubts that the Bostonian, for 17 years a highly partisan majority leader, would be equal to filling the speakership have faded. Now he enjoys wide respect from both sides of the political aisle.

John McCormack was clearly at the peak of his political power, but there was some foreshadowing of how difficult the next year would be. However, little did John realize that he was about to face the four most troubling years of his political and personal life. The upcoming 90th Congress would be a painful one. President Johnson and Speaker

McCormack both knew that there would be little if any expansion of the initiatives they had created in the previous three years, but could they defend the ones that they had now put in place?

Notes

1 Drew Pearson and Jack Anderson, *The Case against Congress: A Compelling Indictment of Corruption on Capitol Hill* (New York: Simon & Schuster, 1968), p. 283.
2 Wilfred C. Rogers, "McCormack Now First in Line of Succession," *BG*, November 23, 1963, p. 21.
3 "Rep. McCormack Is Next in Line," *WP*, November 23, 1963, p. A6.
4 Walt Brown, *Treachery in Dallas* (New York: Carroll & Graf, 1995), p. 283.
5 Jim Bishop, *The Day Kennedy Was Shot* (New York: Funk & Wagnalls, 1968), pp. 338–39.
6 Gerald Blaine with Lisa McCubbin, *The Kennedy Detail: JFK's Secret Service Agents Break Their Silence* (New York: Gallery Books, 2010), pp. 264–65.
7 Nate Jones, "Double Take: Lyndon Johnson Was Nearly Shot by Secret Service? A Day after JFK Died," *TIME*, October 20, 2010.
8 Felix Belair, Jr., "Secret Service Faces Changes in Its Procedures as a Result of the Assassination," *NYT*, November 24, 1963, p. 5.
9 C. D. DeLoache FBI Memorandum to Mr. Mohr, November 22, 1963. John W. McCormack's FBI files.
10 C. D. DeLoache FBI Memorandum to Mr. Mohr, November 23, 1963. John W. McCormack's FBI files.
11 Author's interview with the Hon. Jim Wright, Fort Worth, Texas, January 2011.
12 Easily the most definitive retrospective on the years since Kennedy's assassination is the remarkable book by Larry J. Sabato, *The Kennedy Half Century: The Presidency, Assassination, and Lasting Legacy of John F. Kennedy* (New York: Bloomsbury, 2013).
13 William Manchester, *The Death of a President, November 20–November 25, 1963* (New York: Harper & Row, 1967), p. 508.
14 Ibid.
15 Ibid., p. 541.
16 While Ruth Silva's book *Presidential Succession* (Ann Arbor: University of Michigan Press, 1951) was the first to explore the topic, the definitive work is that of John D. Feerick's *The Twenty-Fifth Amendment: Its Complete History and Applications*, 3rd ed. (New York: Fordham University Press, 2014) first published in 1976 and now in its third edition.
17 Michael R. Beschloss, ed., *Taking Charge: The Johnson White House Tapes, 1963–1964* (New York: Simon & Schuster, 1997), photo pages, p. 224ff.
18 McCormack Papers, Gotlieb Archival Research Center, Boston University.
19 In an effort to diminish the likelihood of either of these two men gaining the presidency through the legislated line of succession, a constitutional amendment was proposed by U.S. Senator Birch Bayh (Dem-Ind.). To hammer home his point about the necessity of the amendment, the fateful 1963 photograph of McCormack and Hayden seated behind President Johnson graced the cover of Senator Bayh's book, *One Heartbeat Away: Presidential Disability and Succession* (Indianapolis: Bobbs-Merrill, 1968).

20 The Presidential succession issue was a frequent topic in the Johnson tapes of January 8, 1964. Dick Russell, p. 312, Mike Mansfield, p. 319, James, "Scottie" Reston of *The New York Times*, p. 335, and James Rowe, pp. 340–42. The reference to the "McCormack slap" appears in Kent B. Germany and Robert David Johnson, eds., *Lyndon B. Johnson: The Presidential Recordings* (New York: W. W. Norton, 2005), Vol. III, p. 568.

21 McCormack discussed the job with Don Oberdorfer, "The Job John McCormack Dreads," *Saturday Evening Post*, March 21, 1964, pp. 66–68.

22 LBJ to John McCormack, November 29, 1963, in Max Holland, ed., *Lyndon B. Johnson: The Presidential Recordings* (New York: W. W. Norton, 2005), Vol. I, pp. 302–308. A fuller depiction may be found in Holland's *The Kennedy Assassination Tapes: The White House Conversations of Lyndon B. Johnson Regarding the Assassination, the Warren Commission and the Aftermath* (New York: Alfred A. Knopf, 2004), pp. 161–66.

23 John W. McCormack letter to Lyndon B. Johnson, November 16, 1940, LBJ Library, University of Texas, Austin, Texas.

24 Robert David Johnson and David Shreve, eds., *Lyndon B. Johnson: The Presidential Recordings* (New York: W. W. Norton, 2005), Vol. II, p. 628.

25 LBJ letter to the McCormacks, October 18, 1968, LBJ Library.

26 LBJ letter to John McCormack, December 21, 1967, LBJ Library.

27 Tom McNamara, "The Washington Merry-Go-Round: McCormack Is Loyal Team Man," *WP*, October 23, 1965, p. B11.

28 Anthony Lewis, "Key Domestic Problem for Johnson—Civil Rights," *NYT*, November 24, 1963, p. 91.

29 Roscoe Drummond, "No Wavering: Why Civil Rights Legislation Will Move More Rapidly through Congress," *BG*, November 24, 1963, p. 8.

30 Walter Lippmann, "Conspiracy on Capitol Hill: Congress Refuses to Legislate but Wants to Take over Power Reserved to the President," *BG*, December 26, 1963, p. 10.

31 Congressional Quarterly, *Congress and the Nation 1945–1964* (Washington, DC: CQ Press, 1965), pp. 723–24.

32 See "Wheat Sales to Russia," in Congressional Quarterly, *Congress and the Nation, 1945–1964:* (Washington, DC: Congressional Quarterly, 1965), pp. 723–24. LBJ to Larry O'Brien, November 25, 1963, in Max Holland, ed., *Lyndon B. Johnson: The Presidential Recordings* (New York: W. W. Norton, 2005), Vol. I, pp. 158–59. See also Michael Amrine, *This Awesome Challenge: The Hundred Days of Lyndon Johnson* (New York: Putnam, 1964), pp. 54–55.

33 See President Johnson's account of this event in his book, *The Vantage Point: Perspectives of the Presidency, 1963–1969* (New York: Holt, Rinehart and Winston, 1971), pp. 39–40. The quotation appears on p. 40.

34 John Leonard, "Admirers Greet Barry at N.H. Coffee Klatches," *BG*, January 9, 1964.

35 A vivid depiction of Kennedy's adroit handling of that crisis appears in Christopher Matthews, *Jack Kennedy: Elusive Hero* (New York: Simon & Schuster, 2011), pp. 363–73.

36 "Rep. McCormack Again Urged to Quit as Speaker," *WP*, December 6, 1963, p. A4.

37 "Columnist Charges Plot for McCormack Ouster," *BG*, December 10, 1963, p. 4.

38 Rowland Evans and Robert Novak, "Inside Report: Reluctant Liberals," *WP*, December 17, 1963, p. A17.

39 Chalmers M. Roberts, "Congressional Haggle Highlights '64 Politics," *WP*, December 22, 1963, p. A1.

40   Julian E. Zelizer, *Taxing America: Wilbur D. Mills, Congress and the State, 1945–1975* (New York: Cambridge University Press, 1998), p. 146.

41   Revenue Act of 1964 was approved February 26, 1964 (78 Stat. 19-146). See "Revenue Act of 1964," in *Congress and the Nation, 1945–1964*, pp. 437–42.

42   Notes on the First Congressional Leadership Breakfast, December 3, 1963, from the Presidential Appointment File, LBJ Library from Jonathan Rosenberg and Zachary Karabell, *Kennedy, Johnson, and the Quest for Justice: The Civil Rights Tapes* (New York: W. W. Norton, 2003), p. 216.

43   Eleanor C. Lewis, "The House Committee on Rules and the Legislative Program of the Kennedy and Johnson Administrations," *Capitol Studies*, II (Fall 1978), pp. 27–38. See also two articles by Douglas M. Fox and Charles H. Clapp, "The House Rules Committee's Agenda-Setting Function, 1961–1968," *Journal of Politics*, XXXII (May 1970), pp. 440–43; and "The House Rules Committee and the Programs of the Kennedy and Johnson Administrations," *Midwest Journal of Political Science*, XIV (November 1970), pp. 667–72.

44   Two valuable accounts of the bill's passage through the House are Clay Risen, *The Bill of the Century: The Epic Battle for the Civil Rights Act* (New York: Bloomsbury, 2014); and Todd S. Purdum, *An Idea Whose Time Has Come: Two Presidents, Two Parties, and the Battle for the Civil Rights Act of 1964* (New York: Henry Holt/Picador, 2015).

45   *Congress and the Nation, 1945–1964*, pp. 96A–97A.

46   LBJ to McCormack and Emanuel Celler February 10, 1964, in Robert David Johnson and Kent B. Germany, eds., *Lyndon B. Johnson: The Presidential Recordings* (New York: W. W. Norton, 2005), Vol. IV, p. 442.

47   This account is thanks to Clay Risen, author of *The Bill of the Century: The Epic Battle for the Civil Rights Act*, p. 119.

48   The most comprehensive portrait of the struggle in the Senate may be found in Robert Mann, *The Walls of Jericho: Lyndon Johnson, Hubert Humphrey, Richard Russell, and the Struggle for Civil Rights* (New York: Harcourt, Brace & Co., 1996). Mann underplayed the role of the House in the 1964 battle.

49   *Congress and the Nation, 1945–1964*, p. 1637.

50   The stylistic differences between the two Senate majority leaders are effectively captured in back-to-back essays published in Norman J. Ornstein, ed., *Congress in Change: Evolution and Reform* (New York: Praeger Publishers, 1975), pp. 117–54. The Johnson essay was by Robert D. Novak and Rowland Evans, "Lyndon B. Johnson: The Ascent to Leadership," and was excerpted from their book, *Lyndon B. Johnson: The Exercise of Power* (New York: New American Library, 1966). The Mansfield essay was by Andrew Glass and entitled "Mike Mansfield, Majority Leader," *National Journal* (March 6, 1971), pp. 499–512.

51   "Harris, William Julius," *BDUSC* (1989 ed.), p. 1141; and Josephine Mellichamp, "William J. Harris," in *Senators from Georgia* (Huntsville, AL: The Strode Publishers Inc., 1976), pp. 215–17.

52   "Russell, Richard Brevard, Jr.," *BDUSC* (1989 ed.), p. 1754.

53   James MacGregor Burns, *Edward Kennedy and the Camelot Legacy* (New York: W. W. Norton & Company, 1976), p. 99.

54   Russell's post-Reorganization committee assignments may be found in Nelson with Bensen and Mitchell, *Committees in the United States Congress, 1947–1992*, Volume 2, *Committee Histories and Member Assignments*, pp. 771–72.

55 "1948: Thirtieth Democratic Convention," in Bain and Parris, *Convention Decisions and Voting Records*, rev. ed., p. 276.

56 Steinberg, *Sam Johnson's Boy: A Close-Up of the President from Texas* (New York: Macmillan, 1968), p. 205.

57 Doris Kearns, *Lyndon Johnson and the American Dream* (New York: Harper & Row, 1976), pp. 103–109; and Steinberg, *Sam Johnson's Boy*, pp. 338–41.

58 Clinton Jacob Woods, "Strange Bedfellows: Congressman Howard W. Smith and the Inclusion of Sex Discrimination in the 1964 Civil Rights Act," *Southern Studies*, XVI (Spring–Summer 2009), pp. 1–32; and Jo Freeman, "How 'Sex' Got Into Title VII: Persistent Opportunism as a Maker of Public Policy," *Law and Inequality: A Journal of Theory and Practice*, IX (March 1991), pp. 163–84.

59 Civil Rights Act of 1964, approved July 2, 1964 (78 Stat. 241-268). See also "Civil Rights Act of 1964 Is Signed Into Law," *CQWR*, July 3, 1964, pp. 1331–32.

60 See "Barry Goldwater's Convention: Coup at the Cow Palace," in White, *The Making of the President 1964*, pp. 190–220.; "The Republicans," in W. R. Rorabaugh's excellent *The Real Making of the President: Kennedy, Nixon and the 1960 Election* (Lawrence: University of Kansas Press, 2009), pp. 95–122.

61 White, "Barry Goldwater's Convention: Coup at the Carl Palace," in *The Making of the President 1964*, pp. 190–242.

62 For a fuller account of this election, see chapter 3, "Landslide Lyndon," in Robert Dallek's definitive biography on LBJ, *Flawed Giant: Lyndon Johnson and His Times, 1961–1973* (New York: Oxford University Press, 1998).

63 For a focused account of the occasion, see John C. Skipper's *Showdown at the 1964 Democratic Convention: Lyndon Johnson, Mississippi and Civil Rights* (Jefferson, NC: MacFarland & Company, Inc., 2012); and chapter 6 "Freedom Now—The Negro Revolution" of Theodore H. White's *The Making of the President 1964* (New York: Atheneum Publishers, 1965).

64 'McCormack, Kennedy Factions Vie on Seating Issue," *BG*, August 25, 1964, p. 6.

65 C. R. Owens, "Atlantic City Aftermath: Kennedy and the McCormacks," *BG*, August 30, 1964, p. A4.

66 Gerald Pomper, "The Nomination of Hubert Humphrey for Vice President," *Journal of Politics*, XXVIII (August 1966), pp. 639–59.

67 White, *The Making of the President 1964*, p. 292.

68 Tonkin Gulf Resolution was approved on August 10, 1964 (78 Stat. 384). The dubious legal issues raised by this resolution are explored in William W. Van Alstyne, "Congress, the President, and the Power to Declare War: A Requiem for Vietnam," *University of Pennsylvania Law Review*, CXXI (November 1972), pp. 1–28.

69 See "Congress Backs President in Viet Nam Crisis," *CQWR*, August 7, 1964, pp. 1667–69.

70 Economic Opportunity Act of 1964 was approved August 20, 1964 (78 Stat. 508-534). See "Johnson's Anti-Poverty Bill Coordinated Several Programs," *Congress and the Nation, 1945–1964*, pp. 1326–29.

71 Food Stamp Act of 1964 approved on August 31, 1964 (78 Stat. 703-709). See "Food Stamp Plans," *Congress and the Nation, 1945–1964*, pp. 740–41.

72 Interest Equalization Tax was approved September 2, 1964 (78 Stat. 809-847). See also "Interest Equalization Tax," *CQWR*, August 21, 1964, pp. 1903–04.

73 Wilderness Act of 1964 was approved September 3, 1964 (78 Stat. 890-896). See also "Congress Clears Bill Establishing Wilderness System," *CQWR*, August 28, 1964,

pp. 1969–70; and Land and Water Conservation Fund Act was approved September 3, 1964 (78 Stat. 897-904). See also "Congress Clears Land Conservation Fund," *CQWR*, September 4, 1964, pp. 2023–25.

74	National Defense Education Act Amendments were approved on October 16, 1964 (78 Stat. 1100–09). See also "NDEA, Impacted Areas," *CQWR*, August 7, 1964, pp. 1680–81.

75	Robert C. Albright, "Dying 88th Leaves Record for Critics: Congress Sheds Lethargy Ignores Scandal to Mold Major Legislation," *WP*, August 16, 1964, p. E1.

76	"The Fear & The Facts," *TIME*, September 25, 1964. See also Robert Mann's *Daisy Petals and Mushroom Clouds: LBJ, Barry Goldwater, and the Ad That Changed American Politics* (Louisiana State University Press, 2011).

77	*CQ's Guide to U.S. Elections* (Washington, DC: Congressional Quarterly Press, 1975), p. 290 and 297.

78	"Democrats Score Net Gain of 38 House Seats," *CQWR*, November 6, 1964, pp. 2643–58.

79	For a fuller account of the Goldwater candidacy in the South, see Bernard Cosman's *Five States for Goldwater; Continuity and Change in Southern Presidential Voting Patterns* (Tuscaloosa: University of Alabama Press, 1966).

80	"Congress Grants 57.6% of Johnson's Specific Requests," *CQWR*, October 23, 1964, pp. 2561–69.

81	Robert L. Peabody, "The Ford-Halleck Minority Leadership Contest, 1965," *Leadership in Congress: Stability, Succession, and Change* (Boston: Little, Brown, 1976), pp. 100–48.

82	"Williams, Watson Purge," *CQWR*, January 1, 1965, pp. 3–4, and "House Dixiecrats Stripped of Seniority," *WP*, January 3, 1965, p. A1.

83	"Seating Disputes," *CQWR*, January 8, 1965, pp. 30–31.

84	Vote on H Res.1, *CQWR*, January 8, 1965, pp. 58–59.

85	"Pretenders in Congress," *WP*, January 1, 1965, p. A12; and Robert E. Baker, "Mississippi's Delegates Win Seats in House," *WP*, January 5, 1965, p. A9; Drew Pearson, "Washington Merry-Go-Round: Liberals Force a Roll Call," *WP*, January 8, 1965, p. D13.

86	Drew Pearson, "McCormack's Deal" in "Teacher Kerr's Absence Record," *WP*, May 20, 1965, p. F15.

87	Letter in the Drew Pearson Papers provided by Mr. Tyler Abell in a private email to the author on July 7, 2015.

88	"Inaugural Events," *WP*, January 20, 1965, p. A5.

89	Richard W. Bolling, *House Out of Order* (New York: Dutton, 1965).

90	Joseph S. Clark and other Senators, *The Senate Establishment* (New York: Hill and Wang, 1963).

91	Woodrow Wilson, *Congressional Government* (Boston: Houghton, Mifflin and Company, 1885).

92	Neil MacNeil, *Forge of Democracy: The House of Representatives* (New York: David McKay, 1963).

93	William S. White, *Home Place: The Story of U.S. House of Representatives* (Boston: Houghton Mifflin, 1965).

94	William S. White, *Citadel: The Story of the U.S. Senate* (New York: Harper, 1957).

95	Edward F. Woods, "Rep. Bolling Being Mentioned As Successor to Rayburn; Believed to Be Choice of House Speaker but Many Feel McCormack Has Inside Track," *St. Louis Post-Dispatch*, September 6, 1961, p. 1.

96   "Seniority: Democrats," in *CQ Almanac, 1962* (Washington, DC: Congressional Quarterly Press, 1963), pp. 30–31.

97   See book reviews, by Anthony Lewis, "Bolling Would Have Speaker Name Committee Heads," *NYT,* November 16, 1964, p. 17; and Frank Eleazar, "Congressman, Reporter Give House Unequal Demerits," *WP,* February 11, 1965, p. A26.

98   Data calculated from Morris P. Fiorina, David W. Rohde, and Peter Wissel, eds., "Historical Change in House Turnover," in Norman J. Ornstein ed., *Congress in Change: Evolution and Reform* (New York: Praeger Publishers, 1975), pp. 30–31.

99   Bolling, *House Out of Order*, pp. 73–74.

100 Best described in David J. Garrow, *Protest at Selma: Martin Luther King, Jr., and the Voting Rights Act of 1965* (New Haven, CT: Yale University Press, 1978).

101 Lyndon Johnson, *The Vantage Point: Perspectives of the Presidency, 1963–1969* (New York: Holt, Rinehart and Winston, 1971), p. 164.

102 Ibid.

103 See Goodwin's account of the speech in Richard N. Goodwin, *Remembering America: A Voice form the Sixties* (Boston: Little, Brown, 1988), pp. 326–336. In a well-intended effort to identify with John McCormack, Goodwin contended that McCormack was "born a few blocks from the poor East Boston neighborhood" where his father was raised (p. 331). However, East Boston and South Boston are separated by a channel and the distance between South Boston's Andrew Square and East Boston's Maverick Square is closer to 5 miles.

104 Johnson address on March 15, 1965, to Congress, The Miller Center, University of Virginia, accessed January 15, 2016.

105 Randall B. Woods, *LBJ: Architect of American Ambition* (New York: Free Press, 2006), p. 584; and Goodwin's *Remembering America* states, "In distant Alabama, Martin Luther King cried" (p. 334).

106 Voting Rights Act of 1965 was approved August 6, 1965 (79 Stat. 437-446). See also "Voting Rights Bill Sent to President," *CQWR,* August 6, 1965, pp. 1539–40. See also Gary May, *Bending toward Justice: The Voting Rights Act and the Transformation of American Democracy* (New York: Basic Books, 2013); House Vote on HR 6400, the Voting Rights Act, CQWR, July 16, 1965, pp. 1402–03.

107 "House Barber Shop Integrated," *Los Angeles Times*, October 14, 1965, p. C1.

108 House Vote on H Res. 8, "The 21 day rule," CQWR, January 8, 1965, pp. 58–59.

109 Online Johnson Tape Archives from the Miller Center, University of Virginia.

110 Michael Beschloss, *Reaching for Glory: Lyndon Johnson's Secret White House Tapes, 1964–1965* (New York: Simon & Schuster, 2001), p. 206.

111 Ibid., p. 207.

112 Ibid.

113 Among the valuable books dealing with Johnson's Great Society initiatives that mention John McCormack but give him little credit for its legislative success include John A. Andrew III, *Lyndon Johnson and the Great Society* (Chicago: Ivan R. Dee, 1998); Irving Bernstein, *Guns or Butter: The Presidency of Lyndon Johnson* (New York: Oxford University Press, 1996); Sidney M. Milkis and Jerome M. Mileur, eds., *The Great Society and the High Tide of Liberalism* (Amherst: University of Massachusetts Press, 2005); and Randall B. Woods, *Prisoners of Hope: Lyndon B. Johnson, the Great Society, and the Limits of Liberalism* (New York: Basic Books, 2016). McCormack is not cited in Eli Ginzburg and Robert M. Solow, eds., *The Great Society: Lessons for the*

Future (New York: Basic Books, 1974); and Marshall Kaplan and Peggy L. Cuciti, eds., *The Great Society and Its Legacy* (Durham, NC: Duke University Press, 1986).

114   Appalachian Regional Development Act of 1965, approved March 9, 1965 (79 Stat. 5-23). See also "$1.1 Billion Appalachia Aid Bill Approved," *CQ Almanac, 1965* (Washington, DC: Congressional Quarterly Service, 1966), pp. 788–97.

115   Elementary and Secondary Education Act of 1965, approved April 11, 1965 (79 Stat. 27-58). See also "First General School Aid Bill Enacted," *CQ Almanac, 1965*, pp. 275–93.

116   These changes are well documented in Eugene Eidenberg and Roy D. Morey, *An Act of Congress: The Legislative Process and the Making of Education Policy* (New York: W. W. Norton, 1969), Part II.

117   Excise Tax Reduction Act of 1965 was approved June 21, 1965 (79 Stat. 136-170). See "House Approves Excise Tax Reductions," *CQWR*, June 4, 1965, pp. 1045–46 and "Excise Tax Reduction Bill Sent to President," *CQWR*, June 18, 1965, pp. 1145–47.

118   The 25th Amendment was approved July 6, 1965 and ratified by the requisite number of States February 10, 1967 (79 Stat. 1327-1328). See also "Presidential Continuity Amendment Sent to States," *CQWR*, July 9, 1965, p. 1319.

119   Older Americans Act was approved July 14, 1965 (79 Stat. 218-226). See: "Agency for the Elderly," *CQ Almanac, 1965*, pp. 356–57.

120   See "Senate Select and Special Committees, 1993–2011," in Garrison Nelson and Charles Stewart III's *Committees in the U.S. Congress, 1993–2010* (Washington, DC: CQ Press, 2011), p. 175; and Val J. Halamandaris, "Aging Committee, House Select," in Donald C. Bacon, Roger H. Davidson, and Morton Keller's *The Encyclopedia of the United States Congress*, Vol. I (New York: Simon & Schuster, 1995), p. 17.

121   Drug Abuse Control Amendments of 1965, approved July 15, 1965 (79 Stat. 226-236). See also "Drug Controls," *CQWR*, July 16, 1965, pp. 1369–70.

122   Social Security Amendments of 1965 (Medicare for the Aged) were approved July 30, 1965 (79 Stat. 286-343). See also "Medical Care-Social Security Bill Sent to the President," *CQWR*, July 30, 1965, pp. 1493–1500.

123   Johnson, *The Vantage Point*, p. 214.

124   Social Security Amendments of 1965 (Medicaid for the Medically Needy) were approved July 30, 1965 (79 Stat. 343-353). See also "Medical Care-Social Security Bill Sent to the President," *CQWR*, July 30, 1965, pp. 1493–500.

125   Illinois Governor Otto Kerner chaired the National Advisory Commission on Civil Disorders and its Report was issued by the Superintendent of Documents (Washington, DC: U.S. Government Printing Office, 1968) and republished in Tom Wicker, ed., *Report of the National Advisory Commission on Civil Disorders* (New York: E.P. Dutton, 1968).

126   Housing and Urban Development Act of 1965 was approved August 10, 1965 (79 Stat. 451-509). See also "Senate Passes Bill to Establish Housing Department," *CQWR*, August 13, 1965, p. 1593.

127   Department of Housing and Urban Development Act was approved September 9, 1965 (79 Stat. 667-671). See also "Department of Housing Approved," *CQ Almanac 1965*, pp. 382–87.

128   President and Vice President Assassination Penalties, approved August 28, 1965 (79 Stat. 580-581). See also "Steps Taken to Follow Up Warren Commission Report," *CQ Almanac 1965*, pp. 582–84.

129　National Foundation on the Arts and the Humanities Act of 1965, approved September 29, 1965 (79 Stat. 845-855). See also "Foundation on the Arts and Humanities," *CQ Almanac 1965*, pp. 621–27.

130　Immigration and Nationality Act of 1965, approved October 3, 1965 (79 Stat. 911-922). See also "National Quotas for Immigration to End," *CQ Almanac 1965*, pp. 459–82.

131　Highway Beautification Act of 1965, approved October 22, 1965 (79 Stat. 1028-1033). See also "Highway Beautification Act of 1965," *CQ Almanac 1965*, pp. 724–33.

132　Water Quality Act of 1965, approved October 2, 1965 (79 Stat. 903–10). See also "Anti-Water Pollution Law Strengthened," *CQ Almanac 1965*, pp. 743–50.

133　Higher Education Act of 1965, approved November 8, 1965 (79 Stat. 1219-1270). See also "Scholarships Featured in College Aid Bill," *CQ Almanac 1965*, pp. 294–305.

134　Jeffrey R. Biggs and Thomas S. Foley, *Honor in the House: Speaker Tom Foley* (Pullman: Washington State University, 1999), pp. 69–70; and Barbara Sinclair, *Legislators, Leaders, and Lawmaking: The U.S. House of Representatives in the Postreform Era* (Baltimore: The Johns Hopkins University Press, 1995), p. 118.

135　The best-known critique of the Great Society is Charles Murray *Losing Ground: American Social Policy, 1950–1980* (New York: Basic Books, 1995); and a more balanced view is Irwin Unger, *The Best of Intentions: The Triumphs and Failures of the Great Society under Kennedy, Johnson, and Nixon* (New York: Doubleday, 1996)

136　"Congress Unusually Cooperative with President's Program," *CQWR*, November 19, 1965, p. 2341.

137　"Congress Backs Johnson on 93% of Roll-Call Votes," *CQ Almanac, 1965*, pp. 1099–1100.

138　Drew Pearson, "Laws by the Loaf: President's Bread-Breaking and Freshman Idealism Made 89th Congress a Smasher," *WP*, October 24, 1965, p. E7.

139　"Back of the 'Conservative Coalition' is Broken," *CQ Almanac 1965*, p. 1083.

140　Author's telephonic interview with Dr. Martin Sweig, May 1997. "D.J. McCormack Was Brother of U.S. Speaker," *BG*, January 8, 1966, p. 20.

141　A letter to the author from Mr. John Kelley, the Business Agent of the Boston Catholic Cemetery Association, dated April 7, 1997, contains a list of the McCormacks buried in grave 1915—section 2 of Mt. Benedict Cemetery in West Roxbury, Massachusetts, contains the names of: Catherine A. McCormick, 19, buried 10/3/1906; Patrick H. McCormick, 24, buried 3/30/1911; Mary McCormick, 52, buried 5/12/1913; and Donald J. McCormack, 65, buried 1/10/1966.

142　James T. Patterson, *The Eve of Destruction: How 1965 Transformed America* (New York: Basic Books, 2012).

143　See some of the critiques: Ernest M. Collins, "Congress Is Losing Its Grip," *Social Studies*, LVII (March 1966), pp. 104–108.

144　Freedom of Information Act, approved July 4, 1966 (89 Stat. 250-251). See also "Freedom of Information Bill Enacted," *CQ Almanac 1966*, pp. 556–59.

145　Sam Archibald, "The Early Years of the Freedom of Information Act—1955 to 1974," *PS: Political Science and Politics*, XXVI (December 1993), pp. 726–31.

146　Urban Mass Transportation Act of 1966, approved September 8, 1966 (8 Stat. 715-717). See also "Urban Mass Transit Grants Extended," *CQ Almanac 1966*, pp. 802–05.

147　Highway Safety Act of 1966, approved September 9, 1966 (80 Stat. 731-737). See also "Traffic, Auto Safety Act," *CQ Almanac 1966*, pp. 269–78.

148　Department of Transportation Act, approved October 15, 1966 (80 Stat. 931-950). See also "Transportation Department Created," *CQ Almanac 1966*, pp. 773–87.

149   Fair Labor Standards Amendments of 1966, approved September 23, 1966 (80 Stat. 830-845). Certain provisions of this Act were subsequently held unconstitutional in *National League of Cities v. Usery*, 426 U.S. 833 (1976). See also "Expansion of Minimum Wage Law Approved," *CQ Almanac 1966*, pp. 821–30.

150   National Wildlife Refuge System Administration Act, approved October 15, 1966 (80 Stat. 926-930). See also "Threatened Wildlife Species," *CQ Almanac 1966*, p. 660.

151   Clean Water Restoration Act of 1966, approved November 3, 1966 (80 Stat. 1246-1254). See also "Water Pollution Control Funds Expanded," *CQ Almanac 1966*, pp. 632–45.

152   Financial Institution Supervisory Act of 1966, approved October 16, 1966 (80 Stat. 1028-1056). See also "Bank Supervision," *CQ Almanac 1966*, pp. 746–52.

153   Demonstration Cities and Metropolitan Development Act of 1966, approved November 3, 1966 (80 Stat. 1255-1296). See also "Housing, Demonstration Cities Bill Enacted," *CQ Almanac 1966*, pp. 210–30.

154   Rowland Evans and Robert Novak, "The Wallace Rout: Alabama Governor Tried to Stop Poverty War Grant Because of Race and Politics," *WP*, October 17, 1965, p. E7.

155   Richard L. Lyons, "Bay State Democrats Face Blood-Letting in Primary: Kennedy Leadership Still Lacking," *WP*, June 12, 1966, p. A9.

156   Christopher Lydon, "For Governor—M'Cormack Outruns a Strong O'Donnell," *BG*, September 14, 1966, p. 1.

157   Helen O'Donnell, *A Common Good: The Friendship of Robert F. Kennedy and Kenneth P. O'Donnell* (New York: William Morrow and Company, Inc., 1998), pp. 364–71.

158   Ibid., p. 371.

159   Lyndon B. Johnson letter to Edward J. McCormack, Jr., October 1, 1966, LBJ Library.

160   James S. Doyle, "With Ted as State Party Leader Kennedys, McCormacks Unite," *BG*, September 20, 1966, p. 5.

161   *Congressional Quarterly's Guide to U.S. Elections* (1975 ed.), p. 414.

162   Tyler Abell conversations with the author throughout 2015.

163   See the overview of this session in Floyd M. Riddick and Murray Zweben, "American Government and Politics: Eighty-Ninth Congress, Second Session," *Western Political Quarterly*, XX (March 1967), pp. 173–90.

164   "McCormack Denounces 'Quit Viet Nam Notion,'" *BG*, May 24, 1966, p. 3.

165   Jeffrey Cohen, *The President's Legislative Policy Agenda, 1789–2002* (New York: Cambridge University Press, 2012), figure 4.5 on p. 127.

166   John W. McCormack, "McCormack Reviews Session," *BG*, October 23, 1966, p. 21.

167   AIPO, *The Gallup Poll, 1935–1971*, III: pp. 1855, 1922, 2026, 2038.

168   "Heckler, Margaret M.," *BDUSC* (1993 ed.), p. 1165.

169   Bruce J. Dierenfield, *Keeper of the Rules: Congressman Howard W. Smith of Virginia* (Charlottesville: University Press of Virginia, 1987).

170   "McCormack Starts 76th Year Quietly," *BG*, December 21, 1966, p. 11.

22

The Unraveling, 1967–68

With American troop commitments to Vietnam numbering in the hundreds of thousands and widespread summertime eruptions in the nation's urban ghettoes, the positive thrust of Lyndon Johnson's Great Society agenda ran aground. Johnson's popularity began its inexorable downward slide at the close of 1966 as he fell below 50% approval in the Gallup Poll. His liberal congressional allies suffered as well, not enough to lose party control of Congress, but enough to lose philosophical control of it. The 1966 midterm election cost the House Democrats 47 seats and shrunk their margin over the House Republicans from 155 seats (295 to 140) to only 51 (248 to 197).[1] Most Republican gains were in the North and West while many southern Republicans who had first gained seats in the five states carried by Barry Goldwater in 1964 proved to be more electorally resilient and philosophically conservative than the Democrats they had displaced.

When Democratic losses are great, the fall-off among northern and western members is disproportionately high. With their numbers seriously depleted, liberals were justifiably concerned that their agenda had lost its momentum and with war-based jingoistic feelings overtaking the nation, they ruefully realized that they would be hard-pressed to protect the legislative gains of the Great Society and reluctantly relinquished any hope that they could extend them.

Serious fissures developed within the Democratic coalition that had produced a 44-state landslide for the Johnson-Humphrey ticket barely two years earlier. College students opposed to the enlarged military draft launched a number of campus protests throughout the country. Their loud and raucous chant, "Hey, Hey, LBJ, How many kids did you kill today?" highlighted both the casualty rate from the thousands of 19-year-olds drafted into the army and the even larger numbers of Vietnamese children killed in the constant bombing raids. From the great California public universities like UCal-Berkeley and UCLA to the massive land grant universities of the Midwest like Michigan, Wisconsin, and Iowa to the private college bastions of the Northeast-like Harvard, Cornell, Columbia, and Yale, it seemed as if the universities and colleges were at war with the nation. The campus antiwar demonstrations created serious tension between liberals who supported the protests and labor union members whose sons did not have the educational deferments to escape the draft. The old liberal-labor coalition began to crumble as the so-called hard hat defenders of the Vietnam War emerged to confront the protestors.

Liberal Discontent: In its year-end review of the 2nd Session of the 89th Congress, *CQ* headlined, "'Conservative Coalition' Shows New Life."[2] That this summation occurred with the membership elected in the 1964 Johnson landslide was troubling enough but with 47 House and 3 Senate Democratic seats lost in 1966, the Conservative Coalition would be further enhanced and emboldened. This was the unhappy prospect greeting Democratic leaders 75-year-old Speaker John McCormack in the House and 63-year-old Senate Majority Leader Mike Mansfield in the Senate as they swore in the new members of the 90th Congress on January 3, 1967. John was now second in seniority, trailing only his old friend Judiciary Chair Manny Celler, the dean of the House.

Congressional liberals took the 1966 losses especially hard. The estimated loss among House liberals numbered 40. Legislative gains that the DSG had made in 1965–66 were now at risk. The "21-day rule" of the 90th Congress that allowed bills to be reported out of committee regardless of the chair's obstructionist efforts was rescinded by a vote of 233 to 185 on January 10, 1967.[3]

Few congressional analysts understood the tensions within the House during this time better than the University of California's Nelson W. Polsby, whose last published book *How Congress Evolves: Social Bases of Institutional Change* captured the conflict between the emboldened liberals of the DSG and the entrenched southern committee chairs.[4] By allying himself with Dick Bolling, Polsby gained a vantage point on the conflict that few fellow political scientists enjoyed and combined with his command of history and trenchant comments about human behavior his book provided a valuable window on how this tumultuous decade, the last of John McCormack's House career, unfolded.

The 1967 DSG battle against the seniority system took on renewed concern as 11 of the House's 20 committees had chairs from Confederate states—five from Texas alone— with another four from states bordering the Confederacy—Kentucky, Maryland, and West Virginia. The "big three" committees remained southern chaired—Ways and Means with Wilbur Mills of Arkansas; Appropriations with George Mahon of Texas; and Rules with William Colmer of Mississippi. It was the arrival of Colmer that was most troubling. He was as much a segregationist as his pal and predecessor Howard W. Smith, albeit with a lower profile.

Racial tension increased as white support for black gains lessened in the wake of the urban riots. Data in the 1967 National Advisory Commission on Civil Disorders, chaired by Illinois Democratic Governor Otto Kerner, reported that there had been 75 disturbances in 67 cities resulting in 83 deaths and 1,897 injuries.[5] White fears, both north and south, fueled what would be called the "backlash." These were the numbers before the even more widespread riots of 1968 occurred.

Black support for the Great Society coalition also frayed when blacks failed to realize the life improvements that had been presumably promised by the passage of civil rights acts. For Alexis de Tocqueville, the nineteenth-century French social critic and insightful observer of American democracy, this growing discontent could be characterized as "a revolution of rising expectations." The recent promise of legislated equality failed to be delivered to a people who had spent more than two centuries in chattel slavery and another century in the legislated inequality of racial segregation. Unlike the inchoate early protests of the college campuses, this tension had a specific focus and it was fastened on the most controversial of the more than one hundred African Americans to have served in the U.S. Congress, Adam Clayton Powell, Jr. (Dem-NY), whose chairmanship of the

House Education and Labor Committee was about to be stripped by vote of the House of Representatives. In an effort to undermine the seniority system that had elevated Powell to his chairmanship, a number of DSG members joined with the Conservative Coalition to deny Powell his committee post. It apparently was the hope of some DSG members that a weakened seniority system would make it easier to prevent ultraconservative segregationist Bill Colmer of Mississippi from becoming chair of Rules.[6] Their hopes were dashed and Colmer became chair.

For Speaker John McCormack, this was an echo of his 1949 decision to return Bill Colmer to the Rules Committee over Sam Rayburn's objections while also enabling Bill Dawson of Chicago, the House's second black Democrat to become the first ever African-American chair of a congressional committee. For John McCormack, this was a racial balancing act to limit southern opposition to Dawson's becoming a committee chair, but to a hard-core liberal like Dick Bolling, then a brand new House member, this was a "big mistake" by John that "changed the history of many subsequent Congresses."[7]

The black chair John McCormack sought to protect in 1967 was not the self-effacing Bill Dawson but the grandiose and self-dramatizing Adam Clayton Powell, Jr. While the House was debating to dethrone only its second African-American committee chair, the U.S. Senate was welcoming its first ever popularly elected African-American U.S. Senator, Edward Brooke of Massachusetts. Brooke was a tall, handsome Washington, DC–born, Boston University–educated lawyer who succeeded Eddie McCormack as Massachusetts's attorney general in 1963.

Adam Clayton Powell, Jr.: The Reverend Adam Clayton Powell Jr. was the son of mixed-race parents with his mother presumed to be of American Indian ancestry.[8] His father, Adam Clayton Powell, Sr., with a postgraduate degree from Yale, became the pastor of Harlem's largest Baptist church and paved the way for his son's political career. Adam, Jr. with degrees from Colgate and Columbia succeeded his father as pastor of the huge Abyssinian Baptist Church. First elected unopposed to the House in 1944 from New York City's heavily black Harlem 22nd Congressional District, Powell was only the third Democratic black to serve in the House and its first from the Northeast. Unlike John McCormack's ally Bill Dawson of Chicago, who preceded him by two years, Powell did not accept the deferential role expected of many blacks in white majority institutions. Powell was tall, good-looking, and relatively light-skinned leading him to "pass for white" early in his time at Colgate. He had a full head of hair that was slicked back and a thin mustache most common to movie villains of the 1930s and 1940s. Smoking ever-present cigarillos, Powell had a rakish swagger and the effect on women in his district and elsewhere was readily discernible. Claude Brown, the Harlem-born author of the acclaimed autobiography *Manchild in the Promised Land*, wrote that the women of Harlem voted for Powell "through their legs."[9]

Powell's House career began with service on the Labor and Indian Affairs Committees in 1945. The Legislative Reorganization Act of 1946 joined Labor to the Education Committee while Indian Affairs was one of five committees incorporated within the renamed Public Lands Committee. Two years later as a member of the depleted Democratic minority in the 80th Congress, Powell was fifth ranked on Education and Labor, relatively high for a second-term member. It was his primary assignment. That was when Powell would make the acquaintance of two newcomers to the committee—Democrat Jack Kennedy of Massachusetts and Republican Dick Nixon of California—both of whom he outranked and both of whom he bedeviled over the next two decades. Although not a member of the 1947 reconstituted Public Lands Committee or its 1951 reincarnation as Interior and Insular Affairs, Powell rejoined the committee in 1955 and served on it for six years, 1955–61. The Interior and Insular Affairs Committee had legislative jurisdiction over the affairs of Puerto Rico, whose thousands of immigrants to New York City had become an increasingly large portion of his Harlem district. It made political sense.

Demography was at work in Powell's life as his redrawn 16th District was changing with Spanish-speaking Puerto Ricans moving into East Harlem displacing the European immigrant Italian, Jewish, German, and Irish families that had settled there earlier. Parts of this district had once been represented in the House by the legendary Fiorello La Guardia and later by the Italian-descended American Labor Party leader Vito Marcantonio. By the 1950s, much of the area would become known as Spanish Harlem. Powell accommodated the change by returning to the renamed committee and taking Yvette Flores Diagio, a native of Puerto Rico, as his third wife in 1960.

Powell's nemesis, the 64-year-old North Carolinian Graham Barden, retired at the close of the 86th Congress, surrendering his chairmanship of Education and Labor to the 52-year-old Powell in 1961 at the start of the Kennedy-Johnson Administration. Barden's disdain for Powell was obvious to the House as Powell was regularly bypassed for subcommittee chairmanships during his first 14 years on the committee in spite of his being ranked third, 1951–59, and second, 1959–61, on the committee.[10] Throughout the 1950s, Powell angered the southern committee chairs and exasperated the House Democratic leadership by regularly sponsoring "Powell Amendments" which were civil rights riders to legislative appropriations bills. Virtually all were discarded by Virginia segregationist Howard Smith's Rules Committee but they slowed the appropriations process while impressing civil rights activists. In 1956, Powell's visibility increased when he chose to endorse the Republican Eisenhower-Nixon ticket over the Democratic Stevenson-Kefauver one. The fact that more than one hundred Democratic members of the Congress had committed themselves in the "Southern Manifesto" to the perpetuation of racial segregation was more than enough to estrange Powell from his own political party. The efforts of Resolutions Chair John McCormack and Bill Dawson at the 1956 Democratic Convention to work out a viable platform compromise on this most divisive issue were dismissed by Powell.

In 1961, Powell's time had come and as chair, he was eager to play a major role by pushing President Kennedy, his old Education and Labor Committee seatmate, into more progressive social legislation through the committee. However, his flamboyant lifestyle was replete with too many wives and multiple girlfriends, some of whom appeared on the committee's payroll but not always in its offices, and it hindered his role as a key legislative spokesman.

It was a minor crisis that bothered him the most. In a 1963 televised interview, Powell referred to a local female critic as "a bag woman" for interests opposed to him. She sued for slander and won. Powell's refusal to pay the court-ordered judgment to her made him subject to arrest and he began limiting his visits to Harlem on Sundays when he would give sermons at the Abyssinian Baptist Church. His haughty disdain for judicial process fueled his enemies, and dressing in African dashikis while publicly shouting out his pet phrase of "Keep the Faith, Baby" made him even more vulnerable to congressional censure.

Powell was entering his 23rd year of service when the 90th Congress commenced in 1967. He had been reelected in 1966 by more than 74% of the vote. Unlike his constituents, few fellow congressmen were enamored of him. The committee's legislative output had slipped because of his many absences and news accounts of payroll abuses had surfaced.

Several members had promised in the waning days of the 89th Congress to introduce measures to deny Powell his seat at the beginning of the 90th Congress. Particularly upset were fellow members of his Education and Labor Committee, who had successfully worked behind the scenes in the 89th Congress to change committee rules, depriving Powell of some of his power as chair. Liberals who might have supported him were perplexed and angered when Powell refused to vote for the Voting Rights Act of 1965 and the Civil Rights Bill of 1966 on grounds that they did not go far enough. Even greater tension was created when Powell held a meeting in late 1966 in committee chambers to plan for a conference on "black power."

Fellow legislators publicly complained of excessive travel at taxpayers' expense, nepotism, absenteeism, and the use of his power as chair of Education and Labor to prevent bills that he opposed from passing. Also hovering over Powell were several legal problems, including charges of tax evasion and a libel suit. Because he had failed to appear in court for the latter charge, Powell was held in contempt of court, for which he faced a jail term if he returned to his home state of New York. This was not a pleasing prospect for the House.

On January 9, 1967, the Democratic Caucus voted to strip Powell of his chairmanship of the Education and Labor Committee.[11] The last time a standing committee chair had been deprived of his title was in 1925. The Democratic Caucus turned the chairmanship over to the second-ranking Democrat, Carl Perkins of Kentucky, a white southerner.

The next day, House Resolution 1 was passed. As amended by Minority Leader Gerald R. Ford, Jr., it denied Powell his House seat pending the outcome of an investigation into his affairs. It was passed overwhelmingly, 363–65.[12] The investigation was to be undertaken by a select committee of nine. They were given five weeks to issue a report and recommend whether or not to allow Powell to take his seat in the 90th Congress. In the meantime, Powell was allowed to draw his regular salary.

As defined in the resolution[13]:

From House Resolution 1, as amended, 90th Congress, First Session, January 10, 1967: [Paragraph 1]

That the question of the right of Adam Clayton Powell to be sworn in as a Representative from the State of New York in the Ninetieth Congress, as well as his final right to a seat therein as such Representative, be referred to a special committee.... Until such committee shall report upon and the House staff decides such question and right, the said Adam Clayton Powell shall not be sworn in or permitted to occupy a seat in this House.

Speaker McCormack appointed nine members to this committee on January 19, 1967—five Democrats and four Republicans.[14] The chair was longtime McCormack ally Manny Celler, chair of the Judiciary Committee and the ranking minority member was Arch A. Moore (Rep-W.Va.). In the fourth majority slot was the committee's lone African-American member, John Conyers, Jr. of Detroit, and in the fifth majority slot was second-term Democrat Andy Jacobs of Indiana who was sympathetic to Powell and published a book-length history of the committee's activities, *The Powell Affair: Freedom Minus One.*[15]

Several reporters noticed McCormack's reluctance to remove Powell from the House, as evidenced in Associated Press articles such as "Feuding Over Powell: McCormack Soothes Demos" and "Powell Backed by McCormack."[16] As a supporter of the seniority rule, John McCormack was hesitant to kick out any member of the U.S. House, and the Powell case was no exception as reported by *Congressional Quarterly*[17]:

> Speaker John W. McCormack (D Mass.) apparently viewed this question as one of exclusion rather than expulsion. He ruled, in response to a parliamentary inquiry, that, if Powell's fitness to serve were brought to a vote after the investigation proposed by the [Morris] Udall resolution only a simple majority would be required, in spite of the fact that Powell would have been sworn in. McCormack did not elaborate on his ruling. No expulsions have been voted by the House since the representatives of the secessionist Southern states were expelled at the outbreak of the Civil War.

Powell's well-publicized difficulties with Congress had been noticed by 88% of people surveyed by Gallup in a poll released on February 5, 1967. A clear majority of those polled believed that Powell should not be allowed to keep his seat; however, "among Negroes, the opinion is 2 to 1 that the 58-year-old congressman should be allowed to retain his seat."[18]

The select committee was terminated upon the filing of its final report, House Report 27 (90–91), on February 23, 1967. The committee found that Powell's "conduct and behavior" had "reflected adversely on the integrity and reputation of the House and its Members."[19] It recommended that he be allowed to take his seat, but stripped of all his seniority, censured and condemned by the House, and pay an unprecedented fine of $40,000 to the House.

On March 1, 1967, the full House cast five separate votes in the Powell matter. Despite McCormack's hopes and the select committee's recommendations, the full House voted 307–116 on the resolution amended by Missouri Republican Thomas B. Curtis that Powell "be excluded as a member of the 90th Congress."[20] The New York Congressman then took the House of Representatives to court on March 8, arguing that the legislative body had acted unconstitutionally. The ironic defendant in the case was Powell defender Speaker John W. McCormack, and the case was known as *Powell v. McCormack.*

In the April 11 special election to fill his vacancy, Powell won going away with a landslide 86.3% of the vote.[21] The lower federal courts refused to hear Powell's case, afraid of passing judgment on a politically charged issue involving the members of the legislative branch. Their decisions sent the case to the Supreme Court. Before a decision could be handed down, the 90th Congress expired in January 1969. Powell was reelected once again by his loyal constituency to the 91st Congress. The House allowed Powell to take his seat in 1969, but stripped him of all seniority and fined him $25,000.

On June 16, 1969, in the final week of Chief Justice Earl Warren's tenure, the Supreme Court ruled 7–1 in favor of Powell with only Justice Potter Stewart, an Eisenhower-appointee, dissenting; declaring that the House had no power to deny him his seat if he met the constitutional requirements of age, citizenship, and residency.[22] Appropriately, it was his constituents, voting for Charles B. Rangel in the 1970 Democratic primary, that finally ended Powell's 26-year House career removing him permanently from the House of Representatives.

Almost conterminous with the House's wrestling with the Powell case was a Senate case involving financial mismanagement charges against Connecticut Democrat Thomas J. Dodd. Based upon information from Dodd's Senate staff, charges were leveled by investigative reporters Drew Pearson and Jack Anderson that Dodd had converted hundreds of thousands of dollars in campaign contributions for his personal use.[23] Dodd was investigated by the Senate's Select Committee on Standards and Conduct that recommended that he be censured by the Senate. On June 23, the Senate voted to censure Dodd by a vote of 51 to 45 but he was allowed to remain in his Senate seat[24] unlike the treatment accorded Powell by the House which voted to exclude Powell from membership in the 90th Congress.

House Committee on Standards of Official Conduct: The House had no permanent ethics committee comparable to that of the Senate and it was Jack Anderson's contention that John McCormack was disinclined to see one created.[25] Late in 1966, the House created the relatively toothless temporary House Select Committee on Standards and Conduct to prepare a code of conduct for House members. It was the powerful public impact of the Powell case that pushed the House into creating an ethics committee with standing status and a clear mandate. On April 13, 1967, the House by a vote of 400–0 finally created a 12-member bipartisan standing Committee on Standards of Official Conduct.[26]

Pearson and Anderson would later contend that "Speaker John McCormack, D-Mass., loaded the committee with members who could be depended upon not to embarrass their colleagues.[27] He gave the committee stern, private instructions to confine its investigation to altruistic generalities."

Johnson Popularity, 1967: John McCormack saw his primary mission as Speaker as moving Lyndon Johnson's program through the House of Representatives. President Johnson's success rate in the House was so high that conservative columnist Robert Novak contended that Speaker McCormack was virtually on Johnson's staff.[28] Unfortunately for McCormack, Johnson's popularity plateaued throughout the

Table 22.1 Gallup Poll Approval Ratings of President Johnson, 1967

Survey Dates	Release Date	Approve (%)	Disapprove (%)	No Opinion (%)
January 26–31, 1967	February 19	46	37	17
April 19–24, 1967	May 7	48	37	15
June 2–7, 1967	July 5	52	35	13
June 22–27, 1967	September 6	40	48	12
October 27 to November 1, 1967	November 5	38	50	12
November 16–21, 1967	November 26	41	49	10
December 7–12, 1967	December 31	46	41	13

Source: *American Institute of Public Opinion, The Gallup Poll, 1935-1971*, Vol. 3, passim.

year with a high of 52% approval in Gallup's July 5 release and 38% approval in its November 5 release. That Johnson's initial 1967 approval of 46% was identical to his last one concealed the volatility of his 1967 ratings.

What this meant for John McCormack was that he could no longer draw on the well of Lyndon Johnson's popularity to secure the passage of bills that the president wanted.

The 90th Congress: The contentious start to the 90th Congress made it clear that there would be no massive outpouring of legislation as had occurred in the 89th Congress. The 47-seat loss in the 1966 House elections shrunk the Democratic margin over the Republicans from 155 to 60.[29] In the Senate, the Democratic slippage was less with a net Democratic loss of 4 seats including a special election that shrank the Democrats' margin from 36 seats to 28 seats.

The Senate Democratic leadership team of Majority Leader Mike Mansfield of Montana and Majority Whip Russell Long of Louisiana remained in place, but there were signs that the thoughtful liberal Mansfield was not as comfortable with the heir of the Louisiana Hayride, Russell Long, "the Princefish," as he had been with former Whip and now Vice President Hubert Humphrey.

Historically, the party that lost a substantial number of seats in House elections often experienced major floor leadership disruptions. This had been true twice during the past decade when the House Republicans overthrew Minority Leader Joe Martin in 1959 following an embarrassing defeat in the 1958 congressional elections and again in 1965 when the 1964 Goldwater debacle depleted their ranks and they overthrew Minority Leader Charlie Halleck. Halleck was the beneficiary of the discontent in 1959 and the victim of it in 1965.

The House Republicans had a lengthy history of leadership battles that often occurred without congressional losses to inspire them. Majority status or minority status, seats gained or seats lost, the House Republicans were a far more contentious lot than the House Democrats.[30] So Speaker John McCormack and his team of Majority Leader Carl Albert and Majority Whip Hale Boggs were relatively immune from being overthrown within the Democratic Caucus. The Democratic House coalition was fragile enough without adding internecine leadership battles to the mix. But the

House Democratic liberals were frustrated. The loss of their two-to-one margin in the House over the Republicans meant that they had once again lost philosophical control of the chamber to the Conservative Coalition of Republicans and southern Democrats.

The Powell case had been disturbing to the House liberals. Many wanted Powell to be punished and hoped to show that they did not have one standard for white members who violated House rules and another standard for black members who were similarly guilty. Once Powell brought his case to the Supreme Court, the matter hung heavily over the chamber. For white liberals outside the House, it seemed as if Powell was being punished more for his public flamboyance than for his actual misdeeds.

What this meant for legislation was that it would be hard for John McCormack to focus on the task at hand, namely expediting Lyndon Johnson's legislation through this Congress. The Conservative Coalition was well aware of the growing discord within the House Democrats against McCormack, and it was able to thwart much of Johnson's programs and pass their own conservative-backed legislation. The *Congressional Quarterly Weekly Report*'s year-end assessment reported in December 29, 1967, that "House 'Conservative Coalition' Dominates Session."[31]

Despite the bad press, President Johnson's admiration of Speaker McCormack remained strong. On John's 76th birthday that year, LBJ praised him once more for his public service[32]:

> Dear John:
>
> The long friendship that you and [Miss] Harriet have so generously given me over these many years is among the best recurring gifts on every passing birthday—and one for which I am always deeply grateful.
>
> I appreciate the traditional thoughtfulness that prompts your message, but I assure you that what I value most is the selfless effort and unstinting counsel which you so readily lend to the difficult but dear public trust we share.
>
> Please accept my heartfelt thanks for your birthday wish—and for the American wish that you daily help fulfill.
>
> Sincerely,
> *LBJ*

Campus and Ghetto Uprisings: College campuses had been the major venue for demonstrations against the escalating war in Vietnam and the military draft was its primary focus. Anti-Johnson chants echoed through college campuses that year and harsh effigies of the beleaguered president appeared at many college demonstrations. Congress attempted to alleviate some of the tension when it changed the name of the 1951 Universal Military Training and Service Act to the Military Service Act of 1967.[33] Approved June 30, 1967, it extended the president's authority to induct men into the armed services through July 1, 1971, and it prohibited the president from instituting a draft lottery or other means of random selection of draftees without the specific approval of Congress. No surprise that in a May 31, 1967, Gallup Poll on President Johnson's popularity, 38% of students approved of LBJ, while 53% disapproved.[34]

As had occurred in the three previous summers, the nation's urban ghettoes veered into violent eruptions. The bloodiest ghetto uprisings in 1967 were in Newark, New Jersey, and Detroit, Michigan. The Newark riots of July 12–17 left 26 dead and hundreds wounded, while the Detroit riot of July 23–27 resulted in 43 deaths, 1,189 injured, and thousands of destroyed buildings.[35] As white sympathy for black difficulties evaporated, a counter movement gained political traction. Watching in Montgomery, Alabama, was former Governor George C. Wallace who planned to ride this angry white "backlash" wave into the White House in the 1968 presidential election.

Early Legislation: Gains made by conservatives in the 1966 elections manifested themselves quickly in the 1st Session. Approved on June 13, 1967, Congress passed the pro-business Investment Tax Credit Act that restored the 7% investment credit on the purchase of machinery and equipment and the allowance of accelerated depreciation in the case of certain real property.[36]

A little-noticed bill passed by the Congress late in the year would later have a major impact upon how Americans would receive their news. The act was known as the Public Broadcasting Act of 1967. Approved November 7, 1967, it established a public corporation to provide financial assistance for noncommercial educational television and radio broadcasting and authorized $9 million for fiscal 1968.[37]

One impact of the Vietnam War was to reinvigorate old isolationist impulses in the Congress culminating in the passage of the Foreign Assistance Act of 1967 that reduced the annual authorization for the foreign aid program to the lowest level in the history of foreign aid.[38] Approved November 14, 1967, it attached several restrictive amendments that curbed the president's authority to conduct foreign policy and prohibited all forms of aid under the foreign assistance acts to countries that traded with North Vietnam.

Two pieces of legislation that closed out the 1st Session were very evocative of the old Progressive Era laws. One was the Air Quality Control Act of 1967 that greatly enlarged existing federal responsibility for air pollution control in the absence of meaningful state action.[39] Approved November 21, 1967, it authorized the expansion of existing federal grants to states and local governments to assist in planning the implementation of air quality standards and provided for the establishment of federal interstate air quality planning agencies and expanded research and development programs for the control of pollution. In tones reminiscent of the muckrakers of the opening decade of the century, Congress passed the Wholesale Meat Act, approved December 15, 1967, which declared it "essential in the public interest that the health and welfare of the consumers be protected by assuring that the meat and meat food products distributed to them are wholesome, not adulterated, and properly marked, labeled, and packaged."[40]

Speaker John McCormack turned 76 on December 21, 1967. He was still younger than Sam Rayburn, who had died at the age of 79 holding the chair, but John McCormack's grasp on the office became more tenuous with each birthday. However, the Democratic majority which he was obliged to manage was not the relatively quiescent set of members that Rayburn had presided over.

The "Bobby Kennedy Law": Congress had grown weary of managing the U.S. Post Office and it instituted legislation to remove itself from the lobbying efforts of postal workers with the passage of the innocuously titled Postal Revenue and Federal Salary Act of 1967. Approved December 16, 1967, this act combined three measures: postal increases on all classes of mail, a raise for federal employees, and a liberalized federal employee life insurance plan.[41] Most importantly, the act provided for automatic future pay increases that would not require congressional action. It became Public Law 90–206.

Following the expected language on postage rates and size and weight limits was Section 221 amending Chapter 31 of Title 5 United States Code under the heading "Employment of relatives; restrictions." This was an anti-nepotism law sponsored by Iowa Democrat Neal Smith stating that "a public official may not appoint, employ, promote, advance, or advocate for appointment, employment promotion, or advancement in or to a civilian position in the agency in which he exercises jurisdiction or control any individual who is a relative of the public individual."[42] The list was exhaustive with 27 categories of relatives included.

The act easily passed the House on October 11 by a vote of 319–89.[43] It was informally known as the "Bobby Kennedy law." With JFK having appointed his brother as attorney general in January 1961 and his brother-in-law R. Sargent Shriver to be the first director of the Peace Corps in March 1961, President Kennedy would have been a two-time violator of this law. Much as the anti-third term 22nd Amendment passed in 1947 was a posthumous rebuke of FDR by the Republican-dominated 80th Congress, so too the Conservative Coalition–dominated 90th Congress chose to posthumously rebuke Kennedy for naming both his brother and his brother-in-law to posts over which "he exercises jurisdiction." The major difference was that Bob Kennedy was still alive and serving in the 90th Congress as the Junior Senator from New York State alongside his brother, Ted, the Senior Senator from Massachusetts. President Johnson took no position on the bill but may have appreciated the discomfit that it caused Bob Kennedy.

Congress also augmented the financial rewards of military service with the passage of the Military Pay Bill of 1967 that increased the monthly pay of servicemen, retroactive to October 1, 1967, by 4.5% for "regular compensation which included basic pay, quarters, and subsistence allowances."[44] Approved December 16, 1967, it also provided for automatic military pay raises in the future that would correspond to similar increases for federal civilian employees unless Congress took separate action on servicemen's salaries.

As members waited for the 2nd Session to convene on January 15, 1968, the Elementary and Secondary Education Amendments of 1967 were approved January 2, 1968, authorizing appropriations totaling $9,249,860,644 for fiscal 1969 and 1970 and adding an additional $132,884,000 to existing authorizations for fiscal 1968.[45] New programs under the law authorized a bilingual education project from non–English-speaking backgrounds, with additional fellowships awarded for teachers of these children; pilot projects to develop effective programs to prevent school dropouts; and technical assistance to rural schools that wished to apply for federal aid. There still were some Great Society glimmers in the air.

1967 Post-Mortem: In its session-ending assessment, the *CQ Weekly Report* issued a thirteen-page article on the Conservative Coalition, in which it analyzed the 1967 House Coalition victories[46]:

E-110,118
NOV 4 1967

REP. BOLLING
SAYS HOUSE OF
REPRESENTATIVES
NEEDS NEW
LEADER

McCORMACK

© 1967 HERBLOCK
THE WASHINGTON P

"Nonsense — I Have A Firm Grip On The Reins"

Figure 22.1 Herblock cartoon critical of Speaker McCormack, November 4, 1967 (Permission Herblock Foundation).

The House had its way on numerous important issues in addition to the major coalition victories on anti-poverty, model cities, rent supplements, spending cuts, crime control and foreign aid. . . . In all, the coalition won 34 domestic and four foreign policy victories.

Dick Bolling's anti-McCormack crusade never relented (Figure 22.1). In an interview with Joe Lastelic of his hometown *The Kansas City Star*, Bolling said of McCormack[47]:

"We haven't had very effective leadership," Bolling said. "Speaker McCormack is a very fine person who tries very hard, but he just does not have the skill to anticipate trouble. I would hope that John McCormack, who is a fine man, a fine Democrat, and has rendered many services to his party, would feel that seven years in the speakership was long enough by January, 1969, and he would step aside for a younger man."

With 205 of his 431 proposals approved, President Johnson had a 1967 Box score of 47.6%.[48] It was lower than any of his previous three years but it exceeded eight of the ten non–LBJ scores in the years from 1954 to 1963. For John McCormack, there were some triumphs and that year's was the passage of the Social Security Amendments of 1967 that provided an across-the-board increase of 13% to all beneficiaries under old-age, survivors and disability insurance programs.[49] Approved January 2, 1968, it raised the monthly minimum benefit from $44 to $55 and increased and liberalized retirement benefits to persons 72 and over who had not met Social Security requirements, and provided additional benefits to certain widows, widowers, and dependent children who had lost their parents.

Democrats in Distress: Congress concluded the 1st Session of the 90th Congress on December 15 but there was little optimism among congressional Democrats for the upcoming 1968 election. With LBJ's popularity in decline and opposition to the war growing daily, anxious Democrats hoped to pressure Johnson to reduce his steadfast commitment to the conflict by sponsoring challenges to his renomination. The logical choice was Bob Kennedy but he demurred. Days later on December 17, it would be Senator Eugene McCarthy of Minnesota who announced that he would enter the April 25 Massachusetts primary in hopes of gaining support from Massachusetts liberals who planned a January caucus to nominate an antiwar challenger to Johnson.[50]

On January 3, 1968, the Gallup Poll released its first survey of the year, indicating that a plurality of Americans disapproved of the way that Johnson was handling the situation in Vietnam, with 39% approving and 49% disapproving.[51] American troop strength in Vietnam hit its peak of 536,100 in 1968 and with no notice to congressional leaders, Johnson called up the military reserves on January 25.[52] Three days later, on January 28, 1968, Gallup released a poll saying Johnson's overall approval rating was at 48% to 39% disapproving.[53] It would get worse. The North Vietnamese and their Viet Cong allies launched the Tet Offensive on January 30 and 31. A week of intense fighting occurred in the capital city of Saigon, with multiple buildings targeted, including the American Embassy.[54] Americans had been repeatedly assured that "there was light at the end of the tunnel" in Vietnam, but were now horrified to see enemy soldiers storming the Embassy on television. When the vaguely competent General William Westmoreland announced that there was a need for another 211,000 troops that would have brought the overall force level to three-quarters of a million Americans in Vietnam, the disillusionment was instant. In the next poll, Johnson's overall numbers flipped to 41% approving and 47% disapproving.[55] The failures of the Vietnam policy were never more clearly revealed than in that dramatic week.

As LBJ's political altitude began to sink so too did that of his ally John McCormack. On February 26, John Herbers of the *New York Times* wrote a lengthy article entitled, "Move On to Have Albert Replace McCormack as Speaker."[56] Featured prominently in the piece was John's longtime nemesis Dick Bolling who was already sharpening his knives. However, the story also contained a fascinating contrary anecdote from an unnamed senior member who described John as looking like "an English undertaker" but was clearly impressed by John's vigor as he recalled, "I saw the Speaker rushing down the hall. He said he needed votes and was going after some member and off he went leaping up the stairs to get members to vote. The Speaker of the House, mind you, running up and down the stairs to get members to the floor."

The 1968 primaries and new tragedies

Unsurprisingly, it was in Massachusetts that speculation about LBJ's candidacy came to a head as the primary filing date fast approached. As they had in 1964, LBJ's operatives sought surrogates to run in his stead to ward off the McCarthy challenge. Syndicated columnists Rowland Evans and Robert Novak reported on March 3 that Senator Ted Kennedy passed on the offer as did both Larry O'Brien and John McCormack, "neither of whom relishes this onerous chore."[57]

Shortly afterward, political observers were stunned as the *Times* reported on March 6 that "President Johnson has decided not to enter any of the 15 Presidential primaries except those three where state law would make his candidacy automatic."[58] With the upcoming March 12 primary, New Hampshire's regular Democrats organized a write-in campaign for President Johnson, who once again demonstrated his long-standing aversion to primaries. With many hundreds of college students coming from nearby Massachusetts and shaving their beards, they became "clean for Gene." State party leaders loyal to the president engineered a massive write-in campaign for Johnson, replete with "loyalty" cards that one could sign and send to the White House indicating one's commitment to the beleaguered president. McCarthy captured 23,263 Democratic votes and 5,511 Republican votes for a total of 28,774 votes. Johnson's showing was slightly better: 27,520 Democratic votes and 1,778 Republican votes, totaling 29,298 votes.[59] Although Johnson had a 49.6% to 41.9% edge in the Democratic primary, his local supporters had overloaded the write-in ballot with more names than delegate slots. Consequently, McCarthy won the majority of the New Hampshire delegate votes, 20 to 6.[60]

U.S. Senator Robert F. Kennedy, who had passed on multiple pleas to engage Johnson in this battle, announced that he would run as well. Gene McCarthy was stunned by Kennedy's decision, and a clearly aggravated McCarthy New Hampshire volunteer remarked, "We woke up after the New Hampshire primary like it was Christmas day. . . . And when we went down to the tree, we found Bobby Kennedy had stolen our presents."[61] This was the battle that Lyndon Johnson had long anticipated. Jeff Shesol quoting W. DeVier Pierson's oral history with Johnson reported him saying, "I had been expecting this."[62] This was a contest that John McCormack feared but he knew exactly whom he would not support. Yet again, he would find himself opposing another Kennedy. And before long, John McCormack would soon lose his best-placed and most supportive ally, President Lyndon B. Johnson.

On Sunday, March 31, two days before the Wisconsin primary and an anticipated clear victory for Gene McCarthy, President Lyndon Johnson announced at the close of a televised address[63]:

> I have concluded that I should not permit the Presidency to become involved in the partisan divisions that are developing in this political year.
>
>   With America's sons in the fields far away, with America's future under challenge right here at home, with our hopes and the world's hopes for peace in the balance every day, I do not believe that I should devote an hour or a day of my time to any

personal partisan causes or to any duties other than the awesome duties of this office—the Presidency of your country.

. . .

Accordingly, I shall not seek, and I will not accept, the nomination of my party for another term as your President.

Thank you for listening.

Good night and God bless all of you.

A shock wave hit the nation and the world. To John McCormack, it was a "tremendous surprise" as he described it to T. Harrison Baker:[64]

I was sent a copy of what he was going to say. And Mrs. McCormack and I were in our apartment and were listening to him . . . then I got a telephone call from Barefoot Sanders [of the White House staff] as to the addition the President was going to say. That he was not going to be a candidate again. That's the first time I knew anything about it.

With no LBJ in the contest the antiwar forces had gained the upper hand in the party. McCormack was especially dismayed with the Bob Kennedy candidacy and on April 17, he called LBJ's Appointments Secretary and de facto Chief of Staff Marvin Watson and said[65]:

I have found that the people at home know the newspapers slander news against the President. I find that the people are behind the President. Certainly, you know my sentiments. I am a supporter of the President. The people know that that the President's policy of peace with justice is right. People do not want softness. Kennedy is not acceptable to them.

In a last plaintive plea, John said to Watson, "Besides that, I haven't given up hope on the President. I believe he will still be my candidate" (Figure 22.2).

Resurgent Riots: Four days after LBJ's announcement, the Reverend Martin Luther King Jr., the nation's most important civil rights leader and the youngest man ever to win the Nobel Peace Prize, was shot to death while standing on a motel balcony in Memphis, Tennessee. City after city braced for the riotous outrage that they knew would follow in the wake of the assassination of Dr. King. It came.

The prolonged morass of the Vietnam War, the rippling waves of protest among college students, the eruption of the nation's black ghettoes, and the strident racism of "backlashing" among many whites led to serious questions about the viability of American political institutions. Ghetto riots in Los Angeles, New York, Detroit, Newark, and many other cities left almost 2,000 injured and close to one hundred dead. Racial antagonism erupted throughout the nation.

As in 1964, when the Birmingham riots created support for the 1964 Civil Rights Act and the Selma March opened the way for the 1965 Voting Rights Act, the murder of Martin Luther King, Jr. generated congressional sympathy for African Americans,

Figure 22.2 McCormack and Johnson in the Cabinet Room, April 3, 1968 (Lyndon B. Johnson Library and Museum).

leading to the passage of the Civil Rights Act of 1968. Housing discrimination became the next agenda item for the civil rights movement, and Congress moved to address it with the Civil Rights Act of 1968. Approved April 11, 1968, this act prohibited discrimination in the sale or rental of about 80% of all housing.[66] It also broadened civil rights by providing criminal penalties for injuring or interfering with an individual's right to vote, to serve on a jury, to participate in government and government-aided programs, to work, to attend school, and to enjoy public accommodations. In a belated burst of congressional sensitivity, American Indians were included in the act's provisions.[67]

With both Senators McCarthy and Kennedy in the primary contest, there were two liberal northern antiwar Catholics challenging one another and hammering away daily at the Johnson Administration's policy in Vietnam. Their first direction confrontation was in Indiana. Bob Kennedy met with angry blacks and shared with them the painful memories of the murder of his own brother as a way of identifying with these people who had just lost their beloved leader. Kennedy was able to mollify their rage which had led many to take to the streets in violent protest. Kennedy won Indiana but the lateness of his candidacy prevented him from gaining ballot access in the Pennsylvania and Massachusetts primaries that McCarthy would win. While McCarthy and Kennedy battled each other, the party's best-known southern governor, Alabama's George Wallace, was preparing to run an independent presidential campaign on the basis of resistance to black gains during the Kennedy and Johnson Administrations.

Throughout the spring, Kennedy and McCarthy vied for Democratic support with Kennedy winning Nebraska and McCarthy winning Oregon breaking a long streak of Kennedy presidential primary successes dating back to Jack's 1960 victories. They had their final showdown in the winner-take-all California primary, the largest of the primary season.

Northern California liberals gave Senator McCarthy the early lead, but when the results from southern California's black ghettoes and Latino barrios came in, Senator Robert Kennedy had won California. A brief speech to his jubilant supporters from the rostrum at Los Angeles's Ambassador Hotel, a brief walk through the hotel's kitchen, and it was over. An assassin's bullet ended another Kennedy's life. The murder of yet another iconic leader deepened the despair felt by American liberals who felt the nation's center of political gravity moving from under their feet.

Loss of liberal momentum

Liberal legislative victories began to diminish further. One of the only liberal victories in Congress that year was passage of the Consumer Credit Protection Act (Truth in Lending Act). It was in the late 1960s that the "consumer movement" emerged and it had the power of the purse to affect changes through purchases. It gained congressional legitimacy as the act required that buyers be told the cost of loans and installment purchase plans in terms of annual rate calculated under certain specified procedures by all lenders and creditors.[68] The act established a National Commission on Consumer Finance to study and make recommendations on the need for further regulation of the consumer finance industry.

Ghetto riots in the nation's cities led to a major overhaul of the criminal justice system. The Omnibus Crime Control and Safe Streets Act of 1968 established a three-member Law Enforcement Assistance Administration within the Justice Department to administer grant programs for training, education, research, and demonstration projects.[69] Approved June 19, 1968, it authorized law enforcement assistance grants to educate the public for riot control and prevention, to combat organized crime, on confessions, wiretapping, and firearms control. The act was designed to assist state and local governments in reducing the incidence of crime, to increase the effectiveness, fairness, and coordination of law enforcement and criminal justice systems at all levels of government.

At last, President Johnson had to face the inevitable reality that the nation could not have a "guns and butter" economy. The war in Vietnam was depleting the economy and the president asked for and Congress obliged with the Revenue and Expenditures Control Act of 1968, approved June 28, 1968, which imposed a 10% surcharge on personal and corporate income taxes.[70]

The session continued on. Legislation passed in the last year of a president's term tends not to be very far-reaching, and so it was with the Johnson Administration. The Vocational Rehabilitation Amendments of 1968 were passed, enlarging the scope of vocational education to permit assistance to disadvantaged, as well as physically and mentally handicapped persons, and it was approved July 7, 1968.[71]

Continuing the conservation thrust of Interior Secretary Stewart Udall, Congress passed the Land and Water Conservation Fund Act of 1968. Approved July 15, 1968, this act provided additional revenue, up to a total of $200 million, for the Land and Conservation Fund and stipulated that the responsibility for fixing and collecting admission and user fees be returned to individual federal agencies.[72]

The increased reports of juvenile crime, some in the wake of the urban riots, led to the passage of the Juvenile Delinquency Prevention and Control Act, approved July 31, 1968, which authorized a three-year, $150 million program of block grants to plan and operate projects to prevent juvenile delinquency and rehabilitate young offenders.[73]

The only ambitious undertaking of the Congress in the closing summer months of the Johnson Administration was to provide more funding for the newly established Department of Housing and Urban Development. The Housing and Urban Act of 1968 enlarged the authorization for the rent supplement program in the model cities undertaking.[74] Approved August 1, 1968, it authorized a $5.3 billion, three-year housing program designed to provide more than 1.7 million units of new and rehabilitated housing for low-income families.

Having made meat safe in the previous session, Congress next passed the Wholesome Poultry Products Act, approved August 18, 1968, which authorized the secretary of agriculture to work with state agencies to establish poultry inspection programs which were to be at least equal to federal standards and established a criminal penalty provision for persons convicted of violating the act.[75]

The National Conventions

The summer of 1968 saw more antiwar protests and George Wallace gaining angry white urban votes in the North as well as the South. Unlike Strom Thurmond's 1948 Dixiecrat candidacy, Wallace sought to mobilize the voters of the urban white working class who had been left behind in the decaying cities as the white middle class fled to the suburbs, leaving these other whites to fight for jobs and housing with blacks and Latinos. The cities were combustible.

Republicans held the first 1968 convention in Miami. Violence erupted, and two were killed. The convention nominated Richard Nixon on his comeback trail over the slow-developing candidacies of New York Governor Nelson A. Rockefeller and California Governor Ronald Reagan. That Nixon was able to win the nomination without the delegate votes of California, his birth state, and New York, his present state of residence, was a testament to the breadth of Nixon's support among the nation's Republicans. After gaining the nomination on the first ballot, Nixon chose Maryland Governor Spiro T. Agnew as his running mate. A former Democrat, Agnew had defeated a blatant racist Democrat, George P. Mahoney, in the 1966 gubernatorial contest, giving Agnew a reputation as somewhat of a racial moderate. While the Republican Convention may have produced two fatalities, the Democratic Convention came close to destroying the party itself.

The 1968 Democratic Convention was to be held in Chicago in late August so that it would be in session for President Johnson's birthday on August 27. It was anticipated at the time of selecting the date and the site of the 1968 Democratic Convention that President Johnson would have another uncontested renomination, a coronation, and go on to vanquish the Republicans again. Yet another dashed dream.

The city of Chicago was anticipating chaos. Riots in the wake of the King assassination and antidraft protests on college campuses led Chicago city officials to prepare themselves for what trouble might ensue[76]: "In his welcoming address, Richard J. Daley asserted that 'as long as I am mayor of this town; there will be law and order in Chicago.' Several thousand antiwar demonstrators had arrived for the convention, and Chicago's 11,900 police were supplemented by 7,500 Army regulars, 7,500 Illinois National Guardsmen, and 1,000 FBI and Secret Service agents."

This would be no ordinary convention. Incumbent President Johnson, nominated by acclamation four years earlier, chose not to show his face at the convention. The murders of the two liberal icons, the Rev. Martin Luther King, Jr. and Senator Robert F. Kennedy, fueled fears of assassination. This was a risk LBJ chose not to take.

Because nominating conventions operate under similar rules and procedures to the House of Representatives, congressional leaders often serve as permanent chairs of the conventions. Wisely, Democrats chose not to have 76-year-old Speaker John McCormack preside at this convention as he had four years earlier. With young Americans more angered than ever at the military morass in Vietnam, being reminded that it was old men sending young men off to war would doom Democratic presidential prospects. Instead, Democrats chose 60-year-old House Majority Leader Carl Albert to be this year's permanent chair.[77] This too would not be a happy choice. The diminutive Albert, at 5'4" and barely 150 pounds, was dwarfed by the convention's rostrum. As demonstrations inside the convention hall became more raucous, it was hard to see Albert above the rostrum or hear him over the microphone.

Back at his ranch, an agitated Lyndon Johnson made phone calls to the podium requesting that the gavel be removed from Carl Albert's hands. While Albert and Chicago Representative Dan Rostenkowski's accounts differ, the one that has received the most traction was recounted by Albert himself: "big Dan Rostenkowski had wrestled the gavel out of the hands of little Carl Albert because only big Dan Rostenkowski could bring order to that convention."[78] Albert was built like a jockey, whereas Rosty was built like a football tight-end, 6'3" and well over 230 solid pounds. Rosty, a former car salesman was a senior member of the Ways and Means Committee, but was best known on Capitol Hill as Mayor Daley's legislative "enforcer." His signaling to the Chicago officials in the stadium brought some semblance of order to the convention.

Rosty's public embarrassing of Carl Albert would later cost him a House leadership slot. Among the lowlights of the convention were the beating of news reporters on the convention floor and Mayor Daley shouting anti-Semitic epithets at Connecticut's U.S. Senator Abraham Ribicoff, who complained that Gestapo tactics were being used to quell the demonstrations.

Demonstrations outside the convention hall in the week before the convention made it clear that the president's security could not be guaranteed, and demonstrations on the floor by embittered antiwar activists loyal to the candidacies of Senators McCarthy and Kennedy led to confrontations with the Chicago police. Conflicts spilled out onto the streets when the police and the Illinois National Guard held off the demonstrators, many of whom were convention delegates, with bayoneted rifles and tear gas. It was arguably the worst moment in the modern political history of the United States.

To Theodore H. White, the best-known election chronicler of the 1960s, this foretaste of the future was disturbing[79]: "At Chicago, for the first time, the most delicate process of American politics was ruptured by violence, the selection of Presidents stained with blood. 1968, throughout, was a year in which the ghosts of America's past returned to haunt the present; but at Chicago the goblins of America's future first appeared to haunt tomorrow."

Vice President Hubert Humphrey of Minnesota received 67.1% of the delegates without competing in a single primary. It was this massive disconnect between the party's primary voters and its convention delegates that would lead the 1972 Democratic Convention to operate under the far-reaching reforms proposed by the McGovern-Fraser Commission. Humphrey named U.S. Senator Edmund S. Muskie of Maine as his vice presidential running mate and the two of them tried mightily to hold the Democratic Party together. Muskie received 74.1% of the convention vote, while 23% of the delegates chose not to vote. This was not a happy send-off for Hubert Humphrey, who had been labeled this generation's "happy warrior."[80]

While Teddy White seemed overwhelmed by the spectacle of the Democratic Party meltdown, three British authors caught the full essence of what the convention's chaos would mean for the future of American politics in their wonderful book, *An American Melodrama*.[81] The nation's oldest political party had fallen to its knees and was near collapse. The election would be anticlimactic.

LBJ's last legislative gasp

The last few major pieces of Johnson Administration legislation included the Wild and Scenic Rivers Act, approved October 2, 1968, that established a National Wild and Scenic Rivers System to preserve outstanding stretches of rivers from incompatible water resource development, pollution, or commercialization.[82] Also approved October 2, 1968, was the National Trails System Act that established a nationwide system of scenic trails, recreational trails, and side trails.[83]

Tidying up loose ends, Congress passed the Vocational Education Act of 1968, amending the Vocational Education Act of 1963 by increasing the funds available for and extending the length of certain programs available to students engaged in vocational education.[84] Approved October 16, 1968, it required that the states devote 40% of these funds for education of the physically handicapped and the disadvantaged and for post-high school courses.

In closing out the legislative history of the Johnson Administration, Congress got caught in the ongoing feud between the National Rifle Association (NRA) and advocates of gun control. The murders earlier in the year of the Reverend King and U.S. Senator Bob Kennedy spurred gun control advocates to push Congress into a stance which it liked to avoid, namely, confronting this well-funded grass-roots NRA. But confront it they did, and the act passed was the watered-down Gun Control Act of 1968, that banned most interstate shipments of long guns to individuals and prohibited individuals with few exceptions from buying guns except in their own states.[85] Approved October 22, 1968, it prohibited sale of rifles, shotguns, or ammunition to persons under 18 and sales of handguns or handgun ammunition to persons less than 21 years of age, and importation of foreign-made military surplus firearms into the United States. The sad irony that the last piece of legislation passed while Lyndon Johnson was president dealt with gun control was lost on most observers. It was the lack of an interstate ban on long guns in 1963 Texas that led to the Kennedy murder that first installed Lyndon Johnson in the White House five years earlier.

In November 1968, the *CQ Weekly Report* analyzed the thrust of Johnson's 1968 legislative agenda, contending that most of the recently passed legislation could be attributed to the Conservative Coalition.[86] The summary of the Coalition's divergence from President Johnson and Speaker McCormack is as follows[87]:

The over-all victory score of the conservative coalition for the four years of the full Johnson Administration was 54 percent, but there was a sharp divergence between its scores in the liberal 89th Congress, which was elected in the 1964 Democratic landslide, and the more conservative 90th Congress, which brought a shift of 47 House seats to the Republicans as a result of the 1966 elections. In the 89th Congress, the coalition was successful on only 39 percent of its votes, while in the 90th it was successful on 68 percent of its votes.

Vietnam Impact: By October 1968, the last Gallup Poll on the Vietnam War during the Johnson Administration, support for the war had cratered at 38%—a full 41-point drop from the 79% of Americans who supported the war in November 1965 at the end of Johnson's second year in office.[88]

In spite of the growing national disenchantment with the war, John McCormack remained committed to it. John's deep-seated Catholicism would not let a nation like South Vietnam with an active Catholic minority fall prey to the oft-repeated refrain of "Godless atheistic Communism." In this regard, he was joined by Carl Vinson's successor as chair of the Armed Services Committee, L. Mendel Rivers of South Carolina, described as "a combative man with a heavy shock of white hair that fell to his collar in the back, who at times kept a loaded derringer on his desk."[89] As recounted by Alvin Josephy.[90]

Rivers had a considerable hold over Speaker McCormack, and the two men worked together to keep the House militantly behind the presidential war policy and bury any dove-like sentiment under an avalanche of loyal votes. Year after year as the war dragged on and disillusionment and opposition arose among the American people, McCormack and Rivers held the Democrats in line.

That it would take seven more years for the United States to finally extricate itself from this foreign policy disaster is a bizarre testament to the inability of American leaders to concede defeat.

The 1968 election results

The combination of Wallace defections in the South was too great and the bitterness of the antiwar movement was too deep for Humphrey to overcome completely the early double-digit lead of former Vice President Richard Nixon. In spite of all the catastrophes he faced, the Johnson war policy being its worst, the Humphrey candidacy closed to within 512,000 votes of overtaking Nixon. The Electoral College split of 31 states for Nixon yielded 301 electoral votes; Humphrey's 13 states plus DC gave him a total of 191 electoral votes; while the five states won by George Wallace—Alabama, Arkansas, Georgia, Louisiana, and Mississippi—provided him with 46 electoral votes.

Like Wallace, Nixon also carried five of the eleven Confederate states with Florida, North Carolina, Tennessee, Virginia, and surprisingly, South Carolina, a state that had supported native son Dixiecrat Strom Thurmond in 1948 and Republican Barry Goldwater in 1964 but Thurmond's joining the Republican Party that year kept South Carolina in the Republican column.[91] Only LBJ's Texas cast its electoral votes for the Humphrey-Muskie ticket. As Nixon surveyed the southern lineup, he knew that his next step was to win over the Wallace voters if he wished to secure his reelection in 1972. Thus, was born "the Southern Strategy."[92]

The congressional elections were a mixed bag with Republicans winning seven Democratic seats while Democrats captured two Republican ones for a net GOP gain of five and a new Senate split of 58 Democrats to 42 Republicans. In one of the more unusual developments, the Republican net gain in the House was only four seats as the GOP gained nine seats and lost five to the Democrats providing a new House party split of 243 Democrats to 192 Republicans. While Nixon's coattails generated five seats in the Senate, the four seats gained in the House was the smallest net gain for a winning presidential candidate in the twentieth century.

Divided government had returned to Washington with the House and Senate Democrats obliged to serve under Republican President Nixon. Majority Whip Hale Boggs of Louisiana considered a challenge to John McCormack's reelection as Speaker in the upcoming 91st Congress. Boggs, a highly visible and voluble member of the Ways and Means Committee, put the contest aside, but it was well-known enough on the Hill to lessen John's trust of Boggs as a loyal lieutenant.[93]

With relatively few freshmen in this new cohort, the House of the 91st Congress looked and behaved very much like the House of the 90th Congress with the Conservative Coalition in command of much of the agenda and querulous liberal Democrats seeking new ways to overthrow Speaker John McCormack.

Not only was the Conservative Coalition back, it had returned to command the agenda. Once again frustrated DSG liberals angrily watched the House leadership team of McCormack-Albert-Boggs fail to prevent the Coalition's hijacking of the liberal agenda.

Bolling's *Power in the House*

In October, John McCormack's speakership was challenged in print by yet another book from Dick Bolling of the Rules Committee. Entitled *Power in the House*,[94] Bolling compared McCormack negatively to Sam Rayburn and contended that McCormack was under the control of the conservative committee chairs. Bolling did not mince words in his disdain for McCormack, and he considered the Powell episode to be the most blatant example of McCormack's failings as Speaker and gave no credit to McCormack for the legislative successes of 1965–66, as he wrote[95]:

> Legislative output during 1965–1966 was a direct bequest of the Goldwater candidacy. Thus, up to 1967, the weakness of McCormack's leadership had not yet been clearly demonstrated to the country.
>
> . . .
>
> The Powell affair is a classic example of Speaker McCormack's inability to anticipate trouble. When he finally could not avoid seeing trouble, his countermoves were poorly thought out and badly implemented.

John's initial reaction took issue with Bolling's preference for a strong, single-minded Speaker who would enforce party discipline through committee assignments. Comparing himself to Republican Speaker Uncle Joe Cannon of Illinois who ruled the House from 1903 to 1911 until his autocratic rule led to the emasculation of the speakership, an indignant McCormack declared: "I don't operate that way. I believe in treating people like human beings. Cannon believed in punishing the members who didn't fall in line."

Although John McCormack never read political science professional journals, he would have agreed completely with the superb 1981 analysis of the transformation of House leadership presented by Joseph Cooper and David Brady.[96] The Cooper-Brady article tracked the disintegration of House leadership power from the hierarchical speakership of Joe Cannon to the bargaining speakership of Sam Rayburn who was obliged to deal with the widespread decentralization and diffusion of power within the House. Remarkably, Rayburn made it work. Sam's knowledge of the House rules, his clear-eyed assessments of the personalities and temperaments of its key actors, and the tight personal links that he was able to forge with the succession of Presidents Franklin D. Roosevelt, Harry Truman, Dwight Eisenhower, and even John F. Kennedy made him unique among leaders of the House. Sam's uniqueness may have led observers to believe that the decentralized House of the 1960s could be effectively managed by the Speaker. Sadly for himself and his fellow Democrats of this decade, John McCormack was not up to that challenge. These were shoes that no one could fill. Dick Bolling knew it and his book revealed it to a national audience.

The book infuriated McCormack, yet even after hearing Bolling's criticism of his legislative skills in a televised interview, John responded with characteristic coolness as the *Boston Globe* reported[97]: "McCormack replied by saying all House members have been long aware of Bolling's 'Keen disappointment' at not being elected to a position of leadership in Congress. 'I am not going to lower the dignity of the office of Speaker by noticing his presumptuous remarks,' McCormack said."

For McCormack, Bolling's continued onslaught was that of a sore loser who failed in his bid to become Majority Leader in 1962. Ironically, the man Bolling was pushing to replace Speaker McCormack was Carl Albert, who won the post of Majority Leader that he so craved. Buried in a footnote of *Power in the House*, Bolling acknowledged[98]: "In fairness to Albert it should be noted that he is and has been entirely loyal to Speaker McCormack and has indicated that he would support him for that position as long as he sought reelection."

Dick Bolling had skewered the House's committee hierarchy in his earlier book, *House Out of Order*, so criticism emanating from his corner of the House was not surprising.[99] But the House of the 1960s was an institution where its members seldom spoke ill of it. These were the days before C-SPAN and Cable News Network gave House members any glimpse of public recognition. The print media generally ignored House debates, and the only members of Congress to enjoy any coverage were U.S. Senators. Insecurities were high enough among House members without their fellows joining in the dismissive chorus.

For many of those who watched Congress closely, Bolling's first book was a sour grapes response to his withdrawal from the 1962 majority leadership contest. The second book was clearly motivated by Bolling's sheer frustration with and contempt for John McCormack's speakership. To Dick Bolling, John McCormack was no Sam Rayburn, and to John McCormack, Dick Bolling was no friend. In John Farrell's biography of Tip O'Neill, he recounted that Dan Rostenkowski regularly visited McCormack's office to "[fill] the Speaker's head with tales of Bolling's disloyalty until McCormack was taut with fury."[100] As Farrell observed, Rosty chose to be Iago to McCormack's Othello. To his credit, Tip O'Neill who sat beside Bolling on the Rules Committee for 16 years and undoubtedly learned of various Bolling-Thompson plots to overthrow McCormack was considerate enough not to unsettle John with these tales.

No surprise that it was O'Neill and not Rostenkowski who would be placed on the "leadership ladder." Tattletales seldom impress the secretive Boston Irish.

In the sixteen pages of Bolling's chapter 6 in *Power in the House*, titled "The 90th Congress: A Study in Frustration,"[101] words used to describe McCormack include "inability," "constitutional mistake," "ineffective," "struck out," "failed," "incompetence," and "awoke belatedly"; and in an understated sentence: "My assessment of McCormack's abilities had been less than enthusiastic."[102] This chapter is arguably the single-most damning published critique of a Speaker of the U.S. House by a sitting member of his or her own party.

President Johnson had a dissimilar view. In a congratulation letter to Speaker McCormack on his November 1968 reelection, LBJ again praised John for his character and performance over his lifetime[103]:

Dear Mr. Speaker:

Lady Bird joins me in sending our warmest congratulations on your re-election.

When I consider the subject of government continuity—which is in my thoughts much these days—I am comforted by the knowledge that one of our greatest living citizens will be back in Washington to help steer America's course.

I can never repay what you have done for me as President. But please know that I will always remain your devoted and admiring friend.

Sincerely,
LBJ

Sadly, that would be the last year in Congress shared between the two men.

Harriet: In his efforts to give Lyndon Johnson's last year as president a successful legislative send-off, John had to navigate through the difficult shoals of the growing success of the Conservative Coalition, while being undermined daily by the DSG liberals. He was also reminded each day of the increased fragility of his beloved wife Harriet, now 84. In this extraordinarily tense year of 1968, John sat in the Speaker's office and using his official stationary, he sent a handwritten love letter on June 10 to Harriet, the most important person in his life and his marital partner of 48 years[104]:

> *Darling Harriet:*
>> *My love for you is deep and intense. With your love,*
>> *God has Blessed me during our married life.*
>> *I again repeat my unlimited love for you.*

Your Sweetheart,
John

Harriet's worsening health preoccupied John to the point that the difficulties he was facing as Speaker had less and less relevance. He began to rely more and more on his staff to conduct the business of his office. It would not be a wise move.

Notes

1 "1966 Elections: A Major Republican Comeback: GOP Gains Eight New Governorships, Three Senate Seats and 47 House Seats," *CQWR*, November 11, 1966, pp. 2773–75.

2 "'Conservative Coalition' Shows New Life," *CQWR*, December 30, 1966, pp. 3078–90.

3 *CQWR*, January 13, 1967, p. 39.

4 Nelson W. Polsby, *How Congress Evolves: Social Bases of Institutional Change* (New York: Oxford University Press, 2004).

5 Best known as the Kerner Commission, the *Report of National Advisory Commission on Civil Disorders* (New York: E.P. Dutton, 1968), p. 115. The data in this portion of the report was provided by the U.S. Senate's Permanent Subcommittee on Investigations of the Government Operations Committee, 90th Congress, 1st Session.

6 Charles Stafford, "It's Decision Day for Powell, Colmer in House," *Chicago Tribune*, January 8, 1967.

7 As quoted in Anthony Champagne, Douglas B. Harris, James W. Riddlesperger, Jr., and Garrison Nelson, *The Austin-Boston Connection*, p. 126.

8	Books on Adam Clayton Powell, Jr. include *Adam by Adam: The Autobiography of Adam Clayton Powell, Jr.* (New York: Dial Press, 1971); Charles V. Hamilton, *Adam Clayton Powell, Jr.: The Political Biography of an American Dilemma* (New York: Collier, 1991); and Wil Haygood, *King of the Cats: The Life and Times of Adam Clayton Powell, Jr.* (Boston: Houghton Mifflin, 1993).

9	Claude Brown, *Manchild in the Promised Land* (New York: Macmillan, 1965), p. 191.

10	Andre E. Reeves, *Congressional Committee Chairmen: Three Who Made an Evolution* (Lexington: University of Kentucky Press, 1993), pp. 43 and 72.

11	*CQWR*, January 13, 1967, p. 47.

12	Ibid., p. 84.

13	*Congressional Record*, 90th Congress, First Session, pp. 14–15.

14	"House Select Committee: In Re Adam Clayton Powell, Jr.," in Garrison Nelson, *Committees in the U.S. Congress, 1947–1992* (Washington, DC: CQ Press, 1993), Vol. 1, p. 806.

15	Andy Jacobs, *The Powell Affair: Freedom Minus One* (Indianapolis: The Bobbs-Merrill Company, 1973).

16	Associated Press, "Feuding Over Powell: McCormack Soothes Demos," *The Cocoa (Fla.) Tribune*, January 6, 1967, p. E12; and "Powell Backed by McCormack," *The Lawton (Okla.) Constitution*, January 6, 1967, p. E15. These clippings are from the Richard W. Bolling Papers at the library of the University of Missouri-Kansas City.

17	*CQWR*, "Powell Loses Chairmanship; Seat in Doubt," January 13, 1967, p. 47.

18	AIPO, *The Gallup Poll: Public Opinion 1935–1971*, Vol. III (New York: Random House, 1972), p. 2048.

19	Debates about the seating of Powell led to a number of law review articles concerning the seating of members, including U.S. Representative Thomas B. Curtis (Rep-Mo.), "Power of the House of Representatives to Judge the Qualifications of Its Members," *Texas Law Review*, XLV (July 1967), pp. 1199–204; Neill Fleishman, "Power of Congress to Exclude Persons Duly Elected," *North Carolina Law Review*, XLVIII (April 1970), pp. 655–66; and Gerald T. McLaughlin., "Congressional Self-Discipline: The Power to Expel, to Exclude and to Punish," *Fordham Law Review*, XLI (October 1972), pp. 43–66.

20	"House Excludes Powell from Membership in the 90th Congress, Rejects Milder Punishment Recommended by Committee," *CQWR*, March 3, 1967, pp. 332–33.

21	*Congressional Quarterly's Guide to U.S. Elections* (5th ed., 2005), II: 1185.

22	*Powell v. McCormack*, 395 U.S. 486 (1969).

23	Pearson and Anderson, "Portrait of a Senator," *The Case against Congress*, pp. 27–97.

24	Andrew J. Glass, "Senate Censures Dodd by 92 to 5 Vote: 2d Charge Is Rejected in Voting; Senator Found Guilty of Using Donations; Will Keep Seat, Rights," *Washington Post*, June 24, 1967, pp. A1, A10.

25	Jack Anderson, "Washington Merry-Go-Round: House Speaker Resists Ethics Move," *Washington Post*, June 4, 1966, p. C7.

26	H.Res. 97-418, April 13, 1967. See Mildred Amer, *The House Committee on Standards of Official Conduct: A Brief History of Its Evolution and Jurisdiction*, Congressional Research Service Report for Congress, 92–686 (1992).

27	Pearson and Anderson, *The Case against Congress*, p. 21.

28	Robert D. Novak, *The Prince of Darkness: 50 Years of Reporting in Washington* (New York: Crown Forum, 2007), p. 301.

29 John F. Bibby, "Political Parties," in Donald C. Bacon, Roger H. Davidson, Morton Keller, eds., *The Encyclopedia of the United States Congress*, Vol. III (New York: Simon & Schuster, 1995), p. 1558.

30 Garrison Nelson, "Partisan Patterns of House Leadership Change, 1789–1977," *APSR*, LXXI (September 1977), pp. 918–39.

31 *CQWR*, December 29, 1967, pp. 2649–61.

32 LBJ letter to John McCormack, August 30, 1967, LBJ Library in Austin, Texas.

33 Military Service Act of 1967 was approved June 30, 1967 (81 Stat. 100-106). See also "Congress Extends Selective Service Law for Four Years, But Rejects Proposals for Comprehensive Draft Reform," *CQ Almanac 1967*, pp. 260–80.

34 AIPO, *The Gallup Poll: 1935–1971*, Vol. III, p. 2065.

35 Walter C. Rucker and James N. Upton, eds., *Encyclopedia of American Race Riots: Greenwood Milestones in African-American History* (Westport, CT: Greenwood, 2007).

36 Investment Tax Credit Act was approved June 13, 1967 (81 Stat. 57-58). See also "Congress Restores Investment Tax Credit for Business; Suspends Operation of Presidential Campaign Fund Law," *CQ Almanac 1967*, pp. 283–300.

37 Public Broadcasting Act of 1967 was approved November 7, 1967 (81 Stat. 365-373). See also "Congress Creates Public Broadcasting Corporation," *CQ Almanac 1967*, pp. 1042–50.

38 Foreign Assistance Act of 1967 was approved November 14, 1967 (81 Stat. 445-463). See also "1967 Aid Authorization Lowest in History," *CQ Almanac 1967*, pp. 679–97.

39 Air Quality Control Act of 1967 was approved November 21, 1967 (81 Stat. 485-507). See also "Congress Strengthens Air Pollution Control Powers," *CQ Almanac 1967*, pp. 875–87.

40 Wholesale Meat Act was approved December 15, 1967 (81 Stat. 584-601). See also "Nation's Meat Inspection Requirements Tightened," *CQ Almanac 1967*, pp. 705–13.

41 Postal Revenue and Federal Salary Act of 1967 was approved December 16, 1967 (81 Stat. 613-648). See also "Postal Rates, Federal Pay Increased in Single Bill," *CQ Almanac 1967*, pp. 589–609.

42 Smith's amendment is mentioned, *CQ Almanac 1967*, pp. 591 and 603. Senate Historian Betty Koed provided a copy of the act.

43 Ibid., House Vote 159 HR7977, October 11, 1967, pp. 72H–73H.

44 Military Pay Bill of 1967 was approved December 16, 1967 (81 Stat. 649-655). See also "Military Pay Increase," *CQ Almanac 1967*, pp. 1055–57.

45 Elementary and Secondary Education Amendments of 1967 was approved January 2, 1968 (81 Stat. 783-820). See also "Two-Year Elementary School Aid Bill Enacted," *CQ Almanac 1967*, pp. 611–26.

46 *CQWR*, "House 'Conservative Coalition' Dominates Session," December 29, 1967, p. 2651.

47 Joe Lastelic, "Bolling Wants McCormack Out: Speaker Should Step Down, He Asserts in Talk: In Favor of Albert: Missourian Leads Group Disappointed with Leadership," *Kansas City Star*, October 28, 1967, p. 1. See also "Bolling Is Right," *New Republic*, November 11, 1967, pp. 8–9.

48 *CQ Almanac 1967*, p. 161.

49 Social Security Amendments of 1967 were approved January 2, 1968 (81 Stat. 821-935). Certain provisions of this Act were subsequently held unconstitutional in *Richardson v. David*, 409 U.S. 1069 (1972), *Richardson v. Griffin*, 409 U.S. 1069 (1972), and *Califano v. Westcott*, 443 U.S. 76 (1978). See also "Social Security Aid Raised; Welfare Pay Restricted," *CQ Almanac 1967*, pp. 892–916.

50 Bill Kovach, "McCarthy, Casually Enters the '72 Race," *NYT*, December 17, 1967, p. 1.

51 AIPO, *The Gallup Poll: Public Opinion, 1935–1971*, Vol. III, p. 2099.

52 Marjorie Hunter, "Leaders in Capitol Not told by Johnson," *NYT*, January 25, 1968, p. 1.

53 AIPO, *The Gallup Poll*, Vol. III, p. 2103.

54 James H. Willbanks, *The Tet Offensive: A Concise History* (New York: Columbia University Press, 2007), pp. 34–37.

55 AIPO, *The Gallup Poll*, Vol. III, p. 2106.

56 John Herbers, "Move On to Have Albert Replace McCormack as Speaker," *NYT*, February 26, 1968, p, 33.

57 Rowland Evans and Robert Novak, "The President's Boston Blues: Lyndon Johnson's Habits of Procrastination Hurt Chances of Squashing McCarthy," *Washington Post*, March 3, 1968, p. B7.

58 John Herbers, "Johnson Rejects Primary Contests: Bars All but Three Required by State Laws—Rift With Kennedys May Widen," *NYT*, March 7, 1968, p. 1.

59 *CQ Guide to U.S. Elections* (1975 ed.), p. 343.

60 Richard C. Bain and Judith H. Parris, *Convention Decisions and Voting Records* (Washington, DC: The Brookings Institution, 1973), pp. 350ff.

61 Jeff Shesol, *Mutual Contempt: Lyndon Johnson, Robert Kennedy, and the Feud That Defined a Decade* (New York: W. W. Norton & Company, 1997), p. 424.

62 Ibid., p. 427.

63 *Public Papers of the Presidents of the United States: Lyndon B. Johnson, 1968–69* (Washington, DC: Government Printing Office, 1970), Vol. I, pp. 475–76.

64 John McCormack interview with T. Harrison Baker of the LBJ Library, September 23, 1968, p. 44.

65 John McCormack phone call to Marvin Watson, April 17, 1968, LBJ Library.

66 Civil Rights Act of 1968, approved April 11, 1968 (82 Stat. 73-92). See also "Congress Enacts Open Housing Legislation," *CQ Almanac 1968*, pp. 152–68.

67 See Donald L. Burnett, "An Historical Analysis of the 1968 'Indian Civil Rights' Act," *Harvard Journal on Legislation*, IX (May 1972), pp. 557–626.

68 Consumer Credit Protection Act (Truth in Lending Act), approved May 29, 1968 (82 Stat. 146-167). See also "Congress Enacts Strong Truth-in-Lending Law," *CQ Almanac 1968*, pp. 205–11.

69 Omnibus Crime Control and Safe Streets Act of 1968, approved June 19, 1968 (82 Stat. 197-239). See also "Congress Passes Extensive Anticrime Legislation," *CQ Almanac 1968*, pp. 225–37.

70 Revenue and Expenditures Control Act of 1968, approved June 28, 1968 (82 Stat. 251-274). See also "Congress Votes Surtax with Expenditure Controls," *CQ Almanac 1968*, pp. 263–78.

71 Vocational Rehabilitation Amendments of 1968, approved July 7, 1968 (82 Stat. 297-306). See also "New Vocational Rehabilitation Program Established," *CQ Almanac 1968*, pp. 391–93.

72 Land and Water Conservation Fund Act of 1968, approved July 15, 1968 (82 Stat. 354-356). See also "Congress Provides Revenues for Conservation Fund," *CQ Almanac 1968*, pp. 291–99.

73 Juvenile Delinquency Prevention and Control Act, approved July 31, 1968 (82 Stat. 462-474). See also "Juvenile Delinquency," *CQ Almanac 1968*, pp. 307–09.

74 Housing and Urban Act of 1968 was approved on August 1, 1968 (82 Stat. 476-611). See also "Housing Bill Provides Home-Buying, Riot, Other Aid," *CQ Almanac 1968*, pp. 313–35.

75 Wholesome Poultry Products Act was approved on August 18, 1968 (82 Stat. 791-808). See also "Federal Poultry Inspection Standards Extended," *CQ Almanac 1968*, pp. 395–99.

76 Bain and Parris eds., *Convention Decisions and Voting Records*, p. 323.

77 Carl Albert's own recollection of this episode is in his autobiography *Little Giant: The Life and Times of Speaker Carl Albert* (Norman, OK: University of Oklahoma Press, 1990), pp. 206–302.

78 Richard E. Cohen, *Rostenkowski: The Pursuit of Power and the End of Old Politics* (Chicago: Ivan R. Dee, 1999), p. 76.

79 See Theodore H. White, "The Chicago Convention: The Furies in the Street," *The Making of the President 1968* (New York: Atheneum, 1969), p. 257. The agony of American liberal intellectuals at this time is captured in a revealing interview with historian Richard Hofstadter, "The Age of Rubbish," *Newsweek*, LXXVI (July 6, 1970), pp. 20–23.

80 Bain and Parris, eds., *Convention Decisions and Voting Records*, pp. 350ff.

81 Lewis Chester, Godfrey Hodgson, and Bruce Page, *An American Melodrama: The Presidential Campaign of 1968* (New York: Viking Press, 1969).

82 Wild and Scenic Rivers Act, approved October 2, 1968 (82 Stat. 906-918). See also "Scenic Rivers," *CQ Almanac 1968*, pp. 485–89.

83 National Trails System Act, approved October 2, 1968 (82 Stat. 919-926). See also "Scenic Trails," *CQ Almanac 1968*, pp. 477–79.

84 Vocational Education Act of 1968, approved October 16, 1968 (82 Stat. 1064-1098). See also "Vocational Education," *CQ Almanac 1968*, pp. 500–504.

85 Gun Control Act of 1968, approved October 22, 1968 (82 Stat. 1213-1236). See also "Gun Controls Extended to Long Guns, Ammunition," *CQ Almanac 1968*, pp. 549–62.

86 *CQWR*, "Conservative Coalition Shaped Major 1968 Bills," November 1, 1968, pp. 2983–90.

87 Ibid., p. 2984.

88 "Table A.1. Support for the Wars by Party, Education, and Age," from John E. Mueller, *War, Presidents, and Public Opinion* (New York: John Wiley, 1973), p. 273.

89 Alvin M. Josephy, Jr., *On the Hill: A History of the American Congress* (New York: Simon & Schuster, 1979), p. 361. A thoughtful depiction of John's pro–Vietnam War leadership may be found in Matthew N. Green's *The Speaker of the House: A Study of Leadership* (New Haven, CT: Yale University Press, 2010), pp. 83–86.

90 Josephy, *On the Hill*, p. 361.

91 Theodore H. White, *The Making of the President 1968* (New York: Atheneum, 1969), pp. 387–411.

92 An early journalistic account of Nixon's effort in the South early in his administration may be found in Reg Murphy and Hal Gulliver, *The Southern Strategy* (New York: Scribner's, 1971); and an academic treatment focused on South Carolina may be found in Bruce H. Kalk, *The Origins of the Southern Strategy: Two Party Competition in South Carolina, 1950–1972* (Lanham, MD: Lexington Books, 2001).

93 As contended in Patrick J. Maney's "Hale Boggs: The Southerner as National Democrat," in Roger D. Davidson, Susan Webb Hammond, Raymond W. Smock, eds., *Masters of the House: Congressional Leadership over Two Centuries* (Boulder, CO: Westview Press, 1998), p. 243.

94 Richard Bolling, *Power in the House: A History of the Leadership in the House of Representatives* (New York: Dutton, 1968).

95 Ibid., pp. 238 and 243.

96   Joseph Cooper and David W. Brady, "Institutional Context and Leadership Style: The House from Cannon to Rayburn," *APSR*, LXXV (June 1981), pp. 411–25.

97   "McCormack Answers Critics," *Boston Globe*, October 29, 1967, p. 6.

98   Bolling, *Power in the House*, p. 254.

99   Richard Bolling, *House Out of Order* (New York: Dutton, 1965).

100   Farrell, *Tip O'Neill*, p. 279.

101   Bolling, *Power in the House*, pp. 239–54.

102   Ibid., p. 248.

103   LBJ letter to John McCormack, November 21, 1968, LBJ Library in Austin, TX.

104   John McCormack letter to Harriet McCormack, June 10, 1968, in the Paul Wright Papers at UMass-Boston.

23

It's Time, Mr. Speaker

On December 21, 1968, John McCormack turned 77, still younger than his dear friend Speaker Sam Rayburn who was 79 when he left the House to return home to die in Texas. However, Sam Rayburn remained an effective leader of the House in his last year of life; John McCormack was less fortunate. That was quickly revealed as the 91st Congress opened with a new highly partisan Republican president and a restive House Democratic membership. It did not bode well for Speaker McCormack.

Estrangement from the Newer Members: More than a generation separated John from the new members of the House who were elected in the age of television campaigning. They were better educated, better dressed, better groomed, better coiffed, and much slicker than the members with whom he had served for the previous 40 years. Few had come from the farming communities of many of his southern colleagues nor had many come from the ethnic enclaves of the big-city Democratic machines. Most were suburban self-starters who had paid fewer dues in their political ascents than their predecessors. To many of them, John McCormack was a relic of a bygone era.

By this time, John's life in the Capitol had evolved into a predictable pattern. Once the House closed for business late on weekday afternoons, John would return to the Hotel Washington for dinner alone with Harriet. John had closed down the alcohol-fueled "Board of Education," Sam's Capitol hideaway in Room H-128 which was created more than 40 years earlier by Republican House Speaker Nick Longworth as a place inside the Capitol where a select few members could consume alcohol during the Prohibition Era.[1] The teetotaling John McCormack did not join his younger colleagues in early evening "happy hour" alcoholic retreats. Arizona Representative Morris Udall who would challenge McCormack in 1969 contended that John was "stand-offish, high-handed, not warm at all. He's blunt and brusque, doesn't mix with the boys or go out and get drunk with them."[2] It's doubtful if Mo Udall had any awareness of the loss of John McCormack's father and his oldest brother to the scourge of alcoholism. But private men like John McCormack did not share their family histories with others, particularly if they had a personal family history at variance with their public one.

John McCormack's lifestyle choices were spartan and dissimilar from most House members. He never owned a home. He rented a three-room suite in the Hotel Washington where he and Harriet lived for 42 years and a second-floor flat in a modest two-story home in Dorchester, Massachusetts, and the Cadillac he drove was provided to him by the House of Representatives. This would clearly indicate that John was as far from financial corruption as anyone who has ever served in Congress. John McCormack had learned the harsh lessons taught by the damaged reputations of rival Boston Irish gatekeepers John Fitzgerald and James Michael Curley. His stable half-century marriage to Harriet indicated that he did not succumb to the flirtations with other women that would undermine Honey Fitz's reputation, and his steadfastness in refusing to gain financially from his office permitted him to escape the tawdriness of James Michael Curley's money-grubbing impulses. John did not steal and he did not cheat. In many ways, it may have made it difficult for newer members of the House, a number of whom apparently indulged in one or both of these behaviors, to identify with John.

A caucus challenge

The Democrats' loss of the presidency in 1968 in the brutal three-way contest to their most hated adversary, Richard Nixon, led to a panic among the party's congressional wing. The increasingly unpopular Vietnam War continued. The liberal coalition was crumbling and the party's most public face was that of the white-haired, gaunt 77-year-old John McCormack.

Mike Mansfield, the Senate Majority Leader, was 12 years younger and his opposition to the war had earned him liberal support. However, Mike Mansfield did not sit behind the president during those addresses to the nation which then were the only times that Congress was televised. It was Speaker McCormack who was the televised embodiment of the Democratic Party. It was an image of aging and disconnection from the youth of America that many in the congressional wing feared.

The challenge to John McCormack's reelection as Speaker came from fourth-termer Morris Udall, the younger brother of Stewart Udall, who had served as secretary of the interior in the Kennedy and Johnson Administrations. Udall was a lanky former professional basketball player with a quick wit and the self-deprecating humor reporters enjoy. It was the first challenge to a sitting Speaker since 1923, when Progressive Republicans forced Speaker Frederick Gillett (Rep-Mass.) into a nine-ballot vote to retain his seat.[3] Many liberal House Democrats who failed to help Vice President Hubert Humphrey win the White House sought to assuage their guilt by dislodging Speaker John McCormack, this remnant of Congress past.

In a collection of Udall's newsletters, edited by Robert L. Peabody of Johns Hopkins University, Udall contended that he was making "a symbolic challenge" to McCormack and if he won, he would let an open contest for the speakership occur. Before Congress opened for business in January, Morris Udall readied his challenge to John McCormack[4]:

> On Christmas Eve day, 1968, Mo Udall telephoned Old John McCormack in South Boston to announce that after only eight years in the back row, he would run against him when the Democrats caucused in January. It was difficult, because the old man kept hoo-hawing season's greetings. "I finally took a deep breath," Udall says, "and told him. He did not keep me on the line long."

Figure 23.1 Speaker John McCormack with U.S. Representative Morris Udall (Dem-Ariz.) (The University of Arizona Libraries Digital Collections).

House Democrats had not toppled a sitting Speaker since 1807 when President Thomas Jefferson nudged Speaker Nathaniel Macon of North Carolina out of the post for continuing to name Jefferson nemesis John Randolph of Roanoke to chair the Ways and Means Committee.[5] History was on the side of John McCormack (Figure 23.1). The contest was not close. McCormack buried Udall 178 to 58 in the caucus with four votes cast for Wilbur Mills, chair of Ways and Means.[6] Because there are no roll calls in caucus votes, inferences are speculative, but it appears that the Democrats of the big cities and the South, the original Austin-Boston connection, rescued John's speakership. An ambitious effort by Matthew Green to tease out where the votes came from cites Udall's votes as originating in members most likely liberal, young, and newly elected in the large class of 1964.[7] However, their numbers had been shredded by the elections of 1966 and 1968. John's support came from the Democrats safe in their big-city districts and his southern allies—who Armed Services Chair Mendel Rivers called "McCormacrats." It was a difficult and costly fight for Speaker McCormack. Many old favors had to be collected and promises were made to members that would be very hard to deliver in this, the first Congress of the Nixon era. One promise that John and Majority Leader Carl Albert reluctantly chose to honor was to institute regular monthly meetings of the Democratic Caucus.[8] McCormack's grasp on power continued to weaken.

There was now no friend in the White House. The narrowness of Richard Nixon's victory—less than 1%—eight years after his even narrower loss to John Kennedy—placed the Nixon White House on ever-constant alert. Inside the White House, "enemies' lists" were compiled to keep track of the administration's critics. Outside the White House, Vice President Spiro Agnew denounced the president's critics as unpatriotic and disloyal to the nation.

The war in Vietnam dragged on.

The last Congress

The 91st Congress would be John McCormack's last. It is not certain if John McCormack knew that it would be so, but a series of negative circumstances were about to converge upon the Speaker's life to speed his departure from the chair. The 91st Congress was a "divided government," one in which the Republican president would confront both the House and the Senate in the hands of the opposition Democrats. This was a repeat of the last three Congresses—the 84th through the 86th—in the Eisenhower Administration a decade earlier. But there was a major difference in the personalities of the key actors and the level of staunch partisanship each brought to the table.

In the 1950s, President Eisenhower, a professional military man, wearied quickly of partisan rhetoric and bickering and found tiresome all of the entreaties of fellow Republicans that he should turn up the volume of partisan discourse in order to further drive Democrats from the seats of power. Fortunately for Eisenhower, he had an eager surrogate in the person of Vice President Richard Nixon. Nixon's commitment to the partisan aspects of the Republican agenda freed Eisenhower to engage in the bipartisan aspects of the office, such as the formation and implementation of foreign and defense policy. Ike let Nixon lead ferocious attacks on the congressional Democrats while he remained detached and above the fray. It was a conscious decision on Ike's part. Nixon's intense partisanship won him the deep loyalty of Republican Party activists and the undying enmity of most Democrats.

Eight years after 1960 when the no-third-term 22nd Amendment had claimed the Eisenhower Administration as its first casualty, the Republicans were back in the White House. For Democrats, their worst fears had been realized. Now it was Nixon himself operating from the Oval Office. President Nixon would have loved to emulate the Eisenhower model of a president above the political fray and have a Vice President Nixon serving as a partisan attack dog, but such was not the case. Nixon delegated much of the attacking rhetoric to Vice President Spiro T. Agnew, but Nixon couldn't contain himself. He regularly slipped off the nonpartisan perch to attack his "enemies" by besmirching the reputations and impugning the motivations of anyone who saw the world differently from him. Despite all of the many "new Nixon's" which had been promised to the nation, the "old Nixon" always resurfaced. It was his most enduring role.

The decade of the 1960s had also altered the House. The Supreme Court's 1964 ruling in *Wesberry v. Sanders* obliged states to redraw their congressional districts so that they would be approximately equal in population.[9] This meant that a number of the smaller homogenous districts that had provided safe electoral havens for many senior members would now disappear. Sam Rayburn's 4th Texas District which had less than one-quarter of the population in Dallas Republican Bruce Alger's adjacent 5th District would be dramatically changed as would so many other electoral sinecures.

The House was a far more contentious chamber in the 1960s than it had ever been in the 1950s. Neither President Eisenhower nor Speaker Rayburn was temperamentally inclined to engage in hand-to-hand combat with one another. However, both men knew that loyal party operatives needed to have their fires stoked on occasion, so each made use of surrogates. President Eisenhower relied upon Vice President Nixon to fulfill the role of partisan slasher and Speaker Rayburn used Majority Leader McCormack. John McCormack relished the partisan aspects of the job. He reveled in floor battles. Given the opportunity to wage verbal warfare on the Republicans and eviscerate their philosophical positions, John McCormack was ferocious and much more like his first House mentor "Cactus Jack" Garner than Sam Rayburn, who shied away from this type of House discourse.

John McCormack found sitting in the Speaker's chair much too constraining.[10] He vastly preferred the post of floor leader to Speaker because it gave him the opportunity to debate and challenge anew the Republicans' regular assertions of financial catastrophe should this or that Democratic piece of legislation be enacted. John McCormack was more temperamentally suited as a passionate advocate for his positions than as a dispassionate presiding officer.

No longer was the partisan battler John McCormack speaking on the House floor for the Democrats in this first Nixon Congress; rather it was Oklahoma's Carl Albert, who was more like Sam Rayburn and sought to mute partisanship. The tough liberals who ran the Democratic Study Group pushed Carl Albert into a more aggressive partisan stance. The DSG's hard-nosed Dick Bolling, Frank Thompson, and Jim O'Hara were eager to delineate more clearly the differences between Democrats and liberals on one side versus Republicans and conservatives on the other. The presence within the Democratic Party of a sizable group of southern conservatives was onerous to the DSG, and it sought to minimize their influence by undermining the seniority rule which the DSG saw as granting the southerners disproportionate power. The accommodating efforts of Carl Albert to halve the difference between the House Democratic Party's competing wings were not viewed favorably by the DSG. A convert to the DSG's more aggressive liberal partisanship stance was House Democratic Whip Hale Boggs of Louisiana. John's protégé Tip O'Neill who would serve in all three of the leadership posts was a DSG member but not one of its vocal spokesmen.[11]

While the government was technically divided in partisan terms, the nation was riven badly by the continuance of the Vietnam War. The pace of protests escalated, and the Nixon White House hoped to find a way to extricate the nation from the war without appearing to have surrendered to the forces of North Vietnam.

The Nixon agenda

Henry Kissinger, the latest Cold War intellectual to be tapped as national security advisor, said the conflict between the United States and the Soviet Union was the only one worth confronting; everything else was merely a sideshow. To Kissinger, the Vietnam War created unnecessary noise for what he had hoped would be an era of "detente" between the two greatest superpowers. Kissinger was able to achieve the 91st Congress's first major legislative achievement with the passage of the Nuclear Non-Proliferation Treaty, which banned the spread of nuclear weapons, provided for safeguard arrangements, and ensured nondiscriminatory access to peaceful uses of nuclear energy.[12] On July 1, 1969, the treaty was concluded with signatures from the United States, the Soviet Union, and 60 other nations.

President Nixon had far less of a domestic policy agenda than was realized at the time.[13] Consequently, his legislative proposals were few in number and his victories were limited. Unlike Lyndon Johnson, Richard Nixon had no intention of letting history judge him on the basis of a legislative legacy. Nixon hoped to be judged on foreign policy success as declared in his first inaugural, "The greatest honor history can bestow is the title of peacemaker."[14]

Two domestic items passed by Congress in 1969, which had echoes of the previous administration, dealt with children's toys and the environment. The first of these was the Child Protection and Toy Safety Act of 1969 that provided a one-step regulation process for prohibiting the sale of children's articles and toys which presented electrical, mechanical, or other thermal hazards and was approved November 6, 1969.[15] The other domestic piece was the National Environmental Policy Act of 1969, which declared that the federal government would "use all practicable means and measures, including financial and technical assistance, in a manner calculated to foster and promote the general welfare, to create and maintain conditions under which man and nature can exist in productive harmony, and fulfill the social, economic, and other requirements of present and future generations of Americans."[16] Approved January 1, 1970, it established a three-member Council on Environmental Quality to advise the president on environmental matters.

President Nixon, like most Republicans, felt that taxation had become excessive and at his urging, Congress passed the Tax Reform Act of 1969. It was the most comprehensive reform of the nation's tax statutes in history and the largest tax cut since the Lyndon Johnson–sponsored and Wilbur Mills–drafted Revenue Act of 1964. Approved December 30, 1969, it increased personal income tax exemptions, lowered tax rates for single persons, repealed the 7% investment tax credit for machinery and equipment purchased, placed a minimum 10% tax on such income estate depreciation deductions, and increased Social Security benefits by 15%.[17]

To close out the year, Congress acceded to the president's wishes on foreign aid with the passage of the Foreign Assistance Act of 1969. Approved December 30, 1969, this act authorized foreign economic and military aid appropriations of $1,972,525,000 in fiscal 1970 and $1,936,525,000 in fiscal 1971.[18] It created an Overseas Private

Investment Corporation to assume investment promotion functions carried on by the Agency for International Development (AID).

On November 4, Nixon addressed the nation to declare a policy of "Vietnamization" that presumably would allow the United States to declare a "just peace" and extricate itself from this military quagmire.[19] In an effort to show his support for the war's continuance, McCormack had Sam Rayburn protégé Jim Wright of Fort Worth introduce a bill supporting the Nixon Vietnam agenda on the pretext that bipartisan support for the war would remove it as a source of contention in the upcoming 1970 election. It backfired badly as Evans and Novak reported that "DSG members view leadership handling of the resolution as another political blunder by McCormack, displaying insensitivity to [the] political needs of rank and file congressmen."[20]

Dr. Martin Sweig

Earlier in 1965, a crisis occurred in John McCormack's Capitol Hill office as Eugene T. Kinnaly, his longtime chief of staff, had taken ill and would never fully recover. John had hired the 39-year-old Kinnaly in 1928 to continue the work that he had ably provided John's predecessor, the late U.S. Representative James Gallivan (Dem-Mass.) who had defeated John in the 1926 primary. Following Gallivan's death in 1928, John ran again and in his campaign flyer, he stated that he would retain Gene Kinnaly should he be elected. It was a wise move. It kept Kinnaly from challenging him for the open seat and pleased Gallivan's supporters. Kinnaly served with John for 41 years until his own death in 1969.

Kinnaly's incapacity led John's number two, Dr. Martin Sweig to become his lead assistant. Marty Sweig was the son of an immigrant Jewish Kosher butcher from Winthrop, one of Boston's less affluent neighboring communities.[21] After graduating from Georgetown University in 1943, he was hired as a clerk in John's office at the age of 22 and as a very bright young man he steadily gained the confidence of John's key assistants, James V. "Buster" Hartrey in Boston and Gene Kinnaly in Washington. He was very ambitious and chose to continue graduate studies in history at Georgetown. After completing his comprehensive exams, Sweig had intended to write on the Spanish Civil War, but when his research indicated that General Francisco Franco, supported by conservative landowners and the Catholic Church, was the probable villain in that event, he began to tilt toward the leftist-leaning Republican cause. John McCormack, a devout Roman Catholic, told Sweig that he would not be writing a dissertation with that thesis in his office. Sweig compromised by writing on the Boer War in South Africa and supporting the Boers against the British, the common enemy of the Germans and the Irish. Sweig's pro-Boer stance led him to angrily confront former British Prime Minister Winston Churchill, a Boer War veteran, when he visited the Capitol in 1959.[22]

John's Washington office was run as a very loose ship and his staff took advantage of it. During the 1958 investigation of Boston industrialist Bernard Goldfine, there is a passing reference in a *Boston Globe* article to Christmas gifts given to McCormack senior staff members Gene Kinnaly and Joe Feeney by Goldfine.[23] John was relatively casual about it, "I don't ask my employees who they get Christmas gifts from. I wouldn't think of it."[24] John waved it aside with no follow-up. By contrast, when President Eisenhower learned of the extravagant gifts, including a Vicuna fur coat, given by Goldfine to his chief of staff Sherman Adams, a former New Hampshire governor, he requested and received Adams's resignation.

House Speakers have two offices—the formal ceremonial one in the Capitol Building where John McCormack spent most of his time carrying out his duties and a district office in one of the three House Office Buildings. In John's case, the seldom used district office was in the recently completed Rayburn House Office Building on the other side of Independence Avenue.[25] Perhaps the most telling observation was made by E. W. Kenworthy for the *New York Times* describing McCormack's dual office arrangement, "Neither of the Speaker's offices conveys the sense that here is a center of national business. Rather, the whole atmosphere is that of a local political headquarters. Evidently it was an atmosphere that Dr. Sweig found congenial to his talents and temperament."[26]

A Personal Encounter: I first encountered Marty Sweig in the Speaker's Capitol office on the Friday afternoon before the Labor Day weekend in 1968 in hopes of meeting Speaker McCormack to further my doctoral research on leadership in the U.S. House. Like many PhDs not on college campuses, Marty enjoyed being called "Doctor Sweig," and that was how he was addressed in the office apparently at his insistence. As I stood at the receptionist's desk, Sweig took the telephone from her hand and identified himself to the caller as "Speaker McCormack." Both the receptionist and the secretary seated behind her shrugged their shoulders and rolled their eyes in a manner that led me to believe that this was a common occurrence. (While this behavior would be denied at Sweig's trial, a number of witnesses recalled talking to someone purporting to be Speaker McCormack.)[27]

After a short wait I was ushered into Speaker McCormack's office and we exchanged pleasantries. I was especially interested in how he was able to obtain a seat on the powerful House Ways and Means Committee in only his third year in office. He told me at length that incoming Speaker John Nance Garner had wanted to name John as chair of that term's Democratic Caucus but since he had not yet arrived in Washington, Bill Arnold of Illinois was named instead. John's goal on meeting with Garner was to be moved from his minor committee assignments to the Judiciary Committee upon which he had served in the Massachusetts legislature. But Jack Garner had bigger plans for him and urged John to run for election to the Ways and Means Committee. Garner indicated that the Texans would support him and he should get the senior member of the Massachusetts delegation, Billy Connery of Lynn to "blow his nose at you." As a native of Lynn myself, I was very familiar with the Connery name with both a public school and the local American Legion Post named for him.

The Speaker was delighted when I shared that information with him and I was rewarded with one of his cigars. We had a rambling hour-long conversation until Marty arrived to tell the Speaker that Mrs. McCormack had arrived at the Capitol and wished to be driven back to their apartment at the Hotel Washington. I was invited to join them at the parking garage in the basement of the Capitol. We exchanged parting remarks and I was brought back to Marty's office.

As it was the Friday afternoon before a holiday, Marty brought out bottles of bourbon and Scotch and offered me a drink. We discussed graduate school experiences; he in history at Georgetown and me in political science at the University of Iowa. He tossed a German-language book at me and asked me to translate a few sentences. I demurred. While PhD candidates in history were expected to be conversant in French and German, political science candidates at Big Ten universities were expected to be skilled in statistics and research methods. In spite of his disappointment, I was invited to dinner. Marty who was sightless in one eye did not drive so one of his associates drove us to various ethnic restaurants in the city as more alcohol flowed in my direction, far beyond my tolerance level. I was driven back to my hotel before midnight and the following morning, Marty called my room to learn of my condition.

Although we never met again, I remained in touch with Marty by telephone when I needed clarification about the Speaker's allies. I found him to be quite helpful in clarifying details regarding John's career but he was stunned to learn what I had discovered about the Scottish Canadian ancestry of John's father. It was during one of those conversations that he said that John McCormack was "the most secretive" person that he had ever met.

Temptation: Like many congressional staffers (and members), Marty got to hobnob regularly with the rich and powerful people of the Washington community. It was difficult for staff members, who were generally overworked and underpaid, to find themselves in the company of those with enormous wealth and connection. Given the influence that many of the staff members, particularly the chiefs of staff, had over these powerful offices, it was easy to succumb to temptation. No longer overseen by Gene Kinnaly with whom he had shared an office and with his salary increased from $24,000 to $36,000, Marty was freer to succumb to temptation and a reading of his FBI file indicates his indulgence appeared to be European travel.[28] In his FBI files, there are multiple accounts of Marty traveling to Europe first class on high-end luxury ocean liners. Some entries appear:

> November, 1964: Sweig in Germany returning to the US "travelling first class on a return trip from Naples to the U.S. in November, 1964 aboard the ocean liner 'Leonardo daVinci'"
> November 16, 1966: Sweig in Paris en route to Munich
> December 5, 1966: Sweig in Rome, Athens, and Paris will be returning on the "Queen Mary"
> November 6, 1968: Sweig in Rome and Naples traveling on "the Italian liner 'Michelangelo'"

One fascinating assessment appeared in a May 14, 1965, letter to the FBI from a Texas couple that encountered Marty on one of his voyages. The FBI report recounted:

> A prominent El Paso couple, during a trip to Europe last fall, met an individual who did not ring true to them. This individual was Dr. MARTIN SWEIG, a German,

claimed residence in Boston, Mass., who identified himself as a member of the staff of the Speaker of the House of Representatives. This individual was traveling first class on a return trip from Naples to the U.S. in November, 1964, aboard the Italian liner "Leonardo daVinci." He claimed to have been back to Germany for eye surgery, was Jewish, 40 years of age, 5'7" tall, 150 pounds, dark complected. He spoke English well with an accent, was single and associated with very few people. Because this man wore good clothes in poor taste, was obviously unattractive, had poor table manners, and because he was a strange individual, people could not believe that he could be a member of the Speaker's staff. His conversation did not reflect any specific disloyalty.

With first-class travel on oceangoing luxury liners and extended stays in Europe, Marty would easily have spent close to a year's salary but he had another source of income—one that was less aboveboard.

By the mid-1960s, John McCormack was squeezed between the escalating expectations of the legislatively ambitious Lyndon Johnson and the growing frustration of the DSG liberals who felt that he was much too accommodating to the southern committee chairs. With his attention bifurcated in this manner, John began to rely more heavily on Sweig's management of his office, particularly with the growing but necessary demands of constituency service.

Within his Capitol Hill office, McCormack had allowed Sweig to act on his behalf. Not just signing letters as was done in virtually every congressional office, Marty was also capable of imitating the Speaker's voice. Eddie McCormack asserted that Marty's skill at imitating John's voice, while appreciated on occasion by John, had become a gag in Washington when John would be in someone else's office and they would call the Speaker, hearing Marty Sweig imitate John on the phone.[29] It seemed to be relatively harmless and it expedited business by apparently letting the Speaker be in two places at once.

Jack Anderson columns

With John McCormack struggling to deliver LBJ's last pieces of legislation while fending off his liberal DSG critics, John's office and Marty Sweig also drew the attention of longtime Washington investigative journalist Jack Anderson, who had inherited Drew Pearson's "Washington Merry-Go-Round" syndicated column.[30] With John's concentration fragmented between his House responsibilities and his concerns over Harriet's increasing frailty, Marty had become even more central to running the office. No longer supervised by Gene Kinnaly, Marty's hubris led him to proclaim openly to a group of Oxford-bound Rhodes Scholars that "he had absolute control over the Speaker's appointment schedule and implied that he also had a lot of control over the decision-making . . . that he was the most powerful man on the Hill."[31] It appeared that Marty had become bored with simply running the office and broadened his reach into less estimable ventures.

With his skill at imitating the Speaker's voice, he was able to wrest favors from various government officials and to facilitate the lucrative influence peddling career of Nathan Voloshen, a New York attorney who had become a successful Washington "fixer." One of Voloshen's more ambitious schemes was to lean on the Securities and Exchange Commission (SEC) to benefit the Parvin-Dohmann Company that the SEC had banned from trading on the American Stock Exchange for which he had been paid $50,000.[32] Another was to threaten the University of Delaware with the loss of a government contract from NASA if they failed to admit the son of a convicted labor racketeer.[33] Sweig would make the contacts and Voloshen would seal the deals and get the payoffs.

Anderson's major source was David Detweiler, a paid investigator who posed as an intern in John McCormack's Capitol Hill office for a few months in 1968. It was around the time that I had personally witnessed Marty pretend to be John McCormack on the phone, thus confirming my original observation. Detweiler alerted Anderson to a major Sweig-Voloshen scam, that of impersonating John's voice on calls to the Federal Bureau of Prisons on behalf of criminals. These were not only white-collar ones jailed for fraud, embezzlement, and money-laundering who had not used weapons in their criminal pursuits but even for some heavily mobbed-up hardened criminals who did use weapons.[34] Their jail terms would either be shortened, or moved to less secure venues, or in some cases, they would even be released on parole. Their grateful families would pay off Voloshen. While John McCormack made similar calls to the Bureau of Prisons on behalf of constituents, including those for the notorious South Boston mob boss, James "Whitey" Bulger, John's efforts were uncompensated constituent service whereas the Sweig-Voloshen enterprise was a profit-making one.

With my wariness increased, I called Jack Anderson, then semiretired, at his home in Bethesda, Maryland.[35] I told him that I was about to embark on the writing of a John McCormack biography but I needed to know if John McCormack was "dirty." If he was, I would not proceed with it. In our lengthy conversation, Anderson said emphatically that John McCormack was "clean" but the people around him were "dirty," most notably Marty Sweig and Nathan Voloshen. Anderson told me that John was "much too trusting."

With Marty Sweig operating out of the Capitol office, Voloshen used John's less public district one in the Rayburn Building, but it appears that he did most of his business from the office of the semi-reputable Adam Clayton Powell. The story gained its greatest traction when *LIFE* magazine published a five-page article by William Lambert entitled, "The Murky Men from the Speaker's Office."[36] The investigation had begun midsummer in the Federal District Court for Eastern New York in New York City. Assigned to handle the case was a young attorney, Richard Ben-Veniste, a graduate of Pennsylvania's Muhlenberg College—named for the Muhlenberg family that had produced the first Speaker of the House, Frederick A. C. Muhlenberg. The 26-year-old Ben-Veniste with law degrees from Columbia and Northwestern Universities began his distinguished career as a prosecutor with this case[37] and it launched a career that eventually led to his involvement in the Watergate Scandal of 1973–74, the House's Abscam Scandal of 1979–80, the Senate Whitewater Committee of 1995–96, and his appointment to the 9/11 Commission of 2002.

The crisis broke wide open when Marty Sweig returned from the grand jury's deliberations on October 16, 1969. The case against Sweig was very strong and ultimately he and Voloshen would be named in fifteen indictable counts. As noted in court records[38]:

> The fifteen-count indictment in this case charged Sweig and Nathan Voloshen with conspiracy and related offense of false personation, conflict of interest, and perjury. . . . [They] conspired to defraud the United States by using the influence of the Speaker's office to benefit Voloshen's clients who had matters pending before various federal departments and agencies by applying and attempting to apply improper influence upon individuals in departments and agencies.

Sweig knew that he had been caught and had brought dishonor to the man who had employed him for a quarter century. Personal mortification engulfed Sweig and he agreed to a suspension from his post if John McCormack was to retain any semblance of authority in the speakership.

On that October night, the Washington press corps was in full pursuit of the story. Reporters clambered over one another eager to confront the Speaker with news of Sweig's disclosures. How would he react? Would Sweig resign? Would McCormack resign? How much longer could he hold on? The questions peppered the Speaker.

In the midst of this evening, arguably the longest and most stressful of John McCormack's half-century political career, the door to his office was pushed open. Harriet, the 85-year-old wife of the Speaker, entered, pushing her walker before her. She was completely oblivious to the raucous tumult in the corridor outside the Speaker's office and the controversy surrounding her husband. John McCormack moved away from all the reporters in his office seeking information, his fellow House Democrats pressing their own ambitions, and the members of his staff needing reassurance about their own jobs. He escorted Harriet to a comfortable chair. After she was seated, she looked up and asked simply, "John, I thought we were going out for ice cream."[39]

His decision had been made. This would not be the time to announce it; there would be a better time. At this moment, only Harriet's concerns mattered. It was a fateful combination of the failing health of Mrs. McCormack, the undermining of his authority by Dick Bolling and the DSG, and the problems of navigating a Democratic Party alternative to President Nixon's legislative agenda that took its toll. As his 78th birthday approached on December 21, 1969, John was simply worn out.

The year's end brought an accounting. Nixon's congressional box score for the 1st Session of the 91st Congress noted him as receiving 32.2% of his requests.[40] That number was well below President Johnson's two sessions of the 90th Congress, 48% in 1967 and 56% in 1968 when both Houses of the 90th Congress were ostensibly controlled by Democrats, albeit impacted by the Conservative Coalition. Yet in its year-end summary, *Congressional Quarterly* reported that Nixon had an overall percentage of successful House floor votes of 72.3%, just three points below that of LBJ's 75.6% score in 1967. Given that the Democrats controlled both the House and Senate, this was remarkably high, and comparable to Ike's divided sessions in 1956 at 73.5% and

1958 at 74.0%.[41] As before, the Conservative Coalition left a very heavy imprint upon this session, as it had in the previous three years.[42]

Changes: With the invaluable Marty Sweig gone from the office and a criminal trial on the horizon, the McCormack office changed. John Monahan, a loyal staff member since 1961, moved into Marty's slot after Sweig was sent to jail.[43] There was little love lost between Sweig and Monahan and it was he and not Sweig who John assigned the responsibility of protecting the national security documents that John was asked to review during the fourteen months when he was next in line to President Johnson.[44] According to Anderson, "McCormack stubbornly refused to give the FBI permission to poke into the doctor's affairs. Another man, Sweig's junior, was subsequently chosen."

With his electoral career ended, Eddie McCormack joined Stan Bregman and Tyler Abell in a Washington law firm and was able to play a more prominent role in John's office. Others aiding John at this time were mutual friends of the McCormack's, Bill and Dorothy McSweeny who had become very close to John and Harriet McCormack and dined frequently with them in those later years.[45] Bill McSweeny was from Haverhill, a worker's city north of Boston close to New Hampshire. He was an award-winning reporter who had become vice president of Armand Hammer's Occidental Petroleum Company. McSweeny and his vivacious wife Dorothy were well connected to the Washington social scene. Bill even became John's "dollar-a-year" man who saw his job as shepherding John through this difficult transition and preparing him for a life after the U.S. House. The McSweenys prepared a set of oral history tapes for Boston University's Gotlieb Archival Research Center filled with John's reminiscences. They remained very protective of John McCormack's reputation.

Others were less protective. Charges were directed at John McCormack in the 1972 book *The Washington Pay-off* by Robert Winter-Berger, a slick New York con man. Winter-Berger was described by the office of New York State Attorney General Louis J. Lefkowitz as selling stock "in a company [that] never existed and all tests on the [presumed company's] product were a complete failure."[46] While Winter-Berger's association with the office of House Minority Leader Gerry Ford was true,[47] his assertions about John McCormack defied credulity. Two stand out: he contended that he was brought to the office to help John gain the 1964 nomination for vice president with LBJ.[48] Given that John was then 72 years old with an 80-year-old wife, and a well-known antipathy toward publicity and a deeper aversion to travel, any thought that McCormack would seek the high-profile post of vice president made no sense. John had already spent months as next in line to the presidency and it was not a period of time he enjoyed or wished to continue. Winter-Berger's other contention that he lunched twice a week with McCormack for five years never appears in any account of John's luncheon partners, who were generally fellow Irish-descended members of the House, his personal "Irish mafia." Other Winter-Berger accusations of payoffs to Gerry Ford were dismissed as noncredible by the Senate Rules Committee. It would appear that Winter-Berger sought to deflect prosecution by piling accusations on John McCormack. Sweig prosecutor Richard Ben-Veniste concluded that Winter-Berger had little of substance to contribute to his investigation as did syndicated political reporters Rowland Evans and Robert Novak who thought the claims held no merit.[49]

The Crisis Builds: Efforts to remove McCormack from the speakership became more visible and public as national columnists Evans and Novak rattled off different scenarios that would likely replace John with Majority Leader Carl Albert or Ways and Means Chair Wilbur Mills. Morris Udall, the year's earlier challenger was discussed in passing as was DSG leader and senior Rules Committee member Dick Bolling.[50] It was McCormack's support for President Nixon's war-related surtax and the White House's hawkish stance on Vietnam that ratcheted up further opposition as John was seen as increasingly out of touch with the House's newer Democrats.[51]

There was no concealing the disarray in John's office following Marty Sweig's departure. House members knew how dependent John was upon Sweig's management of his office. Any member who dealt with the McCormack office was fully aware that Marty had total control of access to the Speaker and many were sympathetic with what they saw as a betrayal of an old man's trust. Some others couldn't have cared less.

The Last Session: The Second Session of the 91st Congress would be John McCormack's last year in the U.S. House of Representatives. It was a divided government with a Republican president who had been historically hostile to many of the items on the Democratic agenda. There would also be a congressional election in November 1970, the long-term consequences of which would impact both parties. The strategic choices were simple: should the congressional parties confront President Nixon with legislation favorable to their agenda and dare the president to veto it so that the congressional Democrats would have a set of issues upon which they could build a greater majority, or should they cooperate with this president to show the nation that divided government can work effectively and that the Democrats could put patriotism and the national interest above partisan advantage? Wartime Congresses historically have strained for bipartisanship. Much to the surprise of many analysts, the Democratic Congress chose to cooperate with President Nixon and passed a substantial number of bills in 1970.

Early in 1970, one junior member, second-termer Jerome Waldie of California made a grandstanding effort to declare a vote of "no confidence" in John.[52] Since this was not the British House of Commons where "votes of no confidence" matter but the U.S. House of Representatives where they don't, Waldie's motion was simply gratuitous. John McCormack was nominated by the Democratic Caucus but was elected Speaker by the House itself. Only the full House could remove him from office. The Waldie motion was tabled by a vote of 192 to 23 in the caucus. Not only did John's caucus opponent Mo Udall vote against it, but Dick Bolling moved to table it in order "to avoid a phony vote of confidence."[53]

John sought to tamp down speculation about his future by hinting that he would run again for the speakership in 1971. His hints only infuriated a group of 19 young House liberals led by Waldie who opened up a frontal assault on the seniority system on March 19.[54] Listed among the nineteen were John Conyers. Jr. of Michigan, who John was able to name the first African American on the House Judiciary Committee and California's Robert L. Leggett who hired Marty Sweig as an assistant long enough to have Marty qualify for a congressional pension.

House Business: Amid the leadership chaos, the House continued to move bills to the floor. Environmental legislation received favorable hearings in Congress and the first act passed in the second session was the Federal Water Quality Improvement Act of 1970, approved April 3, 1970. This act authorized the federal government to clean up disastrous oil spills which jeopardized the nation's waters and beaches, with the polluter paying the costs, and placing new controls on sewage coming from vessels which fouled many of the nation's marinas, harbors, and ports.[55] It also created an Office of Environmental Quality that had first been supported by Congress in 1969.

Transportation interests were especially pleased with the passage of the Airport and Airway Development Act of 1970 that provided federal aid for aviation facilities and authorized a new low-range program for expansion of U.S. airport and airway systems.[56] Approved May 21, 1970, this program was to be financed in major part by new taxes on users of the aviation system. The revenues from the user charges would be paid into a trust fund in the U.S. Treasury similar to the existing Highway Trust Fund.

In May 1970 another crisis emerged. As the Vietnam War dragged on, college campuses erupted anew as the isolated president in the White House broadened the war into Cambodia while his staff compiled lists of "enemies" among his countrymen. The horrendous vision of four dead students at Ohio's Kent State University had been televised repeatedly until it was lodged firmly in the minds of Americans.

Youthful demonstrators against the Vietnam War raised serious questions about the age of voter eligibility. The most often chanted expression regarding this was "Old enough to fight; old enough to vote." Given the fact that most Americans drafted to fight in Vietnam were only 19 and ineligible to vote in most states, Congress moved to address this issue. Approved June 22, 1970, Congress passed the Voting Rights Act Amendments of 1970 which extended the Voting Rights Act of 1965 until 1975 and granted the right to vote in federal, state, and local elections to citizens between the ages of 18 and 21.[57] This would result in the passage and ultimate ratification of the 26th Amendment to the Constitution, lowering the voting age to 18. Leading the charge for 18-year-olds to get the vote was 78-year-old Speaker John McCormack, the House's last World War I veteran.[58]

The Announcement: On May 20, John formally announced that he would resign at the end of the 91st Congress.[59] The office was filled with supportive members. Hale Boggs and Wright Patman were photographed listening to the announcement while seated on the floor in John's office was his nephew Eddie and nearby was Ted Kennedy (Figure 23.2). It would be the first announced resignation from the speakership since 1925 when embattled Republican Frederick Gillett of Massachusetts left the House for a seat in the Senate. Since then, five of McCormack's predecessors had left the House feet first: Nick Longworth, Henry Rainey, Joe Byrns, Will Bankhead, and Sam Rayburn.

One of the ironies of this session of Congress was that it was on President Nixon's watch that Congress passed the Newspaper Preservation Act, approved July 24, 1970, which exempted from the antitrust laws certain combinations and arrangements necessary for the survival of failing newspapers, and allowed competing newspapers in the same city to pool their printing and business operations if one of them was in danger of failing.[60] The president's well-known hatred for newspapers was most obvious in his well-publicized "last press conference" following his bitter defeat for governor of California in 1962. Nixon signed the bill into law and may have come to

Figure 23.2 John McCormack announces his retirement, May 20, 1970 (Carl Albert Congressional Research Center, University of Oklahoma).

regret it a few years later when the *Washington Post* launched the investigation of his reelection campaign's activities that obliged him to resign from office in 1974.

The Postal Reorganization Act reorganized the Post Office Department as an independent agency, the United States Postal Service.[61] Approved August 12, 1970, it was widely viewed as the final stage of an effort to reestablish the ailing postal system on an efficient financial and businesslike basis. Lyndon Johnson had increased the Cabinet by two departments—Housing and Urban Development and Transportation—during his presidency, and Richard Nixon reduced the Cabinet by one.

No other single issue had helped Nixon gain the White House than his tough stance on "law and order," and he was eager to get legislation passed which delivered on his campaign promises. One of these laws was the Organized Crime Control Act that was intended to strengthen the legal tools of those engaged in the evidence-gathering process involving organized crime by writing new witness-immunity guidelines.[62] Criminal enterprises could no longer provide income for investment in legitimate businesses.

John's retirement at the close of the 91st Congress would bring to an end the 30-year reign of the Rayburn-McCormack era in the speakership. With John McCormack's impending retirement, the DSG liberals envisioned a reformed House that would no longer be dominated by a leadership beholden to the seniority-protected southern committee barons. Eager liberals saw an opportunity to implement key reforms. Not since the Legislative Reorganization Act of 1946 had any serious reform moves been made. Their efforts were only partially realized with the passage of the Legislative Reorganization Act of 1970 that revised committee procedures in the House and Senate, required that teller votes be recorded by name, and made committee votes public.[63] Approved October 26, 1970, it also created a Joint Committee on Congressional Operations to continue the study of operations and organization of Congress and to recommend improvements.

The 1970 Election: The endless Vietnam War not only split the country, it also split Congress. The Senate was "dovish" as antiwar speeches and resolutions emanated from Democratic Senators George McGovern of South Dakota, Bill Fulbright of Arkansas, Frank Church of Idaho, and Republican Senators Mark Hatfield of Oregon, John Sherman Cooper of Kentucky, and Charles Goodell of New York. Across the Capitol, the House remained solidly in the grip of its prowar "hawkish" leadership.[64]

Eager to remove liberal Democrats from the U.S. Senate, President Nixon and Vice President Agnew engaged in an unprecedented campaign from coast to coast. Their theme was "law and order." The deaths in May 1970 of four Kent State University students protesting the expansion of the Vietnam War into Cambodia was seen as evidence of how liberal challenges to the administration's Vietnam policy were unraveling the nation's social and political fabric.

Rather than defeating liberal U.S. Senators, the Nixon-Agnew attack backfired and the Republicans suffered a net loss of eleven governorships, including seven incumbents.[65] The public seemed to know that "law and order" involved a state's police power. It was not a senatorial issue but a gubernatorial one. The congressional results were mixed. The election confirmed the Democrats' hold on the House as they picked up eleven new seats. However, in the Senate, the Democrats lost three seats and their margin over Nixon's Republicans had shrunk from fourteen to ten.[66]

Closing Legislation: Having been unable to seriously wound one another in the election, President Nixon and the congressional Democrats put aside partisan rhetoric and went back to the nation's legislative agenda. Surprisingly, the closing weeks of 1970 saw an extraordinary amount of legislative output. Divided government seemed to have no impact on the productivity of the 91st Congress.[67]

A far-reaching regulatory thrust into the activities of the nation's workplaces was contained in the Occupational Safety and Health Act of 1970, approved December 29, 1970, giving the secretary of labor the authority to set and enforce safety standards for the protection of workers and created a three-member commission to enforce regulations.[68]

The Securities Investor Protection Act of 1970, approved December 30, 1970, established a private nonprofit Securities Investor Protection Corporation (SLPC) to oversee the activities of registered brokers and dealers and members of national securities exchanges.[69] It also created an insurance fund to protect investors against losses. This fund was to be financed through a combination of existing stock exchange trust funds, assessments, and lines of bank credit. Later in the 1970s, banks would insist upon deregulation, but as long as old-time populist Wright Patman of Texas chaired the House Banking Committee, the activities of banks would continue to be scrutinized regularly. Patman managed to gain passage of the Bank Holding Company Act Amendments of 1970 that placed holding companies that controlled a single bank under the regulatory authority of the Federal Reserve Board and required that they divest themselves of most nonbanking business.[70] Approved December 31, 1970, it extended the Bank Holding Company Act of 1956, which provided for regulation of holding companies controlling more than one bank, to the one-bank companies.

News accounts of product tampering led to the passage of the Poisoning Prevention Packing Act of 1970 that required special packing of potentially dangerous household goods to protect children from serious injury or illness resulting from handling, using, or ingesting such substances.[71] It was approved December 30, 1970. The regulatory impulses of the 91st Congress continued with the passage of the Clean Air Amendments of 1970 that established specific deadlines for 90% reduction of certain pollutants from new automobiles.[72] Approved December 31, 1970, it provided for new research programs, establishment of national air quality standards, fuel limitations, and standards for new stationary sources of pollution.

To close out the 91st Congress, Democrats took care to protect two of their key constituencies—the cities and the poor. For the cities, Congress passed the Housing and Urban Development Act of 1970 that authorized the secretary of housing and urban development to write insurance against such crimes as theft, burglary, and robbery when state and federal reinsurance programs were unavailable or where existing rates were prohibitive.[73] Approved December 31, 1970, it also established a maximum rent of 25% of a family's income for public housing and annual federal contributions to cover the difference between the rent income and operating costs.

The poor received some relief with the passage of the Food Stamp Act of 1964 Amendments that enlarged the food stamp program and extended it for an additional three years.[74] Approved January 11, 1971, the amendments included a new administration proposal for free stamps for families with monthly incomes below $30, and contained a restrictive new work requirement. It required that recipients register for and accept employment as a condition of receiving stamps.

Nor was presidential authority ignored in the closing moments of this Congress. Even though a Republican now sat in the White House, the congressional Democrats could not resist their post–New Deal impulses to expand executive authority. Two reorganization plans were passed. While President Nixon may not have fully availed himself of the powers which they were about to grant him, the congressional Democrats hoped that the 1972 election would place a fellow Democrat in the White House who would fully appreciate these regulatory gifts. The Reorganization Plan No. 3 of 1970, transmitted July 1970, consolidated all major programs to combat pollution in a single independent Environmental Protection Agency.[75] The other was the Reorganization Plan No. 4 of 1970, transmitted July 9, 1970, which created a National Oceanic and Atmospheric Administration in the Commerce Department, consolidating agencies from multiple departments.[76] It went into effect October 3, 1970.

Much of the legislative success was attributed, once again, to the Conservative Coalition.[77] The House Democratic leadership team of McCormack-Albert-Boggs put up relatively little resistance to the Coalition, and Richard Nixon's support score on floor votes was 84.6%, the highest ever for a divided government House in the 60 years that *Congressional Quarterly* had been computing that statistic.[78]

Preserving the Austin-Boston succession

Leadership Continuity: As legislation churned its way through the House, John McCormack's May 20 announcement publicly confirmed the decision that he had made months earlier. He was now in his 79th year on earth, his forty-second in the House, and his ninth in the Speaker's chair. His closest friends were deceased or long retired. Martin Sweig, his longtime legislative aide and chief of staff, had just been convicted of "influence peddling" and was sentenced to 30 months in federal prison. There were serious portents of an ignominious end to a glorious career.

How could John McCormack step down without seeming to surrender to the double distress of office scandal and the unfriendly machinations of the Republican president? Neither really mattered at that point. A man who lived as modestly as he did would never be accused of personal dishonesty, only of getting too old and being too trusting. Leaving Richard Nixon's Washington would be no hardship. For John McCormack, it was the failing health of his beloved Harriet that was his greatest concern at that time; not his reputation.

There had to be a succession; a continuity in the line. The path to the House speakership under the Democrats had become an orderly process. Called simply the "leadership ladder," it worked to minimize party conflict and to subdue ambition. One was named as Democratic Whip by the senior-most party officials, and if one was successful in that capacity, then you would likely be moved up to the elected post of Majority Floor Leader. And majority it was. By this time, the Democrats had held a House majority for eighteen of the twenty Congresses since 1930 and would hold it for another twelve consecutive Congresses, the longest period of one-party domination of an elected political institution in American history.

The floor leadership post was the only one that regularly engendered opposition in the Democratic Caucus. Once that hurdle had been passed, the elevation from Floor Leader to Speaker was automatic and rendered without opposition. John McCormack had held one of the three top posts among the House Democrats for 30 years, longer than anyone in congressional history, and no one more than he appreciated the subtle intricacies that lay below the surface of this seemingly automatic operation of the succession.

Carl Albert of Oklahoma, the Majority Floor Leader, and Hale Boggs of Louisiana, the Majority Whip, joined Speaker John McCormack in the Democratic leadership. They were an unlikely trio. It is doubtful if they would have sought each other's company in the world beyond Capitol Hill. John McCormack, the tall, gaunt, and ascetic 78-year-old Speaker from Boston, who dined every evening for 50 years with his wife, was a man of modest tastes and regular habits. Carl Albert, the small, quick-witted 62-year-old Majority Leader educated in a one-room rural Oklahoma schoolhouse and as a Rhodes Scholar at Oxford University, was a bundle of energy and insecurity. Hale Boggs, the handsome, florid-faced, robust 56-year-old majority whip, who had gone to Tulane and married into one of New Orleans's aristocratic families, was as well connected to Washington's social life as McCormack was isolated from it.

Dissimilar as they were, these three leaders had guided the House through the tumultuous 1960s, which had seen the near catastrophic confrontation with the Soviet Union over nuclear missiles in Cuba, the assassination of the young, beloved President John F. Kennedy, the ascension to the presidency of their mutual friend Lyndon Johnson, the enormous legislative success of LBJ's ambitious Great Society programs, the growth of the American presence in Vietnam to more than 530,000 troops, the urban riots in the black ghettoes, the murders of both the Reverend Martin Luther King, Jr. and Senator Robert Kennedy of New York, the unruly antiwar protests of the college campuses, and now the election of Richard Nixon. Through it all, they had maintained the Democratic majority in the House. It was no easy task.

With the world beyond Capitol Hill becoming more dangerous and unpredictable, it was important that the House half of Capitol Hill remain safe and predictable. They had serious business to do. Speaker McCormack would announce his retirement on May 20. Majority Leader Albert would present himself to the Democratic Caucus as the party's candidate for Speaker, and Majority Whip Boggs would present himself as the candidate for Majority Leader. They would decide among themselves who would be whip.

President Richard Nixon, ever sensitive to electoral advantage, knew that race was the great fault line within the Democratic Party. He sought to move disaffected white Democrats to his party through the "Southern strategy," by downplaying the Republican Party's historic commitment to civil rights, and give white southerners an electoral haven from rising black expectations. In contemporary parlance, Nixon was playing the "race card." Nixon strategist, the 29-year-old Kevin Phillips, author of the prophetic 1969 book *The Emerging Republican Majority*, would be quoted in the *New York Times* saying[79]: "Republicans would be shortsighted if they weakened enforcement of the Voting Rights Act. The more Negroes who register as Democrats in the South, the sooner the Negrophobes will quit the Democratic Party and become Republican. That's where the voters are."

Should the congressional Democrats address the race question by further pushing civil rights to expand the opportunities of their black constituents and consolidate the party's hold on this massive well-placed bloc? Or should they finesse race politics by pushing other legislative agenda items such as economic growth or entitlement expansion that were nonracial in character? These were difficult questions. They too hung over the succession. It was disturbing that 62 votes in the Democratic Caucus had been cast in 1969 against a sitting Speaker. The signs of unrest were there. This would not be an easy succession. It had to be done with care.

Majority Leader Albert's succession to Speaker would likely meet with the least difficulty. Traditionally, the movement from leader to Speaker had been unopposed and Albert was "safe." He had served on the coalition-building Agriculture Committee from 1948 through 1961 and as Speaker Sam Rayburn's whip from 1955 to 1961. Democratic whips maintained their committee assignments even while serving in the leadership; floor leaders seldom did. Speaker Rayburn's northeast Texas district was just across the Red River from Albert's district in southeastern Oklahoma, and Mr. Rayburn felt comfortable with him when he first placed Albert in the leadership. Carl Albert was a very well-known commodity.

Carl Albert's ascension from whip to majority leader in 1962 was to have been challenged by the brilliant but abrasive liberal Richard Bolling of Missouri, also a Rayburn favorite. But Dick Bolling smelled the coffee, counted the votes, and withdrew his likely challenge. For his 16 years of loyal service to the party leadership, Albert was fulsomely endorsed in Speaker McCormack's retirement announcement.[80]

The succession of Majority Whip Boggs to Majority Leader was less certain. Traditionally, it was the office of floor leader that had been the most closely contested, and Boggs was "less safe." Hale Boggs was one of the most talented legislators in the House, but his ambitions sometimes engendered distrust. In 1952, Boggs had lost a primary battle for Governor of Louisiana. It had not jeopardized Boggs's slot on the Ways and Means Committee, but it had kept him from being fully trusted by other House members. John McCormack was more forgiving, and he placed Boggs on the leadership ladder by naming him majority whip in 1962.

Boggs himself was a wonderful anomaly. He was a "poor boy" whose father had been a Mississippi bank teller. As a scholarship student at Tulane University, Boggs had parlayed his good looks and easy sociability into a prominent role on campus and won the hand of the beautiful, talented, and well-connected Marie Corinne "Lindy" Morrison Claiborne. He was a white southerner, but also a Roman Catholic like McCormack, and he came from an urban district in New Orleans which was more than a third black and had developed a personal and liberal commitment to civil rights. Boggs was a living embodiment of all the peculiar and contradictory elements of the Democratic Party.[81]

Boggs had southern opponents who distrusted him on race questions and northern opponents who distrusted southerners no matter how liberal. Questions were also raised about his temperament and his behavior, but Boggs was well placed. He was the second-ranking Democrat on the House's most important panel, the tax-writing Ways and Means Committee whose fifteen Democratic members served as the "committee on committees" for all of the other House Democrats' committee assignments. Boggs had helped fellow House members by rescuing them from dead-end assignments that could shorten their careers and by moving talented junior members into places of committee prominence generally reserved for more senior members. John McCormack was also an alumnus of the Ways and Means Committee and well aware that Ways and Means had produced more Speakers than any other House committee.

McCormack did not endorse Boggs in his May 20 retirement speech or anyone else running for Majority Leader. He had no intention of making new enemies from old friends in his closing months in the House. John had also heard from his House confidants that Boggs had considered a challenge to John in 1969, so there would be no early endorsement of Boggs.

Apparently, the DSG liberals took too much obvious joy in John's imminent retirement and he put aside his earlier intention not to intervene in the leadership succession. In late July, Evans and Novak reported that John "lashed out at congressional Democratic liberals" contending that they talked big and produced little.[82] To McCormack, they were a bunch of "phonies" and "fakers." Evans and Novak reported that John would support Boggs for Majority Leader and Chicago's Dan Rostenkowski for whip, although he "lacks experience in floor debate so necessary for a majority leader." "[It] would end all chance of the liberals electing a floor leader. The team of Boggs, 56, and Rostenkowski, 42, would extend far into the future the Southern-big city axis which has led House Democrats for so long. Thus would John McCormack's last hurrah deeply affect his party and the Congress."

That may have been McCormack's hope but the prospect of the first truly open majority leadership contest in the 30 years since McCormack himself defeated Virginia's Clifton Woodrum in 1940 was too important to ignore. Ultimately, there would be five candidates in the final lineup: Hale Boggs, the majority whip, who was the best positioned; the leading challenger and liberal favorite Morris Udall of Arizona, who had lost the 1969 speakership battle to McCormack; the blustery and bullying Wayne Hays of Ohio, who was slotted to chair the House Administration Committee; B. F. "Bernie" Sisk of California, a senior member of the Rules Committee and transplanted southerner from Texas who had moved west to escape the devastating dust storms of the 1930s; and James G. O'Hara of Michigan, the DSG candidate most favored by organized labor. Representatives Hays, Sisk, and O'Hara were all junior to Boggs and senior to Udall. They were relative long shots, but each hoped to capitalize on a deadlock between Boggs, the "establishment" candidate, and Udall, the "insurgent" candidate.

Throughout the summer and the fall of 1970, the competitors battled for advantage. A key bargaining chip was the job of majority whip. Unlike the House Republicans who began electing their whips in the 1920s, the House Democrats appointed theirs.[83] It was one way of containing conflict and of bringing into the leadership a younger member who could be socialized into maintaining the long-term goals of the party leadership.

The McCormack-Albert-Boggs triumvirate gathered in the Speaker's district office in the Rayburn Building away from the Capitol. It was now the end of October, and an ice storm had whipped across the Capitol. Washington is a city regularly immobilized by the weather. Anything that cannot be legislated, lobbied, appropriated, or taxed stops the city in its tracks.

Majority Leader Albert was secure in the knowledge that no serious challenge to his speakership elevation would be mounted. By this time, Majority Whip Boggs felt better about his prospects for succeeding Albert as Majority Leader, but he still was no lock for the job.

Hale Boggs wanted to fill the job of majority whip with Dan "Rosty" Rostenkowski of Illinois. Rosty was young at 42, a northern Catholic with a heavily black constituency, and he was the trusted congressional lieutenant of Chicago Mayor Richard Daley. Not lost in Boggs's assessment of Rosty's virtues was the fact that the twelve Illinois Democrats represented the fifth largest House party delegation. Rostenkowski of Illinois had already been a beneficiary of Boggs's assistance.[84] In May 1964 at the age of 36, Rosty had been moved onto Ways and Means in only his third term of service. It was not a record—then-Chair of Ways and Means Wilbur Mills (Dem.-Ark.) had joined the committee at the age of 33—but Rosty's assignment was a sign of distinction to the other members.

The policy impact of the Boggs-Rostenkowski pairing would be immediate. With two members of the House Democratic leadership being Catholic white men familiar with urban racial problems, the question of race would be directly addressed. There was also a personal dimension: Boggs had promised Rostenkowski the job.

It would not be an easy sell. Majority Leader and future Speaker Carl Albert had doubts about Rostenkowski, some political and some personal. On the political level, placing a Daley lieutenant in the job of majority whip would seem to legitimate the brutal roughhouse tactics of the Chicago police during the 1968 Democratic convention. This move would infuriate the liberals. On the personal level, it was 6'3" Dan Rostenkowski who allegedly seized the gavel from the 5'4" Carl Albert at the convention when the antiwar delegates took their protests to the floor. It was a moment of publicly televised personal mortification for Albert that he would not forgive.

Speaker McCormack listened quietly while various names were tossed out for discussion and qualms overtook each of them—some were too lazy, some had questionable morals, while others were electorally vulnerable. The Speaker then spoke. He went on at length about the prominence of Massachusetts's members in the leadership of each chamber. He rattled off the names of former Massachusetts Speakers, committee chairs, and Senate leaders. "What about Tom?" asked the Speaker.[85]

Tip O'Neill: "Tom" was Thomas P. O'Neill, Jr, from Cambridge, Massachusetts. Known to virtually everyone else in the House as "Tip," Representative O'Neill had been a longtime protégé of John McCormack's. They regularly met for coffee after John breakfasted with Harriet and after dinner with Harriet, McCormack and O'Neill would occasionally make the rounds of the evening parties that are a staple of Washington social life. O'Neill was not mentioned on any of the early speculative lists attempting to handicap the leadership races. More interest was shown in his longtime roommate Eddie Boland from Springfield in western Massachusetts, a senior member of the Appropriations Committee, the largest committee in the House.

Tip was a member of the "Tuesday-to-Thursday Club"—East Coast members who seldom spent their weekends in Washington and who flew into Washington for midweek legislative business and flew back home to be with their constituents and families on weekends. Tip had a wife, Millie, back home in Cambridge where she was the primary parent for the couple's five children. For Tip, the apartment was just for sleeping. For longtime bachelor Eddie Boland, with his dark hair and quick-moving eyes, the apartment was more central to his life. Boland's Appropriations Committee was the hardest working and the least partisan one in the House, and Eddie always brought work home with him. As a break from his tedious homework tallying federal government expenditures, Eddie would clean the floors and the drapes of the apartment.

Tip served on the 15-member Rules Committee, which was the "traffic cop" for the House floor. The Rules Committee decided procedural questions such as whether or not bills could be amended and the length of time for floor debate. There were no specific subject matters which the Rules Committee had to deal with, so homework was slight. This was why Tip could hang out with Speaker McCormack in the evening after his dinners with Harriet, and Eddie would not.

Eddie Boland's other problem was dynastic. In 1962, at the Massachusetts State Democratic Convention, he had made the major nominating speech for Ted Kennedy, the president's youngest brother, contributing to the convention's endorsement of Teddy over Massachusetts Attorney General Edward "Eddie" McCormack, Jr., the childless Speaker's nephew. The ensuing Teddy-Eddie primary fight was brutal and left many lasting wounds.

McCormack nemesis Dick Bolling of Missouri once asked why Tip was named whip and Eddie Boland was not. He was told that Boland had nominated Ted Kennedy for U.S. Senate at the 1962 state convention and not Eddie McCormack. Even though John McCormack had been dead for four years, Bolling exploded and slammed his fist down on his desk, declaring[86]: "The son of a bitch would never have forgiven him!"

O'Neill faced difficulty back home. His Cambridge and Boston constituency was filled with college students. The antiwar protests emanating from Harvard, MIT, Boston University, Boston College, Tufts, and Brandeis pushed him into the difficult position of having to choose between the "hawkishness" of John McCormack's House leadership team and the "dovishness" of his constituents.[87] It was not an easy line to walk. O'Neill's ties to the House were fraying and the expense of maintaining a large family and two residences 400 miles apart gnawed at him. But the whip's job paid more, and O'Neill would now be in a position where he could set the timing of floor votes and gain more control over his life.

Carl Albert was delighted at the prospect of someone other than Rostenkowski working with him. John McCormack was pleased to maintain a Massachusetts tie to the leadership and to reward Tom O'Neill, his loyal protégé. Hale Boggs, now outvoted two to one, chose not to tell Rostenkowski the bad news. Boggs's own elevation was no certainty and he had just failed his first test at delivering on a promise. Meanwhile, race politics would be finessed, but not addressed.

It was Bill McSweeny who was in John's district office when the whip decision was made and was asked to deliver the good news to Tip. McSweeny went to Duke Zeibert's legendary restaurant at Connecticut Avenue and L Street where he found Tip and Rosty enjoying each other's company.[88] He motioned Tip aside and told him that he would be the next whip but that he could not share the news with Rosty lest those twelve Illinois Democrats became angry and choose not to vote for Hale Boggs as Majority Leader. Tip's skills at dealing with dueling rivals were put to use once again. He would later exhibit them in the Jimmy Carter-Ted Kennedy conflicts of 1979–80 and again in his own dealings with President Ronald Reagan.[89]

An unofficial slate was now set: Albert for Speaker, Boggs for Majority Floor Leader, and O'Neill for Majority Whip. The meeting ended. Carl Albert and Hale Boggs bundled up and went out to face the ice storm while the Speaker awaited the arrival of his limousine. The limousine arrived, and Speaker John McCormack was driven back to the Hotel Washington to have another quiet dinner alone with Mrs. McCormack.

Sweig trials and aftermath

There were two trials of Marty Sweig, one in New York City, the other in Miami.[90] Only Martin Sweig was on trial when the first case went to court on July 2, 1970. Nathan Voloshen chose to plead guilty and on November 24, 1970, with his health failing, the 72-year-old Voloshen was fined $10,000 with a one-year suspended sentence. He would die nine months later.

Ben-Veniste's most vivid memory of the New York trial was when he called John McCormack as a government witness. McCormack, a seasoned criminal defense attorney, entered the courtroom with a shambling gait that Ben-Veniste believed was intended to elicit sympathy from the jury. Once John saw Marty, he lifted his arms and clasped them together as a boxer would after a successful bout. Sweig responded by getting up from his chair and bowed in John's direction. At this point, Ben-Veniste realized that most of the case was now lost.[91] John testified that Marty "was very devoted to me. He worked all hours of the day, until 2 or 3 in the morning and Saturdays." During his testimony, John contended that he never inquired what Sweig and Voloshen were up to because, "I am not a curious fellow."[92] One juror told reporters that John "helped Dr. Sweig more than he hurt."[93] As a result, the conspiracy charge was dropped and Sweig was convicted on only one of the six perjury charges. He would eventually be sentenced in September 1970 to 30 months in prison and fined $2,000.

A later trial in Miami was more successful for the government after Voloshen gave Ben-Veniste the name of Florida lobbyist Mike Silbert who rewarded Sweig with $5,000 for interventions on his clients' behalf and by paying the rent on Marty's comfortable Capitol Hill apartment.[94] This was de facto evidence of bribery and Ben-Veniste reported that Marty was found "guilty on three counts of conspiracy and bribery as charged in the indictment."[95] Marty was sentenced to three years in prison but the Florida judge agreed to let this sentence run concurrently with the New York one. Sweig appealed his conviction and lost in the Court of Appeals for the Second Circuit and his certiorari appeal for the Supreme Court was rejected.[96]

On July 18, 1972, Sweig was released on parole from the Lewisburg (Pa.) Federal Penitentiary. "I was a model prisoner," Sweig said to reporters on his release.[97]

Most puzzling to Ben-Veniste in his 2009 memoirs published 30 years after the trials was McCormack's attitude during the trials:

> I found it hard to understand how McCormack could have been both unaware of what had gone on and still willing to stand up for Sweig. Where was the outrage, or at least the disappointment and disapproval? . . . Was it simply loyalty that brought McCormack to Miami to testify on Sweig's behalf, or did the old man have something to fear if Sweig felt abandoned? I didn't know the answer then and I don't know the answer now.

There was a simple answer and one deeply rooted in the code of the South Boston Irish: friends don't send friends to jail.

In the months following John's departure from the House, President Nixon heaped public praise upon him while at the same time Justice Department officials launched further investigations of the conduct of John's office during his speakership. Jack Anderson who had come to respect John's honesty and probity considered Nixon's behavior to be hypocritical and exposed it in his columns.[98]

It's Time, Mr. Speaker: The joy had left the McCormack speakership. Squabbles from within the party sapped the Speaker's energy. Partisan battles with Minority Leader Gerald Ford acting on behalf of the Nixon White House ground the Speaker down.

McCormack was now in the last portion of his eighth decade on earth and his greatest friends and allies in the House were long gone. Some of his allies remained, but not enough to help him withstand the perpetual challenges.

Tom Foley of Washington State, who served as Speaker from 1989 to 1995, vividly recalled a John McCormack speech about when to leave[99]:

> It was John McCormack who once said we should always feel very proud to be the representatives of half-a-million or so of our fellow Americans. That it was one of the great honors in American life to be a Representative in Congress. And that when we came to work in the morning, and when we first caught glimpse of the Capitol from east or west, north or south, in rain or shine, in sun or shade, however it appeared, if it didn't give us a sense of thrill, a sense of not only personal satisfaction, but very deep gratitude to our constituents for the honor of letting us represent them, we should simply quit. Those members who no longer felt that thrill had stayed too long.

It was time. On May 20, 1970, Speaker John McCormack announced his retirement, after serving nine consecutive years in the chair, the longest consecutive stint in American history to that point. And then it was over. With the close of business on January 3, 1971, Speaker John McCormack's 43rd year representing the citizens of Boston in the nation's largest legislative assembly had come to an end. On John's last day as Speaker, Bill McSweeny recalled that the House galleries were filled with congressional wives there to honor arguably the greatest husband in House history.

The Death of Mrs. McCormack and the Loneliest Years: John McCormack did not live to see the end of the Austin-Boston speakership of which he was an integral part. As he left the House in 1971, he was consumed with more personal concerns. His beloved wife Harriet had begun to fail. News accounts of her illness demonstrated the intense devotion John had to her, especially in her final year[100]:

> at [Washington's] Providence Hospital where she had been a patient for more than a year and where the former speaker had spent every night and most days in an adjoining room with a door cut through the wall separating them . . .
>
> When friends and nurses offered to take up the vigil and free him from the hospital for a time, McCormack refused. "This is not a sacrifice," he was quoted as saying. "And it is not a duty. I want to be with Harriet, and I will be."

On December 2, 1971, M. Harriet Joyce McCormack died in Providence Hospital at the age of 87. A *Boston Globe* article from December 4 describes Harriet's last homecoming[101]:

> McCormack was assisted from the aircraft by his nephew, then, with relatives and friends, stood silent until the simple grey metal casket was carried out by a nine-man Air Force honor guard. He refused to enter the waiting limousine and stood, head bared, until the coffin was placed in a waiting hearse.

Then summoning newsmen to lean in the window, he told them how his wife of 51 years had "asked thousands of times: 'When are we going home?' When we passed over South Boston I told her: 'You're home again, my dear.'"

Harriet's funeral service took place at St. Margaret's Church on Columbia Road, now the Blessed Mother Teresa Parish, just blocks away from their second-floor flat on the same road, where they had lived for the entirety of their married life. Attending the service was former President Lyndon B. Johnson, there to pay his respects to the ever-loyal wife of John McCormack, his greatest congressional ally in fashioning the Great Society, and 1,000 others.[102]

President Johnson, more than any other of John McCormack's contemporaries, knew how central Harriet was in John's life. There is little doubt that when Johnson's younger daughter Luci chose to become a Catholic, the Johnsons spoke with the McCormacks about her new religion, one that the Protestants LBJ and Lady Bird were not particularly familiar with. When the Johnson presidency drew to a close in 1968, their affinity for one another remained strong[103]:

Dear Miss Harriet:

I know that neither of us needs any souvenirs of the long and happy years our families have shared. But let this little album speak always for my gratitude to you and your good John. Lady Bird and I know the strength you give him, so he can apply it with courage and wisdom to America's purpose. Every American is proud to thank you for that.

God bless you always.

Sincerely,
LBJ

John McCormack lived for almost a decade after his retirement from the House. He accepted awards and made speeches, but his active involvement in the destiny of the Democrats in the House and the state of Massachusetts had ended. He gave a few retrospective interviews[104] including one to the *Boston Herald* in which he admitted that "five or six of [his siblings] lived to be 17, 18, 19" and not the infants that he told South Boston 60 years earlier during his political ascent.[105] What did it matter now?

John went to Washington infrequently and according to the manager of the Hotel Washington, he would never stay in the room where he and Harriet had lived for 42 years and it was only when John left the speakership that the room was finally remodeled. It was a quiet time of regular lunches and dinners at Jimmy's Harborside Restaurant overlooking Boston Harbor. Greek-born Jimmy Doulos, who had owned the restaurant for years, felt indebted to John McCormack for expediting his naturalization papers, and he set aside a regular table for John to take his lunches and dinners while holding court for all of the regular patrons who always knew where to find him at those times of the day. For John McCormack, whose longevity seemed linked to establishing routines in his life, this was an ideal situation. After he left the house on Columbia Road in Dorchester, he moved to a one-bedroom apartment at

Jamaica Towers in Jamaica Plain where his nephew Eddie and his wife Emily lived. Only cigars, orange juice, and chocolate bars could be found in his refrigerator, so these twice daily trips to Jimmy's for meals were essential.

Another of his rituals was to watch the Boston Red Sox take the city on their regular roller-coaster rides. For much of the 1970s, the Red Sox had tantalized this city which had seen no World Series title since 1918 and the trading of Babe Ruth to the hated Yankees of New York City. Always coming close to a World Series victory, the Red Sox had become like Sisyphus of ancient mythology coming close but never quite getting the boulder to the crest of the mountain. For more philosophical types, the Red Sox's flirtation with success and ultimate failure was treated as an allegory in which this Puritanical "city on a hill" had succumbed to the material blandishments of the Sodom to the south and had to suffer for its sin of sending its best ball player to New York City. To John McCormack, for whom allegory was just intellectual effluvia, the Red Sox were simply chokers.

At 2:05 p.m. on November 22, 1980, at Eastwood, the Nursing Home in Dedham, Massachusetts, John William McCormack died. The cause of death was "cardiovascular arrest of 5 minutes duration; and arteriosclerotic cardiovascular disease of 10 year's duration."[106] It was 17 years to the day that John F. Kennedy had been murdered in Dallas, Texas, a tragedy that had placed John McCormack a heartbeat away from the presidency.

John McCormack's body was returned to his old South Boston neighborhood where a Funeral Mass was held at St. Monica's Church. The eulogy was delivered by South Boston's own Massachusetts Senate President William M. "Billy" Bulger. The leading dignitary was Vice President-elect George H. W. Bush. Although elected from Texas, Bush was a native of nearby Milton, Massachusetts. Also present were U.S. Senator Edward M. Kennedy, the House's former Speaker Carl Albert and its present one Tip O'Neill as well as Republican leader John Rhodes of Arizona.[107] St. Monica's is one of the smaller neighborhood Catholic churches but it faces the original Old Harbor Village, the federal housing project sponsored by John in the 1930s and is just across from Vinton Street, where John had last lived with his sainted mother Mary Ellen and his brothers. He had truly come home. John W. McCormack was buried beside his beloved Harriet at St. Joseph's Cemetery in West Roxbury.

Notes

1 "Since Speaker McCormack was not a bachelor and didn't drink, the room fell into disuse as a place where the Speaker's key advisers gathered to plot strategy and unwind from a legislative day." Robert L. Peabody, *Leadership in Congress: Stability, Succession, and Change* (Boston: Little, Brown, 1967), p. 189.
2 Quoted in Champagne et al., *The Austin-Boston Connection*, p. 128.
3 Robert Remini, *The House: The History of the House of Representatives* (New York: Smithsonian Books in association with HarperCollins, 2006), p. 296; and Jeffery A. Jenkins and Charles Stewart III, *Fighting for the Speakership: The House and the Rise of Party Government* (Princeton, NJ: Princeton University Press, 2013), pp. 284–86, 359.

4   Robert L. Peabody, ed., *Education of a Congressman: The Newsletters of Morris K. Udall* (Indianapolis: Bobbs-Merrill, 1972), p. 296.

5   Noble E. Cunningham, Jr., *The Jeffersonian Republicans in Power: Party Operations, 1801–1809* (Chapel Hill, NC: University of North Carolina Press, 1963), p. 88. Macon was a candidate for election as Speaker in the 11th Congress in 1809 and lost to Joseph Varnum of Massachusetts on the second ballot, 45 to 65, *Annals of Congress*, 11th Congress, 1st Session, p. 56.

6   Richard L. Lyons, "McCormack Beats Back House Revolt," *WP*, January 3, 1969, p. A1.

7   The fullest account of this contest can be found in Matthew N. Green's "McCormack Versus Udall: Explaining Intraparty Challenges to the Speaker of the House," *Americans Politics Research*, XXXIV, January 2006, pp. 3–21.

8   Burton D. Sheppard, *Rethinking Congressional Reform: The Reform Roots of the Special Interest Congress* (Cambridge, MA: Schenkman, 1985), p. 42; and Ronald M. Peters, Jr., *The American Speakership: The Office in Historical Perspective*, 2nd ed. (Baltimore, MA: The Johns Hopkins University Press, 1997), pp. 153–55.

9   *Wesberry v. Sanders*, 376 U.S. 1 (1964).

10 Author's telephonic interview with the Hon. John W. McCormack, April 1977.

11 Sheppard, *Rethinking Congressional Reform*, pp. 51–52.

12 Nuclear Non-Proliferation Treaty, concluded July 1, 1969 (21 UST 483-566). See also "Senate Ratifies Nuclear Nonproliferation Treaty," *CQ Almanac 1969*, pp. 162–68.

13 Paul C. Light, *The President's Agenda: Domestic Policy Choice from Kennedy to Clinton*, 3rd ed. (Baltimore, MD: The Johns Hopkins University Press, 1999), pp. 115–18; and Fred I. Greenstein, *The Presidential Difference: Leadership Style from FDR to Barack Obama*, 3rd ed. (Princeton, NJ: Princeton University Press, 2009), pp. 99–109.

14 Richard M. Nixon. "Inaugural Address," January 20, 1969, American Presidency Project, accessed September 7, 2015.

15 Child Protection and Toy Safety Act of 1969, approved November 6, 1969 (83 Stat. 187-190). See also "Toy Safety," *CQ Almanac 1969*, pp. 248–50.

16 National Environmental Policy Act of 1969, approved January 1, 1970 (83 Stat. 852-856). See "Environmental Quality Council," *CQ Almanac 1969*, pp. 525–27.

17 Tax Reform Act of 1969, approved December 30, 1969 (83 Stat. 487-472). See "Congressionally Initiated Tax Reform Bill Enacted," *CQ Almanac 1969*, pp. 589–649.

18 Foreign Assistance Act of 1969, approved December 30, 1969 (83 Stat. 805-826). See "Foreign Aid Authorization Lowest in Program's History," *CQ Almanac 1969*, pp. 434–47.

19 Chalmers M. Roberts, "Nixon Says Speech Has Wide Support: Nixon Claims Wide Support for Speech Support for Withdrawal," *WP*, November 5, 1969, p. A1.

20 Rowland Evans and Robert Novak, "McCormack's Blunder in Springing of Viet Trap Angers Party Liberals," *WP*, December 1, 1969, p. A23.

21 Richard J. Connolly, "Sweig: Quiet Man," *BG*, October 18, 1969, p. 2.

22 The 1959 Churchill-Sweig encounter is described in Richard J. Connolly, "Sweig: An Unofficial Envoy; But McCormack Aide Angered Churchill," *WP*, October 19, 1969, p. 8.

23 "No Party Slant in Goldfine Gifts," *BG*, July 4, 1958, pp. 1, 7.

24 "Goldfine Gifts OK at Yule: McCormack," *BG*, July 8, 1958, p. 5.

25 A March 2016 telephone conversation with former McCormack assistant John Monahan questioned the existence of the second office but it was referenced in the Kenworthy *New York Times* article and in a telephone conversation with Bill McSweeny.

26 E. W. Kenworthy, "Dual Office Setup Linked to Voloshen Case," *NYT*, November 2, 1969, p. 72.

27 Edith Evans Asbury, "Sweig Trial Here Told He Posed as McCormack: Witnesses Also Say Voloshen Let Phone Callers Think Speaker Was on Line," *NYT*, July 8, 1970, p. 38.

28 FBI File of Dr. Martin T. Sweig.

29 This was an Eddie McCormack observation, October 1995.

30 The most recent assessment of Jack Anderson's career and influence may be found in Mark Feldstein's *Poisoning the Press, Richard Nixon, Jack Anderson, and the Rise of Washington's Scandal Culture* (New York: Farrar, Straus and Giroux, 2010). Now a professor at the University of Maryland, Mr. Feldstein was interviewed in the summer of 2014.

31 Jack Anderson, "The Washington Merry-Go-Round: Nixon Tax Veto Threat Is No Bluff," *WP*, December 12, 1969, p. D17. Other Anderson columns in the *Post* featuring Sweig were "McCormack's Aide Held Potent Spot," *WP*, October 20, 1969, p. B11; "Speaker Never Took Money for Favors," *WP*, October 30, 1969, p. G11; and "Firing Aide Was Painful to Speaker," *WP*, October 23, 1969, p. F9.

32 Richard H. Stewart, "$50,000 for 5 Hours of Work: Jury Told of Voloshen's Fee for Arranging Meeting," *BG*, June 27, 1970, p. 2. Sweig was at the meeting in the account of Edith Evans Asbury, "S.E.C. Head Tells of Sweig Meeting: Says Defendant Sought Aid for Client of Voloshen," *NYT*, June 27, 1970, p. 13.

33 Richard H. Stewart, "College 'Pressured,' Sweig Jury Told," *BG*, July 1, 1970, p. 2; and Jack Anderson, "Sweig Trial Witness Testifies NASA Funds Used as Club," *WP*, July 1, 1970, p. A3.

34 Associated Press, "Sweig Case Figure's Body Found Dumped in Car Trunk," *BG*, October 8, 1970, p. 68. Salvatore (Sally Burns) Granello, an associate of Mafia kingpins Vito Genovese and Thomas (Three-Finger Brown) Lucchese, paid Voloshen for help in preventing his transfer from Danbury (Ct.) Federal Prison to a tougher place. While Sweig's name was mentioned in testimony, this was one of the dismissed counts. Joseph F. Fried, "Ex-Convict's Body Found in Car Here: Granello Had Been Linked to Gambling and Racketeering," *NYT*, October 7, 1970, p. 41.

35 Author's phone call to Jack Anderson, Bethesda, MD, March 2002.

36 William Lambert, "The Murky Men from the Speaker's Office," *LIFE*, October 31, 1969, pp. 52ff.

37 Richard Ben-Veniste, "United States v. Sweig and Voloshen," in his *The Emperor's New Clothes: Exposing the Truth from Watergate to 9/11* (New York: Thomas Dunne Books, 2009), pp. 51–93.

38 From the United States Court of Appeals for the Second Circuit, in *United States of America v. Martin Sweig*, argued March 25, 1971, Appendix A, p. 46.

39 Author's phone conversations with Mr. Bill McSweeny, Washington, DC, Fall 1998.

40 "Congress Approves One-Third of Nixon's Requests," *CQ Almanac 1969*, pp. 115–23.

41 "Presidential Victories on Votes in Congress, 1953–2007," in Norman J. Ornstein, Thomas E. Mann, and Michael J. Malbin, eds., *Vital Statistics on Congress, 2008* (Washington, DC: The Brookings Institution, CQ Press, 2008), pp. 144–45, and updated with annual *Congressional Quarterly Almanacs*.

42 "Conservative Coalition Remains Potent in Congress," *CQ Almanac 1969*, pp. 1052–59.

43 Phone interview with John Monahan, March 2016.

44 Jack Anderson, "McCormack's Aide Held Potent Spot," *WP*, October 20, 1969, p. B11.

45 Multiple conversations with Eddie McCormack in Boston and Bill McSweeny in Washington, 1995–97.

46 News release from the office of New York Attorney General Louis J. Lefkowitz, June 6, 1960.

47 Jack Anderson, "Rep. Ford Closely Linked to Lobbyist," *WP*, July 20, 1972), p. F7.

48 Robert N. Winter-Berger, *The Washington Pay-Off: An Insider's View of Corruption in Government* (New York: Lyle Stuart, 1972), pp. 32–33.

49 Rowland Evans and Robert Novak, "Another Mystery Book," *WP*, March 26, 1972, p. B7.

50 Rowland Evans and Robert Novak, "Drive to Purge McCormack Grows Stronger," *BG*, September 3, 1969, p. 15; and "Liberal Democrats Conclude Albert Is Best Bet to Topple McCormack," *WP*, September 5, 1969, p. A23.

51 Rowland Evans and Robert Novak, "Democrats v. McCormack, At First Party Caucus, Speaker Appears Impervious to Rank-and-File Discontent in House," *WP*, January 25, 1970, p. B7.

52 Richard L. Lyons, "Rep' Waldie Asks Removal of McCormack as Speaker," *WP*, February 4, 1970, p. A2.

53 "Challenge to McCormack," *CQWR*, February 20, 1970, p. 577.

54 Richard L. Lyons, "19 in House Threaten Revolt Over Seniority," *WP*, March 20, 1970, p. A4.

55 Federal Water Quality Improvement Act of 1970 was approved April 3, 1970 (84 Stat. 91-115). See also "Comprehensive Water Pollution Control Act Cleared," *CQ Almanac 1970*, pp. 175–78.

56 Airport and Airway Development Act of 1970 was approved May 21, 1970 (84 Stat. 219-253). See also "Congress Passes Airport and Airway Development Act," *CQ Almanac 1970*, pp. 168–74.

57 Voting Rights Act Amendments of 1970 were approved June 22, 1970 (84 Stat. 314-319). Subsequently, the Supreme Court on December 21, 1970, by a 5–4 decision, held that Congress had the power to lower the voting age to 18 for federal but not state and local elections. *Oregon v. Mitchell*, 400 U.S. 112 (1970). See also "Congress Lowers Voting Age, Extends Voting Rights Act," *CQ Almanac 1970*, pp. 192–99.

58 Richard L. Lyons, "Vote at 18 Change Is Asked: Nixon Request Stirs Hill Row on Rights Bill," *WP*, April 28, 1970, p. A1.

59 Newspaper accounts of John McCormack's retirement, include Martin F. Nolan and S. J. Micciehe, "McCormack Will Retire This Year," *BG*, May 21, 1970, pp. 1, 18; Richard L. Lyons, "McCormack Retirement Ends Turn-of-Century Political Era," *WP*, May 21, 1970, p. A13; and Marjorie Hunter, "McCormack Says He Will Not Seek New House Term; Speaker , 78, to Retire This year Amid Increasing Political Challenges," *NYT*, May 21, 1970, p. 1.

60 Newspaper Preservation Act, approved July 24, 1970 (84 Stat. 466-467). See also "Congress Enacts Bill to Preserve Ailing Newspapers," *CQ Almanac 1970*, pp. 238–43.

61 Postal Reorganization Act, approved August 12, 1970 (84 Stat. 719-787). See also "Congress Clears Landmark Postal Reorganization Plan," *CQ Almanac 1970*, pp. 341–65.

62 Organized Crime Control Act (84 Stat. 922-962). See also "Congress Clears 1970 Organized Crime Control Bill," *CQ Almanac 1970*, pp. 545–53.

63 Legislative Reorganization Act of 1970. approved October 26, 1970 (84 Stat. 1140-1204). See also "First Congressional Reform Bill Enacted since 1946," *CQ Almanac 1970*, pp. 447–61.

64 Garrison Nelson, "Nixon's Silent House of Hawks: A Documented Analysis of the Anti-war Voting Records of Republicans and Democrats in Strategic Districts," *The Progressive*, XXXIV (August 1970), pp. 13–20.

65   "Democrats take 13 Governorships from Republicans," *Congressional Quarterly Weekly Report*, XLV (November 6, 1970), pp. 2748–49, and 2770. Republicans picked up two state governorships, so the net loss was eleven. It was the largest loss of governorships for any party since 1938.

66   "The Election: In the Nation, a Popular Win," *WP*, November 5, 1970, p. A16.

67   David R. Mayhew, *Divided We Govern: Party Control, Lawmaking and Investigations, 1946–1990* (New Haven, CT: Yale University Press, 1991), pp. 61–66 and 75–76.

68   Occupational Safety and Health Act of 1970, approved December 29, 1970 (84 Stat. 1590-1620). Certain provisions of this Act were subsequently held unconstitutional in *Marshall v. Barlow's Inc.*, 436 U.S. 307 (1978). See also "Passage of Job Safety Bill Ends Three-Year Dispute," *CQ Almanac 1970*, pp. 675–82.

69   Securities Investor Protection Act of 1970, approved December 30, 1970 (84 Stat. 1636-1657). See also "Congress Clear Securities Investor Protection Bill," *CQ Almanac 1970*, pp. 865–73.

70   Bank Holding Company Act Amendments of 1970, approved December 31, 1970 (84 Stat. 1760-1769). See also "Regulation Extended to One-Bank Holding Companies," *CQ Almanac 1970*, pp. 874–82.

71   Poisoning Prevention Packing Act of 1970, approved December 30, 1970 (84 Stat. 1670-1674). See also "Hazardous Substances," *CQ Almanac 1970*, p. 630.

72   Clean Air Amendments of 1970, approved December 31, 1970 (84 Stat. 1676-1713). See also "Clean Air Bill Created with Auto Emission Deadline," *CQ Almanac 1970*, pp. 472–86.

73   Housing and Urban Development Act of 1970, approved December 31, 1970 (84 Stat. 1770-1817). See also "Congress Authorizes $2.9 Billion for Housing Programs," *CQ Almanac 1970*, pp. 726–41.

74   Food Stamp Act of 1964 Amendments. Approved January 11, 1971 (84 Stat. 2048-2052). Certain provisions of this Act were subsequently held unconstitutional in *Department of Agriculture v. Moreno*, 413 U.S. 528 (1973), and *Department of Agriculture v. Murray*, 413 U.S. 508 (1973). See also "Food Stamps," *CQ Almanac 1970*, pp. 764–67.

75   Reorganization Plan No. 3 of 1970. Transmitted July 1970 (84 Stat. 2086-2089). See also "Congress Accepts Four Executive Reorganization Plans," *CQ Almanac 1970*, pp. 462–67.

76   Reorganization Plan No. 4 of 1970, transmitted July 9, 1970. Effective October 3, 1970 (84 Stat. 2090-2093). See also "Congress Accepts Four Executive Reorganization Plans," *CQ Almanac 1970*, pp. 462–67.

77   "Conservative Coalition Scores Victories in Congress," *CQ Almanac 1970*, pp. 1144–49.

78   Ornstein, Mann, and Malbin, eds., *Vital Statistics on Congress, 2008*, p. 144.

79   James Boyd, "Nixon's Southern Strategy 'It's All in the Charts,'" *NYT*, May 17, 1970, pp. 215ff.

80   Richard L. Lyons, "McCormack to Quit at End of Session; Nixon Hails His Service to Country," *WP*, May 21, 1970, p. A1; and Margaret Crimmins, "Carl Albert: 'Shoo-In' For Speaker," *WP*, May 21, 1970, p. C2.

81   Patrick Maney, "Hale Boggs: The Southerner as National Democrat," in Roger D. Davidson, Susan Webb Hammond, Raymond W. Smock, eds., *Masters of the House: Congressional Leadership Over Two Centuries* (Westview Press, 1998), pp. 223–58.

82   Rowland Evans and Robert Novak, "McCormack Aims to Thwart Liberals by Supporting Boggs, Rostenkowski," *WP*, July 20, 1969, p. A23.

83   Randall B. Ripley, "The Party Whip Organizations in the United States House of Representatives," *APSR*, LVIII (September 1964), pp. 561–76.

84   Richard E. Cohen, *Rostenkowski: The Pursuit of Power and the End of Old Politics* (Chicago: Ivan R. Dee, 1999), pp. 36–37.

85   Information from the author's informal conversations with Occidental Petroleum vice president and then-McCormack aide William McSweeny in the fall of 1998.

86   Author's interview with the Hon. Richard W. Bolling, Washington, DC, April 1984.

87   See chapter 10, "Vietnam, Kooks, and Commies," in John A. Farrell's marvelous *Tip O'Neill and the Democratic Century: A Biography* (Boston: Little, Brown, 2001), pp. 204–40.

88   Informal conversations with McSweeny in the fall of 1998 and spring 1999. Robert L. Peabody's version has Hale Boggs telephoning O'Neill with the news, in *Leadership in Congress: Stability, Succession, and Change* (Boston: Little Brown & Co., 1976), p. 219.

89   Christopher Matthews, *Tip and the Gipper: When Politics Mattered* (New York: Simon and Schuster, 2013).

90   Richard Ben-Veniste, "United States v. Sweig and Voloshen," in his *The Emperor's New Clothes: Exposing the Truth from Watergate to 9/11* (New York: Thomas Dunne Books, 2009), pp. 52–93.

91   Author's telephonic interview with Richard Ben-Veniste, December 2015.

92   UPI, "New Probe Due in Speaker's Office," *BG*, November 26, 1970, p. 6.

93   Edith Evans Asbury, "A Handwritten Memo by Sweig Persuaded Jury to Convict Him," *NYT*, July 11, 1970, p. 16.

94   "Martin Sweig Named in New Indictment," *WP*, November 4, 1971, p. A10; and AP, "U.S. Charges Ex-House Aide Accepted Bribe," *BG*, January 28, 1972, p. 5.

95   Sweig's Miami trial is described in *The Emperor's New Clothes*, pp. 83–92, with the verdict reported on pp. 91–92, and "Sweig Bribery," *WP*, March 4, 1972, p. D12.

96   *Martin Sweig, Petitioner v. United States of America, Respondent*, Supreme Court of the United States, October Term, 1970, Case No. 1702. Morris M. Goldings and Erwin N. Griswold, eds., *Sweig (Martin) v. U.S. Supreme Court Transcript of Record with Supporting Pleadings*, U.S. Supreme Court Records and Briefs, 1832–1978 .

97   AP, "Sweig Wins Parole after Serving Year," *WP*, July 18, 1972, p. A3.

98   Don Oberdorfer, "Nixon Denies Move against McCormack," *WP*, January 8, 1971, p. A2; and two articles by Jack Anderson, "Washington Merry-Go-Round: Witch-Hunt by Justice Is Suspected," *WP*, September 1, 1971, p. B9; and "McCormack Hounded Despite Denial," *WP*, November 1, 1971, p. B13.

99   Jeffrey R. Biggs and Thomas S. Foley, *Honor in the House: Speaker Tom Foley* (Pullman: Washington State University Press, 1999), p. 260.

100 Richard L. Lyons, "Speaker McCormack's Wife Dies," *WP*, December 3, 1971, p. B18.

101 Robert L. Ward, "'You're home again, my dear,' McCormack Assures His Harriet," *BG*, December 4, 1971, p. 3.

102 "1,000 Mourn Ex-Speaker's Wife at Rites," *WP*, December 7, 1971, p. C4.

103 LBJ letter to Harriet McCormack, February 29, 1968, LBJ Library in Austin, Texas.

104 John W. McCormack, "America: Today and Yesterday, as Speaker McCormack Sees Things after 42 Years in Congress," *U.S. News and World Report*, July 27, 1970, pp. 58–62.

105   Susan V. Hand, "Men Grown Old, Recall Childhoods," *Boston Herald*, January 1, 1978, p. 1.

106   Commonwealth of Massachusetts, Death Certificate of John W. McCormack, November 22, 1980.

107   "Dignitaries to Attend Mass for Speaker McCormack," *BG*, November 25, 1980, p. 42; Wilfred C. Rodgers's account of the wake, "They came to hail the Speaker, last of a venerable line," *BG*, November 24, 1980, p. 1.

Epilogue: Closing the Book

The Austin-Boston Connection Continues: As the 91st Congress closed on January 2, 1971, so too did John McCormack's 42-year congressional career. But it was not the end for the Austin-Boston connection. The House Democratic "leadership ladder" worked to elevate Carl Albert, McCormack's long-serving Majority Leader, to the speakership. Opposition was minimal as Detroit's John Conyers (Dem-Mich.), a leader of the Congressional Black Caucus, challenged Albert's selection in both 1971 and 1973, losing 220–20 in his initial effort[1] and 202–25 in his subsequent one.[2]

While Albert's nomination for Speaker was mildly challenged, Majority Whip Hale Boggs would need two caucus ballots to win over his four rivals—Morris Udall of Arizona, Jim O'Hara of Michigan, B. F. Sisk of California, and Wayne Hays of Ohio. The contest quickly devolved into a two-man battle between Boggs, the "establishment" choice, and Udall, the "insurgent," with O'Hara, Sisk, and Hays hoping for a deadlock that would open the door to their selections. Carl Albert wisely remained neutral in this battle but John McCormack came out for Boggs as would fellow Ways and Means member Chair Wilbur Mills of Arkansas.[3] Most pre-caucus news accounts contended that Udall was ahead of Boggs but there would be no first ballot victory for anyone. However, it was Boggs who would lead on the first ballot with 95 votes, trailed by Udall 69, Sisk 31, Hays 28, and O'Hara 25.[4] On the second ballot, Hays and O'Hara withdrew and Boggs doubled his margin over Udall with a 140 to 88 victory as Sisk's votes dropped to 17. Udall's 1969 challenge to John McCormack was not forgotten by John's loyalists.

The longtime Massachusetts roommates and McCormack protégés Tip O'Neill and Eddie Boland split in this contest with O'Neill supporting Boggs while Boland made the nominating speech for Udall,[5] an echo of 1962's Teddy-Eddie Senate pre-primary convention when Boland placed Ted Kennedy's name in nomination against John McCormack's nephew Eddie. When the dust settled, the 92nd Congress opened with Carl Albert as Speaker, Hale Boggs as Majority Floor Leader, and Tip O'Neill, whose 8th Massachusetts District was across the Charles River from John's 9th District, as Majority Whip named by Boggs.[6] The "Austin-Boston connection" would be preserved.[7]

During the 1972 election, tragedy struck. In an effort to bolster the campaign of freshman Representative Nick Begich, Majority Leader Hale Boggs flew to Alaska. Flying from Anchorage to Juneau in a twin-engine Cessna, the plane disappeared on one of those perilous Alaska flights. The remains of Boggs, Begich, his aide Russell Brown, and pilot Don Jonz were never found.[8]

The Democratic Caucus met to fill the vacant majority leadership. Tip O'Neill was elevated to Majority Floor Leader without opposition as Sam Gibbons of Florida told him, "Tip, I can tell you something that nobody else in this room can. You haven't got an enemy in this room."[9] At the same time, California's John McFall, a Roman Catholic native of Buffalo, New York, was named by Albert and O'Neill to fill the post of majority whip.[10] John Brademas of Indiana, a Harvard graduate who like Albert was a Rhodes Scholar, was named deputy whip and shortly afterward, Tip received a call from Boston. It was 81-year-old John McCormack urging Tip to name another deputy whip. John said,[11] "The party has always had a special Boston-Austin connection. There was Rayburn and myself. There was Kennedy and Johnson. Now that you're in the leadership, I'd like you to call Albert that I would appreciate it if he would keep the Austin-Boston axis going."

The member John had in mind was Jim Wright of Fort Worth, another young north Texas Sam Rayburn protégé who now named as a deputy whip had been placed on the lowest rung of the leadership ladder. When Tip became Speaker in 1977 following Carl Albert's retirement, Jim Wright was elected Majority Leader and served for the entirety of Tip's decade in the chair. Jim would gain the speakership in 1987 when Tip resigned the post at the age of 74.

Jim Wright's speakership was short-lived, lasting only thirty months from January 1987 to June 1989 when Wright was forced to resign the speakership as a result of ethics charges brought against him by the bumptious junior Republican member from Georgia, Newt Gingrich.[12] Wright's departure led to a new House leadership team of Speaker Tom Foley of Washington State, Majority Leader Dick Gephardt of Missouri, and Bill Gray of Pennsylvania, the first African American in House leadership. And for the first time since 1937 more than a half century earlier—one quarter of the nation's 200-year history—none of the top House leadership posts were held by anyone from Texas or Massachusetts. The House reign of the Austin-Boston connection had ended.

The impact of John McCormack's House departure

When John McCormack left the House in 1971, the Austin-Boston connection was still in place and it continued to hold major leadership posts for the next eighteen years (Figure E.1). It would be tempting to conclude that very little happened in the following years. That would be an ill-advised assumption. There were a number of major changes that occurred both in Washington and in Boston. The Washington changes involved House reforms that diminished the power of its committee system while also altering the relationship of the House to the presidency.

Committee Reform Arrives: John McCormack was well aware that his departure from the House would enable the reformers to gain power and implement their proposals to weaken the seniority system and rein in the unbridled power of the committee chairs. As described by Julian Zelizer,[13] "Between 1948 and 1970, two pivotal developments propelled Congress into a new stage in its evolution: the formation of a liberal coalition that promoted congressional reform and a shift in the institutional environment surrounding Congress. These developments created an unfavorable political climate for the committee-era Congress."

Figure E.1 Austin-Boston continues: John McCormack returns to the House with Speaker Carl Albert and Majority Leader Thomas P. O'Neill in 1973 (Carl Albert Congressional Research Center, University of Oklahoma).

John knew that the House that he and Sam Rayburn had managed for three decades was changing[14] and he had no objection to the DSG-led reform effort which created the Democratic Organization, Study, and Review Committee in January 1971.[15] While the heavy drinker and womanizer Phil Burton from San Francisco took over the DSG, the study committee would be chaired by moderate Julia Butler Hansen, a well-regarded Appropriations Committee member from Washington State. This gave the reform movement a formal location within the Democratic Caucus and its suggestions focused on ways to lessen the role of seniority in the selection of chairs and to modernize voting procedures. However, its recommendations were primarily advisory.

Two years later, Speaker Albert and Majority Leader O'Neill named Dick Bolling to be chair of the ten-member Select Committee on Committees on January 31, 1973.[16] This may have been an effort to prevent Bolling from eviscerating them in his next book or it may have been a legitimate effort to accommodate the growing numbers of House reformers who saw Bolling as their champion.[17] A longtime and well-known critic of House procedure, Bolling worked to thwart the seniority system by moving Democratic committee assignments away from Ways and Means and allowing committee members to vote on chairs.[18] With John McCormack no longer a member of the House, it was easier for John's protégés and his nemesis to work together.

While the post-1970 House committees were not as transformed as they were by the 1946 Legislative Reorganization Act, many of the House reforms like recorded teller votes and electronic voting contained in the "Subcommittee Bill of Rights" continue to the present day.[19] Although it was leaders of the DSG who championed them and junior Democratic members who embraced the concepts of greater transparency and accountability from the committee chairs, House Republicans also accepted those changes and extended them following their long overdue capture of the House in 1994.[20] The days when autocratic House chairs silenced junior members and stopped legislation that they opposed from leaving their committees are long gone. It is too much to claim that John McCormack's departure removed the last impediment to reform but with him gone, his allies among the southern chairs knew that the House leadership would no longer protect their prerogatives.

House Deference to the Presidency Ends: John McCormack's speakership was characterized by obvious deference to the White House. Having first gained inside power during the years of FDR's New Deal, John saw his role as expediting the legislative agenda of the presidents with whom he served. This was definitely true for Democrats Franklin Roosevelt whom he greatly admired; Harry Truman with whom he played poker; and Lyndon Johnson with whom he shared deep affection for LBJ's mentor Sam Rayburn. It was also true for the two years of his speakership with Jack Kennedy with whom he fought back in Massachusetts. Even Republican President Richard Nixon who John personally disliked was a legislative beneficiary of John's White House deference.

This may be seen clearly in the presidential support scores on House roll call floor votes that have been computed by *Congressional Quarterly* since 1953.[21] Looking first at the eight years when the House and the presidency were held by fellow Democrats, it was not surprising that the Kennedy/Rayburn 1st Session of the 87th Congress in 1961 had a presidential support score of 83.1%. Similarly, and in spite of the personal tension between them, the two years of the Kennedy/McCormack years had scores of 85.0% in 1962 and 83.1% in 1963 for an 84.0% average of House support. It was in the Johnson/McCormack years, 1964–68, that the scores became stratospheric. Three of the five highest support scores among the 62 reported by *CQ* occurred in the Johnson/McCormack years of 1964 (88.5%), 1965 (93.8%), and 1966 (91.3%). Overall, the five-year average for the Johnson/McCormack years was 86.5%, the highest ever for a President/Speaker combination in the 62 years of this computation.

When John McCormack was asked why the 1965 session had been so successful, he attributed it wholly to Lyndon Johnson[22] "not only within the walls of this Chamber, but beyond it. . . . For first, there was the dynamic, insistent, unrelenting, tireless . . . leadership of President Lyndon Baines Johnson . . . leadership on the highest standards of Presidential relationship between the executive and the legislative branches of our government."

In retrospect, John's deference to the White House echoed that of Democratic Speakers Henry Rainey and Joe Byrns who surrendered the House's authority to the presidency in FDR's first term during John's early years in the House, 1933–36.

Not only did presidents in united governments benefit from John McCormack's White House deference and that of Carl Albert who succeeded him as Speaker in 1971 but so did Republican Richard Nixon in the two congresses of his first term. House support scores for Nixon in 1969–72 easily exceeded the three divided government Congresses of the Eisenhower presidency with Rayburn as Speaker and John as Majority Leader which had a six-year presidential support average of 65.0%. Nixon's first term with Speaker John McCormack and Majority Leader Carl Albert in the 91st

Congress had a 78.4% average support score and the combination of Speaker Albert and Majority Leader Hale Boggs in the 92nd Congress gave Nixon a score of 81.8% for a first-term support score average of 80.1% on bills that received floor votes. These were the highest support scores ever recorded for presumably divided governments.

Tip O'Neill Restores the Balance: Ironically, the key change agent was Tip O'Neill, John McCormack's favorite protégé who had no intention of following in John's deferential footsteps. Succeeding Boggs in 1973, Tip became Majority Leader at the start of Nixon's second term. His animus toward Nixon was genuine. In spite of Nixon's 49-state triumph in the 1972 presidential election, he received little support in the O'Neill-led House. With O'Neill now leading the House Democrats and the unfolding Watergate scandal gripping the nation, Nixon's presidential support score in the 93rd Congress was 48.0% in 1973 and 67.9% in 1974, producing an unweighted average of 58.0% support well below his first four years in office. The presidency of former vice president and House Minority Leader Gerald Ford, O'Neill's golfing buddy, fared worse with even lower support scores of 59.3% in 1974; 50.6% in 1975; and 43.1% in 1976—an average of 51.0%. The House was reasserting itself and it was noticed.

For John McCormack who had been out of the House for six years and living in Boston this was not a House stance toward the presidency that he would have ever envisioned. It would not get much better with the arrival in Washington of the newly elected Democratic President Jimmy Carter of Georgia.

This became clear when syndicated conservative columnist Robert Novak wrote, "The new Speaker, Thomas P. (Tip) O'Neill, suggested Carter was too conservative for congressional Democrats ... and made it clear that he was not modeling his speakership after that of fellow Massachusetts Democrat John McCormack."[23] This change was best portrayed in James Sundquist's insightful analysis *The Decline and Resurgence of Congress*[24] as the post-reform House now came closer to the role envisioned for it by the Founding Fathers when they chose to lodge the revenue power in the more representative of the two congressional chambers.[25]

Tip O'Neill remakes the speakership

Carl Albert's 1976 retirement led to the uncontested ascension of Majority Leader Tip O'Neill to the speakership who became the eighth Massachusetts member to occupy the Speaker's chair. Tip would hold the chair for the next ten consecutive years 1977–87, breaking John McCormack's record of nine consecutive years in the chair. Chosen without opposition in all five of his caucus nominations,[26] O'Neill transformed the speakership into an office that his mentor John McCormack would not recognize.

With O'Neill becoming Speaker, the majority leadership post came open once again and a spirited four-way contest emerged between the two Californians, Democratic Whip John McFall and Caucus Chair Phil Burton along with Rules Committee Chair Dick Bolling of Missouri and Jim Wright of Texas, then a deputy whip. Phil Burton, O'Neill's least favored contender, tried to tilt the contest in his favor by knocking McFall and Bolling out of the fray.[27] But it was O'Neill who let everyone know how he marked his own ballot on the third and final vote cast as Jim Wright won the closest contest in House history by a single vote, 148–147.[28] The Austin-Boston connection that John McCormack and Sam Rayburn had forged in 1940 was still in business and it was in place at the time of John's 1980 passing.

The Public Speakership: While John McCormack's reinvented life story led him to eschew publicity and hide in plain sight by becoming the least interesting major public figure in Washington, the media-savvy Tip O'Neill embraced the limelight with multiple appearances on television and in the movies. As well described by Douglas Harris, O'Neill created the "public speakership"[29]—one that was originally intended to counter the high media visibility of President Ronald Reagan, a former movie and television star. While neither Democratic Speaker Tom Foley of Washington nor Republican Denny Hastert of Illinois seemed comfortable in that role, four of O'Neill's other speakership successors have emulated it—Democrats Jim Wright of Texas and Nancy Pelosi of California as well as Republicans Newt Gingrich of Georgia and John Boehner of Ohio.

As Speaker, O'Neill gained control over the Democratic Caucus and moved the committee assignment power from the Ways and Means Committee to the Steering and Policy Committee that he chaired, per Bolling's recommendation.[30] It was a degree of power that John McCormack never possessed, but given the difference in their personalities, it is doubtful if McCormack would have wanted it. Too many personnel decisions and too many personal enemies would have cost John the affection of the House that he so cherished.

When O'Neill became Speaker in 1977, Democrat Jimmy Carter was sworn in as president. In O'Neill's best-selling memoirs, *Man of the House*, he opened his chapter on "The Carter Years" by declaring, "When it came to the politics of Washington, DC, he never really understood how the system worked. And . . . he didn't want to learn about it either."[31] It was hard for O'Neill to muster support for Carter initiatives and Carter's presidential support scores were mediocre, much as his presidency has been retroactively assessed. The House floor vote scores for Carter's four years were: 74.7% in 1977; 69.6% in 1978; 71.7% in 1979; and 76.9% in 1980 for an overall support average of 73.2% more than twelve points below the 85.5% success of the Jack Kennedy and Lyndon Johnson years. The Democrats of the House of Representatives were no longer beholden to the Democrats of the White House.

The ideological impact of the Austin-Boston connection

During its half-century run, the Austin-Boston connection was able to maintain a relatively low level of ideological distance between the floor leaders of the two congressional parties. The selection of Austin-Boston leaders and other ideological "middlemen" served to mute interparty disagreement during Congress's "textbook" era. Compared to the earlier years of the twentieth century and the years after 1989 and the end of the connection, the mid-twentieth-century Congress is noted for its diminished partisanship. When coupled with the 20 years of Massachusetts moderate Republican Joe

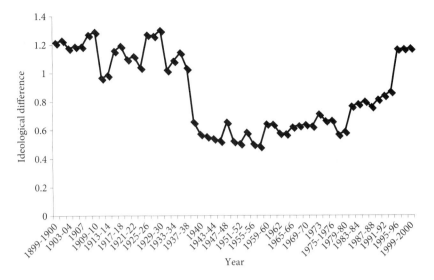

Figure E.2 Ideological Difference Between House Party Leaders, 1899–2000.

Martin as its leader, 1939–59, the creation of the Democrats' Austin-Boston alliance in 1940 served to decrease the ideological gulf between the two parties' House floor leaders.[32] This may be seen in the following chart utilizing the DW-NOMINATE scores developed by Professors Keith T. Poole of the University of Georgia and Howard Rosenthal of New York University presented on their voteview.com website[33] (Figure E.2).

It is not surprising that Newt Gingrich, the conservative Georgia Republican whose onslaught on Speaker Jim Wright's ethics ended both the Wright speakership and the Austin-Boston connection would be the major beneficiary of its collapse. Gingrich's aggressive leadership of the House Republicans led them to gain control of the House in the 1994 election after 40 years in the minority. With Newt Gingrich elected the new Speaker in 1995, levels of partisan and ideological contention intensified and the moderating role of congressional "middlemen" disappeared.[34] This was an unfortunate return to the harsh partisan and ideological battles of the early twentieth century and every indication of the present Congress is that those levels have increased and not abated. For John McCormack this would have brought back unpleasant memories from his earliest days in the House and may be the reason why he made every effort to transform it.

An unfortunate local postscript: The Bulger Brothers

Serving their constituents well is what keeps elected politicians in office and with a half-century in elective politics, John McCormack understood that better than most and one of those responsibilities was assisting constituents with problems arising from government agencies.[35] Those efforts can have unforeseen consequences and none were less foreseen or more unfortunate for John McCormack's reputation than his office's involvement with the Bulger family of South Boston—Massachusetts State Senator William M. "Billy" Bulger, his older brother the notorious mobster, James J. "Whitey" Bulger, Jr., and the Federal Bureau of Prisons.

Although the older Bulger children were born elsewhere in the city, they were raised in South Boston's Old Harbor Village, New England's first public housing project and one created through John McCormack's congressional efforts to better the living conditions of his poorer neighbors. For a number of years, it was renamed the Mary Ellen McCormack Housing Project. While Whitey regularly flouted the law and left school in the ninth grade, Billy became a "triple eagle" as a graduate of Boston College High School with degrees from both Boston College and its law school. The apparent contrast of their dissimilar careers became a regular feature of the multiple books and articles written about the Bulger brothers.[36]

Whitey's lengthy rap sheet led the FBI to label him a "habitual criminal." While other crimes were listed, it was his three convictions for armed bank robbery that led to his imprisonment in the Atlanta Federal Penitentiary in 1956.[37] Communications between the McCormack office and the Bureau of Prisons regarding Whitey first appear in 1957. Whitey was placed in "maximum custody" in 1959 after he provided a hacksaw blade for three inmates who sought to escape. Among the more than 1,000 pages in Whitey's Bureau of Prisons file are at least thirty communications referencing the McCormack office including a February 2, 1959, letter to McCormack responding to a Billy Bulger inquiry about the "irregularity of the mail" from his brother. The prison apologetically informed the McCormack office that Whitey had been "returned to the general population" and that there would be "no difficulty" in receiving mail.

Whitey's involvement in the escape plan led him to be moved in November 1959 from Atlanta to the federal penitentiary on Alcatraz Island, "the Rock" as it was known in the prison system. Alcatraz inmates gain a high level of cachet or "street cred" among fellow criminals and Whitey was no exception.[38] After only 28 months in Alcatraz, less than half of the eight-year average of most inmates and more Billy Bulger induced correspondence from the McCormack office, and Whitey was moved to Leavenworth in Kansas in 1962 and ultimately to Lewisburg in Pennsylvania from where he would be released in 1965 after nine years behind bars. Whitey's imminent parole was a happy event that John announced to Billy.[39]

As Whitey moved through the federal prison system, Billy Bulger began a public career that would eventuate in his being elected a State Representative from South Boston in 1961; State Senator in 1971; and president of the Massachusetts State Senate from 1978 to 1996.[40] It was a career trajectory that closely mirrored John McCormack's and John described the Bulgers as "very close and dear and valued friends of mine and a very fine family—an outstanding family" in a December 15, 1964, letter to the U.S. Board of Parole on file in the Gotlieb Archives at Boston University.[41]

John and Knocko, the McCormack brothers, were very sympathetic to the aspirations of young Irish-descended kids who grew up in "the projects."[42] It was easy to identify with them and perhaps to turn a blind eye to their less noble pursuits. Billy apparently convinced John that his relationship with Whitey was similar to John's relationship with Knocko as the good brother/not so good brother. This was an off-hand observation that Billy shared with me after reading a much earlier draft of this manuscript during my time as a senior fellow at the University of Massachusetts-Boston. Billy Bulger also convinced John (and himself) that all of Whitey's convictions were due to fellow gangsters implicating Whitey in exchange for lighter sentences for themselves. These assertions were similar to those made by then-jailed Boston Mayor Jim Curley in 1947 when John McCormack successfully circulated a petition in the House to get Curley a pardon from President Harry Truman.

The Mob Boss: A free man in 1966, Whitey resumed his associations with Boston's criminal underworld and within a few years he would become a member and eventually the leader of the notorious Irish-American Winter Hill Gang.[43] As Whitey's stature grew, he became edgier, more aggressive, and more violent leading to increased incidents of extortion, loan sharking, drug dealing, and murder. It was in 1971 that Whitey was approached by the FBI for help in undermining the Boston branch of the Providence-based Italian-American Patriarca crime family.[44] With Whitey's help the FBI's woefully misguided but successful efforts to arrest and convict Patriarca's Boston *capo* Gennaro Angiulo created a vacuum within the Boston underworld that led the Irish mob to gain dominance in the city.[45] Unlike South Boston's Gustin Gang of the 1920s that foolishly and fatally sought to supplant the North End Italian mob with an armed attack, the Winter Hill Gang was able to use the FBI to achieve its criminal hegemony in Boston.

Whitey Bulger became the most powerful mob boss in the city and his relationship with the FBI appeared to give him carte blanche to continue his criminal enterprise in Boston even extending his reach into Florida and Oklahoma. Ultimately, Whitey would be indicted for nineteen murders—most were rival criminals or suspected informants but one was a prominent Oklahoma businessman Roger Wheeler, owner of the World Jai Lai Corporation, and two were young Boston women—Deborah Hussey and Debra Davis. Both women were linked to Stevie "the Rifleman" Flemmi, Whitey's closest associate. It was feared that they would "rat out" Winter Hill's clandestine ties to the FBI. Flemmi lived with Deborah Hussey's mother and became her lover while Debra Davis who Flemmi hoped to marry sought to leave him for another man. Under oath, Flemmi said that both women were strangled by Whitey. However, the jury did not convict Whitey on the Davis allegation or on seven of the other murder charges.

Whitey's key "inside" ally was John Connolly, known as "Zip" to Whitey because of their shared Zip code. Connolly was also an Old Harbor-raised Irish-descended guy with Boston College (BC) and Harvard Kennedy School degrees who was hired by the FBI thanks in part to an August 1, 1968, letter on his behalf sent by John McCormack's office. Growing up in Old Harbor, Connolly idolized both Bulger brothers and it was Billy who encouraged him to attend BC. During his FBI career it was Connolly who kept Whitey informed of whom was giving evidence against him that would lead to six of the nineteen murders. And it was Connolly's warnings that led to Whitey's flight from Boston and his 16-year evasion from justice.

FBI Files: In the course of researching John McCormack's life and its reinvention, I made FOIA (Freedom of Information Act) requests for the FBI files of John McCormack, David K. Niles, and Martin Sweig. I was curious to learn if the FBI's Director J. Edgar Hoover knew of John McCormack's family link to Canada given the fact that John was next in the line of presidential succession to Lyndon Johnson during the 14 months between JFK's murder in November 1963 and Hubert Humphrey's vice presidential oath-taking in January 1965. Many Canadians believed (and still do) that John was born in Prince Edward Island which would have rendered him as a non-natural born citizen and likely ineligible to be in the line of presidential succession. There is no evidence in John's extensive FBI files that Hoover ever explored that possibility.

FOIA requests produced two sets of files concerning John McCormack. The larger file consisted of correspondence between McCormack and FBI officials, most of which are with J. Edgar Hoover personally. The first letter in the larger FBI file is dated June 1, 1936, and it is a simple request for copies of speeches given by the director. There are 169 letters between the two men, mostly very cordial—McCormack's birthdays and reelection victories were frequently acknowledged by Hoover while John commended Hoover on his growing collection of awards. Having read the two sets of documents a number of times as well as hundreds of other McCormack letters, it was easy to discern which letters from the McCormack office were written by John and which were not.

The Connolly Letter: The two best fact-based books exploring Whitey Bulger's criminal career are Kevin Cullen and Shelley Murphy's *Whitey Bulger: America's Most Wanted Gangster and the Manhunt That Brought Him to Justice* and Dick Lehr and Gerard O'Neill's *Whitey: The Life of America's Most Notorious Mob Boss*. Both Kevin Cullen and Gerard O'Neill received Pulitzer Prizes as members of the *Boston Globe's* esteemed Spotlight Team.

Both books mention the frequent correspondence between the McCormack office and the Federal Bureau of Prisons regarding Whitey and both ascribe those efforts to steady pressure emanating from Whitey's brother Billy, the State Senator and Knocko McCormack protégé. The one piece of correspondence that both books fasten on is the August 1, 1968, letter from the McCormack office to J. Edgar Hoover which appears to be a request for a personal favor between two old friends. This is the recommendation letter from the McCormack office urging the FBI to hire John Connolly. Given Connolly's deep complicity in Whitey's post-prison criminal rampage, this is the presumed "smoking gun" that brings John McCormack's later career into disrepute. John had been out of office for two years when Whitey's first murder occurred. But there can be no denying that the McCormack office was compromised by the Bulger saga.

While the Connolly letter is on Speaker McCormack's letterhead, there are a number of questions as to its true authorship: Doubts include: (1) the letter is not in John's FBI file; (2) it is not signed; (3) the addressee is John Edgar Hoover, not J. Edgar Hoover as in the letters personally written by John; (4) the salutation to Hoover is "Dear John," a salutation never used in a McCormack letter; (5) McCormack used the salutation

"Dear Edgar" in every letter to Hoover from 1946 on. (Someone edited that letter in both Whitey Bulger and John Connolly's *Wikipedia* entries and changed "Dear John" to "Dear Edgar"—a salutation that is not on the original letter.); (6) John's personal letters were double-spaced, replete with typographical and punctuation errors that are missing from this well-typed letter; and (7) there is no reference to John's wife Harriet that was common in John's personal correspondence. While John may not have written the letter himself, it is clearly consistent with John's general sentiments about struggling Irish-descended Southie kids who aspired to a better life.

South Boston troubles and John's successors

During the 1970s, John McCormack's last decade on earth, his beloved South Boston was embroiled in a bitterly divisive battle over school desegregation. The Great and General Court passed a Racial Imbalance Law in 1965 to overcome patterns of racial discrimination in the state's public schools. In an effort to address the imbalance in Boston, Federal District Judge W. Arthur Garrity, an Irish-descended native of Worcester, Massachusetts, and a graduate of Holy Cross and Harvard Law mandated in 1974 that students from predominantly black Roxbury and predominantly white South Boston should be bussed to each other's high schools. It was a moment in time that gave South Boston a negative image throughout much of the United States and increased its antipathy toward outsiders. This is the one neighborhood within the city that the Irish did not surrender to the oncoming rush of other ethnic groups. Southie is their haven, their fortress, and any criticism, no matter how slight, is resented deeply.[46]

The blatant ugliness of South Boston's vehement opposition to school integration was broadcast nationwide and gave the city a black eye but it deepened the defensiveness of Southie's mostly Irish-descended residents. The conflict spawned a number of books, the best known being 1985's *Common Ground: A Turbulent Decade in the Lives of Three American Families* by J. Anthony Lukas that won both the Pulitzer Prize and the National Book Award.[47]

Leading the South Boston opposition were Billy Bulger and Louise Day Hicks, a Boston University–trained lawyer and daughter of a local judge. As a school board member she denied that the schools were segregated and hoped that her opposition to integration would win her the mayoralty in 1967 against Mayor Kevin White. After that loss, she became chair of the school committee and in 1970, Hicks ran for Congress and won John McCormack's vacated House seat. The seat was redistricted for the 1972 contest and she lost her reelection to former State Senator Joe Moakley who ran against her as an independent.

Joe Moakley: Yet another Irish-descended House member from South Boston, Joe Moakley grew up with the Bulger brothers in Old Harbor Village. A graduate of Suffolk Law and onetime boxer, Moakley served in both the state's House of Representatives, 1953–61 and Senate, 1965–71.[48] Both seats would later be occupied by Billy Bulger. A tough guy who lied about his age to enlist in the wartime U.S. Navy, Moakley quickly became a Tip O'Neill favorite. He was assigned to Tip's former committee, the prestigious and powerful House Rules Committee in 1975 on which he served until his death in 2001, serving as its senior Democrat for 12 years, as chair, 1989–95, and as its ranking minority member, 1995–2001. Joe Moakley was a far more appropriate successor to John McCormack than Mrs. Hicks.

Eddie McCormack's Plan: There was one person best positioned to mediate this dispute and it was South Boston's Eddie McCormack, Knocko McCormack's son and John McCormack's nephew. After his defeat for governor in 1966, Eddie established a Washington law firm with Stanley Bregman and Tyler Abell, Drew Pearson's stepson and the husband of Bess Abell, Lady Bird Johnson's social secretary. His close friendship with U.S. Senator Walter Mondale, Vice President Humphrey's protégé, lodged Eddie in the inner circle of Humphrey's 1968 presidential bid against Richard Nixon. Had Humphrey won, Eddie would have been well placed in the Justice Department. Similarly, Eddie's closeness to Boston Mayor Kevin White would have been rewarded had White been nominated and elected as George McGovern's vice presidential running mate in 1972. With both of his national plans thwarted by Nixon victories, Eddie refocused his efforts on Boston. The city's ambitious downtown revitalization led to the building of corporate skyscrapers and waterfront hotels. Eddie as Mayor White's legal ally became one of the city's most successful development attorneys but he did not leave South Boston behind.

Eddie was clearly troubled by the conflict that engulfed South Boston. Rather than encouraging total resistance, Ed McCormack's life membership in the NAACP and his years as a progressive attorney general had sensitized him to the plight of Boston's blacks and he sought a path of moderation. He had been appointed a "master" to prepare a plan that would facilitate the integration of the city's public schools. Ed McCormack's more measured plan called for a small number of African-American students to be bussed into the schools of South Boston and it was to be implemented over a longer period of time.[49] But Judge Garrity rejected the McCormack compromise and the city's broader school desegregation plan was put in place. It was a disaster. The sight of white Irish-descended residents of South Boston throwing rocks and yelling racial epithets at the black school children bussed into the community evoked vivid memories 20 years earlier of the violent opposition to school integration in Little Rock, Arkansas.

Eddie's efforts to be more like his uncle John and less like his dad, Knocko, did not sit well with many of his neighbors and old school chums. To longtime Southie resident Anna Murphy and her fellow Southies, Eddie Jr. was aloof and self-absorbed. "Eddie didn't do shit for South Boston," she recounted to me one afternoon. What many missed was that Eddie was fundamentally shy and scholarly and had politics not been the family business he would have been happy as a successful attorney and teaching at one of the city's many law schools. After all he topped his class at BU Law and edited its law review. But politics was the family business and Eddie had the scars to prove it. At Eddie McCormack's 1997 wake in South Boston, sentiments were muted for a native son who had once scaled the heights of Massachusetts's politics and had even bloodied the nose of a Kennedy but it was Billy Bulger yet again who would deliver a McCormack eulogy.

Retrospective assessments

John McCormack's political career has been memorialized in Boston with three public buildings: one for state offices – the 22 floor McCormack Building at 1 Ashburton Place on Beacon Hill; one for federal offices – the John W. McCormack U.S. Post Office and Courthouse at 5 Post Office Square, and the John W. McCormack Hall at the University of Massachusetts-Boston. The campus building at UMass-Boston is in very close proximity to the John F. Kennedy Presidential Library and Museum on Dorchester's Columbia Point. A few hundred yards apart, these concrete and brink memorials are a joint testament to the enormous influence that these two descendants of the Boston Irish have had upon the nation and its politics.

However, John McCormack's nine-year speakership has not been celebrated. John did not want to be Speaker. In an April 1977 interview with McCormack, he told me that he preferred being Majority Leader working the floor and assembling voting coalitions than presiding at a distance from the Speaker's chair.[50] In a postscript to a letter to H. G. Dulaney, Sam Rayburn's former secretary, McCormack wrote in 1967, six years after Sam's death, "I miss very much our late friend, Speaker Sam Rayburn. I wish he was here—he as Speaker and I as Majority Leader."[51]

In Randall Ripley's *Party Leaders in the House of Representatives*, he classified the McCormack speakership as "collective" in his leadership style, indicating that he shared power with others unlike the "individualistic" leadership style of his longtime ally Sam Rayburn[52] and his own protégé Tip O'Neill. Regarding John's "use of powers," Ripley placed him in the category of "conservative," indicating that John neither expanded the power of the office nor lost power for it during his tenure. On balance, it would place his speakership in an average category.

Ripley's later book *Majority Party Leadership in Congress* rightly contended that to be effective party leaders should have some control over standing committee assignments. However, his comparison of "the absolute control of Speaker Cannon in the Fifty-eighth Congress [1903–1905] to the spot control of Speaker McCormack in the Eighty-eighth Congress [1963–65]"[53] obscures the fact that Cannon lost that power in the later 61st Congress (1909–11) and by the time John McCormack became Speaker in 1962, that the assignments of both chairs and members had become firmly entrenched thanks to a half century inviolability of seniority.

Other more contemporary assessments like that in *The American Speakership: The Office in Historical Perspective* by Ronald Peters, founder of the Carl Albert Congressional Research and Studies Center at the University of Oklahoma, saw the McCormack and Albert speakerships as "transitional."[54] Their speakerships were caught between what Peters considered to be the aptly named "feudal system" of Sam Rayburn with its alliance between the speakership and the powerful dukes and barons who comprised the committee chairs and the DSG reformers' activist thrust to rid the House of its rigid seniority rules.[55]

Peters offered an assessment of McCormack based on an interview with John E. Barriere, a longtime staff member of the House Banking and Currency Committee: "[John's] personality was as outgoing as Rayburn's was reserved. McCormack loved to be around people, loved to debate, and was happiest when surrounded by a throng."[56] However, this was during the legislative day. Once the House closed for business late in the afternoon, John would return to the Hotel Washington for dinner alone with Harriet.

Robert Bales's Interaction Process Analysis introduced the concept of task leaders and social leaders to describe leader interactions within groups.[57] That distinction was skillfully applied to Chief Justices of the Supreme Court by David Danelski[58] and it fits perfectly with the Rayburn-McCormack pairing. Sam was the gruff no-nonsense "task leader" keeping the House focused on legislation presented before the chamber. It was Sam Rayburn as chair of the powerful Interstate and Foreign Commerce Committee in the 1930s who floor managed FDR's far-reaching securities legislation to gain control of post-crash Wall Street. Sam socialized with a small circle of House members. Hill old-timers told me that Sam only knew the names of the Texans and the committee chairs while John, who never chaired a standing committee, was the voluble "social leader" of the House whose remarkable ability to remember the names of most House members facilitated the informal interactions that a collective body of widely diverse backgrounds and personalities needs in order to pass legislation.

Matthew Green's 2010 valuable monograph, *The Speaker of the House: A Study of Leadership*, devoted a full chapter to examining how the two speakerships of Rayburn and McCormack operated in a number of legislative contexts. Even though the two men were not always on the same page philosophically (e.g., civil rights) Green points out their leadership styles were more similar than dissimilar: "A careful analysis of both Speakers' tenures reveals that Rayburn and McCormack were quite willing and able to shape policy outcomes, although it might have required going to the House floor to do it" (p. 61); and "Both Speakers Rayburn and McCormack exercised legislative leadership on behalf of a variety of goals, not merely the objective of securing their leadership positions in the House" (p. 99).[59] Green's balanced assessment is a valuable corrective to the stark Rayburn-McCormack contrast found in Dick Bolling's two volumes.

Jeffery Jenkins and Charles Stewart III in *Fighting for the Speakership: The House and Party Government*, their expansive and definitive 2013 assessment of speakership elections in the party caucuses and on the House floor, characterize the last twelve decades of speakership elections as the persistence of the "Organizational Cartel" with the respective congressional parties maintaining firm control over the floor votes for their selected speakership nominees.[60] It certainly was true for the seventeen speakership elections—twelve for Rayburn, 1940–61 and five for McCormack, 1962–69—that occurred in the three-decade span between 1940 and 1969. During the years when Sam Rayburn and John McCormack held the top two Democratic leadership posts in the House, 1941–61, they were never opposed in the nominating Democratic Caucus nor were there any Democratic votes against them when their names were presented to the House floor. Even after the highly contentious 1969 Democratic Caucus when 62 members challenged John's renomination, none chose to vote against him when his name was presented to the floor.[61]

Legacy difficulties

There are a number of reasons of varying weights to explain why John McCormack's speakership has not been celebrated and has been relegated to a lesser role: (1) As noted earlier John was much too deferential to the presidency. Presidential support scores on House floor votes during the nine years of John's speakership averaged 84.2%, the highest among the eleven Speakers who have served since 1953 when *Congressional Quarterly* began calculating that measurement. That may account for the high regard that John received from Democratic Presidents Franklin D. Roosevelt, Harry Truman, and Lyndon Johnson. However, it placed the House in a subordinate role and not the coequal one envisioned by the framers of the Constitution who gave the all-important taxing power to the House.

(2) John's deep-seated belief that it was the political alliance of Democrats in the big cities and the South that FDR had created in the 1930s which insured the success of the economic and social reforms of the New Deal committed him to the continuance of that alliance. He remained committed in spite of the fact that: (a) the politically volatile suburbs replaced the big cities as the locus of more American citizens and their officials were better educated and more philosophically liberal than the partisan city Democrats; and (b) the South's increasing price for remaining in the coalition was to resist any congressional reforms that would lessen the ability of its white citizens to maintain political power over its black ones. This was at the heart of John's resistance to changing the seniority system.

Unfortunately, for John McCormack's reputation, it was in the 1950s and 1960s that prominent southern Democrats like Howard Smith, Bill Colmer, and Mendel Rivers were publicly supporting segregation. This was compounded by the sad fact that many of John's South Boston anti-busing constituents became emblematic of northern white opposition to racial integration.

(3) John's hawkish defense and foreign policy views also clashed with those of newer House members. They were shaped by two factors: (a) the 1930s when totalitarian regimes ran roughshod throughout much of Europe, Asia, and Africa while American isolationists resisted any congressional effort at military preparedness leading John to support any and all Defense Department requests, even beyond those of the Pentagon itself; and (b) his anti-Communist Catholicism that led him to support the continuance in power of anti-Communist Catholic dictators. Three come immediately to mind: Francisco Franco in Spain, Rafael Trujillo in the Dominican Republic, and the Diem brothers in South Vietnam. However, these dictators were also supported by each of the presidents with whom John served and whose financial foreign aid requests he delivered for them.

(4) There was one person who would not even designate John's speakership as "average," and that would be his bitter enemy, Dick Bolling of Missouri, who never attained the leadership posts that he felt his brilliance warranted. In Bolling's Papers at the University of Missouri-Kansas City Library, there are three jam-packed legal-size folders of McCormack's failings that indicate the depth and persistence of Bolling's

animus toward McCormack. Every harsh editorial cartoon depicting McCormack as feeble and out of touch may be found in those folders. Bolling's intense dislike of McCormack blinded him to the high regard that Presidents Roosevelt, Truman, and Johnson as well as Bolling's idol Speaker Sam Rayburn and substantial numbers of House members held for McCormack.

Bolling was a prolific writer and an effective public Speaker, skills that a private man like John McCormack either did not possess or chose not to display. This was a one-sided fight. Bolling's two widely read books, *House Out of Order* (1965) and *Power in the House* (1968), eviscerated John. Both books were often adopted in collegiate courses on the U.S. Congress and undoubtedly contributed to the negative assessments of John's speakership.[62] It surprised few on Capitol Hill that when Bolling was asked in 1970 for names of who might replace McCormack, the UPI reported in the *New York Times*, "Bolling Suggests Bolling as Speaker."[63] There is no doubt that Bolling blamed John McCormack for the fact that his extensive and discernible talents had been insufficiently rewarded in the U.S. House.

I personally encountered Bolling's hostility toward John in two meetings in Bolling's Washington office when John's name came up in discussion even after John had passed away. Bolling had no problem "speaking ill of the dead." John, on the other hand, a devout Roman Catholic who believed in the afterlife, was careful not to speak ill of his departed colleagues, fearing that he might be obliged to spend eternity with those he had maligned on earth. His harshest insult was to hold a member in "minimum high regard." In my two lengthy conversations with McCormack, he spoke favorably of all of his colleagues with one exception—John O'Connor of New York, a man he described as "arrogant"—and with whom he squabbled in the 1930s. John's only complaint to me about Bolling was that he needed the Rules Committee to vote on a bill but that Bolling would not bestir himself from a vacation to return to Washington to vote. However, he was able to solicit a positive vote from Mississippi's Bill Colmer on that measure.

(5) The Kennedy factor also contributed to the disparagement of John's leadership career. He had a lengthy and complex history with the Fitzgerald and Kennedy families. John's association, albeit at arm's length, with Boston's disreputable Mayor James Michael Curley, the man who destroyed the electoral career of Rose Kennedy's father, John "Honey Fitz" Fitzgerald, did not endear him to that clan. In 1940, John publicly touted Joe Kennedy for president until FDR revealed his third-term plans to him. That relationship was not helped in the 1940s when FDR soured on Joe and John replaced Kennedy as FDR's favorite Boston Irishman. John's long and complicated relationship with Jack Kennedy that covered 17 years from the date of Jack's 1947 arrival in the House through the years 1962–63 when these two men held the highest elective offices in the nation added to the negative assessment, one that was punctuated by the bitter 1962 Senate primary battle between the president's brother Ted and the Speaker's nephew Eddie.

(6) John's personal self-effacing style kept him out of the Washington limelight. His lifelong devotion to his wife Harriet and his personal commitment to dinnertime

meals with her for more than a half century placed himself well out of the "hail fellow, well met" behaviors of most members of Congress. Having successfully reinvented his family history to obtain public office in Boston, a city deeply divided by religious, ethnic, and social class fissures, John chose to avoid public scrutiny. It would be impossible to achieve that today in a time of easy internet searches on the backgrounds of public officials.

The fairest retrospective account of John McCormack's career appears in Warren Weaver's 1972 book, *Both Your Houses: The Truth about Congress*[64]:

> Speaker John McCormack was a classic example of a good man that the House wore out before it gave him power. Elected from his Boston district at thirty-seven, he became a vigorous floor leader and strong-hearted liberal. But he did not make it to the Speakership until he was seventy, a feeble, confused, and ineffectual old man. Only scandals touching his employees persuaded him into retirement at seventy-eight. Strictly speaking, McCormack's rise was not a product of the seniority system, for he was chosen Speaker in an open, competitive election. But the dead hand of seniority reaches even to such choices, all but dictating the advancement of the next man on the ladder, whatever his qualifications at the time.

John McCormack's speakership career will never be as well regarded as those of his closest ally Sam Rayburn and his favorite protégé Tip O'Neill but it should not be forgotten that John was a leader in the fight for Social Security in the 1930s; served as Majority Leader throughout World War II, the Korean Conflict, and most of the Cold War; and was Speaker of the House when Lyndon Johnson's Great Society was passed with its legacy of Medicare and Medicaid, the Immigration and Nationality Act that ended the discriminatory "national origins" clause, and the nation's most far-reaching Civil Rights acts.[65] In spite of those achievements, this modest man's common decency and his deep compassion for people whose lives and circumstances were clouded by poverty, disease, and discrimination led him to push for progressive legislation that would alleviate these troubling burdens. Because of John's fateful decision to reinvent his early life in order to gain public office in South Boston a half century earlier, he eschewed publicity, and deftly working behind the scenes, he left a legislative legacy that few others could ever claim.

Among those legacies was John McCormack's successful floor management of multiracial Hawaii's 1959 admission to the Union over the opposition of Sam Rayburn and most of his southern Democratic allies. Hawaii's Spark Matsunaga who burst into tears on the announcement of John's retirement remembered John McCormack as "a good, great man, who lived by a code which he himself best expressed: 'If I were given a choice, I would rather be known as a good man than a great man.'"[66]

John McCormack's estimable life and remarkable political career may never be as celebrated as those of his contemporaries, but it is the intent of this book to make sure that John McCormack's life and career will not be forgotten.

Notes

1   *Los Angeles Times*, January 20, 1971, p. A4 and *NYT*, January 20, 1971, p. 1.

2   *CQWR*, January 6, 1973, p. 5; and *NYT*, January 3, 1973, p. 1.

3   Charles Bartlett, "Democrats Unity Faces Two Tests," *Washington Star*, December 20, 1970.

4   Robert L. Peabody, "The Campaigns for House Majority Leader, 1970–71," *Leadership in Congress* (Boston: Little, Brown, 1976), pp. 177–204; and Larry L. King, "The Road to Power in Congress," *Harper's Magazine*, CCXLII (June 1971), pp. 39–63.

5   Peabody, *Leadership in Congress,* pp. 201–202.

6   "Rep. O'Neill Picked as Majority Whip," *Washington Post*, January 23, 1971, p. A1.

7   "Back to Boston: Tip O'Neill," in Anthony Champagne et al., *The Austin-Boston Connection: Five Decades of House Democratic Leadership, 1937–1989*, chapter 7.

8   UPI, "Rep. Boggs Missing on Alaska Flight; Rep Boggs Lost in Alaska on Flight With Rep. Begich," *Washington Post*, October 17, 1972, p. A1.

9   Peabody, *Leadership in Congress*, p. 258; and "Back to Boston: Tip O'Neill," in Champagne et al., *The Austin-Boston Connection*, chapter 7.

10 Peabody, "The Choice of a House Majority Leader and Whip, 1973," in *Leadership in Congress*, pp. 234–65.

11 Tip O'Neill with William Novak, *Man of the House: The Life and Political Memoirs of Speaker Tip O'Neill* (New York: Random House, 1987), p. 226.

12 The story is well told in John M. Barry's monumental *The Ambition and the Power: The Fall of Jim Wright: A True Story of Washington* (New York: Viking, 1989). See also Wright's account in his *Balance of Power: Presidents and Congress from the Era of McCarthy to the Age of Gingrich* (Atlanta: Turner Publishing, 1996), pp. 475–91.

13 See Julian E. Zelizer's thoughtful *On Capitol Hill: The Struggle to Reform Congress and Its Consequences, 1948–2000* (New York: Cambridge University Press, 2004), p. 5. See also Judy Schneider, *Reorganization of the House of Representatives: Modern Reform Efforts* (Washington, DC: Congressional Research Service, 2003).

14 The most effective depiction of how the House changed during the Rayburn era may be found in Joseph Cooper and David W. Brady, "Institutional Context and Leadership Style: The House from Cannon to Rayburn," *APSR*, LXXV (June 1981), pp. 411–25.

15 Roger H. Davidson and Walter J. Oleszek, *Congress against Itself* (Bloomington: Indiana University Press, 1977), pp. 44–47.

16 The committee was created by House Resolution 112, 93rd Congress, 1st Session, January 11, 1973, and terminated on December 20, 1974.

17 References to Bolling's active reformist role are replete throughout Zelizer's *On Capitol Hill*. See also David W. Rohde, *Parties and Leaders in the Postreform House* (Chicago: University of Chicago Press, 1991).

18 "House Select Committee on Committees I (Bolling)," in Garrison Nelson, *Committees in the U.S. Congress: 1947–1992: Committee Histories and Member Assignments* (Washington, DC: CQ Press, 1994), pp. 1026–27.

19 David W. Rohde, "Committee Reform in the House of Representatives and the Subcommittee Bill of Rights," *Annals of the American Academy of Political and Social Science*, CDXI (January 1974), pp. 39–47; and Norman J. Ornstein, "Causes and Consequences of Congressional Change: Subcommittee Reforms in the House of Representatives, 1970–73," in Norman J. Ornstein, ed., *Congress in Change: Evolution and Reform* (New York: Praeger, 1975), pp. 88–114.

20 Eric Schickler, Eric McGhee, and John Sides, "Remaking the House and Senate: Personal Power, Ideology, and the 1970s Reforms," *Legislative Studies Quarterly*, XXVIII (August 2003), pp. 297–331.

21 "Presidential Victories on Votes in Congress, 1953–2007," in Norman J. Ornstein, Thomas E. Mann, and Michael J. Malbin, eds., *Vital Statistics on Congress, 2008* (Washington, DC: The Brookings Institution, CQ Press, 2008), pp. 144–45, and updated with annual *Congressional Quarterly Almanacs*.

22 John W. McCormack speech, *Congressional Record*, 89th Congress, 1st Session, October 22, 1965, p. 2869.

23 Robert D. Novak, *The Prince of Darkness: 50 Years of Reporting in Washington* (New York: Crown Forum, 2007), p. 301.

24 James L. Sundquist, *The Decline and Resurgence of Congress* (Washington, DC: The Brookings Institution, 1981).

25 Daniel J. Palazzolo, *The Speaker and the Budget: Leadership in the Post-Reform House of Representatives* (Pittsburgh: University of Pittsburgh Press, 1992).

26 Jeffery A. Jenkins and Charles Stewart III, *Fighting for the Speakership: The House and the Rise of Party Government* (Princeton, NJ: Princeton University Press, 2013), pp. 416–17.

27 John Aloysius Farrell, *Tip O'Neill and the Democratic Century* (Boston: Little, Brown, 2001), pp. 411–15; and Bruce I. Oppenheimer and Robert L. Peabody, "How the Race for House Majority Leader Was Won—By One Vote," *The Washington Monthly*, IX (November 1977), pp. 46–56.

28 "Jim Wright: The Last Texan," in Champagne et al., *The Austin-Boson Connection*, pp. 243–46; and Farrell, *Tip O'Neill*, p. 414.

29 Douglas B. Harris, "The Rise of the Public Speakership," *Political Science Quarterly*, CXIII (Summer 1998), pp. 193–212.

30 The revised House committee assignment system is recounted in Scott A. Frisch and Sean Q. Kelly, *Committee Assignment Politics in the U.S. House of Representatives* (Norman: University of Oklahoma Press, 2006).

31 O'Neill with William Novak, *Man of the House*, p. 297.

32 Champagne et al., *The Austin-Boston Connection: Five Decades of House Democratic Leadership, 1937–1989*, pp. 254–56.

33 The data was accessed from Howard L. Rosenthal and Keith T. Poole, *United States Congressional Roll Call Voting Records, 1789–1990*. Their first major work was Keith T. Poole and Howard Rosenthal, *Congress: A Political Economic History of Roll Call Voting* (New York: Oxford University Press, 1997), and is continually updated on their voteview.com website.

34 Douglas B. Harris and Garrison Nelson, "Middlemen No More? Emergent Patterns in Congressional Leadership Selection," *P.S.: Political Science and Politics*, XLI (January 2008), pp. 49–55.

35 This linkage is best articulated in Morris P. Fiorina's small classic *Congress: Keystone of the Washington Establishment*, 2nd ed. (New Haven: Yale University Press, 1989) and the centrality of reelection receives its fullest statement in David R. Mayhew's influential *Congress: The Electoral Connection*, 2nd ed. (New Haven, CT: Yale University Press, 2004).

36 A highly critical book that contends that the brothers were more similar than dissimilar is Howie Carr's *The Brothers Bulger: How They Terrorized and Corrupted Boston for a Quarter Century* (Lebanon, IN: Warner Books, 2006).

37 The source for most of this information was the lengthy file on Bulger kept by the Federal Bureau of Prisons and made available by the National Archives.
38 A remarkable set of interviews with Whitey were conducted by researcher Michael Esslinger in *Letters from Alcatraz* (San Francisco: Ocean View Publishing, 2015), pp. 132–75, esp. pp. 147–65. Mr. Esslinger was also interviewed for this book.
39 Letter to Billy Bulger from the McCormack office, announcing Whitey's impending release from Lewisburg in the Howard Gotlieb Archival Research Center at Boston University.
40 The primary source for Billy Bulger's career comes from his autobiography, *While the Music Lasts: My Life in Politics* (Boston: Houghton Mifflin, 1996).
41 Letters from John McCormack to the Bureau of Prisons and U.S. Board of Parole concerning Whitey Bulger, 1964–65, in the Gotlieb Archival Research Center at Boston University provided by Mr. Charles Niles.
42 Billy lists Knocko McCormack as his political mentor in *While the Music Lasts*, pp. 14–16.
43 The best sources for Whitey's post-prison criminal career are Kevin Cullen and Shelley Murphy's *Whitey Bulger: America's Most Wanted Gangster and the Manhunt That Brought Him to Justice* (New York: W. W. Norton & Company, 2013); and Dick Lehr and Gerard O'Neill's *Whitey: The Life of America's Most Notorious Mob Boss* (New York: Broadway Books. 2013). The most telling of the books by Bulger's associates is *Brutal; My Life Inside Whitey Bulger's Irish Mob* by Kevin Weeks and Phyllis Karas (New York: ReganBooks, 2006).
44 The FBI's complicity in the Whitey Bulger saga is vividly captured in Dick Lehr and Gerard O'Neill's *Black Mass: The Irish Mob, the FBI and a Devils' Deal* (New York: Public Affairs, 2000).
45 See O'Neill and Lehr's *The Underboss: The Rise and Fall of a Mafia Family* (New York: St. Martin's Press, 1989).
46 See the insightful treatment by Boston College historian and South Boston native, Thomas H. O'Connor, *South Boston: My Home Town: The History of an Ethnic Neighborhood*, new ed. (Boston: Northeastern University Press, 1994).
47 J. Anthony Lukas, *Common Ground: A Turbulent Decade in the Lives of Three American Families* (New York: Knopf, 1985). In addition to Lukas's book, see also Alan Lupo, *Liberty's Chosen Home: The Politics of Violence in Boston* (Boston: Beacon Press, 1977); Ronald P. Formisano, *Boston against Busing: Race, Class and Ethnicity in the 1960s and 1970s* (Chapel Hill: University of North Carolina Press, 1991); and a first-person account by Ione Malloy, "*Southie Won't Go:*" *A Teacher's Diary of the Desegregation of South Boston High School* (Urbana: University of Illinois Press, 1986).
48 Biographical material from Mark R. Schneider, *Joe Moakley's Journey: From South Boston to El Salvador* (Boston: Northeastern University Press, 2013).
49 The Eddie McCormack plan is discussed in Lukas, *Common Ground*, pp. 244, 248–51.
50 Author's telephonic interview with the Hon. John W. McCormack, April 1977.
51 Letter from John W. McCormack to H. G. Dulaney, quoted in Champagne et al., *The Austin-Boston Connection*, p. 130.
52 Randall B. Ripley, *Party Leaders in the House of Representatives* (Washington, DC: The Brookings Institution, 1967), p. 16. The O'Neill designation is mine.
53 Randall B. Ripley, *Majority Party Leadership in Congress* (Boston: Little, Brown, 1969), p. 177.

54 Ronald M. Peters, Jr., *The American Speakership: The Office in Historical Perspective* (Baltimore: The Johns Hopkins University Press, 1990), p. 147.

55 Ibid., pp. 146–59.

56 Ibid., p. 147.

57 The classic "task leader-social leader" distinction is described in Robert F. Bales, "Task Roles and Social Roles in Problem-Solving Groups," in Eleanor E. Maccoby, Theodore M. Newcomb, and Eugene L. Hartley, eds., *Readings in Social Psychology*, 3rd ed. (New York: Holt, Rinehart and Winston, 1958), pp. 437–47. A political science application of this distinction using Chief Justices of the Supreme Court may be found in David J. Danelski, "Task Group and Social Group on the Supreme Court," in John H. Kessel, George F. Cole, and Robert G. Seddig, eds., *Micropolitics: Individual and Group Level Concepts* (New York: Holt, Rinehart and Winston, Inc., 1970), pp. 266–74.

58 Matthew N. Green, *The Speaker of the House: A Study of Leadership* (New Haven, CT: Yale University Press, 2010), p. 109.

59 Matthew N. Green, *The Speaker of the House: A Study of Leadership* (New Haven, CT: Yale University Press, 2010), p. 109.

60 Jenkins and Stewart III, *Fighting for the Speakership*, chapter 9. See the listing of Speaker and Majority Leader names in "Democratic balancing in caucus, 72nd–103rd Congresses," p. 294.

61 "House Elects McCormack as Speaker," *CQWR*, January 10, 1969, pp. 80–81. The Democratic vote for McCormack was 241–0 with northern Democrats voting 153–0 and southern Democrats voting 88–0.

62 Peters, *The American Speakership*, p. 149.

63 UPI, "Bolling Suggests Bolling as Speaker," *NYT*, January 19, 1970, p. 27.

64 Warren Weaver, Jr., *Both Your Houses: the Truth about Congress* (New York: Praeger Publishers, 1972), p. 72.

65 John Farrell's succinct assessment of the McCormack legacy is especially positive in his *Tip O'Neill*, p. 151.

66 Dedication in Spark M. Matsunaga and Ping Chen's *Rulemakers of the House* (Urbana: University of Illinois Press, 1976).

Sources

A note on sources

This is the first ever full-length biography of John W. McCormack, 1891–1980, who at the time of his death weeks from his 89th birthday was then the second longest-lived Speaker of the U.S. House of Representatives. McCormack was one of the very few political leaders who openly resisted a biography written about him even going so far as to repeatedly warn his office staff about preparing a manuscript of their service with him. As Dr Martin Sweig, his longtime assistant once contended to me, "John McCormack was the most secretive man I ever met." Consequently, the search for sources documenting his life and political career had to go well beyond his apparently sanitized congressional papers located at Boston University's Howard Gotlieb Archival Research Center. Secretiveness also characterized many of John McCormack's South Boston constituents. South Boston had been the focus of negative press during the school busing crisis of the 1970s and the Southies were not eager to share information with an outsider like myself. I lived in South Boston for a few months and traveled frequently to that unique peninsula. During that time, I learned many McCormack family stories, most of which were about Knocko and his sons Jocko and Eddie but very few were about John. Most of those sources refused to let me name them in print but the stories were too revealing to excise from the book so they are included in spite of many not able to be fully fact-checked.

Unpublished doctoral dissertations and theses

Brannen, Ralph Neal. *John McDuffie: State Legislator, Congressman, Federal Judge, 1883-1950*, Ph.D. Dissertation, Auburn University, 1975.

Coffey, Ellen. *The Impact of the New Deal on Boston Politics: The Early Career of John W. McCormack*, Senior Honors Thesis, Palo Alto, CA: Stanford University, 1994.

Goldstein, Jenny. *Transcending Boundaries: Boston's Catholics and Jews, 1929-1965*, Senior Thesis, Waltham, MA: Brandeis University, 2001.

Gordon, Lester Ira. *John McCormack and the Roosevelt Era*, Ph.D. Dissertation. Boston: Boston University, 1976.

Greene, Harry F. *The McCormacks of Massachusetts*, Senior Thesis, Cambridge, MA: Harvard University, 1963.

Hasenfus, William A. *Managing Partner: Joseph W. Martin, Jr., Republican Leader of the United States House of Representatives, 1939-1959*, Ph.D. dissertation, Boston College, 1986.

Hedlund, Richard. *Congress and the British Loan, 1945-1946,* Ph.D. dissertation, University of Kentucky, 1976.

Imler, Joseph A. *The First One Hundred Days of the New Deal: The View from Capitol Hill,* Ph.D. Dissertation, Indiana University, 1975.

Sachar, David B. *David K. Niles and United States Foreign Policy Toward Palestine: A Case Study in American Foreign Policy,* Senior Honors Thesis, Cambridge, MA: Harvard University, 1960.

Document sources

Church documents

McCormack family Canadian birth and baptismal records originally located at St. Columba Roman Catholic Church in Fairfield, Prince Edward Island, were moved to St. Margaret of Scotland Roman Catholic Church in St. Peters, PEI. Later McCormack records are at St. Mary's Roman Catholic Church in Souris, PEI. Massachusetts church records of the Archdiocese of Boston have been relocated from the Chestnut Hill campus of Boston College to Braintree, Massachusetts Baptismal records for McCormack family members may be found in South Boston churches Gate of Heaven and St. Augustine's. Marriage records of Joseph McCormack and Mary Ellen O'Brien may be found at St. James the Greater in Boston. Marriage records of John McCormack and Harriet Joyce may be found at St. Augustine (now St. Theresa of Calcutta) in South Boston. Harriet's funeral took place at St. Augustine's and John's took place at St. Monica's. Burial records for Joe McCormack are in the Rural Cemetery in Waldoboro, Maine. McCormack family members were buried in various Boston-area cemeteries— Sandbanks in Watertown, Mount Benedict in West Roxbury, New Calvary in Waltham, and St. Joseph's in West Roxbury.

Government documents

Massachusetts:

Boston City Charters

City of Boston, *City Directory* (commercially printed and published annually)

Debates in the Massachusetts Constitutional Convention 1917-1918.

Secretary of the Commonwealth of Massachusetts, *Registers of Vital Records—Indexes, 1841-1920,* Massachusetts Archives. Boston, Massachusetts. Also available at the Secretary's office were primary and general election returns for McCormack's fifty-plus year electoral career.

Legislative Journals of the Great and General Court of the Commonwealth of Massachusetts: House of Representatives 1920–23 and Senate 1923–26.

Maine: Office of Vital Records, State Archives, Augusta, Maine.

Texas: Department of Health, Bureau of Vital Statistics, Austin, Texas.

U.S. Congress

Biographical Directory of the United States Congress, Bicentennial Edition, 1774-1989 (Washington, DC: U.S. Government Printing Office, 1969). Referenced in the footnotes as *BDUSC*; *Black Americans in Congress*, 1870–2007 (Washington, DC: United States: Office of History and Preservation, Office of the Clerk, U.S. House of Representatives, 2009); U.S. Congress, *Congressional Directories* (Washington, DC: Government Printing Office, 1928–70); U.S. Congress, *Congressional Record, 70th-91st Congresses* (Washington, DC: Government Printing Office, 1928–71); Congressional Research Service, William G. Whittaker, *Davis-Bacon: The Act and the Literature*, Report 94-908 (2007); U.S. Congress, *Journal of the U.S. House of Representatives* (Washington, DC: U.S. Government Printing Office, 1928–71). "Democratic Caucus Chairmen (1849 to present)," History Art & Archives, U.S. House of Representatives; also relevant congressional hearings referenced in the notes.

U.S. President

Presidential documents and speeches were found in *Public Papers of the President* published in Washington, D.C. by the U.S. Government Printing Office: *Franklin D. Roosevelt, 1933-1945* (13 vols. published 1938–50); *Harry S. Truman, 1945-1953* (8 vols. published 1961–66); *Dwight D. Eisenhower, 1953-1961* (8 vols. published, 1958–61); *John F. Kennedy, 1961-1963* (3 vols. published 1962–64); *Lyndon B. Johnson, 1963-1969* (10 vols., published 1965–70), and *Richard M. Nixon, 1968-1974* (6 vols. published 1971–75).

U.S. Supreme Court

Martin Sweig, Petitioner v. United States of America, Respondent, Supreme Court of the United States, October Term, 1970, Case No. 1702.

U.S. Bureau of the Census, *U.S. Census Returns, 1880-1980.*

U.S. Federal Bureau of Investigation

Freedom of Information requests (FOIA) provided FBI files for John W. McCormack, David K. Niles, and Dr. Martin Sweig. The McCormack-Hoover correspondence includes 169 letters in thirty-four years from 1936 to 1970 that are very cordial. The Niles and Sweig files are more investigatory.

U.S. Federal Bureau of Prisons and U.S. Board of Parole

National Archives provided the U.S. Bureau of Prisons file for James "Whitey" Bulger Jr., 1956–66 and U.S. Board of Parole, 1965–67 from the Gotlieb Archival Research Center.

Canada: Department of Health, Division of Vital Statistics at the Prince Edward Island Provincial Archives, Charlottetown, PEI.

German Foreign Ministry: *Documents on German Foreign Policy, 1918-1945* from the Archives of the German Foreign Ministry (Washington, DC: Government Printing Office, 1951), Series D (1937–45), Volume I, *From Neurath to Ribbentrop (September 1937-September 1938)*; and Volume IV, *The Aftermath of Munich, October 1938-March 1939.*

Archives for documents and oral histories

John McCormack Papers, Gotlieb Archival Research Center, Boston University, Boston, Mass. Extensive John McCormack congressional correspondence from 1950 on, including correspondence with Massachusetts State Senate President William Bulger. Pre-1950 materials are less complete. There are valuable taped congressional interviews of John McCormack with Dr. Lester Gordon for his dissertation *John McCormack and the Roosevelt Era* Band those of Bill and Dorothy McSweeny. Also useful are the Ralph G. Martin papers with notes for *Front Runner, Dark Horse* (Garden City, NY: Doubleday, 1960), including Ed Plaut's interviews with: Representative Dick Bolling – Mike Feldman – Joe Healy – Professor Arthur Holcomb – U,S. Senator Jack Javits – U.S. Senator Estes Kefauver – U.S. Senator Jack Kennedy – Larry O'Brien – John Powers – Ted Riordan – Arthur Schlesinger (Jr.) – U.S. Senator George Smathers – Sargent Shriver – Ted Sorensen – Wilton Vaugh.

Eddie McCormack Family Papers: The boxes in this collection contained medals and gavels that were given to John McCormack, extensive newspaper clippings, family photos, and mostly personal correspondence apparently withheld from the Gotlieb Archives.

Paul Wright Papers, University of Massachusetts-Boston: News accounts of Harriet Joyce's singing career, U.S. Census Records, Massachusetts birth and death notices. Taped interviews with many South Boston neighbors, most valuable are those with James "Buster" Hartrey, who ran McCormack's district office in Boston and John's sister-in-law, Mary T. Coffey McCormack, the wife of Edward "Knocko" McCormack.

Massachusetts Archival Collections: The Boston Public Library has the papers of Boston Republican boss Charles H. Innes who helped McCormack pass the bar examination and was an informal mentor in his early state legislative career. The BPL also has the largest microfilm collection of Boston newspapers that provided a daily record of the city's vibrant politics. Included were the *Boston Globe*, the *Boston Herald Traveler*, the *Boston Record-American* (now all subsumed as the *Boston Herald*), and the defunct *Boston Post*. I was also able to spend days in the *Globe's* huge clippings file. The papers of Augustus Peabody Loring who was helpful to McCormack at the Massachusetts Constitutional Convention, 1917–19 may be found at the Harvard

University Law School in Cambridge. The Massachusetts Historical Society in Boston contains the papers of Henry Lee Shattuck, the quintessential Boston Brahmin who mentored McCormack in his State House career and urged John to run for mayor in 1937. It also contains a collection of files from Nigel Hamilton's *JFK: Reckless Youth* (New York: Random House, 1992). The most complete collection of photographs of McCormack ally and four-time Boston Mayor James Michael Curley may be found in the archives of the College of the Holy Cross in Worcester. The David K. Niles papers at the Robert D. Farber Archives, Brandeis University in Waltham emphasize the efforts to gain U.S. recognition for the State of Israel and include anti-Semitic jabs at McCormack. The Niles papers were assembled by Dr. Abram Sacher, a Niles protégé, who was the founding President of Brandeis. Also helpful but not used extensively were the papers of longtime Republican House leader, U.S. House Speaker Joseph W. Martin, Jr. at Stonehill College in Easton and those of McCormack protégé U.S. House Speaker Thomas P. O'Neill, Jr. at Boston College in Chestnut Hill.

President Franklin D. Roosevelt Library and Museum, Hyde Park, NY: Papers of President Franklin D. Roosevelt and Anna Eleanor Roosevelt as well as correspondence with John Boettinger, Oscar Cox, Robert D. Graff, Harry Hopkins, Gardner Jackson, Isidor Lubin, John McCormack, David K. Niles, Sam Rayburn, James Rowe, and the Democratic National Committee.

Jonathan Daniels Papers, University of North Carolina, Chapel Hill, NC: One of FDR's original Special Assistants to the President along with David K. Niles, his files have notes for his diary, *White House Witness, 1942-1945* (Garden City, NY: Doubleday, 1975) regarding Niles, Sam Rayburn, John McCormack and Joe Casey.

President Harry S. Truman Library and Museum, Independence, MO: The President's Day, 1945–52 and White House Central Files, 1945–53. *Transcribed Oral Histories*: Eben A. Ayers – Hon. Andrew J. Biemiller – Hon. Richard W. Bolling – Hon. Tom C. Clark – Matthew Connelly – Oscar R. Ewing – Hon. Walter H. Judd – Joseph E. Keenan – Frank K. Kelly – Leon H. Keyserling – Charles S. Murphy – Charles G. Ross – Stephen J. Spingarn – Roger Tubby – Robert K. Walsh. The complete David K. Niles Files are at the Truman Library.

President Dwight D. Eisenhower Library and Museum, Abilene, KS: Eisenhower had minimal involvement with McCormack during his administration, 1953–61 as may be seen in Ike's Daily Appointment Calendar.

President John F. Kennedy Library and Museum, Dorchester, MA: Especially valuable were news clippings files recording Kennedy's elections and service in the U.S. House, 1946–53. Also the Kennedy Library granted me access to correspondence between McCormack and Ambassador Joseph P. Kennedy that shed light on the complex relationship between these two powerful families. *Transcribed Oral Histories*: Hon. Carl Albert – Hon. J. Lindsay Almond – Hon. Clinton P. Anderson – Hon. Wayne N. Aspinall – Ruth M. Batson – Professor Samuel H. Beer – Edward C. Berube – Hon. Andrew J. Biemiller – Hon. Corinne "Lindy" Boggs – Hon. T. Hale Boggs – Jim Grant

Bolling – Hon. Richard Bolling – Samuel Bornstein – Thomas Broderick – Grace Burke – Hon. James A. Burke – Professor James MacGregor Burns – Hon. Garrett Byrne – John F. Cahill– Hon. Joseph Casey – Hon. Emanuel Celler – James G. Colbert – Hon. Tom Costin – Richard Cardinal Cushing – Mary Davis – Hon. John E. Fogarty – Hon. Gerald R. Ford, Jr. – Hon. Foster Furcolo – John T. Galvin – Hon. Albert Gore, Sr. – Hon. Edith Green – Hon. Charles A. Halleck – Hon. Oren Harris – Hon. Brooks Hays – Hon. Chet Holifield – Hon. Hubert H. Humphrey – Hon. Jacob Javits – Hon. Robert E. Jones, Jr. – Hon. Michael J. Kirwan – Fletcher Knebel – Hon. Phil M. Landrum – Evelyn Lincoln – Hon. Henry Cabot Lodge, Jr. – Henry R. Luce – Hon. Torbert H. MacDonald – Hon. Mike Mansfield – Hon. John W. McCormack – Hon. George F. Miller – Hon. Wilbur Mills – Francis X. Morrissey – Hon. John Moss – Patsy Mulkern – Dr. Philleo Nash – Clement A. Norton – Hon. Thomas P. "Tip" O'Neill, Jr. – David F. Powers – John E. Powers – Hon. James Quigley – Hon. Jennings Randolph – Hon. Thomas M. Rees – Hon. Henry Reuss – Chalmers Roberts – Hon. Paul G. Rogers – Joseph Russo – Hon. Leverett Saltonstall – Hon. John Sparkman – William Sutton – Hon. Stuart Symington – Hon. Olin Teague – Frank Thompson – Wilton Vaugh – Hon. Robert Wagner – Hon. Ralph W. Yarborough. Also Presidential Recordings 1961–63.

President Lyndon B. Johnson Library and Museum, Austin, TX: Multiple letters, many handwritten, between LBJ and Mrs. Lady Bird Johnson to John and Harriet McCormack indicating strong personal regards between the two families. One of the best McCormack oral histories in these archives is with T. Harrison Baker of the University of Texas Oral History Project, LBJ Library, September 23, 1968. The most accessible Johnson oral histories are *The Presidential Recordings: Lyndon B Johnson*, Philip Zelikow, Ernest May, and Timothy Naftali, general editors, assembled by the Miller Center of Public Affairs at the University of Virginia in eight volumes from November 22, 1963 to July 4, 1964 and published by W. W. Norton, Inc., 2005–11.

Sam Rayburn Library and Museum, Bonham, TX: *Transcribed Interviews*: Some are duplicates from the Kennedy Library but most interviews were done by Professor Anthony Champagne, University of Texas-Dallas. They are: Hon. Carl Albert – Robert S. Allen – Robert E. Baker – Hon. T. Hale Boggs –Hon. Corinne (Lindy) Boggs – Hon. Richard Bolling – Hon. John Brademas – Hon. Jack Brooks – Hon. Edward Edmondson – Hon. John Dingell – D. B. Hardeman – Hon. Daniel Inouye – Hon. Henry M. Jackson – Hon. Melvin Laird – Hon. George Mahon – Hon. John W. McCormack – Hon. Wright Patman – Hon. Bob Poage – Cokie Roberts – Barefoot Sanders – Hon. Homer Thornberry – Hon. Jim Wright.

Carl Albert Congressional Research Center, University of Oklahoma, Norman, OK: The most valuable source in this collection is the very lengthy and surprisingly candid set of seven taped interviews of Speaker Albert, from May 9, 1979 to May 29, 1979 with Professor Ronald M. Peters, Jr. of the University of Oklahoma, who was the founding director of the Carl Albert Congressional Research Center. While there is relatively little direct correspondence between McCormack and Albert, there are valuable news clippings, some of which document the tension between Albert and Hale Boggs that occurred following McCormack's retirement from the House.

Richard W. Bolling Papers, University of Missouri-Kansas City, MO: Bolling's long-time animus toward McCormack may be seen in the three jam-packed legal folders in his papers that contain every published article critical of McCormack as well as a collection of editorial cartoons portraying John as feeble and out of touch. Notes for his two books are included: *House Out of Order* (New York: E.P. Dutton, 1965) and *Power in the House: A History of the Leadership of the House of Representatives* (New York: E.P. Dutton, 1968).

State of Alabama Department of Archives and History, "Statement and Tabulations of General Election, November 8, 1960," Alabama Official and Statistical Register 1963 (Montgomery: Walker Printing Co., 1963).

Bibliography

This bibliography is more extensive than most because of the inclusion of items in the notes that are intended for further reading on the topic. One never ceases to be a teacher. Speeches, remarks, and roll call votes from congressional documents such as the *Congressional Record*, and the *Journals* of the U.S. House of Representatives and U.S. Senate will not be cited specifically.

U.S. House election returns may be found in Congressional Quarterly's original *Guide to U.S. Elections* (Washington, DC, 1975) and updated with the 6th edition, 2010. The best single source for legislative histories is Stephen J. Stathis, *Landmark Legislation, 1774-2002: Major U.S. Acts and Treaties* (Washington, DC: CQ Press, 2003) augmented with congressional session reviews by Arthur W. Macmahon, O. R. Altman, E. Pendleton Herring, and Floyd M. Riddick, published in the *American Political Science Review, South Atlantic Quarterly*, and *Western Political Quarterly*. Congressional committee assignments originally located in the various issues of the *Congressional Directory* have been compiled in the six volumes by Garrison Nelson, *Committees in the U.S. Congress, 1947-1992: Committee Jurisdictions and Member Rosters* (Washington, DC: CQ Press, 1993), Garrison Nelson, Clark H. Bensen, and Mary T. Mitchell, *Committees in the United States Congress, 1947-1992, Committee Histories and Member Assignments* (Washington, DC: CQ Press, 1994), and David T. Canon, Garrison Nelson, and Charles Stewart III, *Committees in the U.S. Congress, 1789-1946,* 4 vols. (Washington, DC: Congressional Quarterly, 2002).

Books cited in the text

Acacia, John, *Clark Clifford: The Wise Man of Washington* (Lexington, KY: University Press of Kentucky, 2009).

Acheson, Sam H., *Joe Bailey: The Last Democrat* (New York: Macmillan, 1932).

Ackerman, Kenneth D., *Dark Horse: The Surprise Election and Political Murder of President James A. Garfield* (New York: Carroll & Graf, 2003).

Ackerman, Bruce, *We the People: Transformations* (Cambridge, MA: Harvard University Press, 1998).

Acts and Resolves of the General Court of Massachusetts, 1947 (Boston: Secretary of the Commonwealth, 1947).

Adams, Cindy, and Susan Crimp, *Iron Rose: The Story of Rose Fitzgerald Kennedy and Her Dynasty* (Beverly Hills, CA: Dove, 1995).

Adams, Henry H., *Harry Hopkins: A Biography* (New York: G. P. Putnam's Sons, 1977).

Adams, John R., *Edward Everett Hale* (Boston: Twayne, 1977).

Adams, W. F., *Ireland and the Irish Emigration to the New World from 1815 to the Famine* (New Haven, CT: Yale University Press, 1932).

Ainley, Leslie G., *Boston Mahatma* (Boston: Brice Humphries, 1949).

Albert, Carl, *Little Giant: The Life and Times of Speaker Carl Albert* (Norman, OK: University of Oklahoma Press, 1990).

Albright, Alice Hope, *Cissy Patterson* (New York: Random House, 1966).

Alexander, Charles C., *Holding the Line: The Eisenhower Era, 1952-1961* (Bloomington: Indiana University Press, 1976).

Allen, Edward, *Sam Rayburn: Leading the Lawmakers* (Chicago: Encyclopedia Press, 1963).

Allen, Robert S., and Drew Pearson, *Washington Merry Go-Round* (New York: Blue Ribbon Books, 1932).

Allison, Graham T., *Essence of Decision: Explaining the Cuban Missile Crisis* (Boston: Little, Brown, 1971).

Allison, Robert J., *James Michael Curley: A Short Biography with Personal Reminiscences* (Beverly, MA: Commonwealth Editions, 2009).

Alperovitz, Gar, *Atomic Diplomacy: Hiroshima and Potsdam* (New York: Simon & Schuster, 1965).

Alperovitz, Gar, *The Decision to Use the Atomic Bomb and the Architecture of an American Myth* (New York: Alfred A. Knopf, 1995).

Ambrose, Stephen E., *Eisenhower: The President*, Vol. 2 (New York: Simon & Schuster, 1984).

Amer, Mildred, *The House Committee on Standards of Official Conduct: A Brief History of Its Evolution and Jurisdiction* (Congressional Research Service Report 1992).

Amory, Cleveland, *The Proper Bostonians* (New York: E. P. Dutton, 1947).

Amrine, Michael, *This Awesome Challenge: The Hundred Days of Lyndon Johnson* (New York: Putnam, 1964).

Anderson, Jack, and Drew Pearson, *The Case Against Congress* (New York: Simon & Schuster, 1968).

Anderson, J. W., *Eisenhower, Brownell, and the Congress: The Tangled Origins of the Civil Rights Bill of 1956-1957* (Tuscaloosa, AL: University of Alabama Press, 1964).

Anderson, Virginia DeJohn, *New England's Generation: The Great Migration and the Formation of Society and Culture in the Seventeenth Century* (Cambridge, G.B.: Cambridge University Press, 1991).

Andres, Charles H., *Our Earliest Colonial Settlements: Their Diversities of Origin and Later Characteristics* (New York: New York University Press, 1933).

Andrew, John A. III, *Lyndon Johnson and the Great Society* (Chicago: Ivan R. Dee, 1998).

Angly, Edward, *Fifty Billion Dollars: My Thirteen Years with the RFC, 1932-1945* (New York: Macmillan, 1951).

Archer, Jules, *The Plot to Seize the White House* (New York: Hawthorne Books, 1973).

Arnett, Alex M., *Claude Kitchin and the Wilson War Policies* (Boston: Little, Brown, 1937).

Arnold, James R., *The First Domino: Eisenhower, the Military, and America's Intervention in Vietnam* (New York: William Morrow, 1991).

Arsenault, Raymond, *Freedom Riders: 1961 and the Struggle for Racial Justice* (New York: Oxford University Press, 2006).

Arsenault, Raymond, *The Sound of Freedom: Marian Anderson, the Lincoln Memorial, and the Concert that Awakened America* ((New York: Bloomsbury Press, 2009).

Atkinson, Charles R., *The Committee on Rules and the Overthrow of Speaker Cannon* (New York: Columbia University Press, 1911).

Aull, Ruth, and Daniel M. Ogden, eds., *Official Proceedings of the Democratic National Convention 1956* (Richmond, VA: Beacon Press, 1956).

Avrich, Paul, *Sacco and Vanzetti: The Anarchist Background* (Princeton, NJ: Princeton University Press, 1996).

Bacon, Donald C., Roger H. Davidson, and Morton H. Keller, eds., *The Encyclopedia of the United States Congress* (New York: Simon & Schuster, 1995).

Bailey, Stephen K., *Congress Makes a Law: The Story Behind the Employment Act of 1946* (New York: Columbia University Press, 1950).

Bailey, Stephen K., and Howard D. Samuel, *Congress at Work* (New York: Henry Holt & Co., 1952).

Bain, Richard C., and Judith H. Parris, *Convention Decisions and Voting Records*, 2nd ed. (Washington, DC: The Brookings Institution, 1973).

Baker, Kelly J., *Gospel According to the Klan: The KKK's Appeal to Protestant America, 1915-1930* (Lawrence: University Press of Kansas, 2011).

Baker, Bobby, and Larry L. King, *Wheeling and Dealing: Confessions of a Capitol Hill Operator* (New York: W. W. Norton, 1978).

Baltzell, E. Digby, *Puritan Boston and Quaker Philadelphia* (New York: The Free Press, 1979).

Bankhead, Tallulah, *Tallulah: My Autobiography* (New York: Harper and Brothers, 1952).

Barber, Lucy C., *Marching on Washington: The Forging of an American Tradition* (Berkeley: University of California Press, 2002).

Barkley, Alben, That *Reminds Me: The Autobiography of the Veep* (Garden City, NY: Doubleday, 1954).

Barrett, David M., *The CIA and Congress: The Untold Story from Truman to Kennedy* (Lawrence, KS: University Press of Kansas, 2005).

Barry, John, *The Ambition and the Power: The Fall of Jim Wright: A True Story of Washington* (New York: Viking, 1989).

Bartlett, Bruce, *Wrong on Race: The Democratic Party's Buried Past* (New York: Palgrave Macmillan, 2008).

Bartlett, John H., *The Bonus March and the New Deal* (Chicago, MA: Donaghue & Co., 1937).

Bayh, Birch, *One Heartbeat Away: Presidential Disability and Succession* (Indianapolis: Bobbs-Merrill, 1968).

Bayor, Ronald, *The Columbia Documentary History of Race and Ethnicity in America* (New York: Columbia University Press, 2004).

Bayor, Ronald H., *Race and the Shaping of Twentieth Century Atlanta* (Chapel Hill: University of North Carolina Press, 1996).

Bayor, Ronald, and Timothy J. Meagher, *The New York Irish* (Baltimore: Johns Hopkins University Press, 1996).

Bearse, Ray, and Anthony Read, *Conspirator: The Untold Story of Tyler Kent* (New York: Doubleday, 1991).

Beatty, Jack, *The Rascal King: The Life and Times of James Michael Curley (1874-1958)* (Reading, MA: Addison-Wesley, 1992).

Beauchamp, Cari, *Joseph P. Kennedy Presents: The Hollywood Years* (New York: Alfred A, Knopf, 2009).

Beck, Emily Morison, *Bartlett's Familiar Quotations*, 15th edn (Boston: Little, Brown, 1980).

Bellush, Bernard, *The Failure of the NRA* (New York: Norton, 1975).

Ben-Veniste, Richard, *The Emperor's New Clothes: Exposing the Truth from Watergate to 9/11* (New York: Thomas Dunne Books, 2009).

Bendix, Reinhard, and Seymour Martin Lipset, eds., *Class, Status, and Power* (Glencoe, IL: The Free Press, 1953).

Bennett, Lerone Jr., *Before the Mayflower: A History of Black America* (New York: Penguin Books, 1984).

Berman, Daniel M., *A Bill Becomes a Law: The Civil Rights Act of 1960* (New York: Macmillan, 1962).

Bernstein, Irving, *Guns or Butter: The Presidency of Lyndon Johnson* (New York: Oxford University Press, 1996).

Beschloss, Michael R., *Kennedy and Roosevelt: The Uneasy Alliance* (New York: W. W. Norton, 1980).

Beschloss, Michael R., ed., *Reaching for Glory: Lyndon Johnson's Secret White House Tapes, 1964-1965* (New York: Simon & Schuster, 2001).

Beschloss, Michael R., *Taking Charge: The Johnson White House Tapes, 1963-1964* (New York: Simon & Schuster, 1997).

Benzaquin, Paul, *Holocaust! Fire in Boston's Cocoanut Grove* (Boston: Braden Press, 1967).

Biger, Gideon, *The Boundaries of Modern Palestine, 1840-1947* (London: Routledge.2004)

Biggs, Jeffrey R., and Thomas S. Foley, *Honor in the House: Speaker Tom Foley* (Pullman, WA: Washington State University Press, 1999).

Billings-Yun, Melanie, *Decision Against War: Eisenhower and Dien Bien Phu, 1954* (New York: Columbia University Press, 1988).

Biographical Directory of the United States Congress, 1774-1989 (Washington, DC: U.S. Government Printing Office, 1989), referenced as BDUSC.

Bird, Kai, and Martin J. Sherwin, *American Prometheus: The Triumph and Tragedy of Robert Oppenheimer* (New York: Alfred Knopf, 2005).

Bishop, Jim, *FDR's Last Year, April 1944-April 1945* (New York: William Morrow, 1974).

Bishop, Jim, *The Day Kennedy Was Shot* (New York: Funk & Wagnalls, 1968).

Black, Conrad, *Franklin Delano Roosevelt: Champion of Freedom* (New York: Public Affairs, 2003).

Blackorby, Edward C., *Prairie Rebel: The Public Life of William Lemke* (Lincoln: University of Nebraska Press, 1963).

Blaine, Gerald, and Lisa McCubbin, *The Kennedy Detail: JFK's Secret Service Agents Break Their Silence* (New York: Gallery Books, 2010).

Blair, Joan and Clay, *The Search for JFK* (New York: Berkley Publishing, 1976).

Bloom, Sol, *The Autobiography of Sol Bloom* (New York: Putnam House, 1948).

Boggs, Lindy, *Washington Through a Purple Veil: Memoirs of a Southern Woman* (New York: Harcourt, Brace, 1994).

Boller, Paul F., *Presidential Campaigns* (New York: Oxford University Press, 1984).

Bolles, Blair, *Tyrant from Illinois: Uncle Joe's Experiment with Personal Power* (New York: Norton, 1957).

Bolling, Richard, *House Out of Order* (New York: E. P. Dutton, 1965).

Bolling, Richard, *Power in the House: A History of the Leadership of the House of Representatives* (New York: E. P. Dutton, 1968).

Boyer, Paul, *Purity in Print: Book Censorship in America from the Gilded Age to the Computer Age* (Madison: University of Wisconsin Press, 2002).

Branch, Taylor, *Parting the Waters: America in the King Years, 1954-63* (New York: Simion & Schuster, 1988).

Brand, H. W., *Traitor to His Class: The Privileged Life and Radical Presidency of Franklin Delano Roosevelt* (New York: Doubleday, 2008).

Brebner, John Bartlet, *New England's Outpost: Acadia before the Conquest of Canada* (New York: 1927).

Breslin, Jimmy, *How the Good Guys Finally Won: Notes from an Impeachment Summer* (New York: Viking, 1975).

Bridgman, Arthur Milnor, *A Souvenir of the Massachusetts Constitutional Convention, Boston, 1917-18-19* (Stoughton, MA: A.M. Bridgman, 1919).

Brinkley, Alan, *The End of Reform: New Deal Liberalism in Recession and War* (New York: Alfred A. Knopf, 1995).)

Brinkley, Alan, *The Publisher: Henry Luce and His American Century* (New York: Alfred A. Knopf, 2010).

Brinkley, Alan, *Voices of Protest: Huey Long, Father Coughlin, and the Great Depression* (New York: Vintage Books, 1984).

Broadwater, Jeff, *Adlai Stevenson and American Politics: The Odyssey of a Cold War Liberal* (New York: Twayne, 1994).

Brooks, Van Wyck, *The Flowering of New England* (New York: E. P. Dutton, 1936).

Brown, Claude, *Manchild in the Promised Land* (New York: Macmillan, 1965).

Brown, Walt, *Treachery in Dallas* (New York: Carroll & Graf Publishing, Inc., 1995).

Brown, Walter J., *James F, Byrnes of South Carolina: A Remembrance* (Macon, GA: Mercer University Press, 1992).

Browning, Christopher, *The Origins of the Final Solution: The Evolution of Nazi Jewish Policy: September 1939-March 1942* (Lincoln: University of Nebraska Press, 2004).

Bryant, Nick, *The Bystander: John F. Kennedy and the Struggle for Black Equality* (New York: Basic Books, 2006).

Bulger, William M., *While the Music Lasts: My Life in Politics* (Winchester, MA: Faber and Faber, 1997).

Burner, David, *The Politics of Provincialism: The Democratic Party in Transition, 1918-1932* (New York: Knopf, 1968).

Burner, David, and Thomas R. West, *The Torch is Passed: The Kennedy Brothers and American Liberalism.* (New York: Athenaeum, 1984).

Burns, James MacGregor, *Edward Kennedy and the Camelot Legacy* (New York: W. W. Norton & Company, 1976).

Burns, James MacGregor, *John F. Kennedy: A Political Profile* (New York: Harcourt, Brace & World, 1960).

Burns, James MacGregor, *Roosevelt: The Lion and the Fox* (New York: Harcourt Brace, 1956).

Burns, James MacGregor, *Roosevelt: The Soldier of Freedom* (New York: Harcourt Brace Jovanoich, 1970).

Burns, James MacGregor, *Running Alone: Presidential Leadership – from JFK to Bush II: Why It has Failed and How We Can Fix It* (New York: Basic Books, 2006).

Burns, James MacGregor, *The Deadlock of Democracy: Four-Party Politics in America* (Englewood Cliffs, NJ: Prentice-Hall, 1963).

Busbey, L. White, *Uncle Joe Cannon: Story of a Pioneer American* (New York: Henry Holt, 1927).

Bush, Vannevar, *Pieces of the Action* (New York: William Morrow, 1970).

Bussmann, Walter, *From Neurath to Ribbentrop, September 1937-September 1938* (Göttingen: Vandenhoeck & Ruprecht, 1950).

Butler, Smedley D., *War is a Racket* (New York: Round Table Books, 1935).

Byrnes, James F., *All in One Lifetime* (New York: Harper's, 1958).

Cahill, Thomas, *How the Irish Saved Civilization: The Untold Story of Ireland's Heroic Role from the Fall of Rime to the Rise of Medieval Europe* (New York: Doubleday, 1995).

Campbell, Angus, Philip Converse, Warren E. Miller, and Donald Stokes, *Elections and the Political Order* (New York: John Wiley, 1966).

Canon, David, *Race, Redistricting, and Representation: The Unintended Consequences of Black Majority Districts* (Chicago: University of Chicago Press, 1999).

Canon, David T., Garrison Nelson, and Charles Stewart III, *Committees in the U.S. Congress, 1789-1946*, 4 vols (Washington, DC: Congressional Quarterly, 2002).

Carlyle, Thomas, *The Correspondence of Thomas Carlyle and Ralph Waldo Emerson, 1834-1872* (Boston: Ticknor. 1886).

Caro, Robert A., *The Years of Lyndon Johnson: Master of the Senate* (New York: Alfred A. Knopf, 2002).

Caro, Robert A., *The Years of Lyndon Johnson: Means of Ascent* (New York: Alfred A. Knopf, 1990).

Caro, Robert A., *The Years of Lyndon Johnson: The Path to Power* (New York: Alfred A. Knopf, 1982).

Carr, Howie, *The Brothers Bulger: How They Terrorized and Corrupted Boston for a Quarter Century* (Lebanon, IN: Warner Books, 2006).

Carroll, Holbert N., *The House of Representatives and Foreign Affairs*, rev. edn (Boston: Little, Brown, 1966).

Casey, Shaun A., *The Making of a Catholic President: Kennedy vs. Nixon, 1960* (New York: Oxford University Press, 2009).

Catalogue of the Public Latin School in Boston. October, 1903.

Catledge, Turner, *The 168 Days* (Garden City, NY: Doubleday, Doran, 1938).

Central Intelligence Agency, *The Secret Cuban Missile Documents* (New York: Brassey's. 1994).

Chace, James, *1912: Wilson, Roosevelt, Taft & Debs—The Election That Changed the Country* (New York: Simon & Schuster, 2004).

Chambers, John Whiteclay II, *To Raise an Army: The Draft Comes to Modern America* (New York: Free Press, 1987).

Champagne, Anthony, *Congressman Sam Rayburn* (New Brunswick, NJ: Rutgers University Press, 1984).

Champagne, Anthony, *Sam Rayburn: A Bio-bibliography* (New York: Greenwood Press, 1988).

Champagne, Anthony, Douglas B. Harris, James W. Riddlesperger, Jr., and Garrison Nelson, *The Austin-Boston Connection: Five Decades of House Democratic Leadership* (College Station: Texas A&M University Press, 2009).

Charles, Searle F., *Minister of Relief: Harry Hopkins and the Depression* (Syracuse, NY: Syracuse University Press, 1963).

Chen, Ping, and Spark M. Matsunaga, *Rulemakers of the House* (Urbana: University of Illinois Press, 1976).

Cheney, Lynne V., and Richard B. Cheney, *Kings of the Hill: Power and Personality in the House of Representatives* (New York: Simon & Schuster, 1996).

Chepesiuk, Ronald, *The Scotch-Irish: From North of Ireland to the Making of America* (Jefferson, NC: McFarland, 2000).

Chester, Lewis, Godfrey Hodgson, and Bruce Page, *An American Melodrama: The Presidential Campaign of 1968* (New York: Viking Press, 1969).

Clancy, Paul, and Shirley Elder, *Tip: A Biography of Thomas P. O'Neill, Speaker of the House* (New York: Macmillan, 1980).

Clark, Joseph S., *The Senate Establishment* (New York: Hill and Wang, 1963).

Clarke, Thurston, JFK's *Last Hundred Days: The Transformation of a Man and the Emergence of a Great President* (New York: Penguin, 2013).

Clough, Bryan, *State Secrets: The Kent-Wolkoff Affair* (East Sussex, G.B.: Hideaway Publications Ltd., 2005).

Clark, Champ, *My Quarter Century of American Politics* (New York: Harper & Bros., 1920).

Clayton, Edward, *The Negro Politician* (Chicago: John Publishing, 1964).

Clifford, Clark M., and Richard C. Holbrooke, *Counsel to the President: A Memoir* (New York: Random House, 1991).

Clifford, J. Garry, and Samuel R. Spencer Jr., *The First Peacetime Draft* (Lawrence: University Press of Kansas, 1986).

Clifford, J. Garry, and Theodore A. Wilson, *Presidents, Diplomats, and Other Mortals: Essays Honoring Robert Ferrell* (Columbia: University of Missouri Press, 2007).

Clinch, Nancy Gager, *The Kennedy Neurosis* (New York: Grosset & Dunlap, 1973).

Cohen, Andrew, *Two Days in June: John F. Kennedy and the 48 Hours that Made History* (Toronto: Signal, McClelland & Stewart, 2014).

Cohen Jeffrey, *The President's Legislative Policy Agenda, 1789-2002* (New York: Cambridge University Press, 2012).

Cohen, Richard E., *Rostenkowski: Pursuit of Power and the End of Old Politics* (Chicago: Ivan R. Dee, 1999).

Cohodas, Nadine, *And the Band Played Dixie; Race And the Liberal Conscience of Ole Miss* (New York: Free Press, 1999).

Cole, Wayne S., *Charles A. Lindbergh and the Battle against American Intervention in World War Two* (New York: Harcourt Brace Jovanovich, 1974), pp. 49–50 and 53–56.

Cole, Wayne S., *Roosevelt and the Isolationists* (Lincoln: University of Nebraska Press, 1983).

Collier, Peter, and David Horowitz, *The Kennedys: An American Drama* (New York: McGraw-Hill, 1984).

Congressional Quarterly, *American Leaders: A Biographical Summary, 1789-1991* (Washington, DC: Congressional Quarterly, 1991).

Congressional Quarterly Inc., *Congress and the Nation, 1945-1964: A Review of Government and Politics in the Postwar Years* (Washington, DC: Congressional Quarterly Service, 1965).

Congressional Quarterly Inc., *Congressional Quarterly Almanac, 1947* (Washington, DC: Congressional Quarterly, 1948).

Congressional Quarterly Inc., *Congressional Quarterly Almanac, 1948* (Washington, DC: Congressional Quarterly, 1949).

Congressional Quarterly Inc., *Congressional Quarterly Almanac, 1949* (Washington, DC: Congressional Quarterly, 1950).

Congressional Quarterly Inc., *Congressional Quarterly Almanac, 1950* (Washington, DC: Congressional Quarterly, 1951).

Congressional Quarterly Inc., *Congressional Quarterly Almanac, 1951* (Washington, DC: Congressional Quarterly, 1952).

Congressional Quarterly Inc., *Congressional Quarterly Almanac, 1954* (Washington, DC: CQ Press, 1955).

Congressional Quarterly Inc., *Congressional Quarterly's Guide to U.S. Elections* (Washington, DC: Congressional Quarterly, 1975).

Congressional Quarterly Inc., *Congressional Quarterly's Guide to U.S. Elections*, 5th edn (Washington, DC: CQ Press, 2005), Vol. 2.

Congressional Quarterly Inc., *Presidential Elections, 1789-1992* (Washington, DC: Congressional Quarterly, 1995).

Connally, John B. with Mickey Herskowitz, *In History's Shadow: An American Odyssey* (New York: Hyperion, 1993).

Connally, Tom, *My Name is Tom Connally* (New York: Crowell, 1954).

Connolly, James J., *The Triumph of Ethnic Progressivism: Urban Political Culture in Boston, 1900-1925* (Cambridge, MA: Harvard University Press, 1998).

Connolly, S. J., *Oxford Companion to Irish History* (New York: Oxford University Press, 2004).

Cook, James F., *Carl Vinson: Patriarch of the Armed Forces* (Macon, GA: Merver University Press, 2004).

Cooney, John, *The American Pope: The Life and Times of Francis Cardinal Spellman* (New York: Dell, 1986).

Cordery, Stacy A., *Alice: Alice Roosevelt Longworth from White House Princess to Washington Power Broker* (New York: Viking, 2007).

Cosman, Bernard, *Five States for Goldwater; Continuity and Change in Southern Presidential Voting Patterns* (Tuscaloosa, AL: University of Alabama Press, 1966).

Craig, Bruce R., *Treasonable Doubt: The Harry Dexter White Spy Case* (Lawrence, KS: University Press of Kansas, 2004).

Cray, Ed, *Chief Justice: A Biography of Earl Warren* (New York: Simon & Schuster, 1997).

Cressy, David, *Coming Over: Migration and Communication between England and New England* (Cambridge, England: Cambridge University Press, 1980).

Cullen, James Bernard, *The Story of the Irish in Boston* (Boston: James Bernard Cullen, 1889).

Cullen, Kevin, and Shelley Murphy, *Whitey Bulger: America's Most Wanted Gangster and the Manhunt that Brought Him to Justice* (New York: W. W. Norton, 2013).

Culver, John C., and John Hyde, *American Dreamer: The Life and Times of Henry A. Wallace* (New York: W. W. Norton, 2000).

Cunningham, Maurice T., and Edmund Beard, *The Re-Segregation of America: The Racial Politics of Legislative Redistricting* (Boston: University of Massachusetts Boston, 1993).

Cunningham, Noble E, Jr., *The Jeffersonian Republicans in Power: Party Operations, 1801-1809* (Chapel Hill, NC: University of North Carolina Press, 1963).

Curran, Michael P., *Life of Patrick A. Collins* (Norwood, MA: Norwood Press, 1906).

Curley, James Michael, *I'd Do It Again: A Record of All My Uproarious Years* (Englewood Cliffs, NJ: Prentice-Hall, 1957).

Cutler, John Henry, *Cardinal Cushing of Boston* (New York: Hawthorn Books, 1970).

Cutler, John Henry, *"Honey Fitz;" Three Steps to the White House* (Indianapolis: Bobbs-Merrill, 1962).

Dale, Edwin L., *Conservatives in Power: A Study in Frustration* (Garden City, NY: Doubleday, 1960).

Dalfiume, Richard M., *Desegregation of the U.S. Armed Forces: Fighting on Two Fronts* (Columbia: University of Missouri Press, 1969).

Dallek, Robert, *An Unfinished Life: John F. Kennedy, 1917-1963* (Boston: Little, Brown, 2003).

Dallek, Robert, *Flawed Giant: Lyndon Johnson and His Times, 1961-1973* (New York: Oxford University Press, 1998).

Dallek, Robert, *Franklin D. Roosevelt and American Foreign Policy, 1932-1945* (New York: Oxford University Press, 1979).

Dallek, Robert, *Lone Star Rising: Lyndon Johnson and His Times* (New York: Oxford University Press, 1991).

Dallin, David J., *Soviet Foreign Policy, 1939-1942* (New Haven: Yale University Press, 1942).

Dalton, Cornelius, John Wirkkala, and Anne Thomas, *Leading the Way: A History of the Massachusetts General Court, 1629-1980* (Boston: Office of the Massachusetts Secretary of State, 1984).

Dalzell, Robert, *Enterprising Elite: The Boston Associates and the World They Made* (Cambridge, MA: Harvard University Press, 1987).

Daniels, Roger, *The Bonus March: An Episode of the Great Depression* (Westport, CT: Greenwood, 1971).

Daniels, Jonathan, *White House Witness, 1942-1945: An Intimate Diary of the Years with F.D.R.* (Garden City, NY: Doubleday & Co., 1975).

Dangerfield, George, *The Damnable Question: A Study in Anglo-Irish Relations* (Boston: Little, Brown, 1976).

Danwer, Leo P., *I Remember Southie* (Boston: Christopher Publishing House, 1976).

David, Paul T., Ralph M. Goldman, and Richard C. Bain, *The Politics of National Nominating Conventions* (Washington, DC: The Brookings Institution, 1960).

Davidson, Roger H., and Walter J. Oleszek, *Congress Against Itself* (Bloomington: Indiana University Press, 1977).

Davidson, Roger H., Susan Webb Hammond, and Raymond W. Smock, *Congressional Leadership over Two Centuries* (Boulder, CO: Westview Press, 1998).

Davis, Daniel S., *Mr. Black Labor: The Story of A. Philip Randolph, Father of the Civil Rights Movement* (New York: Dutton, 1972).

Davis, James W., *Presidential Primaries: The Road to the White House* (New York: Thomas Y. Crowell, 1967).

Davis, John H., *The Kennedys: Dynasty and Disaster, 1848-1983* (New York: McGraw-Hill, 1984).

Davis, Kenneth S., *F.D.R.: The New Deal Years, 1933-1937, A History* (New York: Random House, 1979).

Dawson, Raymond H., *The Decision to Aid Russia: Foreign Policy and Domestic Politics* (Chapel Hill: University of North Carolina Press, 1959).

Daynes, Byron W., *Franklin D. Roosevelt and Congress: The New Deal and Its Aftermath* (Armonk, NY: M.E. Sharpe, 2001).

De Antonio, Emilio, and Daniel Talbot, *Point of Order!: A Documentary of the Army-McCarthy Hearings* (New York: W. W. Norton, 1964).

de Chambrun, Clara Longworth, *The Making of Nicholas Longworth: Annals of an American Family* (Freeport, NY: Books for Libraries, 1971).

Delaforce, Patrick, *The Battle of the Bulge: Hitler's Final Gamble* (New York: Pearson Higher Education, 2004).

Democratic National Convention, *Proceedings (1940-1968)*.

Denton, Sally, *The Plots Against the President: FDR, A Nation in Crisis, and the Rise of the American Right* (New York: Bloomsbury, 2012).

Detzer, David, *The Brink: Cuban Missile Crisis, 1962* (New York: Thomas Y. Crowell, 1970).

Dever, Joseph, *Cushing of Boston: A Candid Portrait* (Boston: Brice Humphries, 1965).

Diamond, Sander, *The Nazi Movement in the United States, 1924-1941* (Ithaca, NY: Cornell University Press, 1974).

Dierenfield, Bruce J., *Keeper of the Rules: Congressman Howard W. Smith of Virginia* (Charlottesville: University Press of Virginia, 1987).

Dies, Martin, *Martin Dies Story* (New York: Bookmailer, 1963).

Dies, Martin, *The Trojan Horse in America* (New York: Dodd, Mead, 1940).

Dinneen, Joseph F., *The Kennedy Family* (Boston: Little, Brown, 1959).

Dinneen, Joseph, *The Purple Shamrock: The Hon. James M. Curly of Boston* (New York: W. W. Norton, 1949).

Dinneen, Joseph, *Ward Eight* (New York: reprinted by Arno Press, 1976).

Dionisopoulos, Allan P., *Rebellion, Racism, and Representation* (DeKalb, IL: Northern Illinois University Press, 1970).

Dirksen, Herbert von, *Moscow, Tokyo, London: Twenty Years of German Foreign Policy* (Norman: University of Oklahoma Press, 1952).

Divine, Robert A., *The Illusion of Neutrality* (Chicago: University of Chicago Press, 1962).

Dodd, Lawrence C., and Bruce I. Oppenheimer, *Congress Reconsidered* (New York: Praeger, 1977).

Domosh, Mona, *Invented Cities: The Creation of the 19th Century Landscape* (New Haven, CT: Yale University Press, 1996).

Donahue, Bernard F., *Private Plans and Public Dangers: The Story of FDR's Third Nomination* (Notre Dame, IN: University of Notre Dame Press, 1965).

Donald, David H., *Charles Sumner and the Coming of the Civil War* (New York: Alfred A. Knopf, 1960).

Donaldson, Gary A., *The First Modern Campaign: Kennedy, Nixon, and the Election of 1960* (Lanham, MD: Rowman & Littlefield, 2007).

Donovan, Robert J., *Conflict and Crisis: The Presidency of Harry S. Truman, 1945-1948* (New York: W. W. Norton, 1977).

Donovan, Robert J., *My First Fifty Years in Politics* (New York: McGraw-Hill, 1960).

Dorough, C. Dwight, *Mr. Sam* (New York: Random House, 1962).

Douglass, Frederick, *Narrative of the Life of Frederick Douglass, An American Slave Written by Himself* (Boston: Published at the Anti-Slavery Office, 1845).

Doyle, William, *An American Insurrection: The Battle of Oxford, Mississippi, 1962* (New York: Doubleday, 2001).

Duffy, James P., *Lindbergh vs. Roosevelt: The Rivalry that Divided America* (Washington, DC: Regnery, 2010).

Dulaney, H. G., and Edward Haake Phillips, *Speak, Mister Speaker* (Bonham, TX: Sam Rayburn Foundation, 1978).

Dunn, Susan, *1940: FDR, Willkie, Lindbergh, Hitler—the Election and the Storm* (New Haven, CT: Yale University Press, 2013).

Dunn, Susan, *Roosevelt's Purge: How FDR Fought to Change the Democratic Party* (Cambridge, MA: The Belknap Press of Harvard University, 2010).

Dwyer, Ryle T., *Irish Neutrality and the USA: 1939-1947* (Dublin: Gill and Macmillan, 1977).

Eagles, Charles W., *The Price of Defiance: James Meredith and the Integration of Ole Miss* (Chapel Hill: University of North Carolina Press, 2009).

Eby, Cecil D., *Comrades and Commissars: The Lincoln Battalion in the Spanish Civil War* (University Park: Pennsylvania State University Press, 2007).

Edsall, Thomas Byrne, Mary D. Edsall, *Chain Reaction: The Impact of Race, Rights, and Taxes on American Politics* (New York: W. W. Norton & Co., 1991).

Ehrmann, Herbert B., *The Case That Will Not Die: Commonwealth vs. Sacco and Vanzetti* (Boston: Little, Brown, 1969).

Eidenberg, Eugene, and Roy D. Morey, *An Act of Congress: The Legislative Process and the Making of Education Policy* (New York: W. W. Norton, 1969).

Eisenger, Peter K., *The Politics of Displacement: Racial and Ethnic Transition in Three American Cities* (New York: Academic Press, 1980).

Eisler, Kim Isaac, *A Justice for All: William J. Brennan, Jr. and the Decisions that Transformed America* (New York: Simon & Schuster, 1993).

Eliot, Thomas H., ed. by Frank O'Brien, *Public and Personal* (St. Louis, MO: Washington University Press, 1971).

Eliot, Thomas H., *Recollections of the New Deal: When People Mattered* (Boston: Northeastern University Press, 1992).

Elliot, Bruce S., Irish *Migrants in the Canadas: A New Approach* (Kingston: McGill-Queen's University Press, 1988).

Ellis, Edward R., The *Epic of New York City* (New York: Coward-McCann, 1966).

English, T. J., Paddy *Whacked: The Untold Story of the Irish American Gangster* (New York: Regan Books, 2005).

Esposito, John C., Fire *in the Grove: The Cocoanut Grove Tragedy and Its Aftermath* (Cambridge, MA: Da Capo Press, 2005).

Esslinger, Michael, *Letters from Alcatraz* (San Francisco: Ocean View Publishing, 2015).

Evans, Hugh E., *The Hidden Campaign: FDR's Health and the 1944 Election* (Armonk, NY: M.E. Sharpe, 2002).

Ewen, David, *Encyclopedia of the Opera* (New York: Hill and Wang, 1955).

Ewing, Cortez A. M., *Congressional Elections, 1896-1944: The Sectional Basis of Political Democracy in the House of Representatives* (Norman: University of Oklahoma Press, 1947).

Fairbanks, Douglas Jr., *The Salad Days* (New York: Doubleday, 1988).

Farley, Jim, *Jim Farley's Story: The Roosevelt Years* (New York: Whittlesey House, 1948).

Farrell, John Aloysius, *Tip O'Neill and the Democratic Century* (Boston: Little, Brown, 2001).

Faulkner, Harold U., From *Versailles to the New Deal: A Chronicle of the Harding, Coolidge, Hoover Era* (New Haven, CT: Yale University Press, 1950).

Fay, Paul Jr., *The Pleasure of His Company* (New York: Harper & Co., 1963).

Feerick, John D., *The Twenty-fifth Amendment: Its Complete History and Applications* (New York: Fordham University Press, 2014).

Feldstein, Mark, *Poisoning the Press, Richard Nixon, Jack Anderson, and the Rise of Washington's Scandal Culture* (New York: Farrar, Straus and Giroux, 2010).

Felsenthal, Carol, *Alice Roosevelt Longworth* (New York: G. P. Putnam's Sons, 1988).

Fenno, Richard F., *Congressmen in Committees* (Boston: Little, Brown, 1973).

Fenno, Richard F., *Home Style: House Members in Their Districts* (Boston: Little, Brown & Co., 1978).

Fenno, Richard F., *The Power of the Purse: Appropriations Politics in Congress* (Boston: Little, Brown, 1973).

Fenton, John H., *People and Parties in Politics: Unofficial Makers of Public Policy* (Glenview, IL: Scott, Foresman, 1966).

Ferguson, Karen Jane, *Black Politics in New Deal Atlanta* (Chapel Hill: University of North Carolina Press, 2002).

Ferrell, Robert H., *Choosing Truman: The Democratic Convention of 1944* (Columbia: University of Missouri Press, 1994).

Ferrell, Robert H., *The Dying President: Franklin D. Roosevelt, 1944-1945* (Columbia: University of Missouri Press, 1998).

Ferrell, Robert H., *Harry S. Truman: A Life* (Columbia: University of Missouri Press, 1994).

Ferrell, Robert H., *Truman in the White House: The Diary of Eben A. Ayers* (Columbia: University of Missouri Press, 1991).

Finkelman, Paul, *Beneath the Image of the Civil Rights Movement and Race Relations: Atlanta, Georgia, 1946-1981* (New York: Routledge, 1996).

Finley, Keith M., *Delaying the Dream: Southern Senators and the Fight Against Civil Rights, 1938-1965* (Baton Rouge: Louisiana State University Press, 2008).

Fiorina, Morris P., *Congress: Keystone of the Washington Establishment,* 2nd edn (New Haven: Yale University Press, 1989).

Fischer, David Hackett, *Albion's Seed: Four British Folkways in America* (New York: Oxford University Press, 1989).

Fleming, Thomas, *The New Dealers' War: F.D.R, and the War within World War II* (New York: Basic Books, 2001).

Flynn, Edward J., *You're the Boss: My Story of a Life in Practical Politics* (New York: Viking, 1947).

Flynn, George Q., *Roosevelt and Romanism: Catholics and American Diplomacy, 1937-1945* (Westport, CT: Greenwood Press, 1976).

Flynn, George Q., *The Draft, 1940-1973* (Lawrence: University Press of Kansas, 1993).

Follett, Mary Parker, *The Speaker of the House of Representatives* (New York: Longmans, Green, 1909).

Foner, Philip S., *History of the Labor Movement in the United States, Vol. 8. Postwar Struggles, 1918-1920* (New York: International Publishers, 1947).

Ford, Henry James, *The Scotch-Irish in America* (Princeton, NJ: Princeton University Press, 1915).

Formisano, Ronald P., *Boston Against Busing: Race, Class and Ethnicity in the 1960s and 1970s* (Chapel Hill: University of North Carolina Press, 1991).

Formisano, Ronald P., and Constance K. Burns, eds., *Boston 1700-1980: The Evolution of Urban Politics* (Westport, CT: Greenwood Press, 1984).

Fowler, Gene, *Beau James: The Life and Times of Jimmy Walker* (New York: Viking, 1949).

Fox, Craig, *Everyday Klansfolk: White Protestant Life and the KKK in 1920s Michigan* (East Lansing, MI: Michigan State University Press, 2011).

Fox, Stephen, *Blood and Power: Organized Crime in Twentieth Century America* (New York: William Morrow, 1989).

Frankfurter, Felix, *The Case of Sacco and Vanzetti: A Critical Analysis for Lawyers and Laymen* (Boston: Little, Brown, 1927).

Frankfurter, Marion Denman, and Gardner Jackson, eds., *The Letters of Sacco and Vanzetti* (New York: Vanguard Press, 1930).

Fraser, Steve, and Gary Gerstle, *The Rise of the New Deal Order* (Princeton, NJ: Princeton University Press, 1989).

Frederickson, Kari, *The Dixiecrat Revolt and the End of the Solid South, 1932-1968* (Chapel Hill: University of North Carolina Press, 2001).

Fried, Albert, *FDR and His Enemies* (New York: St. Martins, 1999).

Fried, Richard M., *Nightmare in Red: The McCarthy Era in Perspective* (New York: Oxford University Press, 1990).

Frisch, Scott A., and Sean Q. Kelly, *Committee Assignment Politics in the U.S. House of Representatives* (Norman: University of Oklahoma Press, 2006).

Fuchs, Lawrence H., *The Political Behavior of American Jews* (Glencoe, IL: The Free Press, 1956).

Fuller, Helen, *Year of Trial: Kennedy's Crucial Decisions* (New York: Harcourt, Brace & World, Inc., 1962).

Furcolo, Foster, *Rendezvous at Katyn* (Boston: Marlborough House, 1973).

Gabler, Neal, *An Empire of Their Own: How the Jews Invented Hollywood* (New York: Crown, 1988).

Gaddis, John L., *Strategies of Containment: A Critical Appraisal of Postwar American National Security Policy* (New York, NY: Oxford University Press, 2005).

Galambos, Louis, and Daun Van Ee, eds., *The Papers of Dwight David Eisenhower, The Presidency: The Middle Way* (Baltimore: The Johns Hopkins Press, 1970).

Galbraith, John Kenneth, *The Great Crash, 1929* (Boston: Houghton Mifflin, 1954).

Galloway, George B., *Congress at the Crossroads* (New York: Thomas Y. Corwell, Co., 1946).

Gallup, George H., American Institute of Public Opinion, *The Gallup Poll: Public Opinion, 1935-1971* (New York: Random House, 1972).

Galvin, John T., *The Gentleman Mr. Shattuck: A Biography of Henry Lee Shattuck, 1870-1971* (Boston: Tontine Press, 1996).

Games, Alison, *Migration and the Origins of the English Atlantic World* (Cambridge, MA: Harvard University Press, 1999).

Gamm, Gerald H., *The Making of New Deal Democrats: Voting Behavior and Realignment in Boston, 1920-1940* (Chicago: University of Chicago Press, 1989).

Gamm, Gerald H., *Urban Exodus: Why the Jews Left Boston and the Catholics Stayed* (Cambridge, MA: Harvard University Press, 1999).

Garfinkel, Herbert, *When Negroes March: The March on Washington in the Organizational Politics for FEPC* (New York: Atheneum, 1969).

Garraty, John A., *Henry Cabot Lodge: A Biography* (New York: Knopf, 1953).

Garrow, David J., *Protest at Selma: Martin Luther King, Jr., and the Voting Rights Act of 1965* (New Haven, CT: Yale University Press, 1978).

Gelfand, Mark I., *A Nation of Cities: The Federal Government and Urban America, 1933-1965* (New York: Oxford University Press, 1975).

Gellman, Irwin F., *The Contender: Richard Nixon: The Congress Years, 1946-1952* (New York: Free Press, 1999).

Gentile, Richard H., *Dictionary of American Biography, Supplement Ten, 1975-1980* (New York: Charles Scribner's Sons, 1995).

Gentry, Curt, *J. Edgar Hoover: The Man and the Secrets* (New York: W. W. Norton, 1991).

Germany, Kent B., and Robert David Johnson, eds., *Lyndon B. Johnson: The Presidential Recordings* (New York: W. W. Norton, 2005) Vol. III.

Germany, Kent B., and Robert David Johnson, eds., *Lyndon B. Johnson: The Presidential Recordings* (New York: W. W. Norton, 2005) Vol. IV.

Gilbert, Robert E., *The Tormented President: Calvin Coolidge, Death, and the Clinical Depression* (Westport, CT: Praeger, 2003).

Gingrich, Newt, *Lessons Learned the Hard Way: A Personal Report* (New York: HarperCollins, 1998).

Ginzburg, Eli and Robert M. Solow, eds., *The Great Society: Lessons for the Future* (New York: Basic Books, 1974).

Glass, Carter, *An Adventure in Constructive Finance* (Garden City, NY: Doubleday, 1927).

Goble, Danney, *Little Giant: The Life and Times of Speaker Carl Albert* (Norman: University of Oklahoma Press, 1990).

Goehlert, Robert U., Fenton S. Martin, and John R. Sayre, *Members of Congress: A Bibliography* (Washington, DC: Congressional Quarterly, 1996).

Goldberg, Lawrence G., and Lawrence J. White, eds., *The Deregulation of the Banking and Security Industries* (Lexington, MA: Lexington Books, 1979).

Goldings, Morris M., and Erwin N. Griswold, eds., *Sweig (Martin) v. U.S. Supreme Court Transcript of Record with Supporting Pleadings*, U.S. Supreme Court Records and Briefs, 1832–1978.

Goldsmith, John A., *Colleagues, Richard B. Russell and His Apprentice Lyndon B. Johnson* (Macon, GA: Mercer University Press, 1998).

Goodman, Walter, *The Committee: The Extraordinary Career of the House Committee on Un-American Activities* (New York: Farrar, Straus and Giroux, 1968).

Goodwin, Doris Kearns, *Lyndon Johnson and the American Dream* (New York: Harper & Row, 1976).

Goodwin, Doris Kearns, *No Ordinary Time: Franklin and Eleanor Roosevelt: The Home Front in World War II* (New York: Simon & Schuster, 1994).

Goodwin, Doris Kearns, *The Kennedys and the Fitzgeralds: An American Saga* (New York: Simon & Schuster, 1987).

Goodwin, Richard N., *Remembering America: A Voice form the Sixties* (Boston: Little, Brown, 1988).

Gosnell, Harold F., *Champion Campaigner: Franklin D. Roosevelt* (New York: Macmillan, 1952).

Graham, Hugh D., *The Uncertain Triumph: Federal Education Policy in the Kennedy and Johnson Years* (Chapel Hill: University of North Carolina Press, 1984).

Grantham, Dewey W., *The Democratic South* (New York: W. W. Norton & Co., 1963).

Green, Matthew N., *The Speaker of the House: A Study of Leadership* (New Haven, CT: Yale University Press, 2010).

Grodzins, Morton, *Americans Betrayed: Politics and the Japanese Evacuation* (Chicago: University of Chicago Press, 1949).

Grossman, Lawrence, *The Democratic Party and the Negro: Northern and National Politics, 1868-92* (Urbana: University of Illinois Press, 1976).

Groves, Leslie R., *Now It Can Be Told: The Story of the Manhattan Project* (New York: Harper & Row, 1962).

Guilfoyle, James H., *On the Trail of the Forgotten Man: A Journal of the Roosevelt Presidential Campaign* (Boston: Peabody Master Printers, 1933).

Guinsberg, Thomas N., *The Pursuit of Isolationism in the United States Senate from Versailles to Pearl Harbor* (New York: Garland, 1982).

Guttman, Allen, *The Wound in the Heart: America and the Spanish Civil War* (New York: The Free Press of Glencoe, 1962).

Gwinn, William Rea., *Uncle Joe Cannon: Archfoe of Insurgency* (New York: Bookman Associates, 1957).

Halberstam, David, *The Best and the Brightest* (New York: Random House, 1972).

Hale, Edward E., *Letters on Irish Emigration First Published in the Boston Daily Advertiser* (Boston: Phillips, Samson & Co., 1852).

Hall, Clayton C., *The Lords Baltimore and the Maryland Palatinate: Six Lectures on Maryland's Colonial History* (Baltimore: Johns Hopkins University Press, 1902).

Hamilton, Charles V., *Adam Clayton Powell, Jr.: The Political Biography of An American Dilemma* (New York: Atheneum, 1991).

Hamilton, Nigel, *JFK: Reckless Youth* (New York: Random House, 1992).

Hand, Samuel B., *Consent and Advise: A Political Biography of Samuel I. Rosenman* (New York: Garland, 1979).

Handlin, Oscar, *Boston's Immigrants: A Study in Acculturation, 1790-1880, New and Revised Edition* (New York: Atheneum, 1969).

Hardeman, D. B., and Donald C. Bacon, *Rayburn: A Biography* (Austin: Texas Monthly Press, 1987).

Hartz, Louis, *The Liberal Tradition in America: An Interpretation of American Political Thought Since the Revolution* (New York: Harcourt, Brace, & World Inc., 1955).

Harvard, William C., *The Changing Politics of the South* (Baton Rouge: Louisiana State University Press, 1972).

Hatch, Alden, *The Lodges of Massachusetts* (New York: Hawthorn Books, 1973).

Haygood, Wil, *King of the Cats: The Life and Times of Adam Clayton Powell, Jr.* (Boston: Houghton Mifflin, 1993).

Haynes, John Earl, and Harvey Klehr, *Alexander Vassiliev's Notebooks: Provenance and Documentation of Soviet Intelligence Activities in the United States* (Washington, DC: Cold War International History Project, Woodrow Wilson Center, 2007).

Haynes, John Earl, and Harvey Klehr, *Venona: Decoding Soviet Espionage in America* (New Haven, CT: Yale University Press, 1999).

Healy, Paul F., *Cissy: The Biography of Eleanor M. "Cissy" Patterson* (Garden City, NY: Doubleday, 1966).

Heard, Alexander, *Southern Politics in State and Nation* (New York: Alfred A. Knopf, 1949).

Hechler, Kenneth, *Insurgency: Personalities and Politics of the Taft Era* (New York: Columbia University Press, 1940).

Hecht, Ben, *A Child of the Century* (New York: Simon & Schuster, 1964).

Hening, George C., *Aid to Russia, 1941-1946: Strategy, Diplomacy and the Origins of the Cold War* (New York: Columbia University Press, 1973).

Hennessy, Michael E., *Four Decades of Massachusetts Politics, 1890-1935* (Norwood, MA: Norwood Press, 1935).

Hersh, Seymour M., *The Dark Side of Camelot* (Boston: Little, Brown, 1997).

Hewlett, Richard G., and Oscar E. Anderson, *The New World, A History of the Atomic Energy Commission, Volume 1, 1939/1946* (University Park, PA: Pennsylvania State University Press, 1962).

Higham, John, *Strangers in the Land: Patterns of American Nativism, 1860-1925* (New Brunswick, NJ: Rutgers University Press, 1955).

Hilberg, Raul, *The Destruction of the European Jews* (Chicago: Quadrangle Books, 1961).

Hilberg, Raul, Stanislaw Staron, and Josef Kermisz, *The Warsaw Diary of Adam Czerniakow: Prelude to Doom*, (New York: Stein and Day, 1979).

Hill, William, and M. B. Schnapper, eds., *The New Frontiersmen: Profiles of the Men around Kennedy* (Washington, DC: Public Affairs Press, 1961).

Himmelberg, Robert F., *The Origins of the National Recovery Administration: Business, Government, and the Trade Association Issue, 1921-1933*, 2nd edn (New York: Fordham University Press, 1976).

Hinckley, Barbara, *The Seniority System in Congress* (Bloomington: Indiana University Press, 1971).

Hodgson, Geoffrey, *The Colonel: The Life and Wars of Henry Stimson, 1867-1950* (New York: Alfred A. Knopf, 1990).

Holland, Max, *The Kennedy Assassination Tapes: The White House Conversations of Lyndon B. Johnson Regarding the Assassination, the Warren Commission and the Aftermath* (New York: Alfred A. Knopf, 2004).

Holland, Max, ed., *Lyndon B. Johnson: The Presidential Recordings* (New York: W. W. Norton, 2005) Vol. I.

Hollett, Dave, *Passage to the New World: Packet Ships and Irish Famine Emigrants* (Abergavenny, Gwent: P.M. Heaton, 1995).

Holli, Melvin G., and Peter d'A. Jones, *Biographical Dictionary of American Mayors, 1820-1980: Big City Mayors, Baltimore, Boston, Buffalo, Chicago, Cincinnati, Cleveland, Detroit, Los Angeles, Milwaukee, New Orleans, New York, Philadelphia, Pittsburgh, San Francisco, St. Louis* (Westport, CT: Greenwood Press, 1981).

Holmes, Oliver Wendell, *The Autocrat at the Breakfast Table* (Boston: Phillips, Sampson and Co., 1858).

Holt, James, *Congressional Insurgents and the Party System* (Cambridge, MA: Harvard University Press, 1967).

Holt, Michael F., *The Political Crisis of the 1850s* (New York: W. W. Norton, 1978).

Houston, Cecil J., and William J. Smyth, *Irish Emigration and Canadian Settlement: Patters, Links, and Letters* (Toronto: University of Toronto Press, 1990).

Hughes, Emmet J., *The Ordeal of Power: A Political Memoir of the Eisenhower Years* (New York: Atheneum, 1962).

Humphrey, Hubert H., *The Education of a Public Man: My Life and Politics* (Garden City, NY: Doubleday, 1976).

Hunter, Stephen, *American Gunfight: The Plot to Kill Harry Truman—And the Shootout That Stopped It* (New York: Simon & Schuster, 2005).

Huthmacher, J. Joseph, *Massachusetts People and Politics: 1919-1933* (New York: Atheneum, 1969).

Hyman, Sidney, *The Lives of William Benton* (Chicago: University of Chicago Press, 1969).

Ickes, Harold, *The Secret Diary of Harold L. Ickes: The First Thousand Days* (Cambridge: Da Capo Press, 1974).

Iganatiev, Noel, *How the Irish Became White* (New York: Routledge Classics, 2008).

Jackson, Carlton, *A Social History of the Scotch-Irish* (Lanham, MD: Madison Books, 1993).

Jackson, Kenneth T., *The Ku Klux Klan in the City 1915-1930* (New York: Oxford University Press, 1967).

Jacobs, Andy, *The Powell Affair: Freedom Minus One* (Indianapolis: Bobbs-Merrill, 1973).

Jacobs, John, *A Rage for Justice: The Passion and Politics of Phillip Burton* (Berkeley: University of California Press, 1995).

Jaffe, Harry S., and Tom Sherwood, *Dream City: Race, Power, and the Decline of Washington D.C.* (New York: Simon & Schuster. 1994).

James, Rawn, *The Double V: How Wars, Protest, and Harry Truman Desegregated America's Military* (New York: Bloomsbury, 2013).

James, Robert Rhodes, *Winston S. Churchill: The Complete Speeches*, Vol. *VII, 1943-1949* (New York: Chelsea House, 1974).

Janis, Irving L., *Groupthink: Psychological Studies of Policy Decisions and Fiascoes* (Boston: Houghton Mifflin, 1983).

Jaher, Frederick Cople, *The Urban Establishment: Upper Strata in Boston, New York, Charleston, Chicago, and Los Angeles* (Urbana: University of Illinois Press, 1982).

Jeffares, A. Norman, and Martin Gray, *A Dictionary of Quotations* (New York: Barnes and Noble, 1997).

Jenkins, Jeffery A., and Charles Stewart III, *Fighting for the Speakership: The House and the Rise of Party Government* (Princeton, NJ: Princeton University Press, 2013).

Johnson, Alvin Page, *Franklin D. Roosevelt's Colonial Ancestors: Their Part in the Making of American History* (Boston: Lothrop, Lee & Shepard, 1933).

Johnson, Donald Bruce, *The Republican Party and Wendell Willkie* (Urbana: University of Illinois Press, 1960).

Johnson, Lyndon B., *The Vantage Point: Perspectives of the Presidency, 1963-1969* (New York: Holt, Rinehart and Winston, 1971).

Johnson, Robert David, and David Shreve, eds., *Lyndon B. Johnson: The Presidential Recordings* (New York: W. W. Norton, 2005) Vol. II.

Jonas, Manfred, *Isolationism in America, 1935-1941* (Ithaca, NY: Cornell University Press, 1966).

Jones, Charles O., *Every Second Year: Congressional Behavior and the Two Year Term* (Washington, DC: The Brookings Institution, 1967).

Jones, Robert Hudson, *The Roads to Russia: United States Lend-Lease to the Soviet Union* (Norman: University of Oklahoma Press, 1969).

Jordan, David M., *FDR, Dewey, and the Election of 1944* (Bloomington: Indiana University Press, 2011).

Josephson, Matthew, and Hannah, *Al Smith: Hero of the Cities: A Political Portrait Drawing on the Papers of Frances Perkins* (Boston: Houghton Mifflin Co., 1969).

Josephy, Alvin M. Jr., *On the Hill: A History of the American Congress* (New York: Simon & Schuster, 1979).

Journal of the Constitutional Convention of the Commonwealth of Massachusetts, 1917 (Boston: Wright & Potter, 1917).

Journals of the [Massachusetts] House of Representatives (Boston: Massachusetts Great and General Court, 1921–23).

Journals of the [Massachusetts] Senate (Boston: Massachusetts Great and General Court, 1923–28).

Juravich, Tom, William F. Hartford, and James H. Green, *Commonwealth of Toil: Chapters in the History of Massachusetts Workers and Their Unions* (Amherst: University of Massachusetts Press, 1996).

Kaiser, David E., *Postmortem: New Evidence in the Case of Sacco and Vanzetti* (Amherst: University of Massachusetts Press, 1985).

Kalk, Bruce H., *The Origins of the Southern Strategy. Two Party Competition in South Carolina, 1950-1972 (*Lanham, MD: Lexington Books, 2001).

Kallina, Edmund F. Jr., *Kennedy v. Nixon: The Presidential Election of 1960* (Gainesville, FL: University of Florida Press, 2010).

Kaplan, Marshall, and Peggy L. Cuciti, eds., *The Great Society and Its Legacy* (Durham, NC: Duke University Press, 1986).

Karabell, Zachary, *The Last Campaign: How Harry Truman Won the 1948 Election* (New York: Knopf, 2000).

Katula, Richard A., *The Eloquence of Edward Everett: America's Greatest Orator* (New York: Peter Lang, 2010).

Katznelson, Ira, *When Affirmative Action Was White: An Untold History of Racial Inequality in Twentieth-Century America* (New York: W. W. Norton, 2006).

Katznelson, Ira, *Fear Itself: The New Deal and the Origins of Our Time* (New York: Livewright, 2013).

Keegan, Gerald ed. by James J. Mangan, *Famine Diary: Journey to a New World* (Dublin: Wolfhound Press, 1991).

Keller, Frances Richardson, *Fictions of U.S. History: A Theory & Four Illustrations* (Bloomington, IN: Indiana University Press, 2002).

Keller, Morton, and Phyllis Keller, *Harvard's Jews, Women, and Blacks: Making Harvard Modern* (New York: Oxford University Press, 2001).

Kempe, Frederick, *Berlin 1961: Kennedy, Khrushchev, and the Most Dangerous Place on Earth* (New York: G. P. Putnam's Sons, 2011).

Kenneally, James J., *A Compassionate Conservative: A Political Biography of Joseph W. Martin, Jr., Member of the U.S. House of Representatives* (Lanham, MD: Lexington Books, 2003).

Kennedy, Ambrose, *American Orator, Bourke Cockran: His Life and Politics* (Boston: Humphries, 1948).

Kennedy, David M., *Freedom from Fear: The American People in Depression and War, 1929-1956* (New York: Oxford University Press, 2005).

Kennedy, Edward M., *True Compass: A Memoir* (New York: Twelve, 2009).

Kennedy Jacqueline, and Michael R. Beschloss, eds., *Jacqueline Kennedy: Historic Conversations on Life with John F. Kennedy* (New York: Hyperion, 2011).

Kennedy, John F., *Public Papers of the Presidents of the United States, 1963* (Washington, DC: U.S. Government Printing Office, 1964).

Kennedy, John F., *The Kennedy Presidential Press Conferences* (New York: Coleman Enterprises, 1978).

Kennedy, John F., *To Turn the Tide: A Selection from President Kennedy's Public Statements* (New York: Harper, 1962).

Kennedy, John F., *Why England Slept* (New York: Wilfred Funk, 1940).

Kennedy, Joseph P., *I'm for Roosevelt* (New York: Reynal & Hitchcock, 1936).

Kennedy, Lawrence W., *Planning the City Upon a Hill: Boston Since 1630* (Amherst: University of Massachusetts Press, 1992).

Kennedy, Robert F., *Robert Kennedy: In His Own Words, the Unpublished Recollections of the Kennedy Years* (Toronto: Bantam Books, 1988).

Kennedy, Robert F., *Thirteen Days: A Memoir of the Cuban Missile Crisis* (New York: W. W. Norton, 1969).

Kennedy, Rose Fitzgerald, *Times to Remember* (Garden City, NY: Doubleday, 1974).

Kennon, Donald R., *The Speakers of the U.S. House of Representatives: A Bibliography* (Baltimore: The Johns Hopkins University Press, 1986).

Kennon, Donald R., and Rebecca M. Rogers, *The Committee on Ways and Means: A Bicentennial History, 1789-1989* (Washington, DC: U.S. House of Representatives, 1989).

Kenny, Kevin, *The American Irish: A History* (New York: Longman, 2000).

Kessel, John H., George F. Cole, and Robert G. Seddig, eds., *Micropolitics: Individual and Group Level Concepts* (New York: Holt, Rinehart and Winston, Inc., 1970).

Kessler, Ronald, *The Sins of the Father: Joseph P. Kennedy and the Dynasty He Founded* (New York: Warner Books, 1996).

Key, V. O. Jr. and Alexander Heard, *Southern Politics in State and Nation* (New York: Knopf, 1949).

Keyes, Edward, *Cocoanut Grove* (New York: Atheneum, 1984).

Keyes, Francis Parkinson, *Capital Kaleidoscope: The Story of a Washington Hostess* (New York: Harper and Brothers, 1937).

Kimball, Warren, *Churchill and Roosevelt: The Complete Correspondence* (Princeton, NJ: Princeton University Press, 1984).

Kimball, Warren, *Forged in War: Roosevelt, Churchill, and the Second World War* (New York: William Morrow).

Kimball, Warren, *The Most Unsordid Act: Lend-Lease, 1939-1941* (Baltimore: The Johns Hopkins Press, 1969).

King, Martin Luther, Jr., *Stride Toward Freedom: The Montgomery Story* (New York: Ballantine Books, 1958).

Klein, Maury, *Rainbow's End: The Crash of 1929* (New York: Oxford University Press, 2001).

Klingaman, William K., *1929: The Year of the Great Crash* (New York: Harper & Row, 1989).

Kohn, Hans, *American Nationalism: An Interpretive Essay* (New York: Collier Books, 1961).

Kornitzer, Bela, *American Fathers and Sons* (New York: Hermitage House, 1952).

Kosoff, David, *Joseph P. Kennedy: A Life and Times* (Englewood Cliffs, NJ: Prentice-Hall, 1974).

Krock Arthur, *Memoirs; Sixty Years on the Firing Line* (New York: Funk & Wagnalls, 1968).

Kunetka, James, *The General and the Genius: Groves and Oppenheimer—The Unlikely Partnership that Built the Atom Bomb* (Washington, DC: Regnery History, 2015).

Lader, Lawrence, *The Bold Brahmins: New England's War against Slavery* (New York: E. P. Dutton, 1961).

Lapham, Lewis J., *Party Leadership and the House Committee on Rules* (New York: Garland, 1988).

Lapomarda, Vincent A., *The Boston Mayor Who Became Truman's Secretary of Labor: Maurice J. Tobin and the Democratic Party* (Bern: Peter Lang Publishing, 1995).

Lash, Joseph P., *Dealers and Dreamers: A New Look at the New Deal* (New York: Doubleday, 1988).

Lash, Joseph P., *From the Diaries of Felix Frankfurter* (New York: W. W. Norton, 1975).

Lash, Joseph P., *Roosevelt and Churchill, 1939-1945: The Partnership that Saved the West* (New York: W. W. Norton, 1976).

Lasky, Victor, *J.F.K.: The Man and the Myth* (New York: Macmillan, 1963).

Lasse, William, *Benjamin V. Cohen, Architect of the New Deal* (New Haven, CT: A Century Foundation Book, Yale University Press, 2002).

Latham, Earl, *The Communist Conspiracy in Washington from the New Deal to McCarthy* (Cambridge, MA: Harvard University Press, 1966).

Latham, Edward C., *Meet Calvin Coolidge: The Man Behind the Myth* (Brattleboro, VT: Stephen Greene Press, 1960).

Lawrence F. O'Brien, *No Final Victories: A Life in Politics from John F. Kennedy to Watergate* (New York: Ballantine Books, 1974).

Laxton, Edward, *The Famine Ships: The Irish Exodus to America, 1846-51* (London: Bloomsbury, 1996).

Leamer, Lawrence, The *Kennedy Men 1901-1963* (New York: William Morrow, 2001).

Leighton, Isabel, ed., *The Aspirin Age, 1919-1941* (New York: American Ltd., 1949).

Lehr, Dick, and Gerard O'Neill, *Black Mass: The Irish Mob, the FBI and a Devil's Deal* (New York: Public Affairs, 2000).

Lehr, Dick, and Gerard O'Neill, *Whitey: The Life of America's Most Notorious Mob Boss* (New York: Broadway Books, 2013).

Levin, Murray B., *Kennedy Campaigning: The System and the Style as Practiced by Senator Edward Kennedy* (Boston: Beacon Press, 1966).

Levin, Murray B. with George Blackwood, *The Compleat Politician: Political Strategy in Massachusetts* (Indianapolis: Bobbs-Merrill, 1962).

Levine, Edward M., *The Irish and Irish Politicians: A Study of Cultural and Social Alienation* (Notre Dame, IN: University of Notre Dame Press, 1966).

Levine, Hillel, and Lawrence Harmon, *The Death of An American Jewish Community: A Tragedy of Good Intentions* (New York: The Free Press, 1992).

Lewis, Anthony, *Gideon's Trumpet* (New York: Alfred A. Knopf, 1964).

Lipset, Seymour Martin, and Earl Rabb, *The Politics of Unreason: Right Wing Extremism in America, 1790-1970* (New York: Harper & Row, 1970).

Leyburn, James G., *The Scotch-Irish: A Social History* (Chapel Hill: University of North Carolina Press, 1962).

Lichtman, Alan J., *Prejudice and the Old Politics: The Presidential Election of 1928* (Chapel Hill: University of North Carolina Press, 1979).

Lieberman, Robert C., *Shifting the Color Line: Race and the American Welfare State* (Cambridge, MA: Harvard University Press, 1995).

Lincoln, Evelyn, *Kennedy and Johnson* (New York: Holt, Reinhart and Winston, 1968).

Lindbergh, Charles A., *The Wartime Journals of Charles A. Lindbergh* (New York: Harcourt Brace Jovanovich, 1970), September 29, 1938, p. 79.

Litt, Edgar, *The Political Cultures of Massachusetts* (Cambridge, MA:. MIT Press, 1965).

Loewenheim, Francis L., Harold D. Langley, and Manfred Jonas, *Roosevelt and Churchill: Their Secret Wartime Correspondence* (New York: Saturday Review Press, 1975).

Lockard, Duane, *New England State Politics* (Princeton, NJ: Princeton University Press, 1959).

Longworth, Alice Roosevelt, *Crowded Hours: Reminiscences of Alice Roosevelt Longworth* (New York: Arno Press, 1980).

Lubell, Samuel, *The Future of American Politics*, 3rd rev. edn (New York: Harper Colophon, 1965).

Lubell, Samuel, *The Hidden Crisis in American Politics* (New York: W. W. Norton, 1971).

Lukas, J. Anthony, *Common Ground: A Turbulent Decade in the Lives of Three American Families* (New York: Knopf, 1985).

Lukas, Robert C., *Eagles East: The Army Air Forces and the Soviet Union, 1941-1945* (Tallahassee: Florida State University Press, 1970).

Lupo, Alan, *Liberty's Chosen Home: The Politics of Violence in Boston*, rev. edn (Boston: Beacon Press, 1988).

Luthin, Reinhard H., *American Demagogues: Twentieth Century* (Boston: The Beacon Press, 1954).

Lyons, Louis M., *Newspaper Story: One Hundred Years of the Boston Globe* (Cambridge, MA: Belknap Press of Harvard University Press, 1971).

Maccoby, Eleanor E., Theodore M. Newcomb, and Eugene L. Hartley, eds., *Readings in Social Psychology* (New York: Holt, Rinehart, and Winston, 1958).

MacCormack, John R., *Highland Heritage & Freedom's Quest: Three Centuries of MacCormacks in Ireland, Scotland, Prince Edward Island and West Lake Ainslie, Nova Scotia* (Halifax, Nova Scotia, Canada: Kinloch Books, 1998).

MacKay, Kenneth Campbell, *The Progressive Movement of 1924* (New York: Columbia University Press, 1947).

MacKay, W. Donald, *Flight from Famine: The Coming of the Irish to Canada* (Toronto: McClelland and Stewart, 1990).

Mackie, J. D., *A History of Scotland*, 2nd rev. edn, by Bruce Lenman and Geoffrey Parker (London: Penguin Books. 1978).

MacManus, Seamus, *The Story of the Irish Race: A Popular History of Ireland* (Old Greenwich, CT: Devin-Adair, 1966).

MacNeil, Neil, *Forge of Democracy: The House of Representatives* (New York: David McKay, 1963).

Maddox, Robert James, *Hiroshima in History: The Myths of Revisionism* (Columbia: University of Missouri Press, 2007).

Maddox, Robert James, *Weapons for Victory: The Hiroshima Decision Fifty Years Later* (Columbia: University of Missouri Press, 2004).

Magdol, Edward, *The Antislavery Rank and File: A Social History of the Abolitionist's Constituency* (Westport, CT: Greenwood Press, 1986).

Mahaffie, Charles D. Jr., *A Land of Discord Always: Acadia from the Beginning to the Expulsion of Its People, 1604-1755* (Camden, ME: Down East Books, 1995).

Maier, Thomas, *The Kennedys: America's Emerald Kings* (New York: Basic Books, 2003).

Malloy, Ione, *"Southie Won't Go:" A Teacher's Diary of the Desegregation of South Boston High School* (Urbana: University of Illinois Press, 1986).

Malloy, Sean L., *Atomic Tragedy: Henry L. Stimson and the Decision to Use the Atomic Bomb Against Japan* (Ithaca, NY: Cornell University Press, 2008).

Manchester, William, *The Death of a President, November 20-November 25, 1963* (New York: Harper & Row, 1967).

Manley, John F., *The Politics of Finance: The House Committee on Ways and Means* (Boston: Little, Brown & Co., 1970).

Mann, Arthur, *Yankee Reformers in the Urban Age: Social Reform in Boston, 1880-1900* (New York: Harper Torchbooks edition, 1966).

Mann, Robert, *Daisy Petals and Mushroom Clouds: LBJ, Barry Goldwater, and the Ad That Changed American Politics* (Baton Rouge: Louisiana State University Press, 2011).

Mann, Robert, *The Walls of Jericho: Lyndon Johnson, Hubert Humphrey, Richard Russell, and the Struggle for Civil Rights* (New York: Harcourt, Brace & Co., 1996).

Mann, Thomas E., *Unsafe at Any Margin: Interpreting Congressional Elections* (Washington, DC: American Enterprise Institute for Policy Research, 1978).

Manners, William, *TR and Will: The Friendship That Split the Republican Party* (New York: Harcourt, Brace & World, 1969).

Manning, Christopher, *William L. Dawson and the Limits of Black Electoral Leadership* (Dekalb: Northern Illinois Press, 2009).

Marcus, Sheldon, *Father Coughlin: The Tumultuous Life of the Priest: Charles Coughlin, the Father of Hate Radio* (New York: The Free Press, 1996).

Marquis, Albert Nelson, *Who's Who in New England* (Chicago: A. N. Marquis, 1938).

Martel, Leon, *Lend-Lease, Loans, and the Coming of the Cold War; A Study of the Implementation of Foreign Policy* (Boulder, CO: Westview, 1979).

Martin, Joseph W., Jr. as told to Robert J. Donovan, *My First Fifty Years in Politics* (New York: McGraw-Hill, 1960).

Martin, Ralph G., *A Hero for Our Time: An Intimate Story of the Kennedy Years* (New York: Macmillan, 1983).

Martin, Ralph G., *Ballots & Bandwagons* (Chicago: Rand, McNally, 1964).

Martin, Ralph G., *Cissy: The Extraordinary Life of Eleanor Medill Patterson* (New York: Simon & Schuster, 1979).

Martin, Ralph G., *Front Runner, Dark Horse* (Garden City, NY: Doubleday, 1960).

Martin, Ralph, *Jennie: The Life of the American Beauty Who Became the Toast—and Scandal—of Two Continents, Ruled an Age and Raised a Son-Winston Churchill-Who Shaped History* (Englewood Cliffs, NJ: Prentice-Hall, 1969).

Martin, Ralph G., *Seeds of Destruction: Joe Kennedy and His Sons* (New York: G. P. Putnam's Sons, 1995).

Martis, Kenneth, ed., with Ruthe Anderson Rowles, *The Historical Atlas of the United States Congressional Districts, 1789-1983* (New York: Free Press; London: Collier Macmillan, 1982).

Matsunaga, Spark M., and Ping Chen, *Rulemakers of the House* (Urbana: University of Illinois Press, 1976).

Mathews, Christopher, *Kennedy & Nixon: The Rivalry that Shaped Postwar America* (New York, NY: Simon & Schuster, 1996).

Matthews, Christopher, *Jack Kennedy: Elusive Hero* (New York: Simon & Schuster, 2011).

Matthews, Chris, *Tip and the Gipper: When Politics Worked* (New York: Simon & Schuster, 2013).

Matthiesen, F. O., *American Renaissance: Art and Expression in the Era of Emerson and Whitman* (London and New York: Oxford University Press, 1941).

May, Ernest R., and Philip D. Zelikow, *The Kennedy Tapes: Inside the White House During the Cuban Missile Crisis* (Cambridge, MA: The Belknap Press of Harvard University Press, 1997).

May, Gary, *Bending Toward Justice: The Voting Rights Act and the Transformation of American Democracy* (New York: Basic Books, 2013).

Mayhew, David R., *Divided We Govern: Party Control, Lawmaking and Investigations, 1946-1990* (New Haven, CT: Yale University Press, 1991).

Mayhew, David R., *Congress: The Electoral Connection* (New Haven, CT: Yale University Press, 1974).

Mayors of Boston: An Illustrated Epitome of Who the Mayors Have Been and What They Have Done (Boston: State Street Trust Company, 1914).

Mazo, Earl, *Richard Nixon: A Political & Personal Portrait* (New York: Harper, 1958).

McCoy, Donald R., and Richard T. Ruetten, *Quest and Response: Minority Rights and the Truman Administration* (Lawrence: University Press of Kansas, 1973).

McCullough, David M., *Truman* (New York: Simon & Schuster, 1995).

McDaniel, Rodger, *Dying for Joe McCarthy's Sins: The Suicide of Wyoming Senator Lester Hunt* (Cockermouth: WordsWorth, 2013).

McGinniss, Joe, *The Last Brother* (New York: Simon & Schuster, 1993).

McGuerin, James, *Bourke Cockran, a Free Lance in American Politics* (New York: Scribner's, 1948).

McJimsey, George T., *Harry Hopkins: Ally of the Poor and Defender of Democracy* (Cambridge, MA: Harvard University Press, 1987).

McKean, David, *Peddling Influence: Thomas "Tommy the Cork" Corcoran and the Birth of Modern Lobbying* (Hanover, NH: Steerforth Press, 2004).

Meacham, Jon, *Franklin and Winston: An Intimate Portrait of an Epic Friendship* (New York: Random House, 2003).

Mellichamp, Josephine, *Senators from Georgia* (Huntsville, AL: The Strode Publishers Inc., 1976).

Meredith, James H., *Three Years in Mississippi* (Bloomington: Indiana University Press, 1966).

Merrill, Milton R., *Reed Smoot: Apostle in Politics* (Logan: Utah State Press, 1990).

Michie, Allan A., and Frank Ryhlick, *Dixie Demagogues* (New York: Vanguard Press, 1939).

Miles, Donna, *Battle of the Bulge Remembered 60 Years Later* (Arlington, VA: United States Department of Defense, 2004).

Milkis, Sidney M., and Jerome M. Mileur, eds., *The Great Society and the High Tide of Liberalism* (Amherst: University of Massachusetts Press, 2005).

Milkis, Sidney M., *The President and the Parties: The Transformation of the American Party System Since the New Deal* (New York: Oxford University Press, 1993).

Miller, Kerby A., *Emigrants and Exiles: Ireland and the Irish Exodus to North America* (New York: Oxford University Press, 1985).

Miller, Merle, *Plain Speaking: An Oral Biography of Harry S. Truman* (New York: Berkley Books, 1974).

Miller, Neil, *Banned in Boston: The Watch and Ward Society's Crusade against Books, Burlesque, and the Social Evil* (Boston: Beacon Press, 2010).

Miller, Perry, *Errand into the Wilderness* (Cambridge, MA: Belknap Press of Harvard University Press, 1956).

Miller, Perry, *Orthodoxy in Massachusetts, 1630-1650; A Genetic Study* (Cambridge, MA: Harvard University Press, 1933).

Miller, William L., *Two Americans: Truman, Eisenhower, and a Dangerous World* (New York: Alfred A. Knopf, 2012).

Miller, William, and Frances Spatz Leighton, *Fishbait* (Englewood Cliffs, NJ: Prentice-Hall, 1977).

Miscamble, Wilson D., *The Most Controversial Decision: Truman, the Atomic Bombs, and the Defeat of Japan* (New York: Cambridge University Press, 2011).

Mitgang, Herbert, *The Man Who Rode the Tiger: The Life and Times of Samuel Seabury* (Philadelphia: J. B. Lippincott, 1963).

Moe, Richard, *Roosevelt's Second Act: The Election of 1940 and the Politics of War* (New York: Oxford University Press, 2013).

Mooney, Booth, *Mr. Speaker: Four Men Who Shaped the United States House of Representatives* (Chicago: Follett, 1964).

Mooney, Booth, *Roosevelt and Rayburn: A Political Partnership* (Philadelphia: J. B. Lippincott, 1971).

Moore, Leonard J., *Citizen Klansmen: The Ku Klux Klan in Indiana, 1921-1928* (Chapel Hill: University of North Carolina Press, 1991).

Moore, William H., *The Kefauver Committee and the Politics of Crime, 1950-1952* (Columbia: University of Missouri Press, 1974).

Morgan, Anne H., *Robert S. Kerr: The Senate Years* (Norman, OK: University of Oklahoma Press, 1977).

Morgan, Edmund S., *The Puritan Family: Religion and Domestic Relationships in the 17th Century New England* (New York: Harper & Row, 1944).

Morris, Edmund, *The Rise of Theodore Roosevelt* (New York: Coward, McCann & Geoghegan, 1979).

Morrow, Lance, *The Best Years of Their Lives: Kennedy, Johnson, and Nixon in 1948: Learning the Secrets of Power* (New York: Basic Books, 2005).

Mott, Frank Luther, *Golden Multitudes: The Story of Best Sellers in the United States* (New York: Macmillan, 1947).

Moynihan, Daniel P., *Secrecy: The American Experience* (New Haven, CT: Yale University Press, 1998).

Mueller, John E., *War, Presidents, and Public Opinion* (New York: John Wiley, 1973).

Mulkern, John R., *The Know-Nothing Party in Massachusetts: The Rise and Fall of a People's Movement* (Boston: Northeastern University Press, 1990).

Munger, Frank J., and Richard F. Fenno, Jr., *National Politics in Federal Aid to Education* (Syracuse, NY: Syracuse University Press, 1962).

Munson, Richard, *The Cardinals of Capitol Hill: The Men and Women Who Control Government Spending* (New York: Grove Press, 1993).

Murphy, Bruce Allen, *Wild Bill: The Legend and Life of William O. Douglas* (New York: Random House, 2003).

Murphy, Reg, and Hal Gulliver, *The Southern Strategy* (New York: Scribner's, 1971).

Murray, Robert K., *Red Scare: A Study in National Hysteria* (Minneapolis: University of Minnesota Press, 1955).

Murray, Robert K., *The 103rd Ballot: Democrats and the Disaster in Madison Square Garden* (New York: Harper & Row, 1976).

Nasaw, David, *The Patriarch: The Remarkable Life and Turbulent Times of Joseph P. Kennedy* (New York: Penguin Books, 2012).

Neal, Steve, *Dark Horse: A Biography of Wendell Willkie* (Garden City, NY: Doubleday, 1984).

Neal, Steve, *Happy Days Are Here Again: The 1932 Democratic Convention, the Emergence of FDR- and How America Was Changed Forever* (New York: HarperCollins, 2004).

Nelson, Garrison, *Committees in the U.S. Congress, 1947-1992: Committee Jurisdictions and Member Rosters* (Washington, DC: CQ Press, 1993).

Nelson, Garrison, *Pathways to the U.S. Supreme Court: From the Arena to the Monastery* (New York: Palgrave Macmillan, 2013).

Nelson, Garrison, Clark H. Bensen, and Mary T. Mitchell, *Committees in the United States Congress, 1947-1992,* Volume 2, *Committee Histories and Member Assignments* (Washington, DC: CQ Press, 1993).

Nelson, Garrison, and Charles Stewart III, *Committees in the U.S. Congress, 1993-2010* (Washington, DC: CQ Press, 2010).

Newton, Michael, *The Ku Klux Klan in Mississippi: A History* (Jefferson, NC: McFarland, 2010).

Nixon, Richard, *RN: The Memoirs of Richard Nixon* (New York: Touchstone, 1990).

Noble, G. Bernard, *Christian A. Herter* (New York: Cooper Square, 1970).

Nordin, Dennis S., *The New Deal's Black Congressman: A Life of Arthur Wergs Mitchell* (Columbia: University of Missouri Press, 1997).

Novak, Robert D., *The Prince of Darkness: 50 Years of Reporting in Washington* (New York: Crown Forum, 2007).

Novak, Robert D., and Rowland Evans, *Lyndon B. Johnson: The Exercise of Power* (New York: New American Library, 1966).

O'Brien, Larry, *No Final Victories: A Life in Politics from John F. Kennedy to Watergate* (New York: Ballantine Books, 1975).

O'Brien, Michael, *John F. Kennedy: A Biography* (New York: Thomas Dunne Books/St. Martin's Press, 2005).

O'Connor, Edwin, *The Last Hurrah* (Boston: Little, Brown & Co., 1956).

O'Connor, Thomas H., *Lords of the Loom, the Cotton Whigs and the Coming of the Civil War* (New York: Scribner's, 1968).

O'Connor, Thomas H., *The Athens of America: Boston, 1825-1845* (Amherst: University of Massachusetts Press, 2006).

O'Connor, Thomas H., *South Boston, My Home Town: The History of an Ethnic Neighborhood,* 2nd edn (Boston: Northeastern University Press, 1994).

O' Connor, Thomas H., *The Boston Irish: A Political History* (Boston: Northeastern University Press, 1995).

O'Donnell, Helen, *A Common Good: The Friendship of Robert F. Kennedy and Kenneth P. O'Donnell* (New York: William Morrow and Company, Inc., 1998).

O'Donnell, Kenneth P., and David F. Powers with Joe McCarthy, *Johnny, We Hardly Knew Ye: Memories of John Fitzgerald Kennedy* (Boston: Little, Brown, 1970).

Ogden, August Raymond, *The Dies Committee: A Study of the Special House Committee for the Investigation of Un-American Activities, 1938-1944* (Washington, DC: Catholic University of America, 1945).

Okrent, Daniel, *Last Call: The Rise and Fall of Prohibition* (New York: Scribner's, 2010).

O'Leary, Louis, *Memorial Volume, 1772-1922: The Arrival of the First Scottish Catholic Emigrants in Prince Edward Island and After* (Summerside, P.E.I.: Journal Publishing Co., 1922).

Olson, Lynne, *Those Angry Days: Roosevelt, Lindbergh, and America's Fight Over World War II, 1939-1941* (New York: Random House, 2013).

O'Neill, Gerard, *Rogues and Redeemers: When Politics was King in Irish Boston* (New York: Crown, 2012).

O'Neill, Gerard, and Dick Lehr, *The Underboss: The Rise and Fall of a Mafia Family* (New York: St. Martin's Press, 1989).

O'Neill, Tip with Gary Hymel, *All Politics is Local and Other Rules of the Game* (New York: Times Books, 1994).

O'Neill, Tip with William Novak, *Man of the House: The Life and Political Memoirs of Speaker Tip O'Neill* (New York: Random House, 1987).

O'Reilly, Kenneth, *Nixon's Piano: Presidents and Racial Politics from Washington to Clinton* (New York: The Free Press, 1995).

Ornstein, Norman J., ed,. *Congress in Change: Evolution and Reform* (New York: Praeger, 1975).

Ornstein, Norman J., Thomas E. Mann, and Michael J. Malbin, eds., *Vital Statistics on Congress, 1987-1988* (Washington, DC: CQ Press, 1987).

Ornstein, Norman J,, Thomas E. Mann, and Michael J. Malbin, eds., *Vital Statistics on Congress, 2008* (Washington, DC: The Brookings Institution, CQ Press, 2008).

Oshinsky, David M., *A Conspiracy So Immense: The World of Joe McCarthy* (New York: The Free Press, 1983).

O'Sullivan, John, *From Voluntarism to Conscription: Congress and Selective Service, 1940-1945* (New York: Garland, 1982).

O'Toole, David, *Outing the Senator: Sex, Spies and Videotape* (Privately Published, 2005).

O'Toole, James M., *Militant and Triumphant: William Henry O'Connell and the Catholic Church in Boston, 1859-1944* (Notre Dame, IN: University of Notre Dame Press, 1992).

Palazzalo, Daniel J., *The Speaker and the Budget: Leadership in the Post-Reform House of Representatives* (Pittsburgh: University of Pittsburgh Press, 1992).

Palmer, James E., *Carter Glass: Unreconstructed Rebel* (Roanoke, VA: Institute of American Biography, 1938).

Pappé, Ilan, *A History of Modern Palestine: One Land, Two Peoples* (New York: Cambridge University Press, 2004).

Parker, Robert with Richard Rashke, *Capitol Hill in Black and White* (New York: Dodd, Mead, 1986).

Parmet, Herbert S., *Jack: The Struggles of John F. Kennedy* (New York: Doubleday Books, 1983).

Parmet, Herbert S., *JFK: The Presidency of John F. Kennedy* (New York: The Dial Press, 1983).

Parmet, Herbert S., *The Democrats: The Years After FDR* (New York: Oxford University Press, 1976).

Parmet, Herbert S., and Marie B. Hecht, *Never Again: A President Runs for a Third Term* (New York: Macmillan, 1968).

Parris, Judith H., *The Convention Problem* (Washington, DC: The Brookings Institution, 1972).

Parrish, Michael E., *Securities Regulation and the New Deal* (New Haven, CT: Yale University Press, 1970).

Parrish, Thomas, *Roosevelt and Marshall: Partners in Politics and War* (New York: William Morrow, 1989).

Patterson, James T., *Congressional Conservatism and the New Deal: The Growth of the Conservative Coalition in Congress, 1933-1939* (Knoxville: University of Kentucky Press, 1967).

Patterson, James T., *The Eve of Destruction: How 1965 Transformed America* (New York: Basic Books, 2012).

Peabody, Robert L., ed., *Education of a Congressman: The Newsletters of Morris K. Udall* (Indianapolis: Bobbs-Merrill, 1972).

Peabody, Robert L., *Leadership in Congress: Stability, Succession, and Change* (Boston: Little, Brown, 1967).

Peabody, Robert L., and Nelson W. Polsby, eds., *New Perspectives on the House of Representatives* (Chicago: Rand McNally, 1963).

Peabody, Robert L., and Nelson W. Polsby, eds., *New Perspectives on the House of Representatives*, 4th ed. (Baltimore, MD: Johns Hopkins University Press, 1992).

Pearson, Drew, *Drew Pearson's Diaries, 1949-1959* (New York: Holt, Rinehart and Winston, 1974).

Pearson, Drew, and Robert S. Allen, *Washington Merry-go-Round* (New York: Horace Liveright, 1931).

Pearson, Drew, and Jack Anderson, *The Case Against Congress: A Compelling Indictment of Corruption on Capitol Hill* (New York: Simon & Schuster, 1968).

Peirce, Neil R., *New England States: People, Politics, and Power in the Six New England States* (New York: Norton, 1976).

Pegram, Thomas R., *One Hundred Percent American: The Rebirth and Decline of the Ku Klux Klan in the 1920s* (Chicago: Ivan R. Dee, 2011).

Perret, Geoffrey, *Jack: A Life Like No Other* (New York: Random House, 2001).

Perry, Barbara A., *Rose Kennedy: The Life and Times of a Political Matriarch* (New York: W. W. Norton, 2013).

Pessen, Edward, *The Log Cabin Myth: The Social Backgrounds of the Presidents* (New Haven, CT: Yale University Press, 1984).

Peters, Ronald M., *The American Speakership: The Office in Historical Perspective*, 2nd edn, Baltimore, MD: The Johns Hopkins University Press, 1997).

Petersen, Svend, *A Statistical History of the American Presidential Elections* (New York: Frederick Ungar, 1963).

Pietrusza, David, *1920: The Year of the Six Presidents* (New York: Carroll and Graf, 2007).

Pietrusza, David, *1960 LBJ vs. JFK vs. Nixon: The Epic Campaign That Forged Three Presidencies* (New York: Union Square, 2008).

Poen, Monte M., *Letters Home by Harry Truman* (New York: G.P. Putnam's Sons, 1984).

Polsby, Nelson W., *How Congress Evolves: Social Bases of Institutional Change* (New York: Oxford University Press, 2004).

Poole, Keith T., and Howard Rosenthal, *Congress: A Political Economic History of Roll Call Voting* (New York: Oxford University Press, 1997).

Poole, Mary, The *Segregated Origins of Social Security: African Americans and the Welfare State* (Chapel Hill: University of North Carolina Press, 2006).

Porter, David L., *Congress and the Waning of the New Deal* (Port Washington, NY: Kennikat Press, 1979).

Porter, David L., *The Seventy-Sixth Congress and World War II, 1939-1940* (Columbia: University of Missouri Press, 1979).

Porter, Kirk H,. and Donald B., Johnson, eds., *National Party Platforms, 1840-1968* (Urbana: University of Illinois Press, 1970).

Porter, Noah, *Evangeline: The Place, the Story, and the Poem* (New York: Cassell, Petter, Galpin, 1892).

Powell, Adam Clayton Jr., *Adam by Adam: The Autobiography of Adam Clayton Powell, Jr.* (New York: Dial Press, 1971).

Pratico, Dominick, *Eisenhower and Social Security: The Origins of the Disability Program* (Bloomington, IN: iUniverse, 2001).

Prebble, John, *The Highland Clearances* (London: Penguin Books, 1963).

President's Commission on Higher Education, *Higher Education for Democracy: A Report of the President's Commission on Higher Education. Vol. 1, Establishing the Goals* (New York: Harper & Brothers, 1947).

Pressman, Jeffrey, *House vs. Senate: Conflict in the Appropriations Process* (New Haven, CT: Yale University Press, 1966).

Purdum, Todd S., *An Idea Whose Time Has Come: Two Presidents, Two Parties, and the Battle for the Civil Rights Act of 1964* (New York: Henry Holt/Picador, 2015).

Putnam, William Lowell, *A Yankee Image: The Life and Times of Roger Lowell Putnam* (West Kennebunk, ME: Published for the Lowell Observatory by Phoenix Publishers, 1991).

Rabb, T. K., *Enterprise and Empire: Merchant and Gentry Investment in the Expansion of England* (Cambridge, MA: Harvard University Press, 1967).

Reed, Christopher R., *The Chicago NAACP and the Rise of Black Professional Leadership, 1910-1966* (Bloomington: Indiana University Press, 1997).

Rees, Jim, *A Farewell to Famine* (Arklow, Ireland: Dee-Jay Publications, 1995).

Reeves, Andre E., *Congressional Committee Chairmen: Three Who Made an Evolution* (Lexington: University of Kentucky Press, 1993).

Reeves, Richard, *President Kennedy: Profile of Power* (New York: Simon & Schuster, 1993).

Reeves, Thomas C., *A Question of Character: A Life of John F. Kennedy* (New York: The Free Press, 1991).

Reeves, Thomas C., *The Life and Times of Joe McCarthy: A Political Biography* (New York: Stein and Day, 1982).

Remini, Robert, *The House: The History of the House of Representatives* (New York: Smithsonian Books in association with HarperCollins, 2006).

Renehan, Edward J., *The Kennedys at War, 1939-1945* (New York: Doubleday, 2002).

Rice, Madeleine H., *American Catholic Opinion in the Slavery Controversy* (New York: Columbia University Press, 1944).

Riddle, Donald H., *The Truman Committee: A Study in Congressional Responsibility* (New Brunswick, NJ: Rutgers University Press, 1964).

Riddlesperger, James W., Anthony Champagne, and Dan Williams, *The Wright Stuff: Reflections on People and Politics* (Forth Worth, TX: Texas Christian University Press, 2013).

Rieselbach, Leroy, *The Roots of Isolationism: Congressional Voting and Presidential Leadership in Foreign Policy* (Indianapolis, IN: Bobbs-Merrill, 1966).

Ripley, Randall B., *Party Leaders of the House of Representatives* (Washington, DC: Brookings Institution, 1967).

Ripley, Randall B., *Majority Party Leadership in Congress* (Boston: Little, Brown, 1969).

Risen, Clay, *The Bill of the Century: The Epic Battle for the Civil Rights Act* (New York: Bloomsbury Press, 2014).

Roberts, Gary Boyd, *Ancestors of American President* (Santa Clarita, CA: Carl Boyer, 3rd Publishing, 1995).

Robertson, David, *Sly and Able: A Political Biography of James F. Byrnes* (New York: W. W. Norton, 1994).

Robinson, James A., *The House Rules Committee* (Indianapolis: Bobbs-Merrill Co., 1963).

Rogers, Nicholas, *Halloween: from Pagan Ritual to Party Night* (New York: Oxford University Press, 2002).

Rohde, David W., *Parties and Leaders in the Postreform House* (Chicago: University of Chicago Press, 1991).

Romerstein, Herbert, and Eric Breindel, *The VENONA Secrets: Exposing Soviet Espionage and America's Traitors* (Washington, DC: Regnery Publishing, 2000).

Rorabaugh, W. R., *The Real Making of the President: Kennedy, Nixon and the 1960 Election* (Lawrence: University of Kansas Press, 2009).

Roseboom, Eugene H., *A History of Presidential Elections: From George Washington to Richard Nixon*, 3rd edn (New York: Macmillan, 1970).

Rosenberg, Jonathan, and Zachary Karabell, *Kennedy, Johnson, and the Quest for Justice: The Civil Rights Tapes* (New York: W. W. Norton, 2003).

Ross, Irwin, *The Loneliest Campaign: The Truman Victory of 1948* (New York: New American Library, 1968).

Rubin, Richard L., *Party Dynamics: The Democratic Coalition and the Politics of Change* (New York: Oxford University Press, 1976).

Rucker, Walter C, and James N. Upton, *Encyclopedia of American Race Riots: Greenwood Milestones in African-American History* (Westport, CT: Greenwood, 2007).

Rudin, James, *Cushing, Spellman, and O'Connor: The Surprising Story of How Three American Cardinals Transformed Catholic-Jewish Relations* (Grand Rapids, MI: W. B. Eerdmans, 2012).

Runyon, John H, Jennifer Verdini, and Sally S. Runyon, comps., *Source Book of American Presidential Campaigns and Election Statistics, 1948-1968* (New York: Frederick Ungar Publishing, 1971).

Rushton, William Faulkner, *The Cajuns: From Acadia to Louisiana* (New York: Farrar Straus Giroux, 1979).

Russell, Francis, *A City in Terror: 1919 The Boston Police Strike* (New York: Viking Press, 1975).

Russell, Francis, *A City in Terror: 1919 Calvin Coolidge and the Boston Police Strike* (Boston: Beacon Press, 2005).

Russell, Francis, *The Knave of Boston and Other Ambiguous Massachusetts Characters* (Boston: Quinlan Press, 1987).

Russell, Francis, *The President Makers: From Mark Hanna to Joseph P. Kennedy* (Boston: Little, Brown, 1976).

Russell, Francis, *Tragedy in Dedham: The Story of the Sacco-Vanzetti Case* (New York: McGraw-Hill, 1962).

Russell, Francis, *Tragedy in Dedham with Sacco and Vanzetti: The Case Resolved* (New York: Harper & Row, 1986).

Sabato, Larry J., *The Kennedy Half Century: The Presidency, Assassination, and Lasting Legacy of John F. Kennedy* (New York: Bloomsbury, 2013).

Sabato, Larry J., *Towards the Millennium: The Elections of 1996* (Boston: Allyn and Bacon, 1997).

Sachar, Abram L., *The Redemption of the Unwanted: From the Liberation of the Death Camps to the Founding of Israel* (New York: St Martin's Marek, 1983).

Safire, William, *Safire's New Political Dictionary: The Definitive Guide to the New Language of Politics* (New York: Random House, 1993).

Salter, J. T., *Public Men In and Out of Office* (Chapel Hill: University of North Carolina Press, 1946).

Saltonstall, Leverett as told to Edward Weeks, *Salty: Recollections of a Yankee in Politics* (Boston: The Boston Globe, 1976).

Searle, Charles F., *Minister of Relief: Harry Hopkins and the Depression* (Syracuse, NY: Syracuse University Press, 1963).

Scarry, John, *John McCormack: His Own Life Story* (New York: Vienna House, 1973).

Schantz, Harvey L., ed., *Politics in an Era of Divided Government: Elections and Governance in the Second Clinton Administration* (New York: Routledge, 2001).

Schattschneider, E. E., *Politics, Pressures and the Tariff: A Study of Free Private Enterprise in Pressure Politics, as Shown in the 1929-1930 Revision of the Tariff* (New York: Prentice-Hall, 1935).

Schecter, Jerrold, and Leona Schecter, *Sacred Secrets: How Soviet Intelligence Operations Changed American History* (Washington, DC: Brassey's, 2002).

Scheman, L. Ronald, *The Alliance for Progress: A Retrospective* (New York: Praeger, 1988).

Schlesinger, Arthur M., *A Thousand Days: John F. Kennedy in the White House* (Boston: Houghton, Mifflin, 1965).

Schlesinger, Arthur M., *Jacqueline Kennedy: Historic Conversations on Life with John F. Kennedy* (New York: Hyperion, 2011).

Schlesinger, Arthur M., *Robert Kennedy and His Times* (Boston: Houghton Mifflin, 1978).

Schlesinger, Arthur M., *The Crisis of the Old Order* (Boston: Houghton, Mifflin, 1967).

Schlesinger, Arthur M., *The Politics of Upheaval, 1935-1936, The Age of Roosevelt* (Boston: Houghton, Mifflin, 1960).

Schlesinger, Arthur M., and Roger Burns, *Congress Investigates: A Documented History, 1792-1974* (New York: Chelsea House, 1975).

Schneider, Judy, *Reorganization of the House of Representatives: Modern Reform Efforts* (Washington, DC: Congressional Research Service, 2003).

Schmidt, Hans, *Maverick Marine: General Smedley D. Butler and the Contradictions of American Military History* (Lexington: University of Kentucky Press, 1998).

Schneider, Mark R., *Joe Moakley's Journey: From South Boston to El Salvador* (Boston: Northeastern University Press, 2013).

Schooley, C. Herschel, *Missouri's Cannon in the House* (Marcelline, MO: Walsworth Publishing, 1977).

Schultz, Nancy Lusignan, *Fire and Roses: The Burning of the Charlestown Convent* (Boston: Northeastern University Press, 2002).

Schwartz, Bernard, *Super Chief: Earl Warren and His Supreme Court: A Judicial Biography* (New York: New York University Press, 1983).

Schwartz, Bernard B., and Robert B. Stevens, eds., *Income Security, Vol.3 of Statutory History of the United States* (New York: Chelsea House, 1970).

Schwarz, Jordan A., *The Interregnum of Despair: Hoover, Congress and the Depression* (Urbana: University of Illinois Press, 1970).

Schwarz, Ted, *Joseph P. Kennedy: The Mogul, the Mob, the Statesman, and the Making of an American Myth* (Hoboken, NJ: John Wiley & Sons, 2003).

Scott, Otto J., *The Secret Six: John Brown and the Abolitionist Movement* (New York: New York Times Books, 1979).

Searls, Hank, *The Lost Prince: Young Joe, The Forgotten Kennedy, The Story of the Oldest Brother* (New York: World, 1969).

Secretary of the Commonwealth, *Number of Assessed Polls, Registered Voters and Persons Who Voted in Each Voting Precinct at the State, City and Town Elections* (Boston: Multiple years).

Secretary of the Commonwealth, *Primaries and Elections 1928,* Boston, 1929.

Secretary of the Commonwealth, *Election Statistics: The Commonwealth of Massachusetts 1960* (Boston: Office of the Secretary of State, 1961).

Seebohm, Caroline, *No Regrets: The Life of Marietta Tree* (New York: Simon & Schuster, 1997).

Shannon, William V., *The American Irish* (New York: Macmillan, 1966).

Shapiro, Edward S., *A Time for Healing: America Jewry Since World War II* (Baltimore: Johns Hopkins University, 1992).

Shaw, John T., *JFK in the Senate: Pathway to the Presidency* (New York: Palgrave Macmillan, 2013).

Shelley, Mack C., *The Permanent Majority: The Conservative Coalition in Congress* (Tuscaloosa, AL: University of Alabama Press, 1983).

Sheppard, Burton D., *Rethinking Congressional Reform: The Reform Roots of the Special Interest Congress* (Cambridge, MA: Schenkman, 1985).

Shepsle, Kenneth A., *The Giant Jigsaw Puzzle: Democratic Committee Assignments in the Modern House* (Chicago: University of Chicago Press, 1978).

Sherwood, Robert E., *Roosevelt and Hopkins: An Intimate History* (New York: Harper & Bros., 1938).

Shesol, Jeff, *Mutual Contempt: Lyndon Johnson, Robert Kennedy, and the Feud that Defined a Decade* (New York: W. W. Norton, 1997).

Shogun, Robert, *Backlash: The Killing of the New Deal* (Chicago: Ivan R. Dee, 2006).

Siff, Ted, and Alan Weil, *Ruling Congress: How the House and Senate Rules Govern the Legislative Process* (New York: Grossman, 1975).

Sinclair, Barbara, *Legislators, Leaders, and Lawmaking: The U.S. House of Representatives in the Postreform Era* (Baltimore, MD: The Johns Hopkins University Press, 1995).

Silva, Ruth, *Presidential Succession* (Ann Arbor: University of Michigan Press, 1951).

Silva, Ruth B., *Rum, Romanism and Votes: 1928 Reexamined* (College Park: Pennsylvania State University Press, 1962).

Skidelsky, Robert, *John Maynard Keynes: Fighting for Britain, 1937-1946* (London: Macmillan, 2000).

Skipper, John C., *Showdown at the 1964 Democratic Convention: Lyndon Johnson, Mississippi and Civil Rights* (Jefferson, NC: MacFarland & Company, Inc. 2012).

Smith, Amanda, *Hostages to Fortune: The Private Letters of Joseph P. Kennedy* (New York: Viking, 2001).

Smith, Richard Norton, *Thomas E. Dewey and His Times* (New York: Simon & Schuster, 1982).

Smith, Arthur, *Tiger in the Senate: The Biography of Wayne Morse* (Garden City, NY: Doubleday, 1962).

Smith, Jean E., *Eisenhower in War and Peace* (New York: Random House, 2012).

Smith, Rixey, and Norman Beasley, *Carter Glass: A Biography* (New York: Longmans Green, 1939).

Smith, William H., *Speakers of the House of Representatives of the United States* (New York: AMS Press, reprint 1971).

Sobel, Robert, *Biographical Directory of the United States Executive Branch, 1774-1977* (Westport, CT: Greenwood Press, 1977).

Sobel, Robert, and John Raimo, eds., *Biographical Directory of the Governors of the United States, 1789-1978* (Westport, CT: Meckler Books, 1978).

Sokol, Jason, *All Eyes Are Upon Us: Race and Politics from Boston to Brooklyn* (New York: Basic Books, 2014).

Solomon, Barbara Miller, *Ancestors and Immigrants: A Changing New England Tradition* (New York: John Wiley & Sons, 1965).

Sorensen, Theodore C., *Counselor: A Life at the Edge of History* (New York: Harper, 2000).

Sorensen, Theodore C., *Kennedy: The Classic Biography* (New York: Bantam, 1966).

Special House Committee on Un-American Activities Authorized to Investigate Nazi Propaganda and Certain Other Propaganda Activities, *Investigation of Nazi and Other Propaganda*, House Report 74-153. February 15, 1935.

Spohn, Richard, and Charles McCollum, dirs., *The Revenue Committees: A Study of the House Ways and Means and Senate Finance Committees and the House and Senate Appropriations Committees* (New York: Grossman Publishers, 1975).

Stack, John F. Jr., *International Conflict in an American City: Boston's Irish, Italians, and Jews 1935-1944* (Westport, CT: Greenwood Press, 1979).

Stanley, Harold W., and Richard G. Niemi, eds., *Vital Statistics on American Politics,* 2nd edn (Washington, DC: Congressional Quarterly, 1990).

Stathis, Stephen J., *Landmark Legislation, 1774-2002: Major U.S. Acts and Treaties* (Washington, DC: CQ Press, 2003).

Steil, Benn, *The Battle of Bretton Woods: John Maynard Keynes, Harry Dexter White, and the Making of a New World Order* (Princeton: Princeton University Press, 2013).

Steinberg, Alfred, *Sam Johnson's Boy: A Close-Up of the President from Texas* (New York: Macmillan, 1968).

Steinberg, Alfred, *Sam Rayburn: A Biography* (New York: Hawthorn Books, 1975).

Steinberg, Alfred, *The Bosses* (New York: Macmillan, 1972).

Stern, Fritz, *The Politics of Cultural Despair: A Study in the Rise of the Germanic Ideology* (New York: Anchor Books, 1965).

Stern, Sheldon, *Averting "The Final Failure": John F. Kennedy and the Secret Cuban Missile Crisis Meetings* (Stanford, CA: Stanford University Press, 2003).

Stern, Sheldon, *The Cuban Missile Crisis in American Memory: Myths Versus Reality* (Stanford, CA: Stanford University Press, 2012).

Stern, Sheldon, *The Week the World Stood Still; Inside the Secret Cuban Missile Crisis* (Stanford, CA: Stanford University Press, 2005).

Stettinius, Edward R. Jr., *Lend-Lease: Weapon for Victory* (New York: Macmillan, 1944).

Stevens, Robert B., *Income Security, Vol. 3 of Statutory History of the United States* (New York: Chelsea House, 1970).

Stewart, Charles III, *Budget Reform Politics: The Design of the Appropriations Process 1865-1921* (Cambridge, UK: Cambridge University Press, 1989).

Stimson, Henry L., and McGeorge Bundy, *On Active Service in Peace and War* (New York: Harper & Bros., 1947).

Strahan, Randall, *The New Ways and Means: Reform and Change in a Congressional Committee* (Chapel Hill: University of North Carolina Press, 1990).

Story, Ronald, *The Forging of an Aristocracy: Harvard and the Boston Upper Class, 1800-1870* (Middletown, CT: Wesleyan University Press, 1980).

Stowe, Charles Edward, *Harriet Beecher Stowe: The Story of Her Life* (New York: Houghton, Mifflin, 1911).

Stowe, Harriet Beecher, *Uncle Tom's Cabin or Life Among the Lowly* (Boston: John P. Jewett & Co., 1852).

Sullivan, Alexander M., *New Ireland* (London: S. Low, Marston, Searle, and Rivington, 1878).

Sullivan, William C. with Bill Brown, *The Bureau: My Thirty Years in Hoover's FBI* (New York: Norton, 1979).

Summers, Anthony, *Official and Confidential: The Secret Life of J. Edgar Hoover* (New York: G. P. Putnam's Sons, 1993).

Sundquist, James L., *Politics and Policy: the Eisenhower, Kennedy, and Johnson Years* (Washington, DC: The Brookings Institution, 1968).

Sundquist, James L., *The Decline and Resurgence of Congress* (Washington, DC: The Brookings Institution, 1981).

Sweeney, Emily. *Boston Organized Crime*, Images of America Series (Charleston, SC: Arcadia Publishing. 2012).

Swift, Will, *The Kennedys Amidst the Gathering Storm: A Thousand Days in London, 1938-1940* (Washington, DC: Smithsonian Books/New York: Collins. 2008).

Tanzer, Lester ed., *The Kennedy Circle* (Washington, DC: Luce Books, 1961).

Taylor, Edward T., *History of the Committee on Appropriations* (Washington, DC: U.S. Government Printing Office, 1941).

Taylor, Jon E., *Freedom to Serve: Truman Civil Rights, and Executive Order 9981* (New York: Routledge, 2013).

Tejada, Susan, *Double Lives, Troubled Times, and the Massachusetts Murder Case that Shook the World* (Boston: Northeastern University Press, 2011).

Temin, Peter, *Engines of Enterprise: An Economic History of New England* (Cambridge, MA: Harvard University Press, 2000).

Timmons, Bascom N., *Garner of Texas: A Personal History* (New York: Harper & Bros., 1948).

Timmons, Bascom N., *Jesse H. Jones: The Man and the Statesman* (New York: Holt, 1956).

Thernstrom, Stephan, *Harvard Encyclopedia of American Ethnic Groups, 1972-1980* (Cambridge: Belknap Press of Harvard University Press, 1980).

Thomas, Hugh, *The Spanish Civil War*, 3rd edn (New York: Harper & Row, 1986).

Thomson, Charles A. H., and Francis M. Shattuck, eds., *The 1956 Presidential Campaign* (Washington, DC: The Brookings Institution, 1960).

Thoreau, Henry David, *The Variorum Walden* (New York: Twayne, 1962).

Thurber, Timothy N., *The Politics of Equality: Hubert H Humphrey and the African American Freedom Struggle* (New York: Columbia University Press, 1999).

Townshend, Adele, *Ten Farms Become a Town: A History of Souris, Prince Edward Island, 1700-1920* (Town of Souris: 1986, Reprinted 1997).

Trout, Charles H., *Boston, the Great Depression, and the New Deal* (New York: Oxford University Press, 1977).

Truman, Harry S., *Memoirs by Harry S. Truman, Year of Decisions* (Garden City, NY: Doubleday, 1955).

Truman, Harry S. *Memoirs by Harry S. Truman, Years of Trial and Hope* (Garden City, NY: Doubleday, 1956).

Tucker, Cynthia Grant, *No Silent Witness: The Eliot Parsonage Women and Their Unitarian World* (New York: Oxford University Press, 2010).

Tull, Charles J., *Father Coughlin and the New Deal* (Syracuse, NY: Syracuse University Press, 1965).

Tunney, Kiernan, *Tallulah: Darling of the Gods* (New York: E. P. Dutton, 1973).

U.S. Census Office, *Population of the United States in 1860* from the 8th Census (Washington, DC, 1864).

U.S. Department of Commerce, *Congressional District Data Book* (Washington, DC: U.S. Government Printing Office, 1961).

U.S. Department of the Army, "Army Battle Casualties and Nonbattle Deaths in World War II," Combines Arms Research Library, June 25, 1953.

U.S. House of Representatives, Committee on Appropriations, A History of the Committee on Appropriations, House of Representatives, H. Doc. 77-299, 77th Congress, 1st Session, 1941.

U.S. House of Representatives, *A History of the Committee on Rules, 1st to 97th Congress, 1789-1981* (House Committee Print, 97th Congress, 2nd Session, 1983).

U.S. Senate Armed Services Committee, *Hearings on Universal Military Training* (Washington, DC: U.S. Government Printing Office, 1948).

Vale, Lawrence J., *From the Puritans to the Projects: Public Housing and Public Neighbors* (Cambridge, MA: Harvard University Press, 2000).

Vann, Barry, *In Search of Ulster-Scots Land: The Birth and Geotheological Imagings of a Transatlantic People, 1603-1703* (Columbia: University of South Carolina Press, 2008).

Van Tuyll, Hubert P., *Feeding the Bear: American Aid to the Soviet Union* (Westport, CT: Greenwood Press, 1989).

Wakin, Edward, *Enter the Irish-American* (New York: Crowell, 1976).

Waller, Robert A., *Rainey of Illinois: A Political Biography, 1903-34* (Urbana: University of Illinois Press, 1977).

Waring, Dorothy, *American Defender* (New York: Robert Speller, Inc. 1935).

Warner, Sam Bass, *Streetcar Suburbs: The Process of Growth in Boston (1870-1900)*. (Cambridge, MA: Harvard University Press, 1978).

Warren, Earl, *The Memoirs of Earl Warren* (Garden City, NY: Doubleday, 1977).

Watson, Bruce, *Sacco and Vanzetti: The Men, the Murders, and the Judgment of Mankind* (New York: Viking Press, 2007).

Watson, John F., *Annals of Philadelphia and Pennsylvania in the Olden Time,* revised by Willis P. Hazard (Philadelphia: E. S. Stuart, 1905).

Wayman, Dorothy G., *Cardinal O'Connell of Boston: A Biography of William Henry O'Connell, 1895-1944* (New York: Farrar, Strauss and Young, 1955).

Wayman, Dorothy G., *David I. Walsh: Citizen-Patriot* (Milwaukee: Bruce Publishing, 1952).

Weaver, Warren, Jr., *Both Your Houses: The Truth about Congress* (New York: Praeger Publishers, 1972).

Webb, James, *Born Fighting: How the Scots-Irish Shaped America* (New York: Broadway Books, 2004).

Weber, Nicholas Fox, *The Clarks of Cooperstown: Their Singer Sewing Machine Fortune, Their Great and Influential Art Collections, Their Forty year Freud* (New York: Alfred A. Knopf, 2007).

Weeks, Kevin, and Phyllis Karas, *Brutal; My Life Inside Whitey Bulger's Irish Mob* (New York: Regan Books, 2006).

Weinstein, Allen, and Alexander Vassiliev, *The Haunted Wood: Soviet Espionage in America-The Stalin Era* (New York: Random House, 1999).

Weiss, Nancy J., *Farewell to the Party of Lincoln: Black Politics in the Age of FDR* (Princeton, NJ: Princeton University Press, 1983).

Whalen, Richard J., *The Founding Father: The Story of Joseph P. Kennedy* (New York: New American Library, 1964).

Whalen, Thomas J., *Kennedy versus Lodge: The 1952 Massachusetts Senate Race* (Boston: Northeastern University Press, 2000).

White, G. Edward, *Earl Warren: A Public Life* (New York: Oxford University Press, 1982).

White, Harry Dexter, *The French International Accounts, 1880-1913* (Cambridge, MA: Harvard University Press, 1933).

White, Theodore, *America in Search of Itself: The Making of the President, 1956-1980* (New York: Warner Books, 1982).

White, Theodore H., *The Making of the President, 1964* (New York: Atheneum, 1965).

White, William S., *Citadel: The Story of the U.S. Senate* (New York: Harper, 1957).

White, William S., *Home Place: The Story of U.S. House of Representatives* (Boston: Houghton Mifflin, 1965).

Whitehill, Walter Muir, *Boston: A Topographical History*, 2nd edn (Cambridge, MA: Harvard University Press, 1978).

Whyte, Robert, *The Ocean Plague or A Voyage to Quebec in an Irish Emigrant Vessel* (Boston: Coolidge and Willey, 1848).

Wicker, Tom, *Report of the National Advisory Commission on Civil Disorders* (New York: E. P. Dutton, 1968).

Widenour, William C., *Henry Cabot Lodge and the Search for an American Foreign Policy* (Berkeley: University of California Press, 1980).

Wilkins, Lee, *Wayne Morse: A Bio-Bibliography* (Westport, CT: Greenwood Press, 1985).

Williams, Selma R., *Kings, Commoners, and Colonists: Puritan Politics in Old and New England, 1603-1660* (New York: Atheneum, 1974).

Wills, Gary, *The Kennedy Imprisonment: A Meditation on Power* (Boston: Little, Brown, 1981).

Wilson, Augusta E., *Liberal Leader in the House, Frank Thompson, Jr. of New Jersey* (Washington: Acropolis Cooks, 1968).

Wilson, James Q., *The Amateur Democrat: Club Politics in Three Cities* (Chicago: University of Chicago Press, 1961).

Wilson, Woodrow, *Congressional Government: A Study in American Politics* (New York: Meridian Books, 1955).

Winter-Berger, Robert N., *The Washington Pay-Off: A Lobbyist's Own Story of Corruption in Government* (Secaucus, NJ: Lyle Stuart, 1972).

Witcover, Jules, *Crapshoot: Rolling the Dice on the Vice Presidency* (New York: Crown, 1992).

Witte, Edward E., *The Development of the Social Security Act: A Memorandum on the History of the Committee on Economic Security and Drafting and Legislative History of the Social Security Act* (Madison: University of Wisconsin Press, 1963).

Wittke, Carl, *We Who Built America: The Saga of the Immigrant* (Cleveland: Case Western Reserve University, 1967).

Wolfskill, George, *The Revolt of the Conservatives: A History of the American Liberty League, 1934-1940* (Boston: Houghton Mifflin, 1962).

Wood, Robert C., *Suburbia: Its People and Their Politics* (Boston: Houghton Mifflin, 1958).

Woodham-Smith, Cecil, *The Great Hunger: Ireland 1845-1849* (London: Hamish Hamilton, 1962).

Woods, Randall B., *LBJ: Architect of American Ambition* (New York: Free Press, 2006).

Woods, Randall B., *Prisoners of Hope: Lyndon B. Johnson, the Great Society, and the Limits of Liberalism* (New York: Basic Books, 2016).

Woolner, David B., and Richard G. Kurial, *FDR, the Vatican, and the Roman Catholic Church in America, 1933-1945* (New York: Palgrave Macmillan, 2003).

Wright, Jim, *Balance of Power: Presidents and Congress from the Era of McCarthy to the Age of Gingrich* (Atlanta: Turner Publishing, 1996).

Wright, Jim, *Of Swords and Plowshares: A Collection of the Best Short Writings of Congressman Jim Wright* (Fort Worth, TX: Stafford-Lowdon, 1967).

Wright, Jim, *Reflections of a Public Man* (Fort Worth, TX: Allied, 1984).

Wright, Jim, *Worth It All: My War for Peace* (New York: Brasseys, 1993).

Wright, Jim, *You and Your Congressman* (New York: G. P. Putnam, 1976).

Yalof, David A., *Pursuit of Justices* (Chicago: University of Chicago Press, 2001).

Yarncll, Allen, *Democrats and Progressives: The 1948 Presidential Election As A Test of Post-War Liberalism* (Berkeley: University of California Press, 1974).

Ybarra, Michael J., *Washington Gone Crazy: Senator Pat McCarran and the Great American Communist Hunt* (Hanover, NH: Steerforth Press, 2004).

Young, Jeff C., *Fathers of American Presidents: From Augustine Washington to William Blythe and Roger Clinton* (Jefferson, NC: McFarland & Co., 1997).

Young, Nancy Beck, *Wright Patman: Populism, Liberalism, and the American Dream* (Dallas, TX: Southern Methodist University, 2000).

Young, Robert J., *The Aftermath of Munich: The Course of French Diplomacy, October 1938-March 1939* (Durham, NC: Duke University Press, 1973).

Young, Ronald A., *Congressional Politics in the Second World War* (New York: Columbia University Press, 1956).

Young, Valton Joseph, *The Speaker's Agent* (New York: Vantage Press, 1956).

Zelizer, Julian E., *On Capitol Hill: The Struggle to Reform Congress and Its Consequences, 1948-2000* (New York: Cambridge University Press, 2004).

Zelizer, Julian E., *Taxing America: Wilbur D. Mills, Congress and the State, 1945-1975* (New York: Cambridge University Press, 1998).

Zink, Harold, *City Bosses in the United States: A Study of Twenty Municipal Bosses* (Durham, NC: Duke University Press, 1930).

Zinn, Howard, *LaGuardia in Congress* (Ithaca, NY: Cornell University Press, 1959).

Zobel, Hiller B., *The Boston Massacre* (New York: W. W. Norton, 1970).

Book chapters, scholarly and newspaper articles

Common abbreviations: APSR: *American Political Science Review*
BG: *Boston Globe and Boston Daily Globe*
CQWR: *Congressional Quarterly Weekly Report*
NYT: *The New York Times*
WP: *Washington Post and Times Herald*
N.B. Page numbers were not included for the newspaper and the *CQ Weekly Report* citations.

A.F.C., "Backstage in Washington," *Outlook and Independent*, April 22, 1931, p. 555.

"A Breach is Closed: McCormack Gets a Special Invitation to White House," *NYT,* March 12, 1959.

Abram, Michael, and Joseph Cooper, "The Rise of the Seniority in the House of Representatives," *Polity,* I (Fall, 1958), pp. 52-84.

"Accelerated Public Works," *CQWR*, September 14, 1962.

"Acts of Congress Held Unconstitutional in Whole or in Part by the Supreme Court of the United States," *The Constitution of the United States: Analysis and Interpretation* (Washington, D.C.: U.S. Government Printing Office, 2004).

"Aged Fighters Bury Hatchet," *Statesville (N.C.) Landmark*, June 3, 1949.

"Agency for the Elderly," *CQ Almanac 1965*, pp. 356-357.

Albright, Robert C., "Democratic Floor Leader Contest Beginning to Boil," *WP,* December 4, 1961.

Albright, Robert C., "Dying 88th Leaves Record for Critics: Congress Sheds Lethargy Ignores Scandal to Mold Major Legislation," *WP*, August 16, 1964.

Albright, Robert C., "Halleck Plans a Big Bridge Across Aisle," *WP*, January 25, 1959.

Albright, Robert C., "House Organizes with Old Officers; Bankhead Re-elected Speaker with 250 Votes to 167 for Martin, Republican," *NYT*, January 4, 1939.

Albright, Robert C., "Study Election, New Deal Laws, Bankhead Urges; Re-nominated, He Says Modification May Be Necessary; Martin Minority Leader," *WP*, January 3, 1939.

Albright, Robert C., "Truman Forces Win Significant Opening Battle: Rules Committee Curbed by House," *WP*, January 4, 1949.

Albright, Robert C., "88th Congress Set for Battle at Bang of Gavel," *WP*, January 6, 1963.

Alsop, Stewart, "The Failure of Congress," *Saturday Evening Post* (December 7, 1963), pp. 23–25.

Alter, Jonathan, "The Power and the Glitz," *Newsweek*, CXXXI, May 25, 1998, p. 64B.

Altman, O. R., "Second Session of the Seventy-Fourth Congress, (January 3, 1936 to June 20, 1936)," *APSR*, XXX (December, 1936), pp. 1086–1107.

Altman, O. R., "First Session of the Seventy-Fifth Congress: January 5, 1937 to August 21, 1937," *APSR*, XXXI (December, 1937), pp. 1071–93.

Altman, O. R., "Second and Third Sessions of the Seventy-Fifth Congress, 1937-38," *APSR*, XXXI (December, 1937), pp. 1071–93.

"America: Today and Yesterday," *U.S. News and World Report*, July 27, 1970.

"Anatomy of a Traitor: What Makes Americans Defect?" *Newsweek*, September 19, 1960, pp. 33–37.

Anderson, Jack, "Firing Aide Was Painful to Speaker," *WP*, October 23, 1969.

Anderson, Jack, "McCormack's Aide Held Potent Spot," *WP*, October 20, 1969.

Anderson, Jack, "McCormack Hounded Despite Denial," *WP*, November 1, 1971.

Anderson, Jack, "Rep. Ford Closely Linked to Lobbyist," *WP*, July 20, 1972.

Anderson, Jack, "Speaker Never Took Money for Favors," *WP*, October 30, 1969.

Anderson, Jack, "Sweig Trial Witness Testifies NASA Funds Used as Club," *WP*, July 1, 1970.

Anderson, Jack, "Washington Merry-Go-Round: House Speaker Resists Ethics Move," *WP*, June 4, 1966.

Anderson, Jack, "Washington Merry-Go-Round: Nixon Tax Veto Threat is No Bluff," *WP*, December 12, 1969.

Anderson, Jack, "Washington Merry-Go-Round: Witch-Hunt by Justice is Suspected," *WP*, September 1, 1971.

"Anti-Water Pollution Law Strengthened," *CQ Almanac 1965*, pp. 743–50.

"'Anxiety' is Voiced on M'Cormack View," *NYT*, November 18, 1961.

Arbogast, William F., "Religious Dispute Lurks in House Speaker's Race," *Indiana Evening Gazette* (November 21, 1961).

Archibald, Sam, "The Early Years of the Freedom of Information Act-1955 to 1974," *PS: Political Science and Politics* XXVI (December, 1993), pp. 726–31.

Asbury, Edith Evans, "A Handwritten Memo by Sweig Persuaded Jury to Convict Him," *NYT*, July 11, 1970.

Asbury, Edith Evans, "Sweig Trial He Told He Posed as McCormack: Witnesses Also Say Voloshen Let Phone Callers Think Speaker Was on Line," *NYT*, July 8, 1970.

Ash, Philip, "The 'Liberalism' of Congressmen Voting for and Against the Taft-Hartley Act," *Journal of Applied Psychology*, XXXII (December, 1948), pp. 636–64.

"Asks Congressional Nomination as Wet; State Senator McCormack Candidate in 12th; Favors Light Wines and Beers, Also Stimulants as Medicine," *BG*, July 19, 1926.

"Assails Stimson on Lodge Letter; McCormack Charges Secretary Took 'Pernicious Political Action' in Massachusetts Race," *NYT*, July, 1942.

"Asserts Wallace Not Hold-up Man: Filling Station Attendant Describes Robbery, Dentist on Stand as Alibi Witness for Defendant," *BG*, November 4, 1927.

Associated Press, "Chamber of Commerce Names Union Leader on List of Greats," *Lawrence (Mass.) Tribune*, January 20, 1947.

Associated Press, "Feuding Over Powell: McCormack Soothes Demos," *The Cocoa (Fla.) Tribune*, January 6, 1967.

Associated Press, "Hiss Will Give Address at Princeton April 26," *WP*, April 7, 1956.

Associated Press, "House Cheers McCormack as Lane Hails Candidacy," *Boston Post,* April 11, 1948.

Associated Press, "Kennedy Has Sister as Capitol Hostess," *Concord (N.H.) Monitor and New Hampshire Patriot,* January 19, 1950.

Associated Press, "Powell Backed by McCormack," *The Lawton (Okla.) Constitution*, January 6, 1967.

Associated Press, "Princeton Backs Students on Plans for Hiss Speech," *WP,* April 11, 1956.

Associated Press, "'Promise You Won't Scuttle School Aid', McCormack Urged," *BG*, November 27, 1961.

Associated Press, "Rayburn to Shun Post as Minority Leader," *NYT*, November 7, 1946.

Associated Press, "Senator Kerr Hails M'Cormack Candidacy," *Boston Post*, April 12, 1956.

Associated Press, "Sweig Case Figure's Body Found Dumped in Car Trunk," *BG*, October 9, 1970.

Associated Press, "Sweig Wins Parole After Serving Year," *WP*, July 18, 1972.

Associated Press, "U.S. Charges Ex-House Aide Accepted Bribe," *BG*, January 28, 1972.

Armstrong, Sinclair, "Congress and the Securities and Exchange Commission," *Virginia Law Review*, XLV (October, 1959), pp. 795–816.

Austin, Brent J., "The Southern Manifesto and Southern Opposition to Desegregation," *Arkansas Historical Quarterly*, LV (September, 1996), pp. 173–93.

"Award of $1300 in Promise Suit—Jury Acts on Default of Defendant—Miss Palatnick says Goldfarb Refused to Marry Her—Mansfield Denies Promise to Elizabeth Ryan," *BG*, November 7, 1913.

"Back of the 'Conservative Coalition' is Broken," *CQ Almanac 1965*, p. 1083.

"Back of the Yards Mourns Loss, A Patriot and Father Eulogized by Friend," *Back of the Yards Journal*, October 6, 1982.

Badger, Tony, "Southerners Who Refused to Sign the Southern Manifesto," *The Historical Journal*, XLII (June, 1999), pp. 517–34.

Badger, Tony, "'The Forerunner of Our Opposition': Arkansas and the Southern Manifesto of 1956," *Arkansas Historical Quarterly*, LVI (Autumn, 1997), pp. 353–60.

Baker, Robert E., "Mississippi's Delegates Win Seats in House," *WP*, January 5, 1965.

Baker, Russell, and Tom Wicker, "Kennedy and the Congress; Some Major Duels Are Forecast; President has Modified Many of his Earlier Goals but Conservatives Are Expected to Fight Hard Against Trade and Medical Care Bills," *NYT*, January 7, 1962.

"Bailey to Lead No More," *NYT*, March 4, 1899.

Bales, Robert F., "Task Roles and Social Roles in Problem-Solving Groups," in Eleanor E. Maccoby, Theodore M. Newcomb, and Eugene L. Hartley, eds., *Readings in Social Psychology*, 3rd edn (New York: Holt, Rinehart and Winston, 1958), pp. 437–47.

"Bank Supervision," *CQ Almanac 1966*, pp. 746–52.

Bankhead, Tallulah, "My Life with Father," *Coronet, XXXI* (November, 1951), pp. 56–60.

Barone, Michael, "Franklin D. Roosevelt; A Protestant Patrician in a Catholic Party," in David B. Woolner and Richard G. Kurial, eds., *FDR, the Vatican, and the Roman Catholic Church in America, 1933-1945* (New York: Palgrave Macmillan, 2003), pp. 3–11.

Barrett, J. R., "Why Paddy Drank: The Social Importance of Whiskey in Pre-Famine Ireland," *Journal of Popular Culture*, XI (1977), pp. 155–56.

Bartlett, Charles, "Civil Rights Bill May Be Too Strong," *BG*, October 6, 1963.

Bartlett, Charles, "Democrats Unity Faces Two Tests," *Washington Star*, December 20, 1970.

Bartlett, Charles, "End's Well—So All's Well: Congress and President Are Happy: Session Ends on a Note of Harmony," *BG*, October 8, 1962.

"Bay State Democrats to Fete Kennedy and McCormack," *BG*, September 12, 1957.

Beecher, William, "Crime Crackdown: Robert Kennedy Plans Multi-Agency Drive Against Top Racketeer; He'll Stress Size of Cases, Not Quantity; His Tie to President Will Be an Aid but He Faces Old Hurdles," *Wall Street Journal*, January 23, 1961.

Belair, Felix Jr., "Secret Service Faces Changes in Its Procedures as a Result of the Assassination," *NYT*, November 24, 1963.

"Benjamin Smith II, 75, U.S. Senator in 1960s," *NYT*, September 28, 1991.

"Berlin to Head Civil Rights Div. For McCormack," *BG*, October 28, 1958.

Beswick, Ellen, "My Fifty Years in Government," *Boston Herald Traveler*, December 13, 1970.

Bibby, John F., "Political Parties," in Donald C. Bacon, Roger H. Davidson, Morton Killer, eds., *The Encyclopedia of the United States Congress*, Vol. III (New York, Simon & Schuster, 1995), pp. 1557–58.

"Bid for Khrushchev Capitol Speech Now Opposed by Supporters of Visit," *WP*, September 3, 1959.

Bishop, Jim, "Hail and Farewell [to Jocko McCormack]," King Features, *Reading (Pa.) Eagle*, October 20, 1982, p. 7.

Blackorby, Edward C., "William Lemke: Agrarian Radical and Union Party Presidential Candidate," *Mississippi Valley Historical Review*, XLIX (June, 1962), pp. 67–84.

Block, Marvin W., "Henry T. Rainey of Illinois," *Journal of the Illinois State Historical Society*, LXV (Summer, 1972), pp. 142–57.

"Bolling is Right," *New Republic*, November 11, 1967, pp. 8–9.

Bone, Hugh A., "Sol Bloom: Supersalesman of Patriotism," in J. T. Salter, ed., *Public Men in and Out of Office* (Chapel Hill: University of North Carolina Press, 1946), pp. 225–39.

"Boston Boxers Take Five of the New England Titles," *Boston Daily Globe*, March 19, 1918.

Boyd, James, "Nixon's Southern Strategy 'It's All in the Charts,'" *NYT*, May 17, 1970.

Boxerman, Burton A., "Adolph Joachim Sabath in Congress: The Early Years, 1907-1932," *Journal of the Illinois State Historical Society*, LXVI (Autumn, 1973), pp. 327–30.

Boxerman, Burton A., "Adolph Joachim Sabath in Congress: The Roosevelt and Truman Years," *Journal of the Illinois State Historical Society*, LXVI (Winter, 1973), pp. 428–43.

Briggs, Philip J., "Congress and Collective Security: The Resolutions of 1943," *World Affairs*, CXXXII (March, 1970), pp. 332–44.

Brinkley, Alan, "Huey Long, the Share Our Wealth Movement and the Limits of Depression Dissidence," *Louisiana History*, XXII (Spring, 1981), pp. 117–34.

Bruner, Jerome S., and Sheldon J. Korchin, "The Boss and the Vote; Case Study in City Politics," *Public Opinion Quarterly*, X (Spring, 1946), pp. 1–23.

Buchanan, Scott, "The Dixiecrat Rebellion: Long-Term Partisan Implications in the Deep South," *Politics and Policy*, XXXIII (2005), pp. 754–69.

Buckley, Kerry W., "Great Silent Majority: Bruce Barton's Construction of Calvin Coolidge," *New England Quarterly*, LXXVI (December, 2003), pp. 593–628.

Buckley, Frank, "Thoreau and the Irish," *New England Quarterly*, XIII (1940), pp. 389–400.

Bullock, Paul, "Rabbits and Radicals: Richard Nixon's 1946 Campaign Against Jerry Voorhis," *Southern California Quarterly*, LV (Fall, 1973), pp. 319–49.

Burke, Vince J., "Question in House Elections: 88th Be Friendlier to Kennedy?" *WP*, October 31, 1962.

Burnett, Donald L., "An Historical Analysis of the 1968 'Indian Civil Rights' Act," *Harvard Journal on Legislation*, IX (May, 1972), pp. 557–626.

Caldeira, Gregory A., "Public Opinion and the U.S. Supreme Court: FDR's Court-Packing Plan," *APSR*, LXXXI (December, 1987), pp. 1139–53.

Campbell, Angus, "Surge and Decline: A Study of Electoral Change," *Public Opinion Quarterly*, XXIV (Autumn, 1960), pp. 397–418.

Campbell, Angus, Philip Converse, Warren Miller, and Donald E. Stokes, "A Classification of the Presidential Elections," in Angus Campbell, et al., *Elections and the Political Order* (New York: John Wiley, 1966), pp. 63–78.

Cantril, Hadley, and John Harding, "The 1942 Elections: A Case Study in Political Psychology," *Public Opinion Quarterly*, VII (Summer, 1943), pp. 222–41.

Carpenter, Leslie, "McCormack May Miss Speakership," *Boston Herald,* June 25, 1961.

Carper, Elise, "Fear of Home Rule by Southerners Seen in Naming District Committee; Local Leaders Sense Double-Cross," *WP*, January 31, 1963.

"Challenge to McCormack," *CQWR*, February 20, 1970.

Champagne, Anthony, "Hatton Sumners and the 1937 Court-Packing Plan," *East Texas Historical Journal 26* (Spring, 1988), pp. 46–49.

Champagne, Anthony, "John Nance Garner," in Roger H. Davidson, Susan Webb Hammond, and Raymond W. Smock, eds., *Masters of the House: Congressional Leadership Over Two Centuries* (Boulder, CO: Westview Press, 1998), pp. 145–80.

"Charley Innes Producer of Teaching Law Than of Being a 'Political Boss,'" *Boston Sunday Advertiser,* April 9, 1933.

"Cheering Democrats Organize House Under Garner as 72nd Congress Opens; Party Leaders Are Ready for Big Job," *NYT,* December 8, 1931.

Chen, Phillip, "Religious Liberty in American Foreign Policy, 1933-1941: Aspects of Public Argument Between FDR and American Roman Catholics," in Woolner and Kurial, eds., *FDR, the Vatican, and the Roman Catholic Church in America, 1933-1945,* pp. 121–39.

Childs, Marquis, "The High Stakes in House Battle," *WP,* December 29, 1961.

"Civil Rights Act of 1964 is Signed into Law," *CQWR*, July 3, 1964.

"Clean Air Bill Created with Auto Emission Deadline," *CQ Almanac 1970*, pp. 472–86.

"Clem Norton Says," *Everett (Mass.) News-Gazette*, December 21, 1947.

Clifford, Garry J., and Theodore A. Wilson, "Blundering on the Brink, 1941: FDR and the 203-202 Vote Reconsidered," in J. Gary Clifford and Theodore A. Wilson, eds., *Presidents, Diplomats, and other Mortals: Essays Honoring Robert Ferrell* (Columbia: University of Missouri Press, 2007), pp. 99–115.

Clopton, Willard, "Stormy Career Ends for Gardner Jackson," *WP*, April 18, 1965.

"Coffin Ships: Death and Pestilence on the Atlantic," www.Irish-Genealogy-Toolkit.com.

Cohen, Richard E., "Campaigning for Congress: The Echo of 1994," in Larry Sabato, ed., *Towards the Millennium: The Elections of 1996* (Boston: Allyn and Bacon, 1997), pp. 174–77.

Cohen, Wilbur J., Robert M. Ball, and Robert J. Myers, 'Social Security Act Amendments of 1954: A Summary and Legislative History," *Social Security Bulletin* (September, 1954), pp. 3–18.

Colbert, James W., "McCormack Halted Stampede to Adlai," *Boston Sunday Post*, April 25, 1956.

Colbert, James, "22 Articles on McCormack's 1956 Presidential Bid," *Boston Post*, April 4 to April 25.

Collins, Edwin, "McCormack's Wards Give Vote to Dever Over Putnam," *BG,* June 19, 1946.

Collins, Ernest M., "Congress is Losing Its Grip," *Social Studies*, LVII (March, 1966), pp. 104–08.

Collins, Ross, "Furcolo Switch Seen as Stride to Governor's Chair or Senate," *BG,* July 6, 1952.

"Columnist Charges Plot for McCormack Ouster," *BG,* December 10, 1963.

"Communications Satellites," *CQWR*, May 4, 1962.

"Comprehensive Water Pollution Control Act Cleared," *CQ Almanac 1970*, pp. 175–78.

"Cong. Javirs Coming Here to Aid G.O.P," *BG*, October 13, 1952.

"Congress Accepts Four Executive Reorganization Plans," *CQ Almanac 1970*, pp. 462–67.

"Congress Approves Manpower Retraining Bill," *CQWR,* March 16, 1962.

"Congress Approves One-third of Nixon's Requests," CQ Almanac 1969, pp. 115–23.

"Congress Authorizes $2.9 Billion for Housing Programs," *CQ Almanac 1970*, pp. 726–41.

"Congress Backs Johnson on 93% of Roll-Call Votes," *CQ Almanac 1965*, pp. 1099–1100.

"Congress Backs President in Vietnam Crisis," *CQWR*, August 7, 1964.

"Congress Backs President on 85.4% of Tests in 1962," *CQWR*, October 26, 1962.

"Congress Clears Bill Establishing Wilderness System," *CQWR*, August 28, 1964.

"Congress Clears Land Conservation Fund," *CQWR*, September 4, 1964.

"Congress Clears Landmark Postal Reorganization Plan," *CQ Almanac 1970*, pp. 341–65.

"Congress Clears Securities Investor Protection Bill," *CQ Almanac 1970*, pp. 865–73.

"Congress Clears Welfare Revisions Bill," *CQWR*, July 21, 1962.

"Congress Clears 1970 Organized Crime Control Bill," *CQ Almanac 1970*, pp. 545–53.

"Congress Clears $375 Million mass Transportation Bill," *CQWR,* July 3, 1964.

"Congress Creates Public Broadcasting Corporation," *CQ Almanac 1967*, pp. 1042–50.

"Congress Enacts Bill to Preserve Ailing Newspapers," *CQ Almanac, 1967*, pp. 192–99.

"Congress Enacts Open Housing Legislation," *CQ Almanac 1968*, pp. 152–68.

"Congress Enacts Strong Truth-in-Lending Law," *CQ Almanac 1968*, pp. 205–11.

"Congress Extends Selective Service Law for Four Years, But Rejects Proposals for Comprehensive Draft Reform," *CQ Almanac 1967,* pp. 260–80,

"Congress Grants 57.6% of Johnson's Specific Requests," *CQWR,* October 23, 1964.

"Congress Lowers Voting Age, Extends Voting Rights Act," *CQ Almanac 1970*, pp. 192–99.

"Congress Passes Airport and Airway Development Act," *CQ Almanac 1970*, pp. 168–74.

"Congress Passes Extensive Anticrime Legislation," *CQ Almanac 1968*, pp. 263–78.

"Congress Provides Revenues for Conservation Fund," *CQ Almanac 1968*, pp. 291–99.

"Congress: Reaper's Return," *TIME,* June 15, 1936, pp. 13–14.

"Congress Restores Investment Tax Credit for Business; Suspends Operation of Presidential Campaign Fund Law," *CQ Almanac 1967*, pp. 283–300.

"Congress Strengthens Air Pollution Control Powers," *CQ Almanac 1967*, pp. 875–87.

"Congress Unusually Cooperative with President's Program," *CQWR,* November 19, 1965.

"Congress Votes Surtax with Expenditure Controls," *CQ Almanac 1968*, pp. 263–78.

"Congress Votes 3.9 Billion in Foreign Aid," *CQWR*, October 11, 1962.

Congressional Quarterly, "Rights, Tax Bills Share Top Priority," *WP,* July 10, 1963.

"Congressionally Initiated Tax Reform Bill Enacted," *CQ Almanac 1969*, pp. 589–649.

"Congressman Hopeful on Khrushchev Visit," *WP,* August 4, 1959.

Connell, Maureen, "Remembrances of Those Who Died on November 22 . . . Especially John W. McCormack," *Boston Irish Echo*, November 21, 1981.

Connolly, Richard J., "Sweig: An Unofficial Envoy; But McCormack Aide Angered Churchill," *WP,* October 19, 1969.

Connolly, Richard J., "Sweig: Quiet Man," *BG,* October 18, 1969.

"Conservative Coalition Remains Potent in Congress," *CQ Almanac,* 1969, pp. 1052–59.

"Conservative Coalition Scores Victories in Congress," *CQ Almanac 1970,* pp. 1144–49.

"Conservative Coalition Shaped Major 1968 Bills," *CQWR,* November 1, 1968.

"'Conservative Coalition' Shows New Life," *CQWR,* December 20, 1966.

Cooke, Edward F., "Drafting the 1952 Platforms," *Western Political Quarterly*, IX (September, 1956), pp. 699–712.

Cooper, Joseph, and David W. Brady, "Institutional Context and Leadership Style: The House from Cannon to Rayburn," *APSR,* LXXV (June, 1981), pp. 411–25.

Crass, Scott, "Men of the House: O'Neill's Roommate, JFK's Roommate, and Speaker McCormack," Themoderatevoice.com.

Crews, Watson Jr., "Eunice and the Kennedy Tradition," *The American Weekly,* a Sunday supplement to the *Lowell (Mass.) Sun*, July 31, 1947.

Crimmins, Margaret, "Carl Albert: 'Shoo-In' For Speaker," *WP,* May 21, 1970.

Crow, John C., "The Role of Congress and the Federal Judiciary in the Deportation of Aliens," *Missouri Law Review,* XXIII (November, 1958), pp. 491–502.

Curtis, Thomas B., "Power of the House of Representatives to Judge the Qualifications of Its Members," *Texas Law Review*, XLV (July, 1967), pp. 1199–1204.

Cutler, Samuel B., "Burke Confirmed as Port Collector," *BG,* November 23, 1944.

Danelski, David J., "Task Group and Social Group on the Supreme Court," in John H. Kessel, George F. Cole, and Robert G. Seddig, eds., *Micropolitics: Individual and Group Level Concepts* (New York: Holt, Rinehart and Winston, Inc., 1970), pp. 266–74.

Davies, Gareth, and Martha Derthick, "Race and Social Welfare Policy: The Social Security Act of 1935," *Political Science Quarterly*, CXII (Summer, 1997), pp. 217–35.

Davis, Frank S., "Sabotage Charged: Timidity, Weakness and Short Sightedness Are Laid to Republicans," *NYT,* October 29, 1940.

Davis, Polly, "Cort Reform and Alben W. Barkley's Election as Majority Leader," *Southern Quarterly*, XV (1976), pp. 15–31.

"Democratic Harmony," *Boston Traveler*, February 5, 1956.

"Democrats Elect Burke Chairman of State Committee," *BG*, September 17, 1939.

"Democrats Name Rayburn Speaker: Anderson of New Mexico Wins Contest for Ways and Means-Martin Minority Leader," *NYT*, January 3, 1945.

"Democrats Score Net Gain of 38 House Seats," *CQWR*, November 6, 1964.

"Democrats Take 13 Governorships from Republicans," *CQWR*, XLV (November 6, 1970).

"Department of Housing Approved," *CQ Almanac 1965*, pp. 382–87.

DeWitt, Larry, "The Decision to Exclude Agricultural and Domestic Workers from the 1935 Social Security," *Social Security Bulletin*, LXX (2010), pp. 49–68.

Diamond, A. N., and Alfred Letzier, "The New Frazier-Lemke Act: A Study," *Columbia Law Review*, XXXVII (November, 1937), pp. 1092–1135.

"Dignitaries to Attend Mass for Speaker McCormack," *BG*, November 25, 1980.

Dinnerstein, Leonard, "Anti-Semitism in the Eightieth Congress: The Displaced Persons Act of 1948," *Capitol Studies*, VI (Fall, 1978), pp. 11–26.

"Disputes Box View on 'Smith Forces,'" *NYT*, January 29, 1929.

Dixon, George, "Washington Scene: Sob Sisters May Get Revenge on 'Smart Halleck,'" *WP*, January 20, 1959.

Doenecke, Justus D., "Non-intervention of the Left: The Keep America Out of the War Congress, 1938-41," *Journal of Contemporary History*, XII (April, 1977), pp. 231–36.

Donaldson, Gary A., "Who Wrote the Clifford Memo? The Origins of Campaign Strategy in the Truman Administration," *Presidential Studies Quarterly*, XXIII (Fall, 1993), pp. 747–54.

Donovan, John C., "Congressional Isolationists and the Roosevelt Foreign Policy," *World Politics*, III (April, 1951), pp. 299–316.

Donovan, Robert J., "Dilatory Congress May Have to Stay After School," *BG*, September 2, 1963).

Dorris, Henry N., "House Democrats Name McCormack as Their Leader," *NYT*, September 26, 1940.

Dorris, Henry N., "Push Plan to Defer House Leader Test," *NYT*, September 19, 1940.

Douglas, Paul H., "Three Saints in Politics," *American Scholar*, XL (Spring, 1971), pp. 223–32.

"Dow Jones Industrial Average All-Time Largest One Day Gains and Losses," *The Wall Street Journal*, retrieved December 11, 2012.

Druks, Herbert, "Harry S. Truman and the Recognition of Israel," *Journal of Thought*, XVI (Winter, 1981), pp. 15–16.

Dugger, Ronnie, "Squabbling in Democratic Party Clouds Kennedy Tour of Texas," *WP*, November 20, 1963.

Dutton, William S., "Prince Edward—The Island Where There is No Divorce and No Crime," *The American Magazine* (December, 1929), pp. 48ff.

"Drug Bill," *CQWR*, October 5, 1962.

"Drug Controls," *CQWR*, July 16, 1965.

Drummond, Roscoe, "No Wavering: Why Civil Rights Legislation Will Move More Rapidly Through Congress," *BG*, November 24, 1963.

Drury, Allen, "Hallek Unseats Martin as G.O.P. Leader in House: Congress to Open Today," *NYT*, January 7, 1959.

"Edelstein Dies after House Talk," *NYT*, June 5, 1941.

Edwards, Franklin R., "Banks and Securities Activities: Legal and Economic Perspectives," in Lawrence G. Goldberg and J. White, eds., *The Deregulation of the Banking and Security Industries* (Lexington, MA: Lexington Books, 1979), pp. 273–91.

Eisenger, Peter K., "Ethnic Political Transition in Boston, 1884-1933: Some Lessons for Contemporary Cities," *Political Science Quarterly*, XCIII (1978), pp. 217–39.

Eldersveld, Samuel J., "The Influence of Metropolitan Party Pluralities in Presidential Elections: A Study of Twelve Key Cities," *APSR*, XLIII (December, 1949), pp. 1189–1206.

Eleazar, Frank, "Congressman, Reporter Give House Unequal Demerits," *WP*, February 11, 1965.

Eliot, Thomas H., "In Defense of Congress," *Common Sense,* X (December 10, 1941, pp. 372–73.

"Environmental Quality Council," *CQ Almanac, 1969*, pp. 525–27.

Essary, Frederick J., "The Split in the Democratic Party," *Atlantic Monthly*, CLX (December, 1937), pp. 651–58.

Evans, Rowland, and Robert Novak, "Another Mystery Book," *WP*, March 26, 1972.

Evans, Rowland, and Robert Novak, "Democrats v. McCormack, At First Party Caucus, Speaker Appears Impervious To Rank-and-File Discontent in House," *WP*, January 25, 1970, p. B7.

Rowland Evans, and Robert Novak, "Drive to Purge McCormack Grows Stronger," *BG*, September 3, 1969, p. 15.

Evans, Rowland, and Robert Novak, "Inside Report: Reluctant Liberals," *WP*, December 22, 1963.

Evans, Rowland, and Robert Novak, "Inside Report: Pressuring the Speaker," *WP*, August 9, 1963.

Evans, Rowland, and Robert Novak, "Liberal Democrats Conclude Albert Is Best Bet to Topple McCormack," *WP*, September 5, 1969, p. A23.

Evans, Rowland, and Robert Novak, "Lyndon B. Johnson: The Ascent to Leadership," reprinted in Norman J. Ornstein, ed., *Congress in Change: Evolution and Reform* (New York: Praeger, 1975), pp. 117–41.

Evans, Rowland, and Robert Novak, "McCormack Aims to Thwart Liberals By Supporting Boggs, Rostenkowski," *WP*, July 20, 1969, p. A23.

Evans, Rowland, and Robert Novak, "The President's Boston Blues: Lyndon Johnson's Habits of Procrastination Hurt Chances of Squashing McCarthy," *WP*, March 3, 1968.

Evans, Rowland, and Robert Novak, "The Wallace Rout: Alabama Governor Tried to Stop Poverty War Grant Because of Race and Politics," *WP*, October 17, 1965.

"Excerpts from the Testimony of Robert Kennedy Before Senate Panel," *NYT,* January 14, 1961.

"Excise Tax Reduction Bill Send to President," *CQWR*, June 18, 1965.

"FDR Talks Frankly—About Foreign Policy, His Opponent, the Voters and the Polls," *American Heritage*, XXXIII (February/March, 1982), accessed May 1, 2015.

Feeney, Mark, "Longtime Congressman Edward Boland Dies," *BG*, November 6, 2001.

Feeney, Mark, "Robert L. Healy, at 84; Globe editor, Columnist, Political Insider," *BG*, June 7, 2010.

Fenno, Richard F., "House Appropriations Committee as a Political System: The Problem of Integration," *APSR*, LVI (June, 1962), pp. 310–24.

Fenno, Richard F., "The House of Representatives and Federal Aid to Education," in Robert L. Peabody and Nelson W. Polsby, eds., *New Perspectives on the House of Representatives*, 2nd edn (Chicago: Rand, McNally, 1969), pp. 283–323.

Ferrell, Robert H., and Francis H. Heller, Francis H., "Plain Faking?" *American Heritage*, XLVI (May/June, 1995), accessed June 11, 2015.

Fesler, James W., "The Brownlow Committee: Fifty Years Later," *Public Administration Review*, XLVII (August, 1987), pp. 292–96.

Field, Walter T., "The Amherst Illustrious: Speaker Rainey," *Amherst Graduates Quarterly*, XXIV (November. 1934), pp. 22–24.

"Fight Over Voting ᶠ ⸴ House Leader—McCormack, Whom President is Said to Back, Has Odds if Balloting is Open," *NYT*, September 18, 1940.

Fiorina, Morris P., David W. Rohde, and Peter Wissel eds., "Historical Change in House Turnover," in Norman J. Ornstein, ed., *Congress in Change: Evolution and Reform* (New York: Praeger, 1975), pp. 24–57.

"First Congressional Reform Bill Enacted Since 1946," *CQ Almanac 1970*, pp. 447–61.

"First General School Aid Bill Enacted," *CQ Almanac 1965*, pp. 275–93.

Fishwick, Marshall, "The Rise and Fall of Horatio Alger," *Saturday Review*, November 17, 1965.

Fleeson, Doris, "McCormack Rescuing His State or His Nephew? Bill to Hike Membership," *BG*, February 14, 1962.

Fleishman, Neill, "Power of Congress to Exclude Persons Duly Elected," *North Carolina Law Review*, XLVIII (April, 1970), pp. 656–66.

"Floridian with Gavel: LeRoy Collins," *NYT*, July 15, 1960.

Folliard, Edward T., "Texas Feud to Test Kennedy's Political Skill During Visit," *WP*, November 21, 1963.

"Food Stamps," *CQ Almanac 1970*, pp. 764–67.

Ford, Aaron I., "The Legislative Reorganization Act of 1946," *American Bar Association Journal*, XXXII (November, 1946), pp. 741–44.

"Foreign Aid Authorization Lowest in Program's History," *CQ Almanac 1969*, pp. 434–47.

"Foreign Policy Day Set by Democrats—McCormack Says the Platform Makers Will Devote All of Wednesday to This Issue," *NYT*, July 17, 1944.

"Foundation of the Arts and Humanities," *CQ Almanac 1965*, pp. 621–27.

"14-Member Democratic Committee Seeks to Fill Top Convention Posts," *WP*, April 9, 1960.

Fox, Douglas M., and Charles H. Clapp, "The House Rules Committee's Agenda-Setting Function, 1961-1968," *Journal of Politics*, XXXII (May, 1970), pp. 440–43.

Fox, Douglas M., and Charles H. Clapp, "The House Rules Committee and the Programs of the Kennedy and Johnson Administrations," *Midwest Journal of Political Science*, XIV (November, 1970), pp. 667–72.

Frady, Marshall, "Wilbur Mills," *LIFE*, LXXI (July 16, 1971), pp. 52ff.

Frankfurter, Felix, "The Case of Sacco and Vanzetti," *Atlantic Monthly*, CXXXICX (March, 1927), acceded March 22, 2015.

"Freedom of Information Bill Enacted," *CQ Almanac 1966*, pp. 556–59.

Fried, Joseph F., "Ex-Convict's Body Found in Car Here: Granello Had Been Linked to Gambling and Racketeering," *NYT*, October 7, 1970.

Fuchs, Lawrence, "Presidential Politics in Boston: The Irish Response to Stevenson," *New England Quarterly*, XXX (December, 1957), pp. 435–47.

"Gallivan and Rival Cheered and Hissed; Debate in South Boston is Enlivened by Crowd; McCormack Loses Rebuttal Chance as Congressman Presides," *Boston Globe*, August 29, 1926, p. B10.

"Gallivan Reviews Work Against Volstead's Bill," *BG*, September 12, 1926.

"Gallivan Turns Fire on Rival's Absence; Asserts McCormack Missed More Roll Call Than He," *BG*, September 5, 1926.

Galloway, J. M., "Speaker Joseph W. Byrns: Party Leader in the New Deal," *Tennessee Historical Quarterly*, XXV (1966), pp. 63–76.

Galvin, John T., "One Man Pulls the Strings in Wild 1925 Mayor's Race," *BG*, August 21, 1983.

Garrow, David J., "The FBI and Martin Luther King," *TheAtlantic.com*, July/August, 2002.

Gazell, James A., "Arthur H. Vandenberg, Internationalism, and the United Nations," *Political Science Quarterly*, LXXXVIII (September, 1973, pp. 375–94).

"The Gentleman at the Keyhole. 'Nicked!'," *Collier's*, December, 1929, p. 44.

Gentile, Richard H., "John William McCormack," in Kenneth T. Jackson, ed., *Dictionary of American Biography, Supplement Ten, 1975-1980* (New York: Charles Scribner's Sons, 1995), pp. 483–87.

"Gift of 600,000 by Kennedy Tops Diocesan Record," *BG*, August 13, 1946.

Gilfond, Duff, "Mr. Speaker," *American Mercury*, XI (August, 1927), pp. 451–58.

Glaeser, Edward L., and Andrei Shleifer, "The Curley Effect: The Economics of Shaping the Electorate," *Journal of Law, Economics and Organization*, XXI (April, 2005), pp. 1–19.

Glass, Andrew J., "Mike Mansfield, Majority Leader," *National Journal* (March 6, 1971), pp. 499–512.

Glass, Andrew J., "Senate Censures Dodd by 92 to 5 Vote: 2nd Charge is Rejected in Voting; Senator Found Guilty of Using Donations; Will Keep Seat, Rights," *WP*, June 24, 1967.

Gold, Allan R., "First Blacks Moving to Boston Project," *NYT*, July 2, 1988.

Goldberg, Carey, "As Promised: Long-Lost Lahey Memo on FDR," *BG*, April 11, 2011.

"Goldfine Gifts OK at Yule: McCormack," *BG*, July 8, 1958.

Goodwin, George, "Seniority System in Congress," *APSR*, LIII (June, 1959), pp. 412–36.

Gould, Lewis L., and Nancy Beck Young, "The Speaker and the Presidents: Sam Rayburn, the White House, and the Legislative Process, 1941-1961," in Roger H. Davidson, Susan Webb Hammond, and Raymond W. Smock, eds., *Masters of the House: Congressional Leaders over Two Centuries* (Boulder, CO: Westview Press, 1998), pp. 181–221.

"Governor Tells Plan to Meet with Knowland," *Los Angeles Times*, March 12, 1958.

Grant, Philip A, Jr., "President Harry S. Truman and the British Loan Act of 1946," *Presidential Studies Quarterly*, XXV (Summer 1995), pp. 489–96.

Grant, Philip A, Jr., "The Mississippi Congressional Delegation and the Formation of the Conservative Coalition," *Journal of Mississippi History*, L (February, 1988), pp. 21–28.

Green, Matthew N., "McCormack Versus Udall: Explaining Intraparty Challenges to the Speaker of the House," *American Politics Research*, XXXIV (January 2006), pp. 3–21.

Groves, Charles S., "Southern Democrats Reported Seeking to Displace McCormack," *BG*, November 17, 1946.

Grubbs, Donald H., "Gardner Jackson, That 'Socialist' Tenant Farmer's Union and the New Deal," *Agricultural History*, XLII (April, 1968), pp. 125–37.

"Gun Controls Extend to Long Guns, Ammunition," *CQ Almanac 1968*, pp. 549–62.

Hagerty, James A., "Wallace Backers in Chicago Gloomy . . . Brief Platform Sought—McCormack and Mrs. Norton Put It at 500 to 1,000 Words—Foreign Policy Stressed," *NYT*, July 15, 1944.

Halamandaris, Val J., "Aging Committee, House Select," in Donald C. Bacon, Roger H. Davidson, and Morton Keller's eds., *The Encyclopedia of the United States Congress*, Vol. I (New York: Simon & Schuster, 1995), p. 17.

Hand, Susan V., "Men Grown Old, Recall Childhoods," *Boston Herald*, January 1, 1978.

Hanna, William F., "The Boston Draft Riot," *Civil War History*, XXXVI (September, 1990), pp. 262–73.

Hanson, David J., "National Prohibition and Repeal in Massachusetts," An entry on the Alcohol Problems and Solutions website, accessed October 1, 2014.

Hard, William, "Nicholas Longworth," *Nation*, XXIII (January 1924), pp. 88–89.

Hard, William, "Nicholas Longworth: A Contradictory Floor Leader of the House," *Current Opinion*, LXXVI (April, 1924).

Harding, John, "The 1942 Congressional Elections," *APSR*, XXXVIII (February, 1944), pp. 41–58

Harris, Douglas B., "The Rise of the Public Speakership," *Political Science Quarterly*, CXIII (Summer, 1998), pp. 193–212.

Harris, Douglas B., and Garrison Nelson, "Middlemen No More? Emergent Patterns in Congressional Leadership Selection," *P.S.: Political Science and Politics*, XLV (January 2008), pp. 49–55.

Harris, Joseph P., "The Reorganization of Congress," *Public Administration Review*, VI (Summer, 1946), pp. 267–82.

Harris, John G., "Curley Yields to McCormack: Step Aside as Leader of Convention Slate When Congressman Objects to Support of MacArthur," *BG*, March 19, 1948.

Harris, John, "McCormack Tops Herter by 30,000," *BG*, November 5, 1958.

Harris, John G., "People's Lobby: Furcolo's Innovation Interests Congress," *BG*, January 16, 1949.

Harris, John, "Platform Drafters Search for Civil Rights Formula," *BG*, August 12, 1956.

Harris, John, "Political Notebook: Adlai's Agent in State Seems to be Dever," *BG*, November 29, 1955.

Harris, John G., "Politics and Politicians," *BG*, February 18, 1940.

Harris, John G., "Politics and Politicians: 2 Bay State Men May Learn F.D.'s Third Term Stand," *BG*, July 7, 1940.

Hart, Henry C., "Legislative Abdication in Regional Development," *Journal of Politics*, XIII (August, 1951), pp. 393–417.

"Hats in the Ring: Monsignor Jim," *New Republic*, CII (March 11, 1940).

"Hazardous Substances," *CQ Almanac 1970*, p. 630.

Heacock, Walter J., "William B. Bankhead and the New Deal," *Journal of Southern History*, XXI (August, 1955), pp. 347–59.

Healy, Robert F., "Kennedy Won't Budge on School Aid Issue: Holds Firm Despite Church Opposition," *BG*, March 12, 1961.

Healy, Robert F., "Ted Kennedy Tells About Harvard Examination Incident," *BG*, June 7, 2010.

Healy, Robert F., "The Political Circuit: How Ted Fared in State Poll," *BG*, July 15, 1962.

Hedlund, Richard, "Brent Spence and the Bretton Woods Legislation," *Register of the Kentucky Historical Society*, LXXIX (Winter, 1981), pp. 40–56.

Hennessy, M. E., "Ely Quits Chicago, Undecided on 'Walk': 'I Don't Know Willkie,'" He
Says on Shift to G.O.P.," *BG,* July 19, 1940.

Hennessy, M. E., "Martin Rates High in G.O.P. Leadership: Reason for Success and Views
on Campaign Revealed," *BG,* September 9, 1935.

Herbers, John, "Johnson Rejects Primary Contests: Bars All but Three Required by State
Laws-Rift with Kennedys May Widen," *NYT,* March 7, 1968.

Herbers, John, "Move On to Have Albert Replace McCormack as Speaker," *NYT,* February
26, 1968.

Herbers, John, "Wallace Urges Radical 'Reality'; Scores the Advice of 'Theorists,'" *NYT,*
September 6, 1963.

Herring, E. Pendleton, "First Session of the Seventy-Fourth Congress," *APSR,* XXIX
(December, 1935), pp. 985–1005.

Herring, E. Pendleton, "Seventy-Second Congress, First Session, December 7, 1931 to July
16, 1932," *APSR,* XXVI (October, 1932), pp. 845–74.

Herring, E. Pendleton, "Seventy-Third Congress, First Session, March 9, 1933," *APSR,*
XXVIII (February, 1934), pp. 65–83.

Herring, E. Pendleton, "Seventy-Third Congress, Second Session, January 3, 1934 to June
18, 1934," *APSR,* XXVIII (October, 1934), pp. 852–66.

Hersey, John, "Survival (A Reporter at Large)," *The New Yorker,* June 17, 1944, pp. 27–38.

Hersey, John, "Survival: From a PT base in the Solomons Comes this Nightmare Epic of
the Will-to-Live," *Reader's Digest,* XLV (August, 1944), pp. 75–80.

High, Stanley, "Whose Party Is It?" *Saturday Evening Post,* CCIX (February 6, 1937), pp. 10ff.

"Highway Authorizations," *CQWR,* October 19, 1962.

"Highway Beautification Act of 1965," *CQ Almanac 1965,* pp. 724–33.

Hill, Thomas Michael, "Senator Arthur H. Vandenberg, the Politics of Bipartisanship, and
the Origins of Anti-Soviet Consensus, 1941-1946," *World Affairs,* CXXXVIII (Winter,
1975–76), pp. 219–41.

Hinckley, Barbara, "Congressional Leadership Selection and Support: A Comparative
Analysis," *Journal of Politics,* XXXII (May, 1970), pp. 268–87.

Hinckley, Barbara, "Seniority in the Committee Leadership Selection of Congress,"
American Journal of Political Science, XIII (November, 1969), pp. 613–30.

Hoffman, Malcom A., "Congress Streamlined," *Federal Bar Association Journal,* VII (July,
1946), pp. 378–83.

Hofstader, Richard, "The Age of Rubbish," *Newsweek,* LXXVI (July 6, 1970), pp. 20–23.

Hogarty, Richard A., and Garrison Nelson, "Redistricting on Beacon Hill and Political
Power on Capitol Hill," *New England Journal of Public Policy,* XVII (Fall/Winter,
2001–02), pp. 91–104.

Holbrook, Stewart, "Frank Merriwell at Yale Again and Again and Again," *American
Heritage,* XII (June, 1961), pp. 24–27.

Hollcroft, Temple B., ed., "Congressman's Letter on the Speaker's Election in the Thirty-fourth
Congress," *Mississippi Valley Historical Review,* XLIII (December, 1956), pp. 444–58.

"Honoring Son's Memory with Memorial Alter," *Lawrence (Mass.) Daily Eagle,* August 15,
1946.

"House Approves Excise Tax Reductions," *CQWR,* June 4, 1965.

"House Barber Shop Integrated," *Los Angeles Times,* October 14, 1965.

"House 'Conservative Coalition' Dominates Session," *CQWR,* December 29, 1967.

"House Democrats as One Pick Garner," *NYT,* December 6, 1931.

"House Elects McCormack as Speaker," *CQWR*, January 10, 1969.

"House Excludes Powell from Membership in the 90th Congress, Rejects Milder Punishment Recommended by Committee," *CQWR*, March 3, 1967.

"House Passes Administration Tax Bill, 219-196," *CQWR,* March 30, 1962.

"House Passes Foreign Aid Authorization," *CQWR*, July 13, 1962.

"House Rejects Compromise Education Bill," *CQWR*, XIX (September 1, 1961).

"Housing, Demonstration Cites Bill Enacted," *CQ Almanac 1966*, pp. 210–30.

"Housing Bill Provides Home-Buying, Riot, Other Aid," *CQ Almanac 1968*, pp. 313–35.

"How Adlai Won: Harry's Bitter Week," *TIME,* August 27, 1956.

"How Adlai Won: PLATFORMS: Something to Live With," *TIME.*

"How the President Persuades Congress," *NYT*, October 27, 1963.

Huertas, Thomas F., "The Economic Brief Against Glass-Steagall," *Journal of Bank Research*, XV (1984), pp. 148–49.

Huitt, Ralph K., "The Morse Committee Assignment Controversy: A Study in Senate Norms," *APSR*, LI (June, 1957), pp. 313–29.

"Hunt for Hanson, Walsh is Bailed, Former Gland Doctor Accused as Accessory in Disposing of Edith Greene's Body, Five Relatives Provide Bonds for Roxbury Physician After His Day in Cell," *BG*, July 18, 1926.

Hunter, Marjorie, "Leaders in Capitol Not told by Johnson," *NYT*, January 25, 1968.

Hunter, Marjorie, "McCormack Says He Will Not Seek New House Term; Speaker, 78, to Retire This year Amid Increasing Political Challenges," *NYT*, May 21, 1970, p. 1.

Hurd, Charles, "House Democrats Act to Free Bills from Rules Block; Caucus Votes 176-48 in Favor of Change to Force Measures to Floor When Stymied; Rayburn Again Speaker; McCormack Will Head Majority-Parley Avoids Decision on Un-American Group," *NYT,* January 2, 1949.

Hurd, Charles, "House Rebels at Speed on Reorganization Bill; Vote Off Until Next Week; Foes are Hopeful; Leaders Defeated, 191 to 149, in Attempt to Force Quick Action, O'Connor Leads battle, He Tells Congress of Letters Threatening 'Bloodshed' and 'Resort to Arms,'" *NYT,* April 1, 1938.

Hyman, Sidney, "Nine Tests for the Presidential Hopeful," *NYT Magazine* (January 4, 1959), pp. 11ff.

"Important Dates in Gibbons' Life," *BG,* September 3, 1958.

"Inaugural Events," *WP*, January 20, 1965.

"Innes, Charles H," *Who's Who in New England* (Chicago: A. N. Marquis, 1938), Vol. 3, p. 686.

"Interest Equalization Tax," *CQWR*, August 21, 1964.

Jaher, Cople, "The Politics of the Boston Brahmins, 1800-1860," in Ronald P. Formisano and Constace K. Burns, eds., *Boston 1700-1980: The Evolution of Urban Politics* (Westport, CT: Greenwood Press, 1984), pp. 59–86.

Jensen, Richard, "'No Irish Need Apply': A Myth of Victimization," *Journal of Social History*, XXXVI (Winter, 2002), pp. 405–29.

"Jimmy's Friends Mourn His Death—Streets Thronged," *BG*, April 6, 1928.

"John F. Kennedy: Democrats' Man Out Front," *TIME*, LXX (December 2, 1957), pp. 17–21.

"John W. (Jocko) McCormack, 62, Vending Machine Representative," *BG*, September 28, 1982.

"John J. Sparkman," in the online *Encyclopedia of Alabama*, accessed August 28, 2014.

"John William McCormack (1891-1980)," in Donald R. Kennon, ed., *The Speakers of the U.S. House of Representatives: A Bibliography, 1789-1984* (Baltimore: Johns Hopkins University Press, 1986), pp. 266–71.

"Johnson, Nixon 'Strongest' Candidates to Editors and Members of Congress in CQ Poll," *CQWR*, July 1, 1960.

"Johnson Victory Snuffs Out California Delegate Revolt," *Los Angeles Times*, July 15, 1960.

Jones, Charles O., "Joseph G. Cannon and Howard W. Smith: An Essay on the Limits of Leadership in the House of Representatives," *Journal of Politics*, XXX (August, 1968), pp. 617–46.

Jones, Charles O., "Representation in Congress: The Case of the House Agriculture Committee," *APSR*, LV (June, 1961), pp. 358–67.

Johnson, Claudius O., "Jerry Voorhis," in John T. Salter, ed., *Public Men In and Out of Office* (Chapel Hill: University of North Carolina Press, 1946), pp. 322–43.

Jones, Nate, "Double Take: Lyndon Johnson Was Nearly Shot by Secret Service? A Day After JFK Died," *TIME*, October 20, 2010.

Jones, Terry L., "An Administration Under Fire: The Long-Farley Affair of 1935," *Louisiana History*, XXVIII (Winter, 1987), pp. 5–17.

"Juvenile Delinquency," *CQ Almanac 1968*, pp. 307–09.

Kahn, Michael A., "Shattering the Myth about President Eisenhower's Supreme Court Appointments," *Presidential Studies Quarterly*, XXII (Winter, 1992), pp. 47–56.

Katznelson, Ira, Kim Geiger, and Daniel Kryder, "Limiting Liberalism: The Southern Veto in Congress," *Political Science Quarterly*, CVIII (Summer, 1993), pp. 283–306.

Kefauver, Estes, "Congressional Reorganization: Better Teamwork between the Legislative and Executive Branches of Government is Essential," *Journal of Politics*, IX (February, 1947), pp. 96–107.

"Kennedy, Curley in Heated Clash on Seaway at Democratic Dinner," *BG*, January 24, 1954.

"Kennedy is Hostile to Curley Bid," *Lynn (Mass.) Telegram-News*, July 9, 1947.

"Kennedy, Lindbergh, Roosevelt, and Munich," in Wayne S. Cole, ed., *Roosevelt & The Isolationists* (Lincoln: University of Nebraska Press, 19830, pp. 274–90).

"Kennedy-McCormack Donnybrook Brews," *CQWR*, October 12, 1961.

Kennedy, John F, "Where Democrats Should Go From Here," *LIFE*, XLII (March 11, 1957), pp. 164–66, 171–79.

Kennedy, Paul, "6 Hecklers Ejected, Wallace Goes in Garden Back Door," *BG,* September 19, 1948.

"Kennedy Rebuffs Curley Petition," *New Bedford (Mass.) Standard-Times*, July 9, 1947.

"Kennedy Refuses to Aid Curley," *Worcester (Mass.) Gazette*, July 8, 1947.

Kennedy, Joseph P., "Present Policy is Politically and Morally Bankrupt: United Nations Not a Vehicle to Enforce Peace," delivered at the University of Virginia Law Forum, Charlottesville, Virginia, December 12, 1950, from *Vital Speeches of the Day*, XVII (January, 1951), pp. 170–74.

Kenworthy, E. W., "Dual Office Setup Linked to Voloshen Case," *NYT,* November 2, 1969.

Key, V. O. Jr. "A Theory of Critical Elections," *Journal of Politics*, XVII (February, 1955), pp. 3–18.

Kimball, Warren, "1776: Lend-Lease Gets a Number," *New England Quarterly*, XLII (June 1969), pp. 260–67.

Kimball, Warren, and Bruce Bartlett, "Roosevelt and Prewar Commitments to Churchill: The Tyler Kent Affair," *Diplomatic History, V* (Fall, 1981), pp. 291–311.

King, Larry L., "The Road to Power in Congress," *Harper's Magazine*, CCXLII (June, 1971), pp. 39–63.

"Knocko McCormack Dies, Ending an Era; Politician was 67," *BG*, November 18, 1983.

Kofmehl, Kenneth, "The Institutionalization of a Voting Bloc," *Western Political Science Quarterly*, XVII (June, 1964), pp. 256–72.

Kovach, Bill, "McCarthy, Casually Enters the'72 Race," *NYT*, December 7, 1967.

Krock, Arthur, "In the Nation: Consistency by Mr. Truman That is Also Fun," *NYT*, February 7, 1947.

Krock, Arthur, "Rayburn's Successor: Absence of Intervention by Kennedy Makes McCormack Likely Choice," *NYT*, November 19, 1961.

Kurtz, Howard, "Marshall Had Harsh Words About Eisenhower, RFK," *WP*, January 31, 1993.

La Follette, Robert M., "Congress Wins a Victory Over Congress: The Legislative Reorganization Act of 1946," *NYT Magazine* (August 4, 1946), pp. 11, 45–46.

Lambert, William, "The Murky Men from the Speaker's Office," *LIFE* (October 31, 1969), pp. 52ff.

Landis, James M., "The Legislative History of the Securities Act of 1933," *George Washington Law Review*, XXVIII (1959), pp. 29–49.

Lapomarda, Vincent A., "A New Deal Democrat in Boston," *Essex Institute Historical Collections*, CVIII (April, 1972), pp. 135–52.

Lapomarda, Vincent A., "Maurice Joseph Tobin: The Decline of Bossism in Boston," *New England Quarterly*, XLIII (September, 1970), pp. 355–81.

Lastelic, Joe, "Bolling Wants McCormack Out: Speaker Should Step Down, He Asserts in Talk: In Favor of Albert: Missourian Leads Group Disappointed with Leadership," *Kansas City Star*, October 28, 1967.

Lawrence, Eric D., Forrest Maltzman, and Paul J. Wahlbeck, "The Politics of Speaker Cannon's Committee Assignments," *American Journal of Political Science*, XLV (July, 2001), pp. 551–62.

"Leaders of the New Congress," *NYT*, January 3, 1953.

Lemmon, Sarah McCulloh, "Ideology of the Dixiecrat Movement," *Social Forces*, XXX (December, 1951), pp. 162–71.

Leonard, John, "Admirers Greet Barry at N.H. Coffee Klatches," *Boston Globe*, January 9, 1964.

Leuchtenburg, William E., "FDR's Court-Packing Plan: A Second Life, a Second Death," *Duke Law Journal* (June to September, 1985), pp. 673–89.

Leuchtenburg, William E., "New Faces of 1946," *Smithsonian Magazine*, XXVII (November 2006), pp. 46–54.

Levin, Harry, "The Private Life of F.O. Matthiessen," *New York Review of Books*, XXV (July 20, 1978), pp. 42–46.

Lewis, Anthony, "Bolling Would Have Speaker Name Committee Heads," *NYT*, November 16, 1964.

Lewis, Anthony, "Key Domestic Problem for Johnson—Civil Rights," *NYT*, November 24, 1963.

Lewis, Eleanor G., "The House Committee on Rules and the Legislative Program of the Kennedy and Johnson Administrations," *Capitol Studies*, II (Fall, 1978), pp. 27–38.

Lewis, William J., "Aspirants All Slugging in State Political Fight," *BG*, October 11, 1956.

Lewis, William J., "Kennedy's Forces Win, Democrats Pick Lynch; Burke Out as State Committee Chairman; Defeated 47-31 Says He'll Run Against Senator," *BG,* May 20, 1956.

Lewis, William J., "McCormack Picked for Interim Post: Legislators Select Boston Democrat, Party Nominee Will Finish ate Atty. Gen. Fingold's Term," *BG,* September 12, 1958.

Lewis, William J., "Ward Wins; McCormack Walks Out, Councilor's Action Causes Uproar at Democratic Parley; Murphy Named," *BG,* June 10, 1956.

"Liberal House Democrats Organize for Action," *CQWR,* January 8, 1960.

Lippmann, Walter, "Conspiracy on Capitol Hill: Congress Refuses to Legislate but Wants to Take Over Power Reserved to the President," *BG,* December 26, 1963.

"Limit of Two Terms for Any President Approved by House," *NYT,* February 6, 1947.

"Limit on Tenure of a President Hit," *NYT,* February 2, 1947.

Lomasney, "5th Suffolk, Boston, Born There of Irish Parents, Dec 3, 1859," in *A Souvenir of the Massachusetts Constitutional Convention; Boston, 1917-18-19* (Stoughton, MA: A.M. Bridgman, 1919).

"Lone Star Flag Leads Parade: Johnson's Nomination Touches Off Jubilant Demonstration," *Los Angeles Times,* July 15, 1960.

Lucy, William H., "Polls, Primaries, and Presidential Nominations," *Journal of Politics,* XXXV (November, 1973), pp. 830–48.

Luedde, Henry W., "New Limitations on the Power of Congress: The A.A.A. Decision," *St. Louis Law Review,* XXI (February, 1936), pp. 149–60.

Lydon, Christopher, "For Governor-M'Cormack Outruns a Strong O'Donnell," *BG,* September 14, 1966.

Lyons, Richard L., "Bay State Democrats Face Blood-Letting in Primary: Kennedy Leadership Still Lacking," *WP,* June 12, 1966.

Lyons, Richard L., "GOP Leaders Join Democrats of South in Rules Unit Battle," *WP,* January 8, 1963.

Lyons, Richard L., "McCormack Beats Back House Revolt," *WP,* January 3, 1969.

Lyons, Richard L., "McCormack Retirement Ends Turn-of-Century Political Era," *WP,* May 21, 1970, p. A13.

Lyons, Richard L., "McCormack to Quit at End of Session; Nixon Hails His Service to Country," *WP,* May 21, 1970.

Lyons, Richard L., "19 in House Threaten Revolt Over Seniority," *WP,* March 20, 1970, p. A4.

Lyons, Richard L., "Rep. Bolling Quits Race for Leader," *WP,* January 4, 1962.

Lyons, Richard L., "Rep. Waldie Asks Removal of McCormack as Speaker," *WP,* February 4, 1970.

Lyons, Richard L., "Speaker McCormack's Wife Dies," *WP,* December 3, 1971.

Lyons, Richard L., "The Next Speaker; McCormack is Next in Line Is Last of Passing Breed," *WP,* December 5, 1961.

Lyons, Richard L., "Vote at 18 Change is Asked: Nixon Request Stirs Hill Row on Rights Bill," *WP,* April 28, 1970.

Lyons, Richard L., "2 Proven Supporters of Kennedy Named to Ways and Means Committee," *WP,* January 15, 1963.

Lyons, Richard L., "28 Republicans Join in Backing Administration," *WP,* January 10, 1963.

Macmahon, Arthur W., "American Government and Politics: Second Session of the Seventy-First Congress, December 2, 1929 to July 3, 1930; Special Session of the Senate, July 7-21," *APSR*, XXIV (November, 1930), pp. 913–46.

Macmahon, Arthur W., "American Government and Politics: Seventy-First Congress, Third Session, December 1, 1930 to March 4, 1931," *APSR*, XXV (November, 1931), pp. 932–55.

"Major Officials Named for the 88th Congress," *NYT*, January 10, 1963.

Mallan, John P., and George Blackwood, "The Tax That Beat a Governor: The Ordeal of Massachusetts," in Alan Westin, ed., *The Uses of Power: 7 Cases in American Politics* (New York: Harcourt. Brace & World, 1962), pp. 285–322.

Maney, Patrick J., "Hale Boggs: The Southerner as National Democrat," in Davidson, Hammond, and Smock, eds., *Masters of the House: Congressional Leadership over Two Centuries*, pp. 223–58.

Manley, John F., "The Conservative Coalition in Congress," *American Behavioral Scientist*, XVII (November to December, 1973), pp. 233–47.

Manley, John F., "The House Committee on Ways and Means: Conflict Management in a Congressional Committee," *APSR*, LIX (December, 1964), pp. 927–39.

Manley, John F., "Wilbur D. Mills: A Study in Congressional Influence," *APSR*, LXII (June, 1969), pp. 442–64.

Mansfield, Harvey C., "Legislative Veto and the Deportation of Aliens," *Public Administration Review*, I (Spring, 1941), pp. 281–86.

Marecello, Ronald, "Senator Josiah Bailey, Harry Hopkins, and the WPA: A Prelude to the Conservative Coalition," *Southern Studies*, XXII (Winter 1983), pp. 321–29.

Markey, Morris, "The Mysterious Death of Starr Faithfull," in Isabel Leighton, ed., *The Aspirin Age, 1919-1941* (New York: Simon & Schuster, 1949), pp. 258–74.

"Martin Sweig Named in New Indictment," *WP*, November 4, 1971.

Masters, Nicholas A., "House Committee Assignments," *APSR* (June, 1961), pp. 345–57.

McAndrews, Lawrence, "The Avoidable Conflict: Kennedy, the Bishops, and Federal Aid to Education," *Catholic Historical Review*, LXXV (April, 1990), pp. 278–93.

McCormack, John W., 'America: Today and Yesterday, as Speaker McCormack Sees Things after 42 Years in Congress," *U.S. News and World Report*, July 27, 1970, pp. 58–62.

McCormack, John W., "Communism—Its Method," *National Republic*, XXIV (June, 1936), p. 1.

McCormack, John W., "I Remember When I was Thirteen," in Leo P. Danwer, ed., *I Remember Southie* (Boston: Christopher Publishing House, 1976), pp. 119–21.

McCormack, John W., "Should Congress Enact a Federal Sedition Law?," *Congressional Digest*, XIV (October, 1935), pp. 236–53.

McCormack, John W., "Personal Liberty," *Annals of the American Academy of Political and Social Science*, CLXXXV (May, 1936), pp. 154–61.

"McCormack Again Attacks Gallivan Failure to Vote," *BG*, September 5, 1926.

"McCormack Aids Dawson: Steps Aside to Open Committee Chairmanship to Negro," *NYT*, January 1, 1949.

"McCormick [sic] Announces for Senate; Won't Defer to Anyone," *BG*, March 6, 1962.

"McCormack Answers Critics," *BG*, October 29, 1967.

"McCormack Asks Collaboration," *NYT*, July 10, 1944.

"McCormack in Whip Post," *NYT*, January 8, 1947.

"McCormack, Kennedy Factions Vie on Seating Issue," *BG*, August 30, 1964.

"McCormack Rejects Bid to Ike Briefing," *WP*, November 12, 1959.

"McCormack Reviled in Anti-Semitic 'Ode,'" *BG*, November 23, 1943.

"McCormack Rites Thronged in Dorchester," *BG*, January 12, 1966.

"McCormack Seeks Seat in Congress; Opposed Gallivan for Nomination Last Term; Kinnaly to Be Secretary if Nomination is Won," *Boston Globe*, June 12, 1928.

"McCormack Statement on Democratic Hassle," *BG*, May 18, 1956.

"McCormack Sure His Religion Won't Hurt His Chances," *BG*, July 10, 1948.

McGeary, Martin N., "Congressional Investigations During Franklin D. Roosevelt's First Term," *APSR*, XXXI (August, 1937), pp. 680–94.

McGrory, Mary, "Pair of Contrasting Bostonians," *Hammond (Ind.) Times*, October 12, 1961.

McGrory, Mary, "Strange Coalition Behind Scenes Hopes to Beat [McCormack]," *BG*, December 3, 1961.

McGrory, Mary, "The Right-Hand Men—Pierre Salinger, Lawrence O'Brien, and Kenneth P. O'Donnell," in Lester Tanzer, ed., *The Kennedy Circle* (Washington, DC: Luce Books, 1961), pp. 68–75.

McLaughlin, Gerald T., "Congressional Self-Discipline: The Power to Expel, to Exclude and to Punish," *Fordham Law Review*, XLI (October, 1972), pp. 43–66.

McNair, Marie, "'Mr. Sam' Shares 77th With Colleague," *WP*, January 7, 1959.

McNamara, Tom, "The Washington Merry-Go-Round: McCormack is Loyal Team Man," *WP*, October 23, 1965.

McNaughton, Frank, "Anti-Semitism in Congress," *TIME*, September 12, 1941.

McNaughton, Frank, "Congress Takes a Rest," *TIME*, McNaughton Papers, Truman Library.

McNaughton, Frank, "House Appropriations' Committee Chairmanship," *TIME* September 4, 1941, Truman Library.

McNaughton, Frank, "Roosevelt Endorsement of La Guardia," *TIME*, October 24, 1941.

"M'Cormack Grateful to Voters and Post," *Boston Sunday Post*, April 25, 1956.

"M'Cormack Rift Denied by Kennedy," *Boston Post*, August 29, 1956.

"Means and Ways," *WP*, January 16, 1963.

"Medical Care-Social Security Bill Sent to the President," *CQWR*, July 30, 1965.

Meehan, Thomas, "A Forgettable Century—Horatio Alger's," *NYT Magazine*, June 18, 1964.

Meggison, Michael T., "The P.E.I. Scottish and Irish Ancestry of John William McCormack, Speaker of the U.S. House of Representatives," *P.E.I. Genealogical Society's Records*, 2000.

Meier, Hank, "Hunting for the Middle Ground: Arthur Vandenberg and the Mackinac Charter, 1943," *Michigan Historical Review*, XIX (Fall, 1993), pp. 1–21.

"Military Pay Increase," *CQ Almanac 1967*, pp. 1055–57.

Miller, Bryon S., "A Law is Passed: The Atomic Energy Act of 1946," *University of Chicago Law Review*, XV (Summer, 1948), pp. 799–821.

Moore, John, "Senator Josiah Bailey and the 'Conservative Manifesto' of 1937," *Journal of Southern History, XXXI* (February, 1965), pp. 22–23, 27.

Morgan, Anne H., "Robert Samuel Kerr (1896-1963)," Online *Encyclopedia of Oklahoma History and Culture*, accessed January 5, 2014.

Morgan, Edwin B., "A Congressman's Letters on the Speaker Election in the Thirty-Fourth Congress," *Mississippi Valley Historical Review*, XLIII (December, 1956), pp. 444–58.

Morgan, Robert, "State Moves to Strengthen Civil Rights," *BG*, February 5, 1959.

Morgenthau, Henry, Jr., "Statement on Economic Security Act," Hearings of the House Ways and Means Committee, 74th Congress, 1st Session (1935).

Moritz, Charles, ed., "John W. McCormack," in *Current Biography, 1962* (New York: H. W. Wilson, 1963), pp. 275–77.

Morris, John D., "Albert Assured of Leader's Post, Rep. Bolling Formally Quits House Democratic Race," *NYT,* January 4, 1962.

Morris, John D., "Congress Ends Longest Session Since Korea War: Battle Over Appropriations Brings Attack on Leaders by Cannon of Missouri; Return Set of Jan 9; Kennedy Won a Few Major Battles, Lost Others and Made Compromises," *NYT,* October 14, 1962.

Morris, John D., "Limit of Two Terms for Any President Approved by House," *NYT,* February 6, 1947.

Morris, John D., "Upper Hand Held by Conservatives: Key Goals Eluded Kennedy and Johnson During the Post-Convention Session," *NYT,* September 1, 1960.

Morrison, Geoffrey F., "Champ Clark and the Rules Revolution of 1910," *Capitol Studies,* II (Winter, 1974), pp. 43–56.

Morris, Richard B., "Where Success Begins: Rags to Riches—Myth and Reality," *The Saturday Review,* XXXVI (November 21, 1953), pp. 15–16, 65–71.

"Move Grows to Nominate McCormack Vice President," *BG,* July 8, 1948.

"Mr. Speaker," *TIME,* January 19, 1962, p. 17.

Mullins, W. E., "Dever Faces Tough Primary Test," *Boston Herald,* April 13, 1946.

Mullins, W. E., "This Is How I See it: Obscure Post for Veteran McCormack, Key Task for Freshman Kennedy Two X's of New Congress," *Boston Herald,* January 17, 1947.

Nadel, Mark, Douglas Harbit, Judith Lichten, Thomas Lichten, and Bruce G. Rosenthal, "The House Science and Astronautics Committee and the Senate Aeronautical and Space Science Committee," in the Ralph Nader Congress Project, *The Environment Committees: A Study of the House and Senate Interior, Agriculture, and Science Committees* (New York: Grossman, 1975), pp. 281–357.

"Nation's Meat Inspection Requirements Tightened," *CQ Almanac 1967,* pp. 705–13.

"National Affairs: The Wide-Open Winner," *TIME,* August 27, 1956.

"National and World Challenges Ignored by 1962 Session," *ADA World,* October, 1962, Congressional Supplement.

"National Quotas for Immigration to End," *CQ Almanac 1965,* pp. 459–82.

"NDEA, Impacted Areas," *CQWR,* August 7, 1964.

Nelson, Garrison, "Change and Continuity in the Recruitment of U.S. House Leaders, 1789-1975," in Norman J. Ornstein, ed., *Congress in Change: Evolution and Reform* (New York: Praeger, 1975), pp. 155–83.

Nelson, Garrison, "In the Shadows of John McCormack's Past Lie New Truths about His Life," *Boston Sunday Globe, Focus,* July 25, 1999.

Nelson, Garrison, "Irish Identity Politics: The Reinvention of Speaker John W. McCormack," *New England Journal of Public Policy,* XV (Fall/Winter 1999/2000), pp. 7–34.

Nelson, Garrison, "Leadership Position-Holding in the United States House of Representatives," *Capitol Studies,* IV (Fall, 1976), pp. 11–36.

Nelson, Garrison, "New England and the Presidency: Voting Bloc Shrinks as Educational Role Grows," *Boston Sunday Globe, Ideas,* December 28, 2003.

Nelson, Garrison, "Nixon's Silent House of Hawks: A Documented Analysis of the Anti-War Voting Records of Republicans and Democrats in Strategic Districts," *The Progressive,* XXXIV (August, 1970), pp. 13–20.

Nelson, Garrison, "Partisan Patterns of House Leadership Change, 1789-1977," *APSR*, LXII (September, 1977), pp. 918–39.

Nelson, Garrison, "Running from New England: Will it Ever Lead the Nation Again?" *New England Journal of Political Science*, III (Fall, 2009), pp. 112–65.

Nelson, Garrison, "Sideshows and Strategic Separations: The Impact of Presidential Year Politics on Congressional Elections," in Harvey L. Schantz, ed., *Politics in an Era of Divided Government: Elections and Governance in the Second Clinton Administration* (New York: Routledge, 2001), pp. 105–27.

Nelson, Garrison, "Unraveling the Reinvention of Speaker John W. McCormack," in Burdett A. Loomis, ed., *Extension of Remarks of the Legislative Studies Section of the American Political Science Association*, January, 2000, pp. 2–7.

Nelson, Garrison, "White House Inheritors and Climbers: Presidential Kin, Class and Performance, 1789-2002," *New England Journal of Public Policy*, XVIII (Spring/Summer 2003), pp. 11–38.

Nelson, Michael, "The President and the Court: Reinterpreting the Court-packing Episode of 1937," *Political Science Quarterly*, 103, no. 2 (Summer, 1988), pp. 267–93.

Neuberger, Richard L., "Progressives in Congress," *Common Sense*, XI (March, 1942), pp. 83–86.

"New Members Back Bankhead Drive in House; Dark Horse Chance Seen Better Due to Close Fight Impending," *NYT,* January 1, 1935.

"New Vocational Rehabilitation Program Established," *CQ Almanac 1968*, pp. 391–93.

"Nicholas Longworth: A Contradictory Floor Leader of the House," *Current Opinion*, LXXVI (April, 1924), pp. 414–16.

"1966 Elections: A Major Republican Comeback: GOP Gains Eight New Governorships, Three Senate Seats and 47 House Seats," *CQWR*, November 11, 1966.

"1967 Aid Authorization Lowest in History," *CQ Almanac 1967*, pp. 679–97.

"No Big Fight in Primary Expected by McCormack," *BG,* June 29, 1958.

"No Party Slant in Goldfine Gifts," *BG,* July 4, 1958.

Nolan, Martin F. and S. J. Micciehe, "McCormack Will Retire This Year," *BG,* May 21, 1970, pp. 1 and 18.

Norris, Curt, "New England Mysteries: Shady Doctor Leaves Trail of Horror," *Quincy (Mass.) Patriot Ledger*, October 27, 1984.

Oberdorfer, Don, "Nixon Denies Move Against McCormack," *WP*, January 8, 1971.

Oberdorfer, Don, "The Job John McCormack Dreads," *Saturday Evening Post* (March 21, 1964), pp. 66–68.

"O'Brien Puts Oil in Kennedy Machine," *Los Angeles Times*, July 13, 1960.

O'Connor, "Principal Legislation of the Seventy-Fourth Congress," *U.S. Law Review*, LXIX (September, 1935), pp. 466–73.

O'Connor, Richard W., "From Andrew Square to Speaker's Chair," *Yankee*, 40 (April, 1976), pp. 90–95, 132–34.

O'Donnell, John, "Capitol Stuff," *Washington Daily News*, March 22, 1943.

Oliver, Myrna, "Rep. Edward Boland, 90; Opposed Aid to Contras," *Los Angeles Times*, November 6, 2011.

Oliver, William W., "Vinson in Congress," *Northwestern Law Review*, XLIX (March/April, 1954), pp. 62–75.

O'Neill, Tip as told to Mary McSherry, "Unforgettable John McCormack," *Reader's Digest*, May, 1981, pp. 123–27.

"1.1 Billion Appalachia Aid Bill Approved," *CQ Almanac 1965*, pp. 788–97.

Oppenheimer, Bruce I., and Robert L. Peabody, "How the Race for House Majority Leader was Won—By One Vote," *Washington Monthly*, IX (November 1977), pp. 46–56.

Ornstein, Norman J., "Causes and Consequences of Congressional Change: Subcommittee Reforms in the House of Representatives, 1970-73," in Norman J. Ornstein, ed., *Congress in Change: Evolution and Reform* (New York: Praeger, 1975), pp. 88–114.

Owens, Cornelius, "Bay Staters to Vote McCormack to the End," *United Press*, July 11, 1948.

Owens, Cornelius, "McCormack Too Late, Barkley Out in Front," *BG*, July 13, 1948.

Owens, Cornelius, "Rep. McCormack Quits Race for Vice President," *BG*, July 13, 1948.

Owens, C. R., "Atlantic City Aftermath: Kennedy and the McCormacks," *BG*, August 30, 1964.

Owens, C. R., "Democratic Plight: Many Avoid Adlai but-Who else is There?" *BG*, January 15, 1956.

Owens, C. R., "Jack's Pep Talk Revives Orphaned Bay State Bloc," *BG*, July 12, 1960.

Owens, C. R., "[Eddie] McCormack Nears Win on Democrats' 3rd Ballot: Lacks 9 Votes for Choice as Atty Gen. Sen Kennedy, Furcolo Win by Acclamation," *BG*, June 22, 1958.

Owens, C. R., "Politics' New Look: Old Pros Pulled Their Weight on the Convention Floor, but Ivy Leaguers, the Status seekers, Were Tops," *BG*, July 17, 1960.

Page, William Tyler, "Mr. Speaker Longworth," *Scribner's*, LXXXIII (March, 1928), pp. 272–80.

Page, William Tyler, "The Speaker of the House," *Review of Reviews*, LXXVII (March, 1928), 320–21.

"Party Perplexity after Longworth," *Literary Digest*, April 25, 1931, p. 11.

"Party's Film Aids Kennedy's Drive; Senator, Star of Movie, Gets First Demonstration—Other 2nd Place Seekers Gain," *NYT,* August 14, 1956.

"Passage of Job Safety Bill Ends Three-Year-Dispute," *CQ Almanac 1970*, pp. 675–82.

Paterson, Thomas G., and William J. Brophy, "October Missiles and November Elections: The Cuban Missile Crisis and American Politics, 1962," *Journal of American History*, LXXIII (June, 1986), pp. 87–119.

Patterson, James T., "Conservative Coalition Forms in Congress: 1933-1939," *Journal of American History*, LII (March, 1966), pp. 757–72.

Patterson, James T., "Eating Humble Pie: A Note on Roosevelt, Congress, and Neutrality Revision in 1939," *Historian*, XXXI (May, 1969), pp. 407–13.

Peabody, Robert L., "Party Leadership Change in the United States House of Representatives," *APSR*, LXI (September, 1961), pp. 675–93.

Pearson, Drew, "Kennedy Has Three Reasons for Sidetraking McCormack," *The Charleston (S.C.) Gazette*, October 11, 1961.

Pearson, Drew, "Laws by the Loaf: President's Bread-Breaking and Freshman Idealism Made 89th Congress a Smasher," *WP*, October 24, 1965.

Pearson, Drew, "McCormack's Deal" in "Teacher Kerr's Absence Record," *WP,* January 8, 1965.

Pearson, Drew, "Odd Alliance Delays School Bill: Backstage Factor Strange Alignment," *WP*, June 26, 1961.

Pearson, Drew, "Old Feud Mars Speaker Race," *Charleston (S.C.) Gazette*, October 13, 1961.

Pearson, Drew, "Potent McCormack Pokes Finger," *WP*, June 14, 1961.

Pearson, Drew, "The House Misses Mister Sam," *WP*, March 17, 1962.

Pearson, Drew, "Washington Merry-Go-Round: Albert's in the Middle of House Troika," *WP*, February 19, 1963.

Pearson, Drew, "Washington Merry-Go-Round: 'Boycott' of K. Worries Officials," *WP*, August 22, 1959.

Pearson, Drew, "Washington Merry-Go-Round: Cannon Still Blasts Sen. Hayden," *WP*, July 15, 1962.

Pearson, Drew, "Washington Merry-Go-Round: Exit 'Congress of the Old Men,'" *WP*, October 15, 1962.

Pearson, Drew, "Washington Merry-Go-Round: Liberals Force a Roll Call," *WP*, January 8, 1965.

Pearson, Drew, "Washington Merry-Go-Round: McCormack-Smith Pact Reported," *WP*, December 29, 1961.

Pearson, Drew, "Washington Merry-Go-Round: Why Kennedy Hedged School Stand: An Important Record," *WP*, June 27, 1961.

Peppard, Alan, "JFK Traveled to Sam Rayburn's Side in Final Hours," *Dallas Morning News*, Updated December 22, 2010.

Perros, George P., "Introduction," *Preliminary Inventory of the Special House Committee on Un-American Activities Authorized to Investigate Nazi Propaganda and Certain Other Propaganda Activities Under the Authority of H. Res. 198, 73rd Congress*.

"Petition for a Caucus to Fill Rayburn Post," *NYT*, September 20, 1940.

Philpott, A. J., "Eamon De Valera Pleads Irish Cause at Fenway Park," *BG*, June 30, 1919.

Pika, Joseph W., "Interest Groups and the White House under Roosevelt and Truman," *Political Science Quarterly*, CII (Winter, 1987–88), pp. 647–68.

"Platform Builder; John William McCormack," *NYT*, August 7, 1956.

Plesur, Milton, "Republican Congressional Comeback of 1938," *Review of Politics*, XXIV (October, 1962), pp. 525–62.

Polenberg, Richard, "Franklin Roosevelt and the Purge of John O'Connor: The Impact of Urban Change on Political Parties," *New York History*, XLIX (July, 1968), pp. 306–26.

"Political Notes: Promise Kept," *TIME*, (July 1, 1946), p. 23.

"Political Party Affiliations in Congress and the Presidency, 1789-1974," *Congressional Quarterly's Guide to U.S. Elections* (Washington, DC: Congressional Quarterly, 1975), pp. 928–29.

Pollock, James K., "The Seniority Rule in Congress," *North American Review*, CCXXII (December, 1925), pp. 235–45.

"Polish Exiles Honor Katyn Investigators," *BG*, March 29, 1953.

Polk, Judd, and Gardner Patterson, "The British Loan," *Foreign Affairs*, XXIV (April, 1946), pp. 429–40.

Polsby, Nelson W., "Two Strategies of Influence: Choosing a Majority Leader, 1962," in Robert L. Peabody and Nelson W. Polsby, eds., *New Perspectives on the House of Representatives*, (Chicago: Rand, McNally, 1963), pp. 237–70.

Polsby, Nelson W., Miriam Gallaher, and Barry S. Rundquist, "Growth of the Seniority System in the U.S. House of Representatives," *APSR*, LXIII (September, 1969), pp. 787–807.

Pomper, Gerald, "Labor and Congress: The Repeal of Taft-Hartley," *Labor History*, II (Fall, 1961), pp. 323–43.

Pomper, Gerald, "The Nomination of Hubert Humphrey for Vice President," *Journal of Politics*, XXVIII (August, 1966), pp. 639–59.

Porter, David L., "Representative Lindsay Warren, the Water Bloc, and the Transportation Act of 1940," *North Carolina Historical Review* (Summer, 1973), pp. 273–88.

Porter, David L., "The Battle of the Texas Giants: Hatton Sumners, Sam Rayburn, and the Logan-Walter Bill of 1939," *Texana*, XII (1974), pp. 349–81.

Porter, David L., "Senator Carl Hatch and the Hatch Act of 1939," *New Mexico Historical Review*, XLVIII (April, 1973), pp. 151–63.

"Postal Rates, Federal Pay Increased in Single Bill," *CQ Almanac 1967*, pp. 589–609.

"Powell Loses Chairmanship; Seat in Doubt," *CQWR*, January 13, 1967.

Powell, Thomas Reed, "Commerce, Congress, and the Supreme Court, 1922-1925," *Columbia Law Review*, XXV (April to May 1926), pp. 396–431, 521–49.

"Presidency Limit of 8 Years Asked," *NYT,* February 3, 1947.

"President Orders an Even Break for Minorities in Defense Jobs, He Issues an Order That Defense Contract Holders Not Allow Discrimination Against Negroes or Any Worker," *NYT,* June 26, 1941.

"President Suffers Defeat in House Minimum Wage Report," *CQWR*, March 31, 1961.

"Presidential Approval: Harry Truman," Roper Center Public Opinion Archives, University of Connecticut, Accessed at rcweb@ropercenter.uconn.edu.

"Presidential Continuity Amendment Sent to States," *CQWR,* July 9, 1965.

"Presidential Popularity—Harry S. Truman," *Gallup Opinion Index*, 1976.

"Presidential Press Conference, March 1, 1961," in *The Kennedy Presidential Press Conferences* (New York: Coleman Enterprises, 1978).

"Presidential Succession Bill Approved by House Committee" *NYT,* June 27, 1945.

"Pretenders in Congress," *WP*, January 1, 1965.

Preuss, Lawrence, "The International Court of Justice, the Senate, and Matters of Domestic Jurisdiction," *American Journal of International Law*, XL (October, 1946), pp. 720–36.

Prewitt, Kenneth W., "Social Bias in Leadership Selection, Political Recruitment and Electoral Context," *Journal of Politics*, XXXIII (May, 1971), pp. 293–315.

Price, Charles M., and Joseph Boskin, "The Roosevelt 'Purge': A Reappraisal," *Journal of Politics*, XXVIII (August, 1966), pp. 660–70.

Price, Hugh Douglas, "Race, Religion, and the Rules Committee: The Kennedy Aid-to-Education Bills," in Alan F. Westin, ed., *The Uses of Power: 7 Cases in American Politics* (New York: Harcourt, Brace & World, 1962), pp. 1–71.

Prior, Betty, "McCormack Says Missing NSA Pair Took Valuable Code Secrets to Soviet," *WP*, August 17, 1960.

Purdum, Todd S., "Sex in the Senate: Bobby Baker's Salacious Secret History of Capitol Hill," *POLITICO*, November 19, 2013.

"Question of Leadership," *WP*, February 4, 1963.

"Rankin Shakes Fist at Cellar in House," *NYT,* February 8, 1945.

"Rayburn Draft Growing," Unidentified Newspaper, November 12, 1946.

"Rayburn Elected in House Tradition—Choice of Texan as Speaker is Made by Acclamation Before the Body of Bankhead," *NYT,* September 17, 1940.

"Rayburn to Back McCormack for Minority Leader," *BG,* November 28, 1946.

"Refusal of Rayburn to Be Party Leader in House Opens Contest," *BG,* November 22, 1946.

Reilly, John F., "Is Congress Outmoded?: A Study of Proposals for Reorganization," *Georgetown Law Journal*, XXXIV (January, 1946), pp. 201–19.

"Regulation Extended to One-Bank Holding Companies," *CQ Almanac 1970*, pp. 874–82.

Renehan, Edward J., "Joseph Kennedy and the Jews," in the website of the History News Network for April 29, 2002.

"Rep. Kennedy Will Not Sign Curley Plea," *Boston Traveler*, July 8, 1947.

"Rep. McCormack Again Urged to Quit as Speaker," *WP*, December 6, 1963.

"Rep. McCormack is Next in Line," *WP*, November 23, 1963.

"Rep. O'Neill Picks as Majority Whip," *WP*, January 23, 1971.

"Reservations," *TIME*, March 19, 1945.

Reston, James, "Washington: Who Runs the Democrats? Kennedy or McCormack," *NYT*, April 28, 1963.

"Retirement for Rayburn, "*TIME*", May 5, 1961, accessed May 4, 2015.

Rhodes, Jack A., "Congressional Committee Reorganization in 1946," *Southwestern Social Science Quarterly*, XXVIII (June, 1947), pp. 36–52.

Riddick, Floyd M., "American Government and Politics: The First Session of the Seventy-Sixth Congress: January 3, 1939 to August 5, 1939," *APSR*, XXXIII (December, 1939), pp. 1022–43.

Riddick, Floyd M., "American Government and Politics: Third Session of the Seventy-Sixth Congress, January 3, 1940 to January 3, 1941," *APSR*, XXXV (April, 1941), pp. 284–303.

Riddick, Floyd M., "American Government and Politics: First Session of the Seventy-Seventh Congress: January 3, 1941 to January 2, 1942," *APSR*, XXXVI (April, 1942), pp. 290–302.

Riddick, Floyd M., "American Government and Politics: The Second Session of the Seventy-Seventh Congress, January 6 to December 16, 1942," *APSR*, XXXVII (April, 1943), pp. 290–305.

Riddick, Floyd M., "American Government and Politics: First Session of the Seventy-Eighth Congress," *APSR*, XXXVIII (April, 1944), pp. 301–17.

Riddick, Floyd M., "American Government and Politics: The Second Session of the Seventy-Eighth Congress," *ASPR*, XXXIX (April, 1945), pp. 317–36.

Riddick, Floyd M., "American Government and Politics: The First Session of the Seventy-Ninth Congress," *APSR*, XL (April, 1946), pp. 256–71.

Riddick, Floyd M., "American Government and Politics: The Second Session of the Seventy-Ninth Congress," *APSR*, XLI (February, 1947), pp. 12–27.

Riddick, Floyd M., "American Government and Politics: The First Session of the Eightieth Congress," *APSR*, XLII (August, 1948), pp. 677–93.

Riddick, Floyd M., "American Government and Politics: The Second Session of the Eightieth Congress," *APSR*, XLIII (1949), pp. 483–92.

Riddick, Floyd M., "House Versus the Senate in the Third Session of the Seventy-Sixth Congress," *South Atlantic Quarterly*, XL (April, 1941), pp. 169–84.

Riddick, Floyd M., "The Eighty-First Congress: First and Second Sessions," *Western Political Quarterly*, IV (March, 1951), pp. 48–66.

Riddick, Floyd M., "The Eighty-Second Congress: Second Session," *Western Political Quarterly* V (December, 1952), pp. 619–34.

Riddick, Floyd M., "The Eighty-Ninth Congress: Second Session," *Western Political Quarterly*, XX (March, 1967), pp. 173–90.

Ripley, Randall B., "Party Whip Organizations in the United States House of Representatives," *APSR*, LVIII (September, 1964), pp. 561–76.

Roberts, Chalmers M., "Congressional Haggle Highlights'64 Politics," *WP*, December 22, 1963.

Robinson, John, "Among Friends, Truman Liked to Visit Boston," *BG,* December 23, 1973.

Robinson, N. T. N., "Democrats Claim House on Eve of New Congress," *Congressional Digest,* X (December, 1931), pp. 289–90.

Roche, John P., "John McCormack, One of a Kind," *Columbus (Ind.) Republic,* December 1, 1980.

Rodgers, Wilfrid C., "McCormack Now First in Line of Succession," *BG,* November 23, 1963.

Rodgers, Wilfrid C., "McCormack Pitches for JFK's Programs," *BG,* January 6, 1963.

Rodgers, Wilfrid C., "McCormack Romps to Speaker Victory: Formal Vote Today Paces Way for Firm Reign," *BG,* January 10, 1962.

Rodgers, Wilfrid C., "They Came to Hail the Speaker, Last of a Venerable Line," *BG,* November 25, 1980.

Rodgers, Wilfrid, "White House Sings Praise of 'Old Pro' McCormack," *BG,* April 8, 1962.

Rohde, David W., "Committee Reform in the House of Representatives and the Subcommittee Bill of Rights," *Annals of the American Academy of Political and Social Science,* CDXI (January, 1974), pp. 39–47.

Ross, Irwin, "The True Story of Joseph P. Kennedy," *New York Post,* Article IV, January 12, 1961.

Ross, William G., "When Did the Switch in Time Actually Occur? Re-Discovering the Supreme Court's Forgotten Decisions of 1936-37," February 25, 2005. SSRN.com.

Rudwick, Elliott M., "Oscar De Priest and the Jim Crow Restaurant in the U.S. House of Representatives," *Journal of Negro Education,* XXXV (Winter, 1966), pp. 77–82.

Russell, Francis, "John the Bold: Boston's John F. 'Honey Fitz' Fitzgerald," in *The Knave of Boston and Other Ambiguous Massachusetts Characters* (Boston: Quinlan Press, 1987), pp. 20–45.

Russell, Francis, "The Art of the Double Deal: 'Dapper Dan' Coakley and the 'Toodles Ryan' Case," in Peter F. Stevens, ed., *Hidden History of the Boston Irish: Little-known Stories from Ireland's "Next Parish Over"* (Charleston, SC: The History Press, 2008), pp. 51–54.

Russell, Francis, "The Strike That Made a President," *American Heritage* (October, 1963), pp. 44–47, 90–94.

Sargent, James E., "Clifton A. Woodrum of Virginia: A Southern Progressive in Congress, 1923-1945," *Virginia Magazine of History and Biography,* LXXXIX (July, 1981), pp. 341–64.

Sargent, James E., "Roosevelt's Economy Act: Fiscal Conservatism and the Early New Deal," *Congressional Studies,* VII (Winter, 1980), pp. 33–52.

Sargent, James E., "Woodrum's Economy Bloc: The Attack on Roosevelt's WPA," *Virginia Magazine of History,* L (February, 1988), pp. 175–207.

"Says He Saw 4 Kiss Miss Ryan: Mullen Accused of Lying—Ex-Mayor Fitzgerald Brands Ferncroft Episode Silly and False," *Boston Post,* January 20, 1915.

"Senate Ratifies Nuclear Nonproliferation Treaty," *CQ Almanac 1969,* pp. 162–98.

"Senate Votes $556.8 Million Federal Pay Raise," *CQWR,* July 10, 1964.

"Seniority: Democrats," *CQ Almanac 1962,* pp. 30–31.

"Scenic Rivers," *CQ Almanac 1968,* pp. 485–89.

"Scenic Trails," *CQ Almanac 1968,* pp. 477–79.

Schell, Ruth, "Swamp Yankee," *American Speech,* XXXVIII (1963), pp. 121–23.

Scher, Seymour, "Politics of Agency Organization: The Taft-Hartley Congress and NLRB Bifurcation," *Western Political Quarterly*, XV (June, 1962), pp. 328–44.

Schickler, Eric, Eric McGhee, and John Sides, "Remaking the House and Senate: Personal Power, Ideology, and the 1970s Reforms," *Legislative Studies Quarterly*, XXVIII (August, 2003), pp. 297–331.

Schickler, Eric, and Kathryn Pearson, "Agenda Control, Majority Party Power, and the House Committee on Rules, 1937-52," *Legislative Studies Quarterly*, XXXIV (November, 2009), pp. 455–91.

Schlesinger, Arthur M., "Gardner Jackson, 1897-1965," *New Republic*, May 1, 1965.

Schmidt, John F., "International Organization and the Senate," *Tennessee Law Review*, XIX (October, 1945, pp. 29–39).

"Scholarships Featured in College Aid Bill," *CQ Almanac 1965*, pp. 294–305.

Schussbaum, Morton J., "Federal Housing Acts," in Bacon, Davidson, and Keller, eds., *The Encyclopedia of the United States Congress*, Vol. II, pp. 812–14.

Schweikart, Larry, "Banking Act of 1933(Glass-Steagall Act)," in Bacon, Davidson and Keller, eds., *The Encyclopedia of United States Congress*, Vol. II, pp. 136–37.

Schweikart, Larry, "Emergency Baking Relief Act," in Bacon, Davidson, and Keller, eds., *The Encyclopedia of the United States Congress*, Vol. II, pp. 734–35.

Scobie, Ingrid W., "Helen Gahagan Douglas and Her 1950 Senate Race with Richard M. Nixon," *Southern California Quarterly*, LVII (Spring, 1976), pp. 113–26.

Scobie, Ingrid W., "Helen Gahagan Douglas: Broadway Star as a California Politician," *California History*, LXVI (December, 1987), pp. 242–61, 310–413.

"Seating Disputes," *CQWR*, January 8, 1965.

"Senate Passes Bill to Establish Housing Department," *CQWR*, August 13, 1965.

"Senate Passes Communications Satellite Bill," *CQWR*, August 24, 1962.

Shull, Charles W., "The Legislative Reorganization Act of 1946," *Temple Law Quarterly*, XX (January, 1947), pp. 275–306.

Siegel, Arthur, "Combatants Swap Punches for Pillows," *BG*, September 6, 1962.

"Slate for Farley Meets with Dissension in State: Walsh, Dever Prefer Group Unpledged, Others Would Wait Until Roosevelt Announces Move," *BG*, February 13, 1940.

Slayton, Robert A., "Al and Frank: The Great Smith-Roosevelt Feud," in Woolner and Kurial, eds., *FDR, The Vatican and the Roman Catholic Church in America, 1933-1945*, pp. 55–66.

"Snell Beats Tilson in Speakership Race," *NYT*, December 1, 1931.

"Social Security Aid Raised; Welfare Pay Restricted," *CQ Almanac 1967*, pp. 892–916.

"Spellman Denies Political Report, He and Cushing Call Rivalry a 'Fabrication'—Backing of Nixon Disclaimed," *NYT*, November 5, 1960.

Spivak, John L., "Wall Street's Fascist Conspiracy, Testimony that the Dickstein Committee Suppressed," *New Masses*, p. 10.

Squire, Peverill, "Why the 1936 Literary Digest Poll Failed," *Public Opinion Quarterly*, LII (1988), pp. 123–33.

"Speaker H.T. Rainey Dies of Pneumonia and Heart Attack: End Comes Quickly," *NYT*, August 20, 1934.

"Speakers: Joe Byrns Dies and an Old Friend Gets His Job," *Newsweek*, June 13, 1936.

"Speakership Won, Byrns Declares, Sufficient Votes Pledged to Assure his Election in House, He Says; Mead Gains for Leader; Buffalo Member Seems to Have Better Chance than O'Connor or McCormack," *NYT*, November 25, 1934.

Stafford, Charles, "It's Decision Day for Powell, Colmer in House," *Chicago Tribune,* January 8, 1967.

Steinberg, Alfred, "James Michael Curley: The Joyous Scourge of Boston," in *The Bosses* (New York: Macmillan, 1972), pp. 144–46.

Steinberg, Alfred, "Mr. Truman's Mystery Man," *Saturday Evening Post,* CCII (December, 1949, pp. 24, 69ff).

Steinberg, David, "Dr. Lahey's Dilemma," *Boston Globe Sunday Magazine,* May 29, 2011.

"Steps Taken to Follow Up Warren Commission Report," *CQ Almanac 1965,* pp. 582–84.

Stevens, Arthur G. Jr., Arthur H. Miller, and Thomas E. Mann, "Mobilization of Liberal Strength in the House, 1955-1970: The Democratic Study Group," *APSR,* LXVIII (June, 1964), pp. 667–81.

Stewart, Richard H., "College 'Pressured,' Sweig Jury Told," *BG,* July 1, 1970.

Stewart, Richard H., "$50,000 for 5 Hours of Work: Jury Told of Voloshen's Fee for Arranging Meeting," *BG,* June 27, 1970.

Storke, Thomas L., "Forced into the Open: Hopkins Protégé Directs 1944 Drive for F.D," *Washington Daily News,* March 11, 1943.

"Stock Market Crash Heralds Great Depression, October 29, 1929," from the MassMoments website, accessed July 25, 2014.

Strong, Donald S., "Alabama: Transition and Alienation," in William C. Harvard, ed., *The Changing Politics of the South* (Baton Rouge: Louisiana State University Press, 1972), p. 458.

"Sweig Bribery," *WP,* March 4, 1972.

Tanenhaus, Sam, "Investigating Un-American Activities, Now and Then," *NYT,* March 9, 2011.

Ter Horst, J. F., "House Wage Bill Defeat Lands McCormack in Kennedy Doghouse," *BG Files,* March 28, 1961.

"The Age of Rubbish," *Newsweek,* LXXVI, July 6, 1970.

"The Black Vote, 1936-2012," Blackdemographics.com, accessed March 5, 2014.

"The Congress: Mr. Speaker," *TIME,* January 19, 1962.

"The Congress: 'Mr. Will' Goes Home," *TIME,* September 30, 1940.

"The Election: In the Nation, a Popular Win," *WP,* November 5, 1970.

"The Fear & The Facts," *TIME,* September 25, 1964.

"The President's Day," September 20, 1947, Truman Library.

"The Southern Manifesto," *TIME,* March 26, 1956.

"The Speaker," *TIME,* September 23, 1940.

"1,000 Mourn Ex-Speaker's Wife at Rites," *WP,* December 7, 1971.

"1,028 Economists Ask Hoover to Veto Pending Tariff Bill": Professors in 179 Colleges and Other Leaders Assail Rise in Rates as Harmful to Country and Sure to Bring Reprisals," *NYT,* May 5, 1930.

"Threatened Wildlife Species," *CQ Almanac 1966,* p. 660.

"Tobin Accepts Cabinet Post; Drops from Race for Bay State Governor, Notifies Dever He'll Back Him in November," *BG,* August 12, 1948.

"Toy Safety," *CQ Almanac 1969,* pp. 248–50.

"Traffic, Auto Safety Act," *CQ Almanac 1966,* pp. 269–78.

"Transportation Department Created," *CQ Almanac 1966,* pp. 773–87.

Trussell, C. P., "Close is Democratic; Truman Gets Contracts Powers. And 20 Billion is Granted for Arms; Faith in America Voiced; Peace Hope a Major Theme—Party Meetings Name Chiefs for 82nd, Opening Today," *NYT,* January 3, 1951.

Trussell, C. P., "Rayburn Elected as Speaker Again: Texan is Named Record 8th Time as House Organizes—Urges Responsibility," *NYT,* January 4, 1957.

Tucker, Ray T., "Tiger from Texas," *Outlook and Independent,* XXVI (November, 1930), p. 492.

Treadway, Allen T., "The Amherst Illustrious: The Congressional Leaders—Rainey, '83 and Snell, '94," *Amherst Graduates Quarterly,* XXII (May, 1933), pp. 208–18.

Trout, Charles H., "Curley of Boston: The Search for Irish Legitimacy," in Formisano and Burns, Boston, *1789-1980: The Evolution of Urban Politics,* pp. 165–95.

"Two Arrests in Cambridge Holdup, Messenger of Bank Robbed, South Boston and Cambridge Men Arraigned," *BG,* May 29, 1924.

"240 Votes Pledged to McCormack as Speaker," *BG,* December 28, 1961.

"2000 Pay Last Tribute to Edw. M'Cormack Sr.," *BG,* November 21, 1963.

"Two Year School Aid Bill Enacted," *CQ Almanac 1967,* pp. 611–26.

"Up from South Boston: The Rise & Fall of John Fox," *TIME,* July 7, 1958.

United Press, "Rayburn to Back McCormack for Minority Leader," *BG,* November 28, 1946.

"Urban Mass Transit Grants Extended," *CQ Almanac 1966,* pp. 802-805.

"U.S. Moving Again, Kennedy Asserts: He Says His Talks in 1961 'Awakened' the Nation," *NYT,* December 24, 1961.

"United Nations Loan," *CQWR,* September 21, 1962.

United Press International, "Bolling Suggests Bolling as Speaker," *NYT,* January 19, 1970.

United Press International, "Church-State Separatists Don't Want McCormack," *BG,* November 21, 1961.

United Press International, "New Probe Due in Speaker's Office," *BG,* November 26, 1970.

United Press International, "Rep. Boggs Missing on Alaska Flight, Rep Bogs Lost in Alaska On Flight with Rep. Begich," *WP,* October 17, 1972.

"Unusual Coalition Eyes Rains for Speaker," *CQWR,* December 8, 1961.

U.S. House Historical Office. "Historical Highlights: The Repeal of the Twenty-One Day Rule, January 3, 1951."

U.S. Senate Historical Office, "September 4, 1934, 'Merchants of Death.'"

U.S. Senate Historical Office, "The Uncrowned King of the Senate."

Van Alstyne, William W., "Congress, the President, and the Power to Declare War: A requiem for Vietnam," *University of Pennsylvania Law Review,* CXXI (November, 1972), pp. 1–28.

"Vice Presidential Bid May Go to McCormack," BG, July 6, 1948.

Viorst, Milton, "Nixon of the O.P.A," *NYT Magazine,* October 3, 1971.

"Vocational Education," *CQ Almanac 1968,* pp. 500–04.

Vollaro, Daniel R., "Lincoln, Stowe, and the 'Little Woman/Great War' Story: The Making, and Breaking of a Great American Anecdote," *Journal of the Abraham Lincoln Association,* XXX (Winter, 2009), pp. 1ff.

"Vote on H Res. 8," *CQWR,* January 8, 1965.

"Voting Rights Bill Send to President," *CQWR,* August 6, 1965.

"Wallace in Boston Today; Socialists to Picket Garden Rally," *BG,* September 18, 1948.

"Walter F. George," in the online *New Georgia Encyclopedia* accessed June 14, 2015.

Walsh, Robert E., "Labor Notebook: 87th Congress Did More Than It Didn't, AFL-CIO Dept. Finds," *BG,* October 21, 1962.

Ward, John William. "The Common Weal and the Public Trust," 350 Forum. October 21, 1980.

Ward, Robert L., "'You're Home Again, My Dear,' McCormack Assures His Harriet," *BG,* December 4, 1971.

"Was in Boston, Witnesses Say, Testify for McCormack in Cambridge Robbery Case," *Boston Daily Globe*, November 21, 1924.

"Water Pollution Control Funds Expanded," *CQ Almanac 1966*, pp. 632-645.

"Way, William T.," *Who's Who in New England* (Chicago: A.N. Marquis, 1916). Vol. 2, p. 1112.

Wayman, Dorothy G., "Journalist Refutes Charges of Anti-Semitism Laid to Boston," *The Pilot,* October 14, 1944.

Wechsler, James A., "Pat Jackson," *New York Post*, April 10, 1965.

Wechsler, James A., "The Passionate Spirit of Gardner Jackson," *BG,* April 21, 1965.

"What Went Wrong With The Polls: None of Straw Votes Got Exactly the Right Answer—Why?" *The Literary Digest*, November 14, 1936.

White, Eugene N., "Before the Glass-Steagall Act: An Analysis of the Investment Banking Activities of National Banks," *Explorations in Economic History*, XXIII (January, 1986), pp. 33–55.

White, William S., "House GOP Selects Halleck; Democrats 'Draft' Rayburn," *NYT,* January 3, 1947.

White, William S., "Manifesto Splits Democrats Again: Southern Pledge to Fight Integration Ends Truce on Civil Rights Issue," *NYT,* March 13, 1956.

White, William S., "Rayburn Rejects Leadership 'Draft': Southern Democrats Seek to Block McCormack for Post-Thomason Next Choice," *NYT,* December 31, 1946.

White, William S., "The Invisible Gentleman from Kansas City," *Harpers* (May, 1961), pp. 83–87.

Wilcox, Francis O., "The Neutrality Fight in Congress: 1939," *APSR*, XXXIII (October, 1939, pp. 811–25).

Willard, Donald L., "1000 Homes Being Built by Uncle Sam on What Was South Boston Dump," *BG,* November 15, 1936.

"Williams, Watson Purge," *CQWR*, January 1, 1965.

Wilson, Theodore, "The Truman Committee, 1941" in Arthur M. Schlesinger, Jr. and Roger Bruns, eds., *Congress Investigates: A Documentary History, 1792-1974* (New York: Chelsea House, 1975), pp. 3115–3262.

Witney, Fred, "Taft-Hartley and the Eighty-Third Congress," *Labor Law Journal, V* (January, 1954), pp. 76–79.

Wohl, Richard, "Horatio Alger, Jr., and the Gilded Age," in Richard Weiss, ed., The *American Myth of Success: From Horatio Alger to Norman Vincent Peale* (New York: Basic Books, 1969), pp. 48–64.

Wohl, Richard, "The 'Rags to Riches' Story: An Episode of Secular Idealism" in Reinhard Bendix and Seymour Martin Lipset, eds., *Class, Status, and Power* (Glencoe, IL: The Free Press, 1953), pp. 388–93.

Wolf, Thomas Philip, "The 1938 Purge: A R-Examination," in Thomas P. Wolf, William D. Pederson, and Byron W. Daynes, eds., *Franklin D. Roosevelt and Congress: The New Deal and Its Aftermath* (Armonk, NY: M. E. Sharpe, 2001), pp. 108–21.

Woods, Edward F., "Rep. Bolling Being Mentioned as Successor to Rayburn: Believed to be Choice of House but Many Feel McCormack Has Inside Track," *St Louis Post-Dispatch,* September 6, 1961.

Wreszin, Michael, "The Dies Committee 1938," in Arthur M. Schlesinger, Jr. and Roger Bruns, eds., *Congress Investigates: A Documented History, 1792-1974* (New York: Chelsea House in association with R.R. Bowker, 1975). Vol. 4, p. 2927.

X. [George F. Kennan], "The Sources of Soviet Conduct" *Foreign Affairs*, XXV (July, 1947, pp. 566–82).

"You Can't Help Liking Nick," *Literary Digest*, XXI (November, 1925, pp. 44–48.

Young, Jeff C., "Joseph P. Kennedy Sr. (1888-1969)," in *Fathers of American Presidents: From Augustine Washington to William Blythe and Roger Clinton* (Jefferson, NC: McFarland & Co., 1997), pp. 180–89.

"Young Man with Tough Questions: Bob Kennedy," *LIFE*, XLIII (July 1, 1957), pp. 81–82 and 84.

Zelizer, Julian E., "When Liberals Were Organized," *The American Prospect*, Winter, 2015.

Index